CLASSICS

OF

WESTERN PHILOSOPHY

Classics

OF

Western Philosophy

SECOND EDITION

Edited by

STEVEN M. CAHN

HACKETT PUBLISHING COMPANY

INDIANAPOLIS

Library of Congress Cataloging in Publication Data
Main entry under title:

Classics of Western Philosophy.

   Includes bibliographical references.
   1. Philosophy—Addresses, essays, lectures.
I. Cahn, Steven M.
B29.C536   1985   190   84-22391
ISBN 0-915145-94-4
ISBN 0-915145-93-6 (pbk.)

Printed in the United States of America
Cover design by Jackie Lacy
Interior design by James N. Rogers
For further information, address the publisher,
Box 44937, Indianapolis, Indiana 46204

To Marilyn

Contents

Preface to the Second Edition

This revision contains three major additions: Book II of Aristotle's *Physics,* an expanded selection from Locke's *Essay,* and the complete text of Berkeley's *Three Dialogues Between Hylas and Philonous.* For suggestions regarding the choice of chapters from Locke's *Essay,* I am grateful to Hilary Kornblith. I remain indebted to my publisher, William H. Y. Hackett, for his kind support and wise counsel.

STEVEN M. CAHN
Provost and Professor
 of Philosophy
The Graduate School and
 University Center
The City University of New York

September 1984

Preface

Here in one volume are the complete texts of twenty immortal philosophical works along with selections from seven other masterpieces whose original length precludes unabridged reprinting. Sixteen of the world's greatest philosophers are represented, their writings spanning more than two millenia. Crucial fields of philosophy are explored in depth: metaphysics, epistemology, ethics, political philosophy, and philosophy of religion. An introduction to each author contains biographical data, philosophical commentary, and bibliographical guides. Annotations are provided to clarify textual references.

What is the value of philosophy? Different philosophers have answered this question in different ways, but perhaps no reply is more inspirational, even to those who view it in part figuratively, than that provided by one of our century's intellectual giants, Bertrand Russell, at the close of a classic work, *The Problems of Philosophy.*

"Philosophy is to be studied, not for the sake of any definite answers to its questions, since no definite answers can, as a rule, be known to be true, but rather for the sake of the questions themselves; because these questions enlarge our conception of what is possible, enrich our intellectual imagination and diminish the dogmatic assurance which closes the mind against speculation; but above all because, through the greatness of the universe which philosophy contemplates, the mind also is rendered great, and becomes capable of that union with the universe which constitutes its highest good."*

The Problems of Philosophy (1912; rpt. New York: Oxford University Press, 1959), p. 161.

Acknowledgments

I very much appreciate the assistance of my colleagues at the University of Vermont: Robert W. Hall, Patricia W. Kitcher, Philip S. Kitcher, William E. Mann, and George Sher. They have contributed many of the introductions, thereby providing expert commentary on the writings of each philosopher. Professor Mann, who advised me on numerous editorial matters, kindly granted permission for use of his new translation of Anselm's *Proslogion*. He also furnished many of the translations of Latin textual references. Professor Sher, with whom I frequently consulted, aided me in abridging Locke's *Essay*.

For suggestions regarding the contents of the book, I am also grateful to my friends of many years, John O'Connor and James Rachels. Thanks are also proffered to James N. Rogers for his editorial assistance and help in seeing the book into print, and to Patric F. O'Keeffe for his painstaking research and tasteful choice of illustrations.

A special debt is owed William H. Y. Hackett, whose foresight, philosophical understanding, and commitment to the highest standards of publishing, have made this work possible.

Steven M. Cahn

PLATO—Roman copy of
a bust by Silanion

THE DEATH OF SOCRATES
(J. L. David)

PLATO WITH STUDENTS
(mosaic from Pompei)

PLATO

Plato (c.427–c.347 B.C.) was born of a noble and probably wealthy Athenian family. Although little is known about his early years, at a young age he undoubtedly became well acquainted with Socrates. Plato played an active role in the last years of the Peloponnesian War, and afterwards his unhappy tastes of political life, which included the execution of Socrates, led him to conclude that with his high moral standards and decided bent towards speculative thought, a career in the political arena was unsuitable. But he was by no means a man of inaction. After returning from a visit to Italy, he founded his famed Academy, which would endure for nine hundred years. His purpose seems to have been the training of future political leaders who would furnish an environment in which his own moral ideals could be implemented. During two visits to Sicily he attempted to put those ideals into practice but was stymied by the impetuous young King Dionysius. Plato died at the age of eighty, his legacy the philosophical ideas which would shape Western thought.

Although Socrates wrote nothing, we know something about his thought from what appears in the early dialogues of Plato as well as from other authors such as the Greek historian Xenophon (c.430–c.355 B.C.). Plato's use of Socrates as a principal character in the dialogues should not mislead us into thinking that Plato is always a spokesman for his great teacher. Thus, a distinction should be drawn between the historical Socrates and the Socrates of Plato's dialogues. The former served, as he put it, only as a midwife for others, helping bring to birth their views. While some of the dialogues contain elements of the historical Socrates, most reflect Plato's own thought.

The dialogues are divided by most scholars into three groups: early, middle, and late. Each of the early dialogues, including the *Euthyphro,* is an investigation of an ethical issue using the method, perhaps devised by the historical Socrates, of *elenchus,* or refutation. In this method, some individual claims to possess complete knowledge about a virtue such as courage, temperance, or piety, while Socrates professes to be in the dark on the matter. After putting a series of questions to his respondent and eliciting what seem to be promising answers, Socrates brings his partner to offer what appears to be a proper definition of the particular virtue. Then, with constant reference to homely examples such as carpentry, shoemaking, and the like, Socrates poses questions to test the truth of the initial definition. Through these questions and the resulting answers, it gradually becomes clear to all that the original definition has been refuted. The dialogue usually concludes in *aporia;* that is, with a negativity or inconclusiveness which frustrates the reader as well as the once-confident respondent.

1

The purpose of *elenchus* as practised by Socrates is to show that he who claims to know everything about a particular virtue knows nothing at all. Socrates developed this method in trying to find out what the Delphic Oracle meant by saying that he, Socrates, was the wisest man in Athens. After investigating others with a reputation for wisdom, Socrates concluded that the Oracle meant that he was the only person who *knew* that he knew nothing about what constituted the *aretê*, or excellence, of man.

Through *elenchus* Socrates hoped that once a person's ignorance had been demonstrated and he had been purged of the conceit of knowledge, together they could embark on a cooperative quest for the truth. However, not only did the effects of *elenchus* leave its victim numb and speechless, as in the *Meno,* and also a subject of ridicule and amusement for bystanders; they often left him angry and bitter as well. Presumably the effects of the *elenchus* were so devastating as to have the Athenians clamoring for Socrates' death on trumped-up charges.

The *Apology* and *Crito* are not so much exemplifications of *elenchus* as they are Socrates' last will and testament, his justification for the kind of life he led, and his refusal to escape the consequences of his actions by disobeying the law of Athens. Of the early dialogues, these two are probably the most faithful to the content of the historical Socrates' teaching.

The middle dialogues, including the *Meno* and the *Phaedo,* are in part Socratic since they consider many of the same questions as in the earlier dialogues, but they are Platonic in their development of the answers. The search for definitions evolves into the creation of the Theory of Forms, thereby resulting in the dualism between appearance and reality which has always plagued the history of philosophy. The Socratic concern for the care of the soul and the Socratic agnosticism concerning personal immortality is deepened and transformed, leading to the conviction that the soul is immortal and acquires knowledge only through recollection.

In the late dialogues, the dramatic element is pushed to the rear, and Socrates becomes a silent onlooker or is even absent all together. Since these late works are concerned with critical discussions of method and sophisticated consideration of logical and epistemological matters, Plato may have felt that Socrates, with his intense interest in practical matters confronting the individual in the mainstream of life, was an inappropriate spokesman for ideas foreign to his everyday concerns as a historical person.

One approach to Plato's thought is to consider the dialogues individually in chronological order as with Paul Shorey, *What Plato Said* (1933; rpt. Chicago: University of Chicago Press, 1965) or A.E. Taylor, *Plato: The Man and His Work* (1926; rpt. New York: Meridian Books, 1956) and more recently W.K.C. Guthrie, *A History of Greek Philosophy,* vol. IV (Cambridge: Cambridge University Press, 1975) which deals with the dialogues up to and including the *Republic.* A second approach deals systematically with various philosophical problems arising from the dialogues as with G.M.A. Grube, *Plato's Thought* (1935; rpt. Indianapolis: Hackett, 1984); G.C. Field, *The Philosophy of Plato* (1949; rpt. Oxford: Oxford University Press, 1969), and R.M. Hare, *Plato* (Oxford: Oxford University Press, 1982).

An interesting and significant, although controversial, approach to Plato's thought is Werner Jaeger, *Paideia,* vols. II and III (New York: Oxford University Press, 1943-44) which seeks to place Plato's thought within the context of Jaeger's interpretation of Greek thought as *Paideia* or culture. Studies of the historical Socrates and his thought include W.K.C. Guthrie, *Socrates* (1969; rpt. Cambridge: Cambridge University Press, 1971); A.E. Taylor, *Socrates: The Man and His Thought* (1933; rpt. Garden City: Doubleday, 1952); and Norman Gulley, *The Philosophy of Socrates* (London: Macmillan, 1968). Treatment by contemporary philosophers of various issues in the philosophies of Socrates and Plato is to be found in Gregory Vlastos, ed., *The Philosophy of Socrates: A Collection of Critical Essays* (Garden City: Doubleday, 1971), and Gregory Vlastos, ed., *Plato: A Collection of Critical Essays*, vols. I and II (Garden City: Doubleday, 1971).

R.W.H.

MENO

70 MENO: Can you tell me, Socrates, can virtue[1] be taught? Or is it not teachable but the result of practice, or is it neither of these, but men possess it by nature or in some other way?

SOCRATES: Before now, Meno, Thessalians had a high reputation among the
b Greeks and were admired for their horsemanship and their wealth, but now. it seems to me, they are also admired for their wisdom, not least the fellow citizens of your friend Aristippus of Larissa. The responsibility for this reputation of yours lies with Gorgias,[2] for when he came to your city he found that the leading Aleuadae, your lover Aristippus among them, loved him for his wisdom, and so did the leading Thessalians. He accustomed you to give a bold and grand answer to any question
c you may be asked, as experts are likely to do, as he himself was ready to answer any Greek who wished to question him, and every question was answered. But here in Athens, my dear Meno, the opposite is the case, as if there were a dearth of wisdom,
71 and wisdom seems to have departed hence to go to you. If then you want to ask one of us that sort of question, everyone will laugh and say: "Good stranger, you must think me happy indeed if you think I know whether virtue can be taught or how it comes to be; I am so far from knowing whether virtue can be taught or not that I do not even have any knowledge of what virtue itself is."

b I myself, Meno, am as poor as my fellow citizens in this matter, and I blame myself for my complete ignorance about virtue. If I do not know what something is, how could I know what qualities it possesses? Or do you think that someone who does not know at all who Meno is could know whether he is good-looking or rich or well-born, or the opposite of these? Do you think that is possible?

M: I do not; but, Socrates, do you really not know what virtue is? Are we to re-
c port this to the folk back home about you?

S: Not only that, my friend, but also that, as I believe, I have never yet met anyone else who did know.

M: How so? Did you not meet Gorgias when he was here?

Reprinted from Plato's *Meno*, translated by G.M.A. Grube (Indianapolis: Hackett Publishing Company, 1976), by permission of the publisher. The translation follows Burnet's Oxford text. The only liberty taken is where the answers to Socrates' questions are very brief, merely indicating assent or the like. In such instances "he said," the so-frequent repetition of which reads awkwardly in English, has been replaced by a dash, to indicate a change of speaker.

1. [The Greek word is *aretê*. It can refer to specific virtues such as moderation, courage, et cetera, but it is also used for *the* virtue or conglomeration of virtues that makes a man virtuous or good. In this dialogue it is mostly used in this more general sense. Socrates himself at times (e.g., 93b ff.) uses "good" as equivalent to virtuous—G.M.A.G.]

2. [Gorgias was perhaps the most famous of the earlier generation of Sophists, those traveling teachers who arose in the late fifth century to fill the need for higher education. They all taught rhetoric, or the art of speaking, but as Meno tells us, Gorgias concentrated on this more than the others and made fewer general claims for his teaching (95c). He visited Athens in 427 B.C., and his rhetorical devices gave him an immediate success. Plato named one of his dialogues after him. Fairly substantive fragments of his writings are extant.]

S: I did.

M: Did you then not think that he knew?

S: I do not altogether remember, Meno, so that I cannot tell you now what I thought then. Perhaps he does know; you know what he used to say, so you remind me of what he said. You tell me yourself, if you are willing, for surely you share his views. — I do.   d

S: Let us leave Gorgias out of it, since he is not here. But Meno, by the gods, what do you yourself say that virtue is? Speak and do not begrudge us, so that I may have spoken a most unfortunate untruth when I said that I had never met anyone who knew, if you and Gorgias are shown to know.

M: It is not hard to tell you, Socrates. First, if you want the virtue of a man, it is   e easy to say that a man's virtue consists of being able to manage public affairs and in so doing to benefit his friends and harm his enemies and to be careful that no harm comes to himself; if you want the virtue of a woman, it is not difficult to describe: she must manage the home well, preserve its possessions, and be submissive to her husband; the virtue of a child, whether male or female, is different again, and so is that of an elderly man, if you want that, or if you want that of a free man or a slave. And there are very many other virtues, so that one is not at a loss to say what virtue   72 is. There is virtue for every action and every age, for every task of ours and every one of us—and Socrates, the same is true for wickedness.

S: I seem to be in great luck, Meno; while I am looking for one virtue, I have found you to have a whole swarm of them. But, Meno, to follow up the image of swarms, if I were asking you what is the nature of bees, and you said that they are of   b all kinds, what would you answer if I asked you: "Do you mean that they are many and varied and different from one another in so far as they are bees? Or are they no different in that regard, but in some other respect, in their beauty, for example, or their size or in some other such way?" Tell me, what would you answer if thus questioned?

M: I would say that they do not differ from one another in being bees.

S: If I went on to say: "Tell me, what is this very thing, Meno, in which they   c are all the same and do not differ from one another?" Would you be able to tell me?

M: I would.

S: The same is true in the case of the virtues. Even if they are many and various, all of them have one and the same form[3] which makes them virtues, and it is right to look to this when one is asked to make clear what virtue is. Or do you not understand what I mean?   d

M: I think I understand, but I certainly do not grasp the meaning of the question as fully as I want to.

S: I am asking, whether you think it is only in the case of virtue that there is one for man, another for woman and so on, or is the same true in the case of health and size and strength? Do you think that there is one health for man and another

---

3. [The Greek term is *eidos*, which Plato was to use for his separately existing eternal Forms. Its common meaning is stature or appearance. Socrates felt that if we apply the same name or epithet to a number of different things or actions, they must surely have a common characteristic to justify the use of the same term. A definition is then a description of this "form" or appearance, which it presents to the mind's eye. In the earlier dialogues however, as here, this form is not thought of as having a separate existence, but as immanent.]

for woman? Or, if it is health, does it have the same form everywhere, whether in
e   man or in anything else whatever?

M: The health of a man seems to me the same as that of a woman.

S: And so with size and strength? If a woman is strong, that strength will be
the same and have the same form, for by "the same" I mean that strength is no
different as far as being strength, whether in a man or a woman. Or do you think
there is a difference?

M: I do not think so.

73   S: And will there be any difference in the case of virtue, as far as being virtue is
concerned, whether it be in a child or an old man, in a woman or in a man?

M: I think, Socrates, that somehow this is no longer like those other cases.

S: How so? Did you not say that the virtue of a man consists of managing the
city well,[4] and that of a woman of managing the household? — I did.

S: Is it possible to manage a city well, or a household, or anything else, while
not managing it moderately and justly? — Certainly not.

b   S: Then if they manage justly and moderately, they must do so with justice and
moderation? — Necessarily.

S: So both the man and the woman, if they are to be good, need the same
things, justice and moderation. — So it seems.

S: What about a child and an old man? Can they possibly be good if they are
intemperate and unjust? — Certainly not.

S: But if they are moderate and just? — Yes.

c   S: So all men are good in the same way, for they become good by acquiring the
same qualities. — It seems so.

S: And they would not be good in the same way if they did not have the same
virtue. — They certainly would not be.

S: Since then the virtue of all is the same, try to tell me and to remember what
Gorgias, and you with him, said that that same thing is.

d   M: What else but to be able to rule over men, if you are seeking one description
to fit them all.

S: That is indeed what I am seeking, but Meno, is virtue the same in the case
of a child or a slave, namely, for them to be able to rule over a master, and do you
think that he who rules is still a slave? — I do not think so at all, Socrates.

S: It is not likely, my good man. Consider this further point: you say that virtue is to be able to rule. Shall we not add to this *justly and not unjustly?*

M: I think so, Socrates, for justice is virtue.

e   S: Is it virtue, Meno, or a virtue? — What do you mean?

S: As with anything else. For example, if you wish, take roundness, about

----

4. [When discussing goodness or morality, social and political virtues would be more immediately
present to the Greek mind than they are to ours. In both Plato and Aristotle a good man is above all a
good citizen, whereas the modern mind thinks of goodness mainly in more individual terms, such as
sobriety or sexual morals. An extreme example of this occurred in a contemporary judge's summation
to the jury in the case of a woman of loose sexual behaviour who was accused of murdering her husband.
He actually said: "This is a case of murder, not of morals. The morals of the accused have nothing to do
with it."]

which I would say that it is a shape, but not simply that it is shape. I would not so speak of it because there are other shapes.

M: You are quite right. So I too say that not only justice is a virtue but there are many other virtues.

S: What are they? Tell me, as I could mention other shapes to you if you bade 74 me do so, so do you mention other virtues.

M: I think courage is a virtue, and moderation, wisdom, and munificence, and very many others.

S: We are having the same trouble again, Meno, though in another way; we have found many virtues while looking for one, but we cannot find the one which covers all the others.

M: I cannot yet find, Socrates, what you are looking for, one virtue for them all, b as in the other cases.

S: That is likely, but I am eager, if I can, that we should make progress, for you understand that the same applies to everything. If someone asked you what I mentioned just now: "What is shape, Meno?" and you told him that it was roundness, and if then he said to you what I did: "Is roundness shape or a shape?" you would surely tell him that it is a shape? — I certainly would.

S: That would be because there are other shapes? — Yes. c

S: And if he asked you further what they were, you would tell him? — I would.

S: So too, if he asked you what colour is, and you said it is white, and your questioner interrupted you "Is white colour or a colour?" you would say that it is a colour, because there are also other colours? — I would.

S: And if he bade you mention other colours, you would mention others that are no less colours than white is? — Yes.

S: Then if he pursued the argument as I did and said: "We always arrive at the many; do not talk to me in that way, but since you call all these many by one name, and say that no one of them is not a shape even though they are opposites, tell me what this is which applies as much to the round as to the straight and which you call shape, as you say the round is as much a shape as the straight." Do you not say that? e — I do.

S: When you speak like that, do you assert that the round is no more round than it is straight, and that the straight is no more straight than it is round?

M: Certainly not, Socrates.

S: Yet you say that the round is no more a shape than the straight is, nor the one more than the other. — That is true.

S: What then is this to which the name shape applies? Try to tell me. If then you answered the man who was questioning about shape or colour: "I do not under- 75 stand what you want, my man, nor what you mean," he would probably wonder and say: "You do not understand that I am seeking that which is the same in all these cases?" Would you still have nothing to say, Meno, if one asked you: "What is this which applies to the round and the straight and the other things which you call shapes and which is the same in them all?" Try to say, that you may practise for your answer about virtue.

M: No, Socrates, but you tell me. b

S: Do you want me to do you this favour?

M: I certainly do.

S: And you will then be willing to tell me about virtue?

M: I will.

S: We must certainly press on. The subject is worth it.

M: It surely is.

S: Come then, let us try to tell you what shape is. See whether you will accept that it is this: Let us say that shape is that which alone of existing things always follows colour. Is that satisfactory to you, or do you look for it in some other way? I should be satisfied if you defined virtue in this way.

M: But that is foolish, Socrates.

S: How do you mean?

M: That shape, you say, always follows colour. Well then, if someone were to say that he did not know what colour is, but that he had the same difficulty as he had about shape, what do you think your answer would be?

S: A true one, surely, and if my questioner was one of those clever and disputatious debaters, I would say to him: "I have given my answer; if it is wrong, it is your job to refute it." Then, if they are friends as you and I are, and want to discuss with each other, they must answer in a manner more gentle and more proper to discussion. By this I mean that the answers must not only be true, but in terms admittedly known to the questioner. I too will try to speak in these terms. Do you call something "the end?" I mean such a thing as a limit or boundary, for all those are, I say, the same thing. Prodicus[5] might disagree with us, but you surely call something "finished" or "completed"—that is what I want to express, nothing elaborate.

M: I do, and I think I understand what you mean.

S: Further, you call something a plane, and something else a solid, as in geometry?

M: I do.

S: From this you may understand what I mean by shape, for I say this of every shape, that a shape is that which limits a solid; in a word, a shape is the limit of a solid.

M: And what do you say colour is, Socrates?

S: You are outrageous, Meno. You bother an old man to answer questions, but you yourself are not willing to recall and to tell me what Gorgias says that virtue is.

M: After you have answered this, Socrates, I will tell you.

S: Even someone who was blindfolded would know from your conversation that you are handsome and still have lovers.

M: Why so?

S: Because you are forever giving orders in a discussion, as spoiled people do,

5. [Prodicus was a well-known Sophist who was especially keen on the exact meaning of words, and he was fond of making the proper distinctions between words of similar but not identical meanings. We see him in action in the *Protagoras* of Plato (especially 337a–c) where he appears with two other distinguished Sophists, Protagoras and Hippias. His insistence on the proper definition of words would naturally endear him to Socrates who, in Plato, always treats him with more sympathy than he does the other Sophists. The point here is that Prodicus would object to "end," "limit," and "boundary" being treated as "all the same thing."]

who behave like tyrants as long as they are young. And perhaps you have recognized that I am at a disadvantage with handsome people, so I will do you the favour   c
of an answer.

M: By all means do me that favour.

S: Do you want me to answer after the manner of Gorgias, which you would most easily follow?

M: Of course I want that.

S: Do you both say there are effluvia of things as Empedocles[6] does? — Certainly.

S: And that there are channels through which the effluvia make their way? — Definitely.

S: And some effluvia fit some of the channels, while others are too small or too   d
big? — That is so.

S: And there is something which you call sight? — There is.

S: From this, "comprehend what I state," as Pindar said, for colour is an effluvium from a shape which fits the sight and is perceived.

M: That seems to me to be an excellent answer, Socrates.

S: Perhaps it was given in the manner to which you are accustomed. At the same time I think that you can deduce from this answer what sound is, and smell, and many such things. — Quite so.

   e

S: It is a theatrical answer[7] so it pleases you, Meno, more than that about shape. — It does.

S: It is not better, son of Alexidemus, but I am convinced that the other is, and I think you would agree, if you did not have to go away before the mysteries as you told me yesterday, but could remain and be initiated.

M: I would stay, Socrates, if you could tell me many things like these.   77

S: I shall certainly not be lacking in eagerness to tell you such things, both for your sake and my own, but I may not be able to tell you many. Come now, you too try to fulfill your promise to me and tell me the nature of virtue as a whole and stop making many out of one, as jokers say whenever someone breaks something, but allow virtue to remain whole and sound, and tell me what it is, for I have given you   b
examples.

M: I think, Socrates, that virtue is, as the poet says, "to find joy in beautiful things and have power." So I say that virtue is to desire beautiful things and have the power to acquire them.

S: Do you mean that the man who desires beautiful things desires good things? — Most certainly.

S: Do you assume that there are people who desire bad things, and others who desire good things? Do you not think, my good man, that all men desire good   c
things?

---

6. [Empedocles (c.493–433 B.C.) of Acragas in Sicily was a famous physical philosopher. For him there were four eternal elements (earth, water, air, and fire), the intermingling and separation of which produced the physical phenomena. The reference here is to his theories of sense perception.]

7. [Theatrical because it brings in the philosophical theories of Empedocles and a quotation from Pindar, instead of being in simple terms such as Socrates' definition of shape.]

M: I do not.

S: But some desire bad things? — Yes.

S: Do you mean that they believe the bad things to be good, or that they know they are bad and nevertheless desire them? — I think there are both kinds.

S: Do you think, Meno, that anyone, knowing that bad things are bad, nevertheless desires them? — I certainly do.

S: What do you mean by desiring? Is it to secure for oneself? — What else?

d   S: Does he think that the bad things benefit him who possesses them, or does he know they harm him?

M: There are some who believe that the bad things benefit them, others who know that the bad things harm them.

S: And do you think that those who believe that bad things benefit them know that they are bad?

M: No, that I cannot altogether believe.

S: It is clear then that those who do not know things to be bad do not desire
e   what is bad, but they desire those things that they believe to be good but that are in fact bad. It follows that those who have no knowledge of these things and believe them to be good clearly desire good things. Is that not so? — It is likely.

S: Well then, those who you say desire bad things, believing that bad things harm their possessor, know that they will be harmed by them? — Necessarily.

78   S: And do they not think that those who are harmed are miserable to the extent that they are harmed? — That too is inevitable.

S: And that those who are miserable are unhappy? — I think so.

S: Does anyone wish to be miserable and unhappy? — I do not think so, Socrates.

S: No one then wants what is bad, Meno, unless he wants to be such. For what else is being miserable but to desire bad things and secure them?

b   M: You are probably right, Socrates, and no one wants what is bad.

S: You said just now that virtue is to desire good things and have the power to secure them. — Yes, I did.

S: The desiring part of this statement is common to everybody, and one man is no better than another in this? — So it appears.

S: Clearly then, if one man is better than another, he must be better at securing them. — Quite so.

c   S: This then is virtue according to your argument, the power of securing good things.

M: I think, Socrates, that the case is altogether as you now understand it.

S: Let us see then whether what you say is true, for you may well be right. You say that the capacity to acquire good things is virtue? — I do.

S: And by good things you mean, for example, health and wealth?

M: Yes, and also to acquire gold and silver, also honours and offices in the city.

S: By good things you do not mean other goods than these?

M: No, but I mean all things of this kind.

d   S: Very well. According to Meno, the hereditary guest friend of the Great

King, virtue is the acquisition of gold and silver. Do you add to this acquiring, Meno, the words justly and piously, or does it make no difference to you but even if one secures these things unjustly, you call it virtue none the less?

M: Certainly not, Socrates.

S: You would then call it wickedness? — Indeed I would.

S: It seems then that the acquisition must be accompanied by justice or moderation or piety or some other part of virtue; if it is not, it will not be virtue, even though it provides good things.

e

M: How could there be virtue without these?

S: Then failing to secure gold and silver, whenever it would not be just to do so, either for oneself or another, is not this failure to secure them also virtue?

M: So it seems.

S: Then to provide these goods would not be virtue any more than not to provide them, but whatever is done with justice will be virtue, and what is done without anything of the kind is wickedness?

79

M: I think it must necessarily be as you say.

S: We said a little while ago that each of these things was a part of virtue, namely justice and moderation and all such things? — Yes.

S: Then you are playing with me, Meno. — How so, Socrates?

S: Because I begged you just now not to break up or fragment virtue, and I gave examples of how you should answer. You paid no attention, but you tell me that virtue is to be able to secure good things with justice, and this, you say, is a part of virtue.

b

M: I do.

S: It follows then from what you agree to, that to act in whatever you do with a part of virtue is virtue, for you say that justice is a part of virtue, as are all such qualities. Why do I say this? Because when I begged you to tell me about virtue as a whole, you are far from telling me what it is. Rather, you say that every action is virtue if it is performed with a part of virtue, as if you had told me what virtue as a whole is, and I would already know that, even if you fragment it into parts.[8] I think you must face the same question from the beginning, my dear Meno, namely, what is virtue, if every action performed with a part of virtue is virtue? For that is what one is saying when he says that every action performed with justice is virtue. Do you not think you should face the same question again, or do you think one knows what a part of virtue is if one does not know virtue itself? — I do not think so.

c

S: If you remember, when I was answering you about shape, we rejected the kind of answer that tried to answer in terms still being the subject of inquiry and not yet agreed upon. — And we were right to reject them.

d

S: Then surely, my good sir, you must not think, while the nature of virtue as a whole is still under inquiry, that by answering in terms of the parts of virtue you can make its nature clear to anyone or make anything else clear by speaking in this way, but only that the same question must be put to you again—what do you take the nature of virtue to be when you say what you say? Or do you think there is no point in what I am saying? — I think what you say is right.

e

8. [That is, Meno is including the term to be defined in the definition.]

S: Answer me again then from the beginning: What do you and your friend say that virtue is?

M: Socrates, before I even met you I used to hear that you are always in a state of perplexity and that you bring others to the same state, and now I think you are bewitching and beguiling me, simply putting me under a spell, so that I am quite perplexed. Indeed, if a joke is in order, you seem, in appearance and in every other way, to be like the broad torpedo fish, for it too makes anyone who comes close and touches it feel numb, and you seem to have had that kind of effect on me, for both my mind and my tongue are numb, and I have no answer to give you. Yet I have made many speeches about virtue before large audiences on a thousand occasions, very good speeches as I thought, but now I cannot even say what it is. I think you are wise not to sail away from Athens to go and stay elsewhere, for if you were to behave like this as a stranger in another city, you would be driven away for practising sorcery.

S: You are a rascal, Meno, and you nearly deceived me.

M: Why so particularly, Socrates?

S: I know why you drew this image of me.

M: Why do you think I did?

S: So that I should draw an image of you in return. I know that all handsome men rejoice in images of themselves; it is to their advantage, for I think that the images of beautiful people are also beautiful, but I will draw no image of you in turn. Now if the torpedo fish is itself numb and so makes others numb, then I resemble it, but not otherwise, for I myself do not have the answer when I perplex others, but I am more perplexed than anyone when I cause perplexity in others. So now I do not know what virtue is; perhaps you knew before you contacted me, but now you are certainly like one who does not know. Nevertheless, I want to examine and seek together with you what it may be.

M: How will you look for it, Socrates, when you do not know at all what it is? How will you aim to search for something you do not know at all? If you should meet with it, how will you know that this is the thing that you did not know?

S: I know what you want to say, Meno. Do you realize what a debater's argument you are bringing up, that a man cannot search either for what he knows or for what he does not know? He cannot search for what he knows—since he knows it, there is no need to search—nor for what he does not know, for he does not know what to look for.

M: Does that argument not seem sound to you, Socrates?

S: Not to me.

M: Can you tell me why?

S: I can. I have heard wise men and women talk about divine matters. . . .

M: What did they say?

S: What was, I thought, both true and beautiful.

M: What was it, and who were they?

S: The speakers were among the priests and priestesses whose care it is to be able to give an account of their practices. Pindar too says it, and many others of the divine among our poets. What they say is this; see whether you think they speak the truth: They say that the human soul is immortal; at times it comes to an end, which they call dying, at times it is reborn, but it is never destroyed, and one must therefore live one's life as piously as possible:

> Persephone will return to the sun above in the ninth year the souls of those from whom she will exact punishment for old miseries, and from these come noble kings, mighty in strength and greatest in wisdom, and for the rest of time men will call them sacred heroes.

As the soul is immortal, has been born often and has seen all things here and in the underworld, there is nothing which it has not learned; so it is in no way surprising that it can recollect the things it knew before, both about virtue and other things. As the whole of nature is akin, and the soul has learned everything, nothing prevents a man, after recalling one thing only—a process men call learning—discovering everything else for himself, if he is brave and does not tire of the search, for searching and learning are, as a whole, recollection. We must, therefore, not believe that debater's argument, for it would make us idle, and fainthearted men like to hear it, whereas my argument makes them energetic and keen on the search. I trust that this is true, and I want to inquire along with you into the nature of virtue.

M: Yes, Socrates, but how do you mean that we do not learn, but that what we call learning is recollection? Can you teach me that this is so?

S: As I said just now, Meno, you are a rascal. You now ask me if I can teach you, when I say there is no teaching but recollection, in order to show me up at once as contradicting myself.

M: No, by Zeus, Socrates, that was not my intention when I spoke, but just a habit. If you can somehow show me that things are as you say, please do so.

S: It is not easy, but I am nevertheless willing to do my best for your sake. Call one of these many attendants of yours, whichever you like that I may prove it to you in his case.

M: Certainly. You there, come forward.

S: Is he a Greek? Does he speak Greek?

M: Very much so. He was born in my household.

S: Pay attention then whether you think he is recollecting or learning from me.

M: I will pay attention.

S: Tell me now, boy, you know that a square figure is like this? — I do.

S: A square then is a figure in which all these four sides are equal? — Yes indeed.

S: And it also has these lines through the middle equal?[9] — Yes.

9. [Socrates draws a square ABCD. The sides are of course equal, and the "lines through the middle" are the lines joining the middle points of these sides, which also go through the center of the square, namely EF and G.H. He then assumes the sides to be two feet.]

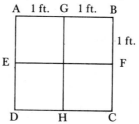

S: And such a figure could be larger or smaller? — Certainly.

S: If then this side were two feet, and this other side two feet, how many feet would the whole be? Consider it this way: if it were two feet this way, and only one foot that way, the figure[10] would be once two feet? — Yes.

d   S: But if it is two feet also that way, it would surely be twice two feet? — Yes.

S: How many feet is twice two feet? Work it out and tell me. — Four, Socrates.

S: Now let us have another figure twice the size of this one, with the four sides equal like this one. — Yes.

S: How many feet will that be? — Eight.

S: Come, now try to tell me how long each side of this will be. The side of this
e   is two feet. What about each side of the one which is its double? — Obviously, Socrates, it will be twice the length.

S: You see, Meno, that I am not teaching the boy anything, but all I do is question him. And now he thinks he knows the length of the line on which an eight-foot figure is based. Do you agree? — I do.

S: And does he know? — Certainly not.

S: He thinks it is a line twice the length? — Yes.

S: Watch him now recollecting things in order, as one must recollect. Tell me,
boy, do you say that a figure double the size is based on a line double the length?
83   Now I mean such a figure as this, not long on one side and short on the other, but equal in every direction like this one, and double the size, that is, eight feet. See whether you still believe that it will be based on a line double the length. — I do.

S: Now the line becomes double its length if we add another of the same length here? — Yes indeed.

S: And the eight-foot square will be based on it, if there are four lines of that length? — Yes.

b   S: Well, let us draw from it four equal lines, and surely that is what you say is the eight-foot square? — Certainly.

S: And within this figure are four squares, each of which is equal to the four-foot square? — Yes.

S: How big is it then? Is it not four times as big? — Of course.

S: Is this square then, which is four times as big, its double? — No, by Zeus.

S: How many times bigger is it? — Four times.

c   S: Then, my boy, the figure based on a line twice the length is not double but four times as big? — You are right.

S: And four times four is sixteen, is it not? — Yes.

S: On how long a line then should the eight-foot square be based? Is it not based on this double line? — Yes. — Now this four-foot square is based on a line half the length? — Yes.

S: Very well. Is the eight-foot square not double this one and half that one?[11] — Yes.

10. [I.e., the rectangle ABFE, which is obviously two square feet.]

11. [I.e., the eight-foot square is double the four-foot square and half the sixteen-foot square, double the square based on a line two feet long, and half the square based on a four-foot side, so it must be

S: Will it not be based on a line longer than this one and shorter than that one? Is that not so? — I think so.

S: Good, you answer what you think. And tell me, was this one not two feet long, and that one four feet? — Yes.

S: The line on which the eight-foot square is based must then be longer than this one of two feet, and shorter than that one of four feet? — It must be.

S: Try to tell me then how long a line you say it is. — Three feet.

S: Then if it is three feet, let us add the half of this one, and it will be three feet? For these are two feet, and the other is one. And here, similarly, these are two feet and that one is one foot, and so the figure you mention comes to be? — Yes.

S: Now if it is three feet this way and three feet that way, will the whole figure be three times three feet? — So it seems.

S: How much is three times three feet? — Nine feet.

S: And the double square was to be how many feet? — Eight.

S: So the eight-foot figure cannot be based on the three-foot line? — Clearly not.

S: But on how long a line? Try to tell us exactly, and if you do not want to work it out, show me from what line. — By Zeus, Socrates, I do not know.

S: You realize, Meno, what point he has reached in his recollection. At first he did not know what the basic line of the eight-foot square was; even now he does not yet know, but then he thought he knew, and answered confidently as if he did know, and he did not think himself at a loss, but now he does think himself at a loss, and as he does not know, neither does he think he knows. — That is true.

S: So he is now in a better position with regard to the matter he does not know?

M: I agree with that too.

S: Have we done him any harm by making him perplexed and numb as the torpedo fish does? — I do not think so.

S: Indeed, we have probably achieved something relevant to finding out how matters stand, for now, as he does not know, he would be glad to find out, whereas before he thought he could easily make many fine speeches to large audiences about the square of double size and said that it must have a base twice as long. — So it seems.

S: Do you think that before he would have tried to find out that which he thought he knew though he did not, before he fell into perplexity and realized he did not know and longed to know? — I do not think so, Socrates.

S: Has he then benefitted from being numbed? — I think so.

S: Look then how he will come out of his perplexity while searching along with me. I shall do nothing more than ask questions and not teach him. Watch whether you find me teaching and explaining things to him instead of asking for his opinion.

S: You tell me, is this not a four-foot figure? You understand? — I do.

S: We add to it this figure which is equal to it? — Yes.

---

based on a line between two and four feet in length. The slave naturally suggests three feet, but that gives a nine-foot square, and is still wrong. (83e).]

S: And we add this third figure equal to each of them? — Yes.

S: Could we then fill in the space in the corner? — Certainly.[12]

S: So we have these four equal figures? — Yes.

e   S: Well then, how many times is the whole figure larger than this one?[13] — Four times.

S: But we should have had one that was twice as large, or do you not remember? — I certainly do.

85   S: Does not this line from one corner to the other cut each of these figures in two?[14] — Yes.

S: So these are four equal lines which enclose this figure? — They are.

S: Consider now: how large is the figure? — I do not understand.

S: Each of these lines cuts off half of each of the four figures inside it, does it not? — Yes.

S: How many of this size are there in this figure? — Four.

S: How many in this? — Two.

b   S: What is the relation of four to two? — Double.

S: How many feet in this? — Eight.

S: Based on what line? — This one.

S: That is, on the line that stretches from corner to corner of the four-foot figure? — Yes. — Clever men call this the diagonal, so that if diagonal is its name, you say that the double figure would be that based on the diagonal? — Most certainly, Socrates.

S: What do you think, Meno? Has he, in his answers, expressed any opinion
c   that was not his own?

M: No, they were all his own.

S: And yet, as we said a short time ago, he did not know? — That is true.

S: So these opinions were in him, were they not? — Yes.

S: So the man who does not know has within himself true opinions about the things that he does not know? — So it appears.

S: These opinions have now just been stirred up like a dream, but if he were repeatedly asked these same questions in various ways, you know that in the end his
d   knowledge about these things would be as accurate as anyone's. — It is likely.

S: And he will know it without having been taught but only questioned, and find the knowledge within himself? — Yes.

S: And is not finding knowledge within oneself recollection? — Certainly.

12. [Socrates now builds up his sixteen-foot square by joining three four-foot squares. Filling "the space in the corner" will give another four-foot square, which completes the sixteen-foot square containing four four-foot squares.]

13. ["This one" is any one of the inside squares of four feet.]

14. [Socrates now draws the diagonals of the four inside squares, namely FH, HE, EG and GF, which together form the square GFHEG. We should note that Socrates here introduces a new element, which is not the result of a question but of his own knowledge, though the answer to the problem follows from questions. The new square contains four halves of a four-foot square, and is therefore eight feet.]

S: Must he not either have at some time acquired the knowledge he now possesses, or else have always possessed it? — Yes.

S: If he always had it, he would always have known. If he acquired it, he cannot have done so in his present life. Or has someone taught him geometry? For he will perform in the same way about all geometry, and all other knowledge. Has someone taught him everything? You should know, especially as he has been born and brought up in your house.

M: But I know that no one has taught him.

S: Yet he has these opinions, or doesn't he?

M: That seems indisputable, Socrates.

S: If he has not acquired them in his present life, is it not clear that he had them and had learned them at some other time? — It seems so.

S: Then that was the time when he was not a human being? — Yes.

S: If then, during the time he exists and is not a human being he will have true opinions which, when stirred by questioning, become knowledge, will not his soul have learned during all time? For it is clear that during all time he exists, either as a man or not. — So it seems.

S: Then if the truth about reality is always in our soul, the soul would be immortal so that you should always confidently try to seek out and recollect what you do not know at present—that is, what you do not recollect?[15]

M: Somehow, Socrates, I think that what you say is right.

S: I think so too, Meno. I do not insist that my argument is right in all other respects, but I would contend at all costs both in word and deed as far as I could that we will be better men, braver and less idle, if we believe that one must search for the things one does not know, rather than if we believe that it is not possible to find out what we do not know and that we must not look for it.

M: In this too I think you are right, Socrates.

S: Since we are of one mind that one should seek to find out what one does not know, shall we try to find out together what virtue is?

M: Certainly. But Socrates, I should be most pleased to investigate and hear your answer to my original question, whether we should try on the assumption that virtue is something teachable, or is a natural gift, or in whatever way it comes to men.

S: If I were directing you, Meno, and not only myself, we would not have investigated whether virtue is teachable or not before we had investigated what virtue itself is. But because you do not even attempt to rule yourself, in order that you may be free, but you try to rule me and do so, I will agree with you—for what can I do? So we must, it appears, inquire into the qualities of something the nature of which we do not yet know. However, please relax your rule a little bit for me and agree to investigate whether it is teachable or not by means of a hypothesis. I mean the way geometers often carry on their investigations. For example, if they are asked whether this triangle can be inscribed within this circle, one of them might say: "I do not yet know whether this triangle is of that kind, but I think I have, as it were, a hypothesis that is relevant to the problem, namely this: "If this triangle is such that,

e

86

b

c

d

e

87

---

15. [This is what the whole passage on recollection with the slave is intended to prove, namely, that the sophism introduced by Meno—that one cannot find out what one does not know—is false.]

when laid along the given line, it is short by a space as large as the figure laid along it, then I think one thing follows, whereas another thing follows if this cannot be done. So

b   I am willing to tell you on this hypothesis about inscribing it in the circle, whether it is impossible or not." So let us speak about virtue also, since we do not know either what it is or what qualities it possesses, and let us investigate whether it is teachable or not by means of a hypothesis, and say this: Among the things existing in the soul, of what sort is virtue, that it should be teachable or not? First, if it is another sort than knowl-edge, is it teachable or not, or, as we were just saying, recollectable? Let it make no

c   difference to us which term we use: is it teachable? Or is it plain to anyone that men cannot be taught anything but knowledge? — I think so.

S: But, if virtue is a kind of knowledge, it can clearly be taught? — Of course.

S: We have dealt with that question quickly, that if it is of one kind it can be taught, if it is of a different kind, it cannot. — We have indeed.

S: The next point to consider seems to be whether virtue is knowledge or

d   something else. — That does seem to be the next point to consider.

S: Well now, do we say that virtue is itself something good, and will this hypothesis stand firm for us, that it is something good? — Of course.

S: If then there is anything else good that is different and separate from knowl-edge, virtue might well not be a kind of knowledge, but if there is nothing good that knowledge does not encompass, we would be right to suspect that it is a kind of knowledge. — That is so.

e   S: Surely virtue makes us good? — Yes.

S: And if we are good, we are beneficent, for all that is good is beneficial. Is that not so? — Yes.

S: So virtue is something beneficial?

M: That necessarily follows from what has been agreed.

S: Let us then examine what kinds of things benefit us, taking them up one by one: health, we say, and strength, and beauty, and also wealth. We say that these things, and others of the same kind, benefit us, do we not? — We do.

88   S: Yet we say that these same things also sometimes harm one. Do you agree or not? — I do.

S: Look then, what directing factor determines in each case whether these things benefit or harm us? Is it not the right use of them that benefits us, and the wrong use that harms us? — Certainly.

S: Let us now look at the qualities of the soul. There is something you call moderation, and justice, courage, intelligence, memory, munificence, and all such things? — There is.

b   S: Consider whichever of these you believe not to be knowledge but different from it; do they not at times harm us, at other times benefit us? Courage, for exam-ple, when it is not wisdom but like a kind of recklessness: when a man is reckless without understanding, he is harmed, when with understanding, he is benefitted. — Yes.

S: The same is true of moderation and mental quickness; when they are learned and disciplined with understanding they are beneficial, but without under-standing they are harmful? — Very much so.

c   S: Therefore, in a word, all that the soul undertakes and endures, if directed by wisdom, ends in happiness, but if directed by ignorance, it ends in the opposite? — That is likely.

S: If then virtue is something in the soul and it must be beneficial, it must be knowledge, since all the qualities of the soul are in themselves neither beneficial nor harmful, but accompanied by wisdom or folly they become harmful or beneficial. This argument shows that virtue, being beneficial, must be a kind of wisdom. — I agree.

d

S: Furthermore, those other things we were mentioning just now, wealth and the like, are at times good and at times harmful. Just as for the rest of the soul the direction of wisdom makes things beneficial, but harmful if directed by folly, so in these cases, if the soul uses and directs them right it makes them beneficial, but bad use makes them harmful? — Quite so.

e

S: The wise soul directs them right, the foolish soul wrongly? — That is so.

S: So one may say this about everything: all other human activities depend on the soul, and those of the soul itself depend on wisdom if they are to be good. According to this argument the beneficial would be wisdom, and we say that virtue is beneficial? — Certainly.

89

S: Virtue then, as a whole or in part, is wisdom?

M: What you say, Socrates, seems to me quite right.

S: Then, if that is so, the good are not so by nature? — I do not think they are.

S: For if they were, this would follow: if the good were so by nature, we would have people who knew which among the young were by nature good; we would take those whom they had pointed out and guard them in the Acropolis, sealing them up there much more carefully than gold so that no one could corrupt them, and when they reached maturity they would be useful to their cities. — Reasonable enough, Socrates.

b

S: Since the good are not good by nature, does learning make them so?

c

M: Necessarily, as I now think, Socrates, and clearly, on our hypothesis if virtue is knowledge, it can be taught.

S: Perhaps, by Zeus, but may it be that we were not right to agree to this?

M: Yet it seemed to be right at the time.

S: We should not only think it right at the time, but also now and in the future if it is to be at all sound.

M: What is the difficulty? What do you have in mind that you do not like about it and doubt that virtue is knowledge?

d

S: I will tell you, Meno, I am not saying that it is wrong to say that virtue is teachable if it is knowledge, but look whether it is reasonable of me to doubt whether it is knowledge. Tell me this: if not only virtue but anything whatever can be taught, should there not be of necessity people who teach it and people who learn it? — I think so.

S: Then again, if on the contrary there are no teachers or learners of something, we should be right to assume that the subject cannot be taught?

e

M: Quite so, but do you think that there are no teachers of virtue?

S: I have often tried to find out whether there were any teachers of it, but in spite of all my efforts I cannot find any. I have searched for them with the help of many people, especially those whom I believed to be most experienced in this matter. And now, Meno, Anytus[16] here has opportunely come to sit down by us. Let us share our search with him. It would be reasonable for us to do so, for Anytus, in the first place, is the son of Anthemion, a man of wealth and wisdom, who did not become rich automatically or as the result of a gift like Ismenias the Theban, who recently acquired the possessions of Polycrates, but through his own wisdom and efforts. Further, he was not an arrogant or puffed up or offensive citizen in other ways, but he was a well-mannered and well-behaved man. Also he gave our friend here a good upbringing and education, as the majority of Athenians believe, for they elected him to the highest offices. It is right then to look for the teachers of virtue with the help of men such as he, whether there are any and if so who they are. Do you therefore, Anytus, join me and your guest friend Meno here, in our inquiry as to who are the teachers of virtue. Look at it in this way: if we wanted Meno to become a good physician, to what teachers would we send him? Would we not send him to the physicians? — Certainly.

S: And if we wanted him to be a good shoemaker, to shoemakers? — Yes.

S: And so with other pursuits? — Certainly.

S: Tell me again on this same topic, like this: we say that we would be right to send him to the physicians if we want him to become a physician; whenever we say that, we mean that it would be reasonable to send him to those who practise the craft rather than to those who do not, and to those who exact fees for this very practice and have shown themselves to be teachers of anyone who wishes to come to them and learn. It is not with this in mind that we would be right to send him? — Yes.

S: And the same is true about flute-playing and the other crafts? It would be very foolish for those who want to make someone a flute-player to refuse to send him to those who profess to teach the craft and make money at it, but to send him to make trouble for others by seeking to learn from those who do not claim to be teachers or have a single pupil in that subject which we want the one we send to learn from them? Do you not think it very unreasonable to do so? — By Zeus I do, and also very ignorant.

S: Quite right. However, you can now deliberate with me about our guest friend Meno here. He has been telling me for some time, Anytus, that he longs to acquire that wisdom and virtue which enables men to manage their households and their cities well, to take care of their parents, to know how to welcome and to send away both citizens and strangers as a good man should. Consider to whom we should be right to send him to learn this virtue. Or is it obvious in view of what was said just now that we should send him to those who profess to be teachers of virtue and have shown themselves to be available to any Greek who wishes to learn, and for this fix a fee and exact it?

A: And who do you say these are, Socrates?

S: You surely know yourself that they are those whom men call sophists.

A: By Heracles, hush, Socrates. May no one of my household or friends,

---

16. [Anytus was a successful democratic politician in Athens. His success must have come after the restoration of democratic government in Athens in 403 B.C., whereas Meno himself joined the expedition of Cyrus in 401 and never came back to Greece. So the conversation must have taken place about 402. Anytus was one of Socrates' accusers in 399, and Plato obviously expects his readers to have this in mind.]

whether citizen or stranger, be mad enough to go to these people and be harmed by them, for they clearly cause the ruin and corruption of their followers.

S: How do you mean, Anytus? Are these people, alone of those who claim the knowledge to benefit one, so different from the others that they not only do not benefit what one entrusts to them but on the contrary corrupt it, even though they obviously expect to make money from the process? I find I cannot believe you, for I d know that one man, Protagoras, made more money from this knowledge of his than Phidias who made such notably fine works, and ten other sculptors. Surely what you say is extraordinary, if those who mend old sandals and restore clothes would be found out within the month if they returned the clothes and sandals in a worse state e than they received them; if they did this they would soon die of starvation, but the whole of Greece has not noticed for forty years that Protagoras corrupts those who frequent him and sends them away in a worse moral condition than he received them. I believe that he was nearly seventy when he died and had practised his craft for forty years. During all that time to this very day his reputation has stood high; and not only Protagoras but a great many others, some born before him and some 92 still alive today. Are we to say that you maintain that they deceive and harm the young knowingly, or that they themselves are not aware of it? Are we to deem those whom some people consider the wisest of men to be so mad as that?

A: They are far from being mad, Socrates. It is much rather those among the young who pay their fees who are mad, and even more the relatives who entrust their young to them and most of all the cities who allow them to come in and do not b drive out any citizen or stranger who attempts to behave in this manner.

S: Has some sophist wronged you, Anytus, or why are you so hard on them?

A: No, by Zeus, I have never met one of them, nor would I allow any one of my people to do so.

S: Are you then altogether without any experience of these men?

A: And may I remain so.

S: How then, my good sir, can you know whether there is any good in their in- c struction or not, if you are altogether without experience of it?

A: Easily, for I know who they are, whether I have experience of them or not.

S: Perhaps you are a wizard, Anytus, for I wonder, from what you yourself say, how else you know about these things. However, let us not try to find out who the men are whose company would make Meno wicked—let them be the sophists if you d like—but tell us, and benefit your family friend here by telling him, to whom he should go in so large a city to acquire, to any worthwhile degree, the virtue I was just now describing.

A: Why did you not tell him yourself?

S: I did mention those whom I thought to be teachers of it, but you say I am wrong, and perhaps you are right. You tell him in your turn to whom among the e Athenians he should go. Tell him the name of anyone you want.

A: Why give him the name of one individual? Any Athenian gentleman he may meet, if he is willing to be persuaded, will make him a better man than the sophists would.

S: And have these gentlemen become virtuous automatically, without learning from anyone, and are they able to teach others what they themselves never learned? 93

A: I believe that these men have learned from those who were gentlemen before them; or do you not think that there are many good men in this city?

S: I believe, Anytus, that there are many men here who are good at public affairs, and that there have been as many in the past, but have they been good teachers of their own virtue? That is the point we are discussing, not whether there are good men here or not, or whether there have been in the past, but we have been
b   investigating for some time whether virtue can be taught. And in the course of that investigation we are inquiring whether the good men of today and of the past knew how to pass on to another the virtue they themselves possessed, or whether a man cannot pass it on or receive it from another. This is what Meno and I have been investigating for some time. Look at it this way, from what you yourself have said.
c   Would you not say that Themistocles was a good man? — Yes. Even the best of men.

S: And therefore a good teacher of his own virtue if anyone was?

A: I think so, if he wanted to be.

S: But do you think he did not want some other people to be worthy men, and especially his own son? Or do you think he begrudged him this, and deliberately
d   did not pass on to him his own virtue? Have you not heard that Themistocles taught his son Cleophantus to be a good horseman? He could remain standing upright on horseback and shoot javelins from that position and do many other remarkable things which his father had him taught and made skillful at, all of which required good teachers. Have you not heard this from your elders? — I have.

S: So one could not blame the poor natural talents of the son for his failure in
e   virtue? — Perhaps not.

S: But have you ever heard anyone, young or old, say that Cleophantus, the son of Themistocles, was a good and wise man at the same pursuits as his father? — Never.

S: Are we to believe that he wanted to educate his son in those other things but not to do better than his neighbors in that skill which he himself possessed, if indeed virtue can be taught? — Perhaps not, by Zeus.

S: And yet he was, as you yourself agree, among the best teachers of virtue in
94   the past. Let us consider another man, Aristides, the son of Lysimachus. Do you not agree that he was good? — I very definitely do.

S: He too gave his own son Lysimachus the best Athenian education in matters which are the business of teachers, and do you think he made him a better man than anyone else? For you have been in his company and seen the kind of man he is. Or
b   take Pericles, a man of such magnificent wisdom. You know that he brought up two sons, Paralus and Xanthippus? — I know.

S: You also know that he taught them to be as good horsemen as any Athenian, that he educated them in the arts, in gymnastics, and in all else that was a matter of skill not to be inferior to anyone, but did he not want to make them good men? I think he did, but this could not be taught. And lest you think that only a few most inferior Athenians are incapable in this respect, reflect that Thucydides[17] too
c   brought up two sons, Melesias and Stephanus, that he educated them well in all

17. [Not the historian but Thucydides, the son of Melesias, an Athenian statesman who was an opponent of Pericles and who was ostracized in 440 B.C.]

other things. They were the best wrestlers in Athens—he entrusted the one to Xanthias and the other to Eudorus, who were thought to be the best wrestlers of the day, or do you not remember?

A: I remember I have heard that said.

S: It is surely clear that he would not have taught his boys what it costs money to teach, but have failed to teach them what costs nothing—making them good men—if that could be taught? Or was Thucydides perhaps an inferior person who had not many friends among the Athenians and the allies? He belonged to a great house; he had great influence in the city and among the other Greeks, so that if virtue could be taught he would have found the man who could make his sons good men, be it a citizen or a stranger, if he himself did not have the time because of his public concerns. But, friend Anytus, virtue can certainly not be taught.

A: I think, Socrates, that you easily speak ill of people. I would advise you, if you will listen to me, to be careful. Perhaps also in another city, and certainly here, it is easier to injure people than to benefit them. I think you know that yourself.

S: I think, Meno, that Anytus is angry, and I am not at all surprised. He thinks, to begin with, that I am slandering those men, and then he believes himself to be one of them. If he ever realizes what slander is, he will cease from anger, but he does not know it now. You tell me, are there not worthy men among your people? — Certainly.

S: Well now, are they willing to offer themselves to the young as teachers? Do they agree they are teachers, and that virtue can be taught?

M: No, by Zeus, Socrates, but sometimes you would hear them say that it can be taught, at other times, that it cannot.

S: Should we say that they are teachers on this subject, when they do not even agree on this point? — I do not think so, Socrates.

S: Further, do you think that these sophists, who along profess to be so, are teachers of virtue?

M: I admire this most in Gorgias, Socrates, that you would never hear him promising this. Indeed, he ridicules the others when he hears them making this claim. He thinks one should make people clever speakers.

S: You do not think then that the sophists are teachers?

M: I cannot tell, Socrates; like most people, at times I think they are, at other times I think they are not.

S: Do you know that not only you and the other public men at times think that it can be taught, at other times that it cannot, but that the poet Theognis[18] says the same thing? — Where?

S: In his elegiacs: "Eat and drink with these men, and keep their company. Please those whose power is great, for you will learn goodness from the good. If you mingle with bad men you will lose even what wit you possess." You see that here he speaks as if virtue can be taught? — So it appears.

S: Elsewhere, he changes somewhat: "if this could be done" he says, "and intelligence could be instilled," somehow those who could do this "would collect large and numerous fees," and further: "Never would a bad son be born of a good

18. [Theognis was a poet of mid-sixth century B.C. A collection of poems is extant (about twelve hundred lines), but the authenticity of a good deal of it is doubtful.]

father, for he would be persuaded by wise words, but you will never make a bad man good by teaching." You realize that the poet is contradicting himself on the same subject? — He seems to be.

S: Can you mention any other subject of which those who claim to be teachers not only are not recognized to be teachers of others but are not recognized to have knowledge of it themselves, and are thought to be poor in the very matter which they profess to teach? Or any other subject of which those who are recognized as worthy teachers at one time say it can be taught and at other times that it cannot? Would you say that people who are so confused about a subject can be effective teachers of it? — No, by Zeus, I would not.

S: If then neither the sophists nor the worthy people themselves are teachers of this subject, clearly there would be no others? — I do not think there are.

S: If there are no teachers, neither are there pupils? — As you say.

S: And we agreed that a subject that has neither teachers nor pupils is not teachable? — We have so agreed.

S: Now there seem to be no teachers of virtue anywhere? — That is so.

S: If there are no teachers, there are no learners? — That seems so.

S: Then virtue cannot be taught?

M: Apparently not, if we have investigated this correctly. I certainly wonder, Socrates, whether there are no good men either, or in what way good men come to be.

S: We are probably poor specimens, you and I, Meno. Gorgias has not adequately educated you, nor Prodicus me. We must then at all costs turn our attention to ourselves and find someone who will in some way make us better. I say this in view of our recent investigation, for it is ridiculous that we failed to see that it is not under the guidance of knowledge that men succeed in their affairs, and that is perhaps why the knowledge of how good men come to be escapes us.

M: How do you mean, Socrates?

S: I mean this: we were right to agree that good men must be beneficent, and that this could not be otherwise. Is that not so? — Yes.

S: And that they will be beneficent and useful if they give us correct guidance in our affairs. To this too we were right to agree? — Yes.

S: But that one cannot guide correctly if one does not have knowledge, to this our agreement is likely to be incorrect. — How do you mean?

S: I will tell you. A man who knew the way to Larissa, or anywhere else you like, and went there and guided others would surely lead them well and correctly? — Certainly.

S: What if someone had had a correct opinion as to which was the way but had not gone there nor indeed had knowledge of it, would he not also lead correctly? — Certainly.

S: And as long as he has the right opinion about that of which the other has knowledge, he will not be a worse guide than the one who knows, as he has a true opinion, though not knowledge. — In no way worse.

S: So true opinion is in no way a worse guide to correct action than knowledge? It is this that we omitted in our investigation of the nature of virtue, when we said that only knowledge can lead to correct action, for true opinion can do so also. — So it seems.

S: So correct opinion is no less useful than knowledge?

M: Yes, to this extent, Socrates. But the man who has knowledge will always succeed, whereas he who has true opinion will only succeed at times.

S: How do you mean? Will he who has the right opinion not always succeed, as long as his opinion is right?

M: That appears to be so of necessity, and it makes me wonder, Socrates, this being the case, why knowledge is prized far more highly than right opinion, and why they are different.   d

S: Do you know why you wonder, or shall I tell you? — By all means tell me.

S: It is because you have paid no attention to the statues of Daedalus, but perhaps there are none in Thessaly.

S: What do you have in mind when you say this?

S: That they too run away and escape if one does not tie them down but remain in place if tied down. — So what?   e

S: To acquire an untied work of Daedalus is not worth much, like acquiring a runaway slave, for it does not remain, but it is worth much if tied down, for his works are very beautiful. What am I thinking of when I say this? True beliefs. For true beliefs, as long as they remain, are a fine thing and all they do is good, but they are not willing to remain long, and they escape from a man's mind, so that they are   98 not worth much until one ties them down by (giving) an account of the reason why. And that, Meno my friend, is recollection, as we previously agreed. After they are tied down, in the first place they become knowledge, and then they remain in place. That is why knowledge is prized higher than correct opinion, and knowledge differs from correct opinion in being tied down.

M: Yes, by Zeus, Socrates, it seems to be something like that.

S: Indeed, I too speak as one who does not have knowledge but is guessing.   b However, I certainly do not think I am guessing that right opinion is a different thing than knowledge. If I claim to know anything else—and I would make that claim about few things—I would put this down as one of the things I know. — Rightly so, Socrates.

S: Well then, is it not correct that when true opinion guides the course of every action, it does no worse than knowledge? — I think you are right in this too.

S: Correct opinion is then neither inferior to knowledge nor less useful in di-   c recting actions, nor is the man who has it less so than he who has knowledge. — That is so.

S: And we agreed that the good man is beneficent? — Yes.

S: Since then it is not only through knowledge but also through right opinion that men are good, and beneficial to their cities when they are, and neither knowledge nor true opinion come to men by nature but are acquired—or do you think   d either of these comes by nature? — I do not think so.

S: Then if they do not come by nature, men are not so by nature either. — Surely not.

S: As goodness does not come by nature, we inquired next whether it could be taught. — Yes.

S: We thought it could be taught, if it was knowledge? — Yes.

S: And that it was knowledge if it could be taught? — Quite so.

e   S: And that if there were teachers of it, it could be taught, but if there were not, it was not teachable? — That is so.

S: And then we agreed that there were no teachers of it? — We did.

S: So we agreed that it was neither teachable nor knowledge? — Quite so.

S: But we certainly agree that virtue is a good thing? — Yes.

S: And that which guides correctly is both useful and good? — Certainly.

99   S: And that only these two things, true belief and knowledge, guide correctly, and that if a man possesses these he gives correct guidance. The things that turn out right by some chance are not due to human guidance, but where there is correct human guidance it is due to two things, true belief or knowledge. — I think that is so.

S: Now because it cannot be taught, virtue no longer seems to be knowledge? — It seems not.

b   S: So one of the two good and useful things has been excluded, and knowledge is not the guide in public affairs? — I do not think so.

S: So it is not by some kind of wisdom, or by being wise, that such men lead their cities, those such as Themistocles and those mentioned by Anytus just now? That is the reason why they cannot make others be like themselves, because it is not knowledge which makes them what they are.

M: It is likely to be as you say, Socrates.

S: Therefore, if it is not through knowledge, the only alternative is that it is

c   through right opinion that statesmen follow the right course for their cities. As regards knowledge, they are no different from soothsayers and prophets. They too say many true things when inspired, but they have no knowledge of what they are saying. — That is probably so.

S: And so, Meno, is it right to call divine these men who, without any understanding, are right in much that is of importance in what they say and do? — Certainly.

S: We should be right to call divine also those soothsayers and prophets whom

d   we just mentioned, and all the poets, and we should call no less divine and inspired those public men who are no less under the gods' influence and possession, as their speeches lead to success in many important matters, though they have no knowledge of what they are saying. — Quite so.

S: Women too, Meno, call good men divine, and the Spartans, when they eulogize someone, say "This man is divine."

e   M: And they appear to be right, Socrates, though perhaps Anytus here will be annoyed with you for saying so.

S: I do not mind that; we shall talk to him again, but if we were right in the way in which we spoke and investigated in this whole discussion, virtue would be neither an inborn quality nor taught, but comes to those who possess it as a gift from the gods which is not accompanied by understanding, unless there is someone

100   among our statesmen who can make another into a statesman. If there were one, he could be said to be among the living as Homer said Teiresias was among the dead, namely, that "he alone retained his wits while the others flitted about like shadows." In the same manner such a man would, as far as virtue is concerned, here also be the only true reality compared, as it were, with shadows.

M: I think that is an excellent way to put it, Socrates.

S: It follows from this reasoning, Meno, that virtue apears to be present in those of us who may possess it as a gift from the gods. We shall have clear knowledge of this when, before we investigate how it comes to be present in men, we first try to find out what virtue in itself is. But now the time has come for me to go. You convince your guest friend Anytus here of these very things of which you have yourself been convinced, in order that he may be more amenable. If you succeed, you will also confer a benefit upon the Athenians.

EUTHYPHRO

2   EUTHYPHRO:[1]   What's new, Socrates, to make you leave your usual haunts in the Lyceum and spend your time here by the king-archon's court? Surely you are not prosecuting any one before the king archon as I am?

    SOCRATES: The Athenians do not call this a prosecution but an indictment, Euthyphro.

b   E: What is this you say? Someone must have indicted you, for you are not going to tell me that you have indicted someone else.

    S: No indeed.

    E: But someone else has indicted you?

    S: Quite so.

    E: Who is he?

    S: I do not really know him myself, Euthyphro. He is apparently young and unknown. They call him Meletus, I believe. He belongs to the Pitthean deme, if you know anyone from that deme called Meletus, with long hair, not much of a beard, and a rather aquiline nose.

    E: I don't know him, Socrates. What charge does he bring against you?

c   S: What charge? A not ignoble one I think, for it is no small thing for a young man to have knowledge of such an important subject. He says he knows how our young men are corrupted and who corrupts them. He is likely to be wise, and when he sees my ignorance corrupting his contemporaries, he proceeds to accuse me to d the city as to their mother. I think he is the only one of our public men to start out the right way, for it is right to care first that the young should be as good as possible, just as a good farmer is likely to take care of the young plants first, and of the others later. So, too, Meletus first gets rid of us who corrupt the growth of the young, as he 3 says, and then afterwards he will obviously take care of the older and become a source of great blessings for the city, as seems likely to happen to one who started out this way.

    E: I could wish this were true, Socrates, but I fear the opposite may happen. He seems to me to start out by harming the very heart of the city by attempting to wrong you. Tell me, what does he say you do to corrupt the young?

b   S: Strange things, to hear him tell it, for he says that I am a maker of gods, and on the ground that I create new gods while not believing in the old gods, he has indicted me for their sake, as he puts it.

    E: I understand, Socrates. This is because you say that the divine sign keeps

Reprinted from *The Trial & Death of Socrates,* translated by G.M.A. Grube (Indianapolis: Hackett Publishing Company, 1975), by permission of the publisher.

1. [We know nothing about Euthyphro except what we can gather from this dialogue. He is obviously a professional priest who considers himself an expert on ritual and on piety generally, and, it seems, is generally so considered. One Euthyphro is mentioned in Plato's *Cratylus* (396d) who is given to *enthousiasmos,* inspiration or possession, but we cannot be sure that it is the same person.—G.M.A.G.]

coming to you.[2] So he has written this indictment against you as one who makes innovations in religious matters, and he comes to court to slander you, knowing that such things are easily misrepresented to the crowd. The same is true in my case. Whenever I speak of divine matters in the assembly and foretell the future, they laugh me down as if I were crazy; and yet I have foretold nothing that did not happen. Nevertheless, they envy all of us who do this. One need not worry about them, but meet them head on.

S:　My dear Euthyphro, to be laughed at does not matter perhaps, for the Athenians do not mind anyone they think clever, as long as he does not teach his own wisdom, but if they think that he makes others to be like himself they get angry, whether through envy, as you say, or for some other reason.

E:　I have certainly no desire to test their feelings toward me in this matter.

S:　Perhaps you seem to make yourself but rarely available, and not to be willing to teach your own wisdom, but my liking for people makes them think that I pour out to anybody anything I have to say, not only without charging a fee but appearing glad to reward anyone who is willing to listen. If then they were intending to laugh at me, as you say they laugh at you, there would be nothing unpleasant in their spending their time in court laughing and jesting, but if they are going to be serious, the outcome is not clear except to you prophets.

E:　Perhaps it will come to nothing, Socrates, and you will fight your case as you think best, as I think I will mine.

S:　What is your case, Euthyphro? Are you the defendant or the prosecutor?

E:　The prosecutor.

S:　Whom do you prosecute?

E:　One whom I am thought crazy to prosecute.

S:　Are you pursuing someone who will easily escape you?

E:　Far from it, for he is quite old.

S:　Who is it?

E:　My father.

S:　My dear sir! Your own father?

E:　Certainly.

S:　What is the charge? What is the case about?

E:　Murder, Socrates.

S:　Good heavens! Certainly, Euthyphro, most men would not know how they could do this and be right. It is not the part of anyone to do this, but of one who is far advanced in wisdom.

E:　Yes by Zeus, Socrates, that is so.

S:　Is then the man your father killed one of your relatives? Or is that obvious, for you would not prosecute your father for the murder of a stranger.

E:　It is ridiculous, Socrates, for you to think that it makes any difference whether the victim is a stranger or a relative. One should only watch whether the

---

2. [In Plato, Socrates always speaks of his divine sign or voice as intervening to prevent him from doing or saying something (e.g., *Apology* 31d), but never positively. The popular view was that it enabled him to foretell the future, and Euthyphro here represents that view. Note, however, that Socrates dissociates himself from "you prophets" (3e).]

killer acted justly or not; if he acted justly, let him go, but if not, one should prosecute, even if the killer shares your hearth and table. The pollution is the same if you knowingly
c   keep company with such a man and do not cleanse yourself and him by bringing him to justice. The victim was a dependent of mine, and when we were farming in Naxos he was a servant of ours. He killed one of our household slaves in drunken anger, so my father bound him hand and foot and threw him in a ditch, then sent a man here to enquire from the priest what should be done. During that time he gave no thought or care to the bound man, as being a killer, and it was no matter if he died, which he did. Hunger and cold and
d   his bonds caused his death before the messenger came back from the seer. Both my father and my other relatives are angry that I am prosecuting my father for murder on behalf of a murderer, when he hadn't even killed him, they say, and even if he had, the dead man does not deserve a thought, since he was a killer. For, they say, it is impious for a son to prosecute his father for murder. But their ideas of the divine attitude to piety and impiety
e   are wrong, Socrates.

S: Whereas, by Zeus, Euthyphro, you think that your knowledge of the divine, and of piety and impiety, is so accurate that, when those things happened as you say, you have no fear of having acted impiously in bringing your father to trial?

E: I should be of no use, Socrates, and Euthyphro would not be superior to the
5   majority of men, if I did not have accurate knowledge of all such things.

S: It is indeed most important, my admirable Euthyphro, that I should become your pupil, and as regards this indictment challenge Meletus about these very things and say to him: that in the past too I considered knowledge about the divine to be most important, and that now that he says that I improvise and innovate about the gods I have become your pupil. I would say to him: "If, Meletus, you agree that
b   Euthyphro is wise in these matters, consider me, too, to have the right beliefs and do not bring me to trial. If you do not think so, then prosecute that teacher of mine for corrupting the older men, me and his own father, by teaching me and by exhorting and punishing him. If he is not convinced, does not discharge me, or indicts you instead of me, I shall repeat the same challenge in court.

E: Yes by Zeus, Socrates, and, if he should try to indict me, I think I would find
c   his weak spots and the talk in court would be about him rather than about me.

S: It is because I realize this that I am eager to become your pupil, my dear friend. I know that other people as well as this Meletus do not even seem to notice you, whereas he sees me so sharply and clearly that he indicts me for ungodliness. So tell me now, by Zeus, what you just now maintained you clearly knew: what kind
d   of thing do you say that godliness and ungodliness are, both as regards murder and other things; or is the pious not the same and alike in every action, and the impious the opposite of all that is pious and like itself, and everything that is to be impious presents us with one form[3] or appearance in so far as it is impious?

E: Most certainly, Socrates.

---

3. [This is the kind of passage that makes it easier for us to follow the transition from Socrates' universal definitions to the Platonic theory of separately existent eternal universal Forms. The words *eidos* and *idea*, the technical terms for the Platonic Forms, commonly mean physical stature or bodily appearance. As we apply a common epithet, in this case pious, to different actions or things, these must have a common characteristic, present a common appearance or form, to justify the use of the same term; but in the early dialogues, as here, it seems to be thought of as immanent in the particulars and without separate existence. The same is true of 6d where the word "Form" is also used.]

S: Tell me then, what is the pious, and what the impious, do you say?

E: I say that the pious is to do what I am doing now, to prosecute the wrongdoer, be it about murder or temple robbery or anything else, whether the wrongdoer is your father or your mother or anyone else; not to prosecute is impious. And observe, Socrates, that I can quote the law as a great proof that this is so. I have already said to others that such actions are right, not to favour the ungodly, whoever they are. These people themselves believe that Zeus is the best and most just of the gods, yet they agree that he bound his father because he unjustly swallowed his sons, and that he in turn castrated his father for similar reasons. But they are angry with me because I am prosecuting my father for his wrongdoing. They contradict themselves in what they say about the gods and about me.

S: Indeed, Euthyphro, this is the reason why I am a defendant in the case, because I find it hard to accept things like that being said about the gods, and it is likely to be the reason why I shall be told I do wrong. Now, however, if you, who have full knowledge of such things, share their opinions, then we must agree with them too, it would seem. For what are we to say, we who agree that we ourselves have no knowledge of them? Tell me, by the god of friendship, do you really believe these things are true?

E: Yes, Socrates, and so are even more surprising things, of which the majority has no knowledge.

S: And do you believe that there really is war among the gods, and terrible enmities and battles, and other such things as are told by the poets, and other sacred stories such as are embroidered by good writers and by representations of which the robe of the goddess is adorned when it is carried up to the Acropolis. Are we to say these things are true, Euthyphro?

E: Not only these, Socrates, but, as I was saying just now, I will, if you wish, relate many other things about the gods which I know will amaze you.

S: I should not be surprised, but you will tell me these at leisure some other time. For now, try to tell me more clearly what I was asking just now, for, my friend, you did not teach me adequately when I asked you what the pious was, but you told me that what you are doing now, prosecuting your father for murder, is pious.

E: And I told the truth, Socrates.

S: Perhaps. You agree, however, that there are many other pious actions.

E: There are.

S: Bear in mind then that I did not bid you tell me one or two of the many pious actions but that form itself that makes all pious actions pious, for you agreed that all impious actions are impious and all pious actions pious through one form, or don't you remember?

E: I do.

S: Tell me then what this form itself is, so that I may look upon it, and using it as a model, say that any action of yours or another's that is of that kind is pious, and if it is not that it is not.

E: If that is how you want it, Socrates, that is how I will tell you.

S: That is what I want.

E: Well then, what is dear to the gods is pious, what is not is impious.

S: Splendid, Euthyphro! You have now answered in the way I wanted.

Whether your answer is true I do not know yet, but you will obviously show me that what you say is true.

E: Certainly.

S: Come then, let us examine what we mean. An action or a man dear to the gods is pious, but an action or a man hated by the gods is impious. They are not the same, but opposites, the pious and the impious. Is that not so?

E: It is indeed.

S: And that seems to be a good statement?

b   E: I think so, Socrates.

S: We have also stated that the gods are in a state of discord, that they are at odds with each other, Euthyphro, and that they are at enmity with each other. Has that, too, been said?

E: It has.

S: What are the subjects of difference that cause hatred and anger? Let us look at it this way. If you and I were to differ about numbers as to which is the greater, would this difference make us enemies and angry with each other, or would we pro-

c   ceed to count and soon resolve our difference about this?

E: We would certainly do so.

S: Again, if we differed about the larger and the smaller, we would turn to measurement and soon cease to differ.

E: That is so.

S: And about the heavier and the lighter, we would resort to weighing and be reconciled.

E: Of course.

S: What subject of difference would make us angry and hostile to each other if we were unable to come to a decision? Perhaps you do not have an answer ready,

d   but examine as I tell you whether these subjects are the just and the unjust, the beautiful and the ugly, the good and the bad. Are these not the subjects of difference about which, when we are unable to come to a satisfactory decision, you and I and other men become hostile to each other whenever we do?

E: That is the difference, Socrates, about those subjects.

S: What about the gods, Euthyphro? If indeed they have differences, will it not be about these same subjects?

E: It certainly must be so.

e   S: Then according to your argument, my good Euthyphro, different gods consider different things to be just, beautiful, ugly, good and bad, for they would not be at odds with one another unless they differed about these subjects, would they?

E: You are right.

S: And they like what each of them considers beautiful, good, and just, and hate the opposites of these?

E: Certainly.

S: But you say that the same things are considered just by some gods and

8   unjust by others, and as they dispute about these things they are at odds and at war with each other. Is that not so?

E: It is.

S: The same things then are loved by the gods and hated by the gods, and would be both god-loved and god-hated.

E: It seems likely.

S: And the same things would be both pious and impious, according to this argument?

E: I'm afraid so.

S: So you did not answer my question, you surprising man. I did not ask you what same thing is both pious and impious, and it appears that what is loved by the gods is also hated by them. So it is in no way surprising if your present action, name- b ly punishing your father, may be pleasing to Zeus but displeasing to Kronos and Ouranos, pleasing to Hephaestus but displeasing to Hera, and so with any other gods who differ from each other on this subject.

E: I think, Socrates, that on this subject no gods would differ from one another, that whoever has killed anyone unjustly should pay the penalty.

S: Well now, Euthyphro, have you ever heard any man maintaining that one c who has killed or done anything else unjustly should not pay the penalty?

E: They never cease to dispute on this subject, both elsewhere and in the courts, for when they have committed many wrongs they do and say anything to avoid the penalty.

S: Do they agree they have done wrong, Euthyphro, and in spite of so agreeing do they nevertheless say they should not be punished?

E: No, they do not agree on that point.

S: So they do not say or do anything. For they do not venture to say this, or dispute that they must not pay the penalty if they have done wrong, but I think they deny doing wrong. Is that not so? d

E: That is true.

S: Then they do not dispute that the wrongdoer must be punished, but they may disagree as to who the wrongdoer is, what he did and when.

E: You are right.

S: Do not the gods have the same experience, if indeed they are at odds with each other about the just and the unjust, as your argument maintains? Some assert that they wrong one another, while others deny it, but no one among gods or men ventures to say that the wrongdoer must not be punished. e

E: Yes, that is true, Socrates, as to the main point.

S: And those who disagree, whether men or gods, dispute about each action, if indeed the gods disagree. Some say it is done justly, others unjustly. Is that not so?

E: Yes indeed.

S: Come now, my dear Euthyphro, tell me, too, that I may become wiser, what 9 proof you have that all the gods consider that man to have been killed unjustly who became a murderer while in your service, was bound by the master of his victim, and died in his bonds before the one who bound him found out from the seers what was to be done with him, and that it is right for a son to denounce and to prosecute his father on behalf of such a man. Come, try to show me a clear sign that all the gods definitely believe this action to be right. If you can give me adequate proof of b this, I shall never cease to extol your wisdom.

E: This is perhaps no light task, Socrates, though I could show you very clearly.

S: I understand that you think me more dull-witted than the jury, as you will obviously show them that these actions were unjust and that all the gods hate such actions.

E: I will show it to them clearly, Socrates, if only they will listen to me.

c   S: They will listen if they think you show them well. But this thought came to me as I was speaking, and I am examining it, saying to myself: "If Euthyphro shows me conclusively that all the gods consider such a death unjust, to what greater extent have I learned from him the nature of piety and impiety? This action would then, it seems, be hated by the gods, but the pious and the impious were not thereby now defined, for what is hated by the gods has also been shown to be loved by them." So I will not insist on this point; let us assume, if you wish, that all the gods

d   consider this unjust and that they all hate it. However, is this the correction we are making in our discussion, that what all the gods hate is impious, and what they all love is pious, and that what some gods love and others hate is neither or both? Is that how you now wish us to define piety and impiety?

E: What prevents us from doing so, Socrates?

S: For my part nothing, Euthyphro, but you look whether on your part this proposal will enable you to teach me most easily what you promised.

e   E: I would certainly say that the pious is what all the gods love, and the opposite, what all the gods hate, is the impious.

S: Then let us again examine whether that is a sound statement, or do we let it pass, and if one of us, or someone else, merely says that this is so, do we accept that it is so? Or should we examine what the speaker means?

E: We must examine it, but I certainly think that this is now a fine statement.

10   S: We shall soon know better whether it is. Consider this: Is the pious loved by the gods because it is pious, or is it pious because it is loved by the gods?

E: I don't know what you mean, Socrates.

S: I shall try to explain more clearly: we speak of something being carried[4] and something carrying, of something being led and something leading, of something being seen and something seeing, and you understand that these things are all different from one another and how they differ?

E: I think I do.

S: So there is something being loved and something loving, and the loving is a different thing.

E: Of course.

---

4. [This is the present participle form of the verb *pheromenon*, literally *being-carried*. The following passage is somewhat obscure, especially in translation, but the general meaning is clear. Plato points out that this participle simply indicates the object of an action of carrying, seeing, loving, etc. It follows from the action and adds nothing new, the action being prior to it, not following from it, and a thing is said to be loved because someone loves it, not vice versa. To say therefore that the pious is being loved by the gods says no more than that the gods love it. Euthyphro, however, also agrees that the pious is loved by the gods because of its nature (because it is pious), but the fact of its being loved by the gods does not define that nature, and as a definition is therefore unsatisfactory. It only indicates a quality or affect of the pious, and the pious is therefore still to be defined (11a7).]

S: Tell me then whether that which is being carried is being carried because someone carries it or for some other reason.

E: No, that is the reason.

S: And that which is being led is so because someone leads it, and that which is being seen because someone sees it?

E: Certainly.

S: It is not seen by someone because it is being seen but on the contrary it is being seen because someone sees it, nor is it because it is being led that someone leads it but because someone leads it that it is being led; nor does someone carry an object because it is being carried, but it is being carried because someone carries it. Is what I want to say clear, Euthyphro? I want to say this, namely, that if anything comes to be, or is affected, it does not come to be because it is coming to be, but it is coming to be because it comes to be; nor is it affected because it is being affected but because something affects it. Or do you not agree?

E: I do.

S: What is being loved is either something that comes to be or something that is affected by something?

E: Certainly.

S: So it is in the same case as the things just mentioned; it is not loved by those who love it because it is being loved, but is being loved because they love it?

E: Necessarily.

S: What then do we say about the pious, Euthyphro? Surely that it is loved by all the gods, according to what you say?

E: Yes.

S: Is it loved because it is pious, or for some other reason?

E: For no other reason.

S: It is loved then because it is pious, but it is not pious because it is loved?[5]

E: Apparently.

S: And because it is loved by the gods it is being loved and is dear to the gods?

E: Of course.

S: The god-beloved is then not the same as the pious, Euthyphro, nor the pious the same as the god-beloved, as you say it is, but one differs from the other.

E: How so, Socrates?

S: Because we agree that the pious is beloved for the reason that it is pious, but it is not pious because it is loved. Is that not so?

b

c

d

e

---

5. [I quote an earlier comment of mine on this passage: "it gives in a nutshell a point of view from which Plato never departed. Whatever the gods may be, they must by their very nature love the right because it is right." They have no choice in the matter. "This separation of the dynamic power of the gods from the ultimate reality, this setting up of absolute values above the gods themselves was not as unnatural to a Greek as it would be to us . . . The gods who ruled on Olympus . . . were not creators but created beings. As in Homer, Zeus must obey the balance of Necessity, so the Platonic gods must conform to an eternal scale of values. They did not create them, cannot alter them, cannot indeed wish to do so." (*Plato's Thought*, Boston: Beacon Press, 1958, pp. 152–3.)]

E: Yes.

S: And that the god-beloved, on the other hand, is so because it is loved by the gods, by the very fact of being loved, but it is not loved because it is god-beloved.

E: True.

S: But if the god-beloved and the pious were the same, my dear Euthyphro, and the pious were loved because it was pious, then the god-beloved would be loved because it was god-beloved, and if the god-beloved was god-beloved because it was loved by the gods, then the pious would also be pious because it was loved by the gods; but now you see that they are in opposite cases as being altogether different from each other: the one is of a nature to be loved because it is loved, the other is loved because it is of a nature to be loved. I'm afraid, Euthyphro, that when you were asked what piety is, you did not wish to make its nature clear to me, but you told me an affect or quality of it, that the pious has the quality of being loved by all the gods, but you have not yet told me what the pious is. Now, if you will, do not hide things from me but tell me again from the beginning what piety is, whether loved by the gods or having some other quality—we shall not quarrel about that— but be keen to tell me what the pious and the impious are.

E: But Socrates, I have no way of telling you what I have in mind, for whatever proposition we put forward goes around and refuses to stay put where we establish it.

S: Your statements, Euthyphro, seem to belong to my ancestor, Daedalus. If I were stating them and putting them forward, you would perhaps be making fun of me and say that because of my kinship with him my conclusions in discussion run away and will not stay where one puts them. As these propositions are yours, how- ever, we need some other jest, for they will not stay put for you, as you say yourself.

E: I think the same jest will do for our discussion, Socrates, for I am not the one who makes them go round and not remain in the same place; it is you who are the Daedalus; for as far as I am concerned they would remain as they were.

S: It looks as if I was cleverer than Daedalus in using my skill, my friend, in so far as he could only cause to move the things he made himself, but I can make other people's move as well as my own. And the smartest part of my skill is that I am clever without wanting to be, for I would rather have my arguments remain unmoved than possess the wealth of Tantalus as well as the cleverness of Daedalus. But enough of this. Since I think you are making unnecessary difficulties, I am as eager as you are to find a way to teach me about piety, and do not give up before you do. See whether you think all that is pious is of necessity just.

E: I think so.

S: And is then all that is just pious? Or is all that is pious just, but not all that is just pious, but some of it is and some is not?

E: I do not follow what you are saying, Socrates.

S: Yet you are younger than I by as much as you are wiser. As I say, you are making difficulties because of your wealth of wisdom. Pull yourself together, my dear sir, what I am saying is not difficult to grasp. I am saying the opposite of what the poet said who wrote:

You do not wish to name Zeus, who had done it, and who made all things grow, for where there is fear there is also shame.

I disagree with the poet. Shall I tell you why?

E: Please do.

S: I do not think that "where there is fear there is also shame," for I think that many people who fear disease and poverty and many other such things feel fear, but are not ashamed of the things they fear. Do you not think so?

E: I do indeed.

S: But where there is shame there is also fear. Does anyone feel shame at something who is not also afraid at the same time of a reputation for wickedness?

E: He is certainly afraid.

S: It is then not right to say "where there is fear there is also shame," but that where there is shame there is also fear, for fear covers a larger area than shame. Shame is a part of fear just as odd is a part of number, with the result that it is not true that where there is number there is also oddness, but that where there is oddness there is also number. Do you follow me?

E: Surely.

S: This is the kind of thing I was asking before, whether where there is piety there is also justice, but where there is justice there is not always piety, for the pious is a part of justice. Shall we say that, or do you think otherwise?

E: No, but like that, for what you say appears to be right.

S: See what comes next: if the pious is a part of the just, we must, it seems, find out what part of the just it is. Now if you asked me something of what we mentioned just now, such as what part of number is the even, and what number that is, I would say it is the number that is divisible into two equal, not unequal parts. Or do you not think so?

E: I do.

S: Try in this way to tell me what part of the just the pious is, in order to tell Meletus not to wrong us any more and not to indict me for ungodliness, since I have learned from you sufficiently what is godly and pious and what is not.

E: I think, Socrates, that the godly and pious is the part of the just that is concerned with the care of the gods, while that concerned with the care of men is the remaining part of justice.

S: You seem to me to put that very well, but I still need a bit of information. I do not know yet what you mean by care, for you do not mean the care of the gods in the same sense as the care of other things, as, for example, we say, don't we, that not everyone knows how to care for horses, but the horse breeder does.

E: Yes, I do mean it that way.

S: So horse breeding is the care of horses.

E: Yes.

S: Nor does everyone know how to care for dogs, but the hunter does.

E: That is so.

S: So hunting is the care of dogs.

E. Yes.

S: And cattle raising is the care of cattle.

E: Quite so.

S: While piety and godliness is the care of the gods, Euthyphro. Is that what you mean?

E: It is.

S: Now care in each case has the same effect; it aims at the good and the benefit of the object cared for, as you can see that horses cared for by horse breeders are benefited and become better. Or do you not think so?

E: I do.

c   S: So dogs are benefited by dog breeding, cattle by cattle raising, and so with all the others. Or do you think that care aims to harm the object of its care?

E: By Zeus, no.

S: It aims to benefit the object of its care?

E: Of course.

S: Is piety then, which is the care of the gods, also to benefit the gods and make them better? Would you agree that when you do something pious you make some one of the gods better?

E: By Zeus, no.

S: Nor do I think that this is what you mean—far from it—but that is why I asked you what you meant by the care of gods, because I did not believe you meant

d   this kind of care.

E: Quite right, Socrates, that is not the kind of care I mean.

S: Very well, but what kind of care of the gods would piety be?

E: The kind of care, Socrates, that slaves take of their masters.

S: I understand. It is likely to be a kind of service of the gods.

E: Quite so.

S: Could you tell me to the achievement of what goal service to doctors tends? Is it not, do you think to achieving health?

E: I think so.

e   S: What about service to shipbuilders? To what achievement is it directed?

E: Clearly, Socrates, to the building of a ship.

S: And service to housebuilders to the building of a house?

E;   Yes.

S: Tell me then, my good sir, to the achievement of what aim does service to the gods tend? You obviously know since you say that you, of all men, have the best knowledge of the divine.

E: And I am telling the truth, Socrates.

S: Tell me then, by Zeus, what is that excellent aim that the gods achieve, using us as their servants?

E: Many fine things, Socrates.

14   S: So do generals, my friend. Nevertheless you could tell me their main concern, which is to achieve victory in war, is it not?

E: Of course.

S: The farmers too, I think, achieve many fine things, but the main point of their efforts is to produce food from the earth.

E: Quite so.

S: Well then, how would you sum up the many fine things that the gods achieve?

E: I told you a short while ago, Socrates, that it is a considerable task to acquire any precise knowledge of these things, but, to put it simply, I say that if a man knows how to say and do what is pleasing to the gods at prayer and sacrifice, those are pious actions such as preserve both private houses and public affairs of state. The opposite of these pleasing actions are impious and overturn and destroy everything.   b

S: You could tell me in far fewer words, if you were willing, the sum of what I asked, Euthyphro, but you are not keen to teach me, that is clear. You were on the point of doing so, but you turned away. If you had given that answer, I should now have acquired from you sufficient knowledge of the nature of piety. As it is, the lover of inquiry must follow his beloved wherever it may lead him. Once more then, what do you say that piety and the pious are? Are they a knowledge of how to sacrifice and pray?   c

E: They are.

S: To sacrifice is to make a gift to the gods, whereas to pray is to beg from the gods?

E: Definitely, Socrates.

S: It would follow from this statement that piety would be a knowledge of how to give to, and beg from, the gods.   d

E: You understood what I said very well, Socrates.

S: That is because I am so desirous of your wisdom, and I concentrate my mind on it, so that no word of yours may fall to the ground. But tell me, what is this service to the gods? You say it is to beg from them and to give to them?

E: I do.

S: And to beg correctly would be to ask from them things that we need?

E;   What else?

S: And to give correctly is to give them what they need from us, for it would not be skillful to bring gifts to anyone that are in no way needed.   e

E: True, Socrates.

S: Piety would then be a sort of trading skill between gods and men?

E: Trading yes, if you prefer to call it that.

S   I prefer nothing, unless it is true. But tell me, what benefit do the gods derive from the gifts they receive from us? What they give us is obvious to all. There is for us no good that we do not receive from them, but how are they benefited by what they receive from us? Or do we have such an advantage over them in the trade that we receive all our blessings from them and they receive nothing from us?   15

E: Do you suppose, Socrates, that the gods are benefited by what they receive from us?

S: What could those gifts from us to the gods be, Euthyphro?

E: What else, you think, than honour, reverence, and what I mentioned before, gratitude.

b   S: The pious is then, Euthyphro, pleasing to the gods, but not beneficial or dear to them?

E: I think it is of all things most dear to them.

S: So the pious is once again what is dear to the gods.

E: Most certainly.

S: When you say this, will you be surprised if your arguments seem to move about instead of staying put? And will you accuse me of being Daedalus who makes them move, though you are yourself much more skillful than Daedalus and make them go round in a circle? Or do you not realize that our argument has moved around and come again to the same place? You surely remember that earlier the

c   pious and the god-beloved were shown not to be the same but different from each other. Or do you not remember?

E: I do.

S: Do you then not realize now that you are saying that what is dear to the gods is the pious? Is this not the same as the god-beloved? Or is it not?

E: It certainly is.

S: Either we were wrong when we agreed before, or, if we were right then, we are wrong now.

E: That seems to be so.

S: So we must investigate again from the beginning what piety is, as I shall not willingly give up before I learn this. Do not think me unworthy, but concentrate

d   your attention and tell the truth. For you know it, if any man does, and I must not let you go, like Proteus, before you tell me. If you had no clear knowledge of piety and impiety you would never have ventured to prosecute your old father for murder on behalf of a servant. For fear of the gods you would have been afraid to take the risk lest you should not be acting rightly, and would have been ashamed before men, but now I know well that you believe you have clear knowledge of piety and

e   impiety. So tell me, my good Euthyphro, and do not hide what you think it is.

E: Some other time, Socrates, for I am in a hurry now, and it is time for me to go.

S: What a thing to do, my friend! By going you have cast me down from a great hope I had, that I would learn from you the nature of the pious and the im-

16   pious and so escape Meletus' indictment by showing that I had acquired wisdom in divine matters from Euthyphro, and my ignorance would no longer cause me to be careless and inventive about such things, and that I would be better for the rest of my life.

APOLOGY[1]

I do not know, men of Athens, how my accusers affected you; as for me, I was almost carried away in spite of myself, so persuasively did they speak. And yet, hardly anything of what they said is true. Of the many lies they told, one in particular surprised me, namely that you should be careful not to be deceived by an accomplished speaker like me. That they are not ashamed to be immediately proved wrong by the facts, when I show myself not to be an accomplished speaker at all, that I think is most shameless on their part—unless indeed they call an accomplished speaker the man who speaks the truth. If they mean that, I would agree that I am an orator, but not after their manner, for indeed, as I say, practically nothing they said was true. From me you will hear the whole truth, though not, by Zeus, gentlemen, expressed in embroidered and stylized phrases like theirs, but things spoken at random and expressed in the first words that come to mind, for I put my trust in the justice of what I say, and let none of you expect anything else. It would not be fitting at my age, as it might be for a young man, to toy with words when I appear before you.

One thing I do ask and beg of you, gentlemen: if you hear me making my defence in the same kind of language as I am accustomed to use in the market place by the bankers' tables,[2] where many of you have heard me, and elsewhere, do not be surprised or create a disturbance on that account. The position is this: this is my first appearance in a lawcourt, at the age of seventy; I am therefore simply a stranger to the manner of speaking here. Just as if I were really a stranger, you would certainly excuse me if I spoke in that dialect and manner in which I had been brought up, so too my present request seems a just one, for you to pay no attention to my manner of speech—be it better or worse—but to concentrate your attention on whether what I say is just or not, for the excellence of a judge lies in this, as that of a speaker lies in telling the truth.

It is right for me, gentlemen, to defend myself first against the first lying accusations made against me and my first accusers, and then against the later accusations and the later accusers. There have been many who have accused me to you for many years now, and none of their accusations are true. These I fear much more than I fear Anytus and his friends, though they too are formidable. These earlier ones, however, are more so, gentlemen; they got hold of most of you from childhood, persuaded you and accused me quite falsely, saying that there is a man called Socrates, a wise man, a student of all things in the sky and below the earth, who makes the worse argument the stronger. Those who spread that rumour, gentlemen, are my dangerous accusers, for their hearers believe that those who study these things do

Reprinted from *The Trial & Death of Socrates*, translated by G.M.A. Grube (Indianapolis: Hackett Publishing Company, 1975), by permission of the publisher.

1. [The word *apology* is a transliteration, not a translation, of the Greek *apologia* which means defence. There is certainly nothing apologetic about the speech.—G.M.A.G.]

2. [The bankers or money-changers had their counters in the market place. It seems that this was a favourite place for gossip.]

not even believe in the gods. Moreover, these accusers are numerous and have been at it a long time; also, they spoke to you at an age when you would most readily believe them, some of you being children and adolescents, and they won their case by default, as there was no defence.

d   What is most absurd in all this is that one cannot even know or mention their names unless one of them is a writer of comedies.[3] Those who maliciously and slanderously persuaded you, who, also, when persuaded themselves then persuaded others, all those are most difficult to deal with: one cannot bring one of them into court or refute him; one must simply fight with shadows as it were in making one's defence, and cross-examine when no one answers. I want you to realize too that my accusers are of two kinds: those who have accused me recently, and the old ones I

e   mention; and to think that I must first defend myself against the latter, for you have also heard their accusations first, and to a much greater extent than the more recent.

         Very well then. I must surely defend myself and attempt to uproot from your

19   minds in so short a time the slander that has resided there so long. I wish this may happen, if it is in any way better for you and me, and that my defence may be successful, but I think this is very difficult and I am fully aware of how difficult it is. Even so, let the matter proceed as the god may wish, but I must obey the law and make my defence.

         Let us then take up the case from its beginning. What is the accusation from

b   which arose the slander in which Meletus trusted when he wrote out the charge against me? What did they say when they slandered me? I must, as if they were my actual prosecutors, read the affidavit they would have sworn. It goes something like this: Socrates is guilty of wrongdoing in that he busies himself studying things in the sky and below the earth; he makes the worse into the stronger argument, and he

c   teaches these same things to others. You have seen this yourselves in the comedy of Aristophanes, a Socrates swinging about there, saying he was walking on air and talking a lot of other nonsense about things of which I know nothing at all. I do not speak in contempt of such knowledge, if someone is wise in these things—lest Meletus bring more cases against me—but, gentlemen, I have no part in it, and on this point I call upon the majority of you as witnesses. I think it right that all those

d   of you who have heard me conversing, and many of you have, should tell each other if anyone of you has ever heard me discussing such subjects to any extent at all. From this you will learn that the other things said about me by the majority are of the same kind.

         Not one of them is true. And if you have heard from anyone that I undertake to teach people and charge a fee for it, that is not true either. Yet I think it a fine thing

e   to be able to teach people as Gorgias of Leontini does, and Prodicus of Ceos, and Hippias of Elis.[4] Each of these men can go to any city and persuade the young, who can keep company with anyone of their own fellow-citizens they want without pay-

---

3. [This refers in particular to Aristophanes, whose comedy, *The Clouds*, produced in 423 B.C., ridiculed the (imaginary) school of Socrates.]

4. [These were all well-known Sophists. Gorgias, after whom Plato named one of his dialogues, was a celebrated rhetorician and teacher of rhetoric. He came to Athens in 427 B.C., and his rhetorical tricks took the city by storm. Two dialogues, the authenticity of which has been doubted, are named after Hippias, whose knowledge was encyclopedic. Prodicus was known for his insistence on the precise meaning of words. Both he and Hippias are characters in the *Protagoras* (named after another famous Sophist).]

ing, to leave the company of these, to join with themselves, pay them a fee, and be 20 grateful to them besides. Indeed, I learned that there is another wise man from Paros who is visiting us, for I met a man who has spent more money on Sophists than everybody else, Callias, the son of Hipponicus. So I asked him—he has two sons—"Callias," I said, "if your sons were colts or calves, we could find and engage a supervisor for them who would make them excel in their proper qualities, some b horse breeder or farmer. Now since they are men, whom do you have in mind to supervise them? Who is an expert in this kind of excellence, the human and social kind? I think you must have given thought to this for your sons. Is there such a person," I asked, "or is there not?" "Certainly there is," he said. "Who is he?" I asked, "What is his name, where is he from? and what is his fee?" "His name, Socrates, is Evenus, he comes from Paros, and his fee is five minas." I thought Evenus a happy man, if he really possesses this art, and teaches for so moderate a fee. Certainly I c would pride and preen myself if I had this knowledge, but I do not have it, gentlemen.

One of you might perhaps interrupt me and say: "But Socrates, what is your occupation? From where have these slanders come? For surely if you did not busy yourself with something out of the common, all these rumours and talk would not have arisen unless you did something other than most people. Tell us what it is, that we may not speak inadvisedly about you." Anyone who says that seems to be right, d and I will try to show you what has caused this reputation and slander. Listen then. Perhaps some of you will think I am jesting, but be sure that all that I shall say is true. What has caused my reputation is none other than a certain kind of wisdom. What kind of wisdom? Human wisdom, perhaps. It may be that I really possess this, while those whom I mentioned just now are wise with a wisdom more than human; e else I cannot explain it, for I certainly do not possess it, and whoever says I do is lying and speaks to slander me. Do not create a disturbance, gentlemen, even if you think I am boasting, for the story I shall tell does not originate with me, but I will refer you to a trustworthy source. I shall call upon the god at Delphi as witness to the existence and nature of my wisdom, if it be such. You know Chairephon. He was my friend from youth, and the friend of most of you, as he shared your exile and 21 your return. You surely know the kind of man he was, how impulsive in any course of action. He went to Delphi at one time and ventured to ask the oracle—as I say, gentlemen, do not create a disturbance—he asked if any man was wiser than I, and the Pythian replied that no one was wiser. Chairephon is dead, but his brother will testify to you about this.

Consider that I tell you this because I would inform you about the origin of the b slander. When I heard of this reply I asked myself: "Whatever does the god mean? What is his riddle? I am very conscious that I am not wise at all; what then does he mean by saying that I am the wisest? For surely he does not lie; it is not legitimate for him to do so." For a long time I was at a loss; then I very reluctantly turned to some such investigation as this: I went to one of those reputed wise, thinking that there, if anywhere, I could refute the oracle and say to it: "This man is wiser than I, c but you said I was." Then, when I examined this man—there is no need for me to tell you his name, he was one of our public men—my experience was something like this: I thought that he appeared wise to many people and especially to himself, but he was not. I then tried to show him that he thought himself wise, but that he was not. As a result he came to dislike me, and so did many of the bystanders. So I with- d drew and thought to myself: "I am wiser than this man; it is likely that neither of us knows anything worthwhile, but he thinks he knows something when he does not, whereas when I do not know, neither do I think I know; so I am likely to be wiser to this small extent, that I do not think I know what I do not know." After this I approached another man, one of those thought to be wiser than he, and I thought the same thing, and so I came to be disliked both by him and by many others.

e

After that I proceeded systematically. I realized, to my sorrow and alarm, that I was getting unpopular, but I thought that I must attach the greatest importance to the god's oracle, so I must go to all those who had any reputation for knowledge to examine its meaning. And by the dog,[5] gentlemen of the jury—for I must tell you

22 the truth—I experienced something like this: in my investigation in the service of the god I found that those who had the highest reputation were nearly the most deficient, while those who were thought to be inferior were more knowledgeable. I must give you an account of my journeyings as if they were labours I had undertaken to prove the oracle irrefutable. After the politicians, I went to the poets, the writers of tragedies and dithyrambs and the others, intending in their case to catch

b myself being more ignorant than they. So I took up those poems with which they seemed to have taken most trouble and asked them what they meant, in order that I might at the same time learn something from them. I am ashamed to tell you the truth, gentlemen, but I must. Almost all the bystanders explained the poems better

c than their authors could. I soon realized that poets do not compose their poems with knowledge, but by some inborn talent and by inspiration, like seers and prophets who also say many fine things without any understanding of what they say. The poets seemed to me to have had a similar experience. At the same time I saw that, because of their poetry, they thought themselves very wise men in other respects, which they were not. So there again I withdrew, thinking that I had the same advantage over them as I had over the politicians.

Finally I went to the craftsmen, for I was conscious of knowing practically

d nothing, and I knew that I would find that they had knowledge of many fine things. In this I was not mistaken; they knew things I did not know, and to that extent they were wiser than I. But, gentlemen of the jury, the good craftsmen seemed to me to have the same fault as the poets: each of them, because of success at his craft, thought himself very wise in other most important pursuits, and this error of theirs

e overshadowed the wisdom they had, so that I asked myself, on behalf of the oracle, whether I should prefer to be as I am, with neither their wisdom nor their ignorance, or to have both. The answer I gave myself and the oracle was that it was to my advantage to be as I am.

As a result of this investigation, gentlemen of the jury, I acquired much

23 unpopularity, of a kind that is hard to deal with and is a heavy burden; many slanders came from these people and a reputation for wisdom, for in each case the bystanders thought that I myself possessed the wisdom that I proved that my interlocutor did not have. What is probable, gentlemen, is that in fact that god is wise and that his oracular response meant that human wisdom is worth little or nothing, and

b that when he says this man, Socrates, he is using my name as an example, as if he said: "This man among you, mortals, is wisest who, like Socrates, understands that

---

5. [A curious oath, occasionally used by Socrates, it appears in a longer form in the *Gorgias* (482b) as "by the dog, the god of the Egyptians."]

his wisdom is worthless." So even now I continue this investigation as the gods bade me—and I go around seeking out anyone, citizen or stranger, whom I think wise. Then if I do not think he is, I come to the assistance of the god and show him that he is not wise. Because of this occupation, I do not have the leisure to engage in public affairs to any extent, nor indeed to look after my own, but I live in great poverty because of my service to the god.

Furthermore, the young men who follow me around of their own free will, those who have most leisure, the sons of the very rich, take pleasure in hearing people questioned; they themselves often imitate me and try to question others. I think they find an abundance of men who believe they have some knowledge but know little or nothing. The result is that those whom they question are angry, not with themselves but with me. They say: "That man Socrates is a pestilential fellow who corrupts the young." If one asks them what he does and what he teaches to corrupt them, they are silent, as they do not know, but, so as not to appear at a loss, they mention those accusations that are available against all philosophers, about "things in the sky and things below the earth," about "not believing in the gods" and "making the worse the stronger argument;" they would not want to tell the truth, that they have been proved to lay claim to knowledge when they know nothing. These people are ambitious, violent and numerous; they are continually and convincingly talking about me; they have been filling your ears for a long time with vehement slanders against me. From them Meletus attacked me, and Anytus and Lycon, Meletus being vexed on behalf of the poets, Anytus on behalf of the craftsmen and the politicians, Lycon on behalf of the orators, so that, as I started out by saying, I should be surprised if I could rid you of so much slander in so short a time. That, gentlemen of the jury, is the truth for you. I have hidden or omitted nothing. I know well enough that this very conduct makes me unpopular, and this is proof that what I say is true, that such is the slander against me, and that such are its causes. If you look into this either now or later, this is what you will find.

Let this suffice as a defence against the charges of my earlier accusers. After this I shall try to defend myself against Meletus, that good and patriotic man, as he says he is, and my later accusers. As these are a different lot of accusers, let us again take up their sworn deposition. It goes something like this: Socrates is guilty of corrupting the young and of not believing in the gods in whom the city believes, but in other new divinities. Such is their charge. Let us examine it point by point.

He says that I am guilty of corrupting the young, but I say that Meletus is guilty of dealing frivolously with serious matters, of irresponsibly bringing people into court, and of professing to be seriously concerned with things about none of which he has ever cared, and I shall try to prove that this is so. Come here and tell me, Meletus. Surely you consider it of the greatest importance that our young men be as good as possible?[6] — Indeed I do.

Come then, tell the jury who improves them. You obviously know, in view of your concern. You say you have discovered the one who corrupts them, namely me, and you bring me here and accuse me to the jury. Come, inform the jury and tell them who it is. You see, Meletus, that you are silent and know not what to say. Does this not seem shameful to you and a sufficient proof of what I say, that you have not

6. [Socrates here drops into his usual method of discussion by question and answer. This, no doubt, is what Plato had in mind, at least in part, when he made him ask the indulgence of the jury if he spoke "in his usual manner."]

been concerned with any of this? Tell me, my good sir, who improves our young
men? — The laws.

That is not what I am asking, but what person, who has knowledge of the laws to
begin with? — These jurymen, Socrates.

How do you mean, Meletus? Are these able to educate the young and improve
them? — Certainly.

All of them, or some but not others? — All of them.

Very good, by Hera. You mention a great abundance of benefactors. But what
about the audience? Do they improve the young or not? — They do, too.

What about the members of Council? — The Councillors, also.

But, Meletus, what about the assembly? Do members of the assembly corrupt the
young, or do they all improve them? —They improve them.

All the Athenians, it seems, make the young into fine good men, except me, and I
alone corrupt them. Is that what you mean? — That is most definitely what I mean.

You condemn me to a great misfortune. Tell me: does this also apply to horses do
you think? That all men improve them and one individual corrupts them? Or is
quite the contrary true, one individual is able to improve them, or very few, namely
the horse breeders, whereas the majority, if they have horses and use them, corrupt
them? Is that not the case, Meletus, both with horses and all other animals? Of
course it is, whether you and Anytus say so or not. It would be a very happy state of
affairs if only one person corrupted our youth, while the others improved them.

You have made it sufficiently obvious, Meletus, that you have never had any concern for our youth; you show your indifference clearly; that you have given no
thought to the subjects about which you bring me to trial.

And by Zeus, Meletus, tell us also whether it is better for a man to live among
good or wicked fellow-citizens. Answer, my good man, for I am not asking a difficult question. Do not the wicked do some harm to those who are ever closest to
them, whereas good people benefit them? — Certainly.

And does the man exist who would rather be harmed than benefited by his associates? Answer, my good sir, for the law orders you to answer. Is there any man who
wants to be harmed? — Of course not.

Come now, do you accuse me here of corrupting the young and making them
worse deliberately or unwillingly? — Deliberately.

What follows, Meletus? Are you so much wiser at your age than I am at mine that
you understand that wicked people always do some harm to their closest
neighbours while good people do them good, but I have reached such a pitch of ignorance that I do not realize this, namely that if I make one of my associates wicked
I run the risk of being harmed by him so that I do such a great evil deliberately, as
you say? I do not believe you, Meletus, and I do not think anyone else will. Either I
do not corrupt the young or, if I do, it is unwillingly, and you are lying in either
case. Now if I corrupt them unwillingly, the law does not require you to bring people to court for such unwilling wrongdoings, but to get hold of them privately, to
instruct them and exhort them; for clearly, if I learn better, I shall cease to do what
I am doing unwillingly. You, however, have avoided my company and were unwilling to instruct me, but you bring me here, where the law requires one to bring those
who are in need of punishment, not of instruction.

And so, gentlemen of the jury, what I said is clearly true: Meletus has never been at all concerned with these matters. Nonetheless tell us, Meletus, how you say that I corrupt the young; or is it obvious from your deposition that it is by teaching them not to believe in the gods in whom the city believes but in other new divinities? Is this not what you say I teach and so corrupt them? — That is most certainly what I do say.

b

Then by those very gods about whom we are talking, Meletus, make this clearer to me and to the jury: I cannot be sure whether you mean that I teach the belief that there are some gods—and therefore I myself believe that there are gods and am not altogether an atheist, nor am I guilty of that—not, however, the gods in whom the city believes, but others, and that this is the charge against me, that there are others. Or whether you mean that I do not believe in gods at all, and that this is what I teach to others.

c

— This is what I mean, that you do not believe in gods at all.

You are a strange fellow, Meletus. Why do you say this? Do I not believe, as other men do, that the sun and the moon are gods?

d

— No by Zeus, jurymen, for he says that the sun is stone, and the moon earth.

My dear Meletus, do you think you are prosecuting Anaxagoras? Are you so contemptuous of the jury and think them so ignorant of letters as not to know that the books of Anaxagoras[7] of Clazomenae are full of those theories, and further, that the young men learn from me what they can buy from time to time for a drachma, at most, in the bookshops, and ridicule Socrates if he pretends that these theories are his own, especially as they are so absurd? Is that, by Zeus, what you think of me, Meletus, that I do not believe that there are any gods?

e

— That is what I say, that you do not believe in the gods at all.

You cannot be believed, Meletus, even, I think, by yourself. The man appears to me, gentlemen of the jury, highly insolent and uncontrolled. He has made an insolent, violent and unrestrained deposition. He is like one who composed a riddle and is trying it out: "Will the wise Socrates realize that I am jesting and contradicting myself, or shall I deceive him and others?" I think he contradicts himself in the affidavit, as if he said: "Socrates is guilty of not believing in the gods but believing in the gods," and surely that is the part of a jester!

27

Examine with me how he appears to contradict himself, and you, Meletus, answer us. Remember, gentlemen, what I asked you when I began, not to create a disturbance if I proceed in my usual manner.

b

Does any man, Meletus, believe in human affairs who does not believe in human beings? Make him answer, and not again and again create a disturbance. Does any man who does not believe in horses believe in equine affairs? Or in flute music but not flute-players? No, my good sir, no man could. If you are not willing to answer, I will tell you and the jury. Answer the next question, however. Does any man believe in divine activities who does not believe in divinities? — No one.

c

Thank you for answering, if reluctantly, when the jury made you. Now you say that I believe in divine activities and teach about them, whether new or old, but at

7. [Anaxagoras of Clazomenae, born about the beginning of the fifth century, came to Athens as a young man and spent time in the pursuit of natural philosophy. He claimed that the universe was directed by Nous (Mind), and that matter was indestructible but always combining in various ways. He left Athens after being prosecuted for impiety.]

any rate divine activities according to what you say, and to this you have sworn in your deposition. But if I believe in divine activities I must quite inevitably believe in divine beings. Is that not so? It is indeed. I shall assume that you agree, as you do not answer.
d   Do we not believe divine beings to be either gods or the children of gods? — Of course.

Then since I do believe in divine beings, as you admit, if divine beings are gods, this is what I mean when I say you speak in riddles and in jest, as you state that I do not believe in gods and then again that I do, since I believe in divine beings. If on the other hand the divine beings are children of the gods, bastard children of the gods by nymphs or some other mothers, as they are said to be, what man would believe children of the gods to ex-
e   ist, but not gods? That would be just as absurd as to believe the young of horses and asses, namely mules, to exist, but not to believe in the existence of horses and asses. You must have made this deposition, Meletus, either to test us or because you were at a loss to find any true wrongdoing of which to accuse me. There is no way in which you could per- suade anyone of even small intelligence that it is not the part of one and the same man to
28 believe in the activities of divine beings and gods, and then again the part of one and the same man not to believe in the existence of divinities and gods and heroes.

I do not think, gentlemen of the jury, that it requires a prolonged defence to prove that I am not guilty of the charges in Meletus' deposition, but this is suffi- cient. On the other hand, you know that what I said earlier is true, that I am very unpopular with many people. This will be my undoing, if I am undone, not Meletus
b   or Anytus but the slanders and envy of many people. This has destroyed many and will, I think, continue to do so. There is no danger that it will stop at me.

Someone might say: "Are you not ashamed, Socrates, to have followed the kind of occupation that has led to your being now in danger of death?" However, I should be right to reply to him: "You are wrong, sir, if you think that a man who is any good at all should take into account the risk of life or death; he should look to this only in his actions, whether what he does is right or wrong, whether he is acting like a good or a
c   bad man." According to your view, all the heroes who died at Troy were inferior peo- ple, especially the son of Thetis who was so contemptuous of danger compared with disgrace.[8] When he was eager to kill Hector, his goddess mother warned him, as I be- lieve, in some such words as these: "My child, if you avenge the death of your com- rade, Patroclus, and you kill Hector, you will die yourself, for your death is to follow immediately after Hector's." Hearing this, he despised death and danger and was much more afraid to live a coward who did not avenge his friends. "Let me die at
d   once," he said, "when once I have given the wrongdoer his deserts, rather than remain here, a laughingstock by the curved ships, a burden upon the earth." Do you think he gave thought to death and danger?

This is the truth of the matter, gentlemen of the jury: wherever a man has taken a position that he believes to be best, or has been placed by his commander, there he must I think remain and face danger, without a thought for death or anything else,
e   rather than disgrace. It would have been a dreadful way to behave, gentlemen of the jury, if, at Potidaea, Amphipolis and Delium, I had, at the risk of death, like anyone else, remained at my post where those you had elected to command had ordered me, and then, when the god ordered me, as I thought and believed, to live the life of a philosopher, to examine myself and others, I had abandoned my post for fear of

---

8. [The scene between Thetis and Achilles is from the *Iliad* (18, 94ff.).]

death or anything else. That would have been a dreadful thing, and then I might truly have justly been brought here for not believing in the gods, disobeying the oracle, fearing death, and thinking I was wise when I was not. To fear death, gentlemen, is no other than to think oneself wise when one is not, to think one knows what one does not know. No one knows whether death may not be the greatest of all blessings for a man, yet men fear it as if they knew that it is the greatest of evils. And surely it is the most blameworthy ignorance to believe that one knows what one does not know. It is perhaps on this point and in this respect, gentlemen, that I differ from the majority of men, and if I were to claim that I am wiser than anyone in anything, it would be in this, that, as I have no adequate knowledge of things in the underworld, so I do not think I have. I do know, however, that it is wicked and shameful to do wrong, to disobey one's superior, be he god or man. I shall never fear or avoid things of which I do not know, whether they may not be good rather than things that I know to be bad. Even if you acquitted me now and did not believe Anytus, who said to you that either I should not have been brought here in the first place, or that now I am here, you cannot avoid executing me, for if I should be acquitted, your sons would practise the teachings of Socrates and all be thoroughly corrupted. If you said to me in this regard: "Socrates, we do not believe Anytus now; we acquit you, but only on condition that you spend no more time on this investigation and do not practise philosophy, and if you are caught doing so you will die;" if, as I say, you were to acquit me on those terms, I would say to you: "Gentlemen of the jury, I am grateful and I am your friend, but I will obey the god rather than you, and as long as I draw breath and am able, I shall not cease to practise philosophy, to exhort you and to point out to anyone of you whom I happen to meet: Good Sir, you are an Athenian, a citizen of the greatest city with the greatest reputation for both wisdom and power; are you not ashamed of your eagerness to possess as much wealth, reputation and honours as possible, while you do not care for nor give thought to wisdom or truth, or the best possible state of your soul?" Then, if one of you disputes this and says he does care, I shall not let him go at once or leave him, but I shall question him, examine him and test him, and if I do not think he has attained the goodness that he says he has, I shall reproach him because he attaches little importance to the most important things and greater importance to inferior things, I shall treat in this way anyone I happen to meet, young and old, citizen and stranger, and more so the citizens because you are more kindred to me. Be sure that this is what the god orders me to do, and I think there is no greater blessing for the city than my service to the god. For I go around doing nothing but persuading both young and old among you not to care for your body or your wealth in preference to or as strongly as for the best possible state of your soul, as I say to you: "Wealth does not bring about excellence, but excellence brings about wealth and all other public and private blessings for men."

Now if by saying this I corrupt the young, this advice must be harmful, but if anyone says that I give different advice, he is talking nonsense. On this point I would say to you, gentlemen of the jury: "Whether you believe Anytus or not, whether you acquit me or not, do so on the understanding that this is my course of action, even if I am to face death many times." Do not create a disturbance, gentlemen, but abide by my request not to cry out at what I say but to listen, for I think it will be to your advantage to listen, and I am about to say other things at which you will perhaps cry out. By no means do this. Be sure that if you kill the sort of man I say I am, you will not harm me more than yourselves. Neither Meletus nor Anytus

29

b

c

d

e

30

b

c

d can harm me in any way; he could not harm me, for I do not think it is permitted that a better man be harmed by a worse; certainly he might kill me, or perhaps banish or disfranchise me, which he and maybe others think to be great harm, but I do not think so. I think he is doing himself much greater harm doing what he is doing now, attempting to have a man executed unjustly. Indeed, gentlemen of the jury, I am far from making a defence now on my own behalf, as might be thought, but on yours, to prevent you from wrongdoing by mistreating the god's gift to you

e by condemning me; for if you kill me you will not easily find another like me. I was attached to this city by the god—though it seems a ridiculous thing to say—as upon a great and noble horse which was somewhat sluggish because of its size and needed to be stirred up by a kind of gadfly. It is to fulfill some such function that the god has placed me in the city. I never cease to rouse everyone of you, to persuade and re-

31 proach you all day long and everywhere I find myself in your company.

Another such man will not easily come to be among you, gentlemen, and if you believe me you will spare me. You might easily strike out at me as people do when they are aroused from a doze; if convinced by Anytus you could easily kill me, and then you could sleep on for the rest of your days, unless the god, in his care for you, sent you someone else. That I am the kind of person to be a gift of the god to the city

b you might realize from the fact that it does not seem like human nature for me to have neglected all my own affairs and to have tolerated this neglect now for so many years while I was always concerned with you, approaching each one of you like a father on an elder brother to persuade you to care for virtue. Now if I profited from this by charging a fee for my advice, there would be some sense to it, but you can see for yourselves that, for all their shameless accusations, my accusers have not been able in their impudence to bring forward a witness to say that I have ever received a

c fee or ever asked for one. I, on the other hand, have a convincing witness that I speak the truth, my poverty.

It may seem strange that while I go around and give this advice privately and interfere in private affairs, I do not venture to go to the assembly and there advise the city. You have heard me give the reason for this in many places. I have a divine

d sign from the god which Meletus has ridiculed in his deposition. This began when I was a child. It is a voice, and whenever it speaks it turns me away from something I am about to do, but it never encourages me to do anything. This is what has prevented me from taking part in public affairs, and I think it was quite right to prevent me. Be sure, gentlemen of the jury, that if I had long ago attempted to take part in politics, I should have died long ago, and benefited neither you nor myself.

e Do not be angry with me for speaking the truth; no man will survive who genuinely opposes you or any other crowd and prevents the occurrence of many unjust and

32 illegal happenings in the city. A man who really fights for justice must lead a private, not a public, life if he is to survive for even a short time.

I shall give you great proofs of this, not words but what you esteem, deeds. Listen to what happened to me, that you may know that I will not yield to any man contrary to what is right, for fear of death, even if I should die at once for not yielding. The things I shall tell you are commonplace and smack of the lawcourts, but they

b are true. I have never held any other office in the city, but I served as a member of the Council, and our tribe was presiding at the time when you wanted to try as a body the ten generals who had failed to pick up the survivors of the naval battle.[9]

9. [This was the battle of Arginusae (south of Lesbos) in 406 B.C., the last Athenian victory of the war.

This was illegal, as you all recognized later. I was the only member of the presiding committee to oppose your doing something contrary to the laws, and I voted against it. The orators were ready to prosecute me and take me away, and your shouts were egging them on, but I thought I should run any risk on the side of law and justice rather than join you, for fear of prison or death, when you were engaged in an unjust course.

This happened when the city was still a democracy. When the oligarchy was established, the Thirty[10] summond me to the Hall, along with four others, and ordered us to bring Leon from Salamis, that he might be executed. They gave many such orders to many people, in order to implicate as many as possible in their guilt. Then I showed again, not in words but in action, that, if it were not rather vulgar to say so, death is something I couldn't care less about, but that my whole concern is not to do anything unjust or impious. That government, powerful as it was, did not frighten me into any wrongdoing. When we left the Hall, the other four went to Salamis and brought in Leon, but I went home. I might have been put to death for this, had not the government fallen shortly afterwards. There are many who will witness to these events.

Do you think I would have survived all these years if I were engaged in public affairs and, acting as a good man must, came to the help of justice and considered this the most important thing? Far from it, gentlemen of the jury, nor would any other man. Throughout my life, in any public activity I may have engaged in, I am the same man as I am in private life. I have never come to an agreement with anyone to act unjustly, neither with anyone else nor with any one of those who they slanderously say are my pupils. I have never been anyone's teacher. If anyone, young or old, desires to listen to me when I am talking and dealing with my own concerns, I have never begrudged this to anyone, but I do not converse when I receive a fee and not when I do not. I am equally ready to question the rich and the poor if anyone is willing to answer my questions and listen to what I say. And I cannot justly be held responsible for the good or bad conduct of these people, as I never promised to teach them anything and have not done so. If anyone says that he has learned anything from me, or that he heard anything privately that the others did not hear, be assured that he is not telling the truth.

Why then do some people enjoy spending considerable time in my company? You have heard why, gentlemen of the jury, I have told you the whole truth. They enjoy hearing those being questioned who think they are wise, but are not. And this is not unpleasant. To do this has, as I say, been enjoined upon me by the god, by means of oracles and dreams, and in every other way that a divine manifestation has ever ordered a man to do anything. This is true, gentlemen, and can easily be established.

If I corrupt some young men and have corrupted others, then surely some of them who have grown older and realized that I gave them bad advice when they were

A violent storm prevented the Athenian generals from rescuing their survivors. For this they were tried in Athens and sentenced to death by the assembly. They were tried in a body, and it is this to which Socrates objected in the Council's presiding committee which prepared the business of the assembly. He obstinately persisted in his opposition, in which he stood alone, and was overruled by the majority. Six generals who were in Athens were executed.]

10. [This was the harsh oligarchy that was set up after the final defeat of Athens in 404 B.C. and that ruled Athens for some nine months in 404-3 before the democracy was restored.]

young should now themselves come up here to accuse me and avenge themselves. If they were unwilling to do so themselves, then some of their kindred, their fathers or brothers or other relations should recall it now if their family had been harmed by me. I see many of these present here, first Crito, my contemporary and fellow demesman, the father of Critoboulos here; next Lysanias of Sphettus, the father of Aeschines here; also Antiphon the Cephisian, the father of Epigenes; and others whose brothers spent their time in this way, Nicostratus, the son of Theozotides, brother of Theodotus, and Theodotus has died so he could not influence him; Paralios here, son of Demodocus, whose brother was Theages; there is Adeimantus, son of Ariston, brother of Plato here; Acantidorus, brother of Apollodorus here.

I could mention many others, some one of whom surely Meletus should have brought in as witness in his own speech. If he forgot to do so, then let him do it now; I will yield time if he has anything of the kind to say. You will find quite the contrary, gentlemen. These men are all ready to come to the help of the corruptor, the man who has harmed their kindred, as Meletus and Anytus say. Now those who were corrupted might well have reason to help me, but the uncorrupted, their kindred who are older men, have no reason to help me except the right and proper one, that they know that Meletus is lying and that I am telling the truth.

Very well, gentlemen of the jury. This, and maybe other similar things, is what I have to say in my defence. Perhaps one of you might be angry as he recalls that when he himself stood trial on a less dangerous charge, he begged and implored the jury with many tears, that he brought his children and many of his friends and family into court to arouse as much pity as he could, but that I do none of these things, even though I may seem to be running the ultimate risk. Thinking of this, he might feel resentful and angry and cast his vote in anger. If there is such a one among you—I do not deem there is, but if there is—I think it would be right to say in reply: "My good sir, I too have a household and, in Homer's phrase, I am not born from 'oak or rock' but from men, so that I have a family, indeed three sons, gentlemen of the jury, of whom one is an adolescent while two are children. Nevertheless, I will not beg you to acquit me by bringing them here. Why do I do none of these things? Not through arrogance, gentlemen, nor through lack of respect for you. Whether I am brave in the face of death is another matter, but with regard to my reputation and yours and that of the whole city, it does not seem right to me to do these things, especially at my age and with my reputation. For it is generally believed, whether it be true or false, that in certain respects Socrates is superior to the majority of men. Now if those of you who are considered superior, be it in wisdom or courage or whatever other virtue makes them so, are seen behaving like that, it would be a disgrace. Yet I have often seen them do this sort of thing when standing trial, men who are thought to be somebody, doing amazing things as if they thought it a terrible thing to die, and as if they were to be immortal if you did not execute them. I think these men bring shame upon the city so that a stranger, too, would assume that those who are outstanding in virtue among the Athenians, whom they themselves select from themselves to fill offices of state and receive other honours, are in no way better than women. You should not act like that, gentlemen of the jury, those of you who have any reputation at all, and if we do, you should not allow it. You should make it very clear that you will more readily convict a man who performs these pitiful dramatics in court and so makes the city a laughingstock, than a man who keeps quiet.

Quite apart from the question of reputation, gentlemen, I do not think it right to supplicate the jury and to be acquitted because of this, but to teach and persuade   c them. It is not the purpose of a juryman's office to give justice as a favour to whomever seems good to him, but to judge according to law, and this he has sworn to do. We should not accustom you to perjure yourselves, nor should you make a habit of it. This is irreverent conduct for either of us.

Do not deem it right for me, gentlemen of the jury, that I should act towards you in a way that I do not consider to be good or just or pious, especially, by Zeus, as I   d am being prosecuted by Meletus here for impiety; clearly, if I convinced you by my supplication to do violence to your oath of office, I would be teaching you not to believe in the gods, and my defence would convict me of not believing in them. This is far from being the case, gentlemen, for I do believe in them as none of my accusers do. I leave it to you and the god to judge me in the way that will be best for me and for you.

[The jury now gives its verdict of guilty, and Meletus asks for the penalty of death.]

There are many other reasons for my not being angry with you for convicting me,   e gentlemen of the jury, and what happened was not unexpected. I am much more surprised at the number of votes cast on each side, for I did not think the decision   36 would be by so few votes but by a great many. As it is, a switch of only thirty votes would have acquitted me. I think myself that I have been cleared on Meletus' charges, and it is clear to all that, if Anytus and Lycon had not joined him in accusing me, he would have been fined a thousand drachmas for not receiving a fifth of   b the votes.

He assesses the penalty at death. What counter-assessment should I propose to you, gentlemen of the jury? Clearly it should be a penalty I deserve, and what do I deserve to suffer or to pay because I have deliberately not led a quiet life but have neglected what occupies most people: wealth, household affairs, the position of general or public orator or the other offices, the political clubs and factions that exist in the city? I thought myself too honest to survive if I occupied myself with those things. I did not follow that path that would have made me of no use either to you or to myself, but I   c went to each of you privately and conferred upon him what I say is the greatest benefit, by persuading him not to care for any of his belongings before caring that he himself should be as good and as wise as possible, not to care for the city's possessions more than for the city itself, and to care for other things in the same way. What do I   d deserve for being such a man? Some good, gentlemen of the jury, if I must truly make an assessment according to my deserts, and something suitable. What is suitable for a poor benefactor who needs leisure to exhort you? Nothing is more suitable, gentlemen, than for such a man to be fed in the Prytaneum,[11] much more suitable for him than for anyone of you who has won a victory at Olympia with a pair or a team of horses. The Olympian victor makes you think yourself happy, I make you be happy.   e Besides, he does not need food, but I do. So if I must make a just assessment of what I deserve, I assess it at this: free meals in the Prytaneum.   37

When I say this you may think, as when I spoke of appeals to pity and entreaties, that I speak arrogantly, but that is not the case, gentlemen of the jury, rather it is

11. [The Prytaneum was the magistrates' hall or town hall of Athens in which public entertainments were given, particularly to Olympian victors on their return home.]

like this: I am convinced that I never willingly wrong anyone, but I am not convincing
you of this, for we have talked together but a short time. If it were the law with us, as it

b   is elsewhere, that a trial for life should not last one but many days, you would be convinced, but now it is not easy to dispel great slanders in a short time. Since I am convinced that I wrong no one, I am not likely to wrong myself, to say that I deserve some
evil and to make some such assessment against myself. What should I fear? That I
should suffer the penalty Meletus has assessed against me, of which I say I do not
know whether it is good or bad? Am I then to choose in preference to this something
that I know very well to be an evil and assess the penalty at that? Imprisonment? Why

c   should I live in prison, always subjected to the ruling magistrates? A fine, and imprisonment until I pay it? That would be the same thing for me, as I have no money.
Exile? For perhaps you might accept that assessment.

I should have to be inordinately fond of life, gentlemen of the jury, to be so
unreasonable as to suppose that other men will easily tolerate my company and conversation when you, my fellow citizens, have been unable to endure them, but found

d   them a burden and resented them so that you are now seeking to get rid of them.
Far from it, gentlemen. It would be a fine life at my age to be driven out of one city
after another, for I know very well that wherever I go the young men will listen to
my talk as they do here. If I drive them away, they will themselves persuade their

e   elders to drive me out; if I do not drive them away, their fathers and relations will
drive me out on their behalf.

Perhaps someone might say: But Socrates, if you leave us will you not be able to
live quietly, without talking? Now this is the most difficult point on which to convince some of you. If I say that it is impossible for me to keep quiet because that

38   means disobeying the god, you will not believe me and will think I am being ironi-
cal. On the other hand, if I say that it is the greatest good for a man to discuss virtue
every day and those other things about which you hear me conversing and testing
myself and others, for the unexamined life is not worth living for man, you will believe me even less.

What I say is true, gentlemen, but it is not easy to convince you. At the same

b   time, I am not accustomed to think that I deserve any penalty. If I had money, I
would assess the penalty at the amount I could pay, for that would not hurt me, but
I have none, unless you are willing to set the penalty at the amount I can pay, and
perhaps I could pay you one mina of silver.[12] So that is my assessment.

Plato here, gentlemen of the jury, and Crito and Critoboulus and Apollodorus
bid me put the penalty at thirty minae, and they will stand surety for the money.
Well then, that is my assessment, and they will be sufficient guarantee of payment.

[The jury now votes again and sentences Socrates to death.]

c   It is for the sake of a short time, gentlemen of the jury, that you will acquire the
reputation and the guilt, in the eyes of those who want to denigrate the city, of having killed Socrates, a wise man, for they will say that I am wise even if I am not. If
you had waited but a little while, this would have happened of its own accord. You
see my age, that I am already advanced in years and close to death. I am saying this

12. [One mina was 100 drachmas, equivalent to, say, twenty-five dollars, though in purchasing power
probably five times greater. In any case, a ridiculously small sum under the circumstances.]

not to all of you but to those who condemned me to death, and to these same jurors I   d
say: Perhaps you think that I was convicted for lack of such words as might have
convinced you, if I thought I should say or do all I could to avoid my sentence. Far
from it. I was convicted because I lacked not words but boldness and shamelessness
and the willingness to say to you what you would most gladly have heard from me,
lamentations and tears and my saying and doing many things that I say are unwor-   e
thy of me but that you are accustomed to hear from others. I did not think then that
the danger I ran should make me do anything mean, nor do I now regret the nature
of my defence. I would much rather die after this kind of defence than live after
making the other kind. Neither I nor any other man should, on trial or in war, contrive to avoid death at any cost. Indeed it is often obvious in battle that one could   39
escape death by throwing away one's weapons and by turning to supplicate one's
pursuers, and there are many ways to avoid death in every kind of danger if one will
venture to do or say anything to avoid it. It is not difficult to avoid death, gentlemen
of the jury, it is much more difficult to avoid wickedness, for it runs faster than
death. Slow and elderly as I am, I have been caught by the slower pursuer, whereas   b
my accusers, being clever and sharp, have been caught by the quicker, wickedness.
I leave you now, condemned to death by you, but they are condemned by truth to
wickedness and injustice. So I maintain my assessment, and they maintain theirs.
This perhaps had to happen, and I think it is as it should be.

Now I want to prophesy to those who convicted me, for I am at the point when   c
men prophesy most, when they are about to die. I say gentlemen, to those who
voted to kill me, that vengeance will come upon you immediately after my death, a
vengeance much harder to bear than that which you took in killing me. You did this
in the belief that you would avoid giving an account of your life, but I maintain that
quite the opposite will happen to you. There will be more people to test you, whom
I now held back, but you did not notice it. They will be more difficult to deal with as   d
they will be younger and you will resent them more. You are wrong if you believe
that by killing people you will prevent anyone from reproaching you for not living
in the right way. To escape such tests is neither possible nor good, but it is best and
easiest not to discredit others but to prepare oneself to be as good as possible. With
this prophecy to you who convicted me, I part from you.

I should be glad to discuss what has happened with those who voted for my   e
acquittal during the time that the officers of the court are busy and I do not yet have
to depart to my death. So, gentlemen, stay with me awhile, for nothing prevents us
from talking to each other while it is allowed. To you, as being my friends, I want to
show the meaning of what has occurred. A surprising thing has happened to me,   40
judges—you I would rightly call judges. At all previous times my usual mantic sign
frequently opposed me, even in small matters, when I was about to do something
wrong, but now that, as you can see for yourselves, I was faced with what one might
think and what is generally thought to be, the worst of evils, my divine sign has not
opposed me, either when I left home at dawn, or when I came into court, or at any   b
time that I was about to say something during my speech. Yet in other talks it often
held me back in the middle of my speaking, but now it has opposed no word or deed
of mine. What do I think is the reason for this? I will tell you. What has happened to
me may well be a good thing, and those of us who believe death to be an evil are certainly mistaken. I have convincing proof of this, for it is impossible that my customary sign did not oppose me if I was not about to do what was right.   c

Let us reflect that there is good hope that death is a blessing, for it is one of two things: either the dead are nothing and have no perception of anything, or it is, as we are told, a change for the soul from here to another place. If it is complete lack of perception, like a dreamless sleep, then death would be a great advantage. For I think that if one had to pick out that night during which a man slept soundly and did not dream, put beside it the other nights and days of his life, and then see how many days and nights had been better and more pleasant than that night, not only a private person but the great king would find them easy to count compared with the other days and nights. If death is like this I say it is an advantage, for all eternity would then seem to be no more than a single night. If, on the other hand, death is a change from here to another place, and what we are told is true and all who have died are there, what greater blessing could there be, gentlemen of the jury? If anyone arriving in Hades will have escaped from those who call themselves judges here, and will find those true judges who are said to sit in judgment there, Minos and Radamanthus and Aeacus and Triptolemus and the other demi-gods who have been upright in their own life, would that be a poor kind of change? Again, what would one of you give to keep company with Orpheus and Musaeus, Hesiod and Homer? I am willing to die many times if that is true. It would be a wonderful way for me to spend my time whenever I met Palamedes and Ajax, the son of Telamon, and any other of the men of old who died through an unjust conviction, to compare my experience with theirs. I think it would be pleasant. Most important, I could spend my time testing and examining people there, as I do here, as to who among them is wise, and who thinks he is, but is not.

What would one not give, gentlemen of the jury, for the opportunity to examine the man who led the great expedition against Troy, or Odysseus, or Sisyphus, and innumerable other men and women one could mention. It would be an extraordinary happiness to talk with them, to keep company with them and examine them. In any case, they would certainly not put one to death for doing so. They are happier there than we are here in other respects, and for the rest of time they are deathless, if indeed what we are told is true.

You too must be of good hope as regards death, gentlemen of the jury, and keep this one truth in mind, that a good man cannot be harmed either in life or in death, and that his affairs are not neglected by the gods. What has happened to me now has not happened of itself, but it is clear to me that it was better for me to die now and to escape from trouble. That is why my divine sign did not oppose me at any point. So I am certainly not angry with those who convicted me, or with my accusers. Of course that was not their purpose when they accused and convicted me, but they thought they were hurting me, and for this they deserve blame. This much I ask from them: when my sons grow up, avenge yourselves by causing them the same kind of grief that I caused you, if you think they care for money or anything else more than they care for virtue, or if they think they are somebody when they are nobody. Reproach them as I reproach you, that they do not care for the right things and think they are worthy when they are not worthy of anything. If you do this, I shall have been justly treated by you, and my sons also.

Now the hour to part has come. I go to die, you go to live. Which of us goes to the better lot is known to no one, except the god.

CRITO

SOCRATES: Why have you come so early, Crito? Or is it not still early?   43
CRITO: It certainly is.
S: How early?
C: Early dawn.
S: I am surprised that the warder was willing to listen to you.
C: He is quite friendly to me by now, Socrates. I have been here often and I have given him something.
S: Have you just come, or have you been here for some time?
C: A fair time.
S: Then why did you not wake me right away but sit there in silence?   b
C: By Zeus no, Socrates. I would not myself want to be in distress and awake so long. I have been surprised to see you so peacefully asleep. It was on purpose that I did not wake you, so that you should spend your time most agreeably. Often in the past throughout my life, I have considered the way you live happy, and especially so now that you bear your present misfortune so easily and lightly.
S: It would not be fitting at my age to resent the fact that I must die now.
C: Other men of your age are caught in such misfortunes, but their age does   c not prevent them resenting their fate.
S: That is so. Why have you come so early?
C: I bring bad news, Socrates, not for you, apparently, but for me and all your friends the news is bad and hard to bear. Indeed, I would count it among the hardest.
S: What is it? Or has the ship arrived from Delos, at the arrival of which I must   d die?
C: It has not arrived yet, but it will, I believe, arrive today, according to a message brought by some men from Sunium, where they left it. This makes it obvious that it will come today, and that your life must end tomorrow.
S: May it be for the best. If it so please the gods, so be it. However, I do not think it will arrive today.
C: What indication have you of this?   44
S: I will tell you. I must die the day after the ship arrives.
C: That is what those in authority say.
S: Then I do not think it will arrive on this coming day, but on the next. I take to witness of this a dream I had a little earlier during this night. It looks as if it was the right time for you not to wake me.
C: What was your dream?
S: I thought that a beautiful and comely woman dressed in white approached

Reprinted from *The Trial & Death of Socrates,* translated by G.M.A. Grube (Indianapolis: Hackett Publishing Company, 1975), by permission of the publisher.

b   me. She called me and said: "Socrates, may you arrive at fertile Phthia[1] on the third day."

C: A strange dream, Socrates.

S: But it seems clear enough to me, Crito

C: Too clear it seems, my dear Socrates, but listen to me even now and be saved. If you die, it will not be a single misfortune only for me. Not only will I be deprived of a friend, the like of whom I shall never find again, but many people who
c   do not know you or me very well will think that I could have saved you if I were willing to spend money, but that I did not care to do so. Surely there can be no worse reputation than to be thought to value money more highly than one's friends, for the majority will not believe that you yourself were not willing to leave prison while we were eager for you to do so.

S: My good Crito, why should we care so much for what the majority think? The most reasonable people, to whom one should pay more attention, will believe that things were done as they were done.

d   C: You see, Socrates, that one must also pay attention to the opinion of the majority. Your present situation makes clear that the majority can inflict not the least but pretty well the greatest evils if one is slandered among them.

S: Would that the majority could inflict the greatest evils, for they would then be capable of the greatest good, and that would be fine, but now they cannot do either. They cannot make a man either wise or foolish, but they inflict things haphazardly.

e   C: That may be so. But tell me this, Socrates, are you anticipating that I and your other friends would have trouble with the informers if you escape from here, as having stolen you away, and that we should be compelled to lose all our property or
45   pay heavy fines and suffer other punishment besides? If you have any such fear, forget it. We would be justified in running this risk to save you, and worse, if necessary. Do follow my advice, and do not act differently.

S: I do have these things in mind, Crito, and also many others.

C: Have no such fear. It is not much money that some people require to save you and get you out of here. Further, do you not see that those informers are cheap, and that not much money would be needed to deal with them? My money is available and
b   is, I think, sufficient. If, because of your affection for me, you feel you should not spend any of mine, there are those strangers here ready to spend money. One of them, Simmias the Theban, has brought enough for this very purpose. Kebes, too, and a good many others. So, as I say, do not let this fear make you hesitate to save yourself, nor let what you said in court trouble you, that you would not know what to do with yourself if you left Athens, for you would be welcomed in many places to which you might go.
c   If you want to go to Thessaly, I have friends there who will greatly appreciate you and keep you safe, so that no one in Thessaly will harm you.

Besides, Socrates, I do not think that what you are doing is right, to give up your life when you can save it, and to hasten your fate as your enemies would hasten it,

---

1. [A quotation from the ninth book of the *Iliad* (363). Achilles has rejected all the presents of Agamemnon for him to return to the battle, and threatens to go home. He says his ships will sail in the morning, and with good weather he might arrive on the third day "in fertile Phthia" (which is his home). The dream means, obviously, that on the third day Socrates' soul, after death, will find its home. As always, counting the first member of a series, the third day is the day after tomorrow.—G.M.A.G.]

and indeed have hastened it in their wish to destroy you. Moreover, I think you are betraying your sons by going away and leaving them, when you could bring them up and educate them. You thus show no concern for what their fate may be. They will probably have the usual fate of orphans. Either one should not have children, or one should share with them to the end the toil of upbringing and education. You seem to me to choose the easiest path, whereas one should choose the path a good and courageous man would choose, particularly when one claims throughout one's life to care for virtue.

I feel ashamed on your behalf and on behalf of us, your friends, lest all that has happened to you be thought due to cowardice on our part: the fact that your trial came to court when it need not have done so, the handling of the trial itself, and now this absurd ending which will be thought to have got beyond our control through some cowardice and unmanliness on our part, since we did not save you, or you save yourself, when it was possible and could be done if we had been of the slightest use. Consider, Socrates, whether this is not only evil, but shameful, both for you and for us. Take counsel with yourself, or rather the time for counsel is past and the decision should have been taken, and there is no further opportunity, for this whole business must be ended tonight. If we delay now, then it will no longer be possible, it will be too late. Let me persuade you on every count, Socrates, and do not act otherwise.

S: My dear Crito, your eagerness is worth much if it should have some right aim; if not, then the greater your keenness the more difficult it is to deal with. We must therefore examine whether we should act in this way or not, as not only now but at all times I am the kind of man who listens only to the argument that on reflection seems best to me. I cannot, now that this fate has come upon me, discard the arguments I used; they seem to me much the same. I value and respect the same principles as before, and if we have no better arguments to bring up at this moment, be sure that I shall not agree with you, not even if the power of the majority were to frighten us with more bogeys, as if we were children, with threats of incarcerations and executions and confiscation of property. How should we examine this matter most reasonably? Would it be by taking up first your argument about the opinions of men, whether it is sound in every case that one should pay attention to some opinions, but not to others? Or was that well-spoken before the necessity to die came upon me, but now it is clear that this was said in vain for the sake of argument, that it was in truth play and nonsense? I am eager to examine together with you, Crito, whether this argument will appear in any way different to me in my present circumstances, or whether it remains the same, whether we are to abandon it or believe it. It was said on every occasion by those who thought they were speaking sensibly, as I have just now been speaking, that one should greatly value some people's opinions, but not others. Does that seem to you a sound statement?

You, as far as a human being can tell, are exempt from the likelihood of dying tomorrow, so the present misfortune is not likely to lead you astray. Consider then, do you not think it a sound statement that one must not value all the opinions of men, but some and no others, nor the opinions of all men, but those of some and not of others? What do you say? Is this not well said?

C: It is.

S: One should value the good opinions, and not the bad ones?

C: Yes.

S: The good opinions are those of wise men, the bad ones those of foolish men?

C: Of course.

b
S: Come then, what of statements such as this: Should a man professionally engaged in physical training pay attention to the praise and blame and opinion of any man, or to those of one man only, namely a doctor or trainer?

C: To those of one only.

S: He should therefore fear the blame and welcome the praise of that one man, and not those of the many?

C: Obviously.

S: He must then act and exercise, eat and drink in the way the one, the trainer and the one who knows, thinks right, not all the others?

C: That is so.

c
S: Very well. And if he disobeys the one, disregards his opinion and his praises while valuing those of the many who have no knowledge, will he not suffer harm?

C: Of course.

S: What is that harm, where does it tend, and what part of the man who disobeys does it affect?

C: Obviously the harm is to his body, which it ruins.

S: Well said. So with other matters, not to enumerate them all, and certainly with actions just and unjust, shameful and beautiful, good and bad, about which we are now deliberating, should we follow the opinion of the many and fear it, or that of the one, if there is one who has knowledge of these things and before whom we feel fear and shame more than before all the others. If we do not follow his directions, we shall harm and corrupt that part of ourselves that is improved by just actions and destroyed by unjust actions. Or is there nothing in this?

d

C: I think there certainly is, Socrates.

S: Come now, if we ruin that which is improved by health and corrupted by disease by not following the opinions of those who know, is life worth living for us when that is ruined? And that is the body, is it not?

e

C: Yes.

S: And is life worth living with a body that is corrupted and in bad condition?

C: In no way.

S: And is life worth living for us with that part of us corrupted that unjust action harms and just action benefits? Or do we think that part of us, whatever it is, that is concerned with justice and injustice, is inferior to the body?

48

C: Not at all.

S: It is more valuable?

C: Much more.

S: We should not then think so much of what the majority will say about us, but what he will say who understands justice and injustice, the one, that is, and the truth itself. So that, in the first place, you were wrong to believe that we should care for the opinion of the many about what is just, beautiful, good, and their opposites. "But," someone might say, "the many are able to put us to death."

b
C: That too is obvious, Socrates, and someone might well say so.

S: And, my admirable friend, that argument that we have gone through remains, I think, as before. Examine the following statement in turn as to whether it stays the same or not, that the most important thing is not life, but the good life.

C: It stays the same.

S: And that the good life, the beautiful life, and the just life are the same; does that still hold, or not?

C: It does hold.

S: As we have agreed so far, we must examine next whether it is right for me to try to get out of here when the Athenians have not acquitted me. If it is seen to be right, we will try to do so; if it is not, we will abandon the idea. As for those questions you raise about money, reputation, the upbringing of children, Crito, those considerations in truth belong to those people who easily put men to death and would bring them to life again if they could, without thinking; I mean the majority of men. For us, however, since our argument leads to this, the only valid consideration, as we were saying just now, is whether we should be acting rightly in giving money and gratitude to those who will lead me out of here, and ourselves helping with the escape, or whether in truth we shall do wrong in doing all this. If it appears that we shall be acting unjustly, then we have no need at all to take into account whether we shall have to die if we stay here and keep quiet, or suffer in another way, rather than do wrong.

C: I think you put that beautifully, Socrates, but see what we should do.

S: Let us examine the question together, my dear friend, and if you can make any objection while I am speaking, make it and I will listen to you, but if you have no objection to make, my dear Crito, then stop now from saying the same thing so often, that I must leave here against the will of the Athenians. I think it important to persuade you before I act, and not to act against your wishes. See whether the start of our enquiry is adequately stated, and try to answer what I ask you in the way you think best.

C: I shall try.

S: Do we say that one must never in any way do wrong willingly, or must one do wrong in one way and not in another? Is to do wrong never good or admirable, as we have agreed in the past, or have all these former agreements been washed out during the last few days? Have we at our age failed to notice for some time that in our serious discussions we were no different from children? Above all, is the truth such as we used to say it was, whether the majority agree or not, and whether we must still suffer worse things than we do now, or will be treated more gently, that nonetheless, wrongdoing is in every way harmful and shameful to the wrongdoer? Do we say so or not?

C: We do.

S: So one must never do wrong.

C: Certainly not.

S: Nor must one, when wronged, inflict wrong in return, as the majority believe, since one must never do wrong.

C: That seems to be the case.

S: Come now, should one injure anyone or not, Crito?

C: One must never do so.

S: Well then, if one is oneself injured, is it right, as the majority say, to inflict an injury in return, or is it not?

C: It is never right.

S: Injuring people is no different from wrongdoing.

C: That is true.

S: One should never do wrong in return, nor injure any man, whatever injury one has suffered at his hands. And Crito, see that you do not agree to this, contrary to your belief. For I know that only a few people hold this view or will hold it, and there is no common ground between those who hold this view and those who do not, but they inevitably despise each other's views. So then consider very carefully whether we have this view in common, and whether you agree, and let this be the basis of our deliberation, that neither to do wrong or to return a wrong is ever right, not even to injure in return for an injury received. Or do you disagree and do not share this view as a basis for discussion? I have held it for a long time and still hold it now, but if you think otherwise, tell me now. If, however, you stick to our former opinion, then listen to the next point.

C: I stick to it and agree with you. So say on.

S: Then I state the next point, or rather I ask you: when one has come to an agreement that is just with someone, should one fulfill it or cheat on it?

C: One should fulfill it.

S: See what follows from this: if we leave here without the city's permission, are we injuring people whom we should least injure? And are we sticking to a just agreement, or not?

C: I cannot answer your question, Socrates. I do not know.

S: Look at it this way. If, as we were planning to run away from here, or whatever one should call it, the laws and the state came and confronted us and asked: "Tell me, Socrates, what are you intending to do? Do you not by this action you are attempting intend to destroy us, the laws, and indeed the whole city, as far as you are concerned? Or do you think it possible for a city not to be destroyed if the verdicts of its courts have no force but are nullified and set at naught by private individuals?" What shall we answer to this and other such arguments? For many things could be said, especially by an orator on behalf of this law we are destroying, which orders that the judgments of the courts shall be carried out. Shall we say in answer, "The city wronged me, and its decision was not right." Shall we say that, or what?

C: Yes, by Zeus, Socrates, that is our answer.

S: Then what if the laws said: "Was that the agreement between us, Socrates, or was it to respect the judgments that the city came to?" And if we wondered at their words, they would perhaps add: "Socrates, do not wonder at what we say but answer, since you are accustomed to proceed by question and answer. Come now, what accusation do you bring against us and the city, that you should try to destroy us? Did we not, first, bring you to birth, and was it not through us that your father married your mother and begat you? Tell us, do you find anything to criticize in those of us who are concerned with marriage?" And I would say that I do not criticize them. "Or in those of us concerned with the nurture of babies and the education that you too received? Were those assigned to that subject not right to instruct your father to educate you in the arts and in physical culture?" And I would say that they were right. "Very well," they would continue, "and after you were born and nurtured and educated, could you, in the first place, deny that you are our offspring and servant, both you and your forefathers? If that is so, do you think that we are on an equal footing as regards the right, and that whatever we do to you it is right for you to do to us? You were not on an equal footing with your father as regards the right, nor with your master if you had one, so as to retaliate for anything they did to you, to revile them if they reviled you, to beat them if they beat you, and so with many other things. Do you think you have this right to retaliation against your country and its laws? That if we undertake to destroy you and think it right to do so, you can undertake to destroy us, as far as you can, in return? And will you say that you are right to do so, you who truly care for virtue? Is your wisdom such as not to realize that your country is to be honoured more than your mother, your father and all your ancestors, that it is more to be revered and more sacred, and that it counts for more among the gods and sensible men, that you must worship it, yield to it and placate its anger more than your father's? You must either persuade it or obey its orders, and endure in silence whatever it instructs you to endure, whether blows or bonds, and if it leads you into war to be wounded or killed, you must obey. To do so is right, and one must not give way or retreat or leave one's post, but both in war and in courts and everywhere else, one must obey the commands of one's city and country, or persuade it as to the nature of justice. It is impious to bring violence to bear against your mother or father, it is much more so to use it against your country." What shall we say in reply, Crito, that the laws speak the truth, or not?

C: I think they do.

S: "Reflect now, Socrates," the laws might say, "that if what we say is true, you are not treating us rightly by planning to do what you are planning. We have given you birth, nurtured you, educated you, we have given you and all other citizens a share of all the good things we could. Even so, by giving every Athenian the opportunity, after he has reached manhood and observed the affairs of the city and us the laws, we proclaim that if we do not please him, he can take his possessions and go wherever he pleases. Not one of our laws raises any obstacle or forbids him, if he is not satisfied with us or the city, if one of you wants to go and live in a colony or wants to go anywhere else, and keep his property. We say, however, that whoever of you remains, when he sees how we conduct our trials and manage the city in other ways, has in fact come to an agreement with us to obey our instructions. We say that the one who disobeys does wrong in three ways, first because in us he disobeys his parents, also those who brought him up, and because, in spite of his agreement, he neither obeys us nor, if we do something wrong, does he try to persuade us to do better. Yet we only propose things, we do not issue savage commands to do whatever we order; we give two alternatives, either to persuade us or to do what we say. He does neither. We do say that you too, Socrates, are open to those charges if you do what you have in mind; you would be among not the least but the most guilty of the Athenians." And if I should say "Why so?" they might well be right to upbraid me and say that I am among the Athenians who most definitely came to that agreement with them. They might well say: "Socrates, we have convincing proofs that we and the city were congenial to you. You would not have dwelt here most consistently of all the Athenians if the city had not been exceedingly pleasing to you. You have never left the city, even to see a festival, nor for any other reason except military service; you have never gone to stay in any other city, as people do; you have had no desire to know another city or other laws; we and our city satisfied you.

"So decisively did you choose us and agree to be a citizen under us. Also, you have had children in this city, thus showing that it was congenial to you. Then at your trial you could have assessed your penalty at exile if you wished, and you are now attempting to do against the city's wishes what you could then have done with her consent. Then you prided yourself that you did not resent death, but you chose, as you said, death in preference to exile. Now, however, those words do not make you ashamed, and you pay no heed to us, the laws, as you plan to destroy us, and you act like the meanest type of slave by trying to run away, contrary to your undertakings and your agreement to live as a citizen under us. First then, answer us on this very point, whether we speak the truth when we say that you agreed, not only in words but by your deeds, to live in accordance with us." What are we to say to that, Crito? Must we not agree?

C: We must, Socrates.

S: "Surely," they might say, "you are breaking the undertakings and agreements that you made with us without compulsion or deceit, and under no pressure of time for deliberation. You have had seventy years during which you could have gone away if you did not like us, and if you thought our agreements unjust. You did not choose to go to Sparta or to Crete, which you are always saying are well governed, nor to any other city, Greek or foreign. You have been away from Athens less than the lame or the blind or other handicapped people. It is clear that the city has been outstandingly more congenial to you than to other Athenians, and so have we, the laws, for what city can please without laws? Will you then not now stick to our agreements? You will, Socrates, if we can persuade you, and not make yourself a laughingstock by leaving the city.

"For consider what good you will do yourself or your friends by breaking our agreements and committing such a wrong. It is pretty obvious that your friends will themselves be in danger of exile, disfranchisement and loss of property. As for yourself, if you go to one of the nearby cities—Thebes or Megara, both are well governed—you will arrive as an enemy to their government; all who care for their city will look on you with suspicion, as a destroyer of the laws. You will also strengthen the conviction of the jury that they passed the right sentence on you, for anyone who destroys the laws could easily be thought to corrupt the young and the ignorant. Or will you avoid cities that are well governed and men who are civilized? If you do this, will your life be worth living? Will you have social intercourse with them and not be ashamed to talk to them? And what will you say? The same as you did here, that virtue and justice are man's most precious possession, along with lawful behaviour and the laws? Do you not think that Socrates would appear to be an unseemly kind of person? One must think so. Or will you leave those places and go to Crito's friends in Thessaly? There you will find the greatest license and disorder, and they may enjoy hearing from you how absurdly you escaped from prison in some disguise, in a leather jerkin or some other things in which escapees wrap themselves, thus altering your appearance. Will there be no one to say that you, likely to live but a short time more, were so greedy for life that you transgressed the most important laws? Possibly, Socrates, if you do not annoy anyone, but if you do, many disgraceful things will be said about you.

"You will spend your time ingratiating yourself with all men, and be at their beck and call. What will you do in Thessaly but feast, as if you had gone to a banquet in Thessaly? As for those conversations of yours about justice and the rest of virtue, where will they be? You say you want to live for the sake of your children, that you may bring them up and educate them. How so? Will you bring them up and educate them by taking them to Thessaly and making strangers of them, that they may enjoy that too? Or not so, but they will be better brought up and educated here, while you are alive, though absent? Yes, your friends will look after them. Will they look after them if you go and live in Thessaly, but not if you go away to the underworld? If those who profess themselves your friends are any good at all, one must assume that they will.

"Be persuaded by us who have brought you up, Socrates. Do not value either your children or your life or anything else more than goodness, in order that when you arrive in Hades you may have all this as your defence before the rulers there. If you do this deed, you will not think it better or more just or more pious here, nor will any one of your friends, nor will it be better for you when you arrive yonder. As it is, you depart, if you depart, after being wronged not by us, the laws, but by men; but if you depart after shamefully returning wrong for wrong and injury for injury, after breaking your agreement and contract with us, after injuring those you should injure least—yourself, your friends, your country and us—we shall be angry with you while you are still alive, and our brothers, the laws of the underworld, will not receive you kindly, knowing that you tried to destroy us as far as you could. Do not let Crito persuade you, rather than us, to do what he says."

Crito, my dear friend, be assured that these are the words I seem to hear, as the Corybants hear the music of their flutes, and the echo of these words resounds in me, and makes it impossible for me to hear anything else. As far as my present beliefs go, if you speak in opposition to them, you will speak in vain. However, if you think you can accomplish anything, speak.

C: I have nothing to say, Socrates.

S: Let it be then, Crito, and let us act in this way, since this is the way the god is leading us.

PHAEDO

57   ECHECRATES: Were you with Socrates yourself, Phaedo,[1] on the day when he drank the poison in prison, or did someone else tell you about it?

    PHAEDO: I was there myself, Echecrates.

    E: What are the things he said before he died? And how did he die? I should be glad to hear this. Hardly anyone from Phlius[2] visits Athens nowadays, nor has

b any stranger come from Athens for some time who could give us a clear account of what happened, except that he drank the poison and died, but nothing more.

58   P: Did you not even hear how the trial went?

    E: Yes, someone did tell us about that, and we wondered that he seems to have died a long time after the trial took place. Why was that, Phaedo?

    P: That was by chance, Echecrates. The day before the trial, as it happened, the prow of the ship that the Athenians send to Delos had been crowned with garlands.

    E: What ship is that?

    P: It is the ship in which, the Athenians say, Theseus once sailed to Crete, tak-

b ing with him the two lots of seven victims.[3] He saved them and was himself saved. They vowed then to Apollo, so the story goes, that if they were saved they would send a mission to Delos every year. And from that time to this they send such an annual mission to the god. They have a law to keep the city pure while it lasts, and no execution may take place once the mission has begun until the ship has made its journey to Delos and returned to Athens, and this can sometimes take a long time if the winds delay it. The mission begins when the priest of Apollo crowns the prow of

c the ship, and this happened, as I say, the day before Socrates' trial. That is why Socrates was in prison a long time between his trial and his execution.

    E: What about his actual death, Phaedo? What did he say? What did he do? Who of his friends were with him? Or did the authorities not allow them to be present and he died with no friends present?

d   P: By no means. Some were present, in fact, a good many.

    E: Please be good enough to tell us all that occurred as fully as possible, unless you have some pressing business.

Translated by G.M.A. Grube. The translation follows Burnet's Oxford text except in rare instances. The only liberty taken is where the answers to Socrates' questions are very brief, merely indicating assent or the like. In such instances, "he said," the so-frequent repetition of which reads awkwardly in English, has been replaced by a dash, to indicate a change of speaker.

1. [Phaedo was a young friend of Socrates who later founded a school of philosophy at Elis— G.M.A.G.]

2. [Phlius was a community in the northeastern part of the Peloponnesus where a Pythagorean society flourished about this time. We are told by Diogenes Laertius (early third century A.D.) that Echecrates was a member of that society.]

3. [Legend says that Minos, king of Crete, compelled the Athenians to send seven youths and seven maidens every year to be sacrificed to the Minotaur until Theseus saved them and killed the monster.]

P: I have the time and I will try to tell you the whole story, for nothing gives me more pleasure than to call Socrates to mind, whether talking about him myself, or listening to someone else do so.

E: Your hearers will surely be like you in this, Phaedo. So do try to tell us every detail as exactly as you can.

P: I certainly found being there an astonishing experience. Although I was witnessing the death of one who was my friend, I had no feeling of pity, for the man appeared happy both in manner and words as he died nobly and without fear, Echecrates, so that it struck me that even in going down to the underworld he was going with the gods' blessing and that he would fare well when he got there, if anyone ever does. That is why I had no feeling of pity, such as would seem natural in my sorrow, nor indeed of pleasure, as we engaged in philosophical discussion as we were accustomed to do—for our arguments were of that sort—but I had a strange feeling, an unaccustomed mixture of pleasure and pain at the same time as I reflected that he was just about to die. All of us present were affected in much the same way, sometimes laughing, then weeping; especially one of us, Apollodorus—you know the man and his ways.

E: Of course I do.

P: He was quite overcome; but I was myself disturbed, and so were the others.

E: Who, Phaedo, were those present?

P: Among the local people there was Apollodorus, whom I mentioned, Critoboulos and his father,[4] also Hermogenes, Epigenes, Aeschines and Antisthenes. Ctesippus of Paeane was there, Menexenus and some others. Plato, I believe, was ill.[5]

E: Were there some strangers present?

P: Yes, Simmias from Thebes with Cebes and Phaidondes, and from Megara, Euclides and Terpsion.

E: What about Aristippus and Cleombrotus? Were they there?

P: No. They were said to be in Aegina.

E: Was there anyone else?

P: I think these were about all.

E: Well then, what do you say the conversation was about?

P: I will try to tell you everything from the beginning. On the previous days also both the others and I used to visit Socrates. We foregathered at daybreak at the court where the trial took place, for it was close to the prison, and each day we used

e

59

b

c

d

4. [The father of Critoboulos is Crito, who in the dialogue named after him tries to persuade Socrates to escape from jail. He is also mentioned in *Apology* 33d and plays a prominent part in the death scene at the end of this dialogue. Several of the other friends of Socrates mentioned here also appear in other dialogues. Hermogenes is one of the speakers in the *Cratylus*. Epigenes is mentioned in *Apology* 33d, as is Aeshines. Aeshines was a writer of Socratic dialogues. Menexenus has a part in the *Lysis* and has a dialogue named after him. Simmias and Cebes are mentioned in the *Crito*, 45b, as having come to Athens with enough money to secure Socrates' escape.]

5. [It is interesting to note that Plato makes it clear that he was *not* present on the last day of Socrates' life, whereas in the *Apology* he twice mentions (34a and 38b) that he *was* present at the trial. Whether this has any significance as regards the historical accuracy of the two works is anyone's guess. Probably it just happened to be so, but these are the only instances in which Plato mentions himself in all his works.]

to wait around talking until the prison should open, for it did not open early. When it opened we used to go in to Socrates and spend most of the day with him. On this day we gathered rather early, because when we left the prison on the previous evening we were informed that the ship from Delos had arrived, and so we told each other to come to the usual place as early as possible. When we arrived the gatekeeper who used to answer our knock came out and told us to wait and not go in until he told us to. "The Eleven,"[6] he said, "are freeing Socrates from his bonds and telling him how his death will take place today." After a short time he came and told us to go in. We found Socrates recently released from his chains, and Xanthippe—you know her—sitting by him, holding their baby. When she saw us, she cried out and said the sort of thing that women usually say: "Socrates, this is the last time your friends will talk to you and you to them." Socrates looked at Crito. "Crito," he said, "let someone take her home." And some of Crito's people led her away lamenting and beating her breast.

Socrates sat up on the bed, bent his leg and rubbed it with his hand, and as he rubbed he said: "What a strange thing that which men call pleasure seems to be, and how astonishing the relation it has with what is thought to be its opposite, namely pain! A man cannot have both at the same time. Yet if he pursues and catches the one, he is almost always bound to catch the other also, like two creatures with one head. I think that if Aesop had noted this he would have composed a fable that a god wished to reconcile their opposition but could not do so, so he joined their two heads together, and therefore when a man has the one, the other follows later. This seems to be happening to me. My bonds caused pain in my leg, and now pleasure seems to be following."

Cebes intervened and said: "By Zeus, yes, Socrates, you did well to remind me. Evenus[7] asked me the day before yesterday, as others had done before, what induced you to write poetry after you came to prison, you who had never composed any poetry before, putting the fables of Aesop into verse and composing the hymn to Apollo. If it is of any concern to you that I should have an answer to give to Evenus when he repeats his question, as I know he will, tell me what to say to him."

Tell him the truth, Cebes, he said, that I did not do this with the idea of rivalling him or his poems, for I knew that would not be easy, but I tried to find out the meaning of certain dreams and to satisfy my conscience in case it was this kind of art they were frequently bidding me to practise. The dreams were something like this: the same dream often came to me in the past, now in one shape now in another, but saying the same thing: "Socrates," it said, "practise and cultivate the arts." In the past I imagined that it was instructing and advising me to do what I was doing, such as those who encourage runners in a race, that the dream was thus bidding me do the very thing I was doing, namely, to practise the art of philosophy, this being the highest kind of art, and I was doing that.

But now, after my trial took place, and the festival of the god was preventing my execution, I thought that, in case my dream was bidding me to practise this popular art, I should not disobey it but compose poetry. I thought it safer not to leave here until I had satisfied my conscience by writing poems in obedience to the dream. So I first wrote in honour of the god of the present festival. After that I realized that a

6. [The Eleven were the police commissioners of Athens.]

7. [Socrates refers to Evenus as a Sophist and teacher of the young in *Apology* 20a–b.]

poet, if he is to be a poet, must compose fables, not arguments. Being no teller of fables myself, I took the stories I knew and had at hand, the fables of Aesop, and I versified the first ones I came across. Tell this to Evenus, Cebes, wish him well and bid him farewell, and tell him, if he is wise, to follow me as soon a possible. I am leaving today, it seems, as the Athenians so order it.

Said Simmias: "What kind of advice is this you are giving to Evenus, Socrates? I have met him many times, and from my observation he is not at all likely to follow it willingly."

How so, said he, is Evenus not a philosopher?

I think so, Simmias said.

Then Evenus will be willing, like every man who partakes worthily of philosophy. Yet perhaps he will not take his own life, for that, they say, is not right. As he said this, Socrates put his feet on the ground and remained in this position during the rest of the conversation.

Then Cebes asked: "How do you mean, Socrates, that it is not right to do oneself violence, and yet that the philosopher will be willing to follow one who is dying?"

Come now, Cebes, have you and Simmias, who keep company with Philolaus,[8] not heard about such things?

Nothing definite, Socrates.

Indeed, I too speak about this from hearsay, but I do not mind telling you what I have heard, for it is perhaps most appropriate for one who is about to depart yonder to tell and examine tales about what we believe that journey to be like. What else could one do in the time we have until sunset?

But whatever is the reason, Socrates, for people to say that it is not right to kill oneself? As to your question just now, I have heard Philolaus say this when staying in Thebes and I have also heard it from others, but I have never heard anyone give a clear account of the matter.

Well, he said, we must do our best, and you may yet hear one. And it may well astonish you if this subject, alone of all others, is simple and it is never, as with everything else, better at certain times and for certain people to die than to live. And if this is so, you may well find it astonishing that those for whom it is better to die are wrong to help themselves, and that they must wait for someone else to benefit them.

And Cebes, lapsing into his own dialect laughed quietly and said: "Zeus knows it is."

Indeed, said Socrates, it does seem unreasonable when put like that, but perhaps there is reason to it. There is the explanation that is put in the language of the mysteries, that we men are in a kind of prison, and that one must not free oneself or run away. That seems to me an impressive doctrine and one not easy to understand fully. However, Cebes, this seems to me well expressed, that the gods are our guardians and that men are one of their possessions. Or do you not think so?

I do, said Cebes.

8. [Philolaus was a contemporary Pythagorean. The reference to him here, as well as the fact that the story is told to Echecrates at Phlius, gives the whole dialogue a Pythagorean background, and this seems a recognition on Plato's part of Pythagorean influence regarding the theories that follow, in particular, the theory of Forms and the purification of man's eternal soul through intellectual activity.]

And would you not be angry if one of your possessions killed itself when you had
c   not given any sign that you wished it to die, and if you had any punishment you
could inflict, you would inflict it?

Certainly, he said.

Perhaps then, put in this way, it is not unreasonable that one should not kill
oneself before some god had indicated the necessity to do so, like the necessity now
put upon us.

That seems likely, said Cebes. As for what you were saying, that philosophers
should be willing and ready to die, that seems strange, Socrates, if what we said just
d   now is reasonable, namely that a god is our protector and that we are his possessions. It is not logical that the wisest of men should not resent leaving this service in
which they are governed by the best of masters, the gods, for a wise man cannot believe that he will look after himself better when he is free. A foolish man might easily think so, that he must escape from his master; he would not reflect that one must
e   not escape from a good master but stay with him as long as possible, because it
would be foolish to escape. But the sensible man would want always to remain with
one better than himself. So, Socrates, the opposite of what was said before is likely
to be true; the wise would resent dying, whereas the foolish would rejoice at it.

I thought that when Socrates heard this he was pleased by Cebes' argumentation.
Glancing at us, he said: "Cebes is always on the track of some arguments; he is cer-
63   tainly not willing to be at once convinced by what one says."

Said Simmias: "But actually, Socrates, I think myself that Cebes has a point now.
Why should truly wise men want to avoid the service of masters better than themselves, and leave them easily? And I think Cebes is aiming his argument at you, because you are bearing leaving us so lightly, and leaving those best of masters, as you
say yourself, the gods."

b   You are both justified in what you say, and I think you mean that I must make a
defence against this, as if I were in court.

You certainly must, said Simmias.

Come then, he said, let me try to make my defence to you more convincing than
it was to the jury. For, Simmias and Cebes, I should be wrong not to resent dying if
I did not believe that I should go first to other wise and good gods, and then to men
who have died and are better than men are here. Be assured that, as it is, I expect to
join the company of good men. This last I would not altogether insist on, but if I
c   insist on anything at all in these matters, it is that that I shall come to gods who are
very good masters. That is why I am not so resentful, because I have good hope that
some future awaits men after death, as we have been told for years, a much better
future for the good than for the wicked.

Well now, Socrates, said Simmias, do you intend to keep this belief to yourself as
d   you leave us, or would you share it with us? I certainly think it would be a blessing
for us too, and at the same time it would be your defence if you convince us of what
you say.

I will try, he said, but first let us see what it is that Crito here has, I think, been
wanting to say for quite a while.

What else, Socrates, said Crito, but what the man who is to give you the poison
has been telling me for some time, that I should warn you to talk as little as possible.
People get heated when they talk, he says, and one should not be heated when tak-

ing the poison, as those who do must sometimes drink it two or three times.   e

Socrates replied: "Take no notice of him; only let him be prepared to administer it twice or, if necessary, three times."

I was rather sure you would say that, Crito said, but he has been bothering me for some time.

Let him be, he said. I want to make my argument before you, my judges, as to why I think that a man who has truly spent his life in philosophy is probably right to be of good cheer in the face of death and to be very hopeful that after death he will attain the greatest blessings yonder. I will try to tell you, Simmias and Cebes, how this may be so. I am afraid that other people do not realize that the one aim of   64 those who practise philosophy in the proper manner is to practise for dying and death. Now if this is true, it would be strange indeed if they were eager for this all their lives and then resent it when what they have wanted and practised for a long time comes upon them.

Simmias laughed and said: "By Zeus, Socrates, you made me laugh, though I was in no laughing mood just now. I think that the majority, on hearing this, will think that it describes the philosophers very well, and our people in Thebes would   b thoroughly agree that philosophers are nearly dead and that the majority of men is well aware that they deserve to be."

And they would be telling the truth, Simmias, except for their being aware. They are not aware of the way true philosophers are nearly dead, nor of the way they deserve to be, nor of the sort of death. But never mind them, he said, let us talk among ourselves. Do we believe that there is such a thing as death?   c

Certainly, said Simmias.

Is it anything else than the separation of the soul from the body? Do we believe that death is this, namely, that the body comes to be separated by itself apart from the soul, and the soul comes to be separated by itself apart from the body? Is death anything else than that?

No, that is what it is, he said.

Consider then, my good sir, whether you share my opinion, for this will lead us to a better knowledge of what we are investigating. Do you think it is the part of a philosopher to be concerned with the so-called pleasures of food and drink?   d

By no means.

What about the pleasures of sex?

Not at all.

What of the other pleasures concerned with the service of the body? Do you think such a man prizes them greatly, the acquisition of distinguished clothes and shoes and the other bodily ornaments? Do you think he values these or despises them, except in so far as one cannot do without them?   e

I think the true philosopher despises them.

Do you not think, he said, that in general such a man's concer . is not with the body but that, as far as he can, he turns away from the body to ards the soul?

I do.

So in the first place, such things show clearly that the philosopher much more than other men frees the soul from association with the body as much as possible?   65

Apparently.

A man who finds no pleasure in such things and has no part in them is thought by the majority not to deserve to live and to be close to death; the man, that is, who does not care for the pleasures of the body.

What you say is certainly true.

Then what about the actual acquiring of knowledge? Is the body an obstacle when one associates it in the search for knowledge? I mean, for example, do men find any truth in sight or hearing, or are not even the poets[9] forever telling us that we do not see or hear anything accurately, and surely if those two physical senses are not clear or precise, our other senses can hardly be accurate, as they are all inferior to these. Do you not think so?

I certainly do, he said.

When then, he asked, does the soul grasp the truth? For whenever it attempts to examine anything with the body, it is clearly deceived by it.

True.

Is it not in reasoning if anywhere that any reality becomes clear to the soul?

Yes.

And indeed the soul reasons best when none of these senses trouble it, neither hearing nor sight, nor pain nor pleasure, but when it is as far as possible by itself, taking leave of the body and having no contact or association with it in its search for reality.

That is so.

And it is then that the soul of the philosopher most disdains the body, flees from it and seeks to be by itself?

It appears so.

What about the following, Simmias? Do we say that there is such a thing as the Just itself, or not?

We do say so, by Zeus.

And the Beautiful, and the Good?

Of course.

And have you ever seen any of these things with your eyes?

In no way, he said.

Or have you ever grasped them with any of your bodily senses? I am speaking of all things such as Size, Health, Strength and, in a word, the reality of all other things, that which each of them essentially is. Is what is most true in them contemplated through the body, or is this the position: whoever of us prepares himself best and most accurately to grasp that thing itself which he is investigating will come closest to the knowledge of it?

Obviously.

Then he will do this most perfectly who approaches the object with thought alone, without associating any sight with his thought, or dragging in any sense perception, but who, using pure thought alone, tries to track down each reality pure and by itself, freeing himself as far as possible from eyes and ears, and in a word,

---

9. ["Even the poets" because poetry concerns itself with the world of sense and appeals to the passions and emotions of the lowest part of the soul in the *Republic* (595a ff.), whereas in the *Phaedo* passions and emotions are attributed to the body.]

from the whole body, because the body confuses the soul and does not allow it to acquire truth and wisdom whenever it is associated with it. Will not that man reach reality, Simmias, if anyone does?

What you say, said Simmias, is indeed true.

All these things will necessarily make the true philosophers believe and say to each other something like this: "There is likely to be something such as a path to guide us out of our confusion, because as long as we have a body and our soul is fused with such an evil we shall never adequately attain what we desire, which we affirm to be the truth. The body keeps us busy in a thousand ways because of its need for nurture. Moreover, if certain diseases befall it, they impede our search for the truth. It fills us with wants, desires, fears, all sorts of illusions and much nonsense, so that, as it is said, in truth and in fact no thought of any kind ever comes to us from the body. Only the body and its desires cause war, civil discord and battles, for all wars are due to the desire to acquire wealth, and it is the body and the care of it, to which we are enslaved, which compel us to acquire wealth, and all this makes us too busy to practise philosophy. Worst of all, if we have leisure for some investigation, everywhere in our investigations the body is present and makes for confusion and fear, so that it prevents us from seeing the truth.

It has been shown to us that, if we are ever to have pure knowledge, we must escape from the body and observe matters in themselves with the soul by itself. It seems likely that we shall only then, when we are dead, attain what we desire and whose lovers we claim to be, namely, wisdom, only after death, as our argument shows, not while we live; for if it is impossible to attain any pure knowledge with the body, then of two things, one: either we can never attain knowledge or we can do so after death. Then and not before, the soul is by itself apart from the body. While we live, we shall be closest to knowledge if we refrain as much as possible from association with the body or join with it more than we must, if we are not infected with its nature but purify ourselves from it until the god himself frees us. In this way we shall escape the contamination of the body's folly; we shall be likely to be in the company of people of the same kind, and by our own efforts we shall know all that is pure, which is presumably the truth, for it is not permitted to the impure to attain the pure."

Such are the things, Simmias, that those who love learning in the proper manner must say to one another and believe. Or do you not think so?

I certainly do, Socrates.

And if this is true, my friend, said Socrates, there is good hope that on arriving where I am going, if anywhere, I shall acquire what has been our chief preoccupation in our past life, so that the journey that is ordered for me is full of hope, as it is also for any other man who believes that his mind has been prepared and, as it were, purified.

It certainly is, said Simmias.

And does purification not turn out to be what we mentioned in our argument some time ago, namely, to separate the soul as far as possible from the body and accustom it to gather itself and collect itself out of the body and to dwell by itself as far as it can both now and in the future, freed, as it were, from the bonds of the body?

Certainly, he said.

And that freedom and separation of the soul from the body is called death?

That is altogether so.

It is only those who practise philosophy in the right way, we say, who always most want to free the soul; and this release and separation of the soul from the body is the preoccupation of the philosophers.

So it appears.

Therefore, as I said at the beginning, it would be ridiculous for a man to train himself in life to live in a state as close to death as possible, and then to resent it when it comes?

Ridiculous, of course.

In fact, Simmias, he said, those who practise philosophy in the right way are in training for dying and they fear death least of all men. Consider it from this point of view: if they are altogether estranged from the body and desire to have their soul by itself, would it not be quite absurd for them to be afraid and resentful when this happens? If they did not gladly set out for a place, where, on arrival, they may hope to attain that for which they had yearned during their lifetime, that is, wisdom, and where they would be rid of the presence of that from which they are estranged?

Many men, at the death of their lovers, wives or sons, were willing to go to the underworld, driven by the hope of seeing there those for whose company they longed, and being with them. Will then a true lover of wisdom, who has a similar hope and knows that he will never find it to any extent except in Hades, be resentful of dying and not gladly undertake the journey thither? One must surely think so, my friend, if he is a true philosopher, for he is firmly convinced that he will not find pure knowledge anywhere except there. And if this is so, then, as I said just now, would it not be highly unreasonable for such a man to fear death?

It certainly would, by Zeus, he said.

Then you have sufficient indication, he said, that any man whom you see resenting death was not a lover of wisdom but a lover of the body, and also a lover of wealth or of honours, either or both.

It is certainly as you say.

And, Simmias, he said, does not what is called courage belong to men of this disposition?

Most certainly.

And the quality of moderation which even the majority call by that name, that is, not to get swept off one's feet by one's passions, but to treat them with disdain and orderliness, is this not suited only to those who most of all despise the body and live the life of philosophy?

Necessarily so, he said.

If you are willing to reflect on the courage and moderation of other people, you will find them strange.

In what way, Socrates?

You know that they all consider death a great evil?

Definitely, he said.

And the brave among them face death, when they do, for fear of greater evils?

That is so.

Therefore, it is fear and terror that make all men brave, except the philosophers. Yet it is illogical to be brave through fear and cowardice.

It certainly is.   e

What of the moderate among them? Is their experience not similar? Is it licence of a kind that makes them moderate? We say this is impossible, yet their experience of this unsophisticated moderation turns out to be similar: they fear to be deprived of other pleasures which they desire, so they keep away from some pleasures because they are overcome by others. Now to be mastered by pleasure is what they call license, but what happens to them is that they master certain pleasures because they are mastered by others. This is like what we mentioned just now, that in some way it   69 is a kind of licence that has made them moderate.

That seems likely.

My good Simmias, I fear this is not the right exchange to attain virtue, to exchange pleasures for pleasures, pains for pains and fears for fears, the greater for the less like coins, but that the only valid currency for which all these things should be exchanged is wisdom. With this we have real courage and moderation and justice   b and, in a word, true virtue, with wisdom, whether pleasures and fears and all those things be present or absent. Exchanged for one another without wisdom such virtue is only an illusory appearance of virtue; it is in fact fit for slaves, without soundness or truth, whereas, in truth, moderation and courage and justice are a purging away of all such things, and wisdom itself is a kind of cleansing or purification. It is likely   c that those who established the mystic rites for us were not inferior persons but were speaking in riddles long ago when they said that whoever arrives in the underworld uninitiated and unsanctified will wallow in the mire, whereas he who has been purified and initiated will dwell with the gods. There are indeed, as those concerned with the mysteries say, many who carry the thyrsus but the Bacchants are few.[10] These latter are, in my opinion, no other than those who have practised philosophy   d in the right way. I have in my life left nothing undone in order to be counted among these as far as possible, as I have been eager to be in every way. Whether my eagerness was right and we accomplished anything we shall, I think, know for certain in a short time, god willing, on arriving yonder.

This is my defence, Simmias and Cebes, that I am likely to be right to leave you and my masters here without resentment or complaint, believing that there, as here, I shall find good masters and good friends. If my defence is more convincing to you   e than to the Athenian jury, it will be well.

When Socrates finished, Cebes intervened: Socrates, he said, everything else you said is excellent, I think, but men find it very hard to believe what you said about the soul. They think that after it has left the body it no longer exists anywhere, but   70 that it is destroyed and dissolved on the day the man dies, as soon as it leaves the body; and that, on leaving it, it is dispersed like breath or smoke, has flown away and gone and is no longer anything anywhere. If indeed it gathered itself together and existed by itself and escaped those evils you were recently enumerating, there would then be much good hope, Socrates, that what you say is true; but to believe this requires a good deal of faith and persuasive argument, to believe that the soul   b still exists after a man has died and that it still possesses some capability and intelligence.

What you say is true, Cebes, Socrates said, but what shall we do? Do you want to

10. [That is, the true worshippers of Dionysus, as opposed to those who only carry the external symbols of his worship.]

discuss whether this is likely to be true or not?

Personally, said Cebes, I should like to hear your opinion on the subject.

I do not think, said Socrates, that anyone who heard me now, not even a comic poet, could say that I am babbling and discussing things that do not concern me, so we must examine the question thoroughly, if you think we should do so. Let us examine it in some such a manner as this: whether the souls of men who have died exist in the underworld or not. We recall an ancient theory that souls arriving there come from here, and then again that they arrive here and are born here from the dead. If that is true, that the living come back from the dead, then surely our souls must exist there, for they could not come back if they did not exist, and this is a sufficient proof that these things are so if it truly appears that the living never come from any other source than from the dead. If this is not the case we should need another argument.

Quite so, said Cebes.

Do not, he said, confine yourself to humanity if you want to understand this more readily, but take all animals and all plants into account, and, in short, for all things which come to be, let us see whether they come to be in this way, that is, from their opposites if they have such, as the beautiful is the opposite of the ugly and the just of the unjust, and a thousand other things of the kind. Let us examine whether those that have an opposite must necessarily come to be from their opposite and from nowhere else, as for example when something comes to be larger it must necessarily become larger from having been smaller before.

Yes.

Then if something smaller comes to be, it will come from something larger before, which became smaller?

That is so, he said.

And the weaker comes to be from the stronger, and the swifter from the slower?

Certainly.

Further, if something worse comes to be, does it not come from the better, and the juster from the more unjust?

Of course.

So we have sufficiently established that all things come to be in this way, opposites from opposites?

Certainly.

There is a further point, something such as this, about these opposites: between each of those pairs of opposites there are two processes: from the one to the other and then again from the other to the first; between the larger and the smaller there is increase and decrease, and we call the one increasing and the other decreasing?

Yes, he said.

And so too there is separation and combination, cooling and heating, and all such things, even if sometimes we do not have a name for the process, but in fact it must be everywhere that they come to be from one another, and that there is a process of becoming from each into the other?

Assuredly, he said.

Well then, is there an opposite to living, as sleeping is the opposite of being awake?

Quite so, he said.

What is it?

Being dead, he said.

Therefore, if these are opposites, they come to be from one another, and there are two processes of generation between the two?

Of course.

I will tell you, said Socrates, one of the two pairs I was just talking about, the pair itself and the two processes, and you will tell me the other. I mean, to sleep and to be awake; to be awake comes from sleeping, and to sleep comes from being awake. Of the two processes one is going to sleep, the other is waking up. Do you accept that, or not?   d

Certainly.

You tell me in the same way about life and death. Do you not say that to be dead is the opposite of being alive?

I do.

And they come to be from one another?

Yes.

What comes to be from being alive?

Being dead.

And what comes to be from being dead?

One must agree that it is being alive.

Then, Cebes, living creatures and things come to be from the dead?

So it appears, he said.   e

Then our souls exist in the underworld?

That seems likely.

Then one of the two processes of becoming is clear, for dying is clear enough, is it not?

It certainly is.

What shall we do then? Shall we not supply the opposite process of becoming? Is nature to be lame in this case? Or must we provide a process of becoming opposite to dying?

We surely must.

And what is that?

Coming to life again.

Therefore, he said, if there is such a thing as coming to life again, it would be a   72
process of coming from the dead to the living?

Quite so.

It is agreed between us then that the living come from the dead in this way no less than the dead from the living and, if that is so, it seems to be a sufficient proof that the souls of the dead are somewhere whence they can come back again.

I think, Socrates, he said, that this follows from what we have agreed on.

Consider in this way, Cebes, he said, that, as I think, we were not wrong to agree. If the two processes of becoming did not always balance each other as if they were going round in a circle, but generation proceeded from one point to its opposite in a   b straight line and it did not turn back again to the other opposite or take any turning, do you realize that all things would ultimately have the same form, be affected in the same way, and cease to become?

How do you mean? he said.

It is not hard to understand what I mean. If, for example, there was such a process as going to sleep, but no corresponding process of waking up, you realize that in the end everything would show the story of Endymion[11] to have no meaning. There

c would be no point to it because everything would have the same experience as he, be asleep. And if everything were combined and nothing separated, the saying of Anaxagoras[12] would soon be true, that all things were mixed together. In the same way, my dear Cebes, if everything that partakes of life were to die and remained in that state and did not come to life again, would not everything ultimately be dead

d and nothing alive? Even if the living came from some other source, and all that lived died, how could all things avoid being absorbed in death?

It could not be, Socrates, said Cebes, and I think what you say is altogether true.

I think, Cebes, said he, that this is very definitely the case and that we were not deceived when we agreed on this: coming to life again in truth exists, the living

e come to be from the dead, and the souls of the dead exist.

Furthermore, Socrates, Cebes rejoined, such is also the case if that theory is true that you are accustomed to mention frequently, that for us learning is no other than recollection. According to this, we must at some previous time have learned what we now recollect. This is possible only if our soul existed somewhere before it took

73 on this human shape. So according to this theory too, the soul is likely to be immortal.

Cebes, Simmias interrupted, what are the proofs of this? Remind me, for I do not quite recall them at the moment.

There is one excellent argument, said Cebes, namely that when men are interrogated in the right manner, they always give the right answer of their own accord, and they could not do this if they did not possess the knowledge and the right explanation inside them. Then if one shows them a diagram or something else of that

b kind, this will show most clearly that such is the case.[13]

If this does not convince you, Simmias, said Socrates, see whether you agree if we examine it in some such way as this, for you doubt that what we call learning is recollection.

11. [Endymion was granted eternal sleep by Zeus, in some versions at the request of Selene (the moon).]

12. [Anaxagoras of Clazomenae was born at the beginning of the fifth century B.C. He came to Athens as a young man and spent most of his life there in the study of natural philosophy. He is quoted later in the dialogue as claiming that the universe is directed by Mind (Nous). See 97c ff. The reference here is to his statement that in the original state of the world all its elements were thoroughly commingled.]

13. [In the *Meno* Socrates does precisely that. By means of a geometical diagram and merely by asking Meno's slave questions, he elicits from him the answer that the square on the diagonal of a square is double the original square. There, too, this is taken to prove that knowledge is recollection.]

It is not that I doubt, said Simmias, but I want to experience the very thing we are discussing, recollection, and from what Cebes undertook to say, I am now remembering and am pretty nearly convinced. Nevertheless, I should like to hear the way you were intending to explain it.

This way, he said. We surely agree that if anyone recollects anything, he must have known it before.

Quite so, he said.

Do we not also agree that when knowledge comes to mind in this way, it is recollection? What way do I mean? Like this: when a man sees or hears or in some other way perceives one thing and not only knows that thing but also thinks of another thing of which the knowledge is not the same but different, are we not right to say that he recollects the second thing that comes into his mind?

How do you mean?

Things such as these: to know a man is a different knowledge from knowing a lyre.

Of course.

Well, you know what happens to lovers: whenever they see a lyre, a garment or anything else that their beloved is accustomed to use, they know the lyre, and the image of the boy to whom it belongs comes into their mind. This is recollection, just as someone, on seeing Simmias, often recollects Cebes, and there are thousands of other such occurrences.

Thousands indeed, said Simmias.

Is this kind of thing not recollection of a kind? he said, especially so when one experiences it about things that one had forgotten, because one had not seen them for some time? — Quite so.

Further, he said, can a man seeing the picture of a horse or a lyre recollect a man, or seeing a picture of Simmias recollect Cebes? — Certainly.

Or seeing a picture of Simmias, recollect Simmias himself? — He certainly can.

In all these cases the recollection is occasioned by things that are similar, but it can also be occasioned by things that are dissimilar? — It can.

When the recollection is caused by similar things, must one not of necessity also experience this: to consider whether the similarity to that which one recollects is deficient in any respect or complete? — One must.

Consider, he said, whether this is the case: we say that there is something that is equal. I do not mean a stick equal to a stick or a stone to a stone, or anything of that kind, but something else beyond all these, the Equal itself. Shall we say that this exists or not?

Indeed we shall by Zeus, said Simmias, most definitely.

And do we know precisely what this is? — Certainly.

Whence have we acquired the knowledge of it? Is it not from the things we mentioned just now, from seeing sticks or stones or some other things that are equal we come to think of that other which is different from them? or doesn't it seem to you to be different? Look at it also this way: do not equal stones and sticks sometimes, while remaining the same, appear to one person to be equal and to another to be unequal? — Certainly they do.

c   But what of the equals themselves?[14] Have they ever appeared unequal to you, or Equality to be Inequality?

Never, Socrates.

These equal things and the Equal itself are therefore not the same?

I do not think they are the same at all, Socrates.

But it is definitely from the equal things, though they are different from equality, that you have derived and grasped the knowledge of equality?

Very true, Socrates.

Whether it be like them or unlike them?

Certainly.

It makes no difference. As long as the sight of one thing makes you think of
d   another, whether it be similar or dissimilar, this must of necessity be recollection?

Quite so.

Well then, he said, do we experience something like this in the case of equal sticks and the other equal objects we just mentioned? Do they seem to us to be equal in the same sense as what is Equal itself? Is there some deficiency in their being such as the Equal, or is there not?

A considerable deficiency, he said.

Whenever someone, on seeing something, realizes that that which he now sees wants to be like some other reality but falls short and cannot be like that other since
e   it is inferior, do we agree that the one who thinks this must have prior knowledge of that to which he says it is like, but deficiently so?

Necessarily.

Well, do we also feel this about the equal objects and the Equal itself, or do we not?

Very definitely.

We must then possess knowledge of the Equal before that time when we first saw
75   the equal objects and realized that all these objects strive to be like the Equal but are deficient in this.

That is so.

Then surely we also agree that this conception of ours derives from seeing or touching or some other sense perception, and cannot come into our mind in any other way, for all these senses, I say, are the same.

They are the same, Socrates, at any rate in respect to that which our argument wishes to make plain. Our sense perceptions must surely make us realize that all that we perceive through them is striving to reach that which is Equal but falls short of it; or how do we express it?

Like that.

Then before we began to see or hear or otherwise perceive, we must have possessed knowledge of the nature of the Equal itself if we were about to refer our

14. [The plural is puzzling, as only the Form of Equality, on the one hand, and the (imperfectly) equal "sticks and stones" have been mentioned. Commentators suggest that the plural here refers to mathematical equals such as the angles at the base of an isosceles triangle, Plato must have something of the kind in mind, but it is hard to see how he expects a reader who could not be familiar with his later work to realize it, especially as the "equal things" in the next line again refer to the particulars.]

sense perceptions of equal objects to it, and realized that all of them were eager to be like it, but were inferior.

That follows from what has been said, Socrates.

But we began to see and hear and otherwise perceive right after birth?

Certainly.

We must then have acquired the knowledge of equality before this.　　　c

Yes.

It seems then that we must have possessed it before birth.

It seems so.

Therefore, if we had this knowledge, we knew before birth and immediately after not only the Equal, but the Greater and the Smaller and all such things, for our present argument is no more about the Equal than about the Beautiful itself, the Good itself, the Just, the Pious and, as I say, about all those things to which we can attach the word "itself," both when we are putting questions and answering them.　　d So we must have acquired knowledge of them all before we were born.

That is so.

If, having acquired this knowledge in each case, we have not forgotten it, we remain knowing and have knowledge throughout our life, for to know is to acquire knowledge, keep it and not lose it. Do we not call the losing of knowledge forgetting?

Most certainly, Socrates, he said.　　　e

But, I think, if we acquired this knowledge before birth, then lost it at birth, and then later by the use of our senses in connection with those objects we mentioned, we recovered the knowledge we had before, would not what we call learning be the recovery of our own knowledge, and we are right to call this recollection?

Certainly.

It was seen to be possible for someone to see or hear or otherwise perceive some-　　76 thing, and by this to be put in mind of something else which he had forgotten and which is related to it by similarity or difference. One of two things follows, as I say: either we were born with the knowledge of it, and all of us know it throughout life, or those who later, we say, are learning, are only recollecting, and learning would be recollection.

That is certainly the case, Socrates.

Which alternative do you choose, Simmias? That we are born with this knowledge or that we recollect later the things of which we had knowledge previously?　　b

I have no means of choosing at the moment, Socrates.

Well, can you make this choice? What is your opinion about it? A man who has knowledge would be able to give an account of what he knows, or would he not?

He must certainly be able to do so, Socrates, he said.

And do you think everybody can give an account of the things we were mentioning just now?

I wish they could, said Simmias, but I'm afraid it is much more likely that by this time tomorrow there will be no one left who can do so adequately.

So you do not think that everybody has knowledge of those things?　　c

No indeed.

So they recollect what they once learned?

They must

When did our souls acquire the knowledge of them? Certainly not since we were born as men.

Indeed no.

Before that then?

Yes.

So then, Simmias, our souls also existed apart from the body before they took on human form, and they had intelligence.

Unless we acquire the knowledge at the moment of birth, Socrates, for that time is still left to us.

d   Quite so, my friend, but at what other time do we lose it? We just now agreed that we are not born with that knowledge. Do we then lose it at the very time we acquire it, or can you mention any other time?

I cannot, Socrates. I did not realize that I was talking nonsense.

So this is our position, Simmias? he said. If those realities we are always talking about exist, the Beautiful and the Good and all that kind of reality, and we refer all the things we perceive to that reality, discovering that it existed before and is ours, and we compare these things with it, then, just as they exist, so our soul must exist

e   before we are born. If these realities do not exist, then this argument is altogether futile. Is this the position, that there is an equal necessity for those realities to exist, and for our souls to exist before we were born? If the former do not exist, neither do the latter?

I do not think, Socrates, said Simmias, that there is any possible doubt that it is equally necessary for both to exist, and it is opportune that our argument comes to the conclusion that our soul exists before we are born, and equally so that reality of

77   which you are now speaking. Nothing is so evident to me personally as that all such things must certainly exist, the Beautiful, the Good, and all those you mentioned just now. I also think that sufficient proof of this has been given.

Then what about Cebes? said Socrates, for we must persuade Cebes also.

He is sufficiently convinced I think, said Simmias, though he is the most difficult of men to persuade by argument, but I believe him to be fully convinced that our soul existed before we were born. I do not think myself, however, that it has been

b   proved that the soul continues to exist after death; the opinion of the majority which Cebes mentioned still stands, that when a man dies his soul is dispersed and this is the end of its existence. What is to prevent the soul coming to be and being constituted from some other source, existing before it enters a human body and then, having done so and departed from it, itself dying and being destroyed?

c   You are right, Simmias, said Cebes. Half of what needed proof has been proved, namely, that our soul existed before we were born, but further proof is needed that it exists no less after we have died, if the proof is to be complete.

It has been proved even now, Simmias and Cebes, said Socrates, if you are ready to combine this argument with the one we agreed on before, that every living thing must come from the dead. If the soul exists before, it must, as it comes to life and birth, come from nowhere else than death and being dead, so how could it avoid ex-

isting after death since it must be born again? What you speak of has then even now   d
been proved. However, I think you and Simmias would like to discuss the argument
more fully. You seem to have this childish fear that the wind would really dissolve
and scatter the soul, as it leaves the body, especially if one happens to die in a high
wind and not in calm weather.   e

Cebes laughed and said: "Assuming that we were afraid, Socrates, try and change
our minds, or rather do not assume that we are afraid, but perhaps there is a child in
us who has these fears; try to persuade him not to fear death like a bogey."

You should, said Socrates, sing a charm over him every day until you have
charmed away his fears.

Where shall we find a good charmer for these fears, Socrates, he said, now that
you are leaving us?   78

Greece is a large country, Cebes, he said, and there are good men in it; the tribes
of foreigners are numerous. You should search among them all, sparing neither
trouble nor expense, for there is nothing on which you could spend your money to
greater advantage. You must also search among yourselves, for you might not easily
find people who could do this better than yourselves.

That shall be done, said Cebes, but let us, if it pleases you, go back to the argument where we left it.   b

Of course it pleases me.

Splendid, he said.

We must then ask ourselves something like this: what kind of thing is likely to be
scattered? On behalf of what kind of thing should one fear this, and for what kind of
thing should one not fear it? We should then examine to which class the soul
belongs, and as a result either fear for the soul or be of good cheer.

What you say is true.

Is not anything that is composite and a compound by nature liable to be split up   c
into its component parts, and only that which is noncomposite, if anything, is not
likely to be split up?

I think that is the case, said Cebes.

Are not the things that always remain the same and in the same state most likely
not to be composite, whereas those that vary from one time to another and are never
the same are composite?

I think that is so.

Let us then return to those same things with which we were dealing earlier, to
that reality of whose existence we are giving an account in our questions and answers; are they ever the same and in the same state, or do they vary from one time to   d
another; can the Equal itself, the Beautiful itself, each thing in itself, the real, ever
be affected by any change whatever? Or does each of them that really is, being simple by itself, remain the same and never in any way tolerate any change whatever?

It must remain the same, said Cebes, and in the same state, Socrates.

What of the many beautiful particulars, be they men, horses, clothes, or other
such things, or the many equal particulars, and all those which bear the same name
as those others? Do they remain the same or, in contrast to those other realities, one   e
might say, never remain the same as themselves or in relation to each other?

The latter is the case, they are never in the same state.

79 These latter you could touch and see and perceive with the other senses, but those that always remain the same can only be grasped by the reasoning power of the mind; they are not seen but are invisible?

That is altogether true, he said.

Do you then want us to assume two kinds of existences, the visible and the invisible?

Let us assume this.

And the invisible always remains the same, whereas the visible never does?

Let us assume that too.

b Now one part of ourselves is the body, another part is the soul?

Quite so.

To which class of existence do we say the body is more alike and akin?

To the visible, as anyone can see.

What about the soul? Is it visible or invisible?

It is not visible to men, Socrates, he said.

Well, we meant visible and invisible to human eyes, or any others?

To human eyes.

Then what do we say about the soul? Is it visible or not visible?

Not visible.

So it is invisible? — Yes.

So the soul is more like the invisible than the body, and the body more like the
c visible? — Without any doubt, Socrates.

We have also said some time ago that when the soul makes use of the body, be it hearing or seeing or some other sense—for to investigate something through the senses is to do it through the body—it is dragged by the body to the things that are never the same, and the soul itself strays and is confused and dizzy, as if it were drunk, in so far as it is in contact with that kind of thing?

Certainly.

But when the soul investigates by itself it passes into the realm of what is pure,
d ever existing, immortal and unchanging, and being akin to this, it always stays with it whenever it is by itself and can do so; it ceases to stray and remains in the same state as it is in touch with things of the same kind, and its experience then is what is called wisdom?

Altogether well said and very true, Socrates, he said.

Judging from what we have said before and what we are saying now, to which of
e these two kinds do you think that the soul is more alike and more akin?

I think, Socrates, he said, that any man, even the dullest, would agree that the soul is altogether more like that which always exists in the same state rather than like that which does not.

What of the body?

That is like the other.

Look at it also this way: when the soul and the body are together, nature orders
80 the one to be subject and to be ruled, and the other to rule and be master. Then

again, which do you think is like the divine and which like the mortal? Do you not think that the nature of the divine is to rule and to lead, whereas it is that of the mortal to be ruled and be subject?

I do.

Which does the soul resemble?

Obviously, Socrates, the soul resembles the divine, and the body resembles the mortal.

Consider then, Cebes, whether it follows from all that has been said that the soul is most like the divine, deathless, intelligible, uniform, indissoluble, always the same as itself, whereas the body is most like that which is human, mortal, multiform,   b unintelligible, soluble and never consistently the same. Have we anything else to say to show, my dear Cebes, that this is not the case?

We have not.

Well then, that being so, is it not natural for the body to dissolve easily, and for the soul to be altogether indissoluble, or nearly so?

Of course.   c

You realize, he said, that when a man dies, the visible part, the body, which exists in the visible world, and which we call the corpse, whose natural lot would be to dissolve, fall apart and be blown away, does not immediately suffer any of these things but remains for a fair time, in fact, quite a long time if the man dies with his body in a suitable condition and at a favourable season? If the body is emaciated or embalmed, as in Egypt, it remains almost whole for a remarkable length of time,   d and even if the body decays, some parts of it, namely bones and sinews and the like, are nevertheless, one might say, deathless. Is that not so? — Yes.

Will the soul, the invisible part which makes its way to a region of the same kind, noble and pure and invisible, to Hades in fact, to the good and wise god whither, god willing, my soul must soon be going—will the soul, being of this kind and nature, be scattered and destroyed on leaving the body, as the majority of men say? Far from it, my dear Cebes and Simmias, but what happens is much more like this: if it is pure when it leaves the body and drags nothing bodily with it, as it had no   e willing association with the body in life, but avoided it and gathered itself together by itself and always practised this, which is no other than practising philosophy in the right way, in fact, training to die easily. Or is this not training for death?   81

It surely is.

A soul in this state makes its way to the invisible, which is like itself, the divine and immortal and wise, and arriving there it can be happy, having rid itself of confusion, ignorance, fear, violent desires and the other human ills and, as is said of the initiates, truly spend the rest of time with the gods. Shall we say this, Cebes, or something different?

This, by Zeus, said Cebes.

But I think that if the soul is polluted and impure when it leaves the body, having   b always been associated with it and served it, bewitched by physical desires and pleasures to the point at which nothing seems to exist for it but the physical, which one can touch and see or eat and drink or make use of for sexual enjoyment, and if that soul is accustomed to hate and fear and avoid that which is dim and invisible to the eyes but intelligible and to be grasped by philosophy—do you think such a soul will escape pure and by itself?

c   Impossible, he said.

It is, no doubt, permeated by the physical, which constant intercourse and association with the body, as well as considerable practice, has caused to become ingrained in it?

Quite so.

We must believe, my friend, that this bodily element is heavy, ponderous, earthy and visible. Through it, such a soul has become heavy and is dragged back to the visible region in fear of the unseen, and of Hades. It wanders, as we are told, around graves and monuments, where shadowy phantoms, images that such souls produce,

d   have been seen, souls that have not been freed and purified but share in the visible, and are therefore seen.

That is likely, Socrates.

It is indeed, Cebes. Moreover, these are not the souls of good but of inferior men, which are forced to wander there, paying the penalty for their previous bad upbringing. They wander until their longing for that which accompanies them, the

e   physical, again imprisons them in a body, and they are then, as is likely, bound to such characters as they have practised in their life.

What kind of characters do you say these are, Socrates?

Those, for example, who have carelessly practised gluttony, violence and drunkenness are likely to join a company of donkeys or of similar animals. Do you

82   not think so?

Very likely.

Those who have esteemed injustice highly, and tyranny and plunder will join the tribes of wolves and hawks and kites, or where else shall we say that they go?

Certainly to those, said Cebes.

And clearly, the destination of the others will conform to the way in which they have behaved?

Clearly, of course.

The happiest of these, who will also have the best destination, are those who have practised popular and social virtue, which they call moderation and justice and

b   which was developed by habit and practice, without philosophy or understanding?

How are they the happiest?

Because it is likely that they will again join a social and gentle group, either of bees or wasps or ants, and then again the same kind of human group, and so be moderate men.

That is likely.

No one may join the company of the gods who has not practised philosophy and is not completely pure when he departs from life, no one but the lover of learning. It

c   is for this reason, my friends Simmias and Cebes, that those who practise philosophy in the right way keep away from all bodily passions, master them and do not surrender themselves to them; it is not at all for fear of wasting their substance and of poverty, which the majority and the money-lovers fear, nor for fear of dishonour and ill repute, like the ambitious and lovers of honours, that they keep away from them.

That would not be natural for them, Socrates, said Cebes.

d   By Zeus, no, he said. Those who care for their own soul and do not live for the service of their body dismiss all these things. They do not travel the same road as those who do not know where they are going but, believing that nothing should be done contrary to philosophy and their deliverance and purification, they turn to this and follow wherever philosophy leads.

How so, Socrates?

I will tell you, he said. The lovers of learning know that when philosophy gets hold of their soul, it is imprisoned in and clinging to the body, and that it is forced   e
to examine other things through it as through a cage and not by itself, and that it wallows in every kind of ignorance. Philosophy sees that the worst feature of this imprisonment is that it is due to desires, so that the prisoner is contributing to his own incarceration. As I say, the lovers of learning know that philosophy gets hold of their soul when it is in that state, then gently encourages it and tries to free it by   83
showing them that investigation through the eyes is full of deceit, as is that through the ears and the other senses. Philosophy then persuades the soul to withdraw from the senses in so far as it is not compelled to use them and bids the soul to gather itself together by itself, to trust only itself and whatever reality, existing by itself, the soul by itself understands, and not to consider as true whatever it examines by   b
other means, for this is different in different circumstances and is sensible and visible, whereas what the soul itself sees is intelligible and invisible. The philosopher thinks that this deliverance must not be opposed and so keeps away from pleasures and desires and pains as far as he can; he reflects that violent pleasure or pain or passion does not cause merely such evils as one might expect, such as one suffers when one has been sick or extravagant through desire, but the greatest and most extreme evil, though one does not reflect on this.   c

What is that, Socrates? asked Cebes.

That the soul of every man, when it feels violent pleasure or pain in connection with some object, inevitably believes at the same time that what causes such feelings must be very real and very true, which it is not. Such objects are mostly visible, are they not?

Certainly.

And doesn't such an experience tie the soul to the body most completely?   d

How so?

Because every pleasure and every pain provides, as it were, another nail to rivet the soul to the body and to weld them together. It makes the soul corporeal, so that it believes that truth is what the body says it is. As it shares the beliefs and delights of the body, I think it inevitably comes to share its ways and manner of life and is unable ever to reach Hades in a pure state; it is always full of body when it departs, so that it soon falls back into another body and grows with it as if it had been sewn into it. Because of this, it can have no part in the company of the divine, the pure   e
and uniform.

What you say is very true, Socrates, said Cebes.

This is why genuine lovers of learning are moderate and brave, or do you think it is for the reasons the majority says they are?

I certainly do not.   84

Indeed no. This is how the soul of a philosopher would reason: it would not think that while philosophy must free it, it should while being freed surrender itself to pleasures and pains and imprison itself again, thus labouring in vain like Penelope at her web. The soul of the philosopher achieves a calm from such emotions; it follows reason and ever stays with it contemplating the true, the divine, which is not the object of opinion. Nurtured by this, it believes that one should live in this manner as long as one is alive and, after death, arrive at what is akin and of the same kind, and escape from human evils. After such nurture there is no danger, Simmias and Cebes, that one should fear that, on parting from the body, the soul would be scattered and dissipated by the winds and no longer be anything anywhere.

When Socrates finished speaking there was a long silence. He appeared to be concentrating on what had been said, and so were most of us. But Cebes and Simmias were whispering to each other. Socrates observed them and questioned them: "Come," he said, "do you think there is something lacking in my argument? There are still many doubtful points and many objections for anyone who wants a thorough discussion of these matters. If you are discussing some other subject, I have nothing to say, but if you have some difficulty about this one, do not hesitate to speak for yourselves and expound it if you think the argument could be improved, and if you think you will do better, take me along with you in the discussion."

I will tell you the truth, Socrates, said Simmias. Both of us have been in difficulty for some time, and each of us has been urging the other to question you because we wanted to hear what you would say, but we hesitated to bother you, lest it be displeasing to you in your present misfortune.

When Socrates heard this he laughed quietly and said: "Really, Simmias, it would be hard for me to persuade other people that I do not consider my present fate a misfortune if I cannot persuade even you, and you are afraid that it is more difficult to deal with me than before. You seem to think me inferior to the swans in prophecy. They sing before too, but when they realize that they must die they sing most and most beautifully, as they rejoice that they are about to depart to join the god whose servants they are. But men, because of their own fear of death, tell lies about the swans and say that they lament their death and sing in sorrow. They do not reflect that no bird sings when it is hungry or cold or suffers in any other way, neither the nightingale nor the swallow nor the hoopoe, though they do say that these sing laments when in pain. Nor do the swans, but I believe that as they belong to Apollo, they are prophetic, have knowledge of the future and sing of the blessings of the underworld, sing and rejoice on that day beyond what they did before. As I believe myself to be a fellow servant with the swans and dedicated to the same god, and have received from the same master a gift of prophecy not inferior to theirs, I am no more despondent than they on leaving life. Therefore, you must speak and ask whatever you want as long as the authorities allow it."

Well spoken, said Simmias. I will tell you my difficulty, and then Cebes will say why he does not accept what was said. I believe, as perhaps you do, that precise knowledge on that subject is impossible or extremely difficult in our present life, but that it surely shows a very poor spirit not to examine thoroughly what is said about it, and to desist before one is exhausted by an all-round investigation. One should achieve one of two things, learn the truth about these things or find it for oneself, or, if that is impossible, adopt the best and most irrefutable of men's theories, and, borne upon this, sail through the dangers of life as upon a raft, unless someone should make that journey safer and less risky upon a firmer vessel of some divine doctrine. So even now, since you have said what you did, I will feel no shame at asking questions, and I will not blame myself in the future because I did not say what I think. As I examine what we said, both by myself and with Cebes, it does not seem to me to be adequate.

Said Socrates: "You may well be right, my friend, but tell me how it is inadequate."   e

In this way, as it seems to me, he said: "One might make the same argument about harmony, lyre and strings, that a harmony is something invisible, without body, beautiful and divine in the attuned lyre, whereas the lyre itself and its strings are physical, bodily, composite, earthy and akin to what is mortal. Then if someone   86 breaks the lyre, cuts or breaks the strings and then insists, using the same argument as you, that the harmony must still exist and is not destroyed because it would be impossible for the lyre and the strings, which are mortal, still to exist when the strings are broken, and for the harmony, which is akin and of the same nature as the divine and immortal, to be destroyed before that which is mortal; he would say that   b the harmony itself still must exist and that the wood and the strings must rot before the harmony can suffer. And indeed, Socrates, I think you must have this in mind, that we mostly suppose the soul to be something of this kind; as the body is stretched and held together by the hot and the cold, the dry and the moist and other such things, and our soul is a mixture and harmony of those things when they are mixed with each other rightly and in due measure. If then the soul is a kind of har-   c mony or attunement, clearly, when our body is relaxed or stretched without due measure by diseases and other evils, the soul must immediately be destroyed, even if it be most divine, as are the other harmonies found in music and all the works of artists, and the remains of each body last for a long time until they rot or are burned. Consider what we shall say in answer to one who deems the soul to be a   d mixture of bodily elements and to be the first to perish in the process we call death."

Socrates looked at us keenly, as was his habit, smiled and said: "What Simmias says is quite fair. If one of you is more resourceful than I am, why did he not answer him, for he seems to have handled the argument competently. However, I think that before we answer him, we should hear Cebes' objection, in order that we may have time to deliberate on an answer. When we have heard him we should either   e agree with them, if we think them in tune with us or, if not, defend our own argument. Come then, Cebes. What is troubling you?"

I tell you, said Cebes, the argument seems to me to be at the same point as before and open to the same objection. I do not deny that it has been very elegantly and, if   87 it is not offensive to say so, sufficiently proved that our soul existed before it took on this present form, but I do not believe the same applies to its existing somewhere after our death. Not that I agree with Simmias' objection that the soul is not stronger and much more lasting than the body, for I think it is superior in all these respects. "Why then," the argument might say, "are you still unconvinced? Since you see that when the man dies, the weaker part continues to exist, do you not think that the more lasting part must be preserved during that time?" On this point consider whether what I say makes sense.   b

Like Simmias, I too need an image, for I think this argument is much as if one said at the death of an old weaver that the man had not perished but was safe and sound somewhere, and offered as proof the fact that the cloak the old man had woven himself and was wearing was still sound and had not perished. If one was not convinced, he would be asked whether a man lasts longer than a cloak which is in   c use and being worn, and if the answer was that a man lasts much longer, this would

be taken as proof that the man was definitely safe and sound, since the more temporary thing had not perished. But Simmias, I do not think that is so, for consider
what I say. Anybody could see that the man who said this was talking nonsense.
That weaver had woven and worn out many such cloaks. He perished after many of
d   them, but before the last. That does not mean that a man is inferior and weaker
than a cloak. The image illustrates, I think, the relationship of the soul to the body,
and anyone who says the same thing about them would appear to me to be talking
sense, that the soul lasts a long time while the body is weaker and more short-lived.
He might say that each soul wears out many bodies, especially if it lives many years.
If the body were in a state of flux and perished while the man was still alive, and the
soul wove afresh the body that is worn out, yet it would be inevitable that whenever
e   the soul perished it would be wearing the last body it wove and perish only before
this last. Then when the soul perished, the body would show the weakness of its
nature by soon decaying and disappearing. So we cannot trust this argument and
be confident that our soul continues to exist somewhere after our death. For, if one
88   were to concede, even more than you do, to a man using that argument, if one were
to grant him not only that the soul exists in the time before we are born, but that
there is no reason why the soul of some should not exist and continue to exist after
our death, and thus frequently be born and die in turn, if one were to grant him that
the soul's nature is so strong that it can survive many bodies, but if, having granted
all this, one does not further agree that the soul is not damaged by its many births
and is not, in the end, altogether destroyed in one of those deaths, he might say that
b   no one knows which death and dissolution of the body brings about the destruction
of the soul, since not one of us can be aware of this. And in that case, any man who
faces death with confidence is foolish, unless he can prove that the soul is altogether
immortal. If he cannot, a man about to die must of necessity fear for his soul, lest the
present separation of the soul from the body bring about the complete destruction
of the soul.

When we heard what they said we were all depressed, as we told each other
c   afterwards. We had been quite convinced by the previous argument, and they
seemed to confuse us again, and to drive us to doubt not only what had already been
said but also what was going to be said, lest we be worthless as critics or the subject
itself admitted of no certainty.

ECHECRATES: By the gods, Phaedo, you have my sympathy, for as I listen to
you now I find myself saying to myself: "What argument shall we trust? That of
d   Socrates, which was extremely convincing, has now fallen into discredit; the statement that the soul is some kind of harmony has a remarkable hold on me, now and
always, and when it was mentioned it reminded me that I had myself previously
thought so. And now I am again in need, as if from the beginning, of some other
argument to convince me that the soul does not die along with the man. Tell me
then, by Zeus, how Socrates tackled the argument. Was he obviously distressed, as
e   you say you people were, or was he not, but quietly came to the rescue of his argument, and did he do so satisfactorily or inadequately? Tell us everything as precisely as you can.

PHAEDO: I have certainly often admired Socrates, Echecrates, but never more
than on this occasion. That he had a reply was perhaps not strange. What I won-
89   dered at most in him was the pleasant, kind and admiring way he received the

young men's argument, and how sharply he was aware of the effect the discussion had on us, and then how well he healed our distress and, as it were, recalled us from our flight and defeat and turned us around to join him in the examination of their argument.

E: How did he do this?

P: I will tell you. I happened to be sitting on his right by the couch on a low stool, so that he was sitting well above me. He stroked my head and pressed the hair on the back of my neck, for he was in the habit of playing with my hair at times.   b "Tomorrow, Phaedo," he said, "you will probably cut this beautiful hair."

Likely enough, Socrates, I said.

Not if you take my advice, he said.

Why not? said I.

It is today, he said, that I shall cut my hair and you yours, if our argument dies on us, and we cannot revive it. If I were you, and the argument escaped me, I would take an oath, as the Argives[15] did, not to let my hair grow before I fought again and   c defeated the argument of Simmias and Cebes.

But, I said, they say that not even Heracles could fight two people.

Then call on me as your Iolaus, as long as the daylight lasts.

I shall call on you, but in this case as Iolaus calling on Heracles.

It makes no difference, he said, but first there is a certain experience we must be careful to avoid.

What is that? I asked.

That we should not become misologues, as people become misanthropes. There is   d no greater evil one can suffer than to hate reasonable discourse. Misology and misanthropy arise in the same way. Misanthropy comes when a man without knowledge or skill has placed great trust in someone and believes him to be altogether truthful, sound and trustworthy; then, a short time afterwards he finds him to be wicked and unreliable, and then this happens in another case; when one has frequently had that experience, especially with those whom one believed to be one's closest friends, then, in the end, after many such blows, one comes to hate all men   e and to believe that no one is sound in any way at all. Have you not seen this happen?

I surely have, I said.

This is a shameful state of affairs, he said, and obviously due to to an attempt to have human relations without any skill in human affairs, for such skill would lead one to believe, what is in fact true, that the very good and the very wicked are both   90 quite rare, and that most men are between those extremes.

How do you mean? said I.

The same as with the very tall and the very short, he said. Do you think anything is rarer than to find an extremely tall man or an extremely short one? Or a dog or any thing else whatever? Or again, one extremely swift or extremely slow, ugly or beautiful, white or black? Are you not aware that in all those cases the most extreme at either end are rare and few, but those in between are many and plentiful?

15. [Herodotus (I, 82) tells us that after losing the city of Thyreae to the Spartans, the Argives swore not to let their hair grow again or their women wear golden ornaments until they had recaptured it.]

Certainly, I said.

b Therefore, he said, if a contest of wickedness were established, there too the winners, you think, would be very few?

That is likely, said I.

Likely indeed, he said, but arguments are not like men in this particular. I was merely following your lead just now.[16] The similarity lies rather in this: it is as when one who lacks skill in arguments puts his trust in an argument as being true, then shortly afterwards believes it to be false—as sometimes it is and sometimes it is not—and so with another argument and then another. You know how those in particular who spend their time studying contradiction in the end believe themselves c to have become very wise and that they alone have understood that there is no soundness or reliability in any object or in any argument, but that all that exists simply fluctuates up and down as if it were in the Euripus[17] and does not remain in the same place for any time at all.

What you say, I said, is certainly true.

It would be pitiable, Phaedo, he said, when there is a true and reliable argument and one that can be understood, if a man who has dealt with such arguments as appear at one time true, at another time untrue, should not blame him-d self or his own lack of skill but, because of his distress, in the end gladly shift the blame away from himself to the arguments, and spend the rest of his life hating and reviling reasonable discussion and so be deprived of truth and knowledge of reality?

Yes, by Zeus, I said, that would be pitiable indeed.

This then is the first thing we should guard against, he said. We should not allow into our minds the conviction that argumentation has nothing sound about it; much e rather we should believe that it is we who are not yet sound and that we must take courage and be eager to attain soundness, you and the others for the sake of your whole life still to come, and I for the sake of death itself. I am in danger at this 91 moment of not having a philosophical attitude about this, but like those who are quite uneducated, I am eager to get the better of you in argument, for the uneducated, when they engage in argument about anything, give no thought to the truth about the subject of discussion but are only eager that those present will accept the position they have set forth. I differ from them only to this extent: I shall not be eager to get the agreement of those present that what I say is true, except incidentally, but I shall be very eager that I should myself be thoroughly convinced that things are so. For I am thinking—see in how contentious a spirit—that if what I say b is true, it is a fine thing to be convinced; if, on the other hand, nothing exists after death, at least for this time before I die I shall distress those present less with lamentations and my folly will not continue to exist along with me—that would be a bad thing—but will come to an end in a short time. Thus prepared, Simmias and Cebes, he said, I come to deal with your argument. If you will take my advice, you will give c but little thought to Socrates but much more to the truth. If you think that what I

16. [Socrates presumably means that there are plenty of very bad arguments. It is not clear where he was following Phaedo in the argument.]

17. [The Euripus was the name of the straits between Euboea and Boetia; its currents were both violent and variable.]

say is true, agree with me; if not, oppose it with every argument and take care that in my eagerness I do not deceive myself and you and, like a bee, leave my sting in you when I go.

We must proceed, he said, and first remind me of what you said if I do not appear to remember it. Simmias, as I believe, is in doubt and fears that the soul, though it is more divine and beautiful than the body, yet predeceases it, being a kind of harmony. Cebes agrees with me that the soul lasts much longer than the body, but that no one knows whether the soul often wears out many bodies and then, on leaving its last body, is now itself destroyed. This then is death, the destruction of the soul, since the body is always being destroyed. Are these the questions, Simmias and Cebes, which we must investigate?

They both agreed that they were.

Do you then, he asked, reject all our previous statements, or some but not others?

Some, they both said, but not others.

What, he said, about the statement we made that learning is recollection and that, if this was so, our soul must of necessity exist elsewhere before us, before it was imprisoned in the body?

For myself, said Cebes, I was wonderfully convinced by it at the time and I stand by it now also, more than by any other statement.

That, said Simmias, is also my position, and I should be very surprised if I ever changed my opinion about this.

But you must change your opinion, my Theban friend, said Socrates, if you still believe that a harmony is a composite thing, and that the soul is a kind of harmony of the elements of the body in a state of tension, for surely you will not allow yourself to maintain that a composite harmony existed before those elements from which it had to be composed, or would you?

Never, Socrates, he said.

Do you realize, he said, that this is what you are in fact saying when you state that the soul exists before it takes on the form and body of a man and that it is composed of elements which do not yet exist? A harmony is like that to which you compare it; the lyre and the strings and the notes, though still unharmonized, exist; the harmony is composed last of all, and is the first to be destroyed. How will you harmonize this statement with your former one?

In no way, said Simmias.

And surely, he said, a statement about harmony should do so more than any other.

It should, said Simmias.

So your statement is inconsistent? Consider which of your statements you prefer, that learning is recollection or that the soul is a harmony?

I much prefer the former, Socrates. I adopted the latter without proof, because of a certain probability and plausibility, which is why it appeals to most men. I know that arguments of which the proof is based on probability are pretentious and, if one does not guard against them, they certainly deceive one, in geometry and everything else. The theory of recollection and learning, however, was based on an assumption worthy of acceptance, for our soul was said to exist also before it came into the body, just as its reality is of the kind that we qualify by the words "which

truly is," and I convinced myself that I was quite correct to accept it. Therefore, I
e   cannot accept the theory that the soul is a harmony either from myself or anyone
else.

What of this, Simmias? Do you think it natural for a harmony, or any other com-
93   posite, to be in a different state from that of the elements of which it is composed?

Not at all, said Simmias.

Nor, as I think, can it act or be acted upon in a different way than its elements?

He agreed.

One must therefore suppose that a harmony does not direct its components, but is
directed by them.

He accepted this.

A harmony is therefore far from making a movement, or uttering a sound, or
doing anything else, in a manner contrary to that of its parts.

Far from it indeed, he said.

Does not the nature of each harmony depend on the way it has been harmonized?

I do not understand, he said.

Will it not, if it is more and more fully harmonized, be more and more fully a har-
b   mony, and if it is less and less fully harmonized, it will be less and less fully a harmony?

Certainly.

Can this be true about the soul, that one soul is more and more fully a soul than
another, or is less and less fully a soul, even to the smallest extent?

Not in any way.

Come now, by Zeus, he said. One soul is said to have intelligence and virtue and
to be good, another to have folly and wickedness and to be bad. Are those things
c   truly said?

They certainly are.

What will someone who holds the theory that the soul is a harmony say that those
things are which reside in the soul, that is, virtue and wickedness? Are these some
other harmony and disharmony? That the good soul is harmonized and, being a
harmony, has within itself another harmony, whereas the evil soul is both itself a
lack of harmony and has no other within itself?

I don't know what to say, said Simmias, but one who holds that assumption must
obviously say something of that kind.

d   We have previously agreed, he said, that one soul is not more and not less a soul
than another, and this means that one harmony is not more and more fully, or less
and less fully, a harmony than another. Is that not so?

Certainly.

Now that which is no more and no less a harmony is not more or less harmonized.
Is that so?

It is.

Can that which is neither more nor less harmonized partake more or less of harmony, or does it do so equally?

Equally.

Then if a soul is neither more nor less a soul than another, it has been harmonized   e
to the same extent?

That is so.

If that is so, it would have no greater share of disharmony or of harmony?

It would not.

That being the case, could one soul have more wickedness or virtue than another,
if wickedness is disharmony and virtue harmony?

It could not.

But rather, Simmias, according to correct reasoning, no soul, if it is a harmony,   94
will have any share of wickedness, for harmony is surely altogether this very thing,
harmony, and would never share in disharmony.

It certainly would not.

Nor would a soul, being altogether this very thing, a soul, share in wickedness?

How could it, in view of what has been said?

So it follows from this argument that all the souls of all living creatures will be
equally good, if souls are by nature equally this very thing, souls.

I think so, Socrates.

Does our argument seem right, he said, and does it seem that it should have come
to this, if the hypothesis that the soul is a harmony was correct?   b

Not in any way, he said.

Further, of all the parts of a man, can you mention any other part that rules him
than his soul, especially if it is a wise soul?

I cannot.

Does it do so by following the affections of the body or by opposing them? I
mean, for example, that when the body is hot and thirsty the soul draws him to the
opposite, to not drinking; when the body is hungry, to not eating, and we see a
thousand other examples of the soul opposing the affections of the body. Is that not
so?

It certainly is.   c

On the other hand we previously agreed that the soul, being a harmony, was
never out of tune with the stress and relaxation and the striking of the strings or
anything else done to its composing elements, but that it followed and never
directed them?

We did so agree, of course.

Well, does it now appear to do quite the opposite, ruling over all the elements of
which one says it is composed, opposing nearly all of them throughout life, direc-   d
ting all their ways, inflicting harsh and painful punishment on them at times in
physical culture and medicine, at other times more gently by threats and exhortations, holding converse with desires and passions and fears as if it were one thing
talking to a different one, as Homer wrote somewhere in the *Odyssey* where he says
that Odysseus "struck his breast and rebuked his heart, saying,

'Endure, my heart, you have endured worse than this.' "

Do you think that when he composed this the poet thought that his soul was a   e
harmony, a thing to be directed by the affections of the body? Did he not rather re-

gard it as ruling over them and mastering them, itself a much more divine thing than a harmony?

Yes, by Zeus, I think so, Socrates.

Therefore, my good friend, it is quite wrong for us to say that the soul is a harmony, and in saying so we would disagree both with the divine poet Homer and with ourselves.

That is so, he said.

Very well, said Socrates. Harmonia of Thebes seems somehow reasonably propitious to us. How and by what argument, my dear Cebes, can we propitiate Cadmus?[18]

I think, Cebes said, that you will find a way. You dealt with the argument about harmony in a manner that was quite astonishing to me. When Simmias was speaking of his difficulties I was very much wondering whether anyone would be able to deal with his argument, and I was quite dumbfounded when right away he could not resist your argument's first onslaught. I should not wonder therefore if that of Cadmus suffered the same fate.

My good sir, said Socrates, do not boast, lest some malign influence upset the argument we are about to make. However, we leave that to the care of the god, but let us come to grips with it in the Homeric fashion, to see if there is anything in what you say. The sum of your problem is this: you consider that the soul must be proved to be immortal and indestructible before a philosopher on the point of death, who is confident that he will fare much better in the underworld than if he had led any other kind of life, can avoid being foolish and simple-minded in this confidence. To prove that the soul is strong, that it is divine, that it existed before we were born as men, all this, you say, does not show the soul to be immortal but only long-lasting. That it existed for a very long time before, that it knew much and acted much, makes it no more immortal because of that; indeed, its very entering into a human body was the beginning of its destruction, like a disease; it would live that life in distress and would in the end be destroyed in what we call death. You say it makes no difference whether it enters a body once or many times as far as the fear of each of us is concerned, for it is natural for a man who is no fool to be afraid, if he does not know and cannot prove that the soul is immortal. This, I think, is what you maintain, Cebes; I deliberately repeat it often, in order that no point may escape us, and that you may add or subtract something if you wish.

And Cebes said: "There is nothing that I want to add or subtract at the moment. That is what I say."

Socrates paused for a long time, deep in thought. He then said: "This is no unimportant problem that you raise, Cebes, for it requires a thorough investigation of the cause of generation and destruction. I will, if you wish, give you an account of my experience in these matters. Then if something I say seems useful to you, make use of it to persuade us of your position."

I surely do wish that, said Cebes.

Listen then, and I will, Cebes, he said. When I was a young man I was wonderful-

18. [Harmonia was in legend the wife of Cadmus, the founder of Thebes. Socrates' punning joke is simply that, having dealt with Harmonia (harmony), we must now deal with Cadmus (i.e., Cebes, the other Theban).]

ly keen on that wisdom which they call natural science, for I thought it splendid to know the causes of everything, why it comes to be, why it perishes and why it exists. I was often changing my mind in the investigation, in the first instance, of questions such as these: Are living creatures nurtured when heat and cold produce a kind of   b putrefaction, as some say? Do we think with our blood, or air, or fire, or none of these, and does the brain provide our senses of hearing and sight and smell, from which come memory and opinion, and from memory and opinion which has become stable, comes knowledge? Then again, as I investigated how these things perish and what happens to things in the sky and on the earth, finally I became convinced that I had no natural aptitude at all for that kind of investigation, and of this I will   c give you sufficient proof. This investigation made me quite blind even to those things which I and others thought that I clearly knew before, so that I unlearned what I thought I knew before, about many other things and specifically about how men grew. I thought before that it was obvious to anybody that men grew through eating and drinking, for food adds flesh to flesh and bones to bones, and in the same   d way appropriate parts were added to all other parts of the body, so that the man grew from an earlier small bulk to a large bulk later, and so a small man became big. That is what I thought then. Do you not think it is reasonable?

I do, said Cebes.

Then further consider this: I thought my opinion was satisfactory, that when a large man stood by a small one he was taller by a head, and so a horse was taller than a horse. Even clearer than this, I thought that ten was more than eight because   e two had been added, and that a two-cubit length is larger than a cubit because it surpasses it by half its length.

And what do you think now about those things?

That I am far, by Zeus, from believing that I know the cause of any of those things. I will not even allow myself to say that where one is added to one either the one to which it is added or the one that is added becomes two, or that the one added and the one to which it is added become two because of the addition of the one to the other. I wonder that, when each of them is separate from the other, each of them   97 is one, nor are they then two, but that, when they come near to one another, this the cause of their becoming two, the coming together and being placed closer to one another. Nor can I any longer be persuaded that when one thing is divided, this division is the cause of its becoming two, for just now the cause of becoming two was the opposite. At that time it was their coming close together and one was added   b to the other, but now it is because one is taken away and separated from the other.

I do not any longer persuade myself that I know why a unit or anything else comes to be, or perishes or exists by the old method of investigation, and I do not accept it, but I have a confused method of my own. One day I heard someone reading, as he said, from a book of Anaxagoras, and saying that it is Mind that directs and is the cause of everything. I was delighted with this cause and it seemed to me   c good that Mind should be the cause of all. I thought that if this were so, the directing Mind would direct everything and arrange each thing in the way that was best. If then one wished to know the cause of each thing, why it comes to be or perishes or exists, one had to find what was the best way for it to be, or to be acted upon, or to act. On these premises then it befitted a man to investigate only, about this and   d other things, what is best. The same man must inevitably also know what is worse, for that is part of the same knowledge. As I reflected on this subject I was glad to think that I had found in Anaxagoras a teacher about the cause of things after my own heart, and that he would tell me, first, whether the earth is flat or round, and then would add why it is so of necessity, saying which is better, and that it was better to be so. If he said it was in the middle of the universe, he would go on to show that it was better for it to be in the middle, and if he showed me those things I should be prepared never to desire any other kind of cause. I was ready to find out in the same way about the sun and the moon and the other heavenly bodies, about their relative speed, their turnings and whatever else happened to them, how it is best that each should act or be acted upon. I never thought that Anaxagoras, who said that those things were directed by Mind, would bring in any other cause for them than that it was best for them to be as they are. Once he had given the best for each as the cause for each and the general cause of all, I thought he would go on to explain the common good for all, and I would not have exchanged my hopes for a fortune. I eagerly acquired his books and read them as quickly as I could in order to know the best and the worst as soon as possible.

This wonderful hope was dashed as I went on reading and saw that the man made no use of Mind, nor gave it any responsibility for the management of things, but mentioned as causes air and ether and water and many other strange things. That seemed to me much like saying that Socrates' actions are all due to his mind, and then in trying to tell the causes of everything I do, to say that the reason that I am sitting here is because my body consists of bones and sinews, because the bones are hard and are separated by joints, that the sinews are such as to contract and relax, that they surround the bones along with flesh and skin which hold them together, then as the bones are hanging in their sockets, the relaxation and contraction of the sinews enable me to bend my limbs, and that is the cause of my sitting here with my limbs bent.

Again, he would mention other such causes for my talking to you: sounds and air and hearing, and a thousand other such things, but he would neglect to mention the true causes, that, after the Athenians decided it was better to condemn me, for this reason it seemed best to me to sit here and more right to remain and to endure whatever penalty they ordered. For by the dog, I think these sinews and bones could long ago have been in Megara or among the Boeotians, taken there by my belief as to the best course, if I had not thought it more right and honourable to endure whatever penalty the city ordered rather than escape and run away. To call those things causes is too absurd. If someone said that without bones and sinews and all such things, I should not be able to do what I decided, he would be right, but surely to say that they are the cause of what I do, and not that I have chosen the best course, even though I act with my mind, is to speak very lazily and carelessly. Imagine not being able to distinguish the real cause from that without which the cause would not be able to act as a cause, it is what the majority appear to do, like people groping in the dark; they call it a cause, thus giving it a name that does not belong to it. That is why one man surrounds the earth with a vortex to make the heavens keep it in place, another makes the air support it like a wide lid. As for their capacity of being in the best place they could possibly be put, this they do not look for, nor do they believe it to have any divine force, but they believe that they will some time discover a stronger and more immortal Atlas to hold everything together more, and they do not believe that the truly good and "binding" binds and holds them together. I would gladly become the disciple of any man who taught the workings of that kind of cause. However, since I was deprived and could neither discover it myself nor learn it from another, do you wish me to give you an explanation of how, as a second best, I busied myself with the search for the cause, Cebes?   d

I would wish it above all else, he said.

After this, he said, when I had wearied of investigating things, I thought that I must be careful to avoid the experience of those who watch an eclipse of the sun, for some of them ruin their eyes unless they watch its reflection in water or some such material. A similar thought crossed my mind, and I feared that my soul would be   e altogether blinded if I looked at things with my eyes and tried to grasp them with each of my senses. So I thought I must take refuge in discussions and investigate the truth of things by means of them. However, perhaps this analogy is inadequate, for I certainly do not admit that one who investigates things by means of words is dealing with images, any more than one who looks at facts. However, I started in this   100 manner: taking as my hypothesis in each case the theory that seemed to me the most compelling, I would consider as true, about cause and everything else, whatever agreed with this, and as untrue whatever did not so agree. But I want to put my meaning more clearly for I do not think that you understand me now.

No, by Zeus, said Cebes, not very well.

This, he said, is what I mean. It is nothing new, but what I have never stopped   b talking about, both elsewhere and in the earlier part of our conversation. I am going to try to show you the kind of cause with which I have concerned myself. I turn back to those oft-mentioned things and proceed from them. I assume the existence of a Beautiful, itself by itself, of a Good and a Great and all the rest. If you grant me these and agree that they exist, I hope to show you the cause as a result, and to find the soul to be immortal.

Take it that I grant you this, said Cebes, and hasten to your concluson.   c

Consider then, he said, whether you share my opinion as to what follows, for I think that, if there is anything beautiful besides the Beautiful itself, is is beautiful for no other reason than that it shares in that Beautiful, and I say so with everything. Do you agree to this sort of cause? — I do.

I no longer understand or recognize those other sophisticated causes, and if someone tells me that a thing is beautiful because it has a bright colour or shape or   d any such thing, I ignore these other reasons—for all these confuse me—but I simply, naively and perhaps foolishly cling to this, that nothing else makes it beautiful other than the presence of, or the sharing in, or however you may describe its relationship to that Beautiful we mentioned, for I will not insist on the precise nature of the relationship, but that all Beautiful things are beautiful by the Beautiful. That, I think, is the safest answer I can give myself or anyone else. And if I stick to this I think I shall never fall into error. This is the safe answer for me or anyone else to   e give, namely, that it is through Beauty that beautiful things are made beautiful. Or do you not think so too? — I do.

And that it is through Bigness that big things are big and the bigger are bigger, and that smaller things are made small by Smallness? — Yes.

And you would not accept the statement that one man is taller than another by a head[19] and the shorter man shorter by the same, but you would bear witness that

19. [This is very puzzling in English. In Greek the confusion is due to the double use of the dative, instrumental and casual, so that it could mean, "because of a head" which is nonsense of course, but the ambiguity is there and makes the statement of Socrates possible.]

101   you mean nothing else than that everything that is bigger is made bigger by
       nothing else than by Bigness, and that is the cause of its being bigger, and the
       smaller is made smaller only by Smallness and this is why it is smaller. I think you
       would be afraid that some opposite argument would confront you if you said that
       someone is bigger or smaller by a head, first, because the bigger is bigger and the
       smaller smaller by the same, then because the bigger is bigger by a head which is
 b   small, and this would be strange, namely, that someone is made bigger by some-
       thing small. Would you not be afraid of this?

          I certainly would, said Cebes, laughing.

          Then you would be afraid to say that ten is more than eight by two, and that this
       is the cause of the excess, and not magnitude and because of magnitude, or that two
       cubits is bigger than one cubit by half and not by Bigness, for this is the same
       fear. — Certainly.

          Then would you not avoid saying that when one is added to one it is the addition
 c   and when it is divided it is the division that is the cause of two? And you would
       loudly exclaim that you do not know how else each thing can come to be except by
       sharing in the particular reality in which it shares, and in these cases you do not
       know of any other cause of becoming two except by sharing in Twoness, and that
       the things that are to be two must share in this, as that which is to be one must share
       in Oneness, and you would dismiss these additions and divisions and other such
       subtleties, and leave them to those wiser than yourself to answer. But you, afraid, as
 d   they say, of your own shadow and your inexperience, would cling to the safety of
       your own hypothesis and give that answer. If someone then attacked your
       hypothesis itself, you would ignore him and would not answer until you had ex-
       amined whether the consequences that follow from it agree with one another or
       contradict one another. And when you must give an account of your hypothesis
       itself you will proceed in the same way: you will assume another hypothesis, the one
 e   which seems to you best of the higher ones until you come to something acceptable,
       but you will not jumble the two as the debaters do by discussing the hypothesis and
       its consequences at the same time, if you wish to discover any truth. This they do
       not discuss at all nor give any thought to, but their wisdom enables them to mix
       everything up and yet to be pleased with themselves, but if you are a philosopher I
102   think you will do as I say.

          What you say is very true, said Simmias and Cebes together.

          ECHECRATES: Yes, by Zeus, Phaedo, and they were right, I think he made
       these things wonderfully clear to anyone of even small intelligence.

          PHAEDO: Yes indeed, Echecrates, and all those present thought so too.

          E: And so do we who were not present but hear of it now. What was said after
       that?

          P: As I recall it, when the above had been accepted, and it was agreed that
       each of the Forms existed, and that other things acquired their name by having a
 b   share in them, he followed this up by asking: If you say these things are so, when
       you then say that Simmias is taller than Socrates but shorter than Phaedo, do you
       not mean that there is in Simmias both tallness and shortness? — I do.

          But, he said, do you agree that the words of the statement 'Simmias is taller than
       Socrates' do not express the truth of the matter? It is not the nature of Simmias to
 c   be taller than Socrates because he is Simmias but because of the tallness he happens

to have? Nor is he taller than Socrates because Socrates is Socrates, but because Socrates has smallness compared with the tallness of the other? — True.

Nor is he shorter than Phaedo because Phaedo is Phaedo, but because Phaedo has tallness compared with the shortness of Simmias? — That is so.

So then Simmias is called both short and tall, being between the two, presenting his shortness to be overcome by the tallness of one, and his tallness to overcome the shortness of the other. He smilingly added, I seem to be going to talk like a book, but it is as I say. The other agreed.

My purpose is that you may agree with me. Now it seems to me that not only Tallness itself is never willing to be tall and short at the same time, but also that that tallness in us[20] will never admit the short or be overcome, but one of two things happens: either it flees and retreats whenever its opposite, the short, approaches, or it is destroyed by its approach. It is not willing to endure and admit shortness and be other than it was, whereas I admit and endure shortness and still remain the same person and am this short man. But Tallness, being tall, cannot venture to be small. In the same way, the short in us is unwilling to become or to be tall ever, nor does any other of the opposites become or be its opposite while still being what it was; either it goes away or is destroyed when that happens. — I altogether agree, said Cebes.

When he heard this, someone of those present—I have no clear memory of who it was—said: "By the gods, did we not agree earlier in our discussion[21] to the very opposite of what is now being said, namely, that the larger came from the smaller and the smaller from the larger, and that this simply was how opposites came to be, from their opposites, but now I think we are saying that this would never happen?"

On hearing this, Socrates inclined his head towards the speaker and said: "You have bravely reminded us, but you do not understand the difference between what is said now and what was said then, which was that an opposite thing came from its opposite thing; now we say that the opposite itself could never become its opposite, neither that in us or that in nature. Then, my friend, we were talking of things that have opposite qualities and naming these after them, but now we say that these opposites themselves, from the presence of which in them things get their name, never can tolerate the coming to be from one another." At the same time he looked to Cebes and said: "Does anything of what this man says also disturb you?"

Not at the moment, said Cebes, but I do not deny that many things do disturb me.

We are altogether agreed then, he said, that an opposite will never be its own opposite. — Entirely agreed.

Consider then whether you will agree to this further point. There is something you call hot and something you call cold. — There is.

Are they the same as what you call snow and fire? — By Zeus, no.

So the hot is something other than fire, and the cold is something other than snow? — Yes.

---

20. [The "tallness in us" is not the Form, which is never immanent in the particular, nor need we imagine it to refer to another thing existing between the Form and the particular; it simply refers to the quality of tallness which is clearly inherent in the particulars. The expression could be used without reference to the theory of Forms at all.]

21. [The reference is to 70d–71a above.]

You think, I believe, that being snow it will not admit the hot, as we said before, and remain what it was and be both snow and hot, but when the hot approaches it will either retreat before it or be destroyed. — Quite so.

So fire, as the cold approaches, will either go away or be destroyed; it will never
e   admit coldness and remain what it was, fire and cold. — What you say is true.

It is true then about some of these things that not only the Form itself deserves its own name for all time, but there is something else that is not the Form but has its character whenever it exists. Perhaps I can make my meaning clearer: the Odd must always be given this name we now mention. Is that not so? — Certainly.

Is it the only one of existing things to be called odd? — this is my question — or is
104   there something else than the Odd which one must nevertheless also always call odd, as well as by its own name, because it is such by nature as never to be separated from the Odd? I mean, for example, the number three and many others. Consider three: do you not think that it must always be called both by its own name and by that of the Odd, which is not the same as three? That is the nature of three, and of five, and of half of all the numbers; each of them is odd, but it is not the Odd. Then
b   again, two and four and the whole other column of numbers; each of them, while not being the same as the Even, is always even. Do you not agree? — Of course.

Look now. What I want to make clear is this: not only do those opposites not admit each other, but this is also true of those things which, while not being opposite to each other yet always contain the opposites, and it seems that these do not admit that Form which is opposite to that which is in them; when it approaches them, they either perish or give way. Shall we not say that three will perish or
c   undergo anything before, while remaining three, becoming even? — Certainly, said Cebes.

Yet surely two is not the opposite of three? — Indeed it is not.

It is then not only opposite Forms that do not admit each other's approach, but also some other things that do not admit the onset of opposites. — Very true.

Do you then want us, if we can, to define what these are? — I surely do.

Would they be the things that are compelled by whatever occupies them not only to
d   contain their own Form but also always that of some opposite. — How do you mean?

As we were saying just now, you surely know that what the Form of three occupies must not only be three but also odd. — Certainly.

And we say that the opposite Form to the Form that achieves this result could never come to it. — It could not.

Now it is Oddness that has done this? — Yes.

And opposite to this is the form of the Even? — Yes.
e   So then the Form of the Even will never come to three? — Never.

Then three has no share in the Even? — Never.

So three is uneven? — Yes.

As for what I said we must define, that is, what kind of things, while not being opposites to something, yet do not admit the opposite, as for example the triad, which is not the opposite of the Even, yet does not admit it because it always brings along the opposite of the Even, and so the dyad in relation to the Odd, fire to the Cold, and very
105   many other things, see whether you would define it thus: Not only does the opposite not admit its opposite, but that which brings along some opposite into that which it

occupies, that which brings this along will not admit the opposite to that which it brings along. Refresh your memory, it is no worse for being heard often. Five does not admit the form of the Even, nor will ten, which is twice five, admit the form of the Odd. It is the opposite of something else, yet it will not admit the form of the Odd. Nor does one-and-a-half and other such fractions admit the form of the Whole, nor will one-third and all such, if you follow me and agree to this.

I certainly agree, he said, and I follow you.

Tell me again from the beginning, he said, and do not answer in the words of the question, but do as I do. I say that beyond that safe answer, which I spoke of first, I see another safe answer. If you should ask me what, coming into a body, makes it hot, my reply would not be that safe and ignorant one, that it is heat, but our present argument provides a more sophisticated answer, namely fire, and if you ask me what, on coming into a body, makes it sick, I will not say sickness but fever. Nor, if asked the presence of what in a number makes it odd, I will not say oddness but oneness, and so with other things. See if you now sufficiently understand what I want. — Quite sufficiently.

Answer me then, he said, what is it that, present in a body, makes it living? — A soul.

And is that always so? — Of course.

Whatever the soul occupies, it always brings life to it? — It does.

Is there, or is there not, an opposite to life? — There is.

What is it? — Death.

So the soul will never admit the opposite of that which it brings along, as we agree from what has been said?

Most certainly, said Cebes.

Well, and what do we call that which does not admit the form of the Even? — The uneven.

What do we call that which will not admit the just and that which will not admit the musical?

The unmusical, and the other the unjust.

Very well, what do we call that which does not admit death?

The deathless, he said.

Now the soul does not admit death? — No.

So the soul is deathless? — It is.

Very well, he said. Shall we say that this has been proved, do you think?

Quite adequately proved, Socrates.

Well now, Cebes, he said, if the uneven were of necessity indestructible, surely three would be indestructible? — Of course.

And if the non-hot were of necessity indestructible, then whenever anyone brought heat to snow, the snow would retreat safe and unthawed, for it could not be destroyed, nor again could it stand its ground and admit the heat? — What you say is true.

In the same way, if the non-cold were indestructible, then when some cold attacked the fire, it would neither be quenched nor destroyed, but retreat safely. — Necessarily.

b   Must then the same not be said of the deathless? If the deathless is also indestructible, it is impossible for the soul to be destroyed when death comes upon it. For it follows from what has been said that it will not admit death or be dead, just as three, we
said, will not be even nor will the odd; nor will fire be cold, nor the heat that is in the
fire. But, someone might say, what prevents the odd, while not becoming even as has
c   been agreed, from being destroyed, and the even to come to be instead? We could not
maintain against the man who said this that it is not destroyed, for the uneven is not
indestructible. If we had agreed that it was indestructible we could have maintained
that at the coming of the even, the odd and the three have gone away and the same
would hold for fire and the hot and the other things. — Surely.

And so now, if we are agreed that the deathless is indestructible, the soul, besides
d   being deathless, is indestructible. If not, we need another argument.

— There is no need for one as far as that goes, for hardly anything could resist destruction if the deathless, which lasts forever, would admit destruction.

All would agree, said Socrates, that the god, and the Form of life itself, and anything that is deathless, are never destroyed. — All men would agree, by Zeus, to
that, and the gods, I imagine, even more so.

e   If the deathless is indestructible, then the soul, if it is deathless, would also be
indestructible? — Necessarily.

Then when death comes to man, the mortal part of him dies, it seems, but his
deathless part goes away safe and indestructible, yielding the place to death. — So
it appears.

The soul, Cebes, he said, is most certainly deathless and indestructible and our
107   souls will really dwell in the underworld.

— I have nothing more to say against that, Socrates, said Cebes, nor can I doubt
your arguments. If Simmias here or someone else has something to say, he should
not remain silent, for I do not know to what further occasion other than the present
he could put it off if he wants to say or to hear anything on these subjects.

Certainly, said Simmias, I myself have no remaining grounds for doubt after
what has been said; nevertheless, in view of the importance of our subject and my
b   low opinion of human weakness, I am bound still to have some private misgivings
about what we have said.

You are not only right to say this, Simmias, Socrates said, but our first hypotheses
require clearer examination, even though we find them convincing. And if you analyze them adequately, you will, I think, follow the argument as far as a man can and
if the conclusion is clear, you will look no further. — That is true.

c   It is right to think then, gentlemen, that if the soul is immortal, it requires our
care not only for the time we call our life, but for the sake of all time, and that one is
in terrible danger if one does not give it that care. If death were escape from everything, it would be a great boon to the wicked to get rid of the body and of their
wickedness together with their soul. But now that the soul appears to be immortal,
d   there is no escape from evil or salvation for it except by becoming as good and wise
as possible, for the soul goes to the underworld possessing nothing but its education
and upbringing, which are said to bring the greatest benefit or harm to the dead
right at the beginning of the journey yonder.

We are told that when each person dies the guardian spirit who was alloted to him
in life proceeds to lead him to a certain place, whence those who have been gathered

together there must, after being judged, proceed to the underworld with the guide   e
who has been appointed to lead them thither from here. Having there undergone what
they must and stayed there the appointed time, they are led back here by another
guide after long periods of time. The journey is not as Aeschylus' Telephus[22] describes
it. He says that only one single path leads to Hades, but I think it is neither one nor   108
simple, for then there would be no need of guides; one could not make any mistake if
there were but one path. As it is, it is likely to have many forks and crossroads; and I
base this judgment on the sacred rites and customs here.

The well-ordered and wise soul follows the guide and is not without familiarity
with its surroundings, but the soul that is passionately attached to the body, as I
said before, hovers around it and the visible world for a long time, struggling and   b
suffering much until it is led away by force and with difficulty by its appointed
spirit. When the impure soul which has performed some impure deed joins the
others after being involved in unjust killings or committed other crimes akin to this
or actions of souls of this kind, everybody shuns it and turns away, unwilling to be
its fellow traveller or its guide; such a soul wanders alone completely at a loss until a
certain time arrives and it is forcibly led to its proper dwelling place. On the other   c
hand, the soul that has led a pure and moderate life finds fellow-travellers and gods
to guide it, and each of them dwells in a place suited to it.

There are many strange places upon the earth, and the earth itself is not such as
those who are used to discourse upon it believe it to be in nature or size, as someone
has convinced me.

Simmias said: "What do you mean, Socrates? I have myself heard many things
said about the earth, but certainly not the things that convince you. I should be   d
glad to hear them."

Indeed, Simmias, I do not think it requires the skill of Glaucus[23] to tell you what
they are, but to prove them true requires more than that skill, and I should perhaps
not be able to do so. Also, even if I had the knowledge, my remaining time would
not be long enough to tell the tale. However, nothing prevents my telling you what
I am convinced is the shape of the earth and what its regions are.   e

Even that is sufficient, said Simmias.

Well then, he said, the first thing of which I am convinced is that if the earth is a
sphere in the middle of the heavens, it has no need of air or any other force to
prevent it from falling. The homogeneous nature of the heavens on all sides and the   109
earth's own equipoise are sufficient, for an object balanced in the middle of something homogeneous will have no tendency to incline more in any direction than any
other but will remain unmoved. This, he said, is the first point of which I am persuaded.

And rightly so, said Simmias.

Further, the earth is very large, and we live around the sea in a small portion of it
between Phasis and the pillars of Heracles, like ants or frogs around a swamp; many   b
other peoples live in many such parts of it. Everywhere about the earth there are numerous hollows of many kinds and shapes and sizes into which the water and the

22. [The *Telephus* of Aeschylus is not extant, and little is known about it.]

23. [A proverbial expression meaning that a difficult task required the skill of Glaucus. Its origin is
obscure, for there are several explanations given by the Scholiasts.]

mist and the air have gathered. The earth itself is pure and lies in the pure sky where the stars are situated, which the majority of those who discourse on these sub-
c   jects call the ether. The water and mist and air are the sediment of the ether and they always flow into the hollows of the earth. We, who dwell in the hollows of it, are unaware of this and we think that we live above, on the surface of the earth. It is as if someone who lived deep down in the middle of the ocean thought he was living on its surface. Seeing the sun and the other heavenly bodies through the water, he
d   would think the sea to be the sky; because he is slow and weak, he has never reached the surface of the sea or risen with his head above the water or come out of the sea to our region here, nor seen how much purer and more beautiful it is than his own re-gion, nor has he ever heard of it from anyone who has seen it.

Our experience is the same: living in a certain hollow of the earth, we believe that we live upon its surface; the air we call the heavens, as if the stars made their way through it; this too is the same: because of our weakness and slowness we are not
e   able to make our way to the upper limit of the air; if anyone got to this upper limit, if anyone came to it or reached it on wings and his head rose above it, he would, as, on rising from the sea, the fishes see things in our region, see things there and, if his nature could endure to contemplate them, he would know that there is the true heaven, the true light and the true earth, for the earth here, these stones and the whole region, are spoiled and eaten away, just as things in the sea are by the salt
110   water.

Nothing worth mentioning grows in the sea; nothing, one might say, is fully de-veloped, but there are caves and sand and endless slime and mud wherever there is earth, not comparable in any way with the beauties of our region. So those things above are in their turn far superior to the things we know. Indeed, if this is the moment to tell a tale, Simmias, it is worth hearing about the nature of things on the
b   surface of the earth under the heavens.

At any rate, Socrates, said Simmias, we should be glad to hear this story.

Well, then, my friend, in the first place it is said that the earth, looked at from above, looks like those spherical balls made up of twelve pieces of leather; it is multi-coloured, and of these colours those used by our painters give us an indica-tion; up there the whole earth has these colours, but much brighter and purer than
c   these; one part is sea-green and of marvelous beauty, another is golden, another is white, whiter than chalk or snow; the earth is composed also of the other colours, more numerous and beautiful than any we have seen. The very hollows of the earth, full of water and air, gleaming among the variety of other colours, present a colour
d   of their own so that the whole is seen as a continuum of variegated colours. On the surface of the earth the plants grow with corresponding beauty, the trees and the flowers and the fruits, and so with the hills and the stones, more beautiful in their smoothness and transparency and colour. Our precious stones here are but frag-ments, our cornelians, jaspers, emeralds and the rest. All stones there are of that
e   kind, and even more beautiful. The reason is that there they are pure, not eaten away or spoiled by decay and brine, or corroded by the water and air which have flowed into the hollows here and bring ugliness and disease upon earth, stones, the other animals and plants. The earth itself is adorned with all these things, and also
111   with gold and silver and other metals. These stand out, being numerous and mas-sive and occurring everywhere, so that the earth is a sight for the blessed. There are many other living creatures upon the earth, and also men, some living inland,

others at the edge of the air, as we live on the edge of the sea, others again live on islands surrounded by air close to the mainland. In a word, what water and the sea are to us, the air is to them and the ether is to them what the air is to us. The climate   b is such that they are without disease, and they live much longer than people do here; their eyesight, hearing and intelligence and all such are as superior to ours as air is superior to water and ether to air in purity; they have groves and temples dedicated to the gods, in which the gods really dwell, and they communicate with them by speech and prophecy and by the sight of them; they see the sun and moon and stars as they are, and in other ways their happiness is in accord with this.   c

This then is the nature of the earth as a whole and of its surroundings; around the whole of it there are many regions in the hollows; some are deeper and more open than that in which we live; others are deeper and have a narrower opening than ours, and there are some that have less depth and more width. All these are connected with each other below the surface of the earth in many places by narrow and   d broader channels, and thus have outlets through which much water flows hot and cold from one to another as into mixing bowls; huge rivers of both hot and cold water thus flow beneath the earth eternally, much fire and large rivers of fire, and many of wet mud, both more pure and more muddy, such as those flowing in advance of the lava and the stream of lava itself in Sicily. These streams then fill up   e every and all regions as the flow reaches each, and all these places move up and down with the oscillating movement of the earth. The natural cause of the oscillation is as follows: one of the hollows of the earth, which is also the biggest, pierces through the whole earth; it is that which Homer mentioned when he said: "Far   112 down where is the deepest pit below the earth. . . .", and which he elsewhere, and many other poets, call Tartarus; into this chasm all the rivers flow together, and again flow out of it, and each river is affected by the nature of the land through which it flows. The reason for their flowing into and out of Tartarus is that this   b water has no bottom or solid base but it oscillates up and down in waves, and the air and wind about it do the same, for they follow it when it flows to this or that part of the earth. Just as when people breathe, the flow of air goes in and out, so here the air oscillates with the water and creates terrible winds as it goes in and out. Whenever the water retreats to what we call the lower part of the earth, it flows into those parts   c and fills them up as if the water were pumped in; when it leaves that part for this, it fills these parts again, and the parts filled flow through the channels and through the earth and in each case arrive at the places to which the channels lead and create seas and marshes and rivers and springs. From there the waters flow under the earth again, some flowing around larger and more numerous regions, some round smaller   d and shallower ones, then flow back into Tartarus, some at a point much lower than where they issued forth, others only a little way, but all of them at a lower point, some of them at the opposite side of the chasm, some on the same side; some flow in a wide circle round the earth once or many times like snakes, then go as far down as possible, then go back into the chasm of Tartarus. From each side it is possible to flow down as far as the center, but not beyond, for this part that faces the river flow   e from either side is steep.

There are many large rivers of all kinds, and among these there are four of note: the biggest which flows on the outside (of the earth) in a circle is called Oceanus; opposite it and flowing in the opposite direction is the Acheron, it flows through many other deserted regions and further underground makes its way to the

113   Acherousian lake to which the souls of the majority come after death and, after remaining there for a certain appointed time, longer for some, shorter for others, they
are sent back to birth as living creatures. The third river issues between the first
two, and close to its source it falls into a region burning with much fire and makes a
lake larger than our sea, boiling with water and mud. From there it goes in a circle
and winding on its way it comes, among other places, to the edge of the Acherou-
b   sian lake but does not mingle with its waters; then, coiling many times underground
it flows lower down into Tartarus; this is called the Pyriphlegethon, and its lava
streams throw off fragments of it in various parts of the earth. Opposite this the
c   fourth river issues forth, which is called Stygion, and it is said to flow first into a terrible and wild region, all of it blue-gray in colour, and the lake that this river forms
by flowing into it is called the Styx. As its waters fall into the lake they acquire
dread powers; then diving below and winding round it flows in the opposite direction from the Pyriphlegethon and into the opposite side of the Acherousian lake; its
waters do not mingle with any other; it too flows in a circle and into Tartarus
opposite the Pyriphlegethon. The name of that fourth river, the poets tell us, is
Cocytus.

     Such is the nature of these things. When the dead arrive at the place to which
d   each has been led by his guardian spirit, they are first judged as to whether they
have led a good and pious life. Those who have lived an average life make their way
to the Acheron and embark upon such vessels as there are for them and proceed to
the lake. There they dwell and are purified by penalties for any wrongdoing they
may have committed; they are also suitably rewarded for their good deeds as each
e   deserves. Those who are deemed incurable because of the enormity of their crimes,
having committed many great sacrileges or wicked and unlawful murders and other
such wrongs—their fitting fate is to be hurled into Tartarus never to emerge from it.
Those who are deemed to have committed great but curable crimes, such as doing
violence to their father or mother in a fit of temper but who have felt remorse for the
114   rest of their lives, or who have killed someone in a similar manner, these must of necessity be thrown into Tartarus, but a year later the current throws them out, those
who are guilty of murder by way of Cocytus, and those who have done violence to
their parents by way of the Pyriphlegethon. After they have been carried along to
the Acherousian lake, they cry out and shout, some for those they have killed, others
b   for those they have maltreated, and calling them they then pray to them and beg
them to allow them to step out into the lake and to receive them. If they persuade
them, they do step out and their punishment comes to an end; if they do not, they
are taken back into Tartarus and from there into the rivers, and this does not stop
until they have persuaded those they have wronged, for this is the punishment
which the judges imposed on them.

     Those who are deemed to have lived an extremely pious life are freed and re-
leased from the regions of the earth as from a prison; they make their way up to a
c   pure dwelling place and live on the surface of the earth. Those who have purified
themselves sufficiently by philosophy live in the future altogether without a body;
they make their way to even more beautiful dwelling places which it is hard to describe clearly, nor do we now have the time to do so. Because of the things we have
enunciated, Simmias, one must make every effort to share in virtue and wisdom in
d   one's life, for the reward is beautiful and the hope is great.

     No sensible man would insist that these things are as I have described them, but I

think it is fitting for a man to risk the belief—for the risk is a noble one—that this, or something like this, is true about the future dwelling places of the soul, since the soul is evidently immortal, and a man should repeat this to himself as if it were an incantation, which is why I have been prolonging my tale. That is the reason why a man should be of good cheer about his own soul, if during life he has ignored the pleasures of the body and its ornamentation as of no concern to him and doing him   e
more harm than good, but has seriously concerned himself with the pleasures of learning, and adorned his soul not with alien but with its own ornaments, namely, moderation, righteousness, courage, freedom and truth, and in that state awaits his   115
journey to the underworld.

Now you, Simmias, Cebes and the rest of you, Socrates continued, will each take that journey at some other time but my fated day calls me now, as a tragic character might say, and it is about time for me to have my bath, for I think it better to have it before I drink the poison and save the women the trouble of washing the corpse.

When Socrates had said this Crito spoke: Very well, Socrates, what are your in-   b
structions to me and the others about your children or anything else? What can we do that would please you most?—Nothing new, Crito, said Socrates, but what I am always saying, that you will please me and mine and yourselves by taking good care of your own selves in whatever you do, even if you do not agree with me now, but if you neglect your own selves, and are unwilling to live following the tracks, as it were, of what we have said now and on previous occasions, you will achieve nothing   c
even if you strongly agree with me at this moment.

We shall be eager to follow your advice, said Crito, but how shall we bury you?

In any way you like, said Socrates, if you can catch me and I do not escape you. And laughing quietly, looking at us, he said: I do not convince Crito that I am this Socrates talking to you here and ordering all I say, but he thinks that I am the thing which he will soon be looking at as a corpse, and so he asks how he shall bury me. I   d
have been saying for some time and at some length that after I have drunk the poison I shall no longer be with you but will leave you to go and enjoy the happy mansions of the blessed, but it seems that I have said all this to him in vain in an at-tempt to reassure you and myself too. Give a pledge to Crito on my behalf, he said, the opposite pledge to that he gave the jury. He pledged that I would stay, you must pledge that I will not stay after I die, but that I shall go away, so that Crito will bear it more easily when he sees my body being burned or buried and will not be angry   e
on my behalf, as if I were suffering terribly, and so that he should not say at the funeral that he is laying out, or carrying out, or burying Socrates. For know you well, my dear Crito, that to express oneself badly is not only faulty as far as the language goes, but does some harm to the soul. You must be of good cheer, and say you are burying my body, and bury it in any way you like and think most customary.   116

After saying this he got up and went to another room to take his bath, and Crito followed him and he told us to wait for him. So we stayed, talking among ourselves, questioning what had been said, and then again talking of the great misfortune that had befallen us. We all felt that we had lost a father and would be orphaned for the rest of our lives. When he had washed, his children were brought to him—two of his sons were small and one was older—and the women of his household came to him.   b
He spoke to them before Crito and gave them what instructions he wanted. Then he sent the women and children away, and he himself joined us. It was now close to

sunset, for he had stayed inside for some time. He came and sat down after his bath and conversed for a short while, when the officer of the Eleven came and stood by

c   him and said: "I shall not reproach you as I do the others, Socrates. They are angry with me and curse me when, obeying the orders of my superiors, I tell them to drink the poison. During the time you have been here I have come to know you in other ways as the noblest, the gentlest and the best man who has ever come here. So now too I know that you will not make trouble for me; you know who is responsible and you will direct your anger against them. You know what message I bring. Fare you well, and try to endure what you must as easily as possible." The officer was weep-

d   ing as he turned away and went out. Socrates looked up at him and said: "Fare you well also, we shall do as you bid us." And turning to us he said: "How pleasant the man is! During the whole time I have been here he has come in and conversed with me from time to time, a most agreeable man. And how genuinely he now weeps for me. Come, Crito, let us obey him. Let someone bring the poison if it is ready; if not, let someone prepare it."

e   But Socrates, said Crito, I think the sun still shines upon the hills and has not yet set. I know that others drink the poison quite a long time after they have received the order, eating and drinking quite a bit, and some of them enjoy intimacy with their loved ones. Do not hurry; there is still some time.

It is natural, Crito, for them to do so, said Socrates, for they think they derive

117   some benefit from doing this, but it is not fitting for me. I do not expect any benefit from drinking the poison a little later, except to become ridiculous in my own eyes for clinging to life, and be sparing of it when there is none left. So do as I ask and do not refuse me.

Hearing this, Crito nodded to the slave who was standing near him; the slave went out and after a time came back with the man who was to administer the poison, carrying it made ready in a cup. When Socrates saw him he said: "Well, my good man, you are an expert in this, what must one do?" — "Just drink it and walk around until your legs feel heavy, and then lie down and it will act of itself." And he

b   offered the cup to Socrates who took it quite cheerfully, Echecrates, without a tremor or any change of feature or colour, but looking at the man from under his eyebrows as was his wont, asked: "What do you say about pouring a libation from this drink? It is allowed?" — "We only mix as much as we believe will suffice," said the man.

c   I understand, Socrates said, but one is allowed, indeed one must, utter a prayer to the gods that the journey from here to yonder may be fortunate. This is my prayer and may it be so.

And while he was saying this, he was holding the cup, and then drained it calmly and easily. Most of us had been able to hold back our tears reasonably well up till then, but when we saw him drinking it and after he drank it, we could hold them back no longer; my own tears came in floods against my will. So I covered my face. I was weeping for myself, not for him, but for my misfortune in being deprived of

d   such a comrade. Even before me, Crito was unable to restrain his tears and got up. Appollodorus had not ceased from weeping before, and at this moment his noisy tears and anger made everybody present break down, except Socrates. "What is this," he said, "you strange fellows. It is mainly for this reason that I sent the women away, to avoid such unseemliness, for I am told one should die in good omened

e   silence. So keep quiet and control yourselves."

His words made us ashamed, and we checked our tears. He walked around, and when he said his legs were heavy he lay on his back as he had been told to do, and the man who had given him the poison touched his body, and after a while tested his feet and legs, pressed hard upon his foot and asked him if he felt this, and Socrates said no. Then he pressed his calves, and made his way up his body and showed 118 us that it was cold and stiff. He felt it himself and said that when the cold reached his heart he would be gone. As his belly was getting cold Socrates uncovered his head—he had covered it—and said—these were his last words—"Crito, we owe a cock to Asclepius;[24] make this offering to him and do not forget."—"It shall be done," said Crito "tell us if there is anything else," but there was no answer. Shortly afterwards Socrates made a movement; the man uncovered him and his eyes were fixed. Seeing this Crito closed his mouth and his eyes.

Such was the end of our comrade, Echecrates, a man who, we would say, was of all those we have known the best, and also the wisest and the most upright.

24. [A cock was sacrificed to Asclepius by the sick people who slept in his temples, hoping for a cure. Socrates obviously means that death is a cure for the ills of life.]

ARISTOTLE—Italian School, sixteenth century; Casa Vasari, Venice

ALEXANDER THE GREAT (Lysippus)

THE ACROPOLIS (PROPYLAEA), ATHEN

ARISTOTLE

Aristotle (384–322 B.C.), born in the Ionian colony of Stagira in northern Greece, was the son of a physician to the Macedonian ruler. At eighteen he entered Plato's Academy in Athens, where he remained for two decades until Plato's death. He then taught outside Athens for a dozen years, including three as tutor to the young prince who later became known as Alexander the Great. In 335 Aristotle returned to Athens and founded his own school, the Lyceum, where he did his most productive research. On the death of Alexander in 323, an outbreak of anti-Macedonian feeling swept Athens, and Aristotle withdrew to the city of Chalcis, "lest," he reportedly said, "the Athenians should sin twice against philosophy."

A distinguished historian of philosophy has referred to Aristotle as "the greatest mind produced by the Greeks"; and even those who might not share this judgment would agree that his intellectual achievements were of enormous magnitude. Virtually singlehanded, he founded the study of logic. His philosophical treatises on metaphysics, ethics, politics, and aesthetics remain more than two thousand years later among the most profound works ever written on these subjects. His scientific studies produced groundbreaking results in biology, psychology, zoology, meteorology, and astronomy. Indeed, his later influence was so profound that during the Middle Ages he was often refered to simply as "the Philosopher."

Aristotle rejected Plato's Theory of Forms, arguing that universals have no subsistence apart from particulars. For example, humanity or redness do not exist independently but only as common elements in specific substances. Thus, whereas Plato viewed knowledge as an a priori inquiry into Ideas, for Aristotle the acquisition of understanding involved an empirical investigation of essential structures shared by individual entities.

Aristotle also rejected Plato's view of the soul as separate from the body, arguing instead that the soul is the body in action, just as sight is the activity of the eye. The soul, therefore, cannot exist apart from the body, for the processes of living, sensing, and knowing require an organism that lives, senses, and knows.

The first work from which excerpts are reprinted here, the *Physics,* is a study of the concepts used in physical science. Aristotle identified four causes or modes of explanation. These have come to be known as the material cause, formal cause, efficient cause, and final cause. In the case of a building, for example, its material cause may be bricks and mortar, its formal cause the architectural blueprints, its efficient cause the builders, and its final cause the providing of shelter.

Aristotle stressed the importance of final causes in understanding the world, for in his view nature is teleological, exhibiting purposeful processes. Chance is not to be understood as the absence of causality but as the coincidental achievement of one end while pursuing another, as, for instance, the case of a person who attends a banquet and unexpectedly meets a friend.

As to Aristotle's views on the purpose of human life, these are to be found in his *Nicomachean Ethics*. This work (named after Aristotle's son Nicomachus), is universally considered one of the great books of moral philosophy. It ranges from detailed analyses of such concepts as choosing, deliberating, and wishing, to a vision of man's highest happiness as a life devoted to the exercise of pure reason. The book does possess some organizational difficulties, since, like other of Aristotle's treatises, it consists of texts of his lectures as preserved in his students' notes. However, unity is provided by central themes, among which are the commitment to viewing the good as the fulfillment of human nature; the emphasis upon a close relationship between ethics and the interests of society; and the need to distinguish moral from intellectual virtue.

This latter distinction provides Aristotle with an answer to the question, raised at the opening of Plato's *Meno,* as to the origin of virtue. According to Aristotle, moral virtue, which we might call "goodness of character," is formed by habit. One becomes good by doing good. Repeated acts of justice and self-control result in a just, self-controlled person who not only performs just and self-controlled actions but does so from a fixed character. Intellectual virtue, on the other hand, which we might refer to as "wisdom," is acquired by teaching, and requires foresight and sophisticated intelligence.

In opposition to the Socratic doctrine that a person who knows the good will necessarily do the good, Aristotle insists upon our acknowledging the phenomenon of moral weakness: the situation, so easy to recognize and yet so difficult to explain, in which individuals act contrary to what they believe to be for the best. Typically, he emphasizes that a theory which denies the existence of moral weakness is at variance with observed facts.

Helpful overviews of Aristotle's thought are D. J. Allan, *The Philosophy of Aristotle* (Oxford: Oxford University Press, 1952); John Herman Randall, Jr., *Aristotle* (1960; rpt. New York: Columbia University Press, 1962); volume six of W. K. C. Guthrie, *A History of Greek Philosophy* (Cambridge: Cambridge University Press, 1981); J. L. Ackrill, *Aristotle the Philosopher* (New York: Oxford University Press, 1981); Abraham Edel, *Aristotle and His Philosophy* (Chapel Hill: University of North Carolina Press, 1982); and Jonathan Barnes, *Aristotle* (New York: Oxford University Press, 1982). Detailed analyses of each of Aristotle's major works is provided in the standard commentary by W. D. Ross, *Aristotle: a complete exposition of his works and thought* (1923; rpt. Cleveland: Meridian Books, 1959). An incisive discussion of the *Physics* is Sarah Waterlow, *Nature, Change and Agency in Aristotle's Physics* (Oxford: Clarendon Press, 1982). Two detailed studies of Aristotle's ethics are John M. Cooper, *Reason and Human Good in Aristotle* (Cambridge: Harvard University Press, 1971); and W. F. R. Hardie, *Aristotle's Ethical Theory,* 2nd ed. (Oxford: Oxford University Press, 1981). Helpful articles on the *Ethics* are collected in Amelie O. Rorty, ed., *Essays on Aristotle's Ethics* (Berkeley: University of California Press, 1980).

S. M. C.

PHYSICS
(Book II)
Nature: An Internal Origin of Change

THE DIFFERENCE BETWEEN NATURAL AND ARTIFICIAL OBJECTS

1

Among things that are, some are natural, others are due to other causes. Those that are natural are animals and their parts, plants, and the simple bodies, such as earth, fire, air and water; for we say that these things and things of this sort are natural. All these things are evidently different from things not naturally constituted; for each of them has in itself an origin of change and stability, whether in place, or growth and decay, or alteration.

Compare with these a bed or a cloak, or any other such kind of thing [i.e. any artifact]. So described [as bed etc.] and to the extent that they are products of a craft, they have no innate impulse to change. But insofar as they are coincidentally made of stone or earth or a mixture of these, they have such an innate impulse, and just to that extent. This is because nature is a sort of origin and cause of change and stability, in that to which it primarily belongs in itself and not coincidentally.

(By 'not coincidentally' I mean the following: Someone who is a doctor might come to be a cause of health in himself. But still, it is not insofar as he is being healed that he has the medical science; rather, it is coincidental that the same person is a doctor and is being healed, and that is why the two [functions] are sometimes separated from each other.)

The same applies to everything else that is produced; for none of them has in itself the origin of production. In some—e.g. a house and each of the other products of handicraft—their origin is in other, external things. In others, i.e. those that might come to be coincidental causes for themselves, the origin is in them, but is not in accord with what they are in themselves.

10

15

20

25

30

WHATEVER HAS A NATURE IS A SUBSTANCE

Nature, then, is what we have said; and things have a nature whenever they have this sort of origin. And all these things are substance; for [substance] is a sort of subject, and nature is always in a subject. The things that accord with nature are both these, and whatever belongs to them in themselves, as travelling upwards belongs to fire—for this neither is nor has a nature, but is natural and accords with nature. We have said, then, what nature is and what is natural and accords with nature.

35
193a

THERE IS NO DOUBT OF THE EXISTENCE OF NATURE

An attempt to show that there is such a thing as nature would be ridiculous. For it is evident that there are many things of this sort; and to prove what is evident from what is not is a mark of an inability to discriminate between what is known because of

5

Reprinted by permission of the translators, G. Fine and T. Irwin, from *Aristotle: Selections*, forthcoming 1987 (Indianapolis: Hackett Publishing Company).

The use of square brackets within the text is to indicate the insertion of word(s) not found in the MS.

Headings are those of the translators.

itself and what is not. (It is clearly possible to suffer from this inability; someone blind from birth would [have to] make inferences about colours.) And so such people are bound to argue about [mere] names, and understand nothing.

SOME THINK THAT NATURE IS MATTER

10   Some people think that the nature and substance of a natural object is the primary constituent present in it, but lacking any order in itself — in a bed, e.g., it will be the wood, in a statue the bronze.

It is a sign of this, according to Antiphon,[1] that if you were to bury a bed, and the rotting residue were to become able to sprout, the result would be wood, not a bed;
15   this, he thinks, is because the conventional arrangement, i.e. the craft [making the wood into a bed], is a [mere] coincident of the wood, whereas the substance is the wood that persists continuously while it is affected in these ways.

And if each of these things is related to something else in the same way (bronze and gold, e.g., to water; bones and wood to earth; and so on with anything else), that
20   thing will also be their matter and substance.

This is why some say fire or earth or air or water is the nature of things that are; some say it is some among these, others that it is all of them. Whatever anyone supposed to persist in these cases — one thing or more than one — he takes this or these to
25   be all the substance there is, and all the other things to be affections, states and conditions of them; and these things are held to be everlasting, since they do not change from themselves, but the other things come to be and are destroyed an unlimited number of times.

This, then, is one way in which we speak of nature — as the primary matter that is
30   subject for each thing that has in itself an origin of change and variation.

BUT FORM IS NATURE TOO

In another way nature is the shape, i.e. the form, that accords with the account. For just as we speak of craftsmanship in what accords with craft and is crafted, so also we speak of nature in what accords with nature and is natural. But we would not yet speak of craftsmanship or of a product in accord with craft, if something were only potentially a bed and still lacked the form of a bed; nor would we say anything of the sort about whatever is naturally constituted. For what is only potentially flesh or bone
35
193b   neither has its nature nor is by nature until it acquires the form that accords with the account by which we define flesh or bone and say what it is.

In another way, then, nature is the shape and form of things having in themselves
5   an origin of change; this form is not separable except in account. (What is composed of form and matter, e.g. man, is not nature, but is natural.)

Indeed, the form is nature more than the matter is.

(1) For something is called whatever it is [e.g. a bed or flesh] when it is actually so, more than when it is only potentially so.

(2) Further, a man comes to be from a man, but not a bed from a bed. Indeed, this is why some say that the nature of the bed is not the shape but the wood, because
10   if it were to sprout the result would be wood, not a bed. But if this shows that the

1. [Antiphon (c. 479–411 B.C.) was an Athenian orator — S.M.C.]

wood is nature, then the shape is also nature, since a man comes to be from a man.

(3) Further, nature spoken of as becoming is a road towards nature; for it is not like medical treatment, which is a road not towards medical science but towards health. For it is necessary that medical treatment proceeds *from* medical science, not *towards* medical science. But nature [as becoming] is not related to nature in this way; what is growing, insofar as it is growing, proceeds from something towards something. What is it, then, that grows? Not what it is growing from, but what it is growing into. Therefore, shape is nature.

Shape and nature are spoken of in two ways. For the privation is also form in a way. But we must consider later whether or not there is privation and a contrary in unqualified coming to be.

THE STUDENT OF NATURE, UNLIKE THE MATHEMATICIAN, STUDIES MATTER

2

We have distinguished, then, the different ways in which we speak of nature. Next we should consider how the mathematician differs from the student of nature. [The difference is not obvious.] For natural bodies certainly have surfaces, solids, lengths, and points; and these are what the mathematician studies.

We should also consider whether astronomy is different from the study of nature, or a part of it. [Apparently it is a part of it;] for it would be absurd if the task of a student of nature were to know what the sun or moon is, but not to know any of the intrinsic coincidents—expecially since students of nature evidently also discuss the shape of the sun and moon, particularly whether or not the earth and heaven are spherical.

Now these things are the concern of the mathematician as well as of the student of nature. But the mathematician is not concerned with them insofar as each is the limit of a natural body. Nor does he study the coincidents of a natural body insofar as they belong to a natural body. Hence he also separates them. For they are separable in thought from change, and his separating them makes no difference, since no falsehood results.

Those who say there are ideas do not notice that they also do this; they separate natural objects, though these are less separable than mathematical objects. This would become clear if one tried to state the definitions of both [ideas and mathematical objects]—of the things themselves and of their [intrinsic] coincidents. For odd and even, straight and curved, and also number, line, and point will not involve change, whereas flesh, bones, and man will—we speak of them as we speak of the snub nose [as including matter], not as we speak of the curved.

This is also clear from the parts of mathematics more related to the study of nature—e.g., optics, harmonics, and astronomy. These are in a way the reverse of geometry; for geometry investigates a natural line, but not insofar as it is natural, whereas optics investigates a mathematical line, but insofar as it is natural, not insofar as it is mathematical.

LIKE THE CRAFTSMAN, HOWEVER, HE STUDIES FORM AS WELL AS MATTER

But since we speak of nature in two ways—both as form and as matter—we should

15 study it as though we were investigating what snubness is, and hence we should study natural objects neither without their matter nor [simply] in accord with their matter. For indeed, since there are these two natures, there might be a puzzle about which one the student of nature should study. Perhaps the compound of the two? If so, then each one of them. Then is it the same or a different discipline that knows each one?

Judging by the early thinkers, the student of nature would seem to study matter,
20 since Empedocles[2] and Democritus[3] touched only slightly on form and essence. Grant, however, that craft imitates nature; and grant that [in the crafts] it is the same science that knows the form and the matter up to a point—e.g. the doctor knows health, and also its constituents, bile and phlegm; and similarly the housebuilder
25 knows both the form of the house and that its matter is bricks and wood; and the same is true in the other cases. It follows that it is also a task for the study of nature to know both sorts of nature.

Moreover the same discipline studies both what something is for—i.e. the end—and whatever is for the end. Now nature is an end that something is for; for whenever
30 a continuous change has some end, this sort of terminus is also what the change is for. This is why it was a ludicrous remark when the poet said [of someone's death], 'He has reached the end he was born for.' It was ludicrous because what we mean by 'end' is not every terminus, but only one that is best.

For crafts [study both end and means, since they] produce their matter, some simply producing it, others making it suitable for their work; and we use all things as
35 though they were for our sake, since we are also an end in a way. (For the end that something is for is of two sorts, as we said in *On Philosophy*.)

There are two crafts that control the matter and involve knowledge: (a) the craft
194b that uses [the matter], and (b) the craft that directs this productive craft. Hence (a) the using craft also in a way directs, but with a difference, in that (b) the directing craft knows the form, whereas (a) the craft that directs by being productive knows the
5 matter. For instance, (b) the pilot knows what sort of form the rudder has, and he prescribes [its production], whereas (a) [the boatbuilder] knows what sort of wood and what sorts of changes are needed to make it. With products of a craft, then, we produce the matter for the sake of the product; with natural things, the matter is already present.

10 Further, matter is relative to something; for each form has a different matter.

How much, then, must the student of nature know about form and essence? As much, perhaps, as the doctor knows about sinews, or the smith about bronze—enough to know what something is for. And he must confine himself to things that are separable in form, but are in matter—for a man is born from a man
15 and the sun. But it is a task for first philosophy [not for the study of nature] to determine what is separable and what it is like.

---

2. [Regarding Empedocles, see Plato's *Meno*, n.6.]

3. [Democritus (c. 460–c. 370 B.C.) was a Greek philosopher who held that all things were composed of unchangeable atoms.]

Cause and Chance

3

THE FOUR CAUSES
Now that we have determined these points, we should consider what sorts of causes, and how many, there are. For our inquiry aims at knowledge; and we think we have knowledge only when we find why something is so—i.e. when we find its primary cause. Clearly, then, we must also do this for becoming, destruction and every sort of   20
natural change, so that when we know their origins we can try to refer to these in answering each of our questions.

THE MATERIAL CAUSE
In one way, then, that from which, as a constituent, an object comes into being is said to be its cause—e.g. the bronze and silver, and their genera, are causes of the statue   25
and bowl.

THE FORMAL CAUSE
In another way, the form—i.e. the pattern—is a cause. The form is the account *[logos]* of essence, and the genera of the account (e.g. of an octave, the ratio *[logos]* two to one; and in general number), and the parts that are in the account.

THE EFFICIENT CAUSE
Again, the source of the primary origin of change or stability is a cause; e.g. the adviser caused [the action], and a father his child, and in general the producer causes   30
the product and the initiator of the change causes what is changed.

THE FINAL CAUSE
Again, something's end—i.e. what it is for—is its cause, as health is of walking. For why does he walk? We say, 'To be healthy'; and in saying this we think we have pro-   35
vided the cause. And the same is true of all the intermediate steps that advance the
end, where something else has initiated the change, as slimming, purging, drugs, or   195a
instruments, e.g. advance health; all of these are for the end, though they differ in that some are actions, some instruments.
   We may take these, then, to be the ways we speak of causes.

THE SAME THING MAY HAVE MORE THAN ONE CAUSE
Since causes are spoken of in many ways, it follows that there are many non-   5
coincidental causes of the same thing. Both the sculpting craft and the bronze, e.g., are causes of the statue, not insofar as it is something else, but insofar as it is a statue.
But they are not causes in the same way; the bronze is a cause as matter, the sculpting   10
craft as the source of the change. Some things are causes of each other—labour, e.g. is the cause of fitness, and fitness of labour. But they are not causes in the same way; fitness is the cause as end, and labour as the origin of change. Further, the same thing is the cause of contraries. For sometimes whatever is the cause of something by its

presence is also held to be the cause of the contrary by its absence; e.g. we hold the absence of a pilot to have caused the wreck of the ship, when his presence would have
15   caused its safety.

All the causes just mentioned are of four especially evident types: (1) Letters are the cause of syllables, matter of artifacts, fire and such things of bodies, parts of the whole, and the assumptions of the conclusion, as that out of which. In these cases one
20   thing—e.g. the parts—is cause as subject, while (2) the other thing—the whole, the composition, and the form—is cause as essence. (3) The seed, the doctor, the adviser and, in general, the producer, are all the sources of the origin of change or stability. (4) Other things are causes as the end and the good of other things. For what the
25   other things are for tends to be the best and their end (it does not matter whether we call it the good or the apparent good). These, then, are how many kinds of causes there are.

WAYS IN WHICH CAUSES MAY BE CITED
Though there are many types of causes, they are fewer when they are arranged under heads. For causes are so called in many ways, and even among causes of the same
30   kind some are prior and others posterior. For example, the cause of health is the practitioner of the medical craft and the practitioner of a craft; the cause of an octave is the double and number; and in every case the inclusive [and less specific causes are posterior] to the particular.

Further, some things and their genera are coincidental causes. Polycleitus[4] and the sculptor, e.g., are causes of the statue in different ways, because being Polycleitus is
35   coincidental to the sculptor. What includes the coincident is also a cause—if, e.g., the man, or, quite generally, the animal, is a cause of the statue. Some coincidental
195b   causes are more remote or more proximate than others; e.g. if the pale man or the musician were said to be the cause of the statue [they would be more remote causes than Polycleitus is].

We may speak of any cause, either proper or coincidental, either as having a potentiality or as actualizing it; e.g. we may say either that the housebuilder, or that the
5   housebuilder actually building, is causing the house to be built.

Similar things may also be said about the things of which the causes are causes. For example, [we can speak of the cause] of this statue, or of a statue, or of an image in general; or of this bronze, or of bronze, or of matter in general. The same is true of
10   coincidents.

Further, we may speak in the same way of combinations [of proper and coincidental causes, and of proper and coincidental things caused]; e.g., instead of Polycleitus or a sculptor, Polycleitus the sculptor.

Still, all these ways amount to six, each spoken of in two ways. For there is (1) the particular and (2) the genus; (3) the coincident and (4) the genus of the coincident;
15   and these may be spoken of either (5) in combination or (6) simply. And each of these may be (i) actually or (ii) potentially operating. The difference is the following. (i) Causes that are actual and particular are and are not in being simultaneously with the things they cause—e.g. this one practising medicine with this one being made healthy; and in the same way, this one housebuilding with this thing being built into

_____
4. [Polycleitus was a fifth century B.C. Greek sculptor.]

a house. (ii) But this is not true of every cause referred to as potentially 20
operating—for the house and the housebuilder are not destroyed simultaneously.

Here as elsewhere, we must always seek the most precise cause. A man, e.g., is
building because he is a builder, and he is a builder insofar as he has his building
craft; his building craft, then, is the prior cause, and the same is true in all cases. Fur- 25
ther, we must seek genera as causes of genera, and particulars as causes of particulars; a sculptor, e.g., is the cause of a statue, but this sculptor of this statue. And
we must seek a potentiality as the cause of a potential effect, and something actualilz-
ing a potentiality as the cause of an actual effect.

This, then, is a sufficient determination of the number of causes, and of the ways
they are causes. 30

LUCK AND CHANCE

4

Luck and chance are also said to be causes, and many things are said to be and to
come to be because of them. We must investigate, then, in what way luck and chance
are among the causes we have mentioned; whether luck is or is not the same as
chance; and, in general, what they are. 35

DOUBTS ABOUT THE EXISTENCE OF LUCK
Some people even wonder whether there is any such thing as chance and luck. For,
they say, nothing results from luck; everything said to result from chance or luck has 196a
some definite cause—e.g. when as a result of luck someone comes to the marketplace
and finds there the person he wanted to meet but did not expect, the cause is his
wishing to go to market. The same is true of other things said to result from luck; in 5
every case, they say, it is possible to find some cause other than luck. For if there were
such a thing as luck, it would appear truly strange and puzzling that none of the early
philosophers who discussed the causes of coming into being and destruction ever
determined anything about luck; in fact they also would seem to have thought that 10
nothing results from luck.

THESE DOUBTS ARE UNCONVINCING
But this too is surprising. For many things that come into being and are in being 15
result from luck and chance. Though people know perfectly well that everything that
comes into being can be referred to some cause, as the old argument against luck
says, still they all say that some of these things result from luck, and others do not.

Hence the early philosophers should have mentioned it in some way. But they certainly did not think luck was any of the causes they recognized—e.g. love or strife or
mind or fire or any other such thing. Their position is strange, then, whether they
supposed there was no such thing as luck, or thought there was, but omitted
it—especially strange considering that they sometimes used it. Empedocles, for exam- 20
ple, uses it when he says that air is separated out on top, not always, but as luck has it;
at least, he says in his cosmogony that it happened to run that way at that time, but
often otherwise. And he says that most of the parts of animals result from luck.

BELIEFS ABOUT CHANCE

There are some who also make chance the cause of our heaven and of all worlds. For they say that the vortex, and the motion that separated out and established everything in its present order, resulted from chance. And this is especially amazing. For animals and plants, they say, neither are nor come into being from luck, but rather, nature or mind or something of that sort is the cause, since it is not just any old thing that comes to be from each type of seed, but an olive tree from one type, and a man from another; and yet they say that the heaven and the most divine of visible things result from chance, and that there is no cause of the sort that animals and plants have.

Now if this is so, it deserves attention; and something might well have been said about it. For in addition to the other strange aspects of what they say, it is still stranger to say all this when they see that nothing in the heavens results from chance, whereas many things result from luck in the cases where [they suppose] nothing results from it. Surely the exact opposite would have been likely.

Some[5] indeed suppose that luck is a cause, but take it to be godlike and superhuman, and therefore obscure to the human mind.

So we must consider chance and luck—what each is, whether they are the same or different, and how they fit into the causes we have distinguished.

THE NATURE OF LUCKY EVENTS

5

First, then, we see that some things always, others usually, come about in the same way. Evidently neither luck nor the result of luck is said to be the cause of these—neither of what is of necessity and always nor of what is usually. But besides these classes of things that come to be there is a third class, which everyone says results from luck; evidently, then, there is such a thing as luck and chance, since we know that this third class results from luck, and that the results of luck belong to this class.

Further, some of the things that come to be come to be for something (some in accord with decision, others not, but both classes are for something), and some do not. Clearly, then, it is possible even for some members of the third class—the neither necessary nor usual—to be for something. What is for something includes both the actions that result from thought and also the results of nature. This, then, is the sort of thing that we regard as a result of luck, whenever it comes about coincidentally.

['Coincidental' must be explained.] Just as some things are something in themselves, and others are something coincidentally, so also it is possible for a cause to be of either sort. For example, the cause of a house is in itself the housebuilder, but coincidentally the pale or musical thing. Hence the cause in itself is determinate, but the coincidental cause is indeterminate, since one thing might have indefinitely many coincidents.

As has been said, then, whenever things that come to be for something have this coincidental cause, they are said to result from chance and luck. The difference between these should be defined later; we may take it as evident for the moment that both are found in things that are for something.

---

5. [The reference is to Democritus.]

AN EXAMPLE OF A LUCKY EVENT

[Suppose, for instance, that A wants to collect a debt from B; one day A comes to the market for some other reason, and meets B collecting subscriptions.] A would have come when B was collecting subscriptions, to recover the money from B, if A had known [B would be there]. In fact, however, A did not come to do this; it was a coincidence that A came [when B was there], and did this [i.e. met B] to collect [the money]. And this is so when A frequents the place [for that purpose] neither usually nor from necessity.

The end, the collection, is not a cause [of A's action] in A, but it is something he decides to do as a result of thought. And in this case A's coming is said to result from luck; but if A always or usually frequented the place because he had decided to and for the purpose of collecting the money, it would not result from luck.

HOW LUCK IS A CAUSE: EXPLANATION OF CURRENT BELIEFS

Clearly, then, luck is a coincidental cause in things that are for something and in accord with decision. Hence thought—since decision requires thought—and luck concern the same things.

Now the causes whose results might be matters of luck are bound to be indeterminate. That is why luck also seems to be something indeterminate and obscure to a human being, and why it might seem in one way that nothing results from luck. For, as we might reasonably expect, all these claims are correct.

(1) For in one way things do result from luck, since they are coincidental results, and luck is a coincidental cause. But luck is not the unqualified [and hence non-coincidental] cause of anything. The [unqualified] cause of a house, e.g., is a housebuilder, and the coincidental cause a flute-player; and the man's coming and collecting the money, without having come to collect it, has an indefinite number of coincidental causes—he might have come because he wished to see someone, or was avoiding someone, or was going to see some sight.

(2) It is also correct to say that luck is something contrary to reason. For rational judgement tells us what is always or usually the case; but luck is found in events that are neither.

(3) Hence, since causes of this sort are indeterminate, luck is also indeterminate.

Still, in some cases one might be puzzled about whether just anything might be a cause of luck. [Apparently not. Suppose someone's haircut exposes him to wind and sun, which are good for his health;] the wind or the sun's warmth, but not the haircut, might be the cause of his health—for some coincidental causes are closer than others to what they cause.

HOW LUCK MAKES SOMEONE LUCKY OR UNLUCKY

Luck is called good when something good results, bad when something bad results; we speak of being lucky and unlucky when the results are great. Hence one who just misses great evil or good is lucky or unlucky. For [though in fact he is no better or worse off than he was, he seems to be], because we think of him as already having [the great evil or good he just misses]—the short distance seems to us to be no distance. Further, it is reasonable that being lucky is unstable; for luck is unstable, since no result of luck can be either always or usually the case.

35

197a

5

10

15

20

25

30

Both luck and chance are coincidental causes, then, as we have said, within the class of events that are capable of being neither exceptionless [i.e. always] nor usual, and specifically within the subclass of these that might be for something.

LUCK IS CONFINED TO RATIONAL AGENTS

6

Chance, however, is not the same as luck, since it is broader; for results of luck are
197b also results of chance, but not all chance results result from luck. For luck and its
results are found wherever it is possible to be lucky, and in general to act, and that is
why luck must concern what is achievable by action. A sign of this is the fact that be-
5   ing lucky seems to be the same, or nearly the same, as being happy, and being happy
is a sort of action, since it is doing well in action. Hence what cannot act cannot do
anything by luck either.

Hence neither an inanimate object nor a beast nor a child does anything by luck,
because they do not have decision [which is needed for action]. Nor are they lucky or
10   unlucky, except by a similarity—as Protarchus[6] said that the stones from which altars
are made are lucky, because they are honored, while their fellows are trodden under-
foot. Still, even these things are affected in a way by the results of luck, when an agent
affects them by some lucky action; but otherwise not.

CHANCE, HOWEVER, IS ALSO FOUND IN NATURAL OBJECTS

Chance, on the other hand, belongs to other animals than man and to many in-
15   animate objects—e.g. we say the horse came by chance since it was saved because it
came, although it did not come in order to be saved. And the tripod fell by chance,
because it did not fall in order to be sat on, although it was set up in order to be sat
on.

Hence it is evident that if an event is of the sort that, speaking without qualifica-
20   tion, is for something, (a) we say that it results from chance if it has an external cause
and is not for the sake of its actual result; and (b) we say it results from luck if it
results from chance and is an object of decision for an agent that makes decisions.

A sign of this is the fact that we say an event is pointless [*maten*] if it is [of the sort
that is] for some result, but [in this case] is not for that result. If, e.g., walking is for
25   evacuating the bowels, but when he walked [on this occasion] it was not for that
reason, then we say that he walked pointlessly, and that his walking is pointless. Here
we assume that an event is pointless if it is naturally for something else, but does not
succeed in [being for] what it is naturally for. For if someone said that his washing was
pointless because the sun was not eclipsed, he would be ridiculous, since washing is
not for producing eclipses.

So also, then, an event happens by chance [*automaton*], as the name suggests,
30   whenever it is pointless [*maten*]. For the stone did not fall in order to hit someone; it
fell, then, by chance, because it might have fallen because someone threw it to hit
someone.

The separation of chance from luck is sharpest in natural events. For if an event is

6. [Protarchus was a student of Gorgias, regarding whom see Plato's *Meno*, no.2.]

contrary to nature, we regard it as a result of chance, not luck. But even this is different from [other cases of chance; the other cases] have an external cause, but [the natural cases] an internal. 35

How Luck and Chance Are Related to the Four Causes

We have said, then, what chance and luck are, and how they differ. Each of them 198a falls within the sort of cause that is the source of the origin of change. For they are in every case either among natural causes or among those resulting from thought; and the number of these is indefinite. 5

Chance and luck are causes of events that mind or nature might have caused, whenever they have some coincidental cause. Now nothing coincidental is prior to anything that is in itself; hence clearly no coincidental cause is prior to a cause in 10 itself. Chance and luck are therefore posterior to mind and nature. And so however true it may be that chance is the cause of the heavens, still it is necessary for mind and nature to be prior causes of this universe and of many other things.

7

Connections Between the Four Causes

It is clear, then, that there are causes, and just the number we say there are; for 15 that is the number of answers to the question 'Why?'. For ultimately we refer the why (1) in the case of unchanging things, e.g. in mathematics, to the essence — for we refer ultimately to the definition of straight or commensurate or something else; or (2) to what first initiated change (e.g. why did they go to war? — because the other side raid- 20 ed them); or (3) to what something is for (e.g. to be the rulers); or (4) with things that come to be, to the matter.

It is evident, then, that these are the causes, and that this is their number. Since there are four of them, it is a task for the student of nature to know them all. His answer to the question 'Why?' will be suitable to the study of nature if he refers to all of them — to the matter, the form, the initiator of change, and what something is for.

The last three often come to one; for what something is and what it is for are one, 25 and the first source of the change is the same in kind as these — for man gives birth to man; and the same is true generally of things that initiate change by being changed.

Things that are changeless are outside the scope of the study of nature. For although they change things, they do not change them by having change or an origin of change within themselves, but they are unchanged. Hence there are three in- 30 quiries: one about what is changeless; one about what is changed but imperishable; and one about what is perishable.

And so the why is given by referring to the matter, and to the essence, and to the first initiator of change. For in cases of coming to be, this is the normal way of ex- amining the causes — by asking what comes to be after what, and what first acted or 35 was affected, and so on in order in every case.

There are two sorts of origins that initiate change naturally. One of these origins is not itself natural, since it has no origin of change within itself; this is true of whatever 198b initiates change without itself being changed — e.g. what is completely changeless (i.e. the first of all beings) and also the essence (i.e. the form), since this is the end that something is for. So since nature is for something, this cause too must be known.

5   The why should be given in every way—e.g. this from this necessarily (from this
without qualification [i.e. always] or usually); and if this is to be (as the conclusion
from the premises); and that this is the essence; and because it is better thus—not un-
qualifiedly better, but better in relation to the substance of each thing.

Teleology and Necessity in Nature

Objection: Apparent Teleology in Nature Is Only a Chance Result of Necessity

8

10   We must first say why nature is among the causes that are for something, and then
how necessity applies to natural things. For everyone refers to this cause, saying that
since the hot, the cold and each element are naturally so, these other things are and
15   come to be from necessity. For indeed if they mention any other cause than
necessity—as one thinker[7] mentions love or strife, and another[8] mentions mind—they
just touch on it, then let it go.

Here, then, is a puzzle: why not suppose nature acts not for something or because it
is better, but from necessity? Zeus's rain does not fall in order to make the grain grow,
but from necessity; for it is necessary that what has been drawn up should cool, and
20   that what has cooled and become water should come down, and it is coincidental that
this makes the grain grow. Similarly, if someone's grain is spoiled on the threshing-
floor; it does not rain in order to spoil the grain, but it is coincidental that the rain
spoils the grain.

Why not suppose, then, that the same is true of the parts of organisms in nature? It
will be from necessity, e.g., that the front teeth come up sharp and [coincidentally]
25   suitable for biting, and the back ones broad and useful for chewing food—since this
[useful] result was coincidental, not what they came about for. And the same will be
true of all the other parts when they seem to be for something.

On this view, then, whenever all the parts came about coincidentally as though for
30   something, these animals survived, since their chance constitution made them
suitable for survival. Other animals, however, were differently constituted, and so
were destroyed—indeed they are still being destroyed—as Empedocles says of the
man-headed calves.

Reply to Objection: Not All Natural Regularities Happen by Chance
This argument, then, and others like it, might puzzle someone. In fact, however, it
is impossible for things to be like this. For these [teeth and other parts], and all
35   natural things, come to be as they do either always or usually, whereas no result of
luck or chance does. For we do not regard frequent winter rain or a summer heat-
199a   wave, but only summer rain or a winter heatwave, as a result of luck or coincidence.
If, then, these [teeth, etc.] seem to be either coincidental results or for something,
5   and they cannot be coincidental or chance results, it follows that they are for

7. [The reference is to Empedocles.]

8. [The reference is to Anaxagoras, regarding whom see Plato's *Apology*, n. 7.]

something. Now surely all such things are natural, as even those making these claims [about necessity] would agree. We find, then, that things are for something when they come into being and remain in being naturally.

ARGUMENTS FROM CRAFT TO NATURE SUPPORT NATURAL TELEOLOGY

Further, whenever a sequence has an end, the earlier action and the next in order are done for the end. Surely what is true for action is true for nature, and what is true for nature is true for each action, if nothing prevents it. Now an action is done for   10 something; what is natural, therefore, is for something. For example, if a house came into being naturally, it would do so just as it actually does by craft; and if natural things came into being not only naturally but also by craft, they would come into be-   15 ing just as they do naturally; one thing, then, is for the other. In general, craft either completes the work that nature is unable to complete or imitates nature. If, then, what accords with craft is for something, then clearly what accords with nature is also for something; for there is the same relation of earlier stages to later both in sequences that accord with craft and in those that accord with nature.

This is most evident with animals other than man, since they use neither craft nor   20 inquiry nor deliberation in their production [but nonetheless act for some end]— indeed this is why some are puzzled about whether spiders, ants and other such things operate by understanding or in some other way. If we advance little by little in this way, it is evident that even in plants things come to be that promote the end—leaves,   25 e.g., grow for the protection of the fruit. If, then, it is both naturally and for some end that a swallow makes its nest and a spider its web, and if plants grow leaves for the sake of the fruit, and send roots down rather than up for nourishment, it evident- ly follows that this sort of cause is found in things that come into being and remain in   30 being naturally. And since nature is of two sorts, as matter and as form, and the form is the end, and since everything else is for the end, the form must be the cause that the other things are for.

THESE ARGUMENTS EXPLAIN APPARENT IRREGULARITIES IN NATURE

Errors occur even in what accords with craft—e.g. the grammarian writes incor- rectly, and the doctor gives the wrong medicine. And so clearly errors are also possi-   35 ble in what accords with nature.   199b

Now in some cases that accord with craft, the correct action is for something, and when errors occur, the attempt is for something, but misses the mark. It will be the same, then, in natural things; freaks will be errors missing the end they are for. Hence in [Empedocles'] original formations of things, a defective origin would also have   5 brought the [man-headed] calves into being, if they were unable to reach any definite term and end—as [freaks] come into being now when the seed is defective.

Further, it is necessary for the seed to come into being first, and not the animal right away; and in fact [Empedocles'] 'all-natured first' was seed.

Further, what is for something is present in plants as well as in animals, though it is   10 less articulate. Then what about plants [in Empedocles' beginning]? Did olive-headed vines keep coming into being, as he says [man-headed] calves did? Surely not—that is absurd—but surely [mixed plants] would have to have come into being, if [mixed] animals did.

Further, [on Empedocles' view] coming into being would have to be mere luck

among seeds also. But whoever says this entirely does away with nature and natural
15 things. For things are natural when they are moved continuously from some origin in
themselves and so arrive at some end; and from each origin comes, not the same thing
in each case, but not just any old thing either, and it always proceeds to the same
[end] if nothing prevents it.

Now certainly the end that a process is for and the process that is for the end might
20 also result from luck. We say, e.g., that the friend in the foreign country came by
luck and paid the ransom and then went away, if he does the action as though he had
come to do it, but that was not in fact what he came to do. This [end is achieved]
coincidentally—for luck is one of the coincidental causes, as we also said before. But
25 whenever this [end] comes about always or usually, it is neither coincidental nor a
result of luck. And in natural things it is always so, unless something prevents it.

NOR DOES TELEOLOGY REQUIRE DELIBERATION
Besides, it is strange for people to think that no process comes about for something
unless they see an agent who by deliberating has initiated the change. Even a craft
does not deliberate. Moreover, if the shipbuilding craft were in the wood, it would
produce a ship in the same way that nature would; and so if one thing is for another
30 in craft, it is so in nature too. This is clearest when a doctor applies medical treatment
to himself—that is what nature is like.

It is evident, then, that nature is a cause as the end that something is for.

A COMMON MISCONCEPTION OF NATURAL NECESSITY

9

Is what is necessary necessary only given an assumption, or can it also be uncondi-
35 tional?

The current view is that there is [unconditional] necessity in things that come to be.
It is as though someone supposed that a wall has come into being from [uncondi-
200a tional] necessity, because heavy things naturally move downwards, and light things to
the surface, so that the stones and the foundations are below, while the earth is above
because of its lightness, and the wooden logs are on the very top because they are
lightest of all.

THE REAL RELATION OF NECESSITY TO TELEOLOGY
5 In fact, however, though the wall certainly requires these things, it did not come
into being because of them—except in the way something comes into being because
of its matter—but to give shelter and protection.

The same is true in all other cases where something is for something; though they
require things that have a necessary nature, they do not come about because of these
10 things, except in the way that things come about because of their matter, but for
something. For instance, why is a saw this sort of thing? In order to do this, and for
this [i.e. sawing]. But this end that the saw is for cannot come into being unless the
saw is made of iron; it is necessary, then, for it to be made of iron if there is to be a
saw performing its function. What is necesary, then, is so given the assumption [that
the end is to be achieved], but not necessary as an end; for necessity is in the matter,

whereas the end that the process is for is in the account [containing the function of   15
the saw].

NECESSITY IN NATURE AND IN MATHEMATICS
Necessity is found both in mathematics and in things that come into being in accord with nature; and to some extent the two cases are similar. For instance, since the straight is [defined as] this, it is necessary for a triangle to have angles equal to two right angles. It is not true that since the triangle is so, the straight is so; if, however, the triangle is not so, the straight is not so either.

In things that come to be for something, it is reversed; if the end is or will be, then the previous things are or will be too. Just as, in the mathematical case, if the conclu-   20
sion [about the triangle] is not so, the origin [about the straight] will not be so either, so also in nature if the previous things are not in being, the end that the process is for will not come about either.

[The analogy with mathematics is quite close.] For the end [like the mathematical origin] is also an origin; it is an origin not of action, but of reasoning [about how to achieve the end], and in the mathematical case, the origin is the origin of reasoning, since there is no action.

And so, if there is to be a house, it is necessary for these things to come to be or to   25
be present or, in general, for the matter that is for something to be there—bricks and stones, e.g., if there is to be a house. However, the end is not because of these things, except in the way something is because of its matter; nor will it come about because of them. In general, however, the end—the house or the saw—requires them—the stones or iron. Similarly, in the mathematical case, the origins require the triangle to   30
have two right angles.

BOTH MATTER AND TELEOLOGY CONCERN THE STUDENT OF NATURE
Evidently, then, what is necessary in natural things is what is spoken of as matter, and the changes of matter. The student of nature should mention both causes, but more especially what something is for, since this is the cause of the matter, whereas the matter is not the cause of the end. The end is what something is for, and the   35
origin is from the definition and the account [saying what something is for].   200b

It is the same with things in accord with craft. For instance, since a house is like this, these things must come to be and be present from necessity; and since health is this, these things must come to be and be present from necessity. In the same way, if a man is this, these things must [come to be and be present, from necessity]; and if these, then these.

But [we must not suppose that the account stating the end excludes necessity;] presumably necessity is also present in the account. Suppose, for instance, we define   5
the function of sawing as this sort of cutting; this sort of cutting requires a saw with teeth of this sort; and these require a saw made of iron. [Hence a saw is defined as being made of iron.] For some parts in the account are in it as matter of the account.

NICOMACHEAN ETHICS
(Bks. I–II, III [1–5], VI, VII [1–10], X)

BOOK ONE
The Highest Good: Happiness

THE HIGHEST GOOD IS SUPREME IN THE HIERARCHY OF GOODS

1

Every craft and every investigation, and likewise every action and decision, seems to aim at some good; hence the good has been well described as that at which everything aims. 1094a

However, there is an apparent difference among the ends aimed at. For the end is sometimes an activity, sometimes a product beyond the activity; and when there is an end beyond the action, the product is by nature better than the activity. 5

Since there are many actions, crafts and sciences, the ends turn out to be many as well; for health is the end of medicine, a boat of boatbuilding, victory of generalship, and wealth of household management. 10

But whenever any of these sciences are subordinate to some one capacity—as e.g. bridlemaking and every other science producing equipment for horses is subordinate to horsemanship, while this and every action in warfare is in turn subordinate to generalship, and in the same way other sciences are subordinate to further ones—in each of these the end of the ruling science is more choiceworthy than all the ends 15 subordinate to it, since it is the end for which those ends are also pursued. And here it does not matter whether the ends of the actions are the activities themselves, or some product beyond them, as in the sciences we have mentioned.

THE RULING SCIENCE STUDYING HIGHEST GOOD IS POLITICAL SCIENCE

2

Suppose, then, that (a) there is some end of the things we pursue in our actions which we wish for because of itself, and because of which we wish for the other things; and (b) we do not choose everything because of something else, since (c) if we do, it will go 20 on without limit, making desire empty and futile; then clearly (d) this end will be the good, i.e. the best good.

Then surely knowledge of this good is also of great importance for the conduct of our lives, and if, like archers, we have a target to aim at, we are more likely to hit the right mark. If so, we should try to grasp, in outline at any rate, what the good is, and 25 which science or capacity is concerned with it.

It seems to concern the most controlling science, the one that, more than any other, is the ruling science. And political science apparently has this character.

Reprinted by permission of the translator Terence Irwin, from Aristotle, *Nicomachean Ethics* (Indianapolis: Hackett Publishing Company, 1985).

The use of square brackets within the text is to indicate the insertion of word(s) not found in the M S.

Headings are those of the translator.

1094b   (1) For it is the one that prescribes which of the sciences ought to be studied in cities, and which ones each class in the city should learn, and how far.

(2) Again, we see that even the most honoured capacities, e.g. generalship, household management and rhetoric, are subordinate to it.

5   (3) Further, it uses the other sciences concerned with action, and moreover legislates what must be done and what avoided.

Hence its end will include the ends of the other sciences, and so will be the human good.

[This is properly called political science;] for though admittedly the good is the same for a city as for an individual, still the good of the city is apparently a greater and more complete good to acquire and preserve. For while it is satisfactory to ac-

10   quire and preserve the good even for an individual, it is finer and more divine to acquire and preserve it for a people and for cities. And so, since our investigation aims at these [goods, for an individual and for a city], it is a sort of political science.

THE METHOD OF POLITICAL INQUIRY

3

Our discussion will be adequate if its degree of clarity reflects the subject-matter; for we should not seek the same degree of exactness in all sorts of arguments alike, any more than in the products of different crafts.

15   Moreover, what is fine and what is just, the topics of inquiry in political science, differ and vary so much that they seem to rest on convention only, not on nature. Goods, however, also vary in the same sort of way, since they cause harm to many people; for it has happened that some people have been destroyed because of their wealth, others because of their bravery.

Since these, then, are the sorts of things we argue from and about, it will be

20   satisfactory if we can indicate the truth roughly and in outline; since [that is to say] we argue from and about what holds good usually [but not universally], it will be satisfactory if we can draw conclusions of the same sort.

Each of our claims, then, ought to be accepted in the same way [as claiming to hold good usually], since the educated person seeks exactness in each area to the ex-

25   tent that the nature of the subject allows; for apparently it is just as mistaken to demand demonstrations from a rhetorician as to accept [merely] persuasive arguments from a mathematician.

1095a   Further, each person judges well what he knows, and is a good judge about that; hence the good judge in a particular area is the person educated in that area, and the unconditionally good judge is the person educated in every area.

This is why a youth is not a suitable student of political science; for he lacks experience of the actions in life which political science argues from and about.

5   Moreover, since he tends to be guided by his feelings, his study will be futile and useless; for its end is action, not knowledge. And here it does not matter whether he is young in years or immature in character, since the deficiency does not depend on age, but results from being guided in his life and in each of his pursuits by his feelings; for an immature person, like an incontinent person, gets no benefit from his

knowledge.

If, however, we are guided by reason in forming our desires and in acting, then this   10
knowledge will be of great benefit.

These are the preliminary points about the student, about the way our claims are
to be accepted, and about what we intend to do.

COMMON BELIEFS ABOUT THE HIGHEST GOOD ARE INADEQUATE

4

Let us, then, begin again. Since every sort of knowledge and decision pursues some   15
good, what is that good which we say is the aim of political science? What [in other
words] is the highest of all the goods pursued in action?

As far as its name goes, most people virtually agree [about what the good is], since
both the many and the cultivated call it happiness, and suppose that living well and
doing well are the same as being happy. But they disagree about what happiness is,   20
and the many do not give the same answer as the wise.

For the many think it is something obvious and evident, e.g. pleasure, wealth or
honour, some thinking one thing, others another; and indeed the same person keeps
changing his mind, since in sickness he thinks it is health, in poverty wealth. And
when they are conscious of their own ignorance, they admire anyone who speaks of   25
something grand and beyond them.

[Among the wise,] however, some used to think that besides these many goods there
is some other good that is something in itself, and also causes all these goods to be
goods.

Presumably, then, it is rather futile to examine all these beliefs, and it is enough to
examine those that are most current or seem to have some argument for them.   30

We must notice, however, the difference between arguments from origins and
arguments towards origins. For indeed Plato was right to be puzzled about this, when
he used to ask if [the argument] set out from the origins or led towards them — just as   1095b
on a race course the path may go from the starting-line to the far end, or back again.

For while we should certainly begin from origins that are known, things are known
in two ways; for some are known to us, some known unconditionally [but not
necessarily known to us]. Presumably, then, the origin *we* should begin from is what
is known to *us*.

This is why we need to have been brought up in fine habits if we are to be adequate   5
students of what is fine and just, and of political questions generally. For the origin
we begin from is the belief that something is true, and if this is apparent enough to
us, we will not, at this stage, need the reason why it is true in addition; and if we have
this good upbringing, we have the origins to begin from, or can easily acquire them.
Someone who neither has them nor can acquire them should listen to Hesiod.[1] 'He   10
who understands everything himself is best of all; he is noble also who listens to one
who has spoken well; but he who neither understands it himself nor takes to heart
what he hears from another is a useless man.'

1. [Hesiod was an eighth-century B.C. Greek poet whose works are a rich source of
mythology. — S.M.C.]

5

But let us begin again from [the common beliefs] from which we digressed. For, it
15   would seem, people quite reasonably reach their conception of the good, i.e. of happiness, from the lives [they lead]; for there are roughly three most favoured lives — the
lives of gratification, of political activity, and, third, of study.

The many, the most vulgar, seemingly conceive the good and happiness as
pleasure, and hence they also like the life of gratification. Here they appear com-
20   pletely slavish, since the life they decide on is a life for grazing animals; and yet they
have some argument in their defence, since many in positions of power feel the same
way as Sardanapallus[2] [and also choose this life].

The cultivated people, those active [in politics], conceive the good as honour, since
this is more or less the end [normally pursued] in the political life. This, however, ap-
25   pears to be too superficial to be what we are seeking, since it seems to depend more on
those who honour than on the one honoured, whereas we intuitively believe that the
good is something of our own and hard to take from us.

Further, their aim in pursuing honour is seemingly to convince themselves that
they are good; at any rate, they seek to be honoured by intelligent people, among
people who know them, and for virtue. It is clear, then, that in the view of active peo-
30   ple at least, virtue is superior [to honour].

Perhaps, indeed, one might conceive virtue more than honour to be the end of the
political life. However, this also is apparently too incomplete [to be the good]. For, it
1096a   seems, someone might possess virtue but be asleep or inactive throughout his life; or,
further, he might suffer the worst evils and misfortunes; and if this is the sort of life he
leads, no one would count him happy, except to defend a philosopher's paradox.
Enough about this, since it has been adequately discussed in the popular work also.

5   The third life is the life of study, which we will examine in what follows.

The money-maker's life is in a way forced on him [not chosen for itself]; and clearly
wealth is not the good we are seeking, since it is [merely] useful, [choiceworthy only]
for some other end. Hence one would be more inclined to suppose that [any of] the
goods mentioned earlier is the end, since they are liked for themselves. But apparent-
10   ly they are not [the end] either; and many arguments have been presented against
them. Let us, then, dismiss them.

A PHILOSOPHICAL CONCEPTION OF THE GOOD: PLATO'S THEORY OF 'FORMS' OR 'IDEAS'

6

Presumably, though, we had better examine the universal good, and puzzle out what
is meant in speaking of it. This sort of inquiry is, to be sure, unwelcome to us, when
15   those who introduced the Forms were friends of ours; still, it presumably seems better, indeed only right, to destroy even what is close to us if that is the way to preserve
the truth. And we must especially do this when we are philosophers, [lovers of
wisdom]; for though we love both the truth and our friends, piety requires us to
honour the truth first.

2. [According to legend, Sardanapallus was an Assyrian ruler who lived in great luxury.]

Those who introduced this view did not mean to produce an Idea for any [series] in which they spoke of prior and posterior [members]; that was why they did not mean to establish an Idea [of number] for [the series of] numbers. But the good is spoken of   20
both in the [category of] what-it-is [i.e. substance], and in [the categories of] quality and relative; and what is in itself, i.e. substance, is by nature prior to what is relative, since a relative would seem to be an appendage and coincident of being. And so there is no common Idea over these.

Further, good is spoken of in as many ways as being is spoken of. For it is spoken of in [the category of] what-it-is, as god and mind; in quality, as the virtues; in quantity,   25
as the measured amount; in relative, as the useful; in time, as the opportune moment; in place, as the [right] situation; and so on. Hence it is clear the good cannot be some common [nature of good things] that is universal and single; for if it were, it would be spoken of in only one of the categories, not in them all.

Further, if a number of things have a single Idea, there is also a single science of   30
them; hence [if there were an Idea of Good] there would also be some single science of all goods. But in fact there are many sciences even of the goods under one category; for the science of the opportune moment, e.g. in war is generalship, in disease medicine. And similarly the science of the measured amount in food is medicine, in exertion gymnastics. [Hence there is no single science of the good, and so no Idea.]

One might be puzzled about what [the believers in Ideas] really mean in speaking   35
of The So-and-So Itself, since Man Itself and man have one and the same account of   1096b
man; for in so far as each is man, they will not differ at all. If it is so, then [Good Itself and good have the same account of good]; hence they also will not differ at all in so far as each is good, [hence there is no point in appealing to Good Itself].

Moreover, Good Itself will be no more of a good by being eternal; for a white thing is no whiter if it lasts a long time than if it lasts a day.   5

The Pythagoreans[3] seemingly have a more plausible view about the good, since they place the One in the column of goods. Indeed, Speusippus seems to have followed them. But let us leave this for another discussion.

A dispute emerges about what we have said: 'The arguments [in favor of the Idea]   10
are not concerned with every sort of good. Goods pursued and liked in themselves are spoken of as one species of goods, while those that in some way tend to produce or preserve these goods, or to prevent their contraries, are spoken of as goods because of these and in a different way; clearly, then, goods are spoken of in two ways, and some are goods in themselves, others goods because of these. [And it is claimed only that there is a single Form for all goods in themselves.]'

Let us, then, separate the goods in themselves from the [merely] useful goods, and   15
consider whether goods in themselves are spoken of in correspondence to a single Idea.

Well, what sorts of goods may be regarded as goods in themselves? (a) Perhaps they are those that are pursued even on their own, e.g. intelligence, seeing, some types of pleasures, and honours; for even if we also pursue these because of something else, they may still be regarded as goods in themselves. (b) Or perhaps nothing except the   20

3. [The Pythagoreans were members of a secret religious society established by the Greek philosopher Pythagoras (c. 582–c. 507 B.C.). They believed in the transmigration of souls and considered numbers the basis for all things. Speusippus, a fourth-century B.C. Greek philosopher, succeeded Plato as head of the Academy.]

Idea is good in itself.

[If (b) is true], then the Form will be futile, [since it will not explain the goodness of anything. But if (a) is true], then, since these other things are also goods in themselves, the same account of good will have to turn up in all of them, just as the same account of whiteness turns up in snow and in chalk. In fact, however, honour, 25 intelligence and pleasure have different and dissimilar accounts, precisely in so far as they are goods. Hence the good is not something common which corresponds to a single Idea.

But how after all, then, is good spoken of? For [these goods have different accounts, i.e. are homonymous, and yet] are seemingly not homonymous by mere chance. Perhaps they are homonymous by all being derived from a single source, or by all referring to a single focus. Or perhaps instead they are homonymous by analogy; for as sight is good in the body, so understanding is good in the soul, and other things are good in other cases.

30   Presumably, though, we should leave these questions for now, since their exact treatment is more appropriate for another [branch of] philosophy. And the same is true about the Idea. For even if the good predicated in common is some single thing, or something separated, itself in itself, clearly it is not the sort of good a human being 35 can pursue in action or possess; but that is just the sort we are looking for in our present inquiry.

1097a   'But,' it might seem to some, 'it is better to get to know the Idea with a view to the goods that we can possess and pursue in action; for if we have this as a sort of pattern, we shall also know better about the goods that are goods for us, and if we know about them, we shall hit on them.'

5   This argument, does indeed have some plausibility, but it would seem to clash with the sciences. For each of these, though it aims at some good and seeks to supply what is lacking, proceeds without concern for knowledge of the Idea; and if the Idea were such an important aid, surely it would not be reasonable for all craftsmen to be ignorant and not even to look for it.

Moreover, it is a puzzle to know what the weaver or carpenter will gain for his own 10 craft from knowing this Good Itself, or how anyone will be better at medicine or generalship from having gazed on the Idea Itself. For what the doctor appears to consider is not even health [universally, let alone good universally], but human beings' health, and even more than that, presumably, this human being's health, since it is particular patients he treats.

So much, then, for these questions.

OUR OWN VIEW OF THE GOOD

7

15   But let us return once again to the good we are looking for, and consider just what it could be, since it is apparently one thing in one action or craft, and another thing in another; for it is one thing in medicine, another in generalship, and so on for the rest.

What, then, is the good in each of these cases? Surely it is that for the sake of which 20 the other things are done; and in medicine this is health, in generalship victory, in

housebuilding a house, in another case something else; but in every action and decision it is the end, since it is for the sake of the end that everyone does the other things.

And so, if there is some end of everything that is pursued in action, this will be the
good pursued in action; and if there are more ends than one, these will be the goods
pursued in action.

Our argument has progressed, then, to the same conclusion [as before, that the
highest end is the good]; but we must try to clarify this still more.   25

Though apparently there are many ends, we choose some of them, e.g. wealth,
flutes and, in general, instruments, because of something else; hence it is clear that
not all ends are complete. But the best good is apparently something complete.
Hence, if only one end is complete, this will be what we are looking for; and if more   30
than one are complete, the most complete of these will be what we are looking for.

An end pursued in itself, we say, is more complete than an end pursued because of
something else; and an end that is never choiceworthy because of something else is
more complete than ends that are choiceworthy both in themselves and because of
this end; and hence an end that is always [choiceworthy, and also] choiceworthy in
itself, never because of something else, is complete without reservation.

Now happiness more than anything else seems complete without reservation, since   1097b
we always [choose it, and also] choose it because of itself, never because of something
else.

Honour, pleasure, understanding and every virtue we certainly choose because of
themselves, since we would choose each of them even if it had no further result, but
we also choose them for the sake of happiness, supposing that through them we shall   5
be happy. Happiness, by contrast, no one ever chooses for their sake, or for the sake
of anything else at all.

The same conclusion [that happiness is complete] also appears to follow from self-
sufficiency, since the complete good seems to be self-sufficient.

Now what we count as self-sufficient is not what suffices for a solitary person by
himself, living an isolated life, but what suffices also for parents, children, wife and in   10
general for friends and fellow-citizens, since a human being is a naturally political
[animal]. Here, however, we must impose some limit; for if we extend the good to
parents' parents and children's children and to friends of friends, we shall go on
without limit, but we must examine this another time.

Anyhow, we regard something as self-sufficient when all by itself it makes a life   15
choiceworthy and lacking nothing; and that is what we think happiness does.

Moreover, [the complete good is most choiceworthy, and] we think happiness is
most choiceworthy of all goods, since it is not counted as one good among many. If it
were counted as one among many, then, clearly, we think that the addition of the
smallest of goods would make it more choiceworthy; for [the smallest good] that is
added becomes an extra quantity of goods [so creating a good larger than the original
good], and the larger of two goods is always more choiceworthy. [But we do not think 20
any addition can make happiness more choiceworthy; hence it is most choiceworthy.]

Happiness, then, is apparently something complete and self-sufficient, since it is
the end of the things pursued in action.

But presumably the remark that the best good is happiness is apparently something
[generally] agreed, and what we miss is a clearer statement of what the best good is.

25   Well, perhaps we shall find the best good if we first find the function of a human being. For just as the good, i.e. [doing] well, for a flautist, a sculptor, and every craftsman, and, in general, for whatever has a function and [characteristic] action, seems to depend on its function, the same seems to be true for a human being, if a human being has some function.

30   Then do the carpenter and the leatherworker have their functions and actions, while a human being has none, and is by nature idle, without any function? Or, just as eye, hand, foot and, in general, every [bodily] part apparently has its functions, may we likewise ascribe to a human being some function besides all of theirs?

1098a   What, then, could this be? For living is apparently shared with plants, but what we are looking for is the special function of a human being; hence we should set aside the life of nutrition and growth. The life next in order is some sort of life of sense-perception; but this too is apparently shared, with horse, ox and every animal. The remaining possibility, then, is some sort of life of action of the (part of the soul) that has reason.

5   Now this [part has two parts, which have reason in different ways], one as obeying the reason [in the other part], the other as itself having reason and thinking. [We intend both.] Moreover, life is also spoken of in two ways [as capacity and as activity], and we must take [a human being's special function to be] life as activity, since this seems to be called life to a fuller extent.

      (a) We have found, then, that the human function is the soul's activity that expresses reason [as itself having reason] or requires reason [as obeying reason]. (b) Now the function of F, e.g. of a harpist, is the same in kind, so we say, as the function of an
10   excellent F, e.g. an excellent harpist. (c) The same is true without reservation in every case, when we add to the function the superior achievement that expresses the virtue; for a harpist's function, e.g. is to play the harp, and a good harpist's is to do it well. (d) Now we take the human function to be a certain kind of life, and take this life to be the soul's activity and actions that express reason. (e) [Hence by (c) and (d)] the ex-
15   cellent man's function is to do this finely and well. (f) Each function is completed well when its completion expresses the proper virtue. (g) Therefore [by (d), (e) and (f)] the human good turns out to be the soul's activity that expresses virtue.

      And if there are more virtues than one, the good will express the best and most complete virtue. Moreover, it will be in a complete life. For one swallow does not
20   make a spring, nor does one day; nor similarly, does one day or a short time make us blessed and happy.

DEFENCE OF THE ACCOUNT OF THE GOOD

      This, then, is a sketch of the good; for, presumably, the outline must come first, to be filled in later. If the sketch is good, then anyone, it seems, can advance and articulate it, and in such cases time is a good discoverer or [at least] a good co-worker. That is
25   also how the crafts have improved, since anyone can add what is lacking [in the outline].

      However, we must also remember our previous remarks, so that we do not look for the same degree of exactness in all areas, but the degree that suits the subject-matter
30   in each area and is proper to the investigation. For the carpenter's and the geometer's inquiries about the right angle are different also; the carpenter's is confined to the

right angle's usefulness for his work, whereas the geometer's concerns what, or what sort of thing, the right angle is, since he studies the truth. We must do the same, then, in other areas too, [seeking the proper degree of exactness], so that digressions do not overwhelm our main task.

Nor should we make the same demand for an explanation in all cases. Rather, in some cases it is enough to prove that something is true without explaining why it is true. This is so, e.g. with origins, where the fact that something is true is the first principle, i.e. the origin.

1098b

Some origins are studied by means of induction, some by means of perception, some by means of some sort of habituation, and others by other means. In each case we should try to find them out by means suited to their nature, and work hard to define them well. For they have a great influence on what follows; for the origin seems to be more than half the whole, and makes evident the answer to many of our questions.

5

8

However, we should examine the origin not only from the conclusion and premises [of a deductive argument], but also from what is said about it; for all the facts harmonize with a true account, whereas the truth soon clashes with a false one.

10

Goods are divided, then, into three types, some called external, some goods of the soul, others goods of the body; and the goods of the soul are said to be goods to the fullest extent and most of all, and the soul's actions and activities are ascribed to the soul. Hence the account [of the good] is sound, to judge by this belief anyhow—and it is an ancient belief agreed on by philosophers.

15

Our account is also correct in saying that some sort of actions and activities are the end; for then the end turns out to be a good of the soul, not an external good.

20

The belief that the happy person lives well and does well in action also agrees with our account, since we have virtually said that the end is a sort of living well and doing well in action.

Further, all the features that people look for in happiness appear to be true of the end described in our account. For to some people it seems to be virtue; to others intelligence; to others some sort of wisdom; to others again it seems to be these, or one of these, combined with pleasure or requiring its addition; and others add in external prosperity as well.

25

Some of these views are traditional, held by many, while others are held by a few reputable men; and it is reasonable for each group to be not entirely in error, but correct on one point at least, or even on most points.

First, our account agrees with those who say happiness is virtue [in general] or some [particular] virtue; for activity expressing virtue is proper to virtue. Presumably, though, it matters quite a bit whether we suppose that the best good consists in possessing or in using, i.e. in a state or in an activity [that actualizes the state]. For while someone may be in a state that achieves no good, if, e.g., he is asleep or inactive in some other way, this cannot be true of the activity; for it will necessarily do actions and do well in them. And just as Olympic prizes are not for the finest and strongest, but for contestants, since it is only these who win; so also in life [only] the fine and good people who act correctly win the prize.

30

1099a

5

Moreover, the life of these [active] people is also pleasant in itself. For being pleased is a condition of the soul, [hence included in the activity of the soul]. Further, each type of person finds pleasure in whatever he is called a lover of, or so that a horse, e.g. pleases the horse-lover, a spectacle the lover of spectacles, and similarly what is just pleases the lover of justice, and in general what expresses virtue pleases the lover of virtue. Hence the things that please most people conflict, because they are not pleasant by nature, whereas the things that please lovers of what is fine are things pleasant by nature; and actions expressing virtue are pleasant in this way; and so they both please lovers of what is fine and are pleasant in themselves.

Hence their life does not need pleasure to be added [to virtuous activity] as some sort of ornament; rather, it has its pleasure within itself. For besides the reasons already given, no one is good if he does not enjoy fine actions; for no one would call him just, e.g. if he did not enjoy doing just actions, or generous if he did not enjoy generous actions, and similarly for the other virtues. If this is so, then actions expressing the virtues are pleasant in themselves.

Moreover, these actions are good and fine as well as pleasant; indeed, they are good, fine and pleasant more than anything else, since on this question the excellent person has good judgement, and his judgement agrees with our conclusions.

Happiness, then, is best, finest and most pleasant, and these three features are not distinguished in the way suggested by the Delian inscription: 'What is most just is finest; being healthy is more beneficial; but it is most pleasant to win our heart's desire.' For all three features are found in the best activities, and happiness we say is these activities, or [rather] one of them, the best one.

Nonetheless, happiness evidently also needs external goods to be added [to the activity], as we said, since we cannot, or cannot easily, do fine actions if we lack the resources.

For, first of all, in many actions we use friends, wealth and political power just as we use instruments. Further, deprivation of certain [externals]—e.g. good birth, good children, beauty—mars our blessedness; for we do not altogether have the character of happiness if we look utterly repulsive or are ill-born, solitary or childless, and have it even less, presumably, if our children or friends are totally bad, or were good but have died.

And so, as we have said, happiness would seem to need this sort of prosperity added also; that is why some people identify happiness with good fortune, while others [reacting from one extreme to the other] identify it with virtue.

THE PLACE OF VIRTUE AND OF EXTERNAL GOODS IN HAPPINESS

9

This [question about the role of fortune] raises a puzzle: Is happiness acquired by learning, or habituation, or by some other form of cultivation? Or is it the result of some divine fate, or even of fortune?

First, then, if the gods give any gift at all to human beings, it is reasonable for them to give happiness also; indeed, it is reasonable to give happiness more than any other human [good], in so far as it is the best of human [goods]. Presumably, however, this question is more suitable for a different inquiry.

But even if it is not sent by the gods, but instead results from virtue and some sort   15
of learning or cultivation, happiness appears to be one of the most divine things, since
the prize and goal of virtue appears to be the best good, something divine and
blessed.

Moreover [if happiness comes in this way] it will be widely shared; for anyone who
is not deformed [in his capacity] for virtue will be able to achieve happiness through
some sort of learning and attention.   20

And since it is better to be happy in this way than because of fortune, it is
reasonable for this to be the way [we become] happy. For whatever is natural is
naturally in the finest state possible, and so are the products of crafts and of every
other cause, especially the best cause; and it would be seriously inappropriate to en-   25
trust what is greatest and finest to fortune.

The answer to our question is also evident from our account [of happiness]. For we
have said it is a certain sort of activity of the soul expressing virtue, [and hence not a
product of fortune]; and some of the other goods are necessary conditions [of hap-
piness], others are naturally useful and cooperative as instruments [but are not parts
of it].

Further, this conclusion agrees with our opening remarks. For we took the goal of   30
political science to be the best good; and most of its attention is devoted to the
character of the citizens, to make them good people who do fine actions, [which is
reasonable if happiness depends on virtue, not on fortune].

It is not surprising, then, that we regard neither ox nor horse nor any other kind of
animal as happy, since none of them can share in this sort of activity. And for the   1100a
same reason a child is not happy either, since his age prevents him from doing these
sorts of actions; and if he is called happy, he is being congratulated because of anticipated blessedness, since, as we have said, happiness requires both complete virtue
and a complete life.
                                                                                        5
[Happiness needs a complete life.] For life includes many reversals of fortune, good
and bad, and the most prosperous person may fall into a terrible disaster in old age,
as the Trojan stories tell us about Priam,[4] but if someone has suffered these sorts of
misfortunes and comes to a miserable end, no one counts him happy.

10

Then should we count no human being happy during his lifetime, but follow Solon's[5]   10
advice to wait to see the end? And if we should hold that, can he really be happy during the time after he has died? Surely that is completely absurd, especially when we
say happiness is an activity.

We do not say, then, that someone is happy during the time he is dead, and Solon's   15
point is not this [absurd one], but rather that when a human being has died, we can
safely pronounce [that he was] blessed [before he died], on the assumption that he is
now finally beyond evils and misfortunes.

4. [Priam was the legendary king of Troy at the time of its destruction by the Greeks as related in
Homer's *Iliad.*]

5. [Solon (c. 639–c. 559 B.C.) was an Athenian statesman and lawgiver.]

20   Still, even this claim is disputable. For if a living person has good or evil of which
he is not aware, then a dead person also, it seems, has good or evil when, e.g., he
receives honours or dishonours, and his children, and descendants in general, do well
or suffer misfortune. [Hence, apparently what happens after his death can affect
whether or not he was happy before his death.]

        However, this view also raises a puzzle. For even if someone has lived in blessedness
until old age, and has died appropriately, many fluctuations of his descendants' for-
25   tunes may still happen to him; for some may be good people and get the life they
deserve, while the contrary may be true of others, and clearly they may be as distantly
related to their ancestor as you please. Surely, then, it would be an absurd result if the
dead person's condition changed along with the fortunes of his descendants, so that at
one time he became happy [in his lifetime] and at another time miserable. But it
30   would also be absurd if the condition of descendants did not affect their ancestors at
all or for any length of time.

        But we must return to the previous puzzle, since that will perhaps also show us the
answer to our present question.

        If, then, we must wait to see the end, and must then count someone blessed, not as
being blessed [during the time he is dead] but because he previously was blessed, sure-
35   ly it is absurd if at the time when he is happy we will not truly ascribe to him the happiness he has.

1100b   [We hesitate] out of reluctance to call him happy during his lifetime, because of
the variations, and because we suppose happiness is enduring and definitely not
prone to fluctuate, whereas the same person's fortunes often turn to and fro. For
5   clearly, if we are guided by his fortunes, so that we often call him happy and then
miserable again, we will be representing the happy person as a kind of chameleon in-
securely based.

        But surely it is quite wrong to be guided by someone's fortunes. For his doing well
or badly does not rest on them; though a human life, as we said, needs these added, it
10   is the activities expressing virtue that control happiness, and the contrary activities
that control its contrary.

        Indeed, the present puzzle is further evidence for our account [of happiness]. For
no human achievement has the stability of activities that express virtue, since these
15   seem to be more enduring even than our knowledge of the sciences; and the most
honourable of the virtues themselves are more enduring [than the others] because
blessed people devote their lives to them more fully and more continually than to
anything else—for this [continued activity] would seem to be the reason we do not
forget them.

        It follows, then, that the happy person has the [stability] we are looking for and
keeps the character he has throughout his life. For always, or more than anything
20   else, he will do and study the actions expressing virtue, and will bear fortunes most
finely, in every way and in all conditions appropriately, since he is truly 'good, four-
square and blameless'.[6]

        However, many events are matters of fortune, and some are smaller, some greater.
25   Hence, while small strokes of good or ill fortune clearly will not influence his life,
many great strokes of good fortune will make it more blessed, since in themselves they

_____

        6. [The words of Greek poet Simonides of Ceos (c. 556–c. 468 B.C.).]

naturally add adornment to it, and his use of them proves to be fine and excellent. Conversely, if they are great misfortunes, they oppress and spoil his blessedness, since they involve pain and impede many activities.

And yet, even here what is fine shines through, when he bears many severe misfortunes with good temper, not because he feels no distress, but because he is noble and magnanimous. 30

And since it is activities that control life, as we said, no blessed person could ever become miserable, since he will never do hateful and base actions. For a truly good and intelligent person, we suppose, will bear strokes of fortune suitably, and from his resources at any time will do the finest actions he can, just as a good general will make the best use of his forces in war, and a good shoemaker will produce the finest shoe he can from the hides given him, and similarly for all other craftsmen. 35 1101a 5

If this is so, then the happy person could never become miserable. Still, he will not be blessed either, if he falls into misfortunes as bad as Priam's. Nor, however, will he be inconstant and prone to fluctuate, since he will neither be easily shaken from his happiness nor shaken by just any misfortunes. He will be shaken from it, though, by many serious misfortunes, and from these a return to happiness will take no short time; at best, it will take a long and complete length of time that includes great and fine successes. 10

Then why not say that the happy person is the one who expresses complete virtue in his activities, with an adequate supply of external goods, not for just any time but for a complete life? Or should we add that he will also go on living this way and will come to an appropriate end? 15

The future is not apparent to us, and we take happiness to be the end, and altogether complete in every way; hence we will say that a living person who has, and will keep, the goods we mentioned is blessed, but blessed as a human being is. So much for a determination of this question. 20

11

Still, it is apparently rather unfriendly and contrary to the [common] beliefs to claim that the fortunes of our descendants and all our friends contribute nothing. But since they can find themselves in many and various circumstances, some of which affect us more, some less, it is apparently a long, indeed endless, task to differentiate all the particular cases, and perhaps a general outline will be enough of an answer. 25

Misfortunes, then, even to the person himself, differ, and some have a certain weight and influence on his life, while others are seemingly lighter. The same is true for the misfortunes of his friends; and it matters whether they happen to living or to dead people—much more than it matters whether lawless and terrible crimes are committed before a tragic drama begins or in the course of it. In our reasoning, then, we should also take account of this difference, and even more, presumably, of the puzzle about whether the dead share in any good or evil. 30 35 1106b

For if we consider this, anything good or evil penetrating to the dead would seem to be weak and unimportant, either without reservation or for them; and even if it is not, still its size and character are not enough to make people happy who are not happy, or to take away the blessedness of those who are happy. And so, when friends do well, and likewise when they do badly, it appears to contribute something to the 5 dead, but of a character and size that neither makes happy people not happy nor anything else of this sort.

12

10   Now that we have determined these points, let us consider whether happiness is something praiseworthy, or instead something honourable; for clearly it is not a capacity [which is neither praiseworthy nor honourable].

Whatever is praiseworthy appears to be praised for its character and its state in relation to something. We praise, e.g., the just and the brave person, and in general 15   the good person and virtue, for their actions and achievements; and we praise the strong person, the good runner and each of the others because he naturally has a certain character and is in a certain state in relation to something good and excellent. This is clear also from praises of the gods; for these praises appear ridiculous because 20   they are referred to us, but they are referred to us because, as we said, praise depends on such a reference.

If praise is for these sorts of things, then clearly for the best things there is no praise, but something greater and better. And indeed this is how it appears. For the gods and the most godlike of men are [not praised, but] congratulated for their 25   blessedness and happiness. And the same is true of goods; for we never praise happiness, as we praise justice, but count it blessed, as something better and more godlike [than anything that is praised].

Indeed, Eudoxus[7] seems to have used the correct argument for the victory of pleasure. By not praising pleasure though it is a good, we indicate, so he thought, 30   that it is superior to everything praiseworthy; and [only] the god and the good have this superiority since the other goods are [praised] by reference to them.

[Here he seems to have argued correctly.] For praise is given to virtue, since it makes us do fine actions; but celebrations are for [successful] achievements, either of body or of soul. But an exact treatment of this is presumably more proper for 35   specialists in celebrations. For us, anyhow, it is clear from what has been said that 1102a   happiness is something honourable and complete.

A further reason why this is seemingly correct is that happiness is an origin; for the origin is what we all aim at in all our other actions; and we take the origin and cause of goods to be something honourable and divine.

Introduction to the Account of Virtue

13

5   Since happiness is an activity of the soul expressing complete virtue, we must examine virtue; for that will perhaps also be a way to study happiness better.

Moreover, the true politician seems to have spent more effort on virtue than on 10   anything else, since he wants to make the citizens good and law-abiding. We find an example of this in the Spartan and Cretan legislators and in any others with their concerns. Since, then, the examination of virtue is proper for political science, the in-

----

7. [Eudoxus of Cnidus (c. 408-c. 355 B.C.) was a Greek astronomer and mathematician.]

quiry clearly suits our original decision [to pursue political science].

It is clear that the virtue we must examine is human virtue, since we are also seeking the human good and human happiness. And by human virtue we mean virtue of the soul, not of the body, since we also say that happiness is an activity of the soul. If this is so, then it is clear the politician must acquire some knowledge about the soul, just as someone setting out to heal the eyes must acquire knowledge about the whole body as well. This is all the more true to the extent that political science is better and more honourable than medicine — and even among doctors the cultivated ones devote a lot of effort to acquiring knowledge about the body. Hence the politician as well [as the student of nature] must study the soul.

But he must study it for the purpose [of inquiring into virtue], as far as suffices for what he seeks; for a more exact treatment would presumably take more effort than his purpose requires. [We] have discussed the soul sufficiently [for our purposes] in [our] popular works as well [as our less popular], and we should use this discussion.

We have said, e.g., that one [part] of the soul is nonrational, while one has reason. Are these distinguished as parts of a body and everything divisible into parts are? Or are they two only in account, and inseparable by nature, as the convex and the concave are in a surface? It does not matter for present purposes.

Consider the nonrational [part]. One [part] of it, i.e. the cause of nutrition and growth, is seemingly plant-like and shared [with other living things]: for we can ascribe this capacity of the soul to everything that is nourished, including embryos, and the same one to complete living things, since this is more reasonable than to ascribe another capacity to them.

Hence the virtue of this capacity is apparently shared, not [specifically] human. For this part and capacity more than others seem to be active in sleep, and here the good and the bad person are least distinct, which is why happy people are said to be no better off than miserable people for half their lives.

And this lack of distinction is not surprising, since sleep is inactivity of the soul in so far as it is called excellent or base, unless to some small extent some movements penetrate [to our awareness], and in this way the decent person comes to have better images [in dreams] than just any random person has. Enough about this, however, and let us leave aside the nutritive part, since by nature it has no share in human virtue.

Another nature in the soul seemingly is also nonrational, though in a way it shares in reason.

[Clearly it is nonrational.] For in the continent and the incontinent person we praise their reason, i.e. the [part] of the soul that has reason, because it exhorts them correctly and towards what is best; but they evidently also have in them some other [part] that is by nature something besides reason, conflicting and struggling with reason.

For just as paralysed parts of a body, when we decide to move them to the right, do the contrary and move off to the left, the same is true of the soul; for incontinent people have impulses in contrary directions. In bodies, admittedly, we see the part go astray, whereas we do not see it in the soul; nonetheless, presumably, we should suppose that the soul also has a [part] besides reason, contrary to and countering reason. The [precise] way it is different does not matter.

However, this [part] as well [as the rational part] appears, as we said, to share in reason. At any rate, in the continent person it obeys reason; and in the temperate and the brave person it presumably listens still better to reason, since there it agrees with reason in everything.

30   The nonrational [part], then, as well [as the whole soul] apparently has two parts. For while the plant-like [part] shares in reason not at all, the [part] with appetites and in general desires shares in reason in a way, in so far as it both listens to reason and obeys it.

It listens in the way in which we are said to 'listen to reason' from father or friends, not in the way in which we ['give the reason'] in mathematics.

1103a   The nonrational part also [obeys and] is persuaded in some way by reason, as is shown by chastening, and by every sort of reproof and exhortation.

If we ought to say, then, that this [part] also has reason, then the [part] that has reason, as well [as the nonrational part] will have two parts, one that has reason to the full extent by having it within itself, and another [that has it] by listening to reason as to a father.

The distinction between virtues also reflects this difference. For some virtues are

5   called virtues of thought, other virtues of character; wisdom, comprehension and intelligence are called virtues of thought, generosity and temperance virtues of character.

For when we speak of someone's character we do not say that he is wise or has good comprehension, but that he is gentle or temperate. [Hence these are the virtues of character.] And yet, we also praise the wise person for his state, and the states that are

10   praiseworthy are the ones we call virtues. [Hence wisdom is also a virtue.]

BOOK TWO

Virtues of Character in General

HOW A VIRTUE OF CHARACTER IS ACQUIRED

1

Virtue, then, is of two sorts, virtue of thought and virtue of character. Virtue of

15   thought arises and grows mostly from teaching, and hence needs experience and time. Virtue of character [i.e. of *ethos*] results from habit [ethos]; hence its name 'ethical', slightly varied from '*ethos*'.

20   Hence it is also clear that none of the virtues of character arises in us naturally.

For if something is by nature [in one condition], habituation cannot bring it into another condition. A stone, e.g., by nature moves downwards, and habituation could not make it move upwards, not even if you threw it up ten thousand times to habituate it; nor could habituation make fire move downwards, or bring anything that is by nature in one condition into another condition.

Thus the virtues arise in us neither by nature nor against nature, but we are by 25
nature able to acquire them, and reach our complete perfection through habit.

Further, if something arises in us by nature, we first have the capacity for it, and
later display the activity. This is clear in the case of the senses; for we did not acquire
them by frequent seeing or hearing, but already had them when we exercised them, 30
and did not get them by exercising them.

Virtues, by contrast, we acquire, just as we acquire crafts, by having previously activated them. For we learn a craft by producing the same product that we must produce when we have learned it, becoming builders, e.g. by building and harpists by
playing the harp; so also, then, we become just by doing just actions, temperate by 1103b
doing temperate actions, brave by doing brave actions.

What goes on in cities is evidence for this also. For the legislator makes the citizens
good by habituating them, and this is the wish of every legislator; if he fails to do it 5
well he misses his goal. [The right] habituation is what makes the difference between
a good political system and a bad one.

Further, just as in the case of a craft, the sources and means that develop each virtue also ruin it. For playing the harp makes both good and bad harpists, and it is
analogous in the case of builders and all the rest; for building well makes good 10
builders, building badly, bad ones. If it were not so, no teacher would be needed, but
everyone would be born a good or a bad craftsman.

It is the same, then, with the virtues. For actions in dealings with [other] human
beings make some people just, some unjust; actions in terrifying situations and the ac- 15
quired habit of fear or confidence make some brave and others cowardly. The same is
true of situations involving appetites and anger; for one or another sort of conduct in
these situations makes some people temperate and gentle, others intemperate and
irascible. 20

To sum up, then, in a single account: A state [of character] arises from [the repetition of] similar activities. Hence we must display the right activities, since differences
in these imply corresponding differences in the states. It is not unimportant, then, to
acquire one sort of habit or another, right from our youth; rather, it is very impor- 25
tant, indeed all-important.

2

Our present inquiry does not aim, as our others do, at study; for the purpose of our
examination is not to know what virtue is, but to become good, since otherwise the inquiry would be of no benefit to us. Hence we must examine the right way to act, 30
since, as we have said, the actions also control the character of the states we acquire.

First, then, actions should express correct reason. That is a common [belief], and
let us assume it; later we will say what correct reason is and how it is related to the
other virtues.

But let us take it as agreed in advance that every account of the actions we must do 1104a
has to be stated in outline, not exactly. As we also said at the start, the type of accounts we demand should reflect the subject-matter; and questions about actions and
expediency, like questions about health, have no fixed [and invariable answers].

5   And when our general account is so inexact, the account of particular cases is all
the more inexact. For these fall under no craft or profession, and the agents
themselves must consider in each case what the opportune action is, as doctors and
navigators do.

10   The account we offer, then, in our present inquiry is of this inexact sort; still, we
must try to offer help.

First, then, we should observe that these sorts of states naturally tend to be ruined
by excess and deficiency. We see this happen with strength and health, which we
mention because we must use what is evident as a witness to what is not. For both ex-

15   cessive and deficient exercises ruin strength; and likewise, too much or too little
eating or drinking ruins health, while the proportionate amount produces, increases
and preserves it.

The same is true, then, of temperance, bravery and the other virtues. For if, e.g.,

20   someone avoids and is afraid of everything, standing firm against nothing, he
becomes cowardly, but if he is afraid of nothing at all and goes to face everything, he
becomes rash. Similarly, if he gratifies himself with every pleasure and refrains from
none, he becomes intemperate, but if he avoids them all, as boors do, he becomes

25   some sort of insensible person. Temperance and bravery, then, are ruined by excess
and deficiency but preserved by the mean.

The same actions, then, are the sources and causes both of emergence and growth
of virtues and of their ruin; but further, the activities of the virtues will be found in

30   these same actions. For this is also true of more evident cases, e.g. strength, which
arises from eating a lot and from withstanding much hard labour, and it is the strong
person who is most able to do these very things. It is the same with the virtues.

35   Refraining from pleasures makes us become temperate, and when we have become
1104b temperate we are most able to refrain from pleasures. And it is similar with bravery;
habituation in disdaining what is fearful and in standing firm against it makes us
become brave, and when we have become brave we shall be most able to stand firm.

3

But [actions are not enough]; we must take as a sign of someone's state his pleasure

5   or pain in consequence of his action. For if someone who abstains from bodily pleasures enjoys the abstinence itself, then he is temperate, but if he is grieved by it, he
is intemperate. Again, if he stands firm against terrifying situations and enjoys it,
or at least does not find it painful, then he is brave, and if he finds it painful, he is
cowardly.

[Pleasures and pains are appropriately taken as signs] because virtue of character is
concerned with pleasures and pains.

10   (1) For it is pleasure that causes us to do base actions, and pain that causes us to
abstain from fine ones. Hence we need to have had the appropriate upbringing — right from early youth, as Plato says — to make us find enjoyment or pain in the
right things; for this is the correct education.

(2) Further, virtues are concerned with actions and feelings; but every feeling and

15   every action implies pleasure or pain; hence, for this reason too, virtue is concerned
with pleasures and pains.

(3) Corrective treatment [for vicious actions] also indicates [the relevance of

pleasure and pain], since it uses pleasures and pains; it uses them because such correction is a form of medical treatment, and medical treatment naturally operates through contraries.

(4) Further, as we said earlier, every state of soul is naturally related to and concerned with whatever naturally makes it better or worse; and pleasures and pains 20 make people worse, from pursuing and avoiding the wrong ones, at the wrong time, in the wrong ways, or whatever other distinctions of that sort are needed in an account.

These [bad effects of pleasure and pain] are the reason why people actually define the virtues as ways of being unaffected and undisturbed [by pleasures and pains]. 25 They are wrong, however, because they speak [of being unaffected] without specification, not of being unaffected in the right or wrong way, at the right or wrong time, and the added specifications.

We assume, then, that virtue is the sort of state [with the appropriate specifications] that does the best actions concerned with pleasures and pains, and that vice is the contrary. The following points will also make it evident that virtue and vice are 30 concerned with the same things.

(5) There are three objects of choice—fine, expedient and pleasant—and three objects of avoidance—their contraries, shameful, harmful and painful. About all these, then, the good person is correct and the bad person is in error, and especially about pleasure. For pleasure is shared with animals, and implied by every object of 35 choice, since what is fine and what is expedient appear pleasant as well. 1105a

(6) Further, since pleasure grows up with all of us from infancy on, it is hard to rub out this feeling that is dyed into our lives; and we estimate actions as well [as feelings], some of us more, some less, by pleasure and pain. Hence, our whole inquiry must be 5 about these, since good or bad enjoyment or pain is very important for our actions.

(7) Moreover, it is harder to fight pleasure than to fight emotion, [though that is hard enough], as Heraclitus[8] says. Now both craft and virtue are concerned in every case with what is harder, since a good result is even better when it is harder. Hence, 10 for this reason also, the whole inquiry, for virtue and political science alike, must consider pleasures and pains; for if we use these well, we shall be good, and if badly, bad.

In short, virtue is concerned with pleasures and pains; the actions that are its 15 sources also increase it or, if they are done differently, ruin it; and its activity is concerned with the same actions that are its sources.

4

However, someone might raise this puzzle: 'What do you mean by saying that to become just we must first do just actions and to become temperate we must first do temperate actions? For if we do what is grammatical or musical, we must already be grammarians or musicians. In the same way, then, if we do what is just or temperate, 20 we must already be just or temperate.'

But surely this is not so even with the crafts, for it is possible to produce something grammatical by chance or by following someone else's instructions. To be a grammarian, then, we must both produce something grammatical and produce it in the

8. [Heraclitus (c. 535–c. 475 B.C.) was an influential pre-Socratic philosopher who viewed the world-order as a continuous flux and considered any claim to permanence an illusion of the human senses.]

25 way in which the grammarian produces it, i.e. expressing grammatical knowledge that is in us.

Moreover, in any case what is true of crafts is not true of virtues. For the products of a craft determine by their own character whether they have been produced well; 30 and so it suffices that they are in the right state when they have been produced. But for actions expressing virtue to be done temperately or justly [and hence well] it does not suffice that they are themselves in the right state. Rather, the agent must also be in the right state when he does them. First, he must know [that he is doing virtuous actions]; second, he must decide on them, and decide on them for themselves; and, third, he must also do them from a firm and unchanging state.

1105b As conditions for having a craft these three do not count, except for the knowing itself. As a condition for having a virtue, however, the knowing counts for nothing, or [rather] for only a little, whereas the other two conditions are very important, indeed 5 all-important. And these other two conditions are achieved by the frequent doing of just and temperate actions.

Hence, actions are called just or temperate when they are the sort that a just or temperate person would do. But the just and temperate person is not the one who [merely] does these actions, but the one who also does them in the way in which just or temperate people do them.

10 It is right, then, to say that a person comes to be just from doing just actions and temperate from doing temperate actions; for no one has even a prospect of becoming good from failing to do them.

The many, however, do not do these actions but take refuge in arguments, thinking that they are doing philosophy, and that this is the way to become excellent peo-15 ple. In this they are like a sick person who listens attentively to the doctor, but acts on none of his instructions. Such a course of treatment will not improve the state of his body; any more than will the many's way of doing philosophy improve the state of their souls.

A Virtue of Character Is a State Intermediate Between Two Extremes, and Involving Decision

The Genus

5

Next we must examine what virtue is. Since there are three conditions arising in the 20 soul—feelings, capacities and states—virtue must be one of these.

By feelings I mean appetite, anger, fear, confidence, envy, joy, love, hate, longing, jealousy, pity, in general whatever implies pleasure or pain.

25 By capacities I mean what we have when we are said to be capable of these feelings—capable of, e.g., being angry or afraid or feeling pity.

By states I mean what we have when we are well or badly off in relation to feelings. If, e.g., our feeling is too intense or slack, we are badly off in relation to anger, but if it is intermediate, we are well off; and the same is true in the other cases.

30 First, then, neither virtues nor vices are feelings. (a) For we are called excellent or

base in so far as we have virtues or vices, not in so far as we have feelings. (b) We are neither praised nor blamed in so far as we have feelings; for we do not praise the angry or the frightened person, and do not blame the person who is simply angry but only the person who is angry in a particular way. But we are praised or blamed in so far as we have virtues or vices. (c) We are angry and afraid without decision; but the virtues are decisions of some kind, or [rather] require decision. (d) Besides, in so far as we have feelings, we are said to be moved; but in so far as we have virtues or vices, we are said to be in some condition rather than moved.

For these reasons the virtues are not capacities either; for we are neither called good nor called bad in so far as we are simply capable of feelings. Further, while we have capacities by nature, we do not become good or bad by nature; we have discussed this before.

If, then, the virtues are neither feelings nor capacities, the remaining possibility is that they are states. And so we have said what the genus of virtue is.

6

But we must say not only, as we already have, that it is a state, but also what sort of state it is.

It should be said, then, that every virtue causes its possessors to be in a good state and to perform their functions well; the virtue of eyes, e.g., makes the eyes and their functioning excellent, because it makes us see well; and similarly, the virtue of a horse makes the horse excellent, and thereby good at galloping, at carrying its rider and at standing steady in the face of the enemy. If this is true in every case, then the virtue of a human being will likewise be the state that makes a human being good and makes him perform his function well.

We have already said how this will be true, and it will also be evident from our next remarks, if we consider the sort of nature that virtue has.

In everything continuous and divisible we can take more, less and equal, and each of them either in the object itself or relative to us; and the equal is some intermediate between excess and deficiency.

By the intermediate in the object I mean what is equidistant from each extremity; this is one and the same for everyone. But relative to us the intermediate is what is neither superfluous nor deficient; this is not one, and is not the same for everyone.

If, e.g., ten are many and two are few, we take six as intermediate in the object, since it exceeds [two] and is exceeded [by ten] by an equal amount, [four]; this is what is intermediate by numerical proportion. But that is not how we must take the intermediate that is relative to us. For if, e.g., ten pounds [of food] are a lot for someone to eat, and two pounds a little, it does not follow that the trainer will prescribe six, since this might also be either a little or a lot for the person who is to take it — for Milo[9] [the athlete] a little, but for the beginner in gymnastics a lot; and the same is true for running and wrestling. In this way every scientific expert avoids excess and deficiency and seeks and chooses what is intermediate — but intermediate relative to us, not in the object.

This, then, is how each science produces its product well, by focusing on what is in-

1106a

5

10

15

20

25

30

35

1106b

5

---

9. [Milo was a sixth-century B.C. Greek wrestler of legendary strength.]

10   termediate and making the product conform to that. This, indeed, is why people regularly comment on well-made products that nothing could be added or subtracted, since they assume that excess or deficiency ruins a good [result] while the mean preserves it. Good craftsmen also, we say, focus on what is intermediate when

15   they produce their product. And since virtue, like nature, is better and more exact than any craft, it will also aim at what is intermediate.

By virtue I mean virtue of character; for this [pursues the mean because] it is concerned with feelings and actions, and these admit of excess, deficiency and an intermediate condition. We can be afraid, e.g., or be confident, or have appetites, or

20   get angry, or feel pity, in general have pleasure or pain, both too much and too little, and in both ways not well; but [having these feelings] at the right times, about the right things, towards the right people, for the right end, and in the right way, is the intermediate and best condition, and this is proper to virtue. Similarly, actions also admit of excess, deficiency and the intermediate condition. Now virtue is concerned

25   with feelings and actions, in which excess and deficiency are in error and incur blame, while the intermediate condition is correct and wins praise, which are both proper features of virtue. Virtue, then, is a mean, in so far as it aims at what is intermediate.

Moreover, there are many ways to be in error, since badness is proper to what is

30   unlimited, as the Pythagoreans pictured it, and good to what is limited; but there is only one way to be correct. That is why error is easy and correctness hard, since it is easy to miss the target and hard to hit it. And so for this reason also excess and deficiency are proper to vice, the mean to virtue; 'for we are noble in only one way, but bad in all sorts of ways.'

Virtue, then, is (a) a state that decides, (b) [consisting] in a mean, (c) the mean

1107a   relative to us, (d) which is defined by reference to reason, (e) i.e., to the reason by reference to which the intelligent person would define it. It is a mean between two vices, one of excess and one of deficiency.

It is a mean for this reason also: Some vices miss what is right because they are defi-

5   cient, others because they are excessive, in feelings or in actions, while virtue finds and chooses what is intermediate.

Hence, as far as its substance and the account stating its essence are concerned, virtue is a mean; but as far as the best [condition] and the good [result] are concerned, it is an extremity.

But not every action or feeling admits of the mean. For the names of some

10   automatically include baseness, e.g. spite, shamelessness, envy [among feelings], and adultery, theft, murder, among actions. All of these and similar things are called by these names because they themselves, not their excesses or deficiencies, are base.

Hence in doing these things we can never be correct, but must invariably be in er-

15   ror. We cannot do them well or not well—e.g. by committing adultery with the right woman at the right time in the right way; on the contrary, it is true without reservation that to do any of them is to be in error.

[To think these admit of a mean], therefore, is like thinking that unjust or cowardly

20   or intemperate action also admits of a mean, an excess and a deficiency. For then there would be a mean of excess, a mean of deficiency, an excess of excess and a deficiency of deficiency.

Rather, just as there is no excess or deficiency of temperance or of bravery, since the intermediate is a sort of extreme [in achieving the good], so also there is no mean of these [vicious actions] either, but whatever way anyone does them, he is in error. For in general there is no mean of excess or of deficiency, and no excess or deficiency of a mean.

25

7

However, we must not only state this general account but also apply it to the particular cases. For among accounts concerning actions, though the general ones are common to more cases, the specific ones are truer, since actions are about particular cases, and our account must accord with these. Let us, then, find these from the chart.

30

(1) First, in feelings of fear and confidence the mean is bravery. The excessively fearless person is nameless (and in fact many cases are nameless), while the one who is excessively confident is rash; the one who is excessively afraid and deficient in confidence is cowardly.

1107b

(2) In pleasures and pains, though not in all types, and in pains less than in pleasures, the mean is temperance and the excess intemperance. People deficient in pleasure are not often found, which is why they also lack even a name; let us call them insensible.

5

(3) In giving and taking money the mean is generosity, the excess wastefulness and the deficiency ungenerosity. Here the vicious people have contrary excesses and defects; for the wasteful person spends to excess and is deficient in taking, whereas the ungenerous person takes to excess and is deficient in spending. At the moment we are speaking in outline and summary, and that suffices; later we shall define these things more exactly.

10

15

(4) In questions of money there are also other conditions. Another mean is magnificence; for the magnificent person differs from the generous by being concerned with large matters, while the generous person is concerned with small. The excess is ostentation and vulgarity, and the deficiency niggardliness, and these differ from the vices related to generosity in ways we shall describe later.

20

(5) In honour and dishonour the mean is magnanimity, the excess something called a sort of vanity, and the deficiency pusillanimity.

(6) And just as we said that generosity differs from magnificence in its concern with small matters, similarly there is a virtue concerned with small honours, differing in the same way from magnanimity, which is concerned with great honours. For honour can be desired either in the right way or more or less than is right. If someone desires it to excess, he is called an honour-lover, and if his desire is deficient he is called indifferent to honour, but if he is intermediate he has no name. The corresponding conditions have no name either, except the condition of the honour-lover, which is called honour-loving.

25

30

This is why people at the extremes claim the intermediate area. Indeed, we also sometimes call the intermediate person an honour-lover, and sometimes call him indifferent to honour; and sometimes we praise the honour-lover, sometimes the person indifferent to honour. We will mention later the reason we do this; for the moment,

1108a

let us speak of the other cases in the way we have laid down.

5   (7) Anger also admits of an excess, deficiency and mean. These are all practically nameless; but since we call the intermediate person mild, let us call the mean mildness. Among the extreme people let the excessive person be irascible, and the vice be irascibility, and let the deficient person be a sort of inirascible person, and the deficiency be inirascibility.

10   There are three other means, somewhat similar to one another, but different. For they are all concerned with association in conversations and actions, but differ in so far as one is concerned with truth-telling in these areas, the other two with sources of pleasure, some of which are found in amusement, and the others in daily life in general. Hence, we should also discuss these states, so that we can better observe that

15   in every case the mean is praiseworthy, while the extremes are neither praiseworthy nor correct, but blameworthy. Most of these cases are also nameless, and we must try, as in the other cases also, to make names ourselves, to make things clear and easy to follow.

20   (8) In truth-telling, then, let us call the intermediate person truthful, and the mean truthfulness; pretence that overstates will be boastfulness, and the person who has it boastful; pretence that understates will be self-deprecation, and the person who has it self-deprecating.

      (9) In sources of pleasure in amusements let us call the intermediate person witty,

25   and the condition wit; the excess buffoonery and the person who has it a buffoon; and the deficient person a sort of boor and the state boorishness.

      (10) In the other sources of pleasure, those in daily life, let us call the person who is pleasant in the right way friendly, and the mean state friendliness. If someone goes to excess with no [further] aim he will be ingratiating; if he does it for his own advan-

30   tage, a flatterer. The deficient person, unpleasant in everything, will be a sort of quarrelsome and ill-tempered person.

      (11) There are also means in feelings and concerned with feelings: Shame, e.g., is not a virtue, but the person prone to shame as well as the virtuous person we have described receives praise. For here also one person is called intermediate, and another—the person excessively prone to shame, who is ashamed about

35   everything—is called excessive; the person who is deficient in shame or never feels shame at all is said to have no sense of disgrace; and the intermediate one is called

1108b prone to shame.

      (12) Proper indignation is the mean between envy and spite; these conditions are concerned with pleasure and pain at what happens to our neighbours. For the properly indignant person feels pain when someone does well undeservedly; the envious

5   person exceeds him by feeling pain when anyone does well, while the spiteful person is so deficient in feeling pain that he actually enjoys [other people's misfortunes].

      There will also be an opportunity elsewhere to speak of these [means that are not virtues].

      We must consider justice after these other conditions, and, because it is not spoken of in one way only, we shall distinguish its two types and say how each of them is a mean.

10   Similarly, we must consider the virtues that belong to reason.

8

Among these three conditions, then, two are vices—one of excess, one of deficiency—and one—the mean—is virtue. In a way each of them is opposed to each of the others, since each extreme is contrary both to the intermediate condition and to the other extreme, while the intermediate is contrary to the extremes. For as the equal is greater in comparison to the smaller, and smaller in comparison to the greater, so 15 also the intermediate states are excessive in comparison to the deficiencies and deficient in comparison to the excesses—both in feelings and in actions.

For the brave person, e.g., appears rash in comparison to the coward, and coward- 20 ly in comparison to the rash person; similarly, the temperate person appears intemperate in comparison to the insensible person, and insensible in comparison with the intermperate person, and the generous person appears wasteful in comparison to the ungenerous, and ungenerous in comparison to the wasteful person. That is why each of the extreme people tries to push the intermediate person to the other extreme, so that the coward, e.g., calls the brave person rash, and the rash person calls 25 him a coward, and similarly in the other cases.

Because these conditions of soul are opposed to each other in these ways, the extremes are more contrary to each other than to the intermediate. For they are further from each other than from the intermediate, just as the large is further from the small, and the small from the large, than either is from the equal. 30

Moreover, sometimes one extreme, e.g. rashness or wastefulness, appears somewhat like the intermediate state, e.g. bravery or generosity, but the extremes are most unlike one another; and the things that are furthest apart from each other are defined as contraries. Hence also the things that are further apart are more contrary. 35

In some cases the deficiency, in others the excess, is more opposed to the in- 1109a termediate condition; e.g. it is cowardice, the deficiency, not rashness, the excess, that is more opposed to bravery; on the other hand, it is intemperance, the excess, not insensibility, the deficiency, that is more opposed to temperance. This happens 5 for two reasons.

One reason is derived from the object itself. Since sometimes one extreme is closer and more similar to the intermediate condition, we oppose the contrary extreme, more than this closer one, to the intermediate condition. Since rashness, e.g., seems to be closer and similar to bravery, and cowardice less similar, we oppose cowardice 10 more than rashness to bravery; for what is further from the intermediate condition seems to be more contrary to it. This, then, is one reason, derived from the object itself.

The other reason is derived from ourselves. For when we ourselves have some natural tendency to one extreme more than the other, this extreme appears more opposed to the intermediate condition; since, e.g. we have more of a natural tendency to pleasure, we drift more easily toward intemperance than towards orderliness. 15 Hence we say that an extreme is more contrary if we naturally develop more in that direction; and this is why intemperance is more contrary to temperance, since it is the excess.

Practical Advice on Ways to Achieve the Mean

9

20   We have said enough, then, to show that virtue of character is a mean and what sort of mean it is; that it is a mean between two vices, one of excess and one of deficiency; and that it is a mean because it aims at the intermediate condition in feelings and actions.

25   Hence it is hard work to be excellent, since in each case it is hard work to find what is intermediate; e.g. not everyone, but only one who knows, finds the midpoint in a circle. So also getting angry, or giving and spending money, is easy and anyone can do it; but doing it to the right person, the right amount, at the right time, for the right end, and in the right way is no longer easy, nor can everyone do it. Hence [doing these things] is rare, praiseworthy and fine.

30   Hence if we aim at the intermediate condition we must first of all steer clear of the more contrary extreme, following the advice that Calypso[10] also gives — 'Hold the ship outside the spray and surge.' For since one extreme is more in error, the other less, and since it is hard to hit the intermediate extremely accurately, the second-best tack,
35   as they say, is to take the lesser of the evils. We shall succeed best in this by the method
1109b we describe.

We must also examine what we ourselves drift into easily. For different people have different natural tendencies towards different goals, and we shall come to know our
5   own tendencies from the pleasure or pain that arises in us. We must drag ourselves off in the contrary direction; for if we pull far away from error, as they do in straightening bent wood, we shall reach the intermediate condition.

And in everything we must beware above all of pleasure and its sources; for we are already biased in its favour when we come to judge it. Hence we must react to it as the
10   elders reacted to Helen,[11] and on each occasion repeat what they said; for if we do this, and send it off, we shall be less in error.

In summary, then, if we do these things we shall best be able to reach the intermediate condition. But no doubt this is hard, especially in particular cases, since it
15   is not easy to define the way we should be angry, with whom, about what, for how long; for sometimes, indeed, we ourselves praise deficient people and call them mild, and sometimes praise quarrelsome people and call them manly. Still, we are not
20   blamed if we deviate a little in excess or deficiency from doing well, but only if we deviate a long way, since then we are easily noticed.

But how far and how much we must deviate to be blamed is not easy to define in an account; for nothing perceptible is easily defined, and [since] these [circumstances of virtuous and vicious action] are particulars, the judgment about them depends on perception.

25   All this makes it clear, then, that in every case the intermediate state is praised, but we must sometimes incline towards the excess, sometimes towards the deficiency; for that is the easiest way to succeed in hitting the intermediate condition and [doing] well.

10. [Calypso was a nymph in Homer's *Odyssey*.]

11. [The reference is to Homer's *Iliad*.]

BOOK THREE

The Preconditions of Virtue

VOLUNTARY ACTION

1

Virtue, then, is about feelings and actions; and these receive praise or blame when   30
they are voluntary, but pardon, sometimes even pity, when they are involuntary.
Hence, presumably, in examining virtue we must define the voluntary and the involuntary. This is also useful for legislators, both for honours and for corrective   35
treatments.

What comes about by force or because of ignorance seems to be involuntary. What   1110a
is forced has an external origin, the sort of origin in which the agent or victim contributes nothing — if, e.g., a wind or human beings who control him were to carry
him off.

But now consider actions done because of fear of greater evils, or because of
something fine. Suppose, e.g., a tyrant tells you to do something shameful, when   5
he has control over your parents and children, and if you do it, they will live, but
if not, they will die. These cases raise dispute about whether they are voluntary or
involuntary.

However, the same sort of thing also happens with throwing the cargo overboard in   10
storms; for no one willingly throws cargo overboard, without restriction, but anyone
with any sense throws cargo overboard to save himself and the others, [which is an
added restriction].

These sorts of actions, then, are mixed. But they are seemingly more like voluntary
actions. For at the time they are done they are choiceworthy, and the goal of the action reflects the occasion; hence we should also call the action voluntary or involuntary with reference to the time when he does it. Now in fact he does it willingly; for in   15
these sorts of actions he has within him the origin of the movement of the limbs that
are the instruments [of the action], and when the origin of the actions is in him, it is
also up to him to do them or not to do them. Hence actions of this sort are voluntary,
though presumably the actions without [the appropriate] restriction are involuntary,
since no one would choose any action of this sort in itself.

For such [mixed] actions people are sometimes actually praised, whenever they en-   20
dure something shameful or painful as the price of great and fine results; and if they
do the reverse, they are blamed, since it is a base person who endures what is most
shameful for nothing fine or for only some moderately fine result.

In some cases there is no praise, but there is pardon, whenever someone does a   25
wrong action because of conditions that overstrain human nature, and that no one
would endure. But presumably there are some things that we cannot be compelled to
do, and rather than do them we should suffer the most terrible consequences and accept death; for the things that [allegedly] compelled Euripides' Alcmaeon to kill his

mother appear ridiculous.[12]

30   It is sometimes hard, however, to judge what [goods] should be chosen at the price of what [evils], and what [evils] should be endured as the price of what [goods]. And it is even harder to abide by our judgment, since the results we expect [when we endure] are usually painful, and the actions we are compelled [to endure, when we choose] are usually shameful. That is why those who have been compelled or not 1110b compelled receive praise and blame.

What sorts of things, then, should we say are forced? Perhaps we should say that something is forced without restriction whenever its cause is external and the agent contributes nothing. Other things are involuntary in themselves, but choiceworthy on this occasion and as the price of these [goods], and their origin is in the agent. These are involuntary in themselves, but, on this occasion and as the price of these [goods], 5 voluntary. Still, they are seemingly more like voluntary actions, since actions are particulars, and these [particulars in mixed actions] are voluntary. But what sort of thing should be chosen as the price of what [good] is not easy to answer, since there are many differences in particular cases.

But suppose someone says that pleasant things and fine things force us, since they are outside us and compel us. It will follow that for him everything is forced, since 10 everyone in every action aims at something fine or pleasant.

Moreover, if our action is forced and unwilling, we find it painful; but if something pleasant or fine is its cause, we do it with pleasure.

It is ridiculous, then, for [our opponent] to ascribe responsibility to external 15 [causes] and not to himself, when he is easily snared by such things; and ridiculous to take responsibility for fine actions himself, but to hold pleasant things responsible for his shameful actions.

What is forced, then, is seemingly what has its origin outside the person forced, who contributes nothing.

Everything caused by ignorance is non-voluntary, but what is involuntary also 20 causes pain and regret. For if someone's action was caused by ignorance, but he now has no objection to the action, he has done it neither willingly, since he did not know what it was, nor unwillingly, since he now feels no pain. Hence, among those who act because of ignorance, the agent who now regrets his action seems to be unwilling, while the agent with no regrets may be called non-willing, since he is another case—for since he is different, it is better if he has his own special name.

25   Further, action caused by ignorance is seemingly different from action done in ignorance. For if the agent is drunk or angry, his action seems to be caused by drunkenness or anger, not by ignorance, though it is done in ignorance, not in knowledge.

[This ignorance does not make an action involuntary.] Certainly every vicious person is ignorant of the actions he must do or avoid, and this sort of error makes people 30 unjust, and in general bad. But talk of involuntary action is not meant to apply to [this] ignorance of what is beneficial.

For the cause of involuntary action is not [this] ignorance in the decision, which causes vice; it is not [in other words] ignorance of the universal, since that is a cause

12. [Euripides' play is not extant. According to Greek mythology, Alcmaeon killed his mother to avenge the death of his father.]

for blame. Rather, the cause is ignorance of the particulars which the action consists   1111a
in and is concerned with; for these allow both pity and pardon, since an agent acts involuntarily if he is ignorant of one of these.

Presumably, then, it is not a bad idea to define these particulars, and say what they
are, and how many. They are: (1) who is doing it; (2) what he is doing; (3) about what
or to what he is doing it; (4) sometimes also what he is doing it with, e.g. the instru-   5
ment; (5) for what result, e.g. safety; (6) in what way, e.g. gently or hard.

Now certainly someone could not be ignorant of *all* of these unless he were mad.
Nor, clearly, (1) could he be ignorant of who is doing it, since he could hardly be ignorant of himself. But (2) he might be ignorant of what he is doing, as when someone
says that [the secret] slipped out while he was speaking, or, as Aeschylus said about
the mysteries, that he did not know it was forbidden to reveal it;[13] or, like the person
with the catapult, that he let it go when he [only] wanted to demonstrate it. (3)   10
Again, he might think that his son is an enemy, as Merope did;[14] or (4) that the
barbed spear has a button on it, or that the stone is pumice-stone. (5) By giving someone a drink to save his life we might kill him; (6) and wanting to touch someone, as   15
they do in sparring, we might wound him.

There is ignorance about all of these [particulars] that the action consists in. Hence
someone who was ignorant of one of these seems to have done an action unwillingly,
especially when he was ignorant of the most important of them; these seem to be
(3) what he is doing it to, and (5) the result for which he does it.

Hence it is action called involuntary with reference to *this* sort of ignorance [that   20
we meant when we said that] the agent must, in addition, feel pain and regret for his
action.

Since, then, what is involuntary is what is forced or is caused by ignorance, what is
voluntary seems to be what has its origin in the agent himself when he knows the particulars that the action consists in.

[Our definition is sound.] For it is not correct to say that action caused by emotion   25
or appetite is involuntary.

For, first of all, on this view none of the other animals will ever act voluntarily; nor
will children. [But clearly they do.]

Next, among all the actions caused by emotion or appetite do we do none of them
voluntarily? Or do we do the fine actions voluntarily and the shameful involuntarily?
Surely [the second answer] is ridiculous when one and the same thing [i.e. appetite or
emotion] causes [both fine and shameful actions]. And presumably it is also absurd to   30
say [as the first answer implies] that things we ought to desire are involuntary; and in
fact we ought both to be angry at some things and to have an appetite for some
things, e.g. for health and learning.

Again, what is involuntary seems to be painful, whereas what reflects our appetite
seems to be pleasant.

Moreover, how are errors that reflect emotion any less voluntary than those that
reflect rational calculation? For both sorts of errors are to be avoided; and since non-   1111b
rational feelings seem to be no less human [than rational calculation], actions

13. [The Greek dramatist is said to have been accused but then acquitted of revealing rites of a secret
religious cult.]

14. [In a lost play of Euripides, Merope, not recognizing his son, nearly slays him.]

resulting from emotion or appetite are also proper to a human being; it is absurd, then, to regard them as involuntary.

2

Now that we have defined what is voluntary and involuntary, the next task is to discuss decision; for it seems to be most proper to virtue, and to distinguish [good] characters [from bad] better than actions do.

Decision, then, is apparently voluntary, but not the same as what is voluntary, which extends more widely. For children and the other animals share in what is voluntary, but not in decision; and the actions we do on the spur of the moment are said to be voluntary, but not to express decision.

Those who say that decision is appetite or emotion or wish or some sort of belief are seemingly wrong.

For decision is not shared with non-rational [animals], but appetite and emotion are shared with them.

Further, the incontinent person acts on appetite, not on decision, but the continent person acts on decision, not on appetite.

Again, appetite is contrary to decision, but not to appetite.

Further, appetite's concern is what is pleasant and what is painful, but neither of these is the concern of decision.

Still less is emotion decision; for actions caused by emotion seem least of all to express decision.

But further, it is not wish either, though it is apparently close to it.

For, first, we do not decide to do what is impossible, and anyone claiming to decide to do it would seem a fool; but we do wish for what is impossible, e.g. never to die, as well [as for what is possible].

Further, we wish [not only for results we can achieve], but also for results that are [possible, but] not achievable through our own agency, e.g. victory for some actor or competitor. But what we decide to do is never anything of that sort, but what we think would come about through our own agency.

Again, we wish for the end more [than for what promotes it], but we decide to do what promotes the end. We wish, e.g. to be healthy, but decide to do what will make us healthy; and we wish to be happy, and say so, but could not appropriately say we decide to be happy, since in general, seemingly, what we decide to do is what is up to us.

Nor is it belief.

For, first, belief seems to be about everything, no less about what is eternal and what is impossible [for us] than about what is up to us.

Moreover, beliefs are divided into true and false, not into good and bad, but decisions are divided into good and bad more than into true and false.

1112a   Now presumably no one even claims that decision is the same as belief in general. But it is not the same as any kind of belief either.

For it is our decisions to do what is good or evil, not our beliefs, that make the characters we have.

Again, we decide to take or avoid something good or evil. We believe what it is, whom it benefits or how; but we do not exactly believe to take or avoid.

Further, decision is praised more for deciding on what is right, whereas belief is praised for believing rightly.

Moreover, we decide on something [even] when we know most completely that it is good; but [what] we believe [is] what we do not quite know.

Again, those who make the best decisions do not seem to be the same as those with the best beliefs; on the contrary, some seem to have better beliefs, but to make the   10
wrong decisions because of vice.

We can agree that decision follows or implies belief. But that is irrelevant, since it is not the question we are asking; our question is whether decision is the *same* as some sort of belief.

Then what, or what sort of thing, is decision, since it is none of the things mentioned? Well, apparently it is voluntary, but not everything voluntary is decided.   15
Then perhaps what is decided is the result of prior deliberation. For decision is associated with reason and thought, and even the name itself seems to indicate that [what is decided, *prohaireton*] is chosen [*haireton*], before [*pro*] other things.

3

But do we deliberate about everything, and is everything open to deliberation, or is there no deliberation about some things? By 'open to deliberation', presumably, we   20
should mean what someone with some sense, not some fool or madman, might deliberate about.

Now no one deliberates about eternal things, e.g. about the universe, or that the sides and the diagonal are incommensurable; nor about things that are in movement but always come about the same way, either from necessity or by nature or by some   25
other cause, e.g. the solstices or the rising of the stars; nor about what happens different ways at different times, e.g. droughts and rains; nor about what results from fortune, e.g. the finding of a treasure. For none of these results could be achieved   30
through our agency.

We deliberate about what is up to us, i.e. about the actions we can do; and this is what is left [besides the previous cases]. For causes seem to include nature, necessity and fortune, but besides them mind and everything [operating] through human agency.

However, we do not deliberate about all human affairs; no Spartan, e.g., deliberates about how the Scythians might have the best political system. Rather, each type of human being deliberates about the actions *he* can do.

Now there is no deliberation about the sciences that are exact and self-sufficient,   112b
e.g. about letters, since we are in no doubt about how to write them [in a word]. Rather, we deliberate about what results through our agency, but in different ways on different occasions, e.g. about questions of medicine and money-making; more   5
about navigation than about gymnastics, to the extent that it is less exactly worked out, and similarly with other [crafts]; and more about beliefs than about sciences, since we are more in doubt about them.

Deliberation concerns what is usually [one way rather than the other], where the outcome is unclear and the right way to act is undefined. And we enlist partners in   10
deliberation on large issues when we distrust our own ability to discern [the right

answer].

We deliberate not about ends, but about what promotes ends; a doctor, e.g., does not deliberate about whether he will cure, or an orator about whether he will persuade, or a politician about whether he will produce good order, or any other [expert] about the end [that his science aims at].

Rather, we first lay down the end, and then examine the ways and means to achieve it. If it appears that any of several [possible] means will reach it, we consider which of them will reach it most easily and most finely; and if only one [possible] means reaches it, we consider how that means will reach it, and how the means itself is reached, until we come to the first cause, the last thing to be discovered.

For a deliberator seemingly inquires and analyses in the way described, as though analysing a diagram. [The comparison is apt, since], apparently, all deliberation is inquiry, though not all inquiry, e.g. in mathematics, is deliberation. And seemingly the last thing [found] in the analysis is the first that comes to be.

If we encounter an impossible step — e.g. we need money but cannot raise it — we desist; but if the action appears possible, we undertake it. What is possible is what we could achieve through our agency, including what our friends could achieve for us; for what our friends achieve is, in a way, achieved through our agency, since the origin is in us. [In crafts] we sometimes look for instruments, sometimes [for the way] to use them; so also in other cases we sometimes look for the means to the end, sometimes for the proper use of the means or for the means to that proper use.

As we have said, then, a human being, seemingly, originates action; deliberation is about the actions he can do; and actions are for the sake of other things; hence we deliberate about what promotes an end, not about the end.

Nor do we deliberate about particulars, e.g. about whether this is a loaf or is cooked the right amount; for these are questions for perception, and if we keep on deliberating at each stage we will go on without end.

What we deliberate about is the same as what we decide to do, except that by the time we decide to do it, it is definite, for what we decide to do is what we have judged to be right as a result of deliberation. For each of us stops inquiring how to act as soon as he traces the origin to himself, and within himself to the dominant part; for this is the part that decides. This is also clear from the ancient political systems represented by Homer; there the kings would first decide and then announce it to the people.

We have found, then, that what we decide to do is whatever action among those up to us we deliberate about and desire to do. Hence also decision will be deliberative desire to do an action that is up to us; for when we have judged [that it is right] as a result of deliberation, our desire to do it expesses our wish.

So much, then, for an outline of the sort of thing that decision is about: it is about what promotes the end.

RATIONAL WISH FOR THE END

4

Wish, we have said, is for the end. But to some it seems that wish is for the good, to others that it is for the apparent good.

If we say that the good is what is wished, it follows that what someone wishes if he chooses incorrectly is not wished at all. For if it is wished, then [on this view] it is good; but what he wishes is in fact evil, if it turns out that way. [Hence what he wishes   20 is not wished, which is self-contradictory.]

If, on the other hand, we say that the apparent good is wished, it follows that there is nothing wished by nature. To each person what is wished is what seems [good to him]; but different things, and indeed contrary things, if it turns out that way, appear good to different people. [Hence contrary things will be wished.]

If, then, these results do not satisfy us, should we say that, without restriction and in reality, what is wished is the good, but to each person what is wished is the apparent good?

To the excellent person, then, what is wished will be what is wished in reality, while   25 to the base person what is wished is whatever it turns out to be [that appears to him]. Similarly in the case of bodies, really healthy things are healthy to people in good condition, while other things are healthy to sickly people, and the same is true of what is bitter, sweet, hot, heavy and so on.

For the excellent person judges each sort of thing correctly, and in each case what   30 is true appears to him. For each state [of character] has its own special [view of] what is fine and pleasant, and presumably the excellent person is far superior because he sees what is true in each case, being a sort of standard and measure of what is fine and pleasant.

In the many, however, pleasure seemingly causes deception, since it appears good when it is not; at any rate, they choose what is pleasant because they assume it is   1113b good, and avoid pain because they assume it is evil.

VIRTUE AND VICE ARE IN OUR POWER

5

We have found, then, that we wish for the end, and deliberate and decide about what promotes it; hence the actions concerned with what promotes the end will be volun-   5 tary actions expressing decision. Now the activities of the virtues are concerned with [what promotes the end]; hence virtue is up to us, and so also is vice.

For when acting is up to us, so is not acting, and when No is up to us, so is Yes. Hence if acting, when it is fine, is up to us, then not acting, when it is shameful, is   10 also up to us; and if not acting, when it is fine, is up to us, then acting, when it is shameful, is also up to us. Hence if doing, and likewise not doing, fine or shameful actions is up to us; and if, as we saw, [doing or not doing them] is [what it is] to be a good or bad person; then it follows that being decent or base is up to us.

The claim that no one is willingly vicious or unwillingly blessed is, seemingly, partly   15 true but partly false. For while certainly no one is unwillingly blessed, vice is voluntary. If it is not we must dispute the conclusion just reached, that a human being originates and fathers his own actions as he fathers his children. But if our conclusion appears true, and we cannot trace [actions] back to other origins beyond those in   20 ourselves, then it follows that whatever has its origin in us is itself up to us and voluntary.

Seemingly there is testimony to our views not only in what each of us does privately, but also in what legislators themselves do. For they impose corrective treatments and penalties on anyone who does vicious actions, if he does them neither by force nor because of ignorance that he is not responsible for; and they honour anyone who does fine actions, on the assumption that they will encourage him and restrain the wrong doer. But they never encourage us to do anything that is not up to us and voluntary; they assume it is pointless to persuade us not to get hot or distressed or hungry or anything else of that sort, since persuasion will not stop it happening to us.

Indeed, they also impose corrective treatments on someone for the ignorance itself, if he seems to be responsible for the ignorance. A drunk, e.g., pays a double penalty; for the origin is in him, since he is in control of getting drunk, and his getting drunk is responsible for his ignorance.

They also impose corrective treatment on someone who [does a vicious action] in ignorance of some provision of law that he is required to know and that is not hard [to know]. And they impose it in other cases likewise for any other ignorance that seems to be caused by the agent's inattention; they assume it is up to him not to be ignorant, since he is in control of paying attention.

But presumably his character makes him inattentive. Still, he himself is responsible for having this character, by living carelessly, and similarly for being unjust by cheating, or being intemperate by passing his time in drinking and the like; for each type of activity produces the corresponding character. This is clear from those who train for some contest or action, since they continually practise the appropriate activities. [Only] a totally insensible person would not know that each type of activity is the source of the corresponding state; hence if someone does what he knows will make him unjust, he is willingly unjust.

Moreover, it is unreasonable [to suppose] that someone who acts unjustly or intemperately does not wish to be unjust or intemperate, though this does not mean that if he is unjust and wishes to stop, he will stop and will be just.

For neither does a sick person recover his health [simply by wishing]; nonetheless, he is sick willingly, by living incontinently and disobeying the doctors, if that was how it happened. At that time, then, it was open to him not to be sick, though no longer open to him once he has let himself go, just as it was up to us to throw a stone, since the origin was in us, though we can no longer take it back once we have thrown it.

Similarly, then, it was originally open to the person who is [now] unjust or intemperate not to acquire this character; hence he has it willingly, though once he has acquired it he can no longer get rid of it.

It is not only vices of the soul that are voluntary; vices of the body are also voluntary for some people, who are those we actually censure. For we never censure someone if nature causes his ugliness; but if his lack of training or attention causes it, we do censure him. The same is true for weakness or maiming; for everyone would pity, not reproach someone if he were blind by nature or because of a disease or a wound, but would censure him if his heavy drinking or some other form of intemperance made him blind.

Hence bodily vices that are up to us are censured, while those not up to us are not censured. If so, then in the other cases also the vices that are censured will be up to us.

But someone may say, 'Everyone aims at the apparent good, and does not control how it appears; on the contrary, his character controls how the end appears to him.'

First, then, if each person is in some way responsible for his own state [of character], then he is also himself in some way responsible for how [the end] appears.

If, on the other hand, he is not [responsible for his own state], he is not himself responsible for his own evil actions, but, on the contrary, does them because he is ignorant of the end, and thinks these are the way to reach the best [result] for himself. His aiming at the end [he aims at] is not his own choice; rather, [to aim at the right   5
end] he must by nature have a sort of inborn sense of sight to make him judge finely and choose what is really good.

Whoever has this fine aim by nature has a good nature. For this aim is the greatest and finest thing, and he cannot learn it or acquire it from another; rather, its natural   10
character [determines] the character of the aim he will have, and when it is naturally good and fine, that is true and complete good nature.

If all this is true, then, surely virtue will be no more voluntary than vice? For how the end appears is laid down, by nature or in whatever way, for the good and the bad   15
person alike, and they trace all the other things back to the end in doing whatever actions they do.

Suppose, then, that it is not nature that makes the end appear however it appears to each person, but something also depends on him; or, alternatively, suppose that [how] the end [appears] is natural, but virtue is voluntary because the virtuous person does the other things voluntarily. In either case vice will be no less voluntary than vir-   20
tue; for the bad person, no less than the good, is responsible for his own actions, even if not for [how] the end [appears].

Now the virtues, as we say, are voluntary, since in fact we are ourselves in a way jointly responsible for our states of character, and by having the characters we have we also make the end we lay down the sort of end it is. Hence the vices will also be voluntary, since the same is true of them.   25

We have now discussed the virtues in general. We have described their genus in outline; they are means, and they are states. Certain actions produce them, and they cause us to do these same actions, expressing the virtues themselves, in the way that correct reason prescribes. They are up to us and voluntary.

Actions and states, however, are not voluntary in the same way. For we are in   30
control of actions from the origin to the end, when we know the particulars. With states, however, we are in control of the origin, but do not know, any more than   1115a
with sicknesses, what the cumulative effect of particular actions will be; none the less, since it was up to us to exercise a capacity either this way or another way, states are voluntary.

BOOK SIX

Virtues of Thought

THE DOCTRINE OF THE MEAN; CORRECT REASON; AND VIRTUES OF THOUGHT

1

1138b   Since we have said previously that we must choose the intermediate condition, not the
20   excess or the deficiency, and that the intermediate condition is as correct reason says,
         let us now determine this [i.e. what it says].

         For in all the states of character we have mentioned, as well as in the others, there
         is a target which someone who has reason focusses on when he tightens and relaxes,
         and there is a definition of the means, which we take to be between excess and defi-
25   ciency because they express correct reason.

         To say this is admittedly true, but it is not at all clear. For in other pursuits directed
         by a science it is equally true that we must labour and be idle neither too much nor
         too little, but the intermediate amount prescribed by correct reason. But knowing
30   only this, we would be none the wiser, e.g. about the medicines to be applied to the
         body, if we were told we must apply as many as medical science instructs and in the
         way that the medical scientist applies them.

         Similarly, then, our account of the states of the soul must not only be true up to this
         point; we must also determine what correct reason is, i.e. what its definition is.

35   After we divided the virtues of the soul we said that some are virtues of character
         and some of thought. And so, having finished our discussion of the virtues of
1139a   character, let us now discuss the others as follows, after first discussing the soul.

         Previously, then, we said that there are two parts of the soul, one that has reason,
5   and one non-rational. Now we should divide in the same way the part that has
         reason.

         Let us assume that there are two parts that have reason; one with which we study
         beings whose origins cannot be otherwise than they are, and one with which we study
         beings whose origins can be otherwise. For when the beings are of different kinds, the
10   parts of the soul naturally suited to each of them are also of different kinds, since the
         parts possess knowledge by being somehow similar and appropriate [to their objects].

         Let us call one of these the scientific part, and the other the rationally calculating
         part, since deliberating is the same as rationally calculating, and no one deliberates
15   about what cannot be otherwise. Hence the rationally calculating part is one part of
         the soul that has reason.

         Hence we should find the best state both of the scientific and of the rationally
         calculating part; for this state is the virtue of each of them. And since something's vir-
         tue is relative to its own proper function [we must consider the function of each part].

2

These are three [capacities] in the soul—perception, understanding, desire—that control action and truth. Of these three perception clearly originates no action, since beasts have perception, but no share in action.   20

As assertion and denial are to thought, so pursuit and avoidance are to desire. Now virtue of character is a state that decides; and decision is a deliberative desire. If, then, the decision is excellent, the reason must be true and the desire correct, so that what reason states is what desire pursues.   25

This, then, is thought and truth concerned with action. By contrast, when thought is concerned with study, not with action or production, its good or bad state consists [simply] in being true or false. For truth is the function of whatever thinks; but the function of what thinks about action is truth agreeing with correct desire.   30

Now the origin—the source, not the goal, of the movement—is decision, and the origin of decision is desire, and reason that aims at some goal. Hence decision requires understanding and thought, and also a state of character, since doing well or   35
badly in action requires both intellect and character.

Thought by itself, however, moves nothing; what moves us is thought aiming at some goal and concerned with action. For this is the sort of thought that also   1139b
originates productive thought; for every producer in his production aims at some [further] goal, and the unconditional goal is not the product, which is only the [conditional] goal of some [production], and aims at some [further] goal. [The unconditional goal is] what we achieve in action, since doing well in action is the goal.

Now desire is for the goal. Hence decision is either understanding combined with desire or desire combined with thought; and what originates movement in this way is   5
a human being.

We do not decide to do what is already past; no one decides, e.g. to have sacked Troy. For neither do we deliberate about what is past, but only about what will be and admits [of being or not being]; and what is past does not admit of not having happened. Hence Agathon is correct to say 'Of this alone even a god is deprived—to   10
make what is all over to have never happened.'[15]

Hence the function of each of the understanding parts is truth; and so the virtue of each part will be the state that makes that part grasp the truth most of all.

3

Then let us begin over again, and discuss these states of the soul. Let us say, then, that there are five states in which the soul grasps the truth in its affirmations or   15
denials. These are craft, scientific knowledge, intelligence, wisdom and understanding; for belief and supposition admit of being false.

SCIENTIFIC KNOWLEDGE

What science is is evident from the following, if we must speak exactly and not be guided by [mere] similarities.

15. [Agathon was a fifth-century B.C. Athenian poet.]

20   For we all suppose that what we know scientifically does not even admit of being otherwise; and whenever what admits of being otherwise escapes observation, we do not notice whether it is or is not, [and hence we do not know about it]. Hence what is known scientifically is by necessity. Hence it is eternal; for the things that are by unconditional necessity are all eternal, and eternal things are ingenerable and indestructible.

25   Further, every science seems to be teachable, and what is scientifically knowable is learnable. But all teaching is from what is already known, as we also say in the *Analytics;* for some teaching is through induction, some by deductive inference, [which both require previous knowledge].

Induction [reaches] the origin, i.e. the universal, while deductive inference proceeds from the universals. Hence deductive inference has origins from which it pro-

30   ceeds, but which are not themselves [reached by] deductive inference. Hence they are [reached] by induction.

Scientific knowledge, then, is a demonstrative state, and has all the other features that in the *Analytics* we add to the definition. For someone has scientific knowledge when he has the appropriate sort of confidence, and the origins are known to him; for

35   if they are not better known to him than the conclusion, he will have scientific knowledge only coincidentally.

So much for a definition of scientific knowledge.

CRAFT-KNOWLEDGE

4

1140a   What admits of being otherwise includes what is produced and what is done in action. Production and action are different; about them we rely also on [our] popular discussions. Hence the state associated with reason and concerned with action is different from the state associated with reason and concerned with production. Nor is

5   one included in the other; for action is not production, and production is not action.

Now building, e.g., is a craft, and is essentially a certain state associated with reason and concerned with production; there is no craft that is not a state associated with reason and concerned with production, and no such state that is not a craft.

10   Hence a craft is the same as a state associated with true reason and concerned with production.

Every craft is concerned with coming to be; and the application of the craft is the study of how something that admits of being and not being comes to be, something whose origin is in the producer and not in the product. For a craft is not concerned

15   with things that are or come to be by necessity; or with things that are by nature, since these have their origin in themselves.

And since production and action are different, craft must be concerned with production, not with action.

In a way craft and fortune are concerned with the same things, as Agathon says;

20   'Craft was fond of fortune, and fortune of craft.'

A craft, then, as we have said, is a state associated with true reason and concerned with production. Lack of craft is a state associated with false reason and concerned with production. Both are concerned with what admits of being otherwise.

INTELLIGENCE

5

To grasp what intelligence is we should first study the sort of people we call   25
intelligent.

It seems proper, then, to an intelligent person to be able to deliberate finely about
what is good and beneficial for himself, not about some restricted area — e.g. about
what promotes health or strength — but about what promotes living well as a whole
[without restriction].

A sign of this is the fact that we call people intelligent about some [restricted area]
whenever they calculate well to promote some excellent end, in an area where there is   30
no craft. Hence where [living well] as a whole is concerned, the deliberative person
will also be intelligent.

Now no one deliberates about what cannot be otherwise or about what cannot be
achieved by his action. Hence, if science is associated with demonstration, but there is
no demonstration of anything whose origin can be otherwise, since every such thing
can itself be otherwise; and if we cannot deliberate about what is by necessity; it   35
follows that intelligence is neither a science nor a craft. It is not a science, because   1140b
what is done in action can be otherwise; and it is not a craft, because action and production belong to different kinds.

The remaining possibility, then, is that intelligence is a state grasping the truth,
associated with reason, and concerned with action about what is good or bad for a   5
human being.

For production has its end beyond it; but action does not, since its end is doing well
itself, [and doing well is the concern of intelligence].

Hence Pericles[16] and such people are the ones whom we regard as intelligent,
because they are able to study what is good for themselves and for human beings; and   10
we think that household managers and politicians are such people.

This is also how we come to give temperance (*sōphrosunē*) its name, because we
think that it preserves intelligence, (*sōzousan tēn phronesīn*). This is the sort of supposition that it preserves.

For the sort of supposition that is corrupted and perverted by what is pleasant or
painful is not every sort — not, e.g., the supposition that the triangle does or does not   15
have two right angles — but a supposition about what is done in action.

For the origin of what is done in action is the goal it aims at; and if pleasure or pain
has corrupted someone, the origin cannot appear to him. Hence it will not be apparent that this must be the goal and cause of all his choice and action; for vice cor-   20
rupts the origin.

Hence [since intelligence is what temperance preserves, and what temperance
preserves is a true supposition about action], intelligence must be a state grasping the
truth, associated with reason, and concerned with action about human goods.

16. [Pericles (c. 495–429 B.C.), the eminent Athenian statesman, was renowned for his incorruptible
character and the wisdom of his politics. He was a staunch defender of democracy and a patron of the arts.]

25   Moreover, there is virtue [or vice in the use] of craft, but not in intelligence. Further, in a craft, someone who makes errors voluntarily is more choiceworthy; but with intelligence, as with the virtues, the reverse is true. Clearly, then, intelligence is a virtue, not craft-knowledge.

There are two parts of the soul that have reason. Intelligence is a virtue of one of them, of the part that has belief; for belief is concerned, as intelligence is, with what admits of being otherwise.

Moreover, it is not only a state associated with reason. A sign of this is the fact that such a state is forgotten, but intelligence is not.

UNDERSTANDING

6

30   Scientific knowledge is supposition about universals, things that are by necessity. Further, everything demonstrable and every science have origins, since scientific knowledge is associated with reason.

Hence there can be neither scientific knowledge nor craft-knowledge nor intelligence about the origins of what is scientifically known. For what is scientifically
35   known is demonstrable, [but the origin is not]; and craft and intelligence are about
1141a what admits of being otherwise. Nor is wisdom [exclusively] about origins; for it is proper to the wise person to have a demonstration of some things.

Hence [the states of the soul] by which we always grasp the truth and never make mistakes, about what can or cannot be otherwise, are scientific knowledge, intelligence, wisdom and understanding. But none of the first three — intelligence,
5   scientific knowledge, wisdom — is possible about origins. The remaining possibility, then, is that we have understanding about origins.

WISDOM

10   We ascribe wisdom in crafts to the people who have the most exact [expertise] in the crafts, e.g. we call Pheidias a wise sculptor and Polycleitus a wise portrait-maker, signifying only that wisdom is excellence in a craft. But we also think some people are wise in general, not wise in some [restricted] area, or in some other [specific] way, as
15   Homer says in the Margites: 'The gods did not make him a digger or a ploughman or wise in anything.' Clearly, then, wisdom is the most exact [form] of scientific knowledge.

Hence the wise person must not only know what is derived from the origins of a science, but also grasp the truth about the origins. Therefore wisdom is understanding and scientific knowledge; it is scientific knowledge of the most honourable things that has received [understanding as] its coping-stone.

20   For it would be absurd for someone to think that political science or intelligence is the most excellent science, when the best thing in the universe is not a human being [and the most excellent science must be of the best things].

Moreover, what is good and healthy for human beings and for fish is not the same, but what is white or straight is always the same. Hence everyone would say that the

content of wisdom is always the same, but the content of intelligence is not. For the 25
agent they would call intelligent is the one who studies well each question about his
own [good], and he is the one to whom they would entrust such questions. Hence intelligence is also ascribed to some of the beasts, whenever they are evidently capable
of forethought about their own life.

This also makes it evident that wisdom is not the same as political science. For if
people are to say that [political science] about what is beneficial to themselves [as 30
human beings] counts as wisdom, there will be many types of wisdom [corresponding
to the different species of animals]. For if there is no one medical science about all beings, there is no one [science] about the good of all animals, but a different [science]
about each specific good. [Hence there will be many types of wisdom, contrary to our
assumption that it has the best objects].

And it does not matter if human beings are the best among the animals. For there
are other beings of a far more divine nature than human beings; e.g., the most evi- 1141b
dent are the beings composing the universe.

What we have said makes it clear that wisdom is both scientific knowledge and
understanding about what is by nature most honourable. That is why people say that
Anaxagoras[17] or Thales[18] or that sort of person is wise, but not intelligent, when they 5
see that he is ignorant of what benefits himself. And so they say that what he knows is
extraordinary, amazing, difficult and divine, but useless, because it is not human
goods that he looks for.

INTELLIGENCE COMPARED WITH THE OTHER VIRTUES OF THOUGHT

7

Intelligence, by contrast, is about human concerns, about what is open to delibera- 10
tion. For we say that deliberating well is the function of the intelligent person more
than anyone else; but no one deliberates about what cannot be otherwise, or about
what lacks a goal that is a good achievable in action. The unconditionally good
deliberator is the one whose aim expresses rational calculation in pursuit of the best
good for a human being that is achievable in action.

Nor is intelligence about universals only. It must also come to know particulars, 15
since it is concerned with action and action is about particulars. Hence in other areas
also some people who lack knowledge but have experience are better in action than
some with knowledge. For someone who knows that light meats are digestible and
healthy, but not which sorts of meats are light, will not produce health; the one who 20
knows that bird meats are healthy will be better at producing health. And since intelligence is concerned with action, it must possess both [the universal and the
particular knowledge] or the [particular] more [than the universal]. Here too,
however, [as in medicine] there is a ruling [science].

17. [Anaxagoras (c. 500–428 B.C.) was a Greek philosopher who considered the world-order to have
been produced by reason. His association with Pericles as teacher and friend led to his being brought to trial
by Pericles' opponents on a charge of impiety. He was found guilty by the Athenian jury, but he escaped
and retired to Ionia.]

18. [Thales (c. 636–c. 546 B.C.) is traditionally considered the first of the Greek philosophers. According to legend, he fell into a well while gazing at the stars. He is credited, however, with predicting a solar
eclipse and introducing geometry to the Greeks.]

8

Political science and intelligence are the same state, but their being is not the same.
One part of intelligence about the city is the ruling part; this is legislative science.

The part concerned with particulars [often] monopolizes the name 'political science' that [properly] applies to both parts in common. This part is concerned with action and deliberation, since [it is concerned with decrees] and the decree is to be acted on as the last thing [reached in deliberation]. Hence these people are the only ones who are said to be politically active; for these are the only ones who practise [politics] in the way that handcraftsmen practise [their knowledge].

Now intelligence seems to be concerned most of all with the individual himself; and this [kind of intelligence often] monopolizes the name 'intelligence' that [properly] applies [to all kinds] in common. Among the other kinds one is household science, another legislative, another political, one part of which is deliberative and another judicial.

In fact knowledge of what is [good] for oneself is one species [of intelligence]. But there is much difference [in views] about it.

Someone who knows about himself, and spends his time on his own concerns, seems to be intelligent, while politicians seem to be overactive. Hence Euripides says, 'Surely I cannot be intelligent, when I could have been inactive, numbered among all the many in the army, and have had an equal share. . . . For those who go too far and are too active. . . .'[19]

For people seek what is good for themselves, and suppose that this [inactivity] is the action required [to achieve their good]. Hence this belief has led to the view that these are the intelligent people.

Presumably, however, one's own welfare requires household management and a political system.

Moreover, [another reason for the difference of opinion is this]: It is unclear, and should be examined, how one must manage one's own affairs.

A sign of what has been said [about the unclarity of what intelligence requires] is the fact that whereas young people become accomplished in geometry and mathematics, and wise within these limits, intelligent young people do not seem to be found. The reason is that intelligence is concerned with particulars as well as universals, and particulars become known from experience, but a young person lacks experience, since some length of time is needed to produce it.

Indeed [to understand the difficulty and importance of experience] we might consider why a boy can become accomplished in mathematics, but not in wisdom or natural science. Surely it is because mathematical objects are reached through abstraction, while the origins of the other sciences are reached from experience. Young people, then, [lacking experience], have no real conviction in these other sciences, but only say the words, whereas the nature of mathematical objects is clear to them.

Moreover [intelligence is difficult because it is deliberative and] deliberation may be in error about either the universal or the particular. For [we may wrongly suppose] either that all sorts of heavy water are bad or that this water is heavy.

19. [These lines, spoken by Odysseus, come from the lost play *Philoctetes*.]

Intelligence is evidently not scientific knowledge; for, as we said, it concerns the last thing [i.e. the particular], since this is what is done in action. Hence it is opposed   25
to understanding. For understanding is about the [first] terms, [those] that have no account; but intelligence is about the last thing, an object of perception, not of scientific knowledge.

This is not the perception of special objects, but the sort by which we perceive that the last among mathematical objects is a triangle; for it will stop here too. This is another species [of perception than perception of special objects]; but it is still perception more than intelligence is.   30

GOOD DELIBERATION

9

Inquiry and deliberation are different, since deliberation is a type of inquiry. We must also grasp what good deliberation is, and see whether it is some sort of scientific knowledge, or belief, or good guessing, or some other kind of thing.

First of all, then, it is not scientific knowledge. For we do not inquire for what we   1142b
already know; but good deliberation is a type of deliberation, and a deliberator inquires and rationally calculates.

Moreover, it is not good guessing either. For good guessing involves no reasoning, and is done quickly; but we deliberate a long time, and it is said that we must act quickly on the result of our deliberation, but deliberate slowly. Moreover, quick   5
thinking is different from good deliberation, and quick thinking is a kind of good guessing.

Nor is good deliberation any sort of belief. Rather, since the bad deliberator is in error, and the good deliberator deliberates correctly, good deliberation is clearly some sort of correctness.

But it is not correctness in scientific knowledge or in belief. For there is no correct-   10
ness in scientific knowledge, since there is no error in it either; and correctness in belief consists in truth, [but correctness in deliberation does not].

Further, everything about which there is belief is already determined, [while what is deliberated about is not yet determined].

However, good deliberation requires reason; hence the remaining possibility is that it belongs to thought. For thought is not yet assertion: [and this is why it is not belief]. For belief is not inquiry, but already an assertion; but in deliberating, either well or badly, we inquire for something and rationally calculate about it.   15

But since good deliberation is a certain sort of correctness in deliberation, we must inquire what [this correctness (is) and what it is correctness about].

Now since correctness has several types, clearly not every type will be good deliberation. For the incontinent or base person will use rational calculation to reach what he proposes to see, and so will have deliberated correctly [if that is all it takes], but will have got himself a great evil. Having deliberated well seems, on the contrary,   20
to be some sort of good; for the sort of correctness in deliberation that makes it good deliberation is the sort that reaches a good.

However, we can reach a good as well [as an evil] by a false inference, so that we reach the right thing to do, but by the wrong steps, when the middle term is false.

25 Hence this type of deliberation, leading us by the wrong steps to the right thing to do, is not enough for good deliberation either.

Moreover, one person may deliberate a long time before reaching the right thing to do, while another reaches it quickly. Nor, then, is the first condition enough for good deliberation; good deliberation is correctness that reflects what is beneficial, about the right thing, in the right way and at the right time.

Further, our deliberation may be unconditionally good or good only to the extent

30 that it promotes some [limited] end. Hence unconditionally good deliberation is the sort that correctly promotes the unconditional end [i.e. the highest good], while the [limited] sort is the sort that correctly promotes some [limited] end.

Hence, if having deliberated well is proper to an intelligent person, good deliberation will be the type of correctness that expresses what is expedient for promoting the end about which intelligence is true supposition.

COMPREHENSION

10

We say that comprehension, i.e. good comprehension, makes people comprehend

1143a and comprehend well. It is not the same as scientific knowledge in general. Nor is it the same as belief, since, if it were, everyone would have comprehension. Nor is it any one of the specific sciences [with its own specific area], in the way that medicine is about what is healthy or geometry is about magnitudes.

For comprehension is neither about what always is and is unchanging nor about

5 just anything that comes to be. It is about what we might be puzzled about and might deliberate about. Hence it is about the same things as intelligence.

Still, comprehension is not the same as intelligence. For intelligence is prescriptive, since its end is what must be done or not done in action, whereas comprehension only

10 judges. (For comprehension and good comprehension are the same; and so are people with comprehension and with good comprehension.)

Comprehension is neither having intelligence nor acquiring it. Rather, it is similar to the way learning is called comprehending when someone applies scientific knowledge. In the same way comprehension consists in the application of belief to

15 judge someone else's remarks on a question that concerns intelligence, and moreover it must judge them finely since judging well is the same as judging finely. And that is how the name 'comprehension' was attached to the comprehension that makes people have good comprehension. It is derived from the comprehension found in learning; for we often call learning comprehending.

CONSIDERATION

We say that [the state] called consideration makes people considerate and makes

them have consideration; it is the correct judgment of the decent person. A sign of   20
this is our saying that the decent person more than others is considerate, and that it is
decent to be considerate about some things. Considerateness is the correct consideration that judges what is decent; and correct consideration judges what is true.

INTELLIGENCE AND THE OTHER VIRTUES OF THOUGHT CONCERNED WITH PARTICULARS

11

It is reasonable for all these states to tend to the same point. For we ascribe considera-   25
tion, comprehension, intelligence and understanding to the same people, and say
that these have consideration, and thereby understanding, and that they are intelligent and comprehending. For all these capacities are about the last things, i.e.
particulars. Moreover, someone has comprehension and good consideration, or has
considerateness in his judgments about the concerns of the intelligent person; for   30
what is decent is the common concern of all good people in relations with other
people.

[These states are all concerned with particulars because] whatever is done in action
is one of the particular and last things. For the intelligent person also must recognize
[what is done in action], while comprehension and consideration are concerned with
what is done in action, and this is one of the last things.   35

Understanding is also concerned with the last things, and in both directions. For
there is understanding, not a rational account, about the first terms and the last.

In demonstrations understanding is about the unchanging terms that are first.   1143b

In [premises] about what is done in action understanding is about the last term, the
one that admits of being otherwise, and hence about the minor premise. For these
last terms are the origins of the end to be aimed at, since universals are reached from
particulars. We must, then, have perception of these particulars, and this perception   5
is understanding.

Hence these states actually seem to grow naturally, so that while no one seems to
have natural wisdom, people seem to have natural consideration, comprehension and
judgment. A sign [of their apparent natural character] is our thinking that they also
correspond to someone's age, and the fact that understanding and consideration
belong to a certain age, as though nature were the cause.   10

[Hence understanding is both origin and end. For demonstrations are from these
things, and about them.]

We must attend, then to the undemonstrated remarks and beliefs of experienced
and older people or of intelligent people, no less than to demonstrations. For these
people see correctly because experience has given them their eye.

We have said, then, what intelligence and wisdom are; what each is about; and   15
that each is the virtue of a different part of the soul.

Puzzles About Intelligence and Wisdom

12

20   Someone might, however, be puzzled about what use they are.

For wisdom is not concerned with any sort of coming into being, and hence will not study any source of human happiness.

25   Admittedly intelligence will study this; but what do we need it for?

For knowledge of what is healthy or fit — i.e. of what results from the state, not of what produces it — makes us no readier to act appropriately if we are already healthy; for having the science of medicine or gymnastics makes us no readier to act appropriately. Similarly, intelligence is the science of what is just, fine and good for a human being; but this is what the good man does; and if we are already good, knowledge of them makes us no readier to act appropriately, since virtues are states activated in actions.

If we concede that intelligence is not useful for this, should we say it is useful for
30   becoming good? In that case it will be no use to those who are already excellent. Nor, however, will it be any use to those who are not. For it will not matter to them whether they have it themselves or take the advice of others who have it. The advice of others will be quite adequate for us, just as it is with health, when we wish to be healthy, but still do not learn medical science.

Besides, it would seem absurd for intelligence, inferior as it is to wisdom, to control
35   it as a superior. [But this will be the result,] since the science that produces also rules and prescribes about its product.

1144a   We must discuss these questions; for so far we have only gone through the puzzles about them.

First of all, let us state that both intelligence and wisdom must be choiceworthy in themselves, even if neither produces anything at all; for each is the virtue of one of the two [rational] parts [of the soul].

Second, they do produce something. Wisdom produces happiness, not in the way
5   that medical science produces health, but in the way that health produces [health]. For since wisdom is a part of virtue as a whole, it makes us happy because it is a state that we possess and activate.

Further, we fulfil our function in so far as we have intelligence and virtue of character; for virtue makes the goal correct, and intelligence makes what promotes
10   the goal [correct]. The fourth part of the soul, the nutritive part, has no such virtue [related to our function], since no action is up to it to do or not to do.

13

To answer the claim that intelligence will make us no readier to do fine and just ac-
15   tions, we must begin from a little further back [in our discussion].

Here is where we begin. We say that some people who do just actions are not yet thereby just, if, e.g., they do the actions prescribed by the laws, either unwillingly because of ignorance, or because of some other end, not because of the actions themselves, even though they do the right actions, those that the excellent person ought to do. Equally, however, it is seemingly possible for someone to do each type of action in the state that makes him a good person, i.e. because of decision and for the 20 sake of the actions themselves.

Now virtue makes the decision correct; but the actions that are naturally to be done to fulfil the decision are the concern not of virtue, but of another capacity. We must get to know them more clearly before continuing our discussion.

There is a capacity, called cleverness, of the sort that can do the actions that tend 25 to promote the assumed goal, and can fully achieve them. If, then, the goal is fine, cleverness is praiseworthy, and if the goal is base, cleverness is unscrupulousness; hence both intelligent and unscrupulous people are called clever.

Intelligence is not the same as this capacity [of cleverness], though it requires [clev- 30 erness]. Intelligence, this eye of the soul, cannot reach its fully developed state without virtue, as we have said and as is clear. For inferences about actions have an origin: 'Since the [highest] end and the best good is this sort of thing', whatever it actually is — let it be any old thing for the sake of argument. And this [best good] is apparent only to the good person; for vice perverts us and produces false views about the origins 35 of actions. 1144b

Evidently, then, we cannot be intelligent without being good.

We must, then, also examine virtue over again. For virtue is similar [in this way] to intelligence; as intelligence is related to cleverness, not the same but similar, so natural virtue is related to full virtue.

For each of us seems to possess his type of character to some extent by nature, since 5 we are just, brave, prone to temperance, or have another feature, immediately from birth. However, we still search for some other condition that will be fully good, and expect to possess these features in another way.

For these natural states belong to children and to beasts as well [as to adults], but without understanding they are evidently harmful. At any rate, this much is seeming- 10 ly clear; just as a heavy body moving around sightless suffers a heavy fall because it has no sight, so it is with virtue. [A naturally well-endowed person without under- standing will harm himself.] But if someone acquires understanding, he improves in his action; and the state he now has, though still similar [to the natural one], will now be virtue to the full extent.

And so, just as there are two sorts of conditions, cleverness and intelligence, in the part of the soul that has belief, so also there are two in the part that has character, 15 natural virtue and full virtue. And full virtue is the one that we cannot acquire without intelligence.

This is why some say that all the virtues are [instances of] intelligence, and why Socrates' inquiries were in one way correct, and in another way in error. For since he 20 thought all the virtues are [instances of] intelligence, he was in error; but since he thought they all require intelligence, he was right.

Here is a sign of this: Whenever people now define virtue, and have said what state it is and what it is related to, they all add that it is the state that expresses correct reason. Now correct reason is reason that expresses intelligence; seemingly, then, they 25 all in a way intuitively believe that the sort of state that is virtue is the state that ex- presses intelligence.

Here we must change direction a little. For it is not merely the state expressing correct reason, but the state associated with correct reason, that is virtue. And it is intelligence that is correct reason in this area. Socrates, then, thought that the virtues

30 are [instances of] reason because he thought they are all [instances of] knowledge, whereas we think they are associated with reason.

What we have said, then, makes it clear that we cannot be fully good without intelligence, or intelligent without virtue of character.

In this way we can also solve the dialectical argument that someone might use to show that the virtues are separated from each other. For, [it is argued], since the same

35 person is not naturally best suited for all the virtues, someone will already have one virtue before he has got another.

This is indeed possible with the natural virtues. It is not possible, however, with

1145a [the full virtues], which someone must have to be called unconditionally good; for as soon as he has intelligence, which is a single state, he has all the virtues as well.

And clearly, even if intelligence were useless in action, we would need it because it is the virtue of this part of the soul, and because the decision will not be correct

5 without intelligence or without virtue. For virtue makes us reach the end in our action, while intelligence makes us reach what promotes the end.

Moreover, intelligence does not control wisdom or the better part of the soul, just as medical science does not control health. For it does not use health, but only aims to bring health into being; hence it prescribes for the sake of health, but does not

10 prescribe to health. Besides, [saying that intelligence controls wisdom] would be like saying that political science rules the gods because it prescribes about everything in the city.

BOOK SEVEN

Continence and Incontinence

Conditions Superior to Virtue, Inferior to Vice, and Between Virtue and Vice

1

15 Next we should make a new beginning, and say that there are three conditions of character to be avoided — vice, incontinence and bestiality. The contraries of two of these are clear; we call one virtue and the other continence.

The contrary to bestiality is most suitably called virtue superior to us, a heroic, indeed divine, sort of virtue. Thus Homer made Priam say that Hector was remarkably good; 'nor did he look as though he were the child of a mortal man, but of a god.'[20] Moreover, so they say, human beings become gods because of exceedingly great virtue.

20. [The quotation is from the *Iliad*.]

Clearly, then, this is the sort of state that would be opposite to the bestial state. For   25
indeed, just as a beast has neither virtue nor vice, so neither does a god, but the god's
state is more honourable than virtue, and the beast's belongs to some kind different
from vice.

Now it is rare that a divine man exists. This is what the Spartans habitually call
him; whenever they very much admire someone, they say he is a divine man. Similar-   30
ly, the bestial person is also rare among human beings. He is most often found in
foreigners; but some bestial features also result from diseases and deformities. We
also use this as a term of reproach for people whose vice exceeds the human level.

We must make some remarks about this condition later. We have discussed vice   35
earlier. We must now discuss incontinence, weakness and softness, softness and self-
indulgence, and also continence and resistance; for we must not suppose that con-   1145b
tinence and incontinence are concerned with the same states as virtue and vice, or
that they belong to a different kind.

As in the other cases we must set out the appearance, and first of all go through the
puzzles. In this way we must prove the common beliefs about these ways of being af-   5
fected — ideally, all the common beliefs, but if not all, then most of them, and the
most important. For if the objections are solved, and the common beliefs are left, it
will be an adequate proof.

COMMON BELIEFS ABOUT CONTINENCE AND INCONTINENCE

Continence and resistance seem to be good and praiseworthy conditions, while incontinence and weakness seem to be base and blameworthy conditions.   10

The continent person seems to be the same as the one who abides by his rational
calculation; and the incontinent person seems to be the same as the one who strays
from it.

The incontinent person knows that his actions are base, but does them because of
his feelings, while the continent person knows that his appetites are base, but because
of reason does not follow them.

People think the temperate person is continent and resistant. Some think that every   15
continent and resistant person is temperate, while others do not. Some people say the
incontinent person is intemperate and the intemperate incontinent, with no distinction; others say they are different.

Sometimes it is said that an intelligent person cannot be incontinent; but
sometimes it is said that some people are intelligent and clever, but still incontinent.

Further, people are called incontinent about emotion, honour and gain.   20

PUZZLES ABOUT THE COMMON BELIEFS

2

We might be puzzled about the sort of correct supposition someone has when he acts
incontinently.

First of all, some say he cannot have knowledge at the time. For it would be terri-

ble, Socrates thought, for knowledge to be in someone, but mastered by something
25   else, and dragged around like a slave. For Socrates fought against the account [of in-
continence] in general, in the belief that there is no incontinence; for no one, he
thought, supposes while he acts that his action conflicts with what is best; our action
conflicts with what is best only because we are ignorant [of the conflict].

This argument, then, contradicts things that appear clearly. If ignorance causes
the incontinent person to be affected as he is, then we must look for the type of ig-
30   norance that it turns out to be; for it is evident, at any rate, that before he is affected
the person who acts incontinently does not think [he should do the action he eventually does].

Some people concede some of this, but reject some of it. For they agree that
nothing is superior to knowledge, but deny that no one's action conflicts with what
has seemed better to him. Hence they say that when the incontinent person is over-
35   come by pleasure he has only belief, not knowledge.

In that case, however, if he has belief, not knowledge, and what resists is not a
1146a   strong supposition, but only a mild one, such as people have when they are in doubt,
we will pardon failure to abide by these beliefs against strong appetites. In fact,
however, we do not pardon vice, or any other blameworthy condition [and incontinence is one of these].

5   Then is it intelligence that resists, since it is the strongest? This is absurd. For on
this view the same person will be both intelligent and incontinent; and no one would
say that the intelligent person is the sort to do the worst actions willingly.

Besides, we have shown earlier that the intelligent person acts [on his knowledge],
since he is concerned with the last things, [i.e. particulars], and that he has the other
virtues.

10   Further, if the continent person must have strong and base appetites, the
temperate person will not be continent nor the continent person temperate. For the
temperate person is not the sort to have either excessive or base appetites; but [the
continent person] must have both.

For if his appetites are good, the state that prevents him from following them must
15   be base, so that not all continence is excellent. If, on the other hand, the appetites are
weak and not base, continence is nothing impressive; and if they are base and weak, it
is nothing great.

Besides, if continence makes someone prone to abide by every belief, it is bad, if,
e.g., it makes him abide by a false as well [as a true] belief.

And if incontinence makes someone prone to abandon every belief, there will be an
20   excellent type of incontinence. Neoptolemus, e.g., in Sophocles' *Philoctetes* is
praiseworthy when, after being persuaded by Odysseus, he does not abide by [his
resolve], because he feels pain at lying.

Besides, the sophistical argument is a puzzle. For [the sophists] wish to refute an
[opponent, by showing] that his views have paradoxical results, so that they will be
clever in encounters. Hence the inference that results in a puzzle; for thought is tied
25   up, since it does not want to stand still because the conclusion is displeasing, but it
cannot advance because it cannot solve the argument.

A certain argument, then, concludes that foolishness associated with incontinence
is virtue. For incontinence makes someone act contrary to what he suppoes [is right];

but since he supposes that good things are evil and that it is wrong to do them, he will   30
do the good actions, not the evil.

Further, if someone acts to pursue what is pleasant because this is what he is persuaded and decides to do, he seems to be better than someone who acts not because of rational calculation, but because of incontinence.

For the first person is the easier to cure, because he might be persuaded otherwise;
but the incontinent person illustrates the proverb 'If water chokes us, what must we   35
drink to wash it down?' For if he had been persuaded to do the action he does, he   1146b
would have stopped when he was persuaded to act otherwise; but in fact, though
already persuaded to act otherwise, he still acts [wrongly].

Further, is there incontinence and continence about everything? If so, who is the
simple incontinent? For no one has all the types of incontinence, but we say that some
people are simply incontinent.   5

These, then, are the sorts of puzzles that arise. We must undermine some of these
claims, and leave others intact; for the solution of the puzzle is the discovery.

3

First, then, we must examine whether the incontinent has knowledge or not, and in
what way he has it. Second, what should we take to be the incontinent and the conti-   10
nent person's area of concern—every pleasure and pain, or some definite subclass?
Are the continent and the resistant person the same or different? Similarly we must
deal with the other questions that are relevant to this study.

THE SCOPE OF INCONTINENCE

We begin the examination with this question: Are the continent and the incontinent   15
person distinguished [from others] (i) by their concerns, or (ii) by their attitudes to
these? In other words, is the incontinent person incontinent (i) only by having these
concerns, or instead (ii) by having this attitude; or instead (iii) by both?

[Surely (iii) is right.] For [(i) is insufficient] since the simple incontinent is not concerned with everything, but with the same things as the intemperate person.   20
Moreover, [(ii) is insufficient] since he is not incontinent simply by being inclined
towards these things—that would make incontinence the same as intemperance.
Rather [as (iii) implies], he is incontinent by being inclined towards them in this way.
For the intemperate person acts on decision when he is led on, since he thinks it is
right in every case to pursue the pleasant thing at hand; but the incontinent person
thinks it is wrong to pursue it, yet still pursues it.

WHAT SORT OF KNOWLEDGE DOES THE INCONTINENT PERSON HAVE OR LACK?

It is claimed that the incontinent person's action conflicts with true belief, not with   25
knowledge. But whether it is knowledge or belief that he has does not matter to the
discussion. For some people with belief are in no doubt, but think they have exact
knowledge.

If, then, it is the weakness of their conviction that makes people with belief, not people with knowledge, act in conflict with their supposition, it follows that
30   knowledge will be no different from belief; for, as Heracleitus makes clear, some people's convictions about what they believe are no weaker than other people's convictions about what they know.

But we speak of knowing in two ways, and ascribe it both to someone who has it without using it and to someone who is using it. Hence it will matter whether someone has the knowledge that his action is wrong, without attending to his knowledge, or he
35   both has and attends to it. For this second case seems extraordinary, but wrong action when he does not attend to his knowledge does not seem extraordinary.

1147a   Besides, since there are two types of premises, someone's action may well conflict with his knowledge if he has both types of premises, but uses only the universal premise and not the partial premise. For [the partial premise states the particulars and] it is particular actions that are done.

Moreover, [in both types of premises] there are different types of universal, (a) one type referring to the agent himself, and (b) the other referring to the object. Perhaps, e.g., someone knows that (a1) dry things benefit every human being, and that (a2) he
5   himself is a human being, or that (b1) this sort of thing is dry; but he either does not have or does not activate the knowledge that (b2) this particular thing is of this sort.

Hence these ways [of knowing and not knowing] make such a remarkable difference that it seems quite intelligible [for someone acting against his knowledge] to have the one sort of knowledge [without (b2)], but astounding if he has the other sort [including (b2)].

10   Besides, human beings may have knowledge in a way different from those we have described. For we see that having those we have described. For we see that having without using includes different types of having; hence some people, e.g. those asleep or mad or drunk, both have knowledge in a way and do not have it.

Moreover, this is the condition of those affected by strong feelings. For emotions,
15   sexual appetites and some conditions of this sort clearly [both disturb knowledge and] disturb the body as well, and even produce fits of madness in some people.

Clearly, then [since incontinents are also affected by strong feelings], we should say that they have knowledge in a way similar to these people.

Saying the words that come from knowledge is no sign [of fully having it]. For peo-
20   ple affected in these ways even recite demonstrations and verses of Empedocles. Further, those who have just learnt something do not yet know it, though they string the words together; for it must grow into them, and this needs time.

Hence we must suppose that incontinents say the words in the way that actors do.

HOW INCONTINENCE HAPPENS

25   Further, we may also look at the cause in the following way, referring to [human] nature. One belief (a) is universal; the other (b) is about particulars, and because they are particulars perception controls them. And in the cases where these two beliefs result in (c) one belief, it is necessary in purely theoretical beliefs for the soul to affirm what has been concluded, and in beliefs about production (d) to act at once on what has been concluded.

If, e.g., (a) everything sweet must be tasted, and (b) this, some one particular   30
thing, is sweet, it is necessary (d) for someone who is able and unhindered also to act
on this at the same time.

Suppose, then, that someone has (a) the universal belief, and it hinders him from
tasting; he has (b) the second belief, that everything sweet is pleasant and this is
sweet, and this belief (b) is active; and he also has appetite. Hence the belief (c) tells
him to avoid this, but appetite leads him on, since it is capable of moving each of the   35
[bodily] parts.

The result, then, is that in a way reason and belief make him act incontinently.   1147b
The belief (b) is contrary to correct reason (a), but only coincidentally, not in itself.
For it is the appetite, not the belief, that is contrary [in itself to correct reason].

Hence beasts are not incontinent, because they have no universal supposition, but
[only] appearance and memory of particulars.   5

How is the ignorance resolved, so that the incontinent person recovers his
knowledge? The same account that applies to someone drunk or asleep applies here
too, and is not special to this way of being affected. We must hear it from the natural
scientists.

And since the last premise (b) is a belief about something perceptible, and controls
action, this must be what the incontinent person does not have when he is being af-   10
fected. Or rather the way he has it is not knowledge of it, but, as we saw, [merely] saying the words, as the drunk says the words of Empedocles.

Further, since the last term does not seem to be universal, or expressive of
knowledge in the same way as the universal term, even the result Socrates was looking   15
for seemingly comes about. For the knowledge that is present when someone is affected by incontinence, and that is dragged about because he is affected, is not the
sort that seems to be knowledge to the full extent [in (c)], but only perceptual
knowlege [in (b)].

So much, then, for knowing and not knowing, and for how it is possible to know
and still to act incontinently.

SIMPLE INCONTINENCE

4

Next we must say whether anyone is simply incontinent, or all incontinents are incon-   20
tinent in some partial way; and if someone is simply incontinent, we must say what
sorts of things he is incontinent about.

First of all, both the continent and resistant person and the incontinent and weak
person are evidently concerned with pleasures and pains.

Some sources of pleasure are necessary; others are choiceworthy in themselves, but
can be taken to excess. The necessary one are the bodily conditions, i.e. those that   25
concern food, sexual intercourse, and the sorts of bodily conditions that we took to
concern temperance and intemperance. Other things are not necessary, but are
choiceworthy in themselves, e.g. victory, honour, wealth and similar good and pleas-   30
ant things.

When people go to excess, in conflict with the correct reason in them, in the pursuit of these sources of pleasure, we do not call them simply incontinent, but add the condition that they are incontinent about wealth, gain, honour or emotion, not simply unconditionally incontinent. For we assume that they are different, and called incontinent [only] because of a similarity, just as the Olympic victor named Human was different, since for him the common account [of human being] was only a little different from his special one, but it was different none the less.

A sign in favour of what we say is the fact that incontinence is blamed not only as an error but as a vice, either unconditional or partial, while none of these conditions [is blamed as a vice].

Now consider the people concerned with the bodily gratifications, those that we take to concern the temperate and the intemperate person. Some of these people go to excess in pursuing these pleasant things and avoiding painful things — hunger, thirst, heat, cold and all that concerns touch and taste — not, however, because they have decided on it, but in conflict with their decision and thought.

These are the people called simply incontinent, not with the added condition that they are incontinent about, e.g., anger.

A sign of this is the fact that people are also called soft about these [bodily] pleasures, but not about any of the non-necessary ones.

This is also why we include the incontinent and the intemperate person, and the continent and the temperate person, in the same class, but do not include any of the partial incontinents. It is because the incontinent and the intemperate person are concerned in a way with the same pleasures and pains. In fact they are concerned with the same things, but not in the same way; the intemperate person decides on them, but the incontinent person does not.

Hence, if someone has no appetites, or slight ones, but still pursues excesses and avoids moderate pains, we will take him to be more intemperate than we would if he did it because he had intense appetites. For think of the lengths he would go to if he also acquired vigorous appetites and felt severe pains at the lack of necessities.

Some pleasant things are naturally choiceworthy, some naturally to be avoided, some in between, as we divided them earlier. Hence some appetites and pleasures are for fine and excellent kinds of things, e.g. wealth, profit, victory and honour. About all these and about the things in between people are blamed not for feeling an appetite and love for them, but for doing so in a particular way, namely to excess.

Some people are overcome by, or pursue, some of these naturally fine and good things to an extent that conflicts with reason, e.g. they take honour or children or parents more seriously than is right. For though these are certainly good and people are praised for taking them seriously, still excess about them is also possible. [It is excessive] if someone fights as Niobe fought [for her children], even with the gods, or regards his father as Satyrus, nicknamed the Fatherlover, did — for he seemed to be excessively silly about it.[21]

There is no vice here, for the reason we have given, since each of these things is naturally choiceworthy for itself, though excess about them is bad and to be avoided.

---

21. According to Greek mythology, Niobe boasted that, with her six sons and six daughters (or, according to another account, seven sons and seven daughters), she was at least the equal of the goddess Leto, who had borne only two children, the twins Apollo and Artemis. Thereupon the twins killed all Niobe's children, and Zeus turned Niobe into stone. Satyrus is said to have deified his father after his death.

Similarly, there is no incontinence here either, since incontinence is not merely to be   5
avoided, but also blameworthy [and these conditions are not].

But because it is a similar way of being affected, people call it incontinence, adding the condition that it is incontinence about this or that. Just so they call someone a
bad doctor or a bad actor, though they would never call him simply bad, since each
of these conditions is not vice, but only similar to it by analogy.   10

It is likewise clear that the only condition that we should take to be continence or
incontinence is the one concerned with what concerns temperance and intemperance. We mentioned emotion because of the similarity [to simple incontinence], and
hence add the condition that someone is incontinent about emotion, as when we say
someone is incontinent about honour or gain.

5

Some things are naturally pleasant, and some of these are unconditionally pleasant,   15
while others reflect differences between kinds of animals and of human beings. Other
things are not naturally pleasant, but deformities or habits or degenerate natures
make them pleasant; and we can see states concerned with each of these that are
similar to [states concerned with naturally pleasant things].

By bestial states I mean e.g. the female human being who is said to tear pregnant   20
women apart and devour the children; or some of the savage people around the Pon-
tus who are reputed to enjoy raw flesh and human flesh, while some trade their
children to each other to feast on; or what is said about Phalaris.[22] These states are
bestial.

Other states are caused by attacks of disease, and some by fits of madness—e.g. the   25
person who sacrificed his mother and ate her, and the one who ate the liver of his
fellow-slave.

Other states result from diseased conditions or from habit—e.g. plucking hairs,
chewing nails, even coal and earth, and besides these sexual intercourse between
males. For in some people these result from [a diseased] nature, in others from habit,   30
as, e.g., in those who have suffered wanton [sexual] assault since their childhood.

Whenever nature is the cause, no one would call these people incontinent, any
more than women would be called incontinent for being mounted rather than
mounting. The same applies to those who are in a diseased state because of habit.

Each of these states, then, is outside the limits of vice, just as bestiality is. If some-   1149a
one who has them overcomes them or is overcome by them, that is not simple [con-
tinence or] incontinence, but the type so called from similarity, just as someone who is
overcome by emotion should be called incontinent in his feelings, but not [simply]
incontinent.

Among all the excesses of foolishness, cowardice, intemperance and irritability   5
some are bestial, some diseased. If, e.g., someone's natural character makes him
afraid of anything, even a mouse, he is a coward with a bestial sort of cowardice.
Another person was afraid of a weasel because of an attack of disease.

22. [Phalaris was a sixth-century B.C. Sicilian tyrant known for his cruelty. He was said to have roasted
victims alive inside a brass bull.]

10   Among foolish people also those who naturally lack reason and live only by perception are bestial, as some races of distant foreigners are. Those who are foolish because of attacks of disease, e.g. epilepsy, or because of fits of madness, are diseased.

15   Sometimes it is possible to have some of these conditions without being overcome—e.g. if Phalaris had an appetite to eat a child or for some bizarre sexual pleasure, but restrained it. It is also possible to be overcome by these conditions and not merely to have them.

      One sort of vice is human, and this is called simple vice. Another sort is called vice with an added condition, and is said to be bestial or diseased vice, but not simple vice. Similarly, then, it is also clear that one sort of incontinence is bestial, another dis-
20   eased, but only the incontinence corresponding to human intemperance is simple incontinence.

      It is clear, then, that incontinence and continence apply only to the concerns of intemperance and temperance, and for other things there is another form of incontinence, so called by transference of the name, and not simply.

SIMPLE INCONTINENCE COMPARED WITH INCONTINENCE IN EMOTION

6

25   Moreover, let us observe, incontinence about emotion is less shameful than incontinence about appetites.

      For, first of all, emotion seemingly hears reason a bit, though it mishears it. It is like over-hasty servants who run out before they have heard all their instructions, and then carry them out wrongly, or dogs who bark at any noise at all, before in-
30   vestigating to see if it is a friend. In the same way, since emotion is naturally hot and hasty, it hears, but does not hear the instruction, and rushes off to exact a penalty. For reason or appearance has shown that we are being slighted or wantonly insulted; and emotion, as though it had inferred that it is right to fight this sort of thing, is ir-
35   ritated at once. Appetite, however, only needs reason or perception to say that this is pleasant, and it rushes off for gratification.

1149b Hence emotion follows reason in a way, but appetite does not. Therefore [incontinence about appetite] is more shameful. For if someone is incontinent about emotion, he is overcome by reason in a way; but if he is incontinent about appetite, he is overcome by appetite, not by reason.

5   Besides, it is more pardonable to follow natural desires, since it is also more pardonable to follow those natural appetites that are shared by everyone and to the extent that they are shared. Now emotion and irritability are more natural than the excessive and unnecessary appetites. It is just as the son said in his defence for beating his father; 'He beat his father; and his father beat *his* father before that'; and point-
10   ing to his young son, he said, 'And he will beat me when he becomes a man; it runs in our family.' Similarly, the father being dragged by his son kept urging him to stop at the front door, since that was as far as he had dragged his own father.

      Moreover, those who plot more are more unjust. But the emotional person does not
15   plot, and neither does emotion; it is open. Appetite, however, is like what they say about Aphrodite, 'trick-weaving Cypris', and what Homer says about her em-

broidered girdle: 'Blandishment, which steals the wits even of the very intelligent.'[23]

If, then, incontinence about appetite is more unjust and more shameful than incontinence about emotion, it is simple incontinence, and vice in a way. 20

Further, no one feels pain when he commits wanton aggression; but whatever someone does from anger, he feels pain when he does it, whereas the wanton aggressor does it with pleasure. Now if whatever more justly provokes anger is more unjust, incontinence caused by the appetite is more unjust, since emotion involves no wanton aggression.

INCONTINENCE COMPARED WITH INTEMPERANCE

It is clear, then, how incontinence about appetites is more shameful than incontinence about emotion, and that continence and incontinence are about bodily appetites and pleasures. Now we must grasp the varieties of these. 25

As we said at the beginning, some appetites are human and natural in kind and degree, some bestial, some caused by deformities and diseases. Temperance and intemperance are concerned only with the first of these. 30

This is also why we do not call beasts either temperate or intemperate, except by transference of the name, if one kind of animal exceeds another altogether in wanton aggression, destructiveness and ravenousness. For beasts have neither decision nor rational calculation, but are outside [rational] nature, as the madmen among human beings are. 35 / 1150a

Bestiality is less grave than vice, but more frightening; for the best part is not corrupted, as it is in a human being, but absent altogether. Hence a comparison between the two is like a comparison between a soulless and an ensouled thing to see which is worse. For in each case the badness of something that lacks an internal origin of its badness is less destructive than the badness of something that has such an internal origin; and understanding is such an internal origin. It is similar, then, to a comparison between the injustice [of a beast] and an unjust human being; for in a way each [of these] is worse, since an evil human being can do innumerably more evils than a beast. 5

7

Now consider the pleasures and pains arising through touch and taste, and consider the appetites for the pleasures, and the aversions from the pains. Earlier we defined temperance and intemperance as concerned with these. It is possible for someone to be in the state where he is overcome, even by [pleasure and pains] which most people overcome, and possible to overcome even those that overcome most people. The person who is prone to be overcome by pleasures is incontinent; the one who overcomes is continent; the one overcome by pains is weak; and the one who overcomes them is resistant. The state of most people is in between, though indeed they may lean more towards the worse states. 10 / 15

Now some pleasures are necessary and some are not. [The necessary ones are necessary] to a certain extent, while their excesses and deficiencies are not. The same is true for appetites and pains.

23. [The quotation is from the *Iliad*.]

20   One person pursues excesses of pleasant things because they are excesses and
because he decides on it, for themselves and not for some further result. He is intemperate; for he is bound to have no regrets, and so is incurable, since someone
without regrets is incurable.

The one who is deficient is his opposite, while the intermediate one is temperate.
The same is true for the one who avoids bodily pains not because he is overcome, but
because he decides on it.

25   One of those who does not [act on] decision is led on because of pleasure; the other
is led on because he is avoiding the pain that comes from appetite; hence these two
differ from each other.

Now it would seem to everyone that someone who does a shameful action from no
appetite or a weak one is worse than if he does it from an intense appetite; and
similarly if he wounds another not from anger, he is worse than if he wounds from

30   anger. For [if he can do such evil when he is unaffected by feeling], what would he
have done if he had been strongly affected? Hence the intemperate person is worse
than the incontinent.

One of the states mentioned [being overcome by pain] is more a species of softness,
while the other person is intemperate. The continent person is opposed to the incontinent, and the resistant to the soft. For resistance consists in holding out, and con-

35   tinence in overcoming, but holding out is different from overcoming, just as not being defeated differs from winning; hence continence is more choiceworthy than
resistance.

1150b Someone who is deficient in withstanding what most people withstand, and are
capable of withstanding, is soft and self-indulgent; for self-indulgence is a kind of
softness. This person trails his cloak to avoid the labour and pain of lifting it, and im-

5   itates an invalid, though he does not think he is miserable, but is [merely] similar to a
miserable person.

It is similar with continence and incontinence also. For it is not surprising if someone is overcome by strong and excessive pleasures or pains; on the contrary, this is
pardonable, provided he struggles against them — like Theodectes' Philoctetes bitten

10   by the snake, or Carcinus' Cercyon in the *Alope*,[24] and like those who are trying to
restrain their laughter and burst out laughing all at once, as happened to
Xenophantes.[25] But it is surprising if someone is overcome by what most people can
resist, and is incapable of withstanding it, not because of his hereditary nature or

15   because of disease — as, e.g., the Scythian king's softness is hereditary, and as the
female is distinguished [by softness] from the male.

The lover of amusements also seems to be intemperate, but in fact he is self-
indulgent. For amusement is a relaxation, since it is a release, and the lover of amusement is one of those who go to excess here.

20   One type of incontinence is impetuosity, while another is weakness. For the weak
person deliberates, but then his feeling makes him abandon the result of his deliberation; but the impetuous person is led on by his feelings because he has not
deliberated. For some people are like those who are not tickled themselves if they

24. [Theodectes and Carcinus were both fourth-century Athenian tragic poets.]

25. [Xenophantes is supposed to have been a musician in the court of Alexander the Great.]

tickle someone else first; if they see and notice something in advance, and rouse themselves and their rational calculation, they are not overcome by feelings, no matter whether something is pleasant or painful. 25

Quick-tempered and ardent people are most prone to be impetuous incontinents. For in quick-tempered people the appetite is so fast, and in ardent people so intense, that they do not wait for reason, because they tend to follow appearance.

8

The intemperate person, as we said, is not prone to regret, since he abides by his decision [when he acts]. But every incontinent is prone to regret. Hence the truth is not what we said in raising the puzzles, but in fact the intemperate person is incurable, and the incontinent curable. 30

For vice resembles diseases such as dropsy or consumption, while incontinence is more like epilepsy; vice is a continuous bad condition, while incontinence is not. For the incontinent is similar to those who get drunk quickly from a little wine, and from less than it takes for most people. 35

And in general incontinence and vice are of different kinds, for the vicious person does not notice that he is vicious, while the incontinent person notices that he is incontinent.

Among the incontinent people themselves those who stray [i.e. the impetuous] are better than those [i.e. the weak] who have reason but do not abide by it. For the second type are overcome by a less strong feeling, and do not act without having deliberated, as the first type do. 1151a

Evidently, then, incontinence is not a vice, though presumably it is one in a way. For incontinence conflicts with decision, while vice expresses decision. All the same, it is similar to vice in its actions. Demodocus attacks the Milesians; 'The Milesians are not stupid, but they do what stupid people would do';[26] and in the same way incontinents are not unjust, but will do injustice. 5

Moreover, the incontinent person is the sort to pursue excessive bodily pleasures that conflict with correct reason, but not because he is persuaded [it is best]. The intemperate person, however, is persuaded, because he is the sort of person to pursue them. Hence the incontinent person is easily persuaded out of it, while the intemperate person is not.

For virtue preserves the origin, while vice corrupts it; and in action the end we act for is the origin, as the assumptions are the origins in mathematics. Reason does not teach the origins either in mathematics or about actions; [with actions] it is virtue, either natural or habituated, that teaches correct belief about the origin. 15

The sort of person [with this virtue] is temperate, and the contrary sort intemperate. But there is also someone whose feelings make him go astray in conflict with correct reason. They overcome him far enough so that his actions do not express correct reason, but not so far as to make him the sort of person to be persuaded that it is right to pursue such pleasures without restraint. This is the incontinent person. He is better than the intemperate person, and is not unconditionally bad, since the best thing, the origin, is preserved in him. 20

25

26. [Demodocus, an epigrammatist, lived in the sixth century B.C.]

Another sort of person is contrary to him. [This is the continent person] who abides [by reason] and does not go astray, not because of his feelings at least. It is evident from this that the continent person's state is excellent, and the incontinent person's state is base.

CONTINENCE

9

30 Now is someone continent if he abides by just any sort of reason and any sort of decision, or must he abide by the correct decision? And is someone incontinent if he fails to abide by just any decision and any reason, or must it be reason that is not false, and the correct decision? This was the puzzle raised earlier.

Perhaps in fact the continent person abides by just any decision coincidentally, but abides by the true reason and the correct decision in itself, while the incontinent per-
35 son does not abide by them. For if someone chooses or pursues one thing because of a
1151b second, he pursues and chooses the second in itself and the first coincidentally. Now when we speak of something unconditionally, we speak of it in itself. Hence in one way [i.e. coincidentally] the continent person abides by just any opinion, and the incontinent strays from it; but unconditionally the continent person abides by the true opinion and the incontinent person strays from it.

5 Now there are some other people who tend to abide by their belief. These are the people called stubborn, who are hard to persuade into something and not easy to persuade out of it. These have some similarity to the continent people, just as the wasteful person has to the generous, and the rash to the confident. But they are different on many points.

10 The continent person is not swayed because of feeling and appetite; [but he is not inflexible about everything] since he will be easily persuaded whenever it is appropriate. But stubborn people are not swayed by reason, [but by other things]; for they acquire appetites, and many of them are led on by pleasures.

The stubborn include the stiff-necked, the ignorant and the boorish. The stiff-necked are as they are because of pleasure and pain. For they find enjoyment in win-
15 ning [the argument] if they are not persuaded to change their views, and they feel pain if their opinions are voided, like decreees in the Assembly. Hence they are more like incontinent than like continent people.

There are also some people who do not abide by their resolutions, but not because they are incontinent. Take Neoptolemus, e.g., in Sophocles' *Philoctetes;* though certainly it was pleasure that made him abandon his resolution, it was a fine pleasure,
20 since he found telling the truth pleasant, and Odysseus had persuaded him to lie. [He is not incontinent] for not everyone who does something because of pleasure is either intemperate or base or incontinent, but only someone who does it because of a shameful pleasure.

Now there is also the sort of person who enjoys bodily things less than is right, and
25 does not abide by reason; hence the continent person is intermediate between this person and the incontinent person. For the incontinent person fails to abide by reason because of too much [enjoyment]; and the other person fails because of too little; while the continent person abides and is not swayed because of too much or too little.

If continence is excellent, then both of these contrary states must be base, as indeed

they appear. However, the other state is evident in only a few people on a few occa- 30
sions; and hence continence seems to be contrary only to incontinence, just as
temperance seems to be contrary only to intemperance.

Now many things are called by some name because of similarity [to genuine cases];
hence the continence of the temperate person has also been associated [with genuine
continence] because of similarity. For the continent and the temperate person are 35
both the sort to do nothing in conflict with reason because of bodily pleasures; but the 1152a
continent person has base appetites, and the temperate person lacks them. The
temperate person is the sort to take no pleasure that conflicts with reason; the continent is the sort to take such pleasure, but not to be led by it.

The incontinent and the intemperate person are similar too; though they are different, they both pursue bodily sources of pleasure, but the intemperate person also 5
[pursues them because he] thinks it is right, while the incontinent person does not
think so.

INCONTINENCE AND INTELLIGENCE

10

Nor can the same person be at once both intelligent and incontinent.

For we have shown that an intelligent person must also at the same time be excellent in character, [and the incontinent person is not]. However, a clever person 10
may well be incontinent. Indeed, the reason people sometimes seem to be intelligent
but incontinent is that [really they are only clever and] cleverness differs from intelligence in the way we described in our first discussion; though they are closely 15
related in definition, they differ in so far as intelligence requires the right decision.

Moreover, someone is not intelligent simply by knowing; he must also act on his
knowledge. But the incontinent person does not.

Further, the incontinent person is not in the condition of someone who knows and
is attending [to his knowledge, as he would have to be if he had intelligence], but in
the condition of one asleep or drunk.

He acts willingly; for in a way he acts in knowledge both of what he is doing and of
the end he is doing it for. But he is not base, since his decision is decent; hence he is
half base.

Nor is he unjust, since he is not a plotter. For one type of incontinent person [i.e. 20
the weak] does not abide by the result of his deliberation, while the ardent [i.e. im-
petuous] person is not even prone to deliberate at all.

In fact the incontinent person is like a city that votes for all the right decrees and
has good laws, but does not apply them, as in Anaxandrides' taunt, 'The city willed
it, that cares nothing for laws.'[27] The base person, by contrast, is like a city that applies its laws, but applies bad ones.

Incontinence and continence are concerned with what exceeds the state of most 25
people; the continent person abides [by reason] more than most people are capable of
doing, the incontinent person less.

The [impetuous] type of incontinence found in ardent people is more easily cured

27. [Anaxandrides was a fourth-century B.C. poet from Rhodes.]

than the [weak] type of incontinence found in those who deliberate but do not abide by it.

30   Incontinents through habituation are more easily cured than the natural incontinents; for habit is easier than nature to change. Indeed the reason why habit is also difficult to change is that it is like nature, as Euenus says, 'Habit, I say, is longtime training, my friend, and in the end training is nature for human beings.'[28]

35   We have said, then, what continence and incontinence, resistance and softness are, and how these states are related to each other.

BOOK TEN

Pleasure

THE RIGHT APPROACH TO PLEASURE

1

20   The next task, presumably, is to discuss pleasure. For it seems to be especially proper
1172a to our [animal] kind, and hence when we educate children we steer them by pleasure and pain. Besides, enjoying and hating the right things seems to be more important for virtue of character. For it extends through the whole of our lives, inclining us
25   strongly towards virtue and the happy life, since people decide to do what is pleasant, and they avoid what is painful. Least of all, then, it seems, should these topics be neglected.

This is especially true when they cause much dispute. For some say pleasure is the good, while others, on the contrary, say it is altogether base.

Now presumably some who say it is base say so because they are persuaded that it is
30   so. Others, however, say it because they think it is better for the conduct of our lives to present pleasure as base even if it is not. For, they say, since the many lean towards pleasure and are slaves to pleasures, we must lead them in the contrary direction, because that is the way to reach the intermediate condition.

35   Surely, however, this is wrong. For arguments about actions and feelings are less credible than the facts; hence any conflict between arguments and perceptible [facts]
1172b arouses contempt for the arguments, and moreover undermines the true ones. For if someone blames pleasure, but then has been seen to seek it on *some* occasions, the reason for his lapse seems to be that he approves of *every* type of pleasure; for the many are not the sort to make distinctions.

5   True arguments, then, are the most useful, not only for knowing the truth but also for the conduct of life. For since they harmonize with the facts, they are credible, and so encourage those who comprehend them to live by them.

Enough of this, then; let us now consider what has been said about pleasure.

---

28. [Euenus was a fifth-century B.C. Sophist from the island of Paros.]

THE CASE FOR PLEASURE

2

Eudoxus thought that pleasure is the good.

(1) This was because he saw that (a) all [animals], both rational and non-rational,   10
seek it. (b) In everything, he says, what is choiceworthy is decent, and what is most
choiceworthy is supreme. (c) Each thing finds its own good, just as it finds its own
nourishment. (d) Hence, when all are drawn to the same thing [i.e. pleasure], this indicates that it is best for all. (e) And what is good for all, what all aim at, is the good.   15

Eudoxus' arguments were found credible because of his virtuous character, rather
than on their own [merits]. For since he seemed to be outstandingly temperate, he did
not seem to be saying this because he was afraid of pleasure; rather, it seemed, what
he said was how it really was.

(2) He thought it was no less evident from consideration of the contrary. (a) Pain
in itself is to be avoided for all. (b) Similarly, then, its contrary is choiceworthy for all.   20
(c) What is most choiceworthy is what we choose not because of, or for the sake of,
anything else. (d) And it is agreed that this is the character of pleasure, since we never
ask anyone what his end is in being pleased, on the assumption that pleasure is
choiceworthy in itself.

(3) Moreover, [he argued], when pleasure is added to any other good, e.g. to just
or temperate action, it makes that good more choiceworthy; and good is increased by   25
the addition of itself.

This [third] argument, at least, seemingly presents pleasure as one good among
others, no more a good than any other. For the addition of *any* other good makes a
good more choiceworthy than it is all by itself.

Indeed Plato uses this sort of argument when he undermines the claim of pleasure
to be the good. For, he argues, the pleasant life is more choiceworthy when combined   30
with intelligence than it is without it; and if the mixed [good] is better, pleasure is not
the good, since nothing can be added to the good to make it more choiceworthy.

Nor, clearly, could anything else be the good if it is made more choiceworthy by
the addition of any good in itself. Then what is the good that meets this condition,   35
and that we share in also? That is what we are looking for.

THE CASE AGAINST PLEASURE

When some object that what everything aims at is not good, surely there is nothing in   1173a
what they say. For if things seem [good] to all, we say they *are* [good]; and if someone
undermines confidence in these, what he says will hardly inspire more confidence in
other things. For if [only] beings without understanding desired these things, there
would be something in the objection; but if intelligent beings also desire them, how
can there be anything in it? And presumably even in inferior [animals] there is   5
something superior to themselves, that seeks their own proper good.

The argument [offered against Eudoxus] about the contrary is also seemingly incorrect. For they argue that if pain is an evil, it does not follow that pleasure is a
good, since evil is also opposed to evil, and both are opposed to the neutral condition

[without pleasure or pain].

10   The objectors' general point here is right, but what they say in the case mentioned is false. For if both pleasure and pain were evils, we would also have to avoid both, and if both were neutral, we would have to avoid neither, or else avoid both equally. Evidently, however, we avoid pain as an evil and choose pleasure as a good; hence this must also be the opposition between them.

3

Again, if [as the objectors argue] pleasure is not a quality, it does not follow [as they

15   suppose] that it is not a good. For neither are virtuous activities or happiness qualities.

They say that the good is definite, whereas pleasure is indefinite because it admits of more or less.

If their judgment rests on the actual condition of being pleased, it must also hold for justice and the other virtues, where evidently we are said to have a certain

20   character more and less, and to express the virtues more and less in our actions. For we may be more [and less] just or brave, and may do just or temperate actions more and less.

If, on the other hand, their judgment rests on the [variety of] pleasures, then surely they fail to state the reason [why pleasures admit of more and less], namely that some are unmixed [with pain] and others are mixed.

25   Moreover, just as health admits of more and less, though it is definite, why should pleasure not be the same? For not every [healthy person] has the same proportion [of bodily elements], nor does the same person always have the same, but it may be relaxed and still remain up to a certain limit, and may differ in more and less. The same is quite possible, then, for pleasure also.

30   They suppose that what is good is complete, whereas processes and becomings are incomplete; and they try to show that pleasure is a process and a becoming. Seemingly, however, they are wrong, and pleasure is not even a process.

For quickness or slowness seems to be proper to every process — if not in itself (as, e.g., with the universe), then in relation to something else. But neither of these is true of pleasure.

1173b   For though certainly it is possible to become pleased quickly, as it is possible to become angry quickly, it is not possible to be pleased quickly, not even in relation to something else. But this is possible for walking and growing and all such things [i.e. for processes]. It is possible, then, to pass quickly or slowly into pleasure, but not possible to be [quickly or slowly] in the corresponding activity, i.e. to be pleased quickly [or slowly].

5   And how could pleasure be a becoming? For not just any random thing, it seems, comes to be from any other; but what something comes to be from is what it is dissolved into. Hence whatever pleasure is the becoming of, pain should be the perishing of it.

They do indeed say that pain is the emptying of the natural [condition, and hence the perishing], and that pleasure is its refilling, [and hence the becoming]. Emptying and filling happen to the body; if, then, pleasure is the refilling of something natural,

what has the refilling will also have the pleasure. Hence it will be the body that has   10
pleasure.

This does not seem to be true, however. The refilling, then, is not pleasure, though
someone might be pleased while a refilling is going on, and pained when he is becoming empty.

This belief [that pleasure is refilling] seems to have arisen from pains and pleasures
about food; for first we are empty and suffer pain, and then take pleasure in the   15
refilling. However, the same is not true for all pleasures; for pleasures in
mathematics, and among pleasures in perception those through the sense of smell,
and many sounds, sights, memories and expectations as well, all arise without
[previous] pain. If this is so, what will they be comings-to-be of? For since no emptiness of anything has come to be, there is nothing whose refilling might come to be.   20

Some people cite the disgraceful pleasures [to show that pleasure is not a good].

(1) To them we might reply that these [sources of disgraceful pleasures] are not
pleasant. If things are healthy or sweet or bitter to sick people, we should not suppose
that they are also healthy, or sweet, or bitter, except to them; nor should we suppose
that things appearing white to people with eye disease are pale, except to them.
Similarly, if things are pleasant to people in bad condition, we should not suppose
that they are also pleasant, except to these people.

(2) Or we might say that the pleasures are choiceworthy, but not when they come   25
from these sources, just as wealth is desirable, but not if you have to betray someone
to get it, and health is desirable, but not if it requires you to eat everything.

(3) Or perhaps pleasures differ in species. For those from fine sources are different
from those from shameful sources; and we cannot have the just person's pleasure   30
without being just, any more than we can have the musician's without being musicians, and similarly in the other cases.

The difference between a friend and a flatterer seems to indicate that pleasure is
not good, or else that pleasures differ in species. For in dealings with us the friend
seems to aim at what is good, but the flatterer at what is pleasant; and the flatterer is
reproached, whereas the friend is praised, on the assumption that in their dealings
they have different aims.

Besides, no one would choose to live with a child's [level of] thought for his whole   1174a
life, taking as much pleasure as possible in what pleases children, or to enjoy himself
while doing some utterly shameful action, even if he would never suffer pain for it.

Moreover, there are many things that we would be eager for even if they brought   5
no pleasure, e.g. seeing, remembering, knowing, having the virtues. Even if pleasures
necessarily follow on them, that does not matter, since we would choose them even if
no pleasure resulted from them.

It would seem clear, then, that pleasure is not the good; that not every pleasure is   10
choiceworthy; and that some are choiceworthy in themselves, differing in species or in
their sources [from those that are not]. So much, then, for the things said about
pleasure and pain.

PLEASURE IS AN ACTIVITY, NOT A PROCESS

4

What, then, or what kind of thing, is pleasure? This will become clearer if we take it up again from the beginning.

PLEASURE IS COMPLETE AT ANY TIME

15 Seeing seems to be complete at any time, since it has no need for anything else to complete its form by coming to be at a later time. And pleasure is also like this, since it is some sort of whole, and no pleasure is to be found at any time that will have its form completed by coming to be for a longer time. Hence pleasure is not a process either.

20   For every process, e.g. building [a temple], takes time, and aims at some end, and is complete when it produces the product it seeks, or, [in other words, is complete] in the whole time [that it takes].

Moreover, each process is incomplete during the processes that are its parts, i.e. during the time it goes on, and it consists of processes that are different in form from the whole process and from each other.

For laying stones together and fluting a column are different processes; and both
25 are different from the [whole] production of the temple. For [the whole production] is a complete production, since it needs nothing further [when it is finished] to achieve the proposed goal; but the production of the foundation or the triglyph is an incomplete production, since [when it is finished] it is [the production] of a part.

Hence, [processes that are parts of larger processes] differ in form; and we cannot find a process complete in form at any time [while it is going on], but [only], if at all, in the whole time [that it takes].

30   The same is true of walking and the other [processes]. For if locomotion is a process from one place to another, it includes locomotions differing in form—flying, walking, jumping and so on. And besides these differences, there are differences in walking itself. For the place from and the place to are not the same in the whole racecourse as they are in a part of it, or the same in one part as in another; nor is pass-
1174b ing one line the same as passing another, since what we cross is not just a line, but a line in a [particular] place, and this line and that line are in different places.

Now we have discussed process exactly elsewhere. But, at any rate, a process is seemingly not complete at every time; and the many [constituent] processes are in-
5 complete, and differ in form, since the place from and the place to make the form of a process [and different processes begin and end in different places].

The form of pleasure, by contrast, is complete at any time. Clearly, then, it is different from a process, and is something whole and complete. This also seems true because a process must take time, but being pleased need not; for what [takes no time and hence is wholly present] in an instant is a whole.

10   This also makes it clear that it is wrong to say that there is a process or a coming-to-be of pleasure. For this is not said of everything, but only of what is divisible and not a whole; for seeing, or a point, or a unit, has no coming to be, and none of these is

either a process or a becoming. But pleasure is a whole; hence it also has no coming to be.

PLEASURE COMPLETES AN ACTIVITY

Every faculty of perception is active in relation to its perceptible object, and completely active when it is in good condition in relation to the finest of its perceptible objects. For this above all seems to be the character of complete activity, whether it is ascribed to the faculty or to the subject that has it. Hence for each faculty the best activity is the activity of the subject in the best condition in relation to the best object of the faculty.   15

This activity will also be the most complete and the pleasantest. For every faculty of perception, and every sort of thought and study, has its pleasure; the pleasantest activity is the most complete; and the most complete is the activity of the subject in good condition in relation to the most excellent object of the faculty; and pleasure completes the activity.   20

But the way in which pleasure completes the activity is not the way in which the perceptible object and the faculty of perception complete it when they are both excellent—just as health and the doctor are not the cause of being healthy in the same way.   25

For clearly a pleasure arises that corresponds to each faculty of perception, since we say that sights and sounds are pleasant; and clearly it arises above all whenever the faculty of perception is best, and is active in relation to the best sort of object. When this is the condition of the perceptible object and of the perceiving subject, there will always be pleasure, when the producer and the subject to be affected are both present.   30

Pleasure completes the activity—not, however, as the state does, by being present [in the activity], but as a sort of consequent end, like the bloom on youths.

Hence as long as the objects of understanding or perception and the subject that judges or attends are in the right condition, there will be pleasure in the activity. For as long as the subject affected and the producer remain similar and in the same relation to each other, the same thing naturally arises.   1175a

Then how is it that no one is continuously pleased? Is it not because we get tired? For nothing human is capable of continuous activity, and hence no continuous pleasure arises either, since pleasure is a consequence of the activity.   5

Again, some things delight us when they are new to us, but less later, for the same reason. For at first our thought is stimulated and intensely active towards them, as our sense of sight is when we stare at something; but later the activity becomes lax and careless, so that the pleasure fades also.   10

We might think that everyone desires pleasure, since everyone desires to be alive. Living is a type of activity, and each of us is active towards the objects he likes most and in the ways he likes most. The musician, e.g., activates his hearing in hearing melodies; the lover of learning activates his thought in thinking about objects of study; and so on for each of the others.   15

Pleasure completes their activities, and hence completes life, which they desire. It is reasonable, then, that they also aim at pleasure, since it completes each person's life for him, and life is choiceworthy.

20   Do we choose life because of pleasure, or pleasure because of life? Let us set aside this question for now, since the two appear to be yoked together, and to allow no separation; for pleasure never arises without activity, and, equally, it completes every activity.

PLEASURES DIFFER IN KIND

5

Hence pleasures also seem to be of different species. For we suppose that things of different species are completed by different things. That is how it appears, both with natural things and with artifacts, e.g. with animals, trees, a painting, a statue, a

25   house or an implement; and similarly, activities that differ in species are also completed by things that differ in species. Activities of thought differ in species from activities of the faculties of perception, and so do these from each other; so also, then, do the pleasures that complete them.

30   This is also apparent from the way each pleasure is proper to the activity that it completes. For the proper pleasure increases the activity.

For we judge each thing better and more exactly when our activity is associated with pleasure. If, e.g., we enjoy doing geometry, we become better geometers, and understand each question better; and similarly lovers of music, building and so on

35   improve at their proper function when they enjoy it.

Each pleasure increases the activity; what increases it is proper to it; and since the

1175b   activities are different in species, what is proper to them is also different in species.

This is even more apparent from the way some activities are impeded by pleasures from others. For lovers of flutes, e.g., cannot pay attention to a conversation if they catch the sound of someone playing the flute, because they enjoy flute-playing more

5   than their present activity; and so the pleasure proper to flute-playing destroys the activity in conversation.

The same is true in other cases also, whenever we are engaged in two activities at once. For the pleasanter activity pushes out the other one, all the more if it is much

10   pleasanter, so that we no longer even engage in the other activity. Hence if we are enjoying one thing intensely, we do not do another very much. It is when we are only mildly pleased that we do something else, e.g. people who eat nuts in theatres do this most whenever the actors are bad.

15   Since, then, the proper pleasure makes an activity more exact, longer and better, while an alien pleasure damages it, clearly the two pleasures differ widely.

For an alien pleasure does practically what a proper pain does. For the proper pain destroys activity, so that if, e.g., writing or rational calculation has no pleasure and is in fact painful for us, we do not write or calculate, since the activity is painful.

20   Hence the proper pleasures and pains have contrary effects on an activity; and the proper ones are those that arise from the activity in itself. And as we have said, the effect of alien pleasures is similar to the effect of pain, since they ruin the activity, though not in the same way as pain.

Which Pleasures Are Goods?

Since activities differ in degrees of decency and badness, and some are choiceworthy,   25
some to be avoided, some neither, the same is true of pleasures; for each activity has
its own proper pleasure. Hence the pleasure proper to an excellent activity is decent,
and the one proper to a base activity is vicious; for, similarly, appetites for fine things
are praiseworthy, and appetites for shameful things are blameworthy.

And in fact the pleasure in an activity is more proper to it than the desire for it. For   30
the desire is distinguished from it in time and in nature; but the pleasure is close to
the activity, and so little distinguished from it that disputes arise about whether the
activity is the same as the pleasure.

Still, pleasure is seemingly neither thought nor perception, since that would be ab-   35
surd. Rather, it is because [pleasure and activity] are not separated that to some people they appear the same.

Hence, just as activities differ, so do the pleasures. Sight differs from touch in puri-   1176a
ty, as hearing and smell do from taste; hence the pleasures also differ in the same
way. So also do the pleasures of thought differ from these [pleasures of sense]; and
both sorts have different kinds within them.

Each kind of animal seems to have its own proper pleasure, just as it has its own
proper function; for the proper pleasure will be the one that corresponds to its
activity.

This is apparent if we also study each kind. For a horse, a dog and a human being   5
have different pleasures; and, as Heracleitus says, an ass would choose chaff over
gold, since asses find food pleasanter than gold. Hence animals that differ in species
also have pleasures that differ in species; and it would be reasonable for animals of
the same species to have the same pleasures also.

In fact, however, the pleasures differ quite a lot, in human beings, at any rate. For   10
the same things delight some people, and cause pain to others; and while some find
them painful and hateful, others find them pleasant and lovable. The same is true of
sweet things. For the same things do not seem sweet to a feverish and to a healthy person, or hot to an enfeebled and to a vigorous person; and the same is true of other   15
things.

But in all such cases it seems that what is really so is what appears so to the excellent person. If this is correct, as it seems to be, and virtue, i.e. the good person in so
far as he is good, is the measure of each thing, then pleasures will also be what appear
pleasures to him, and what is pleasant will be what he enjoys.

And if what he finds objectionable appears pleasant to someone, that is nothing   20
surprising, since human beings suffer many sorts of corruption and damage. It is not
pleasant, however, except to these people in these conditions.

Clearly, then, we should say that the pleasures agreed to be shameful are not
pleasures at all, except to corrupted people.

But what about those pleasures that seem to be decent? Which kind, or which par-   25
ticular pleasure, should we take to be the pleasure of a human being? Surely it will be
clear from the activities, since the pleasures are consequences of these.

Hence the pleasures that complete the activities of the complete and blessed man,
whether he has one activity or more than one, will be called the human pleasures to

the fullest extent. The other pleasures will be human in the secondary and even more remote ways that reflect the character of the activities.

HAPPINESS: FURTHER DISCUSSION

RECAPITULATION: HAPPINESS IS AN END IN ITSELF, CONSISTING IN VIRTUOUS ACTION

6

30 We have now finished our discussion of the types of virtue; of friendship; and of pleasure. It remains for us to discuss happiness in outline, since we take this to be the end of human [aims]. Our discussion will be shorter if we first take up again what we said before.

35 We said, then, that happiness is not a state. For if it were, someone might have it and yet be asleep for his whole life, living the life of a plant, or suffer the greatest 1176b misfortunes. If we do not approve of this, we count happiness as an activity rather than a state, as we said before.

Some activities are necesary, i.e. choiceworthy for some other end, while others are choiceworthy in themselves. Clearly, then, we should count happiness as one of those 5 activities that are choiceworthy in themselves, not as one of those choiceworthy for some other end. For happiness lacks nothing, but is self-sufficient; and an activity is choiceworthy in itself when nothing further beyond it is sought from it.

This seems to be the character of actions expressing virtue; for doing fine and excellent actions is choiceworthy for itself.

But pleasant amusements also [seem to be choiceworthy in themselves]. For they 10 are not chosen for other ends, since they actually cause more harm than benefit, by causing neglect of our bodies and possessions.

Moreover, most of the people congratulated for their happiness resort to these sorts of pastimes. Hence people who are witty [participants] in them have a good reputa- 15 tion with tyrants, since they offer themselves as pleasant [partners] in the tyrant's aims, and these are the sort of people the tyrant requires. And also these amusements seem to have the character of happiness because people in supreme power spend their leisure in them.

However, these sorts of people are presumably no evidence. For virtue and understanding, the sources of excellent activities, do not depend on holding supreme 20 power. Further, these powerful people have had no taste of pure and civilized pleasure, and so they resort to bodily pleasures. But that is no reason to think these pleasures are most choiceworthy, since boys also think that what they honour is best. Hence, just as different things appear honourable to boys and to men, it is reasonable that in the same way different things appear honourable to base and to decent people.

25 As we have often said, then, what is honourable and pleasant is what is so to the excellent person; and to each type of person the activity expressing his own proper sta:e is most choiceworthy; hence the activity expressing virtue is most choiceworthy to the excellent person [and hence is most honourable and pleasant].

Happiness, then, is not found in amusement; for it would be absurd if the end were amusement, and our lifelong efforts and sufferings aimed at amusing ourselves. For we choose practically everything for some other end — except for happiness, since it is [the] end; but serious work and toil aimed [only] at amusement appears stupid and excessively childish. Rather, it seems correct to amuse ourselves so that we can do something serious, as Anacharsis says;[29] for amusement is seemingly relaxation, and it is because we cannot toil continuously that we require relaxation. Relaxation, then, is not [the] end, since we pursue it to prepare for activity.

Further, the happy life seems to be the life expressing virtue, which is a life involving serious actions, and not consisting in amusement.

Besides, we say that things to be taken seriously are better than funny things that provide amusement, and that in each case the activity of the better part and the better person is more serious and excellent; and the activity of what is better is superior, and thereby has more the character of happiness.

Moreover, anyone at all, even a slave, no less than the best person, might enjoy bodily pleasures; but no one would allow that a slave shares in happiness, if one does not [also allow that the slave shares in the sort of] life [needed for happiness]. Happiness, then, is found not in these pastimes, but in the activities expressing virtue, as we also said previously.

THEORETICAL STUDY IS THE SUPREME ELEMENT OF HAPPINESS

7

If happiness, then, is activity expressing virtue, it is reasonable for it to express the supreme virtue, which will be the virtue of the best thing.

The best is understanding, or whatever else seems to be the natural ruler and leader, and to understand what is fine and divine, by being itself either divine or the most divine element in us.

Hence complete happiness will be its activity expressing its proper virtue; and we have said that this activity is the activity of study. This seems to agree with what has been said before, and also with the truth.

For this activity is supreme, since understanding is the supreme element in us, and the objects of understanding are the supreme objects of knowledge.

Besides, it is the most continuous activity, since we are more capable of continuous study than of any continuous action.

We think pleasure must be mixed into happiness; and it is agreed that the activity expressing wisdom is the pleasantest of the activities expressing virtue. At any rate, philosophy seems to have remarkably pure and firm pleasures; and it is reasonable for those who have knowledge to spend their lives more pleasantly than those who seek it.

Moreover, the self-sufficiency we spoke of will be found in study above all.

For admittedly the wise person, the just person and the other virtuous people all need the goods necessary for life. Still, when these are adequately supplied, the just person needs others as partners and recipients of his just actions; and the same is true

29. [Anacharsis was a sixth-century B.C. Scythian prince of legendary wisdom.]

Margin line numbers: 30, 35, 1177a, 5, 10, 15, 20, 25, 30

of the temperate person and the brave person and each of the others.

But the wise person is able, and more able the wiser he is, to study even by himself; and though he presumably does it better with colleagues, even so he is more self-sufficient than any other [virtuous person].

Besides, study seems to be liked because of itself alone, since it has no result beyond having studied. But from the virtues concerned with action we try more or less to gain something beyond the action itself.

Happiness seems to be found in leisure, since we accept trouble so that we can be at leisure, and fight wars so that we can be at peace. Now the virtues concerned with action have their activities in politics or war, and actions here seem to require trouble.

This seems completely true for actions in war, since no one chooses to fight a war, and no one continues it, for the sake of fighting a war; for someone would have to be a complete murderer if he made his friends his enemies so that there could be battles and killings.

But the actions of the politician require trouble also. Beyond political activities themselves these actions seek positions of power and honours; or at least they seek happiness for himself and for his fellow-citizens, which is something different from political science itself, and clearly is sought on the assumption that it is different.

Hence among sections expressing the virtues those in politics and war are pre-eminently fine and great; but they require trouble, aim at some [further] end, and are choiceworthy for something other than themselves.

But the activity of understanding, it seems, is superior in excellence because it is the activity of study; aims at no end beyond itself; has its own proper pleasure, which increases the activity; and is self-sufficient, leisured and unwearied, as far [as these are possible] for a human being. And whatever else is ascribed to the blessed person is evidently found in what expresses this activity.

Hence a human being's complete happiness will be this activity, if it receives a complete span of life, since nothing incomplete is proper to happiness.

Such a life would be superior to the human level. For someone will live it not in so far as he is a human being, but in so far as he has some divine element in him. And the activity of this divine element is as much superior to the activity expressing the rest of virtue as this element is superior to the compound. Hence if understanding is something divine in comparison with a human being, so also will the life that expresses understanding be divine in comparison with human life.

We ought not to follow the proverb-writers, and 'think human, since you are human', or 'think mortal, since you are mortal'. Rather, as far as we can, we ought to be pro-immortal, and go to all lengths to live a life that expresses our supreme element; for however much this element may lack in bulk, by much more it surpasses everything in power and value.

Moreover, each person seems to be his understanding, if he is his controlling and better element; it would be absurd, then, if he were to choose not his own life, but something else's.

And what we have said previously will also apply now. For what is proper to each thing's nature is supremely best and pleasantest for it; and hence for a human being the life expressing understanding will be supremely best and pleasantest, if understanding above all is the human being. This life, then, will also be happiest.

The Relation of Study to the Other Virtues in Happiness

8

The life expressing the other kind of virtue [i.e. the kind concerned with action] is [happiest] in a secondary way because the activities expressing this virtue are human.   10

For we do just and brave actions, and the others expressing the virtues, in relation to other people, by abiding by what fits each person in contracts, services, all types of actions, and also in feelings; and all these appear to be human conditions.

Indeed, some feelings actually seem to arise from the body; and in many ways virtue of character seems to be proper to feelings.   15

Besides, intelligence is yoked together with virtue of character, and so is this virtue with intelligence. For the origins of intelligence express the virtues of character; and correctness in virtues of character expresses intelligence. And since these virtues are also connected to feelings, they are concerned with the compound. Since the virtues   20
of the compound are human virtues, the life and the happiness expressing these virtues is also human.

The virtue of understanding, however, is separated [from the compound]. Let us say no more about it, since an exact account would be too large a task for our present project.

Moreover, it seems to need external supplies very little, or [at any rate] less than virtue of character needs them. For grant that they both need necessary goods, and to   25
the same extent, since there will be only a very small difference even though the politican labours more about the body and suchlike. Still, there will be a large difference in [what is needed] for the [proper] activities [of each type of virtue].

For the generous person will need money for generous actions; and the just person will need it for paying debts, since wishes are not clear, and people who are not just   30
pretend to wish to do justice. Similarly, the brave person will need enough power, and the temperate person will need freedom [to do intemperate actions], if they are to achieve anything that the virtue requires. For how else will they, or any other virtuous people, make their virtue clear?

Moreover, it is disputed whether it is decision or action that is more in control of   35
virtue, on the assumption that it depends on both. Hence, clearly, complete virtue   1178b
depends both on decision and on actions. But for actions many external goods are needed, and the greater and finer the actions the more external goods are needed.

But someone who is studying needs none of these goods, for that activity at least; indeed, for study at least, we might say they are even hindrances.

In so far as he is a human being, however, and [hence] lives together with a   5
number of other human beings, he chooses to do the actions expressing virtue. Hence he will need the sorts of external goods [that are needed for the virtues], for living a human life.

In another way also it appears that complete happiness is some activity of study. For we traditionally suppose that the gods more than anyone are blessed and happy;   10
but what sorts of actions ought we to ascribe to them? Just actions? Surely they will appear ridiculous making contracts, returning deposits and so on. Brave actions? Do they endure what [they find] frightening and endure dangers because it is fine?

15   Generous actions? Whom will they give to? And surely it would be absurd for them to have currency or anything like that. What would their temperate actions be? Surely it is vulgar praise to say that they do not have base appetites. When we go through them all, anything that concerns actions appears trivial and unworthy of the gods.

20   However, we all traditionally suppose that they are alive and active, since surely they are not asleep like Endymion.[30] Then if someone is alive, and action is excluded, and production even more, what is left but study? Hence the gods' activity that is superior in blessedness will be in study. And so the human activity that is most akin to the gods' will, more than any others, have the character of happiness.

25   A sign of this is the fact that other animals have no share in happiness, being completely deprived of this activity of study. For the whole life of the gods is blessed, and human life is blessed to the extent that it has something resembling this sort of activity; but none of the other animals is happy, because none of them shares in study at all. Hence happiness extends just as far as study extends, and the more someone studies, the happier he is, not incidentally but in so far as he studies, since study is valuable in itself. And so [on this argument] happiness will be some kind of study.

35   However, the happy person is a human being, and so will need external prosperity also; for his nature is not self-sufficient for study, but he needs a healthy body, and needs to have food and the other services provided.

1179a   Still, even though no one can be blessed without external goods, we must not think that to be happy we will need many large goods. For self-sufficiency and action do not depend on excess, and we can do fine actions even if we do not rule earth and sea; for even from moderate resources we can do the actions expressing virtue. This is evident to see, when many private citizens seem to do decent actions no less than people in power do—even more, in fact. It is enough if moderate resources are provided; for the life of someone whose activity expresses virtue will be happy.

10   Solon surely described the happy people well, when he said they had been moderately supplied with external goods, had done what he regarded as the finest actions, and had lived their lives temperately. For it is possible to have moderate possessions and still to do the right actions.

15   And Anaxagoras seemingly supposed that the happy person was neither rich nor powerful, since he said he would not be surprised if the happy person appeared an absurd sort of person to the many. For the many judge by externals, since these are all they perceive.

Hence the beliefs of the wise seemingly accord with our arguments; and so these also produce confidence.

20   The truth, however, in questions about action is judged from what we do and how we live, since these are what control us. Hence we ought to examine what has been said by applying it to what we do and how we live; and if it harmonizes with what we do, we should accept it, but if it conflicts we should count it mere words.

The person whose activity expresses understanding and who takes care of understanding is seemingly in the best condition, and most loved by the gods. For if
25   the gods pay some attention to human beings, as they seem to, it would be reasonable for them to take pleasure in what is best and most akin to them, namely understand-

---

30. [According to Greek mythology, Endymion was a remarkably beautiful young man who was placed into everlasting sleep by the Moon, so that she might embrace him each night.]

ing; and reasonable for them to benefit in return those who most of all like and honour understanding, on the assumption that these people attend to what is beloved by the gods, and act correctly and finely.

Clearly, all this is true of the wise person more than anyone else; hence he is most 30
loved by the gods. And it is likely that this same person will be happiest; hence the wise person will be happier than anyone else in this way also.

ETHICS, MORAL EDUCATION AND POLITICS

WE MUST STUDY MORAL EDUCATION TO SEE HOW TO MAKE PEOPLE VIRTUOUS

9

We have now said enough in outlines about happiness and the virtues, and about friendship and pleasure also. Should we then think that our decision [to study these] 35
has achieved its end? On the contrary, the aim of studies about action, as we say, is 1179b
surely not to study and know about each thing, but rather to act on our knowledge.
Hence knowing about virtue is not enough, but we must also try to possess and exercise virtue, or become good in any other way.

Now if arguments were sufficient by themselves to make people decent, the rewards 5
they would command would justifiably have been many and large, as Theognis[31]
says, and rightly bestowed. In fact, however, arguments seem to have enough influence to stimulate and encourage the civilized ones among the young people, and perhaps to make virtue occupy a well-born character that truly loves what is fine; but they seem unable to stimulate the many towards being fine and good. 10

For the many naturally obey fear, not shame; they avoid what is base because of the penalties, not because it is disgraceful. For since they live by their feelings, they pursue their proper pleasures and the sources of them, and avoid the opposed pains, 15
and have not even a notion of what is fine and [hence] truly pleasant, since they have had no taste of it.

What argument could reform people like these? For it is impossible, or not easy, to alter by argument what has long been absorbed by habit; but, presumably, we should be satisfied to achieve some share in virtue when we already have what we seem to need to become decent.

Some think it is nature that makes people good; some think it is habit; some that it 20
is teaching.

The [contribution] of nature clearly is not up to us, but results from some divine cause in those who have it, who are the truly fortunate ones.

Arguments and teaching surely do not influence everyone, but the soul of the student needs to have been prepared by habits for enjoying and hating finely, like 25
ground that is to nourish seed. For someone whose life follows his feelings would not even listen to an argument turning him away, or comprehend it [even if he listened]; and in that state how could he be persuaded to change? And in general feelings seem to yield to force, not to argument.

Hence we must already in some way have a character suitable for virtue, fond of 30
what is fine and objecting to what is shameful.

31. [Theognis was a sixth-century B.C. poet from Megara.]

MORAL EDUCATION REQUIRES LEGISLATION

10

But it is hard for someone to be trained correctly for virtue from his youth if he has not been brought up under correct laws, since the many, especially the young, do not find it pleasant to live in a temperate and resistant way. Hence laws must prescribe
35 their upbringing and practices; for they will not find these things painful when they get used to them.

1180a   Presumably, however, it is not enough to get the correct upbringing and attention when they are young; rather, they must continue the same practices and be habituated to them when they become men. Hence we need laws concerned with
5 these things also, and in general with all of life. For the many yield to compulsion more than to argument, and to sanctions more than to what is fine.

This, some think, is why legislators should urge people towards virtue and exhort them to aim at what is fine, on the assumption that anyone whose good habits have prepared him decently will listen to them; but they should impose corrective treatments and penalties on anyone who disobeys or lacks the right nature, and com-
10 pletely expel an incurable. For the decent person, it is assumed, will attend to reason because his life aims at what is fine, while the base person, since he desires pleasure, has to receive corrective treatment by pain, like a beast of burden; that is why it is said that the pains imposed must be those most contrary to the pleasures he likes.

15   As we have said, then, someone who is to be good must be finely brought up and habituated, and then must live in decent practices, doing nothing base either willingly or unwillingly. And this will be true if his life follows some sort of understanding and correct order that has influence over him.

A father's instructions, however, lack this influence and compelling power; and so
20 in general do the instructions of an individual man, unless he is a king or someone like that. Law, however, has the power that compels; and law is reason that proceeds from a sort of intelligence and understanding. Besides, people become hostile to an individual human being who opposes their impulses even if he is correct in opposing them; whereas a law's prescription of what is decent is not burdensome.

25   And yet, only in Sparta, or in a few other cities as well, does the legislator seem to have attended to upbringing and practices. In most other cities they are neglected, and each individual citizen lives as he wishes, 'laying down the rules for his children and wife', like Cyclops.[32]

30   It is best, then, if the community attends to upbringing, and attends correctly. If, however, the community neglects it, it seems fitting for each individual to promote the virtue of his children and his friends — to be able to do it, or at least to decide to do it.

32. [The reference is to Homer's *Odyssey*, in which the Cyclops were portrayed as savage one-eyed giants living without government or laws.]

MORAL EDUCATION NEEDS LEGISLATIVE SCIENCE

11

From what we have said, however, it seems he will be better able to do it if he acquires legislative science. For, clearly, attention by the community works through laws, and 35
decent attention works through excellent laws; and whether the laws are written or 1180b
unwritten, for the education of one or of many, seems unimportant, as it is in music, gymnastics and other practices. For just as in cities the provisions of law and the [prevailing] types of character have influence, similarly a father's words and habits 5
have influence, and all the more because of kinship and because of the benefits he does; for his children are already fond of him and naturally ready to obey.

Moreover, education adapted to an individual is actually better than a common education for everyone, just as individualized medical treatment is better. For though generally a feverish patient benefits from rest and starvation, presumably some pa- 10
tient does not; nor does the boxing instructor impose the same way of fighting on everyone. Hence it seems that treatment in particular cases is more exactly right when each person gets special attention, since he then more often gets the suitable treatment.

Nonetheless a doctor, a gymnastics trainer and everyone else will give the best individual attention if they also know universally what is good for all, or for these sorts. 15
For sciences are said to be, and are, of what is common [to many particular cases].

Admittedly someone without scientific knowledge may well attend properly to a single person, if his experience has allowed him to take exact note of what happens in each case, just as some people seem to be their own best doctors, though unable to help anyone else at all. None the less, presumably, it seems that someone who wants 20
to be an expert in a craft and a branch of study should progress to the universal, and come to know that, as far as possible; for that, as we have said, is what the sciences are about.

Then perhaps also someone who wishes to make people better by his attention, many people or few, should try to acquire legislative science, if we will become good 25
through laws. For not just anyone can improve the condition of anyone, or the person presented to him; but if anyone can it is the person with knowledge, just as in medical science and the others that require attention and intelligence.

Next, then, should we examine whence and how someone might acquire legislative 30
science? Hence, just as in other cases [we go to the practitioner], should we go to the politicians? For, as we saw, legislative science seems to be a part of political science.

But does the case of political science perhaps seem different from the other sciences and capacities? For in others the same people, e.g. doctors or painters, who transmit the capacity to others, actively practise it themselves. By contrast, those who advertise 35
that they teach politics are the sophists, and none of them practices it. Instead, those 1181a
who practice it are the political activists, and they seem to act on some sort of capacity and experience rather than thought.

For evidently they neither write nor speak on such questions, though presumably it would be finer to do this than to compose speeches for the law courts or the Assembly; 5
nor have they made politicians out of their own sons or any other friends of theirs. And yet it would be reasonable for them to do this if they were able; for there is

nothing better than the political capacity that they could leave to their cities, and nothing better that they could decide to produce in themselves, or, therefore, in their closest friends.

10   Certainly experience seemingly contributes quite a lot; otherwise people would not have become better politicians by familiarity with politics. Hence those who aim to know about political science seemingly need experience as well.

By contrast, those of the sophists who advertise [that they teach political science] appear to be a long way from teaching; for they are altogether ignorant about the sort of thing political science is, and the sorts of things it is about. For if they had 15   known what it is, they would not have taken it to be the same as rhetoric, or something inferior to it, or thought it an easy task to assemble the laws with good reputations and then legislate. For they think they can select the best laws, as though the selection itself did not require comprehension, and as though correct judgment were not the most important thing, as it is in music.

20   It is those with experience in each area who judge the products correctly and who comprehend the method or way of completing them, and what fits with what; for if we lack experience, we must be satisfied with noticing that the product is well or bad-1181b   ly made, as with painting. Now laws are seemingly the products of political science; how, then, could someone acquire legislative science, or judge which laws are best, from laws alone? For neither do we appear to become experts in medicine by reading textbooks.

And yet doctors not only try to describe the [recognized] treatments, but also distinguish different states, and try to say how each type of patient might be cured 5   and must be treated. And what they say seems to be useful to the experienced, though useless to the ignorant.

Similarly, then, collections of laws and political systems[33] might also, presumably, be most useful if we are capable of studying them and of judging what is done finely or in the contrary way, and what sorts of [elements] fit with what. Those who lack the 10   [proper] state [of experience] when they go through these collections will not manage to judge finely, unless they can do it all by themselves [without training], though they might come to comprehend them better.

Since, then, our predecessors have left the area of legislation uncharted, it is presumably better to examine it ourselves instead, and indeed to examine political 15   systems in general, and so to complete the philosophy of human affairs, as far as we are able.

First, then, let us try to find out if our predecessors have made sound remarks on particular topics. Then let us study the collected political systems, to see from them 20   what sorts of things preserve and destroy cities, and each type of political system; and what causes some cities to conduct politics well, and some badly.

For when we have studied these questions, we will perhaps grasp better what sort of political system is best; how each political system should be organized so as to be best; and what habits and laws it should follow.

Let us discuss this, then, starting from the beginning.[34]

33. [Aristotle supervised a collection of the constitutional histories of one hundred fifty-eight Greek states, of which only one, the *Constitution of Athens*, is extant.]

34. [Here the *Nicomachean Ethics* ends, reminding us that for Aristotle the study of ethics is inseparable from the study of political philosophy.]

HEAD OF EPICURUS—a Greek sculpture
dating from Hellenistic times

SAMOS, EPICURUS'S BIRTHPLACE

MONUMENT OF LYSICRATES, 334 B.C.

EPICURUS

Epicurus (341–271 B.C.) was born of Athenian parents on the island of Samos, and was thus counted as an Athenian citizen. In order to fulfill his military obligations, he went to Athens in 323, the year in which Aristotle fled Athens, fearing anti-Macedonian sentiment after the death of Alexander the Great. However, even in Aristotle's absence Athens remained the center for philosophical activity, and Epicurus most certainly became familiar with Platonism and Aristotelianism. The death of Alexander brought about a good deal of political turmoil, some of which affected Epicurus directly. While he was in Athens, his family was evicted from Samos by the Macedonians, as were other Athenian colonists. It may be that Epicurus's evident antipathy to politics began with these events. In any case Epicureanism and the public life do not mix: the latter would upset the tranquillity required by the former.

Epicurus's family migrated to Colophon, in Asia Minor, and Epicurus rejoined them in 321. He spent the next ten years in Colophon, where he came under the tutelage of Nausiphanes, who espoused a version of atomism, a philosophy which had been founded by Leucippus (fifth century B.C.) and Democritus of Abdera (c. 460–c.370 B.C.). Epicurus himself became a convert to atomism, but his atomism differed from that of his predecessors.

Epicurus's version of atomism contended that the universe is composed of only two kinds of things: bodies and the void. That bodies exist is a matter of observation. The existence of the void or empty space is necessary in order for bodies to move. Bodies of visible size are compounded out of bodies of invisible size, namely, atoms. It is impossible for anything to come into existence out of nothing, and it is impossible for anything to pass into nothingness. Therefore what exists always has existed and always will exist. Now many visible bodies are not everlasting; they can be cut up and disintegrated. But since it is impossible for anything to come out of or pass into nothingness, it must be that at least the ultimate parts or atoms of a visible body are not subject to creation, decomposition, or disintegration; that is, the atoms are everlasting. (Epicurus's arguments explaining why there should be ultimate parts at all and why, if they do exist, they are too small to be seen, are obscure.)

Epicurus's infinitely many atoms possess only three variable qualities. They can differ from each other in size, shape, and weight. Some atoms are larger than others, although none of them is big enough to be seen, and none is infinitely small. Some atoms are heavier than others, but the differences in weight do not result in differences in velocity among various atoms. In fact, all atoms move at exactly the same velocity as they fall directly downward through infinite space and infinite time. If all atoms followed parallel downward paths at the same speed, however, they would never interact with each other, and thus nothing would ever change. In order to avoid that difficulty, Epicurus claimed that the atoms occasionally swerve in a random way from their downward paths. When atoms swerve, they may strike other atoms, thus setting off whole series of collisions. Visible objects are the results of such collisions. These objects are systems of atoms which, for some time, display cohesiveness due to a kind of dynamic equilibrium. But, insisted Epicurus, such systems of atoms, no matter how large and well behaved, are the result of purely mechanical causes. There is no design or providence in the universe. Everything that exists can be explained in principle by the motions of atoms in empty space. Nor is the present world-order in which we find ourselves everlasting. It is, like every visible object in it, a collection of atoms which for the present time exists in a dynamic equilibrium, but which will eventually disperse.

Epicurus regarded his atomic theory as the key to his moral theory. The moral theory was epitomized in antiquity as follows: the gods are not to be feared, death is not to be feared, pleasure is easy to obtain, and it is easy to endure pain. The gods, who are also nothing more than collections of atoms, are not to be feared because they have utterly no concern for the affairs of humans. To have any concern would be to spoil their divine tranquillity. Death is not to be feared because it is simply the dissolution of the atomic structure which makes up the soul, and when that happens, one ceases to exist. Thus one can be confident that no pain will be experienced after death.

The pursuit of pleasure is natural in humans, according to Epicurus, and in fact, a person ought always to seek pleasure. But an Epicurean is not an epicure, one devoted to pleasing the senses. The pursuit of excessive or violent pleasures can only result in pain; thus, such pleasures should be avoided. Rather, the pleasure to be sought is best characterized as the absence of pain of any kind. The most pleasant condition, according to Epicurus, is that in which one is neither hungry, thirsty, nor apprehensive, yet confident that one will remain in that condition. In this condition, one's atomic structure is unperturbed. Thus, true pleasure for Epicurus does not require extravagance.

From the time Epicurus began teaching in Athens in 306 until his death, he and his followers lived an abstemious life together, but one which they regarded as approaching perfect pleasure. Once the Epicureans' concept of pleasure is understood, one can see why they thought that pleasure is easy to obtain.

Epicurus's attitude toward his own painful terminal illness illustrates the thesis that it is easy to endure pain. In a letter written to a disciple shortly before his death, he said that "there is set over against these pains the joy of my heart at the memory of our happy conversations in the past."

Although Epicurus was a prolific writer, few of his writings survive. His *Letter to Menoeceus* and *Principal Doctrines,* reprinted here, give us the rudiments of his moral theory. An important source of information about Epicureanism is the Roman poet Lucretius (c.99–c.55 B.C.) in *On the Nature of the Universe,* trans. R. E. Latham (Baltimore: Penguin Books, 1951). J. M. Rist, *Epicurus: An Introduction* (Cambridge: Cambridge University Press, 1972) is a well balanced account. David J. Furley, *Two Studies in the Greek Atomists* (Princeton: Princeton University Press, 1967) is a more specialized but provocative work.

W.E.M.

LETTER TO MENOECEUS

Let no one when young delay to study philosophy, nor when he is old grow weary of his study. For no one can come too early or too late to secure the health of his soul. And the man who says that the age for philosophy has either not yet come or has gone by is like the man who says that the age for happiness is not yet come to him, or has passed away. Wherefore both when young and old a man must study philosophy, that as he grows old he may be young in blessings through the grateful recollection of what has been, and that in youth he may be old as well, since he will know no fear of what is to come. We must then meditate on the things that make our happiness, seeing that when that is with us we have all, but when it is absent we do all to win it.

The things which I used unceasingly to commend to you, these do and practise, considering them to be the first principles of the good life. First of all believe that god is a being immortal and blessed, even as the common idea of a god is engraved on men's minds, and do not assign to him anything alien to his immortality or ill-suited to his blessedness: but believe about him everything that can uphold his blessedness and immortality. For gods there are, since the knowledge of them is by clear vision. But they are not such as the many believe them to be: for indeed they do not consistently represent them as they believe them to be. And the impious man is not he who denies the gods of the many, but he who attaches to the gods the beliefs of the many. For the statements of the many about the gods are not conceptions derived from sensation, but false suppositions, according to which the greatest misfortunes befall the wicked and the greatest blessings the good by the gift of the gods. For men being accustomed always to their own virtues welcome those like themselves, but regard all that is not of their nature as alien.

Become accustomed to the belief that death is nothing to us. For all good and evil consists in sensation, but death is deprivation of sensation. And therefore a right understanding that death is nothing to us makes the mortality of life enjoyable, not because it adds to it an infinite span of time, but because it takes away the craving for immortality. For there is nothing terrible in life for the man who has truly comprehended that there is nothing terrible in not living. So that the man speaks but idly who says that he fears death not because it will be painful when it comes, but because it is painful in anticipation. For that which gives no trouble when it comes, is but an empty pain in anticipation. So death, the most terrifying of ills, is nothing to us, since so long as we exist, death is not with us; but when death comes, then we do not exist. It does not then concern either the living or the dead, since for the former it is not, and the latter are no more.

But the many at one moment shun death as the greatest of evils, at another yearn for it as a respite from the evils in life. But the wise man neither seeks to escape life nor fears the cessation of life, for neither does life offend him nor does the absence of life seem to be any evil. And just as with food he does not seek simply the larger share and nothing else, but rather the most pleasant, so he seeks to enjoy not the

Reprinted from *Epicurus, the Extant Remains*, translated by Cyril Bailey (1926), by permission of the Oxford University Press, Oxford.

longest period of time, but the most pleasant.

And he who counsels the young man to live well, but the old man to make a good end, is foolish, not merely because of the desirability of life, but also because it is the same training which teaches to live well and to die well. Yet much worse still is the man who says it is good not to be born, but

'once born make haste to pass the gates of Death'.[1]

For if he says this from conviction why does he not pass away out of life? For it is open to him to do so, if he had firmly made up his mind to this. But if he speaks in jest, his words are idle among men who cannot receive them.

We must then bear in mind that the future is neither ours, nor yet wholly not ours, so that we may not altogether expect it as sure to come, nor abandon hope of it, as if it will certainly not come.

We must consider that of desires some are natural, others vain, and of the natural some are necessary and others merely natural; and of the necessary some are necessary for happiness, others for the repose of the body, and others for very life. The right understanding of these facts enables us to refer all choice and avoidance to the health of the body and the soul's freedom from disturbance, since this is the aim of the life of blessedness. For it is to obtain this end that we always act, namely, to avoid pain and fear. And when this is once secured for us, all the tempest of the soul is dispersed, since the living creature has not to wander as though in search of something that is missing, and to look for some other thing by which he can fulfil the good of the soul and the good of the body. For it is then that we have need of pleasure, when we feel pain owing to the absence of pleasure; but when we do not feel pain, we no longer need pleasure. And for this cause we call pleasure the beginning and end of the blessed life. For we recognize pleasure as the first good innate in us, and from pleasure we begin every act of choice and avoidance, and to pleasure we return again, using the feeling as the standard by which we judge every good.

And since pleasure is the first good and natural to us, for this very reason we do not choose every pleasure, but sometimes we pass over many pleasures, when greater discomfort accrues to us as the result of them: and similarly we think many pains better than pleasures, since a greater pleasure comes to us when we have endured pains for a long time. Every pleasure then because of its natural kinship to us is good, yet not every pleasure is to be chosen: even as every pain also is an evil, yet not all are always of a nature to be avoided. Yet by a scale of comparison and by the consideration of advantages and disadvantages we must form our judgement on all these matters. For the good on certain occasions we treat as bad, and conversely the bad as good.

And again independence of desire we think a great good—not that we may at all times enjoy but a few things, but that, if we do not possess many, we may enjoy the few in the genuine persuasion that those have the sweetest pleasure in luxury who least need it, and that all that is natural is easy to be obtained, but that which is superfluous is hard. And so plain savours bring us a pleasure equal to a luxurious diet, when all the pain due to want is removed; and bread and water produce the highest pleasure, when one who needs them puts them to his lips. To grow accustomed therefore to simple and not luxurious diet gives us health to the full, and

---

1. [The quotation is by Theognis, regarding whom see Aristotle's *Ethics*, n. 111. —S.M.C.]

makes a man alert for the needful employments of life, and when after long intervals we approach luxuries, disposes us better towards them, and fits us to be fearless of fortune.

When, therefore, we maintain that pleasure is the end, we do not mean the pleasures of profligates and those that consist in sensuality, as is supposed by some who are either ignorant or disagree with us or do not understand, but freedom from pain in the body and from trouble in the mind. For it is not continuous drinkings and revellings, nor the satisfaction of lusts, nor the enjoyment of fish and other luxuries of the wealthy table, which produce a pleasant life, but sober reasoning, searching out the motives for all choice and avoidance, and banishing mere opinions, to which are due the greatest disturbance of the spirit.

Of all this the beginning and the greatest good is prudence. Wherefore prudence is a more precious thing even than philosophy: for from prudence are sprung all the other virtues, and it teaches us that it is not possible to live pleasantly without living prudently and honourably and justly, nor, again, to live a life of prudence, honour, and justice without living pleasantly. For the virtues are by nature bound up with the pleasant life, and the pleasant life is inseparable from them. For indeed who, think you, is a better man than he who holds reverent opinions concerning the gods, and is at all times free from fear of death, and has reasoned out the end ordained by nature? He understands that the limit of good things is easy to fulfil and easy to attain, whereas the course of ills is either short in time or slight in pain: he laughs at destiny, whom some have introduced as the mistress of all things. He thinks that with us lies the chief power in determining events, some of which happen by necessity and some by chance, and some are within our control; for while necessity cannot be called to account, he sees that chance is inconstant, but that which is in our control is subject to no master, and to it are naturally attached praise and blame. For, indeed, it were better to follow the myths about the gods than to become a slave to the destiny of the natural philosophers: for the former suggests a hope of placating the gods by worship, whereas the latter involves a necessity which knows no placation. As to chance, he does not regard it as a god as most men do (for in a god's acts there is no disorder), nor as an uncertain cause of all things: for he does not believe that good and evil are given by chance to man for the framing of a blessed life, but that opportunities for great good and great evil are afforded by it. He therefore thinks it better to be unfortunate in reasonable action than to prosper in unreason. For it is better in a man's actions that what is well chosen should fail, rather than that what is ill chosen should be successful owing to chance.

Meditate therefore on these things and things akin to them night and day by yourself, and with a companion like to yourself, and never shall you be disturbed waking or asleep, but you shall live like a god among men. For a man who lives among immortal blessings is not like to a mortal being.

PRINCIPAL DOCTRINES

I. THE blessed and immortal nature knows no trouble itself nor causes trouble to any other, so that it is never constrained by anger or favour. For all such things exist only in the weak.

II. Death is nothing to us: for that which is dissolved is without sensation; and that which lacks sensation is nothing to us.

III. The limit of quantity in pleasures is the removal of all that is painful. Wherever pleasure is present, as long as it is there, there is neither pain of body nor of mind, nor of both at once.

IV. Pain does not last continuously in the flesh, but the acutest pain is there for a very short time, and even that which just exceeds the pleasure in the flesh does not continue for many days at once. But chronic illnesses permit a predominance of pleasure over pain in the flesh.

V. It is not possible to live pleasantly without living prudently and honourably and justly, nor again to live a life of prudence, honour, and justice without living pleasantly. And the man who does not possess the pleasant life, is not living prudently and honourably and justly, and the man who does not possess the virtuous life, cannot possibly live pleasantly.

VI. To secure protection from men anything is a natural good, by which you may be able to attain this end.

VII. Some men wished to become famous and conspicuous, thinking that they would thus win for themselves safety from other men. Wherefore if the life of such men is safe, they have obtained the good which nature craves; but if it is not safe, they do not possess that for which they strove at first by the instinct of nature.

VIII. No pleasure is a bad thing in itself: but the means which produce some pleasures bring with them disturbances many times greater than the pleasures.

IX. If every pleasure could be intensified so that it lasted and influenced the whole organism or the most essential parts of our nature, pleasures would never differ from one another.

X. If the things that produce the pleasures of profligates could dispel the fears of the mind about the phenomena of the sky and death and its pains, and also teach the limits of desires and of pains, we should never have cause to blame them: for they would be filling themselves full with pleasures from every source and never have pain of body or mind, which is the evil of life.

XI. If we were not troubled by our suspicions of the phenomena of the sky and about death, fearing that it concerns us, and also by our failure to grasp the limits of pains and desires, we should have no need of natural science.

XII. A man cannot dispel his fear about the most important matters if he does not know what is the nature of the universe but suspects the truth of some mythical story. So that without natural science it is not possible to attain our pleasures unalloyed.

Reprinted from *Epicurus, the Extant Remains*, translated by Cyril Bailey (1926), by permission of the Oxford University Press, Oxford.

XIII. There is no profit in securing protection in relation to men, if things above and things beneath the earth and indeed all in the boundless universe remain matters of suspicion.

XIV. The most unalloyed source of protection from men, which is secured to some extent by a certain force of expulsion, is in fact the immunity which results from a quiet life and the retirement from the world.

XV. The wealth demanded by nature is both limited and easily procured; that demanded by idle imaginings stretches on to infinity.

XVI. In but few things chance hinders a wise man, but the greatest and most important matters reason has ordained and throughout the whole period of life does and will ordain.

XVII. The just man is most free from trouble, the unjust most full of trouble.

XVIII. The pleasure in the flesh is not increased, when once the pain due to want is removed, but is only varied: and the limit as regards pleasure in the mind is begotten by the reasoned understanding of these very pleasures and of the emotions akin to them, which used to cause the greatest fear to the mind.

XIX. Infinite time contains no greater pleasure than limited time, if one measures by reason the limits of pleasure.

XX. The flesh perceives the limits of pleasure as unlimited and unlimited time is required to supply it. But the mind, having attained a reasoned understanding of the ultimate good of the flesh and its limits and having dissipated the fears concerning the time to come, supplies us with the complete life, and we have no further need of infinite time: but neither does the mind shun pleasure, nor, when circumstances begin to bring about the departure from life, does it approach its end as though it fell short in any way of the best life.

XXI. He who has learned the limits of life knows that that which removes the pain due to want and makes the whole of life complete is easy to obtain; so that there is no need of actions which involve competition.

XXII. We must consider both the real purpose and all the evidence of direct perception, to which we always refer the conclusions of opinion; otherwise, all will be full of doubt and confusion.

XXIII. If you fight against all sensations, you will have no standard by which to judge even those of them which you say are false.

XXIV. If you reject any single sensation and fail to distinguish between the conclusion of opinion as to the appearance awaiting confirmation and that which is actually given by the sensation or feeling, or each intuitive apprehension of the mind, you will confound all other sensations as well with the same groundless opinion, so that you will reject every standard of judgement. And if among the mental images created by your opinion you affirm both that which awaits confirmation and that which does not, you will not escape error, since you will have preserved the whole cause of doubt in every judgement between what is right and what is wrong.

XXV. If on each occasion instead of referring your actions to the end of nature, you turn to some other nearer standard when you are making a choice or an avoidance, your actions will not be consistent with your principles.

XXVI. Of desires, all that do not lead to a sense of pain, if they are not satisfied, are not necessary, but involve a craving which is easily dispelled, when the object is hard to procure or they seem likely to produce harm.

XXVII. Of all the things which wisdom acquires to produce the blessedness of the complete life, far the greatest is the possession of friendship.

XXVIII. The same conviction which has given us confidence that there is nothing terrible that lasts for ever or even for long, has also seen the protection of friendship most fully completed in the limited evils of this life.

XXIX. Among desires some are natural and necessary, some natural but not necessary, and others neither natural nor necessary, but due to idle imagination.

XXX. Wherever in the case of desires which are physical, but do not lead to a sense of pain, if they are not fulfilled, the effort is intense, such pleasures are due to idle imagination, and it is not owing to their own nature that they fail to be dispelled, but owing to the empty imaginings of the man.

XXXI. The justice which arises from nature is a pledge of mutual advantage to restrain men from harming one another and save them from being harmed.

XXXII. For all living things which have not been able to make compacts not to harm one another or be harmed, nothing ever is either just or unjust; and likewise too for all tribes of men which have been unable or unwilling to make compacts not to harm or be harmed.

XXXIII. Justice never is anything in itself, but in the dealings of men with one another in any place whatever and at any time it is a kind of compact not to harm or be harmed.

XXXIV. Injustice is not an evil in itself, but only in consequence of the fear which attaches to the apprehension of being unable to escape those appointed to punish such actions.

XXXV. It is not possible for one who acts in secret contravention of the terms of the compact not to harm or be harmed, to be confident that he will escape detection, even if at present he escapes a thousand times. For up to the time of death it cannot be certain that he will indeed escape.

XXXVI. In its general aspect justice is the same for all, for it is a kind of mutual advantage in the dealings of men with one another: but with reference to the individual peculiarities of a country or any other circumstances the same thing does not turn out to be just for all.

XXXVII. Among actions which are sanctioned as just by law, that which is proved on examination to be of advantage in the requirements of men's dealings with one another, has the guarantee of justice, whether it is the same for all or not. But if a man makes a law and it does not turn out to lead to advantage in men's dealings with each other, then it no longer has the essential nature of justice. And even if the advantage in the matter of justice shifts from one side to the other, but for a while accords with the general concept, it is none the less just for that period in the eyes of those who do not confound themselves with empty sounds but look to the actual facts.

XXXVIII. Where, provided the circumstances have not been altered, actions which were considered just, have been shown not to accord with the general concept in actual practice, then they are not just. But where, when circumstances have changed, the same actions which were sanctioned as just no longer lead to advantage, there they were just at the time when they were of advantage for the dealings of fellow-citizens with one another; but subsequently they are no longer just, when no longer of advantage.

XXXIX. The man who has best ordered the element of disquiet arising from external circumstances has made those things that he could akin to himself and the rest at least not alien: but with all to which he could not do even this, he has refrained from mixing, and has expelled from his life all which it was of advantage to treat thus.

XL. As many as possess the power to procure complete immunity from their neighbours, these also live most pleasantly with one another, since they have the most certain pledge of security, and after they have enjoyed the fullest intimacy, they do not lament the previous departure of a dead friend, as though he were to be pitied.

EPICTETUS—anonymous
engraving, Biblioteque
Nationale, Paris

MARCUS AURELIUS (Campidiglio, Rome)

THE STOA, ATHENS: HOME OF STOIC

EPICTETUS

Stoicism as an organized philosophical movement flourished for a period of approximately five hundred years, from 300 B.C. to A.D. 180. The dates are, respectively, the approximate year in which the founder of Stoicism, Zeno of Citium (c. 344–c. 262 B.C.), began lecturing from a stoa, or porch, in the marketplace in Athens, and the year in which the last famous Stoic, the Roman emperor Marcus Aurelius, died. Although Stoic doctrine did not remain static in those five hundred years, the doctrinal differences between earlier and later Stoics appear for the most part to be minimal. What *is* remarkable is the difference in emphasis which Stoicism underwent. In the second and first centuries B.C., Stoicism was introduced into Roman intellectual circles. It found an audience so receptive that in the first and second centuries A.D., Stoicism was a powerful influence in the life of the Roman Empire, attracting such figures as Seneca (1–65), Epictetus (c.50–c.130), and Marcus Aurelius (121–180).

In the process of change, Stoicism became less of a philosophy and more of a guide to right conduct. The early Stoics had placed equal emphasis on Logic, Physics, and Ethics; but the Roman Stoics were concerned almost exclusively with the ethical and political aspects of Stoicism. It is easy to see why those aspects of Stoicism appealed to a Marcus Aurelius: the Stoic emphasis on duty and the Stoic belief that all people are citizens of one vast city dovetailed nicely with Roman imperialistic policy. But Stoicism also offered consolation to the less fortunate of the time, including Epictetus, a former slave, since it claimed that that which has ultimate value, namely, virtue, is equally open to all; and that such things as wealth, health, and honor are either of no value whatsoever or merely of instrumental value in the attainment of virtue.

The early Stoics saw the three areas of Logic, Physics, and Ethics as intimately related. These early Stoics made significant contributions to logical theory, with much of their work a departure from Aristotelian logic. For their physical theory the early Stoics looked back to what they took to be the teachings of a Pre-Socratic philosopher, Heraclitus of Ephesus, who flourished around 500 B.C. Heraclitus had taught that the universe is a continuously dynamic thing in which nothing remains strictly the same from one moment to the next. Heraclitus had used fire as a symbol for the ceaseless change occurring in the universe; he may also have intended to say that the universe is actually ruled and guided by fire, which would be the noblest kind of matter in nature. The early Stoics interpreted him in this way. Fire was also thought to be the source and seat of human intelligence; thus, if the universe is ruled by fire, the universe is itself intelligent. In fact, the Stoics believed the universe to be a vast rational being which exhibits, through the guidance of fire, order and law-governed behavior. The Stoics thus consciously appealed to a macrocosm–microcosm analogy: the universe is a rational animal writ large, and a person is or should be the universe writ small. This doctrine has four important repercussions for Stoic ethics.

First, since the source of human intelligence is a natural material element, fire, and since intelligence is the hallmark of what it is to be human, it followed for the Stoics that a person is a part of the natural physical universe, and not something over and above it. This belief fit very well with a doctrine that the Stoics adopted from the Cynics, namely, that all persons are "citizens of the world," which implied that all persons are radically equal. Stoic materialism thus provided a metaphysical underpinning for Stoic cosmopolitanism.

Second, if the universe itself is governed by certain laws and if a person is a microcosm of the universe, then it follows that a person is subject to the same laws as those which govern the universe. The laws in question, moreover, were viewed not merely as *descriptive* but as *prescriptive:* they prescribe how things *ought* to behave. These laws might be at variance with the customs and legal conventions of a particular society, and if so, those customs and conventions are wrong. There is, in other words, a "natural law" which supersedes all customary law and which is binding on all persons. Natural Law theories in and after the Middle Ages have their roots in Stoicism.

Third, inasmuch as a person is a microcosm of an inherently rational world, a person ought to live a life in perfect conformity with nature, that is, a life in which reason dominates a person's actions and passions. The Stoic "wise man" will live his life so that he does only that which is in accord with nature; moreover, he will do it simply *because* it is in accord with nature. For the Stoic the value of an action resides not in the happiness or pleasure it may happen to bring about, but solely in the virtuous state of mind of the agent. In this respect Stoic ethics foreshadow the ethical theory of Immanuel Kant.

Finally, the Stoics' insistence on the law-governed nature of the universe committed them to determinism, the thesis that everything that happens is the outcome of the operation of unchangeable and all-pervasive laws. As their critics were quick to point out, this seemed to clash with their belief that humans are free, responsible agents. In order to meet this criticism the Stoics stressed that it is important to see what constitutes human freedom. Epictetus's *Enchiridion*, or "Handbook," reprinted here, besides giving a moving account of the Stoic view of life, attempts to resolve the contradiction between human freedom and determinism.

Not much is known of Epictetus's life. He was born in Hieropolis in Asia Minor, was for some time a slave, but was freed by his Roman master. He was educated by a Stoic philosopher and began to teach philosophy himself in Rome until he was banished by the emperor Domitian. Epictetus moved to Nicopolis, in northwestern Greece, where he taught and practiced Stoicism until his death. No written works survive: the *Enchiridion* was dictated to a disciple.

F. H. Sandbach's *The Stoics* (New York: W. W. Norton, 1975) gives an elementary account of Stoicism. J. M. Rist, *Stoic Philosophy* (Cambridge: Cambridge University Press, 1969) deals topically with many important issues. Benson Mates, *Stoic Logic* (1953; rpt. Berkeley: University of California Press, 1961) and Shmuel Sambursky, *Physics of the Stoics* (1959; rpt. London: Hutchinson, 1971) are classics in their areas. There are several important papers in A. A. Long, ed., *Problems in Stoicism* (London: Athlone Press, 1971).

W.E.M.

ENCHIRIDION

1

Of all existing things some are in our power, and others are not in our power. In our power are thought, impulse, will to get and will to avoid, and, in a word, everything which is our own doing. Things not in our power include the body, property, reputation, office, and, in a word, everything which is not our own doing. Things in our power are by nature free, unhindered, untrammelled; things not in our power are weak, servile, subject to hindrance, dependent on others. Remember then that if you imagine that what is naturally slavish is free, and what is naturally another's is your own, you will be hampered, you will mourn, you will be put to confusion, you will blame gods and men; but if you think that only your own belongs to you, and that what is another's is indeed another's, no one will ever put compulsion or hindrance on you, you will blame none, you will accuse none, you will do nothing against your will, no one will harm you, you will have no enemy, for no harm can touch you.

Aiming then at these high matters, you must remember that to attain them requires more than ordinary effort; you will have to give up some things entirely, and put off others for the moment. And if you would have these also—office and wealth—it may be that you will fail to get them, just because your desire is set on the former, and you will certainly fail to attain those things which alone bring freedom and happiness.

Make it your study then to confront every harsh impression with the words, 'You are but an impression, and not at all what you seem to be'. Then test it by those rules that you possess; and first by this—the chief test of all—'Is it concerned with what is in our power or with what is not in our power?' And if it is concerned with what is not in our power, be ready with the answer that it is nothing to you.

2

Remember that the will to get promises attainment of what you will, and the will to avoid promises escape from what you avoid; and he who fails to get what he wills is unfortunate, and he who does not escape what he wills to avoid is miserable. If then you try to avoid only what is unnatural in the region within your control, you will escape from all that you avoid; but if you try to avoid disease or death or poverty you will be miserable.

Therefore let your will to avoid have no concern with what is not in man's power; direct it only to things in man's power that are contrary to nature. But for the moment you must utterly remove the will to get; for if you will to get something not in man's power you are bound to be unfortunate; while none of the things in man's power that you could honourably will to get is yet within your reach. Impulse to act and not to act, these are your concern; yet exercise them gently and without strain, and provisionally.

Reprinted from *Epictetus, The Discourses and Manual,* translated by P. E. Matheson (1916), by permission of the Oxford University Press, Oxford.

3

When anything, from the meanest thing upwards, is attractive or serviceable or an object of affection, remember always to say to yourself, 'What is its nature?' If you are fond of a jug, say you are fond of a jug; then you will not be disturbed if it be broken. If you kiss your child or your wife, say to yourself that you are kissing a human being, for then if death strikes it you will not be disturbed.

4

When you are about to take something in hand, remind yourself what manner of thing it is. If you are going to bathe put before your mind what happens in the bath—water pouring over some, others being jostled, some reviling, others stealing; and you will set to work more securely if you say to yourself at once: 'I want to bathe, and I want to keep my will in harmony with nature,' and so in each thing you do; for in this way, if anything turns up to hinder you in your bathing, you will be ready to say, 'I did not want only to bathe, but to keep my will in harmony with nature, and I shall not so keep it, if I lose my temper at what happens'.

5

What disturbs men's mind is not events but their judgements on events. For instance, death is nothing dreadful, or else Socrates would have thought it so. No, the only dreadful thing about it is men's judgement that it is dreadful. And so when we are hindered, or disturbed, or distressed, let us never lay the blame on others, but on ourselves, that is, on our own judgements. To accuse others for one's own misfortunes is a sign of want of education; to accuse oneself shows that one's education has begun; to accuse neither oneself nor others shows that one's education is complete.

6

Be not elated at an excellence which is not your own. If the horse in his pride were to say, 'I am handsome', we could bear with it. But when you say with pride, 'I have a handsome horse', know that the good horse is the ground of your pride. You ask then what you can call your own. The answer is—the way you deal with your impressions. Therefore when you deal with your impressions in accord with nature, then you may be proud indeed, for your pride will be in a good which is your own.

7

When you are on a voyage, and your ship is at anchorage, and you disembark to get fresh water, you may pick up a small shellfish or a truffle by the way, but you must keep your attention fixed on the ship, and keep looking towards it constantly, to see if the Helmsman calls you; and if he does, you have to leave everything, or be bundled on board with your legs tied like a sheep. So it is in life. If you have a dear wife or child given you, they are like the shellfish or the truffle, they are very well in their way. Only, if the Helmsman call, run back to your ship, leave all else, and do not look behind you. And if you are old, never go far from the ship, so that when you are called you may not fail to appear.

8

Ask not that events should happen as you will, but let your will be that events should happen as they do, and you shall have peace.

9

Sickness is a hindrance to the body, but not to the will, unless the will consent. Lameness is a hindrance to the leg, but not to the will. Say this to yourself at each event that happens, for you shall find that though it hinders something else it will not hinder you.

10

When anything happens to you, always remember to turn to yourself and ask what faculty you have to deal with it. If you see a beautiful boy or a beautiful woman, you will find continence the faculty to exercise there; if trouble is laid on you, you will find endurance; if ribaldry, you will find patience. And if you train yourself in this habit your impressions will not carry you away.

11

Never say of anything, 'I lost it', but say, 'I gave it back'. Has your child died? It was given back. Has your wife died? She was given back. Has your estate been taken from you? Was not this also given back? But you say, 'He who took it from me is wicked'. What does it matter to you through whom the Giver asked it back? As long as He gives it you, take care of it, but not as your own; treat it as passers-by treat an inn.

12

If you wish to make progress, abandon reasonings of this sort: 'If I neglect my affairs I shall have nothing to live on'; 'If I do not punish my son, he will be wicked.' For it is better to die of hunger, so that you be free from pain and free from fear, then to live in plenty and be troubled in mind. It is better for your son to be wicked than for you to be miserable. Wherefore begin with little things. Is your drop of oil spilt? Is your sup of wine stolen? Say to yourself, 'This is the price paid for freedom from passion, this is the price of a quiet mind.' Nothing can be had without a price. When you call your slave-boy, reflect that he may not be able to hear you, and if he hears you, he may not be able to do anything you want. But he is not so well off that it rests with him to give you peace of mind.

13

If you wish to make progress, you must be content in external matters to seem a fool and a simpleton; do not wish men to think you know anything, and if any should think you to be somebody, distrust yourself. For know that it is not easy to keep your will in accord with nature and at the same time keep outward things; if you attend to one you must needs neglect the other.

14

It is silly to want your children and your wife and your friends to live for ever, for that means that you want what is not in your control to be in your control, and what is not your own to be yours. In the same way if you want your servant to make no mistakes, you are a fool, for you want vice not to be vice but something different. But if you want not to be disappointed in your will to get, you can attain to that.

Exercise yourself then in what lies in your power. Each man's master is the man who has authority over what he wishes or does not wish, to secure the one or to take away the other. Let him then who wishes to be free not wish for anything or avoid anything that depends on others; or else he is bound to be a slave.

15

Remember that you must behave in life as you would at a banquet. A dish is handed round and comes to you; put out your hand and take it politely. It passes you; do not stop it. It has not reached you; do not be impatient to get it, but wait till your turn comes. Bear yourself thus towards children, wife, office, wealth, and one day you will be worthy to banquet with the gods. But if when they are set before you, you do not take them but despise them, then you shall not only share the gods' banquet, but shall share their rule. For by so doing Diogenes[1] and Heraclitus[2] and men like them were called divine and deserved the name.

16

When you see a man shedding tears in sorrow for a child abroad or dead, or for loss of property, beware that you are not carried away by the impression that it is outward ills that make him miserable. Keep this thought by you: 'What distresses him is not the event, for that does not distress another, but his judgement on the event.' Therefore do not hesitate to sympathize with him so far as words go, and if it so chance, even to groan with him; but take heed that you do not also groan in your inner being.

17

Remember that you are an actor in a play, and the Playwright chooses the manner of it: if he wants it short, it is short; if long, it is long. If he wants you to act a poor man you must act the part with all your powers; and so if your part be a cripple or a magistrate or a plain man. For your business is to act the character that is given you and act it well; the choice of the cast is Another's.

18

When a raven croaks with evil omen, let not the impression carry you away, but

1. [Diogenes (c.412–323 B.C.), a Greek philosopher of the Cynic (doggish) school, taught that the virtuous life was the simple life. He flouted custom, living in a tub and discarding all his possessions. When Alexander the Great reportedly visited him and in admiration offered to fulfill any request, Diogenes is said to have replied, "Just step out of my sunlight." —S.M.C.]

2. [Regarding Heraclitus, see Aristotle's *Ethics*, n. 22.]

straightway distinguish in your own mind and say, 'These portents mean nothing to me; but only to my bit of a body or my bit of property or name, or my children or my wife. But for me all omens are favourable if I will, for, whatever the issue may be, it is in my power to get benefit therefrom.'

19

You can be invincible, if you never enter on a contest where victory is not in your power. Beware then that when you see a man raised to honour or great power or high repute you do not let your impression carry you away. For if the reality of good lies in what is in our power, there is no room for envy or jealousy. And you will not wish to be praetor, or prefect or consul, but to be free; and there is but one way to freedom—to despise what is not in our power.

20

Remember that foul words or blows in themselves are no outrage, but your judgement that they are so. So when anyone makes you angry, know that it is your own thought that has angered you. Wherefore make it your first endeavour not to let your impressions carry you away. For if once you gain time and delay, you will find it easier to control yourself.

21

Keep before your eyes from day to day death and exile and all things that seem terrible, but death most of all, and then you will never set your thoughts on what is low and will never desire anything beyond measure.

22

If you set your desire on philosophy you must at once prepare to meet with ridicule and the jeers of many who will say, 'Here he is again, turned philosopher. Where has he got these proud looks?' Nay, put on no proud looks, but hold fast to what seems best to you, in confidence that God has set you at this post. And remember that if you abide where you are, those who first laugh at you will one day admire you, and that if you give way to them, you will get doubly laughed at.

23

If it ever happen to you to be diverted to things outside, so that you desire to please another, know that you have lost your life's plan. Be content then always to be a philosopher; if you wish to be regarded as one too, show yourself that you are one and you will be able to achieve it.

24

Let not reflections such as these afflict you: 'I shall live without honour, and never be of any account'; for if lack of honour is an evil, no one but yourself can involve you in evil any more than in shame. Is it your business to get office or to be invited to an entertainment?

Certainly not.

Where then is the dishonour you talk of? How can you be 'of no account any-where', when you ought to count for something in those matters only which are in your power, where you may achieve the highest worth?

'But my friends,' you say, 'will lack assistance.'

What do you mean by 'lack assistance'? They will not have cash from you and you will not make them Roman citizens. Who told you that to do these things is in our power, and not dependent upon others? Who can give to another what is not his to give?

'Get them then,' says he, 'that we may have them.'

If I can get them and keep my self-respect, honour, magnanimity, show the way and I will get them. But if you call on me to lose the good things that are mine, in order that you may win things that are not good, look how unfair and thoughtless you are. And which do you really prefer? Money, or a faithful, modest friend? Therefore help me rather to keep these qualities, and do not expect from me actions which will make me lose them.

'But my country,' says he, 'will lack assistance, so far as lies in me.'

Once more I ask, What assistance do you mean? It will not owe colonnades or baths to you. What of that? It does not owe shoes to the blacksmith or arms to the shoemaker; it is sufficient if each man fulfils his own function. Would you do it no good if you secured to it another faithful and modest citizen?

'Yes.'

Well, then, you would not be useless to it.

'What place then shall I have in the city?'

Whatever place you can hold while you keep your character for honour and self-respect. But if you are going to lose these qualities in trying to benefit your city, what benefit, I ask, would you have done her when you attain to the perfection of being lost to shame and honour?

25

Has some one had precedence of you at an entertainment or a levée or been called in before you to give advice? If these things are good you ought to be glad that he got them; if they are evil, do not be angry that you did not get them yourself. Remember that if you want to get what is not in your power, you cannot earn the same reward as others unless you act as they do. How is it possible for one who does not haunt the great man's door to have equal shares with one who does, or one who does not go in his train equality with one who does; or one who does not praise him with one who does? You will be unjust then and insatiable if you wish to get these privileges for nothing, without paying their price. What is the price of a lettuce? An obol perhaps. If then a man pays his obol and gets his lettuces, and you do not pay and do not get them, do not think you are defrauded. For as he has the lettuces so you have the obol you did not give. The same principle holds good too in conduct. You were not invited to some one's entertainment? Because you did not give the host the price for which he sells his dinner. He sells it for compliments, he sells it for attentions. Pay him the price then, if it is to your profit. But if you wish to get the one and yet not give up the other, nothing can satisfy you in your folly.

What! you say, you have nothing instead of the dinner?

Nay, you have this, you have not praised the man you did not want to praise, you have not had to bear with the insults of his doorstep.

26

It is in our power to discover the will of Nature from those matters on which we have no difference of opinion. For instance, when another man's slave has broken the wine-cup we are very ready to say at once, 'Such things must happen'. Know then that when your own cup is broken, you ought to behave in the same way as when your neighbour's was broken. Apply the same principle to higher matters. Is another's child or wife dead? Not one of us but would say, 'Such is the lot of man'; but when one's own dies, straightway one cries, 'Alas! miserable am I'. But we ought to remember what our feelings are when we hear it of another.

27

As a mark is not set up for men to miss it, so there is nothing intrinsically evil in the world.

28

If any one trusted your body to the first man he met, you would be indignant, but yet you trust your mind to the chance comer, and allow it to be disturbed and confounded if he revile you; are you not ashamed to do so?

29

In everything you do consider what comes first and what follows, and so approach it. Otherwise you will come to it with a good heart at first because you have not reflected on any of the consequences, and afterwards, when difficulties have appeared, you will desist to your shame. Do you wish to win at Olympia? So do I, by the gods, for it is a fine thing. But consider the first steps to it, and the consequences, and so lay your hand to the work. You must submit to discipline, eat to order, touch no sweets, train under compulsion, at a fixed hour, in heat and cold, drink no cold water, nor wine, except by order; you must hand yourself over completely to your trainer as you would to a physician, and then when the contest comes you must risk getting hacked, and sometimes dislocate your hand, twist your ankle, swallow plenty of sand, sometimes get a flogging, and with all this suffer defeat. When you have considered all this well, then enter on the athlete's course, if you still wish it. If you act without thought you will be behaving like children, who one day play at wrestlers, another day at gladiators, now sound the trumpet, and next strut the stage. Like them you will be now an athlete, now a gladiator, then orator, then philosopher, but nothing with all your soul. Like an ape, you imitate every sight you see, and one thing after another takes your fancy. When you undertake a thing you do it casually and half-heartedly, instead of considering it and looking at it all round. In the same way some people, when they see a philosopher and hear a man speaking like Euphrates (and indeed who can speak as he can?), wish to be philosophers themselves.

Man, consider first what it is you are undertaking; then look at your own powers and see if you can bear it. Do you want to compete in the pentathlon or in wrestling? Look to your arms, your thighs, see what your loins are like. For different men are born for different tasks. Do you suppose that if you do this you can live as you do now—eat and drink as you do now, indulge desire and discontent just as before? Nay, you must sit up late, work hard, abandon your own people, be looked down on by a mere slave, be ridiculed by those who meet you, get the worst of it in everything—in honour, in office, in justice, in every possible thing. This is what you have to consider: whether you are willing to pay this price for peace of mind, freedom, tranquillity. If not, do not come near; do not be, like the children, first a philosopher, then a tax-collector, then an orator, then one of Caesar's procurators. These callings do not agree. You must be one man, good or bad; you must develop either your Governing Principle, or your outward endowments; you must study either your inner man, or outward things—in a word, you must choose between the position of a philosopher and that of a mere outsider.

30

Appropriate acts are in general measured by the relations they are concerned with. 'He is your father.' This means you are called on to take care of him, give way to him in all things, bear with him if he reviles or strikes you.
'But he is a bad father.'
Well, have you any natural claim to a good father? No, only to a father.
'My brother wrongs me.'
Be careful then to maintain the relation you hold to him, and do not consider what he does, but what you must do if your purpose is to keep in accord with nature. For no one shall harm you, without your consent; you will only be harmed, when you think you are harmed. You will only discover what is proper to expect from neighbour, citizen, or praetor, if you get into the habit of looking at the relations implied by each.

31

For piety towards the gods know that the most important thing is this: to have right opinions about them—that they exist, and that they govern the universe well and justly—and to have set yourself to obey them, and to give way to all that happens, following events with a free will, in the belief that they are fulfilled by the highest mind. For thus you will never blame the gods, nor accuse them of neglecting you. But this you cannot achieve, unless you apply your conception of good and evil to those things only which are in our power, and not to those which are out of our power. For if you apply your notion of good or evil to the latter, then, as soon as you fail to get what you will to get or fail to avoid what you will to avoid, you will be bound to blame and hate those you hold responsible. For every living creature has a natural tendency to avoid and shun what seems harmful and all that causes it, and to pursue and admire what is helpful and all that causes it. It is not possible then for one who thinks he is harmed to take pleasure in what he thinks is the author of the harm, any more than to take pleasure in the harm itself. That is why a father is reviled by his son, when he does not give his son a share of what the son regards as good things; thus Polynices and Eteocles were set at enmity with one another by thinking that a king's throne was a good thing.[3] That is why the farmer, and the sailor, and the merchant, and those who lose wife or children revile the gods. For men's religion is bound up with their interest. Therefore he who makes it his concern rightly to direct his will to get and his will to avoid, is thereby making piety his concern. But it is proper on each occasion to make libation and sacrifice and to offer first-fruits according to the custom of our fathers, with purity and not in slovenly or careless fashion, without meanness and without extravagance.

32

When you make use of prophecy remember that while you know not what the issue will be, but are come to learn it from the prophet, you do know before you come what manner of thing it is, if you are really a philosopher. For if the event is not in our control, it cannot be either good or evil. Therefore do not bring with you to the prophet the will to get or the will to avoid, and do not approach him with trembling, but with your mind made up, that the whole issue is indifferent and does not affect you and that, whatever it be, it will be in your power to make good use of it, and no one shall hinder this. With confidence then approach the gods as counsellors, and further, when the counsel is given you, remember whose counsel it is, and whom you will be disregarding if you disobey. And consult the oracle, as Socrates thought men should, only when the whole question turns upon the issue of events, and neither reason nor any art of man provides opportunities for discovering what lies before you. Therefore, when it is your duty to risk your life with friend or country, do not ask the oracle whether you should risk your life. For if the prophet warns you that the sacrifice is unfavourable, though it is plain that this means death or exile or injury to some part of your body, yet reason requires that even at this cost you must stand by your friend and share your country's danger. Wherefore pay heed to the greater prophet, Pythian Apollo, who cast out of his temple the man who did not help his friend when he was being killed.[4]

33

Lay down for yourself from the first a definite stamp and style of conduct, which you will maintain when you are alone and also in the society of men. Be silent for the most part, or, if you speak, say only what is necessary and in a few words. Talk, but rarely, if occasion calls you, but do not talk of ordinary things—of gladiators, or horse-races, or athletes, or of meats or drinks—these are topics that arise everywhere—but above all do not talk about men in blame or compliment or comparison. If you can, turn the conversation of your company by your talk to some fitting subject; but if you should chance to be isolated among strangers, be silent. Do not laugh much, nor at many things, nor without restraint.

3. [According to Greek mythology, Polynices and Eteocles were the sons of Oedipus. After his blinding they insulted him, and he therefore cursed them. The curse was fulfilled when, the two having agreed to reign in alternate years, Eteocles would not relinquish the throne, and the brothers entered into combat and killed each other.]

4. [Reference is to a story about three men sent to Delphi, site of the Oracle housed in the Temple of Apollo. When attacked by robbers, one fled and a second, in attempting to defend the third, accidentally killed him. The Oracle rejected the runaway and absolved the homicide.]

Refuse to take oaths, altogether if that be possible, but if not, as far as circumstances allow.

Refuse the entertainments of strangers and the vulgar. But if occasion arise to accept them, then strain every nerve to avoid lapsing into the state of the vulgar. For know that, if your comrade have a stain on him, he that associates with him must needs share the stain, even though he be clean in himself.

For your body take just so much as your bare need requires, such as food, drink, clothing, house, servants, but cut down all that tends to luxury and outward show.

Avoid impurity to the utmost of your power before marriage, and if you indulge your passion, let it be done lawfully. But do not be offensive or censorious to those who indulge it, and do not be always bringing up your own chastity. If some one tells you that so and so speaks ill of you, do not defend yourself against what he says, but answer, 'He did not know my other faults, or he would not have mentioned these alone.'

It is not necessary for the most part to go to the games; but if you should have occasion to go, show that your first concern is for yourself; that is, wish that only to happen which does happen, and him only to win who does win, for so you will suffer no hindrance. But refrain entirely from applause, or ridicule, or prolonged excitement. And when you go away do not talk much of what happened there, except so far as it tends to your improvement. For to talk about it implies that the spectacle excited your wonder.

Do not go lightly or casually to hear lectures; but if you do go, maintain your gravity and dignity and do not make yourself offensive. When you are going to meet any one, and particularly some man of reputed eminence, set before your mind the thought, 'What would Socrates or Zeno[5] have done?' and you will not fail to make proper use of the occasion.

When you go to visit some great man, prepare your mind by thinking that you will not find him in, that you will be shut out, that the doors will be slammed in your face, that he will pay no heed to you. And if in spite of all this you find it fitting for you to go, go and bear what happens and never say to yourself, 'It was not worth all this'; for that shows a vulgar mind and one at odds with outward things.

In your conversation avoid frequent and disproportionate mention of your own doings or adventures; for other people do not take the same pleasure in hearing what has happened to you as you take in recounting your adventures.

Avoid raising men's laughter; for it is a habit that easily slips into vulgarity, and it may well suffice to lessen your neighbour's respect.

It is dangerous too to lapse into foul language; when anything of the kind occurs, rebuke the offender, if the occasion allow, and if not, make it plain to him by your silence, or a blush or a frown, that you are angry at his words.

34

When you imagine some pleasure, beware that it does not carry you away, like other imaginations. Wait a while, and give yourself pause. Next remember two things: how long you will enjoy the pleasure, and also how long you will afterwards

5. [Zeno of Citium (c.334–c.262 B.C.), a Greek philosopher who had studied under the Cynics, was the founder of Stoicism. He is not to be confused with Zeno of Elea (c.490–430 B.C.), creator of the immortal paradoxes.]

repent and revile yourself. And set on the other side the joy and self-satisfaction you will feel if you refrain. And if the moment seems come to realize it, take heed that you be not overcome by the winning sweetness and attraction of it; set in the other scale the thought how much better is the consciousness of having vanquished it.

35

When you do a thing because you have determined that it ought to be done, never avoid being seen doing it, even if the opinion of the multitude is going to condemn you. For if your action is wrong, then avoid doing it altogether, but if it is right, why do you fear those who will rebuke you wrongly?

36

The phrases, 'It is day' and 'It is night', mean a great deal if taken separately, but have no meaning if combined. In the same way, to choose the larger portion at a banquet may be worth while for your body, but if you want to maintain social decencies it is worthless. Therefore, when you are at meat with another, remember not only to consider the value of what is set before you for the body, but also to maintain your self-respect before your host.

37

If you try to act a part beyond your powers, you not only disgrace yourself in it, but you neglect the part which you could have filled with success.

38

As in walking you take care not to tread on a nail or to twist your foot, so take care that you do not harm your Governing Principle. And if we guard this in everything we do, we shall set to work more securely.

39

Every man's body is a measure for his property, as the foot is the measure for his shoe. If you stick to this limit, you will keep the right measure; if you go beyond it, you are bound to be carried away down a precipice in the end; just as with the shoe, if you once go beyond the foot, your shoe puts on gilding, and soon purple and embroidery. For when once you go beyond the measure there is no limit.

40

Women from fourteen years upwards are called 'madam' by men. Wherefore, when they see that the only advantage they have got is to be marriageable, they begin to make themselves smart and to set all their hopes on this. We must take pains then to make them understand that they are really honoured for nothing but a modest and decorous life.

41

It is a sign of a dull mind to dwell upon the cares of the body, to prolong exercise, eating, drinking, and other bodily functions. These things are to be done by the way; all your attention must be given to the mind.

42

When a man speaks evil or does evil to you, remember that he does or says it because he thinks it is fitting for him. It is not possible for him to follow what seems good to you, but only what seems good to him, so that, if his opinion is wrong, he suffers, in that he is the victim of deception. In the same way, if a composite judgement which is true is thought to be false, it is not the judgement that suffers, but the man who is deluded about it. If you act on this principle you will be gentle to him who reviles you, saying to yourself on each occasion, 'He thought it right.'

43

Everything has two handles, one by which you can carry it, the other by which you cannot. If your brother wrongs you, do not take it by that handle, the handle of his wrong, for you cannot carry it by that, but rather by the other handle—that he is a brother, brought up with you, and then you will take it by the handle that you can carry by.

44

It is illogical to reason thus, 'I am richer than you, therefore I am superior to you', 'I am more eloquent than you, therefore I am superior to you.' It is more logical to reason, 'I am richer than you, therefore my property is superior to yours', 'I am more eloquent than you, therefore my speech is superior to yours.' You are something more than property or speech.

45

If a man wash quickly, do not say that he washes badly, but that he washes quickly. If a man drink much wine, do not say that he drinks badly, but that he drinks much. For till you have decided what judgement prompts him, how do you know that he acts badly? If you do as I say, you will assent to your apprehensive impressions and to none other.

46

On no occasion call yourself a philosopher, nor talk at large of your principles among the multitude, but act on your principles. For instance, at a banquet do not say how one ought to eat, but eat as you ought. Remember that Socrates had so completely got rid of the thought of display that when men came and wanted an introduction to philosophers he took them to be introduced; so patient of neglect was he. And if a discussion arise among the multitude on some principle, keep silent for the most part; for you are in great danger of blurting out some undigested thought. And when some one says to you, 'You know nothing', and you do not let it provoke you, then know that you are really on the right road. For sheep do not bring grass to their shepherds and show them how much they have eaten, but they digest their fodder and then produce it in the form of wool and milk. Do the same yourself; instead of displaying your principles to the multitude, show them the results of the principles you have digested.

47

When you have adopted the simple life, do not pride yourself upon it, and if you are a water-drinker do not say on every occasion, 'I am a water-drinker.' And if you ever want to train laboriously, keep it to yourself and do not make a show of it. Do not embrace statues. If you are very thirsty take a good draught of cold water, and rinse your mouth and tell no one.

48

The ignorant man's position and character is this: he never looks to himself for benefit or harm, but to the world outside him. The philosopher's position and character is that he always look to himself for benefit and harm.

The signs of one who is making progress are: he blames none, praises none, complains of none, accuses none, never speaks of himself as if he were somebody, or as if he knew anything. And if any one compliments him he laughs in himself at his compliment; and if one blames him, he makes no defence. He goes about like a convalescent, careful not to disturb his constitution on its road to recovery, until it has got firm hold. He has got rid of the will to get, and his will to avoid is directed no longer to what is beyond our power but only to what is in our power and contrary to nature. In all things he exercises his will without strain. If men regard him as foolish or ignorant he pays no heed. In one word, he keeps watch and guard on himself as his own enemy, lying in wait for him.

49

When a man prides himself on being able to understand and interpret the books of Chrysippus,[6] say to yourself, 'If Chrysippus had not written obscurely this man would have had nothing on which to pride himself.'

What is my object? To understand Nature and follow her. I look then for some one who interprets her, and having heard that Chrysippus does I come to him. But I do not understand his writings, so I seek an interpreter. So far there is nothing to be proud of. But when I have found the interpreter it remains for me to act on his precepts; that and that alone is a thing to be proud of. But if I admire the mere power of exposition, it comes to this—that I am turned into a grammarian instead of a philosopher, except that I interpret Chrysippus in place of Homer. Therefore, when some one says to me, 'Read me Chrysippus', when I cannot point to actions which are in harmony and correspondence with his teaching, I am rather inclined to blush.

50

Whatever principles you put before you, hold fast to them as laws which it will be impious to transgress. But pay no heed to what any one says of you; for this is something beyond your own control.

6. [Chrysippus (c.279–c.206 B.C.), third leader of the Stoic school, is said to have been one of the greatest logicians of ancient times.]

51

How long will you wait to think yourself worthy of the highest and transgress in nothing the clear pronouncement of reason? You have received the precepts which you ought to accept, and you have accepted them. Why then do you still wait for a master, that you may delay the amendment of yourself till he comes? You are a youth no longer, you are now a full-grown man. If now you are careless and indolent and are always putting off, fixing one day after another as the limit when you mean to begin attending to yourself, then, living or dying, you will make no progress but will continue unawares in ignorance. Therefore make up your mind before it is too late to live as one who is mature and proficient, and let all that seems best to you be a law that you cannot transgress. And if you encounter anything troublesome or pleasant or glorious or inglorious, remember that the hour of struggle is come, the Olympic contest is here and you may put off no longer, and that one day and one action determines whether the progress you have achieved is lost or maintained.

This was how Socrates attained perfection, paying heed to nothing but reason, in all that he encountered. And if you are not yet Socrates, yet ought you to live as one who would wish to be a Socrates.

52

The first and most necessary department of philosophy deals with the application of principles; for instance, 'not to lie'. The second deals with demonstrations; for instance, 'How comes it that one ought not to lie?' The third is concerned with establishing and analysing these processes; for instance, 'How comes it that this is a demonstration? What is demonstration, what is consequence, what is contradiction, what is true, what is false?' It follows then that the third department is necessary because of the second, and the second because of the first. The first is the most necessary part, and that in which we must rest. But we reverse the order: we occupy ourselves with the third, and make that our whole concern, and the first we completely neglect. Wherefore we lie, but are ready enough with the demonstration that lying is wrong.

53

On every occasion we must have these thoughts at hand,

> 'Lead me, O Zeus, and lead me, Destiny,
> Whither ordained is by your decree.
> I'll follow, doubting not, or if with will
> Recreant I falter, I shall follow still.'[7]

> 'Who rightly with necessity complies
> In things divine we count him skilled and wise,'[8]

---

7. [This quotation is by Cleanthes (c.331–232 B.C.), who headed the Stoic school following Zeno. His most famous work is the poem *Hymn to Zeus*.]

8. [These lines are from a fragment by Euripides.]

'Well, Crito, if this be the gods' will, so be it.'[9]

Anytus and Meletus have power to put me to death, but not to harm me.'[10]

9. [The reference is to Plato's *Crito.*]

10. [The reference is to Plato's *Apology.*]

AUGUSTINE—fresco by Botticelli in the Church of Ognissiti, Florence

AUGUSTINE AND HIS MOTHER
(Ary Scheffer, 19th cent.)

TOMB OF ST. AUGUSTINE
(Pavia Cathedral, 1362)

AUGUSTINE

During the second through the fifth centuries or so of the Christian Era, Christian apologists began to graft the shoots of the New Testament onto the roots of Platonism, Aristotelianism, and Stoicism. Such husbandry was the work of the Fathers of the Church; hence, this part of the Christian Era is sometimes called the Patristic Era.

Indisputably the greatest of the Church Fathers was St. Augustine (A.D. 354–430). Born in the north-African town of Thagaste (now Souk-Ahras, Algeria), Augustine was sent to Carthage in 370 to receive an education in rhetoric, preparatory to a career in law. Not only was Carthage then renowned for education in rhetoric and law; it was also, by Augustine's account, famous for its iniquity, in which he indulged himself freely. In Carthage Augustine first heard of Manicheanism, a dualistic Oriental religion he followed for some nine years. Augustine was attracted to the Manicheans by their swift solution to the problem of evil; that is, the problem of why an all-good, all-powerful God permits the existence of evil in the world. The Manicheans held that counterpoised to God is an all-powerful malignant force, and the world continually exhibits the endless strife between these two.

Following his education, Augustine taught rhetoric in Thagaste, Carthage, and Rome, and in 384 secured a position as a professor of rhetoric at Milan. His disenchantment with Manicheanism had been growing through the years, and by then it was complete; but still tormented by the problem of evil, he had settled for skepticism. While in Milan he encountered two influences which had a profound effect on his life: St. Ambrose, then bishop of Milan, and the writings of the Neoplatonists. Augustine heard many of the sermons given by Ambrose and was deeply moved by them. He also read, in Latin translation, some of the writings of such Neoplatonist philosophers as Plotinus (205–270), who claimed to be perfecting the philosophy of Plato. These two sources convinced him that his reservations about Christianity were ill founded. In particular, he now thought he saw a way out of the impasse created by the problem of evil: since everything that exists is created by God, and everything created by God is good, there could be no all-powerful, perfectly malign being continually thwarting God's efforts. It follows, then, according to Augustine, that evil is nonexistent. As Augustine would have it, evil is not the *presence* of something that exists, but rather the *absence* of something, namely, goodness. Augustine finally converted to Christianity in 386, and was baptized in Milan in the next year. After his conversion he returned to Africa, where he was ordained as priest in the city of Hippo. He rose rapidly in the ecclesiastical ranks to become the bishop of Hippo, a position he held until his death. He died in 430 as the Vandals were preparing to lay siege to Hippo.

Augustine's prodigious writings cover virtually every aspect of Christian experience, since he spent much of his adult life seeking to define Christianity and defend it not only from the attacks of nonbelievers but also from the challenges of several types of heretical Christian. For example, in addition to combating the Manicheans, Augustine also wrote several treatises against the members of a schismatic north-African sect, the Donatists, who maintained that the sacraments, if administered by a sinful priest, had no validity. Augustine also took issue with the Pelagians, who denied the doctrine of original sin, claiming that Adam and Eve's sin was not transmitted to their descendants. The Pelagians believed that God's grace was not necessary for human salvation, a proposition vehemently denied by Augustine. His success against Christian heretics was so complete that subsequent Christian theologians generally consider it sufficient merely to cite his authority on many doctrinal issues. Indeed, his authority was so great that it was appealed to by both sides during the Reformation controversies.

It is commonly said that Augustine Platonized Christianity. This statement must be treated cautiously, for Augustine could not have read many, if any, of Plato's dialogues. In fact, he emphatically rejected many of Plato's most characteristic doctrines, including the doctrines of reincarnation (along with the associated Platonic thesis that the body is the prison of the soul, deserved because of the soul's transgressions in a previous life); recollection (which he replaced with a doctrine of divine illumination); and the denial of moral weakness. Nevertheless, there is a Platonic core to Augustine's thinking. Plato's Forms become for Augustine eternal ideas in God's mind; and, like Plato, Augustine makes a sharp distinction between the things that exist in space or time and that which is outside space and time, the latter being perfect, the former imperfect.

Augustine's most comprehensive treatment of the problems of time constitutes Book XI of his *Confessions,* which is reprinted here. The *Confessions* is a unique book, a work which is at once autobiographical, didactic, devotional, and philosophical. The first nine books give a detailed account of Augustine's life up to and including his conversion to Christianity. In Book XI, however, the issues are strictly theological and philosophical. Augustine begins with the question, "What was God doing before He created Heaven and Earth?" His treatment of this question leads him to consider the further question. "How is it possible to measure time?" which invokes the more general question, "What is time?" The honesty and evident self-perplexity with which he grapples with these difficult questions have attracted many contemporary philosophers to this book of the *Confessions.*

A recent, serviceable biography of Augustine's life is Peter Brown, *Augustine of Hippo: A Biography* (Berkeley: University of California Press, 1967), which also contains information about English translations of Augustine's writings. Etienne Gilson, *The Christian Philosophy of Saint Augustine* (New York: Random House, 1960) provides a clear introduction to Augustine's philosophy. R. A. Markus, ed., *Augustine: A Collection of Critical Essays* (Garden City: Doubleday, 1972) contains a valuable collection of papers on Augustine's philosophy.

W.E.M.

CONFESSIONS

BOOK XI

IN THE BEGINNING GOD CREATED . . .

I

But, Lord, since You are in eternity, are You unaware of what I am saying to You? Or do you see in time what takes place in time? But if You *do* see, why am I giving You an account of all these things? Not, obviously, that You should learn them from me; but I excite my own love for You and the love of those who read what I write, that we all may say: *The Lord is great, and exceedingly to be praised.* I have said before and I will say again: "It is for love of Your love that I do it." We pray [for what we want], yet Truth Himself has said: *Your Father knows what is needful for you before you ask Him.* Thus we are laying bare our love for You in confessing to You our wretchedness and Your mercies towards us: that You may free us wholly as You have already freed us in part, so that we may cease to be miserable in ourselves and come to happiness in You. For You have called us to be poor in spirit, to be meek, to mourn, to hunger and thirst after justice, to be merciful and clean of heart and peacemakers.

Thus I have told You many things, with such power and will as I had, because You, O Lord my God, had first willed that I should confess to You: *for Thou art good and Thy mercy endureth forever.*

II

But when will the voice of my pen have power to tell all Your exhortations and all Your terrors, Your consolations and the guidance by which You have brought me to be to Your people a preacher of Your word and a dispenser of Your Sacrament? Even had I the power to set down all these things duly, the drops of my time are too precious.

For a long time now I burn with the desire to meditate upon Your law, and to confess to You both my knowledge of it and my ignorance of it—the first beginnings of Your light and what remains of my own darkness—until my weakness shall be swallowed up in Your strength. And I do not want to see scattered and wasted upon other things such time as I find free from necessary care of the body, intellectual labour, and the service which either I owe men or do not owe but render all the same.

O Lord my God, be attentive to my prayer. Let Thy mercy grant my desire, since it does not burn for myself alone, but longs to serve the charity I have for my brethren: and in my heart Thous seest that it is so. Let me offer in sacrifice to Thee

Reprinted from *Confessions of St. Augustine,* translated by F. J. Sheed (New York: Sheed & Ward, 1943), by permission of the publisher. The words in brackets are amplifications by the translator. The italicized words are Biblical quotations.

the service of my mind and my tongue, and do Thou give me what I may offer Thee. For I am needy and poor, *Thou art rich unto all who call upon Thee.* Thou art free from care for Thyself and full of care for us. Circumcise the lips of my mouth and lips of my mind of all rash speech and lying. May Thy Scriptures be for my chaste delight; let me not deceive others about them nor be myself deceived. O Lord, hearken and have mercy, O Lord my God, Light of the blind and Strength of the weak, but Light too of the clear of sight and Strength of the strong; hearken to my soul, hear it crying from the depths. Unless Thine ears are attentive to us in the abyss, whither shall we go? To whom shall we cry?

Thine is the day, and Thine is the night: at Thy will the moments flow and pass. Grant me, then, space for my meditations upon the hidden things of Thy law, nor close Thy law against me as I knock. Not for nothing hast Thou willed that the deep secrets of all those pages should be written, not for nothing have those woods their *stags,* which retire to them and are restored, walk in them and are fed, lie down in them and ruminate. Complete Thy work in me, O Lord, and open those pages to me. Thy voice is my joy, abounding above all joys. Grant me what I love, for I do love it. And this too is of Thy gift. Do not abandon what Thou hast given, nor scorn Thy grass that is athirst for Thee. Let me confess to thee whatsoever I shall find in Thy books, and *let me hear the voice of thy praise,* and drink of Thee and *consider the wondrous things of Thy law* from the first beginning, when Thou didst make heaven and earth, until our everlasting reign with Thee in Thy holy city.

O Lord have mercy on me and grant what I desire. For, as I think, my desire is not of earth, not of gold and silver and gems or fine raiment or power and glory or the lusts of the flesh or the necessities of my body and of this our earthly pilgrimage: *all these things shall be added unto us who seek the Kingdom of God and Thy justice.*

See, O my God, whence comes my desire. *The wicked have told me fables but not as Thy law.* That is the source of my desire. See, Father: gaze and see and approve: and may it be pleasing in the sight of Thy mercy that I should find grace before Thee, that the inner secret of Thy words may be laid open at my knock. I beseech it by our Lord Jesus Christ Thy Son, *the Man of Thy right hand, the Son of Man, whom Thou hast confirmed for Thyself* as Mediator between Thyself and us: by whom Thou didst seek us when we sought not Thee, didst seek us indeed that we might seek Thee: Thy Word, by which Thou hast made all things and me among them: Thy Only One, by whom Thou hast called the people of the faithful, and me among them, unto adoption. I beseech it by Him who sits at Thy right hand and makes intercession for us, *in whom are hidden all the treasures of wisdom and knowledge.* These treasures are what I seek in Thy books. Moses wrote of Him: this He says, who is Truth.

III

Grant me to hear and understand what is meant by *In the beginning You made heaven and earth.* For so Moses wrote, wrote and went his way: passed from this world to You and is no longer here before me. Were he here, I should lay hold of him, and ask him, and in Your name beg him, to explain the sense of those words to me; I should lend my bodily ear to the sounds that should issue from his mouth. If he spoke in Hebrew, his voice would beat upon my ear to no purpose, nothing of what it said would reach my mind: if he spoke in Latin, I should know what he said. But how should I know that what he said was true? And if I did know it, would it be from him that I knew it? No: but within me, in the inner retreat of my mind, the Truth, which is neither Hebrew nor Greek, nor Latin, nor Barbarian, would tell me, without lips or tongue or sounded syllables: "He speaks truth:" and I (at once assured) would say to Your servant in all confidence: "You speak truth." Since, then, I cannot question him, I ask Thee, the Truth, filled with whom Moses spoke truth: I ask Thee, my God: pardon my sins, and as Thou didst grant to Thy servant to speak those words, grant me to understand them.

IV

We look upon the heavens and the earth, and they cry aloud that they were made. For they change and vary. (If anything was not made and yet exists, there is nothing in it that was not there before: and it is the essence of change and variation that something should be that was not there before.) They cry aloud, too, that they did not make themselves. "We exist, because we were made; but we did not exist before we existed to be able to give ourselves existence!" And their visible presence is itself the voice with which they speak.

It was You, Lord, who made them: for You are beautiful, and they are beautiful: You are good, and they are good: You are, and they are. But they neither are beautiful nor are good nor simply are as You their Creator: compared with You they are not beautiful and are not good and are not. These truths, thanks to You, we know; and our knowledge compared with Your knowledge is ignorance.

V

But *how* did You make heaven and earth? What instrument did You use for a work so mighty? You are not like an artist; for he forms one body from another as his mind chooses; his mind has the power to give external existence to the form it perceives within itself by its inner eye—and whence should it have that power unless You made it? It impresses that form upon a material already existent and having the capacity to be thus formed, such as clay or stone or wood or gold or such like. And how should these things have come to be unless You had made them to be? It was You who made the workman his body, and the mind that directs his limbs, the matter of which he makes what he makes, the intelligence by which he masters his art and sees inwardly what he is to produce exteriorly, the bodily sense by which he translates what he does from his mind to his material, and then informs the mind of the result of his workmanship, so that the mind may judge by that truth which presides within it whether the work is well done.

All these things praise You, the Creator of them all. But how do You create them? How, O God, did You create heaven and earth? Obviously it was not *in* heaven or on earth that You made heaven and earth; nor in the air nor in the waters, since these belong to heaven and earth; nor did You make the universe in the universe, because there was no place for it to be made until it was made. Nor had You any material in Your hand when You were making heaven and earth: for where should You have got what You had not yet made to use as material? What exists, save because You exist? You spoke and heaven and earth were created; in Your word You created them.

VI

But *how* did You speak? Was it perhaps as when that voice sounded from the cloud saying: *This is my beloved Son?* That voice sounded and ceased to sound, had a beginning and an end. The syllables sounded and died away, the second after the first, the third after the second, and so in order, until the last after the rest, and silence after the last. From this it is clear beyond question that that voice was sounded by the movement of something created by You, a movement in time but serving Your eternal will.

These words were uttered in time and the bodily ear conveyed them to the understanding mind, whose spiritual ear is attuned to Your eternal Word. And the mind compared these words sounding in time with Your eternal Word and its silence: and it said: "It is other, far other. These words are far less than I, indeed they are not at all, for they pass away and are no more: but the Word of God is above me and endures for ever."

Thus, had it been by words sounding and passing away that You said "Let heaven and earth be made," and so created heaven and earth, there would have had to be some bodily creature before heaven and earth, by the movement of which in time that voice came and went in time.

But there was no bodily thing before heaven and earth: or if there were then certainly You did not use some still earlier utterance in time to produce it, that by it You might utter in time the decree that heaven and earth should be made. Whatever it may have been that produced such a voice, it must have been made by You, otherwise it would not have existed at all. But to produce the bodily thing capable of uttering those words, what word did You utter?

VII

Clearly You are calling us to the realization of that Word—God with You, God as You are God—which is uttered eternally and by which all things are uttered eternally.

For this is not an utterance in which what has been said passes away that the next thing may be said and so finally the whole utterance be complete: but all in one act, yet abiding eternally: otherwise it would be but time and change and no true eternity, no true immortality.

I know it, O my God, and I give You thanks. I know it, Lord, I confess it to You: and every man knows it as I do and praises You as I do who is not ungrateful for Your sure truth. We know, Lord, we know, that in the degree that anything is no longer what it was, and is now what it once was not, it is in the process of dying and beginning anew. But of Your Word nothing passes or comes into being, for it is truly immortal and eternal. Thus it is by a Word co-eternal with Yourself that in one eternal act You say all that You say, and all things are made that You say are to be made. You create solely by thus saying. Yet all the things You create by saying are not brought into being in one act and from eternity.

VIII

Tell me, O Lord my God, how this can be? In a kind of way I see, but how to express it I do not know: save that whatever comes into being and ceases to be, begins at the moment and ends at the moment when the eternal reason—which has in itself no beginning or ending—knows that it should begin or end. That eternal reason is Your Word, *the Beginning who also speaks unto us.* This He tells us in the Gospel to our bodily ear, this He uttered exteriorly in the ears of men: that we might believe in Him, and seek Him within us and find Him in the eternal Truth, where the one good Master teaches all His disciples.

There it is that I hear Your voice, Lord, telling me that only one who teaches us is speaking to us, and that whoever does not teach us may be speaking, but not to us. Yet who teaches us save Truth unchanging? When from changing creatures we learn anything, we are led to Truth that does not change: and there we truly learn, as we stand and hear Him and rejoice with you for the voice of the bridegroom, returning to the Source of our being. Thus it is that He is the Beginning: unless He remained when we wandered away, there should be no abiding place for our return. But when we return from error, we return by realizing the Truth; that we may realize it, He instructs us for He is the *Beginning who also speaks unto us.*

IX

This then, O God, was the Beginning in which You created Heaven and Earth: marvellously speaking and marvellously creating in Your Word, Who is Your Son and Your Strength and Your Wisdom and Your Truth. Who shall understand this? Who shall relate it? What is that light which shines upon me but not continuously, and strikes upon my heart with no wounding? I draw back in terror: I am on fire with longing: terror in so far as I am different from it, longing in the degree of my likeness to it. It is Wisdom, Wisdom Itself, which in those moments shines upon me, cleaving through my cloud. And the cloud returns to wrap me round once more as my strength is beaten down under its darkness and the weight of my sins: for *my strength is weakened through poverty,* so that I can no longer support my good, until Thou, Lord who art merciful to my iniquities, shalt likewise heal my weakness: redeeming my life from corruption and crowning me with pity and compassion, and filling my desire with good things: *my youth shall be renewed like the eagle's. For we are saved by hope and we wait with patience for Thy promises.*

Let him who can hear Thy voice speaking within him; I, relying upon Thy inspired word, shall cry aloud: *How great are Thy works, O Lord! Thou has made all things in wisdom.* Wisdom is "the Beginning": and it is in that Beginning that You made heaven and earth.

X

Surely those are still in their ancient error who say to us: "What was God doing before He made heaven and earth?" If, they say, He was at rest and doing nothing, why did He not continue to do nothing for ever after as for ever before? If it was a new movement and a new will in God to create something He had never created before, how could that be a true eternity in which a will should arise which did not exist before? For the will of God is not a creature: it is prior to every creature, since nothing would be created unless the will of the Creator first so willed. The will of God belongs to the very substance of God. Now if something arose in the substance of God which was not there before, that substance could not rightly be called eternal; but if God's will that creatures should be is from eternity, why are creatures not from eternity?

XI

Those who speak thus do not yet understand You, O Wisdom of God, Light of minds: they do not yet understand how the things are made that are made by You and in You. They strive for the savour of eternity, but their mind is still tossing about in the past and future movements of things, and is still vain.

Who shall lay hold upon their mind and hold it still, that it may stand a little while, and a little while glimpse the splendour of eternity which stands for ever: and compare it with time whose moments never stand, and see that it is not comparable. Then indeed it would see that a long time is long only from the multitude of movements that pass away in succession, because they cannot co-exist: that in eternity nothing passes but all is present, whereas time cannot be present all at once. It would see that all the past is thrust out by the future, and all the future follows upon the past, and past and future alike are wholly created and upheld in their passage by that which is always present? Who shall lay hold upon the mind of man, that it may stand and see that time with its past and future must be determined by eternity, which stands and does not pass, which has in itself no past or future. Could my hand have the strength [so to lay hold upon the mind of man] or could my mouth by its speaking accomplish so great a thing?

XII

I come now to answer the man who says: "What was God doing before He made Heaven and earth?" I do not give the jesting answer—said to have been given by one who sought to evade the force of the question—"He was getting Hell ready for people who pry too deep." To poke fun at a questioner is not to see the answer. My reply will be different. I would much rather say "I don't know," when I don't, than hold one up to ridicule who had asked a profound question and win applause for a worthless answer.

But, O my God, I say that You are the Creator of all creation, and if by the phrase heaven and earth we mean all creation, then I make bold to reply: Before God made heaven and earth, He did not make anything. For if He had made something, what would it have been but a creature? And I wish I knew all that it would be profitable for me to know, as well as I know that no creature was made before any creature was made.

XIII

But a lighter mind, adrift among images of time and its passing, might wonder that You, O God almighty and all-creating and all-conserving, Maker of heaven and earth, should have abstained from so vast a work for the countless ages that passed before You actually wrought it. Such a mind should awaken and realize how ill-grounded is his wonder.

How could countless ages pass when You, the Author and Creator of all ages, had not yet made them? What time could there be that You had not created? or how could ages pass, if they never were?

Thus, since You are the Maker of all times, if there actually was any time before You made heaven and earth, how can it be said that You were not at work? If there was time, You made it, for time could not pass before You made time. On the other hand, if before heaven and earth were made there was no time, then what is meant by the question "What were You doing then?" If there was not any time, there was not any "then".

It is not in time that You are before all time: otherwise You would not be before all time. You are before all the past by the eminence of Your ever-present eternity: and You dominate all the future in as much as it is still to be: and once it has come it will be past: but *Thou art always the self-same and Thy years shall not fail.* Your years neither go nor come: but our years come and go, that all may come. Your years abide all in one act of abiding: for they abide and the years that go are not thrust out by those that come, for none pass: whereas our years shall not all be, till all are no more. Your years are as a single day; and Your day comes not daily but is today, a today which does not yield place to any tomorrow or follow upon any yesterday. In You today is eternity: thus it is that You begot one co-eternal with Yourself to whom you said: *Today have I begotten Thee.* You are the Maker of all time, and before all time You are, nor was there ever a time when there was no time!

XIV

At no time then had You not made anything, for time itself You made. And no time is co-eternal with You, for You stand changeless; whereas if time stood change-less, it would not be time. What then is time? Is there any short and easy answer to that? Who can put the answer into words or even see it in his mind? Yet what commoner or more familiar word do we use in speech than time? Obviously when we use it, we know what we mean, just as when we hear another use it, we know what he means.

What then *is* time? If no one asks me, I know; if I want to explain it to a questioner, I do not know. But at any rate this much I dare affirm I know: that if nothing passed there would be no past time; if nothing were approaching, there would be no future time; if nothing were, there would be no present time.

But the two times, past and future, how can they *be,* since the past is no more and the future is not yet? On the other hand, if the present were always present and never flowed away into the past, it would not be time at all, but eternity. But if the present is only time, because it flows away into the past, how can we say that it *is?* For it is, only because it will cease to be. Thus we can affirm that time *is* only in that it tends towards not-being.

XV

Yet we speak of a long time or a short time, applying these phrases only to past or future. Thus for example we call a hundred years ago a long time past, and a hundred years hence a long time ahead, and ten days ago a short time past, ten days hence a short time ahead. But in what sense can that which does not exist be long or short? The past no longer is, the future is not yet. Does this mean that we must not say: "It is long," but of the past "It was long," of the future "It will be long?"

O, my Lord, my Light, here too man is surely mocked by Your truth! If we say the past was long, was it long when it was already past or while it was still present? It could be long only while it was in existence to *be* long. But the past no longer exists; it cannot be long, because it is not at all.

Thus we must not say that the past was long: for we shall find nothing in it capable of being long, since, precisely because it is past, it is not at all. Let us say then that a particular time was long while it was present, because in so far as it was present, it was long. For it had not yet passed away and so become non-existent; therefore it still was something, and therefore capable of being long: though once it passed away, it ceased to be long by ceasing to be.

Let us consider, then, O human soul, whether present time can be long: for it has been given you to feel and measure time's spaces. What will you answer me?

Are the present hundred years a long time? But first see whether a hundred years *can* be present. If it is the first year of the hundred, then that year is present, but the other ninety-nine are still in the future, and so as yet are not: if we are in the second year, then one year is past, one year is present, the rest future. Thus whichever year of our hundred-year period we choose as present, those before it have passed away, those after it are still to come. Thus a hundred years cannot be present.

But now let us see if the chosen year is itself present. If we are in the first month, the others are still to come, if in the second, the first has passed away and the rest are not yet. Thus a year is not wholly present while it runs, and if the whole of it is not present, then the year is not present. For a year is twelve months, and the month that happens to be running its course is the only one present, the others either are no longer or as yet are not. Even the current month is not present, but only one day of it: if that day is the first, the rest are still to come; if the last, the rest are passed away; if somewhere between, it has days past on one side and days still to come on the other.

Thus the present, which we have found to be the only time capable of being long, is cut down to the space of scarcely one day. But if we examine this one day, even it is not wholly present. A day is composed of twenty-four hours—day-hours, night-hours: the first hour finds the rest still to come, the last hour finds the rest passed away, any hour between has hours passed before it, hours to come after it. And that one hour is made of fleeing moments: so much of the hour as has fled away is past, what still remains is future. If we conceive of some point of time which cannot be divided into even the minutest parts of moments, that is the only point that can be called present: and that point flees at such lightning speed from being future to being past, that it has no extent of duration at all. For if it were so extended, it would be divisible into past and future: the present has no length.

Where, then, is there a time that can be called long? Is it the future? But we cannot say of the future "It is long" because as yet it is not at all and therefore is not long. We say "It will be long." But when will it be long? While it is still in the future, it will not be long, because it does not yet exist and so cannot be long. Suppose we say, then, that it is to be long only when, coming out of the future [which is not yet], it begins to be and is now present—and thus something, and thus capable of being long. But the present cries aloud, as we have just heard, that it cannot have length.

XVI

Yet, Lord, we are aware of periods of time; we compare one period with another and say that some are longer, some shorter. We measure how much one is longer than another and say that it is double, or triple, or single, or simply that one is as long as the other. But it is time actually passing that we measure by our awareness; who can measure times past which are now no more or times to come which are not yet, unless you are prepared to say that that which does not exist can be measured? Thus while time is passing, it can be perceived and measured; but when it has passed it cannot, for it *is* not.

XVII

I am seeking, Father, not saying: O, my God, aid me and direct me.

Perhaps it might be said that there are not three times, past, present and future, as we learnt in boyhood and have taught boys: but only present, because the other two do not exist. Or perhaps that these two do exist, but that time comes forth from some secret place when from future it becomes present, and departs into some secret place when from present it becomes past. For where have those who prophesied the future seen the future, if it does not yet exist? What does not exist cannot be seen. And those who describe the past could not describe it truly if they did not mentally see it: and if the past were totally without existence it would be totally impossible to see it. Hence both past and future must exist.

XVIII

Suffer me, Lord, to push my inquiry further; O my Hope, let not my purpose go awry.

If the future and the past exist, I want to know where they are. And if I cannot yet know this, at least I do know that wherever they are, they are there not as future or past, but present. If wherever they are they are future, then in that place they are not yet; if past, then they are there no more. Thus wherever they are and whatever they are, they *are* only as present. When we relate the past truly, it is not the things themselves that are brought forth from our memory—for these have passed away: but words conceived from the images of the things: for the things stamped their prints upon the mind as they passed through it by way of the senses. Thus for example my boyhood, which no longer exists, is in time past, which no longer exists; but the likeness of my boyhood, when I recall it and talk of it, I look upon in time present, because it is still present in my memory.

Whether the case is similar with prophecies of things to come—namely that images of things which are not yet are seen in advance as now existent—I confess, O my God, that I do not know. But this I do know, that we ordinarily consider our future actions in advance, and that this consideration is present, but the action we are thinking of does not yet exist, because it is future; when we have actually set about it and have begun to do what we planned, then that action will exist, because then it will not be future but present.

Whatever may be the mode of this mysterious foreseeing of things to come, unless the thing is it cannot be seen. But what now is, is not future but present. Therefore when we speak of seeing the future, obviously what is seen is not the things which are not yet because they are still to come, but their causes or perhaps the signs that foretell them, for these causes and signs do exist here and now. Thus to those who see them now, they are not future but present, and from them things to come are conceived by the mind and foretold. These concepts already exist, and those who foretell are gazing upon them, present within themselves.

Let me take one example from a vast number of such things.

I am looking at the horizon at dawn: I foretell that the sun is about to rise. What I am looking at is present, what I foretell is future—not the sun, of course, for it now is, but its rising which is not yet. But unless I could imagine the actual rising in my mind, as now when I speak of it, I could not possibly foretell it. But the dawn which

I see in the sky is not the sunrise, although it precedes the sunrise; nor is the dawn the image of the sunrise that is in my mind. But both—the dawn and the image of the sunrise—are present and seen by me, so that the sunrise which is future can be told in advance. Thus the future is not yet; and if it is not yet, it is not; and if it is not, then it is totally impossible to see it. But it can be foretold from things present which now exist and are seen.

XIX

But You, O Ruler of Your creation, how is it that you can show souls things that are to come? For such things You have told Your prophets. In what manner do You show the future to man, for whom nothing future yet is? Or do You show only present signs of things to come? For what does not exist obviously cannot be shown. The means You use is altogether beyond my gaze; my eyes have not the strength; of myself I shall never be able to see so deep, but in You I shall be able, when you grant it, O lovely Light of the eyes of my spirit.

XX

At any rate it is now quite clear that neither future nor past actually exists. Nor is it right to say there are three times, past, present and future. Perhaps it would be more correct to say: there are three times, a present of things past, a present of things present, a present of things future. For these three exist in the mind, and I find them nowhere else: the present of things past is memory, the present of things present is sight, the present of things future is expectation. If we are allowed to speak thus, I see and admit that there are three times, that three times truly are.

By all means continue to say that there are three times, past, present and future; for, though it is incorrect, custom allows it. By all means say it. I do not mind, I neither argue nor object: provided that you understand what you are saying and do not think future or past now exists. There are few things that we phrase properly; most things we phrase badly: but what we are trying to say is understood.

XXI

I said a little while ago that we measure time in its passing, so that we are able to say that this period of time is to that as two to one, or that this is of the same duration as that, and can measure and describe any other proportions of time's parts.

Thus, as I said, we measure time *in its passing.* If you ask me how I know this, my answer is that I know it because we measure time, and we cannot measure what does not exist, and past and future do not exist. But how do we measure time present, since it has no extent? It is measured while it is passing; once it has passed, it cannot be measured, for then nothing exists to measure.

But where does time come from, and by what way does it pass, and where does it go, while we are measuring it? Where is it from?—obviously from the future. By what way does it pass?—by the present. Where does it go?—into the past. In other words it passes from that which does not yet exist, by way of that which lacks extension, into that which is no longer.

But how are we measuring time unless in terms of some kind of duration? We cannot say single or double or triple or equal or proportioned in any other way, save of the duration of periods of time. But in what duration do we measure time while it is actually passing? In the future, from which it comes? But what does not yet exist cannot be measured. In the present, then, by which it passes? But that which has no space cannot be measured. In the past, to which it passes? But what no longer exists cannot be measured.

XXII

My mind burns to solve this complicated enigma. O Lord my God, O good Father, for Christ's sake I beseech Thee, do not shut off these obscure familiar problems from my longing, do not shut them off and leave them impenetrable but let them shine clear for me in the light of Thy mercy, O Lord. Yet whom shall I question about them? And to whom more fruitfully than to Thee shall I confess my ignorance: for Thou art not displeased at the zeal with which I am on fire for Thy Scriptures. Grant me what I love: for it is by Your gift that I love. Grant me this gift, Father, *who dost know how to give good gifts to Thy children.* Grant it because I have *studied that I might know and it is a labour in my sight* until Thou shalt open it to me. For Christ's sake I beseech Thee, in the name of Him who is the Holy of Holies, that no one prevent me. *I have believed, therefore have I spoken.* This is my hope; for this do I live, *that I may see the delight of the Lord. Behold Thou hast made my days old,* and they pass away: but how I know not.

We are forever talking of time and of times. "How long did he speak," "How long did it take him to do that," "For how long a time did I fail to see this," "This syllable is double the length of that." So we speak and so we hear others speak, and others understand us, and we them. They are the plainest and commonest of words, yet again they are profoundly obscure and their meaning still to be discovered.

XXIII

I once heard a learned man say that time is simply the movement of the sun and moon and stars. I did not agree. For why should not time rather be the movement of all bodies? Supposing the lights of heaven were to cease and the potter's wheel moved on, would there not be time by which we could measure its rotations and say that these were at equal intervals, or some slower, some quicker, some taking longer, some shorter? And if we spoke thus, should we not ourselves be speaking in time: would there not be in our words some syllables long, some short—because some would sound for a longer time, some for a shorter?

O God, grant unto men to see by some small example the elements in common between small things and great. There are stars and the lights of heaven *to be for signs and for seasons and for days and years.* This is evident; but just as I would not affirm that one turn of that little wooden wheel is a day, neither should my philosopher say that it is no time at all.

What I am trying to come at is the force and nature of time, by which we measure the movement of bodies and say for example that this movement is twice as long as that. A day means not only the length of time that the sun is above the earth—so that we distinguish day from night—but the time of the sun's whole circuit from east to east—as we say that so many days have passed, so many days being used to include their nights, for the nights are not reckoned separately. Thus, since a day is constituted by the movement of the sun and its completed circle from east to east, I wish to know whether a day is that movement itself, or simply the time the movement takes, or both.

If the movement of the sun through one complete circuit were the day, then it would be a day even if the sun sped through its course in a space of time equal to an hour. If the time the sun now takes to complete its circuit is the day, then it would not be a day if between one sunrise and the next there were only the space of an hour: the sun would have to go around twenty-four times to make one day. But if to constitute a day there is needed both the movement of the sun through one circuit and the time the sun now takes, then you would not have a day if the sun completed its whole circuit in an hour, nor again if the sun stood still and as much time passed as the sun normally takes to complete its journey from one morning to the next.

But I shall not at the moment pursue the question of what it is that we call a day. I shall continue to seek what time is, by which we measure the sun's journey: so that we should say that it had gone round in half its accustomed time, if it went round in a space of time equivalent to twelve hours. And comparing its normal time with this twelve-hour time, we should say that the latter was single, the former double; yet the sun would in the one case have made its journey from east to east in the shorter time, in the other in the longer (so that time is something independent of the sun's movement).

Let no one tell me that the movement of the heavenly bodies is time: when at the prayer of a man the sun stood still that he might complete his victory in battle, the sun stood still but time moved on. The battle was continued for the necessary length of time and was finished.

Therefore I see time as in some way extended. But do I see it? Or do I only seem to see it? Thou wilt show me, O Light, O Truth.

XXIV

Would You have me agree with one who said that time is the movement of a body? You would not: for I learn that no body moves save in time: You have said it. But I do not learn that the movement of the body is time: You have not said it. For when a body is in motion, it is by time that I measure how long it is in motion from the beginning of its movement till it ceases to move. And if I did not see when the movement began, and if it moved on without my seeing when it ceased, I should be able to measure only from the moment I began to look until the moment I stopped looking. If I look for a long time, all I can say is that the time is long, but not how long it is, because when we say how long a time, we say it by comparison: as for example: this is as long as that, or this is twice that, and such like. But if we could note the point of space from which a body in motion comes or the point to which it goes, or could distinguish its parts if it is moving on its axis, we should be able to say how much time has elapsed for the movement of the body, or its part, from one place to another.

Thus since the movement of a body is not the same as our measurement of how long the movement takes, who can fail to see which of these is more deserving of the name of time? A body moves at different speeds, and sometimes stands still; but time enables us to measure not only its motion but its rest as well; and we say "It was at rest for the same length of time as it was in motion," or "It was at rest twice or thrice as long as it was in motion" or any other proportion, whether precisely measured or roughly estimated.

Therefore time is not the movement of a body.

XXV

I confess to You, Lord, that I still do not know what time is. And again I confess to You, Lord, that I know that I am uttering these things in time: I have been talking of time for a long time, and this long time would not be a long time unless time had passed. But how do I know this, since I do not know what time is? Or perhaps I do know, but simply do not know how to express what I know. Alas for me, I do not even know what I do not know! See me, O my God, I stand before You and I do not lie: as my speech is, so is my heart. *For Thou lightest my lamp, O Lord; O my God, enlighten my darkness.*

XXVI

Does not my soul speak truly to You when I say that I can measure time? For so it is, O Lord my God, I measure it and I do not know what it is that I am measuring. I measure the movement of a body, using time to measure it by. Do I not then measure time itself? Could I measure the movement of a body—its duration and how long it takes to move from place to place—if I could not measure the time in which it moves?

But if so, what do I use to measure time with? Do we measure a longer time by a shorter one, as we measure a beam in terms of cubits? Thus we say that the duration of a long syllable is measured by the space of a short syllable and is said to be double. Thus we measure the length of poems by the lengths of the lines, and the lengths of the lines by the lengths of the feet, and the lengths of the feet by the lengths of the syllables, and the lengths of long syllables by the lengths of short. We do not measure poems by pages, for that would be to measure space not time; we measure by the way the voice moves in uttering the poem, and we say: "It is a long poem, for it consists of so many lines; the lines are long for they are composed of so many feet; the feet are long for they include so many syllables; this syllable is long for it is the double of a short syllable."

But not by all this do we arrive at an exact measure of time. It may well happen that a shorter line may take longer if it is recited slowly than a longer line hurried through. And the same is true of a poem or a foot or a syllable.

Thus it seems to me that time is certainly extendedness—but I do not know what it is extendedness of: probably of the mind itself. Tell me, O my God, what am I measuring, when I say either, with no aim at precision, that one period is longer than the other, or precisely, that one is double the other? That I measure time, I know. But I do not measure the future, for it is not yet; nor the present, for it is not extended in space; nor the past, which no longer exists. So what do I measure? Is it time in passage but not past? So I have already said.

XXVII

Persevere, O my soul, fix all the power of your gaze. *God is our helper. He made us, and not we ourselves.* Fix your gaze where truth is whitening toward the dawn.

Consider the example of a bodily voice. It begins to sound, it sounds and goes on sounding, then it ceases: and now there is silence, the sound has passed, the sound no longer is. It was future before it began to sound, and so could not be measured, for as yet it did not exist; and now it cannot be measured because now it exists no longer. Only while sounding could it be measured for then it was, and so was measurable. But even then it was not standing still; it was moving, and moving out of existence. Did this make it more measurable? Only in the sense that by its passing it was spread over a certain space of time which made it measurable: for the present occupies no space.

At any rate, let us grant that it could be measured. And now again imagine a voice. It begins to sound and goes on sounding continuously without anything to break its even flow. Let us measure it, while it is sounding. For when it has ceased to sound, it will be past and will no longer be measurable. Let us measure it then and say how long it is. But it is still sounding and can be measured only from its beginning when it began to sound to its end, when it ceased. For what we measure is the interval between some starting point and some conclusion. This means that a sound which is not yet over cannot be measured so that we may say how long or short it is, nor can it be said either to be equal to some other sound or single or double or any other proportion in relation to it. But when it *is* over, it will no longer be. Then how will it be possible to measure it? Yet we do measure time — not that which is not yet, nor that which is no longer, nor that which has no duration, nor that which lacks beginning and end. Thus it seems that we measure neither time future nor time past nor time present nor time passing: and yet we measure time.

Deus creator omnium:[1] This line is composed of eight syllables, short and long alternately: the four short syllables, the first, third, fifth, seventh are single in relation to the four long syllables, the second, fourth, sixth, eighth. Each long syllable has double the time of each short syllable. I pronounce them and I say that it is so, and so it is, as is quite obvious to the ear. As my ear distinguishes I measure a long syllable by a short and I perceive that it contains it twice. But since I hear a syllable only when the one before it has ceased — the one before being short and the one following long — how am I to keep hold of the short syllable, and how shall I set it against the long one to measure it and find that the long one is twice its length — given that the long syllable does not begin to sound until the short one has ceased? And again can I measure the long one while it is present, since I cannot measure it until it is completed? And its completion is its passing out of existence.

What then is it that I measure? Where is the short syllable by which I measure? Where is the long syllable which I measure? Both have sounded, have fled away, have gone into the past, are now no more: yet I do measure, and I affirm with confidence, in so far as a practised sense can be trusted, that one is single, the other double, in the length of time it occupies. And I could not do this unless they had both passed away and ended. Thus it is not the syllables themselves that I measure, for they are now no more, but something which remains engraved in my memory.

It is in you, O my mind, that I measure time. Do not bring against me, do not bring against yourself the disorderly throng of your impressions. In you, I say, I measure time. What I measure is the impress produced in you by things as they pass and abiding in you when they have passed: and it is present. I do not measure the things themselves whose passage produced the impress; it is the impress that I

---

1. [God, the creator of all. —S.M.C.]

measure when I measure time. Thus either that is what time is, or I am not measuring time at all.

But when we measure silences, and say that some particular silence lasted as long as some particular phrase, do we not stretch our mind to measure the phrase as though it were actually sounded, so as to be able to form a judgment of the relation between the space of the silence and that space of time? For without voice or lips we can go through poems and verses and speeches in our minds, and we can allow for the time it takes for their movement, one part in relation to another, exactly as if we were reciting them aloud. If a man decides to utter a longish sound and settles in his mind how long the sound is to be, he goes through that space of time in silence, entrusts it to his memory, then begins to utter the sound, and it sounds until it reaches the length he had fixed for it. Or rather I should say [not that it sounds but] that it has sounded and will sound: for as much of it as has been uttered at a given moment has obviously sounded, and what remains will sound: and so he completes the sound: at every moment his attention, which is present, causes the future to make its way into the past, the future diminishing and the past growing, until the future is exhausted and everything is past.

XXVIII

But how is the future diminished or exhausted, since the future does not yet exist: or how does the past grow, since it no longer is? Only because, in the mind which does all this, there are three acts. For the mind expects, attends and remembers: what it expects passes, by way of what it attends to, into what it remembers. Would anyone deny that the future is as yet not existent? But in the mind there is already an expectation of the future. Would anyone deny that the past no longer exists? Yet still there is in the mind a memory of the past. Would anyone deny that the present time lacks extension, since it is but a point that passes on? Yet the attention endures, and by it that which is to be passes on its way to being no more. Thus it is not the future that is long, for the future does not exist: a long future is merely a long expectation of the future; nor is the past long since the past does not exist: a long past is merely a long memory of the past.

Suppose that I am about to recite a psalm that I know. Before I begin, my expectation is directed to the whole of it; but when I have begun, so much of it as I pluck off and drop away into the past becomes matter for my memory; and the whole energy of the action is divided between my memory, in regard to what I have said, and my expectation, in regard to what I am still to say. But there is a present act of attention, by which what was future passes on its way to becoming past. The further I go in my recitation, the more my expectation is diminished and my memory lengthened, until the whole of my expectation is used up when the action is completed and has passed wholly into my memory. And what is true of the whole psalm, is true for each part of the whole, and for each syllable: and likewise for any longer action, of which the canticle may be only a part: indeed it is the same for the whole life of man, of which all a man's actions are parts: and likewise for the whole history of the human race, of which all the lives of all men are parts.

XXIX

But *Thy mercy is better than lives,* and behold my life is but a scattering. *Thy right hand has held me up* in my Lord, the Son of Man who is the Mediator in many things and in divers manners—that *I may apprehend by Him in whom I am apprehended* and may be set free from what I once was, following your Oneness: *forgetting the things that are behind* and not poured out upon things to come and things transient, but *stretching forth to those that are before* (not by dispersal but by concentration of energy) *I press towards the prize of the supernal vocation,* where *I may hear the voice of Thy praise* and contemplate Thy delight which neither comes nor passes away.

But now my years are wasted in sighs, and Thou, O Lord, my eternal Father, art my only solace; but I am divided up in time, whose order I do not know, and my thoughts and the deepest places of my soul are torn with every kind of tumult until the day when I shall be purified and melted in the fire of Thy love and wholly joined to Thee.

XXX

And I shall stand and be established in You, in my own true form, in Your truth. I shall no longer suffer the questions of men who, by a disease they have merited for their punishment, ever thirst for more than they can drink. Thus they ask: "What was God making before He made Heaven and earth?" "Or how did the idea of creating something come into His mind whereas He had never created anything before?"

Grant them, Lord, to think well what they are saying, and to realize that one cannot use the word "never" when there is no time. If you say that he "never" made anything, obviously this means that He did not make anything "at any time." Let them see then that there can be no time apart from creation, and let them cease to talk such nonsense. *Let them stretch forth to the things that are before,* and let them realize that before all times You are the Eternal Creator of all times, and that no times are co-eternal with You, nor is any creature, even if there were a creature above time.

XXXI

O Lord, My God, how deep is the abyss of Thy secret, and how far from it have the consequences of my sins held me? Cleanse my eyes and let me rejoice in Thy Light. Assuredly if there were a mind of such vast knowledge and fore-knowledge that all the past and all the future were as clearly known to it as some familiar canticle is known to me, such a mind would be marvellous beyond measure, would strike us silent with awe. For to such a mind nothing would be hidden of ages past or ages still to come, any more than when I am singing my canticle anything is unknown to me of what I have sung from the beginning, of what remains to me to sing to the end. Yet far from me be it to think that You, O Creator of the Universe, Creator of souls and bodies, had only such knowledge as that of the future and the past. Far more marvellously, far more mysteriously, do You hold Your knowledge. For when a man is singing a song he knows, or hearing a song he knows, his impressions vary and his senses are divided between the expectation of sounds to come and the memory of sounds already uttered. No such thing happens to You, the immutable and eternal, the eternal Creator of minds. In the beginning You knew heaven and earth without any element of change in your knowledge; and similarly in the beginning You created Heaven and earth without any element of change in Your action.

Let him who understands praise You, and let him who does not understand praise You likewise. You are the highest, and the humble of heart are Your dwelling place. For You *lift up them that are cast down,* and those do not fall who have You for their high place.

ANSELM OF CANTERBURY—from an eighteenth-century engraving

WILLIAM II APPOINTS ANSELM ARCHBISHOP

CANTERBURY CATHEDRAL

ANSELM

Although he is generally referred to as St. Anselm of Canterbury, Anselm (1033–1109) was not an Englishman by birth or education. He was born in the village of Aosta, in the Piedmont area of what is now Italy. Little is known of his early years, but in 1060 he entered the Benedictine monastery at Bec, in Normandy. Then under the mastership of Lanfranc, Bec had a reputation as an excellent school. When Lanfranc left Bec in 1063, his position fell to the evidently precocious Anselm, who eventually became abbot of the monastery. In the meantime Lanfranc followed William the Conqueror to England in 1066, serving as Archbishop of Canterbury until his death in 1089. William's son, William II, allowed the see of Canterbury to remain vacant for four years, after which time Anselm was made archbishop. He may have been chosen because it was thought that given his relatively advanced age and political inexperience, he would be not a bishop but a pawn in the hands of the king and the other bishops. He turned out to be anything but manipulatable.

Most of the disputes into which Anselm entered revolved around the conflicting claims of secular and spiritual authorities in a highly feudalized society; for example, whether a bishop was a feudal servant of the king, and whether the king had the right to invest bishops with the insignia of their office. Anselm's relations with William II and with William's successor, Henry I, were so fitful that he managed to get himself exiled during the reigns of both kings.

Anselm's philosophical and theological talents are so impressive that he has been called by some the "Father of Scholasticism." His careful, painstaking methods and his insistence on the importance of reason to the life of faith anticipate the works of the great thirteenth-century thinkers' teaching in the cathedral schools. Anselm did not write a magnum opus; his writings consist of several short works, almost all devoted to the philosophical investigation of a particular theological topic. Many of the titles reveal his dominant concerns and his willingness to probe a fairly narrow issue in depth: "On Truth," "On the Fall of the Devil," "Epistle concerning the Incarnation of the Word," "Why God Became Man," "On the Virgin Conception and on Original Sin," "On the Harmony of Foreknowledge, Predestination, and the Grace of God with Free Will."

Although Anselm's writings may seem piecemeal, the vision which inspired and suffuses them is global. He was above all a believing Christian, but one who believed that mere belief was not enough. The task imposed by belief was to show that one's beliefs were rational. For Anselm there could be no genuine conflict between Christian faith and the findings of reason. Not to support the claims of Christian faith, however, by the use of cogent arguments would be a kind of intellectual laziness. His confidence in the power of reason—not only to show that Christian belief is *consistent* but to prove that the major tenets of Christianity are true—may strike us as absurdly extreme; even by the thirteenth century we find more cautious enunciations of the of the harmony of faith and reason.

Anselm's *Proslogion*, reprinted in this volume, is his most famous work. In rapid order Anselm argues for the existence of God and His traditionally ascribed divine attributes, such as omnipotence, justice, mercy, simplicity, and timelessness. He concludes by attempting to sketch how great the joy of the blessed will be.

Anselm's attempt to prove the existence of God has attracted the most attention. The argument, now called the ontological argument (a title bestowed on it by Immanuel Kant), is contained in Chapter II (some would include Chapter III) of the *Proslogion.* The ontological argument has been scorned by some philosophers as the most naive of verbal conjuring tricks, and praised by others as sound. Aquinas, Hume, and Kant rejected it, while Descartes, Spinoza, and Leibniz accepted it. One can find contemporary philosophers on both sides. It is hard to think of any philosophical argument that has excited and agitated philosophers more than this one. For one thing, its sheer audacity is breathtaking. Anselm claims that the existence of God can be demonstrated simply by following out the logical implications of a certain characterization of God. Thus if Anselm's argument works, atheism does not just happen to be false; it is a logically impossible position. A second source of the argument's philosophical fascination is that in order either to defend or criticize it intelligently, one is forced to probe some controversial philosophical issues. As a contemporary philosopher puts it, "Many of the most knotty and difficult problems in philosophy meet in this argument." For example, how is it possible to deny the existence of something without presupposing the existence of the very thing whose existence is denied? Is existence a property of things? Are there genuinely different modes of existence, and if so, can the same thing exist in several modes?—and so on.

For a brilliant and judicious account of Anselm's life and times, consult R. W. Southern, *Saint Anselm and His Biographer* (Cambridge: Cambridge University Press, 1963). Jasper Hopkins, *A Companion to the Study of St. Anselm* (Minneapolis: University of Minnesota Press, 1972) provides a knowledgeable discussion of virtually all Anselm's writings, with an informative emphasis on the theological issues with which Anselm was involved.

The literature on the ontological argument is vast. Two useful anthologies are Alvin Plantinga, ed., *The Ontological Argument* (Garden City: Doubleday, 1965) and John H. Hick and Arthur C. McGill, eds., *The Many-Faced Argument* (New York: Macmillan, 1967). The former includes many of the historically important reactions to the argument, along with contemporary assessments. The latter emphasizes the diversity of approaches that have been taken to Anselm's argument.

W.E.M.

PROSLOGION

PREFACE

After I published, at the pressing entreaties of certain brethren, a certain little treatise as an example of one's meditating on the grounds of faith[1] (in the person of someone who investigates, by means of silently reasoning with himself, that which he does not know), considering it to be a connected sequence of many arguments, I began to ask myself whether by chance *one* argument[2] could be discovered, which would require nothing other than itself alone for proving itself, and which would suffice alone for demonstrating (1) that God truly exists, (2) that He is the supreme good, needing nothing else, and Whom all things need in order to be and to be well, and (3) whatever we believe about the divine being. When I would often and eagerly turn my thought to that end, then sometimes that which I sought would appear to me now to be able to be grasped, and at other times it would completely escape the keenness of my mind. At length, despairing, I wanted to give up the inquiry as if it were of a thing impossible to be discovered. But when I wanted to shut out that conception completely from myself, in order not to impede my mind — by occupying it in error — from other thoughts in which I could make progress, then it began to obtrude itself more and more, with a certain importunity, despite my unwillingness and resistance. Then one day, when I was excessively weary of resisting its importunity, in the very conflict of my thoughts that which I had given up thus presented itself, so that I eagerly embraced the conception which I was anxiously repelling.

Judging then that that which it delighted me to have discovered, if it were written down, would be pleasurable to some people reading it, I have written the following little treatise on this very conception and on certain others, as a person trying to raise his mind to the contemplation of God and seeking to understand that which he believes. And seeing that I judged that neither this work nor that work to which I referred above were worthy of the name "book," or to have the author's name set upon them, yet neither did I think that they ought to be sent forth without some title, by which in some way they would invite a person into whose hands they would come to read them. I have given each its own title, so that the former is called

This translation by William E. Mann is published here by permission of the translator. Copyright 1977 by William E. Mann.

1. [Anselm here refers to an earlier and longer work of his, the *Monologion*—W.E.M.]

2. [The Latin word *argumentum* has much the same latitude of meaning as the English word "argument." When Anselm says that he sought "one argument," he could mean either that he sought one pattern of reasoning which would demonstrate that God exists *and* that He is the supreme good, and so forth, or that he sought one sign or token which, when its logical implications were traced out (perhaps involving several different "arguments" in the first sense), would show that God exists and that he is the supreme good, and so forth.]

An Example of Meditating on the Grounds of Faith, and the following is called *Faith Seeking Understanding.*

But when each of these works, under these titles, was transcribed by several readers, several people (especially the reverend Archbishop of Lyons, Hugh, administering the apostolic office in France, who has commanded me by his apostolic authority) have urged me to prefix my name to them. So that it would be more convenient, I have named the former work *Monologion,* that is, a soliloquy; and the latter *Proslogion,* that is, an address.

CHAPTER I

A Wakening of the Mind to the Contemplation of God

Ah now! little man, flee, for a little while, from your affairs; conceal yourself, for a little while, from your tumultuous thoughts. Cast off now the burdensome cares, and postpone the laborious exercises. Make room, for a little while, for God, and rest for a little while in Him. Enter into the chamber of your mind, shut out everything except God and that which would help you in seeking Him, and when you have shut the door, seek Him [Matthew 6:6].[3] Speak now, my whole heart, speak now to God: "I seek Your countenance, Your countenance, Lord, I seek" [Psalm 27:8].

Ah now! thus, Lord my God, instruct my heart where and how to seek You, where and how to discover You. Lord, if You are not here, where shall I seek You, being absent? If however You are everywhere, why do I not see You present? But surely You dwell in inaccessible light [1 Timothy 6:16]. And where is inaccessible light? Or how shall I approach inaccessible light? Or who will lead me and bring me forward into that light, so that I may see You in it? And then, by what signs, in what form, shall I see You? I have never seen You, Lord my God, I do not know Your form. What shall he do, Lord most high, what shall that exile, far removed from You, do? What shall Your servant do, troubled by Your love and cast off far from Your face [Psalm 51:11]? He strives to see You, and Your face is too far away from him. He desires to approach You, and Your dwelling-place is inaccessible. He longs to discover You, and he knows not Your place. He aims to seek You, and he does not know Your countenance. Lord, You are my God, and You are my master, and never have I seen You. You have made me, and You have made me anew, You have conferred upon me all my goods, and I do not yet know You. In short, I was made in order to see You and I have not yet done that for the sake of which I was made.

Oh the miserable lot of man, when he has lost that for which he was made! Oh that hard and fearful Fall! Alas, what has he lost and what has he found, what has gone and what has stayed? He has lost the blessedness for which he was made, and he has found misery, for the sake of which he was not made. That without which

---

3. [Throughout the text Anselm's Biblical allusions have been indicated. No attempt has been made to make the passages conform to any particular translation of the Bible, although in some cases, the King James Version has influenced the choice of words, simply because it is the best known English translation.]

nothing is happy has gone, and that which in itself is nothing but misery has stayed. Then man ate the bread of the angels [Psalm 78:25], for which he now hungers; now he eats the bread of sorrows [Psalm 127:2], of which he then knew nothing. Alas, the common grief of man, the universal lamentation of the sons of Adam! He belched with fulness; we sigh with hunger. He prospered; we go begging. He possessed happily and wretchedly forsook; we have need unhappily and are wretchedly longing, and alas! we remain empty. Why did he not keep for us, when he so easily could have, that which we so badly need? Why did he thus shut out the light from us, and surround us with darkness? For what purpose did he take away our life, and inflict death? Wretches, whence have we been expelled, whither have we been impelled? Whence have we been cast down, whither have we been buried? From our fatherland into exile, from the vision of God into our blindness. From the enjoyment of immortality into the bitterness and horror of death. What a miserable change! From a great good into a great evil! What heavy damage, heavy sorrow—totally heavy!

Alas, as for my wretched self, one of the wretched sons of Eve, far removed from God, what have I attempted, what have I accomplished? Where was I going, where have I arrived? To what was I aspiring, for what do I long? I have sought goodness [Psalm 122:9], and behold trouble [Jeremiah 14:19]. I was going toward God, and I have stumbled upon myself. I was seeking repose in my solitude, and I have discovered tribulation and sorrow in my inmost self [Psalm 116:3]. I wanted to laugh from the joy of my soul, and I am forced to roar from the lamentation of my heart [Psalm 38:8]. Gladness was hoped for, and behold how my sighs are crowded together!

And You, Oh Lord, how long [Psalm 6:3]? How long, Lord, will You forget us, how long will You turn Your face from us [Psalm 13:1]? When will You look back upon us, and hear us? When will You illuminate our eyes [Psalm 13:3] and reveal Your face to us [Psalm 80:3, 7]? When will You restore Yourself to us? Look back upon us, Lord, hear us, illuminate us, reveal Yourself to us! Restore Yourself to us, without Whom now it is so bad for us, so that it may be good for us. Take pity on our labors and strivings toward You, for we have the strength to do nothing without You. You call us: help us [Psalm 79:9]. I beseech You, Lord, let me not be sighing in despair, but rather breathing in hope. I beseech You, Lord, my heart is bitter in its desolation—sweeten it with Your consolation. I beseech You, Lord, I have begun hungering to seek You—let me not leave fasting for You. I have come to you starving—do not let me withdraw unfed. I have come poor to one who is rich, miserable to one who is compassionate—do not let me return empty and despised. And if I sigh before I should eat [Job 3:24], give, even after the sighing, that which I should eat. Lord, being bent over, I cannot look anywhere but downwards—raise me up so that I can stretch upwards. My iniquities have gone over my head: they muffle me, and like a heavy burden they weigh me down [Psalm 38:4]. Untangle me, unburden me: do not let me be pushed into the pit and its mouth come over me [Psalm 69:15]. Allow me to look up to Your light, even from afar, even from the depths. Teach me to seek You, and reveal Yourself to my seeking, since I can neither seek You without Your teaching me, nor discover You without Your revealing Yourself to me. Let me seek You in desiring You, and desire You in seeking You. Let me discover You in loving You, and love You in discovering You.

I confess, Lord, and give thanks, that You have created in me this image of You, so that I may be reminded of You, conceive of You, and love You. But this image is decayed and worn by vices, and darkened by the smoke of sins, so that it could not do that for which it was made, without Your renewing and reforming it. I do not attempt, Lord, to penetrate to Your loftiness, since I in no way compare my understanding to that; but I desire to understand in some way Your truth, which my heart believes and loves. For I do not seek to understand so that I may believe, but rather I believe so that I may understand. For this too I believe: that unless I shall have believed, I may not understand [Isaiah 7:9].

CHAPTER II

That God Truly Exists

Therefore, Lord, You Who give understanding to faith, give to me: insofar as You know it to be advantageous, let me understand that You exist, as we believe, and also that You are that which we believe You to be. And indeed, we believe You to be something than which nothing greater could be conceived. Or is there thus not something of such a nature, since the fool has said in his heart—there is no God [Psalm 14:1, 53:1]. But surely this same fool, when he hears this very thing that I speak—"something than which nothing greater can be conceived"—understands that which he hears, and that which he understands is in his understanding, even if he does not understand it to exist. For it is one thing for a thing to be in the understanding, and another to understand a thing to exist. For when a painter conceives beforehand that which he is to make, he certainly has it in the understanding, but he does not yet understand to exist that which he has not yet made. However, when he has painted it, he both has it in the understanding and understands that that which he has now made exists. Therefore, even the fool is convinced that something than which nothing greater can be conceived is at least in the understanding, since when he hears this, he understands it, and whatever is understood is in the understanding. And surely that than which a greater cannot be conceived cannot be in the understanding alone. For if it is even in the understanding alone, it can be conceived to exist in reality also, which is greater. Thus if that than which a greater cannot be conceived is in the understanding alone, then that than which a greater cannot be conceived itself is that than which a greater can be conceived. But surely this cannot be. Therefore without doubt something than which a greater cannot be conceived exists, both in the understanding and in reality.

CHAPTER III

That God Cannot be Conceived not to Exist

And surely it exists so truly that it could not be conceived not to exist. For something can be conceived to exist which could not be conceived not to exist, which is greater than that which can be conceived not to exist. Thus if that than which a greater cannot be conceived can be conceived not to exist, then that than which a greater cannot be conceived itself is not that than which a greater cannot be conceived, which cannot be made consistent. Thus something than which a greater cannot be conceived exists so truly that it could not be conceived not to exist.

And this You are, Lord our God. Thus so truly do You exist, Lord my God, that You could not be conceived not to exist. And justly so. For if some mind could conceive of something better than You, the creature would rise above the creator and would judge the creator, which is exceedingly absurd. And indeed, whatever is distinct from You alone can be conceived not to exist. Therefore You alone are the truest of all things and thus You have existence as the greatest of all things, since anything else does not exist so truly, and for that reason has less existence. And so why has the fool said in his heart that there is no God, when to a rational mind it would be so obvious that You exist as the greatest of all things? Why, unless because he is stupid and a fool?

CHAPTER IV

How the Fool Has Said in His Heart What Cannot be Conceived

Indeed how has he said in his heart what he has not been able to conceive, or how has he not been able to conceive what he has said in his heart, when to say in the heart and to conceive are the same? If he truly—rather, *since* he truly—both has conceived (since he has spoken in his heart) and has not spoken in his heart (since he has not been able to conceive), then there is not only one way in which something is said in the heart or is conceived. For in one way a thing is conceived when a word signifying it is conceived; in another when that thing itself is understood. In the former way, thus, God can be conceived not to exist; in the latter, not at all. No one, in fact, understanding what God is, can conceive that God does not exist, although he may say these words in his heart, either without significance or with some extraneous significance. For God is that than which a greater cannot be conceived. He who understands this well certainly understands this very being to exist in such a way that it is not able not to exist in conception. Thus he who understands that God so exists, cannot conceive Him not to exist.

I give thanks to You, good Lord, I give thanks to You, because that which before I believed through Your giving to me, I now so understand through Your illuminating me that if I were unwilling to believe that You exist, I would not be able to understand that You exist.

CHAPTER V

That God is Whatever it is Better to be Than not to be, and, Existing through Himself Alone, He Makes Everything Else out of Nothing

What then are You, Lord God, than Whom nothing greater can be conceived? But what are You except that which is supreme over everything, existing only through Yourself, Who made everything else out of nothing? For whatever is not this is less than could be conceived. But this cannot be conceived of You. Therefore, what good is lacking to the supreme good, through which everything good exists? You are thus just, true, blessed, and whatever it is better to be than not to be. For truly it is better to be just than not just, blessed than not blessed.

CHAPTER VI

How He is Able to Perceive although He is not a Body

Indeed, since it is better to be (1) able to perceive, (2) omnipotent, (3) compassionate, and (4) without passion than not to be so, how are You (1) able to perceive if You are not a body, or (2) omnipotent if You cannot do everything, or (3) compassionate and (4) without passion at the same time? For if only bodies are able to perceive, since the senses are around the body and in the body, how are You able to perceive, since You are not a body but the supreme spirit, Who is better than a body?

But if to perceive is only to cognize or is only for the sake of cognizing — for he who perceives cognizes according to the appropriate senses, so that colors are cognized through vision, and flavors through taste — then whatever cognizes in some fashion is not unsuitably said to perceive in some fashion. Thus, Lord, although You are not a body, You are indeed nevertheless able to perceive in the highest degree, in the way that You supremely cognize everything, not in the way that an animal cognizes by its bodily sense.

CHAPTER VII

How He is Omnipotent although He Cannot Do Many Things

And how are You omnipotent, if You cannot do everything? Or if You cannot be corrupted, or lie, or make that which is true to be false, so that that which has been done has not been done, and several similar things: how can You do everything?

Or is it that to be able to do these things is not power, but impotence? For he who can do these things can do that which impedes himself and that which he ought not to do. The more he can do these things, the more adversity and perversity can do against him, and the less he himself can do against them. Therefore he who can so act cannot have power, but impotence. He is therefore not said to be able because he himself can do these things, but because his impotence makes another able against him; or in some other manner of speaking, just as many things are said improperly, as when we put "to be" for "not to be" and "to do" in place of "not to do" or for "to do nothing." For often we say to a person who denies that a certain thing exists, "So it is, just as you say it is," although it would appear more proper to say, "So it is not, just as you say it is not." In like manner we say, "This person sits idly just as that one is doing," or "This person rests just as that one is doing," although "to sit idly" is not a certain kind of doing, and "to rest" is to do nothing. Thus, when someone is said to have the power of doing or suffering that which impedes himself or that which he ought not to do, "impotence" is understood by means of "power," because the more he has this power, the more powerful adversity and perversity are against him, and the more impotent he is against them. Therefore, Lord God, You are then more truly omnipotent because You can do nothing through impotence, and nothing can work against You.

CHAPTER VIII

How He is Compassionate and Passionless

But how are You at the time both compassionate and passionless? For if You are passionless, You do not suffer; if You do not suffer, You do not have a heart made sad out of compassion for the wretched, which is what it is to be compassionate. But if You are not compassionate, whence comes such great consolation for the wretched?

How, then, are You and are You not compassionate, Lord, unless it is because You are compassionate with respect to us, and not with respect to Yourself? In fact You are compassionate according to our way of perceiving, and not according to Your way, since when You look back upon us wretched ones, we experience the effect of compassion, but You do not experience the affection. And thus You are compassionate, because You save the wretched and spare Your sinners, and You are not compassionate, because You are affected by no compassion for misery.

CHAPTER IX

How a Completely Just and Supremely Just Being Spares the Wicked, and that the Wicked are Justly Pitied

Indeed, how do You spare the wicked, if You are completely just and supremely just? For how does a completely and supremely just being do something which is not just? Or what justice is it to give everlasting life to one meriting eternal death? How then, good God, good to the good and to the wicked, how do You save the wicked, if this is not just, and You do not do anything which is not just?

Or since Your goodness is incomprehensible, is this concealed in the inaccessible light in which You dwell [Timothy 6:16]? Truly in the highest and most secret place of Your goodness is concealed the fount, whence flows the river of Your compassion. For although You are completely and supremely just, still for that reason You are beneficent even to the wicked, since You are completely and supremely good. For indeed You would be less good if You were beneficent to none of the wicked. For he who is good both to the good and to the wicked is better than he who is good only to the good. And he who is good to the wicked both by punishing and by sparing is better than he who is good to the wicked by punishing alone. So, then, You are compassionate, since You are completely and supremely good. And although perhaps it may be seen why You might reward goods to the good and evils to the wicked, it is certainly and utterly unfathomable why You, completely just and needing nothing, should bestow goods to the wicked and guilty ones of Yours. Oh, the loftiness of Your goodness, God! Although it can be seen from whence Your compassion comes, it cannot be fully surveyed. It can be discerned from whence the river flows, but the fount from whence it is born cannot be ascertained. For not only are You kind to Your sinners out of the plenitude of goodness, but the reason You are so is concealed in the loftiness of goodness. Indeed, even though You may, out of goodness, reward goods to the good and evils to the wicked, the reason nevertheless is seen in that justice demands this. When, however, You bestow goods to the wicked, it is known because the supreme good has willed to do this, but it is unfathomable why the supremely just being has been able to will this.

Oh compassion, from what opulent sweetness and sweet opulence You flow forth to us! Oh, the immense goodness of God, with what feeling You ought to be loved by sinners! For You save the righteous, with justice accompanying them, but You free those sinners, with justice condemning them. The former by aid of their merits, the latter contrary to their merits. The former by examining the goods that You have given, the latter by overlooking the evils that You detest. Oh immense goodness, which indeed exceeds all understanding, let that compassion come upon me which proceeds from You with such great opulence! Let that which flows forth from You flow into me! Spare me through clemency, in order that You not take vengeance through justice! For although it be difficult to understand how Your compassion is not distinct from Your justice, yet it is necessary to believe that it is, because in no way is that which pours forth out of goodness (which is nothing without justice—on the contrary, it truly agrees with justice) opposed to justice. Indeed, if You are compassionate because You are supremely good, and if You are not supremely good except because You are supremely just, then truly You are compassionate for the reason that you are supremely just. Help me, just and compassionate God, Whose light I seek, help me, so that I may understand what I say. Truly therefore You are compassionate, because You are just.

Is not Your compassion then born out of Your justice? Do You not then spare the wicked out of justice? If it is so, Lord, if it is so, teach me how it is so. Perhaps it is because it is just for You to be so good that You could not be understood to be better, and to work so powerfully that You could not be conceived to be more powerful? For what is more just than this? This, however, would not be so, if You were good merely by means of punishing and not by means of sparing, and if You made good persons only out of persons who are not good, and not also out of wicked persons. And so in this way it is just that You should spare the wicked, and that You should make good persons out of wicked ones. Finally, that which is not done justly ought not to be done, and that which ought not to be done is done unjustly. If, therefore, it were not just for You to pity the wicked, You ought not to pity them, and if You ought not to pity them, it would be unjust for You to pity them. If it is sinful to say that, then it is lawful to believe that You justly pity the wicked.

CHAPTER X

How He Justly Punishes and Justly Spares the Wicked

But it is also just that You should punish the wicked. For what is more just than that the good should receive goods and the wicked evils? How, then, is it both just that You should punish the wicked, and just that You should spare the wicked?

Or do You justly punish the wicked in one way, and justly spare the wicked in another way? For when You punish the wicked, it is just, because it fits with their merits; when indeed You spare the wicked, it is just, not because of their merits, but because it is becoming to Your goodness. For by sparing the wicked in this manner You are just according to Yourself and not according to us, just as You are compassionate according to us and not according to Yourself. Because by saving those of us whom You would justly lose—just as You are compassionate not because You may experience the affection, but because we experience the effect—in this manner You are just, not because You might restore what is owed by us, but because You do that which is fitting to You, a supremely good being. So, accordingly, without inconsistency You justly punish and You justly spare.

CHAPTER XI

How All of the Lord's Ways are Compassion and Truth, and yet the Lord is Just in All His Ways

But is it not also just according to You, Lord, that You should punish the wicked? Surely it is just for You to be so just that You cannot be conceived to be more just, which You would in no way be, if You were only to requite good to the good and not evil to the wicked. For he who repays both the good and the wicked is more just than he who only repays merits to the good. Therefore it is just, according to You, just and beneficent God, both when you punish and when You spare. Truly therefore, "all the Lord's ways are compassion and truth" [Psalm 25:10], and yet "the Lord is just in all His ways" [Psalm 145:17]. And it follows without contradiction, since for those You will to punish, it is not just that they be saved, and to those You will to spare, it is not just that they be damned. For that alone is just which You will, and that alone is not just which You do not will. So therefore Your compassion is begotten from Your justice, since it is just for You to be so good that You are good even in sparing. And perhaps this is why a supremely just being can will good to the wicked. But if in some way it can be grasped how You can will to save the wicked, it can certainly be comprehended by no reason why with respect to similar wicked people, You save these rather than those through supreme goodness, and damn those rather than these through supreme justice.

So, therefore, truly You are able to perceive, omnipotent, compassionate and passionless, just as You are living, wise, good, blessed, eternal, and whatever it is better to be than not to be.

CHAPTER XII

That God is the Very Life Which He Lives, and so for Similar Attributes

But certainly whatever You are You are not through another but rather through Yourself. You are therefore the very life by which You live, the wisdom by which You are wise, the very goodness by which You are good to the good and the wicked, and so for similar attributes.

CHAPTER XIII

How He Alone is Unbounded and Eternal,
even though Other Spirits are Unbounded and Eternal

But all that which is enclosed in some way by place or by time is less than that which no law of place or of time confines. Therefore, since nothing is greater than You, no place or time contains You, but You are everywhere and always. Since that can be said of You alone, You alone are unbounded and eternal. How then are other spirits also said to be unbounded and eternal?

And indeed You alone are eternal, since just as You alone of all things do not cease to exist, so You do not begin to exist. But how are You alone unbounded? Or is it that a created spirit, compared to You, is bounded, and compared to a body, is truly unbounded? Certainly that is wholly bounded which, when it is entirely somewhere, cannot at the same time be elsewhere, a feature which is discerned only of bodies. That is truly unbounded which is entirely everywhere at the same time, a feature which is understood only of You. However, that is bounded and at the same time unbounded which, when it is entirely somewhere, can at the same time be entirely elsewhere, and yet cannot be everywhere, a feature which is recognized of created spirits. For if the soul were not entirely in each separate member of its body, it would not be entirely aware of each separate member.[4] Thus You, Lord, are uniquely unbounded and eternal, and yet other spirits are also unbounded and eternal.

CHAPTER XIV

How and Why God is Seen and is not Seen by Those Seeking Him

Have you discovered, my soul, that which you were seeking? You were seeking God, and you have discovered Him to be something which is the highest of all beings, than which nothing better can be conceived, to be life itself, light, wisdom, goodness, eternal blessedness and blessed eternity, and to be everywhere and always. For if you have not discovered your God, how is it that He is this which you have discovered, and that which you have understood with such certain truth and true certainty? If you have truly discovered Him, why is it that you do not perceive that which you have discovered? Why does my soul not perceive You, Lord God, if it discovers You?

Or has it not discovered that which it has discovered to be light and truth? How indeed has it understood this without seeing light and truth? Or has it been able to

---

4. [Anselm is here adverting to a doctrine held by St. Augustine. According to Augustine, the soul is not a physical thing, that is, it is not a thing characterized by spatial dimensions. Nevertheless, it is somehow united with the body, which is physical. Furthermore, according to Augustine, since the soul is nonphysical, it has no physical parts. Thus it would be a mistake to say that one part of the soul was lodged in the forehead while another part occupied the territory of one's stomach. Yet it is the soul which takes note of simultaneous headache and stomachache. It could not do this, Augustine believed, unless it were somehow at both places at the same time. The generalization of this train of thought is that the soul is present in its entirety simultaneously at all parts of the body.]

understand anything at all about You, except through "Your light and Your truth" [Psalm 43:3]? If then it has seen light and truth, it has seen You. If it has not seen You, it has not seen light or truth. Or is it that it has seen both truth and light, and nevertheless it has not yet seen You, since it has partly seen You, but it has not seen You just as You are [1 John 3:2]?

Lord my God, my former and reformer, say to my desiring soul what else You are than that which it has seen, so that it may see clearly that which it desires. It extends itself in order that it may see more, and it sees nothing but darkness beyond this which it has seen. I should rather say it does not see darkness, of which there is none in You [1 John 1:5], but it sees itself that it cannot see further because of its darkness. Why is this, Lord, why is this? Is its eye darkened by its own infirmity, or is it dazed by Your splendor? But surely it is both darkened in itself and dazed by You. In any case it is both obscured by its own smallness and overwhelmed by Your immensity. Truly it is both constricted by its narrowness and conquered by Your breadth. How great indeed is that light from which gleams every truth which illuminates the rational mind! How great is that truth in which everything that is true exists, and outside of which nothing exists except nothingness and falsity! How immense is that which by one glance sees whatever has been made, and by whom, through whom, and in what way it has been made of nothing! What purity, what simplicity, what certitude and splendor is there! Certainly more than could be understood by a creature.

CHAPTER XV

That He is Greater Than Can be Conceived

Therefore, Lord, not only are You that than which a greater cannot be conceived, but You are also something greater than can be conceived. Indeed, since it is possible to be conceived to be something of this kind, if You are not this very thing, something can be conceived greater than You, which cannot be done.

CHAPTER XVI

That This is the Inaccessible Light in Which He Dwells

Truly, Lord, this is the inaccessible light in which You dwell [1 Timothy 6:16]. For truly there is nothing else which may penetrate this light in order to look upon You there. Truly for that reason I do not see this light, since it is too great for me, and yet whatever I see, I see by means of it, just as an infirm eye sees that which it sees by means of the light of the sun, which light it cannot behold in the sun itself. My understanding is not adequate to that light. It shines too much, it does not grasp it, nor does the eye of my soul bear for very long to extend toward that light. It is dazed by splendor, conquered by breadth, overwhelmed by immensity, confounded by capacity. Oh supreme and inaccessible light, oh complete and blessed truth, how far You are from me, who am so near to You! How remote You are from my sight, whereas I am so present to Your sight! You are everywhere totally present, and I do not see You. In You I am moved and in You I exist [Acts 17:28], and I cannot approach You. You are within me and around me, and I do not perceive you.

CHAPTER XVII

That in God there is Harmony, Fragrance, Sweetness, Gentleness, and Beauty, in His Ineffable Manner

Still You lie hidden, Lord, from my soul in Your light and blessedness, and for that reason it is still swirled about in its darkness and wretchedness. For it looks around, and it does not see Your beauty. It listens, and it does not hear Your harmony. It smells, and it does not perceive Your fragrance. It tastes, and it does not learn of Your sweetness. It touches, and it does not sense Your gentleness. For You have these attributes, in Yourself in Your ineffable manner, Lord God, Who has bestowed them in their sensible manner to things created by You. But the senses of my soul have stiffened and have become stupefied and are obstructed by the ancient sluggishness of sin.

CHAPTER XVIII

That in God and in His Eternity, Which is Himself, there are No Parts

And behold trouble [Jeremiah 14:19] once more, behold once more how one encounters grief and sorrows in seeking joy and gladness! My soul was hoping now for abundance, and behold once more, it is overwhelmed by indigence! It was striving now to devour, and behold, I begin to hunger all the more! I was attempting to rise up to the light of God, and I have been cut down into my darkness. Indeed, not only have I fallen down into it, but I also feel myself enfolded within it. I fell before my mother conceived me [Psalm 51:5]. Surely in that darkness I was conceived [Psalm 51:5], and with the envelopment of this darkness I was born. At one time surely we all fell in him, in whom we all have sinned [Romans 5:12]. In him, who easily possessed and badly lost—both for himself and for us—we all have lost that which when we wish to seek it, we do not know how, when we seek it, we do not discover, and when we discover it, is not that which we are seeking. Help me, because of Your goodness, Lord [Psalm 25:7]. I have sought Your countenance, Your countenance, Lord, I will seek; do not avert Your face from me [Psalm 27:8-9]. Lift me up from myself to You. Cleanse, heal, sharpen, illumine the eye [Psalm 13:3] of my mind, so that it may look upon You. Let my soul gather up its own powers, and by its whole understanding let it once more extend towards You, Lord.

What are You, Lord, what are You, what shall my heart understand You to be? Surely You are life, You are wisdom, You are truth, You are goodness, You are blessedness, You are eternity, and You are every true good. These are many things, and my narrow understanding cannot see so many at one simultaneous glance in order to be delighted by all of them at once. How then, Lord, are You all these things? Are they parts of You, or rather is each one of these entirely what You are?

For whatever is composed of parts is not entirely one, but in a certain way is many and contrary to itself, and can be dissolved either by action or by the understanding; which is foreign to You, than Whom nothing better can be conceived. Therefore there are no parts in You, Lord, nor are You many, but You are so definitely one thing, and so identical to Yourself, that You are dissimilar in nothing from Yourself. Indeed, You are unity itself, divisible by no understanding. Therefore life, wisdom, and the like are not parts of You, but all of them are one, and each one of them is entirely that You are and what all the others are. Since, therefore, neither You have parts nor Your eternity in which You exist, no place and no time is part of You or Your eternity, but You are entirely everywhere and Your eternity exists entirely forever.

CHAPTER XIX

That He is not in Place or Time, but All Things Exist in Him

But if through Your eternity You have been, You are, and You will be, and to have been is not to be going to be, and to be is not to have been or to be going to be, then how is Your eternity entirely forever?

Or does nothing of Your eternity pass away, so that it does not exist now; nor is it something that is going to be, as if it did not exist? Accordingly, You did not exist yesterday, nor will You exist tomorrow, but You exist yesterday and today and tomorrow. Or rather, You exist neither yesterday nor today nor tomorrow, but You simply exist outside all time. For yesterday, today, and tomorrow are nothing other than in time. You, however, although nothing may exist without You, yet You do not exist in place or time, but all things exist in You. For nothing contains You, but You contain all things.

CHAPTER XX

That He is before and beyond All Things, Even Eternal Things

You therefore permeate and embrace all things, and You are before and beyond all things. And indeed You exist before all things, since before they were made, You exist [Psalm 90:2]. How are You truly beyond all things? For how are You beyond those things which will not have an end?

Or is it because those things can exist in no way without You, although You exist, diminished in no way, even if they return into nothingness? For in this particular way You are beyond them. Or even because they can be conceived to have an end, and You truly in no way can? For so indeed they have an end, in a certain way, and You truly in no way do. And certainly that which in no way has an end is beyond that which is ended in some way. Or do You surpass all things, even eternal things, in this way also: because Your and their eternity is entirely present to You, although they do not yet have of their own eternity that which is going to come, just as now they do not have that which has gone by? In such a way indeed You are always beyond them, since You are always present at that place—or rather, since that place is always present to You—to which they have not yet arrived.

CHAPTER XXI

Whether This is the Age of the Age or Ages of Ages

Is this, then, the age of the age or ages of ages?[5] For just as an age of time contains all temporal things, so Your eternity contains even the ages of time themselves. This eternity is indeed an age because of its indivisible unity, and truly ages because of its interminable immensity. And although You are so great, Lord, that all things are filled with You and are in You, yet You are without any spatiality, so that there is neither a middle nor a half nor any part in You.

CHAPTER XXII

That He Alone is What He is and Who He is

You alone, therefore, Lord, are what You are, and You are who You are. For that which is one thing in its totality and another thing in its parts, and in which something is mutable, is not altogether what it is. And as for that which began out of non-being and can be conceived not to exist, and which would return into non-being unless it subsisted through another; and that which has a past existence which does not now exist, and a future existence which does not yet exist: that does not exist properly and absolutely. You truly are what You are, because whatever You are at any time or in anyway, You are this entirely and always.

And You are properly and simply who You are, since (1) neither do You have either a past existence or a future existence, but only a present existence, (2) nor can You be conceived not to exist at any time. And You are life, light, wisdom, blessedness, eternity, and more goods of this kind, and yet You do not exist unless You are the one and supreme good, You who, sufficing utterly unto Yourself, needing nothing, all things need in order to be and in order to be well.

CHAPTER XXIII

*That This Good is Equally Father and Son and Holy Spirit,
and This is One Necessary Being,
Which is Wholly and Entirely and Only Good*

This good is You, God the Father; this is Your Word, that is, Your Son. And indeed, it cannot be other than what You are, or something greater or less than You, to be in the Word by which You utter Yourself, since Your word is as true, in a way, as You

---

5. [In this peculiar chapter, Anselm asks whether it is more appropriate to characterize God's eternity as *"saeculum saeculi"* or *"saecula saeculorum."* Both phrases were used in the Latin Vulgate version of the Bible—for example, the former in Psalm 111:9 (= 112:9), the latter in 1 Peter 4:11. Both phrases are generally translated as "for ever" or "for ever and ever." Anselm's answer, not surprisingly, is that both phrases are appropriate to characterize God's eternity.]

are true; and therefore it is truth itself, just as You are, none other than You. And You are so simple that nothing can be begotten from You other than that which You are. This itself is Love, one and common to You and to Your son, that is, the Holy Spirit, proceeding from both. For the same Love is not unequal to You or to Your son, since You love Yourself and Him, and He loves You and Himself, as much as You and He exist. Nor is that which is not different from You and from Him other than You and than Him, nor can any other thing proceed from supreme simplicity than that which *is* what it proceeds from. Moreover, that which each single one is, is at the same time what the whole Trinity is, Father, Son, and Holy Spirit, since each single one is not different from the supremely simple unity and the supremely unified simplicity, which can neither be multiplied nor be now this and now that.

"Henceforth one thing is necessary" [Luke 10:42]. Henceforth this is that one necessary being in which there is every good—indeed, which is wholly and uniquely and entirely and only good.

CHAPTER XXIV

A Conjecture as to What Kind and How Great This Good is

Awaken now, my soul, and arouse your entire understanding, and conceive, as much as you can, of what kind and how great that good is. For if individual goods are delightful, think attentively about how delightful that good is, which contains the joyfulness of all goods, and not such a joyfulness as we have experienced in created things, but as different as creator differs from creature. For if the life that is created is good, how good is the life that is a creator? If the salvation which has been brought about is joyful, how joyful is the salvation which brings about all salvation? If wisdom in the cognition of things which have been produced is worthy of love, how worthy of love is the wisdom which has produced all things out of nothing? Finally, if many and great pleasures exist in delightful things, what kind and how great a pleasure is in Him Who has made the delightful things themselves?

CHAPTER XXV

Which and How Great are the Goods Had by Those Enjoying This Good

Oh, he who will enjoy this good: what will be his, and what will not be his! Surely whatever he will wish will be, and that which he will not wish will not be. Certainly then there will be goods of the body and of the soul, of such a kind that "neither eye has seen nor ear has heard nor the heart of man" has conceived [1 Corinthians 2:9]. Why then do you wander through many things, little man, seeking the goods of your soul and your body? Love the one good, in which all goods exist, and it is sufficient. Desire the simple good, which is wholly good, and it is enough. For what do you love, my flesh, what do you desire, my soul? There it is, there it is, whatever you love, whatever you desire.

If beauty delights, "the righteous will shine forth as the sun" [Matthew 13:43]. If swiftness or strength, or freedom of the body, to which nothing can oppose: "they will be as the angels of God" [Matthew 22:30] , because "an animal body is sown, and a spiritual body will arise" [1 Corinthians 15:44] surely by a non-natural power. If a long and healthy life: then there is a sound eternity and eternal soundness, because "the righteous will live forever" [Wisdom 5:15] and "the salvation of the righteous is from God" [Psalm 37:39]. If abundance: they will be abundantly supplied when the glory of God will have appeared [Psalm 17:15]. If drunkenness: "they will be drunk from the fulness of the house" [Psalm 36:8] of God. If pleasant song: there choirs of angels sing without end to God. If any pleasure whatsoever, not impure but pure: God "will make them drink from the torrent of His pleasure" [Psalm 36:8].

If wisdom: the wisdom itself of God will display itself to them. If friendship: they will love God more than themselves, and one another as much as themselves, and God will love them more than they will love themselves; because they will love Him and themselves and one another through Him, and He will love Himself and them through Himself [Cf. Matthew 22:37–39]. If harmony: for all of them there will be one will, because for them there will be no other except the will of God alone. If power: they will be omnipotent in their will since God is omnipotent in His will. For just as God will be able to do that which He will will to do through Himself, so they will be able to do that which they will will to do through Him, because just as they will will nothing else than that which He will will, so He will will whatever they will will; and that which He will will will not be able not to be. If honor and riches: God Himself will set His good and faithful servants over many things [Matthew 25:21, 23]. Indeed, "they will be called the children of God" [Matthew 5:9], and gods, and such they will be; and where His Son will be, there they will be also, "heirs indeed of God, joint-heirs moreover of Christ" [Romans 8:17]. If true security: surely they will be as secure in the fact that at no time and in no way will those goods—or rather, that good—be absent from them, as they will be secure that they will not, of their own free will, lose it, and that neither will the loving God carry it off from His lovers, against their will, nor will something more powerful than God separate God and them against God's and their will.

But what kind or how great is the joy where such and so great a good is? Human heart, needful heart, heart tried by tribulation—indeed, overwhelmed by tribulation—how much would you rejoice if you overflowed with all these things? Ask your innermost self whether it could contain its joy of such a great blessedness of its own. But surely if someone else, whom you loved just as completely as yourself, had the same blessedness, your joy would be doubled, since you would rejoice no less for him than for yourself. But if two or three or many more had it, you would rejoice as much for each one as for yourself, if you loved each as much as yourself. Therefore in that perfect love of innumerable blessed angels and men, where no one will love another less than himself, everyone will rejoice no differently for each of the others than for himself. If therefore, the heart of man will barely contain its own joy of such a great good of its own, how capacious will it be from so many and such great joys? And undoubtedly—since to the extent that anyone loves somebody, so he rejoices in his good—just as in that perfect felicity, anyone will love God incomparably more than himself and all others with him, so he will rejoice inestimably more in the felicity of God than in his own and in that of all others with him. But if they will love God with all their heart, all their mind, and all their soul [Matthew 22:37], but so that nevertheless, all their heart, all their mind, and all their soul is not adequate to the dignity of their love, they will surely rejoice with all their heart, all their mind, and all their soul, so that all their heart, all their mind, and all their soul is not adequate to the fulness of their joy.

CHAPTER XXVI

Whether This is the Full Joy Which the Lord Promises

My God and my Lord, my hope and joy of my heart, say to my soul whether this is the joy of which You speak to us through Your Son: "Ask, and you shall receive, so that your joy may be full" [John 16:24]. For I have discovered a certain joy which is full, and more than full. For when the heart is full, when the mind is full, when the soul is full, when the entire man is full of that joy, at that time joy beyond measure will be left over. Therefore not all that joy will enter into the joyful, but all the joyful will enter into joy. Speak, Lord, speak to Your servant from within his heart, whether this is the joy into which Your servants will enter who will "enter into the joys of their Lord" [Matthew 25:21]. But surely that joy, in which Your chosen ones will rejoice, "eye has not seen, nor ear heard, nor has it risen into the heart of man" [Isaiah 64:4; 1 Corinthians 2:9]. Therefore I have not yet said or conceived, Lord, how greatly those blessed ones of Yours will rejoice. Certainly they will rejoice as much as they will love, and they will love as much as they will know. How much will they know You, Lord, at that time, and how greatly will they love You? Surely "eye has not seen nor ear heard, nor has it risen into the heart of man" in this life how much they will know You and love You in that life.

I pray, God, that I may know You and love You, so that I may rejoice in You. And if I cannot do so to the full in this life, let me at least make progress from day to day until that joy shall come to the full. Let the knowledge of You make progress in me here, and there, let it become full; let Your love grow, and there let it be full: so that here my joy may be great in hope, and there it may be full in reality. Lord, through Your Son You command—rather, You counsel—us to ask and You promise that we shall receive, so that our joy may be full [John 16:24]. I ask, Lord, as You do counsel through our wonderful Counsellor [Isaiah 9:6]; let me receive that which You promise through Your truth, so that my joy may be full. In the meantime, let my mind meditate upon it, let my tongue speak about it. Let my heart love it, let my mouth discourse on it. Let my soul hunger for it, let my flesh thirst for it, let my whole substance desire it, until I may enter into the joy of my Lord [Matthew 25:21], Who is God, three and one, blessed for ever. Amen [Romans 1:25].

THOMAS AQUINAS—panel from the Demidorf altar by Carlo Crivelli, fifteenth century

ALBERTUS MAGNUS
(early Italian)

AQUINAS WITH STUDENTS
(Sch. of Fra Angelico)

THOMAS AQUINAS

Aquinas (1225–1274) was born at the castle of Roccasecca, near Aquino, which lay between Rome and Naples. His well-to-do parents apparently intended an ecclesiastical career for him. He was sent to the Benedictine abbey at Monte Cassino for his early education; from there he went to the University of Naples in 1239.

While in Naples Aquinas came under the influence of the newly created Order of Preachers founded by St. Dominic (1170–1221). The Dominicans at the time were, like the Franciscans, mendicant, or begging, friars. Espousing absolute poverty, they saw their vocation as the spreading of the Gospel to the people, both by word and by living example. The apostolic zeal of the mendicant friars captured the imagination and admiration of many; both the Franciscans and the Dominicans were to become successful and powerful. To Aquinas's family, however, the Dominicans must have appeared an appalling bunch of rag-tag ne'er-do-wells, especially in comparison with the Benedictines, who had prestige, power, and corporate wealth. When Aquinas joined the Dominican order in 1243, his family reacted strongly, going so far as to lock him up in the castle. He remained unswayed, spending his time studying the Bible. Legend has it that his family even offered him the blandishments of a prostitute in order to change his mind. Legend also has it that he refused. After attaining his freedom, Aquinas went to Paris in about 1244 and to Cologne in 1248, to study philosophy and theology.

The Dominicans placed considerable value on intellectual pursuits, and Aquinas profited from the teaching of Albertus Magnus (Albert the Great), perhaps the first of a long line of outstanding Dominican intellects. In 1252 Aquinas returned to the University of Paris as a lecturer, receiving his doctorate in theology in 1256. The divinity faculty at Paris, however, was reluctant to confer the license to teach upon mendicant friars. Aquinas the Dominican and St. Bonaventure (1217–1274) the Franciscan argued their case before the Pope, and both were licensed in 1257. From 1259 to 1268 Aquinas taught at several Dominican monasteries in Italy. He then returned to Paris, only to go to Naples in 1272. Summoned to participate at the Council of Lyons in 1274, he died on the way at Fossanova, near the place of his birth.

Aquinas did not spend much of his adult life in any one place, but he managed to write a tremendous amount of material. Several of his works are commentaries on the works of Aristotle, a fact that requires some comment. Aristotle's major works had been lost to the non-Arabic West until the beginning of the thirteenth century. Their reappearance caused a good deal of intellectual ferment. To many, the world-view disclosed in Aristotle's writings seemed to be a pagan threat to Christianity. To others, including Aquinas, Aristotle's works provided an exhilarating cosmological, metaphysical, and epistemological framework on which to build a coherent and all-encompassing Christian world-view. However, although Aristotle was "the Philosopher," he was not infallible, and Aquinas felt free to reject those aspects of his philosophy which conflicted with Christian revelation.

Some of the most characteristic features of Aquinas's philosophy derived from Aristotle include the insistence on the primary role of the senses in the acquisition of natural knowledge, and the metaphysical analysis of things in terms of matter and form. On the other hand, while Aristotle had held out little chance for personal survival after death, Aquinas argued for personal immortality. Aristotle's "God," or unmoved mover, would appear not to care one whit about the world, whereas the God of Christianity, insisted Aquinas, must be a personal God.

Another difference between Aristotle and Aquinas serves to illustrate Aquinas's views on the relation between reason and faith. Aristotle had asserted that the world was eternal—that is, it had always existed, a doctrine which ran contrary to the Christian doctrine that the world was created by God. Aquinas claimed that nothing in our natural knowledge of the world would force one to conclude either that the world was eternal or that it had been created. Aristotle's position, then, was neither confirmed nor refuted by the evidence of our senses and the operation of human reason. But it is refuted by Revelation, that body of knowledge which transcends our rational faculties and which God has chosen to reveal to us. As a result, the Christian will believe as an item of faith that the world was created by God. For Aquinas, reason is powerless to prove such articles of faith given by Revelation. But reason can operate to demonstrate the truth of propositions which are not themselves articles of faith, but are presupposed by the articles of faith. One such proposition is that God exists.

The greatest of Aquinas's philosophical writings is his monumental *Summa Theologica*. It is divided into three major parts, with each part divided into many questions, and each question into articles. The first two questions of the first part are reprinted here. In the first question Aquinas asks whether Christian theology is a science—a question which may seem peculiar until one finds out that by "science" Aquinas means nothing more than any body of knowledge which has first principles. In the second question Aquinas turns to the issue of God's existence. Here he criticizes Anselm's ontological argument but offers five arguments of his own to show that God exists. These "five ways" have attracted lavish philosophical attention through the centuries.

F.C. Copleston's *Aquinas* (Baltimore: Penguin Books, 1955) and Etienne Gilson's *The Christian Philosophy of St. Thomas Aquinas* (New York: Random House, 1956) are two good introductions to Aquinas's philosophy. Anthony Kenny, ed., *Aquinas: A Collection of Critical Essays* (Garden City: Doubleday, 1969) contains several important essays. Anthony Kenny, *The Five Ways* (London: Routledge & Kegan Paul, 1969) provides a detailed examination of Aquinas's arguments for the existence of God.

W.E.M.

SUMMA THEOLOGICA

PART ONE

GOD

Question I

THE NATURE AND DOMAIN OF SACRED DOCTRINE

(In Ten Articles)

To place our purpose within definite limits, we must first investigate the nature and domain of sacred doctrine. Concerning this there are ten points of inquiry:—

(1) Whether sacred doctrine is necessary? (2) Whether it is a science? (3) Whether it is one or many? (4) Whether it is speculative or practical? (5) How it is compared with other sciences? (6) Whether it is a wisdom? (7) Whether God is its subject-matter? (8) Whether it is argumentative? (9) Whether it rightly employs metaphors and similes? (10) Whether the Sacred Scripture of this doctrine may be expounded in different senses?

First Article

WHETHER, BESIDES THE PHILOSOPHICAL SCIENCES, ANY FURTHER DOCTRINE IS REQUIRED?

We proceed thus to the First Article: —

Objection 1. It seems that, besides the philosophical sciences, we have no need of any further knowledge. For man should not seek to know what is above reason: *Seek not the things that are too high for thee* (*Ecclus.* iii 22). But whatever is not above reason is sufficiently considered in the philosophical sciences. Therefore any other knowledge besides the philosophical sciences is superfluous.

Obj. 2. Further, knowledge can be concerned only with being, for nothing can be known, save the true, which is convertible with being. But everything that is, is considered in the philosophical sciences—even God Himself; so that there is a part of philosophy called theology, or the divine science, as is clear from Aristotle. Therefore, besides the philosophical sciences, there is no need of any further knowledge.

On the contrary, It is written (*2 Tim.* iii. 16): *All Scripture inspired of God is profitable*

Reprinted from *Basic Writings of St. Thomas Aquinas,* ed. Anton C. Pegis (New York: Random House, 1945), by permission of the publisher.

to teach, to reprove, to correct, to instruct in justice. Now Scripture, inspired by God, is not a part of the philosophical sciences discovered by human reason. Therefore it is useful that besides the philosophical sciences there should be another science — *i.e.,* inspired of God.

I answer that, It was necessary for man's salvation that there should be a knowledge revealed by God, besides the philosophical sciences investigated by human reason. First, because man is directed to God as to an end that surpasses the grasp of his reason: *The eye hath not seen, O God, besides Thee, what things Thou hast prepared for them that wait for Thee (Isa.* lxiv. 4). But the end must first be known by men who are to direct their thoughts and actions to the end. Hence it was necessary for the salvation of man that certain truths which exceed human reason should be made known to him by divine revelation. Even as regards those truths about God which human reason can investigate, it was necessary that man be taught by a divine revelation. For the truth about God, such as reason can know it, would only be known by a few, and that after a long time, and with the admixture of many errors; whereas man's whole salvation, which is in God, depends upon the knowledge of this truth. Therefore, in order that the salvation of men might be brought about more fitly and more surely, it was necessary that they be taught divine truths by divine revelation. It was therefore necessary that, besides the philosophical sciences investigated by reason, there should be a sacred science by way of revelation.

Reply Obj. 1. Although those things which are beyond man's knowledge may not be sought for by man through his reason, nevertheless, what is revealed by God must be accepted through faith. Hence the sacred text continues, *For many things are shown to thee above the understanding of man (Ecclus.* iii. 25). And in such things sacred science consists.

Reply Obj. 2. Sciences are diversified according to the diverse nature of their knowable objects. For the astronomer and the physicist both prove the same conclusion — that the earth, for instance is round: the astronomer by means of mathematics *(i.e.,* abstracting from matter), but the physicist by means of matter itself. Hence there is no reason why those things which are treated by the philosophical sciences, so far as they can be known by the light of natural reason, may not also be treated by another science so far as they are known by the light of the divine revelation. Hence the theology included in sacred doctrine differs in genus from that theology which is part of philosophy.

Second Article

WHETHER SACRED DOCTRINE IS A SCIENCE?

We proceed thus to the Second Article: —

Objection 1. It seems that sacred doctrine is not a science. For every science proceeds from self-evident principles. But sacred doctrine proceeds from articles of faith which are not self-evident, since their truth is not admitted by all: *For all men have not faith (2 Thess.* iii. 2). Therefore sacred doctrine is not a science.

Obj. 2. Further, science is not of individuals. But sacred doctrine treats of individual facts, such as the deeds of Abraham, Isaac and Jacob, and the like. Therefore sacred doctrine is not a science.

On the contrary, Augustine says that *to this science alone belongs that whereby saving faith is begotten, nourished, protected and strengthened.* But this can be said of no science except sacred doctrine. Therefore sacred doctrine is a science.

I answer that, Sacred doctrine is a science. We must bear in mind that there are two kinds of sciences. There are some which proceed from principles known by the natural light of the intellect, such as arithmetic and geometry and the like. There are also some which proceed from principles known by the light of a higher science: thus the science of optics proceeds from principles established by geometry, and music from principles established by arithmetic. So it is that sacred doctrine is a science because it proceeds from principles made known by the light of a higher science, namely, the science of God and the blessed. Hence, just as music accepts on authority the principles taught by the arithmetician, so sacred science accepts the principles revealed by God.

Reply Obj. 1. The principles of any science are either in themselves self-evident, or reducible to the knowledge of a higher science; and such, as we have said, are the principles of sacred doctrine.

Reply Obj. 2. Individual facts are not treated in sacred doctrine because it is concerned with them principally; they are rather introduced as examples to be followed in our lives (as in the moral sciences), as well as to establish the authority of those men through whom the divine revelation, on which this sacred scripture or doctrine is based, has come down to us.

Third Article

WHETHER SACRED DOCTRINE IS ONE SCIENCE?

We proceed thus to the Third Article:—

Objection 1. It seems that sacred doctrine is not one science, for according to the Philosopher[1] *that science is one which treats only of one class of subjects.* But the creator and the creature, both of whom are treated in sacred doctrine, cannot be grouped together under one class of subjects. Therefore sacred doctrine is not one science.

Obj. 2. Further, in sacred doctrine we treat of angels, corporeal creatures and human morality. But these belong to separate philosophical sciences. Therefore sacred doctrine cannot be one science.

On the contrary, Holy Scripture speaks of it as one science: *Wisdom gave him the knowledge of holy things* (*Wis.* x. 10).

I answer that, Sacred doctrine is one science. The unity of a power or habit is to be gauged by its object, not indeed, in its material aspect, but as regards the formality under which it is an object. For example, man, ass, stone, agree in the one formality of being colored; and color is the formal object of sight. Therefore, because Sacred Scripture (as we have said) considers some things under the formality of being divinely revealed, all things which have been divinely revealed have in common the formality of the object of this science. Hence, they are included under sacred doctrine as under one science.

Reply Obj. 1. Sacred doctrine does not treat of God and creatures equally, but of

1. [Aquinas often refers to Aristotle as "the Philosopher."—S.M.C.]

God primarily, and of creatures only so far as they are referable to God as their beginning or end. Hence the unity of this science is not impaired.

Reply Obj. 2. Nothing prevents inferior powers or habits from being diversified by objects which yet agree with one another in coming together under a higher power or habit; because the higher power or habit regards its own object under a more universal formality. Thus, the object of the *common sense* is the sensible, including, therefore, whatever is visible or audible. Hence the *common sense,* although one power, extends to all the objects of the five senses. Similarly, objects which are the subject-matter of different philosophical sciences can yet be treated by this one single sacred science under one aspect, namely, in so far as they can be included in revelation. So that in this way sacred doctrine bears, as it were, the stamp of the divine science, which is one and simple, yet extends to everything.

Fourth Article

WHETHER SACRED DOCTRINE IS A PRACTICAL SCIENCE?

We proceed thus to the Fourth Article: —

Objection 1. It seems that sacred doctrine is a practical science, for a practical science is that which ends in action, according to the Philosopher. But sacred doctrine is ordained to action: *Be ye doers of the word, and not hearers only* (*Jas.* i. 22). Therefore sacred doctrine is a practical science.

Obj. 2. Further sacred doctrine is divided into the Old and the New Law. But law belongs to moral science, which is a practical science. Therefore sacred doctrine is a practical science.

On the contrary, Every practical science is concerned with the things man can do; as moral science is concerned with human acts, and architecture with buildings. But sacred doctrine is chiefly concerned with God, Who is rather the Maker of man. Therefore it is not a practical but a speculative science.

I answer that, Sacred doctrine, being one, extends to things which belong to the different philosophical sciences, because it considers in each the same formal aspect, namely, so far as they can be known through the divine light. Hence, although among the philosophical sciences some are speculative and others practical, nevertheless, sacred doctrine includes both; as God, by one and the same science, knows both Himself and His works.

Still, it is more speculative then practical, because it is more concerned with divine things than with human acts; though even of these acts it treats inasmuch as man is ordained by them to the perfect knowledge of God, in which consists eternal beatitude.

This is a sufficient answer to the Objections.

Fifth Article

WHETHER SACRED DOCTRINE IS NOBLER THAN OTHER SCIENCES?

We proceed thus to the Fifth Article: —

Objection 1. It seems that sacred doctrine is not nobler than other sciences, for the nobility of a science depends on its certitude. But other sciences, the principles of which cannot be doubted, seem to be more certain than sacred doctrine; for its principles—namely, articles of faith—can be doubted. Therefore other sciences seem to be nobler.

Obj. 2. Further, it is the part of a lower science to draw upon a higher; as music draws upon arithmetic. But sacred doctrine does draw upon the philosophical sciences; for Jerome[2] observes, in his Epistle to Magnus, that *the ancient doctors so enriched their books with the doctrines and thoughts of the philosophers, that thou knowest not what more to admire in them, their profane erudition or their scriptural learning.* Therefore sacred doctrine is inferior to other sciences.

On the contrary, Other sciences are called the handmaidens of this one: *Wisdom sent her maids to invite to the tower* (*Prov.* ix. 3).

I answer that, Since this science is partly speculative and partly practical, it transcends all other sciences, speculative and practical. Now one speculative science is said to be nobler than another either by reason of its greater certitude, or by reason of the higher dignity of its subject-matter. In both these respects this science surpasses other speculative sciences: in point of greater certitude, because other sciences derive their certitude from the natural light of human reason, which can err, whereas this derives its certitude from the light of the divine knowledge, which cannot err; in point of the higher dignity of its subject-matter, because this science treats chiefly of those things which by their sublimity transcend human reason, while other sciences consider only those things which are within reason's grasp. Of the practical sciences, that one is nobler which is ordained to a more final end, as political science is nobler than military science; for the good of the army is directed to the good of the state. But the purpose of this science, in so far as it is practical, is eternal beatitude, to which as to an ultimate end the ends of all the practical sciences are directed. Hence it is clear that from every standpoint it is nobler than other sciences.

Reply Obj. 1. It may well happen that what is in itself the more certain may seem to us the less certain because of the weakness of our intellect, *which is dazzled by the clearest objects of nature; as the owl is dazzled by the light of the sun.* Hence the fact that some happen to doubt about the articles of faith is not due to the uncertain nature of the truths, but to the weakness of the human intellect; yet the slenderest knowledge that may be obtained of the highest things is more desirable than the most certain knowledge obtained of the lowest things, as is said in *De Animalibus* xi.[3]

Reply Obj. 2. This science can draw upon the philosophical sciences, not as though it stood in need of them, but only in order to make its teaching clearer. For it accepts its principles, not from the other sciences, but immediately from God, by revelation. Therefore it does not draw upon the other sciences as upon its superiors, but uses them as its inferiors and handmaidens: even so the master sciences make use of subordinate sciences, as political science of military science. That it thus uses them is not due to its own defect or insufficiency, but to the defect of our intellect, which is more easily led by what is known through natural reason (from which proceed the other sciences), to that which is above reason, such as are the teachings of this science.

---

2. [Jerome (c.347–c.420), a Father of the Church, was the author of the Vulgate translation of the Bible, the official Latin version of the Roman Catholic Church.]

3. [The reference is to a biological work by Aristotle.]

Sixth Article

WHETHER THIS DOCTRINE IS A WISDOM?

We proceed thus to the Sixth Article: —

Objection 1. It seems that this doctrine is not a wisdom. For no doctrine which borrows its principles is worthy of the name of wisdom, seeing that the wise man directs, and is not directed. But this doctrine borrows its principles. Therefore it is not a wisdom.

Obj. 2. Further, it is a part of wisdom to prove the principles of other sciences. Hence it is called the chief of sciences, as is clear in *Ethics* vi.[4] But this doctrine does not prove the principles of other sciences. Therefore it is not a wisdom.

Obj. 3. Further, this doctrine is acquired by study, whereas wisdom is acquired by God's inspiration, and is accordingly numbered among the gifts of the Holy Spirit (*Isa.* xi. 2). Therefore this doctrine is not a wisdom.

On the contrary, It is written (*Deut.* iv. 6): *This is your wisdom and understanding in the sight of nations.*

I answer that, This doctrine is wisdom above all human wisdoms not merely in any one order, but absolutely. For since it is the part of a wise man to order and to judge, and since lesser matters can be judged in the light of some higher cause, he is said to be wise in any genus who considers the highest cause in that genus. Thus in the realm of building, he who plans the form of the house is called wise and architect, in relation to the subordinate labors who trim the wood and make ready the stones: thus it is said, *As a wise architect I have laid the foundation* (*1 Cor.* ii. 10). Again, in order of all human life, the prudent man is called wise, inasmuch as he directs his acts to a fitting end: thus it is said, *Wisdom is prudence to a man* (*Prov.* x. 23). Therefore, he who considers absolutely the highest cause of the whole universe, namely God, is most of all called wise. Hence wisdom is said to be the knowledge of divine things, as Augustine says. But sacred doctrine essentially treats of God viewed as the highest cause, for it treats of Him not only so far as He can be known through creatures just as philosophers knew Him— *That which is known of God is manifest in them* (*Rom.* i. 19) —but also so far as He is known to Himself alone and revealed to others. Hence sacred doctrine is especially called a wisdom.

Reply Obj. 1. Sacred doctrine derives its principles, not from any human knowledge, but from the divine knowledge, by which, as by the highest wisdom, all our knowledge is ordered.

Reply Obj. 2. The principles of the other sciences either are evident and cannot be proved, or they are proved by natural reason in some other science. But the knowledge proper to this science comes through revelation, and not through natural reason. Therefore it is not its business to prove the principles of the other sciences, but only to judge them. For whatsoever is found in the other sciences contrary to the truth of this science must be condemned as false. Hence, it is said: *Destroying counsels and every height that exalteth itself against the knowledge of God* (*2 Cor.* x. 4, 5).

Reply Obj. 3. Since judgment pertains to wisdom, in accord with a twofold manner of judging there is a twofold wisdom. A man may judge in one way by inclination, as

4. [The reference is to Aristotle's *Nicomachean Ethics*.]

whoever has the habit of a virtue judges rightly of what is virtuous by his very inclination towards it. Hence it is the virtuous man, as we read,[5] who is the measure and rule of human acts. In another way, a man may judge by knowledge, just as man learned in moral science might be able to judge rightly about virtuous acts, though he had not virtue. The first manner of judging divine things belongs to that wisdom which is numbered as a gift of the Holy Ghost: *The spiritual man judgeth all things* (1 Cor. ii. 15). And Dionysius says: *Hierotheus is taught not only as one learning, but also as experiencing divine things.* The second manner of judging belongs to this doctrine, inasmuch as it is acquired by study, though its principles are obtained by revelation.

Seventh Article

WHETHER GOD IS THE SUBJECT-MATTER OF THIS SCIENCE?

We proceed thus to the Seventh Article: —

Objection 1. It seems that God is not the subject-matter of this science. For, according to the Philosopher, in every science the essence of its subject is presupposed. But this science cannot presuppose the essence of God, for Damascene says: *It is impossible to express the essence of God.* Therefore God is not the subject-matter of this science.

Obj. 2. Further, whatever conclusions are reached in any science must be comprehended under the subject-matter of that science. But in Holy Scripture we reach conclusions not only concerning God, but concerning many other things, such as creatures and human morality. Therefore God is not the subject-matter of this science.

On the contrary, The subject-matter of a science is that of which it principally treats. But in this science the treatment is mainly about God; for it is called theology, as treating of God. Therefore God is the subject-matter of this science.

I answer that, God is the subject-matter of this science. The relation between a science and its subject-matter is the same as that between a habit or a power and its object. Now properly speaking the object of a power or habit is that under whose formality all things are referred to that power or habit, as man and stone are referred to sight in that they are colored. Hence colored things are the proper object of sight. But in sacred doctrine all things are treated under the aspect of God, either because they are God Himself, or because they refer to God as to their beginning and end. Hence it follows that God is in very truth the subject-matter of this science. This is made clear also from the principles of this science, namely, the articles of faith, for faith is about God. The subject-matter of the principles and of the whole science must be the same, since the whole science is contained virtually in its principles.

Some, however, looking to what is treated in this science, and not to the aspect under which it is treated, have asserted the subject-matter of this science to be something other than God—that is, either things and signs, or the works of salvation, or the whole Christ, that is, the head and members. Of all these things, in truth, we treat in this science, but so far as they are ordered to God.

5. [The reference is to Aristotle's *Nichomachean Ethics.*]

Reply Obj. 1. Although we cannot know in what consists the essence of God, nevertheless in this doctrine we make use of His effects, either of nature or of grace, in the place of a definition, in regard to whatever is treated in this doctrine concerning God; even as in some philosophical sciences we demonstrate something about a cause from its effect, by taking the effect in the place of a definition of the cause.

Reply Obj. 2. Whatever other conclusions are reached in this sacred science are comprehended under God, not as parts or species or accidents, but as in some way ordained to Him.

Eighth Article

WHETHER SACRED DOCTRINE IS ARGUMENTATIVE?

We proceed thus to the Eighth Article: —

Objection 1. It seems this doctrine is not argumentative. For Ambrose[6] says: *Put arguments aside where faith is sought.* But in this doctrine faith especially is sought: *But these things are written that you may believe* (*Jo.* xx. 31). Therefore sacred doctrine is not argumentative.

Obj. 2. Further, if it is argumentative, the argument is either from authority or from reason. If it is from authority, it seems unbefitting its dignity, for the proof from authority is the weakest form of proof according to Boethius.[7] But if from reason, this is unbefitting its end, because, according to Gregory,[8] *faith has no merit in those things of which human reason brings its own experience.* Therefore sacred doctrine is not argumentative.

On the contrary, The Scripture says that a bishop should *embrace that faithful word which is according to doctrine, that he may be able to exhort in sound doctrine and to convince the gainsayers* (*Tit.* i. 9).

I answer that, As the other sciences do not argue in proof of their principles, but argue from their principles to demonstrate other truths in these sciences, so this doctrine does not argue in proof of its principles, which are the articles of faith, but from them it goes on to prove something else; as the Apostle[9] argues from the resurrection of Christ in proof of the general resurrection (*1 Cor.* xv, 12). However, it is to be borne in mind, in regard to the philosophical sciences, that the inferior sciences neither prove their principles nor dispute with those who deny them, but leave this to a higher science; whereas the highest of them, viz., metaphysics, can dispute with one who denies its principles, if only the opponenet will make some concession; but if he concedes nothing, it can have no dispute with him, though it can answer his arguments. Hence Sacred Scripture, since it has no science above itself, disputes

6. [Ambrose (c.340–397) was bishop of Milan and a Father of the Church.]

7. [Boethius (c.480–524) was a Roman philosopher and statesman whose greatest work, *The Consolation of Philosophy,* was written while he was imprisoned prior to his execution on false charges of treason.]

8. [Gregory I (c.540–604), a Father of the Church who served as pope, defended the view that the temporal powers of the emperor and the spiritual powers of the pope were each supreme within separate spheres.]

9. [Aquinas often refers to Paul as "the Apostle."]

argumentatively with one who denies its principles only if the opponent admits some at least of the truths obtained through divine revelation. Thus, we can argue with heretics from texts in Holy Scripture, and against those who deny one article of faith we can argue from another. If our opponent believes nothing of divine revelation, there is no longer any means of proving the articles of faith by argument, but only of answering his objections—if he has any—against faith. Since faith rests upon infallible truth, and since the contrary of a truth can never be demonstrated, it is clear that the proofs brought against faith are not demonstrations, but arguments that can be answered.

Reply Obj. 1. Although arguments from human reason cannot avail to prove what belongs to faith, nevertheless, this doctrine argues from articles of faith to other truths.

Reply Obj. 2. It is especially proper to this doctrine to argue from authority, inasmuch as its principles are obtained by revelation; and hence we must believe the authority of those to whom the revelation has been made. Nor does this take away the dignity of this doctrine, for although the argument from authority based on human reason is the weakest, yet the argument from authority based on divine revelation is the strongest. But sacred doctrine also makes use of human reason, not, indeed, to prove faith (for thereby the merit of faith would come to an end), but to make clear other things that are set forth in this doctrine. Since therefore grace does not destroy nature, but perfects it, natural reason should minister to faith as the natural inclination of the will ministers to charity. Hence the Apostle says: *Bringing into captivity every understanding unto the obedience of Christ* (*2 Cor.* x. 5). Hence it is that sacred doctrine makes use also of the authority of philosophers in those questions in which they were able to know the truth by natural reason, as Paul quotes a saying of Aratus:[10] *As some also of your own poets said: For we are also His offspring* (*Acts* xvii. 28). Nevertheless, sacred doctrine makes use of these authorities as extrinsic and probable arguments, but properly uses the authority of the canonical Scriptures as a necessary demonstration, and the authority of the doctors of the Church as one that may properly be used, yet merely as probable. For our faith rests upon the revelation made to the apostles and prophets, who wrote the canonical books, and not on the revelations (if any such there are) made to other doctors. Hence Augustine says: *Only those books of Scripture which are called canonical have I learned to hold in such honor as to believe their authors have not erred in any way in writing them. But other authors I so read as not to deem anything in their works to be true, merely because of their having so thought and written, whatever may have been their holiness and learning.*

Ninth Article

WHETHER HOLY SCRIPTURE SHOULD USE METAPHORS?

We proceed thus to the Ninth Article: —

Objection 1. It seems that Holy Scripture should not use metaphors. For that which is proper to the lowest science seems not to befit this science, which holds the highest place of all. But to proceed by the aid of various similitudes and figures is

10. [Aratus was a third-century B.C. Greek court poet.]

proper to poetic, the least of all the sciences. Therefore it is not fitting that this science should make use of such similitudes.

Obj. 2. Further, this doctrine seems to be intended to make truth clear. Hence a reward is held out to those who manifest it: *They that explain me shall have life everlasting* (*Ecclus.* xxiv. 31). But by such similitudes truth is obscured. Therefore to put forward divine truths under the likeness of corporeal things does not befit this doctrine.

Obj. 3. Further, the higher creatures are, the nearer they approach to the divine likeness. If therefore any creature be taken to represent God, this representation ought chiefly to be taken from the higher creatures, and not from the lower; yet this is often found in the Scriptures.

On the contrary, It is written (*Osee* xxii. 10): *I have multiplied visions, and I have used similitudes by the ministry of the prophets.* But to put forward anything by means of similitudes is to use metaphors. Therefore sacred doctrine may use metaphors.

I answer that, It is befitting Holy Scripture to put forward divine and spiritual truths by means of comparisons with material things. For God provides for everything according to the capacity of its nature. Now it is natural to man to attain to intellectual truths through sensible things, because all our knowledge originates from sense. Hence in Holy Scripture spiritual truths are fittingly taught under the likeness of material things. This is what Dionysius[11] says: *We cannot be enlightened by the divine rays except they be hidden within the covering of many sacred veils.* It is also befitting Holy Scripture, which is proposed to all without distinction of persons — *To the wise and to the unwise I am a debtor* (*Rom.* i. 14) — that spiritual truths be expounded by means of figures taken from corporeal things, in order that thereby even the simple who are unable by themselves to grasp intellectual things may be able to understand it.

Reply Obj. 1. Poetry makes use of metaphors to produce a representation, for it is natural to man to be pleased with representations. But sacred doctrine makes use of metaphors as both necessary and useful.

Reply Obj. 2. The ray of divine revelation is not extinguished by the sensible imagery wherewith it is veiled, as Dionysius says; and its truth so far remains that it does not allow the minds of those to whom the revelation has been made, to rest in the likenesses, but raises them to the knowledge of intelligible truths; and through those to whom the revelation has been made others also may receive instruction in these matters. Hence those things that are taught metaphorically in one part of Scripture, in other parts are taught more openly. The very hiding of truth in figures is useful for the exercise of thoughtful minds, and as a defense against the ridicule of the unbelievers, according to the words, *Give not that which is holy to dogs* (*Matt.* vii. 6).

Reply Obj. 3. As Dionysius says, it is more fitting that divine truths should be expounded under the figure of less noble than of nobler bodies; and this for three reasons. First, because thereby men's minds are the better freed from error. For then it is clear that these things are not literal descriptions of divine truths, which might have been open to doubt had they been expressed under the figure of nobler bodies, especially in the case of those who could think of nothing nobler than bodies. Sec-

---

11. [Dionysius the Areopagite, who lived during the first century, was traditionally considered the first bishop of Athens.]

ond, because this is more befitting the knowledge of God that we have in this life. For what He is not is clearer to us than what He is. Therefore similitudes drawn from things farthest away from God form within us a truer estimate that God is above whatsoever we may say or think of Him. Third, because thereby divine truths are the better hidden from the unworthy.

Tenth Article

WHETHER IN HOLY SCRIPTURE A WORD MAY HAVE SEVERAL SENSES?

We proceed thus to the Tenth Article: —

Objection 1. It seems that in Holy Scripture a word cannot have several senses, historical or literal, allegorical, tropological or moral, and anagogical. For many different senses in one text produce confusion and deception and destroy all force of argument. Hence no argument, but only fallacies, can be deduced from a multiplicity of propositions. But Holy Scripture ought to be able to state the truth without any fallacy. Therefore in it there cannot be several senses to a word.

Obj. 2. Further, Augustine says that *the Old Testament has a fourfold division: according to history, etiology, analogy, and allegory.* Now these four seem altogether different from the four divisions mentioned in the first objection. Therefore it does not seem fitting to explain the same word of Holy Scripture according to the four different senses mentioned above.

Obj. 3. Further, besides these senses, there is the parabolical, which is not one of these four.

On the contrary, Gregory says: *Holy Scripture by the manner of its speech transcends every science, because in one and the same sentence, while it describes a fact, it reveals a mystery.*

I answer that, The author of Holy Scripture is God, in Whose power it is to signify His meaning, not by words only (as man also can do), but also by things themselves. So, whereas in every other science things are signified by words, this science has the property that the things signified by the words have themselves also a signification. Therefore that first signification whereby words signify things belongs to the first sense, the historical or literal. That signification whereby things signified by words have themselves also a signification is called the spirtual sense, which is based on the literal, and presupposes it. Now this spiritual sense has a threefold division. For as the Apostle says (*Heb.* x. 1) the Old Law is a figure of the New Law, and Dionysius says *the New Law itself is a figure of future glory.* Again, in the New Law, whatever our Head has done is a type of what we ought to do. Therefore, so far as the things of the Old Law signify the things of the New Law, there is the allegorical sense; so far as the things done in Christ, or so far as the things which signify Christ, are signs of what we ought to do, there is the moral sense. But so far as they signify what relates to eternal glory, there is the anagogical sense. Since the literal sense is that which the author intends, and since the author of Holy Scripture is God, Who by one act comprehends all things by His intellect, it is not unfitting, as Augustine says, if, even according to the literal sense, one word in Holy Scripture should have several senses.

Reply Obj. 1. The multiplicity of these senses does not produce equivocation or any other kind of multiplicity, seeing that these senses are not multiplied because one word signifies several things, but because the things signified by the words can be themselves signs of other things. Thus in Holy Scripture no confusion results, for all the senses are founded on one — the literal — from which alone can any argument be drawn, and not from those intended allegorically, as Augustine says. Nevertheless, nothing of Holy Scripture perishes because of this, since nothing necessary to faith is contained under the spiritual sense which is not elsewhere put forward clearly by the Scripture in its literal sense.

Reply Obj. 2. These three — history, etiology, analogy — are grouped under the literal sense. For it is called history, as Augustine expounds, whenever anything is simply related; it is called etiology when its cause is assigned, as when Our Lord gave the reason why Moses allowed the putting away of wives — namely, because of the hardness of men's hearts (*Matt.* xix. 8); it is called analogy whenever the truth of one text of Scripture is shown not to contradict the truth of another. Of these four, allegory alone stands for the three spiritual senses. Thus Hugh of St. Victor[12] includes the anagogical under the allegorical sense, laying down three senses only — the historical, the allegorical and the tropological.

Reply Obj. 3. The parabolical sense is contained in the literal, for by words things are signified properly and figuratively. Nor is the figure itself, but that which is figured, the literal sense. When Scripture speaks of God's arm, the literal sense is not that God has such a member, but only what is signified by this member, namely, operative power. Hence it is plain that nothing false can ever underlie the literal sense of Holy Scripture.

Question II

THE EXISTENCE OF GOD

(In Three Articles)

Because the chief aim of sacred doctrine is to teach the knowledge of God not only as He is in Himself, but also as He is the beginning of things and their last end, and especially of rational creatures, as is clear from what has been already said, therefore, in our endeavor to expound this science, we shall treat: (1) of God; (2) of the rational creature's movement towards God; (3) of Christ Who as man is our way to God.

In treating of God there will be a threefold division: —

For we shall consider (1) whatever concerns the divine essence. (2) Whatever concerns the distinctions of Persons. (3) Whatever concerns the procession of creatures from Him.

Concerning the divine essence, we must consider: —

(1) Whether God exists? (2) The manner of His existence, or, rather, what is *not*

---

12. [Hugh of St. Victor (1096–1141), born in Saxony, was a noted theologian who also wrote numerous mystical works.]

the manner of His existence. (3) Whatever concerns His operations—namely, His knowledge, will, power.

Concerning the first, there are three points of inquiry:—

(1) Whether the proposition *God exists* is self-evident? (2) Whether it is demonstrable? (3) Whether God exists?

First Article

WHETHER THE EXISTENCE OF GOD IS SELF-EVIDENT?

We proceed thus to the First Article:—

Objection 1. It seems that the existence of God is self-evident. For those things are said to be self-evident to us the knowledge of which exists naturally in us, as we can see in regard to first principles. But as Damascene[13] says, *the knowledge of God is naturally implanted in all.* Therefore the existence of God is self-evident.

Obj. 2. Further, those things are said to be self-evident which are known as soon as the terms are known, which the Philosopher says is true of the first principles of demonstration. Thus, when the nature of a whole and of a part is known, it is at once recognized that every whole is greater than its part. But as soon as the signification of the name *God* is understood, it is at once seen that God exists. For by this name is signified that thing than which nothing greater can be conceived. But that which exists actually and mentally is greater than that which exists only mentally. Therefore, since as soon as the name *God* is understood it exists mentally, it also follows that it exists actually. Therefore the proposition *God exists* is self-evident.

Obj. 3. Further, the existence of truth is self-evident. For whoever denies the existence of truth grants that truth does not exist: and, if truth does not exist, then the proposition *Truth does not exist* is true: and if there is anything true there must be truth. But God is truth itself: *I am the way, the truth, and the life* (*Jo.* xiv. 6). Therefore *God exists* is self-evident.

On the contrary, No one can mentally admit the opposite of what is self-evident, as the Philosopher states concerning the first principles of demonstration. But the opposite of the proposition *God is* can be mentally admitted: *The fool said in his heart, There is no God* (*Ps.* lii 1). Therefore, that God exists is not self-evident.

I answer that, A thing can be self-evident in either of two ways: on the one hand, self-evident in itself, though not to us; on the other, self-evident in itself, and to us. A proposition is self-evident because the predicate is included in the essence of the subject: *e.g., Man is an animal,* for animal is contained in the essence of man. If, therefore, the essence of the predicate and subject be known to all, the proposition will be self-evident to all; as is clear with regard to the first principles of demonstration, the terms of which are certain common notions that no one is ignorant of, such as being and non-being, whole and part, and the like. If, however, there are some to whom the essence of the predicate and subject is unknown, the proposition will be self-evident in itself, but not to those who do not know the meaning of the predicate and subject of the proposition. Therefore, it happens, as Boethius says, that there are some notions of the mind which are common and self-evident only to

---

13. [John Damascene (c.675–c.749) was a Syrian theologian and Father of the Church.]

the learned, as that incorporeal substances are not in space. Therefore, I say that this proposition, *God exists,* of itself is self-evident, for the predicate is the same as the subject, because God is His own existence as will be hereafter shown. Now because we do not know the essence of God, the proposition is not self-evident to us, but needs to be demonstrated by things that are more known to us, though less known in their nature—namely, by His effects.

Reply Obj. 1. To know that God exists in a general and confused way is implanted in us by nature, inasmuch as God is man's beatitude. For man naturally desires happiness, and what is naturally desired by man is naturally known by him. This, however, is not to know absolutely that God exists; just as to know that someone is approaching is not the same as to know that Peter is approaching, even though it is Peter who is approaching; for there are many who imagine that man's perfect good, which is happiness, consists in riches, and others in pleasures, and others in something else.

Reply Obj. 2. Perhaps not everyone who hears this name *God* understands it to signify something than which nothing greater can be thought, seeing that some have believed God to be a body. Yet, granted that everyone understands that by this name *God* is signified something than which nothing greater can be thought, nevertheless, it does not therefore follow that he understands that what the name signifies exists actually, but only that it exists mentally. Nor can it be argued that it actually exists, unless it be admitted that there actually exists something than which nothing greater can be thought; and this precisely is not admitted by those who hold that God does not exist.

Reply Obj. 3. The existence of truth in general is self-evident, but the existence of a Primal Truth is not self-evident to us.

Second Article

WHETHER IT CAN BE DEMONSTRATED THAT GOD EXISTS?

We proceed thus to the Second Article:—

Objection 1. It seems that the existence of God cannot be demonstrated. For it is an article of faith that God exists. But what is of faith cannot be demonstrated, because a demonstration produces scientific knowledge, whereas faith is of the unseen, as is clear from the Apostle (*Heb.* xi. 1). Therefore it cannot be demonstrated that God exists.

Obj. 2. Further, essence is the middle term of demonstration. But we cannot know in what God's essence consists, but solely in what it does not consist, as Damascene says. Therefore we cannot demonstrate that God exists.

Obj. 3. Further, if the existence of God were demonstrated, this could only be from His effects. But His effects are not proportioned to Him, since He is infinite and His effects are finite, and between the finite and infinite there is no proportion. Therefore, since a cause cannot be demonstrated by an effect not proportioned to it, it seems that the existence of God cannot be demonstrated.

On the contrary, The Apostle says: *The invisible things of Him are clearly seen, being understood by the things that are made* (*Rom.* i. 20). But this would not be unless the existence of God could be demonstrated through the things that are made; for the first thing we must know of anything is, whether it exists.

I answer that, Demonstration can be made in two ways: One is through the cause, and is called *propter quid,* and this is to argue from what is prior absolutely. The other is through the effect, and is called a demonstration *quia;* this is to argue from what is prior relatively only to us. When an effect is better known to us than its cause, from the effect we proceed to the knowledge of the cause. And from every effect the existence of its proper cause can be demonstrated, so long as its effects are better known to us; because, since every effect depends upon its cause, if the effect exists, the cause must pre-exist. Hence the existence of God, in so far as it is not self-evident to us, can be demonstrated from those of His effects which are known to us.

Reply Obj. 1. The existence of God and other like truths about God, which can be known by natural reason, are not articles of faith, but are preambles to the articles; for faith presupposes natural knowledge, even as grace presupposes nature and perfection the perfectible. Nevertheless, there is nothing to prevent a man, who cannot grasp a proof, from accepting, as a matter of faith, something which in itself is capable of being scientifically known and demonstrated.

Reply Obj. 2. When the existence of a cause is demonstrated from an effect, this effect takes the place of the definition of the cause in proving the cause's existence. This is especially the case in regard to God, because, in order to prove the existence of anything, it is necessary to accept as a middle term the meaning of the name, and not its essence, for the question of its essence follows on the question of its existence. Now the names given to God are derived from His effects, as will be later shown. Consequently, in demonstrating the existence of God from His effects, we may take for the middle term the meaning of the name *God.*

Reply Obj. 3. From effects not proportioned to the cause no perfect knowledge of that cause can be obtained. Yet from every effect the existence of the cause can be clearly demonstrated, and so we can demonstrate the existence of God from His effects; though from them we cannot know God perfectly as He is in His essence.

Third Article

WHETHER GOD EXISTS?

We proceed thus to the Third Article: —

Objection 1. It seems that God does not exist; because if one of two contraries be infinite, the other would be altogether destroyed. But the name *God* means that He is infinite goodness. If, therefore, God existed, there would be no evil discoverable; but there is evil in the world. Therefore God does not exist.

Obj. 2. Further, it is superfluous to suppose that what can be accounted for by a few principles has been produced by many. But it seems that everything we see in the world can be accounted for by other principles, supposing God did not exist. For all natural things can be reduced to one principle, which is nature; and all voluntary things can be reduced to one principle, which is human reason, or will. Therefore there is no need to suppose God's existence.

On the contrary, It is said in the person of God: *I am Who am* (*Exod.* iii. 14).

I answer that, The existence of God can be proved in five ways.

The first and more manifest way is the argument from motion. It is certain, and evident to our senses, that in the world some things are in motion. Now whatever is moved is moved by another, for nothing can be moved except it is in potentiality to that towards which it is moved; whereas a thing moves inasmuch as it is in act. For motion is nothing else than the reduction of something from potentiality to actuality. But nothing can be reduced from potentiality to actuality, except by something in a state of actuality. Thus that which is actually hot, as fire, makes wood, which is potentially hot, to be actually hot, and thereby moves and changes it. Now it is not possible that the same thing should be at once in actuality and potentiality in the same respect, but only in different respects. For what is actually hot cannot simultaneously be potentially hot; but it is simultaneously potentially cold. It is therefore impossible that in the same respect and in the same way a thing should be both mover and moved, *i.e.,* that it should move itself. Therefore, whatever is moved must be moved by another. If that by which it is moved be itself moved, then this also must needs be moved by another, and that by another again. But this cannot go on to infinity, because then there would be no first mover, and, consequently, no other mover, seeing that subsequent movers move only inasmuch as they are moved by the first mover; as the staff moves only because it is moved by the hand. Therefore it is necessary to arrive at a first mover, moved by no other; and this everyone understands to be God.

The second way is from the nature of efficient cause. In the world of sensible things we find there is an order of efficient causes. There is no case known (neither is it, indeed, possible) in which a thing is found to be the efficient cause of itself; for so it would be prior to itself, which is impossible. Now in efficient causes it is not possible to go on to infinity, because in all efficient causes following in order, the first is the cause of the intermediate cause, and the intermediate is the cause of the ultimate cause, whether the intermediate cause be several, or one only. Now to take away the cause is to take away the effect. Therefore, if there be no first cause among efficient causes, there will be no ultimate, nor any intermediate, cause. But if in efficient causes it is possible to go on to infinity, there will be no first efficient cause, neither will there be an ultimate effect, nor any intermediate efficient causes; all of which is plainly false. Therefore it is necessary to admit a first efficient cause, to which everyone gives the name of God.

The third way is taken from possibility and necessity, and runs thus. We find in nature things that are possible to be and not to be, since they are found to be generated, and to be corrupted, and consequently, it is possible for them to be and not to be. But it is impossible for these always to exist, for that which can not-be at some time is not. Therefore, if everything can not-be, then at one time there was nothing in existence. Now if this were true, even now there would be nothing in existence, because that which does not exist begins to exist only through something already existing. Therefore, if at one time nothing was in existence, it would have been impossible for anything to have begun to exist; and thus even now nothing would be in existence—which is absurd. Therefore, not all beings are merely possible, but there must exist something the existence of which is necessary. But every necessary thing either has its necessity caused by another, or not. Now it is impossible to go on to infinity in necessary things which have their necessity caused by another, as has been already proved in regard to efficient causes. Therefore we cannot but admit the existence of some being having of itself its own necessity, and not receiving it from another, but rather causing in others their necessity. This all men speak of as God.

The fourth way is taken from the gradation to be found in things. Among beings there are some more and some less good, true, noble, and the like. But *more* and *less* are predicated of different things according as they resemble in their different ways something which is the maximum, as a thing is said to be hotter according as it more nearly resembles that which is hottest; so that there is something which is truest, something best, something noblest, and consequently, something which is most being, for those things that are greatest in truth are greatest in being, as it is written in *Metaph.* ii.[14] Now the maximum in any genus is the cause of all in that genus, as fire, which is the maximum of heat, is the cause of all hot things, as is said in the same book. Therefore there must also be something which is to all beings the cause of their being, goodness, and every other perfection; and this we call God.

The fifth way is taken from the governance of the world. We see that things which lack knowledge, such as natural bodies, act for an end, and this is evident from their acting always, or nearly always, in the same way, so as to obtain the best result. Hence it is plain that they achieve their end, not fortuitously, but designedly. Now whatever lacks knowledge cannot move towards an end, unless it be directed by some being endowed with knowledge and intelligence; as the arrow is directed by the archer. Therefore some intelligent being exists by whom all natural things are directed to their end; and this being we call God.

Reply Obj. 1. As Augustine says: *Since God is the highest good, He would not allow any evil to exist in His works, unless His omnipotence and goodness were such as to bring good even out of evil.* This is part of the infinite goodness of God, that He should allow evil to exist, and out of it produce good.

Reply Obj. 2. Since nature works for a determinate end under the direction of a higher agent, whatever is done by nature must be traced back to God as to its first cause. So likewise whatever is done voluntarily must be traced back to some higher cause other than human reason and will, since these can change and fail; for all things that are changeable and capable of defect must be traced back to an immovable and self-necessary first principle, as has been shown.

14. [The reference is to Aristotle's *Metaphysics.*]

RENÉ DESCARTES—by Frans Hals;
in the Louvre, Paris

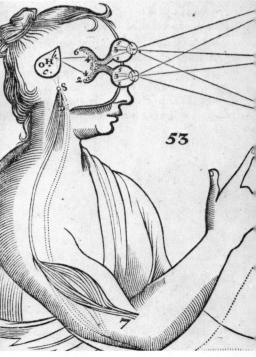

QUEEN CHRISTINA OF SWEDEN

DESCARTES' PERCEPTION OF MOVEME

RENÉ DESCARTES

René Descartes lived in an era of geniuses. In the year of his birth, 1596, Shakespeare was writing *Richard II* and *The Merchant of Venice*. When Descartes died in 1650, Newton was seven. Hobbes and Galileo were near-contemporaries.

Descartes was born in La Haye, now La Haye-Descartes, a small town in Touraine, France, and lived much of his life in virtual seclusion in Holland. His interests were extremely wide-ranging. He made major contributions to anatomy and physiology, optics, mathematics, and of course, philosophy. At the center of his thought lies the view that each science is a branch of one unified science of the world, a science based on mathematics. Thus, Descartes was an early champion of Galileo's doctrine that "the book of nature is written in the language of mathematics." In addition to unifying other sciences through mathematics, Descartes effected a major unification within mathematics when he displayed the relation between the geometry of the ancients and the algebra he helped develop through the use of his Cartesian coordinate system.

The value of mathematics in studying natural science seems obvious to us today. How can mathematics advance the study of philosophy? Like Plato before him, Descartes believes that through training in mathematics the mind becomes capable of engaging in philosophical thought. In mathematics, we encounter absolute certainty, according to Descartes. We recognize that our conclusion cannot be mistaken, because our starting assumptions are obviously true and each step in the chain of reasoning is correct. Further, mathematics introduces us to knowledge gained through the understanding, or through reasoning, rather than through the senses. While children may originally come to accept that $1 + 1 = 2$ by counting cookies, the mature person's belief that $1 + 1 = 2$, always and with no exceptions, seems to have a different basis. Descartes believes that it rests on intellectual understanding: we grasp what a unit is and how the addition operation combines units. It is not mathematical results, but these two striking characteristics of mathematical knowledge, its certainty and its dependence on understanding rather than sensation, that provide illumination for philosophy. Descartes argues that, as with mathematics, certainty must be the touchstone of philosophical truth and the way to that truth must be through the understanding.

The *Meditations on First Philosophy,* reprinted here, is Descartes' most important philosophical treatise. It is an unusual work: rather than lecturing his readers on the virtues of his conclusions, Descartes invites us to come along with him on the journey of discovering those conclusions. What is required of readers is that we too reflect on the issues that intrigue Descartes, that we ask ouselves such questions as, "If I am thinking, is it possible for me to doubt that I exist?"

Recalling that Descartes wished to bring to philosophy the certainty he discerned in mathematics, it is hardly surprising that the First Meditation begins by attempting to doubt all claims. The doubting has two purposes. Descartes wants to show that beliefs based on sensory data are not certain, thereby establishing the superiority of the understanding in acquiring knowledge. He also wants to discover whether any of our beliefs is in fact immune to doubt. In the Second Meditation, Descartes and his readers come to understand through reasoning that there is a claim that cannot be doubted: when one contemplates one's existence, it is not possible to have the slightest doubt that one does in fact exist. This conclusion is neatly captured in the well-known phrase, *cogito, ergo sum,* or "I think, therefore I am" (although these words do not appear in the Meditations). It is crucially important to note that, for Descartes, the "I" in this claim does not refer to a physical person, but to an immaterial mind. "Cartesian dualism" is the view that the world consists of two fundamental types of entities: physical bodies and immaterial minds. Since only minds can think, the *cogito* can only be used to show that a mind exists.

Later in the *Meditations,* Descartes attempts to restore the beliefs that his method of doubt had cast aside, arguing that it is also certain that physical bodies exist. In the Third Meditation, he completes the *cogito* argument and lays the basis for the later arguments concerning the existence of the physical world, contending that any claim which cannot be doubted must actually be true because God exists and would not permit us to be deceived about anything which was completely obvious to us.

Anthony Kenny's *Descartes: A Study of His Philosophy* (New York: Random House, 1968) is designed as an introduction for students but also treats those aspects of Descartes' thought that are of most interest to contemporary philosophers. A number of important papers are collected in Willis Doney, *Descartes: A Collection of Critical Essays* (Garden City: Doubleday, 1967). More recent contributions are collected in Michael Hooker, editor, *Descartes, Critical and Interpretive Essays* (Baltimore: The Johns Hopkins University Press, 1978). Harry Frankfurt, *Demons, Dreamers, and Madmen: The Defense of Reason in Descartes' Meditations* (Indianapolis: Hackett Publishing Company, 1970) offers an excellent discussion of the first two meditations; E.M. Curley, *Descartes Against the Skeptics* (Cambridge, Mass.: Harvard University Press, 1978) provides a clear and interesting discussion of Descartes' relations to some of his contemporaries. When Descartes first published the *Meditations,* he included a series of objections by contemporaries and his replies to them, which is still a wonderful companion to the *Meditations.* These are available along with the other major works of Descartes, including the *Discourse on Method,* the *Principles of Philosophy,* and *The Passions of the Soul,* in *The Philosophical Works of Descartes,* vols. I and II, trans. Elizabeth S. Haldane and G.R.T. Ross (1911; rpt. Cambridge: Cambridge University Press, 1967). An influential contemporary critique of Descartes' position is Gilbert Ryle, *The Concept of Mind* (New York: Barnes & Noble, 1949).

P.W.K.

MEDITATIONS ON FIRST PHILOSOPHY

To the Wisest and Most Dintinguished Men,
the Dean and Doctors of the Faculty of Sacred Theology of Paris
René Descartes Sends Greetings

Such a righteous cause impels me to offer this work to you (and I am confident that you too will regard it as so righteous as to take up its defense, once you have understood the plan of my undertaking) that there is here no better means of commending it than to state briefly what I have sought to achieve in this work.

I have always thought that two questions—that of God and that of the soul—are chief among those that ought to be demonstrated by the aid of philosophy rather than of theology. For although it suffices for believers like ourselves to believe by faith that the soul does not die with the body and that God exists, certainly no unbeliever seems capable of being persuaded of any religion or even any moral virtue, unless these two are first proven to him by natural reason. And since in this life there are often more rewards for vices than for virtues, few would prefer what is right to what is useful, if they neither feared God nor hoped for an afterlife. And although it is utterly true that God's existence is to be believed in because it is taught in the Holy Scriptures, and, on the other hand, that the Holy Scriptures are to be believed because they have God as their source (because, since faith is a gift from God, the very same one who gives the grace that is necessary for believing the rest, can also give us the grace to believe that he exists); nonetheless, this cannot be proposed to unbelievers because they would judge it to be a circle. And truly I have noticed that you, along with all other theologians, affirm not only that the existence of God can be proven by natural reason, but also that one may infer from the Holy Scriptures that the knowledge of him is much easier than the manifold knowledge that we have of created things, and is so utterly easy that those without this knowledge are worthy of blame. For this is clear from Wisdom, Chapter 13 where it is said: "They are not to be excused, for if their capacity for knowing were so great that they could appraise the world, how is it that they did not find the Lord of it even more easily?" And in Romans, Chapter 1, it is said that they are "without excuse." And again in the same text we seem to be warned by these words: "What is known of God is manifest in them": everything that can be known about God can be made manifest by reason drawn from a source none other than our own mind. For this reason I have not thought it unbecoming for me to inquire how it is that this is the case, and by what path God may be known more easily and with greater certainty than the things of this world.

And as to the soul: although many have regarded its nature as incapable of easy inquiry, and some have gone so far as to say that human reasoning convinces them that the soul dies with the body, and that the contrary is to be held on faith alone; never-theless, because the Lateran Council[1] under Leo X, in Session 8, condemned these

Reprinted by permission of the translator Donald A. Cress, from Descartes, *Meditations on First Philosophy* (Indianapolis: Hackett Publishing Company, 1979).

1. [The Council took place between 1512 and 1517.—S.M.C.]

people and explicitly enjoined Christian philosophers to refute their arguments and to use all their abilities to make the truth known, I too have not hesitated to go forward with this.

Moreover, I know that there are many irreligious people who refuse to believe that God exists and that the soul is distinct from the body, for no other reason than that they say that these two doctrines have up to this time not been able to be proven by anybody. Although I am by no means in agreement with these people (on the contrary, I believe that nearly all the arguments which have been brought to bear on these questions by great men have the force of a demonstration, when they are adequately understood, and I am convinced that hardly any arguments could be given that were not previously discovered by others); nevertheless, I judge that there is no greater purpose to fulfill in philosophy than to seek out the best of all these arguments and to exhibit them so carefully and accurately that henceforth all will take them to be true demonstrations. And, finally, because I was very strongly urged to do this by several people, to whom it is known that I practiced a method for solving certain problems in the sciences—not a new one, because nothing is more ancient than the truth, but which I often seemed to use with success in other areas. Thus I believed that I should attempt something on this subject.

Now all that I have been able to accomplish is contained in this treatise. Not that I have begun to gather together in it all the various proofs that can be brought to bear on these matters; that does not seem necessary, except where no proof is sufficiently certain. Rather, I have sought the primary and principal arguments, so that I now dare to propose these as most certain and evident demonstrations. Moreover, these arguments are such that I believe that there is no other way by which human ingenuity can find better ones. For the urgency of the cause, as well as the glory of God to which all this is referred, compel me to speak here on my own behalf somewhat more freely than is my custom. But although I believe my arguments to be certain and obvious, still I am not therefore convinced that they have been accommodated to everybody's power of comprehension. Just as in geometry there are many proofs written by Archimedes, Apollonius,[2] Pappus,[3] and others, that, although they are taken to be obvious and certain (because they manifestly contain nothing which, considered by itself, is not quite easily known, and nothing in which what follows does not square exactly with what precedes), are nevertheless quite lengthy and require a very attentive reader, so that they are understood by only a few; just so, although I believe that the proofs I use here equal and even surpass in certitude and obviousness the demonstrations of geometry, I am nevertheless fearful that they would be inadequately perceived by many people, both because they are quite lengthy, one thing depending on another, and also because they particularly demand a mind quite free from prejudices—a mind that can easily withdraw itself from commerce with the senses. Certainly one is less apt to find people competent to study metaphysics than to study geometry. Moreover, there is a difference in that in geometry everyone is convinced that nothing is customarily written without there being a certain demonstration for it, so that the inexperienced err on the side of assenting to what is false, want-

2. [Apollonius of Perga (c.262–200 B.C.) was a Greek mathematician famed for his study of conic sections.]

3. [Pappus of Alexandria was a fourth-century Greek mathematician whose work exerted an influence on the revival of interest in geometry in the seventeenth century.]

ing as they do to give the appearance of understanding it, more often than of denying what is true. But it is the reverse in philosophy: since nothing is believed concerning which there cannot be a dispute regarding at least one part, few look for truth, and many more, eager to have a reputation for profundity, dare to challenge whatever is the best.

And therefore, however forceful my proofs might be, nevertheless—because they belong to philosophy—I do not expect that what I have accomplished through them will be very significant unless you assist me with your patronage. So great an esteem for your Faculty resides in the minds of all, and so authoritative is the name of the Sorbonne, that, not only in matters of faith, but also in humanistic philosophy, no society, other than the Holy Councils, has been deferred to so much as yours. Nowhere is there thought to be greater sharpness of wit and solid knowledge, or greater integrity and wisdom in delivering judgment. I do not doubt that, if you should deign to pay heed to this work, you would first correct it (for mindful that I am not only human but also ignorant, I do not assert that there are no errors in it); next, that what is lacking may be added, or what is not quite complete may be perfected, or what is in need of further discussion may be more fully laid out, either by yourselves or at least by me, after I have been made aware of it by you; and finally, that, after the arguments contained in it (by which we prove that God exists and that the mind is distinct from the body) will have been brought to that level of sharpness to which I am confident they can be brought, so that these arguments should come to be regarded as the most carefully prepared of demonstrations, should you wish to declare these and attest to them in public. I do not doubt, I say, that, if this should come to pass, all the errors that have ever been entertained regarding these questions will in a short time be erased from the minds of men. For the truth itself easily brings it about that the remaining men of intelligence and learning subscribe to your judgment; and your authority will bring it about that the atheists, who are more accustomed to being dilettantes than brilliant or learned men, shall put aside their spirit of contrariness, and also that perhaps they will defend the arguments which they will know are taken to be demonstrations by men of intelligence, lest they seem not to understand them. And finally, all the others will easily believe in so many testimonies, and there will be no one who would dare call into doubt either the existence of God or the real distinction of the soul from the body. Just how great the usefulness of this thing is, you yourselves can best of all be the judge, in virtue of your singular wisdom; nor does it behoove me to commend the cause of God and religion to you at any greater length, you who have always been the greatest pillar of the Catholic Church.

Preface to the Reader

I have already touched lightly on the question of God and the human mind in my *Discourse on the Method of Rightly Conducting the Reason and Searching for Truth in the Sciences,* published in French in 1637, not for the purpose of giving them an exhaustive treatment there, but only, by sampling opinion, to learn from the judgment of readers how these matters should be subsequently treated. For they seemed to me to be so important that I judged that they ought to be dealt with more than once. And the path I follow in order to explicate these questions is so little trodden and so far removed from everyday use that I did not believe it useful to profess at greater length in a work written in French and read indiscriminately by all sorts of people, lest weaker minds be in a position to believe that they too are to set out on this path.

In the *Discourse* I requested all of those to whom there might occur something in my writings worthy of refutation that they would see fit to warn me of it, and none of the objections, among the questions I received, were worth noting, except two; and I will respond to them here in a few words before I undertake a more careful explanation of them.

The first is that, from the fact that the human mind, being turned in on itself, perceives that it is only a thinking thing, it does not follow that its nature or essence consists only in its being a thinking thing such that the word "only" would exclude everything else which also could perhaps be said to pertain to the nature of the soul. To this objection I answer that I also had no intention in that treatise of excluding those things from the order of the truth of the matter (that is to say, I was not dealing with that order then), but only as far as applies to the order of my perception; thus my meaning was that I am plainly aware of nothing which I know to pertain to my essence, beyond the fact that I am a thinking thing, that is, a thing having within itself the faculty of thinking. But in what ensues I will show how it follows from the fact that I know nothing else that pertains to my essence that nothing else at all really pertains to it.

The second objection is that it does not follow from the fact that I have in myself the idea of a thing more perfect than I, that this idea is more perfect than I, and much less that what is represented by this idea exists. But I answer here that there is an equivocation in the word "idea," for it can be taken either materially, for an operation of the intellect (in this sense one cannot say that this idea is more perfect than I), or else objectively, for the thing represented by means of this operation. This thing, although it is not presumed to exist outside the intellect, nevertheless can be more perfect than I by reason of its essence. But how, from the mere fact that there is in me an idea of something more perfect than I, it follows that this thing truly exists, will be manifested in detail in the ensuing remarks.

Moreover, I have seen two rather long pieces of writing, but in these it was not so much my arguments regarding these things that were attacked by arguments drawn from atheist commonplaces, but the conclusions. And because arguments of this type have no power over those who understand my premises, and because the judgments of most people are so preposterous and silly that they are more likely to be persuaded by the first opinions to come along, however false and alien to reason they may be, than by a true and firm, though subsequently received refutation of them, I do not wish to respond to these works here, lest I have to mention them first. Without going into particulars, I will say only that those considerations that the atheists crudely keep bringing up in order to assail the existence of God always depend on the fact that human sentiments are attributed to God, or that such power and wisdom are claimed for our minds that we begin to determine and grasp what God can and ought to do. And these considerations will cause us no difficulty, provided we only remember that our minds must be considered finite, and that God is incomprehensible and infinite.

But now, after having once and for all put to the test the judgments of men, I here again approach these same questions regarding God and the human mind, and at the same time treat the beginnings of the whole of first philosophy, but in such a way that I have no expectation of approval from the vulgar and no wide audience of readers. Rather, I am an author to none who read these things but those who seriously meditate with me, who have the ability and the desire to withdraw their mind from the senses and at the same time from all prejudices. Such people I know all too well to be few and far between. As to those who do not take care to comprehend the order and series of my reasons but eagerly dispute over single conclusions by themselves, as is the custom for many—those, I say, will derive little benefit from a reading of this treatise; and although perhaps they might find an occasion for quibbling in many spots, still it is not an easy matter for them to raise an objection that is either compelling or worthy of response.

But because I do not promise others that I will satisfy them in all things the first time around, and I do not claim for myself so much that I believe that I can foresee everything that will seem difficult to someone, I will first narrate these very thoughts in the Meditations, by means of which I seem to have arrived at a certain and evident knowledge of the truth, so that I examine whether I can persuade others by the same arguments by which I have been persuaded. Then I will reply to the objections of several naturally gifted and very well-schooled gentlemen, to whom these Meditations have been sent for examination before they were sent to press. For their objections were so many and varied that I have dared to hope that nothing will easily come to mind for any other people—at least nothing of importance—which has not yet already been touched upon by these gentlemen. And thus I also ask the readers not to form a judgment regarding the Meditations before they have designed to read these objections and the replies I have made.

SYNOPSIS OF THE FOLLOWING SIX MEDITATIONS

In the First Meditation the reasons are given why we can doubt all things, especially material things, as long, of course, as we have no other foundations for the sciences than the ones which we have had up until now. Although it is not readily apparent that this doubt is useful, still it is the more so in that it frees us of all prejudices and paves an easy path for leading the mind away from the senses. Finally, it makes it impossible for us to doubt further those things that we shall discover to be true.

In the Second Meditation the mind, by using the freedom peculiar to it, supposes the nonexistence of all those things about whose existence it can have the least doubt, and judges that such a supposition is impossible unless the mind exists during that time. This is also of the greatest utility, since by this means it easily distinguishes what things pertain to it — that is, to an intellectual nature — and what things pertain to a body. But because perhaps many people expected to see proofs for the immortality of the soul here, they are to be put on notice that I believe that I have begun to write in this work only what I have carefully demonstrated. Therefore I was unable to follow any order but the one in use among geometricians, which is to state first everything on which the proposition in question depends, before concluding anything regarding that proposition. But what is required principally and primarily for knowing that the soul is immortal is that we formulate as clear a concept of the soul as possible, patently distinct from any concept of a body. This is what has been done here. Moreover, it is also required that we know that everything that we clearly and distinctly understand is true, in precisely the manner in which we understand them. This could not have been proven before the Fourth Meditation. Moreover, one must have a distinct concept of corporeal nature, which is formulated partly in the Second Meditation, and partly in the Fifth and Sixth. But from all this one ought to conclude that all things clearly and distinctly conceived as diverse substances — as, for example, mind and body are conceived — are indeed substances that are really distinct from one another. This is arrived at in the Sixth Meditation. The same thing is confirmed there from the fact that a body cannot be understood to be anything but divisible, whereas the mind cannot be understood to be anything but indivisible, for we cannot conceive of half a soul, as we can in the case of any body, however small. This is so much the case that the natures of mind and body are acknowledged to be not only diverse but even, in a manner of speaking, to be the contraries of one another. I have not written further on the matter in this treatise, both because these considerations suffice for showing that the annihilation of the mind does not follow from the corrupt state of the body — and therefore for giving mortal men hope in an afterlife — and also because the premises from which the immortality of the mind can be proven depend upon an account of the whole of physics: first, we must know that absolutely all substances, that is, everything that needs to be created by God in order to exist, are by their very nature incorruptible, nor can they ever cease to be, unless by this very same God the denial of whose concurrence to them would reduce them to nothing. Second, we must notice that a body, taken in a general sense, is a substance and that it therefore can never perish. But the human body, insofar as it differs from other bodies, is composed only of a certain configuration of members, together with other accidents of the same sort. But the human mind is not composed of any such accidents, but is a pure substance. For although all its accidents may undergo change — so that it understands some things, wills others, senses others, etc. — the mind does not for this reason become something else. But the human body does become something else, by the mere fact that the shape of some of its parts changes. From these considerations it follows that a body can easily cease to be, whereas the mind by its nature is immortal.

In the Third Meditation I have explained at sufficient length, it seems to me, my principal argument for proving the existence of God. Be that as it may, I sought to use no comparisons drawn from corporeal things, in order to draw the souls of the readers as far as possible from the senses. Thus obscurities may perhaps have remained; but these, I hope, will later be easily removed in my Replies to the Objections. One such obscurity is this: how can the idea that is in us of a supremely perfect being have so much objective reality that it must be from a supremely perfect cause? This is illustrated in the Replies by a comparison with a very ingenious machine, the idea of which is in the mind of the artisan. For, just as the objective ingeniousness of this idea must have some cause (say, the knowledge possessed by the artisan or by someone else from whom he has received knowledge), just so, the idea of God, which is in us, must have God himself for its cause.

In the Fourth Meditation I prove that all that we clearly and distinctly perceive is true; and, at the same time, I explain wherein the nature of falsity consists. These things necessarily ought to be known, as much for reinforcing what has just been said as for understanding what remains. But it should be borne in mind that in that Meditation I have not discussed sin—that is, an error committed in the pursuit of good and evil—but only that error which occurs in the discernment of the true and false. Nor do I examine those matters pertaining to religious faith or to the conduct of life, but only those speculative truths that are known by the aid of the light of nature.

In the Fifth Meditation in addition to explaining corporeal nature in general, I also demonstrate the existence of God by means of a new proof. But again some difficulties arise. These are later resolved in my Replies to the Objections. Finally, I show how it is true that the certitude of geometrical demonstrations depends upon a knowledge of God.

Finally, in the Sixth Meditation I distinguish understanding from imagination; I describe the marks of this distinction. I prove that the mind is really distinct from the body (although I show that the mind is so closely joined to the body, that it forms one thing with the body.) All the errors commonly arising from the senses are presented, along with all the ways in which these errors can be avoided. Finally, I append all the grounds on the basis of which the existence of material things can be inferred. Not that I believe these grounds to be very useful for proving what they prove—namely that there really is a world, that men have bodies, and other such things, concerning which no one of sound mind has ever seriously doubted—but because, by considering these grounds, I recognize that they are neither so firm nor so evident as are the grounds by means of which we arrive at a knowledge of our mind and of God, insofar as these latter grounds are, of all that can be known by the human mind, the most certain and the most evident. Proving this one thing was the goal of these Meditations. For this reason I pass over these other questions, which also will be given treatment in the Meditations at the appropriate occasion.

MEDITATIONS ON FIRST PHILOSOPHY IN WHICH THE EXISTENCE OF GOD AND THE DISTINCTION OF THE SOUL FROM THE BODY ARE DEMONSTRATED

Meditation One: Concerning Those Things That Can Be Called into Doubt

Several years have now passed since I first realized how many were the false opinions that in my youth I took to be true, and thus how doubtful were all the things that I subsequently built upon these opinions. From the time I became aware of this, I realized that for once I had to raze everything in my life, down to the very bottom, so as to begin again from the first foundations, if I wanted to establish anything firm and lasting in the sciences. But the task seemed so enormous that I waited for a point in my life that was so ripe that no more suitable a time for laying hold of these disciplines would come to pass. For this reason, I have delayed so long that I would be at fault were I to waste on deliberation the time that is left for action. Therefore, now that I have freed my mind from all cares, and I have secured for myself some leisurely and carefree time, I withdraw in solitude. I will, in short, apply myself earnestly and openly to the general destruction of my former opinions.

Yet to this end it will not be necessary that I show that all my opinions are false, which perhaps I could never accomplish anyway. But because reason now persuades me that I should withhold my assent no less carefully from things which are not plainly certain and indubitable than I would to what is patently false, it will be sufficient justification for rejecting them all, if I find a reason for doubting even the least of them. Nor therefore need one survey each opinion one after the other, a task of endless proportion. Rather — because undermining the foundations will cause whatever has been built upon them to fall down of its own accord — I will at once attack those principles which supported everything that I once believed.

Whatever I had admitted until now as most true I took in either from the senses or through the senses; however, I noticed that they sometimes deceived me. And it is a mark of prudence never to trust wholly in those things which have once deceived us.

But perhaps, although the senses sometimes deceive us when it is a question of very small and distant things, still there are many other matters which one certainly cannot doubt, although they are derived from the very same senses: that I am sitting here before the fireplace wearing my dressing gown, that I feel this sheet of paper in my hands, and so on. But how could one deny that these hands and that my whole body exist? Unless perhaps I should compare myself to insane people whose brains are so impaired by a stubborn vapor from a black bile that they continually insist that they are kings when they are in utter poverty, or that they are wearing purple robes when they are naked, or that they have a head made of clay, or that they are gourds, or that they are made of glass. But they are all demented, and I would appear no less demented if I were to take their conduct as a model for myself.

All of this would be well and good, were I not a man who is accustomed to sleeping at night, and to undergoing in my sleep the very same things—or now and then even less likely ones—as do these insane people when they are awake. How often has my evening slumber persuaded me of such customary things as these: that I am here, clothed in my dressing gown, seated at the fireplace, when in fact I am lying undressed between the blankets! But right now I certainly am gazing upon this piece of paper with eyes wide awake. This head which I am moving is not heavy with sleep. I extend this hand consciously and deliberately and I feel it. These things would not be so distinct for one who is asleep. But this all seems as if I do not recall having been deceived by similar thoughts on other occasions in my dreams. As I consider these cases more intently, I see so plainly that there are no definite signs to distinguish being awake from being asleep that I am quite astonished, and this astonishment almost convinces me that I am sleeping.

Let us say, then, for the sake of argument, that we are sleeping and that such particulars as these are not true: that we open our eyes, move our heads, extend our hands. Perhaps we do not even have these hands, or any such body at all. Nevertheless, it really must be admitted that things seen in sleep are, as it were, like painted images, which could have been produced only in the likeness of true things. Therefore at least these general things (eyes, head, hands, the whole body) are not imaginary things, but are true and exist. For indeed when painters wish to represent sirens and satyrs by means of bizarre and unusual forms, they surely cannot ascribe utterly new natures to these creatures. Rather, they simply intermingle the members of various animals. And even if they concoct something so utterly novel that its likes have never been seen before (being utterly fictitious and false), certainly at the very minimum the colors from which the painters compose the thing ought to be true. And for the same reason, although even these general things (eyes, head, hands, and the like) can be imaginary, still one must necessarily admit that at least other things that are even more simple and universal are true, from which, as from true colors, all these things—be they true or false—which in our thought are images of things, are constructed.

To this class seems to belong corporeal nature in general, together with its extension; likewise the shape of extended things, their quantity or size, their number; as well as the place where they exist, the time of their duration, and other such things.

Hence perhaps we do not conclude improperly that physics, astronomy, medicine, and all the other disciplines that are dependent upon the consideration of composite things are all doubtful. But arithmetic, geometry, and other such disciplines—which treat of nothing but the simplest and most general things and which are indifferent as to whether these composite things do or do not exist—contain something certain and indubitable. For whether I be awake or asleep, two plus three makes five, and a square does not have more than four sides; nor does it seem possible that such obvious truths can fall under the suspicion of falsity.

All the same, a certain opinion of long standing has been fixed in my mind, namely that there exists a God who is able to do anything and by whom I, such as I am, have been created. How do I know that he did not bring it about that there be no earth at all, no heavens, no extended thing, no figure, no size, no place, and yet all these things should seem to me to exist precisely as they appear to do now? More-over—as I judge that others sometimes make mistakes in matters that they believe they know most perfectly—how do I know that I am not decieved every time I add two and three or count the sides of a square or perform an even simpler operation, if such can be imagined? But perhaps God has not willed that I be thus deceived, for it is said that he is supremely good. Nonetheless, if it were repugnant to his goodness that he should have created me such that I be deceived all the time, it would seem, from this same consideration, to be foreign to him to permit me to be deceived occa-sionally. But we cannot make this last assertion.

Perhaps there are some who would rather deny such a powerful God, than believe that all other matters are uncertain. Let us not put these people off just yet; rather, let us grant that everything said here about God is fictitious. Now they suppose that I came to be what I am either by fate or by chance or by a continuous series of events or by some other way. But because being deceived and being mistaken seem to be im-perfections, the less powerful they take the author of my being to be, the more prob-able it will be that I would be so imperfect as to be deceived perpetually. I have nothing to say in response to these arguments. At length I am forced to admit that there is nothing, among the things I once believed to be true, which it is not permis-sible to doubt—not for reasons of frivolity or lack of forethought, but because of valid and considered arguments. Thus I must carefully withhold assent no less from these things than from the patently false, if I wish to find anything certain.

But it is not enough simply to have made a note of this; I must take care to keep it before my mind. For long-standing opinions keep coming back again and again, almost against my will; they seize upon my credulity, as if it were bound over to them by long use and the claims of intimacy. Nor will I get out of the habit of assenting to them and believing in them, so long as I take them to be exactly what they are, name-ly, in some respects doubtful as by now is obvious, but nevertheless highly probable, so that it is much more consonant with reason to believe them than to deny them. Hence, it seems to me, I would do well to turn my will in the opposite direction, to deceive myself and pretend for a considerable period that they are wholly false and imaginary, until finally, as if with equal weight of prejudice on both sides, no bad habit should turn my judgment from the correct perception of things. For indeed I know that no danger or error will follow and that it is impossible for me to indulge in too much distrust, since I now am concentrating only on knowledge, not on action.

Thus I will suppose not a supremely good God, the source of truth, but rather an evil genius as clever and deceitful as he is powerful, who has directed his entire effort to misleading me. I will regard the heavens, the air, the earth, colors, shapes, sounds, and all external things as nothing but the deceptive games of my dreams, with which he lays snares for my credulity. I will regard myself as having no hands, no eyes, no flesh, no blood, no senses, but as nevertheless falsely believing that I possess all these things. I will remain resolutely fixed in this meditation, and, even if it be out of my power to know anything true, certainly it is within my power to take care resolutely to withhold my assent to what is false, lest this deceiver, powerful and clever as he is, have an effect on me. But this undertaking is arduous, and laziness brings me back to my customary way of living. I am not unlike a prisoner who might enjoy an imaginary freedom in his sleep. When he later begins to suspect that he is sleeping, he fears be-ing awakened and conspires slowly with these pleasant illusions. In just this way, I spontaneously fall back into my old beliefs, and dread being awakened, lest the toilsome wakefulness which follows upon a peaceful rest, have to be spent thenceforward not in the light but among the inextricable shadows of the difficulties now brought forward.

Meditation Two: Concerning the Nature of the Human Mind: That the Mind is More Known Than the Body

Yesterday's meditation filled my mind with so many doubts that I can no longer forget about them—nor yet do I see how they are to be resolved. But, as if I had suddenly fallen into a deep whirlpool, I am so disturbed that I can neither touch my foot to the bottom, nor swim up to the top. Nevertheless I will work my way up, and I will follow the same path I took yesterday, putting aside everything which admits of the least doubt, as if I had discovered it to be absolutely false. I will go forward until I know something certain—or, if nothing else, until I at least know for certain that nothing is certain. Archimedes sought only a firm and immovable point in order to move the entire earth from one place to another. Surely great things are to be hoped for if I am lucky enough to find at least one thing that is certain and indubitable.

Therefore I will suppose that all I see is false. I will believe that none of those things that my deceitful memory brings before my eyes ever existed. I thus have no senses: body, shape, extension, movement, and place are all figments of my imagination. What then will count as true? Perhaps only this one thing: that nothing is certain.

But on what grounds do I know that there is nothing over and above all those which I have just reviewed, concerning which there is not even the least cause for doubt? Is there not a God (or whatever name I might call him) who instills these thoughts in me? But why should I think that, since perhaps I myself could be the author of these things? Therefore am I not at least something? But I have already denied that I have any senses and any body. Still, I hesitate; for what follows from that? Am I so tied to the body and to the senses that I cannot exist without them? But I have persuaded myself that there is nothing at all in the world: no heaven, no earth, no minds, no bodies. Is it not then true that I do not exist? But certainly I should exist, if I were to persuade myself of something. But there is a deceiver (I know not who he is) powerful and sly in the highest degree, who is always purposely deceiving me. Then there is no doubt that I exist, if he deceives me. And deceive me as he will, he can never bring it about that I am nothing so long as I shall think that I am something. Thus it must be granted that, after weighing everything carefully and sufficiently, one must come to the considered judgment that the statement "I am, I exist" is necessarily true every time it is uttered by me or conceived in my mind.

But I do not yet understand well enough who I am—I, who now necessarily exist. And from this point on, I must take care lest I imprudently substitute something else in place of myself; and thus be mistaken even in that knowledge which I claim to be the most certain and evident of all. To this end, I shall meditate once more on what I once believed myself to be before having embarked upon these deliberations. For this reason, then, I will set aside whatever can be refuted even to a slight degree by the arguments brought forward, so that at length there shall remain precisely nothing but what is certain and unshaken.

What therefore did I formerly think I was? A man, of course. But what is a man? Might I not say a rational animal? No, because then one would have to inquire what an "animal" is and what "rational" means. And then from only one question we slide into many more difficult ones. Nor do I now have enough free time that I want to waste it on subtleties of this sort. But rather here I pay attention to what spontaneously and at nature's lead came into my thought beforehand whenever I pondered what I was. Namely, it occurred to me first that I have a face, hands, arms, and this entire mechanism of bodily members, the very same as are discerned in a corpse—which I referred to by the name "body." It also occurred to me that I eat, walk, feel and think; these actions I used to assign to the soul as their cause. But what this soul was I either did not think about or I imagined it was something terribly insubstantial—after the fashion of a wind, fire, or ether—which has been poured into my coarser parts. I truly was not in doubt regarding the body; rather I believed that I distinctly knew its nature, which, were I perhaps tempted to describe it such as I mentally conceived it, I would explain it thus: by "body," I understand all that is suitable for being bounded by some shape, for being enclosed in some place, and thus for filling up space, so that it excludes every other body from that space; for being perceived by touch, sight, hearing, taste, or smell; for being moved in several ways, not surely by itself, but by whatever else that touches it. For I judged that the power of self-motion, and likewise of sensing or of thinking, in no way pertains to the nature of the body. Nonetheless, I used to marvel especially that such faculties were found in certain bodies.

But now what am I, when I suppose that some deceiver—omnipotent and, if I may be allowed to say it, malicious—takes all the pains he can in order to deceive me? Can I not affirm that I possess at least a small measure of all those traits which I already have said pertain to the nature of the body? I pay attention, I think, I deliberate—but nothing happens. I am wearied of repeating this in vain. But which of these am I to ascribe to the soul? How about eating or walking? These are surely nothing but illusions, because I do not have a body. How about sensing? Again, this also does not happen without a body, and I judge that I really did not sense those many things I seemed to have sensed in my dreams. How about thinking? Here I discover that thought is an attribute that really does belong to me. This alone cannot be detached from me. I am; I exist; this is certain. But for how long? For as long as I think. Because perhaps it could also come to pass that if I should cease from all thinking I would then utterly cease to exist. I now admit nothing that is not necessarily true. I am therefore precisely only a thing that thinks; that is, a mind, or soul, or intellect, or reason—words the meaning of which I was ignorant before. Now, I am a true thing, and truly existing; but what kind of thing? I have said it already: a thing that thinks.

What then? I will set my imagination going to see if I am not something more. I am not that connection of members which is called the human body. Neither am I some subtle air infused into these members, not a wind, not a fire, not a vapor, not a breath—nothing that I imagine to myself, for I have supposed all these to be nothing. The assertion stands: the fact still remains that I am something. But perhaps is it the case that, nevertheless, these very things which I take to be nothing (because I am ignorant of them) in reality do not differ from that self which I know? This I do not know. I shall not quarrel about it right now; I can make a judgment only regarding things which are known to me. I know that I exist; I ask now who is this "I" whom I know. Most certainly the knowledge of this matter, thus precisely understood, does not depend upon things that I do not yet know to exist. Therefore, it is not dependent upon any of those things that I feign in my imagination. But this word "feign"[4] warns me of my error. For I would be feigning if I should "imagine" that I am something, because imagining is merely the contemplation of the shape or image of a corporeal thing. But I know now with certainty that I am, and at the same time it could happen that all these images—and, generally, everything that pertains to the nature of the body—are nothing but dreams. When these things are taken into account, I would speak no less foolishly were I to say: "I will imagine so that I might recognize more distinctly who I am," than were I to say: "Now I surely am awake, and I see something true, but because I do not yet see it with sufficient evidence, I will take the trouble of going to sleep so that my dreams might show this to me more truly and more evidently." Thus I know that none of what I can comprehend by means of the imagination pertains to this understanding that I have of myself. Moreover, I know that I must be most diligent about withdrawing my mind from these things so that it can perceive its nature as distinctly as possible.

But what then am I? A thing that thinks. What is that? A thing that doubts, understands, affirms, denies, wills, refuses, and which also imagines and senses.

It is truly no small matter if all of these things pertain to me. But why should they not pertain to me? Is it not I who now doubt almost everything, I who nevertheless understand something, I who affirm that this one thing is true, I who deny other things, I who desire to know more things, I who wish not to be deceived, I who imagine many things against my will, I who take note of many things as if coming from the senses? Is there anything in all of this which is not just as true as it is that I am, even if I am always dreaming or even if the one who created me tries as hard as possible to delude me? Are any of these attributes distinct from my thought? What can be said to be separate from myself? For it is so obvious that it is I who doubt, I who understand, I who will, that there is nothing through which it could be more evidently explicated. But indeed I am also the same one who imagines; for, although perhaps as I supposed before, no imagined thing would be wholly true, the very power of imagining does really exist, and constitutes a part of my thought. Finally, I am the same one who senses or who takes note of bodily things as if through the senses. For example, I now see a light, I hear a noise, I feel heat. These are false, since I am asleep. But I certainly seem to see, hear, and feel. This cannot be false: properly speaking, this is what is called "sensing" in me. But this is, to speak precisely, nothing other than thinking.

From these considerations I begin to know a little better who I am. But it still seems that I cannot hold back from believing that bodily things—whose images are formed by thought, and which the senses themselves examine—are much more distinctly known than this unknown aspect of myself which does not come under the imagination. And yet it would be quite strange if the very things which I consider to be doubtful, unknown, and foreign to me are comprehended by me more distinctly than what is true, what is known—than, in fine, myself. But I see what is happening: my mind loves to wander and does not allow itself to be restricted to the confines of truth. Let it be that way then: let us allow it the freest rein in every respect, so that, when we pull in the reins at the right time a little later, the mind may suffer itself to be ruled more easily.

---

4. [The Latin word 'effingo' means 'to form an image' or 'imagine'.]

Let us consider those things which are commonly believed to be the most distinctly comprehended of all: namely the bodies which we touch and see. But not bodies in general, for these generic perceptions are often somewhat more confused; rather let us consider one body in particular. Let us take, for instance, this piece of wax. It has very recently been taken from the honeycombs; it has not as yet lost all the flavor of its honey. It retains some of the smell of the flowers from which it was collected. Its color, shape, and size are obvious. It is hard and cold. It can easily be touched, and if you rap on it with a knuckle it makes a sound. In short, everything is present in it that appears to be needed in order that a body can be known as distinctly as possible. But notice that while I am speaking, it is brought close to the fire; the remaining traces of the honey flavor are purged; the odor vanishes; the color is changed; the original shape disappears. Its magnitude increases, it becomes liquid and hot, and can hardly be touched; and now, when you knock on it, it does not emit any sound. Up to this point, does the same wax remain? One must confess that it does: no one denies it; no one thinks otherwise. What was there then in the wax that was so distinctly comprehended? Certainly none of the things that I reached by means of the senses. For whatever came under taste or smell or sight or touch or hearing by now has changed, yet the wax remains.

Perhaps the wax was what I now think it is: namely that it really never was the sweetness of the honey or the fragrance of the flowers, not this whiteness, not a figure, not a sound, but a body which a little earlier manifested itself to me in these ways, and now does so in other ways. But just what precisely is this thing which I imagine thus? Let us direct our attention to this and see what remains after we have removed everything which does not belong to the wax: only that it is something extended, flexible, and subject to change. What is this flexible and mutable thing? Is it not the fact that I imagine that this wax can change from a round to a square shape, or from the latter to a rectangular shape? Not at all: for I comprehend that the wax is capable of innumerable changes, yet I cannot survey these innumerable changes by imagining them. Therefore this comprehension is not accomplished by the faculty of imagination. What is this extended thing? Is this thing's extension also unknown? For it becomes larger in wax that is beginning to liquify, greater in boiling wax, and greater still as the heat is increased. And I would not judge rightly what the wax is if I did not believe that this wax can take on even more varieties of extension than I could ever have grasped by the imagination. It remains then for me to concede that I in no way imagine what this wax is, but perceive it by the mind only. I am speaking about this piece of wax in particular, for it is clearer in the case of wax in general. But what is this wax which is perceived only by the mind? It is the same that I see, touch, and imagine; in short it is the same as I took it to be from the very beginning. But we must take note of the fact that the perception of the wax is neither by sight, nor touch, nor imagination, nor was it ever so (although it seemed so before), but rather an inspection on the part of the mind alone. This inspection can be imperfect and confused, as it was before, or clear and distinct, as it is now, according to whether I pay greater or less attention to those things of which the wax consists.

But meanwhile I marvel at how prone my mind is to errors; for although I am considering these things within myself silently and without words, nevertheless I latch onto words themselves and I am very nearly deceived by the ways in which people speak. For we say that we see the wax itself, if it is present, and not that we judge it to be present from its color or shape. Whence I might conclude at once: the wax is therefore known by eyesight, and not by an inspection on the part of the mind alone, unless I perhaps now might have looked out the window at the men crossing the street whom I say I am no less wont to see than the wax. But what do I see over and above the hats and clothing? Could not robots be concealed under these things? But I judge them to be men; thus what I believed I had seen with my eyes, I actually comprehend with nothing but the faculty of judgment which is in my mind.

But a person who seeks to know more than the common crowd should be ashamed of himself if he has come upon doubts as a result of an encounter with the forms of speech devised by the common crowd. Let us then go forward, paying attention to the following question: did I perceive more perfectly and evidently what the wax was when I first saw it and believed I had known it by the external sense — or at least by the common sense, as they say, that is, the imaginative power — than I know it now, after having examined more diligently both what the wax is and how it is known. Surely it is absurd to doubt this matter. For what was there in the first perception that was distinct? What was there that any animal could not have seemed capable of possessing? But when I distinguish the wax from its external forms, as if having taken off its clothes, as it were, I look at the naked wax, even though at this point there can be an error in my judgment; nevertheless I could not perceive it without a human mind.

But what am I to say about this mind, or about myself? For as yet I admit nothing else to be in me over and above my mind. What, I say, am I who seem to perceive this wax so distinctly? Do I not know myself not only much more truly and with more certainty, but also much more distinctly and evidently? For if I judge that the wax exists from the fact that I see it, certainly it follows much more evidently that I myself exist, from the fact that I see the wax. For it could happen that what I see is not truly wax. It could happen that, I have no eyes with which to see anything. But it could not happen that while I see or think I see (I do not now distinguish these two), I who think am not something. Likewise, if I judge that the wax exists from the fact that I touch it, the same thing will again follow: I exist. If from the fact that I imagine, or from whatever other cause, the same thing readily follows. But what I noted regarding the wax applies to all the other things that are external to me. Furthermore, if the perception of the wax seemed more distinct after it became known to me not only from sight or touch, but from many causes, how much more distinctly I must be known to myself; for there are no considerations that can aid in the perception of the wax or any other body without these considerations demonstrating even better the nature of my mind. But there are still so many other things in my mind from which one can draw a more distinct knowledge of the mind, so that those things which emanate from a body seem hardly worth enumerating.

But lo and behold, I have arrived on my own at the place I wanted. Since I know that bodies are not, properly speaking, perceived by the senses or by the faculty of imagination, but only by the intellect, and since, moreover, I know that they are not perceived by being touched or seen, but only insofar as they are expressly understood, nothing can be more easily and more evidently perceived by me than my mind. But because an established habit of belief cannot be put aside so quickly, it is appropriate to stop here, so that by the length of my meditation this new knowledge may be more deeply impressed on my memory.

Meditation Three: Concerning God, That He Exists

Now I will shut my eyes, I will stop up my ears, I will divert all my senses, I will even blot out from my thoughts all images of corporeal things—or at least, since the latter can hardly be done, I will regard these images as nothing, empty and false as indeed they are. And as I converse only with myself and look more deeply into myself, I will attempt to render myself gradually better known and familiar to myself. I am a thing that thinks, that is to say, a thing that doubts, affirms, denies, knows a few things, is ignorant of many things, wills, rejects, and also imagines and senses. As I observed earlier, although these things that I sense or imagine may perhaps be nothing at all outside me, nevertheless I am certain that these modes of thinking—which I call sensations and imaginations—insofar as they are only modes of thinking, are within me.

In these few words I have summed up what I truly know, or at least what, so far, I have observed that I know. Now I will ponder more carefully to see whether perhaps there are other things pertaining to me that, up to this time, I have not yet noticed. I am certain that I am a thing that thinks. But do I not therefore also know what is required so that I may be certain of something? Surely in this first instance of knowing, there is nothing else than a certain clear and distinct perception of what I affirm. Yet this would hardly be sufficient to render me certain of the truth of a thing, if it could ever happen that something that I perceive so clearly and distinctly were false. And thus I now seem to be able to posit as a general rule that what I very clearly and distinctly perceive is true.

Nevertheless, I have previously admitted many things as wholly certain and evident that nevertheless I discovered afterward to be doubtful. What sort of things were these? Why, indeed, the earth, the heavens, the stars, and all the other things that I perceived by means of my senses. But what did I perceive clearly regarding these things? Certainly the ideas or thoughts of these things hovered before my mind. But I do not now deny that these ideas are in me. However, there was something else that I affirmed and that, because of my habit of believing it, I thought was something I clearly perceived, but that, in fact, I did not perceive—namely, that certain things are outside me, things from which those ideas proceed and things to which they were entirely similar. But on this point I was mistaken; or, if I judged truly, this judgment did not result from the force of my perception.

What then? When I considered something very simple and easy in the areas of arithmetic or geometry, for example that two plus three together make five, and the like, did I not intuit them at least clearly enough that I might affirm them to be true? To be sure, I did decide later on that I must doubt these things for no other reason than that it entered my mind that some God could have given me a nature such that I might be deceived—even about matters that seemed most evident. For every time this preconceived opinion about the supreme power of God occurs to me, I am constrained to admit that, if he wishes, it is very easy for him to cause me to err, even in those matters that I think I have intuited as plainly as possible with the eyes of the mind. Yet every time I turn my attention to those very things that I think I perceive with such great clarity, I am so entirely persuaded by these things that I spontaneously burst out with these words: "let him who can deceive me; as long as I think that I am something, he will never bring it about that I am nothing, or one day make it true that I never existed, because it is true now that I am; nor will he ever bring it about that two plus three yield more or less than five, or that similar matters, in which I recognize an obvious contradiction, exist." And, certainly, because I have no occasion for thinking that there is a God who deceives, and because I am not certain whether there even is a God, the reason for doubting—depending as it does on the above hypothesis—is very tenuous and, so to speak, metaphysical. Moreover, in order to remove this doubt, I ought at the first opportunity to inquire if there is a God, and, if there is, whether or not he can be a deceiver. If I am ignorant of these matters, I do not think I can ever be certain of anything else.

Now, however, good order seems to demand that I first arrange all my thoughts into certain classifications, and inquire in which of these truth or falsity properly consists. Some of these thoughts are like images of things. To these alone does the word "idea" properly apply, for example, when I think of a man, a chimera, heaven, an angel, or God. Again, there are other thoughts that take different forms: when I will, when I fear, when I affirm, when I deny, there is always something I grasp as the subject of my thought, yet I comprehend something that is more than the mere likeness of a thing. Some of these thoughts are called volitions or emotions, while others are called judgments.

Now as to what pertains to ideas, if they are considered alone and in their own right, without being referred to something else, they cannot then properly be considered false. For whether I imagine a she-goat or a chimera, it is no less true that I imagine the one than the other. Moreover, we need not fear that falsity exists in the will itself or in the emotions; although I can choose evil things or even things that nowhere exist, it does not follow that it is untrue that I do choose these things. Thus there remain only judgments. I must take care not to be mistaken about these. Now the principal and most frequent error that can be found in judgments consists in the fact that I judge that the ideas, which are in me, are similar to, or in conformity with, certain things outside me. Indeed, if I consider these ideas only as certain modes of my thought, and do not refer them to something else, they can hardly give me any cause for error.

Among these ideas, some seem to me to be innate, some seem to be derived from an external source, and some seem to be produced by me. I understand what a thing is, what truth is, what thought is—I do not seem to have derived these from any source other than from my very own nature. But now I hear a noise, I see the sun, and I feel a fire; until this point I judged that these things proceeded from certain things existing outside me. Finally, I judged that sirens, hippogriffs, and the like have been formed by me. Or perhaps I could also suppose that all of these ideas are derived from an external source, or are innate, or are produced, for I have not yet ascertained clearly their true origin.

But in this meditation those ideas that I believe to be drawn from things existing outside me must especially be investigated. Just what reason is there that moves me so that I believe that these ideas are similar to those objects? Well, I seem to be taught that way by nature. Moreover, I know by experience that these ideas do not depend upon my will, nor consequently upon myself, for often I notice them against my will; as now—whether I will it or not—I feel heat, and therefore I believe that this feeling or idea of heat comes to me from something other than myself, namely from the fire I am near. Nothing is more obvious than the judgment that this object (rather than something else) grafts its likeness on to me.

I will now see whether these reasons are valid enough. When I say in this meditation that I have been taught so by nature, I understand only that I am driven by a spontaneous impulse to believing this position, and not that some light of nature shows me it is true. These two positions are at considerable odds with one another. For whatever this light of nature shows me — for example, that from the fact that I doubt, it follows that I am and so on — cannot in any way be doubtful, because there can be no other faculty in which I may trust as much as the light of nature that could teach which of these positions are not true. As for natural impulses, I have very often judged myself to have been driven by them to the poorer choice, when it was a question of choosing a good; I do not see why I should trust them any more in other matters.

Again, although these ideas do not depend upon my will, it does not therefore follow that they necessarily proceed from things existing outside me. Although these impulses I have discussed are in me, nevertheless they seem to be different from my will. Thus perhaps there is also in me some other faculty, one not yet sufficiently known to me, that produces these ideas, because it has always seemed that these ideas are formed in me when I sleep, without any aid from external things.

Again, even if these ideas do proceed from things other than myself, it does not therefore follow that they must be similar to these objects. Indeed it seems I have frequently noticed a vast difference in many respects. For example, I find within myself two distinct ideas of the sun. One idea derives, as it were, from the senses. Now it is this idea that, among those things I consider to be derived from outside me, is most in need of examination. By means of this idea the sun appears to me to be very small. Yet there is another idea, one derived from the computations of astronomy. This idea is elicited from certain notions innate in me (or is somehow made by me) through which the sun is shown to be several times larger than the earth. Both ideas surely cannot be similar to the same sun existing outside me, and reason convinces me that the one that seems to have emanated from it at such close proximity is the very one that is most dissimilar to the sun.

All of this demonstrates sufficiently that up to this point I have believed not by certain judgment, but only by a blind impulse that things exist outside me that send their ideas or images into me through the sense organs or by some other means.

But still another path occurs to me for inquiring whether there are some objects, from among those things of which there are ideas in me, that exist outside me. Now, insofar as these ideas are merely modes of thought, I do not see any inequality among them; they all seem to proceed from me in the same way. But insofar as one idea represents one thing and another idea another thing, it is obvious that they are very different from one another. There is no question that those ideas that exhibit substances to me are something more and, as I phrase it, contain more objective reality in themselves than those which represent only modes or accidents. Again, the idea that enables me to understand a highest God, one who is eternal, infinite, omniscient, omnipotent, and creator of all things other than himself, has more objective reality in it than those ideas through which finite substances are exhibited.

But it is evident by the light of nature that at the very least there must be as much in the total efficient cause as there is in the effect of that same cause. For, I ask, where can an effect get its reality unless it be from its cause? And how can the cause give that reality to the effect, unless the cause also has that reality? Hence it follows that something cannot come into existence from nothing, nor even can what is more perfect, that is, that contains in itself more reality, come into existence from what contains less. But this is clearly true not merely for those effects whose reality is actual or formal, but also for ideas in which only objective reality is considered. This means, for example, that a stone, which did not exist before, can in no way begin to exist now, unless it be produced by something in which there is, either formally or eminently,[5] everything that is in the stone; nor can heat be introduced into a subject which was not hot before unless it is done by something that is of at least as perfect an order as heat — the same holds true for the rest. Moreover, in me there can be no idea of heat, or of a stone, unless it comes to me from some cause that has at least as much reality as I conceive to be in the heat or in the stone. Although this cause transmits none of its actual or formal reality into my idea, it is not to be thought that the idea must be less real. Rather, the very nature of this idea is such that it needs no formal reality other than itself — except what it borrows from my thought, of which it is a mode. That this idea contains this or that objective reality rather than some other one results from the fact that the idea gets its objective reality from a cause in which there is at least as much formal reality as there is objective reality contained in the idea. For if we posit that something is found in the idea that was not in its cause, then the idea would get it from nothing; but as imperfect a mode of being as this is, by which a thing exists in the intellect objectively through an idea, it nevertheless is surely not nothing; hence it cannot get its existence from nothing.

Also, because the reality that I consider in my ideas is only objective, I should not suspect that there is no need for the same reality to be formally in the causes of these ideas, but that it suffices for it to be in them objectively. To the extent that the objective mode of being pertains to ideas by their very nature, so the formal mode of being belongs to the causes of ideas, at least to the first and preeminent ones, by their very nature. Although one idea can perhaps come into being from another, nevertheless there is no infinite regress here; at length some first idea must be reached whose cause is a sort of archetype that formally contains all the reality that is in the idea only objectively. Thus it is evident to me by the light of nature that my ideas are like images that can easily fail to match the perfection of the things from which they have been drawn, but my ideas cannot contain anything better or more perfect.

But the longer and more attentively I examine all these points, the more clearly and distinctly I know they are true. But what do I finally conclude? Why, if the objective reality of one of my ideas is such that I am certain that the same reality is not formally or eminently in me, and that therefore I myself cannot be the cause of the idea, then it necessarily follows that I am not alone in the world, and that something else — the cause of this idea — also exists. If in fact no such idea is found in me, I shall plainly have no argument to make me certain of the existence of something other than myself. For I have looked at all of these arguments most diligently and so far I have been unable to find any other.

Among my ideas, in addition to the one that represents me to myself — about which there can be no difficulty at this point — there are some that represent God, others that represent inanimate, corporeal objects, others that represent angels, others that represent animals, and finally others that represent men like myself.

As to the ideas that represent other men, animals, or angels, I easily understand that they can be formed from the ideas that I have of myself, of corporeal things, and of God — even if no men except myself, no animals, and no angels were to exist in the

---

5. [By "formal cause" Descartes means one as perfect as its effect; by "eminent cause" he means one more perfect.]

world.

As to the ideas of corporeal things, there is nothing in them which is such that it seems unable to have come from me. For if I investigate thoroughly and if I examine each one individually in the same way that I examined the idea of wax yesterday, I notice that there are only a very few properties that I perceive in them clearly and distinctly: namely, magnitude, or extension in length, breadth, and depth; shape, which arises from the limit of this extension; position, which the various shaped things possess in relation to one another; and motion, or the alteration of this position; to these can be added substance, duration, and number. The remaining properties, however—such as light and colors, sounds, odors, tastes, heat and cold and other tactile qualities—are thought by me only in a very confused and obscure manner, with the result that I do not know whether they are true or false, that is, whether the ideas that I have of these things are ideas of certain things or are not ideas of things. For although a short time ago I noted that falsity properly so called ("formal" falsity) can be found only in judgments, nevertheless there is another kind of falsity (called "material" falsity) in ideas; it occurs whenever judgments present a non-thing as if it were a thing. For example, the ideas I have of heat and cold fall so short of being clear and distinct that I cannot learn from them whether cold is only a privation of heat or whether heat is a privation of cold; whether both are real qualities or neither is. Because ideas can only be ideas of things, and if it is true that cold is nothing more than the privation of heat, then an idea such as this one, that represents something real and positive to me, will not inappropriately be called false—and so too for the other ideas.

Assuredly it is not necessary for me to assign to these ideas an author distinct from me. For if they were false, that is, if they should represent no objects, I know by the light of nature that they proceed from nothing; that is, they are in me for no other reason than that something is lacking in my nature, that my nature is plainly not perfect. If, on the other hand, these ideas are true because they exhibit so little reality to me that I cannot distinguish them from a non-thing, then I see no reason why they cannot get their existence from myself.

As for those things that are the clear and distinct elements in the ideas of corporeal things, I seem able to have borrowed some from the idea of myself: namely, substance, duration, number, and whatever else there may be of this type. For when I think that a stone is a substance, that is to say, a thing that in its own right has an aptitude for existing, and that I too am a substance—although I conceive that I am a thing that thinks and not an extended thing, whereas a stone is an extended thing and not a thing that thinks—there is, accordingly, the greatest diversity between these two concepts, even though they seem to agree with one another when they are considered under the rubric of substance. Furthermore, when I perceive that I exist now and recall that I have previously existed for some time, and when I have several thoughts and know the number of these thoughts, I acquire the ideas of duration and number, which I then apply to everything else. However, all the other elements out of which the ideas of corporeal things are put together (namely extension, shape, position, and motion) are not contained in me formally, because I am only a thing that thinks. But because they are only modes of substance, and I too am a substance, they seem capable of being contained in me eminently.

Thus there remains only the idea of God. We must consider whether there is in this idea something which could not have originated from me. I understand by the word "God" an infinite and independent substance, intelligent and powerful in the highest degree, who created me along with everything else — if in fact there is anything else. Indeed all these qualities are such that, the more diligently I attend to them, the less they seem capable of having arisen from myself alone. Thus, from what has been said above, we must conclude that God necessarily exists.

For although the idea of substance is in me by virtue of the fact that I am a substance, nevertheless it would not for that reason be the idea of an infinite substance, unless it proceeded from some substance which is in fact infinite, because I am finite.

Nor should I think that I do not perceive the infinite by means of a true idea, but only through a negation of the finite, just as I perceive rest and shadows by means of a negation of motion and light. On the contrary, I clearly understand that there is more reality in an infinite substance than there is in a finite one. Thus the perception of the infinite somehow exists in me prior to the perception of the finite, that is, the perception of God exists prior to the perception of myself. Why would I know that I doubt and I desire, that is, that I lack something and that I am not wholly perfect, if there were no idea in me of a more perfect being by comparison with which I might acknowledge my defects?

Nor can it be said that this idea of God is perhaps materially false, and therefore can be from nothing, as I pointed out just now regarding the ideas of heat and cold and the like. On the contrary, because it is the most clear and distinct of all ideas and because it contains more objective reality than any other idea, no idea is truer in its own right, and there is no idea in which less suspicion of falsity is to be found. I maintain that this idea of a being most perfect and infinite is true in the highest degree. Although such a being can perhaps be imagined not to exist, it nevertheless cannot be imagined that this idea shows me nothing real, as was the case with the idea of cold that I referred to earlier. It is also an idea that is clear and distinct in the highest degree; for whatever I clearly and distinctly perceive that is real and true and that contains some perfection is wholly contained in that idea. It is not inconsistent to say that I do not comprehend the infinite or that there are countless other things in God that I can in no way either comprehend or perhaps even touch with thought. For the nature of the infinite is such that it is not comprehended by me, who am finite. And it is sufficient that I understand this very point and judge that all those things that I clearly perceive and that I know to contain some perfection — and perhaps even countless other things of which I am ignorant — are in God either formally or eminently. The result is that, of all those that are in me, the idea that I have of him is the most true, the most clear, and the most distinct.

But perhaps I am something greater than I take myself to be. Perhaps all these perfections that I attribute to God are somehow in me potentially, although they do not yet assert themselves and are not yet reduced to act. For I now observe that my knowledge is gradually being increased; I see nothing that stands in the way of my knowledge being increased more and more to infinity. I see no reason why, with my knowledge thus increased, I cannot acquire all the remaining perfections of God. And, finally, if the potential for producing these perfections is in me already, I see no reason why this potential does not suffice to produce the idea of these perfections.

Yet none of these things can be the case. First, while it is true that my knowledge is gradually increased and that in me there are many elements in potency which do not yet exist in act, nevertheless, none of these elements pertain to the idea of God, in which nothing whatever is potential; this gradual increase is itself a most certain argument for my imperfection. Moreover, although my knowledge might always increase more and more, nevertheless I understand that this knowledge will never by this means be infinite in act, because it will never reach a point where it is incapable of greater increase. On the contrary, I judge God to be infinite in act, with the result that nothing can be added to his perfection. Finally, I perceive that the objective being of an idea cannot be produced by a merely potential being (which, properly speaking, is nothing), but only by an actual or formal being.

Indeed there is nothing in all these matters that is not manifest by the light of nature to a person who is diligent and attentive. But when I am less attentive, and the images of sensible things blind my powers of discernment, I do not so easily recall why the idea of a being more perfect than me necessarily proceeds from a being that really is more perfect. This being the case, it is appropriate to ask further whether I myself who have this idea could exist, if such a being did not exist.

From what sources, then, do I derive my existence? From myself, from my parents, or from whatever other things there are that are less perfect than God. Nothing more perfect than He, nothing even as perfect as He, can be thought or imagined.

But if I were derived from myself, I would not doubt, I would not hope, and I would not lack anything whatever. For I would have given myself all the perfections of which I have some idea; in so doing, I would be God! I must not believe that these things that I lack are perhaps more difficult to acquire than those which I now have. On the contrary, it is evident that it would have been much more difficult for me—that is, a thing or substance that thinks—to emerge from nothing than it would be to acquire the knowledge—something that is only an accident of this substance—of the many things about which I am ignorant. Certainly, if I received this greater quality from myself, I would not have denied myself at least those things that can be had more easily. Nor would I scarcely deny myself any of those other things that I perceive to be contained in the idea of God, because surely nothing seems to me more difficult to make. But if there were any of those other things that were more difficult to make, then they certainly would also seem more difficult to me, assuming, of course, that the remaining ones that I possess I have from myself, because I observe that with them my power is terminated.

Nor do I avoid the cogency of these arguments, if I suppose that perhaps I have always been as I am now, as if it then followed that no author of my existence need be sought. Because the entire period of one's life can be divided into countless parts, each of which in no way depends on the others, it does not follow from the fact that I existed a short while ago that I now ought to exist, unless some cause creates me once again, as it were, at this moment—that is to say, preserves me. For it is obvious to one who is cognizant of the nature of time that the same force and action is needed to preserve anything at all during the individual moments that it lasts as is needed to create that same thing anew—if it should happen not yet to exist. It is one of those things that is manifest by the light of nature that preservation differs from creation solely by virtue of a distinction of reason.

Therefore I ought now to ask myself whether I have some power through which I can bring it about that I myself, who now am, will also exist a little later? Because I am nothing but a thing that thinks—or at least because I am now dealing only with precisely that part of me that is a thing that thinks—if such a power were in me, then I would certainly be aware of it. But I observe that there is no such power; from this fact I know most evidently that I depend upon a being other than myself.

But perhaps this being is not God, and I have been produced either by my parents or by some other causes less perfect than God. Indeed, as I said before, it is evident that there ought to be at least as much in the cause as there is in the effect. Thus, because I am a thing that thinks and because I have within me an idea of God—whatever cause is at length assigned to me—it must be granted that it too is a thing that thinks and has an idea of all the perfections which I attribute to God. And one can again inquire whether it exists through itself or through another. For if it derived from itself, it is evident from what has been said that this thing is God, because, having the power of existing in its own right, it also unquestionably has the power of possessing in act all the perfections whose idea it has in itself—that is, all of those perfections that I conceive as being in God. However, if it is from another cause, one will then once again inquire in a similar fashion about this other thing—whether it is through itself or through another—until finally one arrives at the ultimate cause, which will be God.

For it is apparent enough that there can be no infinite regress, especially since I am dealing here not only with the cause that once produced me, but also and most especially with the cause that preserves me at the present time.

Nor can one imagine that perhaps several partial causes have concurred to bring me into being, and that from one cause I have taken the idea of one of the perfections I attribute to God and from another cause the idea of another perfection; so that all of these perfections are found somewhere in the universe, but not all joined together in one thing, which would be God. On the contrary, unity, simplicity, or the inseparability of all those things which are in God is one of the principal perfections that I understand to be in him. Certainly the idea of the unity of all these perfections could not have been placed in me by a cause from which I do not also have the ideas of the other perfections; for it could not bring it about that I would instantaneously understand them to be joined to one another inseparably, unless it brought it about instantaneoulsy that I recognize which ones these are.

Finally, as to my parents, even if everything that I ever believed about them were true, still they do not preserve me; nor did they bring me into being, insofar as I am a thing that thinks. Rather, they merely placed certain dispositions in the matter in which I judged that I—that is, a mind that is all that I now accept for myself—am contained. And thus there can be no difficulty here concerning these matters. Rather, one has no choice but to conclude that, from the simple fact that I exist and that an idea of a most perfect being, that is, God, is in me, it is most evidently demonstrated that God exists.

There remains only the question of how I received this idea of God. For I did not draw it from the senses, and it never came to me when I did not anticipate it, as the ideas of sensible things are wont to do when these things present themselves—or seem to present themselves—to the organs of the senses. Nor has it been produced by me, for I plainly cannot add or subtract anything from it. It thus remains that it is innate in me, just as the idea of myself is also innate in me.

To be sure it is not astonishing that in creating me, God endowed me with this idea, so that it would be like the sign of an artist impressed upon his work. Nor is it necessary that this sign be something distinct from the work itself. But from this one fact that God created me, it is highly believable that I have somehow been made in his image and likeness, and that I perceive this likeness (in which the idea of God is contained) by means of the same faculty through which I perceive myself. That is, when I turn my powers of discernment toward myself, I not only understand that I am something incomplete and dependent upon another, something aspiring indefinitely for greater and greater or better things, but instantaneously I also understand that the thing on which I depend has in himself all of these greater things—not merely indefinitely and potentially, but infinitely and actually. Thus it is God. The whole force of the argument rests on the fact that I recognize that it is impossible that I should exist, being of such a nature as I am—namely, having the idea of God in me—unless God in fact does exist. God, I say, that same being whose idea is in me: a being having all those perfections that I cannot comprehend, but in some way can touch with my thought, and a being subject to no defects. From these things it is sufficiently obvious that he cannot be a deceiver. For it is manifest by the light of nature that fraud and deception depend on some defect.

But before examining this idea more diligently and at the same time inquiring into the other truths that can be inferred from it, it is appropriate at this point to spend some time contemplating this God, to consider within myself his attributes and the beauty of this immense light, so far as the power of discernment in my darkened wit can carry me, to gaze, to admire, and to adore. For just as we believe by faith that the greatest felicity of the next life consists in nothing more than this contemplation of the divine majesty, so now, from the same—though much less perfect—contemplation we observe that the greatest pleasure of which we are capable in this life can be perceived.

Meditation Four: Concerning the True and the False

Thus have I lately become accustomed to withdrawing the mind from the senses. I have so carefully taken note of the fact that there are very few things that are truly perceived regarding corporeal things, and that a great many more things regarding the human mind—and yet still many more things regarding God—can be known, that with no difficulty do I direct my thinking away from things I can imagine to things that I can only understand, and that are separated from all matter. And I have a manifestly much more distinct idea of the human mind, insofar as it is a thinking thing—not extended in length, breadth or depth—receiving nothing else from a body except the idea of this or that body. And when I direct my attention to the fact that I am doubting, that is, that I am an incomplete and dependent thing, there comes to mind a clear and distinct idea of an independent and complete being, namely, God. And from the mere fact that this idea is in me, or that I who have this idea exist, I plainly conclude that God also exists, and that my existence depends entirely upon him at each and every moment. The result is that I am confident that nothing more evident, nothing more certain can be known by the human mind. From this contemplation of the true God, in whom are hidden all the treasures of knowledge and wisdom, I now seem to see a way by which I might attain knowledge of other matters.

To begin with, I acknowledge that it is impossible for him ever to deceive me; for in every trick or deception some imperfection is found. Although the ability to deceive seems to be an indication of cleverness or power, nevertheless, willful deception evinces maliciousness and weakness. Accordingly, deception is not compatible with God.

Next I observe that there is in me a certain faculty of judgment that I undoubtedly received from God, as is the case with all the other things that are in me. Since he has not wished to deceive me, he certainly has not given me a faculty such that, when I use it properly, I could ever make a mistake.

No doubt regarding this matter remains, except that then it seems to follow that I should never make a mistake, for if all that I have is from God — and he gave me no faculty of making a mistake — I seem incapable of ever erring. So, as long as I think about God alone and direct myself straightforwardly and directly at him, I discover no grounds for error or falsity. But, after I turn my attention back on myself, I nevertheless observe that I am subject to countless errors. Seeking a cause for these errors, I notice that not only a real and positive idea of God (that is, of a being supremely perfect), but also, so to speak, a certain negative idea of nothing (that is, of what is supremely lacking in every perfection) passes before me. I also notice that I have been so constituted as to be some kind of middle ground between God and nothing, or between supreme being and non-being, so that, insofar as I have been created by a supreme being, there is nothing in me by means of which I might be deceived or be led into error; but insofar as I am not the supreme being, I lack quite a few things — so much so that it is not surprising that I am deceived. Thus I certainly understand that error as such is not something real that depends upon God, but rather is only a defect. Nor for that reason is there a need to account for my errors by positing a faculty given to me by God. Rather, it happens that I make mistakes because the faculty of judging the truth, which I have from him, is not infinite in me.

Still, this is not yet altogether satisfactory; for error is not a pure negation, but a privation or a lack of some knowledge that somehow ought to be in me. It does not seem possible to one who attends to the nature of God that he could have placed in me a faculty that is not perfect within its class or that has been deprived of some perfection it ought to have. For if it is true that the more perfect the artisan, the more perfect the works he produces, then what can be made by that supreme creator of all things that is not perfect in all respects? No doubt God could have made me such that I never err; no doubt, again, God always wills what is best; is it not therefore better for me to be deceived than not to be?

While I mull over these things more carefully, it immediately dawns on me that there is no reason to marvel at the fact that God might make things the reasons for which I do not understand; his existence ought not therefore to be doubted, because I might happen to observe that there are other things that were made by him whose "why" and "how" I do not comprehend. Since I know now that my nature is very weak and limited, but that the nature of God is immense, incomprehensible, and infinite, therefore I also know with sufficient evidence that he can make innumerable things whose causes escape me. For this reason alone the whole class of causes, which people customarily derive from a thing's "purpose," I judge to be useless in dealing with matters related to physics. It is not without rashness that I think myself competent to inquire into God's purposes.

It also occurs to me that whenever we ask whether the works of God are perfect, we should examine the whole universe together and not just one creature in isolation from the rest. Something, if all by itself, may rightfully appear very imperfect; but if it is seen in its role as a part in the universe, it is most perfect. However, from having wanted to doubt everything, I know with certainty only that I and God exist; nevertheless, from having taken note of the immense power of God, I am unable to deny that many other things have been made by him, or at least can be made by him, and, what is more, that I would take on the added significance of being a part in the universe of things.

Finally, focusing closer on myself and inquiring into the nature of my errors (the only things that argue for an imperfection in me), I note that these errors depend on the simultaneous concurrence of two causes: the faculty of knowing that is in me, and the faculty of choosing (in other words, the free choice of the will), that is, they depend on the intellect and will at the same time. Through the intellect alone I perceive only ideas concerning which I can make a judgment; no error, properly so-called, is to be found in the intellect thus precisely conceived. For although countless things about which I have no idea perhaps exist, nevertheless I must not be said, properly speaking, to be deprived of them. I am bereft of them only in a negative way, because I can give no argument by which to prove that God ought to have given me a greater faculty of knowing than he has. No matter how expert a craftsman I understand him to be, still I do not therefore believe he ought to have bestowed on each one of his works all the perfections that he can put into some. In fact, I cannot complain that I have received from God an insufficiently ample and imperfect will, or free choice, because I observe that it is limited by no boundaries. And it seems eminently worth noting that nothing else in me is so perfect or so great that I do not understand how they can be even more perfect or greater. If, for example, I consider the faculty of understanding, I immediately recognize that it is very small and quite finite in me, and at the same time I form an idea of another much greater faculty — in fact, the greatest and infinite; and from the fact that I can form an idea of this faculty, I perceive that it pertains to the nature of God. Similarly, if I examine the faculty of memory, imagination, or any other faculty, I manifestly find none, except what in me is feeble and limited, but what in God I understand to be immense. The sole exception is the will or free choice; I observe it to be so great in me that I grasp an idea of nothing greater, to the extent that the will is principally the basis for my understanding that I bear an image and likeness of God. Although it is incomparably greater in God than it is in me, both by virtue of the knowledge and power that are associated with it and that render it more resolute and efficacious — as well as by virtue of its object, for the divine will extends to more things; yet taken formally, will precisely as such, it does not seem greater, because willing is only a matter of being able to do or not do something (that is, of being able to affirm or deny, to pursue or to shun), or better still, the will consists solely in the fact that when something is proposed to us by our intellect either to affirm or deny, to pursue or to shun, we are moved by it in such a way that we sense that no external force could have imposed it on us. In order to be free it is unnecessary for me to be moved in [n]either direction; on the contrary, the more I am inclined toward one direction — either because I evidently grasp that there is in it an aspect of the good and the true, or because God has thus disposed the inner recesses of my thought — the more I choose that direction more freely. Nor indeed does divine grace or natural knowledge ever diminish one's liberty; rather it increases and strengthens it. However, the indifference that I observe when no reason moves me more in one direction than in another is the lowest level of freedom; it evinces no perfection in it, but rather a defect in my knowlege, or a certain negation. Were I always to see clearly what is true and good, I would never deliberate about what is to be judged or chosen. Thus, although I may be entirely free, I could never for that reason be indifferent.

But from these considerations I perceive that the power of willing, which is from God, is not—taken by itself—the cause of my errors, for in its own way it is most ample and perfect. The same goes for the power of understanding. Whatever I understand, because it is from God that I have the power of understanding, I doubtless understand rightly; it is impossible for anything to take place in the intellect that could cause me to be deceived. From what source, therefore, do my errors arise? Solely from the fact that, because the will extends further than the intellect, I do not contain the will within the same boundaries; rather, I even extend it to things I do not understand. Because my will is indifferent to these latter things, it easily turns away from the true and the good; in this way I am deceived and commit sin.

For example, during these last few days when I have been examining whether anything exists in the world, I have noticed that, from the very fact that I had made this examination, it evidently followed that I exist. I could not help judging that what I understood clearly is true; not that I was coerced into holding this judgment because of some external force, but because a great inclination of my will followed from a great light in the intellect—so much so that the more spontaneously and freely I believed it, the less I was indifferent to it. But now I not only know that I, insofar as I am a thing that thinks, exist, but I also know that, having observed some ideas of corporeal nature, I might question whether the thinking nature that is in me—or rather that I am—is something different from this corporeal nature, or whether both natures are the same thing. And I presume that no consideration has as yet occurred to my mind which convinces me of the one more than the other. Thus it certainly follows that I am indifferent about affirming or denying either one, or even about my making any judgment at all in the matter.

Moreover, this indifference extends not only to those things about which the intellect knows absolutely nothing, but generally to everything of which the intellect does not have a keen enough knowledge at the very time when the will is deliberating on them. Although probable guesses might lead me in one direction, all it takes to move me to assent to the very opposite is the knowledge that they are merely guesswork, not certain and indubitable proofs. These last few days I have ample experience of this point, since everything that I had once believed to be as true as it possibly could be, I have now presumed to be utterly false, for the sole reason that I noticed that I could one way or another raise doubts about it.

But if I hold off from making a judgment when I do not perceive with sufficient clarity and distinctness what is in fact true, I clearly would be acting properly and would not be deceived. But were I to make an assertion or a denial, then I would not be using my freedom properly. If I turn in the direction that happens to be false, I am plainly deceived. But if I should embrace either alternative, and in so doing happen upon the truth by accident, I would still not be without fault, for it is manifest by the light of nature that the intellect's perception must always precede the will's being determined. Inherent in this incorrect use of the free will is a privation that constitutes the very essence of error: a privation, I say, is inherent in this operation insofar as the operation proceeds from me, but not in the faculty that was given to me by God, nor even in the operation of the faculty insofar as it depends upon God.

Indeed, I have no cause for complaint on the grounds that God has not given me a greater power of understanding or a greater light of nature than he has given me, for it is of the very essence of a finite intellect not to understand many things, and it is of the very essence of a created intellect to be finite. Actually, rather than think that he has withheld from me or deprived me of those things that he has not given, I ought to thank him, who never owed me anything, for what he has given me.

Again, I have no cause for complaint on the grounds that God has bestowed upon me a will that is open to more things than my intellect; since the will consists of merely one thing, and, as it were, something indivisible, it does not seem that its nature could withstand anything being removed from it. Indeed, the more ample the will is, the more I ought to thank its giver.

Nor again should I complain because God concurs with me in eliciting those acts of the will, or those judgments, in which I am deceived. For those acts are absolutely true and good, insofar as they depend on God; and it is, so to speak, a greater perfection in me in that I can elicit those acts than if I could not do so. But a privation, in which alone the meaning of falsehood and sin is to be found, in no way needs the concurrence of God, for a privation is not a thing; and it is not related to God as its cause; rather, it ought to be called only a negation. For it is no imperfection in God that he gave me the freedom to give or withhold my assent to things of which he has placed no clear and distinct perception in my intelect. But surely it is an imperfection in me that I not use my liberty well and that I make a judgment about what I do not rightly understand. Nevertheless, I see that God could easily have brought it about that, while remaining free and having finite knowledge, I still never err. This result could occur either had he given my intellect a clear and distinct perception of everything about which I would ever deliberate or had he only impressed firmly enough upon my memory—so that I could never forget it—that I should never judge anything that I do not clearly and distinctly understand. I readily understand that, insofar as I am something whole and complete in my own right, I would have been more perfect than I now am, were God to have made me that way. But I cannot therefore deny that it might be, so to speak, a greater perfection in the universe as a whole that some of its parts are not immune to error, while others are, than if they were all alike. And I have no right to complain that God wished to sustain me in the world as a person who is not the principal and most perfect of all.

Furthermore, even if I cannot abstain from errors in the first way, which depends upon the evident perception of everything concerning which one must deliberate, nevertheless I can do so by the second way, which depends solely on my remembering that whenever the truth of a given matter is not apparent, I must abstain from making judgments. Although I observe that there is in me this infirmity, namely that I am unable always to adhere fixedly to one and the same knowledge, nevertheless I can, by attentive and frequently repeated meditation, bring it to pass that I recall it every time the situation demands; thus, I would acquire a habit of not erring.

For this reason, since the greatest and chief perfection of man consists in investigating the cause of error and falsity, I think that today's meditation was quite profitable. Nor can this perfection be anything other than I have described; for whenever I restrain my will in making judgments, so that it extends only to those matters that are clearly and distinctly shown to it by the intellect, it can never happen that I err, because every clear and distinct perception is surely something. Hence it cannot derive its existence from nothing; rather, it necessarily has God for its author — that supremely perfect God, I say, to whom it is repugnant to be a deceiver — thus the perception is surely true. Nor today have I learned only what I must avoid so as not to be deceived; I have also simultaneously learned what I must do to search for the truth. I search for it indeed if only I attend enough to what I perfectly understand, and refrain from the rest that I apprehend more confusedly and more obscurely. I shall give this matter careful attention later.

Meditation Five: Concerning the Essence of Material Things, and Again Concerning God, That He Exists

Many matters still remain for me to examine concerning the attributes of God and of me, that is, concerning the nature of my mind. But perhaps I might take them up at some other time. For now, nothing seems more urgent — having noted what is to be avoided and what is to be done in order to attain the truth — than that I try to free myself from the doubts into which I have recently fallen, and that I see whether or not anything certain can be obtained concerning material things.

Before inquiring whether any such material things exist outside me, surely I ought to consider the ideas of those things, insofar as they are in my thought, and to see which ones are distinct and which ones are confused.

To be sure, I distinctly imagine that quantity, which philosophers commonly call "continuous": namely, the extension of its quantity, or rather the extension of the thing having quantitative dimensions of length, breadth, and depth. I enumerate the thing's various parts. I ascribe to these parts certain sizes, shapes, positions, and movements from place to place; to these movements I ascribe various durations.

Not only have I plainly known and examined those things, viewed thus in a general way, but also I perceive attentively the countless particular aspects of figures, number, movement, and so on. Their truth is open and suitable to my nature to such an extent that, when I first discover them, it is not so much that I seem to learn anything new but that I recall something I already knew. That is, I first notice things that were already in me, although I had not directed a mental gaze toward them.

This is what I believe most needs examination here: I find within me countless ideas of things, that, although perhaps not existing anywhere outside me, still cannot be said to be nothing. Although I somehow think them at will, nevertheless I have not put them together; rather, they have their own true and immutable natures. For example, when I imagine a triangle, although perhaps no such figure exists outside my thought anywhere in the world and never will, still its nature, essence, or form is completely determined, unchangeable, and eternal. I did not produce it and it does not depend on my mind. This point is evident from the fact that many properties can be demonstrated regarding this triangle — namely that its three angles are equal to two right angles, that its longest side is opposite the largest angle, and so on; whether I want to or not, I now clearly acknowledge them, although I had not previously thought of them at all when I imagined a triangle. For this reason, then, I have not produced them.

It is irrelevant to say that perhaps the idea of a triangle came to me from external things through the sense organs, on the grounds that on occasion I have seen triangular-shaped bodies. For I can think of many other figures, concerning which there can be no suspicion of their ever having entered me through the senses, and yet the various properties of these figures, no less than those of the triangle, can be demonstrated. All of these are patently true because they are clearly known by me; thus they are something and not merely nothing. For it is evident that everything that is true is something; I have already demonstrated at length that all that I know clearly is true. Had I not demonstrated this, certainly the nature of my mind is such that I nevertheless must assent to them, at least while I perceive them clearly; I remember that even before now, when I adhered very closely to the objects of the senses, I always took this type of truth to be the most certain of every truth that I evidently knew regarding figures, numbers, or other things pertaining to arithmetic, geometry or, in general, to pure and abstract mathematics.

But if, from the mere fact that I can bring forth from my thought the idea of something, it follows that all that I clearly and distinctly perceive to pertain to something really does pertain to it, then is this not an argument by which to prove the existence of God? Certainly I discover within me an idea of God, that is, of a supremely perfect being, no less than the idea of some figure or number. And I understand clearly and distinctly that it pertains to his nature that he always exists, no less than whatever has been demonstrated about some figure or number also pertains to the nature of this figure or number. Thus, even if everything that I have meditated upon during these last few days were not true, I ought to be at least as certain of the existence of God as I have hitherto been about the truths of mathematics.

Nevertheless, this point is not wholly obvious at first glance, but has the appearance of a sophism. Since in all other matters I am accustomed to distinguishing existence from essence, I easily persuade myself that the essence of God can be separated off from his existence; thus God can be thought of as not existing. Be that as it may, it still becomes obvious to a very diligently attentive person that the existence of God can no more be separated from his essence than the essence of a triangle can be separated from the fact that its three internal angles equal two right angles, or the idea of a valley can be separated from the idea of a mountain. So it is no less repugnant to think of a God (that is, a supremely perfect being) lacking existence (that is, as lacking some perfection), than it is to think of a mountain lacking a valley.

But granted I could no more think of God as not existing than I can think of a mountain without a valley, still it does not follow that a mountain actually exists in the world. Thus, from the fact that I think of God as existing, it does not seem to follow that God exists; for my thought imposes no necessity on things. Just as one can imagine a winged horse, without there being a horse with wings, so in the same way perhaps I can attach existence to God, even though no such God exists.

But there is a sophism lurking here. From the fact that I am unable to think of a mountan except with a valley, it does not follow that a mountain or a valley exists anywhere, but only that, whether they exist or not, a mountain and a valley cannot be separated from one another. But from the fact that I cannot think of God except as existing, it follows that existence is inseparable from God; for this reason he truly exists. Not because my thought brings this situation about, or imposes any necessity on anything; but because the necessity of this thing, namely of the existence of God, forces me to entertain this thought; for I am not free to think of God without existence (that is, the supremely perfect being apart from the supreme perfection), as I am free to imagine a horse with or without wings.

Further, it should not be said here that, having asserted that he has all perfections, I needed to assert that God exists—since existence is one of these perfections—but that my earlier assertion need not have been made. So, I need not believe that all four-sided figures are inscribed in a circle; but assuming that I do believe it, it would then be necessary for me to admit that a rhombus is inscribed in a circle—this is plainly false. Although it is not necessary that I happen upon any thought of God, nevertheless as often as I think of a being first and supreme—and bring forth the idea of God as if from the storehouse of my mind—I must of necessity ascribe all perfections to it, even though I do not at that time enumerate them all, nor take note of them one by one. This necessity plainly suffices so that afterwards, when I consider that existence is a perfection, I rightly conclude that a first and supreme being exists. In the same way, there is no necessity for me ever to imagine a triangle, but as often as I wish to consider a rectilinear figure having but three internal angles, I must ascribe to it those properties from which one rightly infers that the three internal angles of this figure are not greater than two right angles, even though I do not then take notice of this fact. But when I inquire which figures might be inscribed in a circle, there is absolutely no need whatever for my believing that all four-sided figures are of this sort; nor even, for that matter, can I possibly imagine it, as long as I wish to admit only what I clearly and distinctly understand. Consequently, there is a great difference between false beliefs of this sort and true ideas inborn in me, the first and principal of which is the idea of God. For I plainly understand in many ways that it is not an invention dependent upon my thought, but an image of a true and immutable nature. First, because I cannot think of anything but God himself to whose essence belongs existence; next, because I cannot understand two or more Gods of this kind; because, having asserted that one God now exists, I plainly see that it is necessarily the case that he has existed from eternity and will endure forever; finally, because I perceive many other things in God, none of which I can remove or change.

But, indeed, whatever proof I use, it always comes down to the fact that the only things that fully convince me are those that I clearly and distinctly perceive. Although some of those things that I thus perceive are obvious to everyone—while others are discovered only by those who look more closely and inquire more diligently—nevertheless, after they have been discovered, they are considered no less certain than the others. For example, although it is not so readily apparent in the case of a right triangle that the square of the hypotenuse is equal to the square of the other two sides as it is that the hypotenuse is opposite the largest angle; nonetheless, the former is no less believed—once it has been ascertained. However, I acknowledge nothing prior to, or easier than, what pertains to God, unless I am overwhelmed by prejudices or unless images of sensible things besiege my thought from all sides. For what in and of itself is more manifest than that a supreme being exists, or that God, to whose essence alone existence pertains, exists?

But, although I needed to pay close attention in order to perceive this point, nevertheless I not only am now as certain regarding this as I am regarding everything else that seems most certain, but also I observe that the certitude of other things so depends upon this point that without it I am unable ever to know anything perfectly.

Yet I am indeed of such a nature that, while I perceive something very clearly and distinctly, I cannot help but believe it to be true. And yet I am also of such a nature that I cannot keep the gaze of my mind always on the same thing in order to perceive it clearly; the memory of a judgment made earlier often comes to mind, when I no longer fully attend to the reasons for which I judged something. Thus, other reasons can be brought forward that, were I ignorant of God, would easily make me change my opinion; thus I would never have true and certain knowledge of anything, but I would have only vague and changeable opinions. Thus, for example, when I consider the nature of a triangle, it appears most evident to me — steeped as I am in the principles of geometry — that the three internal angles of the triangle are equal to two right angles; I must believe this to be true, as long as I attend to its demonstration. But as soon as I turn my power of discernment from the demonstration, even though I recall that I had looked at it most clearly, nevertheless, were I ignorant of God it can easily happen that I might doubt whether or not it is true. For I can convince myself that I have been so made by nature that I would occasionally be deceived about those things that I believe I quite evidently perceive, especially when I might recall that I have often taken many things to be true and certain, which later, upon bringing other considerations to bear, I have judged to be false.

But once I perceived that there is a God — because at the same time I also understood that all other things depend on him — and that he is no deceiver, I then concluded that everything that I clearly and distinctly perceive is necessarily true. Even if I no longer attend further to the reasons why I judged it to be true, provided that I remember that I did clearly and distinctly observe it, no contrary reason can be brought to bear which might force me to doubt it; rather, I have a true and certain knowledge of this matter. Not just this one either, but also everything else that I recall having once demonstrated, as in geometry, and so on. For what objections can now be raised to me? Have I been made such that I am often deceived? But now I know that I cannot be deceived in those matters that I clearly understand. On other occasions have I not taken many things to be true and certain, but that afterward I recognized as false? However, I did not clearly and distinctly perceive any of them, but — ignorant of this rule of truth — I believe them for other reasons, that I later discovered were less valid. What therefore will be said? Might I perhaps not be dreaming (as I recently objected to myself), or might everything about which I am now thinking be no more true than what passes before the mind of a person sleeping? Be that as it may, it changes nothing; for certainly, although I might be asleep, if something is evident to my intellect, it is wholly true.

And thus I plainly see that the certainty and truth of every science depends upon the knowledge of the true God, to such an extent that, before I had known him, I could not know anything perfectly about any other thing. But now it is possible for me to know certainly and fully countless things — both about God and other intellectual matters, as well as about all corporeal nature, which is the object of pure mathematics.

Meditation Six: Concerning the Existence of Material Things, and the Real Distinction of the Mind from the Body

It remains for me to examine whether material things exist. Indeed I now know that they can exist, at least insofar as they are the object of pure mathematics, because I clearly and distinctly perceive them. For no doubt God is capable of bringing about everything that I am thus capable of perceiving. And I have never judged that God was incapable of something, except when it was incompatible with being perceived by me distinctly. Moreover, from the faculty of imagination, which I observe that I use while I am engaged in dealing with these material things, it seems to follow that they exist; to someone paying very close attention to what imagination is, it appears to be nothing else but an application of the knowing faculty to a body intimately present to it—hence, a body that exists.

And to make this very clear, I first examine the difference between imagination and pure intellection. So, for example, when I imagine a triangle, I not only understand that it is a figure bounded by three lines, but at the same time I also intuit by my powers of discernment these three lines as present—this is what I call "imagining." But if I want to think about a chiliagon, I certainly understand just as well that it is a figure consisting of a thousand sides, and that a triangle is a figure consisting of three lines; but I do not imagine those thousand sides in the same way, that is, I do not intuit them as being present. Albeit that when I think of chiliagon I may perchance represent to myself some figure confusedly—because whenever I think about something corporeal, I always, out of force of habit, imagine something—nevertheless it is evident that it is not a chiliagon. This is so because it is not really different from the figure I would represent to myself if I were to think of a myriagon or any other figure with a large number of sides. Nor is imagination of any help in knowing the properties that differentiate the chiliagon from other polygons. But if it is a question of a pentagon, I surely can understand its form, just as was the case with the chiliagon, without the help of my imagination. But I can also imagine it, that is, by applying the powers of discernment both to its five sides and, at the same time, to the area bounded by those sides; clearly I am aware at this point that I need a peculiar sort of effort on the part of the mind in order to imagine, one that I do not employ in order to understand. This new effort on the part of the mind clearly shows the difference between imagination and pure intellection.

Besides, I believe that this power of imagining that is in me, insofar as it differs from the power of understanding, is not a necessary element of my essence, that is, of the essence of my mind; for although I might lack this power, nonetheless I would undoubtedly remain the same person as I am now. Thus it seems to follow that the power of imagining depends upon something different from me. And I readily understand that were a body to exist to which a mind is so joined that it might direct itself to look at it anytime it wishes, it could happen that by means of this body I intuit corporeal things. The result would be that this mode of thinking differs from pure intellection only in the fact that the mind, when it understands, in a sense turns itself toward itself and gazes upon one of the ideas that are in it. But when it imagines, it turns itself toward the body, and intuits something in the body similar to an idea either understood by the mind or perceived by sense. I say I easily understand that the imagination can function in this way, provided a body does exist. But this is only a probability; although I may investigate everything carefully, nevertheless, I do not yet see how, from the distinct idea of corporeal nature that I find in my imagination, I can draw up an argument that necessarily concludes that some body exists.

But I am in the habit of imagining many other things—over and above the corporeal nature that is the object of pure mathematics—such as colors, sounds, tastes, pain, and so on, but not so distinctly. Inasmuch as I perceive these things better with those senses from which, with the aid of the memory, they seem to have come to the imagination, the same trouble should also be taken concerning the senses, so that I might deal with them more appropriately. It must be seen whether I can obtain any certain argument for the existence of corporeal things from those things that are perceived by the way of thinking that I call "sense."

First I will repeat to myself here what those things were that I believed to be true because I had perceived them by means of the senses and what the grounds were for so believing. Next I will assess the reasons why I called them into doubt. Finally, I will consider what I must now believe concerning these things.

So, first, I sensed that I have a head, hands, feet, and other members that composed this body; I viewed it as a part of me, or perhaps even as the whole of me. I sensed that this body is frequently amid many other bodies, and that these bodies can affect my body in pleasant and unpleasant ways; I gauged what was pleasant by a certain sense of pleasure, and what was unpleasant by a sense of pain. In addition to pain and pleasure, I also sensed in me hunger, thirst, and other such appetites, as well as certain corporeal tendencies to mirth, sadness, anger, and other such feelings. But, as for things external to me—besides the extension, shapes, and motions of bodies—I also sensed their roughness, heat, and other tactile qualities; I sensed, too, the light, colors, odors, tastes, and sounds from whose variety I distinguished the heavens, the earth, the seas, and the other bodies one from the other. Indeed, because of the ideas of all these qualities that presented themselves to my thought and that alone I properly and immediately sensed, it was not wholly without reason that I believed that I sensed things clearly different from my thought, namely, the bodies from which these ideas might proceed. For I knew by experience that they come upon me without my consent, to the extent that, wish as I may, I cannot sense any object unless it be present to the organ of sense, and I cannot fail to sense it when it is present. Since the ideas perceived by sense are much more vivid and clear-cut, and even, in their own way, more "distinct," than any of those that I willingly and knowingly formed by meditation or those that I found impressed on my memory, it seems impossible that they come from myself. Therefore, it remained that they came from other things. Since I had no knowledge of such things except from these ideas themselves, I could not help entertaining the view that these things were similar to those ideas. Also, because I recalled that I had used my senses earlier than my reason, and I saw that the ideas that I myself constructed were not as clear-cut as those that I perceived by means of the senses, I saw that these former ideas were for the most part composed of parts of these latter ideas; I easily convinced myself that I plainly have no idea in the intellect that I did not have beforehand in the sense. Not without reason did I judge that this body, which by a special right I called "mine," belongs more to me than to any other thing, for I could never be separated from it in the same way as I could be from the rest. I sensed all appetites and feelings in it and for it. Finally, I have noticed pain and pleasurable excitement in its parts, but not in other bodies external to it. But why a certain sadness of spirit arises from one feeling of pain or another, and why a certain elation arises from a feeling of excitement, or why some sort of twitching of the stomach, which I call hunger, should warn me to take in nourishment, or why dryness of throat should warn me to take something to drink, and so on—for all these I plainly had no explanation other than that I have been taught so by nature. For there is clearly no affinity, at least none I am aware of, between the twitching of the stomach and the will to take in nourishment, or between the sense of something that causes pain and the thought of the sadness arising from this sense. But nature seems to have taught me everything else that I judged concerning the objects of the senses, because I convinced myself—even before having spent time on any of the arguments that might prove it—that things were this way.

But afterwards many experiences gradually caused all faith that I had in the senses to totter; occasionally towers, which had seemed round from afar, appeared square at close quarters; very large statues, standing on their pinnacles, did not seem large to someone looking at them from ground level; in countless other such things I detected that judgments of the external senses deceived me—not just the external senses, but also the internal senses. What can be more intimate than pain? But I had once heard it said by people whose leg or arm had been amputated that it seems to them that they occasionally sense pain in the very limb that they lacked. Therefore, even in me, it did not seem to be clearly certain that some part of my body was causing me pain, although I did sense pain in it. To these causes of doubt I recently added two quite general ones: first, I believed I never sensed anything while I was awake that I could not believe I also sometimes perceive while asleep. Since I do not believe that what I seem to sense in my dreams comes to me from things external to me, I did not see any reason why I should have these beliefs about things that I seem to sense while I am awake. The second cause of doubt was that, since I was ignorant of the cause of my coming into being (or at least pretended that I was ignorant of it), I saw that nothing prevented my having been so constituted by nature that I should be deceived about even what appeared to me most true. As to the arguments by which I formerly convinced myself of the truth of sensible things, I found no difficulty in responding to them. Since I seemed driven by nature toward many things opposed to reason, I did not think what was taught by nature deserved much credence. Although the perceptions of the senses did not depend on my will, I did not think that we must therefore conclude that they came from things external to me, because perhaps there is in me some faculty, as yet unknown to me, that produces these perceptions.

However, now, after having begun to know better the cause of my coming to be, I believe that I must not rashly admit everything that I seem to derive from the senses. But, then, neither should I call everything into doubt.

First, because I know that all the things that I clearly and distinctly understand can be made by God exactly as I understand them, it is enough that I can clearly and distinctly understand one thing without the other in order for me to be certain that the one thing is different from the other, because at least God can establish them separately. The question of the power by which this takes place is not relevant to their being thought to be different. For this reason, from the fact that I know that I exist, and that meanwhile I judge that nothing else clearly belongs to my nature or essence except that I am a thing that thinks, I rightly conclude that my essence consists in this alone: that I am only a thing that thinks. Although perhaps (or rather, as I shall soon say, to be sure) I have a body that is very closely joined to me, nevertheless, because on the one hand I have a clear and distinct idea of myself—insofar as I am a thing that thinks and not an extended thing—and because on the other hand I have a distinct idea of a body—insofar as it is merely an extended thing, and not a thing that thinks—it is therefore certain that I am truly distinct from my body, and that I can exist without it.

Moreover, I find in myself faculties endowed with certain special modes of thinking—namely the faculties of imagining and sensing—without which I can clearly and distinctly understand myself in my entirety, but not vice versa: I cannot understand them clearly and distinctly without me, that is, without the knowing substance to which they are attached. For in their formal concept they include an act of understanding; thus I perceive that they are distinguished from me just as modes are to be distinguished from the thing of which they are modes. I also recognize certain other faculties—like those of moving from one place to another, of taking on various shapes, and so on—that surely no more can be understood without the substance to which they are attached than those preceding faculties; for that reason they cannot exist without the substance to which they are attached. But it is clear that these faculties, if in fact they exist, must be attached to corporeal or extended substances, but not to a knowing substance, because extension—but certainly not understanding—is contained in a clear and distinct concept of them. But now there surely is in me a passive faculty of sensing, that is, of receiving and knowing the ideas of sensible things; but I cannot use it unless there also exists, either in me or in something else, a certain active faculty of producing or bringing about these ideas. This faculty surely cannot be in me, since it clearly presupposes no intellection, and these ideas are produced without my cooperation and often against my will. Because this faculty is in a substance other than myself, in which ought to be contained—formally or eminently—all the reality that is objectively in the ideas produced by this faculty (as I have just now taken notice), it thus remains that either this substance is a body (or corporeal nature) in which is contained formally all that is contained in ideas objectively or it is God—or some other creature more noble than a body—in which it is all contained eminently. But, since God is not a deceiver, it is absolutely clear that he sends me these ideas neither directly and immediately—nor even through the mediation of any creature, in which the objective reality of these ideas is contained not formally but only eminently. Since he plainly gave me no faculty for making this discrimination—rather, he gave me a great inclination to believe that these ideas proceeded from things—I fail to see why God cannot be understood to be a deceiver, if they proceeded from a source other than corporeal things. For this reason, corporeal things exist. Be that as it may, perhaps not all bodies exist exactly as I grasp them by sense, because this grasp by the senses is in many cases very obscure and confused. But at least everything is in these bodies that I clearly and distinctly understand—that is, everything, considered in a general sense, that is encompassed in the object of pure mathematics.

But as to how this point relates to the other remaining matters that are either merely particular—as, for example, that the sun is of such and such a size or shape, and so on—or less clearly understood—as, for example, light, sound, pain, and so on—although they are very doubtful and uncertain, still, because God is not a deceiver, and no falsity can be found in my opinions, unless there is also in me a faculty given me by God for the purpose of rectifying this falsity, these features provide me with a certain hope of reaching the truth in them. And plainly it cannot be doubted that whatever I am taught by nature has some truth to it; for by "nature," taken generally, I understand only God himself or the coordination, instituted by God, of created things. I understand nothing else by my nature in particular than the totality of all the things bestowed on me by God.

There is nothing that this nature teaches me in a more clear-cut way than that I have a body that is ill-disposed when I feel pain, that it needs food and drink when I suffer hunger or thirst, and so on. Therefore, I ought not to doubt that there is some truth in this.

By means of these feelings of pain, hunger, thirst and so on, nature also teaches that I am present to my body not merely in the way a seaman is present to his ship, but that I am tightly joined and, so to speak, mingled together with it, so much so that I make up one single thing with it. For otherwise, when the body is wounded, I, who am nothing but a thing that thinks, would not then sense the pain. Rather, I would perceive the wound by means of the pure intellect, just as a seaman perceives by means of sight whether anything in the ship is broken. When the body lacks food or drink, I would understand this in a clear-cut fashion; I would not have confused feelings of hunger and thirst. For certainly these feelings of thirst, hunger, pain, and so on are nothing but confused modes of thinking arising from the union and, as it were, the mingling of the mind with the body.

Moreover, I am also taught by nature that many other bodies exist around my body; some of them are to be pursued, and others are to be avoided. And to be sure, from the fact that I sense widely different colors, sounds, odors, tastes, heat, roughness, and so on, I rightly conclude that in the bodies from which these different perceptions of the senses proceed, there are differences corresponding to the different perceptions — although perhaps the former are not similar to the latter. But from the fact that some of these perceptions are pleasant and others unpleasant, it is plainly certain that my body — or rather my whole self, insofar as I am composed of a body and a mind — can be affected by the various agreeable and disagreeeable bodies in the vicinity.

But I have accepted many other things, and, although I seem to have been taught them by nature, still it was not really nature that taught them to me, but a certain habit of making unconsidered judgments. And thus it could easily happen that they are false, as, for example, the belief that any space where there is nothing that moves my senses is empty; or, for example, the belief that in a hot body there is something plainly similar to the idea of heat which is in me; or that in a white or green body there is the same whiteness or greeness that I sense; or in a bitter or sweet thing the same taste, and so on; or the belief that stars and towers, and any other distant bodies have only the same size and shape that they present to the senses — and other examples of the same sort. But lest I not perceive distinctly enough something about this matter, I ought to define more carefully what I properly understand when I say that I am "taught something by nature." For I am using "nature" here in a stricter sense than the totality of everything bestowed on me by God. For in this totality there are contained many things that pertain only to my mind, as, for example, that I perceive that what has been done cannot be undone, and everything else that is known by the light of nature. At the moment the discussion does not center on these matters. There are also many things that pertain only to the body, as, for example, that it tends downward, and so on. I am not dealing with these either, but only with what has been bestowed on me by God, insofar as I am composed of mind and body. Therefore it is nature, thus understood, that teaches me to flee what brings a sense of pain and to pursue what brings a sense of pleasure, and the like. But it does not appear that nature, so conceived, teaches that we conclude from these perceptions of the senses anything in addition to this regarding things external to us unless there previously be an inquiry by the intellect; for it pertains to the mind alone, and not to the composite, to know the truth in these matters. Thus, although a star affects my eye no more than the flame from a small torch, still there is no real or positive tendency in my eye toward believing that the star is any bigger than the flame; rather, ever since my youth, I have made this judgment without reason. Although I feel heat upon drawing closer to the fire, and I feel pain upon drawing even closer to it, there is indeed no argument that convinces me that there is something in the fire that is similar either to the heat or to the pain, but only that there is something in the fire that causes in us these feelings of heat or pain. Although there be nothing in a given space that moves the sense, it does not therefore follow that there is no body in it. I use the perceptions of the senses that properly have been given by nature only for the purpose of signifying to the mind what is agreeable and disagreeable to the composite, of which the mind is a part; within those limits these perceptions are sufficiently clear and distinct. However, I see that I have been in the habit of subverting the order of nature in these and many other matters, because I use the perceptions of the senses as certain rules for immediately discerning what the essence is of the bodies external to us; yet, in respect to this essence, these perceptions still show me nothing but obscurity and confusion.

I have already examined in sufficient detail how it could happen that my judgments are false, the goodness of God notwithstanding. But a new difficulty now comes on the scene concerning those very things that are shown to me by nature as things to be either sought or avoided, as well as concerning the internal senses in which I seem to have detected errors: for example, when a person, deluded by the pleasant taste of food, ingests a poison hidden inside it. But in this case he is impelled by nature only toward desiring the thing in which the pleasant taste is located, but not toward the poison, of which he obviously is unaware. Nothing else can be concluded here except that this nature is not all-knowing. This is not remarkable, since man is a limited being; thus only limited perfection is appropriate to man.

But we often err even in those things to which nature impels us; for example, when those who are ill desire food or drink that will soon be injurious to them. Perhaps it could have been said here that they erred because their nature was corrupt. But this does not remove our difficulty, because a sickly man is no less a creature of God than a healthy one; for that reason it does not seem any less repugnant that the sickly man got a deceiving nature from God. And just as a clock made of wheels and counter-weights follows all the laws of nature no less closely when it has been badly constructed and does not tell time accurately than when it satisfies on all scores the wishes of its maker, just so, if I should consider the body of a man—insofar as it is a kind of mechanism composed of and outfitted with bones, nerves, muscles, veins, blood and skin—even if no mind existed in it, the man's body would still have all the same motions that are in it now except for those motions that proceed either from a command of the will or, consequently, from the mind. I readily recognize that it would be natural for this body, were it, say, suffering from dropsy, to suffer dryness of the throat, which commonly brings a feeling of thirst to the mind, and thus too its nerves and other parts are so disposed by the mind to take a drink with the result that the sickness is increased. It would be no more natural for this body, when there is no such infirmity in it and it is moved by the same dryness, to drink something useful to it. And, from the point of view of the intended purpose of the watch, I could say that it turns away from its nature when it does not tell the right time. Similarly, considering the mechanism of the human body as equipped for the motions that typically occur in it, I might think that it too turns away from its nature, if its throat were dry, when taking a drink would not be beneficial to its continued existence. Nevertheless, I realize well enough that this latter usage of the term "nature" differs greatly from the former. For this latter "nature" is only an arbitrary denomination, extrinsic to the things on which it is predicated and dependent upon my thought, because it compares a man in poor health and a poorly constructed clock with the idea of a man in good health and a well-made clock. But by "nature" taken in the former sense, I understand something that really is in things, and thus it is not without some truth.

When it is said, in the case of the dropsical body, that its "nature" is corrupt—from the fact that this body has a parched throat, and yet does not need a drink—it certainly is only an extrinsic denomination of nature. But be that as it may, in the case of the composite, that is, of a mind joined to such a body, it is not a pure denomination, but a true error of nature that this body should thirst when a drink would be harmful to it. Therefore it remains here to inquire how the goodness of God does not stand in the way of "nature," thus considered, being deceptive.

Now, first, I realize at this point that there is a great difference between a mind and a body, because the body, by its very nature, is something divisible, whereas the mind is plainly indivisible. Obviously, when I consider the mind, that is, myself insofar as I am only a thing that thinks, I cannot distinguish any parts in me; rather, I take myself to be one complete thing. Although the whole mind seems to be united to the whole body, nevertheless, were a foot or an arm or any other bodily part amputated, I know that nothing would be taken away from the mind; nor can the faculties of willing, sensing, understanding, and so on be called its "parts," because it is one and the same mind that wills, senses, and understands. On the other hand, no corporeal or extended thing can be thought by me that I did not easily in thought divide into parts; in this way I know that it is divisible. If I did not yet know it from any other source, this consideration alone would suffice to teach me that the mind is wholly different from the body.

Next, I observe that my mind is not immediately affected by all the parts of the body, but merely by the brain, or perhaps even by just one small part of the brain—namely, by that part in which the "common sense" is said to be found. As often as it is disposed in the same manner, it presents the same thing to the mind, although the other parts of the body can meanwhile orient themselves now this way, now that way, as countless experiments show—none of which need be reviewed here.

I also notice that the nature of the body is such that none of its parts can be moved by another part a short distance away, unless it is also moved in the same direction by any of the parts that stand between them, even though this more distant part does nothing. For example, in the cord ABCD, if the finial part D is pulled, the first part A would be moved in exactly the same direction as it could be moved if one of the intermediate parts, B or C, were pulled and the last part D remained motionless. Just so, when I sense pain in the foot, physics teaches me that this feeling took place because of nerves scattered throughout the foot. These nerves, like cords, are extended from that point all the way to the brain; when they are pulled in the foot, they also pull on the inner parts of the brain to which they are stretched, and produce a certain motion in these parts of the brain. This motion has been constituted by nature so as to affect the mind with a feeling of pain, as if it existed in the foot. But because these nerves need to pass through the tibia, thigh, loins, back, and neck, with the result that they extend from the foot to the brain, it can happen that the part that is in the foot is not stretched; rather one of the intermediate parts is thus stretched, and obviously the same movement will occur in the brain that happens when the foot was badly affected. The necessary result is that the mind feels the same pain. And we must believe the same regarding any other sense.

Finally, I observe that, since each of the motions occurring in that part of the brain that immediately affects the mind occasions only one sensation in it, there is no better way to think about this than that it occasions the sensation that, of all that could be occasioned by it, is most especially and most often conducive to the maintenance of a healthy man. Moreover, experience shows that such are all the senses bestowed on us by nature; therefore, clearly nothing is to be found in them that does not bear witness to God's power and goodness. Thus, for example, when the nerves in the foot are violently and unusually agitated, their motion, which extends through the marrow of the spine to the inner reaches of the brain, gives the mind at that point a sign to feel something—namely, the pain as if existing in the foot. This pain provokes it to do its utmost to move away from the cause, since it is harmful to the foot. But the nature of man could have been so constituted by God that this same motion in the brain might have displayed something else to the mind: either the motion itself as it is in the brain, or as it is in the foot, or in some place in between—or somewhere else entirely different. But nothing else serves so well the maintenance of the body. Similarly, when we need a drink, a certain dryness arises in the throat that moves its nerves, and, by means of them, the inner recesses of the brain. This motion affects the mind with a feeling of thirst, because in this situation nothing is more useful for us to know than that we need a drink to sustain our health; the same holds for the other matters.

From these considerations it is totally clear that, notwithstanding the immense goodness of God, the nature of man—insofar as it is composed of mind and body, cannot help but sometimes be deceived. For if some cause, not in the foot but in some other part through which the nerves are stretched from the foot to the brain—or perhaps even in the brain itself—were to produce the same motion that would normally be produced by a badly affected foot, then the pain will be felt as if it were in the foot, and the senses will naturally be deceived, because it is reasonable that the motion should always show the pain to the mind as something belonging to the foot rather than to some other part, since an identical motion in the brain can bring about only the identical effect and this motion more frequently is wont to arise from a cause that harms the foot than from something existing elsewhere. And if the dryness of the throat does not, as is the custom, arise from the fact that drink aids in the health of the body, but from a contrary cause—as happens in the case of the person with dropsy—then it is far better that it should deceive, than if, on the contrary, it were always deceptive when the body is well constituted. The same goes for the other cases.

This consideration is most helpful, not only for noticing all the errors to which my nature is liable, but also for easily being able to correct or avoid them. To be sure, I know that every sense more frequently indicates what is true than what is false regarding those things that concern the advantage of the body, and I can almost always use more than one sense in order to examine the same thing. Furthermore, I can use memory, which connects present things with preceding ones, plus the intellect, which now has examined all the causes of error. I should no longer fear lest those things that are daily shown me by the senses, are false; rather, the hyperbolic doubts of the last few days ought to be rejected as worthy of derision—especially the principal doubt regarding sleep, which I did not distinguish from being awake. For I now notice that a very great difference exists between these two; dreams are never joined with all the other actions of life by the memory, as is the case with those actions that occur when one is awake. For surely, if someone, while I am awake, suddenly appears to me, and then immediately disappears, as happens in dreams, so that I see neither where he came from or where he went, it is not without reason that I would judge him to be a ghost or a phantom conjured up in my brain, rather than a true man. But when these things happen, regarding which I notice distinctly where they come from, where they are now, and when they come to me, and I connect the perception of them without any interruption with the rest of my life, obviously I am certain that these perceptions have occurred not in sleep but in a waking state. Nor ought I to have even a little doubt regarding the truth of these things, if, having mustered all the senses, memory, and intellect in order to examine them, nothing is announced to me by one of these sources that conflicts with the others. For from the fact that God is no deceiver, it follows that I am in no way deceived in these matters. But because the need to get things done does not always give us the leisure time for such a careful inquiry, one must believe that the life of man is vulnerable to errors regarding particular things, and we must acknowledge the infirmity of our nature.

THOMAS HOBBES—
a contemporary portrait

TITLE PAGE OF *LEVIATHAN*, 1651

CHARLES II AS A BOY (William Dobs

THOMAS HOBBES

Thomas Hobbes (1588–1679) was born in Malmesbury, Wiltshire, England. Raised by a well-to-do uncle, he entered Oxford at the age of fourteen and received his bachelor's degree in 1608. His early interests were largely classical. In 1629, however, on a visit to the continent his imagination was captured by the method of geometry, in which he saw a superior way of arriving at certain truths. In his masterpiece, *Leviathan,* Hobbes remarks that geometry is "the only science that it hath pleased God hitherto to bestow upon mankind." On another continental visit, from 1634 through 1637, Hobbes met Galileo in Italy, conversed frequently with eminent thinkers in Paris, and formulated the outlines of his own philosophical position. Returning to England in 1637, he became increasingly concerned about the impending civil war there. His support of monarchy and his fear of the parliamentarians led him to flee to Holland in 1640. Thereafter, Hobbes remained on the continent for eleven productive years, spending a part of this time tutoring the future Charles II. His final years in England, from 1650 on, were marked by continuing controversy over his views and by the banning of his books.

Hobbes's earlier works include the *Little Treatise,* a discussion of sensation (written between 1630 and 1637), and *Elements of Law* (1640), in which he argues for an undivided sovereignty. His masterpiece, *Leviathan* (1651), is a treatise on "the matter, forme, and power of a commonwealth, ecclesiasticall and civil." Among his other works are a trilogy: *De Cive* (1642), *De Corpore* (1655), and *De Homine* (1657); *Of Liberty and Necessity* (published without his consent in 1654); and a historical work, *Behemoth* (1668).

Although *Leviathan* is best known as a contribution to political philosophy, it is really a multifaceted work, containing important insights into metaphysics and psychology. Since Hobbes recognized that any adequate theory of government must grow out of a sound conception of the governed, he attempted to develop a comprehensive view of man from a mechanistic and materialistic base. *Leviathan* thus begins with the claim that sensation is nothing but motion in the appropriate bodily parts, and that the various forms of imagination which we call 'memory,' 'dream,' and 'apparition' are all echoes of this initial motion. They are, in Hobbes's own vivid phrase, "decaying sense." Associations between thoughts are echoes of connections between past motions; and desire and aversion, the antecedents of action, are the "small beginnings of motion, within the body of man, before they appear in walking, speaking, striking, and other visible actions." Although the details of this materialistic account are crude, the views expressed are recognizable ancestors of views hotly debated today. Even Hobbes's particular brand of materialism, which identifies mental states with occurrences involving parts of physical objects rather than with those objects or parts themselves, continues to find favor.

Hobbes's political philosophy takes as its starting point an extremely pessimistic view of man's nature. According to Hobbes, the basic motivation of mankind is "a perpetual and restless desire of power after power, that ceaseth only in death." Given the universality of this desire for power, life in the state of nature, before the imposition of civil laws backed by sovereign force, must be a perpetual struggle for possessions, supremacy, and glory. In this state, the outcome of one's productive efforts is always uncertain, and life is "solitary, poor, nasty, brutish and short." To avoid this intolerable situation, the law of nature, which dictates self-preservation, commands men to surrender their liberty (although not their ability to defend their lives or persons) to a single sovereign. By covenanting, or contracting, to lend their force to the sovereign's endeavors, they first create the conditions under which the enforcement of laws, and so too the institutions of property and justice, are possible. Thus is born Leviathan, the great artificial being of the commonwealth, whose very soul is sovereignty.

Hobbes's account does not point inevitably to any single form of government. He allows that the sovereignty may reside in a single ruler (monarchy), a group (aristocracy), or the entire population (democracy). He does insist, however, that whatever form the sovereign body takes, its power must be absolute. The reason for this is that the purpose of the original covenant is to create an authority strong enough to protect each member of the populace from the incursions of the others. Given this initial intent, any attempt to separate from the sovereign the abilities to tax, legislate, or deploy the military, to challenge or punish the sovereign's acts, or in any other way to limit his power, must violate the original agreement. There may be a risk that the sovereign will abuse his power; but for Hobbes (though not for Locke) this risk is far outweighed by the secure and orderly existence that that power makes possible.

For a good discussion of Hobbes's life and philosophy, see R. S. Peters, *Hobbes* (Baltimore; Penguin Books, 1956). A number of interesting shorter pieces are collected in Keith Brown, ed., *Hobbes Studies* (Cambridge, Mass: Harvard University Press, 1965). Two important works are Michael Oakshott, *Hobbes on Civil Association* (Berkeley: University of California Press, 1975), and Leo Strauss, *The Political Philosophy of Hobbes* (1936; rpt. Oxford: Oxford University Press, 1963). An influential study of Hobbes's political and moral philosophy is Howard Warrender, *The Political Philosophy of Thomas Hobbes* (Oxford: Oxford University Press, 1957)

LEVIATHAN

(Chs. I–III, VI, XIII–XXI)

THE INTRODUCTION

NATURE, the art whereby God hath made and governs the world, is by the *art* of man, as in many other things, so in this also imitated, that it can make an artificial animal. For seeing life is but a motion of limbs, the beginning whereof is in some principal part within; why may we not say, that all *automata* (engines that move themselves by springs and wheels as doth a watch) have an artificial life? For what is the *heart*, but a *spring;* and the *nerves*, but so many *strings;* and the *joints*, but so many *wheels*, giving motion to the whole body, such as was intended by the artificer? *Art* goes yet further, imitating that rational and most excellent work of nature, *man*. For by art is created that great LEVIATHAN,[1] called a COMMON-WEALTH, or STATE, in Latin CIVITAS, which is but an artificial man; though of greater stature and strength than the natural, for whose protection and defence it was intended; and in which the *sovereignty* is an artificial *soul*, as giving life and motion to the whole body; the *magistrates*, and other *officers* of judicature and execution, artificial *joints; reward* and *punishment*, by which fastened to the seat of the sovereignty every joint and member is moved to perform his duty, are the *nerves*, that do the same in the body natural; the *wealth* and *riches* of all the particular members, are the *strength; salus populi*, the *people's safety*, its *business; counsellors*, by whom all things needful for it to know are suggested unto it, are the *memory; equity*, and *laws*, an artificial *reason* and *will; concord, health, sedition, sickness;* and *civil war, death*. Lastly, the *pacts* and *covenants*, by which the parts of this body politic were at first made, set together, and united, resemble that *fiat*, or the *let us make man*, pronounced by God in creation.

To describe the nature of this artificial man, I will consider.

First, the *matter* thereof, and the *artificer;* both which is *man*.

Secondly, *how*, and by what *covenants* it is made; what are the *rights* and just *power* or *authority* of a *sovereign;* and what it is that *preserveth* or *dissolveth* it.

Thirdly, what is a *Christian commonwealth*.

Lastly, what is the *kingdom of darkness*.

Concerning the first, there is a saying much usurped of late, that *wisdom* is acquired, not by reading of *books*, but of *men*. Consequently whereunto, those persons, that for the most part can give no other proof of being wise, take great delight to show what they think they have read in men, by uncharitable censures of one another behind their backs. But there is another saying not of late understood, by which they might learn truly to read one another, if they would take the pains; that is, *nosce teipsum, read thyself:* which was not meant, as it is now used, to countenance, either the barbarous state of men in power, towards their inferiors; or to encourage men of low degree, to a saucy behaviour towards their betters; but to teach us, that for the similitude of the thoughts and passions of one man, to the thoughts and passions of another, whosoever looketh into himself, and considereth what he doth,

---

1. [The leviathan was a Biblical sea-monster. —S.M.C.]

when he does *think, opine, reason, hope, fear,* &c. and upon what grounds; he shall thereby read and know, what are the thoughts and passions of all other men upon the like occasions. I say the similitude of *passions,* which are the same in all men, *desire, fear, hope,* &c.; not the similitude of the *objects* of the passions, which are the things *desired, feared, hoped,* &c.: for these the constitution individual, and particular education, do so vary, and they are so easy to be kept from our knowledge, that the characters of man's heart, blotted and confounded as they are with dissembling, lying, counterfeiting, and erroneous doctrines, are legible only to him that searcheth hearts. And though by men's actions we do discover their design sometimes; yet to do it without comparing them with our own, and distinguishing all circumstances, by which the case may come to be altered, is to decypher without a key, and be for the most part deceived, by too much trust, or by too much diffidence; as he that reads, is himself a good or evil man.

But let one man read another by his actions never so perfectly, it serves him only with his acquaintance, which are but few. He that is to govern a whole nation, must read in himself, not this or that particular man; but mankind: which though it be hard to do, harder than to learn any language or science; yet when I shall have set down my own reading orderly, and perspicuously, the pains left another, will be only to consider, if he also find not the same in himself. For this kind of doctrine admitteth no other demonstration.

PART ONE

OF MAN

CHAPTER I

Of Sense

CONCERNING the thoughts of man, I will consider them first singly, and afterwards in train, or dependence upon one another. Singly, they are every one a *representation* or *appearance,* of some quality, or other accident of a body without us, which is commonly called an *object.* Which object worketh on the eyes, ears, and other parts of a man's body; and by diversity of working, produceth diversity of appearances.

The original of them all, is that which we call SENSE, for there is no conception in a man's mind, which hath not at first, totally, or by parts, been begotten upon the organs of sense. The rest are derived from that original.

To know the natural cause of sense, is not very necessary to the business now in hand; and I have elsewhere written of the same at large. Nevertheless, to fill each part of my present method, I will briefly deliver the same in this place.

The cause of sense, is the external body, or object, which presseth the organ proper to each sense, either immediately, as in the taste and touch; or mediately, as in seeing, hearing, and smelling; which pressure, by the mediation of the nerves, and other strings and membranes of the body, continued inwards to the brain and heart, causeth there a resistance, or counter-pressure, or endeavour of the heart to deliver itself, which endeavour, because *outward,* seemeth to be some matter without. And this *seeming,* or *fancy,* is that which men call *sense;* and consisteth, as to the eye, in a *light,* or *colour figured;* to the ear, in a *sound;* to the nostril, in an *odour;* to the tongue and palate, in a *savour;* and to the rest of the body, in *heat, cold, hardness, softness,* and such other qualities as we discern by *feeling.* All which qualities, called *sensible,* are in the object, that causeth them, but so many several motions of the matter, by which it presseth our organs diversely. Neither in us that are pressed, are they any thing else, but divers motions; for motion produceth nothing but motion. But their appearance to us is fancy, the same waking, that dreaming. And as pressing, rubbing, or striking the eye, makes us fancy a light; and pressing the ear, produceth a din; so do the bodies also we see, or hear, produce the same by their strong, though unobserved action. For if those colours and sounds were in the bodies, or objects that cause them, they could not be severed from them, as by glasses, and in echoes by reflection, we see they are; where we know the thing we see is in one place, the appearance in another. And though at some certain distance, the real and very object seem invested with the fancy it begets in us; yet still the object is one thing, the image or fancy is another. So that sense, in all cases, is nothing else but original fancy, caused, as I have said, by the pressure, that is, by the motion, of external things upon our eyes, ears, and other organs thereunto ordained.

But the philosophy-schools, through all the universities of Christendom, grounded upon certain texts of Aristotle, teach another doctrine, and say, for the cause of *vision,* that the thing seen, sendeth forth on every side a *visible species,* in English, a *visible show, apparition,* or *aspect,* or *a being seen;* the receiving whereof into the eye, is *seeing.* And for the cause of *hearing,* that the thing heard, sendeth forth an *audible species,* that is an *audible aspect,* or *audible being seen;* which entering at the ear, maketh *hearing.* Nay, for the cause of *understanding* also, they say the thing understood, sendeth forth an *intelligible species,* that is, an *intelligible being seen;* which, coming into the understanding, makes us understand. I say not this, as disproving the use of universities; but because I am to speak hereafter of their office in a commonwealth, I must let you see on all occasions by the way, what things would be amended in them; amongst which the frequency of insignificent speech is one.

CHAPTER II

Of Imagination

THAT when a thing lies still, unless somewhat else stir it, it will lie still for ever, is a truth that no man doubts of. But that when a thing is in motion, it will eternally be in motion, unless somewhat else stay it, though the reason be the same, namely, that nothing can change itself, is not so easily assented to. For men measure, not only other men, but all other things, by themselves; and because they find themselves subject after motion to pain, and lassitude, think every thing else grows weary of motion, and seeks repose of its own accord; little considering, whether it be not some other motion, wherein that desire of rest they find in themselves, consisteth. From hence it is, that the schools say, heavy bodies fall downwards, out of an appetite to rest, and to conserve their nature in that place which is most proper for them; ascribing appetite, and knowledge of what is good for their conversation, which is more than man has, to things inanimate, absurdly.

When a body is once in motion, it moveth, unless something else hinder it, eternally; and whatsoever hindreth it, cannot in an instant, but in time, and by degrees, quite extinguish it; and as we see in the water, though the wind cease, the waves give not over rolling for a long time after: so also it happeneth in that motion, which is made in the internal parts of man, then, when he sees, dreams, &c. For after the object is removed, or the eye shut, we still retain an image of the thing seen, though more obscure than when we see it. And this is it, the Latins call *imagination,* from the image made in seeing; and apply the same, though improperly, to all the other senses. But the Greeks call it *fancy;* which signifies *appearance,* and is as proper to one sense, as to another. IMAGINATION therefore is nothing but *decaying sense;* and is found in men, and many other living creatures, as well sleeping, as waking.

The decay of sense in men waking, is not the decay of the motion made in sense; but an obscuring of it, in such manner as the light of the sun obscureth the light of the stars; which stars do no less exercise their virtue, by which they are visible, in the day than in the night. But because amongst many strokes, which our eyes, ears, and other organs receive from external bodies, the predominant only is sensible; therefore, the light of the sun being predominant, we are not affected with the action of the stars. And any object being removed from our eyes, though the impression it made in us remain, yet other objects more present succeeding, and working on us, the imagination of the past is obscured, and made weak, as the voice of a man is in the noise of the day. From whence it followeth, that the longer the time is, after the sight or sense of any object, the weaker is the imagination. For the continual change of man's body destroys in time the parts which in sense were moved: so that distance of time, and of place, hath one and the same effect in us. For as at a great distance of place, that which we look at appears dim, and without distinction of the smaller parts; and as voices grow weak, and inarticulate; so also, after great distance of time, our imagination of the past is weak; and we lose, for example, of cities we have seen, many particular streets, and of actions, many particular circumstances. This *decaying sense,* when we would express the thing itself, I mean *fancy* itself, we call *imagination,* as I said before: but when we would express the decay, and signify that the sense is fading, old, and past, it is called *memory.* So that imagination and memory are but one thing, which for divers considerations hath divers names.

Much memory, or memory of many things, is called *experience.* Again, imagination being only of those things which have been formerly perceived by sense, either all at once, or by parts at several times; the former, which is the imagining the whole object as it was presented to the sense, is *simple* imagination, as when one imagineth a man, or horse, which he hath seen before. The other is *compounded;* as when, from the sight of a man at one time, and of a horse at another, we conceive in our mind a Centaur. So when a man compoundeth the image of his own person with the image of the actions of another man, as when a man imagines himself a Hercules or an Alexander, which happeneth often to them that are much taken with reading of romances, it is a compound imagination, and properly but a fiction of the mind. There be also other imaginations that rise in men, though waking, from the great impression made in sense: as from gazing upon the sun, the impression leaves an image of the sun before our eyes a long time after; and from being long and vehemently attent upon geometrical figures, a man shall in the dark, though awake, have the images of lines and angles before his eyes; which kind of fancy hath no particular name, as being a thing that doth not commonly fall into men's discourse.

The imaginations of them that sleep are those we call *dreams.* And these also, as all other imaginations, have been before, either totally or by parcels, in the sense. And because in sense, the brain and nerves, which are the necessary organs of sense, are so benumbed in sleep, as not easily to be moved by the action of external objects, there can happen in sleep no imagination, and therefore no dream, but what proceeds from the agitation of the inward parts of man's body; which inward parts, for the connexion they have with the brain, and other organs, when they be distempered, do keep the same in motion; whereby the imaginations there formerly made, appear as if a man were waking; saving that the organs of sense being now benumbed, so as there is no new object, which can master and obscure them with a more vigorous impression, a dream must needs be more clear, in this silence of sense, than our waking thoughts. And hence it cometh to pass, that it is a hard matter, and by many thought impossible, to distinguish exactly between sense and dreaming. For my part, when I consider that in dreams I do not often nor constantly think of the same persons, places, objects, and actions, that I do waking; nor remember so long a train of coherent thoughts, dreaming, as at other times; and because waking I often observe the absurdity of dreams, but never dream of the absurdities of my waking thoughts; I am well satisfied, that being awake, I know I dream not, though when I dream I think myself awake

And seeing dreams are caused by the distemper of some of the inward parts of the body, divers distempers must needs cause different dreams. And hence it is that lying cold breedeth dreams of fear, and raiseth the thought and image of some fearful object, the motion from the brain to the inner parts and from the inner parts to the brain being reciprocal; and that as anger causeth heat in some parts of the body when we are awake, so when we sleep the overheating of the same parts causeth anger, and raiseth up in the brain the imagination of an enemy. In the same manner, as natural kindness, when we are awake, causeth desire, and desire makes heat in certain other parts of the body; so also too much heat in those parts, while we sleep, raiseth in the brain an imagination of some kindness shown. In sum, our dreams are the reverse of our waking imaginations; the motion when we are awake beginning at one end, and when we dream at another.

The most difficult discerning of a man's dream, from his waking thoughts, is then, when by some accident we observe not that we have slept: which is easy to happen to a man full of fearful thoughts, and whose conscience is much troubled; and that sleepeth, without the circumstances of going to bed or putting off his clothes, as one that noddeth in a chair. For he that taketh pains, and industriously lays himself to sleep, in case any uncouth and exorbitant fancy come unto him, cannot easily think it other than a dream. We read of Marcus Brutus, (one that had his life given him by Julius Caesar, and was also his favourite, and notwithstanding murdered him), how at Philippi, the night before he gave battle to Augustus Caesar, he saw a fearful apparition, which is commonly related by historians as a vision; but considering the circumstances, one may easily judge to have been but a short dream. For sitting in his tent, pensive and troubled with the horror of his rash act, it was not hard for him, slumbering in the cold, to dream of that which most affrighted him; which fear, as by degrees it made him wake, so also it must needs make the apparition by degrees to vanish; and having no assurance that he slept, he could have no cause to think it a dream, or any thing but a vision. And this is no very rare accident; for even they that be perfectly awake, if they be timorous and superstitious, possessed with fearful tales, and alone in the dark, are subject to the like fancies, and believe they see spirits and dead men's ghosts walking in churchyards; whereas it is either their fancy only, or else the knavery of such persons as make use of such superstitious fear, to pass disguised in the night, to places they would not be known to haunt.

From this ignorance of how to distinguish dreams, and other strong fancies, from vision and sense, did arise the greatest part of the religion of the Gentiles in time past, that worshipped satyrs, fawns, nymphs, and the like; and now-a-days the opinion that rude people have of fairies, ghosts, and goblins, and of the power of witches. For as for witches, I think not that their witchcraft is any real power; but yet that they are justly punished, for the false belief they have that they can do such mischief, joined with their purpose to do it if they can; their trade being nearer to a new religion than to a craft or science. And for fairies, and walking ghosts, the opinion of them has, I think, been on purpose either taught or not confuted, to keep in credit the use of exorcism, of crosses, of holy water, and other such inventions of ghostly men. Nevertheless, there is no doubt, but God can make unnatural apparitions; but that he does it so often, as men need to fear such things, more than they fear the stay or change of the course of nature, which he also can stay, and change, is no point of Christian faith. But evil men under pretext that God can do any thing, are so bold as to say any thing when it serves their turn, though they think it untrue; it is the part of a wise man, to believe them no farther, that right reason makes that which they say, appear credible. If this superstitious fear of spirits were taken away, and with it, prognostics from dreams, false prophecies, and many other things depending thereon, by which crafty ambitious persons abuse the simple people, men would be much more fitted than they are for civil obedience.

And this ought to be the work of the schools: but they rather nourish such doctrine. For, not knowing what imagination or the senses are, what they receive, they teach: some saying, that imaginations rise of themselves, and have no cause; others, that they rise most commonly from the will; and that good thoughts are blown (inspired) into a man by God, and evil thoughts by the Devil; or that good thoughts are poured (infused) into a man by God, and evil ones by the Devil. Some say the senses receive the species of things, and deliver them to the common sense; and the common sense delivers them over to the fancy, and the fancy to the memory, and the memory to the judgment, like handing of things from one to another, with many words making nothing understood.

The imagination that is raised in man, or any other creature indued with the faculty of imagining, by words, or other voluntary signs, is that we generally call *understanding;* and is common to man and beast. For a dog by custom will understand the call, or the rating of his master; and so will many other beasts. That understanding which is peculiar to man, is the understanding not only his will, but his conceptions and thoughts, by the sequel and contexture of the names of things into affirmations, negations, and other forms of speech; and of this kind of understanding I shall speak hereafter.

CHAPTER III

Of the Consequence or Train of Imaginations

BY *Consequence,* or TRAIN of thoughts, I understand that succession of one thought to another, which is called, to distinguish it from discourse in words, *mental discourse.*

When a man thinketh on any thing whatsoever, his next thought after, is not altogether so casual as it seems to be. Not every thought to every thought succeeds indifferently. But as we have no imagination, whereof we have not formerly had sense, in whole, or in parts; so we have no transition from one imagination to another, whereof we never had the like before in our senses. The reason whereof is this. All fancies are motions within us, relics of those made in the sense: and those motions that immediately succeeded one another in the sense, continue also together after sense: insomuch as the former coming again to take place, and be predominant, the latter followeth, by coherence of the matter moved, in such manner, as water upon a plane table is drawn which way any one part of it is guided by the finger. But because in sense, to one and the same thing perceived, sometimes one thing, sometimes another succeedeth, it comes to pass in time, that in the imagining of any thing, there is no certainty what we shall imagine next; only this is certain, it shall be something that succeeded the same before, at one time or another.

This train of thoughts, or mental discourse, is of two sorts. The first is *unguided, without design,* and inconstant; wherein there is no passionate thought, to govern and direct those that follow, to itself, as the end and scope of some desire, or other passion: in which case the thoughts are said to wander, and seem impertinent one to another, as in a dream. Such are commonly the thoughts of men, that are not only without company, but also without care of any thing; though even then their thoughts are as busy as at other times, but without harmony; as the sound which a lute out of tune would yield to any man; or in tune, to one that could not play. And yet in this wild ranging of the mind, a man may oft-times perceive the way of it, and the dependance of one thought upon another. For in a discourse of our present civil war, what could seem more impertinent, than to ask, as one did, what was the value of a Roman penny? Yet the coherence to me was manifest enough. For the thought of the war, introduced the thought of the delivering up the king to his enemies; the thought of that, brought in the thought of the delivering up of Christ; and that again the thought of the thirty pence, which was the price of that treason; and thence easily followed that malicious question, and all this in a moment of time; for thought is quick.

The second is more constant; as being *regulated* by some desire, and design. For the impression made by such things as we desire, or fear, is strong, and permanent, or, if it cease for a time, of quick return: so strong it is sometimes, as to hinder and break our sleep. From desire, ariseth the thought of some means we have seen produce the like of that which we aim at; and from the thought of that, the thought of means to that mean; and so continually, till we come to some beginning within our own power. And because the end, by the greatness of the impression, comes often to mind, in case our thoughts begin to wander, they are quickly again reduced into the way: which observed by one of the seven wise men, made him give men this precept, which is now worn out, *Respice finem;* that is to say, in all your actions, look often upon what you would have, as the thing that directs all your thoughts in the way to attain it.

The train of regulated thoughts is of two kinds; one, when of an effect imagined we seek the causes, or means that produce it: and this is common to man and beast. The other is, when imagining any thing whatsoever, we seek all the possible effects, that can by it be produced; that is to say, we imagine what we can do with it, when we have it. Of which I have not at any time seen any sign, but in man only; for this is a curiosity hardly incident to the nature of any living creature that has no other passion but sensual, such as are hunger, thirst, lust, and anger. In sum, the discourse of the mind, when it is goverened by design, is nothing but *seeking,* or the faculty of invention, which the Latins called *sagacitas,* and *solertia;* a hunting out of the causes, of some effect, present or past; or of the effects, of some present or past cause. Sometimes a man seeks what he hath lost; and from that place, and time, wherein he misses it, his mind runs back, from place to place, and time to time, to find where, and when he had it; that is to say, to find some certain, and limited time and place, in which to begin a method of seeking. Again, from thence, his thoughts run over the same places and times, to find what action, or other occasion might make him lose it. This we call *remembrance,* or calling to mind: the Latins call it *reminiscentia,* as it were a *re-conning* of our former actions.

Sometimes a man knows a place determinate, within the compass whereof he is to seek; and then his thoughts run over all the parts thereof, in the same manner as one would sweep a room, to find a jewel; or as a spaniel ranges the field, till he find a scent; or as a man should run over the alphabet, to start a rhyme.

Sometimes a man desires to know the event of an action; and then he thinketh of some like action past, and the events thereof one after another; supposing like events will follow like actions. As he that foresees what will become of a criminal, recons what he has seen follow on the like crime before; having this order of thoughts, the crime, the officer, the prison, the judge, and the gallows. Which kind of thoughts, is called *foresight,* and *prudence,* or *providence;* and sometimes *wisdom;* though such conjecture, through the difficulty of observing all circumstances, be very fallacious. But this is certain; by how much one man has more experience of things past, than another, by so much also he is more prudent, and his expectations the seldomer fail him. The *present* only has a being in nature; things *past* have a being in the memory only, but things *to come* have no being at all; the *future* being but a fiction of the mind, applying the sequels of actions past, to the actions that are present; which with most certainty is done by him that has most experience, but not with certainty enough. And though it be called prudence, when the event answereth our expectation; yet in its own nature, it is but presumption. For the foresight of things to come, which is providence, belongs only to him by whose will they are to come. From him only, and supernaturally, proceeds prophecy. The best prophet naturally is the best guesser; and the best guesser, he that is most versed and studied in the matters he guesses at: for he hath most *signs* to guess by.

A *sign* is the evident antecedent of the consequent; and contrarily, the consequent of the antecedent, when the like consequences have been observed, before: and the oftener they have been observed, the less uncertain is the sign. And therefore he that has most experience in any kind of business, has most signs, whereby to guess at the future time; and consequently is the most prudent: and so much more prudent than he that is new in that kind of business, as not to be equalled by any advantage of natural and extemporary wit: though perhaps many young men think the contrary.

Nevertheless it is not prudence that distinguisheth man from beast. There be beasts, that at a year old observe more, and pursue that which is for their good, more prudently, than a child can do at ten.

As prudence is a *presumption* of the *future,* contracted from the *experience* of time *past:* so there is a presumption of things past taken from other things, not future, but past also. For he that hath seen by what courses and degrees a flourishing state hath first come into civil war, and then to ruin; upon the sight of the ruins of any other state, will guess, the like war, and the like courses have been there also. But this conjecture, has the same uncertainty almost with the conjecture of the future; both being grounded only upon experience.

There is no other act of man's mind, that I can remember, naturally planted in him, so as to need no other thing, to the exercise of it, but to be born a man, and live with the use of his five senses. Those other faculties, of which I shall speak by and by, and which seem proper to man only, are acquired and increased by study and industry; and of most men learned by instruction, and discipline; and proceed all from the invention of words, and speech. For besides sense, and thoughts, and the train of thoughts, the mind of man has no other motion; though by the help of speech, and method, the same faculties may be improved to such a height, as to distinguish men from all other living creatures.

Whatsoever we imagine is *finite*. Therefore there is no idea, or conception of any thing we call *infinite*. No man can have in his mind an image of infinite magnitude; nor conceive infinite swiftness, infinite time, or infinite force, or infinite power. When we say any thing is infinite, we signify only, that we are not able to conceive the ends, and bounds of the things named; having no conception of the thing, but of our own inability. And therefore the name of God is used, not to make us conceive him, for he is incomprehensible; and his greatness, and power are unconceivable; but that we may honour him. Also because, whatsoever, as I said before, we conceive, has been perceived first by sense, either all at once, or by parts; a man can have no thought, representing any thing, not subject to sense. No man therefore can conceive any thing, but he must conceive it in some place; and indued with some determinate magnitude; and which may be divided into parts; nor that any thing is all in this place, and all in another place at the same time; nor that two, or more things can be in one, and the same place at once: for none of these things ever have, nor can be incident to sense; but are absurd speeches, taken upon credit, without any signification at all from deceived philosophers, and deceived, or deceiving schoolmen.[2]

CHAPTER VI

Of the Interior Beginnings of Voluntary Motions; Commonly Called the Passions; and the Speeches by which they are Expressed

THERE be in animals, two sorts of *motions* peculiar to them: one called *vital;* begun in generation, and continued without interruption through their whole life; such as are the *course* of the *blood,* the *pulse,* the *breathing,* the *concoction, nutrition, excretion,* &c. to which motions there needs no help of imagination: the other is *animal motion,* otherwise called *voluntary motion; as to go, to speak;* to *move* any of our limbs, in such manner as is first fancied in our minds. That sense is motion in the organs and interior parts of man's body, caused by the action of the things we see, hear, &c.; and that fancy is but the relics of the same motion, remaining after sense, has been already said in the first and second chapters. And because *going, speaking,* and the

2. [The term 'schoolmen' was applied to medieval theologians and philosophers, often with a connotation of pedantry.]

like voluntary motions, depend always upon a precedent thought of *whither, which way,* and *what;* it is evident, that the imagination is the first internal beginning of all voluntary motion. And although unstudied men do not conceive any motion at all to be there, where the thing moved is invisible; or the space it is moved in is, for the shortness of it, insensible; yet that doth not hinder, but that such motions are. For let a space be never so little, that which is moved over a greater space, whereof that little one is part, must first be moved over that. These small beginnings of motion, within the body of man, before they appear in walking, speaking, striking, and other visible actions, are commonly called ENDEAVOR.

This endeavour, when it is toward something which causes it, is called APPETITE, or DESIRE: the latter, being the general name; and the other oftentimes restrained to signify the desire of food, namely *hunger* and *thirst.* And when the endeavour is from-ward something, it is generally called AVERSION. These words, *appetite* and *aversion,* we have from the Latins; and they both of them signify the motions, one of approaching, the other of retiring. So also do the Greek words for the same, which are ὁρμὴ and ἀφορμὴ. For nature itself does often press upon men those truths, which afterwards, when they look for somewhat beyond nature, they stumble at. For the Schools find in mere appetite to go, or move, no actual motion at all: but because some motion they must acknowledge, they call it metaphorical motion; which is but an absurd speech: for though words may be called metaphorical; bodies and motions can not.

That which men desire, they are also said to LOVE: and to HATE those things for which they have aversion. So that desire and love are the same thing; save that by desire, we always signify the absence of the object; by love, most commonly the presence of the same. So also by aversion, we signify the absence; and by hate, the presence of the object.

Of appetites and aversions, some are born with men; as appetite of food, appetite of excretion, and exoneration, which may also and more properly be called aversions, from somewhat they feel in their bodies; and some other appetites, not many. The rest, which are appetites of particular things, proceed from experience, and trial of their effects upon themselves or other men. For of things we know not at all, or believe not to be, we can have no further desire, than to taste and try. But aversion we have for things, not only which we know have hurt us, but also that we do not know whether they will hurt us, or not.

Those things which we neither desire, nor hate, we are said to *contemn;* CON-TEMPT being nothing else but an immobility, or contumacy of the heart, in resisting the action of certain things; and proceeding from that the heart is already moved otherwise, by other more potent objects; or from want of experience of them.

And because the constitution of a man's body is in continual mutation, it is impossible that all the same things should always cause in him the same appetites, and aversions: much less can all men consent, in the desire of almost any one and the same object.

But whatsoever is the object of any man's appetite or desire, that is it which he for his part calleth *good:* and the object of his hate and aversion, *evil;* and of his contempt, *vile* and *inconsiderable.* For these words of good, evil, and contemptible, are ever used with relation to the person that useth them: there being nothing simply and absolutely so; nor any common rule of good and evil, to be taken from the nature of the objects themselves; but from the person of the man, where there is no commonwealth; or, in a commonwealth, from the person that representeth it; or from an arbitrator or judge, whom men disagreeing shall by consent set up, and make his sentence the rule thereof.

The Latin tongue has two words, whose significations approach to those of good and evil; but are not precisely the same; and those are *pulchrum* and *turpe*. Whereof the former signifies that, which by some apparent signs promiseth good; and the latter, that which promiseth evil. But in our tongue we have not so general names to express them by. But for *pulchrum* we say in some things, *fair;* in others, *beautiful,* or *handsome,* or *gallant,* or *honourable,* or *comely,* or *amiable;* and for *turpe, foul, deformed, ugly, base, nauseous,* and the like, as the subject shall require; all which words, in their proper places, signify nothing else but the *mien,* or countenance, that promiseth good and evil. So that good there be three kinds; good in the promise, that is *pulchrum;* good in effect, as the end desired, which is called *jucundum, delightful;* and good as the means, which is called *utile, profitable;* and as many of evil: for *evil* in promise, is that they call *turpe;* evil in effect, and end, is *molestum, unpleasant, troublesome;* and evil in the means, *inutile, unprofitable, hurtful.*

As, in sense, that which is really within us, is, as I have said before, only motion, caused by the action of external objects, but in appearance; to the sight, light and colour; to the ear, sound; to the nostril, odour, &c.: so, when the action of the same object is continued from the eyes, ears, and other organs to the heart, the real effect there is nothing but motion, or endeavour; which consisteth in appetite, or aversion, to or from the object moving. But the apparence, or sense of that motion, is that we either call *delight,* or *trouble of mind.*

This motion, which is called appetite, and for the apparence of it *delight,* and *pleasure,* seemeth to be a corroboration of vital motion, and a help thereunto; and therefore such things as caused delight, were not improperly called *jucunda, à juvando,* from helping or fortifying; and the contrary, *molesta, offensive,* from hindering, and troubling the motion vital.

Pleasure therefore, or *delight,* is the apparence, or sense of good; and *molestation,* or *displeasure,* the apparence, or sense of evil. And consequently all appetite, desire, and love, is accompanied with some delight more or less; and all hatred and aversion, with more or less displeasure and offence.

Of pleasures or delights, some arise from the sense of an object present; and those may be called *pleasure of sense;* the word *sensual,* as it is used by those only that condemn them, having no place till there be laws. Of this kind are all onerations and exonerations of the body; as also all that is pleasant, in the *sight, hearing, smell, taste,* or *touch.* Others arise from the expectation, that proceeds from foresight of the end, or consequence of things; whether those things in the sense please or displease. And these are *pleasures of the mind* of him that draweth those consequences, and are generally called JOY. In the like manner, displeasures are some in the sense, and called PAIN; others in the expectation of consequences, and are called GRIEF.

These simple passions called *appetite, desire, love, aversion, hate, joy,* and *grief,* have their names for divers considerations diversified. As first, when they one succeed another, they are diversely called from the opinion men have of the likelihood of attaining what they desire. Secondly, from the object loved or hated. Thirdly, from the consideration of many of them together. Fourthly, from the alteration or succession itself.

For *appetite,* with an opinion of attaining, is called HOPE.

The same, without such opinion, DESPAIR.

Aversion, with opinion of HURT from the object, FEAR.

The same, with hope of avoiding that hurt by resistance, COURAGE.

Sudden *courage,* ANGER.

Constant *hope,* CONFIDENCE of ourselves.

Constant *despair,* DIFFIDENCE of ourselves.

Anger for great hurt done to another, when we conceive the same to be done by injury, INDIGNATION.

Desire of good to another, BENEVOLENCE, GOOD WILL, CHARITY. If to man generally, GOOD NATURE.

Desire of riches, COVETOUSNESS: a name used always in signification of blame; because men contending for them, are displeased with one another attaining them; though the desire in itself, be to be blamed, or allowed, according to the means by which these riches are sought.

Desire of office, or precedence, AMBITION: a name used also in the worse sense, for the reason before mentioned.

Desire of things that conduce but a little to our ends, and fear of things that are but of little hindrance, PUSILLANIMITY.

Contempt of little helps and hindrances, MAGNANIMITY.

Magnanimity, in danger of death or wounds, VALOUR, FORTITUDE.

Magnanimity in the use of riches, LIBERALTITY.

Pusillanimity in the same, WRETCHEDNESS, MISERABLENESS, or PARSIMONY; as it is liked or disliked.

Love of persons for society, KINDNESS.

Love of persons for pleasing the sense only, NATURAL LUST.

Love of the same, acquired from rumination, that is, imagination of pleasure past, LUXURY.

Love of one singularly, with desire to be singularly beloved, THE PASSION OF LOVE. The same, with fear that the love is not mutual, JEALOUSY.

Desire, by doing hurt to another, to make him condemn some fact of his own, REVENGEFULNESS.

Desire to know why, and how, CURIOSITY; such as is in no living creature but *man:* so that man is distinguished, not only by his reason, but also by this singular passion from other *animals;* in whom the appetite of food, and other pleasures of sense, by predominance, take away the care of knowing causes; which is a lust of the mind, that by a perseverance of delight in the continual and indefatigable generation of knowledge, exceedeth the short vehemence of any carnal pleasure.

Fear of power invisible, feigned by the mind, or imagined from tales publicly allowed, RELIGION: not allowed, SUPERSTITION. And when the power imagined, is truly such as we imagine, TRUE RELIGION.

Fear, without the apprehension of why, or what, PANIC TERROR, called so from the fables, that make Pan the author of them; whereas, in truth, there is always in him that so feareth, first, some apprehension of the cause, though the rest run away by example, every one supposing his fellow to know why. And therefore this passion happens to none but in a throng, or multitude of people.

Joy, from apprehension of novelty, ADMIRATION; proper to man, because it excites the appetite of knowing the cause.

Joy, arising from imagination of a man's own power and ability; is that exultation of the mind which is called GLORYING: which if grounded upon the experience of his own former actions, is the same with *confidence:* but if grounded on the flattery of others; or only supposed by himself, for delight in the consequences of it, is called VAINGLORY: which name is properly given; because a well grounded *confidence* begetteth attempt; whereas the supposing of power does not, and is therefore rightly called *vain.*

Grief, from opinion of want of power is called DEJECTION of mind.

The *vain-glory* which consisteth in the feigning or supposing of abilities in ourselves, which we know are not, is most incident to young men, and nourished by the histories, or fictions of gallant persons; and is corrected oftentimes by age, and employment.

Sudden glory is the passion which maketh those *grimaces* called LAUGHTER; and is caused either by some sudden act of their own, that pleaseth them; or by the apprehension of some deformed thing in another, by comparison whereof they suddenly applaud themselves. And it is incident most to them, that are conscious of the fewest abilities in themselves; who are forced to keep themselves in their own favour, by observing the imperfections of other men. And therefore much laughter at the defects of others, is a sign of pusillanimity. For of great minds, one of the proper works is, to help and free others from scorn; and compare themselves only with the most able.

On the contrary, *sudden dejection,* is the passion that causeth WEEPING; and is caused by such accidents, as suddenly take away some vehement hope, or some prop of their power: and they are most subject to it, that rely principally on helps external, such as are women, and children. Therefore some weep for the loss of friends; others for their unkindness; others for the sudden stop made to their thoughts of revenge, by reconciliation. But in all cases, both laughter, and weeping, are sudden motions; custom taking them both away. For no man laughs at old jests; or weeps for an old calamity.

Grief, for the discovery of some defect of ability, is SHAME, or the passion that discovereth itself in BLUSHING; and consisteth in the apprehension of some thing dishonourable; and in young men, is a sign of the love of good reputation, and commendable: in old men it is a sign of the same; but because it comes too late, not commendable.

The *contempt* of good reputation is called IMPUDENCE.

Grief, for the calamity of another, is PITY; and ariseth from the imagination that the like calamity may befall himself; and therefore is called also COMPASSION, and in the phrase of this present time a FELLOW-FEELING: and therefore for calamity arriving from great wickedness, the best men have the least pity; and for the same calamity, those hate pity, that think themselves least obnoxious to the same.

Contempt, or little sense of the calamity of others, is that which men call CRUELTY; proceeding from security of their own fortune. For, that any man should take pleasure in other men's great harms; without other end of his own, I do not conceive it possible.

Grief, for the success of a competitor in wealth, honour, or other good, if it be

joined with endeavor to enforce our own abilities to equal or exceed him, is called
EMULATION: but joined with endeavour to supplant or hinder a competitor, ENVY.

When in the mind of man, appetites, and aversions, hopes, and fears, concerning
one and the same thing, arise alternately; and divers good and evil consequences of
the doing, or omitting the thing propounded, come successively into our thoughts;
so that sometimes we have an appetite to it; sometimes an aversion from it; sometimes hope to be able to do it; sometimes despair, or fear to attempt it; the whole
sum of desires, aversions, hopes and fears continued till the thing be either done, or
thought impossible, is that we call DELIBERATION.

Therefore of things past, there is no *deliberation;* because manifestly impossible to
be changed: nor of things known to be impossible, or thought so; because men
know, or think such deliberation vain. But of things impossible, which we think possible, we may deliberate; not knowing it is in vain. And it is called *deliberation;* because it is a putting an end to the *liberty* we had of doing, or omitting, according to
our own appetite, or aversion.

This alternate succession of appetites, aversions, hopes and fears, is no less in
other living creatures than in man: and therefore beasts also deliberate.

Every *deliberation* is then said to *end,* when that whereof they deliberate, is either
done, or thought impossible; because till then we retain the liberty of doing, or
omitting; according to our appetite, or aversion.

In *deliberation,* the last appetite, or aversion, immediately adhering to the action,
or to the omission thereof, is that we call the WILL; the act, not the faculty, of *willing.* And beasts that have *deliberation,* must necessarily also have *will.* The definition
of the *will,* given commonly by the Schools, that it is a *rational appetite,* is not good.
For if it were, then could there be no voluntary act against reason. For a *voluntary act*
is that, which proceedeth from the *will,* and no other. But if instead of a rational appetite, we shall say an appetite resulting from a precedent deliberation, then the
definition is the same that I have given here. *Will* therefore *is the last appetite in
deliberating.* And though we say in common discourse, a man had a will once to do a
thing, that nevertheless he forebore to do; yet that is properly but an inclination,
which makes no action voluntary; because the action depends not of it, but of the
last inclination, or appetite. For if the intervenient appetites, make any action
voluntary; then by the same reason all intervenient aversions, should make the same
action involuntary; and so one and the same action, should be both voluntary and
involuntary.

By this it is manifest, that not only actions that have their beginning from
covetousness, ambition, lust, or other appetites to the thing propounded; but also
those that have their beginning from aversion, or fear of those consequences that
follow the omission, are *voluntary actions.*

The forms of speech by which the passions are expressed, are partly the same,
and partly different from those, by which we express our thoughts. And first, generally all passions may be expressed *indicatively;* as *I love, I fear, I joy, I deliberate, I will,
I command:* but some of them have particular expressions by themselves, which
nevertheless are not affirmations, unless it be when they serve to make other
inferences, besides that of the passion they proceed from. Deliberation is expressed
subjunctively; which is a speech proper to signify suppositions, with their consequences: as, *if this be done, then this will follow;* and differs not from the language of
reasoning, save that reasoning is in general words; but deliberation for the most

part is of particulars. The language of desire, and aversion, is *imperative; as do this, forbear that;* which when the party is obliged to do, or forbear, is *command;* otherwise *prayer;* or else *counsel.* The language of vain-glory, of indignation, pity and re-vengefulness, *optative;* but of the desire to know, there is a peculiar expression, called *interrogative;* as, *what is it, when shall it, how is it done,* and *why so?* other language of the passions I find none: for cursing, swearing, reviling, and the like, do not signify as speech; but as the actions of a tongue accustomed.

These forms of speech, I say, are expressions, or voluntary significations of our passions: but certain signs they be not; because they may be used arbitrarily, whether they that use them, have such passions or not. The best signs of passions present, are either in the countenance, motions of the body, actions, and ends, or aims, which we otherwise know the man to have.

And because in deliberation, the appetites, and aversions, are raised by foresight of the good and evil consequences, and sequels of the action whereof we deliberate; the good or evil effect thereof dependeth on the foresight of a long chain of conse-quences of which very seldom any man is able to see to the end. But for so far as a man seeth, if the good in those consequences be greater than the evil, the whole chain is that which writers call *apparent,* or *seeming good.* And contrarily, when the evil exceedeth the good, the whole is *apparent,* or *seeming evil:* so that he who hath by experience, or reason, the greatest and surest prospect of consequences, deliberates best himself; and is able when we will, to give the best counsel unto others.

Continual success in obtaining those things which a man from time to time desireth, that is to say, continual prospering, is that men call FELICITY; I mean the felicity of this life. For there is no such thing as perpetual tranquillity of mind, while we live here; because life itself is but motion, and can never be without desire, nor without fear, no more than without sense. What kind of felicity God hath ordained to them that devoutly honour Him, a man shall no sooner know, than enjoy; being joys, that now are as incomprehensible, as the word of schoolmen *beatifical vision* is unintelligible.

The form of speech whereby men signify their opinion of the goodness of any thing, is PRAISE. That whereby they signify the power and greatness of any thing, is MAGNIFYING. And that whereby they signify the opinion they have of a man's felicity, is by the Greeks called μακαρισμός, for which we have no name in our tongue. And thus much is sufficient for the present purpose, to have been said of the PASSIONS.

CHAPTER XIII

Of the Natural Condition of Mankind as Concerning their Felicity, and Misery

NATURE hath made men so equal, in the faculties of the body, and mind; as that though there be found one man sometimes manifestly stronger in body, or of quicker mind than another; yet when all is reckoned together, the difference be-tween man, and man, is not so considerable, as that one man can thereupon claim to himself any benefit, to which another may not pretend, as well as he. For as to the strength of body, the weakest has strength enough to kill the strongest, either by secret machination, or by confederacy with others, that are in the same danger with himself.

And as to the faculties of the mind, setting aside the arts grounded upon words, and especially that skill of proceeding upon general, and infallible rules, called science; which very few have, and but in few things; as being not a native faculty, born with us; nor attained, as prudence, while we look after somewhat else, I find yet a greater equality amongst men, than that of strength. For prudence, is but experience; which equal time, equally bestows on all men, in those things they equally apply themselves unto. That which may perhaps make such equality incredible, is but a vain conceit of one's own wisdom, which almost all men think they have in a greater degree, than the vulgar; that is, than all men but themselves, and a few others, whom by fame, or for concurring with themselves, they approve. For such is the nature of men, that howsoever they may acknowledge many others to be more witty, or more eloquent, or more learned; yet they will hardly believe there be many so wise as themselves; for they see their own wit at hand, and other men's at a distance. But this proveth rather than men are in that point equal, than unequal. For there is not ordinarily a greater sign of the equal distribution of any thing, than that every man is contented with his share.

From this equality of ability, ariseth equality of hope in the attaining of our ends. And therefore if any two men desire the same thing, which nevertheless they cannot both enjoy, they become enemies; and in the way to their end, which is principally their own conservation, and sometimes their delectation only, endeavour to destroy, or subdue one another. And from hence it comes to pass, that where an invader hath no more to fear, than another man's single power; if one plant, sow, build, or possess a convenient seat, others may probably be expected to come prepared with forces united, to dispossess, and deprive him, not only of the fruit of his labour, but also of his life, or liberty. And the invader again is in the like danger of another.

And from this diffidence of one another, there is no way for any man to secure himself, so reasonable, as anticipation; that is, by force, or wiles, to master the persons of all men he can, so long, till he see no other power great enough to endanger him: and this is no more than his own conservation requireth, and is generally allowed. Also because there be some, that taking pleasure in contemplating their own power in the acts of conquest, which they pursue farther than their security requires; if others, that otherwise would be glad to be at ease within modest bounds, should not by invasion increase their power, they would not be able, long time, by standing only on their defence, to subsist. And by consequence, such augmentation of dominion over men being necessary to a man's conservation, it ought to be allowed him.

Again, men have no pleasure, but on the contrary a great deal of grief, in keeping company, where there is no power able to over-awe them all. For every man looketh that his companion should value him, at the same rate he sets upon himself: and upon all signs of contempt, or undervaluing, naturally endeavours, as far as he dares, (which amongst them that have no common power to keep them in quiet, is far enough to make them destroy each other), to extort a greater value from his contemners, by damage; and from others, by the example.

So that in the nature of man, we find three principal causes of quarrel. First, competition; secondly, diffidence; thirdly, glory.

The first, maketh men invade for gain; the second, for safety; and the third, for reputation. The first use violence, to make themselves masters of other men's persons, wives, children, and cattle; the second, to defend them; the third, for trifles, as a word, a smile, a different opinion, and any other sign of undervalue, either direct in their persons, or by reflection in their kindred, their friends, their nation, their profession, or their name.

Hereby it is manifest, that during the time men live without a common power to keep them all in awe, they are in that condition which is called war; and such a war, as is of every man, against every man. For WAR, consisteth not in battle only, or the act of fighting; but in a tract of time, wherein the will to contend by battle is sufficiently known: and therefore the notion of *time*, is to be considered in the nature of war; as it is in the nature of weather. For as the nature of foul weather, lieth not in a shower or two of rain; but in an inclination thereto of many days together: so the nature of war, consisteth not in actual fighting; but in the known disposition thereto, during all the time there is no assurance to the contrary. All other time is PEACE.

Whatsoever therefore is consequent to a time of war, where every man is enemy to every man; the same is consequent to the time, wherein men live without other security, than what their own strength, and their own invention shall furnish them withal. In such condition, there is no place for industry; because the fruit thereof is uncertain: and consequently no culture of the earth; no navigation, nor use of the commodities that may be imported by sea; no commodious building; no instruments of moving, and removing, such things as require much force; no knowledge of the face of the earth; no account of time; no arts; no letters; no society; and which is worst of all, continual fear, and danger of violent death; and the life of man, solitary, poor, nasty, brutish, and short.

It may seem strange to some man, that has not well weighed these things; that nature should thus dissociate, and render men apt to invade, and destroy one another: and he may therefore, not trusting to this inference, made from the passions, desire perhaps to have the same confirmed by experience. Let him therefore consider with himself, when taking a journey, he arms himself, and seeks to go well accompanied; when going to sleep, he locks his doors; when even in his house he locks his chests; and this when he knows there be laws, and public officers, armed, to revenge all injuries shall be done him; what opinion he has of his fellow-subjects, when he rides armed; of his fellow citizens, when he locks his doors; and of his children, and servants, when he locks his chests. Does he not there as much accuse mankind by his actions, as I do by my words? But neither of us accuse man's nature in it. The desires, and other passions of man, are in themselves no sin. No more are the actions, that proceed from those passions, till they know a law that forbids them: which till laws be made they cannot know: nor can any law be made, till they have agreed upon the person that shall make it.

It may peradventure be thought, there was never such a time, nor condition of war as this; and I believe it was never generally so, over all the world: but there are many places, where they live so now. For the savage people in many places of America, except the government of small families, the concord whereof dependeth on natural lust, have no government at all; and live at this day in that brutish manner, as I said before. Howsoever, it may be perceived what manner of life there would be, where there were no common power to fear, by the manner of life, which men that have formerly lived under a peaceful government, use to degenerate into, in a civil war.

But though there had never been any time, wherein particular men were in a condition of war one against another; yet in all times, kings, and persons of sovereign authority, because of their independency, are in continual jealousies, and in the state and posture of gladiators; having their weapons pointing, and their eyes fixed on one another; that is, their forts, garrisons, and guns upon the frontiers of their kingdoms; and continual spies upon their neighbours; which is a posture of war. But because they uphold thereby, the industry of their subjects; there does not follow from it, that misery, which accompanies the liberty of particular men.

To this war of every man, against every man, this also is consequent; that nothing can be unjust. The notions of right and wrong, justice and injustice have there no place. Where there is no common power, there is no law: where no law, no injustice. Force, and fraud, are in war the two cardinal virtues. Justice, and injustice are none of the faculties neither of the body, nor mind. If they were, they might be in a man that were alone in the world, as well as his senses, and passions. They are qualities, that relate to men in society, not in solitude. It is consequent also to the same condition, that there be no propriety, no dominion, no *mine* and *thine* distinct; but only that to be every man's, that he can get it; and for so long, as he can keep it. And thus much for the ill condition, which man by mere nature is actually placed in; though with a possibility to come out of it, consisting partly in the passions, partly in his reason.

The passions that incline men to peace, are fear of death; desire of such things as are necessary to commodious living; and a hope by their industry to obtain them. And reason suggesteth convenient articles of peace, upon which men may be drawn to agreement. These articles, are they, which otherwise are called the Laws of Nature: whereof I shall speak more particularly, in the two following chapters.

CHAPTER XIV

Of the First and Second Natural Laws, and of Contracts

THE RIGHT OF NATURE, which writers commonly call *jus naturale,* is the liberty each man hath, to use his own power, as he will himself, for the preservation of his own nature; that is to say, of his own life; and consequently, of doing any thing, which in his own judgment, and reason, he shall conceive to be the aptest means thereunto.

By LIBERTY, is understood, according to the proper signification of the word, the absence of external impediments: which impediments, may oft take away part of a man's power to do what he would; but cannot hinder him from using the power left him, according as his judgment, and reason shall dictate to him.

A LAW OF NATURE, *lex naturalis,* is a precept or general rule, found out by reason, by which a man is forbidden to do that, which is destructive of his life, or taketh away the means of preserving the same; and to omit that, by which he thinketh it may be best preserved. For though they that speak of this subject, use to confound *jus,* and *lex, right* and *law:* yet they ought to be distinguished; because RIGHT, consisteth in liberty to do, or to forbear; whereas LAW, determineth, and bindeth to one of them: so that law, and right, differ as much, as obligation, and liberty; which in one and the same matter are inconsistent.

And because the condition of man, as hath been declared in the precedent chapter, is a condition of war of every one against every one: in which case every one is governed by his own reason; and there is nothing he can make use of, that may not be a help unto him, in preserving his life against his enemies; it followeth, that in such a condition, every man has a right to every thing; even to one another's body. And therefore, as long as this natural right of every man to every thing endureth, there can be no security to any man, how strong or wise soever he be, of living out the time, which nature ordinarily alloweth men to live; and consequently it is a precept, or general rule of reason, *that every man, ought to endeavour peace, as far as he has hope of obtaining it; and when he cannot obtain it, that he may seek, and use, all helps, and advantages of war.* The first branch of which rule, containeth the first, and fundamental law of nature; which is, *to seek peace, and follow it.* The second, the sum of the right of nature; which is, *by all means we can, to defend ourselves.*

From this fundamental law of nature, by which men are commanded to endeavour peace, is derived this second law; *that a man be willing, when others are so too, as far-forth, as for peace, and defence of himself he shall think it necessary, to lay down this right to all things; and be contented with so much liberty against other men, as he would allow other men against himself.* For as long as every man holdeth this right, of doing any thing he liketh; so long are all men in the condition of war. But if other men will not lay down their right, as well as he; then there is no reason for any one, to divest himself of his: for that were to expose himself to prey, which no man is bound to, rather than to dispose himself to peace. This is that law of the Gospel; *whatsoever you require that others should do to you, that do ye to them.* And that law of all men, *quod tibi fieri non vis, alteri ne feceris.*

To *lay down* a man's *right* to any thing, is to *divest* himself of the *liberty,* of hindering another of the benefit of his own right to the same. For he that renounceth, or passeth away his right, giveth not to any other man a right which he had not before; because there is nothing to which every man had not right by nature: but only standeth out of his way, that he may enjoy his own original right, without hindrance from him; not without hindrance from another. So that the effect which redoundeth to one man, by another man's defect of right, is but so much diminution of impediments to the use of his own right original.

Right is laid aside, either by simply renouncing it; or by transferring it to another. By *simply* RENOUNCING; when he cares not to whom the benefit thereof redoundeth. By TRANSFERRING; when he intendeth the benefit thereof to some certain person, or persons. And when a man hath in either manner abandoned, or granted away his right; then he is said to be OBLIGED, or BOUND, not to hinder those, to whom such right is granted, or abandoned, from the benefit of it: and that he *ought,* and it is his DUTY, not to make void that voluntary act of his own: and that such hindrance is INJUSTICE, and INJURY, as being *sine jure;* the right being before renounced, or transferred. So that *injury,* or *injustice,* in the controversies of the world, is somewhat like to that, which in the disputations of scholars is called *absurdity.* For as it is there called an absurdity, to contradict what one maintained in the beginning: so in the world, it is called injustice, and injury, voluntarily to undo that, which from the beginning he had voluntarily done. The way by which a man either simply renounceth, or transferreth his right, is a declaration, or signification, by some voluntary and sufficient sign, or signs, that he doth so renounce, or transfer; or hath so renounced, or transferred the same, to him that accepteth it. And these signs are either words only, or actions only; or, as it happeneth most often, both words, and actions. And the same are the BONDS, by which men are bound, and obliged: bonds, that have their strength, not from their own nature, for nothing is more easily broken than a man's word, but from fear of some evil consequence upon that rupture.

Whensoever a man transferreth his right, or renounceth it; it is either in consideration of some right reciprocally transferred to himself; or for some other good he hopeth for thereby. For it is a voluntary act: and of the voluntary acts of every man, the object is some *good to himself.* And therefore there be some rights, which no man can be understood by any words, or other signs, to have abandoned, or transferred. As first a man cannot lay down the right of resisting them, that assault him by force, to take away his life; because he cannot be understood to aim thereby, at any good to himself. The same may be said of wounds, and chains, and imprisonment; both because there is no benefit consequent to such patience; as there is to the patience of suffering another to be wounded, or imprisoned: as also because a man cannot tell, when he seeth men proceed against him by violence, whether they intend his death or not. And lastly the motive, and end for which this renouncing, and transferring of right is introduced, is nothing else but the security of a man's person, in his life, and in the means of so preserving life, as not to be weary of it. And therefore if a man by words, or other signs, seem to despoil himself of the end, for which those signs were intended; he is not to be understood as if he meant it, or that it was his will; but that he was ignorant of how such words and actions were to be interpreted.

The mutual transferring of right, is that which men call CONTRACT.

There is difference between transferring of right to the thing; and transferring, or tradition, that is delivery of the thing itself. For the thing may be delivered together with the translation of the right; as in buying and selling with ready-money; or exchange of goods, or lands: and it may be delivered some time after.

Again, one of the contractors, may deliver the thing contracted for on his part, and leave the other to perform his part at some determinate time after, and in the mean time be trusted; and then the contract on his part, is called PACT, or COVENANT: or both parts may contract now, to perform hereafter: in which cases, he that is to perform in time to come, being trusted, his performance is called *keeping of promise,* or faith; and the failing of performance, if it be voluntary, *violation of faith.*

When the transferring of right, is not mutual: but one of the parties transferreth, in hope to gain thereby friendship, or service from another, or from his friends; or in hope to gain the reputation of charity, or magnanimity; or to deliver his mind from the pain of compassion; or in hope of reward in heaven; this is not contract, but GIFT, FREEGIFT, GRACE: which words signify one and the same thing.

Signs of contract, are either *express,* or *by inference.* Express, are words spoken with understanding of what they signify: and such words are either of the time *present,* or *past;* as, *I give, I grant, I have given, I have granted, I will that this be yours:* or of the future; as, I will give, I will grant: which words of the future are called PROMISE.

Signs by inference, are sometimes the consequence of words; sometimes the consequence of silence; sometimes the consequence of actions; sometimes the consequence of forbearing an action: and generally a sign by inference, of any contract, is whatsoever sufficiently argues the will of the contractor.

Words alone, if they be of the time to come, and contain a bare promise, are an insufficient sign of a free-gift, and therefore not obligatory. For if they be of the time to come, as *tomorrow I will give*, they are a sign I have not given yet, and consequently that my right is not transferred, but remaineth till I transfer it by some other act. But if the words be of the time present, or past, as, *I have given*, or, *do give to be delivered tomorrow*, then is my tomorrow's right given away today; and that by the virtue of the words, though there were no other argument of my will. And there is a great difference in the signification of these words, *volo hoc tuum esse cras*, and *cras dabo;* that is, between *I will that this be thine tomorrow*, and, *I will give it thee tomorrow:* for the word *I will*, in the former manner of speech, signifies an act of the will present; but in the latter, it signifies a promise of an act of the will to come: and therefore the former words, being of the present, transfer a future right; the latter, that be of the future, transfer nothing. But if there be other signs of the will to transfer a right, besides words; then, though the gift be free, yet may the right be understood to pass by words of the future: as if a man propound a prize to him that comes first to the end of a race, the gift is free; and though the words be of the future, yet the right passeth: for if he would not have his words so be understood, he should not have let them run.

In contracts, the right passeth, not only where the words are on the time present, or past, but also where they are of the future: because all contract is mutual translation, or change of right; and therefore he that promiseth only, because he hath already received the benefit for which he promiseth, is to be understood as if he intended the right should pass: for unless he had been content to have his words so understood, the other would not have performed his part first. And for that cause, in buying, and selling, and other acts of contract, a promise is equivalent to a covenant; and therefore obligatory.

He that performeth first in the case of a contract, is said to MERIT that which he is to receive by the performance of the other; and he hath it as *due*. Also when a prize is propounded to many, which is to be given to him only that winneth; or money is thrown amongst many, to be enjoyed by them that catch it; though this be a free gift; yet so to win, or so to catch, is to *merit*, and to have it as DUE. For the right is transferred in the propounding of the prize, and in throwing down the money; though it be not determined to whom, but by the event of the contention. But there is between these two sorts of merit, this difference, that in contract, I merit by virtue of my own power, and the contractor's need; but in this case of free gift, I am enabled to merit only by the benignity of the giver: in contract, I merit at the contractor's hand that he should depart with his right; in this case of gift, I merit not that the giver should part with his right; but that when he has parted with it, it should be mine, rather than another's. And this I think to be the meaning of that distinction of the Schools, between *meritum congrui*, and *meritum condigni*.[3] For God Almighty, having promised Paradise to those men, hoodwinked with carnal desires, that can walk through this world according to the precepts, and limits prescribed by him; they say, he that shall so walk, shall merit Paradise *ex congruo*. But because no man can demand a right to it, by his own righteousness, or any other power in himself, but by the free grace of God only; they say, no man can merit Paradise *ex condigno*. This I say, I think is the meaning of the distinction; but because disputers do not agree upon the signification of their own terms of art, longer than it serves their turn; I

---

3. [Merit by coincidence and merit deserved.]

will not affirm any thing of their meaning: only this I say; when a gift is given indefinitely, as a prize to be contended for, he that winneth meriteth, and may claim the prize as due.

If a covenant be made, wherein neither of the parties perform presently, but trust one another; in the condition of mere nature, which is a condition of war of every man against every man, upon any reasonable suspicion, it is void: but if there be a common power set over them both, with right and force sufficient to compel performance, it is not void. For he that performeth first, has no assurance the other will perform after; because the bonds of words are too weak to bridle men's ambition, avarice, anger, and other passions, without the fear of some coercive power; which in the condition of mere nature, where all men are equal, and judges of the justness of their own fears, cannot possibly be supposed. And therefore he which performeth first, does but betray himself to his enemy; contrary to the right, he can never abandon, of defending his life, and means of living.

But in a civil estate, where there is a power set up to constrain those that would otherwise violate their faith, that fear is no more reasonable; and for that cause, he which by the covenant is to perform first, is obliged so to do.

The cause of fear, which maketh such a covenant invalid, must be always something arising after the covenant made; as some new fact, or other sign of the will not to perform: else it cannot make the covenant void. For that which could not hinder a man from promising, ought not to be admitted as a hindrance of performing.

He that transferreth any right, transferreth the means of enjoying it, as far as lieth in his power. As he that selleth land, is understood to transfer the herbage, and whatsoever grows upon it: nor can he that sells a mill turn away the stream that drives it. And they that give to a man the right of government in sovereignty, are understood to give him the right of levying money to maintain soldiers; and of appointing magistrates for the administration of justice.

To make covenants with brute beasts, is impossible; because not understanding our speech, they understand not, nor accept of any translation of right; nor can translate any right to another: and without mutual acceptation, there is no covenant.

To make covenant with God, is impossible, but by mediation of such as God speaketh to, either by revelation supernatural, or by his lieutenants that govern under him, and in his name: for otherwise we know not whether our covenants be accepted, or not. And therefore they that vow anything contrary to any law of nature, vow in vain; as being a thing unjust to pay such vow. And if it be a thing commanded by the law of nature, it is not the vow, but the law that binds them.

The matter, or subject of a covenant, is always something that falleth under deliberation; for to covenant, is an act of the will; that is to say, an act, and the last act of deliberation; and is therefore always understood to be something to come; and which is judged possible for him that covenanteth, to perform.

And therefore, to promise that which is known to be impossible, is no covenant. But if that prove impossible afterwards, which before was thought possible, the covenant is valid, and bindeth, though not to the thing itself, yet to the value; or, if that also be impossible, to the unfeigned endeavour of performing as much as is possible: for to more no man can be obliged.

Men are freed of their covenants two ways; by performing; or by being forgiven.

For performance, is the natural end of obligation; and forgiveness, the restitution of liberty; as being a retransferring of that right, in which the obligation consisted.

Covenants entered into by fear, in the condition of mere nature, are obligatory. For example, if I covenant to pay a ransom, or service for my life, to an enemy; I am bound by it: for it is a contract, wherein one receiveth the benefit of life; the other is to receive money, or service for it; and consequently, where no other law, as in the condition of mere nature, forbiddeth the performance, the covenant is valid. Therefore prisoners of war, if trusted with the payment of their ransom, are obliged to pay it: and if a weaker prince, make a disadvantageous peace with a stronger, for fear; he is bound to keep it; unless, as hath been said before, there ariseth some new, and just cause of fear, to renew the war. And even in commonwealths, if I be forced to redeem myself from a thief by promising him money, I am bound to pay it, till the civil law discharge me. For whatsoever I may lawfully do without obligation, the same I may lawfully covenant to do through fear: and what I lawfully covenant, I cannot lawfully break.

A former covenant, makes void a later. For a man that hath passed away his right to one man today, hath it not to pass tomorrow to another: and therefore the later promise passeth no right, but is null.

A covenant not to defend myself from force, by force, is always void. For, as I have showed before, no man can transfer, or lay down his right to save himself from death, wounds, and imprisonment, the avoiding whereof is the only end of laying down any right; and therefore the promise of not resisting force, in no covenant transferreth any right; nor is obliging. For though a man may covenant thus, *unless I do so, or so, kill me;* he cannot covenant thus, *unless I do so, or so, I will not resist you, when you come to kill me.* For man by nature chooseth the lesser evil, which is danger of death in resisting; rather than the greater, which is certain and present death in not resisting. And this is granted to be true by all men, in that they lead criminals to execution, and prison, with armed men, notwithstanding that such criminals have consented to the law, by which they are condemned.

A covenant to accuse oneself, without assurance of pardon, is likewise invalid. For in the condition of nature, where every man is judge, there is no place for accusation: and in the civil state, the accusation is followed with punishment; which being force, a man is not obliged not to resist. The same is also true, of the accusation of those, by whose condemnation a man falls into misery; as of a father, wife, or benefactor. For the testimony of such an accuser, if it be not willingly given, is presumed to be corrupted by nature; and therefore not to be received: and where a man's testimony is not to be credited, he is not bound to give it. Also accusations upon torture, are not to be reputed as testimonies. For torture is to be used but as means of conjecture, and light, in the further examination, and search of truth; and what is in that case confessed, tendeth to the ease of him that is tortured; not to the informing of the torturers: and therefore ought not to have the credit of a sufficient testimony: for whether he deliver himself by true, or false accusation, he does it by the right of preserving his own life.

The force of words, being, as I have formerly noted, too weak to hold men to the performance of their covenants; there are in man's nature, but two imaginable helps to strengthen it. And those are either a fear of the consequence of breaking their word; or a glory, or pride in appearing not to need to break it. This latter is a generosity too rarely found to be presumed on, especially in the pursuers of wealth, command, or sensual pleasure; which are the greatest part of mankind. The passion to be reckoned upon, is fear; whereof there be two very general objects: one, the power of spirits invisible; the other, the power of those men they shall therein offend. Of these two, though the former be the greater power, yet the fear of the latter is commonly the greater fear. The fear of the former is in every man, his own religion: which hath place in the nature of man before civil society. The latter hath not so; at least not place enough, to keep men to their promises; because in the condition of mere nature, the inequality of power is not discerned, but by the event of battle. So that before the time of civil society, or in the interruption thereof by war, there is nothing can strengthen a covenant of peace agreed on, against the temptations of avarice, ambition, lust, or other strong desire, but the fear of that invisible power, which they every one worship as God; and fear as a revenger of their perfidy. All therefore that can be done between two men not subject to civil power, is to put one another to swear by the God he feareth: which *swearing,* or OATH, is a *form of speech, added to a promise; by which he that promiseth, signifieth, that unless he perform, he renounceth the mercy of his God, or calleth to him for vengeance on himself.* Such was the heathen form, *Let* Jupiter *kill me else, as I kill this beast.* So is our form, *I shall do thus, and thus, so help me God.* And this, with the rites and ceremonies, which every one useth in his own religion, that the fear of breaking faith might be the greater.

By this it appears, that an oath taken according to any other form, or rite, than his, that sweareth, is in vain; and no oath: and that there is no swearing by any thing which the swearer thinks not God. For though men have sometimes used to swear by their kings, for fear, or flattery; yet they would have it thereby understood, they attributed to them divine honour. And that swearing unnecessarily by God, is but prophaning of his name: and swearing by other things, as men do in common discourse, is not swearing, but an impious custom, gotten by too much vehemence of talking.

It appears also, that the oath adds nothing to the obligation. For a covenant, if lawful, binds in the sight of God, without the oath, as much as with it: if unlawful, bindeth not at all; though it be confirmed with an oath.

CHAPTER XV

Of Other Laws of Nature

FROM that law of nature, by which we are obliged to transfer to another, such rights, as being retained, hinder the peace of mankind, there followeth a third; which is this, *that men perform their covenants made:* without which, covenants are in vain, and but empty words; and the right of all men to all things remaining, we are still in the condition of war.

And in this law of nature, consisteth the fountain and original of JUSTICE. For where no covenant hath preceded, there hath no right been transferred, and every man has right to every thing; and consequently, no action can be unjust. But when a covenant is made, then to break it is *unjust:* and the definition of INJUSTICE, is no other than *the not performance of covenant.* And whatsoever is not unjust, is *just.*

But because covenants of mutual trust, where there is a fear of not performance on either part, as hath been said in the former chapter, are invalid; though the original of justice be the making of covenants; yet injustice actually there can be none, till the cause of such fear be taken away; which while men are in the natural condition of war, cannot be done. Therefore before the names of just, and unjust can have place, there must be some coercive power, to compel men equally to the performance of their covenants, by the terror of some punishment, greater than the benefit they expect by the breach of their covenant; and to make good that propriety, which by mutual contract men acquire, in recompense of the universal right they abandon: and such power there is none before the erection of a commonwealth. And this is also to be gathered out of the ordinary definition of justice in the Schools: for they say, that *justice is the constant will of giving to every man his own.* And therefore where there is no *own*, that is no propriety, there is no injustice; and where there is no coercive power erected, that is, where there is no commonwealth, there is no propriety; all men having right to all things: therefore where there is no commonwealth, there nothing is unjust. So that the nature of justice, consisteth in keeping of valid covenants: but the validity of covenants begins not but with the constitution of a civil power, sufficient to compel men to keep them: and then it is also that propriety begins.

The fool hath said in his heart, there is no such thing as justice; and sometimes also with his tongue; seriously alleging, that every man's conservation, and contentment, being committed to his own care, there could be no reason, why every man might not do what he thought conduced thereunto: and therefore also to make, or not make; keep, or not keep covenants, was not against reason, when it conduced to one's benefit. He does not therein deny, that there be covenants; and that they are sometimes broken, sometimes kept; and that such breach of them may be called injustice, and the observance of them justice: but he questioneth, whether injustice, taking away the fear of God, for the same fool hath said in his heart there is no God, may not sometimes stand with that reason, which dictateth to every man his own good; and particularly then, when it conduceth to such a benefit, as shall put a man in a condition, to neglect not only the dispraise, and revilings, but also the power of other men. The kingdom of God is gotten by violence: but what if it could be gotten by unjust violence? were it against reason so to get it, when it is impossible to receive hurt by it? and if it be not against reason, it is not against justice; or else justice is not to be approved for good. From such reasoning as this, successful wickedness hath obtained the name of virtue: and some that in all other things have disallowed the violation of faith; yet have allowed it, when it is for the getting of a kingdom. And the heathen that believed, that Saturn was deposed by his son Jupiter, believed nevertheless the same Jupiter to be the avenger of injustice: somewhat like to a piece of law in Coke's *Commentaries on Littleton*;[4] where he says, if the right heir of the crown be attainted of treason; yet the crown shall descend to him, and *eo instante* the attainder be void: from which instances a man will be very prone to infer; that when the heir apparent of a kingdom, shall kill him that is in possession, though his father; you may call it injustice, or by what other name you will; yet it can never be against reason, seeing all the voluntary actions of men tend to the benefit of themselves; and those actions are most reasonable, that conduce most to

4. [Edward Coke (1552–1634) was an eminent English jurist who defended common law against encroachments by the crown. Thomas Littleton (c.1442–1481), an English barrister and judge, wrote a work on property law which in an edition expanded by Coke was the standard text on the subject until the nineteenth century.]

their ends. This specious reasoning is nevertheless false.

For the question is not of promises mutual, where there is no security of performance on either side; as when there is no civil power erected over the parties promising; for such promises are no covenants: but either where one of the parties has performed already; or where there is a power to make him perform; there is the question whether it be against reason, that is, against the benefit of the other to perform, or not. And I say it is not against reason. For the manifestation whereof, we are to consider; first, that when a man doth a thing, which notwithstanding any thing can be foreseen, and reckoned on, tendeth to his own destruction, howsoever some accident which he could not expect, arriving may turn it to his benefit; yet such events do not make it reasonably or wisely done. Secondly, that in a condition of war, wherein every man to every man, for want of a common power to keep them all in awe, is an enemy, there is no man who can hope by his own strength, or wit, to defend himself from destruction, without the help of confederates; where every one expects the same defence by the confederation, that any one else does: and therefore he which declares he thinks it reason to deceive those that help him, can in reason expect no other means of safety, than what can be had from his own single power. He therefore that breaketh his covenant, and consequently declareth that he thinks he may with reason do so, cannot be received into any society, that unite themselves for peace and defence, but by the error of them that receive him; nor when he is received, be retained in it, without seeing the danger of their error; which errors a man cannot reasonably reckon upon as the means of his security: and therefore if he be left, or cast out of society, he perisheth; and if he live in society, it is by the errors of other men, which he could not foresee, nor reckon upon; and consequently against the reason of his preservation; and so, as all men that contribute not to his destruction, forbear him only out of ignorance of what is good for themselves.

As for the instance of gaining the secure and perpetual felicity of heaven, by any way; it is frivolous: there being but one way imaginable; and that is not breaking, but keeping of covenant.

And for the other instance of attaining sovereignty by rebellion; it is manifest, that though the event follow, yet because it cannot reasonably be expected, but rather the contrary; and because by gaining it so, others are taught to gain the same in like manner, the attempt thereof is against reason. Justice therefore, that is to say, keeping of covenant, is a rule of reason, by which we are forbidden to do anything destructive to our life; and consequently a law of nature.

There be some that proceed further; and will not have the law of nature, to be those rules which conduce to the preservation of man's life on earth; but to the attaining of an eternal felicity after death; to which they think the breach of covenant may conduce; and consequently be just and reasonable; such are they that think it a work of merit to kill, or depose, or rebel against, the sovereign power constituted over them by their own consent. But because there is no natural knowledge of man's estate after death; much less of the reward that is then to be given to breach of faith; but only a belief grounded upon other men's saying, that they know it supernaturally, or that they know those, that knew them, that knew others, that knew it supernaturally; breach of faith cannot be called a precept of reason, or nature.

Others, that allow for a law of nature, the keeping of faith, do nevertheless make exception of certain persons; as heretics, and such as use not to perform their covenant to others: and this also is against reason. For if any fault of a man, be sufficient to discharge our covenant made; the same ought in reason to have been sufficient to have hindered the making of it.

The names of just, and unjust, when they are attributed to men, signify one thing; and when they are attributed to actions, another. When they are attributed to men, they signify conformity, or inconformity of manners, to reason. But when they are attributed to actions, they signify the conformity, or inconformity to reason, not of manners, or manner of life, but of particular actions. A just man therefore, is he that taketh all the care he can, that his actions may be all just: and an unjust man, is he that neglecteth it. And such men are more often in our language styled by the names of righteous, and unrighteous; than just, and unjust; though the meaning be the same. Therefore a righteous man, does not lose that title, by one, or a few unjust actions, that proceed from sudden passion, or mistake of things, or persons: nor does an unrighteous man, lose his character, for such actions, as he does, or forbears to do, for fear: because his will is not framed by the justice, but by the apparent benefit of what he is to do. That which gives to human actions the relish of justice, is a certain nobleness or gallantness of courage, rarely found, by which a man scorns to be beholden for the contentment of his life, to fraud, or breach of promise. This justice of the manners, is that which is meant, where justice is called a virtue; and injustice a vice.

But the justice of actions denominates men, not just, but *guiltless:* and the injustice of the same, which is also called injury, gives them but the name of *guilty.*

Again, the injustice of manners, is the disposition, or aptitude to do injury and is injustice before it proceed to act; and without supposing any individual person injured. But the injustice of an action, that is to say injury, supposeth an individual person injured; namely him, to whom the covenant was made: and therefore many times the injury is received by one man, when the damage redoundeth to another. As when the master commandeth his servant to give money to a stranger; if it be not done, the injury is done to the master, whom he had before covenanted to obey; but the damage redoundeth to the stranger, to whom he had no obligation; and therefore could not injure him. And so also in commonwealths, private men may remit to one another their debts; but not robberies or other violences, whereby they are endamaged; because the detaining of debt, is an injury to themselves; but robbery and violence, are injuries to the person of the commonwealth.

Whatsoever is done to a man, conformable to his own will signified to the doer, is no injury to him. For if he that doeth it, hath not passed away his original right to do what he please, by some antecedent covenant, there is no breach of covenant; and therefore no injury done him. And if he have; then his will to have it done being signified, is a release of that covenant: and so again there is no injury done him.

Justice of actions, is by writers divided into *commutative,* and *distributive:* and the former they say consisteth in proportion arithmetical; the latter in proportion geometrical. Commutative therefore, they place in the equality of value of the things contracted for; and distributive, in the distribution of equal benefit, to men of equal merit. As if it were injustice to sell dearer than we buy; or to give more to a man than he merits. The value of all things contracted for, is measured by the appetite of the contractors: and therefore the just value, is that which they be contented to give. And merit, besides that which is by covenant, where the performance on one part, meriteth the performance of the other part, and falls under justice commutative, not distributive, is not due by justice; but is rewarded of grace only. And therefore this distinction, in the sense wherein it useth to be expounded, is not right. To speak properly, commutative justice, is the justice, of a contractor; that is, a performance of covenant, in buying, and selling; hiring, and letting to hire; lending, and borrowing; exchanging, bartering, and other acts of contract.

And distributive justice, the justice of an arbitrator; that is to say, the act of defining what is just. Wherein, being trusted by them that make him arbitrator, if he perform his trust, he is said to distribute to every man his own: and this is indeed just distribution, and may be called, though improperly, distributive justice; but more properly equity; which also is a law of nature, as shall be shown in due place.

As justice dependeth on antecedent covenant; so does GRATITUDE depend on antecedent grace; that is to say, antecedent free gift: and is the fourth law of nature; which may be conceived in this form, *that a man which receiveth benefit from another of mere grace, endeavour that he which giveth it, have no reasonable cause to repent him of his good will.* For no man giveth, but with intention of good to himself; because gift is voluntary; and of all voluntary acts, the object is to every man his own good; of which if men see they shall be frustrated, there will be no beginning of benevolence, or trust; nor consequently of mutual help; nor of reconciliation of one man to another; and therefore they are to remain still in the condition of *war;* which is contrary to the first and fundamental law of nature, which commandeth men to *seek peace.* The breach of this law, is called *ingratitude;* and hath the same relation to grace, that injustice hath to obligation by covenant.

A fifth law of nature, is COMPLAISANCE; that is to say, *that every man strive to accommodate himself to the rest.* For the understanding whereof, we may consider, that there is in men's aptness to society, a diversity of nature, rising from their diversity of affections; not unlike to that we see in stones brought together for building of an edifice. For as that stone which by the asperity, and irregularity of figure, takes more room from others, than itself fills; and for the hardness, cannot be easily made plain, and thereby hindereth the building, is by the builders cast away as unprofitable, and troublesome: so also, a man that by asperity of nature, will strive to retain those things which to himself are superfluous, and to others necessary; and for the stubbornness of his passions, cannot be corrected, is to be left, or cast out of society, as cumbersome thereunto. For seeing every man, not only by right, but also by necessity of nature, is supposed to endeavour all he can, to obtain that which is necessary for his conservation; he that shall oppose himself against it, for things superfluous, is guilty of the war that thereupon is to follow; and therefore doth that, which is contrary to the fundamental law of nature, which commandeth *to seek peace.* The observers of this law, may be called SOCIABLE, the Latins call them *commodi;* the contrary, *stubborn, insociable, froward, intractable.*

A sixth law of nature, is this, *that upon caution of the future time, a man ought to pardon the offences past of them that repenting, desire it.* For PARDON, is nothing but granting of peace; which though granted to them that persevere in their hostility, be not peace, but fear; yet not granted to them that give caution of the future time, is sign of an aversion to peace; and therefore contrary to the law of nature.

A seventh is, *that in revenges,* that is, retribution of evil for evil, *men look not at the greatness of the evil past, but the greatness of the good to follow.* Whereby we are forbidden to inflict punishment with any other design, than for correction of the offender, or direction of others. For this law is consequent to the next before it, that commandeth pardon, upon security of the future time. Besides, revenge without respect to the example, and profit to come, is a triumph, or glorying in the hurt of another, tending to no end; for the end is always somewhat to come; and glorying to no end, is vain-glory, and contrary to reason, and to hurt without reason, tendeth to the introduction of war; which is against the law of nature; and is commonly styled by the name of *cruelty.*

And because all signs of hatred, or contempt, provoke to fight; insomuch as most men choose rather to hazard their life, than not to be revenged; we may in the eighth place, for a law of nature, set down this precept, *that no man by deed, word, countenance, or gesture, declare hatred, or contempt of another.* The breach of which law, is commonly called *contumely.*

The question who is the better man, has no place in the condition of mere nature; where, as has been shewn before, all men are equal. The inequality that now is, has been introduced by the laws civil. I know that Aristotle in the first book of his *Politics,* for a foundation of his doctrine, maketh men by nature, some more worthy to command, meaning the wiser sort, such as he thought himself to be for his philosophy; others to serve, meaning those that had strong bodies, but were not philosophers as he; as if master and servant were not introduced by consent of men, but by difference of wit: which is not only against reason; but also against experience. For there are very few so foolish, that had not rather govern themselves, than be governed by others: nor when the wise in their own conceit, contend by force, with them who distrust their own wisdom, do they always, or often, or almost at any time, get the victory. If nature therefore have made men equal, that equality is to be acknowledged: or if nature have made men unequal; yet because men that think themselves equal, will not enter into conditions of peace, but upon equal terms, such equality must be admitted. And therefore for the ninth law of nature, I put this, *that every man acknowledge another for his equal by nature.* The breach of this precept is *pride.*

On this law, dependeth another, *that at the entrance into conditions of peace, no man require to reserve to himself any right, which he is not content should be reserved to every one of the rest.* As it is necessary for all men that seek peace, to lay down certain rights of nature; that is to say, not to have liberty to do all they list: so is it necessary for man's life, to retain some; as right to govern their own bodies; enjoy air, water, motion, ways to go from place to place; and all things else, without which a man cannot live, or not live well. If in this case, at the making of peace, men require for themselves, that which they would not have to be granted to others, they do contrary to the precedent law, that commandeth the acknowledgment of natural equality, and therefore also against the law of nature. The observers of this law, are those we call *modest,* and the breakers *arrogant* men. The Greeks call the violation of this law πλεονεξια; that is, a desire of more than their share.

Also if *a man be trusted to judge between man and man,* it is a precept of the law of nature, *that he deal equally between them.* For without that, the controversies of men cannot be determined but by war. He therefore that is partial in judgment, doth what in him lies, to deter men from the use of judges, and arbitrators; and consequently, against the fundamental law of nature, is the cause of war.

The observance of this law, from the equal distribution to each man, of that which in reason belongeth to him, is called EQUITY, and, as I have said before, distributive justice: the violation, *acception of persons,* προσωπολημψια.

And from this followeth another law, *that such things as cannot be divided, be enjoyed in common, if it can be; and if the quantity of the thing permit, without stint; otherwise pro-*

portionably to the number of them that have right. For otherwise the distribution is un-equal, and contrary to equity.

But some things there be, that can neither be divided, nor enjoyed in common. Then, the law of nature, which prescribeth equity, requireth, *that the entire right; or else, making the use alternate, the first possession, be determined by lot.* For equal distribution, is of the law of nature; and other means of equal distribution cannot be imagined.

Of *lots* there be two sorts, *arbitrary,* and *natural.* Arbitrary, is that which is agreed on by the competitors: natural, is either *primogeniture,* which the Greek calls κλη-ρονομία, which signifies, *given by lot;* or *first seizure.*

And therefore those things which cannot be enjoyed in common, nor divided, ought to be adjudged to the first possessor; and in some cases to the first born, as acquired by lot.

It is also a law of nature, *that all men that mediate peace, be allowed safe conduct.* For the law that commandeth peace, as the *end,* commandeth intercession, as the *means;* and to intercession that means is safe conduct.

And because, though men be never so willing to observe these laws, there may nevertheless arise questions concerning a man's action; first, whether it were done, or not done; secondly, if done, whether against the law, or not against the law, the former whereof, is called a question *of fact;* the latter a question *of right,* therefore unless the parties to the question, covenant mutually to stand to the sentence of another, they are as far from peace as ever. This other to whose sentence they submit is called an ARBITRATOR. And therefore it is of the law of nature, *that they that are at controversy, submit their right to the judgment of an arbitrator.*

And seeing every man is presumed to do all things in order to his own benefit, no man is a fit arbitrator in his own cause; and if he were never so fit; yet equity allowing to each party equal benefit, if one be admitted to be judge, the other is to be admitted also; and so the controversy, that is, the cause of war, remains, against the law of nature.

For the same reason no man in any cause ought to be received for arbitrator, to whom greater profit, or honour, or pleasure apparently ariseth out of the victory of one party, than of the other: for he hath taken, though an unavoidable bribe, yet a bribe; and no man can be obliged to trust him. And thus also the controversy, and the condition of war remaineth, contrary to the law of nature.

And in a controversy of *fact,* the judge being to give no more credit to one, than to the other, if there be no other arguments, must give credit to a third; or to a third and fourth; or more: for else the question is undecided, and left to force, contrary to the law of nature.

These are the laws of nature, dictating peace, for a means of the conservation of men in multitudes; and which only concern the doctrine of civil society. There be other things tending to the destruction of particular men; as drunkenness, and all other parts of intemperance; which may therefore also be reckoned amongst those things which the law of nature hath forbidden; but are not necessary to be mentioned, nor are pertinent enough to this place.

And though this may seem too subtle a deduction of the laws of nature, to be taken notice of by all men; whereof the most part are too busy in getting food, and the rest too negligent to understand; yet to leave all men inexcusable, they have been contracted into one easy sum, intelligible even to the meanest capacity; and that is, *Do not that to another, which thou wouldest not have done to thyself;* which sheweth him, that he has no more to do in learning the laws of nature, but, when weighing the actions of other men with his own, they seem too heavy, to put them into the other part of the balance, and his own into their place, that his own passions, and self-love, may add nothing to the weight; and then there is none of these laws of nature that will not appear unto him very reasonable.

The laws of nature oblige *in foro interno;* that is to say, they bind to a desire they should take place: but *in foro externo;* that is, to the putting them in act, not always. For he that should be modest, and tractable, and perform all he promises, in such time, and place, where no man else should do so, should but make himself a prey to others, and procure his own certain ruin, contrary to the ground of all laws of nature, which tend to nature's preservation. And again, he that having sufficient security, that others shall observe the same laws towards him, observes them not himself, seeketh not peace, but war; and consequently the destruction of his nature by violence.

And whatsoever laws bind *in foro interno,* may be broken, not only by a fact contrary to the law, but also by a fact according to it, in case a man think it contrary. For though his action in this case, be according to the law; yet his purpose was against the law; which, where the obligation is *in foro interno,* is a breach.

The laws of nature are immutable and eternal; for injustice, ingratitude, arrogance, pride, iniquity, acception of persons, and the rest, can never be made lawful. For it can never be that war shall preserve life, and peace destroy it.

The same laws, because they oblige only to a desire, and endeavour, I mean an unfeigned and constant endeavour, are easy to be observed. For in that they require nothing but endeavour, he that endeavoureth their performance, fulfilleth them; and he that fulfilleth the law, is just.

And the science of them, is the true and only moral philosophy. For moral philosophy is nothing else but the science of what is *good,* and *evil,* in the conversation, and society of mankind. *Good,* and *evil,* are names that signify our appetites, and aversions; which in different tempers, customs, and doctrines of men, are different: and divers men, differ not only in their judgment, on the senses of what is pleasant, and unpleasant to the taste, smell, hearing, touch, and sight; but also of what is conformable, or disagreeable to reason, in the actions of common life. Nay, the same man, in divers times, differs from himself; and one time praiseth, that is, called good, what another time he dispraiseth, and calleth evil: from whence arise disputes, controversies, and at last war. And therefore so long as a man is in the condition of mere nature, which is a condition of war, as private appetite is the measure of good, and evil: and consequently all men agree on this, that peace is good, and therefore also the way, or means of peace, which, as I have shewed before, are *justice, gratitude, modesty, equity, mercy,* and the rest of the laws of nature, are good; that is to say; *moral virtues;* and their contrary *vices,* evil. Now the science of virtue and vice, is moral philosophy; and therefore the true doctrine of the laws of nature, is the true moral philosophy. But the writers of moral philosophy, though they acknowledge the same virtues and vices; yet not seeing wherein consisted their goodness; nor that they come to be praised, as the means of peaceable, sociable, and comfortable living, place them in a mediocrity of passions: as if not the cause, but the degree of daring, made fortitude; or not the cause, but the quantity of a gift, made liberality.

These dictates of reason, men used to call by the name of laws, but improperly: for they are but conclusions, or theorems concerning what conduceth to the conservation and defence of themselves; whereas law, properly, is the word of him, that by right hath command over others. But yet if we consider the same theorems, as delivered in the word of God, that by right commandeth all things; then are they properly called laws.

CHAPTER XVI

Of Persons, Authors and Things Personated

A PERSON, is he, *whose words or actions are considered, either as his own, or as representing the words or actions of another man, or of any other thing, to whom they are attributed, whether truly or by fiction.*

When they are considered as his own, then is he called a *natural person:* and when they are considered as representing the words and actions of another, then is he a *feigned* or *artificial person.*

The word person is Latin: instead whereof the Greeks have πρόσωπον, which signifies the *face*, as *persona* in Latin signifies the *disguise,* or *outward appearance* of a man, counterfeited on the stage; and sometimes more particularly that part of it, which disguiseth the face, as a mask or vizard: and from the stage, hath been translated to any representer of speech and action, as well in tribunals, as theatres. So that a *person,* is the same that an *actor* is, both on the stage and in common conversation; and to *personate,* is to *act,* or *represent* himself, or another; and he that acteth another, is said to bear his person, or act in his name; in which sense Cicero useth it where he says, *Unus sustineo tres personas; mei, adversarii, et judicis:* I bear three persons; my own, my adversary's, and the judge's; and is called in divers occasions, diversly; as a *representer,* or *representative,* a *lieutenant,* a *vicar,* an *attorney,* a *deputy,* a *procurator,* an *actor,* and the like.

Of persons artificial, some have their words and actions *owned* by those whom they represent. And then the person is the *actor;* and he that owneth his words and actions, is the AUTHOR: in which case the actor acteth by authority. For that which in speaking of goods and possessions, is called an *owner,* and in Latin *dominus,* in Greek κύριος speaking of actions, is called author. And as the right of possession, is called dominion; so the right of doing any action, is called AUTHORITY. So that by authority, is always understood a right of doing any act; and *done by authority,* done by commission, or licence from him whose right it is.

From hence it followeth, that when the actor maketh a covenant by authority, he bindeth thereby the author, no less than if he had made it himself; and no less subjecteth him to all the consequences of the same. And therefore all that hath been said formerly, (chapter XIV) of the nature of covenants between man and man in their natural capacity, is true also when they are made by their actors, representers, or procurators, that have authority from them, so far forth as is in their commission, but no further.

And therefore he that maketh a covenant with the actor, or representer, not knowing the authority he hath, doth it at his own peril. For no man is obliged by a covenant, whereof he is not author; nor consequently by a covenant made against, or beside the authority he gave.

When the actor doth anything against the law of nature by command of the author, if he be obliged by former covenant to obey him, not he, but the author breaketh the law of nature; for though the action be against the law of nature; yet it is not his: but contrarily, to refuse to do it, is against the law of nature, that forbiddeth breach of covenant.

And he that maketh a covenant with the author, by mediation of the actor, not knowing what authority he hath, but only takes his word: in case such authority be not made manifest unto him upon demand, is no longer obliged: for the covenant made with the author, is not valid, without his counter-assurance. But if he that so covenanteth, knew beforehand he was to expect no other assurance, than the actor's word; then is the covenant valid; because the actor in this case maketh himself the author. And therefore, as when the authority is evident, the covenant obligeth the author, not the actor; so when the authority is feigned, it obligeth the actor only; there being no author but himself.

There are few things, that are incapable of being represented by fiction. Inanimate things, as a church, an hospital, a bridge, may be personated by a rector, master, or overseer. But things inanimate, cannot be authors, nor therefore give authority to their actors: yet the actors may have authority to procure their maintenance, given them by those that are owners, or governors of those things. And therefore, such things cannot be personated, before there by some state of civil government.

Likewise children, fools, and madmen that have no use of reason, may be personated by guardians, or curators; but can be no authors, during that time, of any action done by them, longer than, when they shall recover the use of reason, they shall judge the same reasonable. Yet during the folly, he that hath right of governing them, may give authority to the guardian. But this again has no place but in a state civil, because before such estate, there is no dominion of persons.

An idol, or mere figment of the brain, may be personated; as were the gods of the heathen: which by such officers as the state appointed, were personated, and held possessions, and other goods, and rights, which men from time to time dedicated, and consecrated unto them. But idols cannot be authors: for an idol is nothing. The authority proceeded from the state: and therefore before introduction of civil government, the gods of the heathen could not be personated.

The true God may be personated. As he was; first, by Moses, who governed the Israelites, that were not his, but God's people, not in his own name with *hoc dicit Moses;* but in God's name, with *hoc dicit Dominus.* Secondly, by the Son of man, his own Son, our blessed Saviour Jesus Christ, that came to reduce the Jews, and induce all nations into the kingdom of his father; not as of himself, but as sent from his father. And thirdly, by the Holy Ghost, or Comforter, speaking, and working in the Apostles: which Holy Ghost, was a Comforter that came not of himself; but was sent, and proceeded from them both.

A multitude of men, are made *one* person, when they are by one man, or one person, represented; so that it be done with the consent of every one of that multitude in particular. For it is the *unity* of the representer, not the *unity* of the represented, that maketh the person *one*. And it is the representer than beareth the person, and but one person: and *unity*, cannot otherwise be understood in multitude.

And because the multitude naturally is not *one*, but *many;* they cannot be understood for one; but many authors, of every thing their representative saith, or doth in their name; every man giving their common representer, authority from himself in particular; and owning all the actions the representer doth, in case they give him authority without stint: otherwise, when they limit him in what, and how far he shall represent them, none of them owneth more than they gave him commission to act.

And if the representative consist of many men, the voice of the greater number, must be considered as the voice of them all. For if the lesser number pronounce, for example, in the affirmative, and the greater in the negative, there will be negatives more than enough to destroy the affirmatives; and thereby the excess of negatives, standing uncontradicted, are the only voice the representative hath.

And a representative of even number, especially when the number is not great, whereby the contradictory voices are oftentimes equal, is therefore oftentimes mute, and incapable of action. Yet in some cases contradictory voices equal in number, may determine a question; as in condemning, or absolving, equality of votes, even in that they condemn not, do absolve; but not on the contrary condemn, in that they absolve not. For when a cause is heard; not to condemn, is to absolve: but on the contrary, to say that not absolving, is condemning, is not true. The like it is in a deliberation of executing presently, or deferring till another time: for when the voices are equal, the not decreeing execution is a decree of dilation.

Or if the number be odd, as three, or more, men or assemblies; whereof every one has by a negative voice, authority to take away the effect of all the affirmative voices of the rest, this number is no representative; because by the diversity of opinions, and interests of men, it becomes oftentimes, and in cases of the greatest consequence, a mute person, and unapt, as for many things else, so for the government of a multitude, especially in time of war.

Of authors there be two sorts. The first simply so called; which I have before defined to be him, that owneth the action of another simply. The second is he, that owneth an action, or covenant of another conditionally; that is to say, he undertaketh to do it, if the other doth it not, at, or before a certain time. And these authors conditional, are generally called SURETIES, in Latin *fidejussores*, and *sponsores;* and particularly for debt, *praedes;* and for appearance before a judge, of magistrate, *vades.*

Part Two

OF COMMONWEALTH

CHAPTER XVII

Of the Causes, Generation, and Definition of a Commonwealth

THE final cause, end, or design of men, who naturally love liberty, and dominion over others, in the introduction of that restraint upon themselves, in which we see them live in commonwealths, is the foresight of their own preservation, and of a more contented life thereby; that is to say, of getting themselves out from that miserable condition of war, which is necessarily consequent, as hath been shown in chapter XIII, to the natural passions of men, when there is no visible power to keep them in awe, and tie them by fear of punishment to the performance of their covenants, and observation of those laws of nature set down in the fourteenth and fifteenth chapters.

For the laws of nature, as *justice, equity, modesty, mercy,* and, in sum, *doing to others, as we would be done to,* of themselves, without the terror of some power, to cause them to be observed, are contrary to our natural passions, that carry us to partiality, pride, revenge, and the like. And covenants, without the swords, are but words, and of no strength to secure a man at all. Therefore notwithstanding the laws of nature, which every one hath then kept, when he has the will to keep them, when he can do it safely, if there be no power erected, or not great enough for our security; every man will, and may lawfully rely on his own strength and art, for caution against all other men. And in all places, where men have lived by small families, to rob and spoil one another, has been a trade, and so far from being reputed against the law of nature, that the greater spoils they gained, the greater was their honour; and men observed no other laws therein, but the laws of honour; that is, to abstain from cruelty, leaving to men their lives, and instruments of husbandry. And as small families did then; so now do cities and kingdoms which are but greater families, for their own security, enlarge their dominions, upon all pretences of danger, and fear of invasion, or assistance that may be given to invaders, and endeavour as much as they can, to subdue, or weaken their neighbours, by open force, and secret arts, for want of other caution, justly; and are remembered for it in after ages with honour.

Nor is it the joining together of a small number of men, that gives them this security; because in small numbers, small additions on the one side or the other, make the advantage of strength so great, as is sufficient to carry the victory; and therefore gives encouragement to an invasion. The multitude sufficient to confide in for our security, is not determined by any certain number, but by comparison with the enemy we fear; and is then sufficient, when the odds of the enemy is not of so visible and conspicuous moment, to determine the event of war, as to move him to attempt.

And be there never so great a multitude; yet if their actions be directed according to their particular judgments, and particular appetites, they can expect thereby no defence, nor protection, neither against a common enemy, nor against the injuries of one another. For being distracted in opinions concerning the best use and application of their strength, they do not help but hinder one another; and reduce their strength by mutual opposition to nothing: whereby they are easily, not only subdued by a very few that agree together; but also when there is no common enemy, they make war upon each other, for their particular interests. For if we could suppose a great multitude of men to consent in the observation of justice, and other laws of nature, without a common power to keep them all in awe; we might as well suppose all mankind to do the same; and then there neither would be, nor need to be any civil government, or commonwealth at all; because there would be peace without subjection.

Nor is it enough for the security, which men desire should last all the time of their life, that they be governed, and directed by one judgment, for a limited time; as in one battle, or one war. For though they obtain a victory by their unanimous endeavour against a foreign enemy; yet afterwards when either they have no common enemy, or he that by one part is held for an enemy, is by another part held for a friend, they must needs by the difference of their interests dissolve, and fall again into a war amongst themselves.

It is true, that certain living creatures, as bees, and ants, live sociably one with another, which are therefore by Aristotle numbered amongst political creatures; and yet have no other direction, than their particular judgments and appetites; nor speech, whereby one of them can signify to another, what he thinks expedient for the common benefit: and therefore some man may perhaps desire to know, why mankind cannot do the same. To which I answer.

First, that men are continually in competition for honour and dignity, which these creatures are not; and consequently amongst men there ariseth on that ground, envy and hatred, and finally war; but amongst these not so.

Secondly, that amongst these creatures, the common good differeth not from the private; and being by nature inclined to their private, they procure thereby the common benefit. But man, whose joy consisteth in comparing himself with other men, can relish nothing but what is eminent.

Thirdly, that these creatures, having not, as man, the use of reason, do not see, nor think they see any fault, in the administration of their common business; whereas amongst men, there are very many, that think themselves wiser, and able to govern the public, better than the rest; and these strive to reform and innovate, one this way, another that way; and thereby bring it into distraction and civil war.

Fourthly, that these creatures, though they have some use of voice, in making known to one another their desires, and other affections; yet they want that art of words by which some men can represent to others, that which is good, in the likeness of evil; and evil, in the likeness of good; and augment, or diminish the apparent greatness of good and evil; discontenting men, and troubling their peace at their pleasure.

Fifthly, irrational creatures cannot distinguish between *injury,* and *damage;* and therefore as long as they be at ease, they are not offended with their fellows: whereas man is then most troublesome, when he is most at ease: for then it is that he loves to shew his wisdom, and control the actions of them that govern the commonwealth.

Lastly, the agreement of these creatures is natural; that of men, is by covenant only, which is artificial: and therefore it is no wonder if there by somewhat else required, besides covenant, to make their agreement constant and lasting; which is a common power, to keep them in awe, and to direct their actions to the common benefit.

The only way to erect such a common power, as may be able to defend them from the invasion of foreigners, and the injuries of one another, and thereby to secure them in such sort, as that by their own industry, and by the fruits of the earth, they may nourish themselves and live contentedly; is, to confer all their power and strength upon one man, or upon one assembly of men, that may reduce all their wills, by plurality of voices, unto one will: which is as much as to say, to appoint one man, or assembly of men, to bear their person; and every one to own, and acknowledge himself to be author of whatsoever he that so beareth their person, shall act, or cause to be acted, in those things which concern the common peace and safety; and therein to submit their wills, every one to his will, and their judgments, to his judgment. This is more than consent, or concord; it is a real unity of them all, in one and the same person, made by covenant of every man with every man, in such manner, as if every man should say to every man, *I authorize and give up my right of governing myself, to this man, or to this assembly of men, on this condition, that thou give up thy right to him, and authorize all his actions in like manner.* This done, the multitude so united in one person, is called a COMMONWEALTH, in Latin CIVITAS. This is the generation of the great LEVIATHAN, or rather, to speak more reverently, of that *mortal god,* to which we owe under the *immortal God,* our peace and defence. For by this authority, given him by every particular man in the commonwealth, he hath the use of so much power and strength conferred on him, that by terror thereof, he is enabled to perform the wills of them all, to peace at home, and mutual aid against their enemies abroad. And in him consisteth the essence of the commonwealth; which, to define it, is *one person, of whose acts a great multitude, by mutual covenants one with another, have made themselves every one the author, to the end he may use the strength and means of them all, as he shall think expedient, for their peace and common defence.*

And he that carrieth this person, is called SOVEREIGN, and said to have *sovereign power;* and every one besides, his SUBJECT.

The attaining to this sovereign power, is by two ways. One, by natural force; as when a man maketh his children, to submit themselves, and their children to his government, as being able to destroy them if they refuse; or by war subdueth his enemies to his will, giving them their lives on that condition. The other, is when men agree amongst themselves, to submit to some man, or assembly of men, voluntarily, on confidence to be protected by him against all others. This latter, may be called a political commonwealth, or commonwealth by *institution;* and the former, a commonwealth by *acquisition.* And first, I shall speak of a commonwealth by institution.

CHAPTER XVIII

Of the Rights of Sovereigns by Institution

A *commonwealth* is said to be *instituted,* when a *multitude* of men do agree, and *covenant, every one, with every one,* that to whatsoever *man,* or *assembly of men,* shall be given by the major part, the *right* to *present* the person of them all, that is to say, to be their *representative;* every one, as well he that *voted for it,* as he that *voted against it,* shall *authorize* all the actions and judgments, of that man, or assembly of men, in the same manner, as if they were his own, to the end, to live peaceably amongst themselves, and be protected against other men.

From this institution of a commonwealth are derived all the *rights,* and *faculties* of him, or them, on whom sovereign power is conferred by the consent of the people assembled.

First, because they covenant, it is to be understood, they are not obliged by former covenant to anything repugnant hereunto. And consequently they that have already instituted a commonwealth, being thereby bound by covenant, to own the actions, and judgments of one, cannot lawfully make a new covenant, amongst themselves, to be obedient to any other, in any thing whatsoever, without his permission. And therefore, they that are subjects to a monarch, cannot without his leave cast off monarchy, and return to the confusion of a disunited multitude; nor transfer their person from him that beareth it, to another man, or other assembly of men: for they are bound, every man to every man, to own, and be reputed author of all, that he that already is their sovereign, shall do, and judge fit to be done: so that any one man dissenting, all the rest should break their covenant made to that man, which is injustice: and they have also every man given the sovereignty to him that beareth their person; and therefore if they depose him, they take from him that which is his own, and so again it is injustice. Besides, if he that attempteth to depose his sovereign, be killed, or punished by him for such attempt, he is author of his own punishment, as being by the institution, author of all his sovereign shall do: and because it is unjustice for a man to do anything, for which he may be punished by his own authority, he is also upon that title, unjust. And whereas some men have pretended for their disobedience to their sovereign, a new covenant, made, not with men, but with God; this also is unjust: for there is no covenant with God, but by mediation of somebody that representeth God's person; which none doth by God's lieutenant, who hath the sovereignty under God. But this pretence of covenant with God, is so evident a lie, even in the pretenders' own consciences, that it is not only an act of an unjust, but also of a vile, and unmanly disposition.

Secondly, because the right of bearing the person of them all, is given to him they make sovereign, by covenant only of one to another, and not of him to any of them; there can happen no breach of covenant on the part of the sovereign; and consequently none of his subjects, by any pretence of forfeiture, can be freed from his subjection. That he which is made sovereign maketh no covenant with his subjects beforehand, is manifest; because either he must make it with the whole multitude, as one party to the covenant; or he must make a several covenant with every man. With the whole, as one party, it is impossible; because as yet they are not one person: and if he make so many several covenants as there be men, those covenants after he hath the sovereignty are void; because what act soever can be pretended by any one of them for breach thereof, is the act both of himself, and of all the rest, because done in the person, and by the right of every one of them in particular. Besides, if any one, or more of them, pretend a breach of the covenant made by the sovereign at his institution; and others, or one other of his subjects, or himself alone, pretend there was no such breach, there is in this case, no judge to decide the controversy; it returns therefore to the sword again; and every man recovereth the right of protecting himself by his own strength, contrary to the design they had in the institution. It is therefore in vain to grant sovereignty by way of precedent covenant. The opinion that any monarch receiveth his power by covenant, that is to say, on condition, proceedeth from want of understanding this easy truth, that covenants being but words and breath, have no force to oblige, contain, constrain, or protect any man, but what it has from the public sword; that is, from the untied hands of that man, or assembly of men that hath the sovereignty, and whose actions are avouched by them all, and performed by the strength of them all, in him united. But when an assembly of men is made sovereign; then no man imagineth any such covenant to have passed in the institution; for no man is so dull as to say, for example, the people of Rome made a covenant with the Romans, to hold the sovereignty on such or such conditions; which not performed, the Romans might lawfully depose the Roman people. That men see not the reason to be alike in a monarchy, and in a popular government, proceedeth from the ambition of some, that are kinder to the government of an assembly, whereof they may hope to participate, than of monarchy, which they despair to enjoy.

Thirdly, because the major part hath by consenting voices declared a sovereign; he that dissented must now consent with the rest; that is, be contented to avow all the actions he shall do, or else justly be destroyed by the rest. For if he voluntarily entered into the congregation of them that were assembled, he sufficiently declared thereby his will, and therefore tacitly covenanted, to stand to what the major part should ordain: and therefore if he refuse to stand thereto, or make protestation against any of their decrees, he does contrary to his covenant, and therefore unjustly. And whether he be of the congregation, or not; and whether his consent be asked, or not, he must either submit to their decrees, or be left in the condition of war he was in before; wherein he might without injustice be destroyed by any man whatsoever.

Fourthly, because every subject is by this institution author of all the actions, and judgments of the sovereign instituted; it follows, that whatsoever he doth, it can be no injury to any of his subjects; nor ought he to be by any of them accused of injustice. For he that doth anything by authority from another, doth therein no injury to him by whose authority he acteth: but by this institution of a commonwealth, every particular man is author of all the sovereign doth: and consequently he that complaineth of injury from his sovereign, complaineth of that whereof he himself is author; and therefore ought not to accuse any man but himself; no nor himself of injury; because to do injury to one's self, is impossible. It is true that they that have sovereign power may commit iniquity; but no injustice, or injury in the proper signification.

Fifthly, and consequently to that which was said last, no man that hath sovereign power can justly be put to death, or otherwise in any manner by his subjects punished. For seeing every subject is author of the actions of his sovereign; he punisheth another for the actions committed by himself.

And because the end of this institution, is the peace and defence of them all; and whosoever has right to the end, has right to the means; it belongeth of right, to whatsoever man, or assembly that hath the sovereignty, to be judge both of the means of peace and defence, and also of the hindrances, and disturbances of the same; and to do whatsoever he shall think necessary to be done, both beforehand, for the preserving of peace and security, by prevention of discord at home, and hostility from abroad; and, when peace and security are lost, for the recovery of the same. And therefore,

Sixthly, it is annexed to the sovereignty, to be judge of what opinions and doctrines are averse, and what conducing to peace; and consequently, on what occasions, how far, and what men are to be trusted withal, in speaking to multitudes of people; and who shall examine the doctrines of all books before they be published. For the actions of men proceed from their opinions; and in the well-governing of opinions, consisteth the well-governing of men's actions, in order to their peace, and concord. And though in matter of doctrine, nothing ought to be regarded but the truth; yet this is not repugnant to regulating the same by peace. For doctrine repugnant to peace, can no more be true, than peace and concord can be against the law of nature. It is true, that in a commonwealth, where by the negligence, or unskilfulness of governors, and teachers, false doctrines are by time generally received; the contrary truths may be generally offensive. Yet the most sudden, and rough bursting in of a new truth, that can be, does never break the peace, but only sometimes awake the war. For those men that are so remissly governed, that they dare take up arms to defend, or introduce an opinion, are still in war; and their condition not peace, but only a cessation of arms for fear of one another; and they live, as it were, in the precints of battle continually. It belongeth therefore to him that hath the sovereign power, to be judge, or constitute all judges of opinions and doctrines, as a thing necessary to peace; thereby to prevent discord and civil war.

Seventhly, is annexed to the sovereignty, the whole power of prescribing the rules, whereby every man may know, what goods he may enjoy, and what actions he may do, without being molested by any of his fellow-subjects; and this is it men call *propriety*. For before constitution of sovereign power, as hath already been shown, all men had right to all things; which necessarily causeth war: and therefore this propriety, being necessary to peace, and depending on sovereign power, is the act of that power, in order to the public peace. These rules of propriety, or *meum* and *tuum*, and of *good, evil, lawful,* and *unlawful* in the actions of subjects, are the civil laws; that is to say, the laws of each commonwealth in particular; though the name of civil law be now restrained to the ancient civil laws of the city of Rome; which being the head of a great part of the world, her laws at that time were in these parts the civil law.

Eighthly, is annexed to the sovereignty, the right of judicature; that is to say, of hearing and deciding all controversies, which may arise concerning law, either civil, or natural; or concerning fact. For without the decision of controversies, there is no protection of one subject, against the injuries of another; the laws concerning *meum* and *tuum* are in vain; and to every man remaineth, from the natural and necessary appetite of his own conservation, the right of protecting himself by his private strength, which is the condition of war, and contrary to the end for which every commonwealth is instituted.

Ninthly, is annexed to the sovereignty, the right of making war and peace with other nations, and commonwealths; that is to say, of judging when it is for the public good, and how great forces are to be assembled, armed, and paid for that end; and to levy money upon the subjects, to defray the expenses thereof. For the power by which the people are to be defended, consisteth in their armies; and the strength of an army, in the union of their strength under one command; which command the sovereign instituted, therefore hath; because the command of the *militia*, without other institution, maketh him that hath it sovereign. And therefore whosoever is made general of an army, he that hath the sovereign power is always generalissimo.

Tenthly, is annexed to the sovereignty, the choosing of all counsellors, ministers, magistrates, and officers, both in peace, and war. For seeing the sovereign is charged with the end, which is the common peace and defence, he is understood to have power to use such means, as he shall think most fit for his discharge.

Eleventhly, to the sovereign is committed the power of rewarding with riches, or honour, and of punishing with corporal or pecuniary punishment, or with ignominy, every subject according to the law he hath formerly made; or if there be no law made, according as he shall judge most to conduce to the encouraging of men to serve the commonwealth, or deterring of them from doing disservice to the same.

Lastly, considering what value men are naturally apt to set upon themselves; what respect they look for from others; and how little they value other men; from whence continually arise amongst them, emulation, quarrels, factions, and at last war, to the destroying of one another, and diminution of their strength against a common enemy; it is necessary that there be laws of honour, and a public rate of the worth of such men as have deserved, or are able to deserve well of the commonwealth; and that there be force in the hands of some or other, to put those laws in execution. But it hath already been shown, that not only the whole *militia*, or forces of the commonwealth; but also the judicature of all controversies, is annexed to the sovereignty. To the sovereign therefore it belongeth also to give titles of honour; and to appoint what order of place, and dignity, each man shall hold; and what signs of respect, in public or private meetings, they shall give to one another.

These are the rights, which make the essence of sovereignty; and which are the marks, whereby a man may discern in what man, or assembly of men, the sovereign power is placed, and resideth. For these are incommunicable, and inseparable. The power to coin money, to dispose of the estate and persons of infant heirs; to have preemption in markets; and all other statute prerogatives, may be transferred by the sovereign; and yet the power to protect his subjects be retained. But if he transfer the *militia*, he retains the judicature in vain, for want of execution of the laws: or if he grant away the power of raising money; the *militia* is in vain; or if he give away the government of doctrines, men will be frighted into rebellion with the fear of spirits. And so if we consider any one of the said rights, we shall presently see, that the holding of all the rest will produce no effect, in the conservation of peace and justice, the end for which all commonwealths are instituted. And this division is it, whereof it is said, *a kingdom divided in itself cannot stand:* for unless this division precede, division into opposite armies can never happen. If there had not first been an opinion received of the greatest part of England, that these powers were divided between the King, and the Lords, and the House of Commons, the people had never been divided and fallen into this civil war; first between those that disagreed in politics; and after between the dissenters about the liberty of religion; which have so instructed men in this point of sovereign right, that there be few now in England that do not see, that these rights are inseparable, and will be so generally acknowledged at the next return of peace; and so continue, till their miseries are forgotten; and no longer, except the vulgar be better taught than they have hitherto been.

And because they are essential and inseparable rights, it follows necessarily, that in whatsoever words any of them seem to be granted away, yet if the sovereign power itself be not in direct terms renounced, and the name of sovereign no more given by the grantees to him that grants them, the grant is void: for when he has granted all he can, if we grant back the sovereignty, all is restored, as inseparably annexed thereunto.

This great authority being indivisible, and inseparably annexed to the sovereignty, there is little ground for the opinion of them, that say of sovereign kings, though they be *singulis majores,* of greater power than every one of their subjects, yet they be *universis minores,* of less power than them all together. For if by *all together,* they mean not the collective body as one person, then *all together,* and *every one,* signify the same; and the speech is absurd. But if by *all together,* they understand them as one person, which person the sovereign bears, then the power of all together, is the same with the sovereign's power; and so again the speech is absurd: which absurdity they see well enough, when the sovereignty is in an assembly of the people; but in a monarch they see it not; and yet the power of sovereignty is the same in whomsoever it be placed.

And as the power, so also the honour of the sovereign, ought to be greater, than that of any, or all the subjects. For in the sovereignty is the fountain of honour. The dignities of lord, earl, duke, and prince are his creatures. As in the presence of the master, the servants are equal, and without any honour at all; so are the subjects, in the presence of the sovereign. And though they shine some more, some less, when they are out of his sight; yet in his presence, they shine no more than the stars in the presence of the sun.

But a man may here object, that the condition of subjects is very miserable; as being obnoxious to the lusts, and other irregular passions of him, or them that have so unlimited a power in their hands. And commonly they that live under a monarch, think it the fault of monarchy; and they that live under the government of democracy, or other sovereign assembly, attribute all the inconvenience to that form of commonwealth; whereas the power in all forms, if they be perfect enough to protect them, is the same: not considering that the state of man can never be without some incommodity or other; and that the greatest, that in any form of government can possibly happen to the people in general, is scarce sensible, in respect of the miseries, and horrible calamities, that accompany a civil war, or that dissolute condition of masterless men, without subjection to laws, and a coercive power to tie their hands from rapine and revenge: nor considering that the greatest pressure of sovereign governors, proceedeth not from any delight, or profit they can expect in the damage or weakening of their subjects, in whose vigour, consisteth their own strength and glory; but in the restiveness of themselves, that unwillingly contributing to their own defence, make it necessary for their governors to draw from them what they can in time of peace, that they may have means on any emergent occasion, or sudden need, to resist, or take advantage on their enemies. For all men are by nature provided of notable multiplying glasses, that is their passions and self-love, through which, every little payment appeareth a great grievance; but are destitute of those prospective glasses, namely moral and civil science, to see afar off the miseries that hang over them, and cannot without such payments be avoided.

CHAPTER XIX

Of the Several Kinds of Commonwealth by Institution, and of Succession to the Sovereign Power

THE difference of commonwealths, consisteth in the difference of the sovereign, or the person representative of all and every one of the multitude. And because the sovereignty is either in one man, or in an assembly of more than one; and into that assembly either every man hath right to enter, or not every one, but certain men distinguished from the rest; it is manifest, there can be but three kinds of commonwealth. For the representative must needs be one man, or more: and if more, then it is the assembly of all, or but of a part. When the representative is one man, then is the commonwealth a MONARCHY: when an assembly of all that will come together, then it is a DEMOCRACY, or popular commonwealth: when an assembly of a part only, then it is called an ARISTOCRACY. Other kind of commonwealth there can be none: for either one, or more, or all, must have the sovereign power, which I have shown to be indivisible, entire.

There be other names of government, in the histories, and books of policy; as *tyranny,* and *oligarchy:* but they are not the names of other forms of government, but of the same forms misliked. For they that are discontented under *monarchy,* call it *tyranny;* and they that are displeased with *aristocracy,* call it *oligarchy:* so also, they which find themselves grieved under a *democracy,* call it *anarchy,* which signifies want of government; and yet I think no man believes, that want of government, is any new kind of government: nor by the same reason ought they to believe, that the government is of one kind, when they like it, and another, when they mislike it, or are oppressed by the governors.

It is manifest, that men who are in absolute liberty, may, if they please, give authority to one man, to represent them every one; as well as give such authority to any assembly of men whatsoever; and consequently may subject themselves, if they think good, to a monarch, as absolutely, as to any other representative. Therefore, where there is already erected a sovereign power, there can be no other representative of the same people, but only to certain particular ends, by the sovereign limited. For that were to erect two sovereigns; and every man to have his person represented by two actors, that by opposing one another, must needs divide that power, which, if men will live in peace, is indivisible; and thereby reduce the multitude into the condition of war, contrary to the end for which all sovereignty is instituted. And therefore as it is absurd, to think that a sovereign assembly, inviting the people of their dominion, to send up their deputies, with power to make known their advice, or desires, should therefore hold such deputies, rather than themselves, for the absolute representatives of the people: so it is absurd also, to think the same in a monarchy. And I know not how this so manifest a truth, should of late be so little observed; that in a monarchy, he that had the sovereignty from a descent of six hundred years, was alone called sovereign, had the title of Majesty from every one of his subjects, and was unquestionably taken by them for their king, was notwithstanding never considered as their representative; the name without contradiction passing for the title of those men, which at his command were sent up by the people to carry their petitions, and give him, if he permitted it, their advice. Which may serve as an admonition, for those that are the true, and absolute representative of a people, to instruct men in the nature of that office, and to take heed how they admit of any other general representation upon any occasion whatsoever, if they mean to discharge the trust committed to them.

The difference between these three kinds of commonwealth, consisteth not in the difference of power; but in the difference of convenience, or aptitude to produce the peace, and security of the people; for which end they were instituted. And to compare monarchy with the other two, we may observe; first, that whosoever beareth the person of the people, or is one of that assembly that bears it, beareth also his own natural person. And though he be careful in his politic person to procure the common interest; yet he is more, or no less careful to procure the private good of himself, his family, kindred and friends; and for the most part, if the public interest chance to cross the private, he prefers the private: for the passions of men, are commonly more potent than their reason. From whence it follows, that where the public and private interest are most closely united, there is the public most advanced. Now in monarchy, the private interest is the same with the public. The riches, power, and honour of a monarch arise only from the riches, strength and reputation of his subjects. For no king can be rich, nor glorious, nor secure, whose subjects are either poor, or contemptible, or too weak through want or dissention, to maintain a war against their enemies: whereas in a democracy, or aristocracy, the public prosperity confers not so much to the private fortune of one that is corrupt, or ambitious, as doth many times a perfidious advice, a treacherous action, or a civil war.

Secondly, that a monarch receiveth counsel of whom, when, and where he pleaseth; and consequently may hear the opinion of men versed in the matter about which he deliberates, of what rank or quality soever, and as long before the time of action, and with as much secrecy, as he will. But when a sovereign assembly has need of counsel, none are admitted but such as have a right thereto from the beginning; which for the most part are of those who have been versed more in the acquisition of wealth than of knowledge; and are to give their advice in long discourses, which may, and do commonly excite men to action, but not govern them in it. For the *understanding* is by the flame of the passions, never enlightened, but dazzled. Nor is there any place, or time, wherein an assembly can receive counsel with secrecy, because of their own multitude.

Thirdly, that the resolutions of a monarch, are subject to no other inconstancy, than that of human nature; but in assemblies, besides that of nature, there ariseth an inconstancy from the number. For the absence of a few, that would have the resolution once taken, continue firm, which may happen by security, negligence, or private impediments, or the diligent appearance of a few of the contrary opinion, undoes today, all that was concluded yesterday.

Fourthly, that a monarch cannot disagree with himself, out of envy, or interest; but an assembly may; and that to such a height, as may produce a civil war.

Fifthly, that in monarchy there is this inconvenience; that any subject, by the power of one man, for the enriching of a favourite or flatterer, may be deprived of all he possesseth; which I confess is a great and inevitable inconvenience. But the same may as well happen, where the sovereign power is in an assembly: for their power is the same; and they are as subject to evil counsel, and to be seduced by orators, as a monarch by flatterers; and becoming one another's flatterers, serve one another's covetousness and ambition by turns. And whereas the favourites of monarchs, are few, and they have none else to advance but their own kindred; the favourites of an assembly, are many; and the kindred much more numerous, than of any monarch. Besides, there is no favourite of a monarch, which cannot as well succour his friends, as hurt his enemies: but orators, that is to say, favourites of sovereign assemblies, though they have great power to hurt, have little to save. For to accuse, requires less eloquence, such is man's nature, than to excuse; and condemnation, than absolution more resembles justice.

Sixthly, that it is an inconvenience in monarchy, that the sovereignty may descend upon an infant, or one that cannot discern between good and evil: and consisteth in this, that the use of his power, must be in the hand of another man, or of some assembly of men, which are to govern by his right, and in his name; as curators, and protectors of his person, and authority. But to say there is inconvenience, in putting the use of the sovereign power, into the hand of a man, or an assembly of men; is to say that all government is more inconvenient, than confusion, and civil war. And therefore all the danger that can be pretended, must arise from the contention of those, that for an office of so great honour, and profit, may become competitors. To make it appear, that this inconvenience, proceedeth not from that form of government we call monarchy, we are to consider, that the precedent monarch hath appointed who shall have the tuition of his infant successor, either expressly by testament, or tacitly, by not controlling the custom in that case received: and then such inconvenience, if it happen, is to be attributed, not to the monarchy, but to the ambition, and injustice of the subjects; which in all kinds of government, where the people are not well instructed in their duty, and the rights of sovereignty, is the same. Or else the precedent monarch hath not at all taken order for such tuition; and then the law of nature hath provided this sufficient rule, that the tuition shall be in him, that hath by nature most interest in the preservation of the authority of the infant, and to whom least benefit can accrue by his death, or diminution. For seeing every man by nature seeketh his own benefit, and promotion; to put an infant into the power of those, that can promote themselves by his destruction, or damage, is not tuition, but treachery. So that sufficient provision being taken, against all just quarrel, about the government under a child, if any contention arise to the disturbance of the public peace, it is not to be attributed to the form of monarchy, but to the ambition of subjects, and ignorance of their duty. On the other side, there is no great commonwealth, the sovereignty whereof is in a great assembly, which is not, as to consultations of peace, and war, and making of laws, in the same condition, as if the government were in a child. For as a child wants the judgment to dissent from counsel given him, and is thereby necessitated to take the advice of them, or him, to whom he is committed: so an assembly wanteth the liberty, to dissent from the counsel of the major part, be it good, or bad. And as a child has need of a tutor, or protector, to preserve his person and authority: so also, in great commonwealths, the sovereign assembly, in all great dangers and troubles, have need of *custodes libertatis;* that is of dictators, or protectors of their authority; which are as much as temporary monarchs, to whom for a time, they may commit the entire exercise of their power; and have, at the end of that time, been oftener deprived thereof, than infant kings, by their protectors, regents, or any other tutors.

Though the kinds of sovereignty be, as I have now shown, but three; that is to say, monarchy, where one man has it; or democracy, where the general assembly of subjects hath it; or aristocracy, where it is in an assembly of certain persons nominated, or otherwise distinguished from the rest: yet he that shall consider the particular commonwealths that have been, and are in the world, will not perhaps easily reduce them to three, and may thereby be inclined to think there be other forms, arising from these mingled together. As for example, elective kingdoms; where kings have the sovereign power put into their hands for a time; or kingdoms, wherein the king hath a power limited: which governments, are nevertheless by most writers called monarchy. Likewise if a popular, or aristocratical commonwealth, subdue an enemy's country, and govern the same, by a president, procurator, or other magistrate; this may seem perhaps at first sight, to be a democratical, or aristocratical government. But it is not so. For elective kings, are not sovereigns, but ministers of the sovereign; nor limited kings, sovereigns, but ministers of them that have the sovereign power: nor are those provinces which are in subjection to a democracy, or aristocracy of another commonwealth, democratically or aristocratically governed, but monarchically.

And first, concerning an elective king, whose power is limited to his life, as it is in many places of Christendom at this day; or to certain years or months, as the dictator's power amongst the Romans; if he have right to appoint his successor, he is no more elective but hereditary. But if he have no power to elect his successor, then there is some other man, or assembly known, which after his decease may elect anew, or else the commonwealth dieth, and dissolveth with him, and returneth to the condition of war. If it be known who have the power to give the sovereignty after his death, it is known also that the sovereignty was in them before: for none have right to give that which they have not right to possess, and keep to themselves, if they think good. But if there be none that can give the sovereignty, after the decease of him that was first elected; then has he power, nay he is obliged by the law of nature, to provide, by establishing his successor, to keep those that had trusted him with the government, from relapsing into the miserable condition of civil war. And consequently he was, when elected, a sovereign absolute.

Secondly, that king whose power is limited, is not superior to him, or them that have the power to limit it; and he that is not superior, is not supreme; that is to say not sovereign. The sovereignty therefore was always in that assembly which had the right to limit him; and by consequence the government not monarchy, but either democracy, or aristocracy; as of old time in Sparta; where the kings had a privilege to lead their armies; but the sovereignty was in the Ephori.

Thirdly, whereas heretofore the Roman people governed the land of Judea, for example, by a president; yet was not Judea therefore a democracy; because they were not governed by any assembly, into the which, any of them, had the right to enter; nor an aristocracy; because they were not governed by any assembly, into which, any man could enter by their election: but they were governed by one person, which, though as to the people of Rome, was an assembly of the people, or democracy: yet as to the people of Judea, which had no right at all of participating in the government, was a monarch. For though where the people are governed by an assembly, chosen by themselves out of their own number, the government is called a democracy, or aristocracy; yet when they are governed by an assembly, not of their own choosing, it is a monarchy; not of *one* man, over another man; but of one people, over another people.

Of all these forms of government, the matter being mortal, so that not only monarchs, but also whole assemblies die, it is necessary for the conservation of the peace of men, that as there was order taken for an artificial man, so there be order also taken, for an artificial eternity of life; without which, men that are governed by an assembly, should return into the condition of war in every age; and they that are governed by one man, as soon as their governor dieth. This artificial eternity, is that which men call the right of *succession.*

There is no perfect form of government, where the disposing of the succession is not in the present sovereign. For if it be in any other particular man, or private assembly, it is in a person subject, and may be assumed by the sovereign at his pleasure; and consequently the right is in himself. And if it be in no particular man, but left to a new choice: then is the commonwealth dissolved; and the right is in him that can get it; contrary to the intention of them that did institute the commonwealth, for their perpetual, and not temporary security.

In a democracy, the whole assembly cannot fail, unless the multitude that are to be governed fail. And therefore questions of the right of succession, have in that form of government no place at all.

In an aristocracy, when any of the assembly dieth, the election of another into his room belongeth to the assembly, as the sovereign, to whom belongeth the choosing of all counsellors and officers. For that which the representative doth, as actor, every one of the subjects doth, as author. And though the sovereign assembly may give power to others, to elect new men, for supply of their court; yet it is still by their authority, that the election is made; and by the same it may, when the public shall require it, be recalled.

The greatest difficulty about the right of succession, is in monarchy: and the difficulty ariseth from this, that at first sight, it is not manifest who is to appoint the successor; nor many times, who it is whom he hath appointed. For in both these cases, there is required a more exact ratiocination, than every man is accustomed to use. As to the question, who shall appoint the successor, of a monarch that hath the sovereign authority; that is to say, who shall determine of the right of inheritance, (for elective kings and princes have not the sovereign power in propriety, but in use only), we are to consider, that either he that is in possession, has right to dispose of the succession, or else that right is again in the dissolved multitude. For the death of him that hath the sovereign power in propriety, leaves the multitude without any sovereign at all; that is, without any representative in whom they should be united, and be capable of doing any one action at all: and therefore they are incapable of election of any new monarch; every man having equal right to submit himself to such as he thinks best able to protect him; or if he can, protect himself by his own sword; which is a return to confusion, and to the condition of a war of every man against every man, contrary to the end for which monarchy had its first institution. Therefore it is manifest, that by the institution of monarchy, the disposing of the successor, is always left to the judgment and will of the present possessor.

And for the question, which may arise sometimes, who it is that the monarch in possession, hath designed to the succession and inheritance of his power; it is determined by his express words, and testament; or by other tacit signs sufficient.

By express words, or testament, when it is declared by him in his lifetime, *viva voce,* or by writing; as the first emperors of Rome declared who should be their heirs. For the word heir does not of itself imply the children, or nearest kindred of a man; but whomsoever a man shall any way declare, he would have to succeed him in his estate. If therefore a monarch declare expressly, that such a man shall be his heir, either by word or writing, then is that man immediately after the decease of his predecessor, invested in the right of being monarch.

But where testament, and express words are wanting, other natural signs of the will are to be followed: whereof the one is custom. And therefore where the custom is, that the next of kindred absolutely succeedeth, there also the next of kindred hath right to the succession; for that, if the will of him that was in possession had been otherwise, he might easily have declared the same in his life-time. And likewise where the custom is, that the next of the male kindred succeedeth, there also the right of succession is in the next of the kindred male, for the same reason. And so it is if the custom were to advance the female. For whatsoever custom a man may by a word control, and does not, it is a natural sign he would have that custom stand.

But where neither custom, nor testament hath preceded, there it is to be understood, first, that a monarch's will is, that the government remain monarchical; because he hath approved that government in himself. Secondly, that a child of his own, male, or female, be preferred before any other; because men are presumed to be more inclined by nature, to advance their own children, than the children of other men; and of their own, rather a male than a female; because men, are naturally fitter than women, for actions of labour and danger. Thirdly, where his own issue faileth, rather a brother than a stranger; and so still the nearer in blood, rather than the more remote; because it is always presumed that the nearer of kin, is the nearer in affection; and it is evident that a man receives always, by reflection, the most honour from the greatness of his nearest kindred.

But if it be lawful for a monarch to dispose of the succession by words of contract, or testament, men may perhaps object a great inconvenience: for he may sell, or give his right of governing to a stranger; which, because strangers, that is, men not used to live under the same government, nor speaking the same language, do commonly undervalue one another, may turn to the oppression of his subjects; which is indeed a great inconvenience: but it proceedeth not necessarily from the subjection to a stranger's government, but from the unskilfulness of the governors, ignorant of the true rules of politics. And therefore the Romans when they had subdued many nations, to make their government digestible, were wont to take away that grievance, as much as they thought necessary, by giving sometimes to whole nations, and sometimes to principal men of every nation they conquered, not only the privileges, but also the name of Romans; and took many of them into the senate, and offices of charge, even in the Roman city. And this was it our most wise king, king James, aimed at, in endeavouring the union of his two realms of England and Scotland. Which if he could have obtained, had in all likelihood prevented the civil wars, which make both those kingdoms, at this present, miserable. It is not therefore any injury to the people, for a monarch to dispose of the succession by will; though by the fault of many princes, it hath been sometimes found inconvenient. Of the lawfulness of it, this also is an argument, that whatsoever inconvenience can arrive by giving a kingdom to a stranger, may arrive also by so marrying with strangers, as the right of succession may descend upon them: yet this by all men is accounted lawful.

CHAPTER XX

Of Dominion Paternal, and Despotical

A COMMONWEALTH *by acquisition,* is that, where the sovereign power is acquired by force; and it is acquired by force, when men singly, or many together by plurality of voices, for fear of death, or bonds, do authorize all the actions of that man, or assembly, that hath their lives and liberty in his power.

And this kind of dominion, or sovereignty, differeth from sovereignty by institution, only in this, that men who choose their sovereign, do it for fear of one another, and not of him whom they institute: but in this case, they subject themselves, to him they are afraid of. In both cases they do it for fear: which is to be noted by them, that hold all such covenants, as proceed from fear of death or violence, void: which if it were true, no man, in any kind of commonwealth, could be obliged to obedience. It is true, that in a commonwealth once instituted, or acquired, promises proceeding from fear of death or violence, are no covenants, nor obliging, when the thing promised is contrary to the laws; but the reason is not, because it was made upon fear, but because he that promiseth, hath no right in the thing promised. Also, when he may lawfully perform, and doth not, it is not the invalidity of the covenant, that absolveth him, but the sentence of the sovereign. Otherwise, whensoever a man lawfully promiseth, he unlawfully breaketh: but when the sovereign, who is the actor, acquitteth him, then he is acquitted by him that extorted the promise, as by the author of such absolution.

But the rights, and consequences of sovereignty, are the same in both. His power cannot, without his consent, be transferred to another: he cannot forfeit it: he cannot be accused by any of his subjects, of injury; he cannot be punished by them: he is judge of what is necessary for peace; and judge of doctrines: he is sole legislator; and supreme judge of controversies; and of the times and occasions of war, and peace: to him it belongeth to choose magistrates, counsellors, commanders, and all other officers, and ministers; and to determine of rewards, and punishments, honour, and order. The reasons whereof, are the same which are alleged in the precedent chapter, for the same rights, and consequences of sovereignty by institution.

Dominion is acquired two ways; by generation, and by conquest. The right of dominion by generation, is that, which the parent hath over his children; and is called PATERNAL. And is not so derived from the generation, as if therefore the parent had dominion over his child because he begat him; but from the child's consent, either express, or by other sufficient arguments declared. For as to the generation, God hath ordained to man a helper; and there be always two that are equally parents: the dominion therefore over the child, should belong equally to both; and he be equally subject to both, which is impossible; for no man can obey two masters. And whereas some have attributed the dominion to the man only, as being of the more excellent sex; they misreckon in it. For there is not always that difference of strength, or prudence between the man and the woman, as that the right can be determined without war. In commonwealths, this controversy is decided by the civil law; and for the most part, but not always, the sentence is in favour of the father; because for the most part commonwealths have been erected by the fathers, not by the mothers of families. But the question lieth now in the state of mere nature; where there are supposed no laws of matrimony; no laws for the education of children; but the law of nature, and the natural inclination of the sexes, one to another, and to their children. In this condition of mere nature, either the parents between themselves dispose of the dominion over the child by contract; or do not dispose thereof at all. If they dispose thereof, the right passeth according to the contract. We find in history that the Amazons[5] contracted with the men of the neighbouring countries, to whom they had recourse for issue, that the issue male should be sent back, but the female remain with themselves: so that the dominion of the females was in the mother.

If there be no contract, the dominion is in the mother. For in the condition of mere nature, where there are no matrimonial laws, it cannot be known who is the father, unless it be declared by the mother: and therefore the right of dominion over the child dependeth on her will, and is consequently hers. Again, seeing the infant is first in the power of the mother, so as she may either nourish, or expose it; if she nourish it, it oweth its life to the mother; and is therefore obliged to obey her, rather than any other; and by consequence the dominion over it is hers. But if she expose it, and another find and nourish it, the dominion is in him that nourisheth it. For it ought to obey him by whom it is preserved; because preservation of life being the end, for which one man becomes subject to another, every man is supposed to prom-

5. [According to Greek mythology, the Amazons were a tribe of warlike women.]

ise obedience, to him, in whose power it is to save, or destroy him.

If the mother be the father's subject, the child, is in the father's power: and if the father be the mother's subject, as when a sovereign queen marrieth one of her subjects, the child is subject to the mother; because the father also is her subject.

If a man and woman, monarchs of two several kingdoms, have a child, and contract concerning who shall have the dominion of him, the right of the dominion passeth by the contract. If they contract not, the dominion followeth the dominion of the place of his residence. For the sovereign of each country hath dominion over all that reside therein.

He that hath the dominion over the child, hath dominion also over the children of the child; and over their children's children. For he that hath dominion over the person of a man, hath dominion over all that is his; without which, dominion were but a title, without the effect.

The right of succession to paternal dominion, proceedeth in the same manner, as doth the right of succession of monarchy; of which I have already sufficiently spoken in the precedent chapter.

Dominion acquired by conquest, or victory in war, is that which some writers call DESPOTICAL, from Δεσπότης, which signifieth a *lord,* or *master;* and is the dominion of the master over his servant. And this dominion is then acquired to the victor, when the vanquished to avoid the present stroke of death, covenanteth either in express words, or by other sufficient signs of the will, that so long as his life, and the liberty of his body is allowed him, the victor shall have the use thereof, at his pleasure. And after such covenant made, the vanquished is a SERVANT, and not before: for by the word *servant,* whether it be derived from *servire,* to serve, or from *servare,* to save, which I leave to grammarians to dispute, is not meant a captive, which is kept in prison, or bonds, till the owner of him that took him, or bought him of one that did, shall consider what to do with him: for such men, commonly called slaves, have no obligation at all; but may break their bonds, or the prison; and kill, or carry away captive their master, justly: but one, that being taken, hath corporal liberty allowed him; and upon promise not to run away, nor to do violence to his master, is trusted by him.

It is not therefore the victory, that giveth the right of dominion over the vanquished, but his own covenant. Nor is he obliged because he is conquered; that is to say, beaten, and taken, or put to flight; but because he cometh in, and submitteth to the victor; nor is the victor obliged by an enemy's rendering himself, without promise of life, to spare him for this his yielding to discretion; which obliges not the victor longer, than in his own discretion he shall think fit.

And that which men do, when they demand, as it is now called, *quarter,* which the Greeks called Ζωγρία, *taking alive,* is to evade the present fury of the victor, by submission, and to compound for their life, with ransom, or service: and therefore he that hath quarter, hath not his life given, but deferred till farther deliberation; for it is not a yielding on condition of life, but to discretion. And then only is his life in security, and his service due, when the victor hath trusted him with his corporal liberty. For slaves that work in prisons; or fetters, do it not of duty, but to avoid the cruelty of their task-masters.

The master of the servant, is master also of all he hath: and may exact the use thereof; that is to say, of his goods, of his labour, of his servants, and of his children, as often as he shall think fit. For he holdeth his life of his master, by the covenant of obedience; that is, of owning, and authorizing whatsoever the master shall do. And in case the master, if he refuse, kill him, or cast him into bonds, or otherwise punish him for his disobedience, he is himself the author of the same; and cannot accuse him of injury.

In sum, the rights and consequences of both *paternal* and *despotical* dominion, are the very same with those of a sovereign by institution; and for the same reasons: which reasons are set down in the precedent chapter. So that for a man that is monarch of divers nations, whereof he hath, in one the sovereignty by institution of the people assembled, and in another by conquest, that is by the submission of each particular, to avoid death or bonds; to demand of one nation more than of the other, from the title of conquest, as being a conquered nation, is an act of ignorance of the rights of sovereignty; for the sovereign is absolute over both alike; or else there is no sovereignty at all; and so every man may lawfully protect himself, if he can, with his own sword, which is the condition of war.

By this it appears; that a great family, if it be not part of some commonwealth, is of itself, as to the rights of sovereignty, a little monarchy: whether that family consist of a man and his children; or of a man and his servants; or of a man, and his children, and servants together: wherein the father or master is the sovereign. But yet a family is not properly a commonwealth; unless it be of that power by its own number, or by other opportunities, as not to be subdued without the hazard of war. For where a number of men are manifestly too weak to defend themselves united, every one may use his own reason in time of danger, to save his own life, either by flight, or by submission to the enemy, as he shall think best; in the same manner as a very small company of soldiers, surprised by an army, may cast down their arms, and demand quarter, or run away, rather than be put to the sword. And thus much shall suffice, concerning what I find by speculation, and deduction, of sovereign rights, from the nature, need, and designs of men, in erecting of commonwealths, and putting themselves under monarchs, or assemblies, entrusted with power enough for their protection.

Let us now consider what the Scripture teacheth in the same point. To Moses, the children of Israel say thus: *Speak thou to us, and we will hear thee: but let not God speak to us, lest we die.* (*Exod.* xx, 19.) This is absolute obedience to Moses. Concerning the right of kings, God himself by the mouth of Samuel, saith, (I *Sam.* viii, 11, 12, &c.) *This shall be the right of the king you will have to reign over you. He shall take your sons, and set them to drive his chariots, and to be his horsemen, and to run before his chariots; and gather in his harvest; and to make his engines of war, and instruments of his chariots; and shall take your daughters to make perfumes, to be his cooks, and bakers. He shall take your fields, your vine-yards, and your olive-yards, and give them to his servants. He shall take the tithe of your corn and wine, and give it to the men of his chamber, and to his other servants. He shall take your man-servants, and your maid-servants, and the choice of your youth, and employ them in his business. He shall take the tithe of your flocks; ad you shall be his servants.* This is absolute power, and summed up in the last words, *you shall be his servants.* Again, when the people heard what power their king was to have, yet they consented thereto, and say thus, (*verse* 10) *we will be as all other nations, and our king shall judge our causes, and go before us, to conduct our wars.* Here is confirmed the right that sovereigns have, both to the *militia,* and to all *judicature;* in which is contained absolute power, as one man can possibly transfer to another. Again, the prayer of king Solomon to God, was this (1 *Kings* iii, 9): *Give to thy servant understanding, to judge thy people, and to discern between good and evil.* It belongeth therefore to the sovereign to be *judge*, and to prescribe the rules of *discerning good* and *evil:* which rules are laws; and therefore in him is the legislative power. Saul sought the life of David; yet when it was in his power to slay Saul, and his servants would have done it, David forbad them, saying, (I *Sam.* xxiv, 6) *God forbid I should do such an act against my Lord, the anointed of God.* For obedience of servants St. Paul saith: (*Col.* iii, 22) *Servants obey your masters in all things;* and, (*Col.* iii, 20) *children obey your parents in all things.* There is simple obedience in those that are subject to paternal, or despotical dominion. Again, (*Matt.* xxiii, 2, 3) *The Scribes and Pharisees sit in Moses' chair, and therefore all that they shall bid you observe, that observe and do.* There again is simple obedience. And St. Paul, (*Titus* iii, 2) *Warn them that they subject themselves to princes, and to those that are in authority, and obey them.* This obedience is also simple. Lastly, our Saviour himself acknowledges, that men ought to pay such taxes as are by kings imposed, where he says, *give to Caesar that which is Caesar's;* and paid such taxes himself. And that the king's word, is sufficient to take anything from any subject, when there is need; and that the king is judge of that need: for he himself, as king of the Jews, commanded his disciples to take the ass, and ass's colt to carry him into Jerusalem, saying (*Matt.* xxi, 2, 3) *Go into the village over against you, and you shall find a she ass tied, and her colt with her, untie them, and bring them to me. And if any man ask you, what you mean by it, say the Lord hath need of them: and they will let them go.* They will not ask whether his necessity be a sufficient title; nor whether he be judge of that necessity; but acquiesce in the will of the Lord.

To these places may be added also that of (*Genesis* iii, 5) *Ye shall be as gods, knowing good and evil.* And (*verse* 11) *Who told thee that thou was naked? hast thou eaten of the tree, of which I commanded thee thou shouldest not eat?* For the cognizance or judicature of *good* and *evil*, being forbidden by the name of the fruit of the tree of knowledge, as a trial of Adam's obedience; the devil to inflame the ambition of the woman, to whom that fruit already seemed beautiful, told her that by tasting it, they should be as gods, knowing *good* and *evil.* Whereupon having both eaten, they did indeed take upon them God's office, which is judicature of good and evil; but acquired no new ability to distinguish between them aright. And whereas it is said, that having eaten, they saw they were naked; no man hath so interpreted that place, as if they had been formerly blind, and saw not their own skins: the meaning is plain, that it was then they first judged their nakedness, wherein it was God's will to create them, to be uncomely; and by being ashamed, did tacitly censure God himself. And thereupon God saith; *Hast thou eaten,* &c. as if he should say, doest thou that owest me obedience, take upon thee to judge of my commandments? Whereby it is clearly, though allegorically, signified, that the commands of them that have the right to command, are not by their subjects to be censured, nor disputed.

So that it appeareth plainly, to my understanding, both from reason, and Scripture, that the sovereign power, whether placed in one man, as in monarchy, or in one assembly of men, as in popular, and aristocratical commonwealths, is as great, as possibly men can be imagined to make it. And though of so unlimited a power, men may fancy many evil consequences, yet the consequences of the want of it, which is perpetual war of every man against his neighbour, are much worse. The condition of man in this life shall never be without inconveniences; but there happeneth in no commonwealth any great inconvenience, but what proceeds from the subject's disobedience, and breach of those covenants, from which the commonwealth hath its being. And whosoever thinking sovereign power too great, will seek to make it less, must subject himself, to the power, that can limit it; that is to say, to a greater.

The greatest objection is, that of the practice; when men ask, where, and when, such power has by subjects been acknowledged. But one may ask them again, when, or where has there been a kingdom long free from sedition and civil war. In those nations, whose commonwealths have been long-lived, and not been destroyed but by foreign war, the subjects never did dispute of the sovereign power. But howsoever, an argument from the practice of men, that have not sifted to the bottom, and with exact reason weighed the causes, and nature of commonwealths, and suffer daily those miseries, that proceed from the ignorance thereof, is invalid. For though in all places of the world, men should lay the foundation of their houses on the sand, it could not thence be inferred, that so it ought to be. The skill of making, and maintaining commonwealths, consisteth in certain rules, as doth arithmetic and geometry: not, as tennis-play, on practice only: which rules, neither poor men have the leisure, nor men that have had the leisure, have hitherto had the curiosity, or the method to find out.

CHAPTER XXI

Of the Liberty of Subjects

LIBERTY, or FREEDOM, signifieth, properly, the absence of opposition; by opposition, I mean external impediments of motion; and may be applied no less to irrational, and inanimate creatures, than to rational. For whatsoever is so tied, or environed, as it cannot move but within a certain space, which space is determined by the opposition of some external body, we say it hath not liberty to go further. And so of all living creatures, whilst they are imprisoned, or restrained, with walls, or chains; and of the water whilst it is kept in by banks, or vessels, that otherwise would spread itself into a larger space, we use to say, they are not at liberty, to move in such manner, as without those external impediments they would. But when the impediment of motion, is in the constitution of the thing itself, we use not to say; it wants the liberty; but the power to move; as when a stone lieth still, or a man is fastened to his bed by sickness.

And according to this proper, and generally received meaning of the word, a FREEMAN, *is he, that in those things, which by his strength and wit he is able to do, is not hindered to do what he has a will to.* But when the words *free*, and *liberty*, are applied to any thing but *bodies*, they are abused; for that which is not subject to motion, is not subject to impediment; and therefore, when it is said, for example, the way is free, no liberty of the way is signified, but of those that walk in it without stop. And when we say a gift is free, there is not meant any liberty of the gift, but of the giver, that was not bound by any law or covenant to give it. So when we *speak freely,* it is not the liberty of voice, or pronunciation, but of the man, whom no law hath obliged to speak otherwise than he did. Lastly, from the use of the word *free-will,* no liberty can be inferred of the will, desire, or inclination, but the liberty of the man; which consisteth in this, that he finds no stop, in doing what he has the will, desire, or inclination to do.

Fear and liberty are consistent; as when a man throweth his goods into the sea for *fear* the ship should sink, he doth it nevertheless very willingly, and may refuse to do it if he will: it is therefore the action of one that was *free:* so a man sometimes pays his debt, only for *fear* of imprisonment, which because nobody hindered him from detaining, was the action of a man at *liberty.* And generally all actions which men do in commonwealths, for *fear* of the law, are actions, which the doers had *liberty* to omit.

Liberty, and *necessity* are consistent: as in the water, that hath not only *liberty,* but a *necessity* of descending by the channel: so likewise in the actions which men voluntarily do: which, because they proceed from their will, proceed from *liberty;* and yet, because every act of man's will, and every desire, and inclination proceedeth from some cause, and that from another cause, in a continual chain, whose first link is in the hand of God the first of all causes, proceed from *necessity.* So that to him that could see the connexion of those causes, the *necessity* of all men's voluntary actions, would appear manifest. And therefore God, that seeth, and disposeth all things, seeth also that the *liberty* of man in doing what he will, is accompanied with the *necessity* of doing that which God will, and no more, nor less. For though men may do many things, which God does not command, nor is therefore author of them; yet they can have no passion, nor appetite to anything of which appetite God's will is not the cause. And did not his will assure the *necessity* of man's will, and consequently of all that on man's will dependeth, the *liberty* of men would be a contradiction, and impediment to the omnipotence and *liberty* of God. And this shall suffice, as to the matter in hand, of that natural *liberty,* which only is properly called *liberty.*

But as men, for the attaining of peace, and conservation of themselves thereby, have made an artificial man, which we call a commonwealth; so also have they made artificial chains, called *civil laws,* which they themselves, by mutual covenants, have fastened at one end, to the lips of that man, or assembly, to whom they have given the sovereign power; and at the other end to their own ears. These bonds, in their own nature but weak, may nevertheless be made to hold, by the danger, though not by the difficulty of breaking them.

In relation to these bonds only it is, that I am to speak now, of the *liberty* of *subjects.* For seeing there is no commonwealth in the world, wherein there be rules enough set down, for the regulating of all the actions, and words of men; as being a thing impossible: it followeth necessarily, that in all kinds of actions by the laws praetermitted, men have the liberty, of doing what their own reasons shall suggest, for the most profitable to themselves. For if we take liberty in the proper sense, for corporal liberty; that is to say, freedom from chains and prison; it were very absurd for men to clamour as they do, for the liberty they so manifestly enjoy. Again, if we take liberty, for an exemption from laws, it is no less absurd, for men to demand as they do, that liberty, by which all other men may be masters of their lives. And yet, as absurd as it is, this is it they demand; not knowing that the laws are of no power to protect them, without a sword in the hands of a man, or men, to cause those laws to be put in execution. The liberty of a subject, lieth therefore only in those things, which in regulating their actions, the sovereign hath praetermitted: such as is the liberty to buy, and sell, and otherwise contract with one another; to choose their own abode, their own diet, their own trade of life, and institute their children as they themselves think fit; and the like.

Nevertheless we are not to understand, that by such liberty, the sovereign power of life and death, is either abolished, or limited. For it has been already shown, that nothing the sovereign representative can do to a subject, on what pretence soever, can properly be called injustice, or injury; because every subject is author of every act the sovereign doth; so that he never wanteth right to anything, otherwise, than as he himself is the subject of God, and bound thereby to observe the laws of nature. And therefore it may, and doth often happen in commonwealths, that a subject may be put to death, by the command of the sovereign power; and yet neither do the other wrong: as when Jephtha caused his daughter to be sacrificed:[6] in which, and the like cases, he that so dieth, had liberty to do the action, for which he is nevertheless, without injury put to death. And the same holdeth also in a sovereign prince, that putteth to death an innocent subject. For though the action be against the law of nature, as being contrary to equity, as was the killing of Uriah, by David;[7] yet it was not an injury to Uriah, but to God. Not to Uriah, because the right to do what he pleased was given him by Uriah himself: and yet to God, because David was God's subject, and prohibited all iniquity by the law of nature: which distinction, David himself, when he repented the fact, evidently confirmed, saying, *To thee only have I sinned*. In the same manner, the people of Athens, when they banished the most potent of their commonwealth for ten years, thought they committed no injustice; and yet they never questioned what crime he had done; but what hurt he would do: nay they commanded the banishment of they knew not whom; and every citizen bringing his oystershell into the market place, written with the name of him he desired should be banished, without actually accusing him, sometimes banished an Aristides,[8] for his reputation of justice; and sometimes a scurrilous jester, as Hyperbolus,[9] to make a jest of it. And yet a man cannot say, the sovereign people of Athens wanted right to banish them; or an Athenian the liberty to jest, or to be just.

The liberty, whereof there is so frequent and honourable mention, in the histories, and philosophy of the ancient Greeks, and Romans, and in the writings, and discourse of those that from them have received all their learning in the politics, is not the liberty of particular men; but the liberty of the commonwealth: which is the same with that which every man then should have, if there were no civil laws, nor commonwealth at all. And the effects of it also be the same. For as amongst masterless men, there is perpetual war, of every man against his neighbour; no inheritance, to transmit to the son, nor to expect from the father; no propriety of goods, or lands; no security; but a full and absolute liberty in every particular man: so in states, and commonwealths not dependent on one another, every commonwealth, not every man, has an absolute liberty, to do what it shall judge, that is to say, what that man, or assembly that representeth it, shall judge most conducing to their benefit. But

6. [The reference is to a story related in the Book of Judges according to which the judge Jephthah vowed that if victorious against the Ammonites he would sacrifice whatever first came from the door of his house when he returned. Upon his arrival, after defeating the enemy, he was horrified to be met by his only child, a daughter, whom he then slew as he had sworn he would.]

7. [The reference is to a story related in II Samuel, according to which King David, wishing to marry Bathsheba, arranged for her husband Uriah to be placed in the front line of battle so as to be killed by the enemy.]

8. [Aristides was a fifth-century B.C. Athenian general and statesman who, despite his reputation as a just man, was for a time ostracized at the urging of his rival Themistocles (c.528–462 B.C.), a naval commander.]

9. [Hyperbolus (d.411 B.C.) was an Athenian demagogue who was ridiculed and eventually ostracized.]

withal, they live in the condition of a perpetual war, and upon the confines of battle, with their frontiers armed, and cannons planted against their neighbours round about. The Athenians, and Romans were free; that is, free commonwealths: not that any particular men had the liberty to resist their own representative; but that their representative had the liberty to resist, or invade other people. There is written on the turrets of the city of Lucca[10] in great characters at this day, the word LIBERTAS; yet no man can thence infer, that a particular man has more liberty, or immunity from the service of the commonwealth there, than in Constantinople. Whether a commonwealth be monarchical, or popular, the freedom is still the same.

But it is an easy thing, for men to be deceived, by the specious name of liberty; and for want of judgment to distinguish, mistake that for their private inheritance, and birthright, which is the right of the public only. And when the same error is confirmed by the authority of men in reputation for their writings on this subject, it is no wonder if it produce sedition, and change of government. In these western parts of the world, we are made to receive our opinions concerning the institution, and rights of commonwealths, from Aristotle, Cicero,[11] and other men, Greeks and Romans, that living under popular states, derived those rights, not from the principles of nature, but transcribed them into their books, out of the practice of their own commonwealths, which were popular; as the grammarians describe the rules of language, out of the practice of the time; or the rules of poetry, out of the poems of Homer and Virgil. And because the Athenians were taught, to keep them from desire of changing their government, that they were freemen, and all that lived under monarchy were slaves; therefore Aristotle puts it down in his *Politics, (lib.* 6, *cap.* ii.) *In democracy,* LIBERTY *is to be supposed: for it is commonly held, that no man is* FREE *in any other government.* And as Aristotle; so Cicero, and other writers have grounded their civil doctrine, on the opinions of the Romans, who were taught to hate monarchy, at first, by them that having deposed their sovereign, shared amongst them the sovereignty of Rome; and afterwards by their successors. And by reading of these Greek, and Latin authors, men from their childhood have gotten a habit, under a false show of liberty, of favouring tumults, and of licentious controlling the actions of their sovereigns, and again of controlling those controllers; with the effusion of so much blood, as I think I may truly say, there was never any thing so dearly bought, as these western parts have bought the learning of the Greek and Latin tongues.

To come now to the particulars of the true liberty of a subject; that is to say, what are the things, which though commanded by the sovereign, he may nevertheless, without injustice, refuse to do; we are to consider, what rights we pass away, when we make a commonwealth; or, which is all one, what liberty we deny ourselves, by owning all the actions, without exception, of the man, or assembly we make our sovereign. For in the act of our *submission,* consisteth both our *obligation,* and our *liberty:* which must therefore be inferred by arguments taken from thence; there being no obligation on any man, which ariseth not from some act of his own; for all men equally, are by nature free. And because such arguments, must either be drawn from the express words, *I authorize all his actions,* or from the intention of him that

10. [The city of Lucca is located in Tuscany in central Italy.]

11. [Marcus Tullius Cicero (106–43 B.C.), the statesman and philosopher, was considered the greatest Roman orator.]

submitteth himself to his power, which intention is to be understood by the end for which he so submitteth; the obligation, and liberty of the subject, is to be derived, either from those words, or others equivalent; or else from the end of the institution of sovereignty, namely, the peace of the subjects within themselves, and their defence against a common enemy.

First therefore, seeing sovereignty by institution, is by covenant of every one to every one; and sovereignty by acquisition, by covenants of the vanquished to the victor, or child to the parent; it is manifest, that every subject has liberty in all those things, the right whereof cannot by covenant be transferred. I have shewn before in the 14th chapter, that covenants, not to defend a man's own body, are void. Therefore,

If the sovereign command a man, though justly condemned, to kill, wound, or maim himself; or not to resist those that assault him; or to abstain from the use of food, air, medicine, or any other thing, without which he cannot live; yet hath that man the liberty to disobey.

If a man be interrogated by the sovereign, or his authority, concerning a crime done by himself, he is not bound, without assurance of pardon, to confess it; because no man, as I have shown in the same chapter, can be obliged by covenant to accuse himself.

Again, the consent of a subject to sovereign power, is contained in these words, *I authorize, or take upon me, all his actions;* in which there is no restriction at all, of his own former natural liberty: for by allowing him to *kill me,* I am not bound to kill myself when he commands me. It is one thing to say, *kill me, or my fellow, if you please;* another thing to say, *I will kill myself, or my fellow.* It followeth therefore, that

No man is bound by the words themselves, either to kill himself, or any other man; and consequently, that the obligation a man may sometimes have, upon the command of the sovereign to execute any dangerous, or dishonourable office, dependeth not on the words of our submission; but on the intention, which is to be understood by the end thereof. When therefore our refusal to obey, frustrates the end for which the sovereignty was ordained; then there is no liberty to refuse: otherwise there is.

Upon this ground, a man that is commanded as a soldier to fight against the enemy, though his sovereign have right enough to punish his refusal with death, may nevertheless in many cases refuse, without injustice; as when he substituteth a sufficient soldier in his place: for in this case he deserteth not the service of the commonwealth. And there is allowance to be made for natural timorousness; not only to women, of whom no such dangerous duty is expected, but also to men of feminine courage. When armies fight, there is on one side, or both, a running away; yet when they do it not out of treachery, but fear, they are not esteemed to do it unjustly, but dishonourably. For the same reason, to avoid battle, is not injustice, but cowardice. But he that inrolleth himself a soldier, or taketh imprest money, taketh away the excuse of a timorous nature; and is obliged, not only to go to the battle, but also not to run from it, without his captain's leave. And when the defence of the commonwealth, requireth at once the help of all that are able to bear arms, every one is obliged; because otherwise the institution of the commonwealth, which they have not the purpose, or courage to preserve, was in vain.

To resist the sword of the commonwealth, in defence of another man, guilty, or innocent, no man hath liberty; because such liberty, takes away from the sovereign, the means of protecting us: and is therefore destructive of the very essence of government. But in case a great many men together, have already resisted the sovereign power unjustly, or committed some capital crime, for which every one of them expecteth death, whether have they not the liberty then to join together, and assist, and defend one another? Certainly they have: for they but defend their lives, which the guilty man may as well do, as the innocent. There was indeed injustice in the first breach of their duty; their bearing of arms subsequent to it, though it be to maintain what they have done, is no new unjust act. And if it be only to defend their persons, it is not unjust at all. But the offer of pardon taketh from them, to whom it is offered, the plea of self-defence, and maketh their perseverance in assisting, or defending the rest, unlawful.

As for other liberties, they depend on the silence of the law. In cases where the sovereign has prescribed no rule, there the subject hath the liberty to do, or forbear, according to his own discretion. And therefore such liberty is in some places more, and in some less; and in some times more, in other times less, according as they that have the sovereignty shall think most convenient. As for example, there was a time, when in England a man might enter into his own land and dispossess such as wrongfully possessed it, by force. But in aftertimes, that liberty of forcible entry, was taken away by a statute made, by the king, in parliament. And in some places of the world, men have the liberty of many wives: in other places, such liberty is not allowed.

If a subject have a controversy with his sovereign, of debt, or of right of possession of lands or goods, or concerning any service required at his hands, or concerning any penalty, corporal, or pecuniary, grounded on a precedent law; he hath the same liberty to sue for his right, as if it were against a subject; and before such judges, as are appointed by the sovereign. For seeing the sovereign demandeth by force of a former law, and not by virtue of his power; he declareth thereby, that he requireth no more, than shall appear to be due by that law. The suit therefore is not contrary to the will of the sovereign; and consequently the subject hath the liberty to demand the hearing of his cause; and sentence, according to that law. But if he demand, or take anything by pretence of his power; there lieth, in that case, no action of law; for all that is done by him in virtue of his power, is done by the authority of every subject, and consequently he that brings an action against the sovereign, brings it against himself.

If a monarch, or sovereign assembly, grant a liberty to all, or any of his subjects, which grant standing, he is disabled to provide for their safety, the grant is void; unless he directly renounce, or transfer the sovereignty to another. For in that he might openly, if it had been his will, and in plain terms, have renounced, or transferred it, and did not; it is to be understood it was not his will, but that the grant proceeded from ignorance of the repugnancy between such a liberty and the sovereign power; and therefore the sovereignty is still retained; and consequently all those powers, which are necessary to the exercising thereof; such as are the power of war, and peace, of judicature, of appointing officers, and councillors, of levying money, and the rest named in the 18th chapter.

The obligation of subjects to the sovereign, is understood to last as long, and no longer, than the power lasteth, by which he is able to protect them. For the right men have by nature to protect themselves, when none else can protect them, can by no covenant be relinquished. The sovereignty is the soul of the commonwealth;

which once departed from the body, the members do no more receive their motion from it. The end of obedience is protection; which, wheresoever a man seeth it, either in his own, or in another's sword, nature applieth his obedience to it, and his endeavour to maintain it. And though sovereignty, in the intention of them that make it, be immortal; yet is it in its own nature, not only subject to violent death, by foreign war; but also through the ignorance, and passions of men, it hath in it, from the very institution, many seeds of a natural mortality, by intestine discord.

If a subject be taken prisoner in war; or his person, or his means of life be within the guards of the enemy, and hath his life and corporal liberty given him, on condition to be subject to the victor, he hath liberty to accept the condition; and having accepted it, is the subject of him that took him; because he had no other way to preserve himself. The case is the same, if he be detained on the same terms, in a foreign country. But if a man be held in prison, or bonds, or is not trusted with the liberty of his body; he cannot be understood to be bound by covenant to subjection; and therefore may, if he can, make his escape by any means whatsoever.

If a monarch shall relinquish the sovereignty, both for himself, and his heirs; his subjects return to the absolute liberty of nature; because, though nature may declare who are his sons, and who are the nearest of his kin; yet it dependeth on his own will, as hath been said in the precedent chapter, who shall be his heir. If therefore he will have no heir, there is no sovereignty, nor subjection. The case is the same, if he die without known kindred, and without declaration of his heir. For then there can no heir be known, and consequently no subjection be due.

If the sovereign banish his subject; during the banishment, he is not subject. But he that is sent on a message, or hath leave to travel, is still subject; but it is, by contract between sovereigns, not by virtue of the covenant of subjection. For whosoever entereth into another's dominion, is subject to all the laws thereof; unless he have a privilege by the amity of the sovereigns, or by special licence.

If a monarch subdued by war, render himself subject to the victor; his subjects are delivered from their former obligation, and become obliged to the victor. But if he be held prisoner, or have not the liberty of his own body; he is not understood to have given away the right of sovereignty: and therefore his subjects are obliged to yield obedience to the magistrates formerly placed, governing not in their own name, but in his. For, his right remaining, the question is only of the administration; that is to say, of the magistrates and officers; which, if he have not means to name, he is supposed to approve those, which he himself had formerly appointed.

BARUCH SPINOZA—a portrait by a contemporary artist

SINGEL CANAL, AMSTERDAM (Rembrandt)

THE SYNAGOGUE, AMSTERDAM (Rembran

BARUCH SPINOZA

Baruch Spinoza (1632–1677) was born in Amsterdam, his parents Jewish refugees from the Spanish Inquisition. Educated in the traditional religious studies of his People, he absorbed a profound knowledge of the Bible and Hebrew, later mastering Latin, the language in which he wrote.

Spinoza not only kept abreast of the scientific and philosophical developments of his own time, but as a result of his dissatisfaction with anthropomorphism and mysticism, also studied the works of the important Jewish medieval philosophers who had grappled with these issues—men such as Maimonides (1135–1204), Gersonides (1288–1344), and Crescas (1340–1410). When questioned by a tribunal of his congregation, Spinoza was unwilling to disavow his heterodox theological opinions. Subsequently, the Jewish community of Holland, not at that time entitled to citizenship and fearful of reprisals for permitting such heresies, excommunicated him at the age of twenty-four. For the next four years he stayed in Amsterdam, pursuing his studies while earning a living grinding and polishing lenses. He then moved to the small village of Rijnsburg, near Leyden, and later to Voorburg, outside The Hague, continuing his lonely life as a scholar and lens-grinder. He was offered a chair of philosophy at the University of Heidelberg, but refused it, fearful of losing his freedom of expression. He died at forty-four, the victim of tuberculosis, his frail constitution weakened by arduous labor as well as by the glass dust he had inhaled while practicing his vocation. He was regarded as a person of great courtesy, unusual modesty, and equanimity.

Only two books by Spinoza appeared during his lifetime: *The Principles of Descartes' Philosophy*, an expository volume in geometrical form; and the anonymously published *Theological-Political Treatise*. The latter is perhaps the earliest example of what two centuries later became known as "higher criticism," the study of the Bible as a historical document open to rational interpretation. His posthumous works included an unfinished Hebrew grammar, intended to support his scientific approach to Scriptural exegesis; the *Short Treatise on God, Man, and His Well-Being*, an early, partial draft of his philosophical system; the fragmentary *Treatise on the Correction of the Understanding*, an introduction to his methodology; the incomplete *Political Treatise*, which stresses the value of individual liberty and religious toleration, as well as supporting democracy against the claims of monarchy and aristocracy; and his masterpiece, the *Ethics, Demonstrated in Geometrical Order*, one of the most majestic of all philosophical works.

Spinoza viewed the world as possessing an intelligible structure according to which every event was in principle comprehensible as a necessary part of the whole. The logical order of that whole was to be understood only 'through itself' and was variously termed 'Substance,' 'Nature,' or 'God.' The geometric format of the *Ethics* illustrates this central thesis, since the propositions, corollaries, and notes are all intended as deductions from the initial definitions and axioms which are presented as self-explanatory.

Part I, reprinted in this volume, is complete in itself and contains Spinoza's detailed demonstration of the essence of God. In Part II he offers his solution to the traditional philosophical problem of the relation between mind and body, regarding these not, as Descartes had, as two separate substances, but rather as two aspects of the one Substance. The remainder of the *Ethics*, Parts III, IV, and V, contains Spinoza's moral theory and his view of the ideal life. The terms 'good' and 'bad' are, according to Spinoza, merely words we use to express our own desires. In order to achieve salvation, we need to free ourselves from the bondage of these emotions and strive through reason to achieve knowledge of and identification with the order of the universe, thus coming to possess 'the intellectual love of God' which is 'blessedness.' By thus reinterpreting the concept of God and imparting spirituality to the study of nature, Spinoza fused his commitment to the scientific model of knowledge with the monotheistic vision of his religious heritage.

An excellent, full-length study of Spinoza's work by a leading contemporary philosopher is Stuart Hampshire, *Spinoza* (Middlesex: Penguin Books, 1951). An incisive presentation of Spinoza's philosophical perspective is chapter five of John Herman Randall, Jr., *The Career of Philosophy: From the Middle Ages to the Enlightenment* (1962; rpt. New York: Columbia University Press, 1970). Also useful as a concise presentation of the major themes in Spinoza's system is the essay by P. H. Nidditch in D. J. O'Connor, ed., *A Critical History of Western Philosophy* (Glencoe: The free Press, 1964). A detailed examination of the *Ethics* is Jonathan Bennett, *A Study of Spinoza's ETHICS* (Indianapolis, Hackett Publishing Company, 1984). Four helpful collections of essays are Marjorie Grene, ed., *Spinoza: A Collection of Critical Essays* (Garden City: Doubleday, 1973), Maurice Mandelbaum and Eugene Freeman, eds., *Spinoza: Essays in Interpretation* (LaSalle: Open Court, 1975), Robert W. Shahan and J. I. Biro, eds., *Spinoza: New Perspectives* (Norman: University of Oklahoma Press, 1978), and Richard Kennington, ed., *The Philosophy of Baruch Spinoza* (Washington, D.C.: Catholic University of America Press, 1980). An especially fine essay which penetrates to the heart of Spinoza's thought is the text of a lecture by Frederick J. E. Woodbridge, delivered at Columbia University in 1933 and reprinted in the edition of the *Ethics* edited by James Gutmann (New York: Hafner, 1957). The classic study of the *Ethics* from a historical point of view, exhibiting in immense detail its sources in Hebrew, Latin, and Arabic philosophical literature, as well as its connections to the work of Aristotle, Descartes, and others is Harry Austryn Wolfson, *The Philosophy of Spinoza* (1934; rpt. Cleveland: Meridian Books, 1958).

S.M.C.

THE ETHICS

Part I

CONCERNING GOD

DEFINITIONS

1. By that which is self-caused I mean that whose essence involves existence; or that whose nature can be conceived only as existing.

2. A thing is said to be finite in its own kind *(in suo genere finita)* when it can be limited by another thing of the same nature. For example, a body is said to be finite because we can always conceive of another body greater than it. So, too, a thought is limited by another thought. But body is not limited by thought, nor thought by body.

3. By substance I mean that which is in itself and is conceived through itself; that is, that the conception of which does not require the conception of another thing from which it has to be formed.

4. By attribute I mean that which the intellect perceives of substance as constituting its essence.

5. By mode I mean the affections of substance; that is, that which is in something else and is conceived through something else.

6. By God I mean an absolutely infinite being; that is, substance consisting of infinite attributes, each of which expresses eternal and infinite essence.

Explication

I say 'absolutely infinite,' not 'infinite in its kind.' For if a thing is only infinite in its kind, one may deny that it has infinite attributes. But if a thing is absolutely infinite, whatever expresses essence and does not involve any negation belongs to its essence.

7. That thing is said to be free *(liber)* which exists solely from the necessity of its own nature, and is determined to action by itself alone. A thing is said to be necessary *(necessarius)* or rather, constrained *(coactus),* if it is determined by another thing to exist and to act in a definite and determinate way.

8. By eternity I mean existence itself insofar as it is conceived as necessarily following solely from the definition of an eternal thing.

Explication

For such existence is conceived as an eternal truth, just as is the essence of the thing, and therefore cannot be explicated through duration or time, even if duration be conceived as without beginning and end.

AXIOMS

1. All things that are, are either in themselves or in something else.

Reprinted by permission of the translator, Samuel Shirley, from Spinoza, *The Ethics* and *Selected Letters* (Hackett Publishing Company, 1982).

2. That which cannot be conceived through another thing must be conceived through itself.

3. From a given determinate cause there necessarily follows an effect; on the other hand, if there be no determinate cause it is impossible that an effect should follow.

4. The knowledge of an effect depends on, and involves, the knowledge of the cause.

5. Things which have nothing in common with each other cannot be understood through each other; that is, the conception of the one does not involve the conception of the other.

6. A true idea must agree with that of which it is the idea *(ideatum)*.

7. If a thing can be conceived as not existing, its essence does not involve existence.

PROPOSITION 1

Substance is by nature prior to its affections.

Proof

This is evident from Defs. 3 and 5.

PROPOSITION 2

Two substances having different attributes have nothing in common.

Proof

This too is evident from Def. 3; for each substance must be in itself and be conceived through itself; that is, the conception of the one does not involve the conception of the other.

PROPOSITION 3

When things have nothing in common, one cannot be the cause of the other.

Proof

If things have nothing in common, then (Ax.5) they cannot be understood through one another, and so (Ax.4) one cannot be the cause of the other.

PROPOSITION 4

Two or more distinct things are distinguished from one another either by the difference of the attributes of the substances or by the difference of the affections of the substances.

Proof

All things that are, are either in themselves or in something else (Ax.1); that is (Defs.3 and 5), nothing exists external to the intellect except substances and their affections. Therefore there can be nothing external to the intellect through which several things can be distinguished from one another except substances or (which is the same thing) (Def.4) the attributes and the affections of substances.

PROPOSITION 5

In the universe there cannot be two or more substances of the same nature or attribute.

Proof

If there were several such distinct substances, they would have to be distinguished from one another either by a difference of attributes or by a difference of affections (Pr.4). If they are distinguished only by a difference of attributes, then it will be granted that there cannot be more than one substance of the same attribute. But if they are distinguished by a difference of affections, then, since substance is by nature prior to its affections (Pr.1), disregarding therefore its affections and considering substance in itself, that is (Def.3 and Ax.6) considering it truly, it cannot be conceived as distinguishable from another substance. That is (Pr.4), there cannot be several such substances but only one.

PROPOSITION 6

One substance cannot be produced by another substance.

Proof

In the universe there cannot be two substances of the same attribute (Pr.5), that is (Pr.2) two substances having something in common. And so (Pr.3) one cannot be the cause of the other; that is, one cannot be produced by the other.

Corollary

Hence it follows that substance cannot be produced by anything else. For in the universe there exists nothing but substances and their affections, as is evident from Ax.1 and Defs.3 and 5. But, by Pr.6, it cannot be produced by another substance. Therefore substance cannot be produced by anything else whatsoever.

Another Proof

This can be proved even more readily by the absurdity of the contradictory. For if substance could be produced by something else, the knowledge of substance would have to depend on the knowledge of its cause (Ax.4), and so (Def.3) it would not be substance.

PROPOSITION 7

Existence belongs to the nature of substance.

Proof

Substance cannot be produced by anything else (Cor.Pr.6) and is therefore self-caused *(causa sui);* that is (Def.1), its essence necessarily involves existence; that is, existence belongs to its nature.

PROPOSITION 8

Every substance is necessarily infinite.

Proof

There cannot be more than one substance having the same attribute (Pr.5), and existence belongs to the nature of substance (Pr.7). It must therefore exist either as finite or as infinite. But it cannot exist as finite, for (Def.2) it would have to be limited by another substance of the same nature, and that substance also would have to exist (Pr.7). And so there would exist two substances of the same attribute, which is absurd (Pr.5). Therefore it exists as infinite.

Scholium 1

Since in fact to be finite is in part a negation and to be infinite is the unqualified affirmation of the existence of some nature, it follows from Proposition 7 alone that every substance must be infinite.

Scholium 2

I do not doubt that for those who judge things confusedly and are not accustomed to know things through their primary causes it is difficult to grasp the proof of Proposition 7. Surely, this is because they neither distinguish between the modifications of substances and substances themselves, nor do they know how things are produced. And so it comes about that they ascribe to substances a beginning which they see natural things as having; for those who do not know the true causes of things confuse everything. Without any hesitation they imagine trees as well as men talking and men being formed from stones as well as from seed; indeed, any forms whatsoever are imagined to change into any other forms. So too, those who confuse the divine nature with human nature easily ascribe to God human emotions, especially so long as they are ignorant of how the latter are produced in the mind. But if men were to attend to the nature of substance, they would not doubt at all the truth of Proposition 7; indeed, this Proposition would be an axiom to all and would be ranked among universally accepted truisms. For by substance they would understand that which is in itself and is conceived through itself; that is, that the knowledge of which does not require the knowledge of any other thing. By modifications they would understand that which is in another thing, and whose conception is formed from the thing in which they are. Therefore in the case of non-existent modifications we can have true ideas of them since their essence is included in something else, with the result that they can be conceived through that something else, although they do not exist in actuality externally to the intellect. However, in the case of substances, because they are conceived only through themselves, their truth external to the intellect is only in themselves. So if someone were to say that he has a clear and distinct — that is, a true — idea of substance and that he nevertheless doubts whether such a substance exists, this would surely be just the same as if he were to declare that he has a true idea but nevertheless suspects that it may be false (as is obvious to anyone who gives his mind to it). Or if anyone asserts that substance is created, he at the same time asserts that a false idea has become true, than which nothing more absurd can be conceived. So it must necessarily be admitted that the existence of substance is as much an eternal truth as it is essence.

Hence we can derive in another way that there cannot be more than one substance of the same nature, and I think it worthwhile to set out the proof here. Now to do this in an orderly fashion I ask you to note:

1. The true definition of each thing involves and expresses nothing beyond the nature of the thing defined. Hence it follows that —

2. No definition involves or expresses a fixed number of individuals, since it expresses nothing but the nature of the thing defined. For example, the definition of a triangle expresses nothing other than simply the nature of a triangle, and not a fixed number of triangles.

3. For each single existent thing there must necessarily be a definite cause for its existence.

4. The cause for the existence of a thing must either be contained in the very nature and definition of the existent thing (in effect, existence belongs to its nature) or must have its being independently of the thing itself.

From these premises it follows that if a fixed number of individuals exist in Nature, there must necessarily be a cause why those individuals, and not more or fewer, exist. If, for example, in Nature twenty men were to exist (for the sake of greater clarity I suppose that they exist simultaneously and that no others existed in Nature before them), in order to account for the existence of these twenty men it will not be enough for us to demonstrate the cause of human nature in general; it will furthermore be necessary to demonstrate the cause why not more or fewer than twenty men exist, since (Note 3) there must necessarily be a cause for the existence of each one. But this cause (Notes 2 and 3) cannot be contained in the nature of man, since the true definition of man does not involve the number twenty. So (Note 4) the cause of the existence of these twenty men, and consequently of each one, must necessarily be external to each one, and therefore we can reach the unqualified conclusion that whenever several individuals of a kind exist, there must necessarily be an external cause for their existence. Now since existence belongs to the nature of substance (as has already been shown in this Scholium) the definition of substance must involve necessary existence, and consequently the existence of substance must be concluded solely from its definition. But the existence of several substances cannot follow from the definition of substance (as I have already shown in Notes 2 and 3). Therefore, from the definition of substance it follows necessarily that there exists only one substance of the same nature, as was proposed.

PROPOSITION 9
The more reality or being a thing has, the more attributes it has.

Proof
This is evident from Definition 4.

PROPOSITION 10
Each attribute of one substance must be conceived through itself.

Proof
For an attribute is that which intellect perceives of substance as constituting its essence (Def.4), and so (Def.3) it must be conceived through itself.

Scholium

From this it is clear that although two attributes be conceived as really distinct, that is, one without the help of the other, still we cannot deduce therefrom that they constitute two entities, or two different substances. For it is in the nature of substance that each of its attributes be conceived through itself, since all the attributes it possesses have always been in it simultaneously, and one could not have been produced by another; but each expresses the reality or being of substance. So it is by no means absurd to ascribe more than one attribute to one substance. Indeed, nothing in Nature is clearer than that each entity must be conceived under some attribute, and the more reality or being it has, the more are its attributes which express necessity, or eternity, and infinity. Consequently nothing can be clearer than this, too, that an absolutely infinite entity must necessarily be defined (Def.6) as an entity consisting of infinite attributes, each of which expresses a definite essence, eternal and infinite. Now if anyone asks by what mark can we distinguish between different substances, let him read the following Propositions, which show that in Nature there exists only one substance, absolutely infinite. So this distinguishing mark would be sought in vain.

PROPOSITION 11

God, or substance consisting of infinite attributes, each of which expresses eternal and infinite essence, necessarily exists.

Proof

If you deny this, conceive, if you can, that God does not exist. Therefore (Ax.7) his essence does not involve existence. But this is absurd (Pr.7). Therefore God necessarily exists.

Second Proof

For every thing a cause or reason must be assigned either for its existence or for its non-existence. For example, if a triangle exists, there must be a reason, or cause, for its existence. If it does not exist, there must be a reason or cause which prevents it from existing, or which annuls its existence. Now this reason or cause must either be contained in the nature of the thing or be external to it. For example, the reason why a square circle does not exist is indicated by its very nature, in that it involves a contradiction. On the other hand, the reason for the existence of substance also follows from its nature alone, in that it involves existence (Pr.7). But the reason for the existence or non-existence of a circle or a triangle does not follow from their nature, but from the order of universal corporeal Nature. For it is from this latter that it necessarily follows that either the triangle necessarily exists at this moment or that its present existence is impossible. This is self-evident, and therefrom it follows that a thing necessarily exists if there is no reason or cause which prevents its existence. Therefore if there can be no reason or cause which prevents God from existing or which annuls his existence, we are bound to conclude that he necessarily exists. But if there were such a reason or cause, it would have to be either within God's nature or external to it; that is, it would have to be in another substance of another nature. For if it were of the same nature, by that very fact it would be granted that God exists. But a substance of another nature would have nothing in common with God (Pr.2), and so could neither posit nor annul his existence. Since therefore there cannot be external to God's nature a reason or cause that would annul God's existence, then if indeed he does not exist, the reason or cause must necessarily be in God's nature, which would therefore involve a contradiction. But to affirm this of a Being absolutely infinite and in the highest degree perfect is absurd. Therefore neither in God nor external to God is there any cause or reason which would annul his existence. Therefore God necessarily exists.

A Third Proof

To be able to not exist is weakness; on the other hand, to be able to exist is power, as is self-evident. So if what now necessarily exists is nothing but finite entities, then finite entities are more potent than an absolutely infinite Entity—which is absurd. Therefore either nothing exists, or an absolutely infinite Entity necessarily exists, too. But we do exist, either in ourselves or in something else which necessarily exists (Ax.1 and Pr.7). Therefore an absolutely infinite Entity—that is (Def.6), God—necessarily exists.

Scholium

In this last proof I decided to prove God's existence *a posteriori* so that the proof may be more easily perceived, and not because God's existence does not follow *a priori* from this same basis. For since the ability to exist is power, it follows that the greater the degree of reality that belongs to the nature of a thing, the greater amount of energy it has for existence. So an absolutely infinite Entity, or God, will have from himself absolutely infinite power to exist, and therefore exists absolutely.

But perhaps many will not readily find this proof convincing because they are used to consider only such things as derive from external causes. Of these things they observe that those which come quickly into being—that is, which readily exist—likewise readily perish, while things which they conceive as more complex they regard as more difficult to bring into being—that is, not so ready to exist. However, to free them from these misconceptions I do not need at this point to show what measure of truth there is in the saying; "Quickly come, quickly go," neither need I raise the question whether or not everything is equally easy in respect of Nature as a whole. It is enough to note simply this, that I am not here speaking of things that come into being through external causes, but only of substances, which (Pr.6) cannot be produced by any external cause. For whether they consist of many parts or few, things that are brought about by external causes owe whatever degree of perfection or reality they possess entirely to the power of the external cause, and so their existence has its origin solely in the perfection of the external cause, and not in their own perfection. On the other hand, whatever perfection substance possesses is due to no external cause; therefore its existence, too, must follow solely from its own nature, and is therefore nothing else but its essence. So perfection does not annul a thing's existence: on the contrary, it posits it; whereas imperfection annuls a thing's existence. So there is nothing of which we can be more certain than the existence of an absolutely infinite or perfect Entity; that is, God. For since his essence excludes all imperfection and involves absolute perfection, it thereby removes all reason for doubting his existence and affords the utmost certainty of it. This, I think, must be quite clear to all who give a modicum of attention to the matter.

PROPOSITION 12

No attribute of substance can be truly conceived from which it would follow that substance can be divided.

Proof

The parts into which substance thus conceived would be divided will either retain the nature of substance or they will not. In the first case each part will have to be infinite (Pr.8) and self-caused (Pr.6) and consist of a different attribute (Pr.5); and so several substances could be formed from one substance, which is absurd (Pr.6). Furthermore, the parts would have nothing in common with the whole (Pr.2), and the whole could exist and be conceived without its parts (Def.4 and Pr.10), the absurdity of which none can doubt. But in the latter case where the parts will not retain the nature of substance — then when the whole substance would have been divided into equal parts it would lose the nature of substance and would cease to be. This is absurd (Pr.7).

PROPOSITION 13

Absolutely infinite substance is indivisible.

Proof

If it were divisible, the parts into which it would be divided will either retain the nature of absolutely infinite substance, or not. In the first case, there would therefore be several substances of the same nature, which is absurd (Pr.5). In the second case, absolutely infinite substance can cease to be, which is also absurd (Pr.11).

Corollary

From this it follows that no substance, and consequently no corporeal substance, insofar as it is substance, is divisible.

Scholium

The indivisibility of substance can be more easily understood merely from the fact that the nature of substance can be conceived only as infinite, and that a part of substance can mean only finite substance, which involves an obvious contradiction (Pr.8).

PROPOSITION 14

There can be, or be conceived, no other substance but God.

Proof

Since God is an absolutely infinite being of whom no attribute expressing the essence of substance can be denied (Def.6) and since he necessarily exists (Pr.11), if there were any other substance but God, it would have to be explicated through some attribute of God, and so there would exist two substances with the same attribute, which is absurd (Pr.5). So there can be no substance external to God, and consequently no such substance can be conceived. For if it could be conceived, it would have to be conceived necessarily as existing; but this is absurd (by the first part of this proof). Therefore no substance can be or be conceived external to God.

Corollary 1

Hence it follows quite clearly that God is one: that is (Def.6), in the universe there is only one substance, and this is absolutely infinite, as I have already indicated in Scholium Pr.10.

Corollary 2

It follows that the thing extended and the thing thinking are either attributes of God or (Ax.1) affections of the attributes of God.

PROPOSITION 15
Whatever is, is in God, and nothing can be or be conceived without God.

Proof

Apart from God no substance can be or be conceived (Pr.14), that is (Def.3), something which is in itself and is conceived through itself. Now modes (Def.5) cannot be or be conceived without substance; therefore they can be only in the divine nature and can be conceived only through the divine nature. But nothing exists except substance and modes (Ax.1). Therefore nothing can be or be conceived without God.

Scholium

Some imagine God in the likeness of man, consisting of mind and body, and subject to passions. But it is clear from what has already been proved how far they stray from the true knowledge of God. These I dismiss, for all who have given any consideration to the divine nature deny that God is corporeal. They find convincing proof of this in the fact that by body we understand some quantity having length, breadth and depth, bounded by a definite shape; and nothing more absurd than this can be attributed to God, a being absolutely infinite.

At the same time, however, in other arguments whereby they try to prove their point they show clearly that in this thinking corporeal or extended substance is set completely apart from the divine nature, and they assert that it is created by God. But they have no idea from what divine power it could have been created, which clearly shows that they don't know what they are saying. Now I have clearly proved—at any rate, in my judgment (Cor.Pr.6 and Sch.2 Pr.8)—that no substance can be produced or created by anything else. Furthermore, in Proposition 14 we showed that apart from God no substance can be or be conceived, and hence we deduced that extended substance is one of God's infinite attributes.

However, for a fuller explanation I will refute my opponents' arguments, which all seem to come down to this. Firstly, they think that corporeal substance, insofar as it is substance, is made up of parts, and so they deny that it can be infinite, and consequently that it can pertain to God. This they illustrate with many examples, of which I will take one or two. They say that if corporeal substance is infinite, suppose it to be divided into two parts. Each of these parts will be either finite or infinite. If the former, then the infinite is made up of two finite parts, which is absurd. If the latter, then there is an infinite which is twice as great as another infinite, which is also absurd.

Again, if an infinite length is measured in feet, it will have to consist of an infinite number of feet; and if it is measured in inches, it will consist of an infinite number of inches. So one infinite number will be twelve times greater than another infinite number.

Lastly, if from one point in an infinite quantity two lines, AB and AC be drawn of fixed and determinate length, and thereafter be produced to infinity, it is clear that the distance between B and C continues to increase and finally changes from a determinate distance to an indeterminate distance.

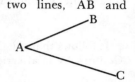

As these absurdities follow, they think, from supposing quantity to be infinite, they conclude that corporeal substance must be finite and consequently cannot pertain to God's essence.

The second argument is also drawn from God's consummate perfection. Since God, they say, is a supremely perfect being, he cannot be that which is acted upon. But corporeal substance, being divisible, can be acted upon. It therefore follows that corporeal substance does not pertain to God's essence.

These are the arguments I find put forward by writers who thereby seek to prove that corporeal substance is unworthy of the divine essence and cannot pertain to it. However, the student who looks carefully into these arguments will find that I have already replied to them, since they are all founded on the same supposition that material substance is composed of parts, and this I have already shown to be absurd (Pr.12 and Cor. Pr.13). Again, careful reflection will show that all those alleged absurdities (if indeed they are absurdities, which is not now under discussion) from which they seek to prove that extended substance is finite do not at all follow from the supposition that quantity is infinite, but that infinite quantity is measurable and is made up of finite parts. Therefore from the resultant absurdities no other conclusion can be reached but that infinite quantity is not measurable and cannot be made up of finite parts. And this is exactly what we have already proved (Pr.12). So the weapon they aimed at us is in fact turned against themselves. If therefore from this 'reductio ad absurdum' argument of theirs they still seek to deduce that extended substance must be finite, they are surely just like one who, having made the supposition that a circle has the properties of a square, deduces therefrom that a circle does not have a center from which all lines drawn to the circumference are equal. For corporeal substance, which can be conceived only as infinite, one, and indivisible (Prs. 8,5 and 12) they conceive as made up of finite parts, multiplex, and divisible, so as to deduce that it is finite. In the same way others, too, having supposed that a line is composed of points, can find many arguments to prove that a line cannot be infinitely divided. Indeed, it is just as absurd to assert that corporeal substance is composed of bodies or parts as that a body is composed of surfaces, surfaces of lines, and lines of points. This must be admitted by all who know clear reason to be infallible, and particularly those who say that a vacuum cannot exist. For if corporeal substance could be so divided that its parts were distinct in reality, why could one part not be annihilated while the others remain joined together as before? And why should all the parts be so fitted together as to leave no vacuum? Surely, in the case of things which are in reality distinct from one another, one can exist without the other and remain in its original state. Since therefore there is no vacuum in Nature (which is discussed elsewhere) and all its parts must so harmonise that there is no vacuum, it also follows that the parts cannot be distinct in reality; that is, corporeal substance, in so far as it is substance, cannot be divided.

If I am now asked why we have this natural inclination to divide quantity, I reply that we conceive quantity in two ways, to wit, abstractly, or superficially—in other words, as represented in the imagination—or as substance, which we do only through the intellect. If therefore we consider quantity as it is presented in the imagination—and this is what we more frequently and readily do—we find it to be finite, divisible, and made up of parts. But if we consider it intellectually and conceive it in so far as it is substance—and this is very difficult—then it will be found to be infinite, one, and indivisible, as we have already sufficiently proved. This will be quite clear to those who can distinguish between the imagination and the intellect, especially if this point also is stressed, that matter is everywhere the same, and there are no distinct parts in it except in so far as we conceive matter as modified in various ways. Then its parts are distinct, not really but only modally. For example, we conceive water to be divisible and to have separate parts in so far as it is water, but not in so far as it is material substance. In this latter respect it is not capable of separation or division. Furthermore, water, qua water, comes into existence and goes out of existence; but qua substance it does not come into existence nor go out of existence [corrumpitur].

I consider that in the above I have also replied to the second argument, since this too is based on the supposition that matter, in so far as it is substance, is divisible and made up of parts. And even though this were not so, I do not know why matter should be unworthy of the divine nature, since (Pr.14) there can be no substance external to God by which it can be acted upon. All things, I repeat, are in God, and all things that come to pass do so only through the laws of God's infinite nature and follow through the necessity of his essence (as I shall later show). Therefore by no manner of reasoning can it be said that God is acted upon by anything else or that extended substance is unworthy of the divine nature, even though it be supposed divisible, as long as it is granted to be eternal and infinite.

But enough of this subject for the present.

PROPOSITION 16

From the necessity of the divine nature there must follow infinite things in infinite ways (modis), (that is, everything that can come within the scope of infinite intellect).

Proof

This proposition should be obvious to everyone who will but consider this point, that from the given definition of any one thing the intellect infers a number of properties which necessarily follow in fact from the definition (that is, from the very essence of the thing), and the more reality the definition of the thing expresses (that is, the more reality the essence of the thing defined involves) the greater the number of its properties. Now since divine nature possesses absolutely infinite attributes (Def.6), of which each one also expresses infinite essence in its own kind, then there must necessarily follow from the necessity of the divine nature an infinity of things in infinite ways (that is, everything that can come within the scope of infinite intellect).

Corollary 1

Hence it follows that God is the efficient cause of all things that can come within the scope of infinite intellect.

Corollary 2

Secondly, it follows that God is the cause through himself, not however *per accidens*.

Corollary 3

Thirdly, it follows that God is absolutely the first cause.

PROPOSITION 17

God acts solely from the laws of his own nature, constrained by none.

Proof

We have just shown that an infinity of things follow, absolutely, solely from the necessity of divine nature, or — which is the same thing — solely from the laws of that same nature (Pr.16); and we have proved (Pr.15) that nothing can be or be conceived without God, but that everything is in God. Therefore there can be nothing external to God by which he can be determined or constrained to act. Thus God acts solely from the laws of his own nature and is constrained by none.

Corollary 1

Hence it follows, firstly, that there is no cause, except the perfection of his nature, which either extrinsically or intrinsically moves God to act.

Corollary 2

It follows, secondly, that God alone is a free cause. For God alone exists solely from the necessity of his own nature (Pr.11 and Cor.1 Pr.14) and acts solely from the necessity of his own nature (Pr.17). So he alone is a free cause (Def.7).

Scholium

Others take the view that God is a free cause because — so they think — he can bring it about that those things which we have said follow from his nature — that is, which are within his power — should not come about, that is, they should not be produced by him. But this is as much as to say that God can bring it about that it should not follow from the nature of a triangle that its three angles are equal to two right angles, or that from a given cause the effect should not follow, which is absurd.

Furthermore, I shall show later on without the help of this proposition that neither intellect nor will pertain to the nature of God. I know indeed that there are many who think they can prove that intellect in the highest degree and free-will belong to the nature of God; for they say they know of nothing more perfect which they may attribute to God than that which is the highest perfection in us. Again, although they conceive of God as having in actuality intellect in the highest degree, they yet do not believe he can bring about the existence of everything which in actuality he understands, for they think they would thereby be nullifying God's power. If, they say, he had created everything that is within his intellect, then he would not have been able to create anything more; and this they regard as inconsistent with God's omnipotence. So they have preferred to regard God as indifferent to everything and as creating nothing but what he has decided, by some absolute exercise of will, to create. However, I think I have shown quite clearly (Pr.16) that from God's supreme power or infinite nature an infinity of things in infinite ways—that is, everything—have necessarily flowed or are always following from that same necessity, just as from the nature of a triangle it follows from eternity to eternity that its three angles are equal to two right angles. Therefore God's omnipotence has from eternity been actual and will remain for eternity in the same actuality. In this way, I submit, God's omnipotence is established as being far more perfect. Indeed my opponents—let us speak frankly—seem to be denying God's omnipotence. For they are obliged to admit that God understands an infinite number of creatable things which nevertheless he can never create. If this were not so, that is, if he were to create all the things that he understands, he would exhaust his omnipotence, according to them, and render himself imperfect. Thus, to affirm God as perfect they are reduced to having to affirm at the same time that he cannot bring about everything that is within the bounds of his power. I cannot imagine anything more absurd than this, or more inconsistent with God's omnipotence.

Furthermore, I have something here to say about the intellect and will that is usually attributed to God. If intellect and will do indeed pertain to the eternal essence of God, one must understand in the case of both these attributes something very different from the meaning widely entertained. For the intellect and will that would constitute the essence of God would have to be vastly different from human intellect and will, and could have no point of agreement except the name. They could be no more alike than the celestial constellation of the Dog and the dog that barks. This I will prove as follows. If intellect does pertain to the divine nature, it cannot, like man's intellect, be posterior to (as most thinkers hold) or simultaneous with the objects of understanding, since God is prior in causality to all things (Cor.1 Pr.16). On the contrary, the truth and formal essence of things is what it is because it exists as such in the intellect of God as an object of thought. Therefore God's intellect, in so far as it is conceived as constituting God's essence, is in actual fact the cause of things, in respect both of their essence and their existence. This seems to have been recognised also by those who have asserted that God's intellect, will and power are one and the same. Since therefore God's intellect is the one and only cause of things, both of their essence and their existence, as we have shown, it must necessarily be different from them both in respect of essence and existence. For that which is caused differs from its cause precisely in what it has from its cause. For example, a man is the cause of the existence of another man, but not of the other's essence; for the essence is an eternal truth. So with regard to their essence the two men can be in full agreement, but they must differ with regard to existence; and for that reason if the existence of the one should cease, the existence of the other would not thereby cease. But if the essence of the one could be destroyed and rendered false, so too would the essence of the other. Therefore a thing which is the cause of the essence and existence of some effect must differ from that effect both in respect of essence and existence. But God's intellect is the cause of the essence and existence of man's intellect. Therefore God's intellect, in so far as it is conceived as constituting the divine essence, differs from man's intellect both in respect of essence and existence, and cannot agree with it in any respect other than name—which is what I sought to prove. In the matter of will, the proof is the same, as anyone can readily see.

PROPOSITION 18
God is the immanent, not the transitive, cause of all things.

Proof
All things that are, are in God, and must be conceived through God (Pr.15), and so (Cor.1 Pr.16) God is the cause of the things that are in him, which is the first point. Further, there can be no substance external to God (Pr.14); that is (Def.3), a thing which is in itself external to God—which is the second point. Therefore God is the immanent, not the transitive, cause of all things.

PROPOSITION 19
God, that is, all the attributes of God, are eternal.

Proof
God is substance (Def.6) which necessarily exists (Pr.11); that is (Pr.7), a thing to whose nature it pertains to exist, or—and this is the same thing—a thing from whose definition existence follows; and so (Def.8) God is eternal. Further, by the attributes of God must be understood that which expresses the essence of the Divine substance (Def.4), that is, that which pertains to substance. It is this, I say, which the attributes themselves must involve. But eternity pertains to the nature of substance (as I have shown in Pr.7). Therefore each of the attributes must involve eternity, and so they are all eternal.

Scholium
This proposition is also perfectly clear from the manner in which I proved the existence of God (Pr.11). From this proof, I repeat, it is obvious that God's existence is, like his essence, an eternal truth. Again, I have also proved God's eternity in another way in Proposition 19 of my *Principles of the Philosophy of Descartes,* and there is no need here to go over that ground again.

PROPOSITION 20
God's existence and his essence are one and the same.

Proof
God and all his attributes are eternal (Pr.19); that is, each one of his attributes expresses existence (Def.8). Therefore the same attributes of God that explicate his eternal essence (Def.4) at the same time explicate his eternal existence; that is, that which constitutes the essence of God at the same time constitutes his existence, and so his existence and his essence are one and the same.

Corollary 1

From this it follows, firstly, that God's existence, like his essence, is an eternal truth.

Corollary 2

It follows, secondly, that God is immutable; that is, all the attributes of God are immutable. For if they were to change in respect of existence, they would also have to change in respect of essence (Pr.20); that is — and this is self-evident — they would have to become false instead of true, which is absurd.

PROPOSITION 21

All things that follow from the absolute nature of any attribute of God must have existed always, and as infinite; that is, through the said attribute they are eternal and infinite.

Proof

Suppose this proposition be denied and conceive, if you can, that something in some attribute of God, following from its absolute nature, is finite and has a determinate existence or duration; for example, the idea of God in Thought. Now Thought, being assumed to be an attribute of God, is necessarily infinite by its own nature (Pr.11). However, in so far as it has the idea of God, it is being supposed as finite. Now (Def.2) it cannot be conceived as finite unless it is determined through Thought itself. But it cannot be determined through Thought itself in so far as Thought constitutes the idea of God, for it is in that respect that Thought is supposed to be finite. Therefore it is determined through Thought in so far as Thought does not constitute the idea of God, which Thought must nevertheless necessarily exist (Pr.11). Therefore there must be Thought which does not constitute the idea of God, and so the idea of God does not follow necessarily from its nature in so far as it is absolute Thought. (For it is conceived as constituting and as not constituting the idea of God.) This is contrary to our hypothesis. Therefore if the idea of God in Thought, or anything in some attribute of God (it does not matter what is selected, since the proof is universal), follows from the necessity of the absolute nature of the attribute, it must necessarily be infinite. That was our first point.

Furthermore, that which thus follows from the necessity of the nature of some attribute cannot have a determinate existence, or duration. If this be denied, suppose that there is in some attribute of God a thing following from the necessity of the nature of the attribute, for example, the idea of God in Thought, and suppose that this thing either did not exist at some time, or will cease to exist in the future. Now since Thought is assumed as an attribute of God, it must necessarily exist, and as immutable (Pr.11 and Cor.2 Pr.20). Therefore outside the bounds of the duration of the idea of God (for this idea is supposed at some time not to have existed, or will at some point cease to exist) Thought will have to exist without the idea of God. But this is contrary to the hypothesis, for it is supposed that when Thought is granted the idea of God necessarily follows. Therefore the idea of God in Thought, or anything that necessarily follows from the absolute nature of some attribute of God, cannot have a determinate existence, but is eternal through that same attribute. That was our second point. Note that the same holds for anything in an attribute of God which necessarily follows from the absolute nature of God.

PROPOSITION 22

Whatever follows from some attribute of God in so far as the attribute is modified by a modification that exists necessarily and as infinite through that same attribute, must also exist both necessarily and as infinite.

Proof

This proposition is proved in the same way as the preceding one.

PROPOSITION 23

Every mode which exists necessarily and as infinite must have necessarily followed either from the absolute nature of some attribute of God or from some attribute modified by a modification which exists necessarily and as infinite.

Proof

A mode is in something else through which it must be conceived (Def.5); that is (Pr.15), it is in God alone and can be conceived only through God. Therefore if a mode is conceived to exist necessarily and to be infinite, both these characteristics must necessarily be inferred or perceived through some attribute of God in so far as that attribute is conceived to express infinity and necessity of existence, or (and by Def.8 this is the same) eternity; that is (Def.6 and Pr.19), in so far as it is considered absolutely. Therefore a mode which exists necessarily and as infinite must have followed from the absolute nature of some attribute of God, either directly (Pr.21) or through the mediation of some modification which follows from the absolute nature of the attribute; that is (Pr.22), which exists necessarily and as infinite.

PROPOSITION 24

The essence of things produced by God does not involve existence.

Proof

This is evident from Def.1. For only that whose nature (considered in itself) involves existence is self-caused and exists solely from the necessity of its own nature.

Corollary

Hence it follows that God is the cause not only of the coming into existence of things but also of their continuing in existence, or, to use a scholastic term, God is the cause of the being of things *(essendi rerum)*. For whether things exist or do not exist, in reflecting on their essence we realise that this essence involves neither existence nor duration. So it is not their essence which can be the cause of either their existence or their duration, but only God, to whose nature alone existence pertains (Cor.1 Pr.14).

PROPOSITION 25

God is the efficient cause not only of the existence of things but also of their essence.

Proof

If this be denied, then God is not the cause of the essence of things, and so (Ax.4) the essence of things can be conceived without God. But this is absurd (Pr.15). Therefore God is also the cause of the essence of things.

Scholium

This proposition follows more clearly from Pr.16; for from that proposition it follows that from the given divine nature both the essence and the existence of things must be inferred. In a word, in the same sense that God is said to be self-caused he must also be said to be the cause of all things. This will be even clearer from the following Corollary.

Corollary

Particular things are nothing but affections of the attributes of God; that is, modes wherein the attributes of God find expression in a definite and determinate way. The proof is obvious from Pr.15 and Def.5.

PROPOSITION 26

A thing which has been determined to act in a particular way has necessarily been so determined by God; and a thing which has not been determined by God cannot determine itself to act.

Proof

That by which things are said to be determined to act in a particular way must necessarily be something positive (as is obvious). So God, from the necessity of his nature, is the efficient cause both of its essence and its existence (Prs. 25 and 16)—which was the first point. From this the second point quite clearly follows as well. For if a thing which has not been determined by God could determine itself, the first part of this proposition would be false, which, as I have shown, is absurd.

PROPOSITION 27

A thing which has been determined by God to act in a particular way cannot render itself undetermined.

Proof

This proposition is evident from Axiom 3.

PROPOSITION 28

Every individual thing, i.e. anything whatever which is finite and has a determinate existence, cannot exist or be determined to act unless it be determined to exist and to act by another cause which is also finite and has a determinate

existence, and this cause again cannot exist or be determined to act unless it be
determined to exist and to act by another cause which is also finite and has a
determinate existence, and so ad infinitum.

Proof

Whatever is determined to exist and to act has been so determined by God (Pr.
26 and Cor.Pr.24). But that which is finite and has a determinate existence cannot
have been produced by the absolute nature of one of God's attributes, for whatever
follows from the absolute nature of one of God's attributes is infinite and eternal
(Pr.21). It must therefore have followed from God or one of his attributes in so far
as that is considered as affected by some mode; for nothing exists but substance and
its modes (Ax.1 and Defs. 3 and 5), and modes (Cor.Pr.25) are nothing but
affections of God's attributes. But neither could a finite and determined thing have
followed from God or one of his attributes in so far as that is affected by a
modification which is eternal and infinite (Pr.22). Therefore, it must have
followed, or been determined to exist and to act, by God or one of his attributes in
so far as it was modified by a modification which is finite and has a determinate
existence. That was the first point. Then again this cause or this mode (the
reasoning is the same as in the first part of this proof) must also have been
determined by another cause, which is also finite and has a determinate existence,
and again this last (the reasoning is the same) by another, and so *ad infinitum.*

Scholium

Since some things must have been produced directly by God (those things, in
fact, which necessarily follow from his absolute nature) and others through the
medium of these primary things (which other things nevertheless cannot be or be
conceived without God) it follows, firstly, that God is absolutely the proximate
cause of things directly produced by him. I say 'absolutely' *(absolute),* and not
'within their own kind' *(suo genere),* as some say. For the effects of God can neither
be nor be conceived without their cause (Pr.15 and Cor.Pr.24). It follows, secondly,
that God cannot properly be said to be the remote cause of individual things, unless
perchance for the purpose of distinguishing these things from things which he has
produced directly, or rather, things which follow from his absolute nature. For by
'remote cause' we understand a cause which is in no way conjoined with its effect.
But all things that are, are in God, and depend on God in such a way that they can
neither be nor be conceived without him.

PROPOSITION 29

Nothing in nature is contingent, but all things are from the necessity of the divine
nature determined to exist and to act in a definite way.

Proof

Whatever is, is in God (Pr.15). But God cannot be termed a contingent thing, for
(Prop.11) he exists necessarily, not contingently. Again, the modes of the divine
nature have also followed from it necessarily, not contingently (Pr.16), and that,
too, whether in so far as the divine nature is considered absolutely (Pr.21) or in so
far as it is considered as determined to act in a definite way (Pr.27). Furthermore,
God is the cause of these modes not only in so far as they simply exist (Cor.Pr.24),

but also in so far as they are considered as determined to a particular action (Pr.26). Now if they are not determined by God (Pr.26), it is an impossibility, not a contingency, that they should determine themselves. On the other hand (Pr.27), if they are determined by God, it is an impossibility, not a contingency, that they should render themselves undetermined. Therefore, all things are determined from the necessity of the divine nature not only to exist but also to exist and to act in a definite way. Thus, there is no contingency.

Scholium

Before I go any further, I wish to explain at this point what we must understand by 'Natura naturans' and 'Natura naturata.' I should perhaps say not 'explain,' but 'remind the reader,' for I consider that it is already clear from what has gone before that by 'Natura naturans' we must understand that which is in itself and is conceived through itself; that is, the attributes of substance that express eternal and infinite essence; or (Cor.1 Pr.14 and Cor.2 Pr.17), God in so far as he is considered a free cause. By 'Natura naturata' I understand all that follows from the necessity of God's nature, that is, from the necessity of each one of God's attributes; or all the modes of God's attributes in so far as they are considered as things which are in God and can neither be nor be conceived without God.

PROPOSITION 30

The finite intellect in act or the infinite intellect in act must comprehend the attributes of God and the affections of God, and nothing else.

Proof

A true idea must agree with its ideate (Ax.6); that is (as is self-evident), that which is contained in the intellect as an object of thought must necessarily exist in Nature. But in Nature (Cor.1 Pr.14) there is but one substance — God — and no other affections (Pr.15) than those which are in God and that can neither be nor be conceived (Pr.15) without God. Therefore, the finite intellect in act or the infinite intellect in act must comprehend the attributes of God and the affections of God, and nothing else.

PROPOSITION 31

The intellect in act, whether it be finite or infinite, as also will, desire, love etc., must be related to Natura naturata, not to Natura naturans.

Proof

By intellect (as is self-evident) we do not understand absolute thought, but only a definite mode of thinking which differs from other modes such as desire, love, etc., and so (Def.5) must be conceived through absolute thought — that is (Pr.15 and Def.6), an attribute of God which expresses the eternal and infinite essence of thought — in such a way that without this attribute it can neither be nor be conceived; and therefore (Sch.Pr.29) it must be related to Natura naturata, not to Natura naturans, just like the other modes of thinking.

Scholium

The reason for my here speaking of the intellect in act is not that I grant there can be any intellect in potentiality, but that, wishing to avoid any confusion, I want to confine myself to what we perceive with the utmost clarity, to wit, the very act of understanding, than which nothing is more clearly apprehended by us. For we can understand nothing that does not lead to a more perfect cognition of the understanding.

PROPOSITION 32

Will cannot be called a free cause, but only a necessary cause.

Proof

Will, like intellect, is only a definite mode of thinking, and so (Pr.28) no single volition can exist or be determined to act unless it is determined by another cause, and this cause again by another, and so ad infinitum. Now if will be supposed infinite, it must also be determined to exist and to act by God, not in so far as he is absolutely infinite substance, but in so far as he possesses an attribute which expresses the infinite and eternal essence of Thought (Pr.23). Therefore in whatever way will is conceived, whether finite or infinite, it requires a cause by which it is determined to exist and to act; and so (Def.7) it cannot be said to be a free cause, but only a necessary or constrained cause.

Corollary 1

Hence it follows, firstly, that God does not act from freedom of will.

Corollary 2

It follows, secondly, that will and intellect bear the same relationship to God's nature as motion-and-rest and, absolutely, as all natural phenomena that must be determined by God (Pr.29) to exist and to act in a definite way. For will, like all the rest, stands in need of a cause by which it may be determined to exist and to act in a definite manner. And although from a given will or intellect infinite things may follow, God cannot on that account be said to act from freedom of will any more than he can be said to act from freedom of motion-and-rest because of what follows from motion-and-rest (for from this, too, infinite things follow). Therefore will pertains to God's nature no more than do other natural phenomena. It bears the same relationship to God's nature as does motion-and-rest and everything else that we have shown to follow from the necessity of the divine nature and to be determined by that divine nature to exist and to act in a definite way.

PROPOSITION 33

Things could not have been produced by God in any other way or in any other order than is the case.

Proof

All things have necessarily followed from the nature of God (Pr.16) and have been determined to exist and to act in a definite way from the necessity of God's nature (Pr.29). Therefore if things could have been of a different nature or been determined to act in a different way so that the order of Nature would have been different, then God's nature, too, could have been other than it now is, and therefore (Pr.11) this different nature, too, would have had to exist, and consequently there would have been two or more Gods, which (Cor.1, Pr.14) is absurd. Therefore things could not have been produced by God in any other way or in any other order than is the case.

Scholium 1

Since I have here shown more clearly than the midday sun that in things there is absolutely nothing by virtue of which they can be said to be 'contingent,' I now wish to explain briefly what we should understand by 'contingent'; but I must first deal with 'necessary' and 'impossible.' A thing is termed 'necessary' either by reason of its essence or by reason of its cause. For a thing's existence necessarily follows either from its essence and definition or from a given efficient cause. Again, it is for these same reasons that a thing is termed 'impossible'—that is, either because its essence or definition involves a contradiction or because there is no external cause determined to bring it into existence. But a thing is termed 'contingent' for no other reason than the deficiency of our knowledge. For if we do not know whether the essence of a thing involves a contradiction, or if, knowing full well that its essence does not involve a contradiction, we still cannot make any certain judgment as to its existence because the chain of causes is hidden from us, then that thing cannot appear to us either as necessary or as impossible. So we term it either 'contingent' or 'possible.'

Scholium 2

It clearly follows from the above that things have been brought into being by God with supreme perfection, since they have necessarily followed from a most perfect nature. Nor does this imply any imperfection in God, for it is his perfection that has constrained us to make this affirmation. Indeed, from its contrary it would clearly follow (as I have just shown) that God is not supremely perfect, because if things had been brought into being in a different way by God, we should have to attribute to God another nature different from that which consideration of a most perfect Being has made us attribute to him.

However, I doubt not that many will ridicule this view as absurd and will not give their minds to its examination, and for this reason alone, that they are in the habit of attributing to God another kind of freedom very different from that which we (Def.7) have assigned to him; that is, an absolute will. Yet I do not doubt that if they were willing to think the matter over and carefully reflect on our chain of proofs they would in the end reject the kind of freedom which they now attribute to God not only as nonsensical but as a serious obstacle to science. It is needless for me here to repeat what was said in the Scholium to Proposition 17. Yet for their sake I shall proceed to show that, even if it were to be granted that will pertains to the essence of God, it would nevertheless follow from his perfection that things could not have been created by God in any other way or in any other order. This will readily be shown if we first consider—as they themselves grant—that on God's decree and will alone does it depend that each thing is what it is. For otherwise God would not be the cause of all things. Further, there is the fact that all God's decrees have been sanctioned by God from eternity, for otherwise he could be accused of imperfection and inconstancy. But since the eternal does not admit of 'when' or 'before' or 'after,' it follows merely from God's perfection that God can never decree otherwise nor ever could have decreed otherwise; in other words, God could not have been prior to his decrees nor can he be without them. "But," they will say, "granted the supposition that God had made a different universe, or that from eternity he had made a different decree concerning Nature and her order, no imperfection in God would follow therefrom." But if they say this, they will be granting at the same time that God can change his decrees. For if God's decrees had been different from what in fact he has decreed regarding Nature and her order — that is, if he had willed and conceived differently concerning Nature — he would necessarily have had a different intellect and a different will from that which he now has. And if it is permissible to attribute to God a different intellect and a different will without any change in his essence and perfection, why should he not now be able to change his decrees concerning created things, and nevertheless remain equally perfect? For his intellect and will regarding created things and their order have the same relation to his essence and perfection, in whatever manner it be conceived.

Then again, all philosophers whom I have read grant that in God there is no intellect in potentiality but only intellect in act. Now since all of them also grant that his intellect and will are not distinct from his essence, it therefore follows from this, too, that if God had had a different intellect in act and a different will, his essence too would necessarily have been different. Therefore — as I deduced from the beginning — if things had been brought into being by God so as to be different from what they now are, God's intellect and will — that is (as is granted), God's essence — must have been different, which is absurd. Therefore since things could not have been brought into being by God in any other way or order — and it follows from God's supreme perfection that this is true — surely we can have no sound reason for believing that God did not wish to create all the things that are in his intellect through that very same perfection whereby he understands them.

"But," they will say, "there is in things no perfection or imperfection; that which is in them whereby they are perfect or imperfect, and are called good or bad, depends only on the will of God. Accordingly, if God had so willed it he could have brought it about that that which is now perfection should be utmost imperfection, and vice versa." But what else is this but an open assertion that God, who necessarily understands that which he wills, can by his will bring it about that he should understand things in a way different from the way he understands them — and this, as I have just shown, is utterly absurd. So I can turn their own argument against them, as follows. All things depend on the power of God. For things to be able to be otherwise than as they are, God's will, too, would necessarily have to be different. But God's will cannot be different (as we have just shown most clearly from the consideration of God's perfection). Therefore neither can things be different.

I admit that this view which subjects everything to some kind of indifferent will of God and asserts that everything depends on his pleasure, diverges less from the truth than the view of those who hold that God does everything with the good in mind. For these people seem to posit something external to God that does not depend upon him, to which in acting God looks as if it were a model, or to which he aims, as if it were a fixed target. This is surely to subject God to fate; and no more absurd assertion can be made about God, whom we have shown to be the first and the only free cause of both the essence and the existence of things. So I need not spend any more time in refuting this absurdity.

PROPOSITION 34

God's power is his very essence.

Proof

From the sole necessity of God's essence it follows that God is self-caused (Pr.11) and the cause of all things (Pr.16 and Cor.). Therefore God's power whereby he and all things are and act, is his very essence.

PROPOSITION 35

Whatever we conceive to be within God's power necessarily exists.

Proof

Whatever is within God's power must be so comprehended in his essence (Pr.34) that it follows necessarily from it, and thus necessarily exists.

PROPOSITION 36

Nothing exists from whose nature an effect does not follow.

Proof

Whatever exists expresses God's nature or essence in a definite and determinate way (Cor. Pr.25); that is (Pr.34), whatever exists expresses God's power, which is the cause of all things, in a definite and determinate way, and so (Pr.16) some effect must follow from it.

APPENDIX

I have now explained the nature and properties of God: that he necessarily exists, that he is one alone, that he is and acts solely from the necessity of his own nature, that he is the free cause of all things and how so, that all things are in God and are so dependent on him that they can neither be nor be conceived without him, and lastly, that all things have been predetermined by God, not from his free will or absolute pleasure, but from the absolute nature of God, his infinite power. Furthermore, whenever the opportunity arose I have striven to remove prejudices that might hinder the apprehension of my proofs. But since there still remain a considerable number of prejudices, which have been, and still are, an obstacle — indeed, a very great obstacle — to the acceptance of the concatenation of things in the manner which I have expounded, I have thought it proper at this point to bring these prejudices before the bar of reason.

Now all the prejudices which I intend to mention here turn on this one point, the widespread belief among men that all things in Nature are like themselves in acting with an end in view. Indeed, they hold it as certain that God himself directs everything to a fixed end; for they say that God has made everything for man's sake and has made man so that he should worship God. So this is the first point I shall consider, seeking the reason why most people are victims of this prejudice and why all are so naturally disposed to accept it. Secondly, I shall demonstrate its falsity; and lastly I shall show how it has been the source of misconceptions about good and bad, right and wrong, praise and blame, order and confusion, beauty and ugliness, and the like.

However, it is not appropriate here to demonstrate the origin of these misconceptions from the nature of the human mind. It will suffice at this point if I take as my basis what must be universally admitted, that all men are born ignorant of the causes of things, that they all have a desire to seek their own advantage, a desire of which they are conscious. From this it follows, firstly, that men believe that they are free, precisely because they are conscious of their volitions and desires; yet concerning the causes that have determined them to desire and will they have not the faintest idea, because they are ignorant of them. Secondly, men act always with an end in view, to wit, the advantage that they seek. Hence it happens that they are always looking only for the final causes of things done, and are satisfied when they find them, having, of course, no reason for further doubt. But if they fail to discover them from some external source, they have no recourse but to turn to themselves, and to reflect on what ends would normally determine them to similar actions, and so they necessarily judge other minds by their own. Further, since they find within themselves and outside themselves a considerable number of means very convenient for the pursuit of their own advantage — as, for instance, eyes for seeing, teeth for chewing, cereals and living creatures for food, the sun for giving light, the sea for breeding fish — the result is that they look on all the things of Nature as means to their own advantage. And realising that these were found, not produced by them, they came to believe that there is someone else who produced these means for their use. For looking on things as means, they could not believe them to be self-created, but on the analogy of the means which they are accustomed to produce for themselves, they were bound to conclude that there was some governor or governors of Nature, endowed with human freedom, who have attended to all their needs and made everything for their use. And having no information on the subject, they also had to estimate the character of these rulers by their own, and so they asserted that the gods direct everything for man's use so that they may bind men to them and be held in the highest honour by them. So it came about that every individual devised different methods of worshipping God as he thought fit in order that God should love him beyond others and direct the whole of Nature so as to serve his blind cupidity and insatiable greed. Thus it was that this misconception developed into superstition and became deep-rooted in the minds of men, and it was for this reason that every man strove most earnestly to understand and to explain the final causes of all things. But in seeking to show that Nature does nothing in vain — that is, nothing that is not to man's advantage — they seem to have shown only this, that Nature and the gods are as crazy as mankind.

Consider, I pray, what has been the upshot. Among so many of Nature's blessings they were bound to discover quite a number of disasters, such as storms, earthquakes, diseases and so forth, and they maintained that these occurred because the gods were angry at the wrongs done to them by men, or the faults committed in the course of their worship. And although daily experience cried out against this and showed by any number of examples that blessings and disasters befall the godly and the ungodly alike without discrimination, they did not on that account abandon their ingrained prejudice. For they found it easier to regard this fact as one among other mysteries they could not understand and thus maintain their innate condition of ignorance rather than to demolish in its entirety the theory they had constructed and devise a new one. Hence they made it axiomatic that the judgment of the gods is far beyond man's understanding. Indeed, it is for this reason, and this reason only, that truth might have evaded mankind forever had not Mathematics, which is concerned not with ends but only with the essences and properties of figures, revealed to men a different standard of truth. And there are other causes too — there is no need to mention them here — which could have made men aware of these widespread misconceptions and brought them to a true knowledge of things.

I have thus sufficiently dealt with my first point. There is no need to spend time in going on to show that Nature has no fixed goal and that all final causes are but figments of the human imagination. For I think that this is now quite evident, both from the basic causes from which I have traced the origin of this misconception and from Proposition 16 and the Corollaries to Proposition 32, and in addition from the whole set of proofs I have adduced to show that all things in Nature proceed from an eternal necessity and with supreme perfection. But I will make this additional point, that this doctrine of Final Causes turns Nature completely upside down, for it regards as an effect that which is in fact a cause, and vice versa. Again, it makes that which is by nature first to be last; and finally, that which is highest and most perfect is held to be the most imperfect. Omitting the first two points as self-evident, Propositions 21, 22 and 23 make it clear that that effect is most perfect which is directly produced by God, and an effect is the less perfect in proportion to the number of intermediary causes required for its production. But if the things produced directly by God were brought about to enable him to attain an end, then of necessity the last things for the sake of which the earlier things were brought about would excel all others. Again, this doctrine negates God's perfection; for if God acts with an end in view, he must necessarily be seeking something that he lacks. And although theologians and metaphysicians may draw a distinction between a purpose arising from want and an assimilative purpose, they still admit that God has acted in all things for the sake of himself, and not for the sake of the things to be created. For prior to creation they are not able to point to anything but God as a purpose for God's action. Thus they have to admit that God lacked and desired those things for the procurement of which he willed to create the means — as is self-evident.

I must not fail to mention here that the advocates of this doctrine, eager to display their talent in assigning purpose to things, have introduced a new style of argument to prove their doctrine, i.e. a reduction, not to the impossible, but to ignorance, thus revealing the lack of any other argument in its favour. For example, if a stone falls from the roof on somebody's head and kills him, by this method of arguing they will prove that the stone fell in order to kill the man; for if it had not fallen for this purpose by the will of God, how could so many circumstances (and there are often many coinciding circumstances) have chanced to concur? Perhaps you will reply that the event occurred because the wind was blowing and the man was walking that way. But they will persist in asking why the wind blew at that time and why the man was walking that way at that very time. If you again reply that the wind sprang up at that time because on the previous day the sea had begun to toss after a period of calm and that the man had been invited by a friend, they will again persist—for there is no end to questions—"But why did the sea toss, and why was the man invited for that time?" And so they will go on and on asking the causes of causes, until you take refuge in the will of God—that is, the sanctuary of ignorance. Similarly, when they consider the structure of the human body, they are astonished, and being ignorant of the causes of such skilful work they conclude that it is fashioned not by mechanical art but by divine or supernatural art, and is so arranged that no one part shall injure another.

As a result, he who seeks the true causes of miracles and is eager to understand the works of Nature as a scholar, and not just to gape at them like a fool, is universally considered an impious heretic and denounced by those to whom the common people bow down as interpreters of Nature and the gods. For these people know that the dispelling of ignorance would entail the disappearance of that sense of awe which is the one and only support for their argument and for the safeguarding of their authority. But I will leave this subject and proceed to the third point that I proposed to deal with.

When men became convinced that everything that is created is created on their behalf, they were bound to consider as the most important quality in every individual thing that which was most useful to them, and to regard as of the highest excellence all those things by which they were most benefited. Hence they came to form these abstract notions to explain the natures of things:—Good, Bad, Order, Confusion, Hot, Cold, Beauty, Ugliness; and since they believe that they are free, the following abstract notions came into being:—Praise, Blame, Right, Wrong. The latter I shall deal with later on after I have treated of human nature; at this point I shall briefly explain the former.

All that conduces to well-being and to the worship of God they call Good, and the contrary, Bad. And since those who do not understand the nature of things, but only imagine things, make no affirmative judgments about things themselves and mistake their imagination for intellect, they are firmly convinced that there is order in things, ignorant as they are of things and of their own nature. For when things are in such arrangement that, being presented to us through our senses, we can readily picture them and thus readily remember them, we say that they are well arranged; if the contrary, we say that they are ill-arranged, or confused. And since those things we can readily picture we find pleasing compared with other things, men prefer order to confusion, as though order were something in Nature other than what is relative to our imagination. And they say that God has created all things in an orderly way, without realizing that they are thus attributing human imagination to God—unless perchance they mean that God, out of consideration for the human imagination, arranged all things in the way that men could most easily imagine. And perhaps they will find no obstacle in the fact that there are any number of things that far surpass our imagination, and a considerable number that confuse the imagination because of its weakness.

But I have devoted enough time to this. The other notions, too, are nothing but modes of imagining whereby the imagination is affected in various ways, and yet the ignorant consider them as important attributes of things because they believe—as I have said—that all things were made on their behalf, and they call a thing's nature good or bad, healthy or rotten and corrupt, according to its effect on them. For instance, if the motion communicated to our nervous system by objects presented through our eyes is conducive to our feeling of well-being, the objects which are its cause are said to be beautiful, while the objects which provoke a contrary motion are called ugly. Those things that we sense through the nose are called fragrant or fetid, through the tongue sweet or bitter, tasty or tasteless, those that we sense by touch are called hard or soft, rough or smooth, and so on. Finally, those that we sense through our ears are said to give forth noise, sound, or harmony, the last of which has driven men to such madness that they used to believe that even God delights in harmony. There are philosophers who have convinced themselves that the motions of the heavens give rise to harmony. All this goes to show that everyone's judgment is a function of the disposition of his brain, or rather, that he mistakes for reality the way his imagination is affected. Hence it is no wonder—as we should note in passing—that we find so many controversies arising among men, resulting finally in scepticism. For although human bodies agree in many respects, there are very many differences, and so one man thinks good what another thinks bad; what to one man is well-ordered, to another is confused; what to one is pleasing, to another is displeasing, and so forth. I say no more here because this is not the place to treat at length of this subject, and also because all are well acquainted with it from experience. Everybody knows those sayings: — "So many heads, so many opinions," "everyone is wise in his own sight," "brains differ as much as palates," all of which show clearly that men's judgment is a function of the disposition of the brain, and they are guided by imagination rather than intellect. For if men understood things, all that I have put forward would be found, if not attractive, at any rate convincing, as Mathematics attests.

We see therefore that all the notions whereby the common people are wont to explain Nature are merely modes of imagining, and denote not the nature of any thing but only the constitution of the imagination. And because these notions have names as if they were the names of entities existing independently of the imagination I call them 'entities of imagination' *(entia imaginationis)* rather than 'entities of reason' *(entia rationis)*. So all arguments drawn from such notions against me can be easily refuted. For many are wont to argue on the following lines: if everything has followed from the necessity of God's most perfect nature, why does Nature display so many imperfections, such as rottenness to the point of putridity, nauseating ugliness, confusion, evil, sin, and so on? But, as I have just pointed out, they are easily refuted. For the perfection of things should be measured solely from their own nature and power; nor are things more or less perfect to the extent that they please or offend human senses, serve or oppose human interests. As to those who ask why God did not create all men in such a way that they should be governed solely by reason, I make only this reply, that he lacked not material for creating all things from the highest to the lowest degree of perfection; or, to speak more accurately, the laws of his nature were so comprehensive as to suffice for the production of everything that can be conceived by an infinite intellect, as I proved in Proposition 16.

These are the misconceptions which I undertook to deal with at this point. Any other misconception of this kind can be corrected by everyone with a little reflection.

GOTTFRIED WILHELM VON LEIBNIZ—from an old engraving

FREDERICK THE GREAT (Anton Graf)

LEIBNIZ IN BERLIN (from an old engraving

GOTTFRIED LEIBNIZ

Gottfried Wilhelm Leibniz (1646–1716) was born in Leipzig, Germany. The son of a professor, Leibniz was precocious and widely read as a youngster, entering the University of Leipzig at fifteen and receiving a doctorate of laws at Altdorf at twenty. After his graduation he declined a professorship, choosing instead to go to Nuremburg, and soon becoming legal counselor in the court of Mainz. In 1672 he was sent to Paris on a diplomatic mission. Remaining there for four years, he conversed with outstanding mathematicians and scientists and learned of recent advances in their fields. During this period, and independently of Newton, he invented the calculus. Upon his return to Germany in 1676, he accepted a position at the court of the Duke of Brunswick in Hanover, where he remained in the service of various nobles for the rest of his life. Throughout his career, Leibniz corresponded widely on philosophical and scientific topics.

Although Leibniz was a prolific writer, many of his major philosophical works were not published during his lifetime. An exception is the *Theodicy,* published in 1710. His important writings include the *Discourse on Metaphysics,* written in 1686; the related *Correspondence With Arnauld* (1686–1690); the *Monadology* (1714); and his *Correspondence With Samuel Clarke* (1715–1716). Also significant is his *New Essays on the Human Understanding* (1704), a critical discussion of Locke's *Essay.*

Leibniz's philosophical system, though comprehensive and wide-ranging, rests on a narrow logical base. Central to this base are his conceptions of the nature of propositions and of substances. According to Leibniz, all propositions assert the inclusion of one concept in another. For example, the statement "Neil Armstrong walked on the moon" asserts that Neil Armstrong's overall concept or essence includes walking on the moon as one of its elements. A substance or 'complete being,' moreover, is one which affords "a conception so complete that the concept shall be sufficient for the understanding of it and for the deduction of all the predicates of which the substance is or may become the subject." Thus, anyone who fully understands Neil Armstrong's concept must know not only that he walked on the moon, but also everything else there is to know about him—his history, current situation, and future. Such full understanding is of course beyond the grasp of our finite minds, but it is not beyond the grasp of God.

From these views about propositions and substances, Leibniz deduced a number of interesting consequences. For one thing, if every fact about Neil Armstrong is included in his concept, then anyone who fully understands that concept will be able to deduce not only who his parents were, but also who their parents were, where his first bite of food was grown, and every other fact about any person or thing ever connected with him. However, any object in the universe is connected to Neil Armstrong in some way or another. For Leibniz, therefore, "every substance is like an entire world and like a mirror of God, or indeed of the whole world which it portrays, each one in its own fashion." Although each substance reflects all the others, no substance can really cause any change in any other. What appears to be causal interaction among substances is really a "pre-established harmony" among them, reflecting the fact that God created each one with an eye to all the rest. Of all the harmoniously evolving substances in the universe, no two are alike in every respect; for if any two were completely alike, they would be one substance rather than two. This last doctrine, that no two things can be completely alike, is widely known as the 'identity of indiscernibles.'

Leibniz's views about substances may appear to raise difficulties about possibility and freedom. If from the beginning it was part of Neil Armstrong's concept to walk on the moon, then it seems to have been impossible for him not to walk on the moon. If this is so, however, then his moon walk (and, by similar reasoning, all other occurrences) must have been necessary or predetermined; and so it appears that human freedom must not exist. Leibniz believed, however, that he could avoid such implications. In his view, God chose the actual world from among many other possibilities. Our world must, therefore, somehow be better than any of the others, for God always chooses what is best. Nevertheless, Leibniz believed that the mere possibility of these other worlds defeats the implication that whatever happens in our world is necessary. Leibniz also thought that he could answer the charge that his views rule out human freedom. Even though a person's concept does contain all his future acts, Leibniz argued, God has decreed that "the will shall always seek the apparent good in certain particular respects . . . he, without at all necessitating our choice, determines it by that which appears most desirable." Since whatever we do stems from our own will, and is done in pursuit of our own vision of the good, it follows according to Leibniz that anything we do is our own responsibility. God "inclines our souls without necessitating them."

The critical literature on Leibniz is voluminous. For a general treatment, see C.D. Broad, *Leibniz: An Introduction* (Cambridge: Cambridge University Press, 1975). Two other recent works of interest are G.H.R. Parkinson, *Logic and Reality in Leibniz' Metaphysics* (Oxford: Oxford University Press, 1965) and Hidé Ishiguro, *Leibniz's Philosophy of Logic and Language* (Ithaca: Cornell University Press, 1972). Bertrand Russell, *A Critical Exposition of the Philosophy of Leibniz* (London: George Allen & Unwin, 1900) remains an important study. An excellent group of short essays is Harry Frankfurt, ed., *Leibniz: A Collection of Critical Essays* (Garden City: Doubleday, 1972).

G.S.

DISCOURSE ON METAPHYSICS

I. Concerning the divine perfection and that God does everything in the most desirable way.

The conception of God which is the most common and the most full of meaning is expressed well enough in the words: God is an absolutely perfect being. The implications, however, of these words fail to receive sufficient consideration. For instance, there are many different kinds of perfection, all of which God possesses, and each one of them pertains to him in the highest degree.

We must also know what perfection is. One thing which can surely be affirmed about it is that those forms or natures which are not susceptible of it to the highest degree, say the nature of numbers or of figures, do not permit of perfection. This is because the number which is the greatest of all (that is, the sum of all the numbers), and likewise the greatest of all figures, imply contradictions. The greatest knowledge, however, and omnipotence contain no impossibility. Consequently power and knowledge do admit of perfection, and in so far as they pertain to God they have no limits.

Whence it follows that God who possesses supreme and infinite wisdom acts in the most perfect manner not only metaphysically, but also from the moral standpoint. And with respect to ourselves it can be said that the more we are enlightened and informed in regard to the works of God the more will we be disposed to find them excellent and conforming entirely to that which we might desire.

II. Against those who hold that there is in the works of God no goodness, or that the principles of goodness and beauty are arbitrary.

Therefore I am far removed from the opinion of those who maintain that there are no principles of goodness or perfection in the nature of things, or in the ideas which God has about them, and who say that the works of God are good only through the formal reason that God has made them. If this position were true, God, knowing that he is the author of things, would not have to regard them afterwards and find them good, as the Holy Scripture witnesses. Such anthropological expressions are used only to let us know that excellence is recognized in regarding the works themselves, even if we do not consider their evident dependence on their author. This is confirmed by the fact that it is in reflecting upon the works that we are able to discover the one who wrought. They must therefore bear in themselves his character. I confess that the contrary opinion seems to me extremely dangerous and closely approaches that of recent innovators[1] who hold that the beauty of the universe and the goodness which we attribute to the works of God are chimeras of human beings who think of God in human terms. In saying, therefore, that things are not good accord-

1. [The reference is to Spinoza, among others. —S.M.C.]

ing to any standard of goodness, but simply by the will of God, it seems to me that one destroys, without realizing it, all the love of God and all his glory; for why praise him for what he has done, if he would be equally praiseworthy in doing the contrary? Where will be his justice and his wisdom if he has only a certain despotic power, if arbitrary will takes the place of reasonableness, and if in accord with the definition of tyrants, justice consists in that which is pleasing to the most powerful? Besides it seems that every act of willing supposes some reason for the willing and this reason, of course, must precede the act. This is why, accordingly, I find so strange those expressions of certain philosophers who say that the eternal truths of metaphysics and Geometry, and consequently the principles of goodness, of justice, and of perfection, are effects only of the will of God. To me it seems that all these follow from his understanding, which does not depend upon his will any more than does his essence.

III. Against those who think that God might have made things better than he has.

Neither am I able to approve of the opinion of certain modern writers who boldly maintain that that which God has made is not perfect in the highest degree, and that he might have done better. It seems to me that the consequences of such an opinion are wholly inconsistent with the glory of God. *Uti minus malum habet rationem boni, ita minus bonum habet rationem mali.*[2] I think that one acts imperfectly if he acts with less perfection than he is capable of. To show that an architect could have done better is to find fault with his work. Furthermore this opinion is contrary to the Holy Scriptures when they assure us of the goodness of God's work. For if comparative perfection were sufficient, then in whatever way God had accomplished his work, since there is an infinitude of possible imperfections, it would always have been good in comparison with the less perfect; but a thing is little praiseworthy when it can be praised only in this way.

I believe that a great many passages from the divine writings and from the holy fathers will be found favoring my position, while hardly any will be found in favor of that of these modern thinkers. Their opinion is, in my judgment, foreign to the writers of antiquity and is a deduction based upon the too slight acquaintance which we have with the general harmony of the universe and with the hidden reasons for God's conduct. In our ignorance, therefore, we are tempted to decide audaciously that many things might have been done better.

These modern thinkers insist upon certain hardly tenable subtleties, for they imagine that nothing is so perfect that there might not have been something more perfect. This is an error. They think, indeed, that they are thus safeguarding the liberty of God. As if it were not the highest liberty to act in perfection according to the sovereign reason. For to think that God acts in anything without having any reason for his willing, even if we overlook the fact that such action seems impossible, is an opinion which conforms little to God's glory. For example, let us suppose that God chooses between A and B, and that he takes A without any reason for preferring it to B. I say that this action on the part of God is at least not praiseworthy, for all praise ought to be founded upon reason which *ex hypothesi* is not present here. My opinion is that God does nothing for which he does not deserve to be glorified.

---

2. [As the lesser evil contains a portion of good, so the lesser good contains a portion of evil. (This translation and the subsequent ones in the *Discourse* are by William E. Mann.)]

IV. That love for God demands on our part complete satisfaction with and acquiescence in that which he has done.

The general knowledge of this great truth that God acts always in the most perfect and most desirable manner possible, is in my opinion the basis of the love which we owe to God in all things; for he who loves seeks his satisfaction in the felicity or perfection of the subject loved and in the perfection of his actions. *Idem velle et idem nolle vera amicitia est.*[3] I believe that it is difficult to love God truly when one, having the power to change his disposition, is not disposed to wish for that which God desires. In fact those who are not satisfied with what God does seem to me like dissatisfied subjects whose attitude is not very different from that of rebels. I hold, therefore, that on these principles, to act conformably to the love of God it is not sufficient to force oneself to be patient, we must be really satisfied with all that comes to us according to his will. I mean this acquiescence in regard to the past; for as regards the future one should not be a quietist with the arms folded, open to ridicule, awaiting that which God will do; according to the sophism which the ancients called λόγον ἀεργον, the lazy reason. It is necessary to act conformably to the presumptive will of God as far as we are able to judge of it, trying with all our might to contribute to the general welfare and particularly to the ornamentation and the perfection of that which touches us, or of that which is nigh and so to speak at our hand. For if the future shall perhaps show that God has not wished our good intention to have its way, it does not follow that he has not wished us to act as we have; on the contrary, since he is the best of all masters, he ever demands only the right intentions, and it is for him to know the hour and the proper place to let good designs succeed.

V. In what the principles of the divine perfection consist, and that the simplicity of the means counterbalances the richness of the effects.

It is sufficient, therefore, to have this confidence in God, that he has done everything for the best and that nothing will be able to injure those who love him. To know in particular, however, the reasons which have moved him to choose this order of the universe, to permit sin, to dispense his salutary grace in a certain manner—this passes the capacity of a finite mind, above all when such a mind has not come into the joy of the vision of God. Yet it is possible to make some general remarks touching the course of providence in the government of things. One is able to say, therefore, that he who acts perfectly is like an excellent Geometer who knows how to find the best construction for a problem; like a good architect who utilizes his location and the funds destined for the building in the most advantageous manner, leaving nothing which shocks or which does not display that beauty of which it is capable; like a good householder who employs his property in such a way that there shall be nothing uncultivated or sterile; like a clever machinist who makes his production in the least difficult way possible; and like an intelligent author who encloses the most of reality in the least possible compass.

Of all beings those which are the most perfect and occupy the least possible space, that is to say those which interfere with one another the least, are the spirits whose perfections are the virtues. That is why we may not doubt that the felicity of

---

3. [To will the same and to reject the same is true friendship.]

the spirits is the principal aim of God and that he puts this purpose into execution, as far as the general harmony will permit. We will recur to this subject again.

When the simplicity of God's way is spoken of, reference is specially made to the means which he employs, and on the other hand when the variety, richness and abundance are referred to, the ends or effects are had in mind. Thus one ought to be proportioned to the other, just as the cost of a building should balance the beauty and grandeur which is expected. It is true that nothing costs God anything, just as there is no cost for a philosopher who makes hypotheses in constructing his imaginary world, because God has only to make decrees in order that a real world come into being; but in matters of wisdom the decrees or hypotheses meet the expenditure in proportion as they are more independent of one another. Reason wishes to avoid multiplicity in hypotheses or principles very much as the simplest system is always preferred in Astronomy.

VI. That God does nothing which is not orderly, and that it is not even possible to conceive of events which are not regular.

The activities or the acts of will of God are commonly divided into ordinary and extraordinary. But it is well to bear in mind that God does nothing out of order. Therefore, that which passes for extraordinary is so only with regard to a particular order established among the created things, for as regards the universal order, everything conforms to it. This is so true that not only does nothing occur in this world which is absolutely irregular, but it is even impossible to conceive of such an occurrence. Because, let us suppose for example that some one jots down a quantity of points upon a sheet of paper helter skelter, as do those who exercise the ridiculous art of Geomancy; now I say that it is possible to find a geometrical line whose concept shall be uniform and constant, that is, in accordnace with a certain formula, and which line at the same time shall pass through all of those points, and in the same order in which the hand jotted them down; also if a continuous line be traced, which is now straight, now circular, and now of any other description, it is possible to find a mental equivalent, a formula or an equation common to all the points of this line by virtue of which formula the changes in the direction of the line must occur. There is no instance of a face whose contour does not form part of a geometric line and which can not be traced entire by a certain mathematical motion. But when the formula is very complex, that which conforms to it passes for irregular. Thus we may say that in whatever manner God might have created the world, it would always have been regular and in a certain order. God, however, has chosen the most perfect, that is to say the one which is at the same time the simplest in hypotheses and the richest in phenomena, as might be the case with a geometric line, whose construction was easy, but whose properties and effects were extremely remarkable and of great significance. I use these comparisons to picture a certain imperfect resemblance to the divine wisdom, and to point out that which may at least raise our minds to conceive in some sort what cannot otherwise be expressed. I do not pretend at all to explain thus the great mystery upon which the whole universe depends.

VII. That miracles conform to the regular order although they go against the subordinate regulations; concerning that which God desires or permits and concerning general and particular intentions.

Now since nothing is done which is not orderly, we may say that miracles are quite within the order of natural operations. We use the term natural of these operations because they conform to certain subordinate regulations which we call the nature of things. For it can be said that this nature is only a custom of God's which he can change on the occasion of a stronger reason than that which moved him to use these regulations. As regards general and particular intentions, according to the way in which we understand the matter, it may be said on the one hand that everything is in accordance with his most general intention, or that which best conforms to the most perfect order he has chosen; on the other hand, however, it is also possible to say that he has particular intentions which are exceptions to the subordinate regulations above mentioned. Of God's laws, however, the most universal, i.e., that which rules the whole course of the universe, is without exceptions.

It is possible to say that God desires everything which is an object of his particular intention. When we consider the objects of his general intentions, however, such as are the modes of activities of created things and especially of the reasoning creatures with whom God wishes to co-operate, we must make a distinction; for if the action is good in itself, we may say that God wishes it and at times commands it, even though it does not take place; but if it is bad in itself and becomes good only by accident through the course of events and especially after chastisement and satisfaction have corrected its malignity and rewarded the ill with interest in such a way that more perfection results in the whole train of circumstances than would have come if that ill had not occurred, —if all this takes place we must say that God permits the evil, and not that he desired it, although he has co-operated by means of the laws of nature which he has established. He knows how to produce the greatest good from them.

VIII. In order to distinguish between the activities of God and the activities of created things we must explain the conception of an individual substance.

It is quite difficult to distinguish God's actions from those of his creatures. Some think that God does everything; others imagine that he only conserves the force that he has given to created things. How far can we say either of these opinions is right?

In the first place since activity and passivity pertain properly to individual substances *(actiones sunt suppositorum)* it will be necessary to explain what such a substance is. It is indeed true that when several predicates are attributes of a single subject and this subject is not an attribute of another, we speak of it as an individual substance, but this is not enough, and such an explanation is merely nominal. We must therefore inquire what it is to be an attribute in reality of a certain subject. Now it is evident that every true predication has some basis in the nature of things, and even when a proposition is not identical, that is, when the predicate is not expressly contained in the subject, it is still necessary that it be virtually contained in it, and this is what the philosophers call *in-esse*, saying thereby that the predicate is in the subject. Thus the content of the subject must always include that of the predicate in such a way that if one understands perfectly the concept of the subject, he will know that the predicate appertains to it also. This being so, we are able to say that this is the nature of an individual substance or of a complete being, namely, to afford a conception so complete that the concept shall be sufficient for the understanding of it and for the deduction of all the predicates of which the substance is or may become the subject. Thus the quality of king, which belonged to Alexander the Great, an abstraction from the subject, is not sufficiently determined to constitute an individual, and does not contain the other qualities of the same subject, nor everything which the idea of this prince includes. God, however, seeing the individual concept, or haecceity, of Alexander, sees there at the same time the basis and the reason of all the predicates which can be truly uttered regarding him; for instance that he will conquer Darius[4] and Porus,[5] even to the point of knowing *a priori* (and not by experience) whether he died a natural death or by poison,—facts which we can learn only through history. When we carefully consider the connection of things we see also the possibility of saying that there was always in the soul of Alexander marks of all that had happened to him and evidences of all that would happen to him and traces even of everything which occurs in the universe, although God alone could recognize them all.

IX. That every individual substance expresses the whole universe in its own manner and that in its full concept are included all its experiences together with all the attendant circumstances and the whole sequence of exterior events.

There follow from these considerations several noticeable paradoxes; among others that it is not true that two substances may be exactly alike and differ only numerically, *solo numero,* and that what St. Thomas says on this point regarding angels and intelligences *(quod ibi omne individuum sit species infima)*[6] is true of all substances, provided that the specific difference is understood as Geometers understand it in the case of figures; again that a substance will be able to commence only through creation and perish only through annihilation; that a substance cannot be divided into two nor can one be made out of two, and that thus the number of substances neither augments nor diminishes through natural means, although they are frequently transformed. Furthermore every substance is like an entire world and like a mirror of God, or indeed of the whole world which it portrays, each one in its own fashion; almost as the same city is variously represented according to the various viewpoints from which it is regarded. Thus the universe is multiplied in some sort as many times as there are substances, and the glory of God is multiplied in the same way by as many wholly different representations of his works. It can indeed be said that every substance bears in some sort the character of God's infinite wisdom and omnipotence, and imitates him as much as it is able to; for it expresses, although confusedly, all that happens in the universe, past, present and future, deriving thus a certain resemblance to an infinite perception or power of knowing. And since all other substances express this particular substance and ac-

4. [Darius III (d. 330 B.C.) was king of Persia.]

5. [Porus (d. 321 B.C.) was a king in India.]

6. [That within them every individual is a unique species.]

commodate themselves to it, we can say that it exerts its power upon all the others in imitation of the omnipotence of the creator.

X. That the belief in substantial forms has a certain basis in fact, but that these forms effect no changes in the phenomena and must not be employed for the explanation of particular events.

It seems that the ancients, able men, who were accustomed to profound meditations and taught theology and philosophy several centuries ago and some of whom recommend themselves to us on account of their piety, had some knowledge of that which we have just said and this is why they introduced and maintained the substantial forms so much decried to-day. But they were not so far from the truth nor so open to ridicule as the common run of our new philosophers imagine. I grant that the consideration of these forms is of no service in the details of physics and ought not to be employed in the explanation of particular phenomena. In regard to this last point, the schoolmen were at fault, as were also the physicists of times past who followed their example, thinking they had given the reason for the properties of a body in mentioning the forms and qualities without going to the trouble of examining the manner of operation; as if one should be content to say that a clock had a certain amount of clockness derived from its form, and should not inquire in what that clockness consisted. This is indeed enough for the man who buys it, provided he surrenders the care of it to someone else. The fact, however, that there was this misunderstanding and misuse of the substantial forms should not bring us to throw away something whose recognition is so necessary in metaphysics. Since without these we will not be able, I hold, to know the ultimate principles nor to lift our minds to the knowledge of the incorporeal natures and of the marvels of God. Yet as the geometer does not need to encumber his mind with the famous puzzle of the composition of the continuum, and as no moralist, and still less a jurist or a statesman has need to trouble himself with the great difficulties which arise in conciliating free will with the providential activity of God (since the geometer is able to make all his demonstrations and the statesman can complete all his deliberations without entering into these discussions which are so necessary and important in Philosophy and Theology), so in the same way the physicist can explain his experiments, now using simpler experiments already made, now employing geometrical and mechanical demonstrations without any need of the general considerations which belong to another sphere, and if he employs the co-operation of God, or perhaps of some soul or animating *Archéus,* or something else of a similar nature, he goes out of his path quite as much as that man who, when facing an important practical question, would wish to enter into profound argumentations regarding the nature of destiny and of our liberty; a fault which men quite frequently commit without realizing it when they cumber their minds with considerations regarding fate, and thus they are even sometimes turned from a good resolution or from some necessary provision.

XI. That the opinions of the theologians and of the so-called scholastic philosophers are not to be wholly despised.

I know that I am advancing a great paradox in pretending to resuscitate in some sort the ancient philosophy, and to recall *postliminio* the substantial forms almost banished from our modern thought. But perhaps I will not be condemned lightly when it is known that I have long meditated over the modern philosophy and that I have devoted much time to experiments in physics and to the demonstrations of geometry and that I, too, for a long time was persuaded of the baselessness of those "beings" which, however, I was finally obliged to take up again in spite of myself and as though by force. The many investigations which I carried on compelled me to recognize that our moderns do not do sufficient justice to Saint Thomas and to the other great men of that period and that there is in the theories of the scholastic philosophers and theologians far more solidity than is imagined, provided that these theories are employed *à propos* and in their place. I am persuaded that if some careful and meditative mind were to take the trouble to clarify and direct their thoughts in the manner of analytic geometers, he would find a great treasure of very important truths, wholly demonstrable.

XII. That the conception of the extension of a body is in a way imaginary and does not constitute the substance of the body.

But to resume the thread of our discussion, I believe that he who will meditate upon the nature of substance, as I have explained it above, will find that the whole nature of bodies is not exhausted in their extension, that is to say, in their size, figure and motion, but that we must recognize something which corresponds to soul, something which is commonly called substantial form, although these forms effect no change in the phenomena, any more than do the souls of beasts, that is if they have souls. It is even possible to demonstrate that the ideas of size, figure and motion are not so distinctive as is imagined, and that they stand for something imaginary relative to our perceptions as do, although to a greater extent, the ideas of color, heat, and the other similar qualities in regard to which we may doubt whether they are actually to be found in the nature of the things outside of us. This is why these latter qualities are unable to constitute "substance" and if there is no other principle of identity in bodies than that which has just been referred to a body would not subsist more than for a moment.

The souls and the substance-forms of other bodies are entirely different from intelligent souls which alone know their actions, and not only do not perish through natural means but indeed always retain the knowledge of what they are; a fact which makes them alone open to chastisement or recompense, and makes them citizens of the republic of the universe whose monarch is God. Hence it follows that all the other creatures should serve them, a point which we shall discuss more amply later.

XIII. As the individual concept of each person includes once for all everything which can ever happen to him, in it can be seen the a priori evidences or the reasons for the reality of each event, and why one happened sooner than the other. But these events, however certain, are nevertheless contingent, being based on the free choice of God and of his creatures. It is true that their choices always have their reasons, but they incline to the choices under no compulsion of necessity.

But before going further it is necessary to meet a difficulty which may arise regarding the principles which we have set forth in the preceding. We have said that the concept of an individual substance includes once for all everything which can ever happen to it and that in considering this concept one will be able to see everything which can truly be said concerning the individual, just as we are able to see in the nature of a circle all the properties which can be derived from it. But does it not seem that in this way the difference between contingent and necessary truths will be destroyed, that there will be no place for human liberty, and that an absolute fatality will rule as well over all our actions as over all the rest of the events of the world? To this I reply that a distinction must be made between that which is certain and that which is necessary. Every one grants that future contingencies are assured since God foresees them, but we do not say just because of that that they are necessary. But it will be objected, that if any conclusion can be deduced infallibly from some definition or concept, it is necessary; and now since we have maintained that everything which is to happen to anyone is already virtually included in his nature or concept, as all the properties are contained in the definition of a circle, therefore, the difficulty still remains. In order to meet the objection completely, I say that the connection or sequence is of two kinds: the one, absolutely necessary, whose contrary implies contradiction, occurs in the eternal verities like the truths of geometry; the other is necessary only *ex hypothesi,* and so to speak by accident, and in itself it is contingent since the contrary is not implied. This latter sequence is not founded upon ideas wholly pure and upon the pure understanding of God, but upon his free decrees and upon the processes of the universe. Let us give an example. Since Julius Caesar will become perpetual Dictator and master of the Republic and will overthrow the liberty of Rome, this action is contained in his concept, for we have supposed that it is the nature of such a perfect concept of a subject to involve everything, in fact so that the predicate may be included in the subject *ut possit inesse subjecto.* We may say that it is not in virtue of this concept or idea that he is obliged to perform this action, since it pertains to him only because God knows everything. But it will be insisted in reply that his nature or form responds to this concept, and since God imposes upon him this personality, he is compelled henceforth to live up to it. I could reply by instancing the similar case of the future contingencies which as yet have no reality save in the understanding and will of God, and which, because God has given them in advance this form, must needs correspond to it. But I prefer to overcome a difficulty rather than to excuse it by instancing other difficulties, and what I am about to say will serve to clear up the one as well as the other. It is here that must be applied the distinction in the kind of relation, and I say that that which happens conformably to these decrees is assured, but that it is not therefore necessary, and if anyone did the contrary, he would do nothing impossible in itself, although it is impossible *ex hypothesi* that that other happen. For if anyone were capable of carrying out a complete demonstration by virtue of which he could prove this connection of the subject, which is Caesar, with the predicate, which is his successful enterprise, he would bring us to see in fact that the future dictatorship of Caesar had its basis in his concept or nature, so that one would see there a reason why he resolved to cross the Rubicon rather than to stop, and why he gained instead of losing the day at Pharsalus,[7] and that it was reasonable and by consequence assured that

7. [Pharsalus was an ancient city in Thessaly, Greece, where in 48 B.C. Caesar defeated Pompey.]

this would occur, but one would not prove that it was necessary in itself, nor that the contrary implied a contradiction, almost in the same way in which it is reasonable and assured that God will always do what is best although what is less perfect is not thereby contradictory. For it would be found that this demonstration of this predicate as belonging to Caesar is not as absolute as are those of numbers or of geometry, but that this predicate supposes a sequence of things which God has shown by his free will. This sequence is based on the first free decree of God which was to do always that which is the most perfect and upon the decree which God made following the first one, regarding human nature, which is that men should always do, although freely, that which appears to be the best. Now every truth which is founded upon this kind of decree is contingent, although certain, for the decrees of God do not change the possibilities of things and, as I have already said, although God assuredly chooses the best, this does not prevent that which is less perfect from being possible in itself. Although it will never happen, it is not its impossibility but its imperfection which causes him to reject it. Now nothing is necessitated whose opposite is possible. One will then be in a position to satisfy these kinds of difficulties, however great they may appear (and in fact they have not been less vexing to all other thinkers who have ever treated this matter), provided that he considers well that all contingent propositions have reasons why they are thus, rather than otherwise, or indeed (what is the same thing) that they have proof *a priori* of their truth, which render them certain and show that the connection of the subject and predicate in these propositions has its basis in the nature of the one and of the other, but he must further remember that such contingent propositions have not the demonstrations of necessity, since their reasons are founded only on the principle of contingency or of the existence of things, that is to say, upon that which is, or which appears to be the best among several things equally possible. Necessary truths, on the other hand, are founded upon the principle of contradiction, and upon the possibility or impossibility of the essences themselves, without regard here to the free will of God or of creatures.

XIV. God produces different substances according to the different views which he has of the world, and by the intervention of God, the appropriate nature of each substance brings it about that what happens to one corresponds to what happens to all the others, without, however, their acting upon one another directly.

After having seen, to a certain extent, in what the nature of substances consists, we must try to explain the dependence they have upon one another and their actions and passions. Now it is first of all very evident that created substances depend upon God who preserves them and can produce them continually by a kind of emanation just as we produce our thoughts, for when God turns, so to say, on all sides and in all fashions, the general system of phenomena which he finds it good to produce for the sake of manifesting his glory, and when he regards all the aspects of the world in all possible manners, since there is no relation which escapes his omniscience, the result of each view of the universe as seen from a different position is a substance which expresses the universe conformably to this view, provided God sees fit to render his thought effective and to produce the substance, and since God's vision is always true, our perceptions are always true and that which deceives us are our judgments, which are of us. Now we have said before, and it follows from what we have just said that each substance is a world by itself, independent of everything else excepting God; therefore, all our phenomena that is all things which are ever able to happen to us, are only consequences of our being. Now as the phenomena maintain a certain order conformably to our nature, or so to speak to the world which is in us (from whence it follows that we can, for the regulation of our conduct, make useful observations which are justified by the outcome of the future phenomena) and as we are thus able often to judge the future by the past without deceiving ourselves, we have sufficient grounds for saying that these phenomena are true and we will not be put to the task of inquiring whether they are outside of us, and whether others perceive them also.

Nevertheless it is most true that the perceptions and expressions of all substances intercorrespond, so that each one following independently certain reasons or laws which he has noticed meets others which are doing the same, as when several have agreed to meet together in a certain place on a set day, they are able to carry out the plan if they wish. Now although all express the same phenomena, this does not bring it about that their expressions are exactly alike. It is sufficient if they are proportional. As when several spectators think they see the same thing and are agreed about it, although each one sees or speaks according to the measure of his vision. It is God alone (from whom all individuals emanate continually, and who sees the universe not only as they see it, but besides in a very different way from them) who is the cause of this correspondence in their phenomena and who brings it about that that which is particular to one, is also common to all, otherwise there would be no relation. In a way, then, we might properly say, although it seems strange, that a particular substance never acts upon another particular substance nor is it acted upon by it. That which happens to each one is only the consequence of its complete idea or concept, since this idea includes all the predicates or events and expresses the whole universe. In fact nothing can happen to us except thoughts and perceptions, and all future thoughts and perceptions are but the consequence, contingent it is true, of our precedent thoughts and perceptions, in such a way that were I able to consider distinctly all that happens or appears to me at the present time, I should be able to see all that will happen to me or that will ever appear to me. This future will not fail me, and will surely appear to me even if all that which is outside of me were destroyed, save only that God and myself were left.

Since, however, we ordinarily attribute to other things an action upon us which brings us to perceive things in a certain manner, it is necessary to consider the basis of this judgment and to inquire what there is of truth in it.

XV. The action of one finite substance upon another consists only in the increase in the degrees of the expression of the first combined with a decrease in that of the second, in so far as God has in advance fashioned them so that they shall act in accord.

Without entering into a long discussion it is sufficient for reconciling the language of metaphysics with that of practical life to remark that we preferably attribute to ourselves, and with reason, the phenomena which we express the most perfectly, and that we attribute to other substances those phenomena which each one expresses the best. Thus a substance, which is of an infinite extension in so far as it expresses all, becomes limited in proportion to its more or less perfect manner of expression. It is thus then that we may conceive of substances as interfering with and limiting one another, and hence we are able to say that in this sense they act upon one another, and that they, so to speak, accommodate themselves to one another. For it can happen that a single change which augments the expression of the one may diminish that of the other. Now the virtue of a particular substance is to express well the glory of God, and the better it expresses it, the less is it limited. Everything when it expresses its virtue or power, that is to say, when it acts, changes to better, and expands just in so far as it acts. When therefore a change occurs by which several substances are affected (in fact every change affects them all) I think we may say that those substances, which by this change pass immediately to a greater degree of perfection, or to a more perfect expression, exert power and act, while those which pass to a lesser degree disclose their weakness and suffer. I also hold that every activity of a substance which has perception implies some pleasure, and every passion some pain, except that it may very well happen that a present advantage will be eventually destroyed by a greater evil, whence it comes that one may sin in acting or exerting his power and in finding pleasure.

XVI. The extraordinary intervention of God is not excluded in that which our particular essences express, because their expression includes everything. Such intervention, however, goes beyond the power of our natural being or of our distinct expression, because these are finite, and follow certain subordinate regulations.

There remains for us at present only to explain how it is possible that God has influence at times upon men or upon other substances by an extraordinary or miraculous intervention, since it seems that nothing is able to happen which is extraordinary or supernatural in as much as all the events which occur to the other substances are only the consequences of their natures. We must recall what was said above in regard to the miracles in the universe. These always conform to the universal law of the general order, although they may contravene the subordinate regulations, and since every person or substance is like a little world which expresses the great world, we can say that this extraordinary action of God upon this substance is nevertheless miraculous, although it is comprised in the general order of the universe in so far as it is expressed by the individual essence or concept of this substance. This is why, if we understand in our natures all that they express, nothing is supernatural in them, because they reach out to everything, an effect always expressing its cause, and God being the veritable cause of the substances. But as that which our natures express the most perfectly pertains to them in a particular manner, that being their special power, and since they are limited, as I have just explained, many things there are which surpass the powers of our natures and even of all limited natures. As a consequence, to speak more clearly, I say that the miracles and the extraordinary interventions of God have this peculiarity that they cannot be foreseen by any created mind however enlightened. This is because the distinct comprehension of the fundamental order surpasses them all, while on the other hand, that which is called natural depends upon less fundamental regulations which the creatures are able to understand. In order then that my words may be as irreprehensible as the meaning I am trying to convey, it will be well to associate certain words with certain significations. We may call that which includes everything that we express and which expresses our union with God himself, nothing going beyond it, our essence. But that which is limited in us may be designated as our nature or our power, and in accordance with this terminology that which goes beyond the natures of all created substances is supernatural.

XVII. An example of a subordinate regulation in the law of nature which demonstrates that God always preserves the same amount of force but not the same quantity of motion: — against the Cartesians and many others.

I have frequently spoken of subordinate regulations, or of the laws of nature, and it seems that it will be well to give an example. Our new philosophers are unanimous in employing that famous law that God always preserves the same amount of motion in the universe. In fact it is a very plausible law, and in times past I held it as indubitable. But since then I have learned in what its fault consists. Monsieur Descartes and many other clever mathematicians have thought that the quantity of motion, that is to say the velocity multiplied by the bulk of the moving body, is exactly equivalent to the moving force, or to speak in mathematical terms that the force varies as the velocity multiplied by the bulk. Now it is reasonable that the same force is always preserved in the universe. So also, looking to phenomena, it will be readily seen that a mechanical perpetual motion is impossible, because the force in such a machine, being always diminished a little by friction and so ultimately destined to be entirely spent, would necessarily have to recoup its losses, and consequently would keep on increasing of itself without any new impulsion from without; and we see furthermore that the force of a body is diminished only in proportion as it gives up force, either to a contiguous body or to its own parts, in so far as they have a separate movement. The mathematicians to whom I have referred think that what can be said of force can be said of the quantity of motion. In order, however, to show the difference I make two suppositions: in the first place, that a body falling from a certain height acquires a force enabling it to remount to the same height, provided that its direction is turned that way, or provided that there are no hindrances. For instance, a pendulum will rise exactly to the height from which it has fallen, provided the resistance of the air and of certain other small particles do not diminish a little its acquired force.

I suppose in the second place that it will take as much force to lift a body A weighing one pound to the height CD, four feet, as to raise a body B weighing four pounds to the height EF, one foot. These two suppositions are granted by our new philosophers. It is therefore manifest that the body A falling from the height CD acquires exactly as much force as the body B falling from the height EF, for the body B at F, having by the first supposition sufficient force to return to E, has therefore the force to carry a body of four pounds to the distance of one foot, EF. And likewise the body A at D, having the force to return to C, has also the force required to carry a body weighing one pound, its own weight, back to C, a distance of four feet. Now by the second supposition the force of these two bodies is equal. Let us now see if the quantity of motion is the same in each case. It is here that we will be surprised to find a very great difference, for it has been proved by Galileo that the velocity acquired by the fall CD is double the velocity acquired by the fall EF, although the height is four times as great. Multiplying, therefore, the body A, whose bulk is 1, by its velocity, which is 2, the product or the quantity of movement will be 2, and on the other hand, if we multiply the body B, whose bulk is 4, by its velocity, which is 1, the product or quantity of motion will be 4. Hence the quantity of the motion of the body A at the point D is half the quantity of motion of the body B at the point F, yet their forces are equal, and there is therefore a great difference between the quantity of motion and the force. This is what we set out to show. We can see therefore how the force ought to be estimated by the quantity of the effect which it is able to produce, for example by the height to which a body of certain weight can be raised. This is a very different thing from the velocity which can be imparted to it, and in order to impart to it double the velocity we must have double the force. Nothing is simpler than this proof and Monsier Descartes has fallen into error here, only because he trusted too much to his thoughts even when they had not been ripened by reflection. But it astonishes me that his disciples have not noticed this error, and I am afraid that they are beginning to imitate little by little certain Peripatetics[8] whom they ridicule, and that they are accustoming themselves to consult rather the books of their master, than reason or nature.

XVIII. The distinction between force and the quantity of motion is, among other reasons, important as showing that we must have recourse to metaphysical considerations in addition to discussions of extension if we wish to explain the phenomena of matter.

This consideration of the force, distinguished from the quantity of motion, is of importance, not only in physics and mechanics for finding the real laws of nature and the principles of motion, and even for correcting many practical errors which have crept into the writings of certain able mathematicians, but also in metaphysics it is of importance for the better understanding of principles. Because motion, if we regard only its exact and formal meaning, that is, change of place, is not something really absolute, and when several bodies change their places reciprocally, it is not possible to determine by considering the bodies alone to which among them movement or repose is to be attributed, as I could demonstrate geometrically, if I wished to stop for it now. But the force, or the proximate cause of these changes is something more real, and there are sufficient grounds for attributing it to one body rather than to another, and it is only through this latter investigation that we can determine to which one the movement must appertain. Now this force is something different from size, from form or from motion, and it can be seen from this consideration that the whole meaning of a body is not exhausted in its extension together with its modifications as our moderns persuade themselves. We are therefore obliged to restore certain beings or forms which they have banished. It appears more and more clear that although all the particular phenomena of nature can be explained mathematically or mechanically by those who understand them, yet nevertheless, the general principles of corporeal nature and even of mechanics are metaphysical rather than geometric, and belong rather to certain indivisible forms or natures as the causes of the appearances, than to the corporeal mass or to exten-

8. [The term 'Peripatetics,' derived from a Greek word meaning 'walking about,' is applied to the followers of Aristotle, since he is said to have taught in this manner.]

sion. In this way we are able to reconcile the mechanical philosophy of the moderns with the circumspection of those intelligent and well-meaning persons who, with a certain justice, fear that we are becoming too far removed from immaterial beings and that we are thus prejudicing piety.

XIX. The utility of final causes in Physics.

As I do not wish to judge people in ill part I bring no accusation against our new philosophers who pretend to banish final causes from physics, but I am nevertheless obliged to avow that the consequences of such a banishment appear to me dangerous, especially when joined to that position which I refuted at the beginning of this treatise. That position seemed to go the length of discarding final causes entirely as though God proposed no end and no good in his activity, or as if good were not to be the object of his will. I hold on the contrary that it is just in this that the principle of all existences and of the laws of nature must be sought, hence God always proposes the best and most perfect. I am quite willing to grant that we are liable to err when we wish to determine the purposes or councils of God, but this is the case only when we try to limit them to some particular design, thinking that he has had in view only a single thing, while in fact he regards everything at once. As for instance, if we think that God has made the world only for us, it is a great blunder, although it may be quite true that he has made it entirely for us, and that there is nothing in the universe which does not touch us and which does not accommodate itself to the regard which he has for us according to the principle laid down above. Therefore when we see some good effect or some perfection which happens or which follows from the works of God we are able to say assuredly that God has purposed it, for he does nothing by chance, and is not like us who sometimes fail to do well. Therefore, far from being able to fall into error in this respect as do the extreme statesmen who postulate too much foresight in the designs of Princes, or as do commentators who seek for too much erudition in their authors, it will be impossible to attribute too much reflection to God's infinite wisdom, and there is no matter in which error is less to be feared provided we confine ourselves to affirmations and provided we avoid negative statements which limit the designs of God. All those who see the admirable structure of animals find themselves led to recognize the wisdom of the author of things and I advise those who have any sentiment of piety and indeed of true philosophy to hold aloof from the expressions of certain pretentious minds who instead of saying that eyes were made for seeing, say that we see because we find ourselves having eyes. When one seriously holds such opinions which hand everything over to material necessity or to a kind of chance (although either alternative ought to appear ridiculous to those who understand what we have explained above) it is difficult to recognize an intelligent author of nature. The effect should correspond to its cause and indeed it is best known through the recognition of its cause, so that it is unreasonable to introduce a sovereign intelligence ordering things, then in place of making use of the wisdom of this sovereign being, to employ only the properties of matter to explain phenomena. As if in order to account for the capture of an important place by a prince, the historian should say it was because the particles of powder in the cannon having been touched by a spark of fire expanded with a rapidity capable of pushing a hard solid body against the walls of the place, while the little particles which composed the brass of the cannon were so well interlaced that they did not separate under this impact,—as if he should account for it in this way instead of making us see how the foresight of the conqueror brought him to choose the time and the proper means and how his ability surmounted all obstacles.

XX. A noteworthy disquisition in Plato's Phaedo against the philosophers who were too materialistic.

This reminds me of a fine disquisition by Socrates in Plato's Phaedo,[9] which agrees perfectly with my opinion on this subject and seems to have been uttered expressly for our too materialistic philosophers. This agreement has led me to a desire to translate it although it is a little long. Perhaps this example will give some of us an incentive to share in many of the other beautiful and well balanced thoughts which are found in the writings of this famous author.

XXI. If the mechanical laws depended upon Geometry alone without metaphysical influences, the phenomena would be very different from what they are.

Now since the wisdom of God has always been recognized in the details of the mechanical structures of certain particular bodies, it should also be shown in the general economy of the world and in the constitution of the laws of nature. This is so true that even in the laws of motion in general, the plans of this wisdom have been noticed. For if bodies were only extended masses, and motion were only a change of place, and if everything ought to be and could be deduced by geometric necessity from these two definitions alone, it would follow, as I have shown elsewhere, that the smallest body on contact with a very large one at rest would impart to it its own velocity, yet without losing any of the velocity that it had. A quantity of other rules wholly contrary to the formation of a system would also have to be admitted. But the decree of the divine wisdom in preserving always the same force and the same total direction has provided for a system. I find indeed that many of the effects of nature can be accounted for in a twofold way, that is to say by a consideration of efficient causes, and again independently by a consideration of final causes. An example of the latter is God's decree always to carry out his plan by the easiest and most determined way. I have shown this elsewhere in accounting for the catoptric and dioptric laws, and I will speak more at length about it in what follows.

XXII. Reconciliation of the two methods of explanation, the one using final causes, and the other efficient causes, thus satisfying both those who explain nature mechanically and those who have recourse to incorporeal natures.

It is worth while to make the preceding remark in order to reconcile those who hope to explain mechanically the formation of the first tissue of an animal and all the interrelation of the parts, with those who account for the same structure by refer-

9. [The section referred to is 97c−99d.]

ring to final causes. Both explanations are good; both are useful not only for the admiring of the work of a great artificer, but also for the discovery of useful facts in physics and medicine. And writers who take these diverse routes should not speak ill of each other. For I see that those who attempt to explain the beauty of divine anatomy ridicule those who imagine that the apparently fortuitous flow of certain liquids has been able to produce such a beautiful variety and that they regard them as overbold and irreverent. These others on the contrary treat the former as simple and superstitious, and compare them to those ancients who regarded the physicists as impious when they maintained that not Jupiter thundered but some material which is found in the clouds. The best plan would be to join the two ways of thinking. To use a practical comparison, we recognize and praise the ability of a workman not only when we show what designs he had in making the parts of his machine, but also when we explain the instruments which he employed in making each part, especially if these instruments are simple and ingeniously contrived. God is also a workman able enough to produce a machine still a thousand times more ingenious than is our body, by employing only certain quite simple liquids purposely composed in such a way that ordinary laws of nature alone are required to develop them so as to produce such a marvellous effect. But it is also true that this development would not take place if God were not the author of nature. Yet I find that the method of efficient causes, which goes much deeper and is in a measure more immediate and *a priori*, is also more difficult when we come to details, and I think that our philosophers are still very frequently far removed from making the most of this method. The method of final causes, however, is easier and can be frequently employed to find out important and useful truths which we should have to seek for a long time, if we were confined to that other more physical method of which anatomy is able to furnish many examples. It seems to me that Snellius, who was the first discoverer of the laws of refraction, would have waited a long time before finding them if he had wished to seek out first how light was formed. But he apparently followed that method which the ancients employed for Catoptrics, that is, the method of final causes. Because, while seeking for the easiest way in which to conduct a ray of light from one given point to another given point by reflection from a given plane (supposing that that was the design of nature) they discovered the equality of the angles of incidence and reflection, as can be seen from a little treatise by Heliodorus of Larissa[10] and also elsewhere. This principle Mons. Snellius,[11] I believe, and afterwards independently of him, M. Fermat,[12] applied most ingeniously to refraction. For since the rays while in the same media always maintain the same proportion of sines, which in turn corresponds to the resistance of the media, it appears that they follow the easiest way, or at least that way which is the most determinate for passing from a given point in one medium to a given point in another medium. That demonstration of this same theorem which M. Descartes has given, using efficient causes, is much less satisfactory. At least we have grounds to think that he would never have

10. [Heliodorus of Larissa was a Greek mathematician of uncertain date who composed a treatise on optics.]

11. [Willebrord Snellius (1591–1626) was a professor of mathematics at the University of Leiden in Holland.]

12. [Pierre de Fermat (1601–1665), a magistrate by profession, was the French mathematician who is credited with founding modern number theory.]

found the principle by that means if he had not learned in Holland of the discovery of Snellius.

XXIII. Returning to immaterial substances we explain how God acts upon the understanding of spirits and asks whether one always keeps the idea of what he thinks about.

I have thought it well to insist a little upon final causes, upon incorporeal natures and upon an intelligent cause with respect to bodies so as to show the use of these conceptions in physics and in mathematics. This for two reasons, first to purge from mechanical philosophy the impiety that is imputed to it, second, to elevate to nobler lines of thought the thinking of our philosophers who incline to materialistic considerations alone. Now, however, it will be well to return from corporeal substances to the consideration of immaterial natures and particularly of spirits, and to speak of the methods which God uses to enlighten them and to act upon them. Although we must not forget that there are here at the same time certain laws of nature in regard to which I can speak more amply elsewhere. It will be enough for now to touch upon ideas and to inquire if we see everything in God and how God is our light. First of all it will be in place to remark that the wrong use of ideas occasions many errors. For when one reasons in regard to anything, he imagines that he has an idea of it and this is the foundation upon which certain philosophers, ancient and modern, have constructed a demonstration of God that is extremely imperfect. It must be, they say, that I have an idea of God, or of a perfect being, since I think of him and we cannot think without having ideas; now the idea of this being includes all perfections and since existence is one of these perfections, it follows that he exists. But I reply, inasmuch as we often think of impossible chimeras, for example of the highest degree of swiftness, of the greatest number, of the meeting of the conchoid with its base or determinant, such reasoning is not sufficient. It is therefore in this sense that we can say that there are true and false ideas according as the thing which is in question is possible or not. And it is when he is assured of the possibility of a thing, that one can boast of having an idea of it. Therefore, the aforesaid argument proves that God exists, if he is possible. This is in fact an excellent privilege of the divine nature, to have need only of a possibility or an essence in order to actually exist, and it is just this which is called self-sufficient being, *ens a se.*

XXIV. What clear and obscure, distinct and confused, adequate and inadequate, intuitive and assumed knowledge is, and the definition of nominal, real, casual and essential.

In order to understand better the nature of ideas it is necessary to touch somewhat upon the various kinds of knowledge. When I am able to recognize a thing among others, without being able to say in what its differences or characteristics consist, the knowledge is confused. Sometimes indeed we may know clearly, that is without being in the slightest doubt, that a poem or a picture is well or badly done because there is in it an "I know not what" which satisfies or shocks us. Such knowledge is not yet distinct. It is when I am able to explain the peculiarities which a thing has, that the knowledge is called distinct. Such is the knowledge of an assayer who discerns the true gold from the false by means of certain tests or marks which make up the definition of gold. But distinct knowledge has degrees, because ordinarily the conceptions which enter into the definitions will themselves be in need of definition, and are only known confusedly. When at length everything which enters into a definition or into distinct knowledge is known distinctly, even back to the primitive conception, I call that knowledge adequate. When my mind understands at once and distinctly all the primitive ingredients of a conception, then we have intuitive knowledge. This is extremely rare as most human knowledge is only confused or indeed assumed. It is well also to distinguish nominal from real definition. I call a definition nominal when there is doubt whether an exact conception of it is possible; as for instance, when I say that an endless screw is a line in three dimensional space whose parts are congruent or fall one upon another. Now although this is one of the reciprocal properties of an endless screw, he who did not know by other means what an endless screw was could doubt if such a line were possible, because the other lines whose ends are congruent (there are only two: the circumference of a circle and the straight line) are plane figures, that is to say they can be described *in plano.* This instance enables us to see that any reciprocal property can serve as a nominal definition, but when the property brings us to see the possibility of a thing it makes the definition real, and as long as one has only a nominal definition he cannot be sure of the consequences which he draws, because if it conceals a contradiction or an impossibility he would be able to draw the opposite conclusions. That is why truths do not depend upon names and are not arbitrary, as some of our new philosophers think. There is also a considerable difference among real definitions, for when the possibility proves itself only by experience, as in the definition of quicksilver, whose possibility we know because such a body, which is both an extremely heavy fluid and quite volatile, actually exists, the definition is merely real and nothing more. If, however, the proof of the possibility is *a priori,* the definition is not only real but also causal as for instance when it contains the possible generation of a thing. Finally, when the definition, without assuming anything which requires a proof *a priori* of its possibility, carries the analysis clear to the primitive conception, the definition is perfect or essential.

XXV. In what cases knowledge is added to mere contemplation of the idea.

Now it is manifest that we have no idea of a conception when it is impossible. And in case the knowledge, where we have the idea of it, is only assumed, we do not visualize it because such a conception is known only in like manner as conceptions internally impossible. And if it be in fact possible, it is not by this kind of knowledge that we learn its possibility. For instance, when I am thinking of a thousand or of a chiliagon, I frequently do it without contemplating the idea. Even if I say a thousand is ten times a hundred, I frequently do not trouble to think what ten and a hundred are, because I assume that I know, and I do not consider it necessary to stop just at present to conceive of them. Therefore it may well happen, as it in fact does happen often enough, that I am mistaken in regard to a conception which I assume that I understand, although it is an impossible truth or at least is incompatible with others with which I join it, and whether I am mistaken or not, this way of assuming our knowledge remains the same. It is, then, only when our knowledge is clear in regard to confused conceptions, and when it is intuitive in regard to those which are distinct, that we see its entire idea.

XXVI. Ideas are all stored up within us. Plato's doctrine of reminiscence.

In order to see clearly what an idea is, we must guard ourselves against a misunderstanding. Many regard the idea as the form or the differentiation of our thinking, and according to this opinion we have the idea in our mind, in so far as we are thinking of it, and each separate time that we think of it anew we have another idea although similar to the preceding one. Some, however, take the idea as the immediate object of thought, or as a permanent form which remains even when we are no longer contemplating it. As a matter of fact our soul has the power of representing to itself any form or nature whenever the occasion comes for thinking about it, and I think that this activity of our soul is, so far as it expresses some nature, form or essence, properly the idea of the thing. This is in us, and is always in us, whether we are thinking of it or no. (Our soul expresses God and the universe and all essences as well as all existences.) This position is in accord with my principles that naturally nothing enters into our minds from outside.

It is a bad habit we have of thinking as though our minds receive certain messengers, as it were, or as if they had doors or windows. We have in our minds all those forms for all periods of time because the mind at every moment expresses all its future thoughts and already thinks confusedly of all that of which it will ever think distinctly. Nothing can be taught us of which we have not already in our minds the idea. This idea is as it were the material out of which the thought will form itself. This is what Plato has excellently brought out in his doctrine of reminiscence, a doctrine which contains a great deal of truth, provided that it is properly understood and purged of the error of pre-existence, and provided that one does not conceive of the soul as having distinctly known and thought at some other time what it learns and thinks now. Plato has confirmed his position by a beautiful experiment.[13] He introduces a boy, whom he leads by short steps, to extremely difficult truths of geometry bearing on incommensurables, all this without teaching the boy anything, merely drawing out replies by a well arranged series of questions. This shows that the soul virtually knows those things, and needs only to be reminded (animadverted) to recognize the truths. Consequently it possesses at least the idea upon which those truths depend. We may say even that it already possesses those truths, if we consider them as the relations of the ideas.

XXVII. In what respect our souls can be compared to blank tablets and how conceptions are derived from the senses.

Aristotle preferred to compare our souls to blank tablets prepared for writing, and he maintained that nothing is in the understanding which does not come through the senses. This position is in accord with the popular conceptions, as Aristotle's approach usually is. Plato thinks more profoundly. Such tenets or practicologies are nevertheless allowable in ordinary use somewhat in the same way as those who accept the Copernican theory still continue to speak of the rising and setting of the sun. I find indeed that these usages can be given a real meaning containing no error, quite in the same way as I have already pointed out that we may truly say particular

13. [The reference is to the *Meno*, 82b–85e.]

substances act upon one another. In this same sense we may say that knowledge is received from without through the medium of the senses because certain exterior things contain or express more particularly the causes which determine us to certain thoughts. Because in the ordinary uses of life we attribute to the soul only that which belongs to it most manifestly and particularly, and there is no advantage in going further. When, however, we are dealing with the exactness of metaphysical truths, it is important to recognize the powers and independence of the soul which extend infinitely further than is commonly supposed. In order, therefore, to avoid misunderstandings it would be well to choose separate terms for the two. These expressions which are in the soul whether one is conceiving of them or not may be called ideas, while those which one conceives of or constructs may be called conceptions, *conceptus.* But whatever terms are used, it is always false to say that all our conceptions come from the so-called external senses, because those conceptions which I have of myself and of my thoughts, and consequently of being, of substance, of action, of identity, and of many others come from an inner experience.

XXVIII. The only immediate object of our perceptions which exists outside of us is God, and in him alone is our light.

In the strictly metaphysical sense no external cause acts upon us excepting God alone, and he is in immediate relation with us only by virtue of our continual dependence upon him. Whence it follows that there is absolutely no other external object which comes into contact with our souls and directly excites perceptions in us. We have in our souls ideas of everything, only because of the continual action of God upon us, that is to say, because every effect expresses its cause and therefore the essences of our souls are certain expressions, imitations or images of the divine essence, divine thought and divine will, including all the ideas which are there contained. We may say, therefore, that God is for us the only immediate external object, and that we see things through him. For example, when we see the sun or the stars, it is God who gives to us and preserves in us the ideas and whenever our senses are affected according to his own laws in a certain manner, it is he, who by his continual concurrence, determines our thinking. God is the sun and the light of souls, *lumen illuminans omnem hominem venientem in hunc mundum,*[14] although this is not the current conception. I think I have already remarked that during the scholastic period many believed God to be the light of the soul, *intellectus agens animae rationalis,*[15] following in this the Holy Scriptures and the fathers who were always more Platonic than Aristotelian in their mode of thinking. The Averroists[16] misused this conception, but others, among whom were several mystic theologians, and William of Saint Amour[17] also, I think, understood this conception in a manner

14. [The light illuminating every man coming into this world.]

15. [The active intellect of the rational soul.]

16. [The Averroists were followers of the Arabic philosopher Averroës (1126–1198), whose commentaries on works of Aristotle were influential in the development of Jewish and Christian thought.]

17. [William of St. Amour was a thirteenth-century philosopher who taught at the University of Paris.]

which assured the dignity of God and was able to raise the soul to a knowledge of its welfare.

XXIX. Yet we think directly by means of our own ideas and not through God's.

Nevertheless I cannot approve of the position of certain able philosophers who seem to hold that our ideas themselves are in God and not at all in us. I think that in taking this position they have neither sufficiently considered the nature of substance, which we have just explained, nor the complete purview and independence of the soul which includes all that happens to it, and expresses God, and with him all possible and actual beings in the same way that an effect expresses its cause. It is indeed inconceivable that the soul should think using the ideas of something else. The soul when it thinks of anything must be affected dynamically in a certain manner, and it must needs have in itself in advance not only the passive capacity of being thus affected, a capacity already wholly determined, but it must have besides an active power by virtue of which it has always had in its nature the marks of the future production of this thought, and the disposition to produce it at its proper time. All of this shows that the soul already includes the idea which is comprised in any particular thought.

XXX. How God inclines our souls without necessitating them; that there are no grounds for complaint; that we must not ask why Judas sinned because this free act is contained in his concept, the only question being why Judas the sinner is admitted to existence, preferably to other possible persons; concerning the original imperfection or limitation before the fall and concerning the different degrees of grace.

Regarding the action of God upon the human will there are many quite different considerations which it would take too long to investigate here. Nevertheless the following is what can be said in general. God in cooperating with ordinary actions only follows the laws which he has established, that is to say, he continually preserves and produces our being so that the ideas come to us spontaneously or with freedom in that order which the concept of our individual substance carries with itself. In this concept they can be foreseen for all eternity. Furthermore, by virtue of the decree which God has made that the will shall always seek the apparent good in certain particular respects (in regard to which this apparent good always has in it something of reality expressing or imitating God's will), he, without at all necessitating our choice, determines it by that which appears most desirable. For absolutely speaking, our will as contrasted with necessity, is in a state of indifference, being able to act otherwise, or wholly to suspend its action, either alternative being and remaining possible. It therefore devolves upon the soul to be on guard against appearances, by means of a firm will, to reflect and to refuse to act or decide in certain circumstances, except after mature deliberation. It is, however, true and has been assured from all eternity that certain souls will not employ their power upon certain occasions.

But who could do more than God has done, and can such a soul complain of anything except itself? All these complaints after the deed are unjust, inasmuch as they would have been unjust before the deed. Would this soul shortly before committing the sin have had the right to complain of God as though he had determined the sin? Since the determinations of God in these matters cannot be foreseen, how would the soul know that it was preordained to sin unless it had already committed the sin? It is merely a question of wishing to or not wishing to, and God could not have set an easier or juster condition. Therefore all judges without asking the reasons which have disposed a man to have an evil will, consider only how far this will is wrong. But, you object, perhaps it is ordained from all eternity that I will sin. Find your own answer. Perhaps it has not been. Now then, without asking for what you are unable to know and in regard to which you can have no light, act according to your duty and your knowledge. But, some one will object; whence comes it then that this man will assuredly do this sin? The reply is easy. It is that otherwise he would not be this man. God foresees from all time that there will be a certain Judas, and in the concept or idea of him which God has, is contained this future free act. The only question, therefore, which remains is why this certain Judas, the betrayer who is possible only because of the idea of God, actually exists. To this question, however, we can expect no answer here on earth excepting to say in general that it is because God has found it good that he should exist notwithstanding that sin which he foresaw. This evil will be more than overbalanced. God will derive a greater good from it, and it will finally turn out that this series of events in which is included the existence of this sinner, is the most perfect among all possible series of events. An explanation in every case of the admirable economy of this choice cannot be given while we are sojourners on earth. It is enough to know the excellence without understanding it. It is here that we must recognize the unfathomable depth of the divine wisdom, without hesitating at a detail which involves an infinite number of considerations. It is clear, however, that God is not the cause of ill. For not only after the loss of innocence by men, has original sin possessed the soul, but even before that there was an original limitation or imperfection in the very nature of all creatures, which rendered them open to sin and able to fall. There is, therefore, no more difficulty in the supralapsarian view than there is in the other views of sin. To this also, it seems to me, can be reduced the opinion of Saint Augustine and of other authors: that the root of evil is in the privation, that is to say, in the lack or limitation of creatures which God graciously remedies by whatever degree of perfection it pleases him to give. This grace of God, whether ordinary or extraordinary, has its degrees and its measures. It is always efficacious in itself to produce a certain proportionate effect and furthermore it is always sufficient not only to keep one from sin but even to effect his salvation, provided that the man co-operates with that which is in him. It has not always, however, sufficient power to overcome the inclination, for, if it did, it would no longer be limited in any way, and this superiority to limitations is reserved to that unique grace which is absolutely efficacious. This grace is always victorious whether through its own self or through the congruity of circumstances.

XXXI. Concerning the motives of election; concerning faith foreseen and the absolute decree and that it all reduces to the question why God has chosen and resolved to admit to existence just such a possible person, whose concept includes just such a sequence of free acts and of free gifts of grace. This at once puts an end to all difficulties.

Finally, the grace of God is wholly unprejudiced and creatures have no claim upon it. Just as it is not sufficient in accounting for God's choice in his dispensations of grace to refer to his absolute or conditional prevision of men's future actions, so it is also wrong to imagine his decrees as absolute with no reasonable motive. As concerns foreseen faith and good works, it is very true that God has elected none but those whose faith and charity he foresees, *quos se fide donaturum praescivit.*[18] The same question, however, arises again as to why God gives to some rather than to others the grace of faith or of good works. As concerns God's ability to foresee not only the faith and good deeds, but also their content and predisposition, or that which a man on his part contributes to them (since there are as truly diversities on the part of men as on the part of grace, and a man although he needs to be aroused to good and needs to become converted, yet acts in accordance with his temperament)—as regards his ability to foresee there are many who say that God, knowing what a particular man will do without grace, that is without his extraordinary assistance, or knowing at least what will be the human contribution, resolves to give grace to those whose natural dispositions are the best, or at any rate are the least imperfect and evil. But if this were the case then the natural dispositions in so far as they were good would still be gifts of grace, since God would have given advantages to some over others; and therefore, since he would well know that the natural advantages which he had given would serve as motives for his grace or for his extraordinary assistance, would not everything be reduced to his mercy? I think, therefore, that since we do not know how much and in what way God regards natural dispositions in the dispensations of his grace, it would be safest and most exact to say, in accordance with our principles and as I have already remarked, that there must needs be among possible beings the person Peter or John whose concept or idea contains all that particular sequence of ordinary and extraordinary manifestations of grace together with the rest of the accompanying events and circumstances, and that it has pleased God to choose him among an infinite number of persons equally possible for actual existence. When we have said this there seems nothing left to ask, and all difficulties vanish. For in regard to that great and ultimate question why it has pleased God to choose him among so great a number of possible persons, it is surely unreasonable to demand more than the general reasons which we have given. The reasons in detail surpass our ken. Therefore, instead of postulating an absolute decree, which being without reason would be unreasonable, and instead of postulating reasons which do not succeed in solving the difficulties and in turn have need themselves of reasons, it will be best to say with St. Paul that there are for God's choice certain great reasons of wisdom and congruity which he follows, which reasons, however, are unknown to mortals and are founded upon the general order, whose goal is the greatest perfection of the world. This is what is meant when the motives of God's glory and of the manifestation of his justice are spoken of, as well as when men speak of his mercy, and his perfection in general; that immense vastness of wealth, in fine, with which the soul of the same St. Paul was to be thrilled.

XXXII. Usefulness of these principles in matters of piety and of religion.

In addition it seems that the thoughts which we have just explained and particu-

---

18. [To whom he has forseen that he would grant faith.]

larly the great principle of the perfection of God's operations and the concept of substance which includes all its changes with all its accompanying circumstances, far from injuring, serve rather to confirm religion, serve to dissipate great difficulties, to inflame souls with a divine love and to raise the mind to a knowledge of incorporeal substances much more than the previous hypotheses. For it appears clearly that all other substances depend upon God just as our thoughts emanate from our own substance; that God is all in all and that he is intimately united to all created things, in proportion however to their perfection; that it is he alone who determines them from without by his influence, and if to act is to determine directly, it may be said in metaphysical language that God alone acts upon me and he alone causes me to do good or ill, other substances contributing only because of his determinations; because God, who takes all things into consideration, distributes his bounties and compels created beings to accommodate themselves to one another. Thus God alone constitutes the relation or communication between substances. It is through him that the phenomena of the one meet and accord with the phenomena of the others, so that there may be a reality in our perceptions. In common parlance, however, an action is attributed to particular causes in the sense that I have explained above because it is not necessary to make continual mention of the universal cause when speaking of particular cases. It can be seen also that every substance has a perfect spontaneity (which becomes liberty with intelligent substances). Everything which happens to it is a consequence of its idea or its being and nothing determines it except God only. It is for this reason that a person of exalted mind and revered saintliness may say that the soul ought often to think as if there were only God and itself in the world. Nothing can make us hold to immortality more firmly than this independence and vastness of the soul which protects it completely against exterior things, since it alone constitutes our universe and together with God is sufficient for itself. It is as impossible for it to perish save through annihilation as it is impossible for the universe to destroy itself, the universe whose animate and perpetual expression it is. Furthermore, the changes in this extended mass which is called our body cannot possibly affect the soul nor can the dissipation of the body destroy that which is indivisible.

XXXIII. Explanation of the relation between the soul and the body, a matter which has been regarded as inexplicable or else as miraculous; concerning the origin of confused perceptions.

We can also see the explanation of that great mystery "the union of the soul and the body," that is to say how it comes about that the passions and actions of the one are accompanied by the actions and passions or else the appropriate phenomena of the other. For it is not possible to conceive how one can have an influence upon the other and it is unreasonable to have recourse at once to the extraordinary intervention of the universal cause in an ordinary and particular case. The following, however, is the true explanation. We have said that everything which happens to a soul or to any substance is a consequence of its concept; hence the idea itself or the essence of the soul brings it about that all of its appearances or perceptions should be born out of its nature and precisely in such a way that they correspond of themselves to that which happens in the universe at large, but more particularly and more perfectly to that which happens in the body associated with it, because it is in a particular way and only for a certain time according to the relation of other bodies to its own body that the soul expresses the state of the universe. This last fact enables us to see how our body belongs to us, without, however, being attached to our essence. I believe that those who are careful thinkers will decide favorably for our principles because of this single reason, viz., that they are able to see in what consists the relation between the soul and the body, a parallelism which appears inexplicable in any other way. We can also see that the perceptions of our senses even when they are clear must necessarily contain certain confused elements, for as all the bodies in the universe are in sympathy, ours receives the impressions of all the others, and while our senses respond to everything, our soul cannot pay attention to every particular. That is why our confused sensations are the result of a variety of perceptions. This variety is infinite. It is almost like the confused murmuring which is heard by those who approach the shore of a sea. It comes from the continual beatings of innumerable waves. If now, out of many perceptions which do not at all fit together to make one, no particular one perception surpasses the others, and if they make impressions about equally strong or equally capable of holding the attention of the soul, they can be perceived only confusedly.

XXXIV. Concerning the difference between spirits and other substances, souls or substantial forms; that the immortality which men desire includes memory.

Supposing that the bodies which constitute a *unum per se*, as human bodies, are substances, and have substantial forms, and supposing that animals have souls, we are obliged to grant that these souls and these substantial forms cannot entirely perish, any more than can the atoms or the ultimate elements of matter, according to the position of other philosophers; for no substance perishes, although it may become very different. Such substances also express the whole universe, although more imperfectly than do spirits. The principal difference, however, is that they do not know that they are, nor what they are. Consequently, not being able to reason, they are unable to discover necessary and universal truths. It is also because they do not reflect regarding themselves that they have no moral qualities, whence it follows that they undergo myriad transformations—as we see a caterpillar change into a butterfly; the result from a moral or practical standpoint is the same as if we said that they perished in each case, and we can indeed say it from the physical standpoint in the same way that we say bodies perish in their dissolution. But the intelligent soul, knowing what it is, having the ability to say that word "I" so full of meaning, not only continues and exists, metaphysically far more certainly than do the others, but it remains the same from the moral standpoint, and constitutes the same personality, for it is its memory or knowledge of this ego which renders it open to punishment and reward. Hence the immortality which is required in morals and in religion does not consist merely in this perpetual existence, which pertains to all substances, for if in addition there were no remembrance of what one had been, immortality would not be at all desirable. Suppose that some individual could suddenly become King of China on condition, however, of forgetting what he had been, as though being born again, would it not amount to the same practically, or as far as the effects could be perceived, as if the individual were annihilated, and a king of China were the same instant created in his place? The individual would have no reason to desire this.

XXXV. The excellence of spirits; that God considers them preferable to other creatures; that the spirits express God rather than the world, while other simple substances express the world rather than God.

In order, however, to prove by natural reasons that God will preserve forever not only our substance, but also our personality, that is to say the recollection and knowledge of what we are (although the distinct knowledge is sometimes suspended during sleep and in swoons) it is necessary to join to metaphysics moral considerations. God must be considered not only as the principle and the cause of all substances and of all existing things, but also as the chief of all persons or intelligent substances, as the absolute monarch of the most perfect city or republic, such as is constituted by all the spirits together in the universe, God being the most complete of all spirits at the same time that he is greatest of all beings. For assuredly the spirits are the most perfect of substances and best express the divinity. Since all the nature, purpose, virtue and function of substances is, as has been sufficiently explained, to express God and the universe, there is no room for doubting that those substances which give the expression, knowing what they are doing and which are able to understand the great truths about God and the universe, do express God and the universe incomparably better than do those natures which are either brutish and incapable of recognizing truths, or are wholly destitute of sensation and knowledge. The difference between intelligent substances and those which are not intelligent is quite as great as between a mirror and one who sees. As God is himself the greatest and wisest of spirits it is easy to understand that the spirits with which he can, so to speak, enter into conversation and even into social relations by communicating to them in particular ways his feelings and his will so that they are able to know and love their benefactor, must be much nearer to him than the rest of created things which may be regarded as mere instruments of spirits. In the same way we see that all wise persons consider far more the condition of a man than of anything else however precious it may be; and it seems that the greatest satisfaction which a soul, satisfied in other respects, can have is to see itself loved by others. However, with respect to God there is this difference that his glory and our worship can add nothing to his satisfaction, the recognition of creatures being nothing but a consequence of his sovereign and perfect felicity and being far from contributing to it or from causing it even in part. Nevertheless, that which is reasonable in finite spirits is found eminently in him and as we praise a king who prefers to preserve the life of a man before that of the most precious and rare of his animals, we should not doubt that the most enlightened and most just of all monarchs has the same preference.

XXXVI. God is the monarch of the most perfect republic composed of all the spirits, and the happiness of this city of God is his principal purpose.

Spirits are of all substances the most capable of perfection and their perfections are different in this that they interfere with one another the least, or rather they aid one another the most, for only the most virtuous can be the most perfect friends. Hence it follows that God who in all things has the greatest perfection will have the greatest care for spirits and will give not only to all of them in general, but even to each one in particular the highest perfection which the universal harmony will permit. We can even say that it is because he is a spirit that God is the originator of existences, for if he had lacked the power of will to choose what is best, there would have been no reason why one possible being should exist rather than any other. Therefore God's being a spirit himself dominates all the consideration which he may have toward created things. Spirits alone are made in his image, being as it were of his blood or as children in the family, since they alone are able to serve him of free will, and to act consciously imitating the divine nature. A single spirit is worth a whole world, because it not only expresses the whole world, but it also knows it and governs itself as does God. In this way we may say that though every substance expresses the whole universe, yet the other substances express the world rather than God, while spirits express God rather than the world. This nature of spirits, so noble that it enables them to approach divinity as much as is possible for created things, has as a result that God derives infinitely more glory from them than from the other beings, or rather the other beings furnish to spirits the material for glorifying him. This moral quality of God which constitutes him Lord and Monarch of spirits influences him so to speak personally and in a unique way. It is through this that he humanizes himself, that he is willing to suffer human woes, and that he enters into social relations with us; as a prince with his subjects so dear to him that the happy and prosperous condition of his empire which consists in the greatest possible felicity of its inhabitants, becomes supreme among his laws. Happiness is to persons what perfection is to beings. And if the dominant principle in the existence of the physical world is the decree to give it the greatest possible perfection, the primary purpose in the moral world or in the city of God which constitutes the noblest part of the universe ought to be to extend the greatest happiness possible. We must not therefore doubt that God has so ordained everything that spirits not only shall live forever, because this is unavoidable, but that they shall also preserve forever their moral quality, so that his city may never lose a person, quite in the same way that the world never loses a substance. Consequently they will always be conscious of their being, otherwise they would be open to neither reward nor punishment, a condition which is the essence of a republic, and above all of the most perfect republic where nothing can be neglected. In fine, God being at the same time the most just and the most debonnaire of monarchs, and requiring only a good will on the part of men, provided that it be sincere and intentional, his subjects cannot desire a better condition. To render them perfectly happy he desires only that they love him.

XXXVII. Jesus Christ has revealed to men the mystery and the admirable laws of the kingdom of heaven, and the greatness of the supreme happiness which God has prepared for those who love him.

The ancient philosophers knew very little of these important truths. Jesus Christ alone has expressed them divinely well, and in a way so clear and simple that the dullest minds have understood them. His gospel has entirely changed the face of human affairs. It has brought us to know the kingdom of heaven, or that perfect republic of spirits which deserves to be called the city of God. He it is who has discovered to us its wonderful laws. He alone has made us see how much God loves us and with what care everything that concerns us has been provided for; how God, inasmuch as he cares for the sparrows, will not neglect reasoning beings, who are infinitely more dear to him; how all the hairs of our heads are numbered; how heaven and earth may pass away but the word of God and that which belongs to the means of our salvation will not pass away; how God has more regard for the least one among intelligent souls than for the whole machinery of the world; how we ought not to fear those who are able to injure the body but are unable to injure the soul, since God alone can render the soul happy or unhappy; and how the souls of the righteous are protected by his hand against all the upheavals of the universe, since God alone is able to act upon them; how none of our acts are forgotten; how everything is to be accounted for, even careless words and even a spoonful of water which is well used; in fact how everything must result in the greatest welfare of the good, for then shall the righteous become like suns and neither our sense nor our minds have ever tasted of anything approaching the joys which God has laid up for those that love him.

MONADOLOGY

1. The *monad* of which we shall here speak is merely a simple substance, which enters into composites; *simple,* that is to say, without parts.

2. And there must be simple substances, since there are composites; for the composite is only a collection or *aggregatum* of simple substances.

3. Now where there are no parts, neither extension, nor figure, nor divisibility is possible. And these monads are the true atoms of nature, and, in a word, the elements of all things.

4. Their dissolution also is not at all to be feared, and there is no conceivable way in which a simple substance can perish naturally.

5. For the same reason there is no conceivable way in which a simple substance can begin naturally, since it cannot be formed by composition.

6. Thus it may be said that the monads can only begin or end all at once, that is to say, they can only begin by creation and end by annihilation; whereas that which is composite begins or ends by parts.

7. There is also no way of explaining how a monad can be altered or changed in its inner being by any other creature, for nothing can be transposed within it, nor can there be conceived in it any internal movement which can be excited, directed, augmented or diminished within it, as can be done in composites, where there is change among the parts. The monads have no windows through which anything can enter or depart. The accidents cannot detach themselves nor go about outside of substances, as did formerly the sensible species of the Schoolmen. Thus neither substance nor accident can enter a monad from outside.

8. Nevertheless, the monads must have some qualities, otherwise they would not even be entities. And if simple substances did not differ at all in their qualities there would be no way of perceiving any change in things, since what is in the compound can only come from the simple ingredients, and the monads, if they had no qualities, would be indistinguishable from one another, seeing also they do not differ in quantity. Consequently, a plenum being supposed, each place would always receive, in any motion, only the equivalent of what it had had before, and one state of things would be indistinguishable from another.

9. It is necessary, indeed, that each monad be different from every other. For there are never in nature two beings which are exactly alike and in which it is not possible to find an internal difference, or one founded upon an intrinsic quality.

10. I take it also for granted that every created being, and consequently the created monad also, is subject to change, and even that this change is continuous in each.

11. It follows from what has just been said, that the natural changes of the monads proceed from an *internal principle,* since an external cause could not influence their inner being.

12. But, besides the principle of change, there must be an individuating *detail of changes,* which forms, so to speak, the specification and variety of the simple substances.

13. This detail must involve a multitude in the unity or in that which is simple. For since every natural change takes place by degrees, something changes and something remains; and consequently, there must be in the simple substance a plurality of affections and of relations, although it has no parts.

14. The passing state, which involves and represents a multitude in unity or in the simple substance, is nothing else than what is called *perception,* which must be distinguished from apperception or consciousness, as will appear in what follows. Here it is that the Cartesians especially failed, having taken no account of the perceptions of which we are not conscious. It is this also which made them believe that spirits only are monads and that there are no souls of brutes or of other entelechies. They, with most people, have failed to distinguish between a prolonged state of unconsciousness and death strictly speaking, and have therefore agreed with the old scholastic prejudice of entirely separate souls, and have even confirmed ill-balanced minds in the belief in the mortality of the soul.

15. The action of the internal principle which causes the change or the passage from one perception to another, may be called *appetition;* it is true that desire cannot always completely attain to the whole perception to which it tends, but it always attains something of it and reaches new perceptions.

16. We experience in ourselves a multiplicity in a simple substance, when we find that the most trifling thought of which we are conscious involves a variety in the object. Thus all those who admit that the soul is a simple substance ought to admit this multiplicity in the monad, and M. Bayle[1] ought not to have found any difficulty in it, as he has done in his Dictionary, article *Rorarius.*

17. It must be confessed, moreover, that *perception* and that which depends on it *are inexplicable by mechanical causes,* that is, by figures and motions. And, supposing that there were a machine so constructed as to think, feel and have perception, we could conceive of it as enlarged and yet preserving the same proportions, so that we might enter it as into a mill. And this granted, we should only find on visiting it, pieces which push one against another, but never anything by which to explain a perception. This must be sought for, therefore, in the simple substance and not in the composite or in the machine. Furthermore, nothing but this (namely, perceptions and their changes) can be found in the simple substance. It is also in this alone that all the *internal activities* of simple substances can consist.

18. The name of *entelechies* might be given to all simple substances or created monads, for they have within themselves a certain perfection; there is a certain sufficiency which makes them the sources of their internal activities, and so to speak, incorporeal automata.

19. If we choose to give the name *soul* to everything that has *perceptions* and *desires* in the general sense which I have just explained, all simple substances or created monads may be called souls, but as feeling is something more than a simple perception, I am willing that the general name of monads or entelechies shall suffice for

1. [Pierre Bayle (1647–1706) was a French skeptical philosopher whose chief work, the *Dictionnaire historique et critique,* contained biographies and detailed critical studies. The article 'Rorarius' attacked Leibniz's theory of monads. —S.M.C.]

those simple substances which have only perception, and that those substances only shall be called *souls* whose perception is more distinct and is accompanied by memory.

20. For we experience in ourselves a state in which we remember nothing and have no distinguishable perception, as when we fall into a swoon or when we are overpowered by a profound and dreamless sleep. In this state the soul does not differ sensibly from a simple monad; but as this state is not continuous and as the soul comes out of it, the soul is something more than a mere monad.

21. And it does not at all follow that in such a state the simple substance is without any perception. This is indeed impossible, for the reasons mentioned above; for it cannot perish, nor can it subsist without some affection, which is nothing else than its perception; but when there is a great number of minute perceptions, in which nothing is distinct, we are stunned; as when we turn continually in the same direction many times in succession, whence arises a dizziness which may make us swoon, and which does not let us distinguish anything. And death may produce for a time this condition in animals.

22. And as every present state of a simple substance is naturally the consequence of its preceding state, so its present is big with its future.

23. Therefore, since on being awakened from a stupor, we are *aware* of our perceptions, we must have had them immediately before, although we were not conscious of them; for one perception can come in a natural way only from another perception, as a motion can come in a natural way only from a motion.

24. From this we see that if there were nothing distinct, nothing, so to speak, in relief and of a higher flavor in our perceptions, we should always be in a dazed state. This is the condition of simply bare monads.

25. We also see that nature has given to animals heightened perceptions, by the pains she has taken to furnish them with organs which collect many rays of light or many undulations of air, in order to render these more efficacious by uniting them. There is something of the same kind in odor, in taste, in touch and perhaps in a multitude of other senses which are unknown to us. And I shall presently explain how that which takes place in the soul represents that which occurs in the organs.

26. Memory furnishes souls with a sort of *consecutiveness* which imitates reason, but which ought to be distinguished from it. We observe that animals, having the perception of something which strikes them and of which they have had a similar perception before, expect, through the representation in their memory, that which was associated with it in the preceeding perception, and experience feelings similar to those which they had had at that time. For instance, if we show dogs a stick, they remember the pain it has caused them and whine and run.

27. And the strong imagination which impresses and moves them, arises either from the magnitude or the multitude of preceding perceptions. For often a strong impression produces all at once the effect of a long-continued *habit*, or of many oft-repeated moderate perceptions.

28. Men act like the brutes, in so far as the association of their perceptions results from the principle of memory alone, resembling the empirical physicians who practice without theory; and we are simple empirics in three-fourths of our actions. For example, when we expect that there will be daylight to-morrow, we are acting as empirics, because that has up to this time always taken place. It is only the astronomer who judges of this by reason.

29. But the knowledge of necessary and eternal truths is what distinguishes us from mere animals and furnishes us with *reason* and the sciences, raising us to a knowledge of ourselves and of God. This is what we call the rational soul or *spirit* in us.

30. It is also by the knowledge of necessary truths, and by their abstractions, that we rise to *acts of reflection*, which make us think of that which calls itself "I", and to observe that this or that is within *us;* and it is thus that, in thinking of ourselves, we think of being, of substance, simple or composite, of the immaterial and of God himself, conceiving that what is limited in us is in him without limits. And these reflective acts furnish the principal objects of our reasonings.

31. Our reasonings are founded on *two great principles, that of contradiction,* in virtue of which we judge that to be *false* which involves contradiction, and that *true,* which is opposed or contradictory to the false.

32. And *that of sufficient reason,* in virtue of which we hold that no fact can be real or existent, no statement true, unless there be a sufficient reason why it is so and not otherwise, although most often these reasons cannot be known to us.

33. There are also two kinds of *truths,* those of *reasoning* and those of *fact.* Truths of reasoning are necessary and their opposite is impossible, and those of *fact* are contingent and their opposite is possible. When a truth is necessary its reason can be found by analysis, resolving it into more simple ideas and truths until we reach those which are primitive.

34. It is thus that mathematicians by analysis reduce speculative *theorems* and practical *canons* to *definitions, axioms* and *postulates.*

35. And there are finally simple ideas, definitions of which cannot be given; there are also axioms and postulates, in a word, *primary principles,* which cannot be proved, and indeed need no proof; and these are *identical propositions,* whose opposite involves an express contradiction.

36. But there must also be a *sufficient reason* for *contingent truths,* or those *of fact,*— that is, for the sequence of things diffused through the universe of created objects— where the resolution into particular reasons might run into a detail without limits, on account of the immense variety of the things in nature and the division of bodies *ad infinitum.* There is an infinity of figures and of movements, present and past, which enter into the efficient cause of my present writing, and there is an infinity of slight inclinations and dispositions, past and present, of my soul, which enter into the final cause.

37. And as all this *detail* only involves other contingents, anterior or more detailed, each one of which needs a like analysis for its explanation, we make no advance: and the sufficient or final reason must be outside of the sequence or *series* of this detail of contingencies, however infinite it may be.

38. And thus it is that the final reason of things must be found in a necessary substance, in which the detail of changes exists only eminently, as in their source; and this is what we call God.

39. Now this substance, being a sufficient reason of all this detail, which also is linked together throughout, *there is but one God, and this God is sufficient.*

40. We may also conclude that his supreme substance, which is unique, universal and necessary, having nothing outside of itself which is independent of it, and being a pure consequence of possible being, must be incapable of limitations and must contain as much of reality as is possible.

41. Whence it follows that God is absolutely perfect, *perfection* being only the magnitude of positive reality taken in its strictest meaning, setting aside the limits or bounds in things which have them. And where there are no limits, that is, in God, perfection is absolutely infinite.

42. It follows also that the creatures have their perfections from the influence of God, but that their imperfections arise from their own nature, incapable of existing without limits. For it is by this that they are distinguished from God.

43. It is also true that in God is the source not only of existences but also of essences, so far as they are real, or of that which is real in the possible. This is because the understanding of God is the region of eternal truths, or of the ideas on which they depend, and because, without him, there would be nothing real in the possibilities, and not only nothing existing but also nothing possible.

44. For, if there is a reality in essences or possibilities or indeed in the eternal truths, this reality must be founded in something existing and actual, and consequently in the existence of the necessary being, in whom essence involves existence, or with whom it is sufficient to be possible in order to be actual.

45. Hence God alone (or the necessary being) has this prerogative, that he must exist if he is possible. And since nothing can hinder the possibility of that which possesses no limitations, no negation, and consequently, no contradiction, this alone is sufficient to establish the existence of God *a priori*. We have also proved it by the reality of the eternal truths. But we have a little while ago[2] proved it also *a posteriori*, since contingent beings exist, which can only have their final or sufficient reason in a necessary being who has the reason of his existence in himself.

46. Yet we must not imagine, as some do, that the eternal truths, being dependent upon God, are arbitrary and depend upon his will, as Descartes seems to have held, and afterwards M. Poiret.[3] This is true only of contingent truths, the principle of which is *fitness* or the choice of the *best*, whereas necessary truths depend solely on his understanding and are its internal object.

47. Thus God alone is the primitive unity or the original simple substance; of which all created or derived monads are the products, and are generated, so to speak, by continual fulgurations of the Divinity, from moment to moment, limited by the receptivity of the creature, to whom limitation is essential.

48. In God is *Power,* which is the source of all; then *Knowledge,* which contains the detail of ideas; and finally *Will,* which effects changes or products according to the principle of the best. These correspond to what in created monads form the subject or basis, the perceptive faculty, and the appetitive faculty. But in God these attributes are absolutely infinite or perfect; and in the created monads or in the *entelechies* (or *perfectihabies* as Hermolaus Barbarus[4] translated the word), they are only imitations proportioned to the perfection of the monads.

49. The creature is said to *act* externally in so far as it has perfection, and to be *acted on* by another in so far as it is imperfect. Thus *action* is attributed to the monad

---

2. [The reference is to secs. 36–39.]

3. [Pierre Poiret (1646–1719) was a French minister and philosopher who defended Calvinism.]

4. [Hermolaus Barbarus (1454–1493) was an Italian diplomat and scholar who translated works of Aristotle into Latin.]

in so far as it has distinct perceptions, and *passivity* in so far as it has confused perceptions.

50. And one creature is more perfect than another, in this that there is found in it that which serves to account *a priori* for what takes place in the other, and it is in this way that it is said to act upon the other.

51. But in simple substances the influence of one monad upon another is purely *ideal* and can have its effect only through the intervention of God, inasmuch as in the ideas of God a monad may demand with reason that God in regulating the others from the commencement of things, have regard to it. For since a created monad can have no physical influence upon the inner being of another, it is only in this way that one can be dependent upon another.

52. And hence it is that the actions and passive reactions of creatures are mutual. For God, in comparing two simple substances, finds in each one reasons which compel him to adjust the other to it, and consequently that which in certain respects is active, is according to another point of view, passive; *active* in so far as that what is known distinctly in it, serves to account for that which takes place in another; and *passive* in so far as the reason for what takes place in it, is found in that which is distinctly known in another.

53. Now, as there is an infinity of possible universes in the ideas of God, and as only one of them can exist, there must be a sufficient reason for the choice of God, which determines him to select one rather than another.

54. And this reason can only be found in the *fitness*, or in the degrees of perfection, which these worlds contain, each possible world having a right to claim existence according to the measure of perfection which it possesses.

55. And this is the cause of the existence of the Best; namely, that his wisdom makes it known to God, his goodness makes him choose it, and his power makes him produce it.

56. Now this *connection*, or this adaptation, of all created things to each and of each to all, brings it about that each simple substance has relations which express all the others, and that, consequently, it is a perpetual living mirror of the universe.

57. And as the same city looked at from different sides appears entirely different, and is as if multiplied *perspectively;* so also it happens that, as a result of the infinite multitude of simple substances, there are as it were so many different universes, which are nevertheless only the perspectives of a single one, according to the different *points of view* of each monad.

58. And this is the way to obtain as great a variety as possible, but with the greatest possible order; that is, it is the way to obtain as much perfection as possible.

59. Moreover, this hypothesis (which I dare to call demonstrated) is the only one which brings into relief the grandeur of God. M. Bayle recognized this, when in his Dictionary (Art. *Rorarius*) he raised objections to it; in which indeed he was disposed to think that I attributed too much to God and more than is possible. But he can state no reason why this universal harmony, which brings it about that each substance expresses exactly all the others, through the relations which it has to them, is impossible.

60. Besides, we can see, in what I have just said, the *a priori* reasons why things could not be otherwise than they are. Because God, in regulating all, has had regard to each part, and particularly to each monad, whose nature being representative,

nothing can limit it to representing only a part of things; although it may be true that this representation is but confused as regards the detail of the whole universe, and can be distinct only in the case of a small part of things, that is to say, in the case of those which are nearest or greatest in relation to each of the monads; otherwise each monad would be a divinity. It is not as regards the object but only as regards the modification of the knowledge of the object, that monads are limited. They all tend confusedly toward the infinite, toward the whole; but they are limited and differentiated by the degrees of their distinct perceptions.

61. And composite substances are analogous in this respect with simple substances. For since the world is a *plenum*, rendering all matter connected, and since in a plenum every motion has some effect on distant bodies in proportion to their distance, so that each body is affected not only by those in contact with it, and feels in some way all that happens to them, but also by their means is affected by those which are in contact with the former, with which it itself is in immediate contact, it follows that this intercommunication extends to any distance whatever. And consequently, each body feels all that happens in the universe, so that he who sees all, might read in each that which happens everywhere, and even that which has been or shall be, discovering in the present that which is removed in time as well as in space; σύμπνοια πάντα, said Hippocrates.[5] But a soul can read in itself only that which is distinctly represented in it. It cannot develop its laws all at once, for they reach into the infinite.

62. Thus, although each created monad represents the entire universe, it represents more distinctly the body which is particularly attached to it, and of which it forms the entelechy; and as this body expresses the whole universe through the connection of all matter in a plenum, the soul also represents the whole universe in representing this body, which belongs to it in a particular way.

63. The body belonging to a monad, which is its entelechy or soul, constitutes together with the entelechy what may be called a *living being*, and together with the soul what may be called an *animal*. Now this body of a living being or of an animal is always organic, for since every monad is in its way a mirror of the universe, and since the universe is regulated in a perfect order, there must also be an order in the representative, that is, in the perceptions of the soul, and hence in the body, through which the universe is represented in the soul.

64. Thus each organic body of a living being is a kind of divine machine or natural automaton, which infinitely surpasses all artificial automata. Because a machine which is made by man's art is not a machine in each one of its parts; for example, the teeth of a brass wheel have parts or fragments which to us are no longer artificial and have nothing in themselves to show the special use to which the wheel was intended in the machine. But nature's machines, that is, living bodies, are machines even in their smallest parts *ad infinitum*. Herein lies the difference between nature and art, that is, between the divine art and ours.

65. And the author of nature has been able to employ this divine and infinitely marvellous artifice, because each portion of matter is not only divisible *ad infinitum*, as the ancients recognized, but also each part is actually endlessly subdivided into parts, of which each has some motion of its own: otherwise it would be impossible for each portion of matter to express the whole universe.

5. [All things agree. Hippocrates (c.460–c.370 B.C.), a Greek physician, became known as "The Father of Medicine."]

66. Whence we see that there is a world of creatures, of living beings, of animals, of entelechies, of souls, in the smallest particle of matter.

67. Each portion of matter may be conceived of as a garden full of plants, and as a pond full of fishes. But each branch of the plant, each member of the animal, each drop of its humors is also such a garden or such a pond.

68. And although the earth and air which lies between the plants of the garden, or the water between the fish of the pond, is neither plant nor fish, they yet contain more of them, but for the most part so tiny as to be imperceptible to us.

69. Therefore there is nothing fallow, nothing sterile, nothing dead in the universe, no chaos, no confusion except in appearance; somewhat as a pond would appear from a distance, in which we might see the confused movement and swarming, so to speak, of the fishes in the pond, without discerning the fish themselves.

70. We see thus that each living body has a ruling entelechy, which in the animal is the soul; but the members of this living body are full of other living beings, plants, animals, each of which has also its entelechy or governing soul.

71. But it must not be imagined, as has been done by some people who have misunderstood my thought, that each soul has a mass or portion of matter belonging to it or attached to it forever, and that consequently it possesses other inferior living beings, destined to its service forever. For all bodies are, like rivers, in a perpetual flux, and parts are entering into them and departing from them continually.

72. Thus the soul changes its body only gradually and by degrees, so that it is never deprived of all its organs at once. There is often a metamorphosis in animals, but never metempsychosis nor transmigration of souls. There are also no entirely *separate* souls, nor *genii* without bodies. God alone is wholly without body.

73. For which reason also, it happens that there is, strictly speaking, neither absolute birth nor complete death, consisting in the separation of the soul from the body. What we call *birth* is envelopment and growth, and what we call *death* is development and diminution.

74. Philosophers have been greatly puzzled over the origin of forms, entelechies, or souls; but to-day, when we know by exact investigations upon plants, insects and animals, that the organic bodies of nature are never products of chaos or putrefaction, but always come from seeds, in which there was undoubtedly some *pre-formation*, it has been thought that not only the organic body was already there before conception, but also a soul in this body, and, in a word, the animal itself; and that by means of conception this animal has merely been prepared for a great transformation, in order to become an animal of another kind. Something similar is seen outside of birth, as when worms become flies, and caterpillars become butterflies.

75. The *animals*, some of which are raised by conception to the grade of larger animals, may be called *spermatic*; but those among them, which remain in their class, that is, the most part, are born, multiply, and are destroyed like the large animals, and it is only a small number of chosen ones which pass to a larger theatre.

76. But this is only half the truth. I have, therefore, held that if the animal never commences by natural means, neither does it end by natural means; and that not only will there be no birth, but also no utter destruction or death, strictly speaking. And these reasonings, made *a posteriori* and drawn from experience, harmonize perfectly with my principles deduced *a priori*, as above.[6]

6. [The reference is to secs. 3–5.]

77. Thus it may be said that not only the soul (mirror of an indestructible universe) is indestructible, but also the animal itself, although its mechanism often perishes in part and takes on or puts off organic coatings.

78. These principles have given me the means of explaining naturally the union or rather the conformity of the soul and the organic body. The soul follows its own peculiar laws and the body also follows its own laws, and they agree in virtue of the *pre-established harmony* between all substances, since they are all representations of one and the same universe.

79. Souls act according to the laws of final causes, by appetitions, ends and means. Bodies act in accordance with the laws of efficient causes or of motion. And the two realms, that of efficient causes and that of final causes, are in harmony with each other.

80. Descartes recognized that souls cannot impart any force to bodies, because there is always the same quantity of force in matter. Nevertheless he believed that the soul could change the direction of bodies. But this was because, in his day, the law of nature which affirms also the conservation of the same total direction in matter, was not known. If he had known this, he would have lighted upon my system of pre-established harmony.

81. According to this system, bodies act as if (what is impossible) there were no souls, and that souls act as if there were no bodies, and that both act as if each influenced the other.

82. As to *spirits* or rational souls, although I find that the same thing which I have stated (namely, that animals and souls begin only with the world and end only with the world) holds good at bottom with regard to all living beings and animals, yet there is this peculiarity in rational animals, that their spermatic animalcules, as long as they remain such, have only ordinary or sensitive souls; but as soon as those which are, so to speak, elected, attain by actual conception to human nature, their sensitive souls are elevated to the rank of reason and to the prerogative of spirits.

83. Among other differences which exist between ordinary souls and minds, some of which I have already mentioned, there is also, this, that souls in general are the living mirrors or images of the universe of creatures, but minds or spirits are in addition images of the Divinity itself, or of the author of nature, able to know the system of the universe and to imitate something of it by architectonic samples, each mind being like a little divinity in its own department.

84. Hence it is that spirits are capable of entering into a sort of society with God, and that he is, in relation to them, not only what an inventor is to his machine (as God is in relation to other creatures), but also what a prince is to his subjects, and even a father to his children.

85. Whence it is easy to conclude that the assembly of all spirits must compose the City of God, that is, the most perfect state which is possible, under the most perfect of monarchs.

86. This City of God, this truly universal monarchy, is a moral world within the natural world, and the highest and most divine of the works of God; it is in this that the glory of God truly consists, for he would have none if his greatness and goodness were not known and admired by spirits. It is, too, in relation to this divine city that he properly has goodness; whereas his wisdom and his power are everywhere manifest.

87. As we have above established a perfect harmony between two natural kingdoms, the one of efficient, the other of final causes, we should also notice here another harmony between the physical kingdom of nature and the moral kingdom of grace; that is, between God considered as the architect of the mechanism of the universe and God considered as monarch of the divine city of spirits.

88. This harmony makes things progress toward grace by natural means. This globe, for example, must be destroyed and repaired by natural means, at such times as the government of spirits may demand it, for the punishment of some and the reward of others.

89. It may be said, farther, that God as architect satisfies in every respect God as legislator, and that therefore sins, by the order of nature and perforce even of the mechanical structure of things, must carry their punishment with them; and that in the same way, good actions will obtain their rewards by mechanical ways through their relations to bodies, although this cannot and ought not always happen immediately.

90. Finally, under this perfect government, there will be no good action unrewarded, no bad action unpunished; and everything must result in the well-being of the good, that is, of those who are not disaffected in this great State, who, after having done their duty, trust in providence, and who love and imitate, as is meet, the author of all good, finding pleasure in the contemplation of his perfections, according to the nature of truly *pure love*, which takes pleasure in the happiness of the beloved. This is what causes wise and virtuous persons to work for all which seems in harmony with the divine will, presumptive or antecedent, and nevertheless to content themselves with that which God in reality brings to pass by his secret, consequent and decisive will, recognizing that if we could sufficiently understand the order of the universe, we should find that it surpasses all the wishes of the wisest, and that it is impossible to render it better than it is, not only for all in general, but also for ourselves in particular, if we are attached, as we should be, to the author of all, not only as to the architect and efficient cause of our being, but also as to our master and final cause, who ought to be the whole aim of our will, and who, alone, can make our happiness.

JOHN LOCKE—an engraving from the portrait by Sir Godfrey Kneller

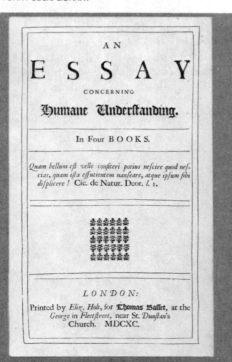

AN

ESSAY

CONCERNING

Humane Understanding.

In Four BOOKS.

Quam bellum eft velle confiteri potius nefcire quod nefcias, quam ifta effutientem naufeare, atque ipfum fibi difplicere ! Cic. de Natur. Deor. *l.* 1.

LONDON:

Printed by *Eliz. Holt,* for **Thomas Baffet,** at the *George* in *Fleetftreet,* near St. *Dunftan's* Church. MDCXC.

TITLE PAGE OF LOCKE'S *ESSAY*

CHRIST CHURCH, OXFORD

JOHN LOCKE

John Locke (1632–1704) was born in Wrington, Somerset, England. He was educated first at Westminster School and then at Oxford, where he received his master's degree in 1658. He remained at Oxford to teach and to study various subjects, among them medicine. In 1667, he went to London with his friend Lord Ashley, later Earl of Shaftsbury, whom he served first as physician and later as secretary and advisor. During this period he began the nearly twenty years' labor which culminated in his major work, *An Essay Concerning Human Understanding*. In 1675 poor health dictated a visit to France, where he spent four years at his studies. Locke returned to England in 1679, but his political fortunes declined along with Shaftsbury's, and he fled to Holland in 1683. He returned to England when William of Orange took the throne in 1689. In 1691 he retired to the serenity of Oates in Essex, where he spent the remainder of his life.

Locke's important philosophical works are two. *An Essay Concerning Human Understanding*, first published in 1690 but largely revised four times, is a massive inquiry into "the original, certainty, and extent of human knowledge, together with the grounds and degrees of belief, opinion, and assent." Lengthy and repetitive, this work is most often reprinted in abridged form, as it is here. *Two Treatises of Government*, also published in 1690, contains a well-known discussion of the foundations of political authority. Other works by Locke include *A Letter Concerning Toleration* (1689), *Some Thoughts Concerning Education* (1693), and *The Reasonableness of Christianity* (1695).

Although its expressed purpose is to discuss human knowledge, Locke's *Essay Concerning Human Understanding* does not address this topic immediately. Rather, the *Essay's* first three books deal with several important related issues. According to Locke, the fundamental element in all intellectual activity is the 'idea,' defined as "whatever it is which the mind can be employed about in thinking." In the first book, Locke argues against the view, held by Descartes and others, that some important ideas and principles are innate, present in the mind from birth. In the second book, he tries to show by several examples that the true source of all our ideas is experience. Each idea, he argues, is acquired either through sensation, or perception of the external world; through reflection, or awareness of the mind's own operation (reflection); or through the combining of ideas derived in one or another of these ways. In the third book, Locke discusses the connection between thinking and language. It is only in the fourth and final book that he turns to the topic of knowledge itself. Thus, *An Essay Concerning Human Understanding* is not a narrow treatise on epistemology, but rather a comprehensive discussion of our intellectual faculties.

Since empiricism is the view that our concepts and knowledge are derived from experience, the *Essay*, with its commitment to the experiential origins of all ideas, is clearly the first great work of the empiricist tradition. Nevertheless, the work also contains clear elements of rationalism, the view that it is reason rather than experience which is the fundamental source of our concepts and knowledge. This rationalistic element emerges in Locke's accounts of such ideas as power and substance, which he represents as containing elements which go beyond the contents of any possible experience. The rationalistic element emerges again and more profoundly in his characterization of knowledge as "the perception of the connection of and agreement, or disagreement and repugnancy of any of our ideas"; in other words, knowledge is acquired by spelling out the deductive consequences of ideas rather than by observing or testing natural phenomena. In these and other ways, the *Essay* occupies an interesting middle point between the rationalism of Descartes and Spinoza, and the later, purer empiricism of Berkeley and Hume.

One of the most striking doctrines in the *Essay* is Locke's view concerning perception. According to Locke, two quite different relations may hold between external objects and ideas acquired through sensation. On the one hand, every such idea is caused by some quality or 'power' of an external object. On the other hand, however, only some ideas of sensation resemble the objects that cause them. Ideas which do resemble objects are called ideas of primary qualities, and include shape, size, motion, and number. Those which do not resemble objects are called ideas of secondary qualities, and include color, taste, and smell. Given the distinction between primary and secondary qualities, it follows that perception does not present a completely accurate picture of the world. In reality, according to Locke the world is an odorless, tasteless, colorless collection of particles in motion. It is, in short, the world of Newtonian science.

Besides the distinction between primary and secondary qualities, Locke's *Essay* contains many other points of continuing interest. These are too numerous to list exhaustively, but they include Locke's view of personal identity (determined, he says, by continuity of consciousness or memory); of freedom (men, but not their wills, can properly be said to be free); and of word meaning (words primarily stand for ideas in our minds).

For general discussion of Locke's works, see R.I. Aaron, *John Locke* (1937; rpt. Oxford: Oxford University Press, 1965). An interesting collection of essays on topics treated by Locke can be found in J.L. Mackie, *Problems from Locke* (Oxford: Clarendon Press, 1976). For discussion of themes common to Locke and the later empiricists, see Jonathan Bennett, *Locke, Berkeley, Hume: Central Themes* (Oxford: Clarendon Press, 1971). A useful collection is C.B. Martin and D.M. Armstrong, eds., *Locke and Berkeley: A Collection of Critical Essays* (Garden City: Doubleday, 1968). For discussion of Locke's political theory, see J.W. Gough, *John Locke's Political Philosophy* (Oxford: Oxford University Press, 1950). An ingenious contemporary reworking of some of Locke's political ideas may be found in Robert Nozick, *Anarchy, State, and Utopia* (New York: Basic Books, 1974).

G.S.

AN ESSAY CONCERNING HUMAN UNDERSTANDING (abridged)

INTRODUCTION

1. *An Inquiry into the Understanding pleasant and useful.* —Since it is the *understanding* that sets man above the rest of sensible beings, and gives him all the advantage and dominion which he has over them; it is certainly a subject, even for its nobleness, worth our labour to inquire into. The understanding, like the eye, whilst it makes us see and perceive all other things, takes no notice of itself; and it requires art and pains to set it at a distance and make it its own object. But whatever be the difficulties that lie in the way of this inquiry; whatever it be that keeps us so much in the dark to ourselves; sure I am that all the light we can let in upon our minds, all the acquaintance we can make with our own understandings, will not only be very pleasant, but bring us great advantage, in directing our thoughts in the search of other things.

2. *Design.* —This, therefore, being my purpose—to inquire into the original, certainty, and extent of *human knowledge,* together with the grounds and degrees of *belief, opinion,* and *assent;*—I shall not at present meddle with the physical consideration of the mind; or trouble myself to examine wherein its essence consists; or by what motions of our spirits or alterations of our bodies we come to have any *sensation* by our organs, or any *ideas* in our understandings; and whether those ideas do in their formation, any or all of them, depend on matter or not. These are speculations which, however curious and entertaining, I shall decline, as lying out of my way in the design I am now upon. It shall suffice to my present purpose, to consider the discerning faculties of a man, as they are employed about the objects which they have to do with. And I shall imagine I have not wholly misemployed myself in the thoughts I shall have on this occasion, if, in this historical, plain method, I can give any account of the ways whereby our understandings come to attain those notions of things we have; and can set down any measures of the certainty of our knowledge; or the grounds of those persuasions which are to be found amongst men, so various, different, and wholly contradictory; and yet asserted somewhere or other with such assurance and confidence, that he that shall take a view of the opinions of mankind, observe their opposition, and at the same time consider the fondness and devotion wherewith they are embraced, the resolution and eagerness wherewith they are maintained, may perhaps have reason to suspect, that either there is no such thing as truth at all, or that mankind hath no sufficient means to attain a certain knowledge of it.

3. *Method.* —It is therefore worth while to search out the bounds between opinion and knowledge; and examine by what measures, in things whereof we have no certain knowledge, we ought to regulate our assent and moderate our persuasion. In order whereunto I shall pursue this following method:—

First, I shall inquire into the original of those *ideas,* notions, or whatever else you please to call them, which a man observes, and is conscious to himself he has in his mind; and the ways whereby the understanding comes to be furnished with them.

Secondly, I shall endeavour to show what *knowledge* the understanding hath by those ideas; and the certainty, evidence, and extent of it.

Thirdly, I shall make some inquiry into the nature and grounds of *faith* or *opinion:* whereby I mean that assent which we give to any proposition as true, of whose truth yet we have no certain knowledge. And here we shall have occasion to examine the reasons and degrees of *assent.*

8. *What Idea stands for.* —Before I proceed on to what I have thought on this subject, I must here in the entrance beg pardon of my reader for the frequent use of the word *idea,* which he will find in the following treatise. It being that term which, I think, serves best to stand for whatsoever is the *object* of the understanding when a man thinks, I have used it to express whatever is meant by *phantasm, notion, species,* or *whatever it is which the mind can be employed about in thinking;* and I could not avoid frequently using it.

I presume it will be easily granted me, that there are such *ideas* in men's minds: every one is conscious of them in himself; and men's words and actions will satisfy him that they are in others.

BOOK I

NEITHER PRINCIPLES NOR IDEAS ARE INNATE

Chapter I

NO INNATE SPECULATIVE PRINCIPLES

1. *The way shown how we come by any knowledge, sufficient to prove it not innate.* —It is an established opinion amongst some men, that there are in the understanding certain *innate principles;* some primary notions, κοιναὶ ἔννοιαι, characters, as it were, stamped upon the mind of man; which the soul receives in its very first being, and brings into the world with it. It would be sufficient to convince unprejudiced readers of the falseness of this supposition, if I should only show (as I hope I shall in the following parts of this Discourse) how men, barely by the use of their natural faculties, may attain to all the knowledge they have, without the help of any innate impressions; and may arrive at certainty, without any such original notions or principles. For I imagine any one will easily grant that it would be impertinent to suppose the ideas of colours innate in a creature to whom God hath given sight, and a power to receive them by the eyes from external objects; and no less unreasonable would it be to attribute several truths to the impressions of nature, and innate characters, when we may observe in ourselves faculties fit to attain as easy and certain knowledge of them as if they were originally imprinted on the mind.

But because a man is not permitted without censure to follow his own thoughts in the search of truth, when they lead him ever so little out of the common road, I shall set down the reasons that made me doubt of the truth of that opinion, as an excuse for my mistake, if I be in one; which I leave to be considered by those who, with me, dispose themselves to embrace truth wherever they find it.

2. *General Assent the great Argument.* —There is nothing more commonly taken for granted than that there are certain *principles,* both *speculative* and *practical,* (for they speak of both), universally agreed upon by all mankind: which therefore, they argue, must needs be the constant impressions which the souls of men receive in their first beings, and which they bring into the world with them, as necessarily and really as they do any of their inherent faculties.

3. *Universal Consent proves nothing innate.* —This argument, drawn from universal consent, has this misfortune in it, that if it were true in matter of fact, that there were certain truths wherein all mankind agreed, it would not prove them innate, if there can be any other way shown how men may come to that universal agreement, in the things they do consent in, which I presume may be done.

4. *'What is, is,' and 'It is impossible for the same Thing to be and not to be,' not universally assented to.* —But, which is worse, this argument of universal consent which is made use of to prove innate principles, seems to me a demonstration that there are none such: because there are none to which all mankind give an universal assent. I shall begin with the speculative, and instance in those magnified principles of demonstration, 'Whatsoever is, is,' and 'It is impossible for the same thing to be and not to be'; which, of all others, I think have the most allowed title to innate. These have so settled a reputation of maxims universally received, that it will no doubt be thought strange if any one should seem to question it. But yet I take liberty to say, that these propositions are so far from having an universal assent, that there are a great part of mankind to whom they are not so much as known.

5. *Not on the Mind naturally imprinted, because not known to Children, Idiots, &c.* — For, first, it is evident, that all children and idiots have not the least apprehension or thought of them. And the want of that is enough to destroy that universal assent which must needs be the necessary concomitant of all innate truths: it seeming to me near a contradiction to say, that there are truths imprinted on the soul, which it perceives or understands not: imprinting, if it signify anything, being nothing else but the making certain truths to be perceived. For to imprint anything on the mind without the mind's perceiving it, seems to me hardly intelligible. If therefore children and idiots have souls, have minds, with those impressions upon them, *they* must unavoidably perceive them, and necessarily know and assent to these truths; which since they do not, it is evident that there are no such impressions. For if they are not notions naturally imprinted, how can they be innate? and if they are notions imprinted, how can they be unknown? To say a notion is imprinted on the mind, and yet at the same time to say, that the mind is ignorant of it, and never yet took notice of it, is to make this impression nothing. No proposition can be said to be in the mind which it never yet knew, which it was never yet conscious of. For if any one may, then, by the same reason, all propositions that are true, and the mind is capable ever of assenting to, may be said to be in the mind, and to be imprinted: since, if any one can be said to be in the mind, which it never yet knew, it must be only because it is capable of knowing it; and so the mind is of all truths it ever shall know. Nay, thus truths may be imprinted on the mind which it never did, nor ever shall know; for a man may live long, and die at last in ignorance of many truths which his mind was capable of knowing, and that with certainty. So that if the capacity of knowing be the natural impression contended for, all the truths a man ever comes to

know will, by this account, be every one of them innate; and this great point will amount to no more, but only to a very improper way of speaking; which, whilst it pretends to assert the contrary, says nothing different from those who deny innate principles. For nobody, I think, ever denied that the mind was capable of knowing several truths. The capacity, they say, is innate; the knowledge acquired. But then to what end such contest for certain innate maxims? If truths can be imprinted on the understanding without being perceived, I can see no difference there can be between any truths the mind is *capable* of knowing in respect of their original: they must all be innate or all adventitious: in vain shall a man go about to distinguish them. He therefore that talks of innate notions in the understanding, cannot (if he intend thereby any distinct sort of truths) mean such truths to be in the understanding as it never perceived, and is yet wholly ignorant of. For if these words 'to be in the understanding' have any propriety, they signify to be understood. So that to be in the understanding, and not to be understood; to be in the mind and never to be perceived, is all one as to say anything is and is not in the mind or understanding. If therefore these two propositions, 'Whatsoever is, is,' and 'It is impossible for the same thing to be and not to be,' are by nature imprinted, children cannot be ignorant of them: infants, and all that have souls, must necessarily have them in their understandings, know the truth of them, and assent to it.

BOOK II

OF IDEAS

Chapter I

OF IDEAS IN GENERAL, AND THEIR ORIGINAL

1. *Idea is the Object of Thinking.* —Every man being conscious to himself that he thinks; and that which his mind is applied about whilst thinking being the *ideas* that are there, it is past doubt that men have in their minds several ideas,—such as are those expressed by the words *whiteness, hardness, sweetness, thinking, motion, man, elephant, army, drunkenness,* and others: it is in the first place then to be inquired, *How he comes by them?*

I know it is a received doctrine, that men have native ideas, and original characters, stamped upon their minds in their very first being. This opinion I have at large examined already; and, I suppose what I have said in the foregoing Book will be much more easily admitted, when I have shown whence the understanding may get all the ideas it has; and by what ways and degrees they may come into the mind;—for which I shall appeal to every one's own observation and experience.

2. *All Ideas come from Sensation or Reflection.* —Let us then suppose the mind to be, as we say, white paper, void of all characters, without any ideas:—How comes it to be furnished? Whence comes it by that vast store which the busy and boundless

fancy of man has painted on it with an almost endless variety? Whence has it all the *materials* of reason and knowledge? To this I answer, in one word, from EXPERI-ENCE. In that all our knowledge is founded; and from that it ultimately derives itself. Our observation employed either, about external sensible objects, or about the internal operations of our minds perceived and reflected on by ourselves, is that which supplies our understandings with all the *materials* of thinking. These two are the fountains of knowledge, from whence all the ideas we have, or can naturally have, do spring.

3. *The Objects of Sensation and Source of Ideas.* — First, our Senses, conversant about particular sensible objects, do convey into the mind several distinct perceptions of things, according to those various ways wherein those objects do affect them. And thus we come by those *ideas* we have of *yellow, white, heat, cold, soft, hard, bitter, sweet,* and all those which we call sensible qualities; which when I say the senses convey into the mind, I mean, they from external objects convey into the mind what produces there those perceptions. This great source of most of the ideas we have, depending wholly upon our senses, and derived by them to the understanding, I call our senses, and derived by them to the understanding, I call SENSATION.

4. *The Operations of our Minds, the other Source of them.* —Secondly, the other fountain from which experience furnisheth the understanding with ideas is,—the perception of the operations of our own mind within us, as it is employed about the ideas it has got;—which operations, when the soul comes to reflect on and consider, do furnish the understanding with another set of ideas, which could not be had from things without. And such are *perception, thinking, doubting, believing, reasoning, knowing, willing,* and all the different actings of our own minds;—which we being conscious of, and observing in ourselves, do from these receive into our understandings as distinct ideas as we do from bodies affecting our senses. This source of ideas every man has wholly in himself; and though it be not sense, as having nothing to do with external objects, yet it is very like it, and might properly enough be called *internal sense.* But as I call the other Sensation, so I call this REFLECTION, the ideas it affords being such only as the mind gets by reflecting on its own operations within itself. By reflection then, in the following part of this discourse, I would be understood to mean, that notice which the mind takes of its own operations, and the manner of them, by reason whereof there come to be ideas of these operations in the understanding. These two, I say, viz. external material things, as the objects of SENSA-TION, and the operations of our own minds within, as the objects of REFLECTION, are to me the only originals from whence all our ideas take their beginnings. The term *operations* here I use in a large sense, as comprehending not barely the actions of the mind about its ideas, but some sort of passions arising sometimes from them, such as is the satisfaction or uneasiness arising from any thought.

5. *All our Ideas are of the one or the other of these.* —The understanding seems to me not to have the least glimmering of any ideas which it doth not receive from one of these two. *External objects* furnish the mind with the ideas of sensible qualities, which are all those different perceptions they produce in us; and *the mind* furnishes the understanding with ideas of its own operations.

These, when we have taken a full survey of them, and their several modes, combinations, and relations, we shall find to contain all our whole stock of ideas; and that we have nothing in our minds which did not come in one of these two ways. Let any one examine his own thoughts, and thoroughly search into his understanding;

and then let him tell me, whether all the original ideas he has there, are any other than of the objects of his senses, or of the operations of his mind, considered as objects of his reflection. And how great a mass of knowledge soever he imagines to be lodged there, he will, upon taking a strict view, see that he has not any idea in his mind but what one of these two have imprinted;—though perhaps, with infinite variety compounded and enlarged by the understanding, as we shall see hereafter.

10. *The Soul thinks not always; for this wants Proofs.* —But whether the soul be supposed to exist antecedent to, or coeval with, or some time after the first rudiments of organization, or the beginnings of life in the body, I leave to be disputed by those who have better thought of that matter. I confess myself to have one of those dull souls, that doth not perceive itself always to contemplate ideas; nor can conceive it any more necessary for the soul always to think, than for the body always to move: the perception of ideas being (as I conceive) to the soul, what motion is to the body; not its essence, but one of its operations. And therefore, though thinking be supposed never so much the proper action of the soul, yet it is not necessary to suppose that it should be always thinking, always in action. That, perhaps, is the privilege of the infinite Author and Preserver of all things, who 'never slumbers nor sleeps'; but is not competent to any finite being, at least not to the soul of man. We know certainly, by experience, that we *sometimes* think; and thence draw this infallible consequence,—that there is something in us that has a power to think. But whether that substance *perpetually* thinks or no, we can be no further assured than experience informs us. For, to say that actual thinking is essential to the soul, and inseparable from it, is to beg what is in question, and not to prove it by reason;—which is necessary to be done, if it be not a self-evident proposition. But whether this, 'That the soul always thinks,' be a self-evident proposition, that everybody assents to at first hearing, I appeal to mankind. It is doubted whether I thought at all last night or no. The question being about a matter of fact, it is begging it to bring, as a proof for it, an hypothesis, which is the very thing in dispute: by which way one may prove anything, and it is but supposing that all watches, whilst the balance beats, think, and it is sufficiently proved, and past doubt, that my watch thought all last night. But he that would not deceive himself, ought to build his hypothesis on matter of fact, and make it out by sensible experience, and not presume on matter of fact, because of his hypothesis, that is, because he supposes it to be so; which way of proving amounts to this, that I must necessarily think all last night, because another supposes I always think, though I myself cannot perceive that I always do so.

But men in love with their opinions may not only suppose what is in question, but allege wrong matter of fact. How else could any one make it an inference of mine, that a thing is not, because we are not sensible of it in our sleep? I do not say there is no *soul* in a man, because he is not sensible of it in his sleep; but I do say, he cannot *think* at any time, waking or sleeping, without being sensible of it. Our being sensible of it is not necessary to anything but to our thoughts; and to them it is; and to them it always will be necessary, till we can think without being conscious of it.

Chapter II

OF SIMPLE IDEAS

1. *Uncompounded Appearances.* —The better to understand the nature, manner, and

extent of our knowledge, one thing is carefully to be observed concerning the ideas we have; and that is, that some of them are *simple* and some *complex.*

Though the qualities that affect our senses are, in the things themselves, so united and blended, that there is no separation, no distance between them; yet it is plain, the ideas they produce in the mind enter by the senses simple and unmixed. For, though the sight and touch often take in from the same object, at the same time, different ideas;—as a man sees at once motion and colour; the hand feels softness and warmth in the same piece of wax: yet the simple ideas thus united in the same subject, are as perfectly distinct as those that come in by different senses. The coldness and hardness which a man feels in a piece of ice being as distinct ideas in the mind as the smell and whiteness of a lily; or as the taste of sugar, and smell of a rose. And there is nothing can be plainer to a man than the clear and distinct perception he has of those simple ideas; which, being each in itself uncompounded, contains in it nothing but *one uniform appearance, or conception in the mind,* and is not distinguishable into different ideas.

2. *The Mind can neither make nor destroy them.* —These simple ideas, the materials of all our knowledge, are suggested and furnished to the mind only by those two ways above mentioned, viz. sensation and reflection. When the understanding is once stored with these simple ideas, it has the power to repeat, compare, and unite them, even to an almost infinite variety, and so can make at pleasure new complex ideas. But it is not in the power of the most exalted wit, or enlarged understanding, by any quickness or variety of thought, to *invent* or *frame* one new simple idea in the mind, not taken in by the ways before mentioned: nor can any force of the understanding *destroy* those that are there. The dominion of man, in this little world of his own understanding being muchwhat the same as it is in the great world of visible things; wherein his power, however managed by art and skill, reaches no farther than to compound and divide the materials that are made to his hand; but can do nothing towards the making the least particle of new matter, or destroying one atom of what is already in being. The same inability will every one find in himself, who shall go about to fashion in his understanding one simple idea, not received in by his senses from external objects, or by reflection from the operations of his own mind about them. I would have any one try to fancy any taste which had never affected his palate; or frame the idea of a scent he had never smelt: and when he can do this, I will also conclude that a blind man hath ideas of colours, and a deaf man true distinct notions of sounds.

Chapter III

OF SIMPLE IDEAS OF SENSE

1. *Division of simple Ideas.* —The better to conceive the ideas we receive from sensation, it may not be amiss for us to consider them, in reference to the different ways whereby they make their approaches to our minds, and make themselves perceivable by us.

First, then, There are some which come into our minds *by one sense only.*

Secondly, There are others that convey themselves into the mind *by more senses than one.*

Thirdly, Others that are had from *reflection only.*

Fourthly, There are some that make themselves way, and are suggested to the mind *by all the ways of sensation and reflection.*

We shall consider them apart under these several heads.

Ideas of one Sense. —There are some ideas which have admittance only through one sense, which is peculiarly adapted to receive them. Thus light and colours, as white, red, yellow, blue, with their several degrees or shades and mixtures, as green, scarlet, purple, sea-green, and the rest, come in only by the eyes. All kinds of noises, sounds, and tones, only by the ears. The several tastes and smells, by the nose and palate. And if these organs, or the nerves which are the conduits to convey them from without to their audience in the brain, —the mind's presence-room (as I may so call it) —are any of them so disordered as not to perform their functions, they have no postern to be admitted by; no other way to bring themselves into view, and be perceived by the understanding.

The most considerable of those belonging to the touch, are heat and cold, and solidity: all the rest, consisting almost wholly in the sensible configuration, as smooth and rough; or else, more or less firm adhesion of the parts, as hard and soft, tough and brittle, are obvious enough.

2. *Few simple Ideas have Names.* —I think it will be needless to enumerate all the particular simple ideas belonging to each sense. Nor indeed is it possible if we would; there being a great many more of them belonging to most of the senses than we have names for. The variety of smells, which are as many almost, if not more, than species of bodies in the world, do most of them want names. Sweet and stinking commonly serve our turn for these ideas, which in effect is little more than to call them pleasing or displeasing; though the smell of a rose and violet, both sweet, are certainly very distinct ideas. Nor are the different tastes, that by our palates we receive ideas of, much better provided with names. Sweet, bitter, sour, harsh, and salt are almost all the epithets we have to denominate that numberless variety of relishes, which are to be found distinct, not only in almost every sort of creatures, but in the different parts of the same plant, fruit, or animal. The same may be said of colours and sounds. I shall, therefore, in the account of simple ideas I am here giving, content myself to set down only such as are most material to our present purpose, or are in themselves less apt to be taken notice of though they are very frequently the ingredients of our complex ideas; amongst which, I think, I may well account solidity, which therefore I shall treat of in the next chapter.

Chapter IV

IDEA OF SOLIDITY

1. *We receive this Idea from Touch.* —The idea of *solidity* we receive by our touch: and it arises from the resistance which we find in body to the entrance of any other body into the place it possesses, till it has left it. There is no idea which we receive more constantly from sensation than solidity. Whether we move or rest, in what posture soever we are, we always feel something under us that supports us, and hinders our further sinking downwards; and the bodies which we daily handle make us

perceive that, whilst they remain between them, they do, by an insurmountable force, hinder the approach of the parts of our hands that press them. *That which thus hinders the approach of two bodies, when they are moved one towards another, I call solidity.* I will not dispute whether this acceptation of the word solid be nearer to its original signification than that which mathematicians use it in. It suffices that I think the common notion of solidity will allow, if not justify, this use of it; but if any one think it better to call it *impenetrability,* he has my consent. Only I have thought the term solidity the more proper to express this idea, not only because of its vulgar use in that sense, but also because it carries something more of positive in it than impenetrability; which is negative, and is perhaps more a consequence of solidity, than solidity itself. This, of all other, seems the idea most intimately connected with, and essential to body; so as nowhere else to be found or imagined, but only in matter. And though our senses take no notice of it, but in masses of matter, of a bulk sufficient to cause a sensation in us: yet the mind, having once got this idea from such grosser sensible bodies, traces it further, and considers it, as well as figure, in the minutest particle of matter that can exist; and finds it inseparably inherent in body, wherever or however modified.

2. *Solidity fills Space.* —This is the idea which belongs to body, whereby we conceive it to fill space. The idea of which filling of space is,—that where we imagine any space taken up by a solid substance, we conceive it so to possess it, that it excludes all other solid substances; and will for ever hinder any other two bodies, that move towards one another in a straight line, from coming to touch one another, unless it removes from between them in a line not parallel to that which they move in. This idea of it, the bodies which we ordinarily handle sufficiently furnish us with.

6. *What Solidity is.* —If any one asks me, *What this solidity is,* I send him to his senses to inform him. Let him put a flint or a football between his hands, and then endeavour to join them, and he will know. If he thinks this not a sufficient explication of solidity, what it is, and wherein it consists; I promise to tell him what it is, and wherein it consists, when he tells me what thinking is, or wherein it consists; or explains to me what extension or motion is, which perhaps seems much easier. The simple ideas we have, are such as experience teaches them us; but if, beyond that, we endeavour by words to make them clearer in the mind, we shall succeed no better than if we went about to clear up the darkness of a blind man's mind by talking; and to discourse into him the ideas of light and colours. The reason of this I shall show in another place.

Chapter V

OF SIMPLE IDEAS OF DIVERS SENSES

Ideas received both by seeing and touching. —The ideas we get by more than one sense are, of *space* or *extension, figure, rest,* and *motion.* For these make perceivable impressions, both on the eyes and touch; and we can receive and convey into our minds the ideas of the extension, figure, motion, and rest of bodies, both by seeing and feeling. But having occasion to speak more at large of these in another place, I here only enumerate them.

Chapter VI

OF SIMPLE IDEAS OF REFLECTION

1. *Simple Ideas are the Operations of Mind about its other Ideas.* —The mind receiving the ideas mentioned in the foregoing chapters from without, when it turns its view inward upon itself, and observes its own actions about those ideas it has, takes from thence other ideas, which are as capable to be the objects of its contemplation as any of those it received from foreign things.

2. *The Idea of Perception, and Idea of Willing, we have from Reflection.* —The two great and principal actions of the mind, which are most frequently considered, and which are so frequent that every one that pleases may take notice of them in himself, are these two:—

Perception, or *Thinking;* and
Volition, or *Willing.*

The power of thinking is called the *Understanding,* and the power of volition is called the *Will;* and these two powers or abilities in the mind are denominated faculties.

Of some of the *modes* of these simple ideas of reflection, such as are *remembrance, discerning, reasoning, judging, knowledge, faith,* &c., I shall have occasion to speak hereafter.

Chapter VII

OF SIMPLE IDEAS OF BOTH SENSATION AND REFLECTION

1. *Ideas of Pleasure and Pain.* —There be other simple ideas which convey themselves into the mind by all the ways of sensation and reflection, viz. *pleasure* or *delight,* and its opposite, *pain,* or *uneasiness; power, existence; unity.*

2. *Mix with almost all our other Ideas.* —Delight or uneasiness, one or other of them, join themselves to almost all our ideas both of sensation and reflection: and there is scarce any affection of our senses from without, any retired thought of our mind within, which is not able to produce in us pleasure or pain. By pleasure and pain, I would be understood to signify, whatsoever delights or molests us; whether it arises from the thoughts of our minds, or anything operating on our bodies. For, whether we call it satisfaction, delight, pleasure, happiness, &c., on the one side, or uneasiness, trouble, pain, torment, anguish, misery, &c., on the other, they are still but different degrees of the same thing, and belong to the ideas of pleasure and pain, delight or uneasiness; which are the names I shall most commonly use for those two sorts of ideas.

7. *Ideas of Existence and Unity.* —*Existence* and *Unity* are two other ideas that are suggested to the understanding by every object without, and every idea within. When ideas are in our minds, we consider them as being actually there, as well as we consider things to be actually without us;—which is, that they exist, or have existence. And whatever we can consider as one thing, whether a real being or idea, suggests to the understanding the idea of unity.

8. *Idea of Power.* — *Power* also is another of those simple ideas which we receive from sensation and reflection. For, observing in ourselves that we do and can think, and that we can at pleasure move several parts of our bodies which were at rest; the effects, also, that natural bodies are able to produce in one another, occurring every moment to our senses, — we both these ways get the idea of power.

9. *Idea of Succession.* — Besides these there is another idea, which, though suggested by our senses, yet is more constantly offered to us by what passes in our minds; and that is the idea of *succession.* For if we look immediately into ourselves, and reflect on what is observable there, we shall find our ideas always, whilst we are awake, or have any thought, passing in train, one going and another coming, without intermission.

10. *Simple Ideas the materials of all our Knowledge.* —These, if they are not all, are at least (as I think) the most considerable of those simple ideas which the mind has, and out of which is made all its other knowledge; all which it receives only by the two forementioned ways of sensation and reflection.

Nor let any one think these too narrow bounds for the capacious mind of man to expatiate in, which takes its flight further than the stars, and cannot be confined by the limits of the world; that extends its thoughts often even beyond the utmost expansion of Matter, and makes excursions into that incomprehensible Inane. I grant all this, but desire any one to assign any *simple idea* which is not received from one of those inlets before mentioned, or any *complex idea* not made out of those simple ones. Nor will it be so strange to think these few simple ideas sufficient to employ the quickest thought, or largest capacity; and to furnish the materials of all that various knowledge, and more various fancies and opinions of all mankind, if we consider how many words may be made out of the various composition of twenty-four letters; or if, going one step further, we will but reflect on the variety of combinations that may be made with barely one of the above-mentioned ideas, viz. number, whose stock is inexhaustible and truly infinite: and what a large and immense field doth extension alone afford the mathematicians?

Chapter VIII

SOME FURTHER CONSIDERATIONS CONCERNING OUR SIMPLE IDEAS OF SENSATION

7. *Ideas in the Mind, Qualities in Bodies.* — To discover the nature of our *ideas* the better, and to discourse of them intelligibly, it will be convenient to distinguish them *as they are ideas or perceptions in our minds;* and *as they are modifications of matter in the bodies that cause such perceptions in us:* that so we may not think (as perhaps usually is done) that they are exactly the images and resemblances of something inherent in the subject; most of those of sensation being in the mind no more the likeness of something existing without us, than the names that stand for them are the likeness of our ideas, which yet upon hearing they are apt to excite in us.

8. *Our Ideas and the Qualities of Bodies.* —Whatsoever the mind perceives *in itself,* or is the immediate object of perception, thought, or understanding, that I call *idea;* and the power to produce any idea in our mind, I call *quality* of the subject wherein that power is. Thus a snowball having the power to produce in us the ideas of white,

cold, and round,—the power to produce those ideas in us, as they are in the snow-ball, I call qualities; and as they are sensations or perceptions in our understand-ings, I call them ideas; which *ideas,* if I speak of sometimes as in the things them-selves, I would be understood to mean those qualities in the objects which produce them in us.

9. *Primary Qualities of Bodies.* —Qualities thus considered in bodies are,

First, such as are utterly inseparable from the body, in what state soever it be; and such as in all the alterations and changes it suffers, all the force can be used upon it, it constantly keeps; and such as sense constantly finds in every particle of matter which has bulk enough to be perceived; and the mind finds inseparable from every particle of matter, though less than to make itself singly be perceived by our senses: v.g. Take a grain of wheat, divide it into two parts; each part has still solidity, ex-tension, figure, and mobility: divide it again, and it retains still the same qualities; and so divide it on, till the parts become insensible; they must retain still each of them all those qualities. For division (which is all that a mill, or pestle, or any other body, does upon another, in reducing it to insensible parts) can never take away either solidity, extension, figure or mobility from any body, but only makes two or more distinct separate masses of matter, of that which was but one before; all which distinct masses, reckoned as so many distinct bodies, after division, make a certain number. These I call *original* or *primary qualities* of body, which I think we may observe to produce simple ideas in us, viz. solidity, extension, figure, motion or rest, and number.

10. *Secondary Qualities of Bodies.* —*Secondly,* such qualities which in truth are nothing in the objects themselves but powers to produce various sensations in us by their primary qualities, i.e. by the bulk, figure, texture, and motion of their insensi-ble parts, as colours, sounds, tastes, &c. These I call *secondary qualities.* To these might be added a *third* sort, which are allowed to be barely powers; though they are as much real qualities in the subject as those which I, to comply with the common way of speaking, call qualities, but for distinction, secondary qualities. For the power in fire to produce a new colour, or consistency, in *wax* or *clay,*—by its pri-mary qualities, is as much a quality in fire, as the power it has to produce in *me* a new idea or sensation of warmth or burning, which I felt not before,—by the same primary qualities, viz. the bulk, texture, and motion of its insensible parts.

11. *How Bodies produce Ideas in us.* —The next thing to be considered is, how bodies produce ideas in us; and that is manifestly by impulse, the only way which we can conceive bodies to operate in.

12. *By motions, external, and in our organism.* —If then external objects be not united to our minds when they produce ideas therein; and yet we perceive these *original* qualities in such of them as singly fall under our senses, it is evident that some motion must be thence continued by our nerves, or animal spirits, by some parts of our bodies, to the brains or the seat of sensation, there to produce in our minds the particular ideas we have of them. And since the extension, figure, num-ber, and motion of bodies of an observable bigness, may be perceived at a distance by the sight, it is evident some singly imperceptible bodies must come from them to the eyes, and thereby convey to the brain some motion; which produces these ideas which we have of them in us.

13. *How secondary Qualities produce their ideas.* —After the same manner that the ideas of these original qualities are produced in us, we may conceive that the ideas

of *secondary* qualities are also produced, viz. by the operation of insensible particles on our senses. For, it being manifest that there are bodies and good store of bodies, each whereof are so small, that we cannot by any of our senses discover either their bulk, figure, or motion,—as is evident in the particles of the air and water, and others extremely smaller than those; perhaps as much smaller than the particles of air and water, as the particles of air and water are smaller than peas or hail-stones;— let us suppose at present that the different motions and figures, bulk and number, of such particles, affecting the several organs of our senses, produce in us those different sensations which we have from the colours and smells of bodies; v.g. that a violet, by the impulse of such insensible particles of matter, of peculiar figures and bulks, and in different degrees and modifications of their motions, causes the ideas of the blue colour, and sweet scent of that flower to be produced in our minds. It being no more impossible to conceive that God should annex such ideas to such motions, with which they have no similitude, than that he should annex the idea of pain to the motion of a piece of steel dividing our flesh, with which that idea hath no resemblance.

14. *They depend on the primary Qualities.* —What I have said concerning colours and smells may be understood also of tastes and sounds, and other the like sensible qualities; which, whatever reality we by mistake attribute to them, are in truth nothing in the objects themselves, but powers to produce various sensations in us; and depend on those primary qualities, viz. bulk, figure, texture, and motion of parts as I have said.

15. *Ideas of primary Qualities are Resemblances; of secondary, not.* —From whence I think it easy to draw this observation,—that the ideas of primary qualities of bodies are resemblances of them, and their patterns do really exist in the bodies them- selves, but the ideas produced in us by these secondary qualities have no resem- blance of them at all. There is nothing like our ideas, existing in the bodies them- selves. They are, in the bodies we denominate from them, only a power to produce those sensations in us; and what is sweet, blue, or warm in idea, is but the certain bulk, figure, and motion of the insensible parts, in the bodies themselves, which we call so.

16. *Examples.* —Flame is denominated hot and light; snow, white and cold; and manna, white and sweet, from the ideas they produce in us. Which qualities are commonly thought to be the same in those bodies that those ideas are in us, the one the perfect resemblance of the other, as they are in a mirror, and it would by most men be judged very extravagant if one should say otherwise. And yet he that will consider that the same fire that, at one distance produces in us the sensation of warmth, does, at a nearer approach, produce in us the far different sensation of pain, ought to bethink himself what reason he has to say—that this idea of warmth, which was produced in him by the fire, is *actually in the fire;* and his idea of pain, which the same fire produced in him the same way, is *not* in the fire. Why are whiteness and coldness in snow, and pain not, when it produces the one and the other idea in us; and can do neither, but by the bulk, figure, number, and motion of its solid parts?

17. *The ideas of the Primary alone really exist.* —The particular bulk, number, figure, and motion of the parts of fire or snow are really in them,—whether any one's senses perceive them or no: and therefore they may be called *real* qualities, be- cause they really exist in those bodies. But light, heat, whiteness, or coldness, are no more really in them than sickness or pain is in manna. Take away the sensation of

them; let not the eyes see light or colours, nor the ears hear sounds; let the palate not taste, nor the nose smell, and all colours, tastes, odours, and sounds, *as they are such particular ideas,* vanish and cease, and are reduced to their causes, i.e. bulk, figure, and motion of parts.

18. *The secondary exist in things only as modes of the primary.* —A piece of manna of a sensible bulk is able to produce in us the idea of a round or square figure; and by being removed from one place to another, the idea of motion. This idea of motion represents it as it really is in manna moving: a circle or square are the same, whether in idea or existence, in the mind or in the manna. And this, both motion and figure, are really in the manna, whether we take notice of them or no: this everybody is ready to agree to. Besides, manna, by the bulk, figure, texture, and motion of its parts, has a power to produce the sensations of sickness, and sometimes of acute pains or gripings in us. That these ideas of sickness and pain are *not* in the manna, but effects of its operations on us, and are nowhere when we feel them not; this also every one readily agrees to. And yet men are hardly to be brought to think that sweetness and whiteness are not really in manna; which are but the effects of the operations of manna, by the motion, size, and figure of its particles, on the eyes and palate: as the pain and sickness caused by manna are confessedly nothing but the effects of its operations on the stomach and guts, by the size, motion, and figure of its insensible parts, (for by nothing else can a body operate, as has been proved): as if it could not operate on the eyes and palate, and thereby produce in the mind particular distinct ideas, which in itself it has not, as well as we allow it can operate on the guts and stomach, and thereby produce distinct ideas, which in itself it has not. These ideas, being all effects of the operations of manna on several parts of our bodies, by the size, figure, number, and motion of its parts;—why those produced by the eyes and palate should rather be thought to be really in the manna, than those produced by the stomach and guts; or why the pain and sickness, ideas that are the effect of manna, should be thought to be nowhere when they are not felt; and yet the sweetness and whiteness, effects of the same manna on other parts of the body, by ways equally as unknown, should be thought to exist in the manna, when they are not seen or tasted, would need some reason to explain.

19. *Examples.* —Let us consider the red and white colours in porphyry. Hinder light from striking on it, and its colours vanish; it no longer produces any such ideas in us: upon the return of light it produces these appearances on us again. Can any one think any real alterations are made in the porphyry by the presence or absence of light; and that those ideas of whiteness and redness are really in porphyry in the light, when it is plain *it has no colour in the dark?* It has, indeed, such a configuration of particles, both night and day, as are apt, by the rays of light rebounding from some parts of that hard stone, to produce in us the idea of redness, and from others the idea of whiteness; but whiteness or redness are not in it at any time, but such a texture that hath the power to produce such a sensation in us.

20. Pound an almond, and the clear white colour will be altered into a dirty one, and the sweet taste into an oily one. What real alteration can the beating of the pestle make in any body, but an alteration of the texture of it?

21. *Explains how water felt as cold by one hand may be warm to the other.* —Ideas being thus distinguished and understood, we may be able to give an account how the same water, at the same time, may produce the idea of cold by one hand and of heat by the other: whereas it is impossible that the same water, if those ideas were

really in it, should at the same time be both hot and cold. For, if we imagine *warmth*, as it is in our hands, to be nothing but a certain sort and degree of motion in the minute particles of our nerves or animal spirits, we may understand how it is possible that the same water may, at the same time, produce the sensations of heat in one hand and cold in the other; which yet *figure* never does, that never producing the idea of a square by one hand which has produced the idea of a globe by another. But if the sensation of heat and cold be nothing but the increase or diminution of the motion of the minute parts of our bodies, caused by the corpuscles of any other body, it is easy to be understood, that if that motion be greater in one hand than in the other; if a body be applied to the two hands, which has in its minute particles a greater motion than in those of one of the hands, and a less than in those of the other, it will increase the motion of the one hand and lessen it in the other; and so cause the different sensations of heat and cold that depend thereon.

23. *Three Sorts of Qualities in Bodies.* —The qualities, then, that are in bodies, rightly considered, are of three sorts:—

First, The bulk, figure, number, situation, and motion or rest of their solid parts. Those are in them, whether we perceive them or not; and when they are of that size that we can discover them, we have by these an idea of the thing as it is in itself; as is plain in artifical things. These I call *primary qualities.*

Secondly, The power that is in any body, by reason of its insensible primary qualities, to operate after a peculiar manner on any of our senses, and thereby produce in *us* the different ideas of several colours, sounds, smells, tastes, &c. These are usually called *sensible qualities.*

Thirdly, The power that is in any body, by reason of the particular constitution of its primary qualities, to make such a change in the bulk, figure, texture, and motion of *another body,* as to make it operate on our senses differently from what it did before. Thus the sun has a power to make wax white, and fire to make lead fluid. These are usually called *powers.*

The first of these, as has been said, I think may be properly called real, original, or primary qualities; because they are in the things themselves, whether they are perceived or not: and upon their different modifications it is that the secondary qualities depend.

The other two are only powers to act differently upon other things: which powers result from the different modifications of those primary qualities.

24. *The first are Resemblances; the second thought to be Resemblances, but are not; the third neither are, nor are thought so.* —But, though the two latter sorts of qualities are powers barely, and nothing but powers, relating to several other bodies, and resulting from the different modifications of the original qualities, yet they are generally otherwise thought of. For the *second* sort, viz. the powers to produce several ideas in us, by our senses, are looked upon as real qualities in the things thus affecting us: but the *third* sort are called and esteemed barely powers. v.g. The idea of heat or light, which we receive by our eyes, or touch, from the sun, are commonly thought real qualities existing in the sun, and something more than mere powers in it. But when we consider the sun in reference to wax, which it melts or blanches, we look on the whiteness and softness produced in the wax, not as qualities in the sun, but effects produced by powers in it. Whereas, if rightly considered, these qualities of light and warmth, which are perceptions in me when I am warmed or enlightened by the sun, are no otherwise in the sun, than the changes made in the wax, when it is

blanched or melted, are in the sun. They are all of them equally *powers in the sun, depending on its primary qualities;* whereby it is able, in the one case, so to alter the bulk, figure, texture, or motion of some of the insensible parts of my eyes or hands, as thereby to produce in me the idea of light or heat; and in the other, it is able so to alter the bulk, figure, texture, or motion of the insensible parts of the wax, as to make them fit to produce in me the distinct ideas of white and fluid.

Chapter IX

OF PERCEPTION

1. *Perception the first simple Idea of Reflection.* — PERCEPTION, as it is the first faculty of the mind exercised about our ideas; so it is the first and simplest idea we have from reflection, and is by some called thinking in general. Though thinking, in the propriety of the English tongue, signifies that sort of operation in the mind about its ideas, wherein the mind is active; where it, with some degree of voluntary attention, considers anything. For in bare naked perception, the mind is, for the most part, only passive; and what it perceives, it cannot avoid perceiving.

2. *Reflection alone can give us the idea of what perception is.* — What perception is, every one will know better by reflecting on what he does himself, when he sees, hears, feels, &c., or thinks, than by any discourse of mine. Whoever reflects on what passes in his own mind cannot miss it. And if he does not reflect, all the words in the world cannot make him have any notion of it.

3. *Arises in sensation only when the mind notices the organic impression.* — This is certain, that whatever alterations are made in the body, if they reach not the mind; whatever impressions are made on the outward parts, if they are not taken notice of within, there is no perception. Fire may burn our bodies with no other effect than it does a billet, unless the motion be continued to the brain, and there the sense of heat, or idea of pain, be produced in the mind; wherein consists actual perception.

4. *Impulse on the organ insufficient.* — How often may a man observe in himself, that whilst his mind is intently employed in the contemplation of some objects, and curiously surveying some ideas that are there, it takes no notice of impressions of sounding bodies made upon the organ of hearing, with the same alteration that uses to be for the producing the idea of sound? A sufficient impulse there may be on the organ; but it not reaching the observation of the mind, there follows no perception: and though the motion that uses to produce the idea of sound be made in the ear, yet no sound is heard. Want of sensation, in this case, is not through any defect in the organ, or that the man's ears are less affected than at other times when he does hear: but that which uses to produce the idea, though conveyed in by the usual organ, not being taken notice of in the understanding, and so imprinting no idea in the mind, there follows no sensation. So that wherever there is sense or perception, there some idea is actually produced, and present in the understanding.

8. *Sensations often changed by the Judgment.* — We are further to consider concerning perception, that the ideas we receive by sensation are often, in grown people, altered by the judgment, without our taking notice of it. When we set before our eyes a round globe of any uniform colour, v.g. gold, alabaster, or jet, it is certain

that the idea thereby imprinted on our minds is of a flat circle, variously shadowed, with several degrees of light and brightness coming to our eyes. But we having, by use, been accustomed to perceive what kind of appearance convex bodies are wont to make in us; what alterations are made in the reflections of light by the difference of the sensible figures of bodies;—the judgment presently, by an habitual custom, alters the appearances into their causes. So that from that which is truly variety of shadow or colour, collecting the figure, it makes it pass for a mark of figure, and frames to itself the perception of a convex figure and an uniform colour; when the idea we receive from thence is only a plane variously coloured, as is evident in painting. To which purpose I shall here insert a problem of that very ingenious and studious promoter of real knowledge, the learned and worthy Mr. Molineux,[1] which he was pleased to send me in a letter some months since; and it is this:—'Suppose a man *born* blind, and now adult, and taught by his *touch* to distinguish between a cube and a sphere of the same metal, and nighly of the same bigness, so as to tell, when he felt one and the other, which is the cube, which the sphere. Suppose then the cube and sphere placed on a table, and the blind man be made to see: *quaere*, whether *by his sight, before he touched them*, he could now distinguish and tell which is the globe, which the cube?' To which the acute and judicious proposer answers, 'Not. For, though he has obtained the experience of how a globe, how a cube affects his touch, yet he has not yet obtained the experience, that what affects his touch so or so, must affect his sight so or so; or that a protuberant angle in the cube, that pressed his hand unequally, shall appear to his eye as it does in the cube.'—I agree with this thinking gentleman, whom I am proud to call my friend, in his answer to this problem; and am of opinion that the blind man, at first sight, would not be able with certainty to say which was the globe, which the cube, whilst he only saw them; though he could unerringly name them by his touch, and certainly distinguish them by the difference of their figures felt. This I have set down, and leave with my reader, as an occasion for him to consider how much he may be beholden to experience, improvement, and acquired notions, where he thinks he had not the least use of, or help from them. And the rather, because this observing gentleman further adds, that 'having, upon the occasion of my book, proposed this to divers very ingenious men, he hardly ever met with one that at first gave the answer to it which he thinks true, till by hearing his reasons they were convinced.'

Chapter X

OF RETENTION

1. *Contemplation.* —The next faculty of the mind, whereby it makes a further progress towards knowledge, is that which I call *retention;* or the keeping of those simple ideas which from sensation or reflection it hath received. This is done two ways.

---

1. [William Molineux (1656–1698), a Dubliner who was a Member of Parliament and who published a work on optics, entered into correspondence with Locke, and the two became close friends. The letter Locke refers to was sent in 1693, and the discussion of Molineux's problem was added to the *Essay* in its second edition (1694). —S.M.C.]

First, by keeping the idea which is brought into it, for some time actually in view, which is called *contemplation*.

2. *Memory.* —The other way of retention is, the power to revive again in our minds those ideas which, after imprinting, have disappeared, or have been as it were laid aside out of sight. And thus we do, when we conceive heat or light, yellow or sweet,—the object being removed. This is *memory*, which is as it were the storehouse of our ideas. For, the narrow mind of man not being capable of having many ideas under view and consideration at once, it was necessary to have a repository, to lay up those ideas which, at another time, it might have use of. But, our *ideas* being nothing but actual perceptions in the mind, which cease to be anything when there is no perception of them; this laying up of our ideas in the repository of the memory signifies no more but this,—that the mind has a power in many cases to revive perceptions which it has once had, with this additional perception annexed to them, that *it has had them before*. And in this sense it is that our ideas are said to be in our memories, when indeed they are actually nowhere;—but only there is an ability in the mind when it will to revive them again, and as it were paint them anew on itself, though some with more, some with less difficulty; some more lively, and others more obscurely. And thus it is, by the assistance of this faculty, that we are said to have all those ideas in our understandings which, though we do not actually contemplate, yet we *can* bring in sight, and make appear again, and be the objects of our thoughts, without the help of those sensible qualities which first imprinted them there.

7. *In Remembering, the Mind is often active.* —In this secondary perception, as I may so call it, or viewing again the ideas that are lodged in the memory, the mind is oftentimes more than barely passive; the appearance of those dormant pictures depending sometimes on the *will*. The mind very often sets itself on work in search of some hidden idea, and turns as it were the eye of the soul upon it; though sometimes too they start up in our minds of their own accord, and offer themselves to the understanding; and very often are roused and tumbled out of their dark cells into open daylight, by turbulent and tempestuous passions; our affections bringing ideas to our memory, which had otherwise lain quiet and unregarded. This further is to be observed, concerning ideas lodged in the memory, and upon occasion revived by the mind, that they are not only (as the word *revive* imports) none of them new ones, but also that the mind takes notice of them as of a former impression, and renews its acquaintance with them, as with ideas it had known before. So that though ideas formerly imprinted are not all constantly in view, yet in remembrance they are constantly known to be such as have been formerly imprinted; i.e. in view, and taken notice of before, by the understanding.

Chapter XI

OF DISCERNING, AND OTHER OPERATIONS OF THE MIND

1. *No Knowledge without Discernment.* —Another faculty we may take notice of in our minds is that of *discerning* and *distinguishing* between the several ideas it has. It is not enough to have a confused perception of something in general. Unless the mind had a distinct perception of different objects and their qualities, it would be

capable of very little knowledge, though the bodies that affect us were as busy about us as they are now, and the mind were continually employed in thinking. On this faculty of distinguishing one thing from another depends the evidence and certainty of several, even very general, propositions, which have passed for innate truths; — because men, overlooking the true cause why those propositions find universal assent, impute it wholly to native uniform impressions; whereas it in truth depends upon this clear discerning faculty of the mind, whereby it *perceives* two ideas to be the same, or different. But of this more hereafter.

4. *Comparing.* — The COMPARING them one with another, in respect of extent, degrees, time, place, or any other circumstances, is another operation of the mind about its ideas, and is that upon which depends all that large tribe of ideas comprehended under *relation;* which, of how vast an extent it is, I shall have occasion to consider hereafter.

6. *Compounding.* — The next operation we may observe in the mind about its ideas is COMPOSITION; whereby it puts together several of those simple ones it has received from sensation and reflection, and combines them into complex ones. Under this of composition may be reckoned also that of *enlarging,* wherein, though the composition does not so much appear as in more complex ones, yet it is nevertheless a putting several ideas together, though of the same kind. Thus, by adding several units together, we make the idea of a dozen; and putting together the repeated ideas of several perches, we frame that of a furlong.

8. *Naming.* — When children have, by repeated sensations, got ideas fixed in their memories, they begin by degrees to learn the use of signs. And when they have got the skill to apply the organs of speech to the framing of articulate sounds, they begin to make use of words, to signify their ideas to others. These verbal signs they sometimes borrow from others, and sometimes make themselves, as one may observe among the new and unusual names children often give to things in the first use of language.

9. *Abstraction.* — The use of words then being to stand as outward marks of our internal ideas, and those ideas being taken from particular things, if every particular idea that we take in should have a distinct name, names must be endless. To prevent this, the mind makes the particular ideas received from particular objects to become general; which is done by considering them as they are in the mind such appearances, — separate from all other existences, and the circumstances of real existence, as time, place, or any other concomitant ideas. This is called ABSTRACTION, whereby ideas taken from particular beings become general representatives of all of the same kind; and their names general names, applicable to whatever exists conformable to such abstract ideas. Such precise, naked appearances in the mind, without considering how, whence, or with what others they came there, the understanding lays up (with names commonly annexed to them) as the standards to rank real existences into sorts, as they agree with these patterns, and to denominate them accordingly. Thus the same colour being observed to-day in chalk or snow, which the mind yesterday received from milk, it considers that appearance alone, makes it a representative of all of that kind; and having given it the name *whiteness,* it by that sound signifies the same quality wheresoever to be imagined or met with; and thus universals, whether ideas or terms, are made.

10. *Brutes abstract not.* — If it may be doubted whether beasts compound and enlarge their ideas that way to any degree; this, I think, I may be positive in, — that

the power of abstracting is not at all in them; and that the having of general ideas is that which puts a perfect distinction betwixt man and brutes, and is an excellency which the faculties of brutes do by no means attain to. For it is evident we observe no footsteps in them of making use of general signs for universal ideas; from which we have reason to imagine that they have not the faculty of abstracting, or making general ideas, since they have no use of words, or any other general signs.

11. *Brutes abstract not, yet are not bare machines.* —Nor can it be imputed to their want of fit organs to frame articulate sounds, that they have no use or knowledge of general words; since many of them, we find, can fashion such sounds, and pronounce words distinctly enough, but never with any such application. And, on the other side, men who, through some defect in the organs, want words, yet fail not to express their universal ideas by signs, which serve them instead of general words, a faculty which we see beasts come short in. And, therefore, I think, we may suppose, that it is in this that the species of brutes are discriminated from man: and it is that proper difference wherein they are wholly separated, and which at last widens to so vast a distance. For if they have any ideas at all, and are not bare machines, (as some would have them,[2]) we cannot deny them to have some reason. It seems as evident to me, that they do reason, as that they have sense; but it is only in particular ideas, just as they received them from their senses. They are the best of them tied up within those narrow bounds, and have not (as I think) the faculty to enlarge them by any kind of abstraction.

15. *The true Beginning of Human Knowledge.* —And thus I have given a short, and, I think, true *history of the first beginnings of human knowledge;*—whence the mind has its first objects; and by what steps it makes its progress to the laying in and storing up those ideas, out of which is to be framed all the knowledge it is capable of: wherein I must appeal to experience and observation whether I am in the right: the best way to come to truth being to examine things as really they are, and not to conclude they are, as we fancy of ourselves, or have been taught by others to imagine.

17. *Dark Room.* —I pretend not to teach, but to inquire; and therefore cannot but confess here again,—that external and internal sensation are the only passages I can find of knowledge to the understanding. These alone, as far as I can discover, are the windows by which light is let into this *dark room.* For, methinks, the understanding is not much unlike a closet wholly shut from light, with only some little openings left, to let in external visible resemblances, or ideas of things without: would the pictures coming into such a dark room but stay there, and lie so orderly as to be found upon occasion, it would very much resemble the understanding of a man, in reference to all objects of sight, and the ideas of them.

These are my guesses concerning the means whereby the understanding comes to have and retain simple ideas, and the modes of them, with some other operations about them.

I proceed now to examine some of these simple ideas and their modes a little more particularly.

---

2. [Descartes, for example.]

Chapter XII

OF COMPLEX IDEAS

1. *Made by the Mind out of simple Ones.* —We have hitherto considered those ideas, in the reception whereof the mind is only passive, which are those simple ones received from sensation and reflection before mentioned, whereof the mind cannot make one to itself, nor have any idea which does not wholly consist of them. But as the mind is wholly passive in the reception of all its simple ideas, so it exerts several acts of its own, whereby out of its simple ideas, as the materials and foundations of the rest, the others are framed. The acts of the mind, wherein it exerts its power over its simple ideas, are chiefly these three: (1) Combining several simple ideas into one compound one; and thus all *complex ideas* are made. (2) The second is bringing two ideas, whether simple or complex, together, and setting them by one another, so as to take a view of them at once, without uniting them into one; by which way it gets all its *ideas of relations*. (3) The third is separating them from all other ideas that accompany them in their real existence: this is called abstraction: and thus all its *general ideas* are made. This shows man's power, and its ways of operation, to be much the same in the material and intellectual world. For the materials in both being such as he has no power over, either to make or destroy, all that man can do is either to unite them together, or to set them by one another, or wholly separate them. I shall here begin with the first of these in the consideration of complex ideas, and come to the other two in their due places. As simple ideas are observed to exist in several combinations united together, so the mind has a power to consider several of them united together as one idea; and that not only as they are united in external objects, but as itself has joined them together. Ideas thus made up of several simple ones put together, I call *complex;*—such as are beauty, gratitude, a man, an army, the universe; which, though complicated of various simple ideas, or complex ideas made up of simple ones, yet are, when the mind pleases, considered each by itself, as one entire thing, and signified by one name.

2. *Made voluntarily.* —In this faculty of repeating and joining together its ideas, the mind has great power in varying and multiplying the objects of its thoughts, infinitely beyond what sensation or reflection furnished it with: but all this still confined to those simple ideas which it received from those two sources, and which are the ultimate materials of all its compositions. For simple ideas are all from things themselves, and of these the mind *can* have no more, nor other than what are suggested to it. It can have no other ideas of sensible qualities than what come from without by the senses; nor any ideas of other kind of operations of a thinking substance, than what it finds in itself. But when it has once got these simple ideas, it is not confined barely to observation, and what offers itself from without; it can, by its own power, put together those ideas it has, and make new complex ones, which it never received so united.

3. *Complex ideas are either of Modes, Substances, or Relations.* —*Complex ideas,* however compounded and decompounded, though their number be infinite, and the variety endless, wherewith they fill and entertain the thoughts of men; yet I think they may be all reduced under these three heads:—

1. *Modes.*

2. *Substances.*

3. *Relations.*

4. *Ideas of Modes.* —First, *Modes* I call such complex ideas which, however compounded, contain not in them the supposition of subsisting by themselves, but are considered as dependences on, or affections of substances;—such as are the ideas signified by the words triangle, gratitude, murder, &c. And if in this I use the word mode in somewhat a different sense from its ordinary signification, I beg pardon; it being unavoidable in discourses, differing from the ordinary received notions, either to make new words, or to use old words in somewhat a new signification; the later whereof, in our present case, is perhaps the more tolerable of the two.

5. *Simple and mixed Modes of simple ideas.* —Of these *modes,* there are two sorts which deserve distinct consideration:—

First, there are some which are only variations, or different combinations of the same simple idea, without the mixture of any other;—as a dozen, or score; which are nothing but the ideas of so many distinct units added together, and these I call *simple modes* as being contained within the bounds of one simple idea.

Secondly, there are others compounded of simple ideas of several kinds, put together to make one complex one;—v.g. beauty, consisting of a certain composition of colour and figure, causing delight to the beholder; theft, which being the concealed change of the possession of anything, without the consent of the proprietor, contains, as is visible, a combination of several ideas of several kinds: and these I call *mixed modes.*

6. *Ideas of Substances, single or collective.* —Secondly, the ideas of *substances* are such combinations of simple ideas as are taken to represent distinct *particular* things subsisting by themselves; in which the supposed or confused idea of substance, such as it is, is always the first and chief. Thus if to substance be joined the simple idea of a certain dull whitish colour, with certain degrees of weight, hardness, ductility, and fusibility, we have the idea of lead; and a combination of the ideas of a certain sort of figure, with the powers of motion, thought and reasoning, joined to substance, make the ordinary idea of a man. Now of substances also, there are two sorts of ideas:—one of *single* substances, as they exist separately, as of a man or a sheep; the other of several of those put together, as an army of men, or flock of sheep—which *collective* ideas of several substances thus put together are as much each of them one single idea as that of a man or an unit.

7. *Ideas of Relation.* —Thirdly, the last sort of complex ideas is that we call *relation,* which consists in the consideration and comparing one idea with another.

Of these several kinds we shall treat in their order.

Chapter XXI

OF POWER

1. *This Idea, how got.* —The mind being every day informed, by the senses, of the alteration of those simple ideas it observes in things without; and taking notice how one comes to an end, and ceases to be, and another begins to exist which was not before; reflecting also on what passes within itself, and observing a constant change of its ideas, sometimes by the impression of outward objects on the senses, and sometimes by the determination of its own choice; and concluding from what it has so constantly observed to have been, that the like changes will for the future be made in the same things, by like agents, and by the like ways,—considers in one thing the possibility of having any of its simple ideas changed, and in another the possibility of making that change; and so comes by the idea which we call *power*. Thus we say, Fire has a power to melt gold, i.e. to destroy the consistency of its insensible parts, and consequently its hardness, and make it fluid; and gold has a power to be melted; that the sun has a power to blanch wax, and wax a power to be blanched by the sun, whereby the yellowness is destroyed, and whiteness made to exist in its room. In which, and the like cases, the power we consider is in reference to the change of perceivable ideas. For we cannot observe any alteration to be made in, or operation upon anything, but by the observable change of its sensible ideas; nor conceive any alteration to be made, but by conceiving a change of some of its ideas.

2. *Power, active and passive.* —Power thus considered is two-fold, viz. as able to make, or able to receive any change. The one may be called *active*, and the other *passive* power. Whether matter be not wholly destitute of active power, as its author, God, is truly above all passive power; and whether the intermediate state of created spirits be not that alone which is capable of both active and passive power, may be worth consideration. I shall not now enter into that inquiry, my present business being not to search into the original of power, but how we come by the *idea* of it. But since active powers make so great a part of our complex ideas of natural substances, (as we shall see hereafter,) and I mention them as such, according to common apprehension; yet they being not, perhaps, so truly *active* powers as our hasty thoughts are apt to represent them, I judge it not amiss, by this intimation, to direct our minds to the consideration of God and spirits, for the clearest idea of *active* power.

4. *The clearest Idea of active Power had from Spirit.* —We are abundantly furnished with the idea of *passive* power by almost all sorts of sensible things. In most of them we cannot avoid observing their sensible qualities, nay, their very substances, to be in a continual flux. And therefore with reason we look on them as liable still to the same change. Nor have we of *active* power (which is the more proper signification of the word power) fewer instances. Since whatever change is observed, the mind must collect a power somewhere able to make that change, as well as a possibility in the thing itself to receive it. But yet, if we will consider it attentively, bodies, by our senses, do not afford us so clear and distinct an idea of active power, as we have from reflection on the operations of our minds. For all power relating to action, and there being but two sorts of action whereof we have an idea, viz. thinking and motion, let us consider whence we have the clearest ideas of the powers which produce these

actions. (1) Of thinking, body affords us no idea at all; it is only from reflection that we have that. (2) Neither have we from body any idea of the beginning of motion. A body at rest affords us no idea of any active power to move; and when it is set in motion itself, that motion is rather a passion than an action in it. For, when the ball obeys the motion of a billiard-stick, it is not any action of the ball, but bare passion. Also when by impulse it sets another ball in motion that lay in its way, it only communicates the motion it had received from another, and loses in itself so much as the other received: which gives us but a very obscure idea of an *active* power of moving in body, whilst we observe it only to *transfer*, but not *produce* any motion. For it is but a very obscure idea of power which reaches not the production of the action, but the continuation of the passion. For so is motion in a body impelled by another; the continuation of the alteration made in it from rest to motion being little more an action, than the continuation of the alteration of its figure by the same blow is an action. The idea of the *beginning* of motion we have only from reflection on what passes in ourselves; where we find by experience, that, barely by willing it, barely by a thought of the mind, we can move the parts of our bodies, which were before at rest. So that it seems to me, we have, from the observation of the operation of bodies by our senses, but a very imperfect obscure idea of *active* power; since they afford us not any idea in themselves of the power to begin any action, either motion or thought.

5. *Will and Understanding two Powers in Mind or Spirit.* — This, at least, I think evident, — That we find in ourselves a power to begin or forbear, continue or end several actions of our minds, and motions of our bodies, barely by a thought or preference of the mind ordering, or as it were commanding, the doing or not doing such or such a particular action. This power which the mind has thus to order the consideration of any idea, or the forbearing to consider it; or to prefer the motion of any part of the body to its rest, and *vice versâ*, in any particular instance, is that which we call the *Will*. The actual exercise of that power, by directing any particular action, or its forbearance, is that which we call *volition* or *willing*. The forbearance of that action, consequent to such order or command of the mind, is called *voluntary*. And whatsoever action is performed without such a thought of the mind, is called *involuntary*. The power of perception is that which we call the *Understanding*. Perception, which we make the act of the understanding, is of three sorts: — 1. The perception of ideas in our minds. 2. The perception of the signification of signs. 3. The perception of the connexion or repugnancy, agreement or disagreement, that there is between any of our ideas. All these are attributed to the understanding, or perceptive power, though it be the two latter only that use allows us to say we understand.

7. *Whence the idea of liberty and necessity.* — Everyone, I think, finds in himself a power to begin or forbear, continue or put an end to several actions in himself. From the consideration of the extent of this power of the mind over the actions of the man, which everyone finds in himself, arise the ideas of liberty and necessity.

8. *Liberty, what.* — All the actions that we have any idea of reducing themselves, as has been said, to these two, viz. thinking and motion; so far as a man has power to think or not to think, to move or not to move, according to the preference or direction of his own mind, so far is a man *free*. Wherever any performance or forbearance are not equally in a man's power; wherever doing or not doing will not equally *follow* upon the preference of his mind directing it, there he is not free, though perhaps the action may be voluntary. So, that the idea of *liberty* is, the idea of a power in any agent to do or forbear any particular action, according to the determination or

thought of the mind, whereby either of them is preferred to the other: where either of them is not in the power of the agent to be produced by him according to his volition, there he is not at liberty; that agent is under *necessity.* So that liberty cannot be where there is no thought, no volition, no will; but there may be thought, there may be will, there may be volition, where there is no liberty. A little consideration of an obvious instance or two may make this clear.

9. *Supposes Understanding and Will.* —A tennis-ball, whether in motion by the stroke of a racket, or lying still at rest, is not by any one taken to be a free agent. If we inquire into the reason, we shall find it is because we conceive not a tennis-ball to think, and consequently not to have any volition, or *preference* of motion to rest, or *vice versâ;* and therefore has not liberty, is not a free agent; but all its both motion and rest come under our idea of necessary, and are so called. Likewise a man falling into the water, (a bridge breaking under him,) has not herein liberty, is not a free agent. For though he has volition, though he prefers his not falling to falling; yet the forbearance of that motion not being in his power, the stop or cessation of that motion follows not upon his volition; and therefore therein he is not free. So a man striking himself, or his friend, by a convulsive motion of his arm, which it is not in his power, by volition or the direction of his mind, to stop or forbear, nobody thinks he has in this liberty; every one pities him, as acting by necessity and constraint.

10. *Belongs not to Volition.* —Again: suppose a man be carried, whilst fast asleep, into a room where is a person he longs to see and speak with; and be there locked fast in, beyond his power to get out: he awakes, and is glad to find himself in so desirable company, which he stays willingly in, i.e. prefers his stay to going away. I ask, is not this stay voluntary? I think nobody will doubt it: and yet, being locked fast in, it is evident he is not at liberty not to stay, he has not freedom to be gone. So that liberty is not an idea belonging to volition, or preferring; but to the person having the power of doing, or forbearing to do, according as the mind shall choose or direct. Our idea of liberty reaches as far as that power, and no farther. For wherever restraint comes to check that power, or compulsion takes away that indifferency of ability to act, or to forbear acting, there liberty, and our notion of it, presently ceases.

11. *Voluntary opposed to involuntary, not to necessary.* —We have instances enough, and often more than enough, in our own bodies. A man's heart beats, and the blood circulates, which it is not in his power by any thought or volition to stop; and therefore in respect of these motions, where rest depends not on his choice, nor would follow the determination of his mind, if it should prefer it, he is not a free agent. Convulsive motions agitate his legs, so that though he wills it ever so much, he cannot by any power of his mind stop their motion, (as in that odd disease called *chorea sancti viti*), but he is perpetually dancing; he is not at liberty in this action, but under as much necessity of moving, as a stone that falls, or a tennis-ball struck with a racket. On the other side, a palsy or the stocks hinder his legs from obeying the determination of his mind, if it would thereby transfer his body to another place. In all these there is want of freedom; though the sitting still, even of a paralytic, whilst he prefers it to a removal, is truly voluntary. Voluntary, then, is not opposed to necessary, but to involuntary. For a man may prefer what he can do, to what he cannot do; the state he is in, to its absence or change; though necessity has made it in itself unalterable.

12. *Liberty, what.* —As it is in the motions of the body, so it is in the thoughts of

our minds: where any one is such, that we have power to take it up, or lay it by, according to the preference of the mind, there we are at liberty. A waking man, being under the necessity of having some ideas constantly in his mind, is not at liberty to think or not to think; no more than he is at liberty, whether his body shall touch any other or no: but whether he will remove his contemplation from one idea to another is many times in his choice; and then he is, in respect of his ideas, as much at liberty as he is in respect of bodies he rests on; he can at pleasure remove himself from one to another. But yet some ideas to the mind, like some motions to the body, are such as in certain circumstances it cannot avoid, nor obtain their absence by the utmost effort it can use. A man on the rack is not at liberty to lay by the idea of pain, and divert himself with other contemplations: and sometimes a boisterous passion hurries our thoughts, as a hurricane does our bodies, without leaving us the liberty of thinking on other things, which we would rather choose. But as soon as the mind regains the power to stop or continue, begin or forbear, any of these motions of the body without, or thoughts within, according as it thinks fit to prefer either to the other, we then consider the man as a *free agent* again.

13. *Necessity, what.* —Wherever thought is wholly wanting, or the power to act or forbear according to the direction of thought, there necessity takes place. This, in an agent capable of volition, when the beginning or continuation of any action is contrary to that preference of his mind, is called compulsion; when the hindering or stopping any action is contrary to his volition, it is called restraint. Agents that have no thought, no volition at all, are in everything *necessary agents.*

14. *Liberty belongs not to the Will.* —If this be so, (as I imagine it is,) I leave it to be considered, whether it may not help to put an end to that long agitated, and, I think, unreasonable, because unintelligible question, viz. *Whether man's will be free or no?* For if I mistake not, it follows from what I have said, that the question itself is altogether improper; and it is as insignificant to ask whether man's *will* be free, as to ask whether his sleep be swift, or his virtue square: liberty being as little applicable to the will, as swiftness of motion is to sleep, or squareness to virtue. Every one would laugh at the absurdity of such a question as either of these: because it is obvious that the modifications of motion belong not to sleep, nor the difference of figure to virtue; and when any one well considers it, I think he will as plainly perceive that liberty, which is but a power, belongs only to *agents,* and cannot be an attribute or modification of the will, which is also but a power.

15. *Volition.* —Such is the difficulty of explaining and giving clear notions of internal actions by sounds, that I must here warn my reader, that *ordering, directing, choosing, preferring,* &c., which I have made use of, will not distinctly enough express volition, unless he will reflect on what he himself does when he wills. For example, preferring, which seems perhaps best to express the act of volition, does it not precisely. For though a man would prefer flying to walking, yet who can say he ever wills it? Volition, it is plain, is an act of the mind knowingly exerting that dominion it takes itself to have over any part of the man, by employing it in, or withholding it from, any particular action. And what is the will, but the faculty to do this? And is that faculty anything more in effect than a power; the power of the mind to determine its thought, to the producing, continuing, or stopping any action, as far as it depends on us? For can it be denied that whatever agent has a power to think on its own actions, and to prefer their doing or omission either to other, has that faculty called will? *Will,* then, is nothing but such a power. *Liberty,* on the other side, is the

power a *man* has to do or forbear doing any particular action according as its doing or forbearance has the actual preference in the mind; which is the same thing as to say, according as he himself wills it.

16. *Powers belonging to Agents.* — It is plain then that the will is nothing but one power or ability, and *freedom* another power or ability so that, to ask, whether the will has freedom, is to ask whether one power has another power, one ability another ability; a question at first sight too grossly absurd to make a dispute, or need an answer. For, who is it that sees not that powers belong only to agents, and are attributes only of substances, and not of powers themselves? So that this way of putting the question (viz. whether the will be free) is in effect to ask, whether the will be a substance, an agent, or at least to suppose it, since freedom can properly be attributed to nothing else. If freedom can with any propriety of speech be applied to power, it may be attributed to the power that is in a man to produce, or forbear producing, motion in parts of his body, by choice or preference; which is that which denominates him free, and is freedom itself. But if any one should ask, whether freedom were free, he would be suspected not to understand well what he said; and he would be thought to deserve Midas's ears,[3] who, knowing that rich was a denomination for the possession of riches, should demand whether riches themselves were rich.

21. *But to the Agent or Man.* — To return, then, to the inquiry about liberty, I think the question is not proper, *whether the will be free,* but *whether a man be free.* Thus, I think.

First, That so far as any one can, by the direction or choice of his mind, preferring the existence of any action to the non-existence of that action, and *vice versa,* make *it* to exist or not exist, so far *he* is free. For if I can, by a thought directing the motion of my finger, make it move when it was at rest, or *vice versa,* it is evident, that in respect of that I am free: and if I can, by a like thought of my mind, preferring one to the other, produce either words or silence, I am at liberty to speak or hold my peace: and as far as this power reaches, of acting or not acting, by the determination of his own thought preferring either, so far is a man free. For how can we think any one freer, than to have the power to do what he will? And so far as any one can, by preferring any action to its not being, or rest to any action, produce that action or rest, so far can he do what he will. For such a preferring of action to its absence, is the willing of it: and we can scarce tell how to imagine any being freer, than *to be able to do what he wills.* So that in respect of actions within the reach of such a power in him, a man seems as free as it is possible for freedom to make him.

22. *In respect of willing, a Man is not free.* — But the inquisitive mind of man, willing to shift off from himself, as far as he can, all thoughts of guilt, though it be by putting himself into a worse state than that of fatal necessity, is not content with this: freedom, unless it reaches further than this, will not serve the turn: and it passes for a good plea, that a man is not free at all, if he be not as *free to will* as he is to *act what he wills.* Concerning a man's liberty, there yet, therefore, is raised this further question, *Whether a man be free to will?* which I think is what is meant, when it is disputed whether the will be free. And as to that I imagine.

23. *How a man cannot be free to will.* — Secondly, That willing, or volition, being an action, and freedom consisting in a power of acting or not acting, a man in respect

3. [According to Greek mythology, King Midas argued that Apollo, the god of music, had lost a musical contest, and Apollo then punished Midas by turning his ears into those of an ass.]

of willing or the act of volition, when any action in his power is once proposed to his thoughts, as presently to be done, cannot be free. The reason whereof is very manifest. For, it being unavoidable that the action depending on his will should exist or not exist, and its existence or not existence following perfectly the determination and preference of his will, he cannot avoid willing the existence or non-existence of that action; it is absolutely necessary that he will the one or the other; i.e. prefer the one to the other: since one of them must necessarily follow; and that which does follow follows by the choice and determination of his mind; that is, by his willing it: for if he did not will it, it would not be. So that, in respect of the act of willing, a man in such a case is not free: liberty consisting in a power to act or not to act; which, in regard of volition, a man, upon such a proposal, has not. For it is unavoidably necessary to prefer the doing or forbearance of an action in a man's power, which is once so proposed to his thoughts; a man must necessarily will the one or the other of them; upon which preference or volition, the action or its forbearance certainly follows, and is truly voluntary. But the act of volition, or preferring one of the two, being that which he cannot avoid, a man, in respect of that act of willing, is under a necessity, and so cannot be free; unless necessity and freedom can consist together, and a man can be free and bound at once. Besides to make a man free after this manner, by making the action of willing to depend on his will, there must be another antecedent will, to determine the acts of this will, and another to determine that, and so *in infinitum:* for wherever one stops, the actions of the last will cannot be free. Nor is any being, as far I can comprehend beings above me, capable of such a freedom of will, that it can forbear to will, i.e. to prefer the being or not being of anything in its power, which it has once considered as such.

24. *Liberty is freedom to execute what is willed.* —This, then, is evident, That *a man is not at liberty to will, or not to will, anything in his power that he once considers of:* liberty consisting in a power to act or to forbear acting, and in that only. For a man that sits still is said yet to be at liberty; because he can walk if he wills it. A man that walks is at liberty also, not because he walks or moves; but because he can stand still if he wills it. *But if a man sitting still has not a power to remove himself, he is not at liberty;* so likewise a man falling down a precipice, though in motion, is not at liberty, because he cannot stop that motion if he would. This being so, it is plain that a man that is walking, to whom it is proposed to give off walking, is not at liberty, whether he will determine himself to walk, or give off walking or not: he must necessarily prefer one or the other of them; walking or not walking. And so it is in regard of all other actions in our power so proposed, which are the far greater number. For, considering the vast number of voluntary actions that succeed one another every moment that we are awake in the course of our lives, there are but few of them that are thought on or proposed to the will, till the time they are to be done; and in all such actions, as I have shown, the mind, in respect of willing, has not a power to act or not to act, wherein consists liberty. The mind, in that case, has not a power to forbear *willing;* it cannot avoid some determination concerning them, let the consideration be as short, the thought as quick as it will, it either leaves the man in the state he was before thinking, or changes it; continues the action, or puts an end to it. Whereby it is manifest, that *it* orders and directs one, in preference to, or with neglect of the other, and thereby either the continuation or change becomes *unavoidably* voluntary.

25. *The Will determined by something without it.* —Since then it is plain that, in

most cases, a man is not at liberty, whether he will or no, (for, when an action in his power is proposed to his thoughts, he *cannot* forbear volition; he *must* determine one way or the other;) the next thing demanded is, — *Whether a man be at liberty to will which of the two he pleases, motion or rest?* This question carries the absurdity of it so manifestly in itself, that one might thereby sufficiently be convinced that liberty concerns not the will. For, to ask whether a man be at liberty to will either motion or rest, speaking or silence, which he pleases, is to ask whether a man can will what he wills, or be pleased with what he is pleased with? A question which, I think, needs no answer: and they who can make a question of it must suppose one will to determine the acts of another, and another to determine that, and so on *in infinitum.*

26. *The ideas of* liberty *and* volition *must be defined.* — To avoid these and the like absurdities, nothing can be of greater use than to establish in our minds determined ideas of the things under consideration. If the ideas of liberty and volition were well fixed in our understandings, and carried along with us in our minds, as they ought, through all the questions that are raised about them, I suppose a great part of the difficulties that perplex men's thoughts, and entangle their understandings, would be much easier resolved; and we should perceive where the confused signification of terms, or where the nature of the thing caused the obscurity.

27. *Freedom.* — First, then, it is carefully to be remembered, That freedom consists in the dependence of the existence, or not existence of any *action,* upon our *volition* of it; and not in the dependence of any action, or its contrary, on our *preference.* A man standing on a cliff, is at liberty to leap twenty yards downwards into the sea, not because he has a power to do the contrary action, which is to leap twenty yards upwards, for that he cannot do; but he is therefore free, because he has a power to leap or not to leap. But if a greater force than his, either holds him fast, or tumbles him down, he is no longer free in that case; because the doing or forbearance of that particular action is no longer in his power. He that is a close prisoner in a room twenty feet square, being at the north side of his chamber, is at liberty to walk twenty feet southward, because he can walk or not walk it; but is not, at the same time, at liberty to do the contrary, i.e. to walk twenty feet northward.

In this, then, consists freedom, *viz. in our being able to act or not to act, according as we shall choose or will.*

28. *What Volition and action mean.* — Secondly, we must remember, that *volition* or *willing* is an act of the mind directing its thought to the production of any action, and thereby exerting its power to produce it. To avoid multiplying of words, I would crave leave here, under the word *action,* to comprehend the forbearance too of any action proposed: sitting still, or holding one's peace, when walking or speaking are proposed, though mere forbearances, requiring as much the determination of the will, and being as often weighty in their consequences, as the contrary actions, may, on that consideration, well enough pass for actions too: but this I say, that I may not be mistaken, if (for brevity's sake) I speak thus.

29. *What determines the Will.* — Thirdly, the will being nothing but a power in the mind to direct the operative faculties of a man to motion or rest, as far as they depend on such direction; to the question, What is it determines the will? the true and proper answer is, The mind. For that which determines the general power of directing, to this or that particular direction, is nothing but the agent itself exercising the power it has that particular way. If this answer satisfies not, it is plain the meaning of the question, What determines the will? is this, — What moves the mind, in every par-

ticular instance, to determine its general power of directing, to this or that particular motion or rest? And to this I answer, — *The motive for continuing in the same state or action, is only the present satisfaction in it; the motive to change is always some uneasiness:* nothing setting us upon the change of state, or upon any new action, but some uneasiness. This is the great motive that works on the mind to put it upon action, which for shortness' sake we will call determining of the will, which I shall more at large explain.

48. *The Power to suspend the Prosecution of any Desire makes way for Consideration.* — There being in us a great many uneasinesses, always soliciting and ready to determine the will, it is natural, as I have said, that the greatest and most pressing should determine the will to the next action; and so it does for the most part, but not always. For, the mind having in most cases, as is evident in experience, a power to *suspend* the execution and satisfaction of any of its desires; and so all, one after another; is at liberty to consider the objects of them, examine them on all sides, and weigh them with others. In this lies the liberty man has; and from the not using of it right comes all that variety of mistakes, errors, and faults which we run into in the conduct of our lives, and our endeavours after happiness; whilst we precipitate the determination of our wills, and engage too soon, before due examination. To prevent this, we have a power to suspend the prosecution of this or that desire; as every one daily may experiment in himself. This seems to me the source of all liberty; in this seems to consist that which is (as I think improperly) called *free-will.* For, during this suspension of any desire, before the will be determined to action, and the action (which follows that determination) done, we have opportunity to examine, view, and judge of the good or evil of what we are going to do; and when, upon due examination, we have judged, we have done our duty, all that we can, or ought to do, in pursuit of our happiness; and it is not a fault, but a perfection of our nature, to desire, will, and act according to the last result of a fair examination.

73. *Recapitulation—Liberty of indifferency* — To conclude this inquiry into *human liberty,* which, as it stood before, I myself from the beginning fearing, and a very judicious friend of mine, since the publication, suspecting to have some mistake in it, though he could not particularly show it me, I was put upon a stricter review of this chapter. Wherein lighting upon a very easy and scarce observable slip I had made, in putting one seemingly indifferent word for another that discovery opened to me this present view, which here, in this second edition, I submit to the learned world, and which, in short, is this: *Liberty* is a power to act or not to act, according as the mind directs. A power to direct the operative faculties to motion or rest in particular instances is that which we call the *will.* That which in the train of our voluntary actions determines the will to any change of operation is *some present uneasiness,* which is, or at least is always accompanied with that of *desire.* Desire is always moved by evil, to fly it: because a total freedom from pain always makes a necessary part of our happiness: but every good, nay, every greater good, does not constantly move desire, because it may not make, or may not be taken to make, any necessary part of our happiness. For all that we desire, is only to be happy. But, though this general desire of happiness operates constantly and invariably, yet the satisfaction of any particular desire *can be suspended* from determining the will to any subservient action, till we have maturely examined whether the particular apparent good which we then desire makes a part of our real happiness, or be consistent or inconsistent with it. The result of our judgment upon that examination is what ultimately determines the man; who could not be *free* if his will were determined by anything but his own desire, guided by his own judgment. I know that liberty, by

some, is placed in an indifferency of the man; antecedent to the determination of his will. I wish they who lay so much stress on such an antecedent indifferency, as they call it, had told us plainly, whether this supposed indifferency be antecedent to the thought and judgment of the understanding, as well as to the decree of the will. For it is pretty hard to state it between them, i.e. immediately *after* the judgment of the understanding, and *before* the determination of the will: because the determination of the will immediately follows the judgment of the understanding: and to place liberty in an indifferency, antecedent to the thought and judgment of the understanding, seems to me to place liberty in a state of darkness, wherein we can neither see nor say anything of it; at least it places it in a subject incapable of it, no agent being allowed capable of liberty, but in consequence of thought and judgment. I am not nice about phrases, and therefore consent to say with those that love to speak so, that liberty is placed in indifferency; but it is an indifferency which remains after the judgment of the understanding, yea, even after the determination of the will: and that is an indifferency not of the *man*, (for after he has once judged which is best, viz. to do or forbear, he is no longer indifferent,) but an indifferency of *the operative powers of the man*, which remaining equally able to operate or to forbear operating after as before the decree of the will, are in a state, which, if one pleases, may be called indifferency; and as far as this indifferency reaches, a man is free, and no further: v.g. I have the ability to move my hand, or to let it rest; that operative power is indifferent to move or not to move my hand. I am then, in that respect perfectly free; my will determines that operative power to rest: I am yet free, because the indifferency of that my operative power to act, or not to act, still remains; the power of moving my hand is not at all impaired by the determination of my will, which at present orders rest; the indifferency of that power to act, or not to act, is just as it was before, as will appear, if the will puts it to the trial, by ordering the contrary. But if, during the rest of my hand, it be seized with a sudden palsy, the indifferency of that operative power is gone, and with it my liberty; I have no longer freedom in that respect, but am under a necessity of letting my hand rest. On the other side, if my hand be put into motion by a convulsion, the indifferency of that operative faculty is taken away by that motion; and my liberty in that case is lost, for I am under a necessity of having my hand move. I have added this, to show in what sort of indifferency liberty seems to me to consist, and not in any other, real or imaginary.

74. *Active and passive power, in motions and in thinking.*—Before I close this chapter, it may perhaps be to our purpose, and help to give us clearer conceptions about *power*, if we make our thoughts take a little more exact survey of *action*. I have said above, that we have ideas but of two sorts of action, viz. motion and thinking. These, in truth, though called and counted actions, yet, if nearly considered, will not be found to be always perfectly so. For, if I mistake not, there are instances of both kinds, which, upon due consideration, will be found rather passions than actions; and consequently so far the effects barely of *passive powers* in those subjects, which yet on their accounts are thought agents. For, in these instances, the substance that hath motion or thought receives the impression, whereby it is put into that action, purely from without, and so acts merely by the capacity it has to receive such an impression from some external agent; and such a power is not properly an active power, but a mere passive capacity in the subject. Sometimes the substance or agent puts itself into action by its own power, and this is properly *active power*. Whatsoever modification a substance has, whereby it produces any effect, that is

called action: v.g. a solid substance, by motion, operates on or alters the sensible ideas of another substance, and therefore this modification of motion we call action. But yet this motion in that solid substance is, when rightly considered, but a passion, if it received it only from some external agent. So that the active power of motion is in no substance which cannot begin motion in itself or in another substance when at rest. So likewise in thinking, a power to receive ideas or thoughts from the operation of any external substance is called a power of thinking: but this is but a passive power, or capacity. But to be able to bring into view ideas out of sight at one's own choice, and to compare which of them one thinks fit, this is an active power. This reflection may be of some use to preserve us from mistakes about powers and actions, which grammar, and the common frame of languages, may be apt to lead us into. Since what is signified by verbs that grammarians call active, does not always signify action: v.g. this proposition: I *see* the moon, or a star, or I *feel* the heat of the sun, though expressed by a verb active, does not signify any action in me, whereby I operate on those substances, but only the reception of the ideas of light, roundness, and heat; wherein I am not active, but barely passive, and cannot, in that position of my eyes or body, avoid receiving them. But when I turn my eyes another way, or remove my body out of the sunbeams, I am properly active; because of my own choice, by a power within myself, I put myself into that motion. Such an action is the product of active power.

Chapter XXIII

OF OUR COMPLEX IDEAS OF SUBSTANCES

1. *Ideas of particular Substances, how made.* —The mind being, as I have declared, furnished with a great number of the simple ideas, conveyed in by the senses as they are found in exterior things, or by reflection on its own operations, takes notice also that a certain number of these simple ideas go constantly together; which being presumed to belong to one thing, and words being suited to common apprehensions, and made use of for quick dispatch, are called, so united in one subject, by one name; which, by inadvertency, we are apt afterward to talk of and consider as one simple idea, which indeed is a complication of many ideas together: because, as I have said, not imagining how these simple ideas *can* subsist by themselves, we accustom ourselves to suppose some *substratum* wherein they do subsist, and from which they do result, which therefore we call *substance.*

2. *Our obscure Idea of Substance in general.* —So that if any one will examine himself concerning his notion of pure substance in general, he will find he has no other idea of it at all, but only a supposition of he knows not what *support* of such qualities which are capable of producing simple ideas in us; which qualities are commonly called accidents. If any one should be asked, what is the subject wherein colour or weight inheres, he would have nothing to say, but the solid extended parts; and if he were demanded, what is it that solidity and extension adhere in, he would not be

in a much better case than the Indian before mentioned who, saying that the world was supported by a great elephant, was asked what the elephant rested on; to which his answer was—a great tortoise: but being again pressed to know what gave support to the broad-backed tortoise, replied—*something, he knew not what.* And thus here, as in all other cases where we use words without having clear and distinct ideas, we talk like children: who, being questioned what such a thing is, which they know not, readily give this satisfactory answer, that it is *something:* which in truth signifies no more, when so used, either by children or men, but that they know not what; and that the thing they pretend to know, and talk of, is what they have no distinct idea of at all, and so are perfectly ignorant of it, and in the dark. The idea then we have, to which we give the *general* name substance, being nothing but the supposed, but unknown, support of those qualities we find existing, which we imagine cannot subsist *sine re substante,* without something to support them, we call that support *substantia;* which, according to the true import of the word, is, in plain English, standing under or upholding.

3. *Of the Sorts of Substances.* —An obscure and relative idea of *substance in general* being thus made we come to have the ideas of *particular sorts of substances,* by collecting *such* combinations of simple ideas as are, by experience and observation of men's senses, taken notice of to exist together; and are therefore supposed to flow from the particular internal constitution, or unknown essence of that substance. Thus we come to have the ideas of a man, horse, gold, water, &c.; of which substances, whether any one has any other *clear* idea, further than of certain simple ideas coexistent together, I appeal to every one's own experience. It is the ordinary qualities observable in iron, or a diamond, put together, that make the true complex idea of those substances, which a smith or a jeweller commonly knows better than a philosopher; who, whatever *substantial forms* he may talk of, has no other idea of those substances, than what is framed by a collection of those simple ideas which are to be found in them: only we must take notice, that our complex ideas of substances, besides all those simple ideas they are made up of, have always the confused idea of something to which they belong, and in which they subsist: and therefore when we speak of any sort of substance, we say it is a thing having such or such qualities; as body is a thing that is extended, figured, and capable of motion; spirit, a thing capable of thinking; and so hardness, friability, and power to draw iron, we say, are qualities to be found in a loadstone. These, and the like fashions of speaking, intimate that the substance is supposed always *something besides* the extension, figure, solidity, motion, thinking, or other observable ideas, though we know not what it is.

4. *No clear or distinct idea of Substance in general.* —Hence, when we talk or think of any particular sort of corporeal substances, as horse, stone, &c., though the idea we have of either of them be but the complication or collection of those several simple ideas of sensible qualities, which we used to find united in the thing called horse or stone; yet, *because we cannot conceive how they should subsist alone, nor one in another,* we suppose them existing in and supported by some common subject; which support we denote by the name substance, though it be certain we have no clear or distinct idea of that thing we suppose a support.

5. *As clear an Idea of spiritual substance as of corporeal substance.* —The same thing happens concerning the operations of the mind, viz. thinking, reasoning, fearing, &c., which we concluding not to subsist of themselves, nor apprehending how they can belong to body, or be produced by it, we are apt to think these the actions of

some other *substance,* which we call *spirit;* whereby yet it is evident that, having no other idea or notion of matter, but something wherein those many sensible qualities which affect our senses do subsist; by supposing a substance wherein thinking, knowing, doubting, and a power of moving, &c., do subsist, we have as clear a notion of the substance of spirit, as we have of body; the one being supposed to be (without knowing what it is) the *substratum* to those simple ideas we have from without; and the other supposed (with a like ignorance of what it is) to be the *substratum* to those operations we experiment in ourselves within. It is plain then, that the idea of *corporeal substance* in matter is as remote from our conceptions and apprehensions, as that of *spiritual substance,* or spirit: and therefore, from our not having any notion of the substance of spirit, we can no more conclude its non-existence, than we can, for the same reason, deny the existence of body; it being as rational to affirm there is no body, because we have no clear and distinct idea of the substance of matter, as to say there is no spirit, because we have no clear and distinct idea of the substance of a spirit.

6. *Our ideas of particular Sorts of Substances.* —Whatever therefore be the secret abstract nature of substance in general, all the ideas we have of particular distinct sorts of substances are nothing but several combinations of simple ideas, co-existing in such, though unknown, cause of their union, as makes the whole subsist of itself. It is by such combinations of simple ideas, and nothing else, that we represent particular sorts of substances to ourselves; such are the ideas we have of their several species in our minds; and such only do we, by their specific names, signify to others, v.g. man, horse, sun, water, iron: upon hearing which words, every one who understands the language, frames in his mind a combination of those several simple ideas which he has usually observed, or fancied to exist together under that denomination; all which he supposes to rest in and be, as it were, adherent to that unknown common subject, which inheres not in anything else. Though, in the meantime, it be manifest, and every one, upon inquiry into his own thoughts, will find, that he has no other idea of any substance, v.g. let it be gold, horse, iron, man, vitriol, bread, but what he has barely of those sensible qualities, which he supposes to inhere; with a supposition of such a *substratum* as gives, as it were, a support to those qualities or simple ideas, which he has observed to exist united together. Thus, the idea of the sun,—what is it but an aggregate of those several simple ideas, bright, hot, roundish, having a constant regular motion, at a certain distance from us, and perhaps some other: as he who thinks and discourses of the sun has been more or less accurate in observing those sensible qualities, ideas, or properties, which are in that thing which he calls the sun.

9. *Three sorts of Ideas make our complex ones of Corporeal Substances.* —The ideas that make our complex ones of corporeal substances, are of these three sorts. First, the ideas of the primary qualities of things, which are discovered by our senses, and are in them even when we perceive them not; such are the bulk, figure, number, situation, and motion of the parts of bodies; which are really in them, whether we take notice of them or not. Secondly, the sensible secondary qualities, which, depending on these, are nothing but the powers those substances have to produce several ideas in us by our senses; which ideas are not in the things themselves, otherwise than as anything is in its cause. Thirdly, the aptness we consider in any substance, to give or receive such alterations of primary qualities, as that the substance so altered should produce in us different ideas from what it did before; these are called active and

passive powers: all which powers, as far as we have any notice or notion of them, terminate only in sensible simple ideas. For whatever alteration a loadstone has the power to make in the minute particles of iron, we should have no notion of any power it had at all to operate on iron, did not its sensible motion discover it: and I doubt not, but there are a thousand changes, that bodies we daily handle have a power to cause in one another, which we never suspect, because they never appear in sensible effects.

10. *Powers thus make a great Part of our complex Ideas of particular Substances.* — *Powers* therefore justly make a great part of our complex ideas of substances. He that will examine his complex idea of gold, will find several of its ideas that make it up to be only powers; as the power of being melted, but of not spending itself in the fire; of being dissolved in *aqua regia*, are ideas as necessary to make up our complex idea of gold, as its colour and weight: which, if duly considered, are also nothing but different powers. For, to speak truly, yellowness is not actually in gold, but is a power in gold to produce that idea in us by our eyes, when placed in a due light: and the heat, which we cannot leave out of our ideas of the sun, is no more really in the sun, than the white colour it introduces into wax. These are both equally powers in the sun, operating, by the motion and figure of its sensible parts, so on a man, as to make him have the idea of heat; and so on wax, as to make it capable to produce in a man the idea of white.

11. *The now secondary Qualities of Bodies would disappear, if we could discover the primary ones of their minute Parts.* — Had we senses acute enough to discern the minute particles of bodies, and the real constitution on which their sensible qualities depend, I doubt not but they would produce quite different ideas in us: and that which is now the yellow colour of gold, would then disappear, and instead of it we should see an admirable texture of parts, of a certain size and figure. This microscopes plainly discover to us; for what to our naked eyes produces a certain colour, is, by thus augmenting the acuteness of our senses, discovered to be quite a different thing; and the thus altering, as it were, the proportion of the bulk of the minute parts of a coloured object to our usual sight, produces different ideas from what it did before. Thus, sand or pounded glass, which is opaque, and white to the naked eye, is pellucid in a microscope; and a hair seen in this way, loses its former colour, and is, in a great measure, pellucid, with a mixture of some bright sparkling colours, such as appear from the refraction of diamonds, and other pellucid bodies. Blood, to the naked eye, appears all red; but by a good microscope, wherein its lesser parts appear, shows only some few globules of red, swimming in a pellucid liquor, and how these red globules would appear, if glasses could be found that could yet magnify them a thousand or ten thousand times more, is uncertain.

14. *Our specific Ideas of Substances.* — But to return to the matter in hand, — the ideas we have of substances, and the ways we come by them. I say, our *specific* ideas of substances are nothing else but *a collection of a certain number of simple ideas, considered as united in one thing*. These ideas of substances, though they are commonly simple apprehensions, and the names of them simple terms, yet in effect are complex and compounded. Thus the idea which an Englishman signifies by the name swan, is white colour, long neck, red beak, black legs, and whole feet, and all these of a certain size, with a power of swimming in the water, and making a certain kind of noise, and perhaps, to a man who has long observed this kind of birds, some other properties: which all terminate in sensible simple ideas, all united in one common

subject.

15. *Our Ideas of spiritual Substances, as clear as of bodily Substances.* —Besides the complex ideas we have of material sensible substances, of which I have last spoken, —by the simple ideas we have taken from those operations of our own minds, which we experiment daily in ourselves, as thinking, understanding, willing, knowing, and power of beginning motion, &c., co-existing in some substance, we are able to frame the *complex idea of an immaterial spirit.* And thus, by putting together the ideas of thinking, perceiving, liberty, and power of moving themselves and other things, we have as clear a perception and notion of immaterial substances as we have of material. For putting together the ideas of thinking and willing, or the power of moving or quieting corporeal motion, joined to substance, of which we have no distinct idea, we have the idea of an immaterial spirit; and by putting together the ideas of coherent solid parts, and a power of being moved, joined with substance, of which likewise we have no positive idea, we have the idea of matter. The one is as clear and distinct an idea as the other: the idea of thinking, and moving a body, being as clear and distinct ideas as the ideas of extension, solidity, and being moved. For our idea of substance is equally obscure, or none at all, in both: it is but a supposed I know not what, to support those ideas we call accidents. It is for want of reflection that we are apt to think that our senses show us nothing but material things. Every act of sensation, when duly considered, gives us an equal view of both parts of nature, the corporeal and spiritual. For whilst I know, by seeing or hearing, &c., that there is some corporeal being without me, the object of that sensation, I do more certainly know, that there is some spiritual being within me that sees and hears. This, I must be convinced, cannot be the action of bare insensible matter; nor ever could be, without an immaterial thinking being.

16. *No Idea of abstract Substance either in Body or Spirit.* —By the complex idea of extended, figured, coloured, and all other sensible qualities, which is all that we know of it, we are as far from the idea of the substance of body, as if we knew nothing at all: nor after all the acquaintance and familiarity which we imagine we have with matter, and the many qualities men assure themselves they perceive and know in bodies, will it perhaps upon examination be found, that they have any more or clearer primary ideas belonging to body, than they have belonging to immaterial spirit.

17. *Cohesion of solid parts and Impulse, the primary ideas peculiar to Body.* —The primary ideas we have *peculiar to body,* as contradistinguished to spirit, are the *cohesion of solid, and consequently separable, parts,* and a *power of communicating motion by impulse.* These, I think, are the original ideas proper and peculiar to body; for figure is but the consequence of finite extension.

18. *Thinking and Motivity.* —The ideas we have belonging and *peculiar to spirit,* are *thinking,* and *will,* or *a power of putting body into motion by thought, and, which is consequent to it, liberty.* For, as body cannot but communicate its motion by impulse to another body, which it meets with at rest, so the mind can put bodies into motion, or forbear to do so, as it pleases. The ideas of *existence, duration,* and *mobility,* are common to them both.

37. *Recapitulation.* —And thus we have seen what kind of ideas we have of *substances of all kinds,* wherein they consist, and how we came by them. From whence, I think, it is very evident,

First, That all our ideas of the several *sorts* of substances are nothing but collections of simple ideas: with a supposition of *something* to which they belong, and in which they subsist: though of this supposed something we have no clear distinct idea at all.

Secondly, That all the simple ideas, that thus united in one common *substratum*, make up our complex ideas of several *sorts* of substances, are no other but such as we have received from sensation or reflection. So that even in those which we think we are most intimately acquainted with, and that come nearest the comprehension of our most enlarged conceptions, we cannot go beyond those simple ideas. And even in those which seem most remote from all we have to do with, and do infinitely surpass anything we can perceive in ourselves by reflection; or discover by sensation in other things, we can attain to nothing but those simple ideas, which we originally received from sensation or reflection; as is evident in the complex ideas we have of angels, and particularly of God himself.

Thirdly, That most of the simple ideas that make up our complex ideas of substances, when truly considered, are only *powers*, however we are apt to take them for positive qualities; v.g. the greatest part of the ideas that make our complex idea of *gold* are yellowness, great weight, ductility, fusibility, and solubility in *aqua regia*, &c., all united together in an unknown *substratum:* all which ideas are nothing else but so many relations to other substances; and are not really in the gold, considered barely in itself, though they depend on those real and primary qualities of its internal constitution, whereby it has a fitness differently to operate, and be operated on by several other substances.

Chapter XXVII

OF IDENTITY AND DIVERSITY

1. *Wherein Identity consists.* —Another occasion the mind often takes of comparing, is the very being of things, when, considering *anything as existing at any determined time and place,* we compare it with *itself existing at another time,* and thereon form the ideas of *identity* and *diversity.* When we see anything to be in any place in any instant of time, we are sure (be it what it will) that it is that very thing, and not another which at that same time exists in another place, how like and undistinguishable soever it may be in all other respects: and in this consists *identity,* when the ideas it is attributed to vary not at all from what they were that moment wherein we consider their former existence, and to which we compare the present. For we never finding, nor conceiving it possible, that two things of the same kind should exist in the same place at the same time, we rightly conclude, that, whatever exists anywhere at any time, excludes all of the same kind, and is there itself alone. When therefore we demand whether anything be the *same* or no, it refers always to something that existed such a time in such a place, which it was certain, at that instant, was the same with itself, and no other. From whence it follows, that one thing cannot have two beginnings of existence, nor two things one beginning; it being impossible for two things of the same kind to be or exist in the same instant, in the very same place; or one and the same thing in different places. That, therefore, that

had one beginning, is the same thing; and that which had a different beginning in time and place from that, is not the same, but diverse. That which has made the difficulty about this relation has been the little care and attention used in having precise notions of the things to which it is attributed.

2. *Identity of Substances and of Modes.* —We have the ideas but of three sorts of substances: 1. *God.* 2. *Finite intelligences.* 3. *Bodies.*

First, *God* is without beginning, eternal, unalterable, and everywhere, and therefore concerning his identity there can be no doubt.

Secondly, *Finite spirits* having had each its determinate time and place of beginning to exist, the relation to that time and place will always determine to each of them its identity, as long as it exists.

Thirdly, The same will hold of every *particle of matter,* to which no addition or substraction of matter being made, it is the same. For, though these three sorts of substances, as we term them, do not exclude one another out of the same place, yet we cannot conceive but that they must necessarily each of them exclude any of the same kind out of the same place: or else the notions and names of identity and diversity would be in vain, and there could be no such distinctions of substances, or anything else one from another. For example: could two bodies be in the same place at the same time; then those two parcels of matter must be one and the same, take them great or little; nay, all bodies must be one and the same. For, by the same reason that two particles of matter may be in one place, all bodies may be in one place: which, when it can be supposed, takes away the distinction of identity and diversity of one and more, and renders it ridiculous. But it being a contradiction that two or more should be one, identity and diversity are relations and ways of comparing well founded, and of use to the understanding. All other things being but modes or relations ultimately terminated in substances, the identity and diversity of each particular existence of them too will be by the same way determined: only as to things whose existence is in succession, such as are the actions of finite beings, v.g. *motion* and *thought,* both which consist in a continued train of succession, concerning *their* diversity there can be no question: because each perishing the moment it begins, they cannot exist in different times, or in different places, as permanent beings can at different times exist in distant places; and therefore no motion or thought, considered as at different times, can be the same, each part thereof having a different beginning of existence.

3. *Principium Individuationis.* —From what has been said, it is easy to discover what is so much inquired after, the *principium individuationis;* and that, it is plain, is existence itself; which determines a being of any sort to a particular time and place, incommunicable to two beings of the same kind. This, though it seems easier to conceive in simple substances or modes; yet, when reflected on, is not more difficult in compound ones, if care be taken to what it is applied: v.g. let us suppose an atom, i.e. a continued body under one immutable superficies, existing in a determined time and place; it is evident, that, considered in any instant of its existence, it is in that instant the same with itself. For, being at that instant what it is, and nothing else, it is the same, and so must continue as long as its existence is continued; for so long it will be the same, and no other. In like manner, if two or more atoms be joined together into the same mass, every one of those atoms will be the same, by the foregoing rule: and whilst they exist united together, the mass, consisting of the same atoms, must be the same mass, or the same body, let the parts be ever so

differently jumbled. But if one of these atoms be taken away, or one new one added, it is no longer the same mass or the same body. In the state of living creatures, their identity depends not on a mass of the same particles, but on something else. For in them the variation of great parcels of matter alters not the identity: an oak growing from a plant to a great tree, and then lopped, is still the same oak; and a colt grown up to a horse, sometimes fat, sometimes lean, is all the while the same horse: though, in both these cases, there may be a manifest change of the parts; so that truly they are not either of them the same masses of matter, though they be truly one of them the same oak, and the other the same horse. The reason whereof is, that, in these two cases—a *mass of matter* and a *living body*—identity is not applied to the same thing.

4. *Identity of Vegetables.* — We must therefore consider wherein an oak differs from a mass of matter, and that seems to me to be in this, that the one is only the cohesion of particles of matter any how united, the other such a disposition of them as constitutes the parts of an oak; and such an organization of those parts as is fit to receive and distribute nourishment, so as to continue and frame the wood, bark, and leaves, &c., of an oak, in which consists the vegetable life. That being then one plant which has such an organization of parts in one coherent body, partaking of one common life, it continues to be the same plant as long as it partakes of the same life, though that life be communicated to new particles of matter vitally united to the living plant, in a like continued organization conformable to that sort of plants. For this organization, being at any one instant in any one collection of matter, is in that particular concrete distinguished from all other, and *is* that individual life, which existing constantly from that moment both forwards and backwards, in the same continuity of insensibly succeeding parts united to the living body of the plant, it has that identity which makes the same plant, and all the parts of it, parts of the same plant, during all the time that they exist united in that continued organization, which is fit to convey that common life to all the parts so united.

5. *Identity of Animals.* — The case is not so much different in *brutes* but that any one may hence see what makes an animal and continues it the same. Something we have like this in machines, and may serve to illustrate it. For example, what is a watch? It is plain it is nothing but a fit organization or construction of parts to a certain end, which, when a sufficient force is added to it, it is capable to attain. If we would suppose this machine one continued body, all whose organized parts were repaired, increased, or diminished by a constant addition or separation of insensible parts, with one common life, we should have something very much like the body of an animal; with this difference, That, in an animal the fitness of the organization, and the motion wherein life consists, begin together, the motion coming from within; but in machines the force coming sensibly from without, is often away when the organ is in order, and well fitted to receive it.

6. *The Identity of Man.* — This also shows wherein the identity of the same *man* consists; viz. in nothing but a participation of the same continued life, by constantly fleeting particles of matter, in succession vitally united to the same organized body. He that shall place the identity of man in anything else, but, like that of other animals, in one fitly organized body, taken in any one instant, and from thence continued, under one organization of life, in several successively fleeting particles of matter united to it, will find it hard to make an embryo, one of years, mad and sober, the *same* man, by any supposition, that will not make it possible for Seth, Ismael, Socrates, Pilate, St. Austin, and Caesar Borgia, to be the same man. For if the iden-

tity of *soul alone* makes the same *man;* and there be nothing in the nature of matter why the same individual spirit may not be united to different bodies, it will be possible that those men, living in distant ages, and of different tempers, may have been the same man: which way of speaking must be from a very strange use of the word man, applied to an idea out of which body and shape are excluded. And that way of speaking would agree yet worse with the notions of those philosophers who allow of transmigration, and are of opinion that the souls of men may, for their miscarriages, be detruded into the bodies of beasts, as fit habitations, with organs suited to the satisfaction of their brutal inclinations. But yet I think nobody, could he be sure that the *soul* of Heliogabalus were in one of his hogs, would yet say that hog were a *man* or *Heliogabalus.*

9. *Personal Identity.* —This being premised, to find wherein personal identity consists, we must consider what *person* stands for;—which, I think, is a thinking intelligent being, that has reason and reflection, and can consider itself as itself, the same thinking thing, in different times and places; which it does only by that consciousness which is inseparable from thinking, and, as it seems to me, essential to it: it being impossible for any one to perceive without *perceiving* that he does perceive. When we see, hear, smell, taste, feel, meditate, or will anything, we know that we do so. Thus it is always as to our present sensations and perceptions: and by this every one is to himself that which he calls *self:*—it not being considered, in this case, whether the same self be continued in the same or divers substances. For, since consciousness always accompanies thinking, and it is that which makes every one to be what he calls self, and thereby distinguishes himself from all other thinking things, in this alone consists personal identity, i.e. the sameness of a rational being: and as far as this consciousness can be extended backwards to any past action or thought, so far reaches the identity of that person; it is the same self now it was then; and it is by the same self with this present one that now reflects on it, that that action was done.

10. *Consciousness makes personal Identity.* —But it is further inquired, whether it be the same identical substance. This few would think they had reason to doubt of, if these perceptions, with their consciousness, always remained present in the mind, whereby the same thinking thing would be always consciously present, and, as would be thought, evidently the same to itself. But that which seems to make the difficulty is this, that this consciousness being interrupted always by forgetfulness, there being no moment of our lives wherein we have the whole train of all our past actions before our eyes in one view, but even the best memories losing the sight of one part whilst they are viewing another; and we sometimes, and that the greatest part of our lives, not reflecting on our past selves, being intent on our present thoughts, and in sound sleep having no thoughts at all, or at least none with that consciousness which remarks our waking thoughts, —I say, in all these cases, our consciousness being interrupted, and we losing the sight of our past selves, doubts are raised whether we are the same thinking thing, i.e. the same *substance* or no. Which, however reasonable or unreasonable, concerns not *personal* identity at all. The question being what makes the same person; and not whether it be the same identical substance, which always thinks in the same person, which, in this case, matters not at all: different substances, by the same consciousness (where they do partake in it) being united into one person, as well as different bodies by the same life are united into one animal, whose identity is preserved in that change of sub-

stances by the unity of one continued life. For, it being the same consciousness that makes a man be himself to himself, personal identity depends on that only, whether it be annexed solely to one individual substance, or can be continued in a succession of several substances. For as far as any intelligent being *can* repeat the idea of any past action with the same consciousness it had of it at first, and with the same consciousness it has of any present action; so far it is the same personal self. For it is by the consciousness it has of its present thoughts and actions, that it is *self to itself* now, and so will be the same self, as far as the same consciousness can extend to actions past or to come; and would be by distance of time, or change of substance, no more two persons, than a man be two men by wearing other clothes to-day than he did yesterday, with a long or a short sleep between: the same consciousness uniting those distant actions into the same person, whatever substances contributed to their production.

16. *Consciousness alone unites actions into the same Person.* —But though the same immaterial substance or soul does not alone, wherever it be, and in whatsoever state, make the same *man;* yet it is plain, consciousness, as far as ever it can be extended—should it be to ages past—unites existences and actions very remote in time into the same *person,* as well as it does the existences and actions of the immediately preceding moment: so that whatever has the consciousness of present and past actions, is the same person to whom they both belong. Had I the same consciousness that I saw the ark and Noah's flood, as that I saw an overflowing of the Thames last winter, or as that I write now, I could no more doubt that I who write this now, that saw the Thames overflowed last winter, and that viewed the flood at the general deluge, was the same *self,* —place that self in what *substance* you please—than that I who write this am the same *myself* now whilst I write (whether I consist of all the same substance, material or immaterial, or no) that I was yesterday. For as to this point of being the same self, it matters not whether this present self be made up of the same or other substances—I being as much concerned, and as justly accountable for any action that was done a thousand years since, appropriated to me now by this self-consciousness, as I am for what I did the last moment.

17. *Self depends on Consciousness, not on Substance.* —*Self* is that conscious thinking thing, —whatever substance made up of, (whether spiritual or material, simple or compounded, it matters not)—which is sensible or conscious of pleasure and pain, capable of happiness or misery, and so is concerned for itself, as far as that consciousness extends. Thus every one finds that, whilst comprehended under that consciousness, the little finger is as much a part of himself as what is most so. Upon separation of this little finger, should this consciousness go along with the little finger, and leave the rest of the body, it is evident the little finger would be the person, the same person; and self then would have nothing to do with the rest of the body. As in this case it is the consciousness that goes along with the substance, when one part is separate from another, which makes the same person, and constitutes this inseparable self: so it is in reference to substances remote in time. That with which the consciousness of this present thinking thing *can* join itself, makes the same person, and is one self with it, and with nothing else; and so attributes to itself, and owns all the actions of that thing, as its own, as far as that consciousness reaches, and no further; as every one who reflects will perceive.

18. *Persons, not Substances, the Objects of Reward and Punishment.* —In this personal identity is founded all the right and justice of reward and punishment; happiness and misery being that for which every one is concerned for *himself,* and not

mattering what becomes of any *substance,* not joined to, or affected with that consciousness. For, as it is evident in the instance I gave but now, if the consciousness went along with the little finger when it was cut off, that would be the same self which was concerned for the whole body yesterday, as making part of itself, whose actions then it cannot but admit as its own now. Though, if the same body should still live, and immediately from the separation of the little finger have its own peculiar consciousness, whereof the little finger knew nothing, it would not at all be concerned for it, as a part of itself, or could own any of its actions, or have any of them imputed to him.

20. *Absolute oblivion separates what is thus forgotten from the person, but not from the man.* —But yet possibly it will still be objected, —Suppose I wholly lose the memory of some parts of my life, beyond a possibility of retrieving them, so that perhaps I shall never be conscious of them again; yet am I not the same person that did those actions, had those thoughts that I once was conscious of, though I have now forgot them? To which I answer, that we must here take notice what the word *I* is applied to; which, in this case, is the *man* only. And the same man being presumed to be the same person, I is easily here supposed to stand also for the same person. But if it be possible for the same man to have distinct incommunicable consciousness at different times, it is past doubt the same man would at different times make different persons; which, we see, is the sense of mankind in the solemnest declaration of their opinions, human laws not punishing the mad man for the sober man's actions, nor the sober man for what the mad man did, —thereby making them two persons: which is somewhat explained by our way of speaking in English when we say such an one is 'not himself,' or is 'beside himself'; in which phrases it is insinuated, as if those who now, or at least first used them, thought that self was changed; the self-same person was no longer in that man.

22. But is not a man drunk and sober the same person? why else is he punished for the fact he commits when drunk, though he be never afterwards conscious of it? Just as much the same person as a man that walks, and does other things in his sleep, is the same person, and is answerable for any mischief he shall do in it. Human laws punish both, with a justice suitable to *their* way of knowledge; —because, in these cases, they cannot distinguish certainly what is real, what counterfeit: and so the ignorance in drunkenness or sleep is not admitted as a plea. For, though punishment be annexed to personality, and personality to consciousness, and the drunkard perhaps be not conscious of what he did, yet human judicatures justly punish him; because the fact is proved against him, but want of consciousness cannot be proved for him. But in the Great Day, wherein the secrets of all hearts shall be laid open, it may be reasonable to think, no one shall be made to answer for what he knows nothing of; but shall receive his doom, his conscience accusing or excusing him.

25. *Consciousness unites substances, material or spiritual, with the same personality.* —I agree, that more probable opinion is, that this consciousness is annexed to, and the affection of, one individual immaterial substance.

But let men, according to their diverse hypotheses, resolve of that as they please. This every intelligent being, sensible of happiness or misery, must grant—that there is something that is *himself,* that he is concerned for, and would have happy; that this self has existed in a continued duration more than one instant, and therefore it is possible may exist, as it has done, months and years to come, without any certain bounds to be set to its duration; and may be the same self, by the same consciousness continued on for the future. And thus, by this consciousness he finds himself to be the same self which did such and such an action some years since, by which he comes to be happy or miserable now. In all which account of self, the same numerical *substance* is not considered as making the same self; but the same continued *consciousness,* in which several substances may have been united, and again separated from it, which, whilst they continued in a vital union with that wherein this consciousness then resided, made a part of that same self. Thus any part of our bodies, vitally united to that which is conscious in us, makes a part of ourselves: but upon separation from the vital union by which that consciousness is communicated, that which a moment since was part of ourselves, is now no more so than a part of another man's self is a part of me: and it is not impossible but in a little time may become a real part of another person. And so we have the same numerical substance become a part of two different persons; and the same person preserved under the change of various substances. Could we suppose any spirit wholly stripped of all its memory or consciousness of past actions, as we find our minds always are of a great part of ours, and sometimes of them all; the union or separation of such a spiritual substance would make no variation of personal identity, any more than that of any particle of matter does. Any substance vitally united to the present thinking being is a part of that very same self which now is; anything united to it by a consciousness of former actions, makes also a part of the same self, which is the same both then and now.

BOOK III

OF WORDS

Chapter II

OF THE SIGNIFICATION OF WORDS

1. *Words are sensible Signs, necessary for Communication of Ideas.* —Man, though he have great variety of thoughts, and such from which others as well as himself might receive profit and delight; yet they are all within his own breast, invisible and hidden from others, nor can of themselves be made to appear. The comfort and advantage of society not being to be had without communication of thoughts, it was necessary that man should find out some external sensible signs, whereof those invisible ideas, which his thoughts are made up of, might be made known to others. For this purpose nothing was so fit, either for plenty or quickness, as those articulate sounds, which with so much ease and variety he found himself able to make. Thus we may conceive how *words,* which were by nature so well adapted to that purpose, came to be made use of by men as the signs of their ideas; not by any natural connexion that there is between particular articulate sounds and certain ideas, for then there would be but one language amongst all men; but by a voluntary imposition, whereby such a word is made arbitrarily the mark of such an idea. The use, then, of words, is to be sensible marks of ideas; and the ideas they stand for are their proper and immediate signification.

3. *Examples of this.* —This is so necessary in the use of language, that in this respect the knowing and the ignorant, the learned and the unlearned, use the words they speak (with any meaning) all alike. They, in every man's mouth, stand for the ideas he has, and which he would express by them. A child having taken notice of nothing in the metal he hears called *gold,* but the bright shining yellow colour, he applies the word gold only to his own idea of that colour, and nothing else; and therefore calls the same colour in a peacock's tail gold. Another that hath better observed, adds to shining yellow great weight: and then the sound gold, when he uses it, stands for a complex idea of a shining yellow and a very weighty substance. Another adds to those qualities fusibility: and then the word gold signifies to him a body, bright, yellow, fusible, and very heavy. Another adds malleability. Each of these uses equally the word gold, when they have occasion to express the idea which they have applied it to: but it is evident that each can apply it only to his own idea; nor can he make it stand as a sign of such a complex idea as he has not.

Chapter III

OF GENERAL TERMS

1. *The greatest Part of Words are general terms.* —All things that exist being particulars, it may perhaps be thought reasonable that words, which ought to be conformed to things, should be so too, —I mean in their signification: but yet we find quite the contrary. The far greatest part of words that make all languages are general terms: which has not been the effect of neglect or chance, but of reason and necessity.

2. *That every particular Thing should have a Name for itself is impossible.* —First, It is impossible that every particular thing should have a distinct peculiar name. For, the signification and use of words depending on that connexion which the mind makes between its ideas and the sounds it uses as signs of them, it is necessary, in the application of names to things, that the mind should have distinct ideas of the things, and retain also the particular name that belongs to every one, with its peculiar appropriation to that idea. But it is beyond the power of human capacity to frame and retain distinct ideas of all the particular things we meet with: every bird and beast men saw; every tree and plant that affected the senses, could not find a place in the most capacious understanding. If it be looked on as an instance of a prodigious memory, that some generals have been able to call every soldier in their army by his proper name, we may easily find a reason why men have never attempted to give names to each sheep in their flock, or crow that flies over their heads; much less to call every leaf of plants, or grain of sand that came in their way, by a peculiar name.

3. *And would be useless, if it were possible.* —Secondly, If it were possible, it would yet be useless; because it would not serve to the chief end of language. Men would in vain heap up names of particular things, that would not serve them to communicate their thoughts. Men learn names, and use them in talk with others, only that they may be understood: which is then only done when, by use or consent, the sound I make by the organs of speech, excites in another man's mind who hears it, the idea I apply it to in mine, when I speak it. This cannot be done by names ap-

plied to particular things; whereof I alone having the ideas in my mind, the names of them could not be significant or intelligible to another, who was not acquainted with all those very particular things which had fallen under my notice.

4. *A distinct name for every particular thing, not fitted for enlargement of knowledge.* — Thirdly, But yet, granting this also feasible, (which I think is not,) yet a distinct name for every particular thing would not be of any great use for the improvement of knowledge: which, though founded in particular things, enlarges itself by general views; to which things reduced into sorts, under general names, are properly subservient. These, with the names belonging to them, come within some compass, and do not multiply every moment, beyond what either the mind can contain, or use requires. And therefore, in these, men have for the most part stopped: but yet not so as to hinder themselves from distinguishing particular things by appropriated names, where convenience demands it. And therefore in their own species, which they have most to do with, and wherein they have often occasion to mention particular persons, they make use of proper names; and there distinct individuals have distinct denominations.

5. *What things have proper Names and why.* — Besides persons, countries also, cities, rivers, mountains, and other the like distinctions of place have usually found peculiar names, and that for the same reason; they being such as men have often an occasion to mark particularly, and, as it were, set before others in their discourses with them. And I doubt not but, if we had reason to mention particular horses as often as we have to mention particular men, we should have proper names for the one, as familiar as for the other, and Bucephalus would be a word as much in use as Alexander. And therefore we see that, amongst jockeys, horses have their proper names to be known and distinguished by, as commonly as their servants: because, amongst them, there is often occasion to mention this or that particular horse when he is out of sight.

6. *How general words are made.* — The next thing to be considered is, — How general words come to be made. For, since all things that exist are only particulars, how come we by general terms; or where find we those general natures they are supposed to stand for? Words become general by being made the signs of general ideas: and ideas become general, by separating from them the circumstances of time and place, and any other ideas that may determine them to this or that particular existence. By this way of abstraction they are made capable of representing more individuals than one; each of which having in it a conformity to that abstract idea, is (as we call it) of that sort.

7. *Shown by the way we enlarge our complex ideas from infancy.* — But, to deduce this a little more distinctly, it will not perhaps be amiss to trace our notions and names from their beginning, and observe by what degrees we proceed, and by what steps we enlarge our ideas from our first infancy. There is nothing more evident, than that the ideas of the persons children converse with (to instance in them alone) are like the persons themselves, only particular. The ideas of the nurse and the mother are well framed in their minds; and, like pictures of them there, represent only those individuals. The names they first gave to them are confined to these individuals; and the names of *nurse* and *mamma*, the child uses, determine themselves to those persons. Afterwards, when time and a larger acquaintance have made them observe that there are a great many other things in the world, that in some common agreements of shape, and several other qualities, resemble their father and mother, and those persons they have been

used to, they frame an idea, which they find those many particulars do partake in; and to that they give, with others, the name *man,* for example. And thus they come to have a general name, and a general idea. Wherein they make nothing new; but only leave out of the complex idea they had of Peter and James, Mary and Jane, that which is peculiar to each, and retain only what is common to them all.

8. *And further enlarge our complex ideas, by still leaving out properties contained in them.* —By the same way that they come by the general name and idea of *man,* they easily advance to more general names and notions. For, observing that several things that differ from their idea of man, and cannot therefore be comprehended under that name, have yet certain qualities wherein they agree with man, by retaining only those qualities, and uniting them into one idea, they have again another and more general idea; to which having given a name they make a term of a more comprehensive extension: which new idea is made, not by any new addition, but only as before, by leaving out the shape, and some other properties signified by the name man, and retaining only a body, with life, sense, and spontaneous motion, comprehended under the name animal.

9. *General natures are nothing but abstract and partial ideas of more complex ones.* — That this is the way whereby men first formed general ideas, and general names to them, I think is so evident, that there needs no other proof of it but the considering of a man's self, or others, and the ordinary proceedings of their minds in knowledge. And he that thinks *general natures* or *notions* are anything else but such abstract and partial ideas of more complex ones, taken at first from particular existences, will, I fear, be at a loss where to find them. For let any one effect, and then tell me, wherein does his idea of *man* differ from that of *Peter* and *Paul,* or his idea of *horse* from that of *Bucephalus,* but in the leaving out something that is peculiar to each individual, and retaining so much of those particular complex ideas of several particular existences as they are found to agree in? Of the complex ideas signified by the names *man* and *horse,* leaving out but those particulars wherein they differ, and retaining only those wherein they agree, and of those making a new distinct complex idea, and giving the name *animal* to it, one has a more general term, that comprehends with man several other creatures. Leave out of the idea of *animal,* sense and spontaneous motion, and the remaining complex idea, made up of the remaining simple ones of body, life, and nourishment, becomes a more general one, under the more comprehensive term, *vivens.* And, not to dwell longer upon this particular, so evident in itself; by the same way the mind proceeds to *body, substance,* and at last to *being, thing,* and such universal terms, which stand for any of our ideas whatsoever. To conclude: this whole mystery of genera and species, which make such a noise in the schools, and are with justice so little regarded out of them, is nothing else but *abstract ideas,* more or less comprehensive, with names annexed to them. In all which this is constant and unvariable, that every more general term stands for such an idea, and is but a part of any of those contained under it.

10. *Why the Genus is ordinarily made Use of in Definitions.* —This may show us the reason why, in the defining of words, which is nothing but declaring their signification, we make use of the *genus,* or next general word that comprehends it. Which is not out of necessity, but only to save the labour of enumerating the several simple ideas which the next general word or *genus* stands for; or, perhaps, sometimes the shame of not being able to do it. But though defining by *genus* and *differentia* (I crave leave to use these terms of art, though originally Latin, since they most properly

suit those notions they are applied to), I say, though defining by the *genus* be the shortest way, yet I think it may be doubted whether it be the best. This I am sure, it is not the only, and so not absolutely necessary. For, definition being nothing but making another understand by words what idea the term defined stands for, a defintion is best made by enumerating those simple ideas that are combined in the signification of the term defined: and, if, instead of such an enumeration, men have accustomed themselves to use the next general term, it has not been out of necessity, or for greater clearness, but for quickness and dispatch sake. For I think that, to one who desired to know what idea the word *man* stood for; if it should be said, that man was a solid extended substance, having life, sense, spontaneous motion, and the faculty of reasoning, I doubt not but the meaning of the term man would be as well understood, and the idea it stands for be at least as clearly made known, as when it is defined to be a rational animal: which, by the several definitions of *animal, vivens,* and *corpus,* resolves itself into those enumerated ideas. I have, in explaining the term *man,* followed here the ordinary definition of the schools; which, though perhaps not the most exact, yet serves well enough to my present purpose. And one may, in this instance, see what gave occasion to the rule, that a definition must consist of *genus* and *differentia;* and it suffices to show us the little necessity there is of such a rule, or advantage in the strict observing of it. For, definitions, as has been said, being only the explaining of one word by several others, so that the meaning or idea it stands for may be certainly known; languages are not always so made according to the rules of logic, that every term can have its signification exactly and clearly expressed by two others. Experience sufficiently satisfies us to the contrary; or else those who have made this rule have done ill, that they have given us so few definitions conformable to it. But of definitions more in the next chapter.

11. *General and Universal are Creatures of the Understanding, and belong not to the Real Existence of things.* —To return to general words: it is plain, by what has been said, that *general* and *universal* belong not to the real existence of things; but are the inventions and creatures of the understanding, made by it for its own use, and concern only signs, whether words or ideas. Words are general, as has been said, when used for signs of general ideas, and so are applicable indifferently to many particular things; and ideas are general when they are set up as the representatives of many particular things: but universality belongs not to things themselves, which are all of them particular in their existence, even those words and ideas which in their signification are general. When therefore we quit particulars, the generals that rest are only creatures of our own making; their general nature being nothing but the capacity they are put into, by the understanding, of signifying or representing many particulars. For the signification they have is nothing but a relation that, by the mind of man, is added to them.

12. *Abstract Ideas are the Essences of Genera and Species.* —The next thing therefore to be considered is, What kind of signification it is that general words have. For, as it is evident that they do not signify barely one particular thing; for then they would not be general terms, but proper names, so, on the other side, it is as evident they do not signify a plurality; for *man* and *men* would then signify the same; and the distinction of numbers (as the grammarians call them) would be superfluous and useless. That then which general words signify is a *sort* of things; and each of them does that, by being a sign of an abstract idea in the mind; to which idea, as things existing are found to agree, so they come to be ranked under that name, or, which is all one, be of that sort. Whereby it is evident that the *essences* of the sorts, or, if the

Latin word pleases better, *species* of things, are nothing else but these abstract ideas. For the having the essence of any species, being that which makes anything to be of that species; and the conformity to the idea to which the name is annexed being that which gives a right to that name; the having the essence, and the having that conformity, must needs be the same thing: since to be of any species, and to have a right to the name of that species, is all one. As, for example, to be a *man,* or of the *species* man, and to have right to the *name* man, is the same thing. Again, to be a man, or of the species man, and have the *essence* of a man, is the same thing. Now, since nothing can be a man, or have a right to the name man, but what has a conformity to the abstract idea the name man stands for, nor anything be a man, or have a right to the species man, but what has the essence of that species; it follows, that the abstract idea for which the name stands, and the essence of the species, is one and the same. From whence it is easy to observe, that the essences of the sorts of things, and, consequently, the sorting of things, is the workmanship of the understanding that abstracts and makes those general ideas.

13. *They are the Workmanship of the Understanding, but have their Foundation in the Similitude of Things.* —I would not here be thought to forget, much less to deny, that Nature, in the production of things, makes several of them alike: there is nothing more obvious, especially in the races of animals, and all things propagated by seed. But yet I think we may say, *the sorting of them under names is the workmanship of the understanding, taking occasion, from the similitude it observes amongst them, to make abstract general ideas,* and set them up in the mind, with names annexed to them, as patterns or forms, (for, in that sense, the word *form* has a very proper signification,) to which as particular things existing are found to agree, so they come to be of that species, have that denomination, or are put into that *classis.* For when we say this is a man, that a horse; this justice, that cruelty; this a watch, that a jack; what do we else but rank things under different specific names, as agreeing to those abstract ideas, of which we have made those names the signs? And what are the essences of those species set out and marked by names, but those abstract ideas in the mind; which are, as it were, the bonds between particular things that exist, and the names they are to be ranked under? And when general names have any connexion with particular beings, these abstract ideas are the medium that unites them: so that the essences of species, as distinguished and denominated by us, neither are nor can be anything but those precise abstract ideas we have in our minds. And therefore the supposed real essences of substances, if different from our abstract ideas, cannot be the essences of the species *we* rank things into. For two species may be one, as rationally as two different essences be the essence of one species: and I demand what are the alterations [which] may, or may not be made in a *horse* or *lead,* without making either of them to be of another species? In determining the species of things by *our* abstract ideas, this is easy to resolve, but if any one will regulate himself herein by supposed *real* essences, he will, I suppose, be at a loss: and he will never be able to know when anything precisely ceases to be of the species of a *horse* or *lead.*

14. *Each distinct abstract Idea is a distinct Essence.* —Nor will any one wonder that I say these essences, or abstract ideas (which are the measures of name, and the boundaries of species) are the workmanship of the understanding, who considers that at least the complex ones are often, in several men, different collections of simple ideas; and therefore that is *covetousness* to one man, which is not so to another. Nay, even in substances, where their abstract ideas seem to be taken from the things themselves, they are not constantly the same; no, not in that species which is most

familiar to us, and with which we have the most intimate acquaintance: it having been more than once doubted, whether the *foetus* born of a woman were a *man,* even so far as that it hath been debated, whether it were or were not to be nourished and baptized: which could not be, if the abstract idea or essence to which the name man belonged were of nature's making; and were not the uncertain and various collection of simple ideas, which the understanding put together, and then, abstracting it, affixed a name to it. So that, in truth, every distinct abstract idea is a distinct essence; and the names that stand for such distinct ideas are the names of things essentially different. Thus a circle is as essentially different from an oval as a sheep from a goat; and rain is as essentially different from snow as water from earth: that abstract idea which is the essence of one being impossible to be communicated to the other. And thus any two abstract ideas, that in any part vary one from another, with two distinct names annexed to them, constitute two distinct sorts, or, if you please, *species,* as essentially different as any two of the most remote or opposite in the world.

15. *Several significations of the word Essence.* —But since the essences of things are thought by some (and not without reason) to be wholly unknown, it may not be amiss to consider the several significations of the word *essence.*

First, Essence may be taken for the very being of anything, whereby it is what it is. And thus the real internal, but generally (in substances) unknown constitution of things, whereon their discoverable qualities depend, may be called their essence. This is the proper original signification of the word, as is evident from the formation of it; *essentia,* in its primary notation, signifying properly, being. And in this sense it is still used, when we speak of the essence of *particular* things, without giving them any name.

Secondly, The learning and disputes of the schools having been much busied about *genus* and *species,* the word *essence* has almost lost its primary signification: and, instead of the real constitution of things, has been almost wholly applied to the artificial constitution of *genus* and *species.* It is true, there is ordinarily supposed a real constitution of the sorts of things; and it is past doubt there must be some real constitution, on which any collection of simple ideas co-existing must depend. But, it being evident that things are ranked under names into sorts or species, only as they agree to certain abstract ideas, to which we have annexed those names, the essence of each *genus,* or sort, comes to be nothing but that abstract idea which the general, or sortal (if I may have leave so to call it from sort, as I do general from genus,) name stands for. And this we shall find to be that which the word essence imports in its most familiar use.

These two sorts of essences, I suppose, may not unfitly be termed, the one the *real,* the other *nominal essence.*

16. *Constant Connexion between the Name and nominal Essence.* —Between the *nominal essence* and the *name* there is so near a connexion, that the name of any sort of things cannot be attributed to any particular being but what has this essence, whereby it anwers that abstract idea whereof that name is the sign.

17. *Supposition, that Species are distinguished by their real Essences useless.* — Concerning the *real essences* of corporeal substances (to mention these only) there are, if I mistake not, two opinions. The one is of those who, using the word essence for they know not what, suppose a certain number of those essences, according to which all natural things are made, and wherein they do exactly every one of them partake, and so become of this or that species. The other and more rational opinion is of those

who look on all natural things to have a real, but unknown, constitution of their insensible parts; from which flow those sensible qualities which serve us to distinguish them one from another, according as we have occasion to rank them into sorts, under common denominations. The former of these opinions, which supposes these essences as a certain number of forms or moulds, wherein all natural things that exist are cast, and do equally partake, has, I imagine, very much perplexed the knowledge of natural things. The frequent productions of monsters, in all the species of animals, and of changelings, and other strange issues of human birth, carry with them difficulties, not possible to consist with this hypothesis; since it is as impossible that two things partaking exactly of the same real essence should have different properties, as that two figures partaking of the same real essence of a circle should have different properties. But were there no other reason against it, yet the supposition of essences that cannot be known; and the making of them, nevertheless, to be that which distinguishes the species of things, is so wholly useless and unserviceable to any part of our knowledge, that that alone were sufficient to make us lay it by, and content ourselves with such essences of the sorts or species of things as come within the reach of our knowledge: which, when seriously considered, will be found, as I have said, to be nothing else but, those *abstract* complex ideas to which we have annexed distinct general names.

18. *Real and nominal Essence, the same in simple Ideas and Modes, different in Substances.* — Essences being thus distinguished into nominal and real, we may further observe, that, in the species of simple ideas and modes, they are always the same; but in substances always quite different. Thus, a figure including a space between three lines, is the real as well as nominal essence of a triangle; it being not only the abstract idea to which the general name is annexed, but the very *essentia* or being of the thing itself; that foundation from which all its properties flow, and to which they are all inseparably annexed. But it is far otherwise concerning that parcel of matter which makes the ring on my finger; wherein these two essences are apparently different. For, it is the real constitution of its insensible parts, on which depend all those properties of colour, weight, fusibility, fixedness, &c., which are to be found in it; which constitution we know not, and so, having no particular idea of, having no name that is the sign of it. But yet it is its colour, weight, fusibility, fixedness, &c., which makes it to be gold, or gives it a right to that name, which is therefore its nominal essence. Since nothing can be called gold but what has a conformity of qualities to that abstract complex idea to which that name is annexed. But this distinction of essences, belonging particularly to substances, we shall, when we come to consider their names, have an occasion to treat of more fully.

19. *Essences ingenerable and incorruptible.* — That such abstract ideas, with names to them, as we have been speaking of are essences, may further appear by what we are told concerning essences, viz. that they are all ingenerable and incorruptible. Which cannot be true of the real constitutions of things, which begin and perish with them. All things that exist, besides their Author, are all liable to change; especially those things we are acquainted with, and have ranked into bands under distinct names or ensigns. Thus, that which was grass to-day is to-morrow the flesh of a sheep; and, within a few days after, becomes part of a man: in all which and the like changes, it is evident their real essence — i.e. that constitution whereon the properties of these several things depended — is destroyed, and perishes with them. But essences being taken for ideas established in the mind, with names annexed to them, they are supposed to remain steadily the same, whatever mutations the particular substances

are liable to. For, whatever becomes of *Alexander* and *Bucephalus*, the ideas to which *man* and *horse* are annexed, are supposed nevertheless to remain the same; and so the essences of those species are preserved whole and undestroyed, whatever changes happen to any or all of the individuals of those species. By this means the essence of a species rests safe and entire, without the existence of so much as one individual of that kind. For, were there now no circle existing anywhere in the world, (as perhaps that figure exists not anywhere exactly marked out,) yet the idea annexed to that name would not cease to be what it is; nor cease to be as a pattern to determine which of the particular figures we meet with have or have not a right to the *name* circle, and so to show which of them, by having that essence, was of that species. And though there neither were nor had been in nature such a beast as *unicorn*, or such a fish as a *mermaid*; yet, supposing those names to stand for complex abstract ideas that contained no inconsistency in them, the essence of a mermaid is as intelligible as that of a man; and the idea of an unicorn as certain, steady, and permanent as that of a horse. From what has been said, it is evident, that the doctrine of the immutability of essences proves them to be only abstract ideas; and is founded on the relation established between them and certain sounds as signs of them; and will always be true, as long as the same name can have the same signification.

20. *Recapitulation.* — To conclude. This is that which in short I would say, viz. that all the great business of *genera* and *species*, and their *essences*, amounts to no more but this: — That men making abstract ideas, and settling them in their minds with names annexed to them, do thereby enable themselves to consider things, and discourse of them, as it were in bundles, for the easier and readier improvement and communication of their knowledge, which would advance but slowly were their words and thoughts confined only to particulars.

Chapter IV
OF SIMPLE IDEAS

5. *If all names were definable, it would be a Process* in infinitum. — I will not here trouble myself to prove that all terms are not definable, from that progress *in infinitum*, which it will visibly lead us into, if we should allow that all names could be defined. For, if the terms of one definition were still to be defined by another, where at last should we stop? But I shall, from the nature of our ideas, and the signification of our words, show *why some names can, and others cannot be defined; and which they are.*

6. *What a Definition is.* — I think it is agreed, that a *definition* is nothing else but *the showing the meaning of one word by several other not synonymous terms.* The meaning of words being only the ideas they are made to stand for by him that uses them, the meaning of any term is then showed, or the word is defined, when, by other words, the idea it is made the sign of, and annexed to, in the mind of the speaker, is as it were represented, or set before the view of another; and thus its signification ascertained. This is the only use and end of definitions; and therefore the only measure of what is, or is not a good definition.

7. *Simple Ideas, why undefinable.* — This being premised, I say that the *names of simple ideas, and those only, are incapable of being defined.* The reason whereof is this, That the several terms of a definition, signifying several ideas, they can all together by no means represent an idea which has no composition at all: and therefore a definition, which is properly nothing but the showing the meaning of one word by several others not signifying each the same thing, can in the names of simple ideas have no place.

Chapter VI
OF THE NAMES OF SUBSTANCES

1. *The common Names of Substances stand for Sorts.* — The common names of substances, as well as other general terms, stand for *sorts:* which is nothing else but the being made signs of such complex ideas wherein several particular substances do or might agree, by virtue of which they are capable of being comprehended in one common conception, and signified by one name. I say do or might agree: for though there be but one sun existing in the world, yet the idea of it being abstracted, so that more substances (if there were several) might each agree in it, it is as much a sort as if there were as many suns as there are stars. They want not their reasons who think there are, and that each fixed star would answer the idea the name sun stands for, to one who was placed in a due distance: which, by the way, may show us how much the sorts, or, if you please, *genera* and *species* of things (for those Latin terms signify to me no more than the English word sort) depend on such collections of ideas as men have made, and not on the real nature of things; since it is not impossible but that, in propriety of speech, that might be a sun to one which is a star to another.

2. *The Essence of each Sort of substance is our abstract Idea to which the name is annexed.* — The measure and boundary of each sort or species, whereby it is constituted that particular sort, and distinguished from others, is that we call its *essence,* which is nothing but that abstract idea to which the name is annexed; so that everything contained in that idea is essential to that sort. This, though it be all the essence of natural substances that *we* know, or by which we distinguish them into sorts, yet I call it by a peculiar name, the *nominal essence,* to distinguish it from the real constitution of substances, upon which depends this nominal essence, and all the properties of that sort; which, therefore, as has been said, may be called the *real essence:* v.g. the nominal essence of gold is that complex idea the word gold stands for, let it be, for instance, a body yellow, of a certain weight, malleable, fusible, and fixed. But the real essence is the constitution of the insensible parts of that body, on which those qualities and all the other properties of gold depend. How far these two are different, though they are both called essence, is obvious at first sight to discover.

3. *The nominal and real Essence different.* — For, though perhaps voluntary motion, with sense and reason, joined to a body of a certain shape, be the complex idea to which I and others annex the name *man,* and so be the nominal essence of the species so called: yet nobody will say that complex idea is the real essence and source of all those operations which are to be found in any individual of that sort. The foundation of all those qualities which are the ingredients of our complex idea, is something quite different: and had we such a knowledge of that constitution of man, from which his faculties of moving, sensation, and reasoning, and other powers flow, and on which his so regular shape depends, as it is possible angels have, and it is cer-

tain his Maker has, we should have a quite other idea of his essence than what now is contained in our definition of that species, be it what it will: and our idea of any individual man would be as far different from what it is now, as is his who knows all the springs and wheels and other contrivances within of the famous clock at Strasburg, from that which a gazing countryman has of it, who barely sees the motion of the hand, and hears the clock strike, and observes only some of the outward appearances.

4. *Nothing essential to Individuals.* —That *essence,* in the ordinary use of the word, relates to sorts, and that it is considered in particular beings no further than as they are ranked into sorts, appears from hence: that, take but away the abstract ideas by which we sort individuals, and rank them under common names, and then the thought of anything essential to any of them instantly vanishes: we have no notion of the one without the other, which plainly shows their relation. It is necessary for me to be as I am; God and nature has made me so: but there is nothing I have is essential to me. An accident or disease may very much alter my colour or shape; a fever or fall may take away my reason or memory, or both; and an apoplexy leave neither sense, nor understanding, no, nor life. Other creatures of my shape may be made with more and better, or fewer and worse faculties than I have; and others may have reason and sense in a shape and body very different from mine. None of these are essential to the one or the other, or to any individual whatever, till the mind refers it to some sort of species of things; and then presently, according to the abstract idea of that sort, something is found essential. Let any one examine his own thoughts, and he will find that as soon as he supposes or speaks of essential, the consideration of some species, or the complex idea signified by some general name, comes into his mind; and it is in reference to that that this or that quality is said to be essential. So that if it be asked, whether it be essential to me or any other particular corporeal being, to have reason? I say, no; no more than it is essential to this white thing I write on to have words in it. But if that particular being be to be counted of the sort *man,* and to have the name *man* given it, then reason is essential to it; supposing reason to be a part of the complex idea the name man stands for: as it is essential to this thing I write on to contain words, if I will give it the name *treatise,* and rank it under that species. So that essential and not essential relate only to our abstract ideas, and the names annexed to them; which amounts to no more than this, that whatever particular thing has not in it those qualities which are contained in the abstract idea which any general term stands for, cannot be ranked under that species, nor be called by that name; since that abstract idea is the very essence of that species.

5. *The only essences perceived by us in individual substances are those qualities which entitle them to receive their names.* —Thus, if the idea of *body* with some people be bare extension or space, then solidity is not essential to body: if others make the idea to which they give the name *body* to be solidity and extension, then solidity is essential to body. That therefore, and that alone, is considered as essential, which makes a part of the complex idea the name of a sort stands for; without which no particular thing can be reckoned of that sort, nor be entitled to that name. Should there be found a parcel of matter that had all the other qualities that are in iron, but wanted obedience to the loadstone, and would neither be drawn by it nor receive direction from it, would any one question whether it wanted anything essential? It would be absurd to ask, Whether a thing really existing wanted anything essential to it. Or could it be demanded, Whether this made an essential or specific difference or no, since *we* have no other measure of essential or specific but our abstract ideas? And

to talk of specific differences in *nature*, without reference to general ideas in names, is to talk unintelligibly. For I would ask for any one, What is sufficient to make an essential difference in nature between any two particular beings, without any regard had to some abstract idea, which is looked upon as the essence and standard of a species? All such patterns and standards being quite laid aside, particular beings, considered barely in themselves, will be found to have all their qualities equally essential; and everything in each individual will be essential to it; or, which is more, nothing at all. For, though it may be reasonable to ask, Whether obeying the magnet be essential to iron? yet I think it is very improper and insignificant to ask, whether it be essential to the particular parcel of matter I cut my pen with; without considering it under the name *iron*, or as being of a certain species. And if, as has been said, our abstract ideas, which have names annexed to them, are the boundaries of species, nothing can be essential but what is contained in those ideas.

6. *Even the real essences of individual substances imply potential sorts.* — It is true, I have often mentioned a *real essence*, distinct in substances from those abstract ideas of them, which I call their nominal essence. By this real essence I mean, that real constitution of anything, which is the foundation of all those properties that are combined in, and are constantly found to co-exist with the nominal essence; that particular constitution which everything has within itself, without any relation to anything without it. But essence, even in this sense, *relates to a sort, and supposes a species.* For, being that real constitution on which the properties depend, it necessarily supposes a sort of things, properties belonging only to species, and not to individuals: v.g. supposing the nominal essence of gold to be a body of such a peculiar colour and weight, with malleability and fusibility, the real essence is that constitution of the parts of matter on which these qualities and their union depend; and is also the foundation of its solubility in *aqua regia* and other properties, accompanying that complex idea. Here are essences and properties, but all upon supposition of a sort or general abstract idea, which is considered as immutable; but there is no individual parcel of matter to which any of these qualities are so annexed as to be essential to it or inseparable from it. That which is essential belongs to it as a condition whereby it is of this or that sort: but take away the consideration of its being ranked under the name of some abstract idea, and then there is nothing necessary to it, nothing inseparable from it. Indeed, as to the real essences of substances, we only suppose their being, without precisely knowing what they are; but that which annexes them still to the species is the nominal essence, of which they are the supposed foundation and cause.

7. *The nominal Essence bounds the Species for us.* — The next thing to be considered is, by which of those essences it is that substances are determined into sorts or species; and that, it is evident, is by the nominal essence. For it is that alone that the name, which is the mark of the sort, signifies. It is impossible, therefore, that anything should determine the sorts of things, which *we* rank under general names, but that idea which that name is designed as a mark for; which is that, as has been shown, which we call nominal essence. Why do we say this is a horse, and that a mule; this is an animal, that an herb? How comes any particular thing to be of this or that sort, but because it has that nominal essence; or, which is all one, agrees to that abstract idea, that name is annexed to? And I desire any one but to reflect on his own thoughts, when he fears or speaks any of those or other names of substances, to know what sort of essences they stand for.

8. *The nature of Species, as formed by us.* — And that the species of things to us are nothing but the ranking them under distinct names, according to the complex ideas in *us,* and not according to precise, distinct, real essences in *them,* is plain from hence: — That we find many of the individuals that are ranked into one sort, called by one common name, and so received as being of one species, have yet qualities, depending on their real constitutions, as far different one from another as from others from which they are accounted to differ specifically. This, as it is easy to be observed by all who have to do with natural bodies, so chemists especially are often, by sad experience, convinced of it, when they, sometimes in vain, seek for the same qualities in one parcel of sulphur, antimony, or vitriol, which they have found in others. For, though they are bodies of the same species, having the same nominal essence, under the same name, yet do they often, upon severe ways of examination, betray qualities so different one from another, as to frustrate the expectation and labour of very wary chemists. But if things were distinguished into species, according to their real essences, it would be as impossible to find different properties in any two individual substances of the same species, as it is to find different properties in two circles, or two equilateral triangles. That is properly the essence to *us,* which determines every particular to this or that *classis;* or, which is the same thing, to this or that general name: and what can that be else, but that abstract idea to which that name is annexed; and so has, in truth, a reference, not so much to the being of particular things, as to their general denominations?

9. *Not the real Essence, or texture of parts, which we know not.* — Nor indeed can we rank and sort things, and consequently (which is the end of sorting) denominate them, by their real essences; because we know them not. Our faculties carry us no further towards the knowledge and distinction of substances, than a collection of *those sensible ideas which we observe in them;* which, however made with the greatest diligence and exactness we are capable of, yet is more remote from the true internal constitution from which those qualities flow, than, as I said, a countryman's idea is from the inward contrivance of that famous clock at Strasburg, whereof he only sees the outward figure and motions. There is not so contemptible a plant or animal, that does not confound the most enlarged understanding. Though the familiar use of things about us take off our wonder, yet it cures not our ignorance. When we come to examine the stones we tread on, or the iron we daily handle, we presently find we know not their make; and can give no reason of the different qualities we find in them. It is evident the internal constitution, whereon their properties depend, is unknown to us: for to go no further than the grossest and most obvious we can imagine amongst them, What is that texture of parts, that real essence, that makes lead and antimony fusible, wood and stones not? What makes lead and iron malleable, antimony and stones not? And yet how infinitely these come short of the fine contrivances and inconceivable real essences of plants or animals, every one knows. The workmanship of the all-wise and powerful God in the great fabric of the universe, and every part thereof, further exceeds the capacity and comprehension of the most inquisitive and intelligent man, than the best contrivance of the most ingenious man doth the conceptions of the most ignorant of rational creatures. Therefore we in vain pretend to range things into sorts, and dispose them into certain classes under names, by their real essences, that are so far from our discovery or comprehension. A blind man may as soon sort things by their colours, and he that has lost his smell as well distinguish a lily and a rose by their odours, as by those internal constitutions which he knows not. He that thinks he can distinguish sheep and goats by their real essences,

that are unknown to him, may be pleased to try his skill in those species called *cassiowary* and *querechinchio*; and by their internal real essences determine the boundaries of those species, without knowing the complex idea of sensible qualities that each of those names stand for, in the countries where those animals are to be found.

13. *The Nominal Essence that of the Species, as conceived by us, proved from Water and Ice.* — But to return to the species of corporeal substances. If I should ask any one whether ice and water were two distinct species of things, I doubt not but I should be answered in the affirmative: and it cannot be denied but he that says they are two distinct species is in the right. But if an Englishman bred in Jamaica, who perhaps had never seen nor heard of ice, coming into England in the winter, find the water he put in his basin at night in a great part frozen in the morning, and, not knowing any peculiar name it had, should call it hardened water; I ask whether this would be a new species to him, different from water? And I think it would be answered here, It would not be to him a new species, no more than congealed jelly, when it is cold, is a distinct species from the same jelly fluid and warm; or than liquid gold in the furnace is a distinct species from hard gold in the hands of a workman. And if this be so, it is plain that *our distinct species* are *nothing but distinct complex ideas, with distinct names annexed to them.* It is true every substance that exists has its peculiar constitution, whereon depend those sensible qualities and powers we observe in it; but the ranking of things into species (which is nothing but sorting them under several titles) is done by us according to the ideas that *we* have of them: which, though sufficient to distinguish them by names, so that we may be able to discourse of them when we have them not present before us; yet if we suppose it to be done by their real internal constitutions, and that things existing are distinguished by nature into species, by real essences, according as we distinguish them into species by names, we shall be liable to great mistakes.

14. *Difficulties in the supposition of a certain number of real Essences.* — To distinguish substantial being into species, according to the usual supposition, that there are certain precise essences of forms of things, whereby all the individuals existing are, by nature distinguished into species, these things are necessary: —

15. *A crude supposition.* — First, To be assured that nature, in the production of things, always designs them to partake of certain regulated established essences, which are to be the models of all things to be produced. This, in that crude sense it is usually proposed, would need some better explication, before it can fully be assented to.

16. *Monstrous births.* — Secondly, It would be necessary to know whether nature always attains that essence it designs in the production of things. The irregular and monstrous births, that in divers sorts of animals have been observed, will always give us reason to doubt of one or both of these.

17. *Are monsters really a distinct species?* — Thirdly, It ought to be determined whether those we call monsters be really a distinct species, according to the scholastic notion of the word species; since it is certain that everything that exists has its particular constitution. And yet we find that some of these monstrous productions have few or none of those qualities which are supposed to result from, and accompany, the essence of that species from whence they derive their originals, and to which, by their descent, they seem to belong.

18. *Men can have no ideas of Real Essences.* —Fourthly, The real essences of those things which we distinguish into species, and as so distinguished we name, ought to be known; i.e. we ought to have ideas of them. But since we are ignorant in these four points, the supposed real essences of things stand *us* not in stead for the distinguishing substances into species.

19. *Our Nominal Essences of Substances not perfect collections of the properties that flow from their Real Essences.* —Fifthly, The only imaginable help in this case would be, that, having framed perfect complex ideas of the properties of things flowing from their different real essences, we should thereby distinguish them into species. But neither can this be done. For, being ignorant of the real essence itself, it is impossible to know all those properties that flow from it, and are so annexed to it, that any one of them being away, we may certainly conclude that that essence is not there, and so the thing is not of that species. We can never know what is the precise number of properties depending on the real essence of gold, any one of which failing, the real essence of gold, and consequently gold, would not be there, unless we knew the real essence of gold itself, and by that determined that species. By the word *gold* here, I must be understood to design a particular piece of matter; v.g. the last guinea that was coined. For, if it should stand here, in its ordinary signification, for that complex idea which I or any one else calls gold, i.e. for the nominal essence of gold, it would be jargon. So hard is it to show the various meaning and imperfection of words, when we have nothing else but words to do it by.

20. *Hence names independent of Real Essences.* —By all which it is clear, that our distinguishing substances into species by names, is not at all founded on their real essences; nor can we pretend to range and determine them exactly into species, according to internal essential differences.

21. *But stand for such a collection of simple ideas as we have made the Name stand for.* —But since, as has been remarked, we have need of *general* words, though we know not the real essences of things; all we can do is, to collect such a number of simple ideas as, by examination, we find to be united together in things existing, and thereof to make one complex idea. Which, though it be not the real essence of any substance that exists, is yet the specific essence to which our name belongs, and is convertible with it; by which we may at least try the truth of these nominal essences. For example: there be that say that the essence of body is *extension*; if it be so, we can never mistake in putting the essence of anything for the thing itself. Let us then in discourse put extension for body, and when we would say that body moves, let us say that extension moves, and see how ill it will look. He that should say that one extension by impulse moves another extension, would, by the bare expression, sufficiently show the absurdity of such a notion. The essence of anything in respect of us, is the whole complex idea comprehended and marked by that name; and in substances, besides the several distinct simple ideas that make them up, the confused one of substance, or of an unknown support and cause of their union, is always a part: and therefore the essence of body is not bare extension, but an extended solid thing; and so to say, an extended solid thing moves, or impels another, is all one, and as intelligible, as to say, *body* moves or impels. Likewise, to say that a rational animal is capable of conversation, is all one as to say a man; but no one will say that rationality is capable of conversation, because it makes not the whole essence to which we give the name man.

22. *Our Abstract Ideas are to us the Measures of the Species we make: instance in*

that of Man. —There are creatures in the world that have shapes like ours, but are hairy, and want language and reason. There are naturals amongst us that have perfectly our shape, but want reason, and some of them language too. There are creatures, as it is said, (*sit fides penes authorem,* but there appears no contradiction that there should be such,) that, with language and reason and a shape in other things agreeing with ours, have hairy tails; others where the males have no beards, and others where the females have. If it be asked whether these be all *men* or no, all of human species? it is plain, the question refers only to the nominal essence: for those of them to whom the definition of the word man, or the complex idea signified by that name, agrees, are men, and the other not. But if the inquiry be made concerning the supposed real essence; and whether the internal constitution and frame of these several creatures be specifically different, it is wholly impossible for us to answer, no part of that going into our specific idea: only we have reason to think, that where the faculties or outward frame so much differs, the internal constitution is not exactly the same. But what difference in the real internal constitution makes a specific difference it is in vain to inquire; whilst our measures of species be, as they are, only our abstract ideas, which we know; and not that internal constitution, which makes no part of them. Shall the difference of hair only on the skin be a mark of a different internal specific constitution between a changeling and a drill, when they agree in shape, and want of reason and speech? And shall not the want of reason and speech be a sign to us of different real constitutions and species between a changeling and a reasonable man? And so of the rest, if we pretend that distinction of species or sorts is fixedly established by the real frame and secret constitutions of things.

25. *The specific Essences that are commonly made by Men.* —But supposing that the *real* essences of substances were discoverable by those that would severely apply themselves to that inquiry, yet we could not reasonably think that the ranking of things under general names was regulated by those internal real constitutions, or anything else but their *obvious* appearances; since languages, in all countries, have been established long before sciences. So that they have not been philosophers or logicians, or such who have troubled themselves about forms and essences, that have made the general names that are in use amongst the several nations of men: but those more or less comprehensive terms have, for the most part, in all languages, received their birth and signification from ignorant and illiterate people, who sorted and denominated things by those sensible qualities they found in them; thereby to signify them, when absent, to others, whether they had an occasion to mention a sort or a particular thing.

26. *Therefore very various and uncertain in the ideas of different men.* —Since then it is evident that we sort and name substances by their nominal and not by their real essences, the next thing to be considered is how, and by whom these essences come to be made. As to the latter, it is evident they are made by the mind, and not by nature: for were they Nature's workmanship, they could not be so various and different in several men as experience tells us they are. For if we will examine it, we shall not find the nominal essence of any one species of substances in all men the same: no, not of that which of all others we are the most intimately acquainted with. It could not possibly be that the abstract idea to which the name *man* is given should be different in several men, if it were of Nature's making; and that to one it should be *animal rationale,* and to another, *animal implume bipes latis unguibus.* He that an-

nexes the name man to a complex idea, made up of sense and spontaneous motion, joined to a body of such a shape, has thereby one essence of the species man; and he that, upon further examination, adds rationality, has another essence of the species he calls man: by which means the same individual will be a true man to the one which is not so to the other. I think there is scarce any one will allow this upright figure, so well known, to be the essential difference of the species man; and yet how far men determine of the sorts of animals rather by their shape than descent, is very visible; since it has been more than once debated, whether several human foetuses should be preserved or received to baptism or no, only because of the difference of their outward configuration from the ordinary make of children, without knowing whether they were not as capable of reason as infants cast in another mould: some whereof, though of an approved shape, are never capable of as much appearance of reason all their lives as is to be found in an ape, or an elephant, and never give any signs of being acted by a rational soul. Whereby it is evident, that the outward figure, which only was found wanting, and not the faculty of reason, which nobody could know would be wanting in its due season, was made essential to the human species. The learned divine and lawyer must, on such occasions, renounce his sacred definition of *animal rationale,* and substitute some other essence of the human species. Monsieur Menage[4] furnishes us with an example worth the taking notice of on this occasion: 'When the abbot of Saint Martin,' says he, 'was born, he had so little of the figure of a man, that it bespake him rather a monster. It was for some time under deliberation, whether he should be baptized or no. However, he was baptized, and declared a man provisionally till time should show what he would prove. Nature had moulded him so untowardly, that he was called all his life the Abbot Malotru; i.e. ill-shaped. He was of Caen.' (*Menagiana,* 278, 430.) This child, we see, was very near being excluded out of the species of man, barely by his shape. He escaped very narrowly as he was; and it is certain, a figure a little more oddly turned had cast him, and he had been executed, as a thing not to be allowed to pass for man. And yet there can be no reason given why, if the lineaments of his face had been a little altered, a rational soul could not have been lodged in him; why a visage somewhat longer, or a nose flatter, or a wider mouth, could not have consisted, as well as the rest of his ill figure, with such a soul, such parts, as made him, disfigured as he was, capable to be a dignitary in the church.

27. *Nominal Essences of particular substances are undetermined by nature, and therefore various as men vary.* — Wherein, then, would I gladly know, consist the precise and unmovable boundaries of that species? It is plain, if we examine, there is no such thing made by Nature, and established by her amongst men. The real essence of that or any other sort of substances, it is evident, we know not; and therefore are so undetermined in our nominal essences, which we make ourselves, that, if several men were to be asked concerning some oddly-shaped *foetus,* as soon as born, whether it were a *man* or no, it is past doubt one should meet with different answers. Which could not happen, if the nominal essences whereby we limit and distinguish the species of substances, were not made by man with some liberty; but were exactly copied from precise boundaries set by nature, whereby it distinguished all substances into certain species. Who would undertake to resolve what species that monster was of which is mentioned by Licetus (lib. i. c. 3),[5] with a man's head and

4. [Giles Menage (1613–1690) was a French philologist and critic.]

5. [Fortunato Liceto (1577–1657) was an Italian physician. The reference is to his *De Monstrorum Causis* (Of the Causes of Monsters).]

hog's body? Or those other which to the bodies of men had the heads of beasts, as dogs, horses, &c. If any of these creatures had lived, and could have spoke, it would have increased the difficulty. Had the upper part to the middle been of human shape, and all below swine, had it been murder to destroy it? Or must the bishop have been consulted, whether it were man enough to be admitted to the font or no? As I have been told it happened in France some years since, in somewhat a like case. So uncertain are the boundaries of species of animals to us, who have no other measures than the complex ideas of our own collecting: and so far are we from certainly knowing what a *man* is; though perhaps it will be judged great ignorance to make any doubt about it. And yet I think I may say, that the certain boundaries of that species are so far from being determined, and the precise number of simple ideas which make the nominal essence so far from being settled and perfectly known, that very material doubts may still arise about it. And I imagine none of the definitons of the word *man* which we yet have, nor descriptions of that sort of animal, are so perfect and exact as to satisfy a considerate inquisitive person; much less to obtain a general consent, and to be that which men would everywhere stick by, in the decision of cases, and determining of life and death, baptism or no baptism, in productions that might happen.

28. *But not so arbitrary as Mixed Modes.* — But though these nominal essences of substances are made by the mind, they are not yet made so arbitrarily as those of mixed modes. To the making of any nominal essence, it is necessary, First, that the ideas whereof it consists have such a union as to make but one idea, how compounded soever. Secondly, that the particular ideas so united be exactly the same, neither more nor less. For if two abstract complex ideas differ either in number or sorts of their component parts, they make two different, and not one and the same essence. In the first of these, the mind, in making its complex ideas of substances, only follows nature; and puts none together which are not supposed to have a union in nature. Nobody joins the voice of a sheep with the shape of a horse; nor the colour of lead with the weight and fixedness of gold, to be the complex ideas of any real substances; unless he has a mind to fill his head with chimeras, and his discourse with unintelligible words. Men observing certain qualities always joined and existing together, therein copied nature; and of ideas so united made their complex ones of substances. For, though men may make what complex ideas they please, and give what names to them they will; yet, if they will be understood *when they speak of things really existing,* they must in some degree conform their ideas to the things they would speak of; or else men's language will be like that of Babel,[6] and every man's words, being intelligible only to himself, would no longer serve to conversation and the ordinary affairs of life, if the ideas they stand for be not some way answering the common appearances and agreement of substances as they really exist.

29. *Our Nominal Essences of substances usually consist of a few obvious qualities observed in things.* — Secondly, Though the mind of man, in making its complex ideas of substances, never puts any together that do not really, or are not supposed to, co-exist; and so it truly borrows that union from nature: yet the number it combines depends upon the various care, industry, or fancy of him that makes it. Men generally content themselves with some few sensible obvious qualities; and often, if not

6. [The reference is to a Biblical story related in the Book of Genesis, according to which, at a time when all people spoke the same language, they attempted to build a tower that reached to heaven, but they were prevented from doing so by God, who confounded their language so they could not understand one another.]

always, leave out others as material and as firmly united as those that they take. Of sensible substances there are two sorts: one of organized bodies, which are propagated by seed; and in these the *shape* is that which to us is the leading quality, and most characteristical part, that determines the species. And therefore in vegetables and animals, an extended solid substance of such a certain figure usually serves the turn. For however some men seem to prize their definiton of *animal rationale*, yet should there a creature be found that had language and reason, but partaked not of the usual shape of a man, I believe it would hardly pass for a man, how much soever it were *animal rationale*. And if Balaam's ass[7] had all his life discoursed as rationally as he did once with his master, I doubt yet whether any one would have thought him worthy the name man, or allowed him to be of the same species with himself. As in vegetables and animals it is the shape, so in most other bodies, not propagated by seed, it is the *colour* we most fix on, and are most led by. Thus where we find the colour of gold, we are apt to imagine all the other qualities comprehended in our complex idea to be there also: and we commonly take these two obvious qualities, viz. shape and colour, for so presumptive ideas of several species, that in a good picture, we readily say, this is a lion, and that a rose; this is a gold, and that a silver goblet, only by the different figures and colours represented to the eye by the pencil.

30. *Yet, imperfect as they thus are, they serve for common converse.* — But though this serves well enough for gross and confused conceptions, and inaccurate ways of talking and thinking; yet *men are far enough from having agreed on the precise number of simple ideas or qualities belonging to any sort of things, signified by its name.* Nor is it a wonder; since it requires much time, pains, and skill, strict inquiry, and long examination to find out what, and how many, those simple ideas are, which are constantly and inseparably united in nature, and are always to be found together in the same subject. Most men, wanting either time, inclination, or industry enough for this, even to some tolerable degree, content themselves with some few obvious and outward appearances of things, thereby readily to distinguish and sort them for the common affairs of life: and so, without further examination, give them names, or take up the names already in use. Which, though in common conversation they pass well enough for the signs of some few obvious qualities co-existing, are yet far enough from comprehending, in a settled signification, a precise number of simple ideas, much less all those which are united in nature. He that shall consider, after so much stir about genus and species, and such a deal of talk of specific differences, how few words we have yet settled definitions of, may with reason imagine, that those *forms* which there hath been so much noise made about are only chimeras, which give us no light into the specific natures of things. And he that shall consider how far the names of substances are from having significations wherein all who use them do agree, will have reason to conclude that, though the nominal essences of substances are all supposed to be copied from nature, yet they are all, or most of them, very imperfect. Since the composition of those complex ideas are, in several men, very different: and therefore that these boundaries of species are as men, and not as Nature, makes them, if at least there are in nature any such prefixed bounds. It is true that many particular substances are so made by Nature, that they have agreement and likeness one with another, and so afford a foundation of being ranked into sorts. But the sorting of things by us, or the making of determinate species, being in order to naming and comprehending them under general terms, I cannot see how it can be properly

---

7. [The reference is to a Biblical story related in the Book of Numbers, according to which God gave the power of speech to the prophet Balaam's ass.]

said, that Nature sets the boundaries of the species of things: or, if it be so, our boundaries of species are not exactly conformable to those in nature. For we, having need of general names for present use, stay not for a perfect discovery of all those qualities which would *best* show us their most material differences and agreements; but we ourselves divide them, by certain obvious appearances, into species, that we may the easier under general names communicate our thoughts about them. For, having no other knowledge of any substance but of the simple ideas that are united in it; and observing several particular things to agree with others in several of those simple ideas; we make that collection our specific idea, and give it a general name; that in recording our thoughts, and in our discourse with others, we may in one short word designate all the individuals that agree in that complex idea, without enumerating the simple ideas that make it up; and so not waste our time and breath in tedious descriptions: which we see they are fain to do who would discourse of any new sort of things they have not yet a name for.

31. *Essences of Species under the same Name very different in different minds.* —But however these species of substances pass well enough in ordinary conversation, it is plain that this complex idea, wherein they observe several individuals to agree, is by different men made very differently; by some more, and others less accurately. In some, this complex idea contains a greater, and in others a smaller number of qualities; and so is apparently such as the mind makes it. The yellow shining colour makes gold to children; others add weight, malleableness, and fusibility; and others yet other qualities, which they find joined with that yellow colour, as constantly as its weight and fusibility. For in all these and the like qualities, one has as good a right to be put into the complex idea of that substance wherein they are all joined as another. And therefore different men, leaving out or putting in several simple ideas which others do not, according to their various examination, skill, or observation of that subject, have different essences of gold, which must make therefore be of their own and not of nature's making.

32. *The more general our Ideas of Substances are, the more incomplete and partial they are.* —If the number of simple ideas that make the nominal essence of the lowest species, or first sorting, of individuals, depends on the mind of man, variously collecting them, it is much more evident that they do so in the more comprehensive classes, which, by the masters of logic, are called *genera*. These are complex ideas designedly imperfect: and it is visible at first sight, that several of those qualities that are to be found in the things themselves are purposely left out of generical ideas. For, as the mind, to make general ideas comprehending several particulars, leaves out those of time and place, and such other, that make them incommunicable to more than one individual; so to make other yet more general ideas, that may comprehend different sorts, it leaves out those qualities that distinguish them, and puts into its new collection only such ideas as are common to several sorts. The same convenience that made men express several parcels of yellow matter coming from Guinea and Peru under one name, sets them also upon making of one name that may comprehend both gold and silver, and some other bodies of different sorts. This is done by leaving out those qualities, which are peculiar to each sort, and retaining a complex idea made up of those that are common to them all. To which the name *metal* being annexed, there is a genus constituted; the essence whereof being that abstract idea, containing only malleableness and fusibility, with certain degrees of weight and fixedness, wherein some bodies of several kinds agree, leaves out the colour and other qualities peculiar to gold and silver, and the other sorts comprehended under the name metal.

Whereby it is plain that men follow not exactly the patterns set them by nature, when they make their general ideas of substances; since there is no body to be found which has barely malleableness and fusibility in it, without other qualities as inseparable as those. But men, in making their general ideas, seeking more the convenience of language, and quick dispatch by short and comprehensive signs, than the true and precise nature of things as they exist, have, in the framing their abstract ideas, chiefly pursued that end; which was to be furnished with store of general and variously comprehensive names. So that in this whole business of genera and species, the genus, or more comprehensive, is but a partial conception of what is in the species; and the species but a partial idea of what is to be found in each individual. If therefore any one will think that a man, and a horse, and an animal, and a plant, &c., are distinguished by real essences made by nature, he must think nature to be very liberal of these real essences, making one for body, another for an animal, and another for a horse; and all these essences liberally bestowed upon Bucephalus. But if we would rightly consider what is done in all these genera and species, or sorts, we should find that there is no new thing made, but only more or less comprehensive signs, whereby we may be enabled to express in a few syllables great numbers of particular things, as they agree in more or less general conceptions, which we have framed to that purpose. In all which we may observe, that the more general term is always the name of a less complex idea; and that each genus is but a partial conception of the species comprehended under it. So that if these abstract general ideas be thought to be complete, it can only be in respect of a certain established relation between them and certain names which are made use of to signify them; and not in respect of anything existing, as made by nature.

33. *This all accommodated to the end of Speech.* — This is adjusted to the true end of speech, which is to be the easiest and shortest way of communicating our notions. For thus he that would discourse of things, as they agreed in the complex idea of extension and solidity, needed but use the word *body* to denote all such. He that to these would join others, signified by the words life, sense, and spontaneous motion, needed but use the word *animal* to signify all which partaked of those ideas, and he that had made a complex idea of a body, with life, sense, and motion, with the faculty of reasoning, and a certain shape joined to it, needed but use the short monosyllable *man*, to express all particulars that correspond to that complex idea. This is the proper business of genus and species: and this men do without any consideration of real essences, or substantial forms; which come not within the reach of our knowledge when we think of those things, nor within the signification of our words when we discourse with others.

34. *Instance in Cassowaries.* — Were I to talk with any one of a sort of birds I lately saw in St. James's Park, about three or four feet high, with a covering of something between feathers and hair, of a dark brown colour, without wings, but in the place thereof two or three little branches coming down like sprigs of Spanish broom, long great legs, with feet only of three claws, and without a tail; I must make this description of it, and so may make others understand me. But when I am told that the name of it is *cassuaris*, I may then use that word to stand in discourse for all my complex idea mentioned in that description; though by that word, which is now become a specific name, I know no more of the real essence or constitution of that sort of animals than I did before; and knew probably as much of the nature of that species of birds before I learned the name, as many Englishmen do of swans or herons, which

are specific names, very well known, of sorts of birds common in England.

35. *Men determine the Sorts of Substances, which may be sorted variously.* —From what has been said, it is evident that *men* make sorts of things. For, it being different essences alone that make different species, it is plain that they who make those abstract ideas which are the nominal essences do thereby make the species, or sort. Should there be a body found, having all the other qualities of gold except malleableness, it would no doubt be made a question whether it were gold or not, i.e. whether it were of that species. This could be determined only by that abstract idea to which every one annexed the name gold: so that it would be true gold to him, and belong to that species, who included not malleableness in his nominal essence, signified by the sound gold; and on the other side it would not be true gold, or of that species, to him who included malleableness in his specific idea. And how, I pray, is it that makes these diverse species, even under one and the same name, but men that make two different abstract ideas, consisting not exactly of the same collection of qualities? Nor is it a mere supposition to imagine that a body may exist wherein the other obvious qualities of gold may be without malleableness; since it is certain that gold itself will be sometimes so eager, (as artists call it,) that it will as little endure the hammer as glass itself. What we have said of the putting in, or leaving out of malleableness, in the complex idea the name gold is by any one annexed to, may be said of its peculiar weight, fixedness, and several other the like qualities: for whatever is left out, or put in, it is still the complex idea to which that name is annexed that makes the species: and as any particular parcel of matter answers that idea, so the name of the sort belongs truly to it; and it is of that species. And thus anything is true gold, perfect metal. All which determination of the species, it is plain, depends on the understanding of man, making this or that complex idea.

36. *Nature makes the Similitudes of Substances.* —This, then, in short, is the case: Nature makes many *particular things*, which do agree one with another in many sensible qualities, and probably too in their internal frame and constitution: but it is not this real essence that distinguishes them into species; it is men who, taking occasion from the qualities they find united in them, and wherein they observe often several individuals to agree, range them into sorts, in order to their naming, for the convenience of comprehensive signs; under which individuals, according to their conformity to this or that abstract idea, come to be ranked as under ensigns: so that this is of the blue, that the red regiment; this is a man, that a drill: and in this, I think, consists the whole business of genus and species.

BOOK IV

OF KNOWLEDGE AND PROBABILITY

Chapter I

OF KNOWLEDGE IN GENERAL

1. *Our Knowledge conversant about our Ideas only.* —Since the mind, in all its thoughts and reasonings, hath no other immediate object but its own ideas, which it alone does or can contemplate, it is evident that our knowledge is only conversant about them.

2. *Knowledge is the Perception of the Agreement or Disagreement of two Ideas.* —*Knowledge* then seems to me to be nothing but *the perception of the connexion of and agreement, or disagreement and repugnancy of any of our ideas.* In this alone it consists. Where this perception is, there is knowledge, and where it is not, there, though we may fancy, guess, or believe, yet we always come short of knowledge. For when we know that white is not black, what do we else but perceive, that these two ideas do not agree? When we possess ourselves with the utmost security of the demonstration, that the three angles of a triangle are equal to two right ones, what do we more but perceive, that equality to two right ones does necessarily agree to, and is inseparable from, the three angles of a triangle?

3. *This Agreement or Disagreement may be any of four sorts.* — But to understand a little more distinctly wherein this agreement or disagreement consists, I think we may reduce it all to these four sorts:

    I. *Identity,* or *diversity.*
    II. *Relation.*
    III. *Co-existence,* or *necessary connexion.*
    IV. *Real existence.*

4. *First, Of Identity, or Diversity in ideas.* —As to the first sort of agreement or disagreement, viz. *identity* or *diversity.* It is the first act of the mind, when it has any sentiments or ideas at all, to perceive its ideas; and so far as it perceives them, to know each what it is, and thereby also to perceive their difference, and that one is not another. This is so absolutely necessary, that without it there could be no knowledge, no reasoning, no imagination, no distinct thoughts at all. By this the mind clearly and infallibly perceives each idea to agree with itself, and to be what it is; and all distinct ideas to disagree, i.e. the one not to be the other: and this it does without pains, labour, or deduction; but at first view, by its natural power of perception and distinction. And though men of art have reduced this into those general rules, *What is, is,* and *It is impossible for the same thing to be and not to be,* for ready application in all cases, wherein there may be occasion to reflect on it: yet it is certain that the first exercise of this faculty is about particular ideas. A man infallibly knows, as soon as ever he has them in his mind, that the ideas he calls *white* and *round* are the very ideas they are; and that they are not other ideas which he calls *red*

or *square.* Nor can any maxim or proposition in the world make him know it clearer or surer than he did before, and without any such general rule. This then is the first agreement or disagreement which the mind perceives in its ideas; which it always perceives at first sight: and if there ever happen any doubt about it, it will always be found to be about the names, and not the ideas themselves, whose identity and diversity will always be perceived, as soon and clearly as the ideas themselves are; nor can it possibly be otherwise.

5. *Secondly, Of abstract Relations between ideas.* —The next sort of agreement or dis-agreement the mind perceives in any of its ideas may, I think, be called *relative,* and is nothing but the perception of the *relation* between any two ideas, of what kind soever, whether substances, modes, or any other. For, since all distinct ideas must eternally be known not to be the same, and so be universally and constantly denied one of another, there could be no room for any positive knowledge at all, if we could not perceive any relation between our ideas, and find out the agreement or disagree-ment they have one with another, in several ways the mind takes of comparing them.

6. *Thirdly, Of their necessary Co-existence in Substances.* —The third sort of agree-ment or disagreement to be found in our ideas, which the perception of the mind is employed about, is *co-existence* or *non-co-existence* in the *same subject;* and this belongs particularly to substances. Thus when we pronounce concerning gold, that it is fixed, our knowledge of this truth amounts to no more but this, that fixedness, or a power to remain in the fire unconsumed, is an idea that always accompanies and is joined with that particular sort of yellowness, weight, fusibility, malleableness, and solubility in *aqua regia,* which make our complex idea signified by the word gold.

7. *Fourthly, Of real Existence agreeing to any idea.* —The fourth and last sort is that of *actual real existence* agreeing to any idea.

Within these four sorts of agreement or disagreement is, I suppose, contained all the knowledge we have, or are capable of. For all the inquiries we can make con-cerning any of our ideas, all that we know or can affirm concerning any of them, is, That it is, or is not, the same with some other; that it does or does not always co-ex-ist with some other idea in the same subject; that it has this or that relation with some other idea; or that it has a real existence without the mind. Thus, 'blue is not yellow,' is of identity. 'Two triangles upon equal bases between two parallels are equal,' is of relation. 'Iron is susceptible of magnetical impressions,' is of co-exist-ence. 'God is,' is of real existence. Though identity and co-existence are truly nothing but relations, yet they are such peculiar ways of agreement or disagreement of our ideas, that they deserve well to be considered as distinct heads, and not under relation in general; since they are so different grounds of affirmation and negation, as will easily appear to any one, who will but reflect on what is said in several places of this *Essay.*

Chapter II

OF THE DEGREES OF OUR KNOWLEDGE

1. *Of the degrees, or differences in clearness, of our Knowledge: I. Intuitive.* —All our

knowledge consisting, as I have said, in the view the mind has of its own ideas, which is the utmost light and greatest certainty we, with our faculties, and in our way of knowledge, are capable of, it may not be amiss to consider a little the degrees of its evidence. The different clearness of our knowledge seems to me to lie in the different way of perception the mind has of the agreement or disagreement of any of its ideas. For if we will reflect on our own ways of thinking, we will find, that sometimes the mind perceives the agreement or disagreement of two ideas *immediately by themselves,* without the intervention of any other: and this I think we may call *intuitive knowledge.* For in this the mind is at no pains of proving or examining, but perceives the truth as the eye doth light, only by being directed towards it. Thus the mind perceives that *white* is not *black,* that a *circle* is not a *triangle,* that *three* are more than *two* and equal to *one and two.* Such kinds of truths the mind perceives at the first sight of the ideas together, by bare intuition; without the intervention of any other idea: and this kind of knowledge is the clearest and most certain that human frailty is capable of. This part of knowledge is irresistible, and, like bright sunshine, forces itself immediately to be perceived, as soon as ever the mind turns its view that way; and leaves no room for hesitation, doubt, or examination, but the mind is presently filled with the clear light of it. *It is on this intuition that depends all the certainty and evidence of all our knowledge;* which certainty every one finds to be so great, that he cannot imagine, and therefore not require a greater: for a man cannot conceive himself capable of a greater certainty than to know that any idea in his mind is such as he perceives it to be; and that two ideas, wherein he perceives a difference, are different and not precisely the same. He that demands a greater certainty than this, demands he knows not what, and shows only that he has a mind to be a sceptic, without being able to be so. Certainty depends so wholly on this intuition, that, in the next degree of knowledge which I call demonstrative, this intuition is necessary in all the connexions of the intermediate ideas, without which we cannot attain knowledge and certainty.

2. *II. Demonstrative.* — The next degree of knowledge is, where the mind perceives the agreement or disagreement of any ideas, but not immediately. Though wherever the mind perceives the agreement or disagreement of any of its ideas, there be certain knowledge; yet it does not always happen, that the mind sees that agreement or disagreement, which there is between them, even where it is discoverable; and in that case remains in ignorance, and at most gets no further than a probable conjecture. The reason why the mind cannot always perceive presently the agreement or disagreement of two ideas, is, because those ideas, concerning whose agreement or disagreement the inquiry is made, cannot by the mind be so put together as to show it. In this case then, when the mind cannot so bring its ideas together as by their immediate comparison, and as it were juxta-position or application one to another, to perceive their agreement or disagreement, it is fain, *by the intervention of other ideas* (one or more, as it happens) to discover the agreement or disagreement which it searches; and this is that which we call *reasoning.* Thus, the mind being willing to know the agreement or disagreement in bigness between the three angles of a triangle and two right ones, cannot by an immediate view and comparing them do it: because the three angles of a triangle cannot be brought at once, and be compared with any other one, or two, angles; and so of this the mind has no immediate, no intuitive knowledge. In this case the mind is fain to find out some other angles, to which the three angles of a triangle have an equality; and, finding

those equal to two right ones, comes to know their equality to two right ones.

7. *Each Step in Demonstrated knowledge must have Intuitive Evidence.* —Now, in every step reason makes in demonstrative knowledge, there is an intuitive knowledge of that agreement or disagreement it seeks with the next intermediate idea which it uses as a proof: for if it were not so, that yet would need a proof; since without the perception of such agreement or disagreement, there is no knowledge produced: if it be perceived by itself, it is intuitive knowledge: if it cannot be perceived by itself, there is need of some intervening idea, as a common measure, to show their agreement or disagreement. By which it is plain, that every step in reasoning that produces knowledge, has intuitive certainty; which when the mind perceives, there is no more required but to remember it, to make the agreement or disagreement of the ideas concerning which we inquire visible and certain. So that to make anything a demonstration, it is necessary to perceive the immediate agreement of the intervening ideas, whereby the agreement or disagreement of the two ideas under examination (whereof the one is always the first, and the other the last in the account) is found. This intuitive perception of the agreement or disagreement of the intermediate ideas, in each step and progression of the demonstration, must also be carried exactly in the mind, and a man must be sure that no part is left out: which, because in long deductions, and the use of many proofs, the memory does not always so readily and exactly retain; therefore it comes to pass, that this is more imperfect than intuitive knowledge, and men embrace often falsehood for demonstrations.

14. *III. Sensitive Knowledge of the particular Existence of finite beings without us.* — These two, viz. intuition and demonstration, are the degrees of our *knowledge;* whatever comes short of one of these, with what assurance soever embraced, is but *faith,* or *opinion,* but not knowledge, at least in all general truths. There is, indeed, another perception of the mind, employed about *the particular existence of finite beings without us,* which, going beyond bare probability, and yet not reaching perfectly to either of the foregoing degrees of certainty, passes under the name of *knowledge.* There can be nothing more certain than that the idea we receive from an external object is in our minds: this is intuitive knowledge. But whether there be anything more than barely that idea in our minds; whether we can thence certainly infer the existence of anything without us, which corresponds to that idea, is that whereof some men think there may be a question made; because men may have such ideas in their minds, when no such thing exists, no such object affects their senses. But yet here I think we are provided with an evidence that puts us past doubting. For I ask any one, Whether he be not invincibly conscious to himself of a different perception, when he looks on the sun by day, and thinks on it by night; when he actually tastes wormwood, or smells a rose, or only thinks on that savour or odour? We as plainly find the difference there is between any idea revived in our minds by our own memory, and actually coming into our minds by our senses, as we do between any two distinct ideas. If any one say, a dream may do the same thing, and all these ideas may be produced in us without any external objects; he may please to dream that I make him this answer:—1. That it is no great matter, whether I remove his scruple or no: where all is but dream, reasoning and arguments are of no use, truth and knowledge nothing. 2. That I believe he will allow a very manifest difference between dreaming of being in the fire, and being actually in it. But yet if he be resolved to appear so sceptical as to maintain, that what I call being actually in the fire is nothing but a dream; and that we cannot thereby certainly know, that any

such thing as fire actually exists without us: I answer, That we certainly finding that pleasure or pain follows upon the application of certain objects to us, whose existence we perceive, or dream that we perceive, by our senses; this certainty is as great as our happiness or misery, beyond which we have no concernment to know or to be. So that, I think, we may add to the two former sorts of knowledge this also, of the existence of particular external objects, by that perception and consciousness we have of the actual entrance of ideas from them, and allow these three degrees of knowledge, viz. *intuitive, demonstrative,* and *sensitive:* in each of which there are different degrees and ways of evidence and certainty.

Chapter III

OF THE EXTENT OF HUMAN KNOWLEDGE

1. *First, it extends no further than we have Ideas.* —Knowledge, as has been said, lying in the perception of the agreement or disagreement of any of our ideas, it follows from hence, That,

First, we can have knowledge no further than we have *ideas.*

2. *It extends no further than we can perceive their Agreement or Disagreement.* —Secondly, That we can have no knowledge further than we can have *perception* of that agreement or disagreement. Which perception being: 1. Either by *intuition,* or the immediate comparing any two ideas; or, 2. By *reason,* examining the agreement or disagreement of two ideas, by the intervention of some others; or, 3. By *sensation,* perceiving the existence of particular things: hence it also follows:

3. *Intuitive Knowledge extends itself not to all the relations of all our Ideas.* —Thirdly, That we cannot have an *intuitive knowledge* that shall extend itself to all our ideas, and all that we would know about them; because we cannot examine and perceive all the relations they have one to another, by juxta-position, or an immediate comparison one with another. Thus, having the ideas of an obtuse and an acute angled triangle, both drawn from equal bases, and between parallels, I can, by intuitive knowledge, perceive the one not to be the other, but cannot that way know whether they be equal or no; because their agreement or disagreement in equality can never be perceived by an immediate comparing them: the difference of figure makes their parts incapable of an exact immediate application; and therefore there is need of some intervening qualities to measure them by, which is demonstration, or rational knowledge.

4. *Nor does Demonstrative Knowledge.* —Fourthly, It follows, also, from what is above observed, that our *rational knowledge* cannot reach to the whole extent of our ideas: because between two different ideas we would examine, we cannot always find such mediums as we can connect one to another with an intuitive knowledge in all the parts of the deduction; and wherever that fails, we come short of knowledge and demonstration.

5. *Sensitive Knowledge narrower than either.* —Fifthly, *Sensitive knowledge* reaching no further than the existence of things actually present to our senses, is yet much narrower than either of the former.

6. *Our Knowledge, therefore, narrower than our Ideas.* —Sixthly, From all which it is evident, that the *extent of our knowledge* comes not only short of the reality of things, but even of the extent of our own ideas. Though our knowledge be limited to our ideas, and cannot exceed them either in extent or perfection; and though these be very narrow bounds, in respect of the extent of All-being, and far short of what we may justly imagine to be in some even created understandings, not tied down to the dull and narrow information that is to be received from some few, and not very acute, ways of perception, such as are our senses; yet it would be well with us if our knowledge were but as large as our ideas, and there were not many doubts and inquiries *concerning the ideas we have,* whereof we are not, nor I believe ever shall be in this world resolved. Nevertheless, I do not question but that human knowledge, under the present circumstances of our beings and constitutions, may be carried much further than it has hitherto been, if men would sincerely, and with freedom of mind, employ all that industry and labour of thought, in improving the means of discovering truth, which they do for the colouring or support of falsehood, to maintain a system, interest, or party they are once engaged in. But yet after all, I think I may, without injury to human perfection, be confident, that our knowledge would never reach to all we might desire to know concerning those ideas we have; nor be able to surmount all the difficulties, and resolve all the questions that might arise concerning any of them. We have the ideas of a *square,* a *circle,* and *equality;* and yet, perhaps, shall never be able to find a circle equal to a square, and certainly know that it is so. We have the ideas of *matter* and *thinking,* but possibly shall never be able to know whether any mere material being thinks or no; it being impossible for us, by the contemplation of our own ideas, without revelation, to discover whether Omnipotency has not given to some systems of matter, fitly disposed, a power to perceive and think, or else joined and fixed to matter, so disposed, a thinking immaterial substance: it being, in respect of our notions, not much more remote from our comprehension to conceive that GOD can, if he pleases, superadd to matter a *faculty of thinking,* than that he should superadd to it *another substance with a faculty of thinking;* since we know not wherein thinking consists, nor to what sort of substances the Almighty has been pleased to give that power, which cannot be in any created being, but merely by the good pleasure and bounty of the Creator. For I see no contradiction in it, that the first Eternal thinking Being, or Omnipotent Spirit, should, if he pleased, give to certain systems of created senseless matter, put together as he thinks fit, some degrees of sense, perception, and thought: though, as I think I have proved, lib. iv. ch. 10, § 14, &c., it is no less than a contradiction to suppose matter (which is evidently in its own nature void of sense and thought) should be that Eternal first-thinking Being. What certainty of knowledge can any one have, that some perceptions, such as, v.g., pleasure and pain, should not be in some bodies themselves, after a certain manner modified and moved, as well as that they should be in an immaterial substance, upon the motion of the parts of the body: Body, as far as we can conceive, being able only to strike and affect body, and motion, according to the utmost reach of our ideas, being able to produce nothing but motion; so that when we allow it to produce pleasure or pain, or the idea of a colour or sound, we are fain to quit our reason, go beyond our ideas, and attribute it wholly to the good pleasure of our Maker. For, since we must allow He has annexed effects to motion which we can no way conceive motion able to produce, what reason have we to conclude that He could not order them as well to be produced in a subject we

cannot conceive capable of them, as well as in a subject we cannot conceive the motion of matter can any way operate upon?

But to return to the argument in hand: our knowledge, I say, is not only limited to the paucity and imperfections of the ideas we have, and which we employ it about, but even comes short of that too: but how far it reaches, let us now inquire.

7. *How far our Knowledge reaches.* —The affirmations or negations we make concerning the ideas we have, may, as I have before intimated in general, be reduced to these four sorts, viz. identity, co-existence, relation, and real existence. I shall examine how far our knowledge extends in each of these:

8. *Firstly, Our Knowledge of Identity and Diversity in ideas extends as far as our Ideas themselves.* —First, as to *identity* and *diversity.* In this way of agreement or disagreement of our ideas, our intuitive knowledge is as far extended as our ideas themselves: and there can be no idea in the mind, which it does not, presently, by an intuitive knowledge, perceive to be what it is, and to be different from any other.

9. *Secondly, Of their Co-existence, extends only a very little way.* —As to the second sort, which is the agreement or disagreement of our ideas in *co-existence,* in this our knowledge is very short; though in this consists the greatest and most material part of our knowledge concerning substances. For our ideas of the species of substances being, as I have showed, nothing but certain collections of simple ideas united in one subject, and so co-existing together; v.g. our idea of flame is a body hot, luminous, and moving upward; of gold, a body heavy to a certain degree, yellow, malleable, and fusible: for these, or some such complex ideas as these, in men's minds, do these two names of the different substances, flame and gold, stand for. When we would know anything further concerning these, or any other sort of substances, what do we inquire, but what *other* qualities or powers these substances have or have not? Which is nothing else but to know what *other* simple ideas do, or do not co-exist with those that make up that complex idea?

10. *Because the Connexion between simple Ideas in substances is for the most part unknown.* —This, how weighty and considerable a part soever of human science, is yet very narrow, and scarce any at all. The reason whereof is, that the simple ideas whereof our complex ideas of substances are made up are, for the most part, such as carry with them, in their own nature, no *visible necessary* connexion or inconsistency with any other simple ideas, whose co-existence with them we would inform ourselves about.

11. *Especially of the secondary Qualities of Bodies.* —The ideas that our complex ones of substances are made up of, and about which our knowledge concerning substances is most employed, are those of their secondary qualities; which depending all (as has been shown) upon the primary qualities of their minute and insensible parts; or, if not upon them, upon something yet more remote from our comprehension; it is impossible we should know which have a *necessary* union or inconsistency one with another. For, not knowing the root they spring from, not knowing what size, figure, and texture of parts they are, on which depend, and from which result those qualities which make our complex idea of gold, it is impossible we should know what *other* qualities result from, or are incompatible with, the same constitution of the insensible parts of gold; and so consequently must always co-exist with that complex idea we have of it, or else are inconsistent with it.

12. *Because necessary Connexion between any secondary and the primary Qualities is*

undiscoverable by us. — Besides this ignorance of the primary qualities of the insensible parts of bodies, on which depend all their secondary qualities, there is yet another and more incurable part of ignorance, which sets us more remote from a certain knowledge of the co-existence or *inco-existence* (if I may so say) of different ideas in the same subject; and that is, that there is no discoverable connexion between any secondary quality and those primary qualities which it depends on.

13. *We have no perfect knowledge of their Primary Qualities.* — That the size, figure, and motion of one body should cause a change in the size, figure, and motion of another body, is not beyond our conception; the separation of the parts of one body upon the intrusion of another; and the change from rest to motion upon impulse; these and the like seem to have *some connexion* one with another. And if we knew these primary qualities of bodies, we might have reason to hope we might be able to know a great deal more of these operations of them one upon another: but our minds not being able to discover any connexion betwixt these primary qualities of bodies and the sensations that are produced in us by them, we can never be able to establish certain and undoubted rules of the *consequence* or *co-existence* of any secondary qualities, though we could discover the size, figure, or motion of those invisible parts which immediately produce them. We are so far from knowing *what* figure, size, or motion of parts produce a yellow colour, a sweet taste, or a sharp sound, that we can by no means conceive how *any* size, figure, or motion of any particles, can possibly produce in us the idea of any colour, taste, or sound whatsoever: there is no conceivable connexion between the one and the other.

14. *And seek in vain for certain and universal knowledge of unperceived qualities in substances.* — In vain, therefore, shall we endeavour to discover by our ideas (the only true way of certain and universal knowledge) what other ideas are to be found constantly joined with that of *our* complex idea of any substance: since we neither know the real constitution of the minute parts on which their qualities do depend; nor, did we know them, could we discover any necessary connexion between them and any of the secondary qualities: which is necessary to be done before we can certainly know their necessary co-existence. So, that, let our complex idea of any species of substances be what it will, we can hardly, from the simple ideas contained in it, certainly determine the necessary co-existence of any other quality whatsoever. Our knowledge in all these inquiries reaches very little further than our experience. Indeed some few of the primary qualities have a necessary dependence and visible connexion one with another, as figure necessarily supposes extension; receiving or communicating motion by impulse, supposes solidity. But though these, and perhaps some others of our ideas have: yet there are so few of them that have a visible connexion one with another, that we can by intuition or demonstration discover the co-existence of very few of the qualities that are to be found united in substances: and we are left only to the assistance of our senses to make known to us what qualities they contain. For of all the qualities that are co-existent in any subject, without this dependence and evident connexion of their ideas one with another, we cannot know certainly any two to co-exist, any further than experience, by our senses, informs us. Thus, though we see the yellow colour, and, upon trial, find the weight, malleableness, fusibility, and fixedness that are united in a piece of gold; yet, because no one of these ideas has any evident dependence or necessary connexion with the other, we cannot certainly know that where any four of these are, the fifth will be there also, how highly probable soever it may be; because the

highest probability amounts not to certainty, without which there can be no true knowledge. For this co-existence can be no further known than it is perceived; and it cannot be perceived but either in particular subjects, by the observation of our senses, or, in general, by the necessary connexion of the ideas themselves.

18. *Thirdly, Of Relations between abstracted ideas it is not easy to say how far our knowledge extends.* —As to the third sort of our knowledge, viz. the agreement or disagreement of any of our ideas in any other relation: this, as it is the largest field of our knowledge, so it is hard to determine how far it may extend: because the advances that are made in this part of knowledge, depending on our sagacity in finding intermediate ideas, that may show the relations and habitudes of ideas whose co-existence is not considered, it is a hard matter to tell when we are at an end of such discoveries; and when reason has all the helps it is capable of, for the finding of proofs, or examining the agreement or disagreement of remote ideas. They that are ignorant of Algebra cannot imagine the wonders in this kind are to be done by it: and what further improvements and helps advantageous to other parts of knowledge the sagacious mind of man may yet find out, it is not easy to determine. This at least I believe, that the *ideas of quantity* are not those alone that are capable of demonstration and knowledge; and that other, and perhaps more useful, parts of contemplation, would afford us certainty, if vices, passions, and domineering interest did not oppose or menace such endeavours.

21. *Fourthly, Of the three real Existences of which we have certain knowledge.* —As to the fourth sort of our knowledge, viz. of the *real actual existence of things*, we have an intuitive knowledge of *our own existence*, and a demonstrative knowledge of the existence of a *God:* of the existence of *anything else*, we have no other but a sensitive knowledge; which extends not beyond the objects present to our senses.

Chapter IV

OF THE REALITY OF KNOWLEDGE

1. *Objection.* '*Knowledge placed in our Ideas may be all unreal or chimerical.*' —I doubt not but my reader, by this time, may be apt to think that I have been all this while only building a castle in the air; and be ready to say to me:—

'To what purpose all this stir? Knowledge, say you, is only the perception of the agreement or disagreement of our own ideas: but who knows what those ideas may be? Is there anything so extravagant as the imaginations of men's brains? Where is the head that has no chimeras in it? Or if there be a sober and a wise man, what difference will there be, by your rules, between his knowledge and that of the most extravagant fancy in the world? They both have their ideas, and perceive their agreement and disagreement one with another. If there be any difference between them, the advantage will be on the warm-headed man's side, as having the more ideas, and the more lively. And so, by your rules, he will be the more knowing. If it be true, that all knowledge lies only in the perception of the agreement or disagreement of our own ideas, the visions of an enthusiast and the reasonings of a sober man will be equally certain. It is no matter how things are: so a man observe but the agreement of his own imaginations, and talk conformably, it is all truth, all certainty. Such castles in the air will be as strongholds of truth, as the demonstrations of Euclid. That an harpy is not a centaur is by this way as certain knowledge, and as much a truth, as that a square is not a circle.

'But of what use is all this fine knowledge of *men's own imaginations*, to a man that inquires after the reality of things? It matters not what men's fancies are, it is the knowledge of things that is only to be prized: it is this alone gives a value to our reasonings, and preference to one man's knowledge over another's, that it is of things as they really are, and not of dreams and fancies.'

2. *Answer. Not so, where Ideas agree with Things.* —To which I answer, That if our knowledge of our ideas terminate in them, and reach no further, where there is something further intended, our most serious thoughts will be of little more use than the reveries of a crazy brain; and the truths built thereon of no more weight than the discourses of a man who sees things clearly in a dream, and with great assurance utters them. But I hope, before I have done, to make it evident, that this way of certainty, by the knowledge of our own ideas, goes a little further than bare imagination: and I believe it will appear that all the certainty of general truths a man has lies in nothing else.

3. *But what shall be the criterion of this agreement?* —It is evident the mind knows not things immediately, but only by the intervention of the ideas it has of them. Our knowledge, therefore, is real only so far as there is a *conformity* between our ideas and the reality of things. But what shall be here the criterion? How shall the mind, when it perceives nothing but its own ideas, know that they agree with things themselves? This, though it seems not to want difficulty, yet, I think, there be two sorts of ideas that we may be assured agree with things.

4. *As, First, All Simple Ideas are really conformed to Things.* —The first are simple ideas, which since the mind, as has been showed, can by no means make to itself, must necessarily be the product of things operating on the mind, in a natural way, and producing therein those perceptions which by the Wisdom and Will of our Maker they are ordained and adapted to. From whence it follows, that simple ideas are not fictions of our fancies, but the natural and regular productions of things without us, really operating upon us; and so carry with them all the conformity which is intended; or which our state requires: for they represent to us things under those appearances which they are fitted to produce in us: whereby we are enabled to distinguish the sorts of particular substances, to discern the states they are in, and so to take them for our necessities, and apply them to our uses. Thus, the idea of whiteness, or bitterness, as it is in the mind, exactly answering that power which is in any body to produce it there, has all the real coformity it can or ought to have, with things without us. And this conformity between our simple ideas and the existence of things, is sufficient for real knowledge.

5. *Secondly, All Complex Ideas, except ideas of Substances, are their own archetypes.* — Secondly, All our complex ideas, *except those of substances,* being archetypes of the mind's own making, not intended to be the copies of anything, nor referred to the existence of anything, as to their originals, cannot want any conformity necessary to real knowledge. For that which is not designed to represent anything but itself, can never be capable of a wrong representation, nor mislead us from the true apprehension of anything, by its dislikeness to it: and such, excepting those of substances, are all our complex ideas. Which, as I have showed in another place, are combinations of ideas, which the mind, by its free choice, puts together, without considering any

connexion they have in nature. And hence it is, that in all these sorts the ideas themselves are considered as the archetypes, and things no otherwise regarded, but as they are conformable to them. So that we cannot but be infallibly certain, that all the knowledge we attain concerning these ideas is real, and reaches things themselves. Because in all our thoughts, reasonings, and discourses of this kind, we intend things no further than as they are conformable to our ideas. So that in these we cannot miss of a certain and undoubted reality.

6. *Hence the reality of Mathematical Knowledge.* —I doubt not but it will be easily granted, that the knowledge we have of mathematical truths is not only certain, but real knowledge; and not the bare empty vision of vain, insignificant chimeras of the brain: and yet, if we will consider, we shall find that it is only of our own ideas. The mathematician considers the truth and properties belonging to a rectangle or circle only as they are in idea in his own mind. For it is possible he never found either of them existing mathematically, i.e. precisely true, in his life. But yet the knowledge he has of any truths or properties belonging to a circle, or any other mathematical figure, are nevertheless true and certain, even of real things existing: because real things are no further concerned, nor intended to be meant by any such propositions, than as things really agree to those archetypes in his mind. Is it true of the *idea* of a triangle, that its three angles are equal to two right ones? It is true also of a triangle, wherever it *really exists*. Whatever other figure exists, that it is not exactly answerable to that idea of a triangle in his mind, is not at all concerned in that proposition. And therefore he is certain all his knowledge concerning such ideas is real knowledge: because, intending things no further than they agree with those his ideas, he is sure what he knows concerning those figures, when they have *barely an ideal existence* in his mind, will hold true of them also when they have *a real existence* in matter: his consideration being barely of those figures, which are the same wherever or however they exist.

7. *And of Moral.* —And hence it follows that moral knowledge is as capable of real certainty as mathematics. For certainty being but the perception of the agreement or disagreement of our ideas, and demonstration nothing but the perception of such agreement, by the intervention of other ideas or mediums; our moral ideas, as well as mathematical, being archetypes themselves, and so adequate and complete ideas; all the agreement or disagreement which we shall find in them will produce real knowledge, as well as in mathematical figures.

11. *Thirdly, Our complex Ideas of Substances have their Archetypes without us; and here knowledge comes short.* —*Thirdly,* There is another sort of complex ideas, which, being referred to archetypes without us, may differ from them, and so our knowledge about them may come short of being real. Such are our ideas of substances, which, consisting of a collection of simple ideas, supposed taken from the works of nature, may yet vary from them; by having more or different ideas united in them than are to be found united in the things themselves. From whence it comes to pass, that they may, and often do, fail of being exactly conformable to things themselves.

18. *Recapitulation.* —Wherever we perceive the agreement or disagreement of any of our ideas, there is certain knowledge: and wherever we are sure those ideas agree with the reality of things, there is certain real knowledge. Of which agreement of our ideas with the reality of things, having here given the marks, I think, I have shown *wherein it is that certainty, real certainty, consists.* Which, whatever it was to

others, was, I confess, to me heretofore, one of those desiderata which I found great want of.

Chapter VI
OF UNIVERSAL PROPOSITIONS: THEIR TRUTH AND CERTAINTY.

1. *Treating of Words necessary to Knowledge.* The though the examining and judging of ideas by themselves, their names being quite laid aside, be the best and surest way to clear and distinct knowledge: yet, through the prevailing custom of using sounds for ideas, I think it is very seldom practised. Every one may observe how common it is for names to be made use of, instead of the ideas themselves, even when men think and reason within their own breasts; especially if the ideas be very complex, and made up of a great collection of simple ones. This makes the consideration of *words* and *propositions* so necessary a part of the Treatise of Knowledge, that it is very hard to speak intelligibly of the one, without explaining the other.

2. *General Truths hardly to be understood, but in verbal Propositions.* — All the knowledge we have, being only of particular or general truths, it is evident that whatever may be done in the former of these, the latter, which is that which with reason is most sought after, can never be well made known, and is very seldom apprehended, but as conceived and expressed in words. It is not, therefore, out of our way, in the examination of our knowledge, to inquire into the truth and certainty of universal propositions.

3. *Certainty twofold — of Truth and of Knowledge.* — But that we may not be misled in this case by that which is the danger everywhere, I mean by the doubtfulness of terms, it is fit to observe that certainty is twofold; *certainty of truth* and *certainty of knowledge.* Certainty of truth is, when words are so put together in propositions as exactly to express the agreement or disagreement of the ideas they stand for, as really it is. Certainty of knowledge is to perceive the agreement or disagreement of ideas, as expressed in any proposition. This we usually call knowing, or being certain of the truth of any proposition.

4. *No Proposition can be certainly known to be true, where the real Essence of each Species mentioned is not known.* — Now, because we cannot be certain of the truth of any general proposition, unless we know the precise bounds and extent of the species its terms stand for, it is necessary we should know the essence of each species, which is that which constitutes and bounds it.

This, in all simple ideas and modes, is not hard to do. For in these the real and nominal essence being the same, or, which is all one, the abstract idea which the general term stands for being the sole essence and boundary that is or can be supposed of the species, there can be no doubt how far the species extends, or what things are comprehended under each term; which, it is evident, are all that have an exact conformity with the idea it stands for, and no other.

But in substances, wherein a real essence, distinct from the nominal, is supposed to constitute, determine, and bound the species, the extent of the general word is very uncertain; because, not knowing this real essence, we cannot know what is, or what is not of that species; and, consequently, what may or may not with certainty be affirmed of it. And thus, speaking of a *man,* or *gold,* or any other species of natural substances, as supposed constituted by a precise and real essence which nature regularly imparts to every individual of that kind, whereby it is made to be of that species, we cannot be certain of the truth of any affirmation or negation made of it. For man or gold, taken in this sense, and used for species of things constituted by real essences, different from the complex idea in the mind of the speaker, stand for we know not what; and the extent of these species, with such boundaries, are so unknown and undetermined, that it is impossible with any certainty to affirm, that all men are rational, or that all gold is yellow. But where the nominal essence is kept to, as the boundary of each species, and men extend the application of any general term no further than to the particular things in which the complex idea it stands for is to be found, there they are in no danger to mistake the bounds of each species, nor can be in doubt, on this account, whether any proposition be true or not. I have chosen to explain this uncertainty of propositions in this scholastic way, and have made use of the terms of *essences,* and *species,* on purpose to show the absurdity and inconvenience there is to think of them as of any other sort of realities, than barely abstract ideas with names to them. To suppose that the species of things are anything but the sorting of them under general names, according as they agree to several abstract ideas of which we make those names the signs, is to confound truth, and introduce uncertainty into all general propositions that can be made about them. Though therefore these things might, to people not possessed with scholastic learning, be treated of in a better and clearer way; yet those wrong notions of essences or species having got root in most people's minds who have received any tincture from the learning which has prevailed in this part of the world, are to be discovered and removed, to make way for that use of words which should convey certainty with it.

5. *This more particularly concerns Substances.* — The names of substances, then, whenever made to stand for species which are supposed to be constituted by real essences which we know not, are not capable to convey certainty to the understanding. Of the truth of general propositions made up of such terms we cannot be sure. The reason whereof is plain: for how can we be sure that this or that quality is in gold, when we know what is or is not gold? Since in this way of speaking, nothing is gold but what partakes of an essence, which we, not knowing, cannot know where it is or is not, and so cannot be sure that any parcel of matter in the world is or is not in this sense gold; being incurably ignorant whether *it* has or has not that which makes anything to be called gold; i.e. that real essence of gold whereof we have no idea at all. This being as impossible for us to know as it is for a blind man to tell in what flower the colour of a pansy is or is not to be found, whilst he has no idea of the colour of a pansy at all. Or if we could (which is impossible) certainly know where a real essence, which we know not, is, v.g. in what parcels of matter the real essence of gold is, yet could we not be sure that this or that quality could with truth be affirmed of gold; since it is impossible for us to know that this or that quality or idea has a necessary connexion with a real essence of which we have no idea at all, whatever species that supposed real essence may be imagined to constitute.

6. *The Truth of few universal Propositions concerning Substances is to be known.* — On the other side, the names of substances, when made use of as they should be, for the ideas men have in their minds, though they carry a clear and determinate signification with them, will not yet serve us to make many universal propositions of whose truth we can be certain. Not because in this use of them we are uncertain what things are signified by them, but because the complex ideas they stand for are such

combinations of simple ones as carry not with them any discoverable connexion or repugnancy, but with a very few other ideas.

7. *Because necessary Co-existence of simple Ideas in Substances can in few Cases be known.* —The complex ideas that our names of the species of substances properly stand for, are collections of such qualities as have been observed to co-exist in an unknown substratum, which we call substance; but what other qualities necessarily co-exist with such combinations, we cannot certainly know, unless we can discover their natural dependence; which, in their primary qualities, we can go but a very little way in; and in all their secondary qualities we can discover no connexion at all: for the reasons mentioned, chap. iii. Viz. I. Because we know not the real constitutions of substances, on which each secondary quality particularly depends. 2. Did we know that, it would serve us only for experimental (not universal) knowledge; and reach with certainty no further than that bare instance: because our understandings can discover no conceivable connexion between any secondary quality and any modification whatsoever of any of the primary ones. And therefore there are very few general propositions to be made concerning substances, which can carry with them undoubted certainty.

8. *Instance in Gold.* —'All gold is fixed,' is a proposition whose truth we cannot be certain of, how universally soever it be believed, For if, according to the useless imagination of the Schools, any one supposes the term gold to stand for a species of things set out by nature, by a real essence belonging to it, it is evident he knows not what particular substances are of that species; and so cannot with certainty affirm anything universally of god. But if he makes gold stand for a species determined by its nominal essence, let the nominal essence, for example, be the complex idea of a body of a certain yellow colour, malleable, fusible, and heavier than any other known; — in this proper use of the word gold, there is no difficulty to know what is or is not gold. But yet no other quality can with certainty be universally affirmed or denied of gold, but what hath a *discoverable* connexion or inconsistency with that nominal essence. Fixedness, for example, having no necessary connexion that we can discover, with the colour, weight, or any other simple idea of our complex one, or with the whole combination together; it is impossible that we should certainly know the truth of this proposition, that all gold is fixed.

9. *No discoverable necessary connexion between nominal essence of gold and other simple ideas.* —As there is no discoverable connexion between fixedness and the colour, weight, and other simple ideas of that nominal essence of gold; so, if we make our complex idea of gold, a body yellow, fusible, ductile, weighty, and fixed, we shall be at the same uncertainty concerning solubility in *aqua regia,* and for the same reason. Since we can never, from consideration of the ideas themselves, with certainty affirm or deny of a body whose complex idea is made up of yellow, very weighty, ductile, fusible, and fixed, that it is soluble in *aqua regia:* and so on of the rest of its qualities. I would gladly meet with one general affirmation concerning any quality of gold, that any one can certainly know is true. It will, no doubt, be presently objected, Is not this an universal proposition, *All gold is malleable?* To which I answer, It is a very certain proposition, if malleableness be a part of the complex idea the word gold stands for. But then here is nothing affirmed of gold, but that that sound stands for an idea in which malleableness is contained: and such a sort of truth and certainty as this it is, to say a centaur is four-footed. But if malleableness make not a part of the specific essence the name of gold stands for, it is plain, *all gold is malleable,* is not a certain proposition. Because, let the complex idea of gold be made up of whichsoever

of its other qualities you please, malleableness will not appear to depend on that complex idea, nor follow from any simple one contained in it: the connexion that malleableness has (if it has any) with those other qualities being only by the intervention of the real constitution of its insensible parts; which, since we know not, it is impossible we should perceive that connexion, unless we could discover that which ties them together.

10. *As far as any such Co-existence can be known, so far Universal Propositions may be certain. But this will go but a little way.* — The more, indeed, of these co-existing qualities we unite into one complex idea, under one name, the more precise and determinate we make the signification of that word; but never yet make it thereby more capable of universal certainty, *in respect of other qualities not contained in our complex idea:* since we perceive not their connexion or dependence on one another; being ignorant both of that real constitution in which they are all founded, and also how they flow from it. For the chief part of our knowledge concerning substances is not, as in other things, barely of the relation of two ideas that may exist separately; but is of the necessary connexion and co-existence of several distinct ideas in the same subject, or of their repugnancy so to co-exist. Could we begin at the other end, and discover what it was wherein that colour consisted, what made a body lighter or heavier, what texture of parts made it malleable, fusible, and fixed, and fit to be dissolved in this sort of liquor, and not in another; — if, I say, we had such an idea as this of bodies, and could perceive wherein all sensible qualities originally consist, and how they are produced; we might frame such abstract ideas of them as would furnish us with matter of more general knowledge, and enable us to make universal propositions, that should carry general truth and certainty with them. But whilst our complex ideas of the sorts of substances are so remote from that internal real constitution on which their sensible qualities depend, and are made up of nothing but an imperfect collection of those apparent qualities our senses can discover, there can be few general propositions concerning substances of whose real truth we can be certainly assured; since there are but few simple ideas of whose connexion and necessary co-existence we can have certain and undoubted knowledge. I imagine, amongst all the secondary qualities of substances, and the powers relating to them, there cannot any two be named, whose necessary co-existence, or repugnance to co-exist, can certainly be known; unless in those of the same sense, which necessarily exclude one another, as I have elsewhere showed. No one, I think, by the colour that is in any body, can certainly know what smell, taste, sound, or tangible qualities it has, nor what alterations it is capable to make or receive on or from other bodies. The same may be said of the sound or taste,&c. Our specific names of substances standing for any collections of such ideas, it is not to be wondered that we can with them make very few general propositions of undoubted real certainty. But yet so far as any complex idea of any sort of substances contains in it any simple idea, whose *necessary* co-existence with any other *may* be discovered, so far universal propositions may with certainty be made concerning it: v.g. could any one discover a necessary connexion between malleableness and the colour or weight of gold, or any other part of the complex idea signified by that name, he might make a certain universal proposition concerning gold in this respect; and the real truth of this proposition, that *all gold is malleable,* would be as certain as of this, *the three angles of all right-lined triangles are all equal to two right ones.*

Chapter IX

OF OUR THREEFOLD KNOWLEDGE OF EXISTENCE

1. *General Propositions that are certain concern not Existence.* —Hitherto we have only considered the essences of things; which being only abstract ideas, and thereby removed in our thoughts from particular existence, (that being the proper operation of the mind, in abstraction, to consider an idea under no other existence but what it has in the understanding,) gives us no knowledge of real existence at all. Where, by the way, we may take notice, that universal propositions of whose truth or falsehood we can have certain knowledge concern not existence: and further, that all particular affirmations or negations that would not be certain if they were made general, are only concerning existence; they declaring only the accidental union or separation of ideas in things existing, which, in their abstract natures, have no known necessary union or repugnancy.

2. *A threefold Knowledge of Existence.* —But, leaving the nature of propositions, and different ways of predication to be considered more at large in another place, let us proceed now to inquire concerning our knowledge of the *existence of things,* and how we come by it. I say, then, that we have the knowledge of *our own* existence by intuition; of the existence of *God* by demonstration; and of *other things* by sensation.

3. *Our Knowledge of our own Existence is Intuitive.* —As for *our own existence,* we perceive it so plainly and so certainly, that it neither needs nor is capable of any proof. For nothing can be more evident to us than our own existence. I think, I reason, I feel pleasure and pain: can any of these be more evident to me than my own existence? If I doubt of all other things, that very doubt makes me perceive my own existence, and will not suffer me to doubt of that. For if I know I feel pain, it is evident I have as certain perception of my own existence, as of the existence of the pain I feel: or if I know I doubt, I have as certain perception of the existence of the thing doubting, as of that thought which I *call doubt.* Experience then convinces us, that we have an *intuitive knowledge* of our own existence, and an internal infallible perception that we are. In every act of sensation, reasoning, or thinking, we are conscious to ourselves of our own being; and, in this matter, come not short of the highest degree of certainty.

Chapter X

OF OUR KNOWLEDGE OF THE EXISTENCE OF A GOD

1. *We are capable of knowing certainly that there is a God.* —Though God has given us no innate ideas of himself; though he has stamped no original characters on our minds, wherein we may read his being; yet having furnished us with those faculties our minds are endowed with, he hath not left himself without witness: since we have sense, perception, and reason, and cannot want a clear proof of him, as long as we carry *ourselves* about us. Nor can we justly complain of our ignorance in this great point; since he has so plentifully provided us with the means to discover and know

him; so far as is necessary to the end of our being, and the great concernment of our happiness. But, though this be the most obvious truth that reason discovers, and though its evidence be (if I mistake not) equal to mathematical certainty: yet it requires thought and attention; and the mind must apply itself to a regular deduction of it from some part of our intuitive knowledge, or else we shall be as uncertain and ignorant of this as of other propositions, which are in themselves capable of clear demonstration. To show, therefore, that we are capable of *knowing*, i.e. *being certain* that there is a God, and *how we may come by* this certainty, I think we need go no further than *ourselves*, and that undoubted knowledge we have of our own existence.

2. *For Man knows that he himself exists.* —I think it is beyond question, that man has a clear idea of his own being; he knows certainly he exists, and that he is something. He that can doubt whether he be anything or no, I speak not to; no more than I would argue with pure nothing, or endeavour to convince nonentity that it were something. If any one pretends to be so sceptical as to deny his own existence, (for really to doubt of it is manifestly impossible,) let him for me enjoy his beloved happiness of being nothing, until hunger or some other pain convince him of the contrary. This, then, I think I may take for a truth, which every one's certain knowledge assures him of, beyond the liberty of doubting, viz. that he is *something that actually exists.*

3. *He knows also that Nothing cannot produce a Being; therefore Something must have existed from Eternity.* —In the next place, man knows, by an intuitive certainty, that bare *nothing can no more produce any real being, than it can be equal to two right angles.* If a man knows not that nonentity, or the absence of all being, cannot be equal to two right angles, it is impossible he should know any demonstration in Euclid. If, therefore, we know there is some real being, and that nonentity cannot produce any real being, it is an evident demonstration, that *from eternity there has been something;* since what was not from eternity had a beginning; and what had a beginning must be produced by something else.

4. *And that eternal Being must be most powerful.* —Next, it is evident, that what had its being and beginning from another, must also have all that which is in and belongs to its being from another too. All the powers it has must be owing to and received from the same source. This eternal source, then, of all being must also be the source and original of all power; and so *this eternal Being must be also the most powerful.*

5. *And most knowing.* —Again, a man finds in *himself* perception and knowledge. We have then got one step further; and we are certain now that there is not only some being, but some knowing, intelligent being in the world. There was a time, then, when there was no knowing being, and when knowledge began to be; or else there has been also *a knowing being from eternity.* If it be said, there was a time when no being had any knowledge, when that eternal being was void of all understanding; I reply, that then it was impossible there should ever have been any knowledge: it being as impossible that things wholly void of knowledge, and operating blindly, and without any perception, should produce a knowing being, as it is impossible that a triangle should make itself three angles bigger than two right ones. For it is as repugnant to the idea of senseless matter, that it should put into itself sense, perception, and knowledge, as it is repugnant to the idea of a triangle, that it should put into itself greater angles than two right ones.

6. *And therefore God.* —Thus, from the consideration of ourselves, and what we

infallibly find in our own constitutions, our reason leads us to the knowledge of this certain and evident truth,— *That there is an eternal, most powerful, and most knowing Being;* which whether any one will please to call God, it matters not. The thing is evident; and from this idea duly considered, will easily be deduced all those other attributes, which we ought to ascribe to this eternal Being. If, nevertheless, any one should be found so senselessly arrogant, as to suppose man alone knowing and wise, but yet the product of mere ignorance and chance; and that all the rest of the universe acted only by that blind haphazard; I shall leave with him that very rational and emphatical rebuke of Tully[3] (1. ii. De Leg.), to be considered at his leisure: 'What can be more sillily arrogant and misbecoming, than for a man to think that he has a mind and understanding in him, but yet in all the universe beside there is no such thing? Or that those things, which with the utmost stretch of his reason he can scarce comprehend, should be moved and managed without any reason at all?' *Quid est enim verius, quam neminem esse oportere tam stulte arrogantem, ut in se mentem et rationem putet inesse, in caelo mundoque non putet? Aut ea quae vix summa ingenii ratione comprehendat, nulla ratione moveri putet?*

From what has been said, it is plain to me we have a more certain knowledge of the existence of a God, than of anything our senses have not immediately discovered to us. Nay, I presume I may say, that we more certainly know that there is a God, than that there is anything else without us. When I say we *know,* I mean there is such a knowledge within our reach which we cannot miss, if we will but apply our minds to that, as we do to several other inquiries.

Chapter XI

OF OUR KNOWLEDGE OF THE EXISTENCE OF OTHER THINGS

1. *Knowledge of the existence of other Finite Beings is to be had only by actual Sensation.* —The knowledge of our own being we have by intuition. The existence of a God, reason clearly makes known to us, as has been shown.

The knowledge of the existence of *any other thing* we can have only by *sensation:* for there being no necessary connexion of real existence with any *idea* a man hath in his memory; nor any other existence but that of God with the existence of any particular man: no particular man can know the existence of any other being, but only when, by actual operating upon him, it makes itself perceived by him. For, the having the idea of anything in our mind, no more proves the existence of that thing, than the picture of a man evidences his being in the world, or the visions of a dream make thereby a true history.

2. *Instance: Whiteness of this Paper.* —It is therefore the *actual receiving* of ideas from without that gives us notice of the existence of other things, and makes us know, that something doth exist at that time without us, which causes that idea in us; though perhaps we neither know nor consider how it does it. For it takes not from the certainty of our senses, and the ideas we receive by them, that we know not the

---

3. [Regarding Tully (Cicero), see Hobbes's *Leviathan,* n. 11. Locke's reference is to *De Legibus,* a political dialogue.]

manner wherein they are produced: v.g. whilst I write this, I have, by the paper affecting my eyes, that idea produced in my mind, which, whatever object causes, I call *white;* by which I know that that quality or accident (i.e. whose appearance before my eyes always causes that idea) doth really exist, and hath a being without me. And of this, the greatest assurance I can possibly have, and to which my faculties can attain, is the testimony of my eyes, which are the proper and sole judges of this thing; whose testimony I have reason to rely on as so certain, that I can no more doubt, whilst I write this, that I see white and black, and that something really exists that causes that sensation in me, than that I write or move my hand; which is a certainty as great as human nature is capable of, concerning the existence of anything, but a man's self alone, and of God.

3. *This notice by our Senses, though not so certain as Demonstration, yet may be called Knowledge, and proves the Existence of Things without us.* —The notice we have by our senses of the existing of things without us, though it be not altogether so certain as our intuitive knowledge, or the deductions of our reason employed about the clear abstract ideas of our own minds; yet it is an assurance that deserves the name of *knowledge.* If we persuade ourselves that our faculties act and inform us right concerning the existence of those objects that affect them, it cannot pass for an ill-grounded confidence: for I think nobody can, in earnest, be so sceptical as to be uncertain of the existence of those things which he sees and feels. At least, he that can doubt so far, (whatever he may have with his own thoughts,) will never have any controversy with me; since he can never be sure I say anything contrary to his own opinion. As to myself, I think God has given me assurance enough of the existence of things without me: since, by their different application, I can produce in myself both pleasure and pain, which is one great concernment of my present state. This is certain: the confidence that our faculties do not herein deceive us, is the greatest assurance we are capable of concerning the existence of material beings. For we cannot act anything but by our faculties; nor talk of knowledge itself, but by the help of those faculties which are fitted to apprehend even what knowledge is.

But besides the assurance we have from our senses themselves, that they do not err in the information they give us of the existence of things without us, when they are affected by them, we are further confirmed in this assurance by other concurrent reasons:—

4. *Confirmed by concurrent reasons:* —*First, Because we cannot have ideas of Sensation but by the Inlet of the Senses.* —I. It is plain those perceptions are produced in us by exterior causes affecting our senses: because those that want the *organs* of any sense, never can have the ideas belonging to that sense produced in their minds. This is too evident to be doubted: and therefore we cannot but be assured that they come in by the organs of that sense, and no other way. The organs themselves, it is plain, do not produce them: for then the eyes of a man in the dark would produce colours, and his nose smell roses in the winter: but we see nobody gets the relish of a pineapple, till he goes to the Indies, where it is, and tastes it.

5. *Secondly, Because we find that an Idea from actual Sensation, and another from Memory, are very distinct Perceptions.* —II. Because sometimes I find that *I cannot avoid the having those ideas produced in my mind.* For though, when my eyes are shut, or windows fast, I can at pleasure recall to my mind the ideas of light, or the sun, which former sensations had lodged in my memory; so I can at pleasure lay by *that* idea, and take into my view that of the smell of a rose, or taste sugar. But, if I turn my

eyes at noon towards the sun, I cannot avoid the ideas which the light or sun then produces in me. So that there is a manifest difference between the ideas laid up in my memory, (over which, if they were there only, I should have constantly the same power to dispose of them, and lay them by at pleasure,) and those which force themselves upon me, and I cannot avoid having. And therefore it must needs be some exterior cause, and the brisk acting of some objects without me, whose efficacy I cannot resist, that produces those ideas in my mind, whether I will or no. Besides, there is nobody who doth not perceive the difference in himself between contemplating the sun, as he hath the idea of it in his memory, and actually looking upon it: of which two, his perception is so distinct, that few of his ideas are more distinguishable one from another. And therefore he hath certain knowledge that they are not *both* memory, or the actions of his mind, and fancies only within him; but that actual seeing hath a cause without.

6. *Thirdly, Because Pleasure or Pain, which accompanies actual Sensation, accompanies not the returning of those Ideas without the external Objects.* —III. Add to this, that many of those ideas are *produced in us with pain*, which afterwards we remember without the least offence. Thus, the pain of heat or cold, when the idea of it is revived in our minds, gives us no disturbance; which, when felt, was very troublesome; and is again, when actually repeated: which is occasioned by the disorder the external object causes in our bodies when applied to them: and we remember the pains of hunger, thirst, or the headache, without any pain at all; which would either never disturb us, or else constantly do it, as often as we thought of it, were there nothing more but ideas floating in our minds, and appearances entertaining our fancies, without the real existence of things affecting us from abroad. The same may be said of *pleasure*, accompanying several actual sensations. And though mathematical demonstration depends not upon sense, yet the examining them by diagrams gives great credit to the evidence of our sight, and seems to give it a certainty approaching to that of demonstration itself. For, it would be very strange, that a man should allow it for an undeniable truth, that two angles of a figure, which he measures by lines and angles of a diagram, should be bigger one than the other, and yet doubt of the existence of those lines and angles, which by looking on he makes use of to measure that by.

7. *Fourthly, Because our Senses assist one another's Testimony of the Existence of outward Things, and enable us to predict.* —IV. Our *senses* in many cases *bear witness to the truth of each other's report*, concerning the existence of sensible things without us. He that *sees* a fire, may, if he doubt whether it be anything more than a bare fancy, *feel* it too; and be convinced, by putting his hand in it. Which certainly could never be put into such exquisite pain by a bare idea or phantom, unless that the pain be a fancy too: which yet he cannot, when the burn is well, by raising the idea of it, bring upon himself again.

Thus I see, whilst I write this, I can change the appearance of the paper; and by designing the letters, tell *beforehand* what new idea it shall exhibit the very next moment, by barely drawing my pen over it: which will neither appear (let me fancy as much as I will) if my hands stand still; or though I move my pen, if my eyes be shut: nor, when those characters are once made on the paper, can I choose afterwards but see them as they are; that is, have the ideas of such letters as I have made. Whence it is manifest, that they are not barely the sport and play of my own imagination, when I find that the characters that were made at the pleasure of my own thoughts, do not obey them; nor yet cease to be, whenever I shall fancy it, but continue to affect my senses constantly and regularly, according to the figures I made them. To which if we will add, that the sight of those shall, from another man, draw such sounds as I beforehand design they shall stand for, there will be little reason left to doubt that those words I write do really exist without me, when they cause a long series of regular sounds to affect my ears, which could not be the effect of my imagination, nor could my memory retain them in that order.

8. *This Certainty is as great as our Condition needs.* —But yet, if after all this any one will be so sceptical as to distrust his senses, and to affirm that all we see and hear, feel and taste, think and do, during our whole being, is but the series and deluding appearances of a long dream, whereof there is no reality; and therefore will question the existence of all things, or our knowledge of anything: I must desire him to consider, that, if all be a dream, then he doth but dream that he makes the question, and so it is not much matter that a waking man should answer him. But yet, if he pleases, he may dream that I make him this answer, That the certainty of things existing in *rerum natura* when we have the testimony of our senses for it is not only as great as our frame can attain to, but as our condition needs. For, our faculties being suited not to the full extent of being, nor to a perfect, clear, comprehensive knowledge of things free from all doubt and scruple; but to the preservation of us, in whom they are; and accommodated to the use of life: they serve to our purpose well enough, if they will but give us certain notice of those things, which are convenient or inconvenient to us. For he that sees a candle burning, and hath experimented the force of its flame by putting his finger in it, will little doubt that this is something existing without him, which does him harm, and puts him to great pain: which is assurance enough, when no man requires greater certainty to govern his actions by than what is as certain as his actions themselves. And if our dreamer pleases to try whether the glowing heat of a glass furnace be barely a wandering imagination in a drowsy man's fancy, by putting his hand into it, he may perhaps be wakened into a certainty greater than he could wish, that it is something more than bare imagination. So that this evidence is as great as we can desire, being as certain to us as our pleasure or pain, i.e. happiness or misery; beyond which we have no concernment, either of knowing or being. Such an assurance of the existence of things without us is sufficient to direct us in the attaining the good and avoiding the evil which is caused by them, which is the important concernment we have of being made acquainted with them.

9. *But reaches no further than actual Sensation.* —In fine, then, when our senses do actually convey into our understandings any idea, we cannot but be satisfied that there doth something *at that time* really exist without us, which doth affect our senses, and by them give notice of itself to our apprehensive faculties, and actually produce that idea which we then perceive: and we cannot so far distrust their testimony, as to doubt that such *collections* of simple ideas as we have observed by our senses to be united together, do really exist together. But this knowledge extends as far as the present testimony of our senses, employed about particular objects that do then affect them, and no further. For if I saw such a collection of simple ideas as is wont to be called *man*, existing together one minute since, and am now alone, I cannot be certain that the same man exists now, since there is no *necessary connexion* of his existence a minute since with his existence now: by a thousand ways he may cease to be, since I had the testimony of my senses for his existence.

And if I cannot be certain that the man I saw last to-day is now in being, I can less be certain that he is so who hath been longer removed from my senses, and I have not seen since yesterday, or since the last year: and much less can I be certain of the existence of men that I never saw. And, therefore, though it be highly probable that millions of men do now exist, yet, whilst I am alone, writing this, I have not that certainty of it which we strictly call knowledge; though the great likelihood of it puts me past doubt, and it be reasonable for me to do several things upon the confidence that there are men (and men also of my acquaintance, with whom I have to do) now in the world: but this is but probability, not knowledge.

12. *The Existence of other finite Spirits not knowable, and rests on Faith.* —What ideas we have of spirits, and how we come by them, I have already shown. But though we have those ideas in our minds, and know we have them there, the having the ideas of spirits does not make us know that any such things do exist without us, or that there are any finite spirits, or any other spiritual beings, but the Eternal God. We have ground from revelation, and several other reasons, to believe with assurance that there are such creatures: but our senses not being able to discover them, we want the means of knowing their particular existences. For we can no more know that there are finite spirits really existing, by the idea we have of such beings in our minds, than by the ideas any one has of fairies or centaurs, he can come to know that things answering those ideas do really exist.

And therefore concerning the existence of finite spirits, as well as several other things, we must content ourselves with the evidence of faith; but universal, certain propositions concerning this matter are beyond our reach. For however true it may be, v.g., that all the intelligent spirits that God ever created do still exist, yet it can never make a part of our certain knowledge. These and the like propositions we may assent to, as highly probable, but are not, I fear, in this state capable of knowing. We are not, then, to put others upon demonstrating, nor ourselves upon search of universal certainty in all those matters; wherein we are not capable of any other knowledge, but what our senses give us in this or that particular.

13. *Only particular Propositions concerning concrete Existences are knowable.* —By which it appears that there are two sorts of propositions:—(1) There is one sort of propositions concerning the *existence* of anything answerable to such an idea: as having the idea of an elephant, phoenix, motion, or an angel, in my mind, the first and natural inquiry is, Whether such a thing does anywhere exist? And this knowledge is only of particulars. No existence of anything without us, but only of God, can certainly be known further than our senses inform us. (2) There is another sort of propositions, wherein is expressed the agreement or disagreement of *our abstract ideas,* and their dependence on one another. Such propositions may be universal and certain. So, having the idea of God and myself, of fear and obedience, I cannot but be sure that God is to be feared and obeyed by me: and this proposition will be certain, concerning man in general, if I have made an abstract idea of such a species, whereof I am one particular. But yet this proposition, how certain soever, that 'men ought to fear and obey God' proves not to me the *existence* of *men* in the world; but will be true of all such creatures, whenever they do exist: which certainty of such general propositions depends on the agreement or disagreement to be discovered in those abstract ideas.

Chapter XVIII

OF FAITH AND REASON, AND THEIR DISTINCT PROVINCES

1. *Necessary to know their boundaries.* —It has been above shown, 1. That we are of necessity ignorant, and want knowledge of all sorts, where we want ideas. 2. That we are ignorant, and want rational knowledge, where we want proofs. 3. That we want certain knowledge and certainty, as far as we want clear and determined specific ideas. 4. That we want probability to direct our assent in matters where we have neither knowledge of our own nor testimony of other men to bottom our reason upon.

From these things thus premised, I think we may come to lay down *the measures and boundaries between faith and reason:* the want whereof may possibly have been the cause, if not of great disorders, yet at least of great disputes, and perhaps mistakes in the world. For till it be resolved how far we are to be guided by reason, and how far by faith, we shall in vain dispute, and endeavour to convince one another in matters of religion.

2. *Faith and Reason, what, as contradistinguished.* —I find every sect, as far as reason will help them, make use of it gladly: and where it fails them, they cry out, It is matter of faith, and above reason. And I do not see how they can argue with any one, or ever convince a gainsayer who makes use of the same plea, without setting down strict boundaries between faith and reason; which ought to be the first point established in all questions where faith has anything to do.

Reason, therefore, here, as contradistinguished to *faith,* I take to be the discovery of the certainty or probability of such propositions or truths, which the mind arrives at by deduction made from such ideas, which it has got by the use of its natural faculties; viz. by sensation or reflection.

Faith, on the other side, is the assent to any proposition, not thus made out by the deductions of reason, but upon the credit of the proposer, as coming from God, in some extraordinary way of communication. This way of discovering truths to men, we call *revelation.*

3. *First, No new simple Idea can be conveyed by traditional Revelation.* —First, Then I say, that *no man inspired by God can by any revelation communicate to others any new simple ideas which they had not before from sensation or reflection.* For, whatsoever impressions he himself may have from the immediate hand of God, this revelation, if it be of new simple ideas, cannot be conveyed to another, either by words or any other signs. Because words, by their immediate operation on us, cause no other ideas but of their natural sounds: and it is by the custom of using them for signs, that they excite and revive in our minds latent ideas; but yet only such ideas as were there before. For words, seen or heard, recall to our thoughts those ideas only which to us they have been wont to be signs of, but cannot introduce any perfectly new, and formerly unknown simple ideas. The same holds in all other signs; which cannot signify to us things of which we have before never had any idea at all.

Thus whatever things were discovered to St. Paul, when he was rapt up into the third heaven; whatever new ideas his mind there received, all the description he can make to others of that place, is only this, That there are such things, 'as eye hath not seen, nor ear heard, nor hath it entered into the heart of man to conceive.' And supposing God should discover to any one, supernaturally, a species of creatures inhabiting, for example, Jupiter or Saturn, (for that it is possible there may be such, nobody can deny,) which had six senses; and imprint on his mind the ideas conveyed to theirs by that sixth sense: he could no more, by words, produce in the minds of other men those ideas imprinted by that sixth sense, than one of us could convey the idea of any colour, by the sound of words, into a man who, having the other four senses perfect, had always totally wanted the fifth, of seeing. For our simple ideas, then, which are the foundation, and sole matter of all our notions and knowledge, we must depend wholly on our reason, I mean our natural faculties; and can by no means receive them, or any of them, from traditional revelation. I say, *traditional revelation*, in distinction to *original revelation*. By the one, I mean that first impression which is made immediately by God on the mind of any man, to which we cannot set any bounds; and by the other, those impressions delivered over to others in words, and the ordinary ways of conveying our conceptions one to another.

4. *Secondly, Traditional Revelation may make us know Propositions knowable also by Reason, but not with the same Certainty that Reason doth.* —*Secondly*, I say that *the same truths may be discovered, and conveyed down from revelation, which are discoverable to us by reason, and by those ideas we naturally may have.* So God might, by revelation, discover the truth of any proposition in Euclid; as well as men, by the natural use of their faculties, come to make the discovery themselves. In all things of this kind there is little need or use of revelation, God having furnished us with natural and surer means to arrive at the knowledge of them. For whatsoever truth we come to the clear discovery of, from the knowledge and contemplation of our own ideas, will always be certainer to us than those which are conveyed to us by *traditional revelation*. For the knowledge we have that this revelation came at first from God, can never be so sure as the knowledge we have from the clear and distinct perception of the agreement or disagreement of our own ideas: v.g. if it were revealed some ages since, that the three angles of a triangle were equal to two right ones, I might assent to the truth of that proposition, upon the credit of the tradition, that it was revealed: but that would never amount to so great a certainty as the knowledge of it, upon the comparing and measuring my own ideas of two right angles, and the three angles of a triangle. The like holds in matter of fact knowable by our senses; v.g. the history of the deluge is conveyed to us by writings which had their original from revelation: and yet nobody, I think, will say he has as certain and clear a knowledge of the flood as Noah, that saw it; or that he himself would have had, had he then been alive and seen it. For he has no greater an assurance than that of his senses, that it is writ in the book supposed writ by Moses inspired: but he has not so great an assurance that Moses wrote that book as if he had seen Moses write it. So that the assurance of its being a revelation is less still than the assurance of his senses.

5. *Even Original Revelation cannot be admitted against the clear Evidence of Reason.* — In propositions, then, whose certainty is built upon the clear perception of the agreement or disagreement of our ideas, attained either by immediate intuition, as in self-evident propositions, or by evident deductions of reason in demonstrations we need not the assistance of revelation, as necessary to gain our assent, and introduce them into our minds. Because the natural ways of knowledge could settle them there, or had done it already; which is the greatest assurance we can possibly have of anything, unless where God immediately reveals it to us: and there too our assurance can be no greater than our knowledge is, that it *is* a revelation from God. But yet nothing, I think, can, under that title, shake or overrule plain knowledge; or

rationally prevail with any man to admit it for true, in a direct contradiction to the clear evidence of his own understanding. For, since no evidence of our faculties, by which we receive such revelations, can exceed, if equal, the certainty of our intuitive knowledge, we can never receive for a truth anything that is directly contrary to our clear and distinct knowledge; v.g. the ideas of one body and one place do so clearly agree, and the mind has so evident a perception of their agreement, that we can never assent to a proposition that affirms the same body to be in two distant places at once, however it should pretend to the authority of a divine revelation: since the evidence, first, that we deceive not ourselves, in ascribing it to God; secondly, that we understand it right; can never be so great as the evidence of our own intuitive knowledge, whereby we discern it impossible for the same body to be in two places at once. And therefore *no proposition can be received for divine revelation, or obtain the assent due to all such, if it be contradictory to our clear intuitive knowledge.* Because this would be to subvert the principles and foundations of all knowledge, evidence, and assent whatsoever: and there would be left no difference between truth and falsehood, no measures of credible and incredible in the world, if doubtful propositions shall take place before self-evident; and what we certainly know give way to what we may possibly be mistaken in. In propositions therefore contrary to the clear perception of the agreement or disagreement of any of our ideas, it will be in vain to urge them as matters of faith. They cannot move our assent under that or any other title whatsoever. For faith can never convince us of anything that contradicts our knowledge. Because, though faith be founded on the testimony of God (who cannot lie) revealing any proposition to us: yet we cannot have an assurance of the truth of its being a divine revelation greater than our own knowledge. Since the whole strength of the certainty depends upon our knowledge that God revealed it; which, in this case, where the proposition supposed revealed contradicts our knowledge or reason, will always have this objection hanging to it, viz. that we cannot tell how to conceive that to come from God, the bountiful Author of our being, which, if received for true, must overturn all the principles and foundations of knowledge he has given us; render all our faculties useless; wholly destroy the most excellent part of his workmanship, our understandings; and put a man in a condition wherein he will have less light, less conduct than the beast that perisheth. For if the mind of man can never have a clearer (and perhaps not so clear) evidence of anything to be a divine revelation, as it has of the principles of its own reason, it can never have a ground to quit the clear evidence of its reason, to give a place to a proposition, whose revelation has not a greater evidence than those principles have.

6. *Traditional Revelation much less.* —Thus far a man has use of reason, and ought to hearken to it, even in immediate and original revelation, where it is supposed to be made to himself. But to all those who pretend not to immediate revelation, but are required to pay obedience, and to receive the truths revealed to others, which, by the tradition of writings, or word of mouth, are conveyed down to them, reason has a great deal more to do, and is that only which can induce us to receive them. For matter of faith being only divine revelation, and nothing else, faith, as we use the word, (called commonly *divine faith*), has to do with no propositions, but those which are supposed to be divinely revealed. So that I do not see how those who make revelation alone the sole object of faith can say, That it is a matter of faith, and not of reason, to believe that such or such a proposition, to be found in such or such a book, is of divine inspiration; unless it be revealed that that proposition, or all in that book, was communicated by divine inspiration. Without such a revelation, the

believing, or not believing, that proposition, or book, to be of divine authority, can never be matter of faith, but matter of reason; and such as I must come to an assent to only by the use of my reason, which can never require or enable me to believe that which is contrary to itself: it being impossible for reason ever to procure any assent to that which to itself appears unreasonable.

In all things, therefore, where we have clear evidence from our ideas, and those principles of knowledge I have above mentioned, reason is the proper judge; and revelation, though it may, in consenting with it, confirm its dictates, yet cannot in such cases invalidate its decrees: nor can we be obliged, where we have the clear and evident sentence of reason, to quit it for the contrary opinion, under a pretence that it is matter of faith: which can have no authority against the plain and clear dictates of reason.

7. *Thirdly, Things above Reason are, when revealed, the proper matter of faith.* —But, *Thirdly,* There being many things wherein we have very imperfect notions, or none at all; and other things, of whose past, present, or future existence, by the natural use of our faculties, we can have no knowledge at all; these, as being beyond the discovery of our natural faculties, and *above reason*, are, when revealed, *the proper matter of faith.* Thus, that part of the angels rebelled against God, and thereby lost their first happy state: and that the dead shall rise, and live again: these and the like, being beyond the discovery of reason, are purely matters of faith, with which reason has directly nothing to do.

8. *Or not contrary to Reason, if revealed, are Matter of Faith; and must carry it against probable conjectures of Reason.* —But since God, in giving us the light of reason, has not thereby tied up his own hands from affording us, when he thinks fit, the light of revelation in any of those matters wherein our natural faculties are able to give a probable determination; *revelation,* where God has been pleased to give it, *must carry it against the probable conjectures of reason.* Because the mind not being certain of the truth of that it does not evidently know, but only yielding to the probability that appears in it, is bound to give up its assent to such a testimony which, it is satisfied, comes from one who cannot err, and will not deceive. But yet, it still belongs to reason to judge of the truth of its being a revelation, and of the signification of the words wherein it is delivered. Indeed, if anything shall be thought revelation which is contrary to the plain principles of reason, and the evident knowledge the mind has of its own clear and distinct ideas; there reason must be hearkened to, as to a matter within its province. Since a man can never have so certain a knowledge, that a proposition which contradicts the clear principles and evidence of his own knowledge was divinely revealed, or that he understands the words rightly wherein it is delivered, as he has that the contrary is true, and so is bound to consider and judge of it as a matter of reason, and not swallow it, without examination, as a matter of faith.

9. *Revelation in Matters where Reason cannot judge, or but probably, ought to be hearkened to.* —First, Whatever proposition is revealed, of whose truth our mind, by its natural faculties and notions, cannot judge, that is purely matter of faith, and above reason.

Secondly, All propositions whereof the mind, by the use of its natural faculties, can come to determine and judge, from naturally acquired ideas, are matter of reason: with this difference still, that, in those concerning which it has but an uncertain evidence, and so is persuaded of their truth only upon probable grounds, which still admit a possibility of the contrary to be true, without doing violence to the certain evidence of its own knowledge, and overturning the principles of all reason; in such probable propositions, I say, an evident revelation ought to determine our assent, even against probability. For where the principles of reason have not evidenced a proposition to be certainly true or false, there clear revelation, as another principle of truth and ground of assent, may determine; and so it may be matter of faith, and be also above reason. Because reason, in that particular matter, being able to reach no higher than probability, faith gave the determination where reason came short; and revelation discovered on which side the truth lay.

10. *In Matters where Reason can afford certain Knowledge, that is to be hearkened to.* — Thus far the dominion of faith reaches, and that without any violence or hindrance to reason; which is not injured or disturbed, but assisted and improved by new discoveries of truth, coming from the eternal fountain of all knowledge. Whatever God hath revealed is certainly true: no doubt can be made of it. This is the proper object of faith: but whether it be a *divine* revelation or no, reason must judge; which can never permit the mind to reject a greater evidence to embrace what is less evident, nor allow it to entertain probability in opposition to knowledge and certainty. There can be no evidence that any traditional revelation is of divine original, in the words we receive it, and in the sense we understand it, so clear and so certain as that of the principles of reason: and therefore *Nothing that is contrary to, and inconsistent with, the clear and self-evident dictates of reason, has a right to be urged or assented to as a matter of faith, wherein reason hath nothing to do.* Whatsoever is divine revelation, ought to overrule all our opinions, prejudices, and interest, and hath a right to be received with full assent. Such a submission as this, of our reason to faith, takes not away the landmarks of knowledge: this shakes not the foundations of reason, but leaves us that use of our faculties for which they were given us.

11. *If the Boundaries be not set between Faith and Reason, no Enthusiasm or Extravagancy in Religion can be contradicted.* — If the provinces of faith and reason are not kept distinct by these boundaries, there will, in matters of religion, be no room for reason at all; and those extravagant opinions and ceremonies that are to be found in the several religions of the world will not deserve to be blamed. For, to this crying up of faith in *opposition* to reason, we may, I think, in good measure ascribe those absurdities that fill almost all the religions which possess and divide mankind. For men having been principled with an opinion, that they must not consult reason in the things of religion, however apparently contradictory to common sense and the very principles of all their knowledge, have let loose their fancies and natural superstition; and have been by them led into so strange opinions, and extravagant practices in religion, that a considerate man cannot but stand amazed at their follies, and judge them so far from being acceptable to the great and wise God, that he cannot avoid thinking them ridiculous and offensive to a sober good man. So that, in effect, religion, which should most distinguish us from beasts, and ought most peculiarly to elevate us, as rational creatures, above brutes, is that wherein men often appear most irrational, and more senseless than beasts themselves. *Credo, quia impossibile est:* I believe, because it is impossible, might, in a good man, pass for a sally of zeal; but would prove a very ill rule for men to choose their opinions or religion by.

Chapter XIX

OF ENTHUSIASM

1. *Love of Truth necessary.* —He that would seriously set upon the search of truth, ought in the first place to prepare his mind with a love of it. For he that loves it not, will not take much pains to get it; nor be much concerned when he misses it. There is nobody in the commonwealth of learning who does not profess himself a lover of truth: and there is not a rational creature that would not take it amiss to be thought otherwise of. And yet, for all this, one may truly say, that there are very few lovers of truth, for truth's sake, even amongst those who persuade themselves that they are so. How a man may know whether he be so in earnest, is worth inquiry: and I think there is one unerring mark of it, viz. The not entertaining any proposition with greater assurance than the proofs it is built upon will warrant. Whoever goes beyond this measure of assent, it is plain receives not the truth in the love of it; loves not truth for truth's sake, but for some other bye-end. For the evidence that any proposition is true (except such as are self-evident) lying only in the proofs a man has of it, whatsoever degrees of assent he affords it beyond the degrees of that evidence, it is plain that all the surplusage of assurance is owing to some other affection, and not to the love of truth: it being as impossible that the love of truth should carry my assent above the evidence there is to me, that it is true, as that the love of truth should make me assent to any proposition for the sake of that evidence which it has not, that it is true: which is in effect to love it as a truth, because it is possible or probable that it may not be true. In any truth that gets not possession of our minds by the irresistible light of self-evidence, or by the force of demonstration, the arguments that gain it assent are the vouchers and gage of its probability to us; and we can receive it for no other than such as they deliver it to our understandings. Whatsoever credit or authority we give to any proposition more than it receives from the principles and proofs it supports itself upon, is owing to our inclinations that way, and is so far a derogation from the love of truth as such: which, as it can receive no evidence from our passions or interests, so it should receive no tincture from them.

2. *A Forwardness to dictate another's beliefs, from whence.* —The assuming an authority of dictating to others, and a forwardness to prescribe to their opinions, is a constant concomitant of this bias and corruption of our judgments. For how almost can it be otherwise, but that he should be ready to impose on another's belief, who has already imposed on his own? Who can reasonably expect arguments and conviction from him in dealing with others, whose understanding is not accustomed to them in his dealing with himself? Who does violence to his own faculties, tyrannizes over his own mind, and usurps the prerogative that belongs to truth alone, which is to command assent by only its own authority, i.e. by and in proportion to that evidence which it carries with it.

3. *Force of Enthusiasm, in which reason is taken away.* —Upon this occasion I shall take the liberty to consider *a third ground of assent,* which with some men has the same authority, and is as confidently relied on as either faith or reason; I mean *enthusiasm:* which, laying by reason, would set up revelation without it. Whereby in effect it takes away both reason and revelation, and substitutes in the room of them the ungrounded fancies of a man's own brain, and assumes them for a foundation

both of opinion and conduct.

4. *Reason and Revelation.* —*Reason* is *natural revelation*, whereby the eternal Father of light and fountain of all knowledge, communicates to mankind that portion of truth which he has laid within the reach of their natural faculties: *revelation* is *natural reason enlarged* by a new set of discoveries communicated by God immediately; which reason vouches the truth of, by the testimony and proofs it gives that they come from God. So that he that takes away reason to make way for revelation, puts out the light of both, and does muchwhat the same as if he would persuade a man to put out his eyes, the better to receive the remote light of an invisible star by a telescope.

5. *Rise of Enthusiasm.* —Immediate revelation being a much easier way for men to establish their opinions and regulate their conduct, than the tedious and not always successful labour of strict reasoning, it is no wonder that some have been very apt to pretend to revelation, and to persuade themselves that they are under the peculiar guidance of heaven in their actions and opinions, especially in those of them which they cannot account for by the ordinary methods of knowledge and principles of reason. Hence we see, that, in all ages, men in whom melancholy has mixed with devotion, or whose conceit of themselves has raised them into an opinion of a greater familiarity with God, and a nearer admittance to his favour than is afforded to others, have often flattered themselves with a persuasion of an immediate intercourse with the Deity, and frequent communications from the Divine Spirit. God, I own, cannot be denied to be able to enlighten the understanding by a ray darted into the mind immediately from the fountain of light: this they understand he has promised to do, and who then has so good a title to expect it as those who are his peculiar people, chosen by him, and depending on him?

6. *Enthusiastic impulse.* —Their minds being thus prepared, whatever groundless opinion comes to settle itself strongly upon their fancies, is an illumination from the Spirit of God, and presently of divine authority: and whatsoever odd action they find in themselves a strong inclination to do, that impulse is concluded to be a call or direction from heaven, and must be obeyed: it is a commission from above, and they cannot err in executing it.

7. *What is meant by Enthusiasm.* —This I take to be properly *enthusiasm*, which, though founded neither on reason nor divine revelation, but rising from the conceits of a warmed or overweening brain, works yet, where it once gets footing, more powerfully on the persuasions and actions of men than either of those two, or both together: men being most forwardly obedient to the impulses they receive from themselves; and the whole man is sure to act more vigorously where the whole man is carried by a natural motion. For strong conceit, like a new principle, carries all easily with it, when got above common sense, and freed from all restraint of reason and check of reflection, it is heightened into a divine authority, in concurrence with our own temper and inclination.

8. *Enthusiasm accepts its supposed illumination without search and proof.* —Though the odd opinions and extravagant actions enthusiasm has run men into were enough to warn them against this wrong principle, so apt to misguide them both in their belief and conduct: yet the love of something extraordinary, the ease and glory it is to be inspired, and be above the common and natural ways of knowledge, so flatters many men's laziness, ignorance, and vanity, that, when once they are got into this way of immediate revelation, of illumination without search, and of certainty without proof

and without examination, it is a hard matter to get them out of it. Reason is lost upon them, they are above it: they see the light infused into their understandings, and cannot be mistaken; it is clear and visible there, like the light of bright sunshine; shows itself, and needs no other proof but its own evidence: they feel the hand of God moving them within, and the impulses of the Spirit, and cannot be mistaken in what they feel. Thus they support themselves, and are sure reasoning hath nothing to do with what they see and feel in themselves: what they have a sensible experience of admits no doubt, needs no probation. Would he not be ridiculous, who should require to have it proved to him that the light shines, and that he sees it? It is its own proof, and can have no other. When the Spirit brings light into our minds, it dispels darkness. We see it as we do that of the sun at noon, and need not the twilight of reason to show it us. This light from heaven is strong, clear, and pure; carries its own demonstration with it: and we may as naturally take a glow-worm to assist us to discover the sun, as to examine the celestial ray by our dim candle, reason.

9. *Enthusiasm how to be discovered.* —This is the way of talking of these men: they are sure, because they are sure: and their persuasions are right, because they are strong in them. For, when what they say is stripped of the metaphor of seeing and feeling, this is all it amounts to: and yet these similes so impose on them, that they serve them for certainty in themselves, and demonstration to others.

10. *The supposed internal Light examined.* —But to examine a little soberly this internal light, and this feeling on which they build so much. These men have, they say, clear light, and they see; they have awakened sense, and they feel: this cannot, they are sure, be disputed them. For when a man says he sees or feels, nobody can deny him that he does so. But here let me ask: This seeing, is it the perception of the truth of the proposition, or of this, that it is a revelation from God? This feeling, is it a perception of an inclination or fancy to do something, or of the Spirit of God moving that inclination? These are two very different perceptions, and must be carefully distinguished, if we would not impose upon ourselves. I may perceive the truth of a proposition, and yet not perceive that it is an immediate revelation from God. I may perceive the truth of a proposition in Euclid, without its being, or my perceiving it to be, a revelation: nay, I may perceive I came not by this knowledge in a natural way, and so may conclude it revealed, without perceiving that it is a revelation of God. Because there be spirits which, without being divinely commissioned, may excite those ideas in me, and lay them in such order before my mind, that I may perceive their connexion. So that the knowledge of any proposition coming into my mind, I know not how, is not a perception that it is from God. Much less is a strong persuasion that it is true, a perception that it is from God, or so much as true. But however it be called light and seeing, I suppose it is at most but belief and assurance: and the proposition taken for a revelation, is not such as they *know* to be true, but *take* to be true. For where a proposition is known to be true, revelation is needless: and it is hard to conceive how there can be a revelation to any one of what he knows already. If therefore it be a proposition which they are persuaded, but do not know, to be true, whatever they may call it, it is not seeing, but believing. For these are two ways whereby truth comes into the mind, wholly distinct, so that one is not the other. What I see, I know to be so, by the evidence of the thing itself: what I believe, I take to be so upon the testimony of another. But this testimony I must know to be given, or else what ground have I of believing? I must see that it is God that reveals this to me, or else I see nothing. The question then here is: How do I

know that God is the revealer of this to me; that this impression is made upon my mind by his Holy Spirit; and that therefore I ought to obey it? If I know not this, how great soever the assurance is that I am possessed with, it is groundless; whatever light I pretend to, it is but *enthusiasm*. For, whether the proposition supposed to be revealed be in itself evidently true, or visibly probable, or, by the natural ways of knowledge, uncertain, the proposition that must be well grounded and manifested to be true, is this, That God is the revealer of it, and that what I take to be a revelation is certainly put into my mind by Him, and is not an illusion dropped in by some other spirit, or raised by my own fancy. For, if I mistake not, these men receive it for true, because they presume God revealed it. Does it not, then, stand them upon to examine upon what grounds they presume it to be a revelation from God? or else all their confidence is mere presumption: and this light they are so dazzled with is nothing but an *ignis fatuus*, that leads them constantly round in this circle; *It is a revelation, because they firmly believe it;* and *they believe it, because it is a revelation.*

11. *Enthusiasm fails of Evidence, that the Proposition is from God.* —In all that is of divine revelation, there is need of no other proof but that it is an inspiration from God: for he can neither deceive nor be deceived. But how shall it be known that any proposition in our minds is a truth infused by God; a truth that is revealed to us by him, which he declares to us, and therefore we ought to believe? Here it is that enthusiasm fails of the evidence it pretends to. For men thus possessed, boast of a light whereby they say they are enlightened, and brought into the knowledge of this or that truth. But if they know it to be a truth, they must know it to be so, either by its own self-evidence to natural reason, or by the rational proofs that make it out to be so. If they see and know it to be a truth, either of these two ways they in vain suppose it to be a revelation. For they know it to be true the same way that any other man naturally may know that it is so, without the help of revelation. For thus, all the truths, of what kind soever, that men uninspired are enlightened with, came into their minds, and are established there. If they say they know it to be true, because it is a revelation from God, the reason is good: but then it will be demanded how they know it to be a revelation from God. If they say, by the light it brings with it, which shines bright in their minds, and they cannot resist: I beseech them to consider whether this be any more than what we have taken notice of already, viz. that it is a revelation, because they strongly believe it to be true. For all the light they speak of is but a strong, though ungrounded persuasion of their own minds, that it is a truth. For rational grounds from proofs that it is a truth, they must acknowledge to have none; for then it is not received as a revelation, but upon the ordinary grounds that other truths are received: and if they believe it to be true because it is a revelation, and have no other reason for its being a revelation, but because they are fully persuaded, without any other reason, that it is true, then they believe it to be a revelation only because they strongly believe it to be a revelation; which is a very unsafe ground to proceed on, either in our tenets or actions. And what readier way can there be to run ourselves into the most extravagant errors and miscarriages, than thus to set up fancy for our supreme and sole guide, and to believe any proposition to be true, any action to be right, only because we believe it to be so? The strength of our persuasions is no evidence at all of their own rectitude: crooked things may be as stiff and inflexible as straight: and men may be as positive and peremptory in error as in truth. How come else the untractable zealots in different and opposite parties? For if the light, which every one thinks he has in his mind, which in this

case is nothing but the strength of his own persuasion, be an evidence that it is from God, contrary opinions have the same title to be inspirations; and God will be not only the Father of lights, but of opposite and contradictory lights, leading men contrary ways; and contradictory propositions will be divine truths, if an ungrounded strength of assurance be an evidence that any proposition is a Divine Revelation.

12. *Firmness of Persuasion no Proof that any Proposition is from God.* —This cannot be otherwise, whilst firmness of persuasion is made the cause of believing, and confidence of being in the right is made an argument of truth. St. Paul himself believed he did well, and that he had a call to it, when he persecuted the Christians, whom he confidently thought in the wrong: but yet it was he, and not they, who were mistaken. Good men are men still liable to mistakes, and are sometimes warmly engaged in errors, which they take for divine truths, shining in their minds with the clearest light.

13. *Light in the Mind, what.* —Light, true light, in the mind is, or can be, nothing else but the evidence of the truth of any proposition; and if it be not a self-evident proposition, all the light it has, or can have, is from the clearness and validity of those proofs upon which it is received. To talk of any other light in the understanding is to put ourselves in the dark, or in the power of the Prince of Darkness, and, by our own consent, to give ourselves up to delusion to believe a lie. For, if strength of persuasion be the light which must guide us; I ask how shall any one distinguish between the delusions of Satan, and the inspirations of the Holy Ghost? He can transform himself into an angel of light. And they who are led by this Son of the Morning are as fully satisfied of the illumination, i.e. are as strongly persuaded that they are enlightened by the Spirit of God as any one who is so: they acquiesce and rejoice in it, are actuated by it: and nobody can be more sure, nor more in the right (if their own strong belief may be judge) than they.

14. *Revelation must be judged of by Reason.* —He, therefore, that will not give himself up to all the extravagances of delusion and error must bring this guide of his *light within* to the trial. God when he makes the prophet does not unmake the man. He leaves all his faculties in the natural state, to enable him to judge of his inspirations, whether they be of *divine* original or no. When he illuminates the mind with supernatural light, he does not extinguish that which is natural. If he would have us assent to the truth of any proposition, he either evidences that truth by the usual methods of natural reason, or else makes it known to be a truth which he would have us assent to by his authority, and convinces us that it is from him, by some marks which reason cannot be mistaken in. *Reason must be our last judge and guide in everything.* I do not mean that we must consult reason, and examine whether a proposition revealed from God can be made out by natural principles, and if it cannot, that then we may reject it: but consult it we must, and by it examine whether it be a revelation from God or no: and if reason finds it to be revealed from God, reason then declares for it as much as for any other truth, and makes it one of her dictates. Every conceit that thoroughly warms our fancies must pass for an inspiration, if there be nothing but the strength of our persuasions, whereby to judge of our persuasions: if reason must not examine their truth by something extrinsical to the persuasions themselves, inspirations and delusions, truth and falsehood, will have the same measure, and will not be possible to be distinguished.

GEORGE BERKELEY—Anglican
Bishop of Cloyne

ALEXANDER POPE (engraving by H. Hall)

TRINITY COLLEGE, DUBLIN

GEORGE BERKELEY

George Berkeley (1685–1753) was born in Kilkenney, Ireland. In 1707 he received a master's degree from Trinity College, Dublin, and spent the following six years as a Tutor there. During this period, when still a young man, Berkeley worked out the essential elements of his philosophical position. He left Trinity in 1713, divided his next eleven years between London and the continent, and was appointed Dean of Derry in 1724. Subsequently, he devoted much time and energy to a plan for establishing a college in the Bermudas. In connection with this project, he and his bride settled in Rhode Island in 1729, only to return to England in 1731 when funding for the college did not materialize. He was appointed Bishop of Cloyne in Ireland in 1734, and thereafter took a deep interest in the social problems of his diocese. In 1752 Berkeley moved to Oxford, where he died peacefully the following year.

Berkeley's first published work, *An Essay Towards a New Theory of Vision* (1709), is a study of the way we perceive the distance, magnitude, and position of objects. His second book, *A Treatise Concerning the Principles of Human Knowledge* (1710) is an already mature formulation of the immaterialism for which he is famous. (A second volume, lost in manuscript, was never rewritten.) *Three Dialogues Between Hylas and Philonous* (1713) recapitulates the *Principles* in a more popular dialogue form.

Berkeley's philosophical views are both an extension of, and a reaction against, those of Locke. Berkeley shared Locke's empiricist premise that the objects of human knowledge are all 'ideas', either "actually imprinted on the senses; or else such as are perceived by attending to the passions and operations of the mind; or lastly, ideas formed by the help of memory and imagination. . . ." However, Berkeley saw difficulties with this position that Locke did not fully appreciate. Specifically, Berkeley wondered how, on this view, we can ever know of the existence of anything except our ideas. If all we are acquainted with are collections of colors, sounds, and other sensations, then we cannot get 'outside' these phenomena to compare them with the material objects which, according to Locke, cause and sometimes resemble them. Thus, Locke's view seems to imply that we cannot know anything about tables, chairs, and other ordinary objects. But Berkeley argued that Locke's starting point need not lead to any such skeptical conclusion.

Berkeley's solution to the problem of perceptual knowledge reconciled the two seemingly incompatible claims that (1) all we perceive are ideas, and that (2) we can know of the existence of tables, chairs, and other ordinary things, by arguing that (3) tables, chairs, and other ordinary things *just are* collections of ideas. This view of Berkeley's is known as 'idealism.'

At first glance, Berkeley's idealism may seem an unsatisfactory way of resolving skeptical doubts; for the collections of ideas to which Berkeley reduces tables and chairs seem very different from the real and enduring objects which we ordinarily believe to surround us. However, Berkeley proposed a number of ingenious arguments to show that his collections of ideas have all the features we attribute to ordinary objects. He argued, for example, that his account distinguishes real from imaginary objects exactly as the ordinary person does. A real object, he maintained, is just a collection of ideas which are "more affecting, orderly, and distinct," and which are produced by some other spirit, namely, God, rather than by the mind perceiving them. Again, Berkeley argued that tables and chairs, construed as collections of ideas, do not lack continuous existence, as they might at first seem to. It is true that *I* may cease having table-ish ideas at any moment; but as long as ideas of the right sort continue to exist in the minds of other spirits (again including God), the collection of ideas constituting my writing table will continue to exist.

Although Berkeley attempted to accommodate all the beliefs of ordinary men, he was savage in his attacks on the views of other philosophers. Of special importance are his views concerning the concepts of 'material substance' and 'abstract ideas.' The notion of material substance, or a 'substratum' which underlies and supports the qualities we perceive, had already troubled Locke, who, finding himself unable to form any idea of it, had characterized it negatively as *"something besides* the extension, figure, solidity, motion, thinking, or other observable ideas, though we know not what it is." Against this, Berkeley argues that the claim that substance 'supports' its qualities is unintelligible; that such a claim in no way explains our ideas (since only an active force, or spirit, could generate them); and that external existence is in any event inconceivable, since anything conceived must be conceived as one idea or another. Against the claim that a general word like 'triangle' stands for an abstract triangular idea stripped of all particulars of shape and size, Berkeley argued that he, at least, was quite unable to form any such indeterminate idea. Berkeley's attacks on abstract ideas and material substance are not unconnected. It is, he argued, largely because philosophers have supposed that they can abstract "the existence of sensible objects from their being perceived, so as to conceive them existing unperceived," that they have believed material substance to exist.

For general studies of Berkeley's views, see G.J. Warnock, *Berkeley* (Baltimore: Penguin Books, 1953) and George Pitcher, *Berkeley* (London: Routledge & Kegan Paul, 1977). An excellent concise study is the essay by J.F. Thomson in D.J. O'Connor, ed., *A Critical History of Western Philosophy* (Glencoe: The Free Press, 1964). Other helpful essays are C.B. Martin and D.M. Armstrong, eds., *Locke and Berkeley: A Collection of Critical Essays* (Garden City: Doubleday, 1968). Another worthwhile collection is Gale W. Engle and Gabriele Taylor, eds., *Berkeley's Principles of Human Knowledge: Critical Studies* (Belmont, Calif.: Wadsworth, 1968). For a discussion of continuities with Locke and Hume, see Jonathan Bennett, *Locke, Berkeley, Hume: Central Themes* (Oxford: Clarendon Press, 1971). A more modern version of Berkeley's idealism, known as 'phenomenalism,' is presented in A.J. Ayer, *The Foundations of Empirical Knowledge* (1940; rpt. London: Macmillan, 1961).

G.S.

A TREATISE CONCERNING THE PRINCIPLES OF HUMAN KNOWLEDGE

PREFACE

What I here make public has, after a long and scrupulous inquiry, seemed to me evidently true and not unuseful to be known—particularly to those who are tainted with skepticism or want a demonstration of the existence and immateriality of God or the natural immortality of the soul. Whether it be so or no, I am content the reader should impartially examine, since I do not think myself any further concerned for the success of what I have written than as it is agreeable to truth. But to the end this may not suffer I make it my request that the reader suspend his judgment till he has once at least read the whole through with that degree of attention and thought which the subject matter shall seem to deserve. For as there are some passages that, taken by themselves, are very liable (nor could it be remedied) to gross misinterpretation, and to be charged with most absurd consequences which, nevertheless, upon an entire perusal will appear not to follow from them, so likewise, though the whole should be read over, yet, if this be done transiently, it is very probable my sense may be mistaken; but to a thinking reader, I flatter myself, it will be throughout clear and obvious. As for the characters of novelty and singularity which some of the following notions may seem to bear, it is, I hope, needless to make any apology on that account. He must surely be either very weak or very little acquainted with the sciences who shall reject a truth that is capable of demonstration for no other reason but because it is newly known and contrary to the prejudices of mankind. Thus much I thought fit to premise in order to prevent, if possible, the hasty censures of a sort of men who are too apt to condemn an opinion before they rightly comprehend it.

INTRODUCTION

1. Philosophy being nothing else but the study of wisdom and truth, it may with reason be expected that those who have spent most time and pains in it should enjoy a greater calm and serenity of mind, a greater clearness and evidence of knowledge, and be less disturbed with doubts and difficulties than other men. Yet so it is, we see the illiterate bulk of mankind that walk the high road of plain common sense, and are governed by the dictates of nature, for the most part easy and undisturbed. To them nothing that is familiar appears unaccountable or difficult to comprehend.

They complain not of any want of evidence in their senses, and are out of all danger of becoming skeptics. But no sooner do we depart from sense and instinct to follow the light of a superior principle, to reason, meditate, and reflect on the nature of things, but a thousand scruples spring up in our minds concerning those things which before we seemed fully to comprehend. Prejudices and errors of sense do from all parts discover themselves to our view; and, endeavoring to correct these by reason, we are insensibly drawn into uncouth paradoxes, difficulties, and inconsistencies, which multiply and grow upon us as we advance in speculation, till at length, having wandered through many intricate mazes, we find ourselves just where we were, or, which is worse, sit down in a forlorn skepticism.

2. The cause of this is thought to be the obscurity of things, or the natural weakness and imperfection of our understandings. It is said the faculties we have are few and those designed by nature for the support and comfort of life, and not to penetrate into the inward essence and constitution of things. Besides, the mind of man being finite, when it treats of things which partake of infinity it is not to be wondered at if it run into absurdities and contradictions, out of which it is impossible it should ever extricate itself, it being of the nature of infinite not to be comprehended by that which is finite.

3. But, perhaps, we may be too partial to ourselves in placing the fault originally in our faculties and not rather in the wrong use we make of them. It is a hard thing to suppose that right deductions from true principles should ever end in consequences which cannot be maintained or made consistent. We should believe that God has dealt more bountifully with the sons of men than to give them a strong desire for that knowledge which he had placed quite out of their reach. This were not agreeable to the wonted, indulgent methods of Providence, which, whatever appetites it may have implanted in the creatures, does usually furnish them with such means as, if rightly made use of, will not fail to satisfy them. Upon the whole, I am inclined to think that the far greater part, if not all, of those difficulties which have hitherto amused philosophers and blocked up the way to knowledge, are entirely owing to ourselves—that we have first raised a dust and then complain we cannot see.

4. My purpose therefore is to try if I can discover what those principles are which have introduced all that doubtfulness and uncertainty, those absurdities and contradictions, into the several sects of philosophy—insomuch that the wisest men have thought our ignorance incurable, conceiving it to arise from the natural dullness and limitation of our faculties. And surely it is a work well deserving our pains to make a strict inquiry concerning the first principles of human knowledge, to sift and examine them on all sides, especially since there may be some grounds to suspect that those lets and difficulties which stay and embarrass the mind in its search after truth do not spring from any darkness and intricacy in the objects or natural defect in the understanding so much as from false principles which have been insisted on, and might have been avoided.

5. How difficult and discouraging soever this attempt may seem when I consider how many great and extraordinary men have gone before me in the same designs, yet I am not without some hopes—upon the consideration that the largest views are not always the clearest, and that he who is shortsighted will be obliged to draw the object nearer, and may, perhaps, by a close and narrow survey discern that which had escaped far better eyes.

6. In order to prepare the mind of the reader for the easier conceiving what follows, it is proper to premise somewhat, by way of introduction, concerning the nature and abuse of language. But the unraveling this matter leads me in some measure to anticipate my design by taking notice of what seems to have had a chief part in rendering speculation intricate and perplexed and to have occasioned innumerable errors and difficulties in almost all parts of knowledge. And that is the opinion that the mind has a power of framing *abstract ideas* or notions of things. He who is not a perfect stranger to the writings and disputes of philosophers must needs acknowledge that no small part of them are spent about abstract ideas. These are in a more especial manner thought to be the object of those sciences which go by the name of logic and metaphysics, and of all that which passes under the notion of the most abstracted and sublime learning, in all which one shall scarce find any question handled in such a manner as does not suppose their existence in the mind, and that it is well acquainted with them.

7. It is agreed on all hands that the qualities or modes of things do never really exist each of them apart by itself and separated from all others, but are mixed, as it were, and blended together, several in the same object. But we are told the mind, being able to consider each quality singly, or abstracted from those other qualities with which it is united, does by that means frame to itself abstract ideas. For example, there is perceived by sight an object extended, colored, and moved: this mixed or compound idea the mind, resolving into its simple, constituent parts and viewing each by itself, exclusive of the rest, does frame the abstract ideas of extension, color, and motion. Not that it is possible for color or motion to exist without extension, but only that the mind can frame to itself by *abstraction* the idea of color exclusive of extension, and of motion exclusive of both color and extension.

8. Again, the mind having observed that in the particular extensions perceived by sense there is something common and alike in all, and some other things peculiar, as this or that figure or magnitude, which distinguish them one from another, it considers apart or singles out by itself that which is common, making thereof a most abstract idea of extension, which is neither line, surface, nor solid, nor has any figure or magnitude, but is an idea entirely prescinded from all these. So likewise the mind, by leaving out of the particular colors perceived by sense that which distinguishes them one from another, and retaining that only which is common to all, makes an idea of color in abstract, which is neither red, nor blue, nor white, nor any other determinate color. And, in like manner, by considering motion abstractedly not only from the body moved, but likewise from the figure it describes, and all particular directions and velocities, the abstract idea of motion is framed which equally corresponds to all particular motions whatsoever that may be perceived by sense.

9. And as the mind frames to itself abstract ideas of qualities or modes, so does it, by the same precision or mental separation, attain abstract ideas of the more compounded beings which include several coexistent qualities. For example, the mind, having observed that Peter, James, and John resemble each other in certain common agreements of shape and other qualities, leaves out of the complex or compounded idea it has of Peter, James, and any other particular man that which is peculiar to each, retaining only what is common to all, and so makes an abstract idea wherein all the particulars equally partake—abstracting entirely from and cutting off all those circumstances and differences which might determine it to any particular existence. And after this manner it is said we come by the abstract idea of

man or, if you please, humanity, or human nature; wherein it is true there is included color, because there is no man but has some color, but then it can be neither white, nor black, nor any particular color, because there is no one particular color wherein all men partake. So likewise there is included stature, but then it is neither tall stature, nor low stature, nor yet middle stature, but something abstracted from all these. And so of the rest. Moreover, there being a great variety of other creatures that partake in some parts, but not all, of the complex idea of man, the mind, leaving out those parts which are peculiar to men, and retaining those only which are common to all the living creatures, frames the idea of *animal,* which abstracts not only from all particular men, but also all birds, beasts, fishes, and insects. The constituent parts of the abstract idea of animal are body, life, sense, and spontaneous motion. By "body" is meant body without any particular shape or figure, there being no one shape or figure common to all animals, without covering, either of hair, or feathers, or scales, etc., nor yet naked: hair, feathers, scales, and nakedness being the distinguishing properties of particular animals, and for that reason left out of the *abstract idea.* Upon the same account the spontaneous motion must be neither walking, nor flying, nor creeping; it is nevertheless a motion, but what that motion is it is not easy to conceive.

10. Whether others have this wonderful faculty of abstracting their ideas, they best can tell; for myself I find indeed I have a faculty of imagining, or representing to myself, the ideas of those particular things I have perceived, and of variously compounding and dividing them. I can imagine a man with two heads, or the upper parts of a man joined to the body of a horse. I can consider the hand, the eye, the nose, each by itself abstracted or separated from the rest of the body. But then whatever hand or eye I imagine, it must have some particular shape and color. Likewise the idea of man that I frame to myself must be either of a white, or a black, or a tawny, a straight, or a crooked, a tall, or a low, or a middle-sized man. I cannot by any effort of thought conceive the abstract idea above described. And it is equally impossible for me to form the abstract idea of motion distinct from the body moving, and which is neither swift nor slow, curvilinear nor rectilinear; and the like may be said of all other abstract general ideas whatsoever. To be plain, I own myself able to abstract in one sense, as when I consider some particular parts or qualities separated from others, with which, though they are united in some object, yet it is possible they may really exist without them. But I deny that I can abstract one from another, or conceive separately, those qualities which it is impossible should exist so separated; or that I can frame a general notion by abstracting from particulars in the manner aforesaid—which two last are the two proper acceptations of "abstraction." And there are grounds to think most men will acknowledge themselves to be in my case. The generality of men which are simple and illiterate never pretend to *abstract notions.* It is said they are difficult and not to be attained without pains and study; we may therefore reasonably conclude that, if such there be, they are confined only to the learned.

11. I proceed to examine what can be alleged in defense of the doctrine of abstraction, and try if I can discover what it is that inclines the men of speculation to embrace an opinion so remote from common sense as that seems to be. There has been a late, deservedly esteemed philosopher[1] who, no doubt, has given it very

---

1. [The reference is to John Locke. The two subsequent quotations are from *An Essay Concerning Human Understanding*, Bk. II, ch. XI, secs. 10–11. —S.M.C.]

much countenance by seeming to think the having abstract general ideas is what puts the widest difference in point of understanding betwixt man and beast.—

> The having of general ideas (he says) is that which puts a perfect distinction betwixt man and brutes, and is an excellency which the faculties of brutes do by no means attain unto. For, it is evident we observe no footsteps in them of making use of general signs for universal ideas; from which we have reason to imagine that they have not the faculty of abstracting, or making general ideas, since they have no use of words or any other general signs.

And a little after:

> Therefore, I think, we may suppose that it is in this that the species of brutes are discriminated from men, and it is that proper difference wherein they are wholly separated, and which at last widens to so wide a distance. For, if they have any ideas at all, and are not bare machines (as some would have them), we cannot deny them to have some reason. It seems as evident to me that they do, some of them, in certain instances reason as that they have sense; but it is only in particular ideas, just as they receive them from their senses. They are the best of them tied up within those narrow bounds, and have not (as I think) the faculty to enlarge them by any kind of abstraction.

I readily agree with this learned author that the faculties of brutes can by no means attain to abstraction. But then if this be made the distinguishing property of that sort of animals, I fear that many of those that pass for men must be reckoned into their number. The reason that is here assigned why we have no grounds to think brutes have abstract general ideas is that we observe in them no use of words or any other general signs; which is built on this supposition—that the making use of words implies the having general ideas. From which it follows that men who use language are able to abstract or generalize their ideas. That this is the sense and arguing of the author will further appear by his answering the question he in another place puts: "Since all things that exist are only particulars, how come we by general terms?" His answer is: "Words become general by being made the signs of general ideas."[2] But it seems that a word becomes general by being made the sign, not of an abstract general idea, but of several particular ideas, any one of which it indifferently suggests to the mind. For example, when it is said, "the change of motion is proportional to the impressed force," or that, "whatever has extension is divisible," these propositions are to be understood of motion and extension in general; and nevertheless it will not follow that they suggest to my thoughts an idea of motion without a body moved, or any determinate direction and velocity, or that I must conceive an abstract general idea of extension which is neither line, surface, nor solid, neither great nor small, black, white, nor red, nor of any other determinate color. It is only implied that whatever motion I consider, whether it be swift or slow, perpendicular, horizontal, or oblique, or in whatever object, the axiom concerning it holds equally true. As does the other of every particular extension, it matters not whether line, surface, or solid, whether of this or that magnitude or figure.

12. By observing how ideas become general we may the better judge how words are made so. And here it is to be noted that I do not deny absolutely there are general ideas, but only that there are any *abstract* general ideas; for, in the passages above quoted, wherein there is mention of general ideas, it is always supposed that

2. [The quotation is from Locke's *Essay,* Bk. III, ch. III, sec. 6.]

they are formed by abstraction, after the manner set forth in sections 8 and 9. Now, if we will annex a meaning to our words and speak only of what we can conceive, I believe we shall acknowledge that an idea which, considered in itself, is particular, becomes general by being made to represent or stand for all other particular ideas of the same sort. To make this plain by an example, suppose a geometrician is demonstrating the method of cutting a line in two equal parts. He draws, for instance, a black line of an inch in length: this, which in itself is a particular line, is nevertheless with regard to its signification general, since, as it is there used, it represents all particular lines whatsoever; for that which is demonstrated of it is demonstrated of all lines or, in other words, of a line in general. And, as that *particular* line becomes general by being made a sign, so the *name* "line," which taken absolutely is particular, by being a sign is made general. And as the former owes its generality not to its being the sign of an abstract or general line, but of all particular right lines that may possibly exist, so the latter must be thought to derive its generality from the same cause, namely, the various particular lines which it indifferently denotes.

13. To give the reader a yet clearer view of the nature of abstract ideas, and the uses they are thought necessary to, I shall add one more passage out of the *Essay on Human Understanding,* which is as follows:

> *Abstract ideas* are not so obvious or easy to children or the yet unexercised mind as particular ones. If they seem so to grown men it is only because by constant and familiar use they are made so. For, when we nicely reflect upon them, we shall find that general ideas are fictions and contrivances of the mind, that carry difficulty with them, and do not so easily offer themselves as we are apt to imagine. For example, does it not require some pains and skill to form the general idea of a triangle (which is yet none of the most abstract, comprehensive, and difficult); for it must be neither oblique nor rectangle, neither equilateral, equicrural, nor scalenon, but *all and none* of these at once? In effect, it is something imperfect that cannot exist, an idea wherein some parts of several different and *inconsistent* ideas are put together. It is true the mind in this imperfect state has need of such ideas and makes all the haste to them it can, for the convenience of communication and enlargement of knowledge to both which it is naturally very much inclined. But yet one has reason to suspect such ideas are marks of our imperfection. At least this is enough to show that the most abstract and general ideas are not those that the mind is first and most easily acquainted with, nor such as its earliest knowledge is conversant about.[3]

If any man has the faculty of framing in his mind such an idea of a triangle as is here described, it is in vain to pretend to dispute him out of it, nor would I go about it. All I desire is that the reader would fully and certainly inform himself whether he has such an idea or no. And this, methinks, can be no hard task for anyone to perform. What more easy than for anyone to look a little into his own thoughts, and there try whether he has, or can attain to have, an idea that shall correspond with the description that is here given of the general idea of a triangle, which is "neither oblique nor rectangle, equilateral, equicrural nor scalenon, but all and none of these at once"?

14. Much is here said of the difficulty that abstract ideas carry with them, and the pains and skill requisite to the forming them. And it is on all hands agreed that there is need of great toil and labor of the mind to emancipate our thoughts from

---

3. [Bk. IV, ch. VII, sec. 9.]

particular objects and raise them to those sublime speculations that are conversant about abstract ideas. From all which the natural consequence should seem to be, that so difficult a thing as the forming abstract ideas was not necessary for *communication*, which is so easy and familiar to all sorts of men. But, we are told, if they seem obvious and easy to grown men, "it is only because by constant and familiar use they are made so." Now, I would fain know at what time it is men are employed in surmounting that difficulty and furnishing themselves with those necessary helps for discourse. It cannot be when they are grown up, for then it seems they are not conscious of any such painstaking; it remains, therefore, to be the business of their childhood. And surely the great and multiplied labor of framing abstract notions will be found a hard task for that tender age. Is it not a hard thing to imagine that a couple of children cannot prate together of their sugar plums and rattles and the rest of their little trinkets till they have first tacked together numberless inconsistencies and so framed in their minds abstract general ideas and annexed them to every common name they make use of?

15. Nor do I think them a whit more needful for the *enlargement of knowledge* than for *communication*. It is, I know, a point much insisted on, that all knowledge and demonstration are about universal notions, to which I fully agree; but then it does not appear to me that those notions are formed by abstraction in the manner premised — *universality*, so far as I can comprehend, not consisting in the absolute, positive nature or conception of any thing, but in the relation it bears to the particulars signified or represented by it; by virtue whereof it is that things, names, or notions, being in their own nature *particular*, are rendered *universal*. Thus, when I demonstrate any proposition concerning triangles, it is to be supposed that I have in view the universal idea of a triangle, which ought not to be understood as if I could frame an idea of a triangle which was neither equilateral, nor scalenon, nor equicrural, but only that the particular triangle I consider, whether of this or that sort it matters not, does equally stand for and represent all rectilinear triangles whatsoever, and is in that sense *universal*. All which seems very plain and not to include any difficulty in it.

16. But here it will be demanded how we can know any proposition to be true of all particular triangles, except we have first seen it demonstrated of the abstract idea of a triangle which equally agrees to all? For, because a property may be demonstrated to agree to some one particular triangle, it will not thence follow that it equally belongs to any other triangle which in all respects is not the same with it. For example, having demonstrated that the three angles of an isosceles rectangular triangle are equal to two right ones, I cannot therefore conclude this affection agrees to all other triangles which have neither a right angle nor two equal sides. It seems therefore that, to be certain this proposition is universally true, we must either make a particular demonstration for every particular triangle, which is impossible, or once for all demonstrate it of the abstract idea of a triangle in which all the particulars do indifferently partake and by which they are all equally represented. To which I answer that, though the idea I have in view whilst I make the demonstration be, for instance, that of an isosceles rectangular triangle whose sides are of a determinate length, I may nevertheless be certain it extends to all other rectilinear triangles, of what sort or bigness soever. And that because neither the right angle, nor the equality, nor determinate length of the sides are at all concerned in the demonstration. It is true the diagram I have in view includes all these particulars, but then there is not the least mention made of them in the proof of the propo-

sition. It is not said the three angles are equal to two right ones, because one of them is a right angle, or because the sides comprehending it are of the same length. Which sufficiently shows that the right angle might have been oblique, and the sides unequal, and for all that the demonstration have held good. And for this reason it is that I conclude that to be true of any obliquangular or scalenon which I had demonstrated of a particular right-angled equicrural triangle, and not because I demonstrated the proposition of the abstract idea of a triangle. And here it must be acknowledged that a man may consider a figure merely as triangular, without attending to the particular qualities of the angles or relations of the sides. So far he may abstract, but this will never prove that he can frame an abstract, general, inconsistent idea of a triangle. In like manner we may consider Peter so far forth as man, or so far forth as animal, without framing the forementioned abstract idea either of man or of animal, inasmuch as all that is perceived is not considered.

17. It were an endless as well as a useless thing to trace the Schoolmen,[4] those great masters of abstraction, through all the manifold, inextricable labyrinths of error and dispute which their doctrine of abstract natures and notions seems to have led them into. What bickerings and controversies, and what a learned dust have been raised about those matters, and what mighty advantage has been from thence derived to mankind, are things at this day too clearly known to need being insisted on. And it had been well if the ill effects of that doctrine were confined to those only who make the most avowed profession of it. When men consider the great pains, industry, and parts that have for so many ages been laid out on the cultivation and advancement of the sciences, and that notwithstanding all this the far greater part of them remains full of darkness and uncertainty, and disputes that are like never to have an end, and even those that are thought to be supported by the most clear and cogent demonstrations, contain in them paradoxes which are perfectly irreconcilable to the understandings of men, and that, taking all together, a small portion of them does supply any real benefit to mankind, otherwise than by being an innocent diversion and amusement—I say the consideration of all this is apt to throw them into a despondency and perfect contempt of all study. But this may, perhaps, cease upon a view of the false principles that have obtained in the world, amongst all which there is none, methinks, has a more wide influence over the thoughts of speculative men than this of *abstract* general ideas.

18. I come now to consider the *source* of this prevailing notion, and that seems to me to be language. And surely nothing of less extent than reason itself could have been the source of an opinion so universally received. The truth of this appears, as from other reasons, so also from the plain confession of the ablest patrons of abstract ideas, who acknowledge that they are made in order to naming; from which it is a clear consequence that if there had been no such thing as speech or universal signs there never had been any thought of abstraction. See Bk. III, chap. 6, sec. 39, and elsewhere of the *Essay on Human Understanding*. Let us examine the manner wherein words have contributed to the origin of that mistake: First then, it is thought that every name has, or ought to have, one only precise and settled signification, which inclines men to think there are certain abstract, determinate ideas which constitute the true and only immediate signification of each general name; and that it is by the mediation of these abstract ideas that a general name comes to signify any particular thing. Whereas, in truth, there is no such thing as one precise and definite sig-

---

4. [Regarding the term 'schoolmen,' see Hobbes's *Leviathan*, n. 2.]

nification annexed to any general name, they all signifying indifferently a great number of particular ideas. All which does evidently follow from what has been already said, and will clearly appear to anyone by a little reflection. To this it will be objected that every name that has a definition is thereby restrained to one certain signification. For example, a "triangle" is defined to be "a plane surface comprehended by three right lines," by which that name is limited to denote one certain idea and no other. To which I answer that in the definition it is not said whether the surface be great or small, black or white, nor whether the sides are long or short, equal or unequal, nor with what angles they are inclined to each other; in all which there may be great variety, and consequently there is no one settled idea which limits the signification of the word "triangle." It is one thing for to keep a name constantly to the same definition, and another to make it stand everywhere for the same idea; the one is necessary, the other useless and impracticable.

19. But, to give a further account of how words came to produce the doctrine of abstract ideas, it must be observed that it is a received opinion that language has no other end but the communicating our ideas, and that every significant name stands for an idea. This being so, and it being withal certain that names which yet are not thought altogether insignificant do not always mark out conceivable ideas, it is straightway concluded that they stand for abstract notions. That there are many names in use amongst speculative men which do not always suggest to others determinate, particular ideas is what nobody will deny. And a little attention will discover that it is not necessary (even in the strictest reasonings) that significant names which stand for ideas should, every time they are used, excite in the understanding the ideas they are made to stand for—in reading and discoursing, names being for the most part used as letters in algebra, in which, though a particular quantity be marked by each letter, yet to proceed right it is not requisite that in every step each letter suggest to your thoughts that particular quantity it was appointed to stand for.

20. Besides, the communicating of ideas marked by words is not the chief and only end of language, as is commonly supposed. There are other ends, as the raising of some passion, the exciting to or deterring from an action, the putting the mind in some particular disposition—to which the former is in many cases barely subservient, and sometimes entirely omitted, when these can be obtained without it, as I think does not unfrequently happen in the familiar use of language. I entreat the reader to reflect with himself and see if it does not often happen, either in hearing or reading a discourse, that the passions of fear, love, hatred, admiration, disdain, and the like, arise immediately in his mind upon the perception of certain words, without any ideas coming between. At first, indeed, the words might have occasioned ideas that were fit to produce those emotions; but, if I mistake not, it will be found that, when language is once grown familiar, the hearing of the sounds or sight of the characters is oft immediately attended with those passions which at first were wont to be produced by the intervention of ideas that are now quite omitted. May we not, for example, be affected with the promise of a *good thing*, though we have not an idea of what it is? Or is not the being threatened with danger sufficient to excite a dread, though we think not of any particular evil likely to befall us, nor yet frame to ourselves an idea of danger in abstract? If anyone shall join ever so little reflection of his own to what has been said, I believe that it will evidently appear to him that general names are often used in the propriety of language without the speaker's designing them for marks of ideas in his own, which he would have them raise in the

mind of the hearer. Even proper names themselves do not seem always spoken with a design to bring into our view the ideas of those individuals that are supposed to be marked by them. For example, when a Schoolman tells me, "Aristotle has said it," all I conceive he means by it is to dispose me to embrace his opinion with the deference and submission which custom has annexed to that name. And this effect may be so instantly produced in the minds of those who are accustomed to resign their judgment to the authority of that philosopher, as it is impossible any idea either of his person, writings, or reputation should go before. Innumerable examples of this kind may be given, but why should I insist on those things which everyone's experience will, I doubt not, plentifully suggest unto him?

21. We have, I think, shown the impossibility of abstract ideas. We have considered what has been said for them by their ablest patrons, and endeavored to show they are of no use for those ends to which they are thought necessary. And lastly, we have traced them to the source from whence they flow, which appears to be language. It cannot be denied that words are of excellent use, in that by their means all that stock of knowledge which has been purchased by the joint labors of inquisitive men in all ages and nations may be drawn into the view and made the possession of one single person. But at the same time it must be owned that most parts of knowledge have been strangely perplexed and darkened by the abuse of words, and general ways of speech wherein they are delivered. Since therefore words are so apt to impose on the understanding, whatever ideas I consider, I shall endeavor to take them bare and naked into my view, keeping out of my thoughts so far as I am able those names which long and constant use has so strictly united with them; from which I may expect to derive the following advantages:

22. *First,* I shall be sure to get clear of all controversies purely verbal—the springing up of which weeds in almost all the sciences has been a main hindrance to the growth of true and sound knowledge. *Secondly,* this seems to be a sure way to extricate myself out of that fine and subtle net of *abstract ideas* which has so miserably perplexed and entangled the minds of men; and that with this peculiar circumstance, that by how much the finer and more curious was the wit of any man, by so much the deeper was he likely to be ensnared and faster held therein. *Thirdly,* so long as I confine my thoughts to my own ideas divested of words, I do not see how I can easily be mistaken. The objects I consider I clearly and adequately know. I cannot be deceived in thinking I have an idea which I have not. It is not possible for me to imagine that any of my own ideas are alike or unlike that are not truly so. To discern the agreements or disagreements there are between my ideas, to see what ideas are included in any compound idea and what not, there is nothing more requisite than an attentive perception of what passes in my own understanding.

23. But the attainment of all these advantages does presuppose an entire deliverance from the deception of words, which I dare hardly promise myself—so difficult a thing it is to dissolve a union so early begun and confirmed by so long a habit as that betwixt words and ideas. Which difficulty seems to have been very much increased by the doctrine of *abstraction.* For so long as men thought abstract ideas were annexed to their words, it does not seem strange that they should use words for ideas—it being found an impracticable thing to lay aside the word and retain the *abstract* idea in the mind, which in itself was perfectly inconceivable. This seems to me the principal cause why those men who have so emphatically recommended to others the laying aside all use of words in their meditations, and contemplating their bare ideas, have yet failed to perform it themselves. Of late many

have been very sensible of the absurd opinions and insignificant disputes which grow out of the abuse of words. And, in order to remedy these evils, they advise well that we attend to the ideas signified and draw off our attention from the words which signify them. But, how good soever this advice may be they have given others, it is plain they could not have a due regard to it themselves so long as they thought the only immediate use of words was to signify ideas, and that the immediate signification of every general name was a determinate abstract idea.

24. But, these being known to be mistakes, a man may with greater ease prevent his being imposed on by words. He that knows he has no other than *particular* ideas will not puzzle himself in vain to find out and conceive the *abstract* idea annexed to any name. And he that knows names do not always stand for ideas will spare himself the labor of looking for ideas where there are none to be had. It were, therefore, to be wished that everyone would use his utmost endeavors to obtain a clear view of the ideas he would consider, separating from them all that dress and encumbrance of words which so much contribute to blind the judgment and divide the attention. In vain do we extend our view into the heavens and pry into the entrails of the earth, in vain do we consult the writings of learned men and trace the dark footsteps of antiquity—we need only draw the curtain of words, to behold the fairest tree of knowledge, whose fruit is excellent and within the reach of our hand.

25. Unless we take care to clear the first principles of knowledge from the embarrassment and delusion of words, we may make infinite reasonings upon them to no purpose; we may draw consequences from consequences, and be never the wiser. The further we go, we shall only lose ourselves the more irrecoverably, and be the deeper entangled in difficulties and mistakes. Whoever, therefore, designs to read the following sheets, I entreat him to make my words the occasion of his own thinking and endeavor to attain the same train of thoughts in reading that I had in writing them. By this means it will be easy for him to discover the truth or falsity of what I say. He will be out of all danger of being deceived by my words, and I do not see how he can be led into an error by considering his own naked, undisguised ideas.

OF THE PRINCIPLES OF HUMAN KNOWLEDGE

It is evident to anyone who takes a survey of the *objects* of human knowledge that they are either ideas actually imprinted on the senses, or else such as are perceived by attending to the passions and operations of the mind, or lastly, ideas formed by help of memory and imagination—either compounding, dividing, or barely representing those originally perceived in the aforesaid ways. By sight I have the ideas of light and colors, with their several degrees and variations. By touch I perceive, for example, hard and soft, heat and cold, motion and resistance, and of all these more and less either as to quantity or degree. Smelling furnishes me with odors, the palate with tastes, and hearing conveys sounds to the mind in all their variety of tone and composition. And as several of these are observed to accompany each other, they come to be marked by one name, and so to be reputed as one thing. Thus, for example, a certain color, taste, smell, figure, and consistence having been observed to go together are accounted one distinct thing signified by the name "apple"; other col-

lections of ideas constitute a stone, a tree, a book, and the like sensible things—
which as they are pleasing or disagreeable excite the passions of love, hatred, joy,
grief, and so forth.

2. But, besides all that endless variety of ideas or objects of knowledge, there is
likewise something which knows or perceives them and exercises divers operations,
as willing, imagining, remembering, about them. This perceiving, active being is
what I call "mind," "spirit," "soul," or "myself." By which words I do not denote
any one of my ideas, but a thing entirely distinct from them, wherein they exist or,
which is the same thing, whereby they are perceived—for the existence of an idea
consists in being perceived.

3. That neither our thoughts, nor passions, nor ideas formed by the imagination
exist without the mind is what everybody will allow. And it seems no less evident
that the various sensations or ideas imprinted on the sense, however blended or
combined together (that is, whatever objects they compose), cannot exist otherwise
than in a mind perceiving them.—I think an intuitive knowledge may be obtained
of this by anyone that shall attend to what is meant by the term "exist" when applied to sensible things. The table I write on I say exists, that is, I see and feel it;
and if I were out of my study I should say it existed—meaning thereby that if I was
in my study I might perceive it, or that some other spirit actually does perceive it.
There was an odor, that is, it was smelled; there was a sound, that is to say, it was
heard; a color or figure, and it was perceived by sight or touch. This is all that I can
understand by these and the like expressions. For as to what is said of the absolute
existence of unthinking things without any relation to their being perceived, that
seems perfectly unintelligible. Their *esse* is *percipi*, nor is it possible they should have
any existence out of the minds or thinking things which perceive them.

4. It is indeed an opinion strangely prevailing amongst men that houses, mountains, rivers, and, in a word, all sensible objects have an existence, natural or real,
distinct from their being perceived by the understanding. But with how great an
assurance and acquiescence soever this principle may be entertained in the world,
yet whoever shall find in his heart to call it in question may, if I mistake not, perceive it to involve a manifest contradiction. For what are the forementioned objects
but the things we perceive by sense? And what do we perceive besides our own
ideas or sensations? And is it not plainly repugnant that any one of these, or any
combination of them, should exist unperceived?

5. If we thoroughly examine this tenet it will, perhaps, be found at bottom to
depend on the doctrine of *abstract ideas*. For can there be a nicer strain of abstraction
than to distinguish the existence of sensible objects from their being perceived, so
as to conceive them existing unperceived? Light and colors, heat and cold, extension and figures—in a word, the things we see and feel—what are they but so many
sensations, notions, ideas, or impressions on the sense? And is it possible to separate, even in thought, any of these from perception? For my part, I might as easily
divide a thing from itself. I may, indeed, divide in my thoughts, or conceive apart
from each other, those things which, perhaps, I never perceived by sense so divided.
Thus I imagine the trunk of a human body without the limbs, or conceive the smell
of a rose without thinking of the rose itself. So far, I will not deny, I can abstract—if
that may properly be called "abstraction" which extends only to the conceiving
separately such objects as it is possible may really exist or be actually perceived
asunder. But my conceiving or imagining power does not extend beyond the possibility of real existence or perception. Hence, as it is impossible for me to see or feel

anything without an actual sensation of that thing, so it is impossible for me to conceive in my thoughts any sensible thing or object distinct from the sensation or perception of it.

6. Some truths there are so near and obvious to the mind that a man need only open his eyes to see them. Such I take this important one to be, to wit, that all the choir of heaven and furniture of the earth, in a word, all those bodies which compose the mighty frame of the world, have not any subsistence without a mind—that their *being* is to be perceived or known, that, consequently, so long as they are not actually perceived by me or do not exist in my mind or that of any other created spirit, they must either have no existence at all or else subsist in the mind of some eternal spirit—it being perfectly unintelligible, and involving all the absurdity of abstraction, to attribute to any single part of them an existence independent of a spirit. To be convinced of which, the reader need only reflect, and try to separate in his own thoughts, the *being* of a sensible thing from its *being perceived.*

7. From what has been said it follows there is not any other substance than *spirit*, or that which perceives. But, for the fuller proof of this point, let it be considered the sensible qualities are color, figure, motion, smell, taste, and such like—that is, the ideas perceived by sense. Now, for an idea to exist in an unperceiving thing is a manifest contradiction, for to have an idea is all one as to perceive; that, therefore, wherein color, figure, and the like qualities exist must perceive them; hence it is clear there can be no unthinking substance or *substratum* of those ideas.

8. But, say you, though the ideas themselves do not exist without the mind, yet there may be things like them, whereof they are copies or resemblances, which things exist without the mind in an unthinking substance. I answer, an idea can be like nothing but an idea; a color or figure can be like nothing but another color or figure. If we look but ever so little into our thoughts, we shall find it impossible for us to conceive a likeness except only between our ideas. Again, I ask whether those supposed originals or external things, of which our ideas are the pictures or representations, be themselves perceivable or no? If they are, then they are ideas and we have gained our point; but if you say they are not, I appeal to anyone whether it be sense to assert a color is like something which is invisible; hard or soft, like something which is intangible; and so of the rest.

9. Some there are who make a distinction betwixt *primary* and *secondary* qualities.[5] By the former they mean extension, figure, motion, rest, solidity or impenetrability, and number; by the latter they denote all other sensible qualities, as colors, sounds, tastes, and so forth. The ideas we have of these they acknowledge not to be the resemblances of anything existing without the mind, or unperceived, but they will have our ideas of the primary qualities to be patterns or images of things which exist without the mind, in an unthinking substance which they call "matter." By "matter," therefore, we are to understand an inert, senseless substance, in which extension, figure, and motion do actually subsist. But it is evident from what we have already shown that extension, figure, and motion are only ideas existing in the mind, and that an idea can be like nothing but another idea, and that consequently neither they nor their archetypes can exist in an unperceiving substance. Hence it is plain that the very notion of what is called "matter" or "corporeal substance" involves a contradiction in it.

5. [Locke, for example. See his *Essay*, Bk. II, ch. VIII.]

10. They who assert that figure, motion, and the rest of the primary or original qualities do exist without the mind in unthinking substances do at the same time acknowledge that colors, sounds, heat, cold, and suchlike secondary qualities do not—which they tell us are sensations existing in the mind alone, that depend on and are occasioned by the different size, texture, and motion of the minute particles of matter. This they take for an undoubted truth which they can demonstrate beyond all exception. Now, if it be certain that those original qualities are inseparably united with the other sensible qualities, and not, even in thought, capable of being abstracted from them, it plainly follows that they exist only in the mind. But I desire anyone to reflect and try whether he can, by any abstraction of thought, conceive the extension and motion of a body without all other sensible qualities. For my own part, I see evidently that it is not in my power to frame an idea of a body extended and moved, but I must withal give it some color or other sensible quality which is acknowledged to exist only in the mind. In short, extension, figure, and motion, abstracted from all other qualities, are inconceivable. Where therefore the other sensible qualities are, there must these be also, to wit, in the mind and nowhere else.

11. Again, *great* and *small, swift* and *slow* are allowed to exist nowhere without the mind, being entirely relative, and changing as the frame or position of the organs of sense varies. The extension, therefore, which exists without the mind is neither great nor small, the motion neither swift nor slow; that is, they are nothing at all. But, say you, they are extension in general, and motion in general: thus we see how much the tenet of extended movable substances existing without the mind depends on that strange doctrine of *abstract ideas.* And here I cannot but remark how nearly the vague and indeterminate description of matter or corporeal substance, which the modern philosophers are run into by their own principles, resembles that antiquated and so much ridiculed notion of *materia prima,* to be met with in Aristotle and his followers. Without extension, solidity cannot be conceived; since, therefore, it has been shown that extension exists not in an unthinking substance, the same must also be true of solidity.

12. That number is entirely the creature of the mind, even though the other qualities be allowed to exist without, will be evident to whoever considers that the same thing bears a different denomination of number as the mind views it with different respects. Thus the same extension is one, or three, or thirty-six, according as the mind considers it with reference to a yard, a foot, or an inch. Number is so visibly relative and dependent on men's understanding that it is strange to think how anyone should give it an absolute existence without the mind. We say one book, one page, one line; all these are equally units, though some contain several of the others. And in each instance it is plain the unit relates to some particular combination of ideas arbitrarily put together by the mind.

13. Unity I know some[6] will have to be a simple or uncompounded idea accompanying all other ideas into the mind. That I have any such idea answering the word "unity" I do not find; and if I had, methinks I could not miss finding it; on the contrary, it should be the most familiar to my understanding, since it is said to accompany all other ideas and to be perceived by all the ways of sensation and reflection. To say no more, it is an *abstract idea.*

14. I shall further add that, after the same manner as modern philosophers prove

6. [Locke, for one.]

certain sensible qualities to have no existence in matter, or without the mind, the same thing may be likewise proved of all other sensible qualities whatsoever. Thus, for instance, it is said that heat and cold are affections only of the mind, and not at all patterns of real beings existing in the corporeal substances which excite them, for that the same body which appears cold to one hand seems warm to another. Now, why may we not as well argue that figure and extension are not patterns or resemblances of qualities existing in matter, because to the same eye at different stations, or eyes of a different texture at the same station, they appear various and cannot, therefore, be the images of anything settled and determinate without the mind? Again, it is proved that sweetness is not really in the sapid thing, because, the thing remaining unaltered, the sweetness is changed into bitter, as in case of a fever or otherwise vitiated palate. Is it not as reasonable to say that motion is not without the mind, since if the succession of ideas in the mind become swifter, the motion, it is acknowledged, shall appear slower without any alteration in any external object?

15. In short, let anyone consider those arguments which are thought manifestly to prove that colors and tastes exist only in the mind, and he shall find they may with equal force be brought to prove the same thing of extension, figure, and motion. Though it must be confessed this method of arguing does not so much prove that there is no extension or color in an outward object as that we do not know by sense which is the true extension or color of the object. But the arguments foregoing plainly show it to be impossible that any color or extension at all, or other sensible quality whatsoever, should exist in an unthinking subject without the mind, or, in truth, that there should be any such thing as an outward object.

16. But let us examine a little the received opinion.—It is said extension is a mode or accident of matter, and that matter is the *substratum* that supports it. Now I desire that you would explain what is meant by matter's "supporting" extension. Say you, I have no idea of matter and, therefore, cannot explain it. I answer, though you have no positive, yet, if you have any meaning at all, you must at least have a relative idea of matter; though you know not what it is, yet you must be supposed to know what relation it bears to accidents, and what is meant by its supporting them. It is evident "support" cannot here be taken in its usual or literal sense—as when we say that pillars support a building; in what sense therefore must it be taken?

17. If we inquire into what the most accurate philosophers[7] declare themselves to mean by "material substance," we shall find them acknowledge they have no other meaning annexed to those sounds but the idea of being in general together with the relative notion of its supporting accidents. The general idea of being appears to me the most abstract and incomprehensible of all other; and as for its supporting accidents, this, as we have just now observed, cannot be understood in the common sense of those words; it must, therefore, be taken in some other sense, but what that is they do not explain. So that when I consider the two parts or branches which make the signification of the words "material substance," I am convinced there is no distinct meaning annexed to them. But why should we trouble ourselves any further in discussing this material *substratum* or support of figure and motion and other sensible qualities? Does it not suppose they have an existence without the mind? And is not this a direct repugnancy and altogether inconceivable?

18. But, though it were possible that solid, figured, movable substances may exist

7. [The reference is again to Locke. See his *Essay*, Bk. II, ch. XXIII, sec. 2.]

without the mind, corresponding to the ideas we have of bodies, yet how is it possible for us to know this? Either we must know it by sense or by reason. As for our senses, by them we have the knowledge only of our sensations, ideas, or those things that are immediately perceived by sense, call them what you will; but they do not inform us that things exist without the mind, or unperceived, like to those which are perceived. This the materialists themselves acknowledge. It remains therefore that if we have any knowledge at all of external things, it must be by reason, inferring their existence from what is immediately perceived by sense. But what reason can induce us to believe the existence of bodies without the mind, from what we perceive, since the very patrons of matter themselves do not pretend there is any necessary connection betwixt them and our ideas? I say it is granted on all hands (and what happens in dreams, frenzies, and the like, puts it beyond dispute) that it is possible we might be affected with all the ideas we have now, though no bodies existed without resembling them. Hence it is evident the supposition of external bodies is not necessary for the producing our ideas; since it is granted they are produced sometimes, and might possibly be produced always in the same order we see them in at present, without their concurrence.

19. But though we might possibly have all our sensations without them, yet perhaps it may be thought easier to conceive and explain the manner of their production by supposing external bodies in their likeness rather than otherwise; and so it might be at least probable there are such things as bodies that excite their ideas in our minds. But neither can this be said, for, though we give the materialists their external bodies, they by their own confession are never the nearer knowing how our ideas are produced, since they own themselves unable to comprehend in what manner body can act upon spirit, or how it is possible it should imprint any idea in the mind. Hence it is evident the production of ideas or sensations in our minds can be no reason why we should suppose matter or corporeal substances, since that is acknowledged to remain equally inexplicable with or without this supposition. If therefore it were possible for bodies to exist without the mind, yet to hold they do so must needs be a very precarious opinion, since it is to suppose, without any reason at all, that God has created innumerable things that are entirely useless and serve to no manner of purpose.

20. In short, if there were external bodies, it is impossible we should ever come to know it; and if there were not, we might have the very same reasons to think there were that we have now. Suppose—what no one can deny possible—an intelligence without the help of external bodies, to be affected with the same train of sensations or ideas that you are, imprinted in the same order and with like vividness in his mind. I ask whether that intelligence has not all the reason to believe the existence of corporeal substances, represented by his ideas and exciting them in his mind, that you can possibly have for believing the same thing? Of this there can be no question—which one consideration is enough to make any reasonable person suspect the strength of whatever arguments he may think himself to have for the existence of bodies without the mind.

21. Were it necessary to add any further proof against the existence of matter after what has been said, I could instance several of those errors and difficulties (not to mention impieties) which have sprung from that tenet. It has occasioned numberless controversies and and disputes in philosophy, and not a few of far greater moment in religion. But I shall not enter into the detail of them in this place as well

because I think arguments a posteriori are unnecessary for confirming what has been, if I mistake not, sufficiently demonstrated a priori, as because I shall hereafter find occasion to speak somewhat of them.

22. I am afraid I have given cause to think me needlessly prolix in handling this subject. For to what purpose is it to dilate on that which may be demonstrated with the utmost evidence in a line or two to anyone that is capable of the least reflection? It is but looking into your own thoughts, and so trying whether you can conceive it possible for a sound, or figure, or motion, or color to exist without the mind or unperceived. This easy trial may make you see that what you contend for is a downright contradiction. Insomuch that I am content to put the whole upon this issue: if you can but conceive it possible for one extended movable substance, or, in general, for any one idea, or anything like an idea, to exist otherwise than in a mind perceiving it, I shall readily give up the cause. And, as for all that compages of external bodies which you contend for, I shall grant you its existence, though you cannot either give me any reason why you believe it exists, or assign any use to it when it is supposed to exist. I say the bare possibility of your opinion's being true shall pass for an argument that it is so.

23. But, say you, surely there is nothing easier than to imagine trees, for instance, in a park, or books existing in a closet, and nobody by to perceive them. I answer you may so, there is no difficulty in it; but what is all this, I beseech you, more than framing in your mind certain ideas which you call books and trees, and at the same time omitting to frame the idea of anyone that may perceive them? But do not you yourself perceive or think of them all the while? This therefore is nothing to the purpose; it only shows you have the power of imagining or forming ideas in your mind; but it does not show that you can conceive it possible the objects of your thought may exist without the mind. To make out this, it is necessary that you conceive them existing unconceived or unthought of, which is a manifest repugnancy. When we do our utmost to conceive the existence of external bodies, we are all the while only contemplating our own ideas. But the mind, taking no notice of itself, is deluded to think it can and does conceive bodies existing unthought of or without the mind, though at the same time they are apprehended by or exist in itself. A little attention will discover to anyone the truth and evidence of what is here said, and make it unnecessary to insist on any other proofs against the existence of *material substance*.

24. It is very obvious, upon the least inquiry into our own thoughts, to know whether it be possible for us to understand what is meant by "the absolute existence of sensible objects in themselves, or without the mind." To me it is evident those words mark out either a direct contradiction or else nothing at all. And to convince others of this, I know no readier or fairer way than to entreat they would calmly attend to their own thoughts; and if by this attention the emptiness or repugnancy of those expressions does appear, surely nothing more is requisite for their conviction. It is on this, therefore, that I insist, to wit, that "the absolute existence of unthinking things" are words without a meaning, or which include a contradiction. This is what I repeat and inculcate, and earnestly recommend to the attentive thoughts of the reader.

25. All our ideas, sensations, or the things which we perceive, by whatsoever names they may be distinguished, are visibly inactive—there is nothing of power or agency included in them. So that one idea or object of thought cannot produce or

make any alteration in another. To be satisfied of the truth of this, there is nothing else requisite but a bare observation of our ideas. For since they and every part of them exist only in the mind, it follows that there is nothing in them but what is perceived; but whoever shall attend to his ideas, whether of sense or reflection, will not perceive in them any power or activity; there is, therefore, no such thing contained in them. A little attention will discover to us that the very being of an idea implies passiveness and inertness in it, insomuch that it is impossible for an idea to do anything or, strictly speaking, to be the cause of anything; neither can it be the resemblance or pattern of any active being, as is evident from sec. 8. Whence it plainly follows that extension, figure, and motion cannot be the cause of our sensations. To say, therefore, that these are the effects of powers resulting from the configuration, number, motion, and size of corpuscles must certainly be false.

26. We perceive a continual succession of ideas, some are anew excited, others are changed or totally disappear. There is, therefore, some cause of these ideas, whereon they depend and which produces and changes them. That this cause cannot be any quality or idea or combination of ideas is clear from the preceding section. It must therefore be a substance; but it has been shown that there is no corporeal or material substance: it remains, therefore, that the cause of ideas is an incorporeal, active substance or spirit.

27. A spirit is one simple, undivided, active being—as it perceives ideas it is called "the understanding," and as it produces or otherwise operates about them it is called "the will." Hence there can be no *idea* formed of a soul or spirit; for all ideas whatever, being passive and inert (*vide* sec. 25), they cannot represent unto us, by way of image or likeness, that which acts. A little attention will make it plain to anyone that to have an idea which shall be like that principle of motion and change of ideas is absolutely impossible. Such is the nature of *spirit*, or that which acts, that it cannot be of itself perceived, but only by the effects which it produces. If any man shall doubt of the truth of what is here delivered, let him but reflect and try if he can frame the idea of any power or active being, and whether he has ideas of two principal powers marked by the names "will" and "understanding," distinct from each other as well as from a third idea of substance or being in general, with a relative notion of its supporting or being the subject of the aforesaid powers—which is signified by the name "soul" or "spirit." This is what some hold; but, so far as I can see, the words "will," "soul," "spirit" do not stand for different ideas or, in truth, for any idea at all, but for something which is very different from ideas, and which, being an agent, cannot be like unto, or represented by, any idea whatsoever. Though it must be owned at the same time that we have some notion of soul, spirit, and the operations of the mind, such as willing, loving, hating—in as much as we know or understand the meaning of those words.

28. I find I can excite ideas in my mind at pleasure, and vary and shift the scene as oft as I think fit. It is no more than willing, and straightway this or that idea arises in my fancy; and by the same power it is obliterated and makes way for another. This making and unmaking of ideas does very properly denominate the mind active. Thus much is certain and grounded on experience; but when we talk of unthinking agents or of exciting ideas exclusive of volition, we only amuse ourselves with words.

29. But, whatever power I may have over my own thoughts, I find the ideas actually perceived by sense have not a like dependence on my will. When in broad

daylight I open my eyes, it is not in my power to choose whether I shall see or no, or to determine what particular objects shall present themselves to my view; and so likewise as to the hearing and other senses; the ideas imprinted on them are not creatures of my will. There is therefore some *other* will or spirit that produces them.

30. The ideas of sense are more strong, lively, and distinct than those of the imagination; they have likewise a steadiness, order, and coherence, and are not excited at random, as those which are the effects of human wills often are, but in a regular train or series, the admirable connection whereof sufficiently testifies the wisdom and benevolence of its Author. Now the set rules or established methods wherein the mind we depend on excites in us the ideas of sense are called "the laws of nature"; and these we learn by experience, which teaches us that such and such ideas are attended with such and such other ideas in the ordinary course of things.

31. This gives us a sort of foresight which enables us to regulate our actions for the benefit of life. And without this we should be eternally at a loss; we could not know how to act anything that might procure us the least pleasure or remove the least pain of sense. That food nourishes, sleep refreshes, and fire warms us; that to sow in the seedtime is the way to reap in the harvest; and in general that to obtain such or such ends, such or such means are conducive—all this we know, not by discovering any necessary connection between our ideas, but only by the observation of the settled laws of nature, without which we should be all in uncertainty and confusion, and a grown man no more know how to manage himself in the affairs of life than an infant just born.

32. And yet this consistent, uniform working which so evidently displays the goodness and wisdom of that Governing Spirit whose Will constitutes the laws of nature, is so far from leading our thoughts to Him that it rather sends them awandering after second causes. For when we perceive certain ideas of sense constantly followed by other ideas, and we know this is not of our own doing, we forthwith attribute power and agency to the ideas themselves and make one the cause of another, than which nothing can be more absurd and unintelligible. Thus, for example, having observed that when we perceive by sight a certain, round, luminous figure, we at the same time perceive by touch the idea or sensation called "heat," we do from thence conclude the sun to be the cause of heat. And in like manner perceiving the motion and collision of bodies to be attended with sound, we are inclined to think the latter an effect of the former.

33. The ideas imprinted on the senses by the Author of Nature are called "real things"; and those excited in the imagination, being less regular, vivid, and constant, are more properly termed "ideas" or "images of things" which they copy and represent. But then our sensations, be they never so vivid and distinct, are nevertheless ideas, that is, they exist in the mind, or are perceived by it, as truly as the ideas of its own framing. The ideas of sense are allowed to have more reality in them, that is, to be more strong, orderly, and coherent than the creatures of the mind; but this is no argument that they exist without the mind. They are also less dependent on the spirit, or thinking substance which perceives them, in that they are excited by the will of another and more powerful spirit; yet still they are *ideas;* and certainly no idea, whether faint or strong, can exist otherwise than in a mind perceiving it.

34. Before we proceed any further it is necessary to spend some time in answering objections which may probably be made against the principles hitherto laid down. In doing of which, if I seem too prolix to those of quick apprehensions, I hope it

may be pardoned, since all men do not equally apprehend things of this nature, and I am willing to be understood by everyone.

First, then, it will be objected that by the foregoing principles all that is real and substantial in nature is banished out of the world, and instead thereof a chimerical scheme of *ideas* takes place. All things that exist, exist only in the mind, that is, they are purely notional. What therefore becomes of the sun, moon, and stars? What must we think of houses, rivers, mountains, trees, stones, nay, even of our own bodies? Are all these but so many chimeras and illusions on the fancy? To all which, and whatever else of the same sort may be objected, I answer that by the principles premised we are not deprived of any one thing in nature. Whatever we see, feel, hear, or anywise conceive or understand remains as secure as ever, and is as real as ever. There is a *rerum natura,* and the distinction between realities and chimeras retains its full force. This is evident from secs. 29, 30, and 33, where we have shown what is meant by "real things" in opposition to "chimeras" or ideas of our own framing; but then they both equally exist in the mind, and in that sense they are alike *ideas.*

35. I do not argue against the existence of any one thing that we can apprehend either by sense or reflection. That the things I see with my eyes and touch with my hands do exist, really exist, I make not the least question. The only thing whose existence we deny is that which philosophers call matter or corporeal substance. And in doing of this there is no damage done to the rest of mankind, who, I dare say, will never miss it. The atheist indeed will want the color of an empty name to support his impiety; and the philosophers may possibly find they have lost a great handle for trifling and disputation.

36. If any man thinks this detracts from the existence or reality of things, he is very far from understanding what has been premised in the plainest terms I could think of. Take here an abstract of what has been said: there are spiritual substances, minds, or human souls, which will or excite ideas in themselves at pleasure, but these are faint, weak, and unsteady in respect of others they perceive by sense—which, being impressed upon them according to certain rules or laws of nature, speak themselves the effects of a mind more powerful and wise than human spirits. These latter are said to have more *reality* in them than the former—by which is meant that they are more affecting, orderly, and distinct, and that they are not fictions of the mind perceiving them. And in this sense the sun that I see by day is the real sun, and that which I imagine by night is the idea of the former. In the sense here given of "reality" it is evident that every vegetable, star, mineral, and in general each part of the mundane system, is as much a *real being* by our principles as by any other. Whether others mean anything by the term "reality" different from what I do, I entreat them to look into their own thoughts and see.

37. It will be urged that thus much at least is true, to wit, that we take away all corporeal substances. To this my answer is that if the word "substance" be taken in the vulgar sense—for a combination of sensible qualities, such as extension, solidity, weight, and the like—this we cannot be accused of taking away; but if it be taken in a philosophic sense—for the support of accidents or qualities without the mind—then indeed I acknowledge that we take it away, if one may be said to take away that which never had any existence, not even in the imagination.

38. But, say you, it sounds very harsh to say we eat and drink ideas, and are clothed with ideas. I acknowledge it does so—the word "idea" not being used in

common discourse to signify the several combinations of sensible qualities which are called "things"; and it is certain that any expression which varies from the familiar use of language will seem harsh and ridiculous. But this does not concern the truth of the proposition which, in other words, is no more than to say we are fed and clothed with those things which we perceive immediately by our senses. The hardness or softness, the color, taste, warmth, figure, and suchlike qualities, which combined together constitute the several sorts of victuals and apparel, have been shown to exist only in the mind that perceives them; and this is all that is meant by calling them "ideas," which word if it was as ordinarily used as "thing," would sound no harsher nor more ridiculous than it. I am not for disputing about the propriety, but the truth of the expression. If therefore you agree with me that we eat and drink and are clad with the immediate objects of sense, which cannot exist unperceived or without the mind, I shall readily grant it is more proper or conformable to custom that they should be called "things" rather than "ideas."

39. If it be demanded why I make use of the word "idea," and do not rather in compliance with custom call them "things," I answer I do it for two reasons; first, because the term "thing" in contradistinction to "idea" is generally supposed to denote somewhat existing without the mind; secondly, because "thing" has a more comprehensive signification than "idea," including spirits or thinking things as well as ideas. Since therefore the objects of sense exist only in the mind and are withal thoughtless and inactive, I chose to mark them by the word "idea," which implies those properties.

40. But, say what we can, someone perhaps may be apt to reply he will still believe his senses, and never suffer any arguments, how plausible soever, to prevail over the certainty of them. Be it so; assert the evidence of sense as high as you please, we are willing to do the same. That what I see, hear, and feel does exist— that is to say, is perceived by me—I no more doubt than I do of my own being. But I do not see how the testimony of sense can be alleged as a proof for the existence of anything which is not perceived by sense. We are not for having any man turn skeptic and disbelieve his senses; on the contrary, we give them all the stress and assurance imaginable; nor are there any principles more opposite to skepticism than those we have laid down, as shall be hereafter clearly shown.

41. *Secondly,* it will be objected that there is a great difference betwixt real fire, for instance, and the idea of fire, betwixt dreaming or imagining oneself burned, and actually being so. This and the like may be urged in opposition to our tenets. To all which the answer is evident from what has been already said; and I shall only add in this place that if real fire be very different from the idea of fire, so also is the real pain that it occasions very different from the idea of the same pain, and yet nobody will pretend that real pain either is, or can possibly be, in an unperceiving thing, or without the mind, any more than its idea.

42. *Thirdly,* it will be objected that we see things actually without or at a distance from us, and which, consequently, do not exist in the mind, it being absurd that those things which are seen at the distance of several miles should be as near to us as our own thoughts. In answer to this I desire it may be considered that in a dream we do oft perceive things as existing at a great distance off, and yet for all that those things are acknowledged to have their existence only in the mind.

43. But for the fuller clearing of this point it may be worth while to consider how it is that we perceive distance and things placed at a distance by sight. For that we

should in truth see external space, and bodies actually existing in it, some nearer, others farther off, seems to carry with it some opposition to what has been said of their existing nowhere without the mind. The consideration of this difficulty it was that gave birth to my *Essay Towards a New Theory of Vision,* which was published not long since, wherein it is shown that distance or outness is neither immediately of itself perceived by sight, nor yet apprehended or judged of by lines and angles, or anything that has a necessary connection with it; but that it is only suggested to our thoughts by certain visible ideas and sensations attending vision, which in their own nature have no manner of similitude or relation either with distance or things placed at a distance; but by a connection taught us by experience they come to signify and suggest them to us after the same manner that words of any language suggest the ideas they are made to stand for; insomuch that a man born blind and afterwards made to see would not, at first sight, think the things he saw to be without his mind or at any distance from him. See sec. 41 of the forementioned treatise.

44. The ideas of sight and touch make two species entirely distinct and heterogeneous. The former are marks and prognostics of the latter. That the proper objects of sight neither exist without mind, nor are the images of external things, was shown even in that treatise. Though throughout the same the contrary be supposed true of tangible objects—not that to suppose that vulgar error was necessary for establishing the notion therein laid down, but because it was beside my purpose to examine and refute it in a discourse concerning *vision.* So that in strict truth the ideas of sight, when we apprehend by them distance and things placed at a distance, do not suggest or mark out to us things actually existing at a distance, but only admonish us what ideas of touch will be imprinted in our minds at such and such distances of time, and in consequence of such and such actions. It is, I say, evident from what has been said in the foregoing parts of this treatise, and in sec. 147 and elsewhere of the *Essay Concerning Vision,* that visible ideas are the language whereby the Governing Spirit on whom we depend informs us what tangible ideas he is about to imprint upon us in case we excite this or that motion in our own bodies. But for a fuller information in this point I refer to the *Essay* itself.

45. *Fourthly,* it will be objected that from the foregoing principles it follows things are every moment annihilated and created anew. The objects of sense exist only when they are perceived; the trees, therefore, are in the garden, or the chairs in the parlor, no longer than while there is somebody by to perceive them. Upon shutting my eyes all the furniture in the room is reduced to nothing, and barely upon opening them it is again created. In answer to all which I refer the reader to what has been said in secs. 3, 4, etc., and desire he will consider whether he means anything by the actual existence of an idea distinct from its being perceived. For my part, after the nicest inquiry I could make, I am not able to discover that anything else is meant by those words; and I once more entreat the reader to sound his own thoughts and not suffer himself to be imposed on by words. If he can conceive it possible either for his ideas or their archetypes to exist without being perceived, then I give up the cause; but if he cannot, he will acknowledge it is unreasonable for him to stand up in defense of he knows not what and pretend to charge on me as an absurdity the not assenting to those propositions which at bottom have no meaning in them.

46. It will not be amiss to observe how far the received principles of philosophy are themselves chargeable with those pretended absurdities. It is thought strangely

absurd that upon closing my eyelids all the visible objects around me should be reduced to nothing; and yet is not this what philosophers commonly acknowledge when they agree on all hands that light and colors, which alone are the proper and immediate objects of sight, are mere sensations that exist no longer than they are perceived? Again, it may to some, perhaps, seem very incredible that things should be every moment creating, yet this very notion is commonly taught in the Schools. For the Schoolmen, though they acknowledge the existence of matter, and that the whole mundane fabric is framed out of it, are nevertheless of opinion that it cannot subsist without the divine conservation, which by them is expounded to be a continual creation.

47. Further, a little thought will discover to us that though we allow the existence of matter or corporeal substance, yet it will unavoidably follow, from the principles which are now generally admitted, that the particular bodies of what kind soever do none of them exist whilst they are not perceived. For it is evident from sec. 11 and the following sections that the matter philosophers contend for is an incomprehensible somewhat, which has none of those particular qualities whereby the bodies falling under our senses are distinguished one from another. But, to make this more plain, it must be remarked that the infinite divisibility of matter is now universally allowed, at least by the most approved and considerable philosophers, who on the received principles demonstrate it beyond all exception. Hence it follows that there is an infinite number of parts in each particle of matter which are not perceived by sense. The reason, therefore, that any particular body seems to be of a finite magnitude, or exhibits only a finite number of parts to sense, is not because it contains no more, since in itself it contains an infinite number of parts, but because the sense is not acute enough to discern them. In proportion, therefore, as the sense is rendered more acute, it perceives a greater number of parts in the object; that is, the object appears greater, and its figure varies, those parts in its extremities which were before unperceivable appearing now to bound it in very different lines and angles from those perceived by an obtuser sense. And at length, after various changes of size and shape, when the sense becomes infinitely acute, the body shall seem infinite. During all which there is no alteration in the body, but only in the sense. Each body, therefore, considered in itself, is infinitely extended, and consequently void of all shape or figure. From which it follows that, though we should grant the existence of matter to be ever so certain, yet it is withal as certain—the materialists themselves are by their own principles forced to acknowledge—that neither the particular bodies perceived by sense, nor anything like them, exist without the mind. Matter, I say, and each particle thereof, is according to them infinite and shapeless, and it is the mind that frames all that variety of bodies which compose the visible world, any one whereof does not exist longer than it is perceived.

48. If we consider it, the objection proposed in sec. 45 will not be found reasonably charged on the principles we have premised, so as in truth to make any objection at all against our notions. For though we hold indeed the objects of sense to be nothing else but ideas which cannot exist unperceived, yet we may not hence conclude they have no existence except only while they are perceived by us, since there may be some other spirit that perceives them, though we do not. Wherever bodies are said to have no existence without the mind, I would not be understood to mean this or that particular mind, but all minds whatsoever. It does not therefore follow from the foregoing principles that bodies are annihilated and created every moment or exist not at all during the intervals between our perception of them.

49. *Fifthly,* it may perhaps be objected that if extension and figure exist only in the mind, it follows that the mind is extended and figured, since extension is a mode or attribute which (to speak with the Schools) is predicated of the subject in which it exists. I answer, those qualities are in the mind only as they are perceived by it — that is, not by way of *mode* or *attribute,* but only by way of *idea;* and it no more follows that the soul or mind is extended, because extension exists in it alone, than it does that it is red or blue, because those colors are on all hands acknowledged to exist in it, and nowhere else. As to what philosophers say of subject and mode, that seems very groundless and unintelligible. For instance, in this proposition "a die is hard, extended, and square," they will have it that the word "die" denotes a subject or substance distinct from hardness, extension, and figure which are predicated of it, and in which they exist. This I cannot comprehend; to me a die seems to be nothing distinct from those things which are termed its modes or accidents. And to say a die is hard, extended, and square is not to attribute those qualities to a subject distinct from and supporting them, but only an explication of the meaning of the word "die."

50. *Sixthly,* you will say there have been a great many things explained by matter and motion; take away these and you destroy the whole corpuscular philosophy and undermine those mechanical principles which have been applied with so much success to account for the phenomena. In short, whatever advances have been made, either by ancient or modern philosophers, in the study of nature do all proceed on the supposition that corporeal substance or matter does really exist. To this I answer that there is not any one phenomenon explained on that supposition which may not as well be explained without it, as might easily be made appear by an induction of particulars. To explain the phenomena is all one as to show why, upon such and such occasions, we are affected with such and such ideas. But how matter should operate on a spirit, or produce any idea in it, is what no philosopher will pretend to explain; it is therefore evident there can be no use of matter in natural philosophy. Besides, they who attempt to account for things do it not by corporeal substance, but by figure, motion, and other qualities, which are in truth no more than mere ideas and, therefore, cannot be the cause of anything, as has been already shown. See sec. 25.

51. *Seventhly,* it will upon this be demanded whether it does not seem absurd to take away natural causes and ascribe everything to the immediate operation of spirits? We must no longer say, upon these principles, that fire heats, or water cools, but that a spirit heats, and so forth. Would not a man be deservedly laughed at who should talk after this manner? I answer, he would so; in such things we ought to "think with the learned and speak with the vulgar." They who by demonstration are convinced of the truth of the Copernican system do nevertheless say, "the sun rises," "the sun sets," or "comes to the meridian"; and if they affected a contrary style in common talk it would without doubt appear very ridiculous. A little reflection on what is here said will make it manifest that the common use of language would receive no manner of alteration or disturbance from the admission of our tenets.

52. In the ordinary affairs of life, any phrases may be retained so long as they excite in us proper sentiments or dispositions to act in such a manner as is necessary for our well-being, how false soever they may be if taken in a strict and speculative sense. Nay, this is unavoidable, since, propriety being regulated by custom, language is suited to the received opinions, which are not always the truest. Hence

it is impossible, even in the most rigid, philosophic reasonings, so far to alter the bent and genius of the tongue we speak, as never to give a handle for cavilers to pretend difficulties and inconsistencies. But a fair and ingenuous reader will collect the sense from the scope and tenor and connection of a discourse, making allowances for those inaccurate modes of speech which use has made inevitable.

53. As to the opinion that there are no corporeal causes, this has been heretofore maintained by some of the Schoolmen, as it is of late by others among the modern philosophers[8] who, though they allow matter to exist, yet will have God alone to be the immediate efficient cause of all things. These men saw that amongst all the objects of sense there was none which had any power or activity included in it, and that by consequence this was likewise true of whatever bodies they supposed to exist without the mind, like unto the immediate objects of sense. But then, that they should suppose an innumerable multitude of created beings which they acknowledge are not capable of producing any one effect in nature, and which therefore are made to no manner of purpose, since God might have done everything as well without them—this I say, though we should allow it possible, must yet be a very unaccountable and extravagant supposition.

54. In the *eighth* place, the universal concurrent assent of mankind may be thought by some an invincible argument in behalf of matter, or the existence of external things. Must we suppose the whole world to be mistaken? And if so, what cause can be assigned of so widespread and predominant an error? I answer, first, that, upon a narrow inquiry, it will not perhaps be found so many as is imagined do really believe the existence of matter or things without the mind. Strictly speaking, to believe that which involves a contradiction, or has no meaning in it, is impossible; and whether the foregoing expressions are not of that sort, I refer it to the impartial examination of the reader. In one sense, indeed, men may be said to believe that matter exists, that is, they act as if the immediate cause of their sensations, which affects them every moment and is so nearly present to them, were some senseless unthinking being. But that they should clearly apprehend any meaning marked by those words, and form thereof a settled speculative opinion, is what I am not able to conceive. This is not the only instance wherein men impose upon themselves, by imagining they believe those propositions they have often heard, though at bottom they have no meaning in them.

55. But secondly, though we should grant a notion to be ever so universally and steadfastly adhered to, yet this is but a weak argument of its truth to whoever considers what a vast number of prejudices and false opinions are everywhere embraced with the utmost tenaciousness by the unreflecting (which are the far greater) part of mankind. There was a time when the antipodes and motion of the earth were looked upon as monstrous absurdities even by men of learning; and if it be considered what a small proportion they bear to the rest of mankind, we shall find that at this day those notions have gained but a very inconsiderable footing in the world.

56. But it is demanded that we assign a cause of this prejudice and account for its obtaining in the world. To this I answer that men, knowing they perceived several

---

8. [The reference is to the occasionalists, among them Arnold Geulincx (1624–1669) of Flanders, and Nicolas Malebranche (1638–1715) of France, who maintained that no interaction occurs between mental and physical events nor among events in either realm. They ascribed the appearance of interaction to the intervention of God, whose actions were said to produce regularities.]

ideas whereof they themselves were not the authors—as not being excited from within nor depending on the operation of their wills—this made them maintain those ideas, or objects of perception, had an existence independent of and without the mind, without ever dreaming that a contradiction was involved in those words. But philosophers having plainly seen that the immediate objects of perception do not exist without the mind, they in some degree corrected the mistake of the vulgar, but at the same time run into another which seems no less absurd, to wit, that there are certain objects really existing without the mind or having a subsistence distinct from being perceived, of which our ideas are only images or resemblances, imprinted by those objects on the mind. And this notion of the philosophers owes its origin to the same cause with the former, namely, their being conscious that they were not the authors of their own sensations, which they evidently knew were imprinted from without, and which therefore must have some cause distinct from the minds on which they are imprinted.

57. But why they should suppose the ideas of sense to be excited in us by things in their likeness, and not rather have recourse to *spirit* which alone can act, may be accounted for, first because they were not aware of the repugnancy there is, as well in supposing things like unto our ideas existing without, as in attributing to them power or activity. Secondly, because the supreme spirit which excites those ideas in our minds is not marked out and limited to our view by any particular finite collection of sensible ideas, as human agents are by their size, complexion, limbs, and motions. And thirdly, because His operations are regular and uniform. Whenever the course of nature is interrupted by a miracle, men are ready to own the presence of a superior agent. But when we see things go on in the ordinary course, they do not excite in us any reflection; their order and concatenation, though it be an argument of the greatest wisdom, power, and goodness in their Creator, is yet so constant and familiar to us that we do not think them the immediate effects of a *free spirit,* especially since inconstancy and mutability in acting, though it be an imperfection, is looked on as a mark of *freedom.*

58. *Tenthly,* it will be objected that the notions we advance are inconsistent with several sound truths in philosophy and mathematics. For example, the motion of the earth is now universally admitted by astronomers as a truth grounded on the clearest and most convincing reasons. But on the foregoing principles there can be no such thing. For, motion being only an idea, it follows that if it be not perceived it exists not; but the motion of the earth is not perceived by sense. I answer, that tenet, if rightly understood, will be found to agree with the principles we have premised, for the question whether the earth moves or no amounts in reality to no more than this, to wit, whether we have reason to conclude, from what has been observed by astronomers, that if we were placed in such and such circumstances, and such or such a position and distance both from the earth and sun, we should perceive the former to move among the choir of the planets, and appearing in all respects like one of them; and this, by the established rules of nature which we have no reason to mistrust, is reasonably collected from the phenomena.

59. We may, from the experience we have had of the train and succession of ideas in our minds, often make, I will not say uncertain conjectures, but sure and well-grounded predictions concerning the ideas we shall be affected with pursuant to a great train of actions, and be enabled to pass a right judgment of what would have appeared to us in case we were placed in circumstances very different from those we are in at present. Herein consists the knowledge of nature, which may preserve its

use and certainty very consistently with what has been said. It will be easy to apply this to whatever objections of the like sort may be drawn from the magnitude of the stars or any other discoveries in astronomy or nature.

60. In the *eleventh* place, it will be demanded to what purpose serves that curious organization of plants and the admirable mechanism on the parts of animals; might not vegetables grow and shoot forth leaves and blossoms, and animals perform all their motions as well without as with all that variety of internal parts so elegantly contrived and put together; which, being ideas, have nothing powerful or operative in them, nor have any necessary connection with the effects ascribed to them? If it be a spirit that immediately produces every effect by a fiat or act of his will, we must think all that is fine and artificial in the works, whether of man or nature, to be made in vain. By this doctrine, though an artist has made the spring and wheels, and every movement of a watch, and adjusted them in such a manner as he knew would produce the motions he designed, yet he must think all this done to no purpose, and that it is an Intelligence which directs the index and points to the hour of the day. If so, why may not the Intelligence do it, without his being at the pains of making the movements and putting them together? Why does not an empty case serve as well as another? And how comes it to pass that whenever there is any fault in the going of a watch, there is some corresponding disorder to be found in the movements, which being mended by a skillful hand all is right again? The like may be said of all the clockwork of nature, great part whereof is so wonderfully fine and subtle as scarce to be discerned by the best microscope. In short, it will be asked how, upon our principles, any tolerable account can be given, or any final cause assigned, of an innumerable multitude of bodies and machines, framed with the most exquisite art, which in the common philosophy have very apposite uses assigned them and serve to explain abundance of phenomena?

61. To all which I answer, first, that though there were some difficulties relating to the administration of Providence, and the uses by it assigned to the several parts of nature which I could not solve by the foregoing principles, yet this objection could be of small weight against the truth and certainty of those things which may be proved a priori with the utmost evidence. Secondly, but neither are the received principles free from the like difficulties, for it may still be demanded to what end God should take those roundabout methods of effecting things by instruments and machines which no one can deny might have been effected by the mere command of His will without all that apparatus; nay, if we narrowly consider it, we shall find the objection may be retorted with greater force on those who hold the existence of those machines without the mind, for it has been made evident that solidity, bulk, figure, motion, and the like have no *activity* or *efficacy* in them so as to be capable of producing any one effect in nature. See sec. 25. Whoever, therefore, supposes them to exist (allowing the supposition possible) when they are not perceived does it manifestly to no purpose, since the only use that is assigned to them, as they exist unperceived, is that they produce those perceivable effects which in truth cannot be ascribed to anything but spirit.

62. But, to come nearer the difficulty, it must be observed that though the fabrication of all those parts and organs be not absolutely necessary to the producing any effect, yet it is necessary to the producing of things in a constant regular way according to the laws of nature. There are certain general laws that run through the whole chain of natural effects; these are learned by the observation and study of

nature and are by men applied as well to the framing artificial things for the use and ornament of life as to the explaining the various phenomena—which explication consists only in showing the conformity any particular phenomenon has to the general laws of nature or, which is the same thing, in discovering the *uniformity* there is in the production of natural effects, as will be evident to whoever shall attend to the several instances wherein philosophers pretend to account for appearances. That there is a great and conspicuous use in these regular, constant methods of working observed by the Supreme Agent has been shown in sec. 31. And it is no less visible that a particular size, figure, motion, and disposition of parts are necessary, though not absolutely, to the producing any effect, yet to the producing it according to the standing mechanical laws of nature. Thus, for instance, it cannot be denied that God, or the Intelligence which sustains and rules the ordinary course of things, might, if He were minded to produce a miracle, cause all the motions on the dial-plate of a watch, though nobody has ever made the movements and put them in it; but yet, if He will act agreeably to the rules of mechanism by Him for wise ends established and maintained in the Creation, it is necessary that those actions of the watchmaker, whereby he makes the movements and rightly adjusts them, precede the production of the aforesaid motions, as also that any disorder in them be attended with the perception of some corresponding disorder in the movements, which, being once corrected, all is right again.

63. It may indeed on some occasions be necessary that the Author of Nature display His overruling power in producing some appearance out of the ordinary series of things. Such exceptions from the general rules of nature are proper to surprise and awe men into an acknowledgement of the Divine Being; but then they are to be used but seldom, otherwise there is a plain reason why they should fail of that effect. Besides, God seems to choose the convincing our reason of His attributes by the works of nature, which discover so much harmony and contrivance in their make and are such plain indications of wisdom and beneficence in their Author rather than to astonish us into a belief of His being by anomalous and surprising events.

64. To set this matter in a yet clearer light, I shall observe that what has been objected in sec. 60 amounts in reality to no more than this: ideas are not anyhow and at random produced, there being a certain order and connection between them, like to that of cause and effect; there are also several combinations of them made in a very regular and artificial manner, which seem like so many instruments in the hand of nature that, being hidden, as it were, behind the scenes, have a secret operation in producing those appearances which are seen on the theater of the world, being themselves discernible only to the curious eye of the philosopher. But, since one idea cannot be the cause of another, to what purpose is that connection? And, since those instruments, being barely *inefficacious perceptions* in the mind, are not subservient to the production of natural effects, it is demanded why they are made, or, in other words, what reason can be assigned why God should make us, upon a close inspection into His works, behold so great variety of ideas so artfully laid together, and so much according to rule, it not being credible that He would be at the expense (if one may so speak) of all that art and regularity to no purpose.

65. To all which my answer is, first, that the connection of ideas does not imply the relation of *cause* and *effect,* but only of a mark or *sign* with the thing *signified.* The fire which I see is not the cause of the pain I suffer upon my approaching it, but the mark that forewarns me of it. In like manner, the noise that I hear is not the effect of

this or that motion or collision of the ambient bodies, but the sign thereof. Secondly, the reason why ideas are formed into machines, that is, artificial and regular combinations, is the same with that for combining letters into words. That a few original ideas may be made to signify a great number of effects and actions, it is necessary they be variously combined together. And, to the end their use be permanent and universal, these combinations must be made by *rule* and with *wise contrivance.* By this means abundance of information is conveyed unto us concerning what we are to expect from such and such actions and what methods are proper to be taken for the exciting such and such ideas, which in effect is all that I conceive to be distinctly meant when it is said that, by discerning the figure, texture, and mechanism of the inward parts of bodies, whether natural or artificial, we may attain to know the several uses and properties depending thereon, or the nature of the thing.

66. Hence it is evident that those things which, under the notion of a cause cooperating or concurring to the production of effects, are altogether inexplicable and run us into great absurdities may be very naturally explained and have a proper and obvious use assigned to them when they are considered only as marks or signs for our information. And it is the searching after and endeavoring to understand those signs instituted by the Author of Nature that ought to be the employment of the natural philosopher, and not the pretending to explain things by corporeal causes, which doctrine seems to have too much estranged the minds of men from that active principle, that supreme and wise Spirit "in whom we live, move, and have our being."

67. In the *twelfth* place, it may perhaps be objected that—though it be clear from what has been said that there can be no such thing as an inert, senseless, extended, solid, figured, movable substance existing without the mind, such as philosophers describe matter—yet, if any man shall leave out of his idea of *matter* the positive ideas of extension, figure, solidity, and motion and say that he means only by that word an inert, senseless substance that exists without the mind or unperceived, which is the occasion of our ideas, or at the presence whereof God is pleased to excite ideas in us—it does not appear but that matter taken in this sense may possibly exist. In answer to which I say, first, that it seems no less absurd to suppose a substance without accidents than it is to suppose accidents without a substance. But secondly, though we should grant this unknown substance may possibly exist, yet where can it be supposed to be? That it exists not in the mind is agreed; and that it exists not in place is no less certain—since all extension exists only in the mind, as has been already proved. It remains therefore that it exists nowhere at all.

68. Let us examine a little the description that is here given us of *matter.* It neither acts, nor perceives, nor is perceived, for this is all that is meant by saying it is an inert, senseless, unknown substance; which is a definition entirely made up of negatives, excepting only the relative notion of its standing under or supporting. But then it must be observed that it supports nothing at all, and how nearly this comes to the description of a *nonentity* I desire may be considered. But, say you, it is the *unknown occasion* at the presence of which ideas are excited in us by the will of God. Now I would fain know how anything can be present to us which is neither perceivable by sense nor reflection, nor capable of producing any idea in our minds, nor is at all extended, nor has any form, nor exists in any place. The words "to be present," when thus applied, must needs be taken in some abstract and strange meaning, and which I am not able to comprehend.

69. Again, let us examine what is meant by "occasion." So far as I can gather from the common use of language, that word signifies either the agent which produces any effect or else something that is observed to accompany or go before it in the ordinary course of things. But when it is applied to matter as above described, it can be taken in neither of those senses, for matter is said to be passive and inert, and so cannot be an agent or efficient cause. It is also unperceivable, as being devoid of all sensible qualities, and so cannot be the occasion of our perceptions in the latter sense, as when the burning my finger is said to be the occasion of the pain that attends it. What therefore can be meant by calling matter an "occasion"? This term is either used in no sense at all or else in some sense very distant from its received signification.

70. You will perhaps say that matter, though it be not perceived by us, is nevertheless perceived by God, to whom it is the occasion of exciting ideas in our minds. For, say you, since we observe our sensations to be imprinted in an orderly and constant manner, it is but reasonable to suppose there are certain constant and regular occasions of their being produced. That is to say, that there are certain permanent and distinct parcels of matter, corresponding to our ideas, which, though they do not excite them in our minds or anyways immediately affect us, as being altogether passive and unperceivable to us, they are nevertheless to God, by whom they are perceived, as it were, so many occasions to remind Him when and what ideas to imprint on our minds that so things may go on in a constant uniform manner.

71. In answer to this I observe that, as the notion of matter is here stated, the question is no longer concerning the existence of a thing distinct from *spirit* and *idea*, from perceiving and being perceived, but whether there are not certain ideas of I know not what sort in the mind of God which are so many marks or notes that direct Him how to produce sensations in our minds in a constant and regular method—much after the same manner as a musician is directed by the notes of music to produce that harmonious train and composition of sound which is called a "tune," though they who hear the music do not perceive the notes and may be entirely ignorant of them. But this notion of matter seems too extravagant to deserve a confutation. Besides, it is in effect no objection against what we have advanced, to wit, that there is no senseless, unperceived substance.

72. If we follow the light of reason we shall, from the constant uniform method of our sensations, collect the goodness and wisdom of the spirit who excites them in our minds; but this is all that I can see reasonably concluded from thence. To me, I say, it is evident that the being of a spirit infinitely wise, good, and powerful is abundantly sufficient to explain all the appearances of nature. But, as for *inert, senseless matter*, nothing that I perceive has any the least connection with it or leads to the thoughts of it. And I would fain see anyone explain any the meanest phenomenon in nature by it or show any manner of reason, though in the lowest rank of probability, that he can have for its existence, or even make any tolerable sense or meaning of that supposition. For as to its being an occasion we have, I think, evidently shown that with regard to us it is no occasion. It remains therefore that it must be, if at all, the occasion to God of exciting ideas in us, and what this amounts to we have just now seen.

73. It is worth while to reflect a little on the motives which induced men to suppose the existence of *material substance;* that so having observed the gradual ceasing and expiration of those motives or reasons, we may proportionably withdraw the

assent that was grounded on them. First, therefore, it was thought that color, figure, motion, and the rest of the sensible qualities or accidents did really exist without the mind; and for this reason it seemed needful to suppose some unthinking *substratum* or substance wherein they did exist, since they could not be conceived to exist by themselves. Afterwards, in process of time, men being convinced that colors, sounds, and the rest of the sensible, secondary qualities had no existence without the mind, they stripped this *substratum* or material substance of those qualities, leaving only the primary ones, figure, motion, and suchlike, which they still conceived to exist without the mind, and consequently to stand in need of a material support. But it having been shown that none even of these can possibly exist otherwise than in a spirit or mind which perceives them, it follows that we have no longer any reason to suppose the being of matter; nay, that it is utterly impossible there should be any such thing so long as that word is taken to denote an *unthinking substratum* of qualities or accidents wherein they exist without the mind.

74. But though it be allowed by the materialists themselves that matter was thought of only for the sake of supporting accidents, and, the reason entirely ceasing, one might expect the mind should naturally, and without any reluctance at all, quit the belief of what was solely grounded thereon, yet the prejudice is riveted so deeply in our thoughts that we can scarce tell how to part with it, and are therefore inclined, since the *thing* itself is indefensible, at least to retain the *name*, which we apply to I know not what abstracted and indefinite notions of being, or occasion, though without any show of reason, at least so far as I can see. For what is there on our part, or what do we perceive among all the ideas, sensations, notions which are imprinted on our minds, either by sense or reflection, from whence may be inferred the existence of an inert, thoughtless, unperceived occasion? And, on the other hand, on the part of an all-sufficient Spirit, what can there be that should make us believe or even suspect He is directed by an inert occasion to excite ideas in our minds?

75. It is a very extraordinary instance of the force of prejudice, and much to be lamented, that the mind of man retains so great a fondness, against all the evidence of reason, for a stupid, thoughtless *somewhat,* by the interposition whereof it would as it were screen itself from the Providence of God and remove him farther off from the affairs of the world. But though we do the utmost we can to secure the belief of matter, though, when reason forsakes us, we endeavor to support our opinion on the bare possibility of the thing, and though we indulge ourselves in the full scope of an imagination not regulated by reason to make out that poor possibility, yet the upshot of all is that there are certain *unknown ideas* in the mind of God; for this, if anything, is all that I conceive to be meant by "occasion" with regard to God. And this at the bottom is no longer contending for the thing, but for the name.

76. Whether, therefore, there are such ideas in the mind of God, and whether they may be called by the name "matter," I shall not dispute. But if you stick to the notion of an unthinking substance or support of extension, motion, and other sensible qualities, then to me it is most evidently impossible there should be any such thing, since it is a plain repugnancy that those qualities should exist in or be supported by an unperceiving substance.

77. But, say you, though it be granted that there is no thoughtless support of extension and the other qualities or accidents which we perceive, yet there may, perhaps, be some inert, unperceiving substance or *substratum* of some other quali-

ties, as incomprehensible to us as colors are to a man born blind, because we have not a sense adapted to them. But if we had a new sense, we should possibly no more doubt of their existence than a blind man made to see does of the existence of light and colors. I answer, first, if what you mean by the word "matter" be only the unknown support of unknown qualities, it is no matter whether there is such a thing or no, since it no way concerns us; and I do not see the advantage there is in disputing about we know not *what*, and we know not *why*.

78. But, secondly, if we had a new sense, it could only furnish us with new ideas or sensations; and then we should have the same reason against their existing in an unperceiving substance that has been already offered with relation to figure, motion, color, and the like. Qualities, as has been shown, are nothing else but *sensations* or *ideas*, which exist only in a *mind* perceiving them; and this is true not only of the ideas we are acquainted with at present, but likewise of all possible ideas whatsoever.

79. But, you will insist, what if I have no reason to believe the existence of matter? What if I cannot assign any use to it or explain anything by it, or even conceive what is meant by that word? Yet still it is no contradiction to say that matter exists, and that this matter is in general a *substance*, or *occasion of ideas*, though, indeed, to go about to unfold the meaning or adhere to any particular explication of those words may be attended with great difficulties. I answer, when words are used without a meaning, you may put them together as you please without danger of running into a contradiction. You may say, for example, that twice two is equal to seven, so long as you declare you do not take the words of that proposition in their usual acceptation but for marks of you know not what. And, by the same reason, you may say there is an inert, thoughtless substance without accidents which is the occasion of our ideas. And we shall understand just as much by one proposition as the other.

80. In the *last* place, you will say, What if we give up the cause of material substance and assert that matter is an unknown *somewhat*—neither substance nor accident, spirit nor idea, inert, thoughtless, indivisible, immovable, unextended, existing in no place? For, say you, whatever may be urged against *substance* or *occasion*, or any other positive or relative notion of matter, has no place at all so long as this *negative* definition of matter is adhered to. I answer, You may, if so it shall seem good, use the word "matter" in the same sense as other men use "nothing," and so make those terms convertible in your style. For, after all, this is what appears to me to be the result of that definition, the parts whereof, when I consider with attention, either collectively or separate from each other, I do not find that there is any kind of effect or impression made on my mind different from what is excited by the term "nothing."

81. You will reply, perhaps, that in the foresaid definition is included what does sufficiently distinguish it from nothing—the positive, abstract idea of *quiddity*, *entity*, or *existence*. I own, indeed, that those who pretend to the faculty of framing abstract general ideas do talk as if they had such an idea, which is, say they, the most abstract and general notion of all; that is, to me, the most incomprehensible of all others. That there are a great variety of spirits of different orders and capacities whose faculties both in number and extent are far exceeding those the Author of my being has bestowed on me, I see no reason to deny. And for me to pretend to determine by my own few, stinted, narrow inlets of perception what ideas the inexhaustible power of the Supreme Spirit may imprint upon them were certainly the

utmost folly and presumption—since there may be, for aught that I know, innumerable sorts of ideas or sensations, as different from one another, and from all that I have perceived, as colors are from sounds. But how ready soever I may be to acknowledge the scantiness of my comprehension with regard to the endless variety of spirits and ideas that might possibly exist, yet for anyone to pretend to a notion of entity or existence, *abstracted* from *spirit* and *idea*, from perceiving and being perceived is, I suspect, a downright repugnancy and trifling with words.—It remains that we consider the objections which may possibly be made on the part of religion.

82. Some there are who think that, though the arguments for the real existence of bodies which are drawn from reason be allowed not to amount to demonstration, yet the Holy Scriptures are so clear in the point as will sufficiently convince every good Christian that bodies do really exist, and are something more than mere ideas, there being in Holy Writ innumerable facts related which evidently suppose the reality of timber and stone, mountains and rivers, and cities, and human bodies. To which I answer that no sort of writings whatever, sacred or profane, which use those and the like words in the vulgar acceptation, or so as to have a meaning in them, are in danger of having their truth called in question by our doctrine. That all those things do really exist, that there are bodies, even corporeal substances, when taken in the vulgar sense, has been shown to be agreeable to our principles; and the difference betwixt *things* and *ideas, realities* and *chimeras* has been distinctly explained. See secs. 29, 30, 33, 36, etc. And I do not think that either what philosophers call "matter," or the existence of objects without the mind, is anywhere mentioned in Scripture.

83. Again, whether there be or be not external things, it is agreed on all hands that the proper use of words is the marking out conceptions, or things only as they are known and perceived by us; whence it plainly follows that in the tenets we have laid down there is nothing inconsistent with the right use and significance of *language,* and that discourse, of what kind soever, so far as it is intelligible, remains undisturbed. But all this seems so very manifest, from what has been set forth in the premises, that it is needless to insist any further on it.

84. But it will be urged that miracles do, at least, lose much of their stress and import by our principles. What must we think of Moses' rod? Was it not *really* turned into a serpent, or was there only a change of *ideas* in the minds of the spectators? And can it be supposed that our Saviour did no more at the marriage-feast in Cana than impose on the sight and smell and taste of the guests, so as to create in them the appearance or idea only of wine? The same may be said of all other miracles, which, in consequence of the foregoing principles, must be looked upon only as so many cheats or illusions of fancy. To this I reply that the rod was changed into a real serpent, and the water into real wine. That this does not in the least contradict what I have elsewhere said will be evident from secs. 34 and 35. But this business of *real* and *imaginary* has been already so plainly and fully explained, and so often referred to, and the difficulties about it are so easily answered from what has gone before, that it were an affront to the reader's understanding to resume the explication of it in this place. I shall only observe that if at table all who were present should see, and smell, and taste, and drink wine, and find the effects of it, with me there could be no doubt of its reality, so that at bottom the scruple concerning real miracles has no place at all on ours, but only on the received principles, and consequently makes rather for than against what has been said.

85. Having done with the objections, which I endeavored to propose in the clearest light, and gave them all the force and weight I could, we proceed in the next place to take a view of our tenets in their consequences. Some of these appear at first sight—as that several difficult and obscure questions, on which abundance of speculation has been thrown away, are entirely banished from philosophy: whether corporeal substance can think; whether matter be infinitely divisible; and how it operates on spirit—these and the like inquiries have given infinite amusement to philosophers in all ages, but, depending on the existence of matter, they have no longer any place on our principles. Many other advantages there are, as well with regard to religion as the sciences, which it is easy for anyone to deduce from what has been premised; but this will appear more plainly in the sequel.

86. From the principles we have laid down it follows human knowledge may naturally be reduced to two heads—that of *ideas* and that of *spirits*. Of each of these I shall treat in order.

And, *first*, as to ideas or unthinking things. Our knowledge of these has been very much obscured and confounded, and we have been led into very dangerous errors, by supposing a two-fold existence of the objects of sense—the one *intelligible* or in the mind, the other *real* and without the mind, whereby unthinking things are thought to have a natural subsistence of their own distinct from being perceived by spirits. This, which, if I mistake not, has been shown to be a most groundless and absurd notion, is the very root of skepticism, for so long as men thought that real things subsisted without the mind, and that their knowledge was only so far forth *real* as it was conformable to *real things*, it follows they could not be certain they had any real knowledge at all. For how can it be known that the things which are perceived are conformable to those which are not perceived or exist without the mind?

87. Color, figure, motion, extension, and the like, considered only as so many *sensations* in the mind, are perfectly known, there being nothing in them which is not perceived. But if they are looked on as notes or images, referred to *things* or *archetypes* existing without the mind, then are we involved all in skepticism. We see only the appearances, and not the real qualities of things. What may be the extension, figure, or motion of anything really and absolutely, or in itself, it is impossible for us to know, but only the proportion or the relation they bear to our senses. Things remaining the same, our ideas vary, and which of them, or even whether any of them at all, represent the true quality really existing in the thing, it is out of our reach to determine. So that, for aught we know, all we see, hear, and feel may be only phantom and vain chimera, and not at all agree with the real things existing in *rerum natura*.[9] All this skepticism follows from our supposing a difference between *things* and *ideas*, and that the former have a subsistence without the mind or unperceived. It were easy to dilate on this subject and show how the arguments urged by skeptics in all ages depend on the supposition of external objects.

88. So long as we attribute a real existence to unthinking things, distinct from their being perceived, it is not only impossible for us to know with evidence the nature of any real unthinking being, but even that it exists. Hence it is that we see philosophers distrust their senses and doubt of the existence of heaven and earth, of everything they see or feel, even of their own bodies. And after all their labor and struggle of thought, they are forced to own we cannot attain to any self-evident or

9. [The world itself.]

demonstrative knowledge of the existence of sensible things. But all this doubtfulness which so bewilders and confounds the mind and makes philosophy ridiculous in the eyes of the world vanishes if we annex a meaning to our words and do not amuse ourselves with the terms "absolute," "external," "exist," and suchlike, signifying we know not what. I can as well doubt of my own being as of the being of those things which I actually perceive by sense; it being a manifest contradiction that any sensible object should be immediately perceived by sight or touch and at the same time have no existence in nature, since the very *existence* of an unthinking being consists in *being perceived.*

89. Nothing seems of more importance toward erecting a firm system of sound and real knowledge, which may be proof against the assaults of skepticism, than to lay the beginning in a distinct explication of what is meant by "thing," "reality," "existence"; for in vain shall we dispute concerning the real existence of things or pretend to any knowledge thereof, so long as we have not fixed the meaning of those words. "Thing," or "being" is the most general name of all; it comprehends under it two kinds entirely distinct and heterogeneous, and which have nothing common but the name, to wit, *spirits* and *ideas.* The former are active, indivisible substances; the latter are inert, fleeting, dependent beings which subsist not by themselves, but are supported by or exist in minds or spiritual substances. We comprehend our own existence by inward feeling or reflection, and that of other spirits by reason. We may be said to have some knowledge or notion of our own minds, of spirits and active beings, whereof in a strict sense we have no ideas. In like manner, we know and have a notion of relations between things or ideas—which relations are distinct from the ideas or things related, in as much as the latter may be perceived by us without our perceiving the former. To me it seems that *ideas, spirits,* and *relations* are all in their respective kinds the object of human knowledge and subject of discourse, and that the term "idea" would be improperly extended to signify everything we know or have any notion of.

90. Ideas imprinted on the senses are real things, or do really exist—this we do not deny, but we deny they can subsist without the minds which perceive them, or that they are resemblances of any archetypes existing without the mind, since the very being of a sensation or idea consists in being perceived, and an idea can be like nothing but an idea. Again, the things perceived by sense may be termed "external" with regard to their origin—in that they are not generated from within by the mind itself, but imprinted by a spirit distinct from that which perceives them. Sensible objects may likewise be said to be "without the mind" in another sense, namely, when they exist in some other mind; thus, when I shut my eyes, the things I saw may still exist, but it must be in another mind.

91. It were a mistake to think that what is here said derogates in the least from the reality of things. It is acknowledged, on the received principles, that extension, motion, and, in a word, all sensible qualities have need of a support, as not being able to subsist by themselves. But the objects perceived by sense are allowed to be nothing but combinations of those qualities, and consequently cannot subsist by themselves. Thus far it is agreed on all hands. So that in denying the things perceived by sense an existence independent of a substance or support wherein they may exist, we detract nothing from the received opinion of their *reality,* and are guilty of no innovation in that respect. All the difference is that, according to us, the unthinking beings perceived by sense have no existence distinct from being per-

ceived, and cannot therefore exist in any other substances than those unextended indivisible substances or *spirits* which act and think and perceive them; whereas philosophers vulgarly hold that the sensible qualities exist in an inert, extended, unperceiving substance which they call "matter," to which they attribute a natural subsistence, exterior to all thinking beings, or distinct from being perceived by any mind whatsoever, even the eternal mind of the Creator, wherein they suppose only ideas of the corporeal substances created by him, if indeed they allow them to be at all created.

92. For as we have shown the doctrine of matter or corporeal substance to have been the main pillar and support of skepticism, so likewise, upon the same foundation, have been raised all the impious schemes of atheism and irreligion. Nay, so great a difficulty has it been thought to conceive matter produced out of nothing that the most celebrated among the ancient philosophers, even of these who maintained the being of a God, have thought matter to be uncreated and coeternal with Him. How great a friend *material substance* has been to atheists in all ages were needless to relate. All their monstrous systems have so visible and necessary a dependence on it that, when this cornerstone is once removed, the whole fabric cannot choose but fall to the ground, insomuch that it is no longer worth while to bestow a particular consideration on the absurdities of every wretched sect of atheists.

93. That impious and profane persons should readily fall in with those systems which favor their inclinations by deriding immaterial substance and supposing the soul to be divisible and subject to corruption as the body, which exclude all freedom, intelligence, and design from the formation of things, and instead thereof make a self-existent, stupid, unthinking substance the root and origin of all beings; that they should hearken to those who deny a Providence, or inspection of a Superior Mind over the affairs of the world, attributing the whole series of events either to blind chance or fatal necessity arising from the impulse of one body or another—all this is very natural. And, on the other hand, when men of better principles observe the enemies of religion lay so great a stress on *unthinking matter,* and all of them use so much industry and artifice to reduce everything to it, methinks they should rejoice to see them deprived of their grand support and driven from that only fortress without which your Epicureans, Hobbists, and the like, have not even the shadow of a pretense, but become the most cheap and easy triumph in the world.

94. The existence of matter, or bodies unperceived, has not only been the main support of atheists and fatalists, but on the same principle does idolatry likewise in all its various forms depend. Did men but consider that the sun, moon, and stars, and every other object of the senses are only so many sensations in their minds, which have no other existence but barely being perceived, doubtless they would never fall down and worship their own *ideas,* but rather address their homage to the Eternal Invisible Mind which produces and sustains all things.

95. The same absurd principle, by mingling itself with the articles of our faith, has occasioned no small difficulties to Christians. For example, about the resurrection, how many scruples and objections have been raised by Socinians[10] and others?

---

10. [Socinianism was an anti-Trinitarian religious movement organized in Poland by Faustus Socinus (1539–1604). The Socinians, who viewed Jesus as a human instrument of the divine will and the Holy Spirit as the activity of God, were disbanded as a result of persecution by the Church.]

But do not the most plausible of them depend on the supposition that a body is denominated "the same," with regard not to the form or that which is perceived by sense, but the material substance, which remains the same under several forms? Take away this *material substance,* about the identity whereof all the dispute is, and mean by "body" what every plain, ordinary person means by that word, to wit, that which is immediately seen and felt, which is only a combination of sensible qualities or ideas, and then their most unanswerable objections come to nothing.

96. Matter being once expelled out of nature drags with it so many skeptical and impious notions, such an incredible number of disputes and puzzling questions, which have been thorns in the sides of divines as well as philosophers and made so much fruitless work for mankind, that if the arguments we have produced against it are not found equal to demonstration (as to me they evidently seem), yet I am sure all friends to knowledge, peace, and religion have reason to wish they were.

97. Beside the external existence of the objects of perception, another great source of errors and difficulties with regard to ideal knowledge is the doctrine of *abstract ideas,* such as it has been set forth in the Introduction. The plainest things in the world, those we are most intimately acquainted with and perfectly know, when they are considered in an abstract way, appear strangely difficult and incomprehensible. Time, place, and motion, taken in particular or concrete, are what everybody knows, but, having passed through the hands of a metaphysician, they become too abstract and fine to be apprehended by men of ordinary sense. Bid your servant meet you at such a *time* in such a *place,* and he shall never stay to deliberate on the meaning of those words; in conceiving that particular time and place, or the motion by which he is to get thither, he finds not the least difficulty. But if *time* be taken exclusive of all those particular actions and ideas that diversify the day, merely for the continuation of existence or duration in abstract, then it will perhaps gravel even a philosopher to comprehend it.

98. Whenever I attempt to frame a simple idea of *time,* abstracted from the succession of ideas in my mind, which flows uniformly and is participated by all beings, I am lost and embrangled in inextricable difficulties. I have no notion of it at all, only I hear others say it is infinitely divisible, and speak of it in such a manner as leads me to entertain odd thoughts of my existence; since that doctrine lays one under an absolute necessity of thinking, either that he passes away innumerable ages without a thought or else that he is annihilated every moment of his life, both which seem equally absurd. Time therefore being nothing, abstracted from the succession of ideas in our minds, it follows that the duration of any finite spirit must be estimated by the number of ideas or actions succeeding each other in that same spirit or mind. Hence, it is a plain consequence that the soul always thinks; and in truth whoever shall go about to divide in his thoughts or abstract the *existence* of a spirit from its *cogitation* will, I believe, find it no easy task.

99. So likewise when we attempt to abstract extension and motion from all other qualities, and consider them by themselves, we presently lose sight of them, and run into great extravagances. All which depend on a twofold abstraction; first, it is supposed that extension, for example, may be abstracted from all other sensible qualities; and secondly, that the entity of extension may be abstracted from its being perceived. But whoever shall reflect, and take care to understand what he says, will, if I mistake not, acknowledge that all sensible qualities are alike *sensations* and alike *real;* that where the extension is, there is the color, too, to wit, in his mind,

and that their archetypes can exist only in some other *mind;* and that the objects of sense are nothing but those sensations combined, blended, or (if one may so speak) concreted together; none of all which can be supposed to exist unperceived.

100. What it is for a man to be happy, or an object good, everyone may think he knows. But to frame an abstract idea of happiness, prescinded from all particular pleasure, or of goodness from everything that is good, this is what few can pretend to. So likewise a man may be just and virtuous without having precise ideas of justice and virtue. The opinion that those and the like words stand for general notions, abstracted from all particular persons and actions, seems to have rendered morality difficult, and the study thereof of less use to mankind. And in effect the doctrine of *abstraction* has not a little contributed toward spoiling the most useful parts of knowledge.

101. The two great provinces of speculative science conversant about ideas received from sense and their relations are natural philosophy and mathematics; with regard to each of these I shall make some observations. And first I shall say somewhat of natural philosophy. On this subject it is that the skeptics triumph. All that stock of arguments they produce to depreciate our faculties and make mankind appear ignorant and low are drawn principally from this head, to wit, that we are under an invincible blindness as to the *true* and *real* nature of things. This they exaggerate, and love to enlarge on. We are miserably bantered, say they, by our senses, and amused only with the outside and show of things. The real essence, the internal qualities and constitution of every the meanest object, is hidden from our view; something there is in every drop of water, every grain of sand, which it is beyond the power of human understanding to fathom or comprehend. But it is evident from what has been shown that all this complaint is groundless, and that we are influenced by false principles to that degree as to mistrust our senses and think we know nothing of those things which we perfectly comprehend.

102. One great inducement to our pronouncing ourselves ignorant of the nature of things is the current opinion that everything includes within itself the cause of its properties; or that there is in each object an inward essence which is the source whence its discernible qualities flow, and whereon they depend. Some have pretended to account for appearances by occult qualities, but of late they are mostly resolved into mechanical causes, to wit, the figure, motion, weight, and suchlike qualities of insensible particles; whereas, in truth, there is no other agent or efficient cause than *spirit,* it being evident that motion, as well as all other *ideas,* is perfectly inert. See sec. 25. Hence, to endeavor to explain the production of colors or sounds by figure, motion, magnitude, and the like, must needs be labor in vain. And accordingly we see the attempts of that kind are not at all satisfactory. Which may be said in general of those instances wherein one idea or quality is assigned for the cause of another. I need not say how many hypotheses and speculations are left out, and how much the study of nature is abridged by this doctrine.

103. The great mechanical principle now in vogue is *attraction.* That a stone falls to the earth, or the sea swells toward the moon, may to some appear sufficiently explained thereby. But how are we enlightened by being told this is done by attraction? It is that that word signifies the manner of the tendency, and that it is by the mutual drawing of bodies instead of their being impelled or protruded toward each other? But nothing is determined of the manner or action, and it may as truly (for aught we know) be termed "impulse," or "protrusion," as "attraction." Again, the

parts of steel we see cohere firmly together, and this also is accounted for by attraction; but, in this as in the other instances, I do not perceive that anything is signified besides the effect itself; for as to the manner of the action whereby it is produced, or the cause which produces it, these are not so much as aimed at.

104. Indeed, if we take a view of the several phenomena and compare them together, we may observe some likeness and conformity between them. For example, in the falling of a stone to the ground, in the rising of the sea toward the moon, in cohesion and crystallization, there is something alike, namely, a union or mutual approach of bodies. So that any one of these or the like phenomena may not seem strange or surprising to a man who has nicely observed and compared the effects of nature. For that only is thought so which is uncommon, or a thing by itself, and out of the ordinary course of our observation. That bodies should tend toward the center of the earth is not thought strange, because it is what we perceive every moment of our lives. But, that they should have a like gravitation toward the center of the moon may seem odd and unaccountable to most men, because it is discerned only in the tides. But a philosopher, whose thoughts take in a larger compass of nature, having observed a certain similitude of appearances, as well in the heavens as the earth, that argue innumerable bodies to have a mutual tendency toward each other, which he denotes by the general name "attraction," whatever can be reduced to that he thinks justly accounted for. Thus he explains the tides by the attraction of the terraqueous globe toward the moon, which to him does not appear odd or anomalous, but only a particular example of a general rule or law of nature.

105. If therefore we consider the difference there is betwixt natural philosophers and other men with regard to their knowledge of the phenomena, we shall find it consists not in an exacter knowledge of the efficient cause that produces them—for that can be no other than the *will of a spirit*—but only in a greater largeness of comprehension, whereby analogies, harmonies, and agreements are discovered in the works of nature, and the particular effects explained, that is, reduced to general rules, see sec. 62, which rules, grounded on the analogy and uniformness observed in the production of natural effects, are most agreeable and sought after by the mind; for that they extend our prospect beyond what is present and near to us, and enable us to make very probable conjectures touching things that may have happened at very great distances of time and place, as well as to predict things to come; which sort of endeavor toward omniscience is much affected by the mind.

106. But we should proceed warily in such things, for we are apt to lay too great a stress on analogies, and, to the prejudice of truth, humor that eagerness of the mind whereby it is carried to extend its knowledge into general theorems. For example, gravitation or mutual attraction, because it appears in many instances, some are straightway for pronouncing "universal"; and that to attract and be attracted by every other body is an essential quality inherent in all bodies whatsoever. Whereas it appears the fixed stars have no such tendency toward each other; and so far is that gravitation from being *essential* to bodies that in some instances a quite contrary principle seems to show itself; as in the perpendicular growth of plants, and the elasticity of the air. There is nothing necessary or essential in the case, but it depends entirely on the will of the governing spirit, who causes certain bodies to cleave together or tend toward each other according to various laws, whilst he keeps others at a fixed distance; and to some he gives a quite contrary tendency to fly asunder just as he sees convenient.

107. After what has been premised, I think we may lay down the following conclusions. First, it is plain philosophers amuse themselves in vain when they inquire for any natural efficient cause distinct from a *mind* or *spirit*. Secondly, considering the whole creation is the workmanship of a *wise and good agent*, it should seem to become philosophers to employ their thoughts (contrary to what some hold) about the final causes of things; and I must confess I see no reason why pointing out the various ends to which natural things are adapted, and for which they were originally with unspeakable wisdom contrived, should not be thought one good way of accounting for them, and altogether worthy a philosopher. Thirdly, from what has been premised no reason can be drawn why the history of nature should not still be studied, and observations and experiments made; which, that they are of use to mankind, and enable us to draw any general conclusions, is not the result of any immutable habitudes or relations between things themselves, but only of God's goodness and kindness to men in the administration of the world. See secs. 30 and 31. Fourthly, by a diligent observation of the phenomena within our view, we may discover the general laws of nature, and from them deduce the other phenomena; I do not say "demonstrate," for all deductions of that kind depend on a supposition that the Author of Nature always operates uniformly and in a constant observance of those rules we take for principles, which we cannot evidently know.

108. Those men who frame general rules from the phenomena and afterwards derive the phenomena from those rules seem to consider signs rather than causes. A man may well understand natural signs without knowing their analogy, or being able to say by what rule a thing is so or so. And, as it is very possible to write improperly, through too strict an observance of general grammar rules; so, in arguing from general rules of nature, it is not impossible we may extend the analogy too far, and by that means run into mistakes.

109. As, in reading other books, a wise man will choose to fix his thoughts on the sense and apply it to use, rather than lay them out in grammatical remarks on the language, so, in perusing the volume of nature, it seems beneath the dignity of the mind to affect an exactness in reducing each particular phenomenon to general rules, or showing how it follows from them. We should propose to ourselves nobler views, such as to recreate and exalt the mind with a prospect of the beauty, order, extent, and variety of natural things: hence, by proper inferences, to enlarge our notions of the grandeur, wisdom, and beneficence of the Creator; and lastly, to make the several parts of the Creation, so far as in us lies, subservient to the ends they were designed for—God's glory and the sustentation and comfort of ourselves and fellow creatures.

110. The best key for the aforesaid analogy or natural science will be easily acknowledged to be a certain celebrated treatise of *mechanics*.[11] In the entrance of which justly admired treatise, time, space, and motion are distinguished into *absolute* and *relative, true* and *apparent, mathematical* and *vulgar;* which distinction, as it is at large explained by the author, does suppose these quantities to have an existence without the mind; and that they are ordinarily conceived with relation to sensible things, to which nevertheless in their own nature they bear no relation at all.

111. As for "time," as it is there taken in an absolute or abstracted sense, for the duration or perseverance of the existence of things, I have nothing more to add con-

11. [The work referred to is Isaac Newton's *Philosophiae Naturalis Principia Mathematica* (1687).]

cerning it after what has been already said on that subject. Secs. 97 and 98. For the rest, this celebrated author holds there is an *absolute space,* which, being unperceivable to sense, remains in itself similar and immovable; and relative space to be the measure thereof, which, being movable and defined by its situation in respect of sensible bodies, is vulgarly taken for immovable space. "Place" he defines to be that part of space which is occupied by any body; and according as the space is absolute or relative, so also is the place. "Absolute motion" is said to be the translation of a body from absolute place to absolute place, as relative motion is from relative place to another. And, because the parts of absolute space do not fall under our senses, instead of them we are obliged to use their sensible measures, and so define both place and motion with respect to bodies which we regard as immovable. But it is said in philosophical matters we must abstract from our senses, since it may be that none of those bodies which seem to be quiescent are truly so, and the same thing which is moved relatively may be really at rest; as likewise one and the same body may be in relative rest and motion, or even moved with contrary relative motions at the same time, according as its place is variously defined. All which ambiguity is to be found in the apparent motions, but not at all in the true or absolute, which should therefore be alone regarded in philosophy. And the true we are told are distinguished from apparent or relative motions by the following properties. — First, in true or absolute motion all parts which preserve the same position with respect to the whole partake of the motions of the whole. Secondly, the place being moved, that which is placed therein is also moved; so that a body moving in a place which is in motion does participate in the motion of its place. Thirdly, true motion is never generated or changed otherwise than by force impressed on the body itself. Fourthly, true motion is always changed by force impressed on the body moved. Fifthly, in circular motion, barely relative, there is no centrifugal force which, nevertheless, in that which is true or absolute, is proportional to the quantity of motion.

112. But, notwithstanding what has been said, it does not appear to me that there can be any motion other than *relative;* so that to conceive motion there must be at least conceived two bodies, whereof the distance or position in regard to each other is varied. Hence, if there was one only body in being it could not possibly be moved. This seems evident, in that the idea I have of motion does necessarily include relation.

113. But, though in every motion it be necessary to conceive more bodies than one, yet it may be that one only is moved, namely, that on which the force causing the change of distance is impressed, or, in other words, that to which the action is applied. For, however some may define relative motion, so as to term that body "moved" which changes its distance from some other body, whether the force or action causing that change were applied to it or no, yet as relative motion is that which is perceived by sense, and regarded in the ordinary affairs of life, it should seem that every man of common sense knows what it is as well as the best philosopher. Now I ask anyone whether, in his sense of motion as he walks along the streets, the stones he passes over may be said to *move,* because they change distance with his feet? To me it seems that though motion includes a relation of one thing to another, yet it is not necessary that each term of the relation be denominated from it. As a man may think of somewhat which does not think, so a body may be moved to or from another body which is not therefore itself in motion.

114. As the place happens to be variously defined, the motion which is related to it varies. A man in a ship may be said to be quiescent with relation to the sides of the

vessel, and yet move with relation to the land. Or he may move eastward in respect of the one, and westward in respect of the other. In the common affairs of life, men never go beyond the earth to define the place of any body; and what is quiescent in respect of that is accounted *absolutely* to be so. But philosophers, who have a greater extent of thought, and juster notions of the system of things, discover even the earth itself to be moved. In order therefore to fix their notions, they seem to conceive the corporeal world as finite, and the utmost unmoved walls or shell thereof to be the place whereby they estimate true motions. If we sound our own conceptions, I believe we may find all the absolute motion we can frame an idea of to be at bottom no other than relative motion thus defined. For, as has been already observed, absolute motion, exclusive of all external relation, is incomprehensible; and to this kind of relative motion all the above-mentioned properties, causes, and effects ascribed to absolute motion will, if I mistake not, be found to agree. As to what is said of the centrifugal force, that it does not at all belong to circular relative motion, I do not see how this follows from the experiment which is brought to prove it. See *Philosophiae Naturalis Principia Mathematica, in Schol. Def. VIII.* For the water in the vessel at that time wherein it is said to have the greatest relative circular motion, has, I think, no motion at all; as is plain from the foregoing section.

115. For, to denominate a body "moved" it is requisite, first, that it change its distance or situation with regard to some other body; and secondly, that the force or action occasioning that change be applied to it. If either of these be wanting, I do not think that, agreeably to the sense of mankind, or the propriety of language, a body can be said to be in motion. I grant indeed that it is possible for us to think a body which we see change its distance from some other to be moved, though it have no force applied to it (in which sense there may be apparent motion), but then it is because the force causing the change of distance is imagined by us to be applied or impressed on that body thought to move; which indeed shows we are capable of mistaking a thing to be in motion which is not, and that is all.

116. From what has been said, it follows that the philosophic consideration of motion does not imply the being of an *absolute space,* distinct from that which is perceived by sense and related to bodies; which that it cannot exist without the mind is clear upon the same principles that demonstrate the like of all other objects of sense. And perhaps, if we inquire narrowly, we shall find we cannot even frame an idea of *pure space* exclusive of all body. This I must confess seems impossible, as being a most abstract idea. When I excite a motion in some part of my body, if it be free or without resistance, I say there is *space;* but if I find a resistance, then I say there is *body;* and in proportion as the resistance to motion is lesser or greater, I say the space is more or less *pure.* So that when I speak of pure or empty space, it is not to be supposed that the word "space" stands for an idea distinct from or conceivable without body and motion—though indeed we are apt to think every noun substantive stands for a distinct idea that may be separated from all others; which has occasioned infinite mistakes. When, therefore, supposing all the world to be annihilated besides my own body, I say there still remains *pure space,* thereby nothing else is meant but only that I conceive it possible for the limbs of my body to be moved on all sides without the least resistance; but if that, too, were annihilated, then there could be no motion, and consequently no space. Some, perhaps, may think the sense of seeing does furnish them with the idea of pure space; but it is plain from what we have elsewhere shown, that the ideas of space and distance are not obtained by that sense. See the *Essay Concerning Vision.*

117. What is here laid down seems to put an end to all those disputes and difficulties that have sprung up amongst the learned concerning the nature of *pure space*. But the chief advantage arising from it is that we are freed from that dangerous dilemma to which several who have employed their thoughts on this subject imagine themselves reduced, to wit, of thinking either that real space is God, or else that there is something besides God which is eternal, uncreated, infinite, indivisible, immutable. Both which may justly be thought pernicious and absurd notions. It is certain that not a few divines, as well as philosophers of great note, have, from the difficulty they found in conceiving either limits or annihilation of space, concluded it must be divine. And some of late have set themselves particularly to show that the incommunicable attributes of God agree to it. Which doctrine, how unworthy soever it may seem of the Divine Nature, yet I do not see how we can get clear of it so long as we adhere to the received opinions.

118. Hitherto of natural philosophy: we come now to make some inquiry concerning the other great branch of speculative knowledge, to wit, mathematics. These, how celebrated soever they may be for their clearness and certainty of demonstration, which is hardly anywhere else to be found, cannot nevertheless be supposed altogether free from mistakes, if in their principles there lurks some secret error which is common to the professors of those sciences with the rest of mankind. Mathematicians, though they deduce their theorems from a great height of evidence, yet their first principles are limited by the consideration of quantity; and they do not ascend into any inquiry concerning those transcendental maxims which influence all the particular sciences, each part whereof, mathematics not excepted, does consequently participate of the errors involved in them. That the principles laid down by mathematicians are true, and their way of deduction from those principles clear and incontestable, we do not deny; but we hold there may be certain erroneous maxims of greater extent than the object of mathematics, and for that reason not expressly mentioned, though tacitly supposed throughout the whole progress of that science; and that the ill effects of those secret, unexamined errors are diffused through all the branches thereof. To be plain, we suspect the mathematicians are as well as other men concerned in the errors arising from the doctrine of abstract general ideas and the existence of objects without the mind.

119. Arithmetic has been thought to have for its object abstract ideas of *number*, of which to understand the properties and mutual habitudes is supposed no mean part of speculative knowledge. The opinion of the pure and intellectual nature of numbers in abstract has made them in esteem with those philosophers who seem to have affected an uncommon fineness and elevation of thought. It has set a price on the most trifling numerical speculations which in practice are of no use but serve only for amusement, and has therefore so far infected the minds of some that they have dreamed of mighty mysteries involved in numbers and attempted the explication of natural things by them. But, if we inquire into our own thoughts and consider what has been premised, we may perhaps entertain a low opinion of those high flights and abstractions, and look on all inquiries about numbers only as so many *difficiles nugae*, so far as they are not subservient to practice and promote the benefit of life.

120. Unity in abstract we have before considered in sec. 13, from which and what has been said in the Introduction, it plainly follows there is not any such idea. But, number being defined a "collection of units," we may conclude that, if there be no such thing as unity or unit in abstract, there are no ideas of number in abstract

denoted by the numerical names and figures. The theories therefore in arithmetic, if they are abstracted from the names and figures, as likewise from all use and practice, as well as from the particular things numbered, can be supposed to have nothing at all for their object; hence we may see how entirely the science of numbers is subordinate to practice, and how jejune and trifling it becomes when considered as a matter of mere speculation.

121. However, since there may be some who, deluded by the specious show of discovering abstracted verities, waste their time in arithmetical theorems and problems which have not any use, it will not be amiss if we more fully consider and expose the vanity of that pretense; and this will plainly appear by taking a view of arithmetic in its infancy, and observing what it was that originally put men on the study of that science, and to what scope they directed it. It is natural to think that at first, men, for ease of memory and help of computation, made use of counters, or in writing of single strokes, points, or the like, each whereof was made to signify a unit, that is, some one thing of whatever kind they had occasion to reckon. Afterwards they found out the more compendious ways of making one character stand in place of several strokes or points. And, lastly, the notation of the Arabians or Indians came into use, wherein, by the repetition of a few characters or figures and varying the signification of each figure according to the place it obtains, all numbers may be most aptly expressed; which seems to have been done in imitation of language, so that an exact analogy is observed betwixt the notation by figures and names, the nine simple figures answering the nine first numeral names and places in the former, corresponding to denominations in the latter. And agreeably to those conditions of the simple and local value of figures were contrived methods of finding, from the given figures or marks of the parts, what figures and how placed are proper to denote the whole, or vice versa. And having found the sought figures, the same rule or analogy being observed throughout, it is easy to read them into words; and so the number becomes perfectly known. For then the number of any particular things is said to be known, when we know the name or figures (with their due arrangement) that according to the standing analogy belong to them. For, these signs being known, we can by the operations of arithmetic know the signs of any part of the particular sums signified by them; and, thus computing in signs (because of the connection established betwixt them and the distinct multitudes of things whereof one is taken for a unit), we may be able rightly to sum up, divide, and proportion the things themselves that we intend to number.

122. In arithmetic, therefore, we regard not the *things,* but the *signs,* which nevertheless are not regarded for their own sake, but because they direct us how to act with relation to things, and dispose rightly of them. Now, agreeable to what we have before observed of words in general (sec. 19, Introd.) it happens here likewise that abstract ideas are thought to be signified by numeral names or characters, while they do not suggest ideas of particular things to our minds. I shall not at present enter into a more particular dissertation on this subject, but only observe that it is evident from what has been said, those things which pass for abstract truths and theorems concerning numbers are in reality conversant about no object distinct from particular numerable things, except only names and characters which originally came to be considered on no other account but their being signs, or capable to represent aptly whatever particular things men had need to compute. Whence it follows that to study them for their own sake would be just as wise, and to as good purpose as if a man, neglecting the true use or original intention and subservience of

language, should spend his time in impertinent criticisms upon words, or reasonings and controversies purely verbal.

123. From numbers we proceed to speak of *extension*, which, considered as relative, is the object of geometry. The *infinite* divisibility of *finite* extension, though it is not expressly laid down either as an axiom or theorem in the elements of that science, yet is throughout the same everywhere supposed and thought to have so inseparable and essential a connection with the principles and demonstrations in geometry that mathematicians never admit it into doubt, or make the least question of it. And, as this notion is the source from whence do spring all those amusing geometrical paradoxes which have such a direct repugnancy to the plain common sense of mankind, and are admitted with so much reluctance into a mind not yet debauched by learning; so is it the principal occasion of all that nice and extreme subtlety which renders the study of mathematics so difficult and tedious. Hence, if we can make it appear that no finite extension contains innumerable parts, or is infinitely divisible, it follows that we shall at once clear the science of geometry from a great number of difficulties and contradictions which have ever been esteemed a reproach to human reason, and withal make the attainment thereof a business of much less time and pains than it hitherto has been.

124. Every particular finite extension which may possibly be the object of our thought is an *idea* existing only in the mind, and consequently each part thereof must be perceived. If, therefore, I cannot perceive innumerable parts in any finite extension that I consider, it is certain they are not contained in it; but it is evident that I cannot distinguish innumerable parts in any particular line, surface, or solid, which I either perceive by sense, or figure to myself in my mind: wherefore I conclude they are not contained in it. Nothing can be plainer to me than that the extensions I have in view are no other than my own ideas; and it is no less plain that I cannot resolve any one of my ideas into an infinite number of other ideas, that is, that they are not infinitely divisible. If by "finite extension" be meant something distinct from a finite idea, I declare I do not know what that is, and so cannot affirm or deny anything of it. But if the terms "extension," "parts," and the like, are taken in any sense conceivable, that is, for ideas, then to say a finite quantity or extension consists of parts infinite in number is so manifest a contradiction that everyone at first sight acknowledges it to be so; and it is impossible it should ever gain the assent of any reasonable creature who is not brought to it by gentle and slow degrees, as a converted gentile to the belief of transubstantiation. Ancient and rooted prejudices do often pass into principles; and those propositions which once obtain the force and credit of a *principle* are not only themselves, but likewise whatever is deducible from them, thought privileged from all examination. And there is no absurdity so gross which, by this means, the mind of man may not be prepared to swallow.

125. He whose understanding is prepossessed with the doctrine of abstract general ideas may be persuaded that (whatever be thought of the ideas of sense) extension in *abstract* is infinitely divisible. And one who thinks the objects of sense exist without the mind will perhaps in virtue thereof be brought to admit that a line but an inch long may contain innumerable parts—really existing, though too small to be discerned. These errors are grafted as well in the minds of geometricians as of other men, and have a like influence on their reasonings; and it were no difficult thing to show how the arguments from geometry made use of to support the infinite divisibility of extension are bottomed on them. At present we shall only observe in

general whence it is that the mathematicians are all so fond and tenacious of this doctrine.

126. It has been observed in another place that the theorems and demonstrations in geometry are conversant about universal ideas (sec. 15, Introd.); where it is explained in what sense this ought to be understood, to wit, that the particular lines and figures included in the diagram are supposed to stand for innumerable others of different sizes; or, in other words, the geometer considers them abstracting from their magnitude—which does not imply that he forms an abstract idea, but only that he cares not what the particular magnitude is, whether great or small, but looks on that as a thing indifferent to the demonstration. Hence it follows that a line in the scheme but an inch long must be spoken of as though it contained ten thousand parts, since it is regarded not in itself, but as it is universal; and it is universal only in its signification, whereby it represents innumerable lines greater than itself, in which may be distinguished ten thousand parts or more, though there may not be above an inch in it. After this manner, the properties of the lines signified are (by a very usual figure) transferred to the sign, and thence, through mistake, thought to appertain to it considered in its own nature.

127. Because there is no number of parts so great but it is possible there may be a line containing more, the inch-line is said to contain parts more than any assignable number; which is true, not of the inch taken absolutely, but only for the things signified by it. But men, not retaining that distinction in their thoughts, slide into a belief that the small particular line described on paper contains in itself parts innumerable. There is no such thing as the ten thousandth part of an inch; but there is of a mile or diameter of the earth, which may be signified by that inch. When therefore I delineate a triangle on paper, and take one side not above an inch, for example, in length to be the radius, this I consider as divided into ten thousand or one hundred thousand parts or more; for, though the ten thousandth part of that line considered in itself is nothing at all, and consequently may be neglected without any error or inconvenience, yet these described lines, being only marks standing for greater quantities, whereof it may be the ten thousandth part is very considerable, it follows that, to prevent notable errors in practice, the radius must be taken of ten thousand parts of more.

128. From what has been said the reason is plain why, to the end any theorem may become universal in its use, it is necessary we speak of the lines described on paper as though they contained parts which really they do not. In doing of which, if we examine the matter thoroughly, we shall perhaps discover that we cannot conceive an inch itself as consisting of, or being divisible into, a thousand parts, but only some other line which is far greater than an inch, and represented by it; and that when we say a line is "infinitely divisible" we must mean a line which is infinitely great. What we have here observed seems to be the chief cause why to suppose the infinite divisibility of finite extension has been thought necessary in geometry.

129. The several absurdities and contradictions which flowed from this false principle might, one would think, have been esteemed so many demonstrations against it. But, by I know not what logic, it is held that proofs a posteriori are not to be admitted against propositions relating to infinity, as though it were not impossible even for an infinite mind to reconcile contradictions; or as if anything absurd and repugnant could have a necessary connection with truth or flow from it. But

whoever considers the weakness of this pretense will think it was contrived on purpose to humor the laziness of the mind which had rather acquiesce in an indolent skepticism than be at the pains to go through with a severe examination of those principles it has ever embraced for true.

130. Of late the speculations about infinites have run so high, and grown to such strange notions, as have occasioned no small scruples and disputes among the geometers of the present age. Some there are of great note who, not content with holding that finite lines may be divided into an infinite number of parts, do yet further maintain that each of those infinitesimals is itself subdivisible into an infinity of other parts or infinitesimals of a second order, and so on ad infinitum. These, I say, assert there are infinitesimals of infinitesimals of infinitesimals, without ever coming to an end: so that according to them an inch does not barely contain an infinite number of parts, but an infinity of an infinity of an infinity ad infinitum of parts. Others there be who hold all orders of infinitesimals below the first to be nothing at all; thinking it with good reason absurd to imagine there is any positive quantity or part of extension which, though multiplied infinitely, can ever equal the smallest given extension. And yet on the other hand it seems no less absurd to think the square, cube, or other power of a positive real root should itself be nothing at all; which they who hold infinitesimals of the first order, denying all of the subsequent orders, are obliged to maintain.

131. Have we not therefore reason to conclude that they are *both* in the wrong, and that there is in effect no such thing as parts infinitely small, or an infinite number of parts contained in any finite quantity? But you will say that if this doctrine obtains it will follow the very foundations of geometry are destroyed, and those great men who have raised that science to so astonishing a height have been all the while building a castle in the air. To this it may be replied that whatever is useful in geometry and promotes the benefit of human life does still remain firm and unshaken on our principles; that science considered as practical will rather receive advantage than any prejudice from what has been said. But to set this in a due light may be the subject of a distinct inquiry. For the rest, though it should follow that some of the more intricate and subtle parts of speculative mathematics may be pared off without any prejudice to truth, yet I do not see what damage will be thence derived to mankind. On the contrary, it were highly to be wished that men of great abilities and obstinate application would draw off their thoughts from those amusements, and employ them in the study of such things as lie nearer the concerns of life, or have a more direct influence on the manners.

132. If it be said that several theorems undoubtedly true are discovered by methods in which infinitesimals are made use of, which could never have been if their existence included a contradiction in it, I answer that upon a thorough examination it will not be found that in any instance it is necessary to make use of or conceive infinitesimal parts of finite lines, or even quantities less than the *minimum sensibile;* nay, it will be evident this is never done, it being impossible.

133. By what we have premised it is plain that very numerous and important errors have taken their rise from those false principles which were impugned in the foregoing parts of this treatise; and the opposites of those erroneous tenets at the same time appear to be most fruitful principles, from whence do flow innumerable consequences highly advantageous to true philosophy, as well as to religion. Particularly *matter,* or *the absolute existence of corporeal objects,* has been shown to be that

wherein the most avowed and pernicious enemies of all knowledge, whether human or divine, have ever placed their chief strength and confidence. And surely, if by distinguishing the real existence of unthinking things from their being perceived, and allowing them a subsistence of their own out of the minds of spirits, no one thing is explained in nature, but, on the contrary, a great many inexplicable difficulties arise; if the supposition of matter is barely precarious, as not being grounded on so much as one single reason; if its consequences cannot endure the light of examination and free inquiry, but screen themselves under the dark and general pretense of "infinites being incomprehensible"; if withal the removal of this *matter* be not attended with the least evil consequence; if it be not even missed in the world, but everything as well, nay, much easier conceived without it; if, lastly, both skeptics and atheists are forever silenced upon supposing only spirits and ideas, and this scheme of things is perfectly agreeable both to reason and religion: methinks we may expect it should be admitted and firmly embraced, though it were proposed only as a *hypothesis,* and the existence of matter had been allowed possible, which yet I think we have evidently demonstrated that it is not.

134. True it is that, in consequence of the foregoing principles, several disputes and speculations which are esteemed no mean parts of learning are rejected as useless. But, how great a prejudice soever against our notions this may give to those who have already been deeply engaged and made large advances in studies of that nature, yet by others we hope it will not be thought any just ground of dislike to the principles and tenets herein laid down that they abridge the labor of study, and make human sciences more clear, compendious, and attainable than they were before.

135. Having dispatched what we intended to say concerning the knowledge of *ideas,* the method we proposed leads us in the next place to treat of *spirits*—with regard to which, perhaps human knowledge is not so deficient as is vulgarly imagined. The great reason that is assigned for our being thought ignorant of the nature of spirits is our not having an *idea* of it. But surely it ought not to be looked on as a defect in a human understanding that it does not perceive the idea of spirit if it is manifestly impossible there should be any such idea. And this, if I mistake not, has been demonstrated in section 27; to which I shall here add that a spirit has been shown to be the only substance or support wherein the unthinking beings or ideas can exist; but that this *substance* which supports or perceives ideas should itself be an idea or like an idea is evidently absurd.

136. It will perhaps be said that we want a sense (as some have imagined) proper to know substances withal, which, if we had, we might know our own soul as we do a triangle. To this I answer, that, in case we had a new sense bestowed upon us, we could only receive thereby some new sensations or ideas of sense. But I believe nobody will say that what he means by the terms "soul" and "substance" is only some particular sort of idea or sensation. We may therefore infer, that all things duly considered, it is not more reasonable to think our faculties defective in that they do not furnish us with an idea of spirit or active thinking substance than it would be if we should blame them for not being able to comprehend a *round square.*

137. From the opinion that spirits are to be known after the manner of an idea or sensation have risen many absurd and heterodox tenets, and much skepticism about the nature of the soul. It is even probable that this opinion may have produced a doubt in some whether they had any soul at all distinct from their body, since upon

inquiry they could not find they had an idea of it. That an *idea* which is inactive, and the existence whereof consists in being perceived, should be the image or likeness of an agent subsisting by itself seems to need no other refutation than barely attending to what is meant by those words. But perhaps you will say that though an idea cannot resemble a spirit in its thinking, acting, or subsisting by itself, yet it may in some other respects; and it is not necessary that an idea or image be in all respects like the original.

138. I answer, if it does not in those mentioned, it is impossible it should represent it in any other thing. Do but leave out the power of willing, thinking, and perceiving ideas, and there remains nothing else wherein the idea can be like a spirit. For by the word "spirit" we mean only that which thinks, wills, and perceives; this, and this alone, constitutes the signification of that term. If therefore it is impossible that any degree of those powers should be represented in an idea, it is evident there can be no idea of a spirit.

139. But it will be objected that, if there is no idea signified by the terms "soul," "spirit," and "substance," they are wholly insignificant or have no meaning in them. I answer, those words do mean or signify a real thing, which is neither an idea nor like an idea, but that which perceives ideas, and wills, and reasons about them. What I am myself, that which I denote by the term "I," is the same with what is meant by "soul," or "spiritual substance." If it be said that this is only quarreling at a word, and that, since the immediate significations of other names are by common consent called "ideas," no reason can be assigned why that which is signified by the name "spirit" or "soul" may not partake in the same appellation. I answer, all the unthinking objects of the mind agree in that they are entirely passive, and their existence consists only in being perceived; whereas a soul or spirit is an active being whose existence consists, not in being perceived, but in perceiving ideas and thinking. It is therefore necessary, in order to prevent equivocation and confounding natures perfectly disagreeing and unlike, that we distinguish between *spirit* and *idea*. See sec. 27.

140. In a large sense, indeed, we may be said to have an idea or rather a notion of *spirit;* that is, we understand the meaning of the word, otherwise we could not affirm or deny anything of it. Moreover, as we conceive the ideas that are in the minds of other spirits by means of our own, which we suppose to be resemblances of them, so we know other spirits by means of our own soul—which in that sense is the image or idea of them; it having a like respect to other spirits that blueness or heat by me perceived has to those ideas perceived by another.

141. It must not be supposed that they who assert the natural immortality of the soul are of opinion that it is absolutely incapable of annihilation even by the infinite power of the Creator who first gave it being, but only that it is not liable to be broken or dissolved by the ordinary laws of nature or motion. They indeed who hold the soul of man to be only a thin vital flame, or system of animal spirits, make it perishing and corruptible as the body; since there is nothing more easily dissipated than such a being, which it is naturally impossible should survive the ruin of the tabernacle wherein it is enclosed. And this notion has been greedily embraced and cherished by the worst part of mankind, as the most effectual antidote against all impressions of virtue and religion. But it has been made evident that bodies, of what frame or texture soever, are barely passive ideas in the mind, which is more distant and heterogeneous from them than light is from darkness. We have shown that the

soul is indivisible, incorporeal, unextended, and it is consequently incorruptible. Nothing can be plainer than that the motions, changes, decays, and dissolutions which we hourly see befall natural bodies (and which is what we mean by "the course of nature") cannot possibly affect an active, simple, uncompounded substance; such a being is therefore indissoluble by the force of nature; that is to say, the soul of man is naturally immortal.

142. After what has been said, it is, I suppose, plain that our souls are not to be known in the same manner as senseless, inactive objects, or by way of *idea*. Spirits and *ideas* are things so wholly different that when we say "they exist," "they are known," or the like, these words must not be thought to signify anything common to both natures. There is nothing alike or common in them: and to expect that by any multiplication or enlargement of our faculties we may be enabled to know a spirit as we do a triangle seems as absurd as if we should hope to see a sound. This is inculcated because I imagine it may be of moment toward clearing several important questions and preventing some very dangerous errors concerning the nature of the soul. We may not, I think, strictly be said to have an *idea* of an active being, or of an action, although we may be said to have a *notion* of them. I have some knowledge or notion of my mind, and its acts about ideas, inasmuch as I know or understand what is meant by those words. What I know, that I have some notion of. I will not say that the terms "idea" and "notion" may not be used convertibly, if the world will have it so; but yet it conduces to clearness and propriety that we distinguish things very different by different names. It is also to be remarked that, all relations including an act of the mind, we cannot so properly be said to have an idea, but rather a notion of the relations or habitudes between things. But if, in the modern way, the word "idea" is extended to spirits, and relations, and acts, this is, after all, an affair of verbal concern.

143. It will not be amiss to add that the doctrine of *abstract ideas* has had no small share in rendering those sciences intricate and obscure which are particularly conversant about spiritual things. Men have imagined they could frame abstract notions of the powers and acts of the mind and consider them prescinded as well from the mind or spirit itself as from their respective objects and effects. Hence a great number of dark and ambiguous terms, presumed to stand for abstract notions, have been introduced into metaphysics and morality, and from these have grown infinite distractions and disputes amongst the learned.

144. But nothing seems more to have contributed toward engaging men in controversies and mistakes with regard to the nature and operations of the mind than the being used to speak of those things in terms borrowed from sensible ideas. For example, the will is termed "the motion of the soul": this infuses a belief that the mind of man is as a ball in motion, impelled and determined by the objects of sense, as necessarily as that is by the stroke of a racket. Hence arise endless scruples and errors of dangerous consequence in morality. All which, I doubt not, may be cleared, and truth appear plain, uniform, and consistent, could but philosophers be prevailed on to retire into themselves, and attentively consider their own meaning.

145. From what has been said it is plain that we cannot know the existence of other spirits otherwise than by their operations, or the ideas by them excited in us. I perceive several motions, changes, and combinations of ideas that inform me there are certain particular agents, like myself, which accompany them and concur in their production. Hence, the knowledge I have of other spirits is not immediate, as

is the knowledge of my ideas, but depending on the intervention of ideas, by me referred to agents or spirits distinct from myself, as effects or concomitant signs.

146. But though there be some things which convince us human agents are concerned in producing them, yet it is evident to everyone that those things which are called "the works of nature," that is, the far greater part of the ideas or sensations perceived by us, are not produced by, or dependent on, the wills of men. There is therefore some other spirit that causes them; since it is repugnant that they should subsist by themselves. See sec. 29. But, if we attentively consider the constant regularity, order, and concatenation of natural things, the surprising magnificence, beauty, and perfection of the larger, and the exquisite contrivance of the smaller parts of the creation, together with the exact harmony and correspondence of the whole, but above all the never-enough-admired laws of pain and pleasure, and the instincts or natural inclinations, appetites, and passions of animals; I say if we consider all these things, and at the same time attend to the meaning and import of the attributes: one, eternal, infinitely wise, good, and perfect, we shall clearly perceive that they belong to the aforesaid spirit, "who works all in all," and "by whom all things consist."

147. Hence it is evident that God is known as certainly and immediately as any other mind or spirit whatsoever distinct from ourselves. We may even assert that the existence of God is far more evidently perceived than the existence of men; because the effects of nature are infinitely more numerous and considerable than those ascribed to human agents. There is not any one mark that denotes a man, or effect produced by him, which does not more strongly evince the being of that spirit who is the Author of Nature. For it is evident that in affecting other persons the will of man has no other object than barely the motion of the limbs of his body; but that such a motion should be attended by, or excite any idea in the mind of another, depends wholly on the will of the Creator. He alone it is who, "upholding all things by the word of his power," maintains that intercourse between spirits whereby they are able to perceive the existence of each other. And yet this pure and clear light which enlightens everyone is itself invisible.

148. It seems to be a general pretense of the unthinking herd that they cannot *see* God. Could we but see him, say they, as we see a man, we should believe that he is, and, believing, obey his commands. But alas, we need only open our eyes to see the sovereign Lord of all things, with a more full and clear view than we do any one of our fellow creatures. Not that I imagine we see God (as some will have it) by a direct and immediate view; or see corporeal things, not by themselves, but by seeing that which represents them in the essence of God, which doctrine[12] is, I must confess, to me incomprehensible. But I shall explain my meaning: a human spirit or person is not perceived by sense, as not being an idea; when therefore we see the color, size, figure, and motions of a man, we perceive only certain sensations or ideas excited in our own minds; and these being exhibited to our view in sundry distinct collections, serve to mark out unto us the existence of finite and created spirits like ourselves. Hence it is plain we do not see a man—if by "man" is meant that which lives, moves, perceives, and thinks as we do—but only such a certain collection of ideas as directs us to think there is a distinct principle of thought and motion, like to our-

12. [The reference is to Malebranche's view that what we immediately perceive are Ideas, or archetypes, in the mind of God.]

selves, accompanying and represented by it. And after the same manner we see God; all the difference is that, whereas some one finite and narrow assemblage of ideas denotes a particular human mind, whithersoever we direct our view, we do at all times and in all places perceive manifest tokens of the divinity: everything we see, hear, feel, or anywise perceive by sense, being a sign or effect of the power of God; as is our perception of those very motions which are produced by men.

149. It is therefore plain that nothing can be more evident to anyone that is capable of the least reflection than the existence of God, or a spirit who is intimately present to our minds, producing in them all that variety of ideas or sensations which continually affect us, on whom we have an absolute and entire dependence, in short "in whom we live, and move, and have our being." That the discovery of this great truth, which lies so near and obvious to the mind, should be attained to by the reason of so very few, is a sad instance of the stupidity and inattention of men who, though they are surrounded with such clear manifestations of the Deity, are yet so little affected by them that they seem, as it were, blinded with excess of light.

150. But you will say, has nature no share in the production of natural things, and must they be all ascribed to the immediate and sole operation of God? I answer, if by "nature" is meant only the visible *series* of effects or sensations imprinted on our minds, according to certain fixed and general laws, then it is plain that nature, taken in this sense, cannot produce anything at all. But, if by "nature" is meant some being distinct from God, as well as from the laws of nature, and things perceived by sense, I must confess that word is to me an empty sound without any intelligible meaning annexed to it. Nature, in this acceptation, is a vain chimera, introduced by those heathens who had not just notions of the omnipresence and infinite perfection of God. But it is more unaccountable that it should be received among Christians, professing belief in the Holy Scriptures, which constantly ascribe those effects to the immediate hand of God that heathen philosophers are wont to impute to nature. "The Lord he causeth the vapours to ascend; he maketh lightnings with rain; he bringeth forth the wind out of his treasures." Jerem. 10:13. "He turneth the shadow of death into the morning, and maketh the day dark with night." Amos 5:8. "He visiteth the earth, and maketh it soft with showers: He blesseth the springing thereof, and crowneth the year with his goodness; so that the pastures are clothed with flocks, and the valleys are covered over with corn." See Psalm 65. But notwithstanding that this is the constant language of Scripture, yet we have I know not what aversion from believing that God concerns himself so nearly in our affairs. Fain would we suppose him at a great distance off, and substitute some blind, unthinking deputy in his stead, though (if we may believe Saint Paul) "he be not far from every one of us."

151. It will, I doubt not, be objected that the slow and gradual methods observed in the production of natural things do not seem to have for their cause the immediate hand of an Almighty Agent. Besides, monsters, untimely births, fruits blasted in the blossom, rains failing in desert places, miseries incident to human life, and the like, are so many arguments that the whole frame of nature is not immediately actuated and superintended by a spirit of infinite wisdom and goodness. But the answer to this objection is in a good measure plain from sec. 62; it being visible that the aforesaid methods of nature are absolutely necessary, in order to working by the most simple and general rules, and after a steady and consistent manner; which argues both the wisdom and goodness of God. Such is the artificial contrivance of

this mighty machine of nature that, whilst its motions and various phenomena strike on our senses, the hand which actuates the whole is itself unperceivable to men of flesh and blood. "Verily" (says the prophet) "thou art a God that hidest thyself." Isaiah 45:15. But, though God conceal himself from the eyes of the sensual and lazy, who will not be at the least expense of thought, yet to an unbiased and attentive mind nothing can be more plainly legible than the intimate presence of an all-wise Spirit, who fashions, regulates, and sustains the whole system of being. It is clear, from what we have elsewhere observed, that the operating according to general and stated laws is so necessary for our guidance in the affairs of life, and letting us into the secret of nature, that without it all reach and compass of thought, all human sagacity and design, could serve to no manner of purpose; it were even impossible there should be any such faculties or powers in the mind. See sec. 31. Which one consideration abundantly outbalances whatever particular inconveniences may thence arise.

152. We should further consider that the very blemishes and defects of nature are not without their use, in that they make an agreeable sort of variety and augment the beauty of the rest of the creation, as shades in a picture serve to set off the brighter and more enlightened parts. We would likewise do well to examine whether our taxing the waste of seeds and embryos, and accidental destruction of plants and animals, before they come to full maturity, as an imprudence in the Author of Nature, be not the effect of prejudice contracted by our familiarity with impotent and saving mortals. In man indeed a thrifty management of those things which he cannot procure without much pains and industry may be esteemed wisdom. But we must not imagine that the inexplicably fine machine of an animal or vegetable costs the great Creator any more pains or trouble in its production than a pebble does; nothing being more evident than that an omnipotent spirit can indifferently produce everything by a mere fiat or act of his will. Hence, it is plain that the splendid profusion of natural things should not be interpreted weakness or prodigality in the agent who produces them, but rather be looked on as an argument of the riches of his power.

153. As for the mixture of pain or uneasiness which is in the world, pursuant to the general laws of nature, and the actions of finite, imperfect spirits, this, in the state we are in at present, is indispensably necessary to our well-being. But our prospects are too narrow. We take, for instance, the idea of some one particular pain into our thoughts, and account it *evil;* whereas, if we enlarge our view, so as to comprehend the various ends, connections, and dependencies of things, on what occasions and in what proportions we are affected with pain and pleasure, the nature of human freedom, and the design with which we are put into the world; we shall be forced to acknowledge that those particular things which, considered in themselves, appear to be evil, have the nature of good, when considered as linked with the whole system of beings.

154. From what has been said, it will be manifest to any considering person, that it is merely for want of attention and comprehensiveness of mind that there are any favorers of atheism or the Manichaean heresy[13] to be found. Little and unreflecting

---

13. [Manichaeism, a religion founded by the Persian Mani (c.216–c.276), strongly influenced the development of Christianity. Basic to the Manichaean outlook is the doctrine that the universe is the scene of an eternal struggle between two antagonistic powers, Light and Darkness (or Good and Evil).]

souls may indeed burlesque the works of Providence the beauty and order whereof they have not capacity, or will not be at the pains to comprehend; but those who are masters of any justness and extent of thought, and are withal used to reflect, can never sufficiently admire the divine traces of wisdom and goodness that shine thoughout the economy of nature. But what truth is there which shines so strongly on the mind that by an aversion of thought, a willful shutting of the eyes, we may not escape seeing it? Is it therefore to be wondered at if the generality of men, who are ever intent on business or pleasure, and little used to fix or open the eye of their mind, should not have all that conviction and evidence of the being of God which might be expected in reasonable creatures?

155. We should rather wonder that men can be found so stupid as to neglect, than that neglecting they should be unconvinced of such an evident and momentous truth. And yet it is to be feared that too many of parts and leisure, who live in Christian countries, are, merely through a supine and dreadful negligence, sunk into a sort of atheism. Since it is downright impossible that a soul pierced and enlightened with a thorough sense of the omnipresence, holiness, and justice of that Almighty Spirit should persist in a remorseless violation of his laws. We ought, therefore, earnestly to meditate and dwell on those important points; that so we may attain conviction without all scruple "that the eyes of the Lord are in every place beholding the evil and the good; that he is with us and keepeth us in all places whither we go, and giveth us bread to eat and raiment to put on"; that he is present and conscious to our innermost thoughts; and that we have a most absolute and immediate dependence on him. A clear view of which great truths cannot choose but fill our hearts with an awful circumspection and holy fear, which is the strongest incentive to *virtue* and the best guard against *vice*.

156. For, after all, what deserves the first place in our studies is the consideration of God and our duty; which to promote, as it was the main drift and design of my labors, so shall I esteem them altogether useless and ineffectual if, by what I have said, I cannot inspire my readers with a pious sense of the presence of God; and, having shown the falseness or vanity of those barren speculations which make the chief employment of learned men, the better dispose them to reverence and embrace the salutary truths of the Gospel, which to know and to practice is the highest perfection of human nature.

THREE DIALOGUES

BETWEEN

HYLAS AND PHILONOUS

IN OPPOSITION TO SCEPTICS AND ATHEISTS

THE FIRST DIALOGUE

Philonous. Good morrow, Hylas: I did not expect to find you abroad so early.

Hylas. It is indeed something unusual; but my thoughts were so taken up with a subject I was discoursing of last night, that finding I could not sleep, I resolved to rise and take a turn in the garden.

Phil. It happened well, to let you see what innocent and agreeable pleasures you lose every morning. Can there be a pleasanter time of the day, or a more delightful season of the year? That purple sky, these wild but sweet notes of birds, the fragrant bloom upon the trees and flowers, the gentle influence of the rising sun, these and a thousand nameless beauties of nature inspire the soul with secret transports; its faculties too being at this time fresh and lively, are fit for those meditations, which the solitude of a garden and tranquillity of the morning naturally dispose us to. But I am afraid I interrupt your thoughts: for you seemed very intent on something.

Hyl. It is true, I was, and shall be obliged to you if you will permit me to go on in the same vein; not that I would by any means deprive myself of your company, for my thoughts always flow more easily in conversation with a friend, than when I am alone: but my request is, that you would suffer me to impart my reflections to you.

Phil. With all my heart, it is what I should have requested myself, if you had not prevented me.

Hyl. I was considering the odd fate of those men who have in all ages, through an affection of being distinguished from the vulgar, or some unaccountable turn of thought, pretended either to believe nothing at all, or to believe the most extravagant things in the world. This however might be borne, if their paradoxes and scepticism did not draw after them some consequences of general disadvantage to mankind. But the mischief lies here; that when men of less leisure see them who are supposed to have spent their whole time in the pursuits of knowledge, professing an entire ignorance of all things, or advancing such notions as are repugnant to plain and commonly received principles, they will be tempted to entertain suspicions concerning the most important truths, which they had hitherto held sacred and unquestionable.

Phil. I entirely agree with you, as to the ill tendency of the affected doubts of some philosophers, and fantastical conceits of others. I am even so far gone of late in this way of thinking, that I have quitted several of the sublime notions I had got in their schools for vulgar opinions. And I give it to you on my word, since this revolt from

Reprinted by permission of the editor Robert Merrihew Adams from *Berkeley, Three Dialogues Between Hylas and Philonous* (Indianapolis: Hackett Publishing Company, 1979).

metaphysical notions to the plain dictates of nature and common sense, I find my understanding strangely enlightened, so that I can now easily comprehend a great many things which before were all mystery and riddle.

Hyl. I am glad to find there was nothing in the accounts I heard of you.

Phil. Pray, what were those?

Hyl. You were represented in last night's conversation, as one who maintained the most extravagant opinion that ever entered into the mind of man, to wit, that there is no such thing as *material substance* in the world.

Phil. That there is no such thing as what philosophers call *material substance,* I am seriously persuaded: but if I were made to see anything absurd or sceptical in this, I should then have the same reason to renounce this, that I imagine I have now to reject the contrary opinion.

Hyl. What! Can anything be more fantastical, more repugnant to common sense, or a more manifest piece of scepticism, than to believe there is no such thing as *matter?*

Phil. Softly, good Hylas. What if it should prove, that you, who hold there is, are by virtue of that opinion a greater *sceptic,* and maintain more paradoxes and repugnancies to common sense, than I who believe no such thing?

Hyl. You may as soon persuade me, the part is greater than the whole, as that, in order to avoid absurdity and scepticism, I should ever be obliged to give up my opinion in this point.

Phil. Well, then, are you content to admit that opinion for true, which upon examination shall appear most agreeable to common sense, and remote from scepticism?

Hyl. With all my heart. Since you are for raising disputes about the plainest things in nature, I am content for once to hear what you have to say.

Phil. Pray, Hylas, what do you mean by a *sceptic?*

Hyl. I mean what all men mean, one that doubts of everything.

Phil. He then who entertains no doubt concerning some particular point, with regard to that point cannot be thought a *sceptic.*

Hyl. I agree with you.

Phil. Whether does doubting consist in embracing the affirmative or negative side of a question?

Hyl. In neither; for whoever understands English, cannot but know that *doubting* signifies a suspense between both.

Phil. He then that denies any point, can no more be said to doubt of it, than he who affirms it with the same degree of assurance.

Hyl. True.

Phil. And consequently, for such his denial is no more to be esteemed a *sceptic* than the other.

Hyl. I acknowledge it.

Phil. How comes it then, Hylas, that you pronounce me a *sceptic,* because I deny what you affirm, to wit, the existence of matter? Since, for aught you can tell, I am as peremptory in my denial, as you in your affirmation.

Hyl. Hold, Philonous, I have been a little out in my definition; but every false step a man makes in discourse is not to be insisted on. I said indeed, that a *sceptic* was one who doubted of everything; but I should have added, or who denies the reality and truth of things.

Phil. What things? Do you mean the principles and theorems of sciences? But these you know are universal intellectual notions, and consequently independent of matter; the denial therefore of this doth not imply the denying them.

Hyl. I grant it. But are there no other things? What think you of distrusting the senses, of denying the real existence of sensible things, or pretending to know nothing of them. Is not this sufficient to denominate a man a *sceptic?*

Phil. Shall we therefore examine which of us it is that denies the reality of sensible things, or professes the greatest ignorance of them; since, if I take you rightly, he is to be esteemed the greatest *sceptic?*

Hyl. That is what I desire.

Phil. What mean you by sensible things?

Hyl. Those things which are perceived by the senses. Can you imagine that I mean anything else?

Phil. Pardon me, Hylas, if I am desirous clearly to apprehend your notions, since this may much shorten our inquiry. Suffer me then to ask you this farther question. Are those things only perceived by the senses which are perceived immediately? Or, may those things properly be said to be *sensible,* which are perceived mediately, or not without the intervention of others?

Hyl. I do not sufficiently understand you.

Phil. In reading a book, what I immediately perceive are the letters, but mediately, or by means of these, are suggested to my mind the notions of God, virtue, truth, &c. Now, that the letters are truly sensible things, or perceived by sense, there is no doubt: but I would know whether you take the things suggested by them to be so too.

Hyl. No certainly, it were absurd to think *God* or *virtue* sensible things, though they may be signified and suggested to the mind by sensible marks, with which they have an arbitrary connection.

Phil. It seems then, that by *sensible things* you mean those only which can be perceived immediately by sense.

Hyl. Right.

Phil. Does it not follow from this, that though I see one part of the sky red, and another blue, and that my reason doth thence evidently conclude there must be some cause of that diversity of colors, yet that cause cannot be said to be a sensible thing, or perceived by the sense of seeing?

Hyl. It does.

Phil. In like manner, though I hear variety of sounds yet I cannot be said to hear the causes of those sounds.

Hyl. You cannot.

Phil. And when by my touch I perceive a thing to be hot and heavy, I cannot say with any truth or propriety, that I feel the cause of its heat or weight.

Hyl. To prevent any more questions of this kind, I tell you once for all, that by *sensible things* I mean those only which are perceived by sense, and that in truth the senses perceive nothing which they do not perceive immediately: for they make no inferences. The deducing therefore of causes or occasions from effects and appearances, which alone are perceived by sense, entirely relates to reason.

Phil. This point then is agreed between us, that *sensible things are those only which are immediately perceived by sense.* You will farther inform me, whether we immediately perceive by sight anything beside light, and colors, and figures: or by hearing anything but sounds: by the palate, anything beside tastes: by the smell, beside odors: or by the touch, more than tangible qualities.

Hyl. We do not.

Phil. It seems therefore, that if you take away all sensible qualities, there remains nothing sensible.

Hyl. I grant it.

Phil. Sensible things therefore are nothing else but so many sensible qualities, or combinations of sensible qualities.

Hyl. Nothing else.

Phil. Heat then is a sensible thing.

Hyl. Certainly.

Phil. Does the reality of sensible things consist in being perceived? Or, is it something distinct from their being perceived, and that bears no relation to the mind?

Hyl. To *exist* is one thing, and to be *perceived* is another.

Phil. I speak with regard to sensible things only: and of these I ask, whether by their real existence you mean a subsistence exterior to the mind, and distinct from their being perceived?

Hyl. I mean a real absolute being, distinct from, and without any relation to, their being perceived.

Phil. Heat therefore, if it be allowed a real being, must exist without the mind.

Hyl. It must.

Phil. Tell me, Hylas, is this real existence equally compatible to all degrees of heat, which we perceive: or is there any reason why we should attribute it to some, and deny it to others? And if there be, pray let me know that reason.

Hyl. Whatever degree of heat we perceive by sense, we may be sure the same exists in the object that occasions it.

Phil. What, the greatest as well as the least?

Hyl. I tell you, the reason is plainly the same in respect of both: they are both perceived by sense; nay, the greater degree of heat is more sensibly perceived; and consequently, if there is any difference, we are more certain of its real existence than we can be of the reality of a lesser degree.

Phil. But is not the most vehement and intense degree of heat a very great pain?

Hyl. No one can deny it.

Phil. And is any unperceiving thing capable of pain or pleasure?

Hyl. No, certainly.

Phil. Is your material substance a senseless being, or a being endowed with sense and perception?

Hyl. It is senseless, without doubt.

Phil. It cannot therefore be the subject of pain.

Hyl. By no means.

Phil. Nor consequently of the greatest heat perceived by sense, since you acknowledge this to be no small pain.

Hyl. I grant it.

Phil. What shall we say then of your external object; is it a material substance, or no?

Hyl. It is a material substance with the sensible qualities inhering in it.

Phil. How then can a great heat exist in it, since you own it cannot in a material substance? I desire you would clear this point.

Hyl. Hold, Philonous, I fear I was out in yielding intense heat to be a pain. It should seem rather, that pain is something distinct from heat, and the consequence or effect of it.

Phil. Upon putting your hand near the fire, do you perceive one simple uniform sensation or two distinct sensations?

Hyl. But one simple sensation.

Phil. Is not the heat immediately perceived?

Hyl. It is.

Phil. And the pain?

Hyl. True.

Phil. Seeing therefore they are both immediately perceived at the same time, and the fire affects you only with one simple, or uncompounded idea, it follows that this same simple idea is both the intense heat immediately perceived, and the pain; and consequently, that the intense heat immediately perceived, is nothing distinct from a particular sort of pain.

Hyl. It seems so.

Phil. Again, try in your thoughts, Hylas, if you can conceive a vehement sensation to be without pain, or pleasure.

Hyl. I cannot.

Phil. Or can you frame to yourself an idea of sensible pain or pleasure in general, abstracted from every particular idea of heat, cold, tastes, smells? &c.

Hyl. —I do not find that I can.

Phil. Does it not therefore follow, that sensible pain is nothing distinct from those sensations or ideas, in an intense degree?

Hyl. It is undeniable; and to speak the truth, I begin to suspect a very great heat cannot exist but in a mind perceiving it.

Phil. What! Are you then in that *sceptical* state of suspense, between affirming and denying?

Hyl. I think I may be positive in the point. A very violent and painful heat cannot exist without the mind.

Phil. It has not therefore, according to you, any real being.

Hyl. I own it.

Phil. Is it therefore certain, that there is no body in nature really hot?

Hyl. I have not denied there is any real heat in bodies. I only say, there is no such thing as an intense real heat.

Phil. But did you not say before, that all degrees of heat were equally real: or if there was any difference, that the greater were more undoubtedly real than the lesser?

Hyl. True: but it was, because I did not then consider the ground there is for distinguishing between them, which I now plainly see. And it is this: because intense heat is nothing else but a particular kind of painful sensation; and pain cannot exist but in a perceiving being; it follows that no intense heat can really exist in an unperceiving corporeal substance. But this is no reason why we should deny heat in an inferior degree to exist in such a substance.

Phil. But how shall we be able to discern those degrees of heat which exist only in the mind, from those which exist without it?

Hyl. That is no difficult matter. You know, the least pain cannot exist unperceived; whatever, therefore, degree of heat is a pain, exists only in the mind. But as for all other degrees of heat, nothing obliges us to think the same of them.

Phil. I think you granted before, that no unperceiving being was capable of pleasure, any more than of pain.

Hyl. I did.

Phil. And is not warmth, or a more gentle degree of heat than what causes uneasiness, a pleasure?

Hyl. What then?

Phil. Consequently it cannot exist without the mind in any unperceiving substance, or body.

Hyl. So it seems.

Phil. Since therefore, as well those degrees of heat that are not painful, as those that are, can exist only in a thinking substance; may we not conclude that external bodies are absolutely incapable of any degree of heat whatsoever?

Hyl. On second thoughts, I do not think it so evident that warmth is a pleasure, as that a great degree of heat is a pain.

Phil. I do not pretend that warmth is as great a pleasure as heat is a pain. But if you grant it to be even a small pleasure, it serves to make good my conclusion.

Hyl. I could rather call it an *indolence*. It seems to be nothing more than a privation of both pain and pleasure. And that such a quality or state as this may agree to an unthinking substance, I hope you will not deny.

Phil. If you are resolved to maintain that warmth, or a gentle degree of heat, is no pleasure, I know not how to convince you otherwise than by appealing to your own sense. But what think you of cold?

Hyl. The same that I do of heat. An intense degree of cold is a pain; for to feel a very great cold, is to perceive a great uneasiness: it cannot therefore exist without the mind; but a lesser degree of cold may, as well as a lesser degree of heat.

Phil. Those bodies, therefore, upon whose application to our own, we perceive a moderate degree of heat, must be concluded to have a moderate degree of heat or warmth in them: and those, upon whose application we feel a like degree of cold, must be thought to have cold in them.

Hyl. They must.

Phil. Can any doctrine be true that necessarily leads a man into an absurdity?

Hyl. Without doubt it cannot.

Phil. Is it not an absurdity to think that the same thing should be at the same time both cold and warm?

Hyl. It is.

Phil. Suppose now one of your hands hot, and the other cold, and that they are both at once put into the same vessel of water, in an intermediate state; will not the water seem cold to one hand, and warm to the other?

Hyl. It will.

Phil. Ought we not therefore by your principles to conclude, it is really both cold and warm at the same time, that is, according to your own concession, to believe an absurdity?

Hyl. I confess it seems so.

Phil. Consequently, the principles themselves are false, since you have granted that no true principle leads to an absurdity.

Hyl. But after all, can anything be more absurd than to say, *there is no heat in the fire?*

Phil. To make the point still clearer; tell me, whether in two cases exactly alike, we ought not to make the same judgment?

Hyl. We ought.

Phil. When a pin pricks your finger, does it not rend and divide the fibres of your flesh?

Hyl. It does.

Phil. And when a coal burns your finger, does it any more?

Hyl. It does not.

Phil. Since therefore you neither judge the sensation itself occasioned by the pin, nor anything like it to be in the pin; you should not, conformably to what you have now granted, judge the sensation occasioned by the fire, or anything like it, to be in the fire.

Hyl. Well, since it must be so, I am content to yield this point, and acknowledge, that heat and cold are only sensations existing in our minds: but there still remain qualities enough to secure the reality of external things.

Phil. But what will you say, Hylas, if it shall appear that the case is the same with regard to all other sensible qualities, and that they can no more be supposed to exist without the mind, than heat and cold?

Hyl. Then indeed you will have done something to the purpose; but that is what I despair of seeing proved.

Phil. Let us examine them in order. What think you of tastes, do they exist without the mind, or no?

Hyl. Can any man in his senses doubt whether sugar is sweet, or wormwood bitter?

Phil. Inform me, Hylas. Is a sweet taste a particular kind of pleasure or pleasant sensation, or is it not?

Hyl. It is.

Phil. And is not bitterness some kind of uneasiness or pain?

Hyl. I grant it.

Phil. If therefore sugar and wormwood are unthinking corporeal substances without the mind, how can sweetness and bitterness, that is, pleasure and pain, agree to them?

Hyl. Hold, Philonous, I now see what it was deluded me all this time. You asked whether heat and cold, sweetness and bitterness, were not particular sorts of pleasure and pain; to which I answered simply, that they were. Whereas I should have thus distinguished: those qualities, as perceived by us, are pleasures or pains, but not as existing in the external objects. We must not therefore conclude absolutely, that there is no heat in the fire, or sweetness in the sugar, but only that heat or sweetness, as perceived by us, are not in the fire or sugar. What say you to this?

Phil. I say it is nothing to the purpose. Our discourse proceeded altogether concerning sensible things, which you defined to be the things we *immediately perceived by our senses.* Whatever other qualities therefore you speak of, as distinct from these, I know nothing of them, neither do they at all belong to the point in dispute. You may indeed pretend to have discovered certain qualities which you do not perceive, and assert those insensible qualities exist in fire and sugar. But what use can be made of this to your present purpose, I am at a loss to conceive. Tell me then once more, do you acknowledge that heat and cold, sweetness and bitterness, (meaning those qualities which are perceived by the senses) do not exist without the mind?

Hyl. I see it is to no purpose to hold out, so I give up the cause as to those mentioned qualities. Though I profess it sounds oddly, to say that sugar is not sweet.

Phil. But for your farther satisfaction, take this along with you: that which at other times seems sweet, shall to a distempered palate appear bitter. And nothing can be plainer, than that divers persons perceive different tastes in the same food, since that which one man delights in, another abhors. And how could this be, if the taste was something really inherent in the food?

Hyl. I acknowledge I know not how.

Phil. In the next place, odors are to be considered. And, with regard to these, I would fain know whether what has been said of tastes does not exactly agree to them? Are they not so many pleasing or displeasing sensations?

Hyl. They are.

Phil. Can you then conceive it possible that they should exist in an unperceiving thing?

Hyl. I cannot.

Phil. Or can you imagine, that filth and ordure affect those brute animals that feed on them out of choice, with the same smells which we perceive in them?

Hyl. By no means.

Phil. May we not therefore conclude of smells, as of the other forementioned qualities, that they cannot exist in any but a perceiving substance or mind?

Hyl. I think so.

Phil. Then as to sounds, what must we think of them: are they accidents really inherent in external bodies, or not?

Hyl. That they inhere not in the sonorous bodies, is plain from hence; because a bell struck in the exhausted receiver of an air-pump, sends forth no sound. The air therefore must be thought the subject of sound.

Phil. What reason is there for that, Hylas?

Hyl. Because when any motion is raised in the air, we perceive a sound greater or lesser, to the air's motion; but without some motion in the air, we never hear any sound at all.

Phil. And granting that we never hear a sound but when some motion is produced in the air, yet I do not see how you can infer from thence, that the sound itself is in the air.

Hyl. It is this very motion in the external air, that produces in the mind the sensation of *sound*. For, striking on the drum of the ear, it causes a vibration, which by the auditory nerves being communicated to the brain, the soul is thereupon affected with the sensation called *sound*.

Phil. What! Is sound then a sensation?

Hyl. I tell you, as perceived by us, it is a particular sensation in the mind.

Phil. And can any sensation exist without the mind?

Hyl. No certainly.

Phil. How then can sound, being a sensation, exist in the air, if by the *air* you mean a senseless substance existing without the mind?

Hyl. You must distinguish, Philonous, between sound as it is perceived by us, and as it is in itself; or (which is the same thing) between the sound we immediately perceive and that which exists without us. The former indeed is a particular kind of sensation, but the latter is merely a vibrative or undulatory motion in the air.

Phil. I thought I had already obviated that distinction by the answer I gave when you were applying it in a like case before. But to say no more of that; are you sure then that sound is really nothing but motion?

Hyl. I am.

Phil. Whatever therefore agrees to real sound, may with truth be attributed to motion.

Hyl. It may.

Phil. It is then good sense to speak of *motion*, as of a thing that is *loud, sweet, acute*, or *grave*.

Hyl. I see you are resolved not to understand me. Is it not evident, those accidents or modes belong only to sensible sound, or *sound* in the common acceptation of the word, but not to *sound* in the real and philosophic sense, which, as I just now told you, is nothing but a certain motion of the air?

Phil. It seems then there are two sorts of sound, the one vulgar, or that which is heard, the other philosophical and real.

Hyl. Even so.

Phil. And the latter consists in motion.

Hyl. I told you so before.

Phil. Tell me, Hylas, to which of the senses, think you, the idea of motion belongs: to the hearing?

Hyl. No certainly, but to the sight and touch.

Phil. It should follow then, that according to you, real sounds may possibly be *seen* or *felt*, but never *heard*.

Hyl. Look you, Philonous, you may if you please make a jest of my opinion, but that will not alter the truth of things. I own indeed, the inferences you draw me into, sound something oddly; but common language, you know, is framed by, and for the use of, the vulgar: we must not therefore wonder, if expressions adapted to exact philosophic notions, seem uncouth and out of the way.

Phil. Is it come to that? I assure, you, I imagine myself to have gained no small point, since you make so light of departing from common phrases and opinions; it being a main part of our inquiry, to examine whose notions are widest of the common road, and most repugnant to the general sense of the world. But can you think it no more than a philosophical paradox, to say that *real sounds are never heard,* and that the idea of them is obtained by some other sense. And is there nothing in this contrary to nature and the truth of things?

Hyl. To deal ingenuously, I do not like it. And after the concessions already made, I had as well grant that sounds too have no real being without the mind.

Phil. And I hope you will make no difficulty to acknowledge the same of colors.

Hyl. Pardon me: the case of colors is very different. Can anything be plainer, than that we see them on the objects?

Phil. The objects you speak of are, I suppose, corporeal substances existing without the mind.

Hyl. They are.

Phil. And have true and real colors inhering in them?

Hyl. Each visible object has that color which we see in it.

Phil. How! Is there anything visible but what we perceive by sight.

Hyl. There is not.

Phil. And do we perceive anything by sense, which we do not perceive immediately?

Hyl. How often must I be obliged to repeat the same thing? I tell you, we do not.

Phil. Have patience, good Hylas; and tell me once more, whether there is anything immediately perceived by the senses, except sensible qualities. I know you asserted there was not: but I would now be informed, whether you still persist in the same opinion.

Hyl. I do.

Phil. Pray, is your corporeal substance either a sensible quality, or made up of sensible qualities?

Hyl. What a question that is! Who ever thought it was?

Phil. My reason for asking was, because in saying, *Each visible object has that color which we see in it,* you make visible objects to be corporeal substances; which implies either that corporeal substances are sensible qualities, or else that there is something beside sensible qualities perceived by sight: but as this point was formerly agreed between us, and is still maintained by you, it is a clear consequence, that your corporeal substance is nothing distinct from sensible qualities.

Hyl. You may draw as many absurd consequences as you please, and endeavor to perplex the plainest things; but you shall never persuade me out of my senses. I clearly understand my own meaning.

Phil. I wish you would make me understand it too. But since you are unwilling to have your notion of corporeal substance examined, I shall urge that point no farther. Only be pleased to let me know, whether the same colors which we see, exist in external bodies, or some other.

Hyl. The very same.

Phil. What! Are then the beautiful red and purple we see on yonder clouds, really in them? Or do you imagine they have in themselves any other form, than that of a dark mist or vapor?

Hyl. I must own, Philonous, those colors are not really in the clouds as they seem to be at this distance. They are only apparent colors.

Phil. Apparent call you them? How shall we distinguish these apparent colors from real?

Hyl. Very easily. Those are to be thought apparent, which appearing only at a distance, vanish upon a nearer approach.

Phil. And those I suppose are to be thought real, which are discovered by the most near and exact survey.

Hyl. Right.

Phil. Is the nearest and exactest survey made by the help of a microscope, or by the naked eye?

Hyl. By a microscope, doubtless.

Phil. But a microscope often discovers colors in an object different from those perceived by the unassisted sight. And in case we had microscopes magnifying to any assigned degree; it is certain, that no object whatsoever, viewed through them, would appear in the same color which it exhibits to the naked eye.

Hyl. And what will you conclude from all this? You cannot argue that there are really and naturally no colors on objects: because by artificial managements they may be altered, or made to vanish.

Phil. I think it may evidently be concluded from your own concessions, that all the colors we see with our naked eyes, are only apparent as those on the clouds, since they vanish upon a more close and accurate inspection, which is afforded us by a microscope. Then as to what you say by way of prevention: I ask you, whether the real and natural state of an object is better discovered by a very sharp and piercing sight, or by one which is less sharp?

Hyl. By the former without doubt.

Phil. Is it not plain from *Dioptrics*, that microscopes make the sight more penetrating, and represent objects as they would appear to the eye in case it were naturally endowed with a most exquisite sharpness?

Hyl. It is.

Phil. Consequently the microscopical representation is to be thought that which best sets forth the real nature of the thing, or what it is in itself. The colors, therefore, by it perceived, are more genuine and real, than those perceived otherwise.

Hyl. I confess there is something in what you say.

Phil. Besides, it is not only possible but manifest, that there actually are animals, whose eyes are by nature framed to perceive those things, which by reason of their minuteness escape our sight. What think you of those inconceivably small animals perceived by glasses? Must we suppose they are all stark blind? Or, in case they see, can it be imagined their sight has not the same use in preserving their bodies from injuries, which appears in that of all other animals? And if it hath, is it not evident, they must see particles less than their own bodies, which will present them with a far different view in each object, from that which strikes our senses? Even our own eyes do not always represent objects to us after the same manner. In the *jaundice*, everyone knows that all things seem yellow. Is it not therefore highly probable, those animals in whose eyes we discern a very different texture from that of ours, and whose bodies abound with different humors, do not see the same colors in every object that we do? From all which, should it not seem to follow, that all colors are equally apparent, and that none of those which we perceive are really inherent in any outward object?

Hyl. It should.

Phil. The point will be past all doubt, if you consider, that in case colors were real properties or affections inherent in external bodies, they could admit of no alteration, without some change wrought in the very bodies themselves: but is it not evident from what has been said, that upon the use of microscopes, upon a change happening in the humors of the eye, or a variation of distance, without any manner of real altera-tion in the thing itself, the colors of any object are either changed, or totally disap-pear? Nay, all other circumstances remaining the same, change but the situation of some objects, and they shall present different colors to the eye. The same thing hap-pens upon viewing an object in various degrees of light. And what is more known, than that the same bodies appear differently colored by candle-light from what they do in the open day? Add to these the experiment of a prism, which separating the heterogeneous rays of light, alters the color of any object; and will cause the whitest to appear of a deep blue or red to the naked eye. And now tell me, whether you are still of opinion that every body has its true real color inhering in it: and if you think it has, I would fain know farther from you, what certain distance and position of the object, what peculiar texture and formation of the eye, what degree or kind of light is necessary for ascertaining that true color, and distinguishing it from apparent ones.

Hyl. I own myself entirely satisfied, that they are all equally apparent; and that there is no such thing as color really inhering in external bodies, but that it is altogether in the light. And what confirms me in this opinion is, that in proportion to the light, colors are still more or less vivid; and if there be no light, then are there no colors perceived. Besides, allowing there are colors on external objects, yet how is it possible for us to perceive them? For no external body affects the mind, unless it act first on our organs of sense. But the only action of bodies is motion; and motion can-not be communicated otherwise than by impulse. A distant object therefore cannot act on the eye, nor consequently make itself or its properties perceivable to the soul. Whence it plainly follows, that it is immediately some contiguous substance, which operating on the eye occasions a perception of colors: and such is light.

Phil. How! Is light then a substance?

Hyl. I tell you, Philonous, external light is nothing but a thin fluid substance, whose minute particles being agitated with a brisk motion, and in various manners reflected from the different surfaces of outward objects to the eyes, communicate dif-ferent motions to the optic nerves; which, being propagated to the brain, cause therein various impressions: and these are attended with the sensations of red, blue, yellow, &c.

Phil. It seems then, the light does no more than shake the optic nerves.

Hyl. Nothing else.

Phil. And consequent to each particular motion of the nerves, the mind is affected with a sensation, which is some particular color.

Hyl. Right.

Phil. And these sensations have no existence without the mind.

Hyl. They have not.

Phil. How then do you affirm that colors are in the light, since by *light* you understand a corporeal substance external to the mind?

Hyl. Light and colors, as immediately perceived by us, I grant cannot exist without the mind. But in themselves they are only the motions and configurations of certain insensible particles of matter.

Phil. Colors then, in the vulgar sense, or taken for the immediate objects of sight, cannot agree to any but a perceiving substance.

Hyl. That is what I say.

Phil. Well then, since you give up the point as to those sensible qualities, which are alone thought colors by all mankind beside, you may hold what you please with regard to those invisible ones of the philosophers. It is not my business to dispute about them; only I would advise you to bethink yourself, whether considering the inquiry we are upon, it be prudent for you to affirm, *The red and blue which we see are not real colors, but certain unknown motions and figures which no man ever did or can see are truly so.* Are not these shocking notions, and are not they subject to as many ridiculous inferences, as those you were obliged to renounce before in the case of sounds?

Hyl. I frankly own, Philonous, that it is in vain to stand out any longer. Colors, sounds, tastes, in a word, all those termed *secondary qualities,* have certainly no existence without the mind. But by this acknowledgment I must not be supposed to derogate anything from the reality of matter or external objects, seeing it is no more than several philosophers maintain, who nevertheless are the farthest imaginable from denying matter. For the clearer understanding of this, you must know sensible qualities are by philosophers divided into *primary* and *secondary.*[1] The former are extension, figure, solidity, gravity, motion, and rest. And these they hold exist really in bodies. The latter are those above enumerated; or briefly, all sensible qualities beside the primary, which they assert are only so many sensations or ideas existing nowhere but in the mind. But all this, I doubt not, you are already apprised of. For my part, I have been a long time sensible there was such an opinion current among philosophers, but was never thoroughly convinced of its truth till now.

Phil. You are still then of opinion that extension and figures are inherent in external unthinking substances.

Hyl. I am.

Phil. But what if the same arguments which are brought against secondary qualities, will hold good against these also?

Hyl. Why then I shall be obliged to think, they too exist only in the mind.

Phil. Is it your opinion, the very figure and extension which you perceive by sense, exist in the outward object or material substance?

Hyl. It is.

Phil. Have all other animals as good grounds to think the same of the figure and extension which they see and feel?

Hyl. Without doubt, if they have any thought at all.

---

1. [See Locke's Essay, Bk. II, ch. VIII — S.M.C.]

Phil. Answer me, Hylas. Think you the senses were bestowed upon all animals for their preservation and well-being in life? Or were they given to men alone for this end?

Hyl. I make no question but they have the same use in all other animals.

Phil. If so, is it not necessary they should be enabled by them to perceive their own limbs, and those bodies which are capable of harming them?

Hyl. Certainly.

Phil. A mite therefore must be supposed to see his own foot, and things equal or even less than it, as bodies of some considerable dimension; though at the same time they appear to you scarce discernible, or at best as so many visible points.

Hyl. I cannot deny it.

Phil. And to creatures less than the mite they will seem yet larger.

Hyl. They will.

Phil. Insomuch that what you can hardly discern, will to another extremely minute animal appear as some huge mountain.

Hyl. All this I grant.

Phil. Can one and the same thing be at the same time in itself of different dimensions?

Hyl. That were absurd to imagine.

Phil. But from what you have laid down it follows, that both the extension by you perceived, and that perceived by the mite itself, as likewise all those perceived by lesser animals, are each of them the true extension of the mite's foot; that is to say, by your own principles you are led into an absurdity.

Hyl. There seems to be some difficulty in the point.

Phil. Again, have you not acknowledged that no real inherent property of any object can be changed, without some change in the thing itself?

Hyl. I have.

Phil. But as we approach to or recede from an object, the visible extension varies, being at one distance ten or a hundred times greater than at another. Does it not therefore follow from hence likewise, that it is not really inherent in the object?

Hyl. I own I am at a loss what to think.

Phil. Your judgment will soon be determined, if you will venture to think as freely concerning this quality, as you have done concerning the rest. Was it not admitted as a good argument, that neither heat nor cold was in the water, because it seemed warm to one hand, and cold to the other?

Hyl. It was.

Phil. Is it not the very same reasoning to conclude, there is no extension or figure in an object, because to one eye it shall seem little, smooth, and round, when at the same time it appears to the other, great, uneven, and angular?

Hyl. The very same. But does this latter fact ever happen?

Phil. You may at any time make the experiment, by looking with one eye bare, and with the other. through a microscope.

Hyl. I know not how to maintain it, and yet I am loath to give up *extension*, I see so many odd consequences following upon such a concession.

Phil. Odd, say you? After the concessions already made, I hope you will stick at nothing for its oddness. But on the other hand should it not seem very odd, if the general reasoning which includes all other sensible qualities did not also include extension? If it be allowed that no idea nor anything like an idea can exist in an unperceiving substance, then surely it follows, that no figure or mode of extension, which we can either perceive or imagine, or have any idea of, can be really inherent in matter; not to mention the peculiar difficulty there must be, in conceiving a material substance, prior to and distinct from extension, to be the *substratum* of extension. Be the sensible quality what it will, figure, or sound, or color; it seems alike impossible it should subsist in that which doth not perceive it.

Hyl. I give up the point for the present, reserving still a right to retract my opinion, in case I shall hereafter discover any false step in my progress to it.

Phil. That is a right you cannot be denied. Figures and extension being dispatched, we proceed next to *motion.* Can a real motion in any external body be at the same time both very swift and very slow?

Hyl. It cannot.

Phil. Is not the motion of a body swift in a reciprocal proportion to the time it takes up in describing any given space? Thus a body that describes a mile in an hour, moves three times faster than it would in case it described only a mile in three hours.

Hyl. I agree with you.

Phil. And is not time measured by the succession of ideas in our minds?

Hyl. It is.

Phil. And is it not possible ideas should succeed one another twice as fast in your mind, as they do in mine, or in that of some spirit of another kind.

Hyl. I own it.

Phil. Consequently the same body may to another seem to perform its motion over any space in half the time that it does to you. And the same reasoning will hold as to any other proportion: that is to say, according to your principles (since the motions perceived are both really in the object) it is possible one and the same body shall be really moved the same way at once, both very swift and very slow. How is this consistent either with common sense, or with what you just now granted?

Hyl. I have nothing to say to it.

Phil. Then as for *solidity;* either you do not mean any sensible quality by that word, and so it is beside our inquiry: or if you do, it must be either hardness or resistance. But both the one and the other are plainly relative to our senses: it being evident, that what seems hard to one animal, may appear soft to another, who hath greater force and firmness of limbs. Nor is it less plain, that the resistance I feel is not in the body.

Hyl. I own the very sensation of resistance, which is all you immediately perceive, is not in the *body;* but the cause of that sensation is.

Phil. But the causes of our sensations are not things immediately perceived, and therefore not sensible. This point I thought had been already determined.

Hyl. I own it was; but you will pardon me if I seem a little embarrassed: I know not how to quit my old notions.

Phil. To help you out, do but consider that if extension be once acknowledged to have no existence without the mind, the same must necessarily be granted of motion, solidity, and gravity, since they all evidently suppose extension. It is therefore superfluous to inquire particularly concerning each of them. In denying extension, you have denied them all to have any real existence.

Hyl. I wonder, Philonous, if what you say be true, why those philosophers who deny the secondary qualities any real existence, should yet attribute it to the primary. If there is no difference between them, how can this be accounted for?

Phil. It is not my business to account for every opinion of the philosophers. But among other reasons which may be assigned for this, it seems probable, that pleasure and pain being rather annexed to the former than the latter, may be one. Heat and cold, tastes and smells, have something more vividly pleasing or disagreeable than the ideas of extension, figure, and motion, affect us with. And it being too visibly absurd to hold, that pain or pleasure can be in an unperceiving substance, men are more easily weaned from believing the external existence of the secondary, than the primary qualities. You will be satisfied there is something in this, if you recollect the difference you made between an intense and more moderate degree of heat, allowing the one a real existence, while you denied it to the other. But after all, there is no rational ground for that distinction; for surely an indifferent sensation is as truly *a sensation,* as one more pleasing or painful; and consequently should not any more than they be supposed to exist in an unthinking subject.

Hyl. It is just come into my head, Philonous, that I have somewhere heard of a distinction between absolute and sensible extension. Now though it be acknowledged that *great* and *small,* consisting merely in the relation which other extended beings have to the parts of our own bodies, do not really inhere in the substances themselves; yet nothing obliges us to hold the same with regard to *absolute extension,* which is something abstracted from *great* and *small,* from this or that particular magnitude or figure. So likewise as to motion, *swift* and *slow* are altogether relative to the succession of ideas in our own minds. But it does not follow, because those modifications of motion exist not without the mind, that therefore absolute motion abstracted from them does not.

Phil. Pray what is it that distinguishes one motion, or one part of extension, from another? Is it not something sensible, as some degree of swiftness or slowness, some certain magnitude or figure peculiar to each?

Hyl. I think so.

Phil. These qualities, therefore, stripped of all sensible properties, are without all specific and numerical differences, as the schools call them.

Hyl. They are.

Phil. That is to say, they are extension in general, and motion in general.

Hyl. Let it be so.

Phil. But it is a universally received maxim, that *everything which exists, is particular.* How then can motion in general, or extension in general, exist in any corporeal substance?

Hyl. I will take time to solve your difficulty.

Phil. But I think the point may be speedily decided. Without doubt you can tell, whether you are able to frame this or that idea. Now I am content to put our dispute on this issue. If you can frame in your thoughts a distinct abstract idea of motion or extension, divested of all those sensible modes, as swift and slow, great and small, round and square, and the like, which are acknowledged to exist only in the mind, I will then yield the point you contend for. But if you cannot, it will be unreasonable on your side to insist any longer upon what you have no notion of.

Hyl. To confess ingenuously, I cannot.

Phil. Can you even separate the ideas of extension and motion, from the ideas of all those qualities which they who make the distinction, term *secondary*.

Hyl. What! Is it not an easy matter, to consider extension and motion by themselves, abstracted from all other sensible qualities? Pray how do the mathematicians treat of them?

Phil. I acknowledge, Hylas, it is not difficult to form general propositions and reasonings about those qualities, without mentioning any other; and in this sense to consider or treat of them abstractedly. But how does it follow that because I can pronounce the word *motion* by itself, I can form the idea of it in my mind exclusive of body? Or because theorems may be made of extension and figures, without any mention of *great* or *small*, or any other sensible mode or quality; that therefore it is possible such an abstract idea of extension, without any particular size or figure, or sensible quality, should be distinctly formed, and apprehended by the mind? Mathematicians treat of quantity, without regarding what other sensible qualities it is attended with, as being altogether indifferent to their demonstrations. But when laying aside the words, they contemplate the bare ideas, I believe you will find, they are not the pure abstracted ideas of extension.

Hyl. But what say you to *pure intellect?* May not abstracted ideas be framed by that faculty?

Phil. Since I cannot frame abstract ideas at all, it is plain, I cannot frame them by the help of *pure intellect,* whatsoever faculty you understand by those words. Besides, not to inquire into the nature of pure intellect and its spiritual objects, as *virtue, reason, God,* or the like; thus much seems manifest, that sensible things are only to be perceived by sense, or represented by the imagination. Figures, therefore, and extension, being originally perceived by sense, do not belong to pure intellect. But for your farther satisfaction, try if you can frame the idea of any figure, abstracted from all particularities of size, or even from other sensible qualities.

Hyl. Let me think a little—I do not find that I can.

Phil. And can you think it possible, that should really exist in nature, which implies a repugnancy in its conception?

Hyl. By no means.

Phil. Since therefore it is impossible even for the mind to disunite the ideas of extension and motion from all other sensible qualities, does it not follow, that where the one exist, there necessarily the other exist likewise?

Hyl. It should seem so.

Phil. Consequently the very same arguments which you admitted, as conclusive against the secondary qualities, are, without any farther application of force, against the primary too. Besides, if you will trust your senses, is it not plain, all sensible qualities coexist, or, to them, appear as being in the same place? Do they ever represent a motion, or figure, as being divested of all other visible and tangible qualities?

Hyl. You need say no more on this head. I am free to own, if there be no secret error or oversight in our proceedings hitherto, that all sensible qualities are alike to be denied existence without the mind. But my fear is, that I have been too liberal in my former concessions, or overlooked some fallacy or other. In short, I did not take time to think.

Phil. For that matter, Hylas, you may take what time you please in reviewing the progress of our inquiry. You are at liberty to recover any slips you might have made, or offer whatever you have omitted, which makes for your first opinion.

Hyl. One great oversight I take to be this: that I did not sufficiently distinguish the *object* from the *sensation.* Now though this latter may not exist without the mind, yet it will not thence follow that the former cannot.

Phil. What object do you mean? The object of the senses?

Hyl. The same.

Phil. It is then immediately perceived.

Hyl. Right.

Phil. Make me to understand the difference between what is immediately perceived, and a sensation.

Hyl. The sensation I take to be an act of the mind perceiving; beside which, there is something perceived; and this I call the *object.* For example, there is red and yellow on that tulip. But then the act of perceiving those colors is in me only, and not in the tulip.

Phil. What tulip do you speak of? Is it that which you see?

Hyl. The same.

Phil. And what do you see beside color, figure, and extension?

Hyl. Nothing.

Phil. What you would say then is, that the red and yellow are coexistent with the extension; is it not?

Hyl. That is not all; I would say, they have a real existence without the mind, in some unthinking substance.

Phil. That the colors are really in the tulip which I see, is manifest. Neither can it be denied, that this tulip may exist independent of your mind or mine; but that any immediate object of the senses, that is, any idea, or combination of ideas, should exist in an unthinking substance, or exterior to all minds, is in itself an evident contradiction. Nor can I imagine how this follows from what you said just now, to wit that the red and yellow were on the tulip *you saw,* since you do not pretend to *see* that unthinking substance.

Hyl. You have an artful way, Philonous, of diverting our inquiry from the subject.

Phil. I see you have no mind to be pressed that way. To return then to your distinction between *sensation* and *object;* if I take you right, you distinguish in every perception two things, the one an action of the mind, the other not.

Hyl. True.

Phil. And this action cannot exist in, or belong to, any unthinking thing; but whatever beside is implied in a perception, may.

Hyl. That is my meaning.

Phil. So that if there was a perception without any act of the mind, it were possible such a perception should exist in an unthinking substance.

Hyl. I grant it. But it is impossible there should be such a perception.

Phil. When is the mind said to be active?

Hyl. When it produces, puts an end to, or changes anything.

Phil. Can the mind produce, discontinue, or change anything but by an act of the will?

Hyl. It cannot.

Phil. The mind therefore is to be accounted active in its perceptions, so far forth as volition is included in them.

Hyl. It is.

Phil. In plucking this flower, I am active, because I do it by the motion of my hand, which was consequent upon my volition; so likewise in applying it to my nose. But is either of these smelling?

Hyl. No.

Phil. I act too in drawing the air through my nose; because my breathing so, rather than otherwise, is the effect of my volition. But neither can this be called *smelling:* for if it were, I should smell every time I breathed in that manner.

Hyl. True.

Phil. Smelling then is somewhat consequent to all this.

Hyl. It is.

Phil. But I do not find my will concerned any farther. Whatever more there is, as that I perceive such a particular smell or any smell at all, this is independent of my will, and therein I am altogether passive. Do you find it otherwise with you, Hylas?

Hyl. No, the very same.

Phil. Then as to seeing, is it not in your power to open your eyes, or keep them shut; to turn them this or that way?

Hyl. Without doubt.

Phil. But does it in like manner depend on your will, that in looking on this flower, you perceive *white* rather than any other color? Or directing your open eyes toward yonder part of the heaven, can you avoid seeing the sun? Or is light or darkness the effect of your volition?

Hyl. No, certainly.

Phil. You are then in these respects altogether passive.

Hyl. I am.

Phil. Tell me now, whether *seeing* consists in perceiving light and colors, or in opening and turning the eyes?

Hyl. Without doubt, in the former.

Phil. Since therefore you are in the very perception of light and colors altogether passive, what is become of that action you were speaking of, as an ingredient in every sensation? And does it not follow from your own concessions, that the perception of light and colors, including no action in it, may exist in an unperceiving substance? And is not this a plain contradiction?

Hyl. I know not what to think of it.

Phil. Besides, since you distinguish the *active* and *passive* in every perception, you must do it in that of pain. But how is it possible that pain, be it as little active as you please, should exist in an unperceiving substance? In short, do but consider the point, and then confess ingenuously, whether light and colors, tastes, sounds, &c. are not all equally passions or sensations in the soul. You may indeed call them *external objects,* and give them in words what subsistence you please. But examine your own thoughts, and then tell me whether it be not as I say?

Hyl. I acknowledge, Philonous, that upon a fair observation of what passes in my mind, I can discover nothing else, but that I am a thinking being, affected with variety of sensations; neither is it possible to conceive how a sensation should exist in an unperceiving substance. But then on the other hand, when I look on sensible things in a different view, considering them as so many modes and qualities, I find it necessary to suppose a material *substratum,* without which they cannot be conceived to exist.

Phil. Material substratum call you it? Pray, by which of your senses came you acquainted with that being?

Hyl. It is not itself sensible; its modes and qualities only being perceived by the senses.

Phil. I presume then it was by reflection and reason you obtained the idea of it.

Hyl. I do not pretend to any proper positive idea of it. However I conclude it exists, because qualities cannot be conceived to exist without a support.

Phil. It seems then you have only a relative notion of it, or that you conceive it not otherwise than by conceiving the relation it bears to sensible qualities.

Hyl. Right.

Phil. Be pleased therefore to let me know wherein that relation consists.

Hyl. Is it not sufficiently expressed in the term *substratum,* or *substance?*

Phil. If so, the word *substratum* should import, that it is spread under the sensible qualities or accidents.

Hyl. True.

Phil. And consequently under extension.

Hyl. I own it.

Phil. It is therefore somewhat in its own nature entirely distinct from extension.

Hyl. I tell you, extension is only a mode, and matter is something that supports modes. And is it not evident the thing supported is different from the thing supporting?

Phil. So that something distinct from, and exclusive of, extension, is supposed to be the *substratum* of extension.

Hyl. Just so.

Phil. Answer me, Hylas. Can a thing be spread without extension? Or is not the idea of extension necessarily included in *spreading?*

Hyl. It is.

Phil. Whatsoever therefore you suppose spread under anything, must have in itself an extension distinct from the extension of that thing under which it is spread.

Hyl. It must.

Phil. Consequently every corporeal substance, being the *substratum* of extension, must have in itself another extension by which it is qualified to be a *substratum:* and so on to infinity. And I ask whether this be not absurd in itself, and repugnant to what you granted just now, to wit, that the *substratum* was something distinct from, and exclusive of, extension.

Hyl. Aye but, Philonous, you take me wrong. I do not mean that matter is *spread* in a gross literal sense under extension. The word *substratum* is used only to express in general the same thing with *substance.*

Phil. Well then, let us examine the relation implied in the term *substance.* Is it not that it stands under accidents?

Hyl. The very same.

Phil. But that one thing may stand under or support another, must it not be extended?

Hyl. It must.

Phil. Is not therefore this supposition liable to the same absurdity with the former?

Hyl. You still take things in a strict literal sense: that is not fair, Philonous.

Phil. I am not for imposing any sense on your words: you are at liberty to explain them as you please. Only I beseech you, make me understand something by them. You tell me, matter supports or stands under accidents. How! Is it as your legs support your body?

Hyl. No; that is the literal sense.

Phil. Pray let me know any sense, literal or not literal, that you understand it in. — How long must I wait for an answer, Hylas?

Hyl. I declare I know not what to say. I once thought I understood well enough what was meant by matter's supporting accidents. But now the more I think on it, the less can I comprehend it; in short, I find that I know nothing of it.

Phil. It seems then you have no idea at all, neither relative nor positive of matter; you know neither what it is in itself, nor what relation it bears to accidents.

Hyl. I acknowledge it.

Phil. And yet you asserted, that you could not conceive how qualities or accidents should really exist, without conceiving at the same time a material support of them.

Hyl. I did.

Phil. That is to say, when you conceive the real existence of qualities, you do withal conceive something which you cannot conceive.

Hyl. It was wrong I own. But still I fear there is some fallacy or other. Pray what think you of this? It is just come into my head, that the ground of all our mistake lies in your treating of each quality by itself. Now, I grant that each quality cannot singly subsist without the mind. Color cannot without extension, neither can figure without some other sensible quality. But as the several qualities united or blended together form entire sensible things, nothing hinders why such things may not be supposed to exist without the mind.

Phil. Either, Hylas, you are jesting, or have a very bad memory. Though indeed we went through all the qualities by name one after another; yet my arguments, or rather your concessions, nowhere tended to prove, that the secondary qualities did not subsist each alone by itself; but that they were not *at all* without the mind. Indeed in treating of figure and motion, we concluded they could not exist without the mind, because it was impossible even in thought to separate them from all secondary qualities, so as to conceive them existing by themselves. But then this was not the only argument made use of upon that occasion. But (to pass by all that hath been hitherto said, and reckon it for nothing, if you will have it so) I am content to put the whole upon this issue. If you can conceive it possible for any mixture or combination of qualities, or any sensible object whatever, to exist without the mind, then I will grant it actually to be so.

Hyl. If it comes to that, the point will soon be decided. What more easy than to conceive a tree or house existing by itself, independent of, and unperceived by, any mind whatsoever? I do at this present time conceive them existing after that manner.

Phil. How say you, Hylas, can you see a thing which is at the same time unseen?

Hyl. No, that were a contradiction.

Phil. Is it not as great a contradiction to talk of *conceiving* a thing which is *unconceived?*

Hyl. It is.

Phil. The tree or house therefore which you think of, is conceived by you.

Hyl. How should it be otherwise?

Phil. And what is conceived is surely in the mind.

Hyl. Without question, that which is conceived is in the mind.

Phil. How then came you to say, you conceived a house or tree existing independent and out of all minds whatsoever?

Hyl. That was I own an oversight; but stay, let me consider what led me into it. — It is a pleasant mistake enough. As I was thinking of a tree in a solitary place, where no one was present to see it, methought that was to conceive a tree as existing unperceived or unthought of, not considering that I myself conceived it all the while. But now I plainly see, that all I can do is to frame ideas in my own mind. I may indeed conceive in my own thoughts the idea of a tree, or a house, or a mountain, but that is all. And this is far from proving, that I can conceive them *existing out of the minds of all spirits.*

Phil. You acknowledge then that you cannot possibly conceive, how any one corporeal sensible thing should exist otherwise than in a mind.

Hyl. I do.

Phil. And yet you will earnestly contend for the truth of that which you cannot so much as conceive.

Hyl. I profess I know not what to think, but still there are some scruples remain with me. It is not certain I see things at a distance? Do we not perceive the stars and moon, for example, to be a great way off? Is not this, I say, manifest to the senses?

Phil. Do you not in a dream too perceive those or the like objects?

Hyl. I do.

Phil. And have they not then the same appearance of being distant?

Hyl. They have.

Phil. But you do not thence conclude the apparitions in a dream to be without the mind?

Hyl. By no means.

Phil. You ought not therefore to conclude that sensible objects are without the mind, from their appearance or manner wherein they are perceived.

Hyl. I acknowledge it. But doth not my sense deceive me in those cases?

Phil. By no means. The idea or thing which you immediately perceive, neither sense nor reason informs you that it actually exists without the mind. By sense you only know that you are affected with such certain sensations of light and colors. &c. And these you will not say are without the mind.

Hyl. True: but beside all that, do you not think the sight suggests something of *outness* or *distance?*

Phil. Upon approaching a distant object, do the visible size and figure change perpetually, or do they appear the same at all distances?

Hyl. They are in a continual change.

Phil. Sight therefore does not suggest, or any way inform you, that the visible object you immediately perceive exists at a distance, or will be perceived when you advance farther onward, there being a continued series of visible objects succeeding each other, during the whole time of your approach.

Hyl. It does not; but still I know, upon seeing an object, what object I shall perceive after having passed over a certain distance: no matter whether it be exactly the same or no: there is still something of distance suggested in the case.

Phil. Good Hylas, do but reflect a little on the point, and then tell me whether there be any more in it than this. From the ideas you actually perceive by sight, you have by experience learned to collect what other ideas you will (according to the standing order of nature) be affected with, after such a certain succession of time and motion.

Hyl. Upon the whole, I take it to be nothing else.

Phil. Now is it not plain, that if we suppose a man born blind was on a sudden made to see, he could at first have no experience of what may be suggested by sight.

Hyl. It is.

Phil. He would not then according to you have any notion of distance annexed to the things he saw; but would take them for a new set of sensations existing only in his mind.

Hyl. It is undeniable.

Phil. But to make it still more plain: is not *distance* a line turned endwise to the eye?

Hyl. It is.

Phil. And can a line so situated be perceived by sight?

Hyl. It cannot.

Phil. Does it not therefore follow that distance is not properly and immediately perceived by sight?

Hyl. It should seem so.

Phil. Again, is it your opinion that colors are at a distance?

Hyl. It must be acknowledged, they are only in the mind.

Phil. But do not colors appear to the eye as coexisting in the same place with extension and figures?

Hyl. They do.

Phil. How can you then conclude from sight, that figures exist without, when you acknowledge colors do not; the sensible appearance being the very same with regard to both?

Hyl. I know not what to answer.

Phil. But allowing that distance was truly and immediately perceived by the mind, yet it would not thence follow it existed out of the mind. For whatever is immediately perceived is an idea: and can any *idea* exist out of the mind?

Hyl. To suppose that, were absurd: but inform me, Philonous, can we perceive or know nothing beside our ideas?

Phil. As for the rational deducing of causes from effects, that is beside our inquiry. And by the senses you can best tell, whether you perceive anything which is not immediately perceived. And I ask you, whether the things immediately perceived, are other than your own sensations or ideas? You have indeed more than once, in the course of this conversation, declared yourself on those points; but you seem by this last question to have departed from what you then thought.

Hyl. To speak the truth, Philonous, I think there are two kinds of objects, the one perceived immediately, which are likewise called *ideas;* the other are real things or external objects perceived by the mediation of ideas, which are their images and representations. Now I own, ideas do not exist without the mind; but the latter sort of objects do. I am sorry I did not think of this distinction sooner; it would probably have cut short your discourse.

Phil. Are those external objects perceived by sense, or by some other faculty?

Hyl. They are perceived by sense.

Phil. How! Is there anything perceived by sense, which is not immediately perceived?

Hyl. Yes, Philonous, in some sort there is. For example, when I look on a picture or statue of Julius Caesar, I may be said after a manner to perceive him (though not immediately) by my senses.

Phil. It seems then, you will have our ideas, which alone are immediately perceived, to be pictures of external things: and that these also are perceived by sense, inasmuch as they have a conformity or resemblance to our ideas.

Hyl. That is my meaning.

Phil. And in the same way that Julius Caesar, in himself invisible, is nevertheless perceived by sight; real things, in themselves imperceptible, are perceived by sense.

Hyl. In the very same.

Phil. Tell me, Hylas, when you behold the picture of Julius Caesar, do you see with your eyes any more than some colors and figures, with a certain symmetry and composition of the whole?

Hyl. Nothing else.

Phil. And would not a man, who had never known anything of Julius Caesar, see as much?

Hyl. He would.

Phil. Consequently he hath his sight, and the use of it, in as perfect a degree as you.

Hyl. I agree with you.

Phil. Whence comes it then that your thoughts are directed to the Roman emperor, and his are not? This cannot proceed from the sensations or ideas of sense by you then perceived; since you acknowledge you have no advantage over him in that respect. It should seem therefore to proceed from reason and memory: should it not?

Hyl. It should.

Phil. Consequently it will not follow from that instance, that anything is perceived by sense which is not immediately perceived. Though I grant we may in one acceptation be said to perceive sensible things mediately by sense: that is, when from a frequently perceived connection, the immediate perception of ideas by one sense suggests to the mind others, perhaps belonging to another sense, which are wont to be connected with them. For instance, when I hear a coach drive along the streets, immediately I perceive only the sound; but from the experience I have had that such a sound is connected with a coach. I am said to hear the coach. It is nevertheless evident, that in truth and strictness, nothing can be *heard* but *sound:* and the coach is not then properly perceived by sense, but suggested from experience. So likewise when we are said to see a red-hot bar of iron; the solidity and heat of the iron are not the objects of sight, but suggested to the imagination by the color and figure, which are properly perceived by that sense. In short, those things alone are actually and strictly perceived by any sense, which would have been perceived, in case that same sense had then been first conferred on us. As for other things, it is plain they are only suggested to the mind by experience grounded on former perceptions. But to return to your comparison of Caesar's picture, it is plain, if you keep to that, you must hold the real things, or archetypes of our ideas, are not perceived by sense, but by some internal faculty of the soul, as reason or memory. I would therefore fain know, what arguments you can draw from reason for the existence of what you call *real things* or *material objects*. Or whether you remember to have seen them formerly as they are in themselves? Or if you have heard or read of any one that did.

Hyl. I see, Philonous, you are disposed to raillery; but that will never convince me.

Phil. My aim is only to learn from you, the way to come at the knowledge of *material beings*. Whatever we perceive, is perceived immediately or mediately: by sense, or by reason and reflection. But as you have excluded sense, pray show me what reason you have to believe their existence; or what *medium* you can possibly make use of, to prove it either to mine or your own understanding.

Hyl. To deal ingenuously, Philonous, now I consider the point, I do not find I can give you any good reason for it. But thus much seems pretty plain, that it is at least possible such things may really exist. And as long as there is no absurdity in supposing them, I am resolved to believe as I did, till you bring good reasons to the contrary.

Phil. What! Is it come to this, that you only believe the existence of material objects, and that your belief is founded barely on the possibility of its being true? Then you will have me bring reasons against it: though another would think it reasonable, the proof should lie on him who holds the affirmative. And after all, this very point which you are now resolved to maintain without any reason, is in effect what you have more than once during this discourse seen good reason to give up. But to pass over all this; if I understand you rightly, you say our ideas do not exist without the mind; but that they are copies, images, or representations of certain originals that do.

Hyl. You take me right.

Phil. They are then like external things.

Hyl. They are.

Phil. Have those things a stable and permanent nature independent of our senses; or are they in a perpetual change, upon our producing any motions in our bodies, suspending, exerting, or altering our faculties or organs of sense.

Hyl. Real things, it is plain, have a fixed and real nature, which remains the same, not withstanding any change in our senses, or in the posture and motion of our bodies; which indeed may affect the ideas in our minds, but it were absurd to think they had the same effect on things existing without the mind.

Phil. How then is it possible, that things perpetually fleeting and variable as our ideas, should be copies or images of anything fixed and constant? Or in other words, since all sensible qualities, as size, figure, color, &c., that is, our ideas, are continually changing upon every alteration in the distance, medium, or instruments of sensation; how can any determinate material objects be properly represented or painted forth by several distinct things, each of which is so different from and unlike the rest? Or if you say it resembles some one only of our ideas, how shall we be able to distinguish the true copy from all the false ones?

Hyl. I profess, Philonous, I am at a loss. I know not what to say to this.

Phil. But neither is this all. Which are material objects in themselves, perceptible or imperceptible?

Hyl. Properly and immediately nothing can be perceived but ideas. All material things therefore are in themselves insensible, and to be perceived only by their ideas.

Phil. Ideas then are sensible, and their archetypes or originals insensible.

Hyl. Right.

Phil. But how can that which is sensible be like that which is insensible? Can a real thing in itself *invisible* be like a *color;* or a real thing which is not *audible,* be like a *sound?* In a word, can anything be like a sensation or idea, but another sensation or idea?

Hyl. I must own, I think not.

Phil. Is it possible there should be any doubt in the point? Do you not perfectly know your own ideas?

Hyl. I know them perfectly; since what I do not perceive or know, can be no part of my idea.

Phil. Consider therefore, and examine them, and then tell me if there be anything in them which can exist without the mind: or if you can conceive anything like them existing without the mind.

Hyl. Upon inquiry, I find it is impossible for me to conceive or understand how anything but an idea can be like an idea. And it is most evident, that *no idea can exist without the mind.*

Phil. You are therefore by your principles forced to deny the reality of sensible things, since you made it to consist in an absolute existence exterior to the mind. That is to say, you are a downright *sceptic.* So I have gained my point, which was to show your principles led to scepticism.

Hyl. For the present I am, if not entirely convinced, at least silenced.

Phil. I would fain know what more you would require in order to a perfect conviction. Have you not had the liberty of explaining yourself all manner of ways? Were any little slips in discourse laid hold and insisted on? Or were you not allowed to retract or reinforce anything you had offered, as best served your purpose? Has not everything you could say been heard and examined with all the fairness imaginable? In a word, have you not in every point been convinced out of your own mouth? And if you can at present discover any flaw in any of your former concessions, or think of any remaining subterfuge, any new distinction, color, or comment whatsoever, why do you not produce it?

Hyl. A little patience, Philonous. I am at present so amazed to see myself ensnared, and as it were imprisoned in the labyrinths you have drawn me into, that on the sudden it cannot be expected I should find my way out. You must give me time to look about me, and recollect myself.

Phil. Hark; is not this the college bell?

Hyl. It rings for prayers.

Phil. We will go in then if you please, and meet here again tomorrow morning. In the meantime you may employ your thoughts on this morning's discourse, and try if you can find any fallacy in it, or invent any new means to extricate yourself.

Hyl. Agreed.

THE SECOND DIALOGUE

Hylas. I beg your pardon, Philonous, for not meeting you sooner. All this morning my head was so filled with our late conversation, that I had not leisure to think of the time of the day, or indeed of anything else.

Philonous. I am glad you were so intent upon it, in hopes if there were any mistakes in your concessions, or fallacies in my reasonings from them, you will now discover them to me.

Hyl. I assure you, I have done nothing ever since I saw you, but search after mistakes and fallacies, and with that view have minutely examined the whole series of yesterday's discourse: but all in vain, for the notions it led me into, upon review, appear still more clear and evident; and the more I consider them, the more irresistibly do they force my assent.

Phil. And is not this, think you, a sign that they are genuine, that they proceed from nature, and are conformable to right reason? Truth and beauty are in this alike, that the strictest survey sets them both off to advantage. While the false lustre of error and disguise cannot endure being reviewed, or too nearly inspected.

Hyl. I own there is a great deal in what you say. Nor can any one be more entirely satisfied of the truth of those odd consequences, so long as I have in view the reasonings that lead to them. But when these are out of my thoughts, there seems on the other hand something so satisfactory, so natural and intelligible in the modern way of explaining things, that I profess I know not how to reject it.

Phil. I know not what way you mean.

Hyl. I mean the way of accounting for our sensations or ideas.

Phil. How is that?

Hyl. It is supposed the soul makes her residence in some part of the brain, from which the nerves take their rise, and are thence extended to all parts of the body: and that outward objects, by the different impressions they make on the organs of sense, communicate certain vibrative motions to the nerves; and these being filled with spirits, propagate them to the brain or seat of the soul, which according to the various impressions or traces thereby made in the brain, is variously affected with ideas.

Phil. And call you this an explication of the manner whereby we are affected with ideas?

Hyl. Why not, Philonous, have you anything to object against it?

Phil. I would first know whether I rightly understand your hypothesis. You make certain traces in the brain to be the causes or occasions of our ideas. Pray tell me, whether by the *brain* you mean any sensible thing?

Hyl. What else think you I could mean?

Phil. Sensible things are all immediately perceivable; and those things which are immediately perceivable, are ideas; and these exist only in the mind. Thus much you have, if I mistake not, long since agreed to.

Hyl. I do not deny it.

Phil. The brain therefore you speak of, being a sensible thing, exists only in the mind. Now, I would fain know whether you think it reasonable to suppose, that one idea or thing existing in the mind, occasions all other ideas. And if you think so, pray how do you account for the origin of that primary idea or brain itself?

Hyl. I do not explain the origin of our ideas by that brain which is perceivable to sense, this being itself only a combination of sensible ideas, but by another which I imagine.

Phil. But are not things imagined as truly *in the mind* as things perceived?

Hyl. I must confess they are.

Phil. It comes therefore to the same thing; and you have been all this while accounting for ideas, by certain motions or impressions in the brain, that is, by some alterations in an idea, whether sensible or imaginable, it matters not.

Hyl. I begin to suspect my hypothesis.

Phil. Beside spirits, all that we know or conceive are our own ideas. When therefore you say, all ideas are occasioned by impressions in the brain, do you conceive this brain or no? If you do, then you talk of ideas imprinted in an idea, causing that same idea, which is absurd. If you do not conceive it, you talk unintelligibly, instead of forming a reasonable hypothesis.

Hyl. I now clearly see it was a mere dream. There is nothing in it.

Phil. You need not be much concerned at it: for after all, this way of explaining things, as you called it, could never have satisfied any reasonable man. What connection is there between a motion in the nerves, and the sensations of sound or color in the mind? Or how is it possible these should be the effect of that?

Hyl. But I could never think it had so little in it, as now it seems to have.

Phil. Well then, are you at length satisfied that no sensible things have a real existence; and that you are in truth an arrant *sceptic?*

Hyl. It is too plain to be denied.

Phil. Look! Are not the fields covered with a delightful verdure? Is there not something in the woods and groves, in the rivers and clear springs, that soothes, that delights, that transports the soul? At the prospect of the wide and deep ocean, or some huge mountain whose top is lost in the clouds, or of an old gloomy forest, are not our minds filled with a pleasing horror? Even in rocks and deserts, is there not an agreeable wildness? How sincere a pleasure is it to behold the natural beauties of the earth! To preserve and renew our relish for them, is not the veil of night alternately drawn over her face, and does she not change her dress with the seasons? How aptly are the elements disposed? What variety and use in the meanest productions of nature? What delicacy, what beauty, what contrivance in animal and vegetable bodies? How exquisitely are all things suited, as well to their particular ends, as to constitute apposite parts of the whole! And while they mutually aid and support, do they not also set off and illustrate each other? Raise now your thoughts from this ball of earth, to all those glorious luminaries that adorn the high arch of heaven. The motion and situation of the planets, are they not admirable for use and order? Were those (miscalled *erratic)* globes ever known to stray, in their repeated journeys through the pathless void? Do they not measure areas round the sun ever proportioned to the times? So fixed, so immutable are the laws by which the unseen author of nature actuates the universe. How vivid and radiant is the luster of the fixed stars! How magnificent and rich that negligent profusion, with which they appear to be scattered throughout the whole azure vault! Yet if you take the telescope, it brings into your sight a new host of stars that escape the naked eye. Here they seem contiguous and minute, but to a nearer view immense orbs of light at various distances, far sunk in the abyss of space. Now you must call imagination to your aid. The feeble narrow sense cannot descry innumerable worlds revolving round the central fires; and in those worlds the energy of an all-perfect mind displayed in endless forms. But neither sense nor imagination are big enough to comprehend the boundless extent with all its glittering furniture. Though the laboring mind exert and strain each power to its utmost reach, there still stands out ungrasped a surplusage immeasurable. Yet all the vast bodies that compose this mighty frame, how distant and remote soever, are by some secret mechanism, some divine art and force, linked in a mutual dependence and intercourse with each other, even with this earth, which was almost slipt from my thoughts, and lost in the crowd of worlds. Is not the whole system immense, beautiful, glorious beyond expression and beyond thought! What treatment then do those philosophers deserve, who would deprive these noble and delightful scenes of all reality? How should those principles be entertained, that lead us to think all the visible beauty of the creation a false imaginary glare? To be plain, can you expect this scepticism of yours will not be thought extravagantly absurd by all men of sense?

Hyl. Other men may think as they please: but for your part you have nothing to reproach me with. My comfort is, you are as much a *sceptic* as I am.

Phil. There, Hylas, I must beg leave to differ from you.

Hyl. What! Have you all along agreed to the premises, and do you now deny the conclusion, and leave me to maintain those paradoxes by myself which you led me into? This surely is not fair.

Phil. I deny that I agreed with you in those notions that led to scepticism. You indeed said, the reality of sensible things consisted in an *absolute existence* out of the minds of spirits, or distinct from their being perceived. And pursuant to this notion of reality, you are obliged to deny sensible things any real existence: that is, according to your own definition, you profess yourself a *sceptic*. But I neither said nor thought the reality of sensible things was to be defined after that manner. To me it is evident, for the reasons you allow of, that sensible things cannot exist otherwise than in a mind or spirit. Whence I conclude, not that they have no real existence, but that seeing they depend not on my thought, and have an existence distinct from being perceived by me, *there must be some other mind wherein they exist.* As sure therefore as the sensible world really exists, so sure is there an infinite omnipresent spirit who contains and supports it.

Hyl. What! This is no more than I and all Christians hold; nay, and all others too who believe there is a God, and that he knows and comprehends all things.

Phil. Aye, but here lies the difference. Men commonly believe that all things are known or perceived by God, because they believe the being of a God, whereas I, on the other side, immediately and necessarily conclude the being of a God, because all sensible things must be perceived by him.

Hyl. But so long as we all believe the same thing, what matter is it how we come by that belief?

Phil. But neither do we agree in the same opinion. For philosophers, though they acknowledge all corporeal beings to be perceived by God, yet they attribute to them an absolute subsistence distinct from their being perceived by any mind whatever, which I do not. Besides, is there no difference between saying, *There is a God, therefore he perceives all things:* and saying, *Sensible things do really exist: and if they really exist, they are necessarily perceived by an infinite mind: therefore there is an infinite mind, or God.* This furnishes you with a direct and immediate demonstration, from a most evident principle, of the *being of a God.* Divines and philosophers had proved beyond all controversy, from the beauty and usefulness of the several parts of the creations that it was the workmanship of God. But that setting aside all help of astronomy and natural philosophy, all contemplation of the contrivance, order, and adjustment of things, an infinite mind should be necessarily inferred from the bare existence of the sensible world, is an advantage peculiar to them only who have made this easy reflection: that the sensible world is that which we perceive by our several senses; and that nothing is perceived by the senses beside ideas; and that no idea or archetype of an idea can exist otherwise than in a mind. You may now, without any laborious search into the sciences, without any subtlety of reason, or tedious length of discourse, oppose and baffle the most strenuous advocate for atheism. Those miserable refuges, whether in an eternal succession of unthinking causes and effects, or in a fortuitous concourse of atoms; those wild imaginations of Vanini,[2] Hobbes, and Spinoza; in a word the whole system of atheism, is it not entirely overthrown by this single reflection on the repugnancy included in supposing the whole, or any part, even the most rude and shapeless of the visible world, to exist without a mind? Let any one of those abettors of impiety but look into his own thoughts, and there try if he can conceive how so much as a rock, a desert, a chaos, or confused jumble of atoms; how anything at all, either sensible or imaginable, can exist independent of a mind, and he need go no farther to be convinced of his folly. Can anything be fairer than to put a dispute on such an issue, and leave it to a man himself to see if he can conceive, even in thought, what he holds to be true in fact, and from a notional to allow it a real existence?

Hyl. It cannot be denied, there is something highly serviceable to religion in what you advance. But do you not think it looks very like a notion entertained by some eminent moderns,[3] of *seeing all things in God?*

Phil. I would gladly know that opinion; pray explain it to me.

Hyl. They conceive that the soul, being immaterial, is incapable of being united with material things, so as to perceive them in themselves, but that she perceives them by her union with the substance of God, which being spiritual is therefore purely intelligible, or capable of being the immediate object of a spirit's thought. Besides, the divine essence contains in it perfections correspondent to each created being; and which are for that reason proper to exhibit or represent them to the mind.

Phil. I do not understand how our ideas, which are things altogether passive and inert, can be the essence, or any part (or like any part) of the essence or substance of

2. [Giulio Cesare Lucilio Vanini (1585–1619) was an Italian philosopher burned at the stake at Toulouse, France on charges of atheism and witchcraft.]

3. [The reference is to Nicolas Malebranche (1638–1715), regarding whom see Berkeley's *Treatise*, n. 8.]

God, who is an impassive, indivisible, purely active being. Many more difficulties and objections there are, which occur at first view against this hypothesis; but I shall only add that it is liable to all the absurdities of the common hypotheses, in making a created world exist otherwise than in the mind of a spirit. Beside all which it has this peculiar to itself; that it makes that material world serve to no purpose. And if it pass for a good argument against other hypotheses in the sciences, that they suppose nature or the divine wisdom to make something in vain, or do that by tedious round-about methods, which might have been performed in a much more easy and compendious way, what shall we think of that hypothesis which supposes the whole world made in vain?

Hyl. But what say you, are not you too of opinion that we see all things in God? If I mistake not, what you advance comes near it.

Phil. Few men think, yet all will have opinions. Hence men's opinions are superficial and confused. It is nothing strange that tenets, which in themselves are ever so different, should nevertheless be confounded with each other by those who do not consider them attentively. I shall not therefore be surprised, if some men imagine that I run into the enthusiasm of Malebranche, though in truth I am very remote from it. He builds on the most abstract general ideas, which I entirely disclaim. He asserts an absolute external world, which I deny. He maintains that we are deceived by our senses, and know not the real natures or the true forms and figures of extended beings; of all which I hold the direct contrary. So that upon the whole there are no principles more fundamentally opposite than his and mine. It must be owned I entirely agree with what the holy Scripture saith, *that in God we live, and move, and have our being.*[4] But that we see things in his essence after the manner above set forth, I am far from believing. Take here in brief my meaning. It is evident that the things I perceive are my own ideas, and that no idea can exist unless it be in a mind. Nor is it less plain that these ideas or things by me perceived, either themselves or their archetypes, exist independently of my mind, since I know myself not to be their author, it being out of my power to determine at pleasure, what particular ideas I shall be affected with upon opening my eyes or ears. They must therefore exist in some other mind, whose will it is they should be exhibited to me. The things, I say, immediately perceived, are ideas or sensations, call them which you will. But how can any idea or sensation exist in, or be produced by, anything but a mind or spirit? This indeed is inconceivable; and to assert that which is inconceivable, is to talk nonsense: is it not?

Hyl. Without doubt.

Phil. But on the other hand, it is very conceivable that they should exist in, and be produced by, a spirit; since this is no more than I daily experience in myself, inasmuch as I perceive numberless ideas; and by an act of my will can form a great variety of them, and raise them up in my imagination: though it must be confessed, these creatures of the fancy are not altogether so distinct, so strong, vivid, and permanent, as those perceived by my senses, which latter are called *real things*. From all which I conclude, *there is a mind which affects me every moment with all the sensible impressions I perceive.* And from the variety, order, and manner of these, I conclude the author of them to be *wise, powerful, and good, beyond comprehension.* Mark it well; I do not say, I see things by perceiving that which represents them in the in-

---

4. [The quotation is from *Acts* 17:28.]

telligible substance of God. This I do not understand; but I say, the things by me perceived are known by the understanding, and produced by the will, of an infinite spirit. And is not all this most plain and evident? Is there any more in it, than what a little observation of our own minds, and that which passes in them not only enables us to conceive, but also obliges us to acknowledge?

Hyl. I think I understand you very clearly; and own the proof you give of a diety seems no less evident, than it is surprising. But allowing that God is the supreme and universal cause of all things, yet may not there be still a third nature besides spirits and ideas? May we not admit a subordinate and limited cause of our ideas? In a word, may there not for all that be *matter?*

Phil. How often must I inculcate the same thing? You allow the things immediately perceived by sense to exist nowhere without the mind: but there is nothing perceived by sense, which is not perceived immediately: therefore there is nothing sensible that exists without the mind. The matter therefore which you still insist on, is something intelligible, I suppose; something that may be discovered by reason and not by sense.

Hyl. You are in the right.

Phil. Pray let me know what reasoning your belief of matter is grounded on; and what this matter is in your present sense of it.

Hyl. I find myself affected with various ideas, whereof I know I am not the cause; neither are they the cause of themselves, or of one another, or capable of subsisting by themselves, as being altogether inactive, fleeting, dependent beings. They have therefore some cause distinct from me and them: of which I pretend to know no more, than that is *the cause of my ideas.* And this thing, whatever it be, I call matter.

Phil. Tell me, Hylas, has every one a liberty to change the current proper signification annexed to a common name in any language? For example, suppose a traveller should tell you, that in a certain country men might pass unhurt through the fire; and, upon explaining himself, you found he meant by the word *fire* that which others call *water:* or if he should assert there are trees which walk upon two legs, meaning men by the term *trees.* Would you think this reasonable?

Hyl. No; I should think it very absurd. Common custom is the standard of propriety in language. And for any man to affect speaking improperly, is to pervert the use of speech, and can never serve to a better purpose, than to protract and multiply disputes where there is no difference in opinion.

Phil. And does not *matter,* in the common current acceptation of the word, signify an extended, solid, moveable, unthinking, inactive substance?

Hyl. It does.

Phil. And, has it not been made evident, that no such substance can possibly exist? And though it should be allowed to exist, yet how can that which is *inactive* be a *cause;* or that which is *unthinking* be a *cause of thought?* You may indeed, if you please, annex to the word *matter* a contrary meaning to what is vulgarly received; and tell me you understand by it an unextended, thinking, active being, which is the cause of our ideas. But what else is this, than to play with words, and run into that very fault you just now condemned with so much reason? I do by no means find fault with your reasoning, in that you collect a cause from the *phenomena:* but I deny that the cause deducible by reason can properly be termed matter.

Hyl. There is indeed something in what you say. But I am afraid you do not thoroughly comprehend my meaning. I would by no means be thought to deny that

God or an infinite spirit is the supreme cause of all things. All I contend for, is, that subordinate to the supreme agent there is a cause of a limited and inferior nature, which concurs in the production of our ideas, not by any act of will or spiritual efficiency, but by that kind of action which belongs to matter, *viz. motion.*

Phil. I find, you are at every turn relapsing into your old exploded conceit, of a moveable and consequently an extended substance existing without the mind. What! Have you already forgot you were convinced, or are you willing I should repeat what has been said on that head? In truth this is not fair dealing in you, still to suppose the being of that which you have so often acknowledged to have no being. But not to insist farther on what has been so largely handled, I ask whether all your ideas are not perfectly passive and inert, including nothing of action in them?

Hyl. They are.

Phil. And are sensible qualities anything else but ideas?

Hyl. How often have I acknowledged that they are not?

Phil. But is not motion a sensible quality?

Hyl. It is.

Phil. Consequently it is no action.

Hyl. I agree with you. And indeed it is very plain, that when I stir my finger, it remains passive; but my will which produced the motion, is active.

Phil. Now I desire to know in the first place, whether motion being allowed to be no action, you can conceive any action besides volition: and in the second place, whether to say something and conceive nothing be not to talk nonsense: and lastly, whether having considered the premises, you do not perceive that to suppose any efficient or active cause of our ideas, other than *spirit*, is highly absurd and unreasonable?

Hyl. I give up the point entirely, but though matter may not be a cause, yet what hinders its being an *instrument* subservient to the supreme agent in the production of our ideas?

Phil. An instrument, say you; pray what may be the figure, springs, wheels, and motions of that instrument?

Hyl. Those I pretend to determine nothing of, both the substance and its qualities being entirely unknown to me.

Phil. What? You are then of opinion, it is made up of unknown parts, that it hath unknown motions, and an unknown shape.

Hyl. I do not believe that it hath any figure or motion at all, being already convinced, that no sensible qualities can exist in an unperceiving substance.

Phil. But what motion is it possible to frame of an instrument void of all sensible qualities, even extension itself?

Hyl. I do not pretend to have any notion of it.

Phil. And what reason have you to think, this unknown, this inconceivable Somewhat does exist? Is it that you imagine God cannot act as well as without it, or that you find by experience the use of some such thing, when you form ideas in your own mind?

Hyl. You are always teasing me for reasons of my belief. Pray what reasons have you not to believe it?

Phil. It is to me a sufficient reason not to believe the existence of anything, if I see no reason for believing it. But not to insist on reasons for believing, you will not so much as let me know what it is you would have me believe, since you say you have no manner of notion of it. After all, let me entreat you to consider whether it be like a philosopher, or even like a man of common sense, to pretend to believe you know not what, and you know not why.

Hyl. Hold, Philonous. When I tell you matter is an *instrument,* I do not mean altogether nothing. It is true, I know not the particular kind of instrument; but however I have some notion of *instrument in general,* which I apply to it.

Phil. But what if it should prove that there is something, even in the most general notion of *instrument,* as taken in a distinct sense from *cause,* which makes the use of it inconsistent with the divine attributes?

Hyl. Make that appear, and I shall give up the point.

Phil. What mean you by the general nature or notion of *instrument?*

Hyl. That which is common to all particular instruments composeth the general notion.

Phil. Is it not common to all instruments, that they are applied to the doing those things only, which cannot be performed by the mere act of our wills? Thus for instance, I never use an instrument to move my finger, because it is done by a volition. But I should use one, if I were to remove part of a rock, or tear up a tree by the roots. Are you of the same mind? Or can you show any example where an instrument is made use of in producing an effect immediately depending on the will of the agent?

Hyl. I own, I cannot.

Phil. How therefore can you suppose, that an all-perfect spirit, on whose will all things have an absolute and immediate dependence, should need an instrument in his operations, or not needing it make use of it? Thus it seems to me that you are obliged to own the use of a lifeless inactive instrument, to be incompatible with the infinite perfection of God; that is, by your own confession, to give up the point.

Hyl. It does not readily occur what I can answer you.

Phil. But methinks you should be ready to own the truth, when it has been fairly proved to you. We indeed, who are beings of finite powers, are forced to make use of instruments. And the use of an instrument showeth the agent to be limited by rules of another's prescription, and that he cannot obtain his end, but in such a way and by such conditions. Whence it seems a clear consequence, that the supreme unlimited agent useth no tool or instrument at all. The will of an omnipotent spirit is no sooner exerted than executed, without the application of means, which, if they are employed by inferior agents, it is not upon account of any real efficacy that is in them, or necessary aptitude to produce any effect, but merely in compliance with the laws of nature, or those conditions prescribed to them by the first cause, who is himself above all limitation or prescription whatsoever.

Hyl. I will no longer maintain that matter is an instrument. However, I would not be understood to give up its existence neither; since, notwithstanding what hath been said, it may still be an *occasion.*

Phil. How many shapes is your matter to take? Or how often must it be proved not to exist, before you are content to part with it? But to say no more of this (though by all the laws of disputation I may justly blame you for so frequently changing the signification of the principal term) I would fain know what you mean by affirming that matter is an occasion, having already denied it to be a cause. And when you have shown in what sense you understand *occasion,* pray in the next place be pleased to show me what reason induceth you to believe there is such an occasion of our ideas.

Hyl. As to the first point: by *occasion* I mean an inactive unthinking being, at the presence whereof God excites ideas in our minds.

Phil. And what may be the nature of that inactive unthinking being?

Hyl. I know nothing of its nature.

Phil. Proceed then to the second point, and assign some reason why we should allow an existence to this inactive, unthinking, unknown thing.

Hyl. When we see ideas produced in our minds after an orderly and constant manner, it is natural to think they have some fixed and regular occasions, at the presence of which they are excited.

Phil. You acknowledge then God alone to be the cause of our ideas, and that he causes them at the presence of those occasions.

Hyl. That is my opinion.

Phil. Those things which you say are present to God, without doubt he perceives.

Hyl. Certainly; otherwise they could not be to him an occasion of acting.

Phil. Not to insist now on your making sense of this hypothesis, or answering all the puzzling questions and difficulties it is liable to: I only ask whether the order and regularity observable in the series of our ideas, or the course of nature, be not sufficiently accounted for by the wisdom and power of God; and whether it does not derogate from those attributes, to suppose he is influenced, directed, or put in mind, when and what he is to act, by any unthinking substance. And lastly whether, in case I granted all you contend for, it would make anything to your purpose, it not being easy to conceive how the external or absolute existence of an unthinking substance, distinct from its being perceived, can be inferred from my allowing that there are certain things perceived by the mind of God, which are to him the occasion of producing ideas in us.

Hyl. I am perfectly at a loss what to think, this notion of *occasion* seeming now altogether as groundless as the rest.

Phil. Do you not at length perceive, that in all these different acceptations of *matter,* you have been only supposing you know not what, for no manner of reason, and to no kind of use?

Hyl. I freely own myself less fond of my notions, since they have been so accurately examined. But still, methinks I have some confused perception that there is such a thing as *matter.*

Phil. Either you perceive the being of matter immediately, or mediately. If immediately, pray inform me by which of the senses you perceive it. If mediately, let me know by what reasoning it is inferred from those things which you perceive immediately. So much for the perception. Then for the matter itself, I ask whether it is object, *substratum,* cause, instrument, or occasion? You have already pleaded for each of these, shifting your notions, and making matter to appear sometimes in one shape, then in another. And what you have offered has been disapproved and rejected by yourself. If you have anything new to advance, I would gladly hear it.

Hyl. I think I have already offered all I had to say on those heads. I am at a loss what more to urge.

Phil. And yet you are loath to part with your old prejudice. But to make you quit it more easily, I desire that, beside what has been hitherto suggested, you will farther consider whether, upon supposition that matter exists, you can possibly conceive how you should be affected by it? Or supposing it did not exist, whether it be not evident you might for all that be affected with the same ideas you now are, and consequently have the very same reasons to believe its existence that you now can have.

Hyl. I acknowledge it is possible we might perceive all things just as we do now, though there was no matter in the world; neither can I conceive, if there be matter, how it should produce any idea in our minds. And I do farther grant, you have entirely satisfied me, that it is impossible there should be such a thing as matter in any of the foregoing acceptations. But still I cannot help supposing that there is *matter* in some sense or other. What that is I do not indeed pretend to determine.

Phil. I do not expect you should define exactly the nature of that unknown being. Only be pleased to tell me, whether it is a substance: and if so, whether you can suppose a substance without accidents; or in case you suppose it to have accidents or qualities, I desire you will let me know what those qualities are, at least what is meant by matter's supporting them.

Hyl. We have already argued on those points. I have no more to say to them. But to prevent any farther questions, let me tell you, I at present understand by *matter* neither substance nor accident, thinking nor extended being, neither cause, instrument, nor occasion, but something entirely unknown, distinct from all these.

Phil. It seems then you include in your present notion of matter, nothing but the general abstract idea of *entity*.

Hyl. Nothing else, save only that I superadd to this general idea the negation of all those particular things, qualities, or ideas that I perceive, imagine, or in any wise apprehend.

Phil. Pray where do you suppose this unknown matter to exist?

Hyl. Oh Philonous! now you think you have entangled me; for if I say it exists in place, then you will infer that it exists in the mind, since it is agreed that place or extension exists only in the mind: but I am not ashamed to own my ignorance. I know not where it exists; only I am sure it exists not in place. There is a negative answer for you: and you must expect no other to all the questions you put for the future about matter.

Phil. Since you will not tell me where it exists, be pleased to inform me after what manner you suppose it to exist, or what you mean by its *existence*.

Hyl. It neither thinks nor acts, neither perceives, nor is perceived.

Phil. But what is there positive in your abstracted notion of its existence?

Hyl. Upon a nice observation, I do not find I have any positive notion or meaning at all. I tell you again I am not ashamed to own my ignorance. I know not what is meant by its *existence*, or how it exists.

Phil. Continue, good Hylas, to act the same ingenuous part, and tell me sincerely whether you can frame a distinct idea of entity in general, prescinded from and exclusive of all thinking and corporeal beings, all particular things whatsoever.

Hyl. Hold, let me think a little—I profess, Philonous, I do not find that I can. At first glance methought I had some dilute and airy notion of pure entity in abstract; but upon closer attention it has quite vanished out of sight. The more I think on it, the more am I confirmed in my prudent resolution of giving none but negative

answers, and not pretending to the least degree of any positive knowledge or conception of matter, its *where*, its *how*, its *entity*, or anything belonging to it.

Phil. When therefore you speak of the existence of matter, you have not any notion
in your mind.

Hyl. None at all.

Phil. Pray tell me if the case stands not thus: at first, from a belief of material
substance you would have it that the immediate objects existed without the mind;
then that their archetypes; then causes; next instruments; then occasions: lastly,
something in general, which being interpreted proves *nothing*. So matter comes to
nothing. What think you, Hylas, is not this a fair summary of your whole proceeding?

Hyl. Be that as it will, yet I still insist upon it, that our not being able to conceive a
thing, is no argument against its existence.

Phil. That from a cause, effect, operation, sign, or other circumstance, there may
reasonably be inferred the existence of a thing not immediately perceived, and that it
were absurd for any man to argue against the existence of that thing, from his having
no direct and positive notion of it, I freely own. But where there is nothing of all this;
where neither reason nor revelation induce us to believe the existence of a thing;
where we have not even a relative notion of it; where an abstraction is made from
perceiving and being perceived, from spirit and idea: lastly, where there is not so
much as the most inadequate or faint idea pretended to: I will not indeed thence conclude against the reality of any notion, or existence of anything: but my inference
shall be, that you mean nothing at all: that you employ words to no manner of purpose, without any design or signification whatsoever. And I leave it to you to consider
how mere jargon should be treated.

Hyl. To deal frankly with you, Philonous, your arguments seem in themselves
unanswerable, but they have not so great an effect on me as to produce that entire
conviction, that hearty acquiescence which attends demonstration. I find myself still
relapsing into an obscure surmise of I know not what, *matter*.

Phil. But are you not sensible, Hylas, that two things must concur to take away all
scruple, and work a plenary assent in the mind? Let a visible object be set in never so
clear a light, yet if there is any imperfection in the sight, or if the eye is not directed
towards it, it will not be distinctly seen. And though a demonstration be never so well
grounded and fairly proposed, yet if there is withal a stain of prejudice, or a wrong
bias on the understanding, can it be expected on a sudden to perceive clearly and
adhere firmly to the truth? No, there is need of time and pains: the attention must be
awakened and detained by a frequent repetition of the same thing placed oft in the
same, oft in different lights. I have said it already, and find I must still repeat and inculcate, that it is an unaccountable licence you take in pretending to maintain you
know not what, for you know not what reason, to you know not what purpose? Can
this be paralleled in any art or science, any sect or profession of men? Or is there
anything so barefacedly groundless and unreasonable to be met with even in the
lowest of common conversation? But perhaps you will still say, matter may exist,
though at the same time you neither know what is meant by *matter*, or by its *existence*. This indeed is surprising, and the more so because it is altogether voluntary,
you not being led to it by any one reason; for I challenge you to show me that thing in
nature which needs matter to explain or account for it.

Hyl. The reality of things cannot be maintained without supposing the existence of matter. And is not this, think you, a good reason why I should be earnest in its defence?

Phil. The reality of things! What things, sensible or intelligible?

Hyl. Sensible things.

Phil. My glove, for example?

Hyl. That or any other thing perceived by the senses.

Phil. But to fix on some particular thing; is it not a sufficient evidence to me of the existence of this *glove*, that I see it, and feel it, and wear it? Or if this will not do, how is it possible I should be assured of the reality of this thing, which I actually see in this place, by supposing that some unknown thing, which I never did or can see, exists after an unknown manner, in an unknown place, or in no place at all? How can the supposed reality of that which is intangible, be a proof that anything tangible really exists? or of that which is invisible, that any visible thing, or in general of anything which is imperceptible, that a perceptible exists? Do but explain this, and I shall think nothing too hard for you.

Hyl. Upon the whole, I am content to own the existence of matter is highly improbable; but the direct and absolute impossibility of it does not appear to me.

Phil. But granting matter to be possible, yet, upon that account merely, it can have no more claim to existence than a golden mountain, or a centaur.

Hyl. I acknowledge it; but still you do not deny it is possible; and that which is possible, for aught you know, may actually exist.

Phil. I deny it to be possible; and have, if I mistake not, evidently proved from your own concessions that it is not. In the common sense of the word *matter*, is there any more implied, than an extended, solid, figured, moveable substance existing without the mind? And have not you acknowledged over and over, that you have seen evident reason for denying the possibility of such a substance?

Hyl. True, but that is only one sense of the term *matter*.

Phil. But is it not the only proper genuine received sense? And if matter in such a sense be proved impossible, may it not be thought with good grounds absolutely impossible? Else how could anything be proved impossible? Or indeed how could there be any proof at all one way or other, to a man who takes the liberty to unsettle and change the common signification of words?

Hyl. I thought philosophers might be allowed to speak more accurately than the vulgar, and were not always confined to the common acceptation of a term.

Phil. But this now mentioned is the common received sense among philosophers themselves. But not to insist on that, have you not been allowed to take matter in what sense you pleased? And have you not used this privilege in the utmost extent, sometimes entirely changing, at others leaving out or putting into the definition of it whatever for the present best served your design, contrary to all the known rules of reason and logic? And hath not this shifting unfair method of yours spun out our dispute to an unnecessary length; matter having been particularly examined, and by your own confession refuted in each of those senses? And can any more be required to prove the absolute impossibility of a thing, than the proving it impossible in every particular sense, that either you or any one else understands it?

Hyl. But I am not so thoroughly satisfied that you have proved the impossibility of matter in the last most obscure abstracted and indefinite sense.

Phil. When is a thing shown to be impossible?

Hyl. When a repugnancy is demonstrated between the ideas comprehended in its definition.

Phil. But where there are no ideas, there no repugnancy can be demonstrated between ideas.

Hyl. I agree with you.

Phil. Now in that which you call the obscure indefinite sense of the word *matter*, it is plain, by your own confession, there was included no idea at all, no sense except an unknown sense, which is the same thing as none. You are not therefore to expect I should prove a repugnancy between ideas where there are no ideas; or the impossibility of Matter taken in an *unknown* sense, that is no sense at all. My business was only to show, you meant *nothing*; and this you were brought to own. So that in all your various senses, you have been showed either to mean nothing at all, or if anything, an absurdity. And if this be not sufficient to prove the impossibility of a thing, I desire you will let me know what is.

Hyl. I acknowledge you have proved that matter is impossible; nor do I see what more can be said in defense of it. But at the same time that I give up this, I suspect all my other notions. For surely none could be more seemingly evident than this once was: and yet it now seems as false and absurd as ever it did true before. But I think we have discussed the point sufficiently for the present. The remaining part of the day I would willingly spend, in running over in my thoughts the several heads of this morning's conversation, and tomorrow shall be glad to meet you here again about the same time.

Phil. I will not fail to attend you.

THE THIRD DIALOGUE

Philonous. Tell me, Hylas, what are the fruits of yesterday's meditation? Has it confirmed you in the same mind you were in at parting? Or have you since seen cause to change your opinion?

Hylas. Truly my opinion is, that all our opinions are alike vain and uncertain. What we approve to-day, we condemn tomorrow. We keep a stir about knowledge, and spend our lives in the pursuit of it, when, alas! we know nothing all the while: nor do I think it possible for us ever to know anything in this life. Our faculties are too narrow and too few. Nature certainly never intended us for speculation.

Phil. What! Say you we can know nothing, Hylas?

Hyl. There is not that single thing in the world, whereof we can know the real nature, or what it is in itself.

Phil. Will you tell me I do not really know what fire or water is?

Hyl. You may indeed know that fire appears hot, and water fluid: but this is no more than knowing what sensations are produced in your own mind, upon the application of fire and water to your organs of sense. Their internal constitution, their true and real nature, you are utterly in the dark as to *that*.

Phil. Do I not know this to be a real stone that I stand on, and that which I see before my eyes to be a real tree?

Hyl. Know? No, it is impossible you or any man alive should know it. All you know, is, that you have such a certain idea or appearance in your own mind. But what is this to the real tree or stone? I tell you, that color, figure, and hardness, which you perceive, are not the real natures of those things, or in the least like them. The same may be said of all other real things or corporeal substances which compose the world. They have none of them anything in themselves, like those sensible qualities by us perceived. We should not therefore pretend to affirm or know anything of them, as they are in their own nature.

Phil. But surely, Hylas, I can distinguish gold, for example, from iron: and how could this be, if I knew not what either truly was?

Hyl. Believe me, Philonous, you can only distinguish between your own ideas. That yellowness, that weight, and other sensible qualities, think you they are really in the gold? They are only relative to the senses, and have no absolute existence in nature. And in pretending to distinguish the species of real things, by the appearances in your mind, you may perhaps act as wisely as he that should conclude two men were of a different species, because their clothes were not of the same color.

Phil. It seems then we are altogether put off with the appearances of things, and those false ones too. The very meat I eat, and the cloth I wear, have nothing in them like what I see and feel.

Hyl. Even so.

Phil. But is it not strange the whole world should be thus imposed on, and so foolish as to believe their senses? And yet I know not how it is, but men eat, and drink, and sleep, and perform all the offices of life, as comfortably and conveniently, as if they really knew the things they are conversant about.

Hyl. They do so: but you know ordinary practice does not require a nicety of speculative knowledge. Hence the vulgar retain their mistakes, and for all that, make a shift to bustle through the affairs of life. But philosophers know better things.

Phil. You mean, they know that they *know nothing.*

Hyl. That is the very top and perfection of human knowledge.

Phil. But are you all this while in earnest, Hylas; and are you seriously persuaded that you know nothing real in the world? Suppose you are going to write, would you not call for pen, ink, and paper, like another man; and do you not know what it is you call for?

Hyl. How often must I tell you, that I know not the real nature of any one thing in the universe? I may indeed upon occasion make use of pen, ink, and paper. But what any one of them is in its own true nature, I declare positively I know not. And the same is true with regard to every other corporeal thing. And, what is more, we are not only ignorant of the true and real nature of things, but even of their existence. It cannot be denied that we perceive such certain appearances or ideas; but it cannot be concluded from thence that bodies really exist. Nay, now I think on it, I must agreeably to my former concessions farther declare, that it is impossible any real corporeal thing should exist in nature.

Phil. You amaze me. Was ever anything more wild and extravagant than the notions you now maintain: and is it not evident you are led into all these extravagancies by the belief of *material substance?* This makes you dream of unknown natures in everything. It is this occasions your distinguishing between the reality and sensible appearances of things. It is to this you are indebted for being ignorant of what everybody else knows perfectly well. Nor is this all: you are not only ignorant of the true nature of everything, but you know not whether anything really exists, or whether there are any true natures at all; forasmuch as you attribute to your material beings an absolute or external existence, wherein you suppose their reality consists. And as you are forced in the end to acknowledge such an existence means either a direct repugnancy, or nothing at all, it follows that you are obliged to pull down your own hypothesis of material substance, and positively to deny the real existence of any part of the universe. And so you are plunged into the deepest and most deplorable *scepticism* that ever man was. Tell me, Hylas, is it not as I say?

Hyl. I agree with you. *Material substance* was no more than an hypothesis, and a false and groundless one too. I will no longer spend my breath in defence of it. But whatever hypothesis you advance, or whatsoever scheme of things you introduce in its stead, I doubt not it will appear every whit as false: let me but be allowed to question you upon it. That is, suffer me to serve you in your own kind, and I warrant it shall conduct you through as many perplexities and contradictions, to the very same state of scepticism that I myself am in at present.

Phil. I assure you, Hylas, I do not pretend to frame any hypothesis at all. I am of a vulgar cast, simple enough to believe my senses, and leave things as I find them. To be plain, it is my opinion, that the real things are those very things I see and feel, and perceive by my senses. These I know, and finding they answer all the necessities and purposes of life, have no reason to be solicitous about any other unknown beings. A piece of sensible bread, for instance, would stay my stomach better than ten thousand times as much of that insensible, unintelligible, real bread you speak of. It is likewise my opinion, that colors and other sensible qualities are on the objects. I cannot for my life help thinking that snow is white, and fire hot. You indeed, who by *snow* and *fire* mean certain external, unperceived, unperceiving substances, are in the right to deny whiteness or heat to be affections inherent in them. But I, who understand by those words the things I see and feel, am obliged to think like other folks. And as I am no sceptic with regard to the nature of things, so neither am I as to their existence. That a thing should be really perceived by my senses, and at the same time not really exist, is to me a plain contradiction; since I cannot prescind or abstract, even in thought, the existence of a sensible thing from its being perceived. Wood, stones, fire, water, flesh, iron, and the like things, which I name and discourse of, are things that I know; otherwise I should never have thought of them, or named them. And I should not have known them, but that I perceived them by my senses; and things perceived by the senses are immediately perceived; and things immediately perceived are ideas; and ideas cannot exist without the mind; their existence therefore consists in being perceived; when therefore they are actually perceived, there can be no doubt of their existence. Away then with all that scepticism, all those ridiculous philosophical doubts. What a jest is it for a philosopher to question the existence of sensible things, till he has it proved to him from the veracity of God: or to pretend our knowledge in this point falls short of intuition or demonstration? I might as well doubt of my own being, as of the being of those things I actually see and feel.

Hyl. Not so fast, Philonous: you say you cannot conceive how sensible things should exist without the mind. Do you not?

Phil. I do.

Hyl. Supposing you were annihilated, cannot you conceive it possible, that things perceivable by sense may still exist?

Phil. I can; but then it must be in another mind. When I deny sensible things an existence out of the mind, I do not mean my mind in particular, but all minds. Now it is plain they have an existence exterior to my mind, since I find them by experience to be independent of it. There is therefore some other mind wherein they exist, during the intervals between the times of my perceiving them: as likewise they did before my birth, and would do after my supposed annihilation. And as the same is true, with regard to all other finite created spirits; it necessarily follows, there is an *omnipresent eternal mind,* which knows and comprehends all things, and exhibits them to our view in such a manner, and according to such rules as he himself has ordained, and are by us termed the *laws of nature.*

Hyl. Answer me, Philonous. Are all our ideas perfectly inert beings? Or have they any agency included in them?

Phil. They are altogether passive and inert.

Hyl. And is not God an agent, a being purely active?

Phil. I acknowledge it.

Hyl. No idea therefore can be like unto, or represent the nature of God.

Phil. It cannot.

Hyl. Since therefore you have no idea of the mind of God, how can you conceive it possible, that things should exist in his mind? Or, if you can conceive the mind of God without having an idea of it, why may not I be allowed to conceive the existence of matter, notwithstanding that I have no idea of it?

Phil. As to your first question; I own I have properly no idea, either of God or any other spirit; for these being active, cannot be represented by things perfectly inert, as our ideas are. I do nevertheless know, that I, who am a spirit or thinking substance, exist as certainly, as I know my ideas exist. Farther, I know what I mean by the terms *I* and *myself;* and I know this immediately, or intuitively, though I do not perceive it as I perceive a triangle, a color, or a sound. The mind, spirit, or soul, is that indivisible unextended thing, which thinks, acts, and perceives. I say *indivisible,* because unextended; and *unextended,* because extended, figured, moveable things, are ideas; and that which perceives ideas, which thinks and wills, is plainly itself no idea, nor like an idea. Ideas are things inactive, and perceived: and spirits a sort of beings altogether different from them. I do not therefore say my soul is an idea, or like an idea. However, taking the word *idea* in a large sense, my soul may be said to furnish me with an idea, that is, an image, or likeness of God, though indeed extremely inadequate. For all the notion I have of God, is obtained by reflecting on my own soul, heightening its powers, and removing its imperfections. I have therefore, though not an inactive idea, yet in myself some sort of an active thinking image of the Deity. And though I perceive him not by sense, yet I have a notion of him, or know him by reflection and reasoning. My own mind and my own ideas I have an immediate knowledge of; and by the help of these, do mediately apprehend the possibility of the existence of other spirits and ideas. Farther, from my own being, and from the dependency I find in myself and my ideas, I do, by an act of reason, necessarily infer the existence of a God, and of all created things in the mind of God. So much for your first question. For the second: I suppose by this time you can answer it yourself. For you neither perceive matter objectively, as you do an inactive being or idea, nor know it, as you do yourself, by a reflex act: neither do you mediately apprehend it by similitude of the one or the other; nor yet collect it by reasoning from that which you know immediately. All which makes the case of *matter* widely different from that of the *Deity.*

Hyl. You say your own soul supplies you with some sort of an idea or image of God. But at the same time you acknowledge you have, properly speaking, no idea of your own soul. You even affirm that spirits are a sort of beings altogether different from ideas. Consequently that no idea can be like a spirit. We have therefore no idea of any spirit. You admit nevertheless that there is spiritual substance, although you have no idea of it; while you deny there can be such a thing as material substance, because you have no notion or idea of it. Is this fair dealing? To act consistently, you must either admit matter or reject spirit. What say you to this?

Phil. I say in the first place, that I do not deny the existence of material substance, merely because I have no notion of it, but because the notion of it is inconsistent, or in other words, because it is repugnant that there should be a notion of it. Many things, for aught I know, may exist, whereof neither I nor any other man hath or can have any idea or notion whatsoever. But then those things must be possible, that is, nothing inconsistent must be included in their definition. I say secondly, that although we believe things to exist which we do not perceive; yet we may not believe that any particular thing exists, without some reason for such belief: but I have no reason for believing the existence of matter. I have no immediate intuition thereof: neither can I mediately from my sensations, ideas, notions, actions or passions, infer an unthinking, unperceiving, inactive substance, either by probable deduction, or necessary consequence. Whereas the being of my self, that is, my own soul, mind or thinking principle, I evidently know by reflection. You will forgive me if I repeat the same things in answer to the same objections. In the very notion or definition of material substance, there is included a manifest repugnance and inconsistency. But this cannot be said of the notion of spirit. That ideas should exist in what doth not perceive, or be produced by what doth not act, is repugnant. But it is no repugnancy to say, that a perceiving thing should be the subject of ideas, or an active thing the cause of them. It is granted we have neither an immediate evidence nor a demonstrative knowledge of the existence of other finite spirits; but it will not thence follow that such spirits are on a foot with material substances: if to suppose the one be inconsistent, and it be not inconsistent to suppose the other; if the one can be inferred by no argument, and there is a probability for the other; if we see signs and effects indicating distinct finite agents like ourselves, and see no sign or symptom whatever that leads to a rational belief of matter. I say lastly, that I have a notion of spirit, though I have not, strictly speaking, an idea of it. I do not perceive it as an idea or by means of an idea, but know it by reflection.

Hyl. Notwithstanding all you have said, to me it seems, that according to your own way of thinking, and in consequence of your own principles, it should follow that you are only a system of floating ideas, without any substance to support them. Words are not to be used without a meaning. And as there is no more meaning in spiritual substance than in material substance, the one is to be exploded as well as the other.

Phil. How often must I repeat, that I know or am conscious of my own being; and that I myself am not my ideas, but somewhat else, a thinking active principle that perceives, knows, wills, and operates about ideas. I know that I, one and the same self, perceive both colors and sounds: that a color cannot perceive a sound, nor a sound a color: that I am therefore one individual principle, distinct from color and sound; and, for the same reason, from all other sensible things and inert ideas. But I am not in like manner conscious either of the existence or essence of matter. On the contrary, I know that nothing inconsistent can exist, and that the existence of matter implies an inconsistency. Farther, I know what I mean, when I affirm that there is a spiritual substance or support of ideas, that is, that a spirit knows and perceives ideas. But I do not know what is meant, when it is said, that an unperceiving substance hath inherent in it and supports either ideas or the archetypes of ideas. There is therefore upon the whole no parity of case between spirit and matter.

Hyl. I own myself satisfied in this point. But do you in earnest think, the real existence of sensible things consists in their being actually perceived? If so; how comes it that all mankind distinguish between them? Ask the first man you meet, and he shall tell you, *to be perceived* is one thing, and *to exist* is another.

Phil. I am content, Hylas, to appeal to the common sense of the world for the truth of my notion. Ask the gardener, why he thinks yonder cherry tree exists in the garden, and he shall tell you, because he sees and feels it; in a word, because he perceives it by his senses. Ask him why he thinks an orange tree not be there, and he shall tell you, because he does not perceive it. What he perceives by sense, that he terms a real being, and saith it *is,* or *exists;* but that which is not perceivable, the same, he saith, has no being.

Hyl. Yes, Philonous, I grant the existence of a sensible thing consists in being perceivable, but not in being actually perceived.

Phil. And what is perceivable but an idea? And can an idea exist without being actually perceived? These are points long since agreed between us.

Hyl. But be your opinion never so true, yet surely you will not deny it is shocking, and contrary to the common sense of men. Ask the fellow, whether yonder tree has an existence out of his mind: what answer think you he would make?

Phil. The same that I should myself, to wit, that it does exist out of his mind. But then to a Christian it cannot surely be shocking to say, the real tree existing without his mind is truly known and comprehended by (that is, *exists in*) the infinite mind of God. Probably he may not at first glance be aware of the direct and immediate proof there is of this, inasmuch as the very being of a tree, or any other sensible thing, implies a mind wherein it is. But the point itself he cannot deny. The question between the materialists and me is not, whether things have a real existence out of the mind of this or that person, but whether they have an absolute existence, distinct from being perceived by God, and exterior to all minds. This indeed some heathens and philosophers have affirmed, but whoever entertains notions of the Deity suitable to the Holy Scriptures, will be of another opinion.

Hyl. But according to your notions, what difference is there between real things, and chimeras formed by the imagination, or the visions of a dream, since they are all equally in the mind?

Phil. The ideas formed by the imagination are faint and indistinct; they have, besides, an entire dependence on the will. But the ideas perceived by sense, that is, real things, are more vivid and clear, and being imprinted on the mind by a spirit distinct from us, have not a like dependence on our will. There is therefore no danger of confounding these with the foregoing: and there is as little of confounding them with the visions of a dream, which are dim, irregular, and confused. And though they should happen to be never so lively and natural, yet by their not being connected, and of a piece with the preceding and subsequent transactions of our lives, they might easily be distinguished from realities. In short, by whatever method you distinguish *things* from *chimeras* on your own scheme, the same, it is evident, will hold also upon mine. For it must be, I presume, by some perceived difference, and I am not for depriving you of any one thing that you perceive.

Hyl. But still, Philonous, you hold, there is nothing in the world but spirits and ideas. And this, you must needs acknowledge, sounds very oddly.

Phil. I own the word *idea,* not being commonly used for *thing,* sounds something out of the way. My reason for using it was, because a necessary relation to the mind is understood to be implied by that term; and it is now commonly used by philosophers, to denote the immediate objects of the understanding. But however oddly the proposition may sound in words, yet it includes nothing so very strange or shocking in its sense, which in effect amounts to no more than this, to wit, that there are only things perceiving, and things perceived; or that every unthinking being is necessarily, and from the very nature of its existence, perceived by some mind; if not by any finite created mind, yet certainly by the infinite mind of God, in whom *we live, and move, and have our being.* Is this as strange as to say, the sensible qualities are not on the objects: or, that we cannot be sure of the existence of things, or know anything of their real natures, though we both see and feel them, and perceive them by all our senses?

Hyl. And in consequence of this, must we not think there are no such things as physical or corporeal causes; but that a spirit is the immediate cause of all the *phenomena* in nature? Can there be anything more extravagant than this?

Phil. Yes, it is infinitely more extravagant to say, a thing which is inert, operates on the mind, and which is unperceiving, is the cause of our perceptions, without any regard either to consistency, or the old known axiom: *Nothing can give to another that which it hath not itself.* Besides, that which you hold, I know not for what reason, seems so extravagant, is no more than the Holy Scriptures assert in a hundred places. In them God is represented as the sole and immediate author of all those effects, which some heathens and philosophers are wont to ascribe to nature, matter, fate, or the like unthinking principle. This is so much the constant language of Scripture, that it were needless to confirm it by citations.

Hyl. You are not aware, Philonous, that in making God the immediate author of all the motions in nature, you make him the author of murder, sacrilege, adultery, and the like heinous sins.

Phil. In answer to that, I observe first, that the imputation of guilt is the same, whether a person commits an action with or without an instrument. In case therefore you suppose God to act by the mediation of an instrument, or occasion, called *matter,* you as truly make him the author of sin as I, who think him the immediate agent in all those operations vulgarly ascribed to nature. I farther observe, that sin or moral turpitude does not consist in the outward physical action or motion, but in the internal deviation of the will from the laws of reason and religion. This is plain, in that the killing an enemy in a battle, or putting a criminal legally to death, is not thought sinful, though the outward act be the very same with that in the case of murder. Since therefore sin does not consist in the physical action, the making God an immediate cause of all such actions, is not making him the author of sin. Lastly, I have nowhere said that God is the only agent who produces all the motions in bodies. It is true, I have denied there are any other agents beside spirits: but this is very consistent with allowing to thinking rational beings, in the production of motions, the use of limited powers, ultimately indeed derived from God, but immediately under the direction of their own wills, which is sufficient to entitle them to all the guilt of their actions.

Hyl. But the denying matter, Philonous, or corporeal substance; there is the point. You can never persuade me that this is not repugnant to the universal sense of mankind. Were our dispute to be determined by most voices, I am confident you would give up the point, without gathering the votes.

Phil. I wish both our opinions were fairly stated and submitted to the judgment of men who had plain common sense, without the prejudices of a learned education. Let me be represented as one who trusts his senses, who thinks he knows the things he sees and feels, and entertains no doubts of their existence; and you fairly set forth with all your doubts, your paradoxes, and your scepticism about you, and I shall willingly acquiesce in the determination of any indifferent person. That there is no substance wherein ideas can exist beside spirit, is to me evident. And that the objects immediately perceived are ideas, is on all hands agreed. And that sensible qualities are objects immediately perceived, no one can deny. It is therefore evident there can be no *substratum* of those qualities but spirit, in which they exist, not by way of mode or property, but as a thing perceived in that which perceives it. I deny therefore that there is any unthinking *substratum* of the objects of sense, and in that acceptation that there is any material substance. But if by *material substance* is meant only sensible body, that which is seen and felt, (and the unphilosophical part of the world, I dare say, mean no more) then I am more certain of matter's existence than you, or any other philosopher, pretend to be. If there be anything which makes the generality of mankind averse from the notions I espouse, it is a misapprehension that I deny the reality of sensible things: but as it is you who are guilty of that and not I, it follows that in truth their aversion is against your notions, and not mine. I do therefore assert that I am as certain as of my own being, that there are bodies or corporeal substances, (meaning the things I perceive by my senses) and that granting this, the bulk of mankind will take no thought about, nor think themselves at all concerned in the fate of those unknown natures, and philosophical quiddities, which some men are so fond of.

Hyl. What say you to this? Since, according to you, men judge of the reality of things by their senses, how can a man be mistaken in thinking the moon a plain lucid surface, about a foot in diameter; or a square tower, seen at a distance, round; or an oar, with one end in the water, crooked?

Phil. He is not mistaken with regard to the ideas he actually perceives; but in the inferences he makes from his present perceptions. Thus in the case of the oar, what he immediately perceives by sight is certainly crooked; and so far he is in the right. But if he thence conclude, that upon taking the oar out of the water he shall perceive the same crookedness; or that it would affect his touch, as crooked things are wont to do: in that he is mistaken. In like manner, if he shall conclude from what he perceives in one station, that in case he advances toward the moon or tower, he should still be affected with the like ideas, he is mistaken. But his mistake lies not in what he perceives immediately and at present, (it being a manifest contradiction to suppose he should err in respect of that) but in the wrong judgment he makes concerning the ideas he apprehends to be connected with those immediately perceived: or concerning the ideas that, from what he perceives at present, he imagines would be perceived in other circumstances. The case is the same with regard to the Copernican system. We do not here perceive any motion of the earth: but it were erroneous thence to conclude, that, in case we were placed at as great a distance from that, as we are now from the other planets, we should not then perceive its motion.

Hyl. I understand you; and must needs own you say things plausible enough: but give me leave to put you in mind of one thing. Pray, Philonous, were you not formerly as positive that matter existed, as you are now that it does not?

Phil. I was. But here lies the difference. Before, my positiveness was founded without examination, upon prejudice; but now, after inquiry, upon evidence.

Hyl. After all, it seems our dispute is rather about words than things. We agree in the thing, but differ in the name. That we are affected with ideas from without is evident; and it is no less evident, that there must be (I will not say archetypes, but) powers without the mind, corresponding to those ideas. And as these powers cannot subsist by themselves, there is some subject of them necessarily to be admitted, which I call *matter,* and you call *spirit.* This is all the difference.

Phil. Pray, Hylas, is that powerful Being, or subject of powers, extended?

Hyl. It hath not extension; but it has the power to raise in you the idea of extension.

Phil. It is therefore itself unextended.

Hyl. I grant it.

Phil. Is it not also active?

Hyl. Without doubt: otherwise, how could we attribute powers to it?

Phil. Now let me ask you two questions: *first,* whether it be agreeable to the usage either of philosophers or others, to give the name *matter* to an unextended active being? And *secondly,* whether it be not ridiculously absurd to misapply names contrary to the common use of language?

Hyl. Well then, let it not be called matter, since you will have it so, but some *third nature* distinct from matter and spirit. For, what reason is there why you should call it spirit? Does not the notion of spirit imply, that it is thinking as well as active and unextended?

Phil. My reason is this: because I have a mind to have some notion of meaning in what I say; but I have no notion of any action distinct from volition, neither can I conceive volition to be anywhere but in a spirit: therefore when I speak of an active being, I am obliged to mean a spirit. Beside, what can be plainer than that a thing which hath no ideas in itself, cannot impart them to me; and if it hath ideas, surely it must be a spirit. To make you comprehend the point still more clearly if it be possible: I assert as well as you, that since we are affected from without, we must allow powers to be without in a being distinct from ourselves. So far we are agreed. But then we differ as to the kind of this powerful being. I will have it to be spirit, you matter, or I know not what (I may add too, you know not what) third nature. Thus I prove it to be spirit. From the effects I see produced, I conclude there are actions; and because actions, volitions; and because there are volitions, there must be a will. Again, the things I perceive must have an existence, they or their archetypes, out of my mind: but being ideas, neither they nor their archetypes can exist otherwise than in an understanding: there is therefore an understanding. But will and understanding constitute in the strictest sense a mind or spirit. The powerful cause therefore of my ideas, is in strict propriety of speech a *spirit.*

Hyl. And now I warrant you think you have made the point very clear, little suspecting that what you advance leads directly to a contradiction. Is it not an absurdity to imagine any imperfection in God?

Phil. Without a doubt.

Hyl. To suffer pain is an imperfection.

Phil. It is.

Hyl. Are we not sometimes affected with pain and uneasiness by some other being?

Phil. We are.

Hyl. And have you not said that being is a spirit, and is not that spirit God?

Phil. I grant it.

Hyl. But you have asserted, that whatever ideas we perceive from without, are in the mind which affects us. The ideas therefore of pain and uneasiness are in God; or in other words, God suffers pain: that is to say, there is an imperfection in the divine nature, which you acknowledged was absurd. So you are caught in a plain contradiction.

Phil. That God knows or understands all things, and that he knows among other things what pain is, even every sort of painful sensation, and what it is for his creatures to suffer pain, I make no question. But that God, though he knows and sometimes causes painful sensations in us, can himself suffer pain, I positively deny. We who are limited and dependent spirits, are liable to impressions of sense, the effects of an external agent, which being produced against our wills, are sometimes painful and uneasy. But God, whom no external being can affect, who perceives nothing by sense as we do, whose will is absolute and independent, causing all things, and liable to be thwarted or resisted by nothing; it is evident, such a being as this can suffer nothing, nor be affected with any painful sensation, or indeed any sensation at all. We are chained to a body, that is to say, our perceptions are connected with corporeal motions. By the law of our nature we are affected upon every alteration in the nervous parts of our sensible body: which sensible body, rightly considered, is nothing but a complection of such qualities or ideas, as have no existence distinct from being perceived by a mind: so that this connection of sensations with corporeal motions, means no more than a correspondence in the order of nature between two sets of ideas, or things immediately perceivable. But God is a pure spirit, disengaged from all such sympathy or natural ties. No corporeal motions are attended with the sensations of pain or pleasure in his mind. To know everything knowable is certainly a perfection; but to endure, or suffer, or feel anything by sense, is an imperfection. The former, I say, agrees to God, but not the latter. God knows, or hath ideas; but his ideas are not conveyed to him by sense, as ours are. Your not distinguishing, where there is so manifest a difference, makes you fancy you see an absurdity where there is none.

Hyl. But all this while you have not considered, that the quantity of matter has been demonstrated to be proportioned to the gravity of bodies. And what can withstand demonstration?

Phil. Let me see how you demonstrate that point.

Hyl. I lay it down for a principle, that the moments or quantities of motion in bodies, are in a direct compounded reason of the velocities and quantities of matter contained in them. Hence, where the velocities are equal, it follows, the moments are directly as the quantity of matter in each. But it is found by experience, that all bodies (bating the small inequalities, arising from the resistance of the air) descend with an equal velocity; the motion therefore of descending bodies and consequently their gravity, which is the cause or principle of that motion, is proportional to the quantity of matter; which was to be demonstrated.

Phil. You lay it down as a self-evident principle, that the quantity of motion in any body, is proportional to the velocity and *matter* taken together: and this is made use of to prove a proposition, from whence the existence of *matter* is inferred. Pray is not this arguing in a circle?

Hyl. In the premise I only mean, that the motion is proportional to the velocity, jointly with the extension and solidity.

Phil. But allowing this to be true, yet it will not thence follow, that gravity is proportional to *matter,* in your philosophic sense of the word; except you take it for granted, that unknown *substratum,* or whatever else you call it, is proportional to those sensible qualities; which to suppose, is plainly begging the question. That there is magnitude and solidity, or resistance, perceived by sense, I readily grant; as likewise that gravity may be proportional to those qualities, I will not dispute. But that either these qualities, as perceived by us, or the powers producing them, do exist in a *material substratum;* this is what I deny, and you indeed affirm, but, notwithstanding your demonstration, have not yet proved.

Hyl. I shall insist no longer on that point. Do you think, however, you shall persuade me the natural philosophers have been dreaming all this while; pray what becomes of all their hypotheses and explications of the *phenomena,* which suppose the existence of matter?

Phil. What mean you, Hylas, by the *phenomena?*

Hyl. I mean the appearances which I perceive by my senses.

Phil. And the appearances perceived by sense, are they not ideas?

Hyl. I have told you so a hundred times.

Phil. Therefore, to explain the *phenomena,* is to show how we come to be affected with ideas, in that manner and order wherein they are imprinted on our senses. Is it not?

Hyl. It is.

Phil. Now if you can prove, that any philosopher has explained the production of any one idea in our minds by the help of *matter,* I shall for ever acquiesce and look on all that has been said against it as nothing: but if you cannot, it is vain to urge the explication of *phenomena.* That a being endowed with knowledge and will, should produce or exhibit ideas, is easily understood. But that a being which is utterly destitute of these faculties should be able to produce ideas, or in any sort to affect an intelligence, this I can never understand. This I say, though we had some positive conception of matter, though we knew its qualities, and could comprehend its existence, would yet be so far from explaining things, that it is itself the most inexplicable thing in the world. And yet for all this, it will not follow, that philosophers have been doing nothing; for by observing and reasoning upon the connection of ideas, they discover the laws and methods of nature, which is a part of knowledge both useful and entertaining.

Hyl. After all, can it be supposed God would deceive all mankind? Do you imagine, he would have induced the whole world to believe the being of matter, if there was no such thing?

Phil. That every epidemical opinion arising from prejudice, or passion, or thoughtlessness, may be imputed to God, as the author of it, I believe you will not affirm. Whatsoever opinion we father on him, it must be either because he has discovered it to us by supernatural revelation, or because it is so evident to our natural faculties, which were framed and given us by God, that it is impossible we should withhold our assent from it. But where is the revelation? Or where is the evidence that extorts the belief of matter? Nay, how does it appear, that matter, taken from something distinct from what we perceive by our senses, is thought to exist by all mankind, or indeed by any except a few philosophers, who do not know what they would be at? Your question supposes these points are clear; and when you have cleared them, I shall myself obliged to give you another answer. In the meantime let it suffice that I tell you, I do not suppose God has deceived mankind at all.

Hyl. But the novelty, Philonous, the novelty! There lies the danger. New notions should always be discountenanced; they unsettle men's minds, and nobody knows where they will end.

Phil. Why the rejecting a notion that has no foundation either in sense or in reason, or in divine authority, should be thought to unsettle the belief of such opinions as are grounded on all or any of these, I cannot imagine. That innovations in government and religion, are dangerous, and ought to be discountenanced, I freely own. But is there the like reason why they should be discouraged in philosophy? The making anything known which was unknown before, is an innovation in knowledge: and if all such innovations had been forbidden, men would not have made a notable progress in the arts and sciences. But it is none of my business to plead for novelties and paradoxes. That the qualities we perceive, are not on the objects: that we must not believe our senses: that we know nothing of the real nature of things, and can never be assured even of their existence: that real colors and sounds are nothing but certain unknown figures and motions: that motions are in themselves neither swift nor slow: that there are in bodies absolute extensions, without any particular magnitude or figure: that a thing stupid, thoughtless and inactive, operates on a spirit: that the least particle of body, contains innumerable extended parts. These are the novelties, these are the strange notions which shock the genuine uncorrupted judgment of all mankind; and being once admitted, embarrass the mind with endless doubts and difficulties. And it is against these and the like innovations, I endeavor to vindicate common sense. It is true, in doing this, I may perhaps be obliged to use some *ambages,* and ways of speech not common. But if my motions are once thoroughly understood, that which is most singular in them, will in effect be found to amount to no more than this: that it is absolutely impossible, and a plain contradiction to suppose, any unthinking being should exist without being perceived by a mind. And if this notion be singular, it is a shame it should be so at this time of day, and in a Christian country.

Hyl. As for the difficulties other opinions may be liable to, those are out of the question. It is your business to defend your own opinion. Can anything be plainer, than that you are for changing all things into ideas? You, I say, who are not ashamed to charge me with *scepticism.* This is so plain, there is no denying it.

Phil. You mistake me. I am not for changing things into ideas, but rather ideas into things; since those immediate objects of perception, which according to you, are only appearances of things, I take to be the real things themselves.

Hyl. Things! You may pretend what you please; but it is certain, you leave us nothing but the empty forms of things, the outside only which strikes the senses.

Phil. What you call the empty forms and outside of things, seems to me the very things themselves. Nor are they empty or incomplete otherwise, than upon your supposition, that matter is an essential part of all corporeal things. We both therefore agree in this, that we perceive only sensible forms: but herein we differ, you will have them to be empty appearances, I real beings. In short you do not trust your senses, I do.

Hyl. You say you believe your senses; and seem to applaud yourself that in this you agree with the vulgar. According to you therefore, the true nature of a thing is discovered by the senses. If so, whence comes that disagreement? Why is not the same figure, and other sensible qualities, perceived all manner of ways? And why should we use a microscope, the better to discover the true nature of a body, if it were discoverable to the naked eye?

Phil. Strictly speaking, Hylas, we do not see the same object that we feel; neither is the same object perceived by the microscope, which was by the naked eye. But in case every variation was thought sufficient to constitute a new kind or individual, the endless number or confusion of names would render language impracticable. Therefore to avoid this as well as other inconveniences which are obvious upon a little thought, men combine together several ideas, apprehended by divers senses, or by the same sense at different times, or in different circumstances, but observed however to have some connection in nature, either with respect to co-existence or succession; all which they refer to one name, and consider as one thing. Hence it follows that when I examine by my other senses a thing I have seen, it is not in order to understand better the same object which I had perceived by sight, the object of one sense not being perceived by the other senses. And when I look through a microscope, it is not that I may perceive more clearly what I perceived already with my bare eyes, the object perceived by the glass being quite different from the former. But in both cases my aim is only to know what ideas are connected together; and the more a man knows of the connection of ideas, the more he is said to know of the nature of things. What therefore if our ideas are variable; what if our senses are not in all circumstances affected with the same appearances? It will not thence follow, they are not to be trusted, or that they are inconsistent either with themselves or anything else, except it be with your preconceived notion of (I know not what) one single, unchanged, unperceivable, real nature, marked by each name: which prejudice seems to have taken its rise from not rightly understanding the common language of men speaking of several distinct ideas, as united into one thing by the mind. And indeed there is cause to suspect several erroneous conceits of the philosophers are owing to the same original: while they began to build their schemes, not so much on notions as words, which were framed by the vulgar, merely for conveniency and dispatch in the common actions of life, without any regard to speculation.

Hyl. Methinks I apprehend your meaning.

Phil. It is your opinion, the ideas we perceive by our senses are not real things, but images, or copies of them. Our knowledge therefore is no farther real, than as our ideas are the true representations of those originals. But as these supposed originals are in themselves unknown, it is impossible to know how far our ideas resemble them; or whether they resemble them at all. We cannot therefore be sure we have any real knowledge. Farther, as our ideas are perpetually varied, without any change in the supposed real things, it necessarily follows they cannot all be true copies of them: or if some are, and others are not, it is impossible to distinguish the former from the latter. And this plunges us yet deeper in uncertainty. Again, when we consider the point, we cannot conceive how any idea, or anything like an idea, should have an absolute existence out of a mind: nor consequently, according to you, how there should be any real thing in nature. The result of all which is, that we are thrown into the most hopeless and abandoned *scepticism*. Now give me leave to ask you, *first*, whether your referring ideas to certain absolutely existing unperceived substances, as their originals, be not the source of all this *scepticism?* *Secondly*, whether you are informed, either by sense or reason, of the existence of those unknown originals? And in case you are not, whether it be not absurd to suppose them? *Thirdly*, whether, upon inquiry, you find there is anything distinctly conceived or meant by the *absolute or external existence of unperceiving substances?* *Lastly*, whether the premises considered, it be not the wisest way to follow nature, trust your senses, and laying aside all anxious thought about unknown natures or substances, admit with the vulgar those for real things, which are perceived by the senses?

Hyl. For the present, I have no inclination to the answering part. I would much rather see how you can get over what follows. Pray are not the objects perceived by the senses of one, likewise perceivable to others present? If there were an hundred more here, they would all see the garden, the trees, and flowers as I see them. But they are not in the same manner affected with the ideas I frame in my imagination. Does not this make a difference between the former sort of objects and the latter?

Phil. I grant it does. Nor have I ever denied a difference between the objects of sense and those of imagination. But what would you infer from thence? You cannot say that sensible objects exist unperceived, because they are perceived by many.

Hyl. I own I can make nothing of that objection: but it hath led me into another. Is it not your opinion that by our senses we perceive only the ideas existing in our minds?

Phil. It is.

Hyl. But the same idea which is in my mind, cannot be in yours, or in any other mind. Doth it not therefore follow from your principles, that no two can see the same thing? And is not this highly absurd?

Phil. If the term *same* be taken in the vulgar acceptation, it is certain, (and not at all repugnant to the principles I maintain) that different persons may perceive the same thing; or the same thing or idea exist in different minds. Words are of arbitrary imposition; and since men are used to apply the word *same* where no distinction or variety is perceived, and I do not pretend to alter their perceptions, it follows, that as men have said before, *several saw the same thing*, so they may upon like occasions still continue to use the same phrase, without any deviation either from propriety of language, or the truth of things. But if the term *same* be used in the acceptation of philosophers, who pretend to an abstracted notion of identity, then, according to their sundry definitions of this notion, (for it is not yet agreed wherein that philosophic identity consists) it may or may not be possible for divers persons to perceive the same thing. But whether philosophers shall think fit to call a thing the *same* or not, is, I conceive, of small importance. Let us suppose several men together, all endued with the same faculties, and consequently affected in like sort by their senses, and who had yet never known the use of language; they would without question in their perceptions. Though perhaps, when they came to the use of speech, some regarding the uniformness of what was perceived, might call it the *same* thing: others especially regarding the diversity of persons who perceived, might choose the denomination of *different* things. But who sees not that all the dispute is about a word? to wit, whether what is perceived by different persons, may yet have the term *same* applied to it? Or suppose a house, whose walls or outward shell remaining unaltered, the chambers are all pulled down, and new ones built in their place; and that you should call this the *same,* and I should say it was not the *same* house: would we not for all this perfectly agree in our thoughts of the house, considered in itself? And would not all the differences consist in a sound? If you should say, we differed in our notions; for that you superadded to your ideas of the house the simple abstracted idea of identity, whereas I did not; I would tell you I know not what you mean by that *abstracted idea of identity;* and should desire you to look into your own thoughts, and be sure you understood yourself.—Why so silent, Hylas? Are you not yet satisfied, men may dispute about identity and diversity, without any real difference in their thoughts and opinions, abstracted from names? Take this farther reflexion with you: that whether matter be allowed to exist or no, the case is exactly the same as to the point in hand. For the materialists themselves acknowledge what we immediately perceive by our senses, to be our own ideas. Your difficulty therefore, that no two see the same thing, makes equally against the materialists and me.

Hyl. But they suppose an external archetype, to which referring their several ideas, they may truly be said to perceive the same thing.

Phil. And (not to mention your having discarded those archetypes) so may you suppose an external archetype on my principles; *external,* I mean, to your own mind; though indeed it must be supposed to exist in that mind which comprehends all things; but then this serves all the ends of identity, as well as if it existed out of a mind. And I am sure you yourself will not say, it is less intelligible.

Hyl. You have indeed clearly satisfied me, either that there is no difficulty at bottom in this point; or if there be, that it makes equally against both opinions.

Phil. But that which makes equally against two contradictory opinions, can be a proof against neither.

Hyl. I acknowledge it. But after all, Philonous, when I consider the substance of what you advance against *scepticism,* it amounts to no more than this. We are sure that we really see, hear, feel; in a word, that we are affected with sensible impressions.

Phil. And how are we concerned any farther? I see this *cherry,* I feel it, I taste it: and I am sure *nothing* cannot be seen, or felt, or tasted: it is therefore *real.* Take away the sensations of softness, moisture, redness, tartness, and you take away the *cherry.* Since it is not a being distinct from sensations; a *cherry,* I say, is nothing but a congeries of sensible impressions, or ideas perceived by various senses: which ideas are united into one thing (or have one name given them) by the mind; because they are observed to attend each other. Thus when the palate is affected with such a particular taste, the sight is affected with a red color, the touch with roundness, softness, &c. Hence, when I see, and feel, and taste, in such sundry certain manners, I am sure the *cherry* exists, or is real; its reality being in my opinion nothing abstracted from those sensations. But if by the word *cherry* you mean an unknown nature distinct from all those sensible qualities, and by its existence something distinct from its being perceived; then indeed I own, neither you nor I, nor any one else, can be sure it exists.

Hyl. But what would you say, Philonous, if I should bring the very same reasons against the existence of sensible things in a mind, which you have offered against their existing in a material *substratum?*

Phil. When I see your reasons, you shall hear what I have to say to them.

Hyl. Is the mind extended or unextended?

Phil. Unextended, without doubt.

Hyl. Do you say the things you perceive are in your mind?

Phil. They are.

Hyl. Again, have I not heard you speak of sensible impressions?

Phil. I believe you may.

Hyl. Explain to me now, O Philonous! how it is possible there should be room for all those trees and houses to exist in your mind. Can extended things be contained in that which is unextended? Or are we to imagine impressions made on a thing void of all solidity? You cannot say objects are in your mind, as books in your study: or that things are imprinted on it, as the figure of a seal upon wax. In what sense therefore are we to understand those expressions? Explain me this if you can: and I shall then be able to answer all those queries you formerly put to me about my *substratum*.

Phil. Look you, Hylas, when I speak of objects as existing in the mind or imprinted on the senses; I would not be understood in the gross literal sense, as when bodies are said to exist in a place, or a seal to make an impression upon wax. My meaning is only that the mind comprehends or perceives them; and that it is affected from without, or by some being distinct from itself. This is my explication of your difficulty; and how it can serve to make your tenet of an unperceiving material *substratum* intelligible, I would fain know.

Hyl. Nay, if that be all, I confess I do not see what use can be made of it. But are you not guilty of some abuse of language in this?

Phil. None at all: it is no more than common custom, which you know is the rule of language, has authorised: nothing being more usual, than for philosophers to speak of the immediate objects of the understanding as things existing in the mind, Nor is there anything in this, but what is conformable to the general analogy of language; most part of the mental operations being signified by words borrowed from sensible things; as is plain in the terms *comprehend, reflect, discourse, &c.*, which, being applied to the mind, must not be taken in their gross, original sense.

Hyl. You have, I own, satisfied me in this point: but there still remains one great difficulty, which I know not how you will get over. And indeed it is of such importance, that if you could solve all others, without being able to find a solution for this, you must never expect to make me a proselyte to your principles.

Phil. Let me know this mighty difficulty.

Hyl. The Scripture account of the creation, is what appears to me utterly irreconcilable with your notions. Moses tells us of a creation:[5] a creation of what? Of ideas? No, certainly, but of things, of real things, solid corporeal substances. Bring your principles to agree with this, and I shall perhaps agree with you.

Phil. Moses mentions the sun, moon and stars, earth and sea, plants and animals: that all these do really exist, and were in the beginning created by God, I make no question. If by *ideas,* you mean fictions and fancies of the mind, then these are no ideas. If by *ideas* you mean immediate objects of the understanding, or sensible things which cannot exist unperceived, or out of a mind, then these things are ideas. But whether you do, or do not call them *ideas,* it matters little. The difference is only about a name. And whether that name be retained or rejected, the sense, the truth and reality of things continues the same. In common talk, the objects of our senses are not termed *ideas* but *things.* Call them so still: provided you do not attribute to

---

5. [This and subsequent references are to the first chapter of the Book of Genesis.]

them any absolute external existence, and I shall never quarrel with you for a word. The creation therefore I allow to have been a creation of things, of *real* things. Neither is this in the least inconsistent with my principles, as is evident from what I have now said; and would have been evident to you without this, if you had not forgotten what had been so often said before. But as for solid corporeal substances, I desire you to show where Moses makes any mention of them; and if they should be mentioned by him, or any other inspired writer, it would still be incumbent on you to show those words were not taken in the vulgar acceptation for things falling under our senses, but in the philosophic acceptation, for matter, or an unknown quiddity, with an absolute existence. When you have proved these points, then (and not till then) may you bring the authority of Moses into our dispute.

Hyl. It is in vain to dispute about a point so clear. I am content to refer it to your own conscience. Are you not satisfied there is some peculiar repugnancy between the Mosaic account of the creation, and your notions?

Phil. If all possible sense, which can be put on the first chapter of Genesis, may be conceived as consistently with my principles as any other, then it has no peculiar repugnancy with them. But there is no sense you may not as well conceive, believing as I do. Since, beside spirits, all you conceive are ideas; and the existence of these I do not deny. Neither do you pretend they exist without the mind.

Hyl. Pray let me see any sense you can understand it in.

Phil. Why, I imagine that if I had been present at the creation, I should have seen things produced into being; that is, become perceptible, in the order described by the sacred historian. I ever before believed the Mosaic account of the creation, and now find no alteration in my manner of believing it. When things are said to begin or end their existence, we do not mean this with regard to God, but his creatures. All objects are eternally known by God, or, which is the same thing, have an eternal existence in His mind: but when things, before imperceptible to creatures, are, by a decree of God, made perceptible to them; then are they said to begin a relative existence, with respect to created minds. Upon reading therefore the Mosaic account of the creation, I understand that the several parts of the world became gradually perceivable to finite spirits, endowed with proper faculties; so that whoever such were present, they were in truth perceived by them. This is the literal obvious sense suggested to me, by the words of the Holy Scripture: in which is included no mention or no thought, either of *substratum*, instrument, occasion, or absolute existence. And upon inquiry, I doubt not, it will be found, that most plain honest men, who believe the creation, never think of those things any more than I. What metaphysical sense you may understand it in, you only can tell.

Hyl. But, Philonous, you do not seem to be aware, that you allow created things, in the beginning, only a relative, and, consequently, hypothetical, being: that is to say, upon supposition there were men to perceive them, without which they have no actuality of absolute existence, wherein creation might terminate. Is it not therefore according to you plainly impossible, the creation of any inanimate creatures should precede that of man? And is not this directly contrary to the Mosaic account?

Phil. In answer to that I say, *first*, created beings might begin to exist in the mind of other created intelligences, beside men. You will not therefore be able to prove any contradiction between Moses and my notions, unless you first show, there was no other order of finite created spirits in being before man. I say farther, in case we conceive the creation, as we should at this time a parcel of plants or vegetables of all sorts, produced by an invisible power, in a desert where nobody was present: that this way of explaining or conceiving it, is consistent with my principles, since they deprive you of nothing, either sensible or imaginable: that it exactly suits with the common, natural, undebauched notions of mankind: that it manifests the dependence of all things on God; and consequently has all the good effect or influence, which it is possible that important article of our faith should have in making men humble, thankful, and resigned to their creator. I say moreover, that in this naked conception of things, divested of words, there will not be found any notion of what you call the *actuality of absolute existence.* You may indeed raise a dust with those terms, and so lengthen our dispute to no purpose. But I entreat you calmly to look into your own thoughts, and then tell me if they are not an useless and unintelligible jargon.

Hyl. I own, I have no very clear notion annexed to them. But what say you to this? Do you not make the existence of sensible things consist in their being in a mind? And were not all things eternally in the mind of God? Did they not therefore exist from all eternity, according to you? And how could that which was eternal, be created in time? Can anything be clearer or better connected than this?

Phil. And are not you too of opinion, that God knew all things from eternity?

Hyl. I am.

Phil. Consequently they always had a being in the divine intellect.

Hyl. This I acknowledge.

Phil. By your own confession therefore, nothing is new, or begins to be, in respect of the mind of God. So we are agreed in that point.

Hyl. What shall we make then of the creation?

Phil. May we not understand it to have been entirely in respect of finite spirits; so that things, with regard to us, may properly be said to begin their existence, or be created, when God decreed they should become perceptible to intelligent creatures, in that order and manner which he then established, and we now call the laws of nature? You may call this a *relative,* or *hypothetical existence* if you please. But so long as it supplies us with the most natural, obvious, and literal sense of the Mosaic history of the creation; so long as it answers all the religious ends of that great article; in a word, so long as you can assign no other sense or meaning in its stead; why should we reject this? Is it to comply with a ridiculous sceptical humor of making everything nonsense and unintelligible? I am sure you cannot say, it is for the glory of God. For allowing it to be a thing possible and conceivable, that the corporeal world should have an absolute subsistence extrinsical to the mind of God, as well as to the minds of all created spirits: yet how could this set forth either the immensity or omniscience of the Deity, or the necessary and immediate dependence of all things on him? Nay, would it not rather seem to derogate from those attributes?

Hyl. Well, but as to this decree of God's, for making things perceptible: what say you, Philonous, is it not plain, God did either execute that decree from all eternity, or at some certain time began to will what he had not actually willed before, but only designed to will. If the former, then there could be no creation or beginning of existence in finite things. If the latter, then we must acknowledge something new to befall the Deity; which implies a sort of change: and all change argues imperfection.

Phil. Pray consider what you are doing. Is it not evident, this objection concludes equally against a creation in any sense; nay, against every other act of the Deity, discoverable by the light of nature? None of which can we conceive, otherwise than as performed in time, and having a beginning. God is a being of transcendent and unlimited perfections: his nature therefore is incomprehensible to finite spirits. It is not therefore to be expected, that any man, whether *materialist* or *immaterialist,* should have exactly just notions of the Deity, his attributes, and ways of operation. If then you would infer anything against me, your difficulty must not be drawn from the inadequateness of our conceptions of the divine nature, which is unavoidable on any scheme; but from the denial of matter, of which there is not one word, directly or indirectly, in what you have now objected.

Hyl. I must acknowledge, the difficulties you are concerned to clear, are such only as arise from the non-existence of matter, and are peculiar to that notion. So far you are in the right. But I cannot by any means bring myself to think there is no such peculiar repugnancy between the creation and your opinion; though indeed where to fix it, I do not distinctly know.

Phil. What would you have! Do I not acknowledge a twofold state of things, the one ectypal or natural, the other archetypal and eternal? The former was created in time; the latter existed from everlasting in the mind of God. Is not this agreeable to the common notions of divines? Or is any more than this necessary in order to con-ceive the creation? But you suspect some peculiar repugnancy, though you know not where it lies. To take away all possibility of scruple in the case, do but consider this one point. Either you are not able to conceive the creation on any hypothesis what-soever; and if so, there is no ground for dislike or complaint against my particular opinion on that score: or you are able to conceive it; and, if so, why not on my prin-ciples, since thereby nothing conceivable is taken away? You have all along been allowed the full scope of sense, imagination, and reason. Whatever therefore you could before apprehend, either immediately or mediately by your senses, or by ratio-cination from your senses; whatever you could perceive, imagine, or understand, re-mains still with you. If therefore the notion you have of the creation by other prin-ciples be intelligible, you have it still upon mine; if it be not intelligible, I conceive it to be no notion at all; and so there is no loss of it. And indeed it seems to me very plain, that the supposition of matter, that is, a thing perfectly unknown and in-conceivable, cannot serve to make us conceive anything. And I hope, it need not be proved to you, that if the existence of matter doth not make the creation conceivable, the creation's being without it inconceivable, can be no objection against its non-existence.

Hyl. I confess, Philonous, you have almost satisfied me in this point of the creation.

Phil. I would fain know why you are not quite satisfied. You tell me indeed of a repugnancy between the Mosaic history and immaterialism: but you know not where it lies. Is this reasonable, Hylas? Can you expect I should solve a difficulty without knowing what it is? But to pass by all that, would not a man think you were assured there is no repugnancy between the received notions of materialists and the inspired writings?

Hyl. And so I am.

Phil. Ought the historical part of Scripture to be understood in a plain obvious sense, or in a sense which is metaphysical, and out of the way?

Hyl. In the plain sense, doubtless.

Phil. When Moses speaks of herbs, earth, water, &c. as having been created by God; think you not the sensible things, commonly signified by those words, are sug-gested to every unphilosophical reader?

Hyl. I cannot help thinking so.

Phil. And are not all ideas, or things perceived by sense, to be denied a real existence by the doctrine of the materialists?

Hyl. This I have already acknowledged.

Phil. The creation therefore, according to them, was not the creation of things sensible, which have only a relative being, but of certain unknown natures, which have an absolute being, wherein creation might terminate?

Hyl. True.

Phil. Is it not therefore evident, the asserters of matter destroy the plain obvious sense of Moses, with which their notions are utterly inconsistent; and instead of it obtrude on us I know not what, something equally unintelligible to themselves and me?

Hyl. I cannot contradict you.

Phil. Moses tells us of a creation. A creation of what? Of unknown quiddities, of occasions, or *substratums?* No, certainly; but of things obvious to the senses. You must first reconcile this with your notions, if you expect I should be reconciled to them.

Hyl. I see you can assault me with my own weapons.

Phil. Then as to *absolute existence;* was there ever known a more jejune notion than that? Something it is, so abstracted and unintelligible, that you have frankly owned you could not conceive it, much less explain anything by it. But allowing matter to exist, and the notion of absolute existence to be as clear as light; yet was this ever known to make the creation more credible? Nay, has it not furnished the *atheists* and *infidels* of all ages, with the most plausible argument against a creation? That a corporeal substance, which hath an absolute existence without the minds of spirits, should be produced out of nothing by the mere will of a spirit, has been looked upon as a thing so contrary to all reason, so impossible and absurd, that not only the most celebrated among the ancients, but even divers modern and Christian philosphers have thought matter co-eternal with the Deity. Lay these things together, and then judge you whether materialism disposes men to believe the creations of things.

Hyl. I own, Philonous, I think it does not. This of the *creation* is the last objection I can think of; and I must needs own it has been sufficiently answered as well as the rest. Nothing now remains to be overcome, but a sort of unaccountable backwardness that I find in myself toward your notions.

Phil. When a man is swayed, he knows not why, to one side of the question; can this, think you, be anything else but the effect of prejudice, which never fails to attend old and rooted notions? And indeed in this respect I cannot deny the belief of matter to have very much the advantage over the contrary opinion, with men of a learned education.

Hyl. I confess it seems to be as you say.

Phil. As a balance therefore to this weight of prejudice, let us throw into the scale the great advantages that arise from the belief of immaterialism, both in regard to religion and human learning. The being of a God, and incorruptibility of the soul, those great articles of religion, are they not proved with the clearest and most immediate evidence? When I say the being of a *God,* I do not mean an obscure general cause of things, whereof we have no conception, but *God,* in the strict and proper sense of the word. A being whose spirituality, omnipresence, providence, omniscience, infinite power and goodness, are as conspicuous as the existence of sensible things, of which (notwithstanding the fallacious pretences and affected scruples of *sceptics*) there is no more reason to doubt, than of our own being. Then with relation to human sciences; in natural philosophy, what intricacies, what obscurities, what contradictions, has the belief of matter led men into! To say nothing of the numberless disputes about its extent, continuity, homogeneity, gravity, divisibility, &c. do they not pretend to explain all things by bodies operating on bodies, according to the laws of motion? And yet, are they able to comprehend how any one body should move another? Nay, admitting there was no difficulty in reconciling the notion of an inert being with a cause; or in conceiving how an accident might pass from one body to another; yet by all their strained thoughts and extravagant suppositions, have they been able to reach the mechanical production of any one animal or vegetable body? Can they account, by the laws of motion, for sounds, tastes, smells, or colors, or for the regular course of things? Have they accounted by physical principles for the aptitude and contrivance, even of the most inconsiderable parts of the universe? But laying aside matter and corporeal causes, and admitting only the efficiency of an all-perfect mind, are not all the effects of nature easy and intelligible? If the *phenomena* are nothing else but *ideas;* God is a *spirit,* but matter an unintelligent, unperceiving being. If they demonstrate an unlimited power in their cause; God is active and omnipotent, but matter an inert mass. If the order, regularity, and usefulness of them, can never be sufficiently admired; God is infinitely wise and provident, but matter destitute of all contrivance and design. These surely are great advantages in *physics.* Not to mention that the apprehension of a distant deity, naturally disposes men to a negligence in their *moral* actions, which they would be more cautious of, in case they thought him immediately present, and acting on their minds without the interposition of matter, or unthinking second causes. Then in *metaphysics;* what difficulties concerning entity in abstract, substantial forms, hylarchic principles, plastic natures, [substance and accident], principle of individuation, possibility of matter's thinking, origin of ideas, the manner how two independent substances, so widely different as *spirit* and *matter,* should mutually operate on each other? What difficulties, I say, and endless disquisitions concerning these and innumerable other the like points, do we escape by supposing only spirits and ideas? Even the *mathematics* themselves, if we take away the absolute existence of extended things, become much more clear and easy; the most shocking paradoxes and intricate speculations in those sciences, depending on the infinite divisibility of finite extension, which depends on that supposition. But what need is there to insist on the particular sciences? Is not that opposition to all science whatsoever, that frenzy of ancient and modern *sceptics,* built on the same foundation? Or can you produce so much as one argument against the reality of corporeal things, or in behalf of that avowed utter ignorance of their natures, which does not suppose their reality to consist in an external absolute existence? Upon this supposition indeed, the objections from the change of colors in a pigeon's neck, or the appearances of a broken oar in the water, must be allowed to have weight. But those and the like objections vanish, if we do not maintain the being of absolute external originals, but place the reality of things in ideas, fleeting indeed, and changeable; however not changed at random, but according to the fixed order of nature. For herein consists that constancy and truth of things, which secures all the concerns of life, and distinguishes that which is *real* from the irregular visions of the fancy.

Hyl. I agree to all you have now said, and must own that nothing can incline me to embrace your opinion, more than the advantages I see it is attended with. I am by nature lazy; and this would be a mighty abridgment in knowledge. What doubts, what hypotheses, what labyrinths of amusement, what fields of disputation, what an ocean of false learning, may be avoided by that single notion of *immaterialism?*

Phil. After all, is there anything farther remaining to be done? You may remember you promised to embrace that opinion, which upon examination should appear most agreeable to common sense, and remote from *scepticism.* This by your own confession is that which denies matter, or the absolute existence of corporeal things. Nor is this all; the same notion has been proved several ways, viewed in different lights, pursued in its consequences, and all objections against it cleared. Can there be a greater evidence of its truth? Or is it possible it should have all the marks of a true opinion, and yet be false?

Hyl. I own myself entirely satisfied for the present in all respects. But what security can I have that I shall still continue the same full assent to your opinion, and that no unthought-of objection or difficulty will occur hereafter?

Phil. Pray, Hylas, do you in other cases, when a point is once evidently proved, withhold your assent on account of objections or difficulties it may be liable to? Are the difficulties that attend the doctrine of incommensurable quantities, of the angle of contact, of the asymptotes to curves, or the like, sufficient to make you hold out against mathematical demonstration? Or will you disbelieve the providence of God because there may be some particular things which you know not how to reconcile with it? If there are difficulties attending immaterialism, there are at the same time direct and evident proofs for it. But for the existence of matter, there is not one proof, and far more numerous and insurmountable objections lie against it. But where are those mighty difficulties you insist on? Alas! you know not where or what they are; something which may possibly occur hereafter. If this be a sufficient pretence for withholding your full assent, you should never yield it to any proposition, how free soever from exceptions, how clearly and solidly soever demonstrated.

Hyl. You have satisfied me, Philonous.

Phil. But to arm you against all future objections, do but consider, that which bears equally hard on two contradictory opinions, can be a proof against neither. Whenever therefore any difficulty occurs, try if you can find a solution for it on the hypothesis of the *materialists.* Be not deceived by words; but sound your own thoughts. And in case you cannot conceive it easier by the help of *materialism,* it is plain it can be no objection against *immaterialsim.* Had you proceeded all along by this rule, you would probably have spared yourself abundance of trouble in objecting; since of all your difficulties I challenge you to show one that is explained by matter; nay, which is not more unintelligible with than without that supposition, and consequently makes rather *against* than *for* it. You should consider, in each particular, whether the difficulty arises from the *non-existence of matter.* If it does not, you might as well argue from the infinite divisibility of extension against the divine prescience, as from such a difficulty against *immaterialism.* And yet upon recollection I believe you will find this to have been often, if not always, the case. You should likewise take heed not to argue on a *petitio principii.* One is apt to say, the unknown substances ought to be esteemed real things, rather than the ideas in our minds: and who can tell but the unthinking external substance may concur as a cause or instrument in the production of our ideas? But is not this proceeding on a supposition that there are such external substances? And to suppose this, is it not begging the question? But above all things you should beware of imposing on yourself by that vulgar sophism, which is called *ignoratio elenchi.* You talked often as if you thought I maintained the non-existence of sensible things: whereas in truth no one can be more thoroughly assured of their existence than I am: and it is you who doubt; I should have said, positively deny it. Everything that is seen, felt, heard, or any way perceived by the senses, is, on the principles I embrace, a real being, but not on yours. Remember, the matter you contend for is an unknown somewhat, (if indeed it may be termed *somewhat*) which is quite stripped of all sensible qualities, and can neither be perceived by sense, nor apprehended by the mind. Remember, I say, that it is not any object which is hard or soft, hot or cold, blue or white, round or square, &c. For all these things I affirm do exist. Though indeed I deny they have an existence distinct from being perceived; or that they exist out of all minds whatsoever. Think on these points; let them be attentively considered and still kept in view. Otherwise you will not comprehend the state of the question; without which your objections will always be wide of the mark, and instead of mine, may possibly be directed (as more than once they have been) against your own notions.

Hyl. I must needs own, Philonous, nothing seems to have kept me from agreeing with you more than this same *mistaking the question.* In denying matter, at first glimpse I am tempted to imagine you deny the things we see and feel; but upon reflection find there is no ground for it. What think you therefore of retaining the name *matter,* and applying it to sensible things? This may be done without any change in your sentiments: and believe me it would be a means of reconciling them to some persons, who may be more shocked at an innovation in words than in opinion.

Phil. With all my heart: retain the word *matter,* and apply it to the objects of sense, if you please, provided you do not attribute to them any subsistence distinct from their being perceived. I shall never quarrel with you for an expression. *Matter,* or *material substance,* are terms introduced by philosophers; and, as used by them, imply a sort of independency, or a subsistence distinct from being perceived by a mind: but are never used by common people; or if ever, it is to signify the immediate objects of sense. One would think therefore, so long as the names of all particular things, with the terms *sensible, substance, body, stuff,* and the like, are retained, the word *matter* should be never missed in common talk. And in philosophical discourses it seems the best way to leave it quite out; since there is not perhaps any one thing that hath more favored and strengthened the depraved bent of the mind toward atheism, than the use of that general confused term.

Hyl. Well but, Philonous, since I am content to give up the notion of an unthinking substance exterior to the mind, I think you ought not to deny me the privilege of using the word *matter* as I please, and annexing it to a collection of sensible qualities subsisting only in the mind. I freely own there is no other substance, in a strict sense, than *spirit.* But I have been so long accustomed to the term *matter,* that I know not how to part with it. To say, there is no *matter* in the world, is still shocking to me. Whereas to say, there is no *matter,* if by that term be meant an unthinking substance existing without the mind: but if by *matter* is meant some sensible thing, whose existence consists in being perceived, then there is *matter:* this distinction gives it quite another turn: and men will come into your notions with small difficulty, when they are proposed in that manner. For after all, the controversy about *matter* in the strict acceptation of it, lies altogether between you and the philosophers; whose principles, I acknowledge, are not near so natural, or so agreeable to the common sense of mankind, and Holy Scriptures, as yours. There is nothing we either desire or shun, but as it makes, or is apprehended to make, some part of our happiness or misery.

But what has happiness or misery, joy or grief, pleasure or pain, to do with absolute existence, or with unknown entities, abstracted from all relation to us? It is evident, things regard us only as they are pleasing or displeasing: and they can please or displease, only so far forth as they are perceived. Farther therefore we are not concerned; and thus far you leave things as you found them. Yet still there is something new in this doctrine. It is plain, I do not now think with the philosophers, nor yet altogether with the vulgar. I would know how the case stands in that respect: precisely, what you have added to, or altered in my former notions.

Phil. I do not pretend to be a setter-up of *new notions.* My endeavors tend only to unite, and place in a clearer light, that truth which was before shared between the vulgar and the philosophers: the former being of opinion, that *those things they immediately perceive are the real things;* and the latter, that *the things immediately perceived, are ideas which exist only in the mind.* Which two notions put together, do in effect constitute the substance of what I advance.

Hyl. I have been a long time distrusting my senses; methought I saw things by a dim light, and through false glasses. Now the glasses are removed, and a new light breaks in upon my understanding. I am clearly convinced that I see things in their native forms; and am no longer in pain about their unknown natures or absolute existence. This is the state I find myself in at present: though indeed the course that brought me to it, I do not yet thoroughly comprehend. You set out upon the same principles that Academics, Cartesians, and the like sects, usually do; and for a long time it looked as if you were advancing their philosophical *scepticism;* but in the end your conclusions are directly opposite to theirs.

Phil. You see, Hylas, the water of yonder fountain, how it is forced upwards, in a round column, to a certain height; at which it breaks and falls back into the basin from whence it rose: its ascent as well as descent, proceeding from the same uniform law or principle of *gravitation.* Just so, the same principles which at first view lead to *scepticism,* pursued to a certain point, bring men back to common sense.

FINIS

DAVID HUME—engraving by
W. J. Edwards

THE QUADRANGLE, EDINBURGH UNIVERSITY

NINEWELLS, HUME'S FAMILY ESTATE

DAVID HUME

David Hume was born in 1711 in Edinburgh. At the age of fifteen he had completed his education at Edinburgh University, and he began to study law. Three years later, convinced that he had made a major philosophical discovery, he abandoned his legal studies to devote his entire attention to philosophy. In 1739, Hume published his *Treatise of Human Nature* which, in his own words, "fell deadborn from the press." Disappointed by his failure to obtain an audience for his ideas, Hume decided that the style of the *Treatise* was at fault, and in 1748 he published an abbreviated version of Book I of the *Treatise*. This later work, the *Enquiry Concerning Human Understanding,* is reprinted here. Although more successful than the *Treatise* had been, the *Enquiry* was not the popular introduction to his thought that Hume had hoped it would be.

Hume continued to write on philosophical topics, publishing his *Enquiry Concerning the Principles of Morals* in 1751. He also wrote works on political theory, as well as a history of England; in his own lifetime, his fame rested chiefly on these non-philosophical writings. In addition, Hume was employed at various times as a private tutor, a librarian, and a diplomat. A sociable and witty man, he had numerous friends and, at his death in 1776, he was widely mourned. The *Dialogues Concerning Natural Religion* was published posthumously.

Hume's official aim in the *Enquiry* is to investigate the powers of human reason. Yet from its first page, the work has a very definite thrust. A vigorous opponent of superstition, Hume is interested in disclosing the pretensions of traditional metaphysics, which he regards as providing cover for dogmatism and prejudice.

An important weapon in Hume's attack is his distinction between 'relations of ideas' and 'matters of fact.' In some areas of inquiry we establish our conclusions by reasoning deductively from first principles which merely record the meanings we have given to our terms. Arithmetic and geometry are prime examples of fields of this type, sciences in which, according to Hume's theory, we work out the logical consequences of our definitions. However, not all our knowledge is founded on definition and deduction. The laws of nature discovered by physicists and chemists cannot be deduced from definitions, but are established by experiment and observation. Hume points out that we are not able to deduce these laws from statements which record our observations. Rather, our acceptance of them is based on a kind of inference which is more risky than deduction. In a deductive argument the truth of the premises guarantees the truth of the conclusion. But, as Hume notes, our belief that the sun will rise every morning is founded on our past experience; and even though it may be true that the sun has risen every morning of our lives, that evidence does not guarantee the truth of the thesis that the sun will always rise.

Hume poses for us the problem of how we can reasonably accept statements about the entire course of nature. What justifies us in generalizing, from our own limited experience, about principles which allegedly hold true throughout the universe? In response to this question, Hume offers a simple and devastating argument. We cannot find any a priori guarantee for the orderliness of the universe and thus we cannot show a priori that these ordinary inferences are likely to be reliable. Nor, on pain of arguing in a circle, can we appeal to past experience to support the idea that nature is regular, since such appeal would depend on precisely the mode of inference which is here in question.

Hume's own solution to this problem is to claim that there are no rational justifications to be given for our ordinary nondeductive inferences. We make these inferences through the operation of habit, or, as Hume calls it, custom. A similar operation is at work when we make causal judgments. Hume argues that judgments that one event caused another have a complex logical structure. They assert that the earlier event, which we call the cause, is of a type which we find to be regularly followed by events of the type of the effect, and that custom determines us to expect this regular succession. Hume then applies this analysis of causation to the issue of human freedom. He argues that once we have a clear understanding of what is involved in causation, and once we know what is meant by human freedom, we will recognize that there is no inconsistency between the thesis that all human actions are caused and the claim that humans sometimes act freely.

The final sections of the *Enquiry* are concerned with issues in the philosophy of religion, some of which are tackled more thoroughly in the *Dialogues Concerning Natural Religion*. Hume's principal aim is to show that religious debates are futile. Since we cannot reason deductively to conclusions about the nature and existence of God, our reasoning in this area must be nondeductive. Our inferences would thus have to be based on the workings of custom. However, because we have no direct experience of God, custom is unable to operate here, we have no basis for our inferences, and debates or discussions are inevitably fruitless. Hume illustrates this idea in detail, exhibiting the failure of traditional arguments for the existence of God.

Although during his lifetime Hume's philosophical writings were usually ignored or misunderstood, his influence on the course of philosophy and on contemporary philosophical debate has been immense.

A thorough survey of Hume's entire philosophy is Norman Kemp-Smith, *The Philosophy of David Hume* (1941; rpt. London: Macmillan, 1964). Some enlightening essays on a variety of aspects of Hume's philosophy are included in V. C. Chappell, ed., *Hume: A Collection of Critical Essays* (Garden City: Doubleday, 1966). Interesting accounts of Hume's problem of nondeductive inference and the development of the problem from Hume to the present day can be found in Wesley C. Salmon, *The Foundations of Scientific Inference* (Pittsburgh: University of Pittsburgh Press, 1966), and Brian Skyrms, *Choice and Chance: An Introduction to Inductive Logic* (Belmont, Calif.: Dickenson, 1966). An excellent treatment of Hume's questions and solutions is given by Jonathan Bennett in the last four chapters of his *Locke, Berkeley, Hume: Central Themes* (Oxford: Clarendon Press, 1971). Barry Stroud's *Hume* (London: Routledge & Kegan Paul, 1978) provides a systematic and illuminating discussion of Hume's epistemology.

P.S.K.

AN ENQUIRY CONCERNING HUMAN UNDERSTANDING

SECT I. — *Of the Different Species of Philosophy.*

MORAL philosophy,[1] or the science of human nature, may be treated after two different manners; each of which has its peculiar merit, and may contribute to the entertainment, instruction, and reformation of mankind. The one considers man chiefly as born for action; and as influenced in his measures by taste and sentiment; pursuing one object, and avoiding another, according to the value which these objects seem to possess, and according to the light in which they present themselves. As virtue, of all objects, is allowed to be the most valuable, this species of philosophers paint her in the most amiable colours; borrowing all helps from poetry and eloquence, and treating their subject in an easy and obvious manner, and such as is best fitted to please the imagination, and engage the affections. They select the most striking observations and instances from common life; place opposite characters in a proper contrast; and alluring us into the paths of virtue by the views of glory and happiness, direct our steps in these paths by the soundest precepts and most illustrious examples. They make us *feel* the difference between vice and virtue; they excite and regulate our sentiments; and so they can but bend our hearts to the love of probity and true honour, they think, that they have fully attained the end of all their labours.

The other species of philosophers consider man in the light of a reasonable rather than an active being, and endeavour to form his understanding more than cultivate his manners. They regard human nature as a subject of speculation; and with a narrow scrutiny examine it, in order to find those principles, which regulate our understanding, excite our sentiments, and make us approve or blame any particular object, action, or behaviour. They think it a reproach to all literature, that philosophy should not yet have fixed, beyond controversy, the foundation of morals, reasoning, and criticism; and should for ever talk of truth and falsehood, vice and virtue, beauty and deformity, without being able to determine the source of these distinctions. While they attempt this arduous task, they are deterred by no difficulties; but proceeding from particular instances to general principles, they still push on their enquiries to principles more general, and rest not satisfied till they arrive at

The text of the *Enquiry* is a modernized version, edited by Eric Steinberg, of the original 1777 version.

1. [Hume employs the term "moral" in three different senses throughout his writings. In the present case, "moral philosophy" does not mean, as it might for us today, merely the study of our obligations, standards of right and wrong conduct, and the meaning of ethical concepts, but rather includes all those subjects which have a relation to human nature—politics, history, and ethics are typical examples. In this sense, moral philosophy is opposed to natural philosophy or physical science. In addition to the second contemporary sense noted above, Hume often employs "moral" to mean "based on experience or matters of fact," thereby contrasting "moral" with "demonstrative" or "intuitive." For examples of the last sense, see pp. 629, 668 and 695—E.S.]

those original principles, by which, in every science, all human curiosity must be bounded. Though their speculations seem abstract, and even unintelligible to common readers, they aim at the approbation of the learned and the wise; and think themselves sufficiently compensated for the labour of their whole lives, if they can discover some hidden truths, which may contribute to the instruction of posterity.

It is certain that the easy and obvious philosophy will always, with the generality of mankind, have the preference above the accurate and abstruse; and by many will be recommended, not only as more agreeable, but more useful than the other. It enters more into common life; moulds the heart and affections; and, by touching those principles which actuate men, reforms their conduct, and brings them nearer to that model of perfection which it describes. On the contrary, the abstruse philosophy, being founded on a turn of mind, which cannot enter into business and action, vanishes when the philosopher leaves the shade, and comes into open day; nor can its principles easily retain any influence over our conduct and behaviour. The feelings of our heart, the agitation of our passions, the vehemence of our affections, dissipate all its conclusions, and reduce the profound philosopher to a mere plebeian.

This also must be confessed, that the most durable, as well as justest fame, has been acquired by the easy philosophy, and that abstract reasoners seem hitherto to have enjoyed only a momentary reputation, from the caprice or ignorance of their own age, but have not been able to support their renown with more equitable posterity. It is easy for a profound philosopher to commit a mistake in his subtile reasonings; and one mistake is the necessary parent of another, while he pushes on his consequences, and is not deterred from embracing any conclusion, by its unusual appearance, or its contradiction to popular opinion. But a philosopher, who proposes only to represent the common sense of mankind in more beautiful and more engaging colours, if by accident he falls into error, goes no farther; but renewing his appeal to common sense, and the natural sentiments of the mind, returns into the right path, and secures himself from any dangerous illusions. The fame of CICERO[2] flourishes at present; but that of ARISTOTLE is utterly decayed. LA BRUYERE[3] passes the seas, and still maintains his reputation: But the glory of MALEBRANCHE[4] is confined to his own nation, and to his own age. And ADDISON,[5] perhaps, will be read with pleasure, when LOCKE shall be entirely forgotten.

The mere philosopher is a character, which is commonly but little acceptable in the world, as being supposed to contribute nothing either to the advantage of pleasure of society; while he lives remote from communication with mankind, and is wrapped up in principles and notions equally remote from their comprehension. On the other hand, the mere ignorant is still more despised; nor is any thing deemed a surer sign of an illiberal genius in an age and nation where the sciences flourish, than to be entirely destitute of all relish for those noble entertainments. The most perfect character is supposed to lie between those extremes; retaining an equal abil-

2. [See Hobbes's *Leviathan*, n. 11.]

3. [A French author of character sketches and maxims, Jean de La Bruyère (1645–1696) was also a literary critic.]

4. [See Berkeley's *Treatise*, ns. 8, 12.]

5. [Joseph Addison (1672–1719) was an English poet, essayist, and critic.]

ity and taste for books, company, and business; preserving in conversation that discernment and delicacy which arise from polite letters; and in business, that probity and accuracy which are the natural result of a just philosophy. In order to diffuse and cultivate so accomplished a character, nothing can be more useful than compositions of the easy style and manner, which draw not too much from life, require no deep application or retreat to be comprehended, and send back the student among mankind full of noble sentiments and wise precepts, applicable to every exigence of human life. By means of such compositions, virtue becomes amiable, science agreeable, company instructive, and retirement entertaining.

Man is a reasonable being; and as such, receives from science his proper food and nourishment: But so narrow are the bounds of human understanding, that little satisfaction can be hoped for in this particular, either from the extent or security of his acquisitions. Man is a sociable, no less than a reasonable being: But neither can he always enjoy company agreeable and amusing, or preserve the proper relish for them. Man is also an active being; and from that disposition, as well as from the various necessities of human life, must submit to business and occupation: But the mind requires some relaxation, and cannot always support its bent to care and industry. It seems, then, that nature has pointed out a mixed kind of life as most suitble to human race, and secretly admonished them to allow none of these biasses to *draw* too much, so as to incapacitate them for other occupations and entertainments. Indulge your passion for science, says she, but let your science be human, and such as may have a direct reference to action and society. Abstruse thought and profound researches I prohibit, and will severely punish, by the pensive melancholy which they introduce, by the endless uncertainty in which they involve you, and by the cold reception which your pretended discoveries shall meet with, when communicated. Be a philosopher; but, amidst all your philosophy, be still a man.[6]

Were the generality of mankind contented to prefer the easy philosophy to the abstract and profound, without throwing any blame or contempt on the latter, it might not be improper, perhaps, to comply with this general opinion, and allow every man to enjoy, without opposition, his own taste and sentiment. But as the matter is often carried farther, even to the absolute rejecting of all profound reasonings, or what is commonly called *metaphysics*, we shall now proceed to consider what can reasonably be pleaded in their behalf.

We may begin with observing, that one considerable advantage, which results from the accurate and abstract philosophy, is, its subserviency to the easy and humane; which, without the former, can never attain a sufficient degree of exactness in its sentiments, precepts, or reasonings. All polite letters are nothing but pictures of human life in various attitudes and situations; and inspire us with different sentiments, of praise or blame, admiration or ridicule, according to the qualities of the

6. [The preceding two sentences might well refer to Hume himself, as he concluded Book I of the *Treatise of Human Nature*: "But before I launch out into those immense depths of philosophy, which lie before me, I find myself inclined to stop a moment in my present station, and to ponder that voyage, which I have undertaken . . . I am first affrighted and confounded with that forlorn solitude, in which I am placed in my philosophy, and fancy myself some strange uncouth monster, who not being able to mingle and unite in society, has been expelled all human commerce, and left utterly abandoned and disconsolate . . . I have exposed myself to the enmity of all metaphysicians, logicians and mathematicians, and even theologians; and can I wonder at the insults I must suffer. I have declared my disapprobation of their systems; and can I be surprised, if they should express a hatred of mine and of my person." Hume's personal agony was not alleviated by the book's icy reception.]

object, which they set before us. An artist must be better qualified to succeed in this undertaking, who, besides a delicate taste and a quick apprehension, possesses an accurate knowledge of the internal fabric, the operations of the understanding, the workings of the passions, and the various species of sentiment which discriminate vice and virtue. How painful soever this inward search or enquiry may appear, it becomes, in some measure, requisite to those, who would describe with success the obvious and outward appearances of life and manners. The anatomist presents to the eye the most hideous and disagreeable objects; but his science is useful to the painter in delineating even a VENUS or an HELEN. While the latter employs all the richest colours of his art, and gives his figures the most graceful and engaging airs; he must still carry his attention to the inward structure of the human body, the position of the muscles, the fabric of the bones, and the use and figure of every part or organ. Accuracy is, in every case, advantageous to beauty, and just reasoning to delicate sentiment. In vain would we exalt the one by depreciating the other.

Besides, we may observe, in every art or profession, even those which most concern life or action, that a spirit of accuracy, however acquired, carries all of them nearer their perfection, and renders them more subservient to the interests of society. And though a philosopher may live remote from business, the genius of philosophy, if carefully cultivated by several, must gradually diffuse itself throughout the whole society, and bestow a similar correctness on every art and calling. The politician will acquire greater foresight and subtility, in the subdividing and balancing of power; the lawyer more method and finer principles in his reasonings; and the general more regularity in his discipline, and more caution in his plans and operations. The stability of modern governments above the ancient, and the accuracy of modern philosophy, have improved, and probably will still improve, by similar gradations.

Were there no advantage to be reaped from these studies, beyond the gratification of an innocent curiosity, yet ought not even this to be despised; as being one accession to those few safe and harmless pleasures, which are bestowed on human race. The sweetest and most inoffensive path of life leads through the avenues of science and learning; and whoever can either remove any obstructions in this way, or open up any new prospect, ought so far to be esteemed a benefactor to mankind. And though these researches may appear painful and fatiguing, it is with some minds as with some bodies, which being endowed with vigorous and florid health, require severe exercise, and reap a pleasure from what, to the generality of mankind, may seem burdensome and laborious. Obscurity, indeed, is painful to the mind as well as to the eye; but to bring light from obscurity, by whatever labour, must needs be delightful and rejoicing.

But this obscurity in the profound and abstract philosophy, is objected to, not only as painful and fatiguing, but as the inevitable source of uncertainty and error. Here indeed lies the justest and most plausible objection against a considerable part of metaphysics, that they are not properly a science; but arise either from the fruitless efforts of human vanity, which would penetrate into subjects utterly inaccessible to the understanding, or from the craft of popular superstitions, which, being unable to defend themselves on fair ground, raise these entangling brambles to cover and protect their weakness. Chased from the open country, these robbers fly into the forest, and lie in wait to break in upon every unguarded avenue of the mind, and overwhelm it with religious fears and prejudices. The stoutest antagonist, if he remit his watch a moment, is oppressed. And many, through cowardice and folly, open the gates to the enemies, and willingly receive them with reverence and submission, as their legal sovereigns.

But is this a sufficient reason, why philosophers should desist from such researches, and leave superstition still in possession of her retreat? Is it not proper to draw an opposite conclusion, and perceive the necessity of carrying the war into the most secret recesses of the enemy? In vain do we hope, that men, from frequent disappointment, will at last abandon such airy sciences, and discover the proper province of human reason. For, besides, that many persons find too sensible an interest in perpetually recalling such topics; besides this, I say, the motive of blind despair can never reasonably have place in the sciences; since, however unsuccessful former attempts may have proved, there is still room to hope, that the industry, good fortune, or improved sagacity of succeeding generations may reach discoveries unknown to former ages. Each adventurous genius will still leap at the arduous prize, and find himself stimulated, rather than discouraged, by the failures of his predecessors; while he hopes that the glory of achieving so hard an adventure is reserved for him alone. The only method of freeing learning, at once, from these abstruse questions, is to enquire seriously into the nature of human understanding, and show, from an exact analysis of its powers and capacity, that it is by no means fitted for such remote and abstruse subjects. We must submit to this fatigue, in order to live at ease ever after:[7] And must cultivate true metaphysics with some care, in order to destroy the false and adulterate. Indolence, which, to some persons, affords a safeguard against this deceitful philosophy, is, with others, overbalanced by curiosity; and despair, which, at some moments, prevails, may give place afterwards to sanguine hopes and expectations. Accurate and just reasoning is the only catholic remedy, fitted for all persons and all dispositions; and is alone able to subvert that abstruse philosophy and metaphysical jargon, which, being mixed up with popular superstition, renders it in a manner impenetrable to careless reasoners, and gives it the air of science and wisdom.

Besides this advantage of rejecting, after deliberate enquiry, the most uncertain and disagreeable part of learning, there are many positive advantages, which result from an accurate scrutiny into the powers and faculties of human nature. It is remarkable concerning the operations of the mind, that, though most intimately present to us, yet, whenever they become the object of reflection, they seem involved in obscurity; nor can the eye readily find those lines and boundaries, which discriminate and distinguish them. The objects are too fine to remain long in the same aspect or situation; and must be apprehended in an instant, by a superior penetration, derived from nature, and improved by habit and reflection. It becomes, therefore, no inconsiderable part of science barely to know the different operations of the mind, to separate them from each other, to class them under their proper heads, and to correct all that seeming disorder, in which they lie involved, when made the

7. [The preceding two sentences are almost a paraphrase of John Locke's remarks in the Introduction to his *Essay Concerning Human Understanding* (1690): "If by this inquiry into the nature of the understanding, I can discover the powers thereof; how far they reach; to what things they are in any degree proportionate; and where they fail us, I suppose it may be of use to prevail with the busy mind of man to be more cautious in meddling with things exceeding its comprehension; to stop when it is at the utmost extent of its tether and to sit down in a quiet ignorance of those things which, upon examination, are found to be beyond the reach of our capacities."]

object of reflection and enquiry. This task of ordering and distinguishing, which has
no merit, when performed with regard to external bodies, the objects of our senses,
rises in its value, when directed towards the operations of the mind, in proportion to
the difficulty and labour, which we meet with in performing it. And if we can go no
farther than this mental geography, or delineation of the distinct parts and powers
of the mind, it is at least a satisfaction to go so far;[8] and the more obvious this
science may appear (and it is by no means obvious) the more contemptible still must
the ignorance of it be esteemed, in all pretenders to learning and philosophy.

Nor can there remain any suspicion, that this science is uncertain and chimerical;
unless we should entertain such a scepticism as is entirely subversive of all speculation, and even action. It cannot be doubted, that the mind is endowed with several
powers and faculties, that these powers are distinct from each other, that what is
really distinct to the immediate perception may be distinguished by reflection; and
consequently, that there is a truth and falsehood in all propositions on this subject,
and a truth and falsehood, which lie not beyond the compass of human understanding. There are many obvious distinctions of this kind, such as those between the will
and understanding, the imagination and passions, which fall within the comprehension of every human creature; and the finer and more philosophical distinctions are
no less real and certain, though more difficult to be comprehended. Some instances,
especially late ones, of success in these enquiries,[9] may give us a juster notion of the
certainty and solidity of this branch of learning. And shall we esteem it worthy the
labour of a philosopher to give us a true system of the planets, and adjust the position and order of those remote bodies; while we affect to overlook those, who, with
so much success, delineate the parts of the mind, in which we are so intimately concerned?

But may we not hope, that philosophy, if cultivated with care, and encouraged by
the attention of the public, may carry its researches still farther, and discover, at
least in some degree, the secret springs and principles, by which the human mind is
actuated in its operations? Astronomers had long contented themselves with proving, from the phenomena, the true motions, order, and magnitude of the heavenly
bodies: Till a philosopher, at last, arose,[10] who seems, from the happiest reasoning,
to have also determined the laws and forces, by which the revolutions of the planets
are governed and directed. The like has been performed with regard to other parts
of nature. And there is no reason to despair of equal success in our enquiries concerning the mental powers and economy, if prosecuted with equal capacity and caution. It is probable, that one operation and principle of the mind depends on
another; which, again, may be resolved into one more general and universal: And
how far these researches may possibly be carried, it will be difficult for us, before, or

8. [Hume had been more optimistic in the Introduction to the *Treatise of Human Nature:* "In pretending, therefore, to explain the principles of human nature, we in effect propose a complete system of the
sciences, built on a foundation almost entirely new, and the only one upon which they can stand with
any security." For a further illustration of the more subdued tone of the *Enquiry* and its more moderate
claims, see footnote 11.]

9. [In the Introduction to the *Treatise of Human Nature*, Hume had cited John Locke (1632–1704),
Francis Bacon (1561–1626), Joseph Butler (1692–1752), Francis Hutcheson (1694–1746), Bernard
Mandeville (1670–1733), and Lord Shaftesbury (1671–1713) among those who "have begun to put the
science of man on a new footing."]

10. [Sir Isaac Newton (1642–1721]

even after, a careful trial, exactly to determine.[11] This is certain, that attempts of this kind are every day made even by those who philosophize the most negligently: And nothing can be more requisite than to enter upon the enterprise with thorough care and attention; that, if it lie within the compass of human understanding, it may at last be happily achieved; if not, it may, however, be rejected with some confidence and security. This last conclusion, surely, is not desirable; nor ought it to be embraced too rashly. For how much must we diminish from the beauty and value of this species of philosophy, upon such a supposition? Moralists have hitherto been accustomed, when they considered the vast multitude and diversity of those actions that excite our approbation or dislike, to search for some common principle, on which this variety of sentiments might depend. And though they have sometimes carried the matter too far, by their passion for some one general principle; it must, however, be confessed, that they are excusable in expecting to find some general principles, into which all the vices and virtues were justly to be resolved. The like has been the endeavour of critics, logicians, and even politicians: Nor have their attempts been wholly unsuccessful; though perhaps longer time, greater accuracy, and more ardent application may bring these sciences still nearer their perfection. To throw up at once all pretensions of this kind may justly be deemed more rash, precipitate, and dogmatical, than even the boldest and most affirmative philosophy, that has ever attempted to impose its crude dictates and principles on mankind.

What though these reasonings concerning human nature seem abstract, and of difficult comprehension? This affords no presumption of their falsehood. On the contrary, it seems impossible, that what has hitherto escaped so many wise and profound philosophers can be very obvious and easy. And whatever pains these researches may cost us, we may think ourselves sufficiently rewarded, not only in point of profit but of pleasure, if, by that means, we can make any addition to our stock of knowledge, in subjects of such unspeakable importance.

But as, after all, the abstractedness of these speculations is no recommendation, but rather a disadvantage to them, and as this difficulty may perhaps be surmounted by care and art, and the avoiding of all unnecessary detail, we have, in the following enquiry, attempted to throw some light upon subjects, from which uncertainty has hitherto deterred the wise, and obscurity the ignorant. Happy, if we can unite the boundaries of the different species of philosophy, by reconciling profound enquiry with clearness, and truth with novelty! And still more happy, if, reasoning in this easy manner, we can undermine the foundations of an abstruse philosophy, which seems to have hitherto served only as a shelter to superstition, and a cover to absurdity and error!

SECT II. — *Of the Origin of Ideas.*

EVERY one will readily allow, that there is a considerable difference between the perceptions of the mind, when a man feels the pain of excessive heat, or the pleasure

---

11. [Cf. *Treatise of Human Nature,* Introduction, ". . . . we must endeavor to render all our principles as universal as possible, by tracing up our experiments to the utmost, and explaining all effects from the simplest and fewest causes . . . Where experiments of this kind are judiciously collected and compared, we may hope to establish on them a science, which will not be inferior in certainty, and will be much superior in utility to any other of human comprehension."]

of moderate warmth, and when he afterwards recalls to his memory this sensation, or anticipates it by his imagination. These faculties may mimic or copy the perceptions of the senses; but they never can entirely reach the force and vivacity of the original sentiment. The utmost we say of them, even when they operate with greatest vigour, is, that they represent their object in so lively a manner, that we could *almost* say we feel or see it: But, except the mind be disordered by disease or madness, they never can arrive at such a pitch of vivacity, as to render these perceptions altogether undistinguishable. All the colours of poetry, however splendid, can never paint natural objects in such a manner as to make the description be taken for a real landscape. The most lively thought is still inferior to the dullest sensation.

We may observe a like distinction to run though all the other perceptions of the mind. A man in a fit of anger, is actuated in a very different manner from one who only thinks of that emotion. If you tell me, that any person is in love, I easily understand your meaning, and form a just conception of his situation; but never can mistake that conception for the real disorders and agitations of the passion. When we reflect on our past sentiments and affections, our thought is a faithful mirror, and copies its objects truly; but the colours which it employs are faint and dull, in comparison of those in which our original perceptions were clothed. It requires no nice discernment or metaphysical head to mark the distinction between them.

Here therefore we may divide all the perceptions of the mind into two classes or species, which are distinguished by their different degrees of force and vivacity. The less forcible and lively are commonly denominated THOUGHTS or IDEAS. The other species want a name in our language, and in most others; I suppose, because it was not requisite for any, but philosophical purposes, to rank them under a general term or appellation. Let us, therefore, use a little freedom, and call them IMPRESSIONS; employing that word in a sense somewhat different from the usual.[12] By the term *impression*, then, I mean all our more lively perceptions, when we hear, or see, or feel, or love, or hate, or desire, or will. And impressions are distinguished from ideas, which are the less lively perceptions, of which we are conscious, when we reflect on any of those sensations or movements above mentioned.

Nothing, at first view, may seem more unbounded than the thought of man, which not only escapes all human power and authority, but is not even restrained within the limits of nature and reality. To form monsters, and join incongruous shapes and appearances, costs the imagination no more trouble than to conceive the most natural and familiar objects. And while the body is confined to one planet, along which it creeps with pain and difficulty; the thought can in an instant transport us into the most distant regions of the universe; or even beyond the universe, into the unbounded chaos, where nature is supposed to lie in total confusion. What never was seen, or heard of, may yet be conceived; nor is any thing beyond the power of thought, except what implies an absolute contradiction.

But though our thought seems to possess this unbounded liberty, we shall find,

12. [In Hume's time, the term "impression" was commonly employed to refer to a copy or effect produced on the senses or mind by external causes or objects. In this respect, Hume's use is new. For he claims to be employing the term to refer to perceptions, independent of their origin or causal implications concerning their production— "By the term of impression I would not be understood to express the manner in which our lively perceptions are produced in the soul, but merely the perceptions, themselves." *(Treatise* I, 1, 1, note). Because of this new usage, even things which have no representative character, such as emotions and volitions, are included under the heading of impressions.]

upon a nearer examination, that it is really confined within very narrow limits, and that all this creative power of the mind amounts to no more than the faculty of compounding, transposing, augmenting, or diminishing the materials afforded us by the senses and experience. When we think of a golden mountain, we only join two consistent ideas, *gold*, and *mountain*, with which we were formerly acquainted. A virtuous horse we can conceive; because, from our own feeling, we can conceive virtue; and this we may unite to the figure and shape of a horse, which is an animal familiar to us. In short, all the materials of thinking are derived either from our outward or inward sentiment: The mixture and composition of these belongs alone to the mind and will. Or, to express myself in philosophical language, all our ideas or more feeble perceptions are copies of our impressions or more lively ones.

To prove this, the two following arguments will, I hope, be sufficient. First, when we analyse our thoughts or ideas, however compounded or sublime, we always find, that they resolve themselves into such simple ideas as were copied from a precedent feeling or sentiment. Even those ideas, which, at first view, seem the most wide of this origin, are found, upon a nearer scrutiny, to be derived from it. The idea of God, as meaning an infinitely intelligent, wise, and good Being, arises from reflecting on the operations of our own mind, and augmenting, without limit, those qualities of goodness and wisdom. We may prosecute this enquiry to what length we please; where we shall always find, that every idea which we examine is copied from a similar impression. Those who would assert, that this position is not universally true nor without exception, have only one, and that an easy method of refuting it; by producing that idea, which, in their opinion, is not derived from this source. It will then be incumbent on us, if we would maintain our doctrine, to produce the impression or lively perception, which corresponds to it.

Secondly. If it happen, from a defect of the organ, that a man is not susceptible of any species of sensation, we always find, that he is as little susceptible of the correspondent ideas. A blind man can form no notion of colours; a deaf man of sounds. Restore either of them that sense, in which he is deficient; by opening this new inlet for his sensations, you also open an inlet for the ideas; and he finds no difficulty in conceiving these objects. The case is the same, if the object, proper for exciting any sensation, has never been applied to the organ. A LAPLANDER or NEGRO has no notion of the relish of wine. And though there are a few or no instances of a like deficiency in the mind, where a person has never felt or is wholly incapable of a sentiment or passion, that belongs to his species; yet we find the same observation to take place in a less degree. A man of mild manners can form no idea of inveterate revenge or cruelty; nor can a selfish heart easily conceive the heights of friendship and generosity. It is readily allowed, that other beings may possess many senses of which we can have no conception; because the ideas of them have never been introduced to us, in the only manner, by which an idea can have access to the mind, to wit, by the actual feeling and sensation.

There is, however, one contradictory phenomenon, which may prove, that it is not absolutely impossible for ideas to arise, independent of their correspondent impressions. I believe it will readily be allowed, that the several distinct ideas of colour, which enter by the eye, or those of sound, which are conveyed by the ear, are really different from each other; though, at the same time, resembling. Now if this be true of different colours, it must be no less so of the different shades of the same colour; and each shade produces a distinct idea, independent of the rest. For if this should be denied, it is possible, by the continual gradation of shades, to run a colour insensibly into what is most remote from it; and if you will not allow any of the means to be different, you cannot, without absurdity, deny the extremes to be the same. Suppose, therefore, a person to have enjoyed his sight for thirty years, and to have become perfectly acquainted with colours of all kinds, except one particular shade of blue, for instance, which it never has been his fortune to meet with. Let all the different shades of that colour, except that single one, be placed before him, descending gradually from the deepest to the lightest; it is plain, that he will perceive a blank, where that shade is wanting, and will be sensible, that there is a greater distance in that place between the contiguous colours than in any other. Now I ask, whether it be possible for him, from his own imagination, to supply this deficiency, and raise up to himself the idea of that particular shade, though it had never been conveyed to him by his senses? I believe there are few but will be of opinion that he can: And this may serve as a proof, that the simple ideas are not always, in every instance, derived from the correspondent impressions; though this instance is so singular, that it is scarcely worth our observing, and does not merit, that for it alone we should alter our general maxim.

Here, therefore, is a proposition, which not only seems, in itself, simple and intelligible; but, if a proper use were made of it, might render every dispute equally intelligible, and banish all that jargon, which has so long taken possession of metaphysical reasonings, and drawn disgrace upon them. All ideas, especially abstract ones, are naturally faint and obscure: The mind has but a slender hold of them: They are apt to be confounded with other resembling ideas; and when we have often employed any term, though without a distinct meaning, we are apt to imagine it has a determinate idea, annexed to it. On the contrary, all impressions, that is, all sensations, either outward or inward, are strong and vivid: The limits between them are more exactly determined: Nor is it easy to fall into any error or mistake with regard to them. When we entertain, therefore, any suspicion, that a philosophical term is employed without any meaning or idea (as is but too frequent), we need but enquire, *from what impression is that supposed idea derived?* And if it be impossible to assign any, this will serve to confirm our suspicion. By bringing ideas into so clear a light, we may reasonably hope to remove all dispute, which may arise, concerning their nature and reality.[13]

13. It is probable that no more was meant by those, who denied innate ideas, than that all ideas were copies of our impressions; though it must be confessed, that the terms, which they employed, were not chosen with such caution, nor so exactly defined, as to prevent all mistakes about their doctrine. For what is meant by *innate?* If innate be equivalent to natural, then all the perceptions and ideas of the mind must be allowed to be innate or natural, in whatever sense we take the latter word, whether in opposition to what is uncommon, artificial, or miraculous. If by innate be meant, cotemporary to our birth, the dispute seems to be frivolous; nor is it worth while to enquire at what time thinking begins, whether before, at, or after our birth. Again, the word *idea,* seems to be commonly taken in a very loose sense, by *Locke* and others: as standing for any of our perceptions, our sensations and passions, as well as thoughts. Now in this sense, I should desire to know, what can be meant by asserting, that self-love, or resentment of injuries, or the passion between the sexes is not innate?

But admitting these terms, *impressions* and *ideas,* in the sense above explained, and understanding by *innate,* what is original or copied from no precedent perception, then may we assert, that all our impressions are innate, and our ideas not innate.

To be ingenuous, I must own it to be my opinion, that Locke was betrayed into this question by the schoolmen, who, making use of undefined terms, draw out their disputes to a tedious length, without ever touching the point in question. A like ambiguity and circumlocution seem to run through that great philosopher's reasonings on this as well as most other subjects.

[In Book I of the *Essay Concerning Human Understanding,* Locke had attacked the theory of innate ideas and contended that the mind is a *tabula rasa* or blank slate at birth.]

SECT. III. — *Of the Association of Ideas.*

IT is evident, that there is a principle of connexion between the different thoughts or ideas of the mind, and that, in their appearance to the memory or imagination, they introduce each other with a certain degree of method and regularity. In our more serious thinking or discourse, this is so observable, that any particular thought, which breaks in upon the regular tract or chain of ideas, is immediately re-marked and rejected. And even in our wildest and most wandering reveries, nay in our very dreams, we shall find, if we reflect, that the imagination ran not altogether at adventures, but that there was still a connexion upheld among the different ideas, which succeeded each other. Were the loosest and freest conversation to be trans-cribed, there would immediately be observed something, which connected it in all its transitions. Or where this is wanting, the person, who broke the thread of dis-course, might still inform you, that there had secretly revolved in his mind a succes-sion of thought, which had gradually led him from the subject of conversation. Among different languages, even where we cannot suspect the least connexion or communication, it is found, that the words, expressive of ideas, the most com-pounded, do yet nearly correspond to each other: A certain proof, that the simple ideas, comprehended in the compound ones, were bound together by some univer-sal principle, which had an equal influence on all mankind.

Though it be too obvious to escape observation, that different ideas are con-nected together; I do not find, that any philosopher has attempted to enumerate or class all the principles of association; a subject, however, that seems worthy of curiosity. To me, there appear to be only three principles of connexion among ideas, namely, *Resemblance, Contiguity* in time or place, and *Cause* or *Effect.*

That these principles serve to connect ideas will not, I believe, be much doubted. A picture naturally leads our thoughts to the original:[14] The mention of one apart-ment in a building naturally introduces an enquiry or discourse concerning the others:[15] And if we think of a wound, we can scarcely forbear reflecting on the pain which follows it.[16] But that this enumeration is complete, and that there are no other principles of association, except these, may be difficult to prove to the satisfac-tion of the reader, or even to a man's own satisfaction. All we can do, in such cases, is to run over several instances, and examine carefully the principle, which binds the different thoughts to each other, never stopping till we render the principle as general as possible.[17] The more instances we examine, and the more care we employ, the more assurance shall we acquire, that the enumeration, which we form from the whole, is complete and entire.

14. Resemblance.

15. Contiguity.

16. Cause and Effect.

17. For instance, *Contrast* or *Contrariety* is also a connexion among Ideas: But it may, perhaps, be con-sidered as a mixture of *Causation* and *Resemblance.* Where two objects are contrary, the one destroys the other; that is, the cause of its annihilation, and the idea of the annihilation of an object, implies the idea of its former existence.

SECT. IV.— *Sceptical Doubts concerning the Operations of the Understanding.*

PART I.

ALL the objects of human reason or enquiry may naturally be divided into two kinds, to wit, *Relations of Ideas,* and *Matters of Fact.* Of the first kind are the sciences of Geometry, Algebra, and Arithmetic; and in short, every affirmation, which is either intuitively or demonstratively certain. *That the square of the hypothenuse is equal to the square of the two sides,* is a proposition, which expresses a relation between these figures. *That three times five is equal to the half of thirty,* expresses a relation between these numbers. Propositions of this kind are discoverable by the mere operation of thought, without dependence on what is any where existent in the universe. Though there never were a circle or triangle in nature, the truths, demonstrated by EUCLID, would for ever retain their certainty and evidence.

Matters of fact, which are the second objects of human reason, are not ascertained in the same manner; nor is our evidence of their truth, however great, of a like nature with the foregoing. The contrary of every matter of fact is still possible; because it can never imply a contradiction, and is conceived by the mind with the same facility and distinctness, as if ever so conformable to reality. *That the sun will not rise to-morrow* is no less intelligible a proposition, and implies no more contradiction, than the affirmation, *that it will rise.* We should in vain, therefore, attempt to demonstrate its falsehood. Were it demonstratively false, it would imply a contradiction, and could never be distinctly conceived by the mind.[18]

It may, therefore, be a subject worthy of curiosity, to enquire what is the nature of that evidence, which assures us of any real existence and matter of fact, beyond the present testimony of our senses, or the records of our memory. This part of philosophy, it is observable, has been little cultivated, either by the ancients or moderns; and therefore our doubts and errors, in the prosecution of so important an enquiry, may be the more excusable; while we march through such difficult paths, without any guide or direction. They may even prove useful, by exciting curiosity, and destroying that implicit faith and security, which is the bane of all reasoning and free enquiry. The discovery of defects in the common philosophy, if any such there be, will not, I presume, be a discouragement, but rather an incitement, as is usual, to attempt something more full and satisfactory, than has yet been proposed to the public.

All reasonings concerning matter of fact seem to be founded on the relation of *Cause and Effect.* By means of that relation alone we can go beyond the evidence of our memory and senses. If you were to ask a man, why he believes any matter of

---

18. [Compare the distinction between "relations of ideas" and "matters of fact" with the distinction between two kinds of relations discussed in the *Treatise* I, 3. 1. "Relations may be divided into two classes; into such as depend entirely on the ideas, which we compare together, and such as may be changed without any change in the ideas. 'Tis from the idea of a triangle, that we discover the relation of equality, which its three angles bear to two right ones; and this relation is invariable, as long as our idea remains the same. On the contrary, the relations of *contiguity* and *distance* betwixt two objects may be changed merely by an alteration of their place, without any change on the objects themselves or on their ideas." It is significant to note that although geometry is included in the list of disciplines dealing with "relations of ideas", in editions of the *Enquiry* prior to 1756, the following footnote appeared in Section XII: "In general, we may pronounce, that the ideas of *greater, less,* or *equal,* which are the chief objects of geometry, are far from being so exact or determinate as to be the foundation of such extraordinary inferences. . . ."]

fact, which is absent; for instance, that his friend is in the country, or in FRANCE; he would give you a reason; and this reason would be some other fact; as a letter received from him, or the knowledge of his former resolutions and promises. A man, finding a watch or any other machine in a desert island, would conclude, that there had once been men in that island. All our reasonings concerning fact are of the same nature. And here it is constantly supposed, that there is a connexion between the present fact and that which is inferred from it. Were there nothing to bind them together, the inference would be entirely precarious. The hearing of an articulate voice and rational discourse in the dark assures us of the presence of some person: Why? because these are the effects of the human make and fabric, and closely connected with it. If we anatomize all the other reasonings of this nature, we shall find, that they are founded on the relation of cause and effect, and that this relation is either near or remote, direct or collateral. Heat and light are collateral effects of fire, and the one effect may justly be inferred from the other.

If we would satisfy ourselves, therefore, concerning the nature of that evidence, which assures us of matters of fact, we must enquire how we arrive at the knowledge of cause and effect.

I shall venture to affirm, as a general proposition, which admits of no exception, that the knowledge of this relation is not, in any instance, attained by reasonings *a priori*; but arises entirely from experience, when we find, that any particular objects are constantly conjoined with each other. Let an object be presented to a man of ever so strong natural reason and abilities; if that object be entirely new to him, he will not be able, by the most accurate examination of its sensible qualities, to discover any of its causes or effects. ADAM, though his rational faculties be supposed, at the very first, entirely perfect, could not have inferred from the fluidity, and transparency of water, that it would suffocate him, or from the light and warmth of fire, that it would consume him. No object ever discovers, by the qualities which appear to the senses, either the causes which produced it, or the effects which will arise from it; nor can our reason, unassisted by experience, ever draw any inference concerning real existence and matter of fact.

This proposition, *that causes and effects are discoverable, not by reason, but by experience,* will readily be admitted with regard to such objects, as we remember to have once been altogether unknown to us; since we must be conscious of the utter inability, which we then lay under, of foretelling, what would arise from them. Present two smooth pieces of marble to a man, who has no tincture of natural philosophy; he will never discover, that they will adhere together, in such a manner as to require great force to separate them in a direct line, while they make so small a resistance to a lateral pressure. Such events, as bear little analogy to the common course of nature, are also readily confessed to be known only by experience; nor does any man imagine that the explosion of gunpowder, or the attraction of a loadstone, could ever be discovered by arguments *a priori*. In like manner, when an effect is supposed to depend upon an intricate machinery or secret structure of parts, we make no difficulty in attributing all our knowledge of it to experience. Who will assert, that he can give the ultimate reason, why milk or bread is proper nourishment for a man, not for a lion or a tiger?

But the same truth may not appear, at first sight, to have the same evidence with regard to events, which have become familiar to us from our first appearance in the world, which bear a close analogy to tbe whole course of nature, and which are supposed to depend on the simple qualities of objects, without any secret structure of parts. We are apt to imagine, that we could discover these effects by the mere operation of our reason, without experience. We fancy, that were we brought, on a sudden, into this world, we could at first have inferred, that one Billiard-ball would commmunicate motion to another upon impulse; and that we needed not to have waited for the event, in order to pronounce with certainty concerning it. Such is the influence of custom, that, where it is strongest, it not only covers our natural ignorance, but even conceals itself, and seems not to take place, merely because it is found in the highest degree.

But to convince us, that all the laws of nature, and all the operations of bodies without exception, are known only by experience, the following reflections may, perhaps, suffice. Were any object presented to us, and were we required to pronounce concerning the effect, which will result from it, without consulting past observation; after what manner, I beseech you, must the mind proceed in this operation? It must invent or imagine some event, which it ascribes to the object as its effect; and it is plain that this invention must be entirely arbitrary. The mind can never possibly find the effect in the supposed cause, by the most accurate scrutiny and examination. For the effect is totally different from the cause, and consequently can never be discovered in it. Motion in the second Billiard-ball is a quite distinct event from motion in the first; nor is there any thing in the one to suggest the smallest hint of the other. A stone or piece of metal raised into the air, and left without any support, immediately falls: But to consider the matter *a priori*, is there any thing we discover in this situation, which can beget the idea of a downward, rather than an upward, or any other motion, in the stone or metal?

And as the first imagination or invention of a particular effect, in all natural operations, is arbitrary, where we consult not experience; so must we also esteem the supposed tie or connexion between the cause and effect, which binds them together, and renders it impossible, that any other effect could result from the operation of that cause. When I see, for instance, a Billiard-ball moving in a straight line towards another; even suppose motion in the second ball should by accident be suggested to me, as the result of their contact or impulse; may I not conceive, that a hundred different events might as well follow from that cause? May not both these balls remain at absolute rest? May not the first ball return in a straight line, or leap off from the second in any line or direction? All the suppositions are consistent and conceivable. Why then should we give the preference to one, which is no more consistent or conceivable than the rest? All our reasonings *a priori* will never be able to show us any foundation for this preference.

In a word, then, every effect is a distinct event from its cause. It could not, therefore, be discovered in the cause, and the first invention or conception of it, *a priori*, must be entirely arbitrary. And even after it is suggested, the conjunction of it with the cause must appear equally arbitrary; since there are always many other effects, which, to reason, must seem fully as consistent and natural. In vain, therefore, should we pretend to determine any single event, or infer any cause or effect, without the assistance of observation and experience.

Hence we may discover the reason, why no philosopher, who is rational and modest, has ever pretended to assign the ultimate cause of any natural operation, or to show distinctly the action of that power, which produces any single effect in the universe. It is confessed, that the utmost effort of human reason is, to reduce the principles, productive of natural phenomena, to a greater simplicity, and to resolve the many particular effects into a few general causes, by means of reasonings from analogy, experience, and observation. But as to the causes of these general causes,[19] we should in vain attempt their discovery; nor shall we ever be able to satisfy ourselves, by any particular explication of them. These ultimate springs and principles are totally shut up from human curiosity and enquiry. Elasticity, gravity, cohesion of parts, communication of motion by impulse; these are probably the ultimate causes and principles which we shall ever discover in nature; and we may esteem ourselves sufficiently happy, if, by accurate enquiry and reasoning, we can trace up the particular phenomena to, or near to, these general principles. The most perfect philosophy of the natural kind only staves off our ignorance a little longer: As perhaps the most perfect philosophy of the moral or metaphysical kind serves only to discover larger portions of it. Thus the observation of human blindness and weakness is the result of all philosophy, and meets us, at every turn, in spite of our endeavours to elude or avoid it.

Nor is geometry, when taken into the assistance of natural philosophy, ever able to remedy this effect, or lead us into the knowledge of ultimate causes, by all that accuracy of reasoning, for which it is so justly celebrated. Every part of mixed mathematics[20] proceeds upon the supposition, that certain laws are established by nature in her operations; and abstract reasonings are employed, either to assist experience in the discovery of these laws, or to determine their influence in particular instances, where it depends upon any precise degree of distance and quantity. Thus, it is a law of motion, discovered by experience, that the moment or force of any body in motion is in the compound ratio or proportion of its solid contents and its velocity; and consequently, that a small force may remove the greatest obstacle or raise the greatest weight, if, by any contrivance or machinery, we can increase the velocity of that force, so as to make it an overmatch for its antagonist. Geometry assists us in the application of this law, by giving us the just dimensions of all the parts and figures, which can enter into any species of machine; but still the discovery of the law itself is owing merely to experience, and all the abstract reasonings in the world could never lead us one step towards the knowledge of it. When we reason *a priori*, and consider merely any object or cause, as it appears to the mind, independent of all observation, it never could suggest to us the notion of any distinct object, such as its effect; much less, show us the inseparable and inviolable connection between them. A man must be very sagacious, who could discover by reasoning, that crystal is the effect of heat, and ice of cold, without being previously acquainted with the operation of these qualities.

PART II.

But we have not, yet, attained any tolerable satisfaction with regard to the question first proposed. Each solution still gives rise to a new question as difficult as the foregoing, and leads us on to farther enquiries. When it is asked, *What is the nature of*

---

19. [Compare with p. 633.]

20. [For Hume, "mixed mathematics" is equivalent to what would today be called "applied mathematics", or the application of mathematics or mathematical principles to the physical world and experience, as, for instance, in astronomy, surveying, or the calculation of probabilities.]

all our reasonings concerning matter of fact? the proper answer seems to be, that they are founded on the relation of cause and effect. When again it is asked, *What is the foundation of all our reasonings and conclusions concerning that relation?* it may be replied in one word, EXPERIENCE. But if we still carry on our sifting humour, and ask, *What is the foundation of all conclusions from experience?* this implies a new question, which may be of more difficult solution and explication. Philosophers, that give themselves airs of superior wisdom and sufficiency, have a hard task, when they encounter persons of inquisitive dispositions, who push them from every corner, to which they retreat, and who are sure at last to bring them to some dangerous dilemma. The best expedient to prevent this confusion, is to be modest in our pretensions; and even to discover the difficulty ourselves before it is objected to us. By this means, we may make a kind of merit of our very ignorance.

I shall content myself, in this section, with an easy task, and shall pretend only to give a negative answer to the question here proposed. I say then, that, even after we have experience of the operations of cause and effect, our conclusions from that experience are *not* founded on reasoning, or any process of the understanding. This answer we must endeavour, both to explain and to defend.

It must certainly be allowed, that nature has kept us at a great distance from all her secrets, and has afforded us only the knowledge of a few superficial qualities of objects; while she conceals from us those powers and principles, on which the influence of these objects entirely depends. Our senses inform us of the colour, weight, and consistence of bread; but neither sense nor reason can ever inform us of those qualities, which fit it for the nourishment and support of a human body. Sight or feeling conveys an idea of the actual motion of bodies; but as to that wonderful force or power, which would carry on a moving body for ever in a continued change of place, and which bodies never lose but by communicating it to others; of this we cannot form the most distant conception. But notwithstanding this ignorance of natural powers[21] and principles, we always presume, when we see like sensible qualities, that they have like secret powers, and expect, that effects, similar to those which we have experienced, will follow from them. If a body of like colour and consistence with that bread, which we have formerly eat, be presented to us, we make no scruple of repeating the experiment, and foresee, with certainty, like nourishment and support. Now this is a process of the mind or thought, of which I would willingly know the foundation. It is allowed on all hands, that there is no known connexion between the sensible qualities and the secret powers; and consequently, that the mind is not led to form such a conclusion concerning their constant and regular conjunction, by any thing which it knows of their nature. As to past *Experience*, it can be allowed to give *direct* and *certain* information of those precise objects only, and that precise period of time, which fell under its cognizance: But why this experience should be extended to future times, and to other objects, which for aught we know, may be only in appearance similar; this is the main question on which I would insist. The bread, which I formerly eat, nourished me; that is, a body of such sensible qualities, was, at that time, endued with such secret powers: But does it follow, that other bread must also nourish me at another time, and that like

---

21. ["Power" is used loosely, in a popular sense. A more detailed explanation of the word would lend strength to the argument. See Sect. VII.]

sensible qualities must always be attended with like secret powers? The consequence seems nowise necessary. At least, it must be acknowledged, that there is here a consequence drawn by the mind; that there is a certain step taken; a process of thought, and an inference, which wants to be explained. These two propositions are far from being the same, *I have found that such an object has always been attended with such an effect,* and *I foresee, that other objects, which are, in appearance, similar, will be attended with similar effects.* I shall allow, if you please, that the one proposition may justly be inferred from the other: I know in fact, that it always is inferred. But if you insist, that the inference is made by a chain of reasoning, I desire you to produce that reasoning. The connexion between these propositions is not intuitive. There is required a medium, which may enable the mind to draw such an inference, if indeed it be drawn by reasoning and argument. What that medium is, I must confess, passes my comprehension; and it is incumbent on those to produce it, who assert, that it really exists, and is the origin of all our conclusions concerning matter of fact.

This negative argument must certainly, in process of time, become altogether convincing, if many penetrating and able philosophers shall turn their enquiries this way; and no one be ever able to discover any connecting proposition or intermediate step, which supports the understanding in this conclusion. But as the question is yet new, every reader may not trust so far to his own penetration, as to conclude, because an argument escapes his enquiry, that therefore it does not really exist. For this reason it may be requisite to venture upon a more difficult task; and enumerating all the branches of human knowledge, endeavour to show, that none of them can afford such an argument.

All reasonings may be divided into two kinds, namely demonstrative reasoning, or that concerning relations of ideas, and moral reasoning, or that concerning matter of fact and existence. That there are no demonstrative arguments in the case, seems evident; since it implies no contradiction, that the course of nature may change, and that an object, seemingly like those which we have experienced, may be attended with different or contrary effects. May I not clearly and distinctly conceive, that a body, falling from the clouds, and which, in all other respects, resembles snow, has yet the taste of salt or feeling of fire? Is there any more intelligible proposition than to affirm, that all the trees will flourish in DECEMBER and JANUARY, and decay in MAY and JUNE? Now whatever is intelligible, and can be distinctly conceived, implies no contradiction, and can never be proved false by any demonstrative argument or abstract reasoning *a priori.*

If we be, therefore, engaged by arguments to put trust in past experience, and make it the standard of our future judgment, these arguments must be probable only, or such as regard matter of fact and real existence, according to the division above mentioned. But that there is no argument of this kind, must appear, if our explication of that species of reasoning be admitted as solid and satisfactory. We have said, that all arguments concerning existence are founded on the relation of cause and effect; that our knowledge of that relation is derived entirely from experience; and that all our experimental conclusions proceed upon the supposition, that the future will be conformable to the past. To endeavour, therefore, the proof of this last supposition by probable arguments, or arguments regarding existence, must be evidently going in a circle, and taking that for granted, which is the very point in question.

In reality, all arguments from experience are founded on the similarity, which we discover among natural objects, and by which we are induced to expect effects similar to those, which we have found to follow from such objects. And though none but a fool or madman will ever pretend to dispute the authority of experience, or to reject that great guide of human life; it may surely be allowed a philosopher to have so much curiosity at least, as to examine the principle of human nature, which gives this mighty authority to experience, and makes us draw advantage from that similarity, which nature has placed among different objects. From causes, which appear *similar*, we expect similar effects. This is the sum of all our experimental conclusions. Now it seems evident, that, if this conclusion were formed by reason, it would be as perfect at first, and upon one instance, as after ever so long a course of experience. But the case is far otherwise. Nothing so like as eggs; yet no one, on account of this appearing similarity, expects the same taste and relish in all of them. It is only after a long course of uniform experiments in any kind, that we attain a firm reliance and security with regard to a particular event. Now where is that process of reasoning, which, from one instance, draws a conclusion, so different from that which it infers from a hundred instances, that are nowise different from that single one? This question I propose as much for the sake of information, as with an intention of raising difficulties. I cannot find, I cannot imagine any such reasoning. But I keep my mind still open to instruction, if any one will vouchsafe to bestow it on me.

Should it be said, that, from a number of uniform experiments, we *infer* a connexion between the sensible qualities and the secret powers; this, I must confess, seems the same difficulty, couched in different terms. The question still recurs, on what process of argument this *inference* is founded? Where is the medium, the interposing ideas, which join propositions so very wide of each other? It is confessed, that the colour, consistence, and other sensible qualities of bread appear not, of themselves, to have any connexion with the secret powers of nourishment and support. For otherwise we could infer these secret powers from the first appearance of these sensible qualities, without the aid of experience; contrary to the sentiment of all philosophers, and contrary to plain matter of fact. Here then is our natural state of ignorance with regard to the powers and influence of all objects. How is this remedied by experience? It only shows us a number of uniform effects, resulting from certain objects, and teaches us, that those particular objects, at that particular time, were endowed with such powers and forces. When a new object, endowed with similar sensible qualities, is produced, we expect similar powers and forces, and look for a like effect. From a body of like colour and consistence with bread, we expect like nourishment and support. But this surely is a step or progress of the mind, which wants to be explained. When a man says, *I have found, in all past instances, such sensible qualities conjoined with such secret powers:* And when he says, *similar sensible qualities will always be conjoined with similar secret powers;* he is not guilty of a tautology, nor are these propositions in any respect the same. You say that the one proposition is an inference from the other. But you must confess that the inference is not intuitive; neither is it demonstrative: Of what nature is it then? To say it is experimental, is begging the question. For all inferences from experience suppose, as their foundation, that the future will resemble the past, and that similar powers will be conjoined with similar sensible qualities. If there be any suspicion, that the course of nature may change, and that the past may be no rule for the future, all experience becomes useless, and can give rise to no inference or conclusion. It is impossible, therefore, that any arguments from experience can prove this resemblance of the past to the future; since all these arguments are founded on the supposition of that resemblance. Let the course of things be allowed hitherto ever so regular; that alone, without some new argument or inference, proves not, that, for the future, it will continue so. In vain do you pretend to have learned the nature of bodies from your past experience. Their secret nature, and consequently, all their effects and influence, may change, without any change in their sensible qualities. This happens sometimes, and with regard to some objects: Why may it not happen always, and with regard to all objects? What logic, what process of argument secures you against this supposition? My practice, you say, refutes my doubts. But you mistake the purport of my question. As an agent, I am quite satisfied in the point; but as a philosopher, who has some share of curiosity, I will not say scepticism, I want to learn the foundation of this inference. No reading, no enquiry has yet been able to remove my difficulty, or give me satisfaction in a matter of such importance. Can I do better than propose the difficulty to the public, even though, perhaps, I have small hopes obtaining a solution? We shall at least, by this means, be sensible of our ignorance, if we do not augment our knowledge.

I must confess, that a man is guilty of unpardonable arrogance, who concludes, because an argument has escaped his own investigation, that therefore it does not really exist. I must also confess, that, though all the learned, for several ages, should have employed themselves in fruitless search upon any subject, it may still, perhaps, be rash to conclude positively, that the subject must, therefore, pass all human comprehension. Even though we examine all the sources of our knowledge, and conclude them unfit for such a subject, there may still remain a suspicion, that the enumeration is not complete, or the examination not accurate. But with regard to the present subject, there are some considerations, which seem to remove all this accusation of arrogance or suspicion of mistake.

It is certain, that the most ignorant and stupid peasants, nay infants, nay even brute beasts, improve by experience, and learn the qualities of natural objects, by observing the effects, which result from them. When a child has felt the sensation of pain from touching the flame of a candle, he will be careful not to put his hand near any candle; but will expect a similar effect from a cause, which is similar in its sensible qualities and appearance. If you assert, therefore, that the understanding of the child is led into this conclusion by any process of argument or ratiocination, I may justly require you to produce that argument; nor have you any pretence to refuse so equitable a demand. You cannot say, that the argument is abstruse, and may possibly escape your enquiry; since you confess, that it is obvious to the capacity of a mere infant. If you hesitate, therefore, a moment, or if, after reflection, you produce any intricate or profound argument, you, in a manner, give up the question, and confess, that it is not reasoning which engages us to suppose the past resembling the future, and to expect similar effects from causes, which are, to appearance, similar. This is the proposition which I intended to enforce in the present section. If I be right, I pretend not to have made any mighty discovery. And if I be wrong, I must acknowledge myself to be indeed a very backward scholar; since I cannot now discover an argument, which, it seems, was perfectly familiar to me, long before I was out of my cradle.

SECT. V. — *Sceptical Solution of these Doubts.*

PART I.

The passion for philosophy, like that for religion, seems liable to this inconvenience, that, though it aims at the correction of our manners, and extirpation of our vices, it may only serve, by imprudent management, to foster a predominant inclination, and push the mind, with more determined resolution, towards that side, which already *draws* too much, by the biass and propensity of the natural temper. It is certain, that, while we aspire to the magnanimous firmness of the philosophic sage, and endeavour to confine our pleasures altogether within our own minds, we may, at last, render our philosophy like that of EPICTETUS, and other *Stoics,*[22] only a more refined system of selfishness, and reason ourselves out of all virtue, as well as social enjoyment. While we study with attention the vanity of human life, and turn all our thoughts towards the empty and transitory nature of riches and honours, we are, perhaps, all the while, flattering our natural indolence, which, hating the bustle of the world, and drudgery of business, seeks a pretence of reason, to give itself a full and uncontrolled indulgence. There is, however, one species of philosophy, which seems little liable to this inconvenience, and that because it strikes in with no disorderly passion of the human mind, nor can mingle itself with any natural affection or propensity; and that is the ACADEMIC or SCEPTICAL philosophy.[23] The academics always talk of doubt and suspense of judgment, of danger in hasty determinations, of confining to very narrow bounds the enquiries of the understanding, and of renouncing all speculations which lie not within the limits of common life and practice. Nothing, therefore, can be more contrary than such a philosophy to the supine indolence of the mind, its rash arrogance, its lofty pretensions, and its superstitious credulity. Every passion is mortified by it, except the love of truth; and that passion never is, nor can be carried to too high a degree. It is surprising, therefore, that this philosophy, which, in almost every instance, must be harmless and innocent, should be the subject of so much groundless reproach and obloquy. But, perhaps, the very circumstance, which renders it so innocent, is what chiefly exposes it to the public hatred and resentment. By flattering no irregular passion, it gains few partizans: By

22. [Stoicism, the school of philosophy that spanned at least five centuries, from the third century B.C. to the second century A.D., had as its main ethical tenet that man must live in harmony with nature; nature is construed as inherently rational and man must be rational as well. Epictetus (c.50–c.130 A.D.), an illustrious later Stoic, maintained that living in harmony with nature is a matter of distinguishing those things within our power from those which are not, and seeking to control only the former. This involves purging oneself of desires and strong feelings concerning the latter. As Epictetus noted, "Men are disturbed not by things, but by the view which they take of things" (*Enchiridion* V).]

23. [Academical or skeptical philosophy, the title of Section XII of the *Enquiry,* refers to the philosophy of the Greek Academy founded by Plato, more specifically, to the philosophy of the Academy in the second and third centuries B.C., in which a form of moderate skepticism reputedly was espoused. For example, Carneades (c.213–128 B.C.), one of the leading members of the school, is said to have challenged Stoic doctrines concerning the infallibility of our perceptions and claimed that no perception is infallible or an object of knowledge. All we can be sure of is the nature of the "appearances". Still, the academic skeptics, unlike the Pyrrhonians (see footnote 84), formulated a theory of credible belief according to which some things are more probable than others, and did not advocate a suspension of judgment on all things. Hume is often taken to be advocating a theory of academic or moderate skepticism in the *Enquiry.* For a further discussion of this topic, see Richard H. Popkin, "David Hume: His Pyrrhonism and his Critique of Pyrrhonism" in *Hume;* edited by V.C. Chappell (South Bend, Indiana: 1968).]

opposing so many vices and follies, it raises to itself abundance of enemies, who stigmatize it as libertine, profane, and irreligious.

Nor need we fear, that this philosophy, while it endeavours to limit our enquiries to common life, should ever undermine the reasonings of common life, and carry its doubts so far as to destroy all action, as well as speculation. Nature will always maintain her rights, and prevail in the end over any abstract reasoning whatsoever. Though we should conclude, for instance, as in the foregoing section, that, in all reasonings from experience, there is a step taken by the mind, which is not supported by any argument or process of the understanding, there is no danger, that these reasonings, on which almost all knowledge depends, will ever be affected by such a discovery. If the mind be not engaged by argument to make this step, it must be induced by some other principle of equal weight and authority; and that principle will preserve its influence as long as human nature remains the same. What that principle is, may well be worth the pains of enquiry.

Suppose a person, though endowed with the strongest faculties of reason and reflection, to be brought on a sudden into this world; he would, indeed, immediately observe a continual succession of objects, and one event following another; but he would not be able to discover any thing farther. He would not, at first, by any reasoning, be able to reach the idea of cause and effect; since the particular powers, by which all natural operations are performed, never appear to the senses; nor is it reasonable to conclude, merely because one event, in one instance, precedes another, that therefore the one is the cause, the other the effect. Their conjunction may be arbitrary and casual. There may be no reason to infer the existence of one from the appearance of the other. And in a word, such a person, without more experience, could never employ his conjecture or reasoning concerning any matter of fact, or be assured of any thing beyond what was immediately present to his memory and senses.

Suppose again, that he has acquired more experience, and has lived so long in the world as to have observed similar objects or events to be constantly conjoined together; what is the consequence of this experience? He immediately infers the existence of one object from the appearance of the other. Yet he has not, by all his experience, acquired any idea or knowledge of the secret power, by which the one object produces the other; nor is it, by any process of reasoning, he is engaged to draw this inference. But still he finds himself determined to draw it: And though he should be convinced, that his understanding has no part in the operation, he would nevertheless continue in the same course of thinking. There is some other principle, which determines him to form such a conclusion.

This principle is CUSTOM or HABIT. For wherever the repetition of any particular act or operation produces a propensity to renew the same act or operation, without being impelled by any reasoning or process of the understanding; we always say, that this propensity is the effect of *Custom*. By employing that word, we pretend not to have given the ultimate reason of such a propensity. We only point out a principle of human nature, which is universally acknowledged, and which is well known by its effects. Perhaps, we can push our enquiries no farther, or pretend to give the cause of this cause; but must rest contented with it as the ultimate principle, which we can assign, of all our conclusions from experience. It is sufficient satisfaction, that we can go so far; without repining at the narrowness of our faculties, because they will carry us no farther. And it is certain we here advance a very intelligible propositon at least, if not a true one, when we assert, that, after the constant conjunction of two objects, heat and flame, for instance, weight and solidity, we are determined by custom alone to expect the one from the appearance of the other. This hypothesis seems even the only one, which explains the difficulty, why we draw, from a thousand instances, an inference, which we are not able to draw from one instance, that is, in no respect, different from them. Reason is incapable of any such variation. The conclusions, which it draws from considering one circle, are the same which it would form upon surveying all the circles in the universe. But no man, having seen only one body move after being impelled by another, could infer, that every other body will move after a like impulse. All inferences from experience, therefore, are effects of custom, not of reasoning.[24]

24. Nothing is more usual than for writers, even on *moral, political,* or *physical* subjects, to distinguish between *reason* and *experience,* and to suppose, that these species of argumentation are entirely different from each other. The former are taken for the mere result of our intellectual faculties, which, by considering *a priori* the nature of things, and examining the effects, that must follow from their operation, establish particular principles of science and philosophy. The latter are supposed to be derived entirely from sense and observation, by which we learn what has actually resulted from the operation of particular objects, and are thence able to infer, what will, for the future, result from them. Thus, for instance, the limitations and restraints of civil government, and a legal constitution, may be defended, either from *reason,* which reflecting on the great frailty and corruption of human nature, teaches, that no man can safely be trusted with unlimited authority; or from *experience* and history, which inform us of the enormous abuses, that ambition, in every age and country, has been found to make of so imprudent a confidence.

The same distinction between reason and experience is maintained in all our deliberations concerning the conduct of life; while the experienced statesman, general, physician, or merchant is trusted and followed; and the unpractised novice, with whatever natural talents endowed, neglected and despised. Though it be allowed, that reason may form very plausible conjectures with regard to the consequences of such a particular conduct in such particular circumstances; it is still supposed imperfect, without the assistance of experience, which is alone able to give stability and certainty to the maxims, derived from study and reflection.

But notwithstanding that this distinction be thus universally received, both in the active and speculative scenes of life, I shall not scruple to pronounce, that it is, at bottom, erroneous, at least, superficial.

If we examine those arguments which, in any of the sciences above-mentioned, are supposed to be the mere effects of reasoning and reflection, they will be found to terminate, at last, in some general principle or conclusion, for which we can assign no reason but observation and experience. The only difference between them and those maxims, which are vulgarly esteemed the result of pure experience, is, that the former cannot be established without some process of thought, and some reflection on what we have observed, in order to distinguish its circumstances, and trace its consequences: Whereas in the latter, the experienced event is exactly and fully similar to that which we infer as the result of any particular situation. The history of a TIBERIUS or a NERO makes us dread a like tyranny, were our monarchs freed from the restraints of laws and senates: But the observation of any fraud or cruelty in private life is sufficient, with the aid of a little thought, to give us the same apprehension; while it serves as an instance of the general corruption of human nature, and shows us the danger which we must incur by reposing an entire confidence in mankind. In both cases, it is experience which is ultimately the foundation of our inference and conclusion.

There is no man so young and unexperienced, as not to have formed, from observation, many general and just maxims concerning human affairs and the conduct of life; but it must be confessed, that when a man comes to put these in practice, he will be extremely liable to error, till time and farther experience both enlarge these maxims, and teach him their proper use and application. In every situation or incident, there are many particular and seemingly minute circumstances, which the man of greatest talents is, at first, apt to overlook, though on them the justness of his conclusions, and consequently the prudence of his conduct, entirely depend. Not to mention, that, to a young beginner, the general observations and maxims occur not always on the proper occasions, nor can be immediately applied with due calmness and distinction. The truth is, an unexperienced reasoner could be no reasoner at all, were he absolutely unexperienced; and when we assign that character to any one, we mean it only in a comparative sense, and suppose him possessed of experience, in a smaller and more imperfect degree.

Custom, then, is the great guide of human life. It is that principle alone, which renders our experience useful to us, and makes us expect, for the future, a similar train of events with those which have appeared in the past. Without the influence of custom, we should be entirely ignorant of every matter of fact, beyond what is immediately present to the memory and senses. We should never know how to adjust means to ends, or to employ our natural powers in the production of any effect. There would be an end at once of all action, as well as of the chief part of speculation.

But here it may be proper to remark, that though our conclusions from experience carry us beyond our memory and senses, and assure us of matters of fact, which happened in the most distant places and most remote ages; yet some fact must always be present to the senses or memory, from which we may first proceed in drawing these conclusions. A man, who should find in a desert country the remains of pompous buildings, would conclude, that the country had, in ancient times, been cultivated by civilized inhabitants; but did nothing of this nature occur to him, he could never form such an inference. We learn the events of former ages from history; but then we must peruse the volumes, in which this instruction is contained, and thence carry up our inferences from one testimony to another, till we arrive at the eye-witnesses and spectators of these distant events. In a word, if we proceed not upon some fact, present to the memory or senses, our reasonings would be merely hypothetical; and however the particular links might be connected with each other, the whole chain of inferences would have nothing to support it, nor could we ever, by its means, arrive at the knowledge of any real existence. If I ask, why you believe any particular matter of fact, which you relate, you must tell me some reason; and this reason will be some other fact, connected with it. But as you cannot proceed after this manner, *in infinitum*, you must at last terminate in some fact, which is present to your memory or senses; or must allow that your belief is entirely without foundation.

What then is the conclusion of the whole matter? A simple one; though, it must be confessed, pretty remote from the common theories of philosophy. All belief of matter of fact or real existence is derived merely from some object, present to the memory or senses, and a customary conjunction between that and some other object. Or in other words; having found, in many instances, that any two kinds of objects, flame and heat, snow and cold, have always been conjoined together; if flame or snow be presented anew to the senses, the mind is carried by custom to expect heat or cold, and to *believe*, that such a quality does exist, and will discover itself upon a nearer approach. This belief is the necessary result of placing the mind in such circumstances. It is an operation of the soul, when we are so situated, as unavoidable as to feel the passion of love, when we receive benefits; or hatred, when we meet with injuries. All these operations are a species of natural instincts, which no reasoning or process of the thought and understanding is able, either to produce, or to prevent.

At this point, it would be very allowable for us to stop our philosophical researches. In most questions, we can never make a single step farther; and in all questions, we must terminate here at last, after our most restless and curious enquiries. But still our curiosity will be pardonable, perhaps commendable, if it carry us on to still farther researches, and make us examine more accurately the nature of this *belief*, and of the *customary conjunction*, whence it is derived. By this means we may meet with some explications and analogies, that will give satisfaction; at least to such as love the abstract sciences, and can be entertained with speculations, which, however accurate, may still retain a degree of doubt and uncertainty. As to readers of a different taste; the remaining part of this section is not calculated for them, and the following enquiries may well be understood, though it be neglected.

PART II.

Nothing is more free than the imagination of man; and though it cannot exceed that original stock of ideas, furnished by the internal and external senses, it has unlimited power of mixing, compounding, separating, and dividing these ideas, in all the varieties of fiction and vision. It can feign a train of events, with all the appearance of reality, ascribe to them a particular time and place, conceive them as existent, and paint them out to itself with every circumstance, that belongs to any historical fact, which it believes with the greatest certainty. Wherein, therefore, consists the difference between such a fiction and belief? It lies not merely in any peculiar idea, which is annexed to such a conception as commands our assent, and which is wanting to every known fiction. For as the mind has authority over all its ideas, it could voluntarily annex this particular idea to any fiction, and consequently be able to believe whatever it pleases; contrary to what we find by daily experience. We can, in our conception, join the head of a man to the body of a horse; but it is not in our power to believe, that such an animal has ever really existed.

It follows, therefore, that the difference between *fiction* and *belief* lies in some sentiment or feeling, which is annexed to the latter, not to the former, and which depends not on the will, nor can be commanded at pleasure. It must be excited by nature, like all other sentiments; and must arise from the particular situation, in which the mind is placed at any particular juncture. Whenever any object is presented to the memory or senses, it immediately, by the force of custom, carries the imagination to conceive that object, which is usually conjoined to it; and this conception is attended with a feeling or sentiment, different from the loose reveries of the fancy. In this consists the whole nature of belief. For as there is no matter of fact which we believe so firmly, that we cannot conceive the contrary, there would be no difference between the conception assented to, and that which is rejected, were it not for some sentiment, which distinguishes the one from the other. If I see a billiard-ball moving towards another, on a smooth table, I can easily conceive it to stop upon contact. This conception implies no contradiction; but still it feels very differently from that conception, by which I represent to myself the impulse, and the communication of motion from one ball to another.

Were we to attempt a *definition* of this sentiment, we should, perhaps, find it a very difficult, if not an impossible task; in the same manner as if we should endeavour to define the feeling of cold or passion of anger, to a creature who never had any experience of these sentiments. BELIEF is the true and proper name of this feeling; and no one is ever at a loss to know the meaning of that term; because every man is every moment conscious of the sentiment represented by it. It may not, however, be improper to attempt a *description* of this sentiment; in hopes we may, by that means, arrive at some analogies, which may afford a more perfect explication of it. I say then, that belief is nothing but a more vivid, lively, forcible, firm, steady conception of an object, than what the imagination alone is ever able to attain. This variety of terms, which may seem so unphilosophical, is intended only to express that act of the mind, which renders realities, or what is taken for such, more present to us than fictions, causes them to weigh more in the thought, and gives them a superior influence on the passions and imagination. Provided we agree about the thing, it is needless to dispute about the terms. The imagination has the command over all its ideas, and can join and mix and vary them, in all the ways possible. It may conceive fictitious objects with all the circumstances of place and time. It may set them, in a manner, before our eyes, in their true colours, just as they might have existed. But as it is impossible, that this faculty of imagination can ever, of itself, reach belief, it is evident, that belief consists not in the peculiar nature or order of ideas, but in the *manner* of their conception, and in their *feeling* to the mind. I confess, that it is impossible perfectly to explain this feeling or manner of conception. We may make use of words, which express something near it. But its true and proper name, as we observed before, is *belief;* which is a term, that every one sufficiently understands in common life. And in philosophy, we can go no farther than assert, that *belief* is something felt by the mind, which distinguishes the ideas of the judgment from the fictions of the imagination. It gives them more weight and influence; makes them appear of greater importance; enforces them in the mind; and renders them the governing principle of our actions. I hear at present, for instance, a person's voice, with whom I am acquainted; and the sound comes as from the next room. This impression of my senses immediately conveys my thought to the person, together with all the surrounding objects. I paint them out to myself as existing at present, with the same qualities and relations, of which I formerly knew them possessed. These ideas take faster hold of my mind, than ideas of an enchanted castle. They are very different to the feeling, and have a much greater influence of every kind, either to give pleasure or pain, joy or sorrow.

Let us, then, take in the whole compass of this doctrine, and allow, that the sentiment of belief is nothing but a conception more intense and steady than what attends the mere fictions of the imagination, and that this *manner* of conception arises from a customary conjunction of the object with something present to the memory or senses: I believe that it will not be difficult, upon these suppositions, to find other operations of the mind analogous to it, and to trace up these phenomena to principles still more general.

We have already observed, that nature has established connexions among particular ideas, and that no sooner one idea occurs to our thoughts than it introduces its correlative, and carries our attention towards it, by a gentle and insensible movement. These principles of connexion or association we have reduced to three, namely, *Resemblance, Contiguity,* and *Causation;* which are the only bonds, that unite our thoughts together, and beget that regular train of reflection or discourse, which, in a greater or less degree, takes place among all mankind. Now here arises a question, on which the solution of the present difficulty will depend. Does it happen, in all these relations, that, when one of the objects is presented to the senses or memory, the mind is not only carried to the conception of the correlative, but reaches a steadier and stronger conception of it than what otherwise it would have been able to attain? This seems to be the case with that belief, which arises from the relation of cause and effect. And if the case be the same with the other relations or principles of association, this may be established as a general law, which takes place in all the operations of the mind.

We may, therefore, observe, as the first experiment to our present purpose, that, upon the appearance of the picture of an absent friend, our idea of him is evidently enlivened by the *resemblance,* and that every passion, which that idea occasions, whether of joy or sorrow, acquires new force and vigour. In producing this effect, there concur both a relation and a present impression. Where the picture bears him no resemblance, at least was not intended for him, it never so much as conveys our thought to him: And where it is absent, as well as the person; though the mind may pass from the thought of the one to that of the other; it feels its idea to be rather weakened than enlivened by that transition. We take a pleasure in viewing the picture of a friend, when it is set before us; but when it is removed, rather choose to consider him directly, than by reflection in an image, which is equally distant and obscure.

The ceremonies of the ROMAN CATHOLIC religion may be considered as instances of the same nature. The devotees of that superstition usually plead in excuse for the mummeries, with which they are upbraided, that they feel the good effect of those external motions, and postures, and actions, in enlivening their devotion and quickening their fervour, which otherwise would decay, if directed entirely to distant and immaterial objects. We shadow out the objects of our faith, say they, in sensible types and images, and render them more present to us by the immediate presence of these types, than it is possible for us to do, merely by an intellectual view and contemplation. Sensible objects have always a greater influence on the fancy than any other; and this influence they readily convey to those ideas, to which they are related, and which they resemble. I shall only infer from these practices, and this reasoning, that the effect of resemblance in enlivening the ideas is very common; and as in every case a resemblance and a present impression must concur, we are abundantly supplied with experiments to prove the reality of the foregoing principle.

We may add force to these experiments by others of a different kind, in considering the effects of *contiguity* as well as of *resemblance.* It is certain, that distance diminishes the force of every idea, and that, upon our approach to any object; though it does not discover itself to our senses; it operates upon the mind with an influence, which imitates an immediate impression. The thinking on any object readily transports the mind to what is contiguous; but it is only the actual presence of an object, that transports it with a superior vivacity. When I am a few miles from home, whatever relates to it touches me more nearly than when I am two hundred leagues distant; though even at that distance the reflecting on any thing in the neighbourhood of my friends or family naturally produces an idea of them. But as in this latter case, both the objects of the mind are ideas; notwithstanding there is an easy transition between them; that transition alone is not able to give a superior vivacity to any of the ideas, for want of some immediate impression.[25]

25. [The reference is to Cicero, *de Finibus,* Lib. v.2.: "Should I say that we came by it naturally, he said, or is it because of some delusion that we are more moved when we see those places in which we have heard that many noteworthy people spent their time, than if we were hearing of their deeds or reading one of their writings? And in fact I am myself moved at this moment; for Plato comes to my mind, who was the first, we are told, to make a habit of holding discussions here. And it is not just his memory which those little gardens bring to me—they seem to set the man himself before my eyes. Here is Speusippus, here is Xenocrates, and over there his pupil Polemo—that chair we are looking at was actually Polemo's. Even our own senate house—I mean the Hostilia, not the new one, which seems smaller to me since it was enlarged—I used to look at it and imagine Scipio, Cato, Laelius, and of course my own grandfather most of all. Such is the power of suggestion in places. It is not without good reason that the training of the memory is launched upon this basis."]

No one can doubt but causation has the same influence as the other two relations of resemblance and contiguity. Superstitious people are fond of the relics of saints and holy men, for the same reason, that they seek after types or images, in order to enliven their devotion, and give them a more intimate and strong conception of those exemplary lives, which they desire to imitate. Now it is evident, that one of the best relics, which a devotee could procure, would be the handywork of a saint; and if his clothes and furniture are ever to be considered in this light, it is because they were once at his disposal, and were moved and affected by him; in which respect they are to be considered as imperfect effects, and as connected with him by a shorter chain of consequences than any of those, by which we learn the reality of his existence.

Suppose, that the son of a friend, who had been long dead or absent, were presented to us; it is evident, that this object would instantly revive its correlative idea, and recall to our thoughts all past intimacies and familiarities, in more lively colours than they would otherwise have appeared to us. This is another phenomenon, which seems to prove the principle above-mentioned.

We may observe, that, in these phenomena, the belief of the correlative object is always presupposed; without which the relation could have no effect. The influence of the picture supposes, that we *believe* our friend to have once existed. Contiguity to home can never excite our ideas of home, unless we *believe* that it really exists. Now I assert, that this belief, where it reaches beyond the memory or senses, is of a similar nature, and arises from similar causes, with the transition of thought and vivacity of conception here explained. When I throw a piece of dry wood into a fire, my mind is immediately carried to conceive, that it augments, not extinguishes the flame. This transition of thought from the cause to the effect proceeds not from reason. It derives its origin altogether from custom and experience. And as it first begins from an object, present to the senses, it renders the idea or conception of flame more strong and lively than any loose, floating reverie of the imagination. That idea arises immediately. The thought moves instantly towards it, and conveys to it all that force of conception, which is derived from the impression present to the senses. When a sword is levelled at my breast, does not the idea of wound and pain strike me more strongly, than when a glass of wine is presented to me, even though by accident this idea should occur after the appearance of the latter object? But what is there in this whole matter to cause such a strong conception, except only a present object and a customary transition to the idea of another object, which we have been accustomed to conjoin with the former? This is the whole operation of the mind, in all our conclusions concerning matter of fact and existence; and it is a satisfaction to find some analogies, by which it may be explained. The transition from a present object does in all cases give strength and solidity to the related idea.

Here, then, is a kind of pre-established harmony[26] between the course of nature and the succession of our ideas; and though the powers and forces, by which the

26. [In the philosophy of Leibniz (1646–1716), "pre-established harmony" refers to the fact that as there can be no interaction between one entity or substance and another, whether in perception or action, God must create each entity in the universe so that its states arise from itself and yet in complete harmony or conformity with the states of all other things. Leibniz illustrated this notion by using the example of two clocks. They can be in perfect agreement, not because they mutually influence each other, nor because they are continually adjusted, but because they are manufactured so skillfully that keeping the same time is guaranteed.]

former is governed, be wholly unknown to us; yet our thoughts and conceptions have still, we find, gone on in the same train with the other works of nature. Custom is that principle, by which this correspondence has been effected; so necessary to the subsistence of our species, and the regulation of our conduct, in every circumstance and occurrence of human life. Had not the presence of an object instantly excited the idea of those objects, commonly conjoined with it, all our knowledge must have been limited to the narrow sphere of our memory and senses; and we should never have been able to adjust means to ends, or employ our natural powers, either to the producing of good, or avoiding of evil. Those, who delight in the discovery and contemplation of *final causes,*[27] have here ample subject to employ their wonder and admiration.

I shall add, for a further confirmation of the foregoing theory, that, as this operation of the mind, by which we infer like effects from like causes, and *vice versa,* is so essential to the subsistence of all human creatures, it is not probable, that it could be trusted to the fallacious deductions of our reason, which is slow in its operations; appears not, in any degree, during the first years of infancy; and at best is, in every age and period of human life, extremely liable to error and mistake. It is more conformable to the ordinary wisdom of nature to secure so necessary an act of the mind, by some instinct or mechanical tendency, which may be infallible in its operations, may discover itself at the first appearance of life and thought, and may be independent of all the laboured deductions of the understanding. As nature has taught us the use of our limbs, without giving us the knowledge of the muscles and nerves, by which they are actuated; so has she implanted in us an instinct, which carries forward the thought in a correspondent course to that which she has established among external objects; though we are ignorant of those powers and forces, on which this regular course and succession of objects totally depends.

SECTION VI. — *Of Probability.*[28]

THOUGH there be no such thing as *Chance* in the world; our ignorance of the real cause of any event has the same influence on the understanding, and begets a like species of belief or opinion.

There is certainly a probability, which arises from a superiority of chances on any side; and according as this superiority increases, and surpasses the opposite chances, the probability receives a proportionable increase, and begets still a higher degree of belief or assent to that side, in which we discover the superiority. If a die were marked with one figure or number of spots on four sides, and with another

27. [In the philosophy of Aristotle (384–322 B.C.), a final cause is a structure common to members of a species, which helps to make intelligible the changes of the members and which answers the question: What is the end or goal of the thing? The concept was frequently applied to the universe itself, and it was maintained that the universe had an end state or goal toward which it was heading. See *Enquiry,* Section XI.]

28. Mr. Locke divides all arguments into demonstrative and probable. In this view, we must say, that it is only probable all men must die, or that the sun will rise to-morrow. But to conform our language more to common use, we ought to divide arguments into *demonstrations, proofs,* and *probabilities.* By proofs meaning such arguments from experience as leave no room for doubt or opposition. [For Hume's explanation of "opposition," see Section X.]

figure or number of spots on the two remaining sides, it would be more probable, that the former would turn up than the latter; though, if it had a thousand sides marked in the same manner, and only one side different, the probability would be much higher, and our belief or expectation of the event more steady and secure. This process of the thought or reasoning may seem trivial and obvious; but to those who consider it more narrowly, it may, perhaps, afford matter for curious speculation.

It seems evident, that, when the mind looks forward to discover the event, which may result from the throw of such a die, it considers the turning up of each particular side as alike probable; and this is the very nature of chance, to render all the particular events, comprehended in it, entirely equal. But finding a greater number of sides concur in the one event than in the other, the mind is carried more frequently to that event, and meets it oftener, in revolving the various possibilities or chances, on which the ultimate result depends. This concurrence of several views in one particular event begets immediately, by an inexplicable contrivance of nature, the sentiment of belief, and gives that event the advantage over its antagonist, which is supported by a smaller number of views, and recurs less frequently to the mind. If we allow, that belief is nothing but a firmer and stronger conception of an object than what attends the mere fictions of the imagination, this operation may, perhaps, in some measure, be accounted for. The concurrence of these several views or glimpses imprints the idea more strongly on the imagination; gives it superior force and vigour; renders its influence on the passions and affections more sensible; and in a word, begets that reliance or security, which constitutes the nature of belief and opinion.

The case is the same with the probability of causes, as with that of chance. There are some causes, which are entirely uniform and constant in producing a particular effect; and no instance has ever yet been found of any failure or irregularity in their operation. Fire has always burned, and water suffocated every human creature: The production of motion by impulse and gravity is an universal law, which has hitherto admitted of no exception. But there are other causes, which have been found more irregular and uncertain; nor has rhubarb always proved a purge, or opium a soporific to every one, who has taken these medicines. It is true, when any cause fails of producing its usual effect, philosophers ascribe not this to any irregularity in nature; but suppose, that some secret causes, in the particular structure of parts, have prevented the operation. Our reasonings, however, and conclusions concerning the event are the same as if this principle had no place. Being determined by custom to transfer the past to the future, in all our inferences; where the past has been entirely regular and uniform, we expect the event with the greatest assurance, and leave no room for any contrary supposition. But where different effects have been found to follow from causes, which are to *appearance* exactly similar, all these various effects must occur to the mind in transferring the past to the future, and enter into our consideration, when we determine the probability of the event. Though we give the preference to that which has been found most usual, and believe that this effect will exist, we must not overlook the other effects, but must assign to each of them a particular weight and authority, in proportion as we have found it to be more or less frequent. It is more probable, in almost every country of EUROPE, that there will be frost sometime in JANUARY, than that the weather will continue open throughout that whole month; though this probability varies according to the different climates, and approaches to a certainty in the more northern kingdoms. Here then it seems evident, that, when we transfer the past to the future, in order to determine the effect, which will result from any cause, we transfer all the different events, in the same proportion as they have appeared in the past, and conceive one to have existed a hundred times, for instance, another ten times, and another once. As a great number of views do here concur in one event, they fortify and confirm it to the imagination, beget that sentiment which we call *belief,* and give its object the preference above the contrary event, which is not supported by an equal number of experiments, and recurs not so frequently to the thought in transferring the past to the future. Let any one try to account for this operation of the mind upon any of the received systems of philosophy, and he will be sensible of the difficulty. For my part, I shall think it sufficient, if the present hints excite the curiosity of philosophers, and make them sensible how defective all common theories are in treating of such curious and such sublime subjects.

SECT. VII.— *Of the Idea of Necessary Connexion.*

PART I.

THE great advantage of the mathematical sciences above the moral consists in this, that the ideas of the former, being sensible, are always clear and determinate, the smallest distinction between them is immediately perceptible, and the same terms are still expressive of the same ideas, without ambiguity or variation. An oval is never mistaken for a circle, nor an hyperbola for an ellipsis. The isosceles and scalenum are distinguished by boundaries more exact than vice and virtue, right and wrong. If any term be defined in geometry, the mind readily, of itself, substitutes, on all occasions, the definition for the term defined: Or even when no definition is employed, the object itself may be presented to the senses, and by that means be steadily and clearly apprehended. But the finer sentiments of the mind, the operations of the understanding, the various agitations of the passions, though really in themselves distinct, easily escape us, when surveyed by reflection; nor is it in our power to recall the original object, as often as we have occasion to contemplate it. Ambiguity, by this means, is gradually introduced into our reasonings: Similar objects are readily taken to be the same: And the conclusion becomes at last very wide of the premises.

One may safely, however, affirm, that, if we consider these sciences in a proper light, their advantages and disadvantages nearly compensate each other, and reduce both of them to a state of equality. If the mind, with greater facility, retains the ideas of geometry clear and determinate, it must carry on a much longer and more intricate chain of reasoning, and compare ideas much wider of each other, in order to reach the abstruser truths of that science. And if moral ideas are apt, without extreme care, to fall into obscurity and confusion, the inferences are always much shorter in these disquisitions, and the intermediate steps, which lead to the conclusion, much fewer than in the sciences which treat of quantity and number. In reality, there is scarcely a proposition in EUCLID so simple, as not to consist of more parts, than are to be found in any moral reasoning which runs not into chimera and conceit. Where we trace the principles of the human mind through a few steps, we may be very well satisfied with our progress; considering how soon nature throws a bar to all our enquiries concerning causes, and reduces us to an acknowledgment of our ignorance. The chief obstacle, therefore, to our improvement in the moral or metaphysical sciences is the obscurity of the ideas, and ambiguity of the terms. The principal difficulty in the mathematics is the length of inferences and compass of thought, requisite to the forming of any conclusion. And, perhaps, our progress in natural philosophy is chiefly retarded by the want of proper experiments and phenomena, which are often discovered by chance, and cannot always be found, when requisite, even by the most diligent and prudent enquiry. As moral philosophy seems hitherto to have received less improvement than either geometry or physics, we may conclude, that, if there be any difference in this respect among these sciences, the difficulties, which obstruct the progress of the former, require superior care and capacity to be surmounted.

There are no ideas, which occur in metaphysics, more obscure and uncertain, than those of *power, force, energy,* or *necessary connexion,* of which it is every moment necessary for us to treat in all our disquisitions. We shall, therefore, endeavour, in this section, to fix, if possible, the precise meaning of these terms, and thereby remove some part of that obscurity, which is so much complained of in this species of philosophy.

It seems a proposition, which will not admit of much dispute, that all our ideas are nothing but copies of our impressions, or, in other words, that it is impossible for us to *think* of any thing, which we have not antecedently *felt*, either by our external or internal senses. I have endeavoured[29] to explain and prove this proposition, and have expressed my hopes, that, by a proper application of it, men may reach a greater clearness and precision in philosophical reasonings, than what they have hitherto been able to attain. Complex ideas may, perhaps, be well known by definition, which is nothing but an enumeration of those parts or simple ideas, that compose them. But when we have pushed up definitions to the most simple ideas, and find still some ambiguity and obscurity; what resource are we then possessed of? By what invention can we throw light upon these ideas, and render them altogether precise and determinate to our intellectual view? Produce the impressions or original sentiments, from which the ideas are copied. These impressions are all strong and sensible. They admit not of ambiguity. They are not only placed in a full light themselves, but may throw light on their correspondent ideas, which lie in obscurity. And by this means, we may, perhaps, attain a new microscope or species of optics, by which, in the moral sciences, the most minute, and most simple ideas may be so enlarged as to fall readily under our apprehension, and be equally known with the grossest and most sensible ideas, that can be the object of our enquiry.

To be fully acquainted, therefore, with the idea of power or necessary connexion, let us examine its impression; and in order to find the impression with greater certainty, let us search for it in all the sources, from which it may possibly be derived.

When we look about us towards external objects, and consider the operation of causes, we are never able, in a single instance, to discover any power or necessary connexion; any quality, which binds the effect to the cause, and renders the one an infallible consequence of the other. We only find, that the one does actually, in fact, follow the other. The impulse of one billiard-ball is attended with motion in the second. This is the whole that appears to the *outward* senses. The mind feels no sentiment or *inward* impression from this succession of objects: Consequently, there is

29. Section II. Of the Origin of Ideas.

not, in any single, particular instance of cause and effect, any thing which can suggest the idea of power or necessary connexion.

From the first appearance of an object, we never can conjecture what effect will result from it. But were the power or energy of any cause discoverable by the mind, we could foresee the effect, even without experience; and might, at first, pronounce with certainty concerning it, by the mere dint of thought and reasoning.

In reality, there is no part of matter, that does ever, by its sensible qualities, discover any power or energy, or give us ground to imagine, that it could produce any thing, or be followed by any other object, which we could denominate its effect. Solidity, extension, motion; these qualities are all complete in themselves, and never point out any other event which may result from them. The scenes of the universe are continually shifting, and one object follows another in an uninterrupted succession; but the power or force, which actuates the whole machine, is entirely concealed from us, and never discovers itself in any of the sensible qualities of body. We know, that, in fact, heat is a constant attendant of flame; but what is the connexion between them, we have no room so much as to conjecture or imagine. It is impossible, therefore, that the idea of power can be derived from the contemplation of bodies, in single instances of their operation; because no bodies ever discover any power, which can be the original of this idea.[30]

Since, therefore, external objects as they appear to the senses, give us no idea of power or necessary connexion, by their operation in particular instances, let us see, whether this idea be derived from reflection on the operations of our own minds, and be copied from any internal impression. It may be said, that we are every moment conscious of internal power; while we feel, that, by the simple command of our will, we can move the organs of our body, or direct the faculties of our mind. An act of volition produces motion in our limbs, or raises a new idea in our imagination. This influence of the will we know by consciousness. Hence we acquire the idea of power or energy; and are certain, that we ourselves and all other intelligent beings are possessed of power. This idea, then, is an idea of reflection, since it arises from reflecting on the operations of our own mind, and on the command which is exercised by will, both over the organs of the body and faculties of the soul.

We shall proceed to examine this pretension; and first with regard to the influence of volition over the organs of the body. This influence, we may observe, is a fact, which, like all other natural events, can be known only by experience, and can never be foreseen from any apparent energy or power in the cause, which connects it with the effect, and renders the one an infallible consequence of the other. The motion of our body follows upon the command of our will. Of this we are every moment conscious. But the means, by which this is effected; the energy, by which the will performs so extraordinary an operation; of this we are so far from being immediately conscious, that it must for ever escape our most diligent enquiry.

For *first;* is there any principle in all nature more mysterious than the union of soul with body; by which a supposed spiritual substance acquires such an influence over a material one, that the most refined thought is able to actuate the grossest matter? Were we empowered, by a secret wish, to remove mountains, or control the

---

30. Mr. Locke, in his chapter of power, says, that, finding from experience, that there are several new productions in matter, and concluding that there must somewhere be a power capable of producing them, we arrive at last by this reasoning at the idea of power. But no reasoning can ever give us a new, original, simple idea; as this philosopher himself confesses. This, therefore, can never be the origin of that idea. [The reference is to Locke's *Essay,* Bk. II, ch.XXI.]

planets in their orbit; this extensive authority would not be more extraordinary, nor more beyond our comprehension. But if by consciousness we perceived any power or energy in the will, we must know this power; we must know its connexion with the effect; we must know the secret union of soul and body, and the nature of both these substances; by which the one is able to operate, in so many instances, upon the other.

Secondly, We are not able to move all the organs of the body with a like authority; though we cannot assign any reason besides experience, for so remarkable a difference between one and the other. Why has the will an influence over the tongue and fingers, not over the heart or liver? This question would never embarrass us, were we conscious of a power in the former case, not in the latter. We should then perceive, independent of experience, why the authority of will over the organs of the body is circumscribed within such particular limits. Being in that case fully acquainted with the power or force, by which it operates, we should also know, why its influence reaches precisely to such boundaries, and no farther.

A man, suddenly struck with a palsy in the leg or arm, or who had newly lost those members, frequently endeavours, at first, to move them, and employ them in their usual offices. Here he is as much conscious of power to command such limbs, as a man in perfect health is conscious of power to actuate any member which remains in its natural state and condition. But consciousness never deceives. Consequently, neither in the one case nor in the other, are we ever conscious of any power. We learn the influence of our will from experience alone. And experience only teaches us, how one event constantly follows another; without instructing us in the secret connexion, which binds them together, and renders them inseparable.

Thirdly, We learn from anatomy, that the immediate object of power in voluntary motion, is not the member itself which is moved, but certain muscles, and nerves, and animal spirits,[31] and, perhaps, something still more minute and more unknown, through which the motion is successively propagated, ere it reach the member itself whose motion is the immediate object of volition. Can there be a more certain proof, that the power, by which this whole operation is performed, so far from being directly and fully known by an inward sentiment or consciousness, is, to the last degree, mysterious and unintelligible? Here the mind wills a certain event: Immediately another event, unknown to ourselves, and totally different from the one intended, is produced: This event produces another, equally unknown: Till at last, through a long succession, the desired event is produced. But if the original power were felt, it must be known: Were it known, its effect must also be known; since all power is relative to its effect. And *vice versa,* if the effect be not known, the power cannot be known nor felt. How indeed can we be conscious of a power to move our limbs, when we have no such power; but only that to move certain animal spirits, which, though they produce at last the motion of our limbs, yet operate in such a manner as is wholly beyond our comprehension?

We may, therefore, conclude from the whole, I hope, without any temerity, though with assurance; that our idea of power is not copied from any sentiment or consciousness of power within ourselves, when we give rise to animal motion, or apply our limbs to their proper use and office. That their motion follows the command

---

31. [Fluids or currents in the nerves produced by the warming of the blood. "Animal spirits" was a major concept in seventeenth- and eighteenth-century attempts to explain sensation, bodily motion, and voluntary behavior.]

of the will is a matter of common experience, like other natural events: But the power or energy by which this is effected, like that in other natural events, is unknown and inconceivable.[32]

Shall we then assert, that we are conscious of a power or energy in our own minds, when, by an act or command of our will, we raise up a new idea, fix the mind to the contemplation of it, turn it on all sides, and at last dismiss it for some other idea, when we think that we have surveyed it with sufficient accuracy? I believe the same arguments will prove, that even this command of the will gives us no real idea of force or energy.

First, It must be allowed, that, when we know a power, we know that very circumstance in the cause, by which it is enabled to produce the effect: For these are supposed to be synonymous. We must, therefore, know both the cause and effect, and the relation between them. But do we pretend to be acquainted with the nature of the human soul and the nature of an idea, or the aptitude of the one to produce the other? This is a real creation; a production of something out of nothing: Which implies a power so great, that it may seem, at first sight, beyond the reach of any being, less than infinite. At least it must be owned, that such a power is not felt, nor known, nor even conceivable by the mind. We only feel the event, namely, the existence of an idea, consequent to a command of the will: But the manner, in which this operation is performed; the power, by which it is produced; is entirely beyond our comprehension.

Secondly, The command of the mind over itself is limited, as well as its command over the body; and these limits are not known by reason, or any acquaintance with the nature of cause and effect; but only by experience and observation, as in all other natural events and in the operation of external objects. Our authority over our sentiments and passions is much weaker than that over our ideas; and even the latter authority is circumscribed within very narrow boundaries. Will any one pretend to assign the ultimate reason of these boundaries, or show why the power is deficient in one case not in another.

Thirdly, This self-command is very different at different times. A man in health possesses more of it, than one languishing with sickness. We are more master of our thoughts in the morning than in the evening: Fasting, than after a full meal. Can we give any reason for these variations, except experience? Where then is the power, of which we pretend to be conscious? Is there not here, either in a spiritual or material substance, or both, some secret mechanism or structure of parts, upon which the effect depends, and which, being entirely unknown to us, renders the power or energy of the will equally unknown and incomprehensible?

Volition is surely an act of the mind, with which we are sufficiently acquainted.

---

32. It may be pretended, that the resistance which we meet with in bodies, obliging us frequently to exert our force, and call up all our power, this gives us the idea of force and power. It is this *nisus* or strong endeavour, of which we are conscious, that is the original impression from which this idea is copied. But, first, we attribute power to a vast number of objects, where we never can suppose this resistance or exertion of force to take place; to the Supreme Being, who never meets with any resistance; to the mind in its command over its ideas and limbs, in common thinking and motion, where the effect follows immediately upon the will, without any exertion or summoning up of force; to inanimate matter, which is not capable of this sentiment. *Secondly,* This sentiment of an endeavour to overcome resistance has no known connexion with any event: What follows it, we know by experience; but could not know it *a priori.* It must, however, be confessed, that the animal *nisus,* which we experience, though it can afford no accurate precise idea of power, enters very much into that vulgar, inaccurate idea, which is formed of it.

Reflect upon it. Consider it on all sides. Do you find anything in it like this creative power, by which it raises from nothing a new idea, and with a kind of FIAT, imitates the omnipotence of its Maker, if I may be allowed so to speak, who called forth into existence all the various scenes of nature? So far from being conscious of this energy in the will, it requires as certain experience, as that of which we are possessed, to convince us, that such extraordinary effects do ever result from a simple act of volition.

The generality of mankind never find any difficulty in accounting for the more common and familiar operations of nature; such as the descent of heavy bodies, the growth of plants, the generation of animals, or the nourishment of bodies by food: But suppose, that, in all these cases, they perceive the very force or energy of the cause, by which it is connected with its effect, and is for ever infallible in its operation. They acquire, by long habit, such a turn of mind, that, upon the appearance of the cause, they immediately expect with assurance its usual attendant, and hardly conceive it possible, that any other event could result from it. It is only on the discovery of extraordinary phenomena, such as earthquakes, pestilence, and prodigies of any kind, that they find themselves at a loss to assign a proper cause, and to explain the manner, in which the effect is produced by it. It is usual for men, in such difficulties, to have recourse to some invisible intelligent principle,[33] as the immediate cause of that event, which surprises them, and which they think, cannot be accounted for from the common powers of nature. But philosophers, who carry their scrutiny a little farther, immediately perceive, that, even in the most familiar events, the energy of the cause is as unintelligible as in the most unusual, and that we only learn by experience the frequent CONJUNCTION of objects, without being ever able to comprehend any thing like CONNEXION between them. Here then, many philosophers[34] think themselves obliged by reason to have recourse, on all occasions, to the same principle, which the vulgar never appeal to but in cases, that appear miraculous and supernatural. They acknowledge mind and intelligence to be, not only the ultimate and original cause of all things, but the immediate and sole cause of every event, which appears in nature. They pretend, that those objects, which are commonly denominated *causes,* are in reality nothing but *occasions;* and that the true and direct principle of every effect is not any power or force in nature, but a volition of the Supreme Being, who wills, that such particular objects should, for ever, be conjoined with each other. Instead of saying, that one billiard-ball moves another, by a force, which it has derived from the author of nature; it is the Deity himself, they say, who, by a particular volition, moves the second ball, being determined to this operation by the impulse of the first ball; in consequence of those general laws, which he has laid down to himself in the government of the universe. But philosophers advancing still in their enquiries, discover, that, as we are totally ignorant of the power, on which depends the mutual operation of bodies, we are no less ignorant of that power, on which depends the operation of mind on body, or of body on mind; nor are we able, either from our senses or consciousness, to assign the ultimate principle in one case, more than in the other. The same ignorance, therefore, reduces them to the same conclusion. They assert, that the Deity is the immediate

33. [In Latin, "deus ex machina": In Greek and Roman plays, a deity brought in by stage machinery to intervene in the action or resolve a situation.]

34. [The remainder of this paragraph is a discussion of the views of the "occasionalists", followers of Descartes (1596–1650), whose most famous representative was Nicolas Malebranche (1638–1715).]

cause of the union between soul and body; and that they are not the organs of sense, which, being agitated by external objects, produce sensations in the mind; but that it is a particular volition of our omnipotent Maker, which excites such a sensation, in consequence of such a motion in the organ. In like manner, it is not any energy in the will, that produces local motion in our members: It is God himself, who is pleased to second our will, in itself impotent, and to command that motion, which we erroneously attribute to our own power and efficacy. Nor do philosophers stop at this conclusion. They[35] sometimes extend the same inference to the mind itself, in its internal operations. Our mental vision or conception of ideas is nothing but a revelation made to us by our Maker. When we voluntarily turn our thoughts to any object, and raise up its image in the fancy; it is not the will which creates that idea: It is the universal Creator, who discovers it to the mind, and renders it present to us.

Thus, according to these philosophers, every thing is full of God. Not content with the principle, that nothing exists but by his will, that nothing possesses any power but by his concession: They rob nature, and all created beings, of every power, in order to render their dependence on the Deity still more sensible and immediate. They consider not, that, by this theory, they diminish, instead of magnifying, the grandeur of those attributes, which they affect so much to celebrate. It argues surely more power in the Deity to delegate a certain degree of power to inferior creatures, than to produce every thing by his own immediate volition. It argues more wisdom to contrive at first the fabric of the world with such perfect foresight, that, of itself, and by its proper operation, it may serve all the purposes of providence, than if the great Creator were obliged every moment to adjust its parts, and animate by his breath all the wheels of that stupendous machine.

But if we would have a more philosophical confutation of this theory, perhaps the two following reflections may suffice.

First, It seems to me, that this theory of the universal energy and operation of the Supreme Being, is too bold ever to carry conviction with it to a man, sufficiently apprized of the weakness of human reason, and the narrow limits, to which it is confined in all its operations. Though the chain of arguments, which conduct to it, were ever so logical, there must arise a strong suspicion, if not an absolute assurance, that it has carried us quite beyond the reach of our faculties, when it leads to conclusions so extraordinary, and so remote from common life and experience. We are got into fairy land, long ere we have reached the last steps of our theory; and *there* we have no reason to trust our common methods of argument, or to think that our usual analogies and probabilities have any authority. Our line is too short to fathom such immense abysses. And however we may flatter ourselves, that we are guided, in every step which we take, by a kind of verisimilitude and experience; we may be assured, that this fancied experience has no authority, when we thus apply it to subjects, that lie entirely out of the sphere of experience. But on this we shall have occasion to touch afterwards.[36]

Secondly, I cannot perceive any force in the arguments, on which this theory is founded. We are ignorant, it is true, of the manner in which bodies operate on each other: Their force or energy is entirely incomprehensible: But are we not equally ignorant of the manner or force by which a mind, even the supreme mind, operates

35. [Malebranche, for example]

36. Section XII.

either on itself or on body? Whence, I beseech you, do we acquire any idea of it? We have no sentiment or consciousness of this power in ourselves. We have no idea of the Supreme Being but what we learn from reflection on our own faculties. Were our ignorance, therefore, a good reason for rejecting any thing, we should be led into that principle of denying all energy in the Supreme Being as much as in the grossest matter. We surely comprehend as little the operations of one as of the other. Is it more difficult to conceive, that motion may arise from impulse, than that it may arise from volition? All we know is our profound ignorance in both cases.[37]

PART II.

But to hasten to a conclusion of this argument, which is already drawn out to too great a length: We have sought in vain for an idea of power or necessary connexion, in all the sources from which we could suppose it to be derived. It appears, that, in single instances of the operation of bodies, we never can, by our utmost scrutiny, discover any thing but one event following another; without being able to comprehend any force or power, by which the cause operates, or any connexion between it and its supposed effect. The same difficulty occurs in contemplating the operations of mind on body; where we observe the motion of the latter to follow upon the volition of the former; but are not able to observe or conceive the tie, which binds together the motion and volition, or the energy by which the mind produces this effect. The authority of the will over its own faculties and ideas is not a whit more comprehensible: So that, upon the whole, there appears not, throughout all nature, any one instance of connexion, which is conceivable by us. All events seem entirely loose and separate. One event follows another; but we never can

---

37. I need not examine at length the *vis inertiae* which is so much talked of in the new philosophy, and which is ascribed to matter. We find by experience, that a body at rest or in motion continues for ever in its present state, till put from it by some new cause: And that a body impelled takes as much motion from the impelling body as it acquires itself. These are facts. When we call this a *vis inertiae*, we only mark these facts, without pretending to have any idea of the inert power; in the same manner as, when we talk of gravity, we mean certain effects without comprehending that active power. It was never the meaning of SIR ISAAC NEWTON to rob second causes of all force or energy; though some of his followers have endeavoured to establish that theory upon his authority. On the contrary, that great philosopher had recourse to an ethereal active fluid to explain his universal attraction; though he was so cautious and modest as to allow, that it was a mere hypothesis, not to be insisted on, without more experiments. I must confess, that there is something in the fate of opinions a little extraordinary. DES CARTES insinuated that doctrine of the universal and sole efficacy of the Deity, without insisting on it. MALEBRANCHE and other CARTESIANS made it the foundation of all their philosophy. It had, however, no authority in ENGLAND. LOCKE, CLARKE [Samuel Clarke (1675–1729)], and CUDWORTH [Ralph Cudworth (1617–1688)], never so much as take notice of it, but supposed all along that matter has a real, though subordinate and derived power. By what means has it become so prevalent among our modern metaphysicians?

[The "new philosophy" is Newtonianism. The followers of Newton who might satisfy Hume's description and were also known to him include: George Cheyne (1671–1743), author of *Philosophical Principles of Religion: Natural and Revealed* (1715), and who some think was Hume's physician as a young man; Colin Maclaurin (1698–1746), who taught mathematics at the University of Edinburgh when Hume was a student there, and who wrote *An Account of Sir Isaac Newton's Philosophical Discoveries* (1748); and William Whiston (1667–1752), Newton's successor at Cambridge, and author of *A New Theory of the Earth* (1696). For a discussion of the relation between Hume and Newton see: James Noxon, *Hume's Philosophical Development: a Study of his Methods* (Oxford: 1973); and Robert H. Hurlbutt III, *Hume, Newton, and the Design Argument* (Lincoln, Nebraska: 1965); and Nicholas Capaldi, *David Hume: The Newtonian Philosopher* (Boston: 1975). One "modern metaphysician" would be George Berkeley, who maintained that since objects are merely collections of passive ideas, no agency is to be found in them.]

observe any tie between them. They seem *conjoined,* but never *connected.* And as we can have no idea of any thing, which never appeared to our outward sense or inward sentiment, the necessary conclusion *seems* to be, that we have no idea of connexion or power at all, and that these words are absolutely without any meaning, when employed either in philosophical reasonings, or common life.

But there still remains one method of avoiding this conclusion, and one source which we have not yet examined. When any natural object or event is presented, it is impossible for us, by any sagacity or penetration, to discover, or even conjecture, without experience, what event will result from it, or to carry our foresight beyond that object, which is immediately present to the memory and senses. Even after one instance or experiment, where we have observed a particular event to follow upon another, we are not entitled to form a general rule, or foretell what will happen in like cases; it being justly esteemed an unpardonable temerity to judge of the whole course of nature from one single experiment, however accurate or certain. But when one particular species of event has always, in all instances, been conjoined with another, we make no longer any scruple of foretelling one upon the appearance of the other, and of employing that reasoning, which can alone assure us of any matter of fact or existence. We then call the one object, *Cause;* the other, *Effect.* We suppose, that there is some connexion between them; some power in the one, by which it infallibly produces the other, and operates with the greatest certainty and strongest necessity.

It appears, then, that this idea of a necessary connexion among events arises from a number of similar instances, which occur, of the constant conjunction of these events; nor can that idea ever be suggested by any one of these instances, surveyed in all possible lights and positions. But there is nothing in a number of instances, different from every single instance, which is supposed to be exactly similar; except only, that after a repetition of similar instances, the mind is carried by habit, upon the appearance of one event, to expect its usual attendant, and to believe, that it will exist. This connexion, therefore, which we *feel* in the mind, this customary transition of the imagination from one object to its usual attendant, is the sentiment or impression, from which we form the idea of power or necessary connexion. Nothing farther is in the case. Contemplate the subject on all sides; you will never find any other origin of that idea. This is the sole difference between one instance, from which we can never receive the idea of connexion, and a number of similar instances, by which it is suggested. The first time a man saw the communication of motion by impulse, as by the shock of two billiard-balls, he could not pronounce that the one event was *connected:* but only that it was *conjoined* with the other. After he had observed several instances of this nature, he then pronounces them to be *connected.* What alteration has happened to give rise to this new idea of *connexion?* Nothing but that he now *feels* these events to be *connected* in his imagination, and can readily foretell the existence of one from the appearance of the other. When we say, therefore, that one object is connected with another, we mean only, that they have acquired a connexion in our thought, and give rise to this inference, by which they become proofs of each other's existence: A conclusion, which is somewhat extraordinary; but which seems founded on sufficient evidence. Nor will its evidence be weakened by any general diffidence of the understanding, or sceptical suspicion concerning every conclusion, which is new and extraordinary. No conclusions can be more agreeable to scepticism than such as make discoveries concerning the weakness and narrow limits of human reason and capacity.

And what stronger instance can be produced of the surprising ignorance and weakness of the understanding, than the present? For surely, if there be any relation among objects, which it imports to us to know perfectly, it is that of cause and effect. On this are founded all our reasonings concerning matter of fact or existence. By means of it alone we attain any assurance concerning objects, which are removed from the present testimony of our memory and senses. The only immediate utility of all sciences, is to teach us, how to control and regulate future events by their causes. Our thoughts and enquiries are, therefore, every moment, employed about this relation: Yet so imperfect are the ideas which we form concerning it, that it is impossible to give any just definition of cause, except what is drawn from something extraneous and foreign to it. Similar objects are always conjoined with similar. Of this we have experience. Suitably to this experience, therefore, we may define a cause to be *an object, followed by another, and where all the objects, similar to the first, are followed by objects similar to the second.* Or in other words, *where, if the first object had not been, the second never had existed.* The appearance of a cause always conveys the mind, by a customary transition, to the idea of the effect. Of this also we have experience. We may, therefore, suitably to this experience, form another definition of cause; and call it, *an object followed by another, and whose appearance always conveys the thought to that other.* But though both these definitions be drawn from circumstances foreign to the cause, we cannot remedy this inconvenience, or attain any more perfect definition, which may point out that circumstance in the cause, which gives it a connexion with its effect. We have no idea of this connexion; nor even any distinct notion what it is we desire to know, when we endeavour at a conception of it. We say, for instance, that the vibration of this string is the cause of this particular sound. But what do we mean by that affirmation? We either mean, *that this vibration is followed by this sound, and that all similar vibrations have been followed by similar sounds:* Or, *that this vibration is followed by this sound, and that upon the appearance of one, the mind anticipates the senses, and forms immediately an idea of the other.* We may consider the relation of cause and effect in either of these two lights; but beyond these, we have no idea of it.[38]

---

38. According to these explications and definitions, the idea of *power* is relative as much as that of *cause;* and both have a reference to an effect, or some other event constantly conjoined with the former. When we consider the *unknown* circumstance of an object, by which the degree or quantity of its effect is fixed and determined, we call that its power: And accordingly, it is allowed by all philosophers, that the effect is the measure of the power. But if they had any idea of power, as it is in itself, why could not they measure it in itself? The dispute whether the force of a body in motion be as its velocity, or the square of its velocity; this dispute, I say, needed not be decided by comparing its effects in equal or unequal times; but by a direct mensuration and comparison.

As to the frequent use of the words, Force, Power, Energy, &c. which every where occur in common conversation, as well as in philosophy; that is no proof, that we are acquainted, in any instance, with the connecting principle between cause and effect, or can account ultimately for the production of one thing by another. These words, as commonly used, have very loose meanings annexed to them; and their ideas are very uncertain and confused. No animal can put external bodies in motion without the sentiment of a *nisus* or endeavour; and every animal has a sentiment or feeling from the stroke or blow of an external object, that is in motion. These sensations, which are merely animal, and from which we can *a priori* draw no inference, we are apt to transfer to inanimate objects, and to suppose, that they have some such feelings, whenever they transfer or receive motion. With regard to energies, which are exerted, without our annexing to them any idea of communicated motion, we consider only the constant experienced conjunction of the events; and as we *feel* a customary connexion between the ideas, we transfer that feeling to the objects; as nothing is more usual than to apply to external bodies every internal sensation, which they occasion.

To recapitulate, therefore, the reasonings of this section: Every idea is copied from some preceding impression or sentiment; and where we cannot find any impression, we may be certain that there is no idea. In all single instances of the operation of bodies or minds, there is nothing that produces any impression, nor consequently can suggest any idea, of power or necessary connexion. But when many uniform instances appear, and the same object is always followed by the same event; we then begin to entertain the notion of cause and connexion. We then *feel* a new sentiment or impression, to wit, a customary connexion in the thought or imagination between one object and its usual attendant; and this sentiment is the original of that idea which we seek for. For as this idea arises from a number of similar instances, and not from any single instance; it must arise from that circumstance, in which the number of instances differ from every individual instance. But this customary connexion or transition of the imagination is the only circumstance, in which they differ. In every other particular they are alike. The first instance which we saw of motion, communicated by the shock of two billiard-balls (to return to this obvious illustration) is exactly similar to any instance that may, at present, occur to us; except only, that we could not, at first, *infer* one event from the other; which we are enabled to do at present, after so long a course of uniform experience. I know not, whether the reader will readily apprehend this reasoning. I am afraid, that, should I multiply words about it, or throw it into a greater variety of lights, it would only become more obscure and intricate. In all abstract reasonings, there is one point of view, which, if we can happily hit, we shall go farther towards illustrating the subject, than by all the eloquence and copious expression in the world. This point of view we should endeavour to reach, and reserve the flowers of rhetoric for subjects which are more adapted to them.

SECTION VIII. — *Of Liberty and Necessity.*

PART I.

IT might reasonably be expected, in questions, which have been canvassed and disputed with great eagerness, since the first origin of science and philosophy, that the meaning of all the terms, at least, should have been agreed upon among the disputants; and our enquiries, in the course of two thousand years, been able to pass from words to the true and real subject of the controversy. For how easy may it seem to give exact definitions of the terms employed in reasoning, and make these definitions, not the mere sound of words, the object of future scrutiny and examination? But if we consider the matter more narrowly, we shall be apt to draw a quite opposite conclusion. From this circumstance alone, that a controversy has been long kept on foot, and remains still undecided, we may presume, that there is some ambiguity in the expression, and that the disputants affix different ideas to the terms employed in the controversy. For as the faculties of the mind are supposed to be naturally alike in every individual; otherwise nothing could be more fruitless than to reason or dispute together; it were impossible, if men affix the same ideas to their terms, that they could so long form different opinions of the same subject; especially when they communicate their views, and each party turn themselves on all sides, in search of arguments, which may give them the victory over their antagonists. It is true; if men attempt the discussion of questions, which lie entirely beyond the reach of human capacity, such as those concerning the origin of worlds, or the economy of the intellectual system or region of spirits, they may long beat the air in their fruitless contests, and never arrive at any determinate conclusion. But if the question regard any subject of common life and experience; nothing, one would think, could preserve the dispute so long undecided, but some ambiguous expressions, which keep the antagonists still at a distance, and hinder them from grappling with each other.

This has been the case in the long disputed question concerning liberty and necessity; and to so remarkable a degree, that, if I be not much mistaken, we shall find, that all mankind, both learned and ignorant, have always been of the same opinion with regard to this subject, and that a few intelligible definitions would immediately have put an end to the whole controversy. I own, that this dispute has been so much canvassed on all hands, and has led philosophers into such a labyrinth of obscure sophistry, that it is no wonder, if a sensible reader indulge his ease so far as to turn a deaf ear to the proposal of such a question, from which he can expect neither instruction nor entertainment. But the state of the argument here proposed may, perhaps, serve to renew his attention; as it has more novelty, promises at least some decision of the controversy, and will not much disturb his ease by any intricate or obscure reasoning.

I hope, therefore, to make it appear, that all men have ever agreed in the doctrine both of necessity and of liberty, according to any reasonable sense, which can be put on these terms; and that the whole controversy has hitherto turned merely upon words. We shall begin with examining the doctrine of necessity.

It is universally allowed, that matter, in all its operations, is actuated by a necessary force, and that every natural effect is so precisely determined by the energy of its cause, that no other effect, in such particular circumstances, could possibly have resulted from it. The degree and direction of every motion is, by the laws of nature, prescribed with such exactness, that a living creature may as soon arise from the shock of two bodies, as motion, in any other degree or direction than what is actually produced by it. Would we, therefore, form a just and precise idea of *necessity*, we must consider whence that idea arises, when we apply it to the operation of bodies.

It seems evident, that, if all the scenes of nature were continually shifted in such a manner, that no two events bore any resemblance to each other, but every object was entirely new, without any similitude to whatever had been seen before, we should never, in that case, have attained the least idea of necessity, or of a connexion among these objects. We might say, upon such a supposition, that one object or event has followed another; not that one was produced by the other. The relation of cause and effect must be utterly unknown to mankind. Inference and reasoning concerning the operations of nature would, from that moment, be at an end; and the memory and senses remain the only canals, by which the knowledge of any real existence could possibly have access to the mind. Our idea, therefore, of necessity and causation arises entirely from the uniformity, observable in the operations of nature; where similar objects are constantly conjoined together, and the mind is determined by custom to infer the one from the appearance of the other. These two circumstances form the whole of that necessity, which we ascribe to matter. Beyond the constant *conjunction* of similar objects, and the consequent *inference* from one to the other, we have no notion of any necessity, or connexion.

If it appear, therefore, that all mankind have ever allowed, without any doubt or hesitation, that these two circumstances take place in the voluntary actions of men, and in the operations of mind; it must follow, that all mankind have ever agreed in the doctrine of necessity, and that they have hitherto disputed, merely for not understanding each other.

As to the first circumstance, the constant and regular conjunction of similar events; we may possibly satisfy ourselves by the following considerations. It is universally acknowledged, that there is a great uniformity among the actions of men, in all nations and ages, and that human nature remains still the same, in its principles and operations. The same motives always produce the same actions: The same events follow from the same causes. Ambition, avarice, self-love, vanity, friendship, generosity, public spirit; these passions, mixed in various degrees, and distributed through society, have been, from the beginning of the world, and still are, the source of all the actions and enterprises, which have ever been observed among mankind. Would you know the sentiments, inclinations, and course of life of the GREEKS and ROMANS ? Study well the temper and actions of the FRENCH and EN-GLISH: You cannot be much mistaken in transferring to the former *most* of the observations, which you have made with regard to the latter. Mankind are so much the same, in all times and places, that history informs us of nothing new or strange in this particular. Its chief use is only to discover the constant and universal principles of human nature, by showing men in all varieties of circumstances and situations, and furnishing us with materials, from which we may form our observations, and become acquainted with the regular springs of human action and behaviour. These records of wars, intrigues, factions, and revolutions, are so many collections of experiments, by which the politician or moral philosopher fixes the principles of his science; in the same manner as the physician or natural philosopher becomes acquainted with the nature of plants, minerals, and other external objects, by the experiments, which he forms concerning them. Nor are the earth, water, and other elements, examined by ARISTOTLE, and HIPPOCRATES,[39] more like to those, which at present lie under our observation, than the men, described by the POLYBIUS[40] and TACITUS,[41] are to those, who now govern the world.

Should a traveller, returning from a far country, bring us an account of men, wholly different from any, with whom we were ever acquainted; men, who were entirely divested of avarice, ambition, or revenge; who knew no pleasure but friendship, generosity, and public spirit; we should immediately, from these circumstances, detect the falsehood, and prove him a liar, with the same certainty as if he had stuffed his narration with stories of centaurs and dragons, miracles and prodigies. And if we would explode any forgery in history, we cannot make use of a more convincing argument, than to prove, that the actions, ascribed to any person, are directly contrary to the course of nature, and that no human motives, in such circumstances, could ever induce him to such a conduct. The veracity of QUINTUS CUR-TIUS[42] is as much to be suspected, when he describes the supernatural courage of

39. [See Leibniz's Monadology, n. 5.]

40. [Polybius (c.201–120 B.C.), a Greek historian, wrote of the rise of Rome.]

41. [Tacitus (55–c.117), a Roman historian, wrote about the Germanic tribes and about the luxurious habits of Romans, which he criticized sharply.]

42. [Quintus Curtius Rufus, a first-century Roman author, wrote a history of Alexander the Great.]

ALEXANDER, by which he was hurried on singly to attack multitudes, as when he describes his supernatural force and activity, by which he was able to resist them. So readily and universally do we acknowledge a uniformity in human motives and actions as well as in the operations of body.

Hence likewise the benefit of that experience, acquired by long life and a variety of business and company, in order to instruct us in the principles of human nature, and regulate our future conduct, as well as speculation. By means of this guide, we mount up to the knowledge of men's inclinations and motives, from their actions, expressions, and even gestures; and again, descend to the interpretation of their actions from our knowledge of their motives and inclinations. The general observations, treasured up by a course of experience, give us the clue of human nature, and teach us to unravel all its intricacies. Pretexts and appearances no longer deceive us. Public declarations pass for the specious colouring of a cause. And though virtue and honour be allowed their proper weight and authority, that perfect disinterestedness, so often pretended to, is never expected in multitudes and parties; seldom in their leaders; and scarcely even in individuals of any rank or station. But were there no uniformity in human actions, and were every experiment, which we could form of this kind, irregular and anomalous, it were impossible to collect any general observations concerning mankind; and no experience, however accurately digested by reflection, would ever serve to any purpose. Why is the aged husbandman more skilful in his calling than the young beginner, but because there is a certain uniformity in the operation of the sun, rain, and earth, towards the production of vegetables; and experience teaches the old practitioner the rules, by which this operation is governed and directed?

We must not, however, expect, that this uniformity of human actions should be carried to such a length, as that all men, in the same circumstances, will always act precisely in the same manner, without making any allowance for the diversity of characters, prejudices, and opinions. Such a uniformity in every particular, is found in no part of nature. On the contrary, from observing the variety of conduct in different men, we are enabled to form a greater variety of maxims, which still suppose a degree of uniformity and regularity.

Are the manners of men different in different ages and countries? We learn thence the great force of custom and education, which mould the human mind from its infancy, and form it into a fixed and established character. Is the behaviour and conduct of the one sex very unlike that of the other? It is thence we become acquainted with the different characters, which nature has impressed upon the sexes, and which she preserves with constancy and regularity. Are the actions of the same person much diversified in the different periods of his life, from infancy to old age? This affords room for many general observations concerning the gradual change of our sentiments and inclinations, and the different maxims, which prevail in the different ages of human creatures. Even the characters, which are peculiar to each individual, have a uniformity in their influence; otherwise our acquaintance with the persons and our observation of their conduct, could never teach us their dispositions, or serve to direct our behaviour with regard to them.

I grant it possible to find some actions, which seem to have no regular connexion with any known motives, and are exceptions to all the measures of conduct, which have ever been established for the government of men. But if we would willingly know, what judgment should be formed of such irregular and extraordinary actions; we may consider the sentiments, commonly entertained with regard to those irregular events, which appear in the course of nature, and the operations of external objects. All causes are not conjoined to their usual effects, with like uniformity. An artificer, who handles only dead matter, may be disappointed of his aim, as well as the politician, who directs the conduct of sensible and intelligent agents.

The vulgar, who take things according to their first appearance, attribute the uncertainty of events to such an uncertainty in the causes as makes the latter often fail of their usual influence; though they meet with no impediment in their operation. But philosophers, observing, that, almost in every part of nature, there is contained a vast variety of springs and principles, which are hid, by reason of their minuteness or remoteness, find, that it is at least possible the contrariety of events may not proceed from any contingency in the cause, but from the secret operation of contrary causes. This possibility is converted into certainty by farther observation; when they remark, that, upon an exact scrutiny, a contrariety of effects always betrays a contrariety of causes, and proceeds from their mutual opposition. A peasant can give no better reason for the stopping of any clock or watch than to say that it does not commonly go right: But an artist easily perceives, that the same force in the spring or pendulum has always the same influence on the wheels; but fails of its usual effect, perhaps by reason of a grain of dust, which puts a stop to the whole movement. From the observation of several parallel instances, philosophers form a maxim, that the connexion between all causes and effects is equally necessary, and that its seeming uncertainty in some instances proceeds from the secret opposition of contrary causes.

Thus for instance, in the human body, when the usual symptoms of health or sickness disappoint our expectation; when medicines operate not with their wonted powers; when irregular events follow from any particular cause; the philosopher and physician are not surprised at the matter, nor are ever tempted to deny, in general, the necessity and uniformity of those principles, by which the animal economy is conducted. They know, that a human body is a mighty complicated machine: That many secret powers lurk in it, which are altogether beyond our comprehension: That to us it must often appear very uncertain in its operations: And that therefore the irregular events, which outwardly discover themselves, can be no proof, that the laws of nature are not observed with the greatest regularity in its internal operations and government.

The philosopher, if he be consistent, must apply the same reasoning to the actions and volitions of intelligent agents. The most irregular and unexpected resolutions of men may frequently be accounted for by those, who know every particular circumstance of their character and situation. A person of an obliging disposition gives a peevish answer: But he has the toothache, or has not dined. A stupid fellow discovers an uncommon alacrity in his carriage: But he has met with a sudden piece of good fortune. Or even when an action, as sometimes happens, cannot be particularly accounted for, either by the person himself or by others; we know, in general, that the characters of men are, to a certain degree, inconstant and irregular. This is, in a manner, the constant character of human nature; though it be applicable, in a more particular manner, to some persons, who have no fixed rule for their conduct, but proceed in a continued course of caprice and inconstancy. The internal principles and motives may operate in a uniform manner, notwithstanding these seeming irregularities; in the same manner as the winds, rain, clouds, and other variations of the weather are supposed to be governed by steady principles; though not easily discoverable by human sagacity and enquiry.

Thus it appears, not only that the conjunction between motives and voluntary actions is as regular and uniform, as that between the cause and effect in any part of nature; but also that this regular conjunction has been universally acknowledged among mankind, and has never been the subject of dispute, either in philosophy or common life. Now, as it is from past experience, that we draw all inferences concerning the future, and as we conclude, that objects will always be conjoined together, which we find to have always been conjoined; it may seem superfluous to prove, that this experienced uniformity in human actions is a source, whence we draw *inferences* concerning them. But in order to throw the argument into a greater variety of lights, we shall also insist, though briefly, on this latter topic.

The mutual dependence of men is so great, in all societies, that scarce any human action is entirely complete in itself, or is performed without some reference to the actions of others, which are requisite to make it answer fully the intention of the agent. The poorest artificer, who labours alone, expects at least the protection of the magistrate, to ensure him the enjoyment of the fruits of his labour. He also expects, that, when he carries his goods to market, and offers them at a reasonable price, he shall find purchasers; and shall be able, by the money he acquires, to engage others to supply him with those commodities, which are requisite for his subsistence. In proportion as men extend their dealings, and render their intercourse with others more complicated, they always comprehend, in their schemes of life, a greater variety of voluntary actions, which they expect, from the proper motives, to cooperate with their own. In all these conclusions, they take their measures from past experience, in the same manner as in their reasonings concerning external objects; and firmly believe, that men, as well as all the elements, are to continue, in their operations, the same, that they have ever found them. A manufacturer reckons upon the labour of his servants, for the execution of any work, as much as upon the tools, which he employs, and would be equally surprised, were his expectations disappointed. In short, this experimental inference and reasoning concerning the actions of others enters so much into human life, that no man, while awake, is ever a moment without employing it. Have we not reason, therefore, to affirm, that all mankind have always agreed in the doctrine of necessity, according to the foregoing definition and explication of it?

Nor have philosophers ever entertained a different opinion from the people in this particular. For not to mention, that almost every action of their life supposes that opinion; there are even few of the speculative parts of learning, to which it is not essential. What would become of *history*, had we not a dependence on the veracity of the historian, according to the experience, which we have had of mankind? How could *politics* be a science, if laws and forms of government had not a uniform influence upon society? Where would be the foundation of *morals*, if particular characters had no certain or determinate power to produce particular sentiments, and if these sentiments had no constant operation on actions? And with what pretence could we employ our *criticism* upon any poet or polite author, if we could not pronounce the conduct and sentiments of his actors, either natural or unnatural, to such characters, and in such circumstances? It seems almost impossible, therefore, to engage, either in science or action of any kind, without acknowledging the doctrine of necessity, and this *inference* from motives to voluntary actions; from characters to conduct.

And indeed, when we consider how aptly *natural* and *moral* evidence link together, and form only one chain of argument, we shall make no scruple to allow, that they are of the same nature, and derived from the same principles. A prisoner, who has neither money nor interest, discovers the impossibility of his escape, as well when he considers the obstinacy of the gaoler, as the walls and bars, with which he is surrounded; and, in all attempts for his freedom, chooses rather to work upon the stone and iron of the one, than upon the inflexible nature of the other. The same prisoner, when conducted to the scaffold, foresees his death as certainly from the constancy and fidelity of his guards, as from the operation of the ax or wheel. His mind runs along a certain train of ideas: The refusal of the soldiers to consent to his escape; the action of the executioner; the separation of the head and body; bleeding, convulsive motions, and death. Here is a connected chain of natural causes and voluntary actions; but the mind feels no difference between them, in passing from one link to another: Nor is less certain of the future event than if it were connected with the objects present to the memory or senses, by a train of causes, cemented together by what we are pleased to call a *physical* necessity. The same experienced union has the same effect on the mind, whether the united objects be motives, volition, and actions; or figure and motion. We may change the names of things; but their nature and their operation on the understanding never change.

Were a man, whom I know to be honest and opulent, and with whom I live in intimate friendship, to come into my house, where I am surrounded with my servants, I rest assured, that he is not to stab me before he leaves it, in order to rob me of my silver standish; and I no more suspect this event, than the falling of the house itself which is new, and solidly built and founded. — *But he may have been seized with a sudden and unknown frenzy.* —So may a sudden earthquake arise, and shake and tumble my house about my ears. I shall therefore change the suppositions. I shall say, that I know with certainty, that he is not to put his hand into the fire, and hold it there, till it be consumed: And this event, I think I can foretell with the same assurance, as that, if he throw himself out at the window, and meet with no obstruction, he will not remain a moment suspended in the air. No suspicion of an unknown frenzy can give the least possibility to the former event, which is so contrary to all the known principles of human nature. A man who at noon leaves his purse full of gold on the pavement at Charing-Cross, may as well expect that it will fly away like a feather, as that he will find it untouched an hour after. Above one half of human reasonings contain inferences of a similar nature, attended with more or less degrees of certainty, proportioned to our experience of the usual conduct of mankind in such particular situations.

I have frequently considered, what could possibly be the reason, why all mankind, though they have ever, without hesitation, acknowledged the doctrine of necessity, in their whole practice and reasoning, have yet discovered such a reluctance to acknowledge it in words, and have rather shown a propensity, in all ages, to profess the contrary opinion. The matter, I think, may be accounted for, after the following manner. If we examine the operations of body, and the production of effects from their causes, we shall find, that all our faculties can never carry us farther in our knowledge of this relation, than barely to observe, that particular objects are *constantly conjoined* together, and that the mind is carried, by a *customary transition,* from the appearance of one to the belief of the other. But though this conclusion concerning human ignorance be the result of the strictest scrutiny of this subject, men still entertain a strong propensity to believe, that they penetrate farther into the powers of nature, and perceive something like a necessary connexion between the cause and the effect. When again they turn their reflections towards the operations of their own minds, and *feel* no such connexion of the motive and the action; they are thence apt to suppose, that there is a difference between the effects, which result from material force, and those which arise from thought and intelligence. But being once convinced, that we know nothing farther of causation of any kind, than merely the *constant conjunction* of objects, and the consequent *inference* of the mind from one to another, and finding, that these two circumstances are universally allowed to have place in voluntary actions; we may be more easily led to own the same necessity common to all causes. And though this reasoning may contradict the systems of many philosophers, in ascribing necessity to the determinations of the will, we shall find, upon reflection, that they dissent from it in words only, not in their real sentiment. Necessity, according to the sense, in which it is here taken, has never yet been rejected, nor can ever, I think, be rejected by any philosopher. It may only, perhaps, be pretended, that the mind can perceive, in the operations of matter, some farther connexion between the cause and effect; and a connexion that has not place in the voluntary actions of intelligent beings. Now whether it be so or not, can only appear upon examination; and it is incumbent on these philosophers to make good their assertion, by defining or describing that necessity, and pointing it out to us in the operations of material causes.

It would seem, indeed, that men begin at the wrong end of this question concerning liberty and necessity, when they enter upon it by examining the faculties of the soul, the influence of the understanding, and the operations of the will. Let them first discuss a more simple question, namely, the operations of body and of brute unintelligent matter; and try whether they can there form any idea of causation and necessity, except that of a constant conjunction of objects, and subsequent inference of the mind from one to another. If these circumstances form, in reality, the whole of that necessity, which we conceive in matter, and if these circumstances be also universally acknowledged to take place in the operations of the mind, the dispute is at an end; at least, must be owned to be thenceforth merely verbal. But as long as we will rashly suppose, that we have some farther idea of necessity and causation in the operations of external objects; at the same time, that we can find nothing farther, in the voluntary actions of the mind; there is no possibility of bringing the question to any determinate issue, while we proceed upon so erroneous a supposition. The only method of undeceiving us, is, to mount up higher; to examine the narrow extent of science when applied to material causes; and to convince ourselves, that all we know of them, is, the constant conjunction and inference above mentioned. We may, perhaps, find, that it is with difficulty we are induced to fix such narrow limits to human understanding: But we can afterwards find no difficulty when we come to apply this doctrine to the actions of the will. For as it is evident, that these have a regular conjunction with motives and circumstances and characters, and as we always draw inferences from one to the other, we must be obliged to acknowledge in words, that necessity, which we have already avowed, in every deliberation of our lives, and in every step of our conduct and behaviour.[43]

But to proceed in this reconciling project with regard to the question of liberty and necessity; the most contentious question, of metaphysics, the most contentious science; it will not require many words to prove, that all mankind have ever agreed in the doctrine of liberty as well as in that of necessity, and that the whole dispute, in this respect also, has been hitherto merely verbal. For what is meant by liberty, when applied to voluntary actions? We cannot surely mean, that actions have so little connexion with motives, inclinations, and circumstances, that one does not follow with a certain degree of uniformity from the other, and that one affords no inference by which we can conclude the existence of the other. For these are plain and acknowledged matters of fact. By liberty, then, we can only mean *a power of acting or not acting, according to the determinations of the will;* that is, if we choose to remain at rest, we may; if we choose to move, we also may. Now this hypothetical liberty is universally allowed to belong to every one, who is not a prisoner and in chains. Here then is no subject of dispute.

Whatever definition we may give of liberty, we should be careful to observe two requisite circumstances; *first,* that it be consistent with plain matter of fact; *secondly,* that it be consistent with itself. If we observe these circumstances, and render our definition intelligible, I am persuaded that all mankind will be found of one opinion with regard to it.

It is universally allowed, that nothing exists without a cause of its existence, and that chance, when strictly examined, is a mere negative word, and means not any real power, which has any where, a being in nature. But it is pretended, that some causes are necessary, some not necessary. Here then is the advantage of definitions. Let any one *define* a cause, without comprehending, as a part of the definition, a *necessary connexion* with its effect; and let him show distinctly the origin of the idea, expressed by the definition; and I shall readily give up the whole controversy. But if

---

43. The prevalence of the doctrine of liberty may be accounted for, from another cause, *viz.* a false sensation or seeming experience which we have, or may have, of liberty or indifference, in many of our actions. The necessity of any action, whether of matter or of mind, is not, properly speaking, a quality in the agent, but in any thinking or intelligent being, who may consider the action; and it consists chiefly in the determination of his thoughts to infer the existence of that action from some preceding objects; as liberty, when opposed to necessity, is nothing but the want of that determination, and a certain looseness or indifference, which we feel, in passing, or not passing, from the idea of one object to that of any succeeding one. Now we may observe, that, though, in *reflecting* on human actions, we seldom feel such a looseness or indifference, but are commonly able to infer them with considerable certainty from their motives, and from the dispositions of the agent; yet it frequently happens, that, in *performing* the actions themselves, we are sensible of something like it: And as all resembling objects are readily taken for each other, this has been employed as a demonstrative and even intuitive proof of human liberty. We feel, that our actions are subject to our will, on most occasions; and imagine we feel, that the will itself is subject to nothing, because, when by a denial of it we are provoked to try, we feel, that it moves easily every way, and produces an image of itself, (or a *Velleïty,* as it is called in the schools) even on that side, on which it did not settle. This image, or faint motion, we persuade ourselves, could, at that time, have been completed into the thing itself; because, should that be denied, we find, upon a second trial, that, at present, it can. We consider not, that the fantastical desire of showing liberty, is here the motive of our actions. And it seems certain, that, however we may imagine we feel a liberty within ourselves, a spectator can commonly infer our actions from our motives and character; and even where he cannot, he concludes in general, that he might, were he perfectly acquainted with every circumstance of our situation and temper, and the most secret springs of our complexion and disposition. Now this is the very essence of necessity, according to the foregoing doctrine.

the foregoing explication of the matter be received, this must be absolutely impracticable. Had not objects a regular conjunction with each other, we should never
have entertained any notion of cause and effect; and this regular conjunction produces that inference of the understanding, which is the only connexion, that we can
have any comprehension of. Whoever attempts a definition of cause, exclusive of
these circumstances, will be obliged, either to employ unintelligible terms, or such
as are synonymous to the term, which he endeavours to define.[44] And if the definition above mentioned be admitted; liberty, when opposed to necessity, not to constraint, is the same thing with chance; which is universally allowed to have no existence.

PART II.

There is no method of reasoning more common, and yet none more blamable,
than, in philosophical disputes, to endeavour the refutation of any hypothesis, by a
pretence of its dangerous consequences to religion and morality. When any opinion
leads to absurdities, it is certainly false, but it is not certain that an opinion is false,
because it is of dangerous consequence. Such topics, therefore, ought entirely to be
forborne; as serving nothing to the discovery of truth, but only to make the person
of an antagonist odious. This I observe in general, without pretending to draw any
advantage from it. I frankly submit to an examination of this kind, and shall venture to affirm, that the doctrines, both of necessity and of liberty, as above explained, are not only consistent with morality, but are absolutely essential to its support.

Necessity may be defined two ways, conformably to the two definitions of *cause,* of
which it makes an essential part. It consists either in the constant conjunction of
like objects, or in the inference of the understanding from one object to another.
Now necessity, in both these senses, (which, indeed, are, at bottom, the same) has
universally, though tacitly, in the schools, in the pulpit, and in common life, been
allowed to belong to the will of man; and no one has ever pretended to deny, that
we can draw inferences concerning human actions, and that those inferences are
founded on the experienced union of like actions, with like motives, inclinations,
and circumstances. The only particular, in which any one can differ, is, that either,
perhaps, he will refuse to give the name of necessity to this property of human
actions: But as long as the meaning is understood, I hope the word can do no harm:
Or that he will maintain it possible to discover something farther in the operations
of matter. But this, it must be acknowledged, can be of no consequence to morality
or religion, whatever it may be to natural philosophy or metaphysics. We may here
be mistaken in asserting, that there is no idea of any other necessity or connexion in
the actions of body: But surely we ascribe nothing to the actions of the mind, but
what every one does, and must readily allow of. We change no circumstance in the
received orthodox system with regard to the will, but only in that with regard to
material objects and causes. Nothing therefore can be more innocent, at least, than
this doctrine.

---

44. Thus, if a cause be defined, *that which produces any thing;* it is easy to observe, that *producing* is synonymous to *causing.* In like manner, if a cause be defined, *that by which anything exists;* this is liable to the
same objection. For what is meant by these words, *by which?* Had it been said, that a cause is *that* after
which *anything constantly exists;* we should have understood the terms. For this is, indeed, all we know of
the matter. And this constancy forms the very essence of necessity, nor have we any other idea of it.

All laws being founded on rewards and punishments, it is supposed as a fundamental principle, that these motives have a regular and uniform influence on the mind, and both produce good and prevent the evil actions. We may give to this influence what name we please; but, as it is usually conjoined with the action, it must be esteemed a *cause,* and be looked upon as an instance of that necessity, which we would here establish.

The only proper object of hatred or vengeance, is a person or creature, endowed with thought and consciousness; and when any criminal or injurious actions excite that passion, it is only by their relation to the person, or connexion with him. Actions are, by their very nature, temporary and perishing; and where they proceed not from some *cause* in the character and disposition of the person who performed them, they can neither redound to his honour, if good; nor infamy, if evil. The actions themselves may be blamable; they may be contrary to all the rules of morality and religion: But the person is not answerable for them; and as they proceeded from nothing in him, that is durable and constant, and leave nothing of that nature behind them, it is impossible he can, upon their account, become the object of punishment or vengeance. According to the principle, therefore, which denies necessity, and consequently causes, a man is as pure and untainted, after having committed the most horrid crime, as at the first moment of his birth, nor is his character any wise concerned in his actions; since they are not derived from it, and the wickedness of the one can never be used as a proof of the depravity of the other.

Men are not blamed for such actions, as they perform ignorantly and casually, whatever may be the consequences. Why? but because the principles of these actions are only momentary, and terminate in them alone. Men are less blamed for such actions as they perform hastily and unpremeditately, than for such as proceed from deliberation. For what reason? but because a hasty temper, though a constant cause or principle in the mind, operates only by intervals, and infects not the whole character. Again, repentance wipes off every crime, if attended with a reformation of life and manners. How is this to be accounted for? but by asserting, that actions render a person criminal, merely as they are proofs of criminal principles in the mind; and when, by an alteration of these principles, they cease to be just proofs, they likewise cease to be criminal. But, except upon the doctrine of necessity, they never were just proofs, and consequently never were criminal.

It will be equally easy to prove, and from the same arguments, that *liberty,* according to that definition above mentioned, in which all men agree, is also essential to morality, and that no human actions, where it is wanting, are susceptible of any moral qualities, or can be the objects either of approbation or dislike. For as actions are objects of our moral sentiment, so far only as they are indications of the internal character, passions, and affections; it is impossible that they can give rise either to praise or blame, where they proceed not from these principles, but are derived altogether from external violence.

I pretend not to have obviated or removed all objections to this theory, with regard to necessity and liberty. I can foresee other objections, derived from topics, which have not here been treated of. It may be said, for instance, that, if voluntary actions be subjected to the same laws of necessity with the operations of matter, there is a continued chain of necessary causes, pre-ordained and pre-determined, reaching from the original cause of all, to every single volition of every human creature. No contingency any where in the universe; no indifference; no liberty. While we act, we are, at the same time, acted upon. The ultimate Author of all our volitions is the Creator of the world, who first bestowed motion on this immense machine, and placed all beings in that particular position, whence every subsequent event, by an inevitable necessity, must result. Human actions, therefore, either can have no moral turpitude at all, as proceeding from so good a cause; or if they have any turpitude, they must involve our Creator in the same guilt, while he is acknowledged to be their ultimate cause and author. For as a man, who fired a mine, is answerable for all the consequences, whether the train he employed be long or short; so wherever a continued chain of necessary causes is fixed, that Being, either finite or infinite, who produces the first, is likewise the author of all the rest, and must both bear the blame and acquire the praise, which belong to them. Our clear and unalterable ideas of morality establish this rule, upon unquestionable reasons, when we examine the consequences of any human action; and these reasons must still have a greater force, when applied to the volitions and intentions of a Being, infinitely wise and powerful. Ignorance or impotence may be pleaded for so limited a creature as man; but those imperfections have no place in our Creator. He foresaw, he ordained, he intended all those actions of men, which we so rashly pronounce criminal. And we must therefore conclude, either that they are not criminal, or that the Deity, not man, is accountable for them. But as either of these positions is absurd and impious, it follows, that the doctrine, from which they are deduced, cannot possibly be true, as being liable to all the same objections. An absurd consequence, if necessary, proves the original doctrine to be absurd; in the same manner as criminal actions render criminal the original cause, if the connexion between them be necessary and inevitable.

This objection consists of two parts, which we shall examine separately; *First,* that, if human actions can be traced up, by a necessary chain, to the Deity, they can never be criminal; on account of the infinite perfection of that Being, from whom they are derived, and who can intend nothing but what is altogether good and laudable. Or, *Secondly,* if they be criminal, we must retract the attribute of perfection, which we ascribe to the Deity, and must acknowledge him to be the ultimate author of guilt and moral turpitude in all his creatures.

The answer to the first objection seems obvious and convincing. There are many philosophers, who, after an exact scrutiny of all the phenomena of nature, conclude, that the WHOLE, considered as one system, is, in every period of its existence, ordered with perfect benevolence; and that the utmost possible happiness will, in the end, result to all created beings, without any mixture of positive or absolute ill and misery. Every physical ill, say they, makes an essential part of this benevolent system, and could not possibly be removed, even by the Deity himself, considered as a wise agent, without giving entrance to greater ill, or excluding greater good, which will result from it. From this theory, some philosophers, and the ancient *Stoics* among the rest, derived a topic of consolation under all afflictions, while they taught their pupils, that those ills, under which they laboured, were, in reality, goods to the universe; and that to an enlarged view, which could comprehend the whole system of nature, every event became an object of joy and exultation. But though this topic be specious and sublime, it was soon found in practice weak and ineffectual. You would surely more irritate, than appease a man, lying under the racking pains of the gout, by preaching up to him the rectitude of those general laws, which produced the malignant humours in his body, and led them through the proper canals, to the sinews and nerves, where they now excite such acute torments. These enlarged views may, for a moment, please the imagination of a speculative man, who is placed in ease and security; but neither can they dwell with constancy on his mind, even though undisturbed by the emotions of pain or passion; much less can they maintain their ground, when attacked by such powerful antagonists. The affections take a narrower and more natural survey of their object; and by an economy, more suitable to the infirmity of human minds, regard alone the beings around us, and are actuated by such events as appear good or ill to the private system.

The case is the same with *moral* as with *physical* ill. It cannot reasonably be supposed, that those remote considerations, which are found of so little efficacy with regard to one, will have a more powerful influence with regard to the other. The mind of man is so formed by nature, that, upon the appearance of certain characters, dispositions, and actions, it immediately feels the sentiment of approbation or blame; nor are there any emotions more essential to its frame and constitution. The characters, which engage our approbation, are chiefly such as contribute to the peace and security of human society; as the characters, which excite blame, are chiefly such as tend to public detriment and disturbance: Whence it may reasonably be presumed, that the moral sentiments arise, either mediately or immediately, from a reflection on these opposite interests. What though philosophical meditations establish a different opinion or conjecture; that every thing is right with regard to the WHOLE, and that the qualities, which disturb society, are, in the main, as beneficial, and are as suitable to the primary intention of nature, as those which more directly promote its happiness and welfare? Are such remote and uncertain speculations able to counterbalance the sentiments, which arise from the natural and immediate view of the objects? A man who is robbed of a considerable sum; does he find his vexation for the loss any wise diminished by these sublime reflections? Why then should his moral resentment against the crime be supposed incompatible with them? Or why should not the acknowledgment of a real distinction between vice and virtue be reconcileable to all speculative systems of philosophy, as well as that of a real distinction between personal beauty and deformity? Both these distinctions are founded in the natural sentiments of the human mind: And these sentiments are not to be controlled or altered by any philosophical theory or speculation whatsoever.

The *second* objection admits not of so easy and satisfactory an answer; nor is it possible to explain distinctly, how the Deity can be the mediate cause of all the actions of men, without being the author of sin and moral turpitude. These are mysteries, which mere natural and unassisted reason is very unfit to handle; and whatever system she embraces, she must find herself involved in inextricable difficulties, and even contradictions, at every step which she takes with regard to such subjects. To reconcile the indifference and contingency of human actions with prescience; or to defend absolute decrees, and yet free the Deity from being the author of sin, has been found hitherto to exceed all the power of philosophy. Happy, if she be thence sensible of her temerity, when she pries into these sublime mysteries; and leaving a scene so full of obscurities and perplexities, return, with suitable modesty, to her true and proper province, the examination of common life; where she will find difficulties enough to employ her enquiries, without launching into so boundless an ocean of doubt, uncertainty, and contradiction!

SECTION IX. — *Of the Reason of Animals.*

ALL our reasonings concerning matter of fact are founded on a species of ANALOGY, which leads us to expect from any cause the same events, which we have observed to result from similar causes. Where the causes are entirely similar, the analogy is perfect, and the inference, drawn from it, is regarded as certain and conclusive: Nor does any man ever entertain a doubt, where he sees a piece of iron, that it will have weight and cohesion of parts; as in all other instances, which have ever fallen under his observation. But where the objects have not so exact a similarity, the analogy is less perfect, and the inference is less conclusive; though still it has some force, in proportion to the degree of similarity and resemblance. The anatomical observations, formed upon one animal, are, by this species of reasoning, extended to all animals; and it is certain, that when the circulation of the blood, for instance, is clearly proved to have place in one creature, as a frog, or fish, it forms a strong presumption, that the same principle has place in all. These analogical observations may be carried farther, even to this science, of which we are now treating; and any theory, by which we explain the operations of the understanding, or the origin and connexion of the passions in man, will acquire additional authority, if we find, that the same theory is requisite to explain the same phenomena in all other animals. We shall make trial of this, with regard to the hypothesis, by which, we have, in the foregoing discourse, endeavoured to account for all experimental reasonings; and it is hoped, that this new point of view will serve to confirm all our former observations.

First, It seems evident, that animals, as well as men learn many things from experience, and infer, that the same events will always follow from the same causes. By this principle they become acquainted with the more obvious properties of external objects, and gradually, from their birth, treasure up a knowledge of the nature of fire, water, earth, stones, heights, depths, &c. and of the effects, which result from their operation. The ignorance and inexperience of the young are here plainly distinguishable from the cunning and sagacity of the old, who have learned, by long observation, to avoid what hurt them, and to pursue what gave ease or pleasure. A horse, that has been accustomed to the field, becomes acquainted with the proper height, which he can leap, and will never attempt what exceeds his force and ability. An old greyhound will trust the more fatiguing part of the chase to the younger, and will place himself so as to meet the hare in her doubles; nor are the conjectures, which he forms on this occasion, founded in any thing but his observation and experience.

This is still more evident from the effects of discipline and education on animals, who, by the proper application of rewards and punishments, may be taught any course of action, the most contrary to their natural instincts and propensities. Is it not experience, which renders a dog apprehensive of pain, when you menace him, or lift up the whip to beat him? Is it not even experience, which makes him answer to his name, and infer, from such an arbitrary sound, that you mean him rather than any of his fellows, and intend to call him, when you pronounce it in a certain manner, and with a certain tone and accent?

In all these cases, we may observe, that the animal infers some fact beyond what immediately strikes his senses; and that this inference is altogether founded on past experience, while the creature expects from the present object the same consequences, which it has always found in its observation to result from similar objects.

Secondly, It is impossible, that this inference of the animal can be founded on any process of argument or reasoning, by which he concludes, that like events must follow like objects, and that the course of nature will always be regular in its operations. For if there be in reality any arguments of this nature, they surely lie too abstruse for the observation of such imperfect understandings; since it may well employ the utmost care and attention of a philosophic genius to discover and observe them. Animals, therefore, are not guided in these inferences by reasoning: Neither are children: Neither are the generality of mankind, in their ordinary actions and conclusions: Neither are philosophers themselves, who, in all the active parts of life, are, in the main, the same with the vulgar, and are governed by the same maxims. Nature must have provided some other principle, of more ready, and more general use and application; nor can an operation of such immense consequence in life, as that of inferring effects from causes, be trusted to the uncertain process of reasoning and argumentation. Were this doubtful with regard to men, it seems to admit of no question with regard to the brute creation; and the conclusion being once firmly established in the one, we have a strong presumption, from all the rules of analogy, that it ought to be universally admitted, without any exception or reserve. It is custom alone, which engages animals, from every object, that strikes their senses, to infer its usual attendant, and carries their imagination, from the appearance of the one, to conceive the other, in that particular manner, which we denominate *belief.* No other explication can be given of this operation, in all the higher, as well as lower classes of sensitive beings, which fall under our notice and observation.[45]

45. Since all reasonings concerning facts or causes is derived merely from custom, it may be asked how it happens, that men so much surpass animals in reasoning, and one man so much surpasses another? Has not the same custom the same influence on all?

We shall here endeavour briefly to explain the great difference in human understandings: After which the reason of the difference between men and animals will easily be comprehended.

1. When we have lived any time, and have been accustomed to the uniformity of nature, we acquire a general habit, by which we always transfer the known to the unknown, and conceive the latter to resemble the former. By means of this general habitual principle, we regard even one experiment as the foundation of reasoning, and expect a similar event with some degree of certainty, where the experiment has been made accurately, and free from all foreign circumstances. It is therefore considered as a matter of great importance to observe the consequences of things; and as one man may very much surpass another in attention and memory and observation, this will make a very great difference in their reasoning.

2. Where there is a complication of causes to produce any effect, one mind may be much larger than another, and better able to comprehend the whole system of objects, and to infer justly their consequences.

3. One man is able to carry on a chain of consequences to a greater length than another.

4. Few men can think long without running into a confusion of ideas, and mistaking one for another; and there are various degrees of this infirmity.

5. The circumstance, on which the effect depends, is frequently involved in other circumstances, which are foreign and extrinsic. The separation of it often requires great attention, accuracy, and subtilty.

6. The forming of general maxims from particular observation is a very nice operation; and nothing is more usual, from haste or a narrowness of mind, which sees not on all sides, than to commit mistakes in this particular.

7. When we reason from analogies, the man, who has the greater experience or the greater promptitude of suggesting analogies, will be the better reasoner.

8. Biases from prejudice, education, passion, party, &c. hang more upon one mind than another.

9. After we have acquired a confidence in human testimony, books and conversation enlarge much more the sphere of one man's experience and thought than those of another.

It would be easy to discover many other circumstances that make a difference in the understandings of men.

But though animals learn many parts of their knowledge from observation, there are also many parts of it, which they derive from the original hand of nature; which much exceed the share of capacity they possess on ordinary occasions; and in which they improve, little or nothing, by the longest practice and experience. These we denominate INSTINCTS, and are so apt to admire, as something very extraordinary, and inexplicable by all the disquisitions of human understanding. But our wonder will, perhaps, cease or diminish; when we consider, that the experimental reasoning itself, which we possess in common with beasts, and on which the whole conduct of life depends, is nothing but a species of instinct or mechanical power, that acts in us unknown to ourselves; and in its chief operations, is not directed by any such relations or comparisons of ideas, as are the proper objects of our intellectual faculties. Though the instinct be different, yet still it is an instinct, which teaches a man to avoid the fire; as much as that, which teaches a bird, with such exactness, the art of incubation, and the whole economy and order of its nursery.

SECTION X. — *Of Miracles.*[46]

PART I.

THERE is, in Dr. TILLOTSON'S writings,[47] an argument against the *real presence,*[48] which is as concise, and elegant, and strong as any argument can possibly be supposed against a doctrine, so little worthy of a serious refutation. It is acknowledged on all hands, says that learned prelate, that the authority, either of the scripture or of tradition, is founded merely in the testimony of the apostles, who were eye-witnesses to those miracles of our Saviour, by which he proved his divine mission. Our evidence, then, for the truth of the *Christian* religion is less than the evidence for the truth of our senses; because, even in the first authors of our religion, it was no greater; and it is evident it must diminish in passing from them to their disciples; nor can any one rest such confidence in their testimony, as in the immediate object of his senses. But a weaker evidence can never destroy a stronger; and therefore, were the doctrine of the real presence ever so clearly revealed in scripture, it were directly contrary to the rules of just reasoning to give our assent to it. It contradicts sense, though both the scripture and tradition, on which it is supposed to be built, carry not such evidence with them as sense; when they are considered merely as external evidences, and are not brought home to every one's breast, by the immediate operation of the Holy Spirit.

Nothing is so convenient as a decisive argument of this kind, which must at least

46. [A draft of this section was extant as early as 1737; although Hume had apparently entertained the idea of including it in the *Treatise,* evidence suggests that he withheld it for fear of displeasing Joseph Butler, whose approval of the work he sought. The essay was first published as part of the *Enquiry* and is thought by many to be a direct reply to two influential works, one by Thomas Sherlock (1678–1761), Bishop of London, *Tryal of the Witnesses of the Resurrection of Jesus* (1729); the other was Zachary Pearce's (1690–1774) *Miracles of Jesus Vindicated* (1729).]

47. [John Tillotson (1630–1694), a Presbyterian theologian who became Archbishop of Canterbury in 1691, argued in *Rule of Faith* (1676) and *A Doctrine Against Transubstantiation* (1684) that transubstantiation could never be established as part of Christian doctrine.]

48. [The presence of the body and blood of Christ in the bread and wine of the Eucharist.]

silence the most arrogant bigotry and superstition, and free us from their impertinent solicitations. I flatter myself, that I have discovered an argument of a like
nature, which, if just, will, with the wise and learned, be an everlasting check to all
kinds of superstitious delusion, and consequently, will be useful as long as the world
endures. For so long, I presume, will the accounts of miracles and prodigies be
found in all history, sacred and profane.

Though experience be our only guide in reasoning concerning matters of fact; it
must be acknowledged, that this guide is not altogether infallible, but in some cases
is apt to lead us into errors. One, who in our climate, should expect better weather
in any week of JUNE than in one of DECEMBER , would reason justly, and conformably to experience; but it is certain, that he may happen, in the event, to find himself mistaken. However, we may observe, that, in such a case, he would have no
cause to complain of experience; because it commonly informs us beforehand of the
uncertainty, by that contrariety of events, which we may learn from a diligent
observation. All effects follow not with like certainty, from their supposed causes.
Some events are found, in all countries and all ages, to have been constantly conjoined together: Others are found to have been more variable, and sometimes to disappoint our expectations; so that, in our reasonings concerning matter of fact, there
are all imaginable degrees of assurance, from the highest certainty to the lowest
species of moral evidence.

A wise man, therefore, proportions his belief to the evidence. In such conclusions
as are founded on an infallible experience, he expects the event with the last degree
of assurance, and regards his past experience as a full *proof* of the future existence of
that event. In other cases, he proceeds with more caution: He weighs the opposite
experiments: He considers which side is supported by the greater number of experiments: To that side he inclines, with doubt and hesitation; and when at last he
fixes his judgment, the evidence exceeds not what we properly call *probability*. All
probability, then, supposes an opposition of experiments and observations, where
the one side is found to overbalance the other, and to produce a degree of evidence,
proportioned to the superiority. A hundred instances or experiments on one side,
and fifty on another, afford a doubtful expectation of any event; though a hundred
uniform experiments, with only one that is contradictory, reasonably beget a pretty
strong degree of assurance. In all cases, we must balance the opposite experiments,
where they are opposite, and deduct the smaller number from the greater, in order
to know the exact force of the superior evidence.

To apply these principles to a particular instance; we may observe, that there is
no species of reasoning more common, more useful, and even necessary to human
life, than that which is derived from the testimony of men, and the reports of eye-
witnesses and spectators. This species of reasoning, perhaps, one may deny to be
founded on the relation of cause and effect. I shall not dispute about a word. It will
be sufficient to observe, that our assurance in any argument of this kind is derived
from no other principle than our observation of the veracity of human testimony,
and of the usual conformity of facts to the reports of witnesses. It being a general
maxim, that no objects have any discoverable connexion together, and that all the
inferences, which we can draw from one to another, are founded merely on our experience of their constant and regular conjunction; it is evident, that we ought not
to make an exception to this maxim in favour of human testimony, whose connexion with any event seems, in itself, as little necessary as any other. Were not the
memory tenacious to a certain degree; had not men commonly an inclination to

truth and a principle of probity; were they not sensible to shame, when detected in a falsehood: Were not these, I say, discovered by *experience* to be qualities, inherent in human nature, we should never repose the least confidence in human testimony. A man delirious, or noted for falsehood and villainy, has no manner of authority with us.

And as the evidence, derived from witnesses and human testimony, is founded on past experience, so it varies with the experience, and is regarded either as a *proof* or a *probability*, according as the conjunction between any particular kind of report and any kind of object has been found to be constant or variable. There are a number of circumstances to be taken into consideration in all judgments of this kind; and the ultimate standard, by which we determine all disputes, that may arise concerning them, is always derived from experience and observation. Where this experience is not entirely uniform on any side, it is attended with an unavoidable contrariety in our judgments, and with the same opposition and mutual destruction of argument as in every other kind of evidence. We frequently hesitate concerning the reports of others. We balance the opposite circumstances, which cause any doubt or uncertainty; and when we discover a superiority on any side, we incline to it; but still with a diminution of assurance, in proportion to the force of its antagonist.

This contrariety of evidence, in the present case, may be derived from several different causes; from the opposition of contrary testimony; from the character or number of the witnesses; from the manner of their delivering their testimony; or from the union of all these circumstances. We entertain a suspicion concerning any matter of fact, when the witnesses contradict each other; when they are but few, or of a doubtful character; when they have an interest in what they affirm; when they deliver their testimony with hesitation, or on the contrary, with too violent asseverations. There are many other particulars of the same kind, which may diminish or destroy the force of any argument, derived from human testimony.

Suppose, for instance, that the fact, which the testimony endeavours to establish, partakes of the extraordinary and the marvellous; in that case, the evidence, resulting from the testimony, admits of a diminution, greater or less, in proportion as the fact is more or less unusual. The reason, why we place any credit in witnesses and historians, is not derived from any *connexion,* which we perceive a priori, between testimony and reality, but because we are accustomed to find a conformity between them. But when the fact attested is such a one as has seldom fallen under our observation, here is a contest of two opposite experiences; of which the one destroys the other, as far as its force goes, and the superior can only operate on the mind by the force, which remains. The very same principle of experience, which gives us a certain degree of assurance in the testimony of witnesses, gives us also, in this case, another degree of assurance against the fact, which they endeavour to establish; from which contradiction there necessarily arises a counterpoise, and mutual destruction of belief and authority.

I should not believe such a story were it told me by CATO;[49] was a proverbial saying in ROME, even during the lifetime of that philosophical patriot.[50] The incredibility of a fact, it was allowed, might invalidate so great an authority.

49. [The reference is to Marcus Porcius Cato (Cato the Younger) (95–46 B.C.), a Roman statesman and philosopher.]

50. Plutarch in *Vita Catonis.* [Plutarch (c.46–c.120) was a Greek biographer who vividly portrayed the lives of noted Greeks and Romans. The reference here is to his *Life of Cato.*]

The INDIAN prince,[51] who refused to believe the first relations concerning the effects of frost, reasoned justly; and it naturally required very strong testimony to engage his assent to facts, that arose from a state of nature, with which he was unacquainted, and which bore so little analogy to those events, of which he had had constant and uniform experience. Though they were not contrary to his experience, they were not conformable to it.[52]

But in order to increase the probability against the testimony of witnesses, let us suppose, that the fact, which they affirm, instead of being only marvellous, is really miraculous; and suppose also, that the testimony, considered apart and in itself, amounts to an entire proof; in that case, there is proof against proof, of which the strongest must prevail, but still with a diminution of its force, in proportion to that of its antagonist.

A miracle is a violation of the laws of nature; and as a firm and unalterable experience has established these laws, the proof against a miracle, from the very nature of the fact, is as entire as any argument from experience can possibly be imagined. Why is it more than probable, that all men must die; that lead cannot, of itself, remain suspended in the air; that fire consumes wood, and is extinguished by water; unless it be, that these events are found agreeable to the laws of nature, and there is required a violation of these laws, or in other words, a miracle to prevent them? Nothing is esteemed a miracle, if it ever happen in the common course of nature. It is no miracle that a man, seemingly in good health, should die on a sudden: because such a kind of death, though more unusual than any other, has yet been frequently observed to happen. But it is a miracle, that a dead man should come to life; because that has never been observed, in any age or country. There must, therefore, be a uniform experience against every miraculous event, otherwise the event would not merit that appellation. And as an uniform experience amounts to a proof, there is here a direct and full *proof,* from the nature of the fact, against the existence of any miracle; nor can such a proof be destroyed, or the miracle rendered credible, but by an opposite proof, which is superior.[53]

The plain consequence is (and it is a general maxim worthy of our attention),

51. [A variation of this story appears in Locke's *Essay Concerning Human Understanding* IV. 15., as a story about the King of Siam and a Dutch ambassador. An account closer to Hume's is mentioned by Butler in the Introduction to his *Analogy of Religion, Natural and Revealed, to the Constitution and Course of Nature* (1736).]

52. No INDIAN, it is evident, could have experience that water did not freeze in cold climates. This is placing nature in a situation quite unknown to him; and it is impossible for him to tell *a priori* what will result from it. It is making a new experiment, the consequence of which is always uncertain. One may sometimes conjecture from analogy what will follow; but still this is but conjecture. And it must be confessed, that, in the present case of freezing, the event follows contrary to the rules of analogy, and is such as a rational INDIAN would not look for. The operations of cold upon water are not gradual, according to the degrees of cold; but whenever it comes to the freezing point, the water passes in a moment, from the utmost liquidity to perfect hardness. Such an event, therefore, may be denominated *extraordinary,* and requires a pretty strong testimony, to render it credible to people in a warm climate: But still it is not *miraculous,* nor contrary to uniform experience of the course of nature in cases where all the circumstances are the same. The inhabitants of SUMATRA have always seen water fluid in their own climate, and the freezing of their rivers ought to be deemed a prodigy: But they never saw water in MUSCOVY during the winter; and therefore they cannot reasonably be positive what would there be the consequence.

53. Sometimes an event may not, *in itself, seem* to be contrary to the laws of nature, and yet, if it were real, it might, by reason of some circumstances, be denominated a miracle; because, in *fact,* it is contrary

'That no testimony is sufficient to establish a miracle, unless the testimony be of such a kind, that its falsehood would be more miraculous, than the fact, which it endeavours to establish: And even in that case there is a mutual destruction of arguments, and the superior only gives us an assurance suitable to that degree of force, which remains, after deducting the inferior.' When any one tells me, that he saw a dead man restored to life, I immediately consider with myself, whether it be more probable, that this person should either deceive or be deceived, or that the fact, which he relates, should really have happened. I weigh the one miracle against the other; and according to the superiority, which I discover, I pronounce my decision, and always reject the greater miracle. If the falsehood of his testimony would be more miraculous, than the event which he relates; then, and not till then, can he pretend to command my belief or opinion.

PART II.

In the foregoing reasoning we have supposed, that the testimony, upon which a miracle is founded, may possibly amount to an entire proof, and that the falsehood of that testimony would be a real prodigy: But it is easy to show, that we have been a great deal too liberal in our concession, and that there never was a miraculous event established on so full an evidence.

For *first*, there is not to be found, in all history, any miracle attested by a sufficient number of men, of such unquestioned good-sense, education, and learning, as to secure us against all delusion in themselves; of such undoubted integrity, as to place them beyond all suspicion of any design to deceive others; of such credit and reputation in the eyes of mankind, as to have a great deal to lose in case of their being detected in any falsehood; and at the same time, attesting facts, performed in such a public manner, and in so celebrated a part of the world, as to render the detection unavoidable: All which circumstances are requisite to give us a full assurance in the testimony of men.

Secondly. We may observe in human nature a principle, which, if strictly examined, will be found to diminish extremely the assurance, which we might, from human testimony, have, in any kind of prodigy. The maxim, by which we commonly conduct ourselves in our reasonings, is, that the objects, of which we have no experience, resemble those, of which we have; that what we have found to be most usual is always most probable; and that where there is an opposition of arguments, we ought to give the preference to such as are founded on the greatest number of past observations. But though, in proceeding by this rule, we readily reject any fact

---

to these laws. Thus if a person, claiming a divine authority, should command a sick person to be well, a healthful man to fall down dead, the clouds to pour rain, the winds to blow, in short, should order many natural events, which immediately follow upon his command; these might justly be esteemed miracles, because they are really, in this case, contrary to the laws of nature. For if any suspicion remain, that the event and command concurred by accident, there is no miracle and no transgression of the laws of nature. If this suspicion be removed, there is evidently a miracle, and a transgression of these laws; because nothing can be more contrary to nature than that the voice or command of a man should have such an influence. A miracle may be accurately defined, *a transgression of a law of nature by a particular volition of the Deity, or by the interposition of some invisible agent.* A miracle may either be discoverable by men or not. This alters not its nature and essence. The raising of a house or ship into the air is a visible miracle. The raising of a feather, when the wind wants ever so little of a force requisite for that purpose, is as real a miracle, though not so sensible with regard to us.

which is unusual and incredible in an ordinary degree; yet in advancing farther, the mind observes not always the same rule; but when anything is affirmed utterly absurd and miraculous, it rather the more readily admits of such a fact, upon account of that very circumstance, which ought to destroy all its authority. The passion of *surprise* and *wonder*, arising from miracles, being an agreeable emotion, gives a sensible tendency towards the belief of those events, from which it is derived. And this goes so far, that even those who cannot enjoy this pleasure immediately, nor can believe those miraculous events, of which they are informed, yet love to partake of the satisfaction at second-hand or by rebound, and place a pride and delight in exciting the admiration of others.

With what greediness are the miraculous accounts of travellers received, their descriptions of sea and land monsters, their relations of wonderful adventures, strange men, and uncouth manners? But if the spirit of religion join itself to the love of wonder, there is an end of common sense; and human testimony, in these circumstances, loses all pretensions to authority. A religionist may be an enthusiast, and imagine he sees what has no reality: He may know his narrative to be false, and yet persevere in it, with the best intentions in the world, for the sake of promoting so holy a cause: Or even where this delusion has not place, vanity, excited by so strong a temptation, operates on him more powerfully than on the rest of mankind in any other circumstances; and self-interest with equal force. His auditors may not have, and commonly have not, sufficient judgment to canvass his evidence: What judgment they have, they renounce by principle, in these sublime and mysterious subjects: Or if they were ever so willing to employ it, passion and a heated imagination disturb the regularity of its operations. Their credulity increases his impudence: And his impudence overpowers their credulity.

Eloquence, when at its highest pitch, leaves little room for reason or reflection; but addressing itself entirely to the fancy or the affections, captivates the willing hearers, and subdues their understanding. Happily, this pitch it seldom attains. But what a TULLY[54] or a DEMOSTHENES[55] could scarcely effect over a ROMAN or ATHENIAN audience, every *Capuchin*,[56] every itinerant or stationary teacher can perform over the generality of mankind, and in a higher degree, by touching such gross and vulgar passions.

The many instances of forged miracles, and prophecies, and supernatural events, which, in all ages, have either been detected by contrary evidence, or which detect themselves by their absurdity, prove sufficiently the strong propensity of mankind to the extraordinary and the marvellous, and ought reasonably to beget a suspicion against all relations of this kind. This is our natural way of thinking, even with regard to the most common and most credible events. For instance: There is no kind of report, which rises so easily, and spreads so quickly, especially in country places and provincial towns, as those concerning marriages; insomuch that two young persons of equal condition never see each other twice, but the whole neighbourhood immediately join them together. The pleasure of telling a piece of news so inter-

---

54. [Regarding Tully (Cicero), see Hobbes's *Leviathan*, n. 11.]

55. [Demosthenes (c.384–322 B.C.) was a famous Greek orator.]

56. [The Capuchins, founded in the sixteenth century, were Francescan friars who did extensive preaching and missionary work.]

esting, of propagating it, and of being the first reporters of it, spreads the intelligence. And this is so well known, that no man of sense gives attention to these reports, till he find them confirmed by some greater evidence. Do not the same passions, and others still stronger, incline the generality of mankind to believe and report, with the greatest vehemence and assurance, all religious miracles?

Thirdly. It forms a strong presumption against all supernatural and miraculous relations, that they are observed chiefly to abound among ignorant and barbarous nations; or if a civilized people has ever given admission to any of them, that people will be found to have received them from ignorant and barbarous ancestors, who transmitted them with that inviolable sanction and authority, which always attend received opinions. When we peruse the first histories of all nations, we are apt to imagine ourselves transported into some new world; where the whole frame of nature is disjointed, and every element performs its operations in a different manner, from what it does at present. Battles, revolutions, pestilence, famine, and death, are never the effect of those natural causes, which we experience. Prodigies, omens, oracles, judgments, quite obscure the few natural events, that are intermingled with them. But as the former grow thinner every page, in proportion as we advance nearer the enlightened ages, we soon learn, that there is nothing mysterious or supernatural in the case, but that all proceeds from the usual propensity of mankind towards the marvellous, and that, though this inclination may at intervals receive a check from sense and learning, it can never be thoroughly extirpated from human nature.

It is strange, a judicious reader is apt to say, upon the perusal of these wonderful historians, *that such prodigious events never happen in our days.* But it is nothing strange, I hope, that men should lie in all ages. You must surely have seen instances enough of that frailty. You have yourself heard many such marvellous relations started, which, being treated with scorn by all the wise and judicious, have at last been abandoned even by the vulgar. Be assured, that those renowned lies, which have spread and flourished to such a monstrous height, arose from like beginnings; but being sown in a more proper soil, shot up at last into prodigies almost equal to those which they relate.

It was a wise policy in that false prophet, ALEXANDER, who, though now forgotten, was once so famous, to lay the first scene of his impostures in PAPHLAGONIA, where, as LUCIAN tell us,[57] the people were extremely ignorant and stupid, and ready to swallow even the grossest delusion. People at a distance, who are weak enough to think the matter at all worth enquiry, have no opportunity of receiving better information. The stories come magnified to them by a hundred circumstances. Fools are industrious in propagating the imposture; while the wise and learned are contented, in general, to deride its absurdity, without informing themselves of the particular facts, by which it may be distinctly refuted. And thus the impostor above-mentioned was enabled to proceed, from his ignorant PAPHLAGO-NIANS , to the enlisting of votaries, even among the GRECIAN philosophers, and men of the most eminent rank and distinction in ROME: Nay, could engage the at-

---

57. [In *Alexander, the False Prophet,* the Greek author Lucian (born c.120) relates how Alexander of Abonoteichos was hailed as an oracle because of a hoax perpetrated on the people of Paphlagonia, whereby he made it appear that the god Asclepius was being born in the form of a serpent from a goose's egg. Paphlagonia was an ancient country in Asia Minor located in what is now Turkey.]

tention of that sage emperor MARCUS AURELIUS;[58] so far as to make him trust the success of a military expedition to his delusive prophecies.

The advantages are so great, of starting an imposture among an ignorant people, that, even though the delusion should be too gross to impose on the generality of them *(which, though seldom, is sometimes the case)* it has a much better chance for succeeding in remote countries, than if the first scene has been laid in a city renowned for arts and knowledge. The most ignorant and barbarous of these barbarians carry the report abroad. None of their countrymen have a large correspondence, or sufficient credit and authority to contradict and beat down the delusion. Men's inclination to the marvellous has full opportunity to display itself. And thus a story, which is universally exploded in the place where it was first started, shall pass for certain at a thousand miles distance. But had ALEXANDER fixed his residence at ATHENS, the philosophers of that renowned mart of learning had immediately spread, throughout the whole ROMAN empire, their sense of the matter; which, being supported by so great authority, and displayed by all the force of reason and eloquence, had entirely opened the eyes of mankind. It is true; LUCIAN, passing by chance through PAPHLAGONIA, had an opportunity of performing this good office. But, though much to be wished, it does not always happen, that every ALEXANDER meets with a LUCIAN, ready to expose and detect his impostures.

I may add as a *fourth* reason, which diminishes the authority of prodigies, that there is no testimony for any, even those which have not been expressly detected, that is not opposed by an infinite number of witnesses; so that not only the miracle destroys the credit of testimony, but the testimony destroys itself. To make this the better understood, let us consider, that, in matters of religion, whatever is different is contrary; and that it is impossible the religions of ancient ROME, of TURKEY, of SIAM, and of CHINA should, all of them, be established on any solid foundation. Every miracle, therefore, pretended to have been wrought in any of these religions (and all of them abound in miracles), as its direct scope is to establish the particular system to which it is attributed; so has it the same force, though more indirectly, to overthrow every other system. In destroying a rival system, it likewise destroys the credit of those miracles, on which that system was established; so that all the prodigies of different religions are to be regarded as contrary facts, and the evidences of these prodigies, whether weak or strong, as opposite to each other. According to this method of reasoning, when we believe any miracle of MAHOMET or his successors, we have for our warrant the testimony of a few barbarous ARABIANS: And on the other hand, we are to regard the authority of TITUS LIVIUS,[59] PLUTARCH, TACITUS, and, in short, of all the authors and witnesses, GRECIAN, CHINESE, and ROMAN CATHOLIC, who have related any miracle in their particular religion; I say, we are to regard their testimony in the same light as if they had mentioned that MAHOMETAN miracle, and had in express terms contradicted it, with the same certainty as they have for the miracle they relate. This argument may appear over subtile and refined; but is not in reality different from the reasoning of a judge, who supposes, that the credit of two witnesses, maintaining a crime against any one, is destroyed by the testimony of two others, who affirm him to have been two hundred

---

58. [Marcus Aurelius (121–180) was a Roman Emperor and a major Stoic philosopher.]

59. [Titus Livius (59 B.C.–A.D. 17), commonly known as Livy, was a Roman historian; his major work, the 142-book *History of Rome*, covered Rome's beginnings until his own time.]

leagues distant, at the same instant when the crime is said to have been committed.

One of the best attested miracles in all profane history, is that which TACITUS reports of VESPASIAN,[60] who cured a blind man in ALEXANDRIA, by means of his spittle, and a lame man by the mere touch of his foot; in obedience to a vision of the god SERAPIS who had enjoined them to have recourse to the Emperor, for these miraculous cures. The story may be seen in that fine historian;[61] where every circumstance seems to add weight to the testimony, and might be displayed at large with all the force of argument and eloquence, if any one were now concerned to enforce the evidence of that exploded and idolatrous superstition. The gravity, solidity, age, and probity of so great an emperor, who, through the whole course of his life, conversed in a familiar manner with his friends and courtiers, and never affected those extraordinary airs of divinity assumed by ALEXANDER and DEMETRIUS.[62] The historian, a contemporary writer, noted for candour and veracity, and withal, the greatest and most penetrating genius, perhaps, of all antiquity; and so free from any tendency to credulity, that he even lies under the contrary imputation, of atheism and profaneness: The persons, from whose authority he related the miracle, of established character for judgment and veracity, as we may well presume; eye-witnesses of the fact, and confirming their testimony, after the FLAVIAN family[63] was despoiled of the empire, and could no longer give any reward, as the price of a lie. *Utrumque, qui interfuere, nunc quoque memorant, postquam nullum mendacio pretium.*[64] To which if we add the public nature of the facts, as related, it will appear, that no evidence can well be supposed stronger for so gross and so palpable a falsehood.

There is also a memorable story related by Cardinal DE RETZ,[65] which may well deserve our consideration. When that intriguing politician fled into SPAIN, to avoid the persecution of his enemies, he passed through SARAGOSSA, the capital of ARRAGON, where he was shown, in the cathedral, a man, who had served seven years as a door-keeper, and was well known to every body in town, that had ever paid his devotions at that church. He had been seen, for so long a time, wanting a leg; but recovered that limb by the rubbing of holy oil upon the stump; and the cardinal assures us that he saw him with two legs. This miracle was vouched by all the canons of the church; and the whole company in town were appealed to for a confirmation of the fact; whom the cardinal found, by their zealous devotion, to be

60. [Vespasian (9–79) was emperor of Rome and founder of the Flavian dynasty which ruled from 69 to 96.]

61. Hist. Bk. IV, Chap. 81. SUETONIUS gives nearly the same account in VESP. 7. [The reference to Suetonius is found in *Lives of the Twelve Caesars*, Book VIII. The story is not found in Tacitus exactly as Hume describes it, for Tactitus, himself, seems to have doubted that the cure was "miraculous."]

62. [Demetrius I (c.336–283 B.C.), ruler of Macedonia]

63. [The family that ruled the Roman Empire from 69–96 A.D. and included the emperor Vespasian (9–79), and his sons Titus (40–81) and Domitian (51–96).]

64. [Of each event, those who were present, even now keep speaking, though they get no reward for lying.]

65. [Cardinal de Retz (1613–1679), a French political leader. His memoirs (1717) provide insight into the court life of his time.]

thorough believers of the miracle. Here the relater was also cotemporary to the supposed prodigy, of an incredulous and libertine character, as well as of great genius; the miracle of so *singular* a nature as could scarcely admit of a counterfeit, and the witnesses very numerous, and all of them, in a manner, spectators of the fact, to which they gave their testimony. And what adds mightily to the force of the evidence, and may double our surprise on this occasion, is, that the cardinal himself, who relates the story, seems not to give any credit to it, and consequently cannot be suspected of any concurrence in the holy fraud. He considered justly, that it was not requisite, in order to reject a fact of this nature, to be able accurately to disprove the testimony, and to trace its falsehood, through all the circumstances of knavery and credulity which produced it. He knew, that, as this was commonly altogether impossible at any small distance of time and place; so was it extremely difficult, even where one was immediately present, by reason of the bigotry, ignorance, cunning, and roguery of a great part of mankind. He therefore concluded, like a just reasoner, that such an evidence carried falsehood upon the very face of it, and that a miracle, supported by any human testimony, was more properly a subject of derision than of argument.

There surely never was a greater number of miracles ascribed to one person, than those, which were lately said to have been wrought in FRANCE upon the tomb of Abbé PARIS, the famous JANSENIST, with whose sanctity the people were so long deluded. The curing of the sick, giving hearing to the deaf, and sight to the blind, were every where talked of as the usual effects of that holy sepulchre. But what is more extraordinary; many of the miracles were immediately proved upon the spot, before judges of unquestioned integrity, attested by witnesses of credit and distinction, in a learned age, and on the most eminent theatre that is now in the world. Nor is this all: A relation of them was published and dispersed every where; nor were the *Jesuits,* though a learned body, supported by the civil magistrate, and determined enemies to those opinions, in whose favour the miracles were said to have been wrought, ever able distinctly to refute or detect them.[66] Where shall we find such a

66. This book was writ by Mons. MONTGERRON, counsellor or judge of the parliament of PARIS, a man of figure and character, who was also a martyr to the cause, and is now said to be somewhere in a dungeon on account of his book.

There is another book in three volumes (called *Recueil des Miracles de l'Abbé* PARIS) giving an account of many of these miracles, and accompanied with prefatory discourses, which are very well written. There runs, however, through the whole of these a ridiculous comparison between the miracles of our Saviour and those of the Abbé; wherein it is asserted, that the evidence for the latter is equal to that for the former: As if the testimony of men could ever be put in the balance with that of God himself, who conducted the pen of the inspired writers. If these writers, indeed, were to be considered merely as human testimony, the FRENCH author is very moderate in his comparison: since he might, with some appearance of reason, pretend, that the JANSENIST miracles much surpass the other in evidence and authority. The following circumstances are drawn from authentic papers, inserted in the above-mentioned book.

Many of the miracles of Abbé PARIS were proved immediately by witnesses before the officiality or bishop's court at PARIS, under the eye of cardinal NOAILLES, whose character for integrity and capacity was never contested even by his enemies.

His successor in the archbishopric was an enemy to the JANSENISTS, and for that reason promoted to the see by the court. Yet 22 rectors or *curés* of PARIS, with infinite earnestness, press him to examine those miracles, which they assert to be known to the whole world, and undisputably certain: But he wisely forbore.

The MOLINIST party had tried to discredit these miracles in one instnce, that of Madamoiselle le FRANC. But, besides that their proceedings were in many respects the most irregular in the world, particularly in citing only a few of the JANSENIST witnesses, whom they tampered with: Besides this, I say, they

number of circumstances, agreeing to the corroboration of one fact? And what have we to oppose to such a cloud of witnesses, but the absolute impossibility or miraculous nature of the events, which they relate? And this surely, in the eyes of all reasonable people, will alone be regarded as a sufficient refutation.

---

soon found themselves overwhelmed by a cloud of new witnesses, one hundred and twenty in number, most of them persons of credit and substance in PARIS, who gave oath for the miracle. This was accompanied with a solemn and earnest appeal to the parliament. But the parliament were forbidden by authority to meddle in the affair. It was at last observed, that where men are heated by zeal and enthusiasm, there is no degree of human testimony so strong as may not be procured for the greatest absurdity: And those who will be so silly as to examine the affair by that medium, and seek particular flaws in the testimony, are almost sure to be confounded. It must be a miserable imposture, indeed, that does not prevail in that contest. [The Molinists were Jesuits who followed the teachings of Luis de Molina (1535–1600). Molina's main tenet concerned the problem of reconciling divine grace and human freedom; he claimed that although God has infallible knowledge of whether or not an individual will accept grace, this foreknowledge does not determine the action of the individual. Hence, the efficacy of grace is not a matter of God's will, but of His knowledge, and, ultimately, therefore, a matter of man's acceptance.]

All who have been in FRANCE about that time have heard of the reputation of Mons. HERAUT, the *lieutenant de Police,* whose vigilance, penetration, activity, and extensive intelligence have been much talked of. This magistrate, who by the nature of his office is almost absolute, was invested with full powers, on purpose to suppress or discredit these miracles; and he frequently seized immediately, and examined the witnesses and subjects of them: But never could reach any thing satisfactory against them.

In the case of Madamoiselle THIBAUT he sent the famous DE SYLVA to examine her; whose evidence is very curious. The physician declares, that it was impossible she could have been so ill as was proved by witnesses; because it was impossible she could, in so short a time, have recovered so perfectly as he found her. He reasoned, like a man of sense, from natural causes; but the opposite party told him, that the whole was a miracle, and that his evidence was the very best proof of it.

The MOLINISTS were in a sad dilemma. They durst not assert the absolute insufficiency of human evidence, to prove a miracle. They were obliged to say, that these miracles were wrought by witchcraft and the devil. But they were told, that this was the resource of the JEWS of old.

No JANSENIST was ever embarrassed to account for the cessation of the miracles, when the churchyard was shut up by the king's edict. It was the touch of the tomb, which produced these extraordinary effects; and when no one could approach the tomb, no effects could be expected. God, indeed, could have thrown down the walls in a moment; but he is master of his own graces and works, and it belongs not to us to account for them. He did not throw down the walls of every city like those of JERICHO, on the sounding of the rams' horns, nor break up the prison of every apostle, like that of St. PAUL.

No less a man, than the Duc de CHATILLON, a duke and peer of FRANCE, of the highest rank and family, gives evidence of a miraculous cure, performed upon a servant of his, who had lived several years in his house with a visible and palpable infirmity.

I shall conclude with observing, that no clergy are more celebrated for strictness of life and manners than the secular clergy of FRANCE, particularly the rectors or curés of PARIS, who bear testimony to these impostures.

The learning, genius, and probity of the gentlemen, and the austerity of the nuns of PORT-ROYAL, have been much celebrated all over EUROPE. [Port Royal was the name of a famous Jansenist monastery located not far from Paris and, derivatively, the Jansenist movement associated with the school. Jansenism was a Roman Catholic movement based on the teachings of Cornelius Jansen (1585–1638), a Dutch theologian. Jansen denied freedom of the will and maintained predestination and the infallible efficacy of Divine grace needed for salvation. Blaise Pascal (1623–1662), Jean Racine (1639–1699), Antoine Arnauld (1612–1694), and Pierre Nicole (1625–1695) all were affiliated with the movement. Pascal, Arnauld, and Nicole wrote tracts for the Jansenists and the latter two co-authored the *Logique ou l'art de Penser* (1662), known as the Port Royal Logic. Racine was a student at the monastery and wrote the *Abrégé de l'histoire de Port-Royal* (1742 and 1747), to which Hume refers in this footnote. In addition, Pascal's sister was a nun at the monastery and Arnauld's sister an abbess.] Yet they all give evidence for a miracle, wrought on the niece of the famous PASCAL, whose sanctity of life, as well as extraordinary capacity, is well known. The famous RACINE gives an account of this miracle in his famous history of PORT-ROYAL, and fortifies it with all the proofs, which a multitude of nuns, priests, physicians, and men of the world, all of them of undoubted credit, could bestow upon it. Several men of letters, particularly

Is the consequence just, because some human testimony has the utmost force and authority in some cases, when it relates the battle of PHILIPPI or PHARSALIA[67] for instance; that therefore all kinds of testimony must, in all cases, have equal force and authority? Suppose that the CAESAREAN and POMPEIAN factions had, each of them, claimed the victory in these battles, and that the historians of each party had uniformly ascribed the advantage to their own side; how could mankind, at this distance, have been able to determine between them? The contrariety is equally strong between the miracles related by HERODOTUS[68] or PLUTARCH, and those delivered by MARIANA, BEDE, or any monkish historian.

The wise lend a very academic faith to every report which favours the passion of the reporter; whether it magnifies his country, his family, or himself, or in any other way strikes in with his natural inclinations and propensities. But what greater temptation than to appear a missionary, a prophet, an ambassador from heaven? Who would not encounter many dangers and difficulties, in order to attain so sublime a character? Or if, by the help of vanity and a heated imagination, a man has first made a convert of himself, and entered seriously into the delusion; who ever scruples to make use of pious frauds, in support of so holy and meritorious a cause?

The smallest spark may here kindle into the greatest flame; because the materials are always prepared for it. The *avidum genus auricularum,*[69] the gazing populace, receive greedily, without examination, whatever soothes superstition, and promotes wonder.

How many stories of this nature, have, in all ages, been detected and exploded in their infancy? How many more have been celebrated for a time, and have afterwards sunk into neglect and oblivion? Where such reports, therefore, fly about, the solution of the phenomenon is obvious; and we judge in conformity to regular experience and observation, when we account for it by the known and natural principles

---

the bishop of TOURNAY, thought this miracle so certain, as to employ it in the refutation of atheists and free-thinkers. The queen-regent of FRANCE, who was extremely prejudiced against the PORT-ROYAL, sent her own physician to examine the miracle, who returned an absolute convert. In short, the supernatural cure was so uncontestable, that it saved, for a time, that famous monastery from the ruin with which it was threatened by the JESUITS. Had it been a cheat, it had certainly been detected by such sagacious and powerful antagonists, and must have hastened the ruin of the contrivers. Our divines, who can build up a formidable castle from such despicable materials; what a prodigious fabric could they have reared from these and many other circumstances, which I have not mentioned! How often would the great names of PASCAL, RACINE, ARNAUD, NICOLE, have resounded in our ears? But if they be wise, they had better adopt the miracle, as being more worth, a thousand times, than all the rest of their collection. Besides, it may serve very much to their purpose. For that miracle was really performed by the touch of an authentic holy prickle of the holy thorn, which composed the holy crown, which, &c.

67. [Philippi was a city in eastern Macedonia and the scene of the two battles in 42 B.C. at which Antony and Octavian (Augustus), allies of the slain Caesar, defeated Cassius and Brutus, former supporters of Pompey. Pharsalia was a city in Thessaly in Greece where a battle was fought in 48 B.C. in which Julius Caesar (102–44 B.C.) triumphed over Pompey (106–48 B.C.).]

68. [Herodotus (c.484–c.425 B.C.), was a Greek historian often referred to as "The Father of History." He wrote *The Persian Wars.* Juan de Mariana (c. 1536–c.1623), a Spanish Jesuit and historian, wrote a history of Spain. Bede (673–735), an English historian and Benedictine monk, wrote an ecclesiastical history of England.]

69. [Literally, "a gossip hungry race"; this is an adaptation or misquotation of *Humanum genus est avidum nimus auricularum* "the human race is too gossip-hungry" (Lucretius, *De Rerum Natura,* iv. 594).]

of credulity and delusion. And shall we, rather than have a recourse to so natural a solution, allow of a miraculous violation of the most established laws of nature?

I need not mention the difficulty of detecting a falsehood in any private or even public history, at the place, where it is said to happen; much more when the scene is removed to ever so small a distance. Even a court of judicature, with all the authority, accuracy, and judgment, which they can employ, find themselves often at a loss to distinguish between truth and falsehood in the most recent actions. But the matter never comes to any issue, if trusted to the common method of altercation and debate and flying rumours; especially when men's passions have taken part on either side.

In the infancy of new religions, the wise and learned commonly esteem the matter too inconsiderable to deserve their attention or regard. And when afterwards they would willingly detect the cheat, in order to undeceive the deluded multitude, the season is now past, and the records and witnesses, which might clear up the matter, have perished beyond recovery.

No means of detection remain, but those which must be drawn from the very testimony itself of the reporters: And these, though always sufficient with the judicious and knowing, are commonly too fine to fall under the comprehension of the vulgar.

Upon the whole, then, it appears, that no testimony for any kind of miracle has ever amounted to a probability, much less to a proof; and that, even supposing it amounted to a proof, it would be opposed by another proof; derived from the very nature of the fact, which it would endeavour to establish. It is experience only, which gives authority to human testimony; and it is the same experience, which assures us of the laws of nature. When, therefore, these two kinds of experience are contrary, we have nothing to do but subtract the one from the other, and embrace an opinion, either on one side or the other, with that assurance which arises from the remainder. But according to the principle here explained, this subtraction, with regard to all popular religions, amounts to an entire annihilation; and therefore we may establish it as a maxim, that no human testimony can have such force as to prove a miracle, and make it a just foundation for any such system of religion.

I beg the limitations here made may be remarked, when I say, that a miracle can never be proved, so as to be the foundation of a system of religion. For I own, that otherwise, there may possibly be miracles, or violations of the usual course of nature, of such a kind as to admit of proof from human testimony; though, perhaps, it will be impossible to find any such in all the records of history. Thus, suppose, all authors, in all languages, agree, that, from the first of JANUARY 1600, there was a total darkness over the whole earth for eight days: Suppose that the tradition of this extraordinary event is still strong and lively among the people: That all travellers, who return from foreign countries, bring us accounts of the same tradition, without the least variation or contradiction: It is evident, that our present philosophers, instead of doubting the fact, ought to receive it as certain, and ought to search for the causes whence it might be derived. The decay, corruption, and dissolution of nature, is an event rendered probable by so many analogies, that any phenomenon, which seems to have a tendency towards that catastrophe, comes within the reach of human testimony, if that testimony be very extensive and uniform.

But suppose, that all the historians who treat of ENGLAND, should agree, that, on the first of JANUARY 1600, Queen ELIZABETH died; that both before and after her death she was seen by her physicians and the whole court, as is usual with persons of her rank; that her successor was acknowledged and proclaimed by the parliament; and that, after being interred a month, she again appeared, resumed the throne, and governed ENGLAND for three years: I must confess that I should be surprised at the occurrence of so many odd circumstances, but should not have the least inclination to believe so miraculous an event. I should not doubt of her pretended death, and of those other public circumstances that followed it: I should only assert it to have been pretended, and that it neither was, nor possibly could be real. You would in vain object to me the difficulty, and almost impossibility of deceiving the world in an affair of such consequence; the wisdom and solid judgment of that renowned queen; with the little or no advantage which she could reap from so poor an artifice: All this might astonish me; but I would still reply, that the knavery and folly of men are such common phenomena, that I should rather believe the most extraordinary events to arise from their concurrence, than admit of so signal a violation of the laws of nature.

But should this miracle be ascribed to any new system of religion; men, in all ages, have been so much imposed on by ridiculous stories of that kind, that this very circumstance would be a full proof of a cheat, and sufficient, with all men of sense, not only to make them reject the fact, but even reject it without farther examination. Though the Being to whom the miracle is ascribed, be, in this case, Almighty, it does not, upon that account, become a whit more probable; since it is impossible for us to know the attributes or actions of such a Being, otherwise than from the experience which we have of his productions, in the usual course of nature. This still reduces us to past observation, and obliges us to compare the instances of the violation of truth in the testimony of men, with those of the violation of the laws of nature by miracles, in order to judge which of them is most likely and probable. As the violations of truth are more common in the testimony concerning religious miracles, than in that concerning any other matter of fact; this must diminish very much the authority of the former testimony, and make us form a general resolution, never to lend any attention to it, with whatever specious pretence it may be covered.

Lord BACON seems to have embraced the same principles of reasoning. 'We ought,' says he, 'to make a collection or particular history of all monsters and prodigious births or productions, and in a word of every thing new, rare, and extraordinary in nature. But this must be done with the most severe scrutiny, lest we depart from truth. Above all, every relation must be considered as suspicious, which depends in any degree upon religion, as the prodigies of LIVY : And no less so, every thing that is to be found in the writers of natural magic or alchimy, or such authors, who seem, all of them, to have an unconquerable appetite for falsehood and fable.'[70]

I am the better pleased with the method of reasoning here delivered, as I think it may serve to confound those dangerous friends or disguised enemies to the *Christian Religion*, who have undertaken to defend it by the principles of human reason. Our most holy religion is founded on *Faith*, not on reason; and it is a sure method of exposing it to put it to such a trial as it is, by no means, fitted to endure. To make this more evident, let us examine those miracles, related in scripture; and not to lose ourselves in too wide a field, let us confine ourselves to such as we find in the *Pen-*

---

70. *Novum Organum* lib. ii. aph. 29. [Francis Bacon (1561–1626) was an English philosopher and statesman who stressed the importance of scientific methodology in the acquisition of knowledge, and according to Hume first applied "experimental philosophy to natural subjects."]

tateuch,[71] which we shall examine, according to the principles of these pretended Christians, not as the word or testimony of God himself, but as the production of a mere human writer and historian. Here then we are first to consider a book, presented to us by a barbarous and ignorant people, written in an age when they were still more barbarous, and in all probability long after the facts which it relates, corroborated by no concurring testimony, and resembling those fabulous accounts, which every nation gives of its origin. Upon reading this book, we find it full of prodigies and miracles. It gives an account of a state of the world and of human nature entirely different from the present: Of our fall from that state: Of the age of man, extended to near a thousand years: Of the destruction of the world by a deluge: Of the arbitrary choice of one people, as the favourites of heaven; and that people the countrymen of the author: Of their deliverance from bondage by prodigies the most astonishing imaginable: I desire any one to lay his hand upon his heart, and after a serious consideration declare, whether he thinks that the falsehood of such a book, supported by such a testimony, would be more extraordinary and miraculous than all the miracles it relates; which is, however, necessary to make it be received, according to the measures of probability above established.

What we have said of miracles may be applied, without any variation, to prophecies; and indeed, all prophecies are real miracles, and as such only, can be admitted as proofs of any revelation. If it did not exceed the capacity of human nature to foretell future events, it would be absurd to employ any prophecy as an argument for a divine mission or authority from heaven. So that, upon the whole, we may conclude, that the *Christian Religion* not only was at first attended with miracles, but even at this day cannot be believed by any reasonable person without one. Mere reason is insufficient to convince us of its veracity: And whoever is moved by *Faith* to assent to it, is conscious of a continued miracle in his own person, which subverts all the principles of his understanding, and gives him a determination to believe what is most contrary to custom and experience.

SECTION XI. — *Of a Particular Providence and of a Future State.*

I WAS lately engaged in conversation with a friend who loves sceptical paradoxes; where, though he advanced many principles, of which I can by no means approve, yet as they seem to be curious, and to bear some relation to the chain of reasoning carried on throughout this enquiry, I shall here copy them from my memory as accurately as I can, in order to submit them to the judgment of the reader.

Our conversation began with my admiring the singular good fortune of philosophy, which, as it requires entire liberty above all other privileges, and chiefly flourishes from the free opposition of sentiments and argumentation, received its first birth in an age and country of freedom and toleration, and was never cramped, even in its most extravagant principles, by any creeds, confessions, or penal statutes. For, except the banishment of PROTAGORAS,[72] and the death of SOC-

71. [The Pentateuch, the Five Books of Moses, is the first five books of the Bible: Genesis, Exodus, Leviticus, Numbers, and Deuteronomy.]

72. [Protagoras of Abdera (490(?)–421(?) B.C.), outstanding member of the group of philosophers known as the Sophists, was exiled from Athens because of his religious views, which were said to be impious.]

RATES, which last event proceeded partly from other motives, there are scarcely any instances to be met with, in ancient history, of this bigotted jealousy, with which the present age is so much infested. EPICURUS lived at ATHENS to an advanced age, in peace and tranquillity: EPICUREANS [73] were even admitted to receive the sacerdotal character, and to officiate at the altar, in the most sacred rites of the established religion: And the public encouragement[74] of pensions and salaries was afforded equally, by the wisest of all the ROMAN emperors,[75] to the professors of every sect of philosophy. How requisite such kind of treatment was to philosophy, in her early youth, will easily be conceived, if we reflect, that, even at present, when she may be supposed more hardy and robust, she bears with much difficulty the inclemency of the seasons, and those harsh winds of calumny and persecution, which blow upon her.

You admire, says my friend, as the singular good fortune of philosophy, what seems to result from the natural course of things, and to be unavoidable in every age and nation. This pertinacious bigotry, of which you complain, as so fatal to philosophy, is really her offspring, who, after allying with superstition, separates himself entirely from the interest of his parent, and becomes her most inveterate enemy and persecutor. Speculative dogmas of religion, the present occasions of such furious dispute, could not possibly be conceived or admitted in the early ages of the world; when mankind, being wholly illiterate, formed an idea of religion more suitable to their weak apprehension, and composed their sacred tenets of such tales chiefly as were the objects of traditional belief, more than of argument or disputation. After the first alarm, therefore, was over, which arose from the new paradoxes and principles of the philosophers; these teachers seem ever after, during the ages of antiquity, to have lived in great harmony with the established superstition, and to have made a fair partition of mankind between them; the former claiming all the learned and wise, the latter possessing all the vulgar and illiterate.

It seems then, say I, that you leave politics entirely out of the question, and never suppose, that a wise magistrate can justly be jealous of certain tenets of philosophy, such as those of EPICURUS, which, denying a divine existence, and consequently a providence and a future state, seem to loosen, in a great measure, the ties of morality, and may be supposed, for that reason, pernicious to the peace of civil society.

I know, replied he, that in fact these persecutions never, in any age, proceeded from calm reason, or from experience of the pernicious consequences of philosophy; but arose entirely from passion and prejudice. But what if I should advance farther, and assert, that, if EPICURUS had been accused before the people, by any of the *sycophants* or informers of those days, he could easily have defended his cause, and proved his principles of philosophy to be as salutary as those of his adversaries, who endeavoured, with such zeal, to expose him to the public hatred and jealousy.

I wish, said I, you would try your eloquence upon so extraordinary a topic, and make a speech for EPICURUS, which might satisfy, not the mob of ATHENS, if you will allow that ancient and polite city to have contained any mob, but the more phil-

---

73. LUCIANI συμπ. ἢ λαπίϑαι. 9. [*The Carousel or the Lapiths*]

74. LUCIANI εὐνοῦχος. 3. [*The Eunuch*]

75. Id. & Dio. [*The Eunuch* and Dio Cassius (c.150–c.235), *History of Rome,* Bk. LXXII]

osophical part of his audience, such as might be supposed capable of comprehending his arguments.

The matter would not be difficult, upon such conditions, replied he: And if you please, I shall suppose myself EPICURUS for a moment, and make you stand for the ATHENIAN people, and shall deliver you such an harangue as will fill all the urn with white beans, and leave not a black one to gratify the malice of my adversaries.[76]

Very well: Pray proceed upon these suppositions.

I come hither, O ye ATHENIANS, to justify in your assembly what I maintained in my school, and I find myself impeached by furious antagonists, instead of reasoning with calm and dispassionate enquirers. Your deliberations, which of right should be directed to questions of public good, and the interest of the commonwealth, are diverted to the disquisitions of speculative philosophy; and these magnificent, but perhaps fruitless enquiries, take place of your more familiar but more useful occupations. But so far as in me lies, I will prevent this abuse. We shall not here dispute concerning the origin and government of worlds. We shall only enquire how far such questions concern the public interest. And if I can persuade you, that they are entirely indifferent to the peace of society and security of government, I hope that you will presently send us back to our schools, there to examine, at leisure, the question, the most sublime, but, at the same time, the most speculative of all philosophy.

The religious philosophers, not satisfied with the tradition of your forefathers, and doctrine of your priests (in which I willingly acquiesce), indulge a rash curiosity, in trying how far they can establish religion upon the principles of reason; and they thereby excite, instead of satisfying, the doubts, which naturally arise from a diligent and scrutinous enquiry. They paint, in the most magnificent colours, the order, beauty, and wise arrangement of the universe; and then ask, if such a glorious display of intelligence could proceed from the fortuitous concourse of atoms, or if chance could produce what the greatest genius can never sufficiently admire. I shall not examine the justness of this argument. I shall allow it to be as solid as my antagonists and accusers can desire. It is sufficient, if I can prove, from this very reasoning, that the question is entirely speculative, and that, when, in my philosophical disquisitions, I deny a providence and a future state, I undermine not the foundations of society, but advance principles, which they themselves, upon their own topics, if they argue consistently, must allow to be solid and satisfactory.

You then, who are my accusers, have acknowledged, that the chief or sole argument for a divine existence (which I never questioned) is derived from the order of nature; where there appear such marks of intelligence and design, that you think it extravagant to assign for its cause, either chance, or the blind and unguided force of matter. You allow, that this is an argument drawn from effects to causes. From the order of the work, you infer, that there must have been project and forethought in the workman. If you cannot make out this point, you allow, that your conclusion fails; and you pretend not to establish the conclusion in a greater latitude than the phenomena of nature will justify. These are your concessions. I desire you to mark the consequences.

---

76. [In Athens, beans were used for balloting: white beans signified assent or agreement; black ones, dissent or disagreement. For an examination of the argument, see Hume's *Dialogues Concerning Natural Religion*.]

When we infer any particular cause from an effect, we must proportion the one to the other, and can never be allowed to ascribe to the cause any qualities, but what are exactly sufficient to produce the effect. A body of ten ounces raised in any scale may serve as a proof, that the counterbalancing weight exceeds ten ounces; but can never afford a reason that it exceeds a hundred. If the cause, assigned for any effect, be not sufficient to produce it, we must either reject that cause, or add to it such qualities as will give it a just proportion to the effect. But if we ascribe to it farther qualities, or affirm it capable of producing other effects, we can only indulge the licence of conjecture, and arbitrarily suppose the existence of qualities and energies, without reason or authority.

The same rule holds, whether the cause assigned be brute unconscious matter, or a rational intelligent being. If the cause be known only by the effect, we never ought to ascribe to it any qualities, beyond what are precisely requisite to produce the effect: Nor can we, by any rules of just reasoning, return back from the cause, and infer other effects from it, beyond those by which alone it is known to us. No one, merely from the sight of one of ZEUXIS'S[77] pictures, could know, that he was also a statuary or architect, and was an artist no less skilful in stone and marble than in colours. The talents and taste, displayed in the particular work before us; these we may safely conclude the workman to be possessed of. The cause must be proportioned to the effect; and if we exactly and precisely proportion it, we shall never find in it any qualities, that point farther, or afford an inference concerning any other design or performance. Such qualities must be somewhat beyond what is merely requisite for producing the effect, which we examine.

Allowing, therefore, the gods to be the authors of the existence or order of the universe; it follows, that they possess that precise degree of power, intelligence, and benevolence, which appears in their workmanship; but nothing farther can ever be proved, except we call in the assistance of exaggeration and flattery to supply the defects of argument and reasoning. So far as the traces of any attributes, at present, appear, so far may we conclude these attributes to exist. The supposition of farther attributes is mere hypothesis; much more the supposition, that, in distant regions of space or periods of time, there has been, or will be, a more magnificent display of these attributes, and a scheme of administration more suitable to such imaginary virtues. We can never be allowed to mount up from the universe, the effect, to JUPITER, the cause; and then descend downwards, to infer any new effect from that cause; as if the present effects alone were not entirely worthy of the glorious attributes, which we ascribe to that deity. The knowledge of the cause being derived solely from the effect, they must be exactly adjusted to each other; and the one can never refer to any thing farther, or be the foundation of any new inference and conclusion.

You find certain phenomena in nature. You seek a cause or author. You imagine that you have found him. You afterwards become so enamoured of this offspring of your brain, that you imagine it impossible, but he must produce something greater and more perfect than the present scene of things, which is so full of ill and disorder. You forget, that this superlative intelligence and benevolence are entirely imaginary, or, at least, without any foundation in reason; and that you have no ground to ascribe to him any qualities, but what you see he has actually exerted and displayed

---

77. [Zeuxis was a fifth-century B.C. Greek painter.]

in his productions. Let your gods, therefore, O philosophers, be suited to the present appearances of nature: And presume not to alter these appearances by arbitrary suppositions, in order to suit them to the attributes, which you so fondly ascribe to your deities.

When priests and poets, supported by your authority, O ATHENIANS, talk of a golden or silver age, which preceded the present state of vice and misery, I hear them with attention and with reverence. But when philosophers, who pretend to neglect authority, and to cultivate reason, hold the same discourse, I pay them not, I own, the same obsequious submission and pious deference. I ask; who carried them into the celestial regions, who admitted them into the councils of the gods, who opened to them the book of fate, that they thus rashly affirm, that their deities have executed, or will execute, any purpose beyond what has actually appeared? If they tell me, that they have mounted on the steps or by the gradual ascent of reason, and by drawing inferences from effects to causes, I still insist, that they have aided the ascent of reason by the wings of imagination; otherwise they could not thus change their manner of inference, and argue from causes to effects; presuming, that a more perfect production than the present world would be more suitable to such perfect beings as the gods, and forgetting that they have no reason to ascribe to these celestial beings any perfection or any attribute, but what can be found in the present world.

Hence all the fruitless industry to account for the ill appearances of nature, and save the honour of the gods; while we must acknowledge the reality of that evil and disorder, with which the world so much abounds. The obstinate and intractable qualities of matter, we are told, or the observance of general laws, or some such reason, is the sole cause, which controlled the power and benevolence of JUPITER, and obliged him to create mankind and every sensible creature so imperfect and so unhappy. These attributes, then, are, it seems, beforehand, taken for granted, in their greatest latitude. And upon that supposition, I own, that such conjectures may, perhaps, be admitted as plausible solutions of the ill phenomena. But still I ask; Why take these attributes for granted, or why ascribe to the cause any qualities but what actually appear in the effect? Why torture your brain to justify the course of nature upon suppositions, which, for aught you know, may be entirely imaginary, and of which there are to be found no traces in the course of nature?

The religious hypothesis, therefore, must be considered only as a particular method of accounting for the visible phenomena of the universe: But no just reasoner will ever presume to infer from it any single fact, and alter or add to the phenomena, in any single particular. If you think, that the appearances of things prove such causes, it is allowable for you to draw an inference concerning the existence of these causes. In such complicated and sublime subjects, every one should be indulged in the liberty of conjecture and argument. But here you ought to rest. If you come backward, and arguing from your inferred causes, conclude, that any other fact has existed, or will exist, in the course of nature, which may serve as a fuller display of particular attributes; I must admonish you, that you have departed from the method of reasoning, attached to the present subject, and have certainly added something to the attributes of the cause, beyond what appears in the effect; otherwise you could never, with tolerable sense or propriety, add any thing to the effect, in order to render it more worthy of the cause.

Where, then, is the odiousness of that doctrine, which I teach in my school, or rather, which I examine in my gardens? Or what do you find in this whole question, wherein the security of good morals, or the peace and order of society is in the least concerned?

I deny a providence, you say, and supreme governor of the world, who guides the course of events, and punishes the vicious with infamy and disappointment, and rewards the virtuous with honour and success, in all their undertakings. But surely, I deny not the course itself of events, which lies open to every one's enquiry and examination. I acknowledge, that, in the present order of things, virtue is attended with more peace of mind than vice, and meets with a more favourable reception from the world. I am sensible, that, according to the past experience of mankind, friendship is the chief joy of human life, and moderation the only source of tranquillity and happiness. I never balance between the virtuous and the vicious course of life; but am sensible, that, to a well disposed mind, every advantage is on the side of the former. And what can you say more, allowing all your suppositions and reasonings? You tell me, indeed, that this disposition of things proceeds from intelligence and design. But whatever it proceeds from, the disposition itself, on which depends our happiness or misery, and consequently our conduct and deportment in life, is still the same. It is still open for me, as well as you, to regulate my behaviour, by my experience of past events. And if you affirm, that, while a divine providence is allowed, and a supreme distributive justice in the universe, I ought to expect some more particular reward of the good, and punishment of the bad, beyond the ordinary course of events; I here find the same fallacy, which I have before endeavoured to detect. You persist in imagining, that, if we grant that divine existence, for which you so earnestly contend, you may safely infer consequences from it, and add something to the experienced order of nature, by arguing from the attributes which you ascribe to your gods. You seem not to remember, that all your reasonings on this subject can only be drawn from effects to causes; and that every argument, deduced from causes to effects, must of necessity be a gross sophism; since it is impossible for you to know any thing of the cause, but what you have antecedently, not inferred, but discovered to the full, in the effect.

But what must a philosopher think of those vain reasoners, who, instead of regarding the present scene of things as the sole object of their contemplation, so far reverse the whole course of nature, as to render this life merely a passage to something farther; a porch, which leads to a greater, and vastly different building; a prologue, which serves only to introduce the piece, and give it more grace and propriety? Whence, do you think, can such philosophers derive their idea of the gods? From their own conceit and imagination surely. For if they derived it from the present phenomena, it would never point to anything farther, but must be exactly adjusted to them. That the divinity may *possibly* be endowed with attributes, which we have never seen exerted; may be governed by principles of action, which we cannot discover to be satisfied: All this will freely be allowed. But still this is mere *possibility* and hypothesis. We can never have reason to *infer* any attributes, or any principles of action in him, but so far as we know them to have been exerted and satisfied.

Are there any marks of a distributive justice in the world? If you answer in the affirmative, I conclude, that, since justice here exerts itself, it is satisfied. If you reply in the negative, I conclude, that you have then no reason to ascribe justice, in our sense of it, to the gods. If you hold a medium between affirmation and negation, by saying, that the justice of the gods, at present, exerts itself in part, but not in its full extent;

I answer, that you have no reason to give it any particular extent, but only so far as you see it, *at present*, exert itself.

Thus I bring the dispute, O ATHENIANS, to a short issue with my antagonists. The course of nature lies open to my contemplation as well as to theirs. The experienced train of events is the great standard, by which we all regulate our conduct. Nothing else can be appealed to in the field, or in the senate. Nothing else ought ever to be heard of in the school, or in the closet. In vain would our limited understanding break through these boundaries, which are too narrow for our fond imagination. While we argue from the course of nature, and infer a particular intelligent cause, which first bestowed, and still preserves order in the universe, we embrace a principle, which is both uncertain and useless. It is uncertain; because the subject lies entirely beyond the reach of human experience. It is useless; because our knowledge of this cause being derived entirely from the course of nature, we can never, according to the rules of just reasoning, return back from the cause with any new inference, or making additions to the common and experienced course of nature, establish any new principles of conduct and behaviour.

I observe (said I, finding he had finished his harangue) that you neglect not the artifice of the demagogues of old; and as you were pleased to make me stand for the people, you insinuate yourself into my favour by embracing those principles, to which, you know, I have always expressed a particular attachment. But allowing you to make experience (as indeed I think you ought) the only standard of our judgment concerning this, and all other questions of fact; I doubt not but, from the very same experience, to which you appeal, it may be possible to refute this reasoning, which you have put into the mouth of EPICURUS. If you saw, for instance, a half-finished building, surrounded with heaps of brick and stone and mortar, and all the instruments of masonry; could you not *infer* from the effect, that it was a work of design and contrivance? And could you not return again, from this inferred cause, to infer new additions to the effect, and conclude, that the building would soon be finished, and receive all the further improvements, which art could bestow upon it? If you saw upon the sea-shore the print of one human foot, you would conclude, that a man had passed that way, and that he had also left the traces of the other foot, though effaced by the rolling of the sands or inundation of the waters. Why then do you refuse to admit the same method of reasoning with regard to the order of nature? Consider the world and the present life only as an imperfect building, from which you can infer a superior intelligence; and arguing from that superior intelligence, which can leave nothing imperfect; why may you not infer a more finished scheme or plan, which will receive its completion in some distant point of space or time? Are not these methods of reasoning exactly similar? And under what pretence can you embrace the one, while you reject the other?

The infinite difference of the subjects, replied he, is a sufficient foundation for this difference in my conclusions. In works of *human* art and contrivance, it is allowable to advance from the effect to the cause, and returning back from the cause, to form new inferences concerning the effect, and examine the alterations, which it has probably undergone, or may still undergo. But what is the foundation of this method of reasoning? Plainly this; that man is a being, whom we know by experience, whose motives and designs we are acquainted with, and whose projects and inclinations have a certain connexion and coherence, according to the laws which nature has established for the government of such a creature. When, therefore, we find, that any work has proceeded from the skill and industry of man; as we are otherwise acquainted with the nature of the animal, we can draw a hundred inferences concerning what may be expected from him; and these inferences will all be founded in experience and observation. But did we know man only from the single work or production which we examine, it were impossible for us to argue in this manner; because our knowledge of all the qualities, which we ascribe to him, being in that case derived from the production, it is impossible they could point to any thing farther, or be the foundation of any new inference. The print of a foot in the sand can only prove, when considered alone, that there was some figure adapted to it, by which it was produced: But the print of a human foot proves likewise, from our other experience, that there was probably another foot, which also left its impression, though effaced by time or other accidents. Here we mount from the effect to the cause; and descending again from the cause, infer alterations in the effect; but this is not a continuation of the same simple chain of reasoning. We comprehend in this case a hundred other experiences and observations, concerning the *usual* figure and members of that species of animal, without which this method of argument must be considered as fallacious and sophistical.

The case is not the same with our reasonings from the works of nature. The Deity is known to us only by his productions, and is a single being in the universe, not comprehended under any species or genus, from whose experienced attributes or qualities, we can, by analogy, infer any attribute or quality in him. As the universe shows wisdom and goodness, we infer wisdom and goodness. As it shows a particular degree of these perfections, we infer a particular degree of them, precisely adapted to the effect which we examine. But farther attributes or farther degrees of the same attributes, we can never be authorized to infer or suppose, by any rules of just reasoning. Now, without some such licence of supposition, it is impossible for us to argue from the cause, or infer any alteration in the effect, beyond what has immediately fallen under our observation. Greater good produced by this Being must still prove a greater degree of goodness: A more impartial distribution of rewards and punishments must proceed from a greater regard to justice and equity. Every supposed addition to the works of nature makes an addition to the attributes of the Author of nature; and consequently, being entirely unsupported by any reason or argument, can never be admitted but as mere conjecture and hypothesis.[78]

The great source of our mistake in this subject, and of the unbounded licence of conjecture, which we indulge, is, that we tacitly consider ourselves, as in the place of the Supreme Being, and conclude, that he will, on every occasion, observe the same conduct, which we ourselves, in his situation, would have embraced as rea-

---

78. In general, it may, I think, be established as a maxim, that where any cause is known only by its particular effects, it must be impossible to infer any new effects from that cause; since the qualities, which are requisite to produce these new effects along with the former, must either be different, or superior, or of more extensive operation, than those which simply produced the effect, whence alone the cause is supposed to be known to us. We can never, therefore, have any reason to suppose the existence of these qualities. To say, that the new effects proceed only from a continuation of the same energy, which is already known from the first effects, will not remove the difficulty. For even granting this to be the case (which can seldom be supposed), the very continuation and exertion of a like energy (for it is impossible it can be absolutely the same), I say, this exertion of a like energy, in a different period of space and time, is a very arbitrary supposition, and what there cannot possibly be any traces of in the effects, from which all our knowledge of the cause is originally derived. Let the *inferred* cause be exactly proportioned (as it should be) to the known effect; and it is impossible that it can possess any qualities, from which new or different effects can be *inferred*.

sonable and eligible. But, besides that the ordinary course of nature may convince us, that almost everything is regulated by principles and maxims very different from ours; besides this, I say, it must evidently appear contrary to all rules of analogy to reason, from the intentions and projects of men, to those of a Being so different, and so much superior. In human nature, there is a certain experienced coherence of designs and inclinations; so that when, from any fact, we have discovered one intention of any man, it may often be reasonable, from experience, to infer another, and draw a long chain of conclusions concerning his past or future conduct. But this method of reasoning can never have place with regard to a Being, so remote and incomprehensible, who bears much less analogy to any other being in the universe than the sun to a waxen taper, and who discovers himself only by some faint traces or outlines, beyond which we have no authority to ascribe to him any attribute or perfection. What we imagine to be a superior perfection, may really be a defect. Or were it ever so much a perfection, the ascribing of it to the Supreme Being, where it appears not to have been really exerted, to the full, in his works, savours more of flattery and panegyric, than of just reasoning and sound philosophy. All the philosophy, therefore, in the world, and all the religion, which is nothing but a species of philosophy, will never be able to carry us beyond the usual course of experience, or give us measures of conduct and behaviour different from those which are furnished by reflections on common life. No new fact can ever be inferred from the religious hypothesis; no event foreseen or foretold; no reward or punishment expected or dreaded, beyond what is already known by practice and observation. So that my apology for EPICURUS will still appear solid and satisfactory; nor have the political interests of society any connexion with the philosophical disputes concerning metaphysics and religion.

There is still one circumstance, replied I, which you seem to have overlooked. Though I should allow your premises, I must deny your conclusion. You conclude, that religious doctrines and reasonings *can* have no influence on life, because they *ought* to have no influence; never considering, that men reason not in the same manner you do, but draw many consequences from the belief of a divine Existence, and suppose that the Deity will inflict punishments on vice, and bestow rewards on virtue, beyond what appear in the ordinary course of nature. Whether this reasoning of theirs be just or not, is no matter. Its influence on their life and conduct must still be the same. And, those, who attempt to disabuse them of such prejudices, may, for aught I know, be good reasoners, but I cannot allow them to be good citizens and politicians; since they free men from one restraint upon their passions, and make the infringement of the laws of society, in one respect, more easy and secure.

After all, I may, perhaps, agree to your general conclusion in favour of liberty, though upon different premises from those, on which you endeavour to found it. I think, that the state ought to tolerate every principle of philosophy; nor is there an instance, that any government has suffered in its political interests by such indulgence. There is no enthusiasm among philosophers; their doctrines are not very alluring to the people; and no restraint can be put upon their reasonings, but what must be of dangerous consequence to the sciences, and even to the state, by paving the way for persecution and oppression in points, where the generality of mankind are more deeply interested and concerned.

But there occurs to me (continued I) with regard to your main topic, a difficulty, which I shall just propose to you, without insisting on it; lest it lead into reasonings of too nice and delicate a nature. In a word, I much doubt whether it be possible for a cause to be known only by its effect (as you have all along supposed) or to be of so singular and particular a nature as to have no parallel and no similarity with any other cause or object, that has ever fallen under our observation. It is only when two *species* of objects are found to be constantly conjoined, that we can infer the one from the other; and were an effect presented, which was entirely singular, and could not be comprehended under any known *species*, I do not see, that we could form any conjecture of inference at all concerning its cause. If experience and observation and analogy be, indeed, the only guides which we can reasonably follow in inferences of this nature; both the effect and cause must bear a similarity and resemblance to other effects and causes, which we know, and which we have found, in many instances, to be conjoined with each other. I leave it to your own reflection to pursue the consequences of this principle. I shall just observe, that, as the antagonists of EPICURUS always suppose the universe, an effect quite singular and unparalleled, to be the proof of a Deity, a cause no less singular and unparalleled; your reasonings, upon that supposition, seem, at least, to merit our attention. There is, I own, some difficulty, how we can ever return from the cause to the effect, and, reasoning from our ideas of the former, infer any alteration on the latter, or any addition to it.

SECTION XII. — *Of the Academical or Sceptical Philosophy.*

PART I.

THERE is not a greater number of philosophical reasonings, displayed upon any subject, than those, which prove the existence of a Deity, and refute the fallacies of *Atheists;* and yet the most religious philosophers still dispute whether any man can be so blinded as to be a speculative atheist. How shall we reconcile these contradictions? The knights-errant, who wandered about to clear the world of dragons and giants, never entertained the least doubt with regard to the existence of these monsters.

The *Sceptic* is another enemy of religion, who naturally provokes the indignation of all divines and graver philosophers; though it is certain, that no man ever met with any such absurd creature, or conversed with a man, who had no opinion or principle concerning any subject, either of action or speculation. This begets a very natural question; What is meant by a sceptic? And how far it is possible to push these philosophical principles of doubt and uncertainty?

There is a species of scepticism, *antecedent* to all study and philosophy, which is much inculcated by DES CARTES[79] and others, as a sovereign preservative against

---

79. [In the *Discourse on Method* (1637) and the *Meditations* (1641), Descartes advocated a form of provisional doubt or skepticism in which "as far as the opinions which I had been receiving since my birth were concerned, I could not do better than to reject them completely for once in my lifetime, and to resume them afterwards, or perhaps accept better ones in their place, when I had determined how they fitted into a rational scheme . . . In this I did not wish to imitate the sceptics, who doubted only for the sake of doubting and intended to remain always irresolute; on the contrary, my whole purpose was to achieve greater certainty and to reject the loose earth and sand in favor of rock and clay" (*Discourse on Method* II and III).]

error and precipitate judgment. It recommends an universal doubt, not only of all our former opinions and principles, but also of our very faculties; of whose veracity, say they, we must assure ourselves, by a chain of reasoning, deduced from some original principle, which cannot possibly be fallacious or deceitful. But neither is there any such original principle, which has a prerogative above others, that are self-evident and convincing: Or if there were, could we advance a step beyond it, but by the use of those very faculties, of which we are supposed to be already diffi-dent. The CARTESIAN doubt, therefore, were it ever possible to be attained by any human creature (as it plainly is not) would be entirely incurable; and no reasoning could ever bring us to a state of assurance and conviction upon any subject.

It must, however, be confessed, that this species of scepticism, when more moder-ate, may be understood in a very reasonable sense, and is a necessary preparative to the study of philosophy, by preserving a proper impartiality in our judgments, and weaning our mind from all those prejudices, which we may have imbibed from edu-cation or rash opinion. To begin with clear and self-evident principles, to advance by timorous and sure steps, to review frequently our conclusions, and examine ac-curately all their consequences; though by these means we shall make both a slow and a short progress in our systems; are the only methods, by which we can ever hope to reach truth, and attain a proper stability and certainty in our determina-tions.

There is another species of scepticism, *consequent* to science and enquiry, when men are supposed to have discovered, either the absolute fallaciousness of their mental faculties, or their unfitness to reach any fixed determination in all those curious subjects of speculation, about which they are commonly employed. Even our very senses are brought into dispute, by a certain species of philosophers; and the maxims of common life are subjected to the same doubt as the most profound principles or conclusions of metaphysics and theology. As these paradoxical tenets (if they may be called tenets) are to be met with in some philosophers, and the ref-utation of them in several, they naturally excite our curiosity, and make us enquire into the arguments, on which they may be founded.

I need not insist upon the more trite topics, employed by the sceptics in all ages, against the evidence of *sense;* such as those which are derived from the imperfection and fallaciousness of our organs, on numberless occasions; the crooked appearance of an oar in water; the various aspects of objects, according to their different dis-tances; the double images which arise from the pressing one eye; with many other appearances of a like nature. These sceptical topics, indeed, are only sufficient to prove, that the senses alone are not implicitly to be depended on; but that we must correct their evidence by reason, and by considerations, derived from the nature of the medium, the distance of the object, and the disposition of the organ, in order to render them, within their sphere, the proper *criteria* of truth and falsehood. There are other more profound arguments against the senses, which admit not of so easy a solution.

It seems evident, that men are carried, by a natural instinct or prepossession, to repose faith in their senses; and that, without any reasoning, or even almost before the use of reason, we always suppose an external universe, which depends not on our perception, but would exist, though we and every sensible creature were absent or annihilated. Even the animal creation are governed by a like opinion, and preserve this belief of external objects, in all their thoughts, designs, and actions.

It seems also evident, that, when men follow this blind and powerful instinct of nature, they always suppose the very images, presented by the senses, to be the external objects, and never entertain any suspicion, that the one are nothing but representations of the other. This very table, which we see white, and which we feel hard, is believed to exist, independent of our perception, and to be something external to our mind, which perceives it. Our presence bestows not being on it: Our absence does not annihilate it. It preserves its existence uniform and entire, independent of the situation of intelligent beings, who perceive or contemplate it.

But this universal and primary opinion of all men is soon destroyed by the slightest philosophy, which teaches us, that nothing can ever be present to the mind but an image or perception, and that the senses are only the inlets, through which these images are conveyed, without being able to produce any immediate intercourse between the mind and the object. The table, which we see, seems to diminish, as we remove farther from it: But the real table, which exists independent of us, suffers no alteration: It was, therefore, nothing but its image, which was present to the mind. These are the obvious dictates of reason; and no man, who reflects, ever doubted, that the existences, which we consider, when we say, *this house* and *that tree*, are nothing but perceptions in the mind, and fleeting copies or representations of other existences, which remain uniform and independent.

So far, then, are we necessitated by reasoning to contradict or depart from the primary instincts of nature, and to embrace a new system with regard to the evidence of our senses. But here philosophy finds herself extremely embarrassed, when she would justify this new system, and obviate the cavils and objections of the sceptics. She can no longer plead the infallible and irresistible instinct of nature: For that led us to a quite different system, which is acknowledged fallible and even erroneous. And to justify this pretended philosophical system, by a chain of clear and convincing argument, or even any appearance of argument, exceeds the power of all human capacity.

By what argument can it be proved, that the perceptions of the mind must be caused by external objects, entirely different from them, though resembling them (if that be possible) and could not arise either from the energy of the mind itself, or from the suggestion of some invisible and unknown spirit, or from some other cause still more unknown to us? It is acknowledged, that, in fact, many of these perceptions arise not from any thing external, as in dreams, madness, and other diseases. And nothing can be more inexplicable than the manner, in which body should so operate upon mind as ever to convey an image of itself to a substance, supposed of so different, and even contrary a nature.

It is a question of fact, whether the perceptions of the senses be produced by external objects, resembling them: How shall this question be determined? By experience surely; as all other questions of a like nature. But here experience is, and must be entirely silent. The mind has never any thing present to it but the perceptions, and cannot possibly reach any experience of their connexion with objects. The supposition of such a connexion is, therefore, without any foundation in reasoning.

To have recourse to the veracity of the supreme Being, in order to prove the veracity of our senses, is surely making a very unexpected circuit. If his veracity were at all concerned in this matter, our senses would be entirely infallible; because it is not possible that he can ever deceive. Not to mention, that, if the external world be once called in question, we shall be at a loss to find arguments, by which we may prove the existence of the Being or any of his attributes.

This is a topic, therefore, in which the profounder and more philosophical sceptics will always triumph, when they endeavour to introduce an universal doubt into all subjects of human knowledge and enquiry. Do you follow the instincts and propensities of nature, may they say, in assenting to the veracity of sense? But these lead you to believe, that the very perception or sensible image is the external object. Do you disclaim this principle, in order to embrace a more rational opinion, that the perceptions are only representations of something external? You here depart from your natural propensities and more obvious sentiments; and yet are not able to satisfy your reason, which can never find any convincing argument from experience to prove, that the perceptions are connected with any external objects.

There is another sceptical topic of a like nature, derived from the most profound philosophy; which might merit our attention, were it requisite to dive so deep, in order to discover arguments and reasonings, which can so little serve to any serious purpose. It is universally allowed by modern enquirers, that all the sensible qualities of objects, such as hard, soft, hot, cold, white, black, &c., are merely secondary, and exist not in the objects themselves, but are perceptions of the mind, without any external archetype or model, which they represent. If this be allowed, with regard to secondary qualities, it must also follow, with regard to the supposed primary qualities of extension and solidity; nor can the latter be any more entitled to that denomination than the former. The idea of extension is entirely acquired from the senses of sight and feeling; and if all the qualities, perceived by the senses, be in the mind, not in the object, the same conclusion must reach the idea of extension, which is wholly dependent on the sensible ideas or the ideas of secondary qualities.[80] Nothing can save us from this conclusion, but the asserting, that the ideas of those primary qualities are attained by *Abstraction;* an opinion, which, if we examine it accurately, we shall find to be unintelligible, and even absurd. An extension, that is neither tangible nor visible, cannot possibly be conceived: And a tangible or visible extension, which is neither hard nor soft, black nor white, is equally beyond the reach of human conception. Let any man try to conceive a triangle in general, which is neither *Isoceles* nor *Scalenum,* nor has any particular length or proportion of sides; and he will soon perceive the absurdity of all the scholastic notions with regard to abstraction and general ideas.[81]

Thus the first philosophical objection to the evidence of sense or to the opinion of

---

80. [The distinction between primary and secondary qualities was first made by Robert Boyle (1627–1691), although the basis for the distinction goes back to ancient philosophy and is implicit in the writings of Galileo (1564–1642) and Descartes. The primary qualities are commonly understood to be those qualities of our ideas which truly characterize (or are in) the object; the secondary, those qualities of our ideas which do not truly characterize (or are not in) the object, and are, thus, merely perceptions of the mind.]

81. This argument is drawn from Dr. BERKELEY [*A Treatise Concerning the Principles of Human Knowledge,* Introduction]; and indeed most of the writings of that very ingenious author form the best lessons of scepticism, which are to be found either among the ancient or modern philosophers, BAYLE not excepted. He professes, however, in his title-page (and undoubtedly with great truth) to have composed his book against the sceptics as well as against the atheists and free-thinkers. But that all his arguments, though otherwise intended, are, in reality, merely sceptical, appears from this, *that they admit of no answer and produce no conviction.* Their only effect is to cause that momentary amazement and irresolution and confusion, which is the result of scepticism.

external existence consists in this, that such an opinion, if rested on natural instinct, is contrary to reason, and if referred to reason, is contrary to natural instinct, and at the same time carries no rational evidence with it, to convince an impartial enquirer. The second objection goes farther, and represents this opinion as contrary to reason: at least, if it be a principle of reason, that all sensible qualities are in the mind, not in the object. Bereave matter of all its intelligible qualities, both primary and secondary, you in a manner annihilate it, and leave only a certain unknown, inexplicable *something,* as the cause of our perceptions; a notion so imperfect, that no sceptic will think it worth while to contend against it.

PART II.

It may seem a very extravagant attempt of the sceptics to destroy *reason* by argument and ratiocination; yet is this the grand scope of all their enquiries and disputes. They endeavour to find objections, both to our abstract reasonings, and to those which regard matter of fact and existence.

The chief objection against all *abstract* reasonings is derived from the ideas of space and time; ideas, which, in common life and to a careless view, are very clear and intelligible, but when they pass through the scrutiny of the profound sciences (and they are the chief object of these sciences) afford principles, which seem full of absurdity and contradiction. No priestly *dogmas,* invented on purpose to tame and subdue the rebellious reason of mankind, ever shocked common sense more than the doctrine of the infinite divisibility of extension, with its consequences; as they are pompously displayed by all geometricians and metaphysicians, with a kind of triumph and exultation. A real quantity, infinitely less than any finite quantity, containing quantities infinitely less than itself, and so on *in infinitum;* this is an edifice so bold and prodigious, that it is too weighty for any pretended demonstration to support, because it shocks the clearest and most natural principles of human reason.[82] But what renders the matter more extraordinary, is, that these seemingly absurd opinions are supported by a chain of reasoning, the clearest and most natural; nor is it possible for us to allow the premises without admitting the consequences. Nothing can be more convincing and satisfactory than all the conclusions concerning the properties of circles and triangles; and yet, when these are once received, how can we deny, that the angle of contact between a circle and its tangent is infinitely less than any rectilineal angle, that as you may increase the diameter of the circle *in infinitum,* this angle of contact becomes still less, even *in infinitum,* and that the angle of contact between other curves and their tangents may be infinitely less than those between any circle and its tangent, and so on, *in infinitum?* The demonstration of these principles seems as unexceptionable as that which proves the three angles of a triangle to be equal to two right ones, though the latter opinion be natural and easy, and the former big with contradiction and absurdity. Reason here seems to be thrown into a kind of amazement and suspense, which, without the suggestions of any sceptic, gives her a diffidence of herself, and of the ground on which

---

82. Whatever disputes there may be about mathematical points, we must allow that there are physical points; that is, parts of extension, which cannot be divided or lessened, either by the eye or imagination. These images, then, which are present to the fancy or senses, are absolutely indivisible, and consequently must be allowed by mathematicians to be infinitely less than any real part of extension; and yet nothing appears more certain to reason, than that an infinite number of them composes an infinite extension. How much more an infinite number of those infinitely small parts of extension, which are still supposed infinitely divisible?

she treads. She sees a full light, which illuminates certain places; but that light borders upon the most profound darkness. And between these she is so dazzled and confounded, that she scarcely can pronounce with certainty and assurance concerning any one object.

The absurdity of these bold determinations of the abstract sciences seems to become, if possible, still more palpable with regard to time than extension. An infinite number of real parts of time, passing in succession, and exhausted one after another, appears so evident a contradiction, that no man, one should think, whose judgment is not corrupted, instead of being improved, by the sciences, would ever be able to admit of it.

Yet still reason must remain restless, and unquiet, even with regard to that scepticism, to which she is driven by these seeming absurdities and contradictions. How any clear, distinct idea can contain circumstances, contradictory to itself, or to any other clear, distinct idea, is absolutely incomprehensible; and is, perhaps, as absurd as any proposition, which can be formed. So that nothing can be more sceptical, or more full of doubt and hesitation, than this scepticism itself, which arises from some of the paradoxical conclusions of geometry or the science of quantity.[83]

The sceptical objections to *moral* evidence, or to the reasonings concerning matter of fact, are either *popular* or *philosophical.* The popular objections are derived from the natural weakness of human understanding; the contradictory opinions, which have been entertained in different ages and nations; the variations of our judgment in sickness and health, youth and old age, prosperity and adversity; the perpetual contradiction of each particular man's opinions and sentiments; with many other topics of that kind. It is needless to insist farther on this head. These objections are but weak. For as, in common life, we reason every moment concerning fact and existence, and cannot possibly subsist, without continually employing this species of argument, any popular objections, derived from thence, must be insufficient to destroy that evidence. The great subverter of *Pyrrhonism*[84] or the ex-

---

83. It seems to me not impossible to avoid these absurdities and contradictions, if it be admitted, that there is no such thing as abstract or general ideas, properly speaking; but that all general ideas are, in reality, particular ones, attached to a general term, which recalls, upon occasion, other particular ones, that resemble, in certain circumstances, the idea, present to the mind. Thus when the term Horse, is pronounced, we immediately figure to ourselves the idea of a black or a white animal, of a particular size or figure: But as that term is also usually applied to animals of other colours, figures and sizes, these ideas, though not actually present to the imagination, are easily recalled; and our reasoning and conclusion proceed in the same way, as if they were actually present. If this be admitted (as seems reasonable) it follows that all the ideas of quantity, upon which mathematicians reason, are nothing but particular, and such as are suggested by the senses and imagination, and consequently, cannot be infinitely divisible. It is sufficient to have dropped this hint at present, without prosecuting it any farther. It certainly concerns all lovers of science not to expose themselves to the ridicule and contempt of the ignorant by their conclusions; and this seems the readiest solution of these difficulties.

84. [A form of extreme skepticism named after its first exponent, Pyrrho of Elis (c.360–c.270 B.C.). Unlike the Academic skeptics (see footnote 23), who are represented as having claimed that some things are more credible than others, even if nothing is certain, the Pyrrhonians are typically represented as being skeptical of that and all other doctrines, as recommending suspension of judgment on all things, and in lieu of knowledge, that one live according to nature, custom, or the laws of his country. Michel de Montaigne (1533–1592) presents a graphic view of the Pyrrhonians in his *Apology for Raimond Sebond* (1576): "They do their work with everything. If they win, your proposition is lame; if you win, theirs is. If they lose, they confirm ignorance; if you lose, you confirm it . . . They use their reason to inquire and debate, but not to conclude and choose. Whoever will imagine a perpetual confession of ignorance, a judgment without leaning or inclination, on any occasion whatever, he has a conception of Pyrrhonism."]

cessive principles of scepticism, is action, and employment, and the occupations of common life. These principles may flourish and triumph in the schools; where it is, indeed, difficult, if not impossible, to refute them. But as soon as they leave the shade, and by the presence of the real objects, which actuate our passions and senti-ments, are put in opposition to the more powerful principles of our nature, they vanish like smoke, and leave the most determined sceptic in the same condition as other mortals.

The sceptic, therefore, had better keep within his proper sphere, and display those *philosophical* objections, which arise from more profound researches. Here he seems to have ample matter of triumph; while he justly insists, that all our evidence for any matter of fact, which lies beyond the testimony of sense or memory, is derived entirely from the relation of cause and effect; that we have no other idea of this relation than that of two objects, which have been frequently *conjoined* together; that we have no argument to convince us, that objects, which have, in our experi-ence, been frequently conjoined, will likewise, in other instances, be conjoined in the same manner; and that nothing leads us to this inference but custom or a certain instinct of our nature; which it is indeed difficult to resist, but which, like other in-stincts, may be fallacious and deceitful. While the sceptic insists upon these topics, he shows his force, or rather, indeed, his own and our weakness; and seems, for the time at least, to destroy all assurance and conviction. These arguments might be dis-played at greater length, if any durable good or benefit to society could ever be ex-pected to result from them.

For here is the chief and most confounding objection to *excessive* scepticism, that no durable good can ever result from it; while it remains in its full force and vigour. We need only ask such a sceptic, *What his meaning is? And what he proposes by all these curious researches?* He is immediately at a loss, and knows not what to answer. A COPERNICAN or PTOLEMAIC, who supports each his different system of astronomy, may hope to produce a conviction, which will remain constant and durable, with his audience. A STOIC or EPICUREAN displays principles, which may not only be dura-ble, but which have an effect on conduct and behaviour. But a PYRRHONIAN cannot expect, that his philosophy will have any constant influence on the mind: Or if it had, that its influence would be beneficial to society. On the contrary, he must acknowledge, if he will acknowledge any thing, that all human life must perish, were his principles universally and steadily to prevail. All discourse, all action would immediately cease; and men remain in a total lethargy, till the necessities of nature, unsatisfied, put an end to their miserable existence. It is true; so fatal an event is very little to be dreaded. Nature is always too strong for principle. And though a PYRRHONIAN may throw himself or others into a momentary amazement and confusion by his profound reasonings; the first and most trivial event in life will put to flight all his doubts and scruples, and leave him the same, in every point of action and speculation, with the philosophers of every other sect, or with those who never concerned themselves in any philosophical researches. When he awakes from his dream, he will be the first to join in the laugh against himself, and to confess, that all his objections are mere amusement, and can have no other tendency than to show the whimsical condition of mankind, who must act and reason and believe; though they are not able, by their most diligent enquiry, to satisfy themselves con-cerning the foundation of these operations, or to remove the objections, which may be raised against them.

PART III.

There is, indeed, a more *mitigated* scepticism or *academical* philosophy, which may be both durable and useful, and which may, in part, be the result of this PYRRHON-ISM, or *excessive* scepticism, when its undistinguished doubts are, in some measure, corrected by common sense and reflection. The greater part of mankind are naturally apt to be affirmative and dogmatical in their opinions; and while they see objects only on one side, and have no idea of any counterpoising argument, they throw themselves precipitately into the principles, to which they are inclined; nor have they any indulgence for those who entertain opposite sentiments. To hesitate or balance perplexes their understanding, checks their passion, and suspends their action. They are, therefore, impatient till they escape from a state, which to them is so uneasy; and they think, that they can never remove themselves far enough from it, by the violence of their affirmations and obstinacy of their belief. But could such dogmatical reasoners become sensible of the strange infirmities of human understanding, even in its most perfect state, and when most accurate and cautious in its determinations; such a reflection would naturally inspire them with more modesty and reserve, and diminish their fond opinion of themselves, and their prejudice against antagonists. The illiterate may reflect on the disposition of the learned, who, amidst all the advantages of study and reflection, are commonly still diffident in their determinations: And if any of the learned be inclined, from their natural temper, to haughtiness and obstinacy, a small tincture of PYRRHONISM might abate their pride, by showing them, that the few advantages, which they may have attained over their fellows, are but inconsiderable, if compared with the universal perplexity and confusion, which is inherent in human nature. In general, there is a degree of doubt, and caution, and modesty, which, in all kinds of scrutiny and decision, ought for ever to accompany a just reasoner.

Another species of *mitigated* scepticism, which may be of advantage to mankind, and which may be the natural result of the PYRRHONIAN doubts and scruples, is the limitation of our enquiries to such subjects as are best adapted to the narrow capacity of human understanding. The *imagination* of man is naturally sublime, delighted with whatever is remote and extraordinary, and running, without control, into the most distant parts of space and time in order to avoid the objects, which custom has rendered too familiar to it. A correct *Judgment* observes a contrary method, and avoiding all distant and high enquiries, confines itself to common life, and to such subjects as fall under daily practice and experience; leaving the more sublime topics to the embellishment of poets and orators, or to the arts of priests and politicians. To bring us to so salutary a determination, nothing can be more serviceable, than to be once thoroughly convinced of the force of the PYRRHONIAN doubt, and of the impossibility, that any thing, but the strong power of natural instinct, could free us from it. Those who have a propensity of philosophy, will still continue their researches; because they reflect, that, besides the immediate pleasure, attending such an occupation, philosophical decisions are nothing but the reflections of common life, methodized and corrected. But they will never be tempted to go beyond common life, so long as they consider the imperfection of those faculties which they employ, their narrow reach, and their inaccurate operations. While we cannot give a satisfactory reason, why we believe, after a thousand experiments, that a stone will fall, or fire burn; can we ever satisfy ourselves concerning any determination, which we may form, with regard to the origin of worlds, and the situation of nature, from, and to eternity?

This narrow limitation, indeed, of our enquiries, is, in every respect, so reasonable, that it suffices to make the slightest examination into the natural powers of the human mind, and to compare them with their objects, in order to recommend it to us. We shall then find what are the proper subjects of science and enquiry.

It seems to me, that the only objects of the abstract sciences or of demonstration are quantity and number, and that all attempts to extend this more perfect species of knowledge beyond these bounds are mere sophistry and illusion. As the component parts of quantity and number are entirely similar, their relations become intricate and involved; and nothing can be more curious, as well as useful, than to trace, by a variety of mediums, their equality or inequality, through their different appearances. But as all other ideas are clearly distinct and different from each other, we can never advance farther, by our utmost scrutiny, than to observe this diversity, and, by an obvious reflection, pronounce one thing not to be another. Or if there by any difficulty in these decisions, it proceeds entirely from the undeterminate meaning of words, which is corrected by juster definitions. That *the square of the hypothenuse is equal to the squares of the other two sides,* cannot be known, let the terms be ever so exactly defined, without a train of reasoning and enquiry. But to convince us of this proposition, *that where there is no property, there can be no injustice,* it is only necessary to define the terms, and explain injustice to be a violation of property. This proposition is, indeed, nothing but a more imperfect definition. It is the same case with all those pretended syllogistical reasonings, which may be found in every other branch of learning, except the sciences of quantity and number; and these may safely, I think, be pronounced the only proper objects of knowledge and demonstration.

All other enquiries of men regard only matter of fact and existence; and these are evidently incapable of demonstration. Whatever *is* may *not be.* No negation of a fact can involve a contradiction. The non-existence of any being, without exception, is as clear and distinct an idea as its existence.[85] The proposition, which affirms it not to be, however false, is no less conceivable and intelligible, than that which affirms it to be. The case is different with the sciences, properly so called. Every proposition, which is not true, is there confused and unintelligible. That the cube root of 64 is equal to the half of 10, is a false proposition, and can never be distinctly conceived. But that CAESAR, or the angel GABRIEL, or any being never existed, may be a false proposition, but still is perfectly conceivable, and implies no contradiction.

The existence, therefore, of any being can only be proved by arguments from its cause or its effect; and these arguments are founded entirely on experience. If we reason *a priori,* any thing may appear able to produce any thing. The falling of a pebble may, for aught we know, extinguish the sun; or the wish of a man control the planets in their orbits. It is only experience, which teaches us the nature and bounds of cause and effect, and enables us to infer the existence of one object from

---

85. [Cf. *Treatise* I.2.6: "The idea of existence, then, is the very same with the idea of what we conceive to be existent. To reflect on any thing simply, and to reflect on it as existent, are nothing different from each other. That idea, when conjoined with the idea of any object, makes no addition to it. Whatever we conceive, we conceive to be existent. Any idea we please to form is the idea of a being; and the idea of a being is any idea we please to form."—and Descartes, *Meditations* V: "It is certain that I . . . find the idea of God in my consciousness . . . and I know with not less clearness and distinctness that an actual and eternal existence pertains to his nature, than that all which is demonstrable of any figure or number really belongs to the nature of that figure or number."]

that of another.[86] Such is the foundation of moral reasoning, which forms the greater part of human knowledge, and is the source of all human action and behaviour.

Moral reasonings are either concerning particular or general facts. All deliberations in life regard the former; as also all disquisitions in history, chronology, geography, and astronomy.

The sciences, which treat of general facts, are politics, natural philosophy, physic, chymistry, &c. where the qualities, causes and effects of a whole species of objects are enquired into.

Divinity or Theology, as it proves the existence of a Deity, and the immortality of souls, is composed partly of reasonings concerning particular, partly concerning general facts. It has a foundation in *reason*, so far as it is supported by experience. But its best and most solid foundation is *faith* and divine revelation.

Morals and criticism are not so properly objects of the understanding as of taste and sentiment. Beauty, whether moral or natural, is felt, more properly than perceived. Or if we reason concerning it, and endeavour to fix its standard, we regard a new fact, to wit, the general taste of mankind, or some such fact, which may be the object of reasoning and enquiry.

When we run over libraries, persuaded of these principles, what havoc must we make? If we take in our hand any volume; of divinity or school metaphysics, for instance; let us ask, *Does it contain any abstract reasoning concerning quantity or number?* No. *Does it contain any experimental reasoning concerning matter of fact and existence?* No. Commit it then to the flames: For it can contain nothing but sophistry and illusion.

---

86. That impious maxim of the ancient philosophy, *Ex nihilo, nihil fit* [From nothing, nothing comes], by which the creation of matter was excluded, ceases to be a maxim, according to this philosophy. Not only the will of the supreme Being may create matter; but, for aught we know *a priori*, the will of any other being might create it, or any other cause, that the most whimsical imagination can assign.

DIALOGUES CONCERNING NATURAL RELIGION

Pamphilus to Hermippus

It has been remarked, my Hermippus, that, though the ancient philosophers conveyed most of their instruction in the form of dialogue, this method of composition has been little practised in later ages, and has seldom succeeded in the hands of those who have attempted it. Accurate and regular argument, indeed, such as is now expected of philosophical inquirers, naturally throws a man into the methodical and didactic manner; where he can immediately, without preparation, explain the point at which he aims; and thence proceed, without interruption, to deduce the proofs on which it is established. To deliver a *system* in conversation scarcely appears natural; and while the dialogue writer desires, by departing from the direct style of composition, to give a freer air to his performance, and avoid the appearance of *author* and *reader,* he is apt to run into a worse inconvenience and convey the image of *pedagogue* and *pupil.* Or if he carries on the dispute in the natural spirit of good company, by throwing in a variety of topics and preserving a proper balance among the speakers, he often loses so much time in preparations and transitions that the reader will scarcely think himself compensated, by all the graces of dialogue, for the order, brevity, and precision, which are sacrificed to them.

There are some subjects, however, to which dialogue-writing is peculiarly adapted, and where it is still preferable to the direct and simple method of composition.

Any point of doctrine which is so *obvious* that it scarcely admits of dispute, but at the same time so *important* that it cannot be too often inculcated, seems to require some such method of handling it; where the novelty of the manner may compensate the triteness of the subject, where the vivacity of conversation may enforce the precept, and where the variety of lights, presented by various personages and characters, may appear neither tedious nor redundant.

Any question of philosophy, on the other hand, which is so *obscure* and *uncertain* that human reason can reach no fixed determination with regard to it—if it should be treated at all—seems to lead us naturally into the style of dialogue and conversation. Reasonable men may be allowed to differ where no one can reasonably be positive: Opposite sentiments, even without any decision, afford an agreeable amusement; and if the subject be curious and interesting, the book carries us, in a manner, into company, and unites the two greatest and purest pleasures of human life—study and society.

Happily, these circumstances are all to be found in the subject of *natural religion.* What truth so obvious, so certain, as the *being* of a God, which the most ignorant ages have acknowledged, for which the most refined geniuses have ambitiously striven to produce new proofs and arguments? What truth so important as this, which is the ground of all our hopes, the surest foundation of morality, the firmest support of society, and the only principle which ought never to be a moment absent from our thoughts and meditations? But, in treating of this obvious and important truth, what obscure questions occur concerning the *nature* of that Divine Being; his attributes, his decrees, his plan of providence? These have been always subjected to the disputations of men: Concerning these, human reason has not reached any certain determination. But these are topics so interesting that we cannot restrain our restless inquiry with regard to them; though nothing but doubt, uncertainty, and contradiction have as yet been the result of our most accurate researches.

This I had lately occasion to observe, while I passed, as usual, part of the summer season with Cleanthes, and was present at those conversations of his with Philo and Demea, of which I gave you lately some imperfect account. Your curiosity, you then told me, was so excited that I must, of necessity, enter into a more exact detail of their reasonings, and display those various systems which they advanced with regard to so delicate a subject as that of natural religion. The remarkable contast in their characters still further raised your expectations; while you opposed the accurate philosophical turn of Cleanthes to the careless scepticism of Philo, or compared either of their dispositions with the rigid inflexible orthodoxy of Demea. My youth rendered me a mere auditor of their disputes; and that curiosity, natural to the early season of life, has so deeply imprinted in my memory the whole chain and connection of their arguments, that, I hope, I shall not omit or confound any considerable part of them in the recital.

Part I

After I joined the company, whom I found sitting in Cleanthes' library, Demea paid Cleanthes some compliments on the great care which he took of my education, and on his unwearied perseverance and constancy in all his friendships. The father of Pamphilus, said he, was your intimate friend; the son is your pupil, and may indeed be regarded as your adopted son, were we to judge by the pains which you bestow in conveying to him every useful branch of literature and science. You are no more wanting, I am persuaded, in prudence than in industry. I shall, therefore, communicate to you a maxim which I have observed with regard to my own children, that I may learn how far it agrees with your practice. The method I follow in their education is founded on the saying of an ancient, *"That students of philosophy ought first to learn logics, then ethics, next physics, last of all the nature of the gods."*[1] This science of natural theology, according to him, being the most profound and abstruse of any, required the maturest judgment in its students; and none but a mind enriched with all the other sciences can safely be entrusted with it.

Are you so late, says Philo, in teaching your children the principles of religion? Is there no danger of their neglecting or rejecting altogether those opinions of which they have heard so little during the whole course of their education? It is only as a science, replied Demea, subjected to human reasoning and disputation, that I postpone the study of natural theology. To season their minds with early piety is my chief care; and by continual precept and instruction and I hope too, by example, I

---

1. Chrysippus *apud* Plut., *De repug. Stoicorum.* [Regarding Chrysippus, see Epictetus' *Enchiridion*, n. 6. Regarding Plutarch, see Hume's *Enquiry*, n. 50. The work referred to is *Of the Inconsistencies of the Stoics.* —S.M.C.]

imprint deeply on their tender minds an habitual reverence for all the principles of religion. While they pass through every other science, I still remark the uncertainty of each part; the eternal disputations of men; the obscurity of all philosophy; and the strange, ridiculous conclusions which some of the greatest geniuses have derived from the principles of mere human reason. Having thus tamed their minds to a proper submission and self-diffidence, I have no longer any scruple of opening to them the greatest mysteries of religion, nor apprehend any danger from that assuming arrogance of philosophy, which may lead them to reject the most established doctrines and opinions.

Your precaution, says Philo, of seasoning your children's minds early with piety is certainly very reasonable, and no more than is requisite in this profane and irreligious age. But what I chiefly admire in your plan of education is your method of drawing advantage from the very principles of philosophy and learning which, by inspiring pride and self-sufficiency, have commonly, in all ages, been found so destructive to the principles of religion. The vulgar, indeed, we may remark, who are unacquainted with science and profound inquiry, observing the endless disputes of the learned, have commonly a thorough contempt for philosophy; and rivet themselves the faster, by that means, in the great points of theology which have been taught them. Those who enter a little into study and inquiry, finding many appearances of evidence in doctrines the newest and most extraordinary, think nothing too difficult for human reason; and, presumptuously breaking through all fences, profane the inmost sanctuaries of the temple. But Cleanthes will, I hope, agree with me that, after we have abandoned ignorance, the surest remedy, there is still one expedient left to prevent this profane liberty. Let Demea's principles be improved and cultivated: Let us become thoroughly sensible of the weakness, blindness, and narrow limits of human reason: Let us duly consider its uncertainty and endless contrarieties, even in subjects of common life and practice: Let the errors and deceits of our very senses be set before us; the insuperable difficulties which attend first principles in all systems; the contradictions which adhere to the very ideas of matter, cause and effect, extension, space, time, motion; and, in a word, quantity of all kinds, the object of the only science that can fairly pretend to any certainty or evidence. When these topics are displayed in their full light, as they are by some philosophers and almost all divines, who can retain such confidence in this frail faculty of reason as to pay any regard to its determinations in points so sublime, so abstruse, so remote from common life and experience? When the coherence of the parts of a stone, or even that composition of parts which renders it extended; when these familiar objects, I say, are so inexplicable, and contain circumstances so repugnant and contradictory; with what assurance can we decide concerning the origin of worlds or trace their history from eternity to eternity?

While Philo pronounced these words, I could observe a smile in the countenance both of Demea and Cleanthes. That of Demea seemed to imply an unreserved satisfaction in the doctrines delivered; but in Cleanthes' features I could distinguish an air of finesse, as if he perceived some raillery or artificial malice in the reasonings of Philo.

You propose then, Philo, said Cleanthes, to erect religious faith on philosophical scepticism; and you think that, if certainty or evidence be expelled from every other subject of inquiry, it will all retire to these theological doctrines, and there acquire a superior force and authority. Whether your scepticism be as absolute and sincere as you pretend, we shall learn by and by, when the company breaks up; we shall then see whether you go out at the door or the window, and whether you really doubt if your body has gravity or can be injured by its fall, according to popular opinion derived from our fallacious senses and more fallacious experience. And this consideration, Demea, may, I think, fairly serve to abate our ill-will to this humorous sect of the sceptics. If they be thoroughly in earnest, they will not long trouble the world with their doubts, cavils, and disputes; if they be only in jest, they are, perhaps, bad railers, but can never be very dangerous, either to the state, to philosophy, or to religion.

In reality, Philo, continued he, it seems certain that, though a man in a flush of humor, after intense reflection on the many contradictions and imperfections of human reason, may entirely renounce all belief and opinion, it is impossible for him to persevere in this total scepticism or make it appear in his conduct for a few hours. External objects press in upon him: Passions solicit him: His philosophical melancholy dissipates; and even the utmost violence upon his own temper will not be able, during any time, to preserve the poor appearance of scepticism. And for what reason impose on himself such a violence? This is a point in which it will be impossible for him ever to satisfy himself, consistently with his sceptical principles. So that, upon the whole, nothing could be more ridiculous than the principles of the ancient Pyrrhonians;[2] if, in reality, they endeavored, as is pretended, to extend throughout the same scepticism which they had learned from the declamations of their schools, and which they ought to have confined to them.

In this view, there appears a great resemblance between the sects of the Stoics and Pyrrhonians, though perpetual antagonists; and both of them seem founded on this erroneous maxim: that what a man can perform sometimes, and in some dispositions, he can perform always and in every disposition. When the mind, by Stoical reflections, is elevated into a sublime enthusiasm of virtue and strongly smit with any *species* of honor or public good, the utmost bodily pain and sufferings will not prevail over such a high sense of duty; and it is possible, perhaps, by its means, even to smile and exult in the midst of tortures. If this sometimes may be the case in fact and reality, much more may a philosopher, in his school or even in his closet, work himself up to such an enthusiasm, and support, in imagination, the acutest pain or most calamitous event which he can possibly conceive. But how shall he support this enthusiasm itself? The bent of his mind relaxes and cannot be recalled at pleasure; avocations lead him astray; misfortunes attack him unawares; and the *philosopher* sinks, by degrees, into the *plebeian*.

I allow of your comparison between the Stoics and Sceptics, replied Philo. But you may observe, at the same time, that though the mind cannot, in Stoicism, support the highest flights of philosophy, yet, even when it sinks lower, it still retains somewhat of its former disposition; and the effects of the Stoic's reasoning will appear in his conduct in common life, and through the whole tenor of his actions. The ancient schools, particularly that of Zeno,[3] produced examples of virtue and constancy which seem astonishing to present times.

2. [The reference is to followers of Pyrrho, regarding whom see Hume's *Enquiry*, n. 84.]

3. [Regarding Zeno of Citium, see Epictetus' *Enchiridion*, n. 5.]

Vain Wisdom all and false Philosophy.
Yet with a pleasing sorcery could charm
Pain, for a while, or anguish; and excite
Fallacious Hope, or arm the obdurate breast
With stubborn Patience, as with triple steel.[4]

In like manner, if a man has accustomed himself to sceptical considerations on the uncertainty and narrow limits of reason, he will not entirely forget them when he turns his reflection on other subjects; but in all his philosophical principles and reasoning, I dare not say, in his common conduct, he will be found different from those who either never formed any opinions in the case or have entertained sentiments more favorable to human reason.

To whatever length anyone may push his speculative principles of scepticism, he must act, I own, and live, and converse like other men; and for this conduct he is not obliged to give any other reason than the absolute necessity he lies under of so doing. If he ever carries his speculations farther than this necessity constrains him, and philosophizes either on natural or moral subjects, he is allured by a certain pleasure and satisfaction which he finds in employing himself after that manner. He considers, besides, that everyone, even in common life, is constrained to have more or less of this philosophy; that from our earliest infancy we make continual advances in forming more general principles of conduct and reasoning; that the larger experience we acquire, and the stronger reason we are endued with, we always render our principles the more general and comprehensive; and that what we call *philosophy* is nothing but a more regular and methodical operation of the same kind. To philosophize on such subjects is nothing essentially different from reasoning on common life, and we may only expect greater stability, if not greater truth, from our philosophy on account of its exacter and more scrupulous method of proceeding.

But when we look beyond human affairs and the properties of the surrounding bodies—when we carry our speculations into the two eternities, before and after the present state of things; into the creation and formation of the universe; the existence and properties of spirits; the powers and operations of one universal Spirit existing without beginning and without end, omnipotent, omniscient, immutable, infinite, and incomprehensible—we must be far removed from the smallest tendency to scepticism not to be apprehensive that we have here got quite beyond the reach of our faculties. So long as we confine our speculations to trade, or morals, or politics, or criticism, we make appeals, every moment, to common sense and experience, which strengthen our philosophical conclusions and remove (at least in part) the suspicion, which we so justly entertain with regard to every reasoning, that is very subtle and refined. But in theological reasonings, we have not this advantage; while at the same time we are employed upon objects which, we must be sensible, are too large for our grasp, and of all others, require most to be familiarized to our apprehension. We are like foreigners in a strange country to whom everything must seem suspicious, and who are in danger every moment of transgressing against the laws and customs of the people with whom they live and converse. We know not how far we ought to trust our vulgar methods of reasoning in such a subject, since, even in common life, and in that province which is peculiarly appropriated to them,

---

4. [The quotation is from John Milton's *Paradise Lost.*]

we cannot account for them and are entirely guided by a kind of instinct or necessity in employing them.

All sceptics pretend that, if reason be considered in an abstract view, it furnishes invincible arguments against itself, and that we could never retain any conviction or assurance, on any subject, were not the sceptical reasonings so refined and subtile that they are not able to counterpoise the more solid and more natural arguments derived from the senses and experience. But it is evident, whenever our arguments lose this advantage and run wide of common life, that the most refined scepticism comes to be upon a footing with them, and is able to oppose and counterbalance them. The one has no more weight than the other. The mind must remain in suspense between them; and it is that very suspense or balance which is the triumph of scepticism.

But I observe, says Cleanthes, with regard to you, Philo, and all speculative sceptics that your doctrine and practice are as much at variance in the most abstruse points of theory as in the conduct of common life. Wherever evidence discovers itself, you adhere to it, notwithstanding your pretended scepticism; and I can observe, too, some of your sect to be as decisive as those who make greater professions of certainty and assurance. In reality, would not a man be ridiculous who pretended to reject Newton's explication of the wonderful phenomenon of the rainbow because that explication gives a minute anatomy of the rays of light—a subject, forsooth, too refined for human comprehension? And what would you say to one who, having nothing particular to object to the arguments of Copernicus and Galileo for the motion of the earth, should withhold his assent on that general principle that these subjects were too magnificent and remote to be explained by the narrow and fallacious reason of mankind?

There is indeed a kind of brutish and ignorant scepticism, as you well observed, which gives the vulgar a general prejudice against what they do not easily understand, and makes them reject every principle which requires elaborate reasoning to prove and establish it. This species of scepticism is fatal to knowledge, not to religion; since we find that those who make greatest profession of it give often their assent, not only to the great truths of theism and natural theology, but even to the most absurd tenets which a traditional superstition has recommended to them. They firmly believe in witches, though they will not believe nor attend to the most simple proposition of Euclid. But the refined and philosophical sceptics fall into an inconsistence of an opposite nature. They push their researches into the most abstruse corners of science, and their assent attends them in every step, proportioned to the evidence which they meet with. They are even obliged to acknowledge that the most abstruse and remote objects are those which are best explained by philosophy. Light is in reality anatomized; the true system of the heavenly bodies is discovered and ascertained. But the nourishment of bodies by food is still an inexplicable mystery; the cohesion of the parts of matter is still incomprehensible. These sceptics, therefore, are obliged, in every question, to consider each particular evidence apart, and proportion their assent to the precise degree of evidence which occurs. This is their practice in all natural, mathematical, moral, and political science. And why not the same, I ask, in the theological and religious? Why must conclusions of this nature be alone rejected on the general presumption of the insufficiency of human reason, without any particular discussion of the evidence? Is not such an unequal conduct a plain proof of prejudice and passion?

Our senses, you say, are fallacious; our understanding erroneous; our ideas, even of the most familiar objects—extension, duration, motion—full of absurdities and contradictions. You defy me to solve the difficulties or reconcile the repugnancies which you discover in them. I have not capacity for so great an undertaking: I have not leisure for it: I perceive it to be superfluous. Your own conduct, in every circumstance, refutes your principles, and shows the firmest reliance on all the received maxims of science, morals, prudence, and behavior.

I shall never assent to so harsh an opinion as that of a celebrated writer,[5] who says that the Sceptics are not a sect of philosophers: they are only a sect of liars. I may, however, affirm (I hope without offence) that they are a sect of jesters or railers. But for my part, whenever I find myself disposed to mirth and amusement, I shall certainly choose my entertainment of a less perplexing and abstruse nature. A comedy, a novel, or, at most, a history seems a more natural recreation than such metaphysical subtilties and abstractions.

In vain would the sceptic make a distinction between science and common life, or between one science and another. The arguments employed in all, if just, are of a similar nature and contain the same force and evidence. Or if there be any difference among them, the advantage lies entirely on the side of theology and natural religion. Many principles of mechanics are founded on very abstruse reasoning; yet no man who has any pretensions to science, even no speculative sceptic, pretends to entertain the least doubt with regard to them. The Copernican system contains the most surprising paradox, and the most contrary to our natural conceptions, to appearances, and to our very senses; yet even monks and inquisitors are now constrained to withdraw their opposition to it. And shall Philo, a man of so liberal a genius and extensive knowledge, entertain any general undistinguished scruples with regard to the religious hypothesis, which is founded on the simplest and most obvious arguments and, unless it meets with artificial obstacles, has such easy access and admission into the mind of man?

And here we may observe, continued he, turning himself towards Demea, a pretty curious circumstance in the history of the sciences. After the union of philosophy with the popular religion, upon the first establishment of Christianity, nothing was more usual, among all religious teachers, than declamations against reason, against the senses, against every principle derived merely from human research and inquiry. All the topics of the ancient Academics[6] were adopted by the Fathers, and thence propagated for several ages in every school and pulpit throughout Christendom. The Reformers embraced the same principles of reasoning or rather declamation; and all panegyrics on the excellence of faith were sure to be interlarded with some severe strokes of satire against natural reason. A celebrated prelate, too,[7] of the Romish communion, a man of the most extensive learning, who wrote a demonstration of Christianity, has also composed a treatise which contains all the cavils of the boldest and most determined Pyrrhonism. Locke seems to have been the first

---

5. *L'art de penser.* [This work, the influential *Port-Royal Logic*, was coauthored by Pierre Nicole (1625-1695), a French theologian, and Antoine Arnauld, regarding whom see Hume's *Enquiry*, n. 66.]

6. [Regarding the Academy, see Hume's *Enquiry*, n. 23.]

7. Mons. Huet. [The reference is to Peter Daniel Huet (1630–1721), a renowned French scholar who was bishop of Avranches.]

Christian who ventured openly to assert that *faith* was nothing but a species of *reason;* that religion was only a branch of philosophy; and that a chain of arguments, similar to that which established any truth in morals, politics, or physics, was always employed in discovering all the principles of theology, natural and revealed. The ill use which Bayle and other libertines made of the philosophical scepticism of the Fathers and first Reformers still further propagated the judicious sentiment of Mr. Locke. And it is now in a manner avowed, by all pretenders to reasoning and philosophy, that atheist and sceptic are almost synonymous. And as it is certain that no man is in earnest when he professes the latter principle, I would fain hope that there are as few who seriously maintain the former.

Don't you remember, said Philo, the excellent saying of Lord Bacon[8] on this head? That a little philosophy, replied Cleanthes, makes a man an atheist; a great deal converts him to religion. That is a very judicious remark, too, said Philo. But what I have in my eye is another passage, where, having mentioned David's fool, who said in his heart there is no God, this great philosopher observes that the atheists nowadays have a double share of folly; for they are not contented to say in their hearts there is no God, but they also utter that impiety with their lips, and are thereby guilty of multiplied indiscretion and imprudence. Such people, though they were ever so much in earnest, cannot, methinks, be very formidable.

But though you should rank me in this class of fools, I cannot forbear communicating a remark that occurs to me from the history of the religious and irreligious scepticism with which you have entertained us. It appears to me that there are strong symptoms of priestcraft in the whole progress of this affair. During ignorant ages, such as those which followed the dissolution of the ancient schools, the priests perceived that atheism, deism, or heresy of any kind, could only proceed from the presumptuous questioning of received opinions, and from a belief that human reason was equal to everything. Education had then a mighty influence over the minds of men, and was almost equal in force to those suggestions of the senses and common understanding by which the most determined sceptic must allow himself to be governed. But at present, when the influence of education is much diminished and men, from a more open commerce of the world, have learned to compare the popular principles of different nations and ages, our sagacious divines have changed their whole system of philosophy and talk the language of Stoics, Platonists, and Peripatetics,[9] not that of Pyrrhonians and Academics. If we distrust human reason we have now no other principle to lead us into religion. Thus sceptics in one age, dogmatists in another—whichever system best suits the purpose of these reverend gentlemen in giving them an ascendant over mankind—they are sure to make it their favorite principle and established tenet.

It is very natural, said Cleanthes, for men to embrace those principles by which they find they can best defend their doctrines, nor need we have any recourse to priestcraft to account for so reasonable an expedient. And surely, nothing can afford a stronger presumption that any set of principles are true and ought to be embraced than to observe that they tend to the confirmation of true religion, and serve to confound the cavils of atheists, libertines, and free-thinkers of all denominations.

8. [Regarding Francis Bacon, see Hume's *Enquiry*, n. 70.]

9. [Regarding the Peripatetics, see Leibniz's *Discourse*, n. 8.]

Part II

I must own, Cleanthes, said Demea, that nothing can more surprise me than the light in which you have all along put this argument. By the whole tenor of your discourse, one would imagine that you were maintaining the Being of a God against the cavils of atheists and infidels, and were necessitated to become a champion for that fundamental principle of all religion. But this, I hope, is not by any means a question among us. No man; no man, at least of common sense, I am persuaded, ever entertained a serious doubt with regard to a truth so certain and self-evident. The question is not concerning the *being* but the *nature of God*. This I affirm, from the infirmities of human understanding, to be altogether incomprehensible and unknown to us. The essence of that supreme mind, his attributes, the manner of his existence, the very nature of his duration—these and every particular which regards so divine a being are mysterious to men. Finite, weak, and blind creatures, we ought to humble ourselves in his august presence, and, conscious of our frailties, adore in silence his infinite perfections which eye hath not seen, ear hath not heard, neither hath it entered into the heart of man to conceive. They are covered in a deep cloud from human curiosity; it is profaneness to attempt penetrating through these sacred obscurities; and, next to the impiety of denying his existence, is the temerity of prying into his nature and essence, decrees and attributes.

But lest you should think that my *piety* has here got the better of my *philosophy*, I shall support my opinion, if it needs any support, by a very great authority. I might cite all the divines, almost from the foundation of Christianity, who have ever treated of this or any other theological subject; but I shall confine myself, at present, to one equally celebrated for piety and philosophy. It is Father Malebranche who, I remember, thus expresses himself.[10] "One ought not so much (says he) to call God a spirit in order to express positively what he is, as in order to signify that he is not matter. He is a Being infinitely perfect—of this we cannot doubt. But in the same manner as we ought not to imagine, even supposing him corporeal, that he is clothed with a human body, as the anthropomorphites asserted, under color that that figure was the most perfect of any, so neither ought we to imagine that the spirit of God has human ideas or bears any resemblance to our spirit, under color that we know nothing more perfect than a human mind. We ought rather to believe that as he comprehends the perfections of matter without being material . . . he comprehends also the perfections of created spirits without being spirit, in the manner we conceive spirit: That his true name is *He that is*, or, in other words, Being without restriction, All Being, the Being infinite and universal."

After so great an authority, Demea, replied Philo, as that which you have produced, and a thousand more which you might produce, it would appear ridiculous in me to add my sentiment or express my approbation of your doctrine. But surely, where reasonable men treat these subjects, the question can never be concerning the *being* but only the *nature* of the Deity. The former truth, as you well observe, is unquestionable and self-evident. Nothing exists without a cause; and the original cause of this universe (whatever it be) we call *God*, and piously ascribe to him every species of perfection. Whoever scruples this fundamental truth deserves every

---

10. *Recherche de la Vérité,* liv. 3, cap. 9. [Regarding Malebranche, see Berkeley's *Treatise,* ns. 8, 12. The work referred to is *The Search for Truth.*]

punishment which can be inflicted among philosophers, to wit, the greatest ridicule, contempt, and disapprobation. But as all perfection is entirely relative, we ought never to imagine that we comprehend the attributes of this divine Being, or to suppose that his perfections have any analogy or likeness to the perfections of a human creature. Wisdom, thought, design, knowledge—these we justly ascribe to him because these words are honorable among men, and we have no other language or other conceptions by which we can express our adoration of him. But let us beware lest we think that our ideas anywise correspond to his perfections, or that his attributes have any resemblance to these qualities among men. He is infinitely superior to our limited view and comprehension; and is more the object of worship in the temple than of disputation in the schools.

In reality, Cleanthes, continued he, there is no need of having recourse to that affected scepticism so displeasing to you in order to come at this determination. Our ideas reach no farther than our experience: We have no experience of divine attributes and operations. I need not conclude my syllogism: You can draw the inference yourself. And it is a pleasure to me (and I hope to you, too) that just reasoning and sound piety here concur in the same conclusion, and both of them establish the adorably mysterious and incomprehensible nature of the Supreme Being.

Not to lose any time in circumlocutions, said Cleanthes, addressing himself to Demea, much less in replying to the pious declamations of Philo, I shall briefly explain how I conceive this matter. Look round the world: Contemplate the whole and every part of it: You will find it to be nothing but one great machine, subdivided into an infinite number of lesser machines, which again admit of subdivisions to a degree beyond what human senses and faculties can trace and explain. All these various machines, and even their most minute parts, are adjusted to each other with an accuracy which ravishes into admiration all men who have ever contemplated them. The curious adapting of means to ends, throughout all nature, resembles exactly, though it much exceeds, the productions of human contrivance—of human design, thought, wisdom, and intelligence. Since therefore the effects resemble each other, we are led to infer, by all the rules of analogy, that the causes also resemble, and that the Author of Nature is somewhat similar to the mind of man, though possessed of much larger faculties, proportioned to the grandeur of the work which he has executed. By this argument *a posteriori,* and by this argument alone, do we prove at once the existence of a Deity and his similarity to human mind and intelligence.

I shall be so free, Cleanthes, said Demea, as to tell you that from the beginning I could not approve of your conclusion concerning the similarity of the Deity to men, still less can I approve of the mediums by which you endeavor to establish it. What! No demonstration of the Being of God! No abstract arguments! No proofs *a priori!* Are these which have hitherto been so much insisted on by philosophers all fallacy, all sophism? Can we reach no farther in this subject than experience and probability? I will say not that this is betraying the cause of a Deity; but surely, by this affected candor, you give advantages to atheists which they never could obtain by the mere dint of argument and reasoning.

What I chiefly scruple in this subject, said Philo, is not so much that all religious arguments are by Cleanthes reduced to experience, as that they appear not to be even the most certain and irrefragable of that inferior kind. That a stone will fall, that fire will burn, that the earth has solidity, we have observed a thousand and a thousand times; and when any new instance of this nature is presented, we draw without hesitation the accustomed inference. The exact similarity of the cases gives us a perfect assurance of a similar event, and a stronger evidence is never desired nor sought after. But wherever you depart, in the least, from the similarity of the cases, you diminish proportionably the evidence; and may at last bring it to a very weak *analogy*, which is confessedly liable to error and uncertainty. After having experienced the circulation of the blood in human creatures, we make no doubt that it takes place in Titius and Maevius; but from its circulation in frogs and fishes it is only a presumption, though a strong one, from analogy that it takes place in men and other animals. The analogical reasoning is much weaker when we infer the circulation of the sap in vegetables from our experience that the blood circulates in animals; and those who hastily followed that imperfect analogy are found, by more accurate experiments, to have been mistaken.

If we see a house, Cleanthes, we conclude, with the greatest certainty, that it had an architect or builder because this is precisely that species of effect which we have experienced to proceed from that species of cause. But surely you will not affirm that the universe bears such a resemblance to a house that we can with the same certainty infer a similar cause, or that the analogy is here entire and perfect. The dissimilitude is so striking that the utmost you can here pretend to is a guess, a conjecture, a presumption concerning a similar cause; and how that pretension will be received in the world, I leave you to consider.

It would surely be very ill received, replied Cleanthes; and I should be deservedly blamed and detested did I allow that the proofs of a Deity amounted to no more than a guess or conjecture. But is the whole adjustment of means to ends in a house and in the universe so slight a resemblance? the economy of final causes? the order, proportion, and arrangement of every part? Steps of a stair are plainly contrived that human legs may use them in mounting; and this inference is certain and infallible. Human legs are also contrived for walking and mounting; and this inference, I allow, is not altogether so certain because of the dissimilarity which you remark; but does it, therefore, deserve the name only of presumption or conjecture?

Good God! cried Demea, interrupting him, where are we? Zealous defenders of religion allow that the proofs of a Deity fall short of perfect evidence! And you, Philo, on whose assistance I depended in proving the adorable mysteriousness of the Divine Nature, do you assent to all these extravagant opinions of Cleanthes? For what other name can I give them? or, why spare my censure when such principles are advanced, supported by such an authority, before so young a man as Pamphilus?

You seem not to apprehend, replied Philo, that I argue with Cleanthes in his own way, and, by showing him the dangerous consequences of his tenets, hope at last to reduce him to our opinion. But what sticks most with you, I observe, is the representation which Cleanthes has made of the argument *a posteriori;* and, finding that that argument is likely to escape your hold and vanish into air, you think it so disguised that you can scarcely believe it to be set in its true light. Now, however much I may dissent, in other respects, from the dangerous principle of Cleanthes, I must allow that he has fairly represented that argument, and I shall endeavor so to state the matter to you that you will entertain no further scruples with regard to it.

Were a man to abstract from everything which he knows or has seen, he would be altogether incapable, merely from his own ideas, to determine what kind of scene the universe must be, or to give the preference to one state or situation of things above another. For as nothing which he clearly conceives could be esteemed impossible or implying a contradiction, every chimera of his fancy would be upon an equal footing; nor could he assign just reason why he adheres to one idea or system, and rejects the others which are equally possible.

Again, after he opens his eyes and contemplates the world as it really is, it would be impossible for him at first to assign the cause of any one event, much less the whole of things, or of the universe. He might set his fancy a rambling, and she might bring him in an infinite variety of reports and representations. These would all be possible; but, being all equally possible, he would never of himself give a satisfactory account for his preferring one of them to the rest. Experience alone can point out to him the true cause of any phenomenon.

Now, according to this method of reasoning, Demea, it follows (and is, indeed, tacitly allowed by Cleanthes himself) that order, arrangement, or the adjustment of final causes, is not of itself any proof of design, but only so far as it has been experienced to proceed from that principle. For aught we can know *a priori*, matter may contain the source or spring of order originally within itself, as well as mind does; and there is no more difficulty in conceiving that the several elements, from an internal unknown cause, may fall into the most exquisite arrangement, than to conceive that their ideas, in the great universal mind, from a like internal unknown cause, fall into that arrangement. The equal possibility of both these suppositions is allowed. But, by experience, we find (according to Cleanthes) that there is a difference between them. Throw several pieces of steel together, without shape or form, they will never arrange themselves so as to compose a watch. Stone and mortar and wood, without an architect, never erect a house. But the ideas in a human mind, we see, by an unknown, inexplicable economy, arrange themselves so as to form the plan of a watch or house. Experience, therefore, proves that there is an original principle of order in mind, not in matter. From similar effects we infer similar causes. The adjustment of means to ends is alike in the universe, as in a machine of human contrivance. The causes, therefore, must be resembling.

I was from the beginning scandalized, I must own, with this resemblance which is asserted between the Deity and human creatures, and must conceive it to imply such a degradation of the Supreme Being as no sound theist could endure. With your assistance, therefore, Demea, I shall endeavor to defend what you justly call the adorable mysteriousness of the Divine Nature, and shall refute this reasoning of Cleanthes, provided he allows that I have made a fair representation of it.

When Cleanthes had assented, Philo, after a short pause, proceeded in the following manner.

That all inferences, Cleanthes, concerning fact are founded on experience, and that all experimental reasonings are founded on the supposition that similar causes prove similar effects, and similar effects similar causes, I shall not at present much dispute with you. But observe, I entreat you, with what extreme caution all just reasoners proceed in the transferring of experiments to similar cases. Unless the cases be exactly similar, they repose no perfect confidence in applying their past observation to any particular phenomenon. Every alteration of circumstances occasions a doubt concerning the event; and it requires new experiments to prove certainly that the new circumstances are of no moment or importance. A change in bulk, situation, arrangement, age, disposition of the air, or surrounding bodies—any of these particulars may be attended with the most unexpected consequences. And unless the objects be quite familiar to us, it is the highest temerity to expect with assurance, after any of these changes, an event similar to that which before fell under our observation. The slow and deliberate steps of philosophers here, if anywhere, are distinguished from the precipitate march of the vulgar, who, hurried on by the smallest similitude, are incapable of all discernment or consideration.

But can you think, Cleanthes, that your usual phlegm and philosophy have been preserved in so wide a step as you have taken when you compared to the universe houses, ships, furniture, machines; and, from their similarity in some circumstances, inferred a similarity in their causes? Thought, design, intelligence, such as we discover in men and other animals, is no more than one of the springs and principles of the universe, as well as heat or cold, attraction or repulsion, and a hundred others which fall under daily observation. It is an active cause by which some particular parts of nature, we find, produce alterations on other parts. But can a conclusion, with any propriety, be transferred from parts to the whole? Does not the great disproportion bar all comparison and inference? From observing the growth of a hair, can we learn anything concerning the generation of a man? Would the manner of a leaf's blowing, even though perfectly known, afford us any instruction concerning the vegetation of a tree?

But allowing that we were to take the *operations* of one part of nature upon another for the foundation of our judgment concerning the *origin* of the whole (which never can be admitted), yet why select so minute, so weak, so bounded a principle as the reason and design of animals is found to be upon this planet? What peculiar privilege has this little agitation of the brain which we call *thought,* that we must thus make it the model of the whole universe? Our partiality in our own favor does indeed present it on all occasions, but sound philosophy ought carefully to guard against so natural an illusion.

So far from admitting, continued Philo, that the operations of a part can afford us any just conclusion concerning the origin of the whole, I will not allow any one part to form a rule for another part if the latter be very remote from the former. Is there any reasonable ground to conclude that the inhabitants of other planets possess thought, intelligence, reason, or anything similar to these faculties in men? When nature has so extremely diversified her manner of operation in this small globe, can we imagine that she incessantly copies herself throughout so immense a universe? And if thought, as we may well suppose, be confined merely to this narrow corner and has even there so limited a sphere of action, with what propriety can we assign it for the original cause of all things? The narrow views of a peasant who makes his domestic economy the rule for the government of kingdoms is in comparison a pardonable sophism.

But were we ever so much assured that a thought and reason resembling the human were to be found throughout the whole universe, and were its activity elsewhere vastly greater and more commanding than it appears in this globe; yet I cannot see why the operations of a world constituted, arranged, adjusted, can with any propriety be extended to a world which is in its embryo-state, and is advancing towards that constitution and arrangement. By observation we know somewhat of the economy, action, and nourishment of a finished animal; but we must transfer with great caution that observation to the growth of a foetus in the womb, and still more to the formation of an animalcule in the loins of its male parent. Nature, we find, even from our limited experience, possesses an infinite number of springs and principles which incessantly discover themselves on every change of her position and situation. And what new and unknown principles would actuate her in so new and unknown a situation as that of the formation of a universe, we cannot, without the utmost temerity, pretend to determine.

A very small part of this great system, during a very short time, is very imperfectly discovered to us; and do we thence pronounce decisively concerning the origin of the whole?

Admirable conclusion! Stone, wood, brick, iron, brass, have not, at this time, in this minute globe of earth, an order or arrangement without human art and contrivance; therefore, the universe could not originally attain its order and arrangement without something similar to human art. But is a part of nature a rule for another part very wide of the former? Is it a rule for the whole? Is a very small part a rule for the universe? Is nature in one situation a certain rule for nature in another situation vastly different from the former?

And can you blame me, Cleanthes, if I here imitate the prudent reserve of Simonides,[11] who, according to the noted story, being asked by Hiero,[12] *What God was?* desired a day to think of it, and then two days more; and after that manner continually prolonged the term, without ever bringing in his definition or description? Could you even blame me if I had answered, at first, *that I did not know,* and was sensible that this subject lay vastly beyond the reach of my faculties? You might cry out sceptic and railer, as much as you pleased; but, having found in so many other subjects much more familiar the imperfections and even contradictions of human reason, I never should expect any success from its feeble conjectures in a subject so sublime and so remote from the sphere of our observation. When two *species* of objects have always been observed to be conjoined together, I can *infer,* by custom, the existence of one wherever I *see* the existence of the other; and this I call an argument from experience. But how this argument can have place where the objects, as in the present case, are single, individual, without parallel or specific resemblance, may be difficult to explain. And will any man tell me with a serious countenance that an orderly universe must arise from some thought and art like the human because we have experience of it? To ascertain this reasoning it were requisite that we had experience of the origin of the worlds; and it is not sufficient, surely, that we have seen ships and cities arise from human art and contrivance . . .

Philo was proceeding in this vehement manner, somewhat between jest and earnest, as it appeared to me, when he observed some signs of impatience in Cleanthes, and then immediately stopped short. What I had to suggest, said Cleanthes, is only that you would not abuse terms, or make use of popular expressions to subvert philosophical reasonings. You know that the vulgar often distinguish reason from experience, even where the question relates only to matter of fact and existence, though it is found, where that *reason* is properly analyzed, that it is nothing but a species of experience. To prove by experience the origin of the universe from mind is not more contrary to common speech than to prove the motion of the earth from the same principle. And a caviller might raise all the same objections to the Copernican

11. [Regarding Simonides, see Aristotle's *Ethics,* n. 12.]

12. [The reference is to Hiero I, a fifth-century B.C. ruler of Syracuse noted as a patron of literature.]

system which you have urged against my reasonings. Have you other earths, might he say, which you have seen to move? Have . . .

Yes! cried Philo, interrupting him, we have other earths. Is not the moon another earth, which we see to turn round its center? Is not Venus another earth, where we observe the same phenomenon? Are not the revolutions of the sun also a confirmation, from analogy, of the same theory? All the planets, are they not earths which revolve about the sun? Are not the satellites moons which move round Jupiter and Saturn, and along with these primary planets round the sun? These analogies and resemblances, with others which I have not mentioned, are the sole proofs of the Copernican system; and to you it belongs to consider whether you have any analogies of the same kind to support your theory.

In reality, Cleanthes, continued he, the modern system of astronomy is now so much received by all inquirers, and has become so essential a part even of our earliest education, that we are not commonly very scrupulous in examining the reasons upon which it is founded. It is now become a matter of mere curiosity to study the first writers on that subject who had the full force of prejudice to encounter, and were obliged to turn their arguments on every side in order to render them popular and convincing. But if we peruse Galileo's famous *Dialogues*[13] concerning the system of the world, we shall find that that great genius, one of the sublimest that ever existed, first bent all his endeavors to prove that there was no foundation for the distinction commonly made between elementary and celestial substances. The schools, proceeding from the illusions of sense, had carried this distinction very far; and had established the latter substances to be ingenerable, incorruptible, unalterable, impassible; and had assigned all the opposite qualities to the former. But Galileo, beginning with the moon, proved its similarity in every particular to the earth: its convex figure, its natural darkness when not illuminated, its density, its distinction into solid and liquid, the variations of its phases, the mutual illuminations of the earth and moon, their mutual eclipses, the inequalities of the lunar surface, etc. After many instances of this kind, with regard to all the planets, men plainly saw that these bodies became proper objects of experience, and that the similarity of their nature enabled us to extend the same arguments and phenomena from one to the other.

In this cautious proceeding of the astronomers you may read your own condemnation, Cleanthes; or rather may see that the subject in which you are engaged exceeds all human reason and inquiry. Can you pretend to show any such similarity between the fabric of a house and the generation of a universe? Have you ever seen nature in any such situation as resembles the first arrangement of the elements? Have worlds ever been formed under your eye, and have you had leisure to observe the whole progress of the phenomenon, from the first appearance of order to its final consummation? If you have, then cite your experience and deliver your theory.

Part III

How the most absurd argument, replied Cleanthes, in the hands of a man of ingenuity and invention, may acquire an air of probability! Are you not aware,

---

13. [The reference is to Galileo's *Dialogue Concerning the Two Chief World Systems* (1632).]

Philo, that it became necessary for Copernicus and his first disciples to prove the similarity of the terrestrial and celestial matter because several philosophers, blinded by old systems and supported by some sensible appearances, had denied this similarity; but that it is by no means necessary that theists should prove the similarity of the works of nature to those of art, because this similarity is self-evident and undeniable? The same matter, a like form; what more is requisite to show an analogy between their causes, and to ascertain the origin of all things from a divine purpose and intention? Your objections, I must freely tell you, are no better than the abstruse cavils of those philosophers who denied motion, and ought to be refuted in the same manner—by illustrations, examples, and instances rather than by serious argument and philosophy.

Suppose, therefore, that an articulate voice were heard in the clouds, much louder and more melodious than any which human art could ever reach; suppose that this voice were extended in the same instant over all nations and spoke to each nation in its own language and dialect; suppose that the words delivered not only contain a just sense and meaning, but convey some instruction altogether worthy of a benevolent Being superior to mankind—could you possibly hesitate a moment concerning the cause of this voice, and must you not instantly ascribe it to some design or purpose? Yet I cannot see but all the same objections (if they merit that appellation) which lie against the system of theism may also be produced against this inference.

Might you not say that all conclusions concerning fact were founded on experience; that, when we hear an articulate voice in the dark and thence infer a man, it is only the resemblance of the effects which leads us to conclude that there is a like resemblance in the cause; but that this extraordinary voice, by its loudness, extent, and flexibility to all languages, bears so little analogy to any human voice that we have no reason to suppose any analogy in their causes; and, consequently, that a rational, wise, coherent speech proceeded, you know not whence, from some accidental whistling of the winds, not from any divine reason or intelligence? You see clearly your own objections in these cavils; and I hope too, you see clearly that they cannot possibly have more force in the one case than in the other.

But to bring the case still nearer the present one of the universe, I shall make two suppositions which imply not any absurdity or impossibility. Suppose that there is a natural, universal, invariable language, common to every individual of human race, and that books are natural productions which perpetuate themselves in the same manner with animals and vegetables, by descent and propagation. Several expressions of our passions contain a universal language: All brute animals have a natural speech, which, however limited, is very intelligible to their own species. And as there are infinitely fewer parts and less contrivance in the finest composition of eloquence than in the coarsest organized body, the propagation of an *Iliad* or *Aeneid* is an easier supposition than that of any plant or animal.

Suppose, therefore, that you enter into your library thus peopled by natural volumes containing the most refined reason and most exquisite beauty; could you possibly open one of them and doubt that its original cause bore the strongest analogy to mind and intelligence? When it reasons and discourses; when it expostulates, argues, and enforces its views and topics; when it applies sometimes to the pure intellect, sometimes to the affections; when it collects, disposes, and adorns every consideration suited to the subject; could you persist in asserting that all this, at the bottom, had really no meaning, and that the first formation of this volume in the loins of its original parent proceeded not from thought and design? Your obstinacy, I know, reaches not that degree of firmness; even your sceptical play and wantonness would be abashed at so glaring an absurdity.

But if there be any difference, Philo, between this supposed case and the real one of the universe, it is all to the advantage of the latter. The anatomy of an animal affords many stronger instances of design than the perusal of Livy or Tacitus;[14] and any objection which you start in the former case, by carrying me back to so unusual and extraordinary a scene as the first formation of worlds, the same objection has place on the supposition of our vegetating library. Choose, then, your party, Philo, without ambiguity or evasion; assert either that a rational volume is no proof of a rational cause or admit of a similar cause to all the works of nature.

Let me here observe, too, continued Cleanthes, that this religious argument, instead of being weakened by that scepticism so much affected by you, rather acquires force from it and becomes more firm and undisputed. To exclude all argument or reasoning of every kind is either affectation or madness. The declared profession of every reasonable sceptic is only to reject abstruse, remote, and refined arguments; to adhere to common sense and the plain instincts of nature; and to assent, wherever any reasons strike him with so full a force that he cannot, without the greatest violence, prevent it. Now the arguments for natural religion are plainly of this kind; and nothing but the most perverse, obstinate metaphysics can reject them. Consider, anatomize the eye; survey its structure and contrivance, and tell me, from your own feeling, if the idea of a contriver does not immediately flow in upon you with a force like that of sensation. The most obvious conclusion, surely, is in favor of design; and it requires time, reflection, and study, to summon up those frivolous though abstruse objections which can support infidelity. Who can behold the male and female of each species, the correspondence of their parts and instincts, their passions and whole course of life before and after generation, but must be sensible that the propagation of the species is intended by nature? Millions and millions of such instances present themselves through every part of the universe, and no language can convey a more intelligible, irresistible meaning than the curious adjustment of final causes. To what degree, therefore, of blind dogmatism must one have attained to reject such natural and such convincing arguments?

Some beauties in writing we may meet with which seem contrary to rules, and which gain the affections and animate the imagination in oppostion to all the precepts of criticism and to the authority of the established masters of art. And if the argument for theism be, as you pretend, contradictory to the principles of logic, its universal, its irresistible influence proves clearly that there may be arguments of a like irregular nature. Whatever cavils may be urged, an orderly world, as well as a coherent, articulate speech, will still be received as an incontestable proof of design and intention.

It sometimes happens, I own, that the religious arguments have not their due influence on an ignorant savage and barbarian; not because they are obscure and difficult, but because he never asks himself any question with regard to them. Whence arises the curious structure of an animal? From the copulation of its parents. And these whence? From *their* parents? A few removes set the objects at such a distance that to him they are lost in darkness and confusion; nor is he actuated by any

---

14. [Regarding Livy, see Hume's *Enquiry,* n. 59. Regarding Tacitus, see Hume's *Enquiry,* n. 41.]

curiosity to trace them farther. But this is neither dogmatism nor scepticism, but stupidity: a state of mind very different from your sifting, inquisitive disposition, my ingenious friend. You can trace causes from effects; you can compare the most distant and remote objects; and your greatest errors proceed not from barrenness of thought and invention, but from too luxuriant a fertility which suppresses your natural good sense by a profusion of unnecessary scruples and objections.

Here I could observe, Hermippus, that Philo was a little embarrassed and confounded; but, while he hesitated in delivering an answer, luckily for him, Demea broke in upon the discourse and saved his countenance.

Your instance, Cleanthes, said he, drawn from books and language, being familiar, has, I confess, so much more force on that account; but is there not some danger, too, in this very circumstance, and may it not render us presumptuous, by making us imagine we comprehend the Deity and have some adequate idea of his nature and attributes? When I read a volume, I enter into the mind and intention of the author; I become him, in a manner, for the instant, and have an immediate feeling and conception of those ideas which revolved in his imagination while employed in that composition. But so near an approach we never surely can make to the Deity. His ways are not our ways. His attributes are perfect but incomprehensible. And this volume of nature contains a great and inexplicable riddle, more than any intelligible discourse or reasoning.

The ancient Platonists, you know, were the most religious and devout of all the pagan philosophers; yet many of them, particularly Plotinus,[15] expressly declare that intellect or understanding is not to be ascribed to the Deity, and that our most perfect worship of him consists, not in acts of veneration, reverence, gratitude, or love, but in a certain mysterious self-annihilation or total extinction of all our faculties. These ideas are, perhaps, too far stretched; but still it must be acknowledged that, by representing the Deity as so intelligible and comprehensible, and so similar to a human mind, we are guilty of the grossest and most narrow partiality, and make ourselves the model of the whole universe.

All the *sentiments* of the human mind, gratitude, resentment, love, friendship, approbation, blame, pity, emulation, envy, have a plain reference to the state and situation of man, and are calculated for preserving the existence and promoting the activity of such a being in such circumstances. It seems, therefore, unreasonable to transfer such sentiments to a supreme existence or to suppose him actuated by them; and the phenomena, besides, of the universe will not support us in such a theory. All our *ideas* derived from the senses are confessedly false and illusive, and cannot therefore be supposed to have place in a supreme intelligence. And as the ideas of internal sentiment, added to those of the external senses, compose the whole furniture of human understanding, we may conclude that none of the *materials* of thought are in any respect similar in the human and in the divine intelligence. Now, as to the *manner* of thinking, how can we make any comparison between them or suppose them anywise resembling? Our thought is fluctuating, uncertain, fleeting, successive, and compounded; and were we to remove these circumstances, we absolutely annihilate its essence, and it would in such a case be an abuse of terms to apply to it the name of thought or reason. At least, if it appear more pious and re-

15. [Plotinus (205–270), born in Egypt, developed a complex philosophical system referred to as Neo-Platonism which fused elements of Platonism and mysticism.]

spectful (as it really is) still to retain these terms when we mention the Supreme
Being, we ought to acknowledge that their meaning, in that case, is totally incomprehensible; and that the infirmities of our nature do not permit us to reach any
ideas which in the least correspond to the ineffable sublimity of the Divine attributes.

Part IV

It seem strange to me, said Cleanthes, that you, Demea, who are so sincere in the
cause of religion, should still maintain the mysterious, incomprehensible nature of
the Deity, and should insist so strenuously that he has no manner of likeness or resemblance to human creatures. The Deity, I can readily allow, possesses many
powers and attributes of which we can have no comprehension; but, if our ideas, so
far as they go, be not just and adequate and correspondent to his real nature, I know
not what there is in this subject worth insisting on. Is the name, without any meaning, of such mighty importance? Or how do you *mystics,* who maintain the absolute
incomprehensibility of the Deity, differ from sceptics or atheists, who assert that the
first cause of all is unknown and unintelligible? Their temerity must be very great
if, after rejecting the production by a mind—I mean a mind resembling the human
(for I know of no other)—they pretend to assign, with certainty, any other specific
intelligible cause; and their conscience must be very scrupulous, indeed, if they refuse to call the universal unknown cause a God or Deity, and to bestow on him as
many sublime eulogies and unmeaning epithets as you shall please to require of
them.

   Who could imagine, replied Demea, that Cleanthes, the calm philosophical
Cleanthes, would attempt to refute his antagonists by affixing a nickname to them;
and, like the common bigots and inquisitors of the age, have recourse to invective
and declamation instead of reasoning? Or does he not perceive that these topics are
easily retorted, and that *anthropomorphite* is an appellation as invidious, and implies
as dangerous consequences, as the epithet of *mystic* with which he has honored us?
In reality, Cleanthes, consider what it is you assert when you represent the Deity as
similar to a human mind and understanding. What is the soul of man? A composition of various faculties, passions, sentiments, ideas—united, indeed, into one self or
person, but still distinct from each other. When it reasons, the ideas which are the
parts of its discourse arrange themselves in a certain form or order which is not preserved entire for a moment, but immediately gives place to another arrangement.
New opinions, new passions, new affections, new feelings arise which continually
diversify the mental scene and produce in it the greatest variety and most rapid succession imaginable. How is this compatible with that perfect immutability and
simplicity which all true theists ascribe to the Deity? By the same act, say they, he
sees past, present, and future; his love and hatred, his mercy and justice, are one individual operation; he is entire in every point of space, and complete in every instant of duration. No succession, no change, no acquisition, no diminution. What he
is implies not in it any shadow of distinction or diversity. And what he is this
moment he ever has been and ever will be, without any new judgment, sentiment, or
operation. He stands fixed in one simple, perfect state; nor can you ever say, with
any propriety, that this act of his is different from that other, or that this judgment

or idea has been lately formed and will give place, by succession, to any different judgment or idea.

I can readily allow, said Cleanthes, that those who maintain the perfect simplicity of the Supreme Being, to the extent in which you have explained it, are complete *mystics,* and chargeable with all the consequences which I have drawn from their opinion. They are, in a word, *atheists,* without knowing it. For though it be allowed that the Deity possesses attributes of which we have no comprehension, yet ought we never to ascribe to him any attributes which are absolutely incompatible with that intelligent nature essential to him. A mind whose acts and sentiments and ideas are not distinct and successive, one that is wholly simple and totally immutable, is a mind which has no thought, no reason, no will, no sentiment, no love, no hatred; or, in a word, is no mind at all. It is an abuse of terms to give it that appellation, and we may as well speak of limited extension without figure, or of number without composition.

Pray consider, said Philo, whom you are at present inveighing against. You are honoring with the appellation of *atheist* all the sound, orthodox divines, almost, who have treated of this subject; and you will at last be, yourself, found, according to your reckoning, the only sound theist in the world. But if idolaters be atheists, as, I think, may justly be asserted, and Christian theologians the same, what becomes of the argument, so much celebrated, derived from the universal consent of mankind?

But, because I know you are not much swayed by names and authorities, I shall endeavor to show you, a little more distinctly, the inconveniences of that anthropomorphism which you have embraced, and shall prove that there is no ground to suppose a plan of the world to be formed in the Divine mind, consisting of distinct ideas, differently arranged, in the same manner as an architect forms in his head the plan of a house which he intends to execute.

It is not easy, I own, to see what is gained by this supposition, whether we judge of the matter by *reason* or by *experience.* We are still obliged to mount higher in order to find the cause of this cause which you had assigned as satisfactory and conclusive.

If *reason* (I mean abstract reason derived from inquiries *a priori*) be not alike mute with regard to all questions concerning cause and effect, this sentence at least it will venture to pronounce: that a mental world or universe of ideas requires a cause as much as does a material world or universe of objects; and, if similar in its arrangement, must require a similar cause. For what is there in this subject which should occasion a different conclusion or inference? In an abstract view, they are entirely alike; and no difficulty attends the one supposition which is not common to both of them.

Again, when we will needs force *experience* to pronounce some sentence, even on these subjects which lie beyond her sphere, neither can she perceive any material difference in this particular between these two kinds of worlds, but finds them to be governed by similar principles, and to depend upon an equal variety of causes in their operations. We have specimens in miniature of both of them. Our own mind resembles the one; a vegetable or animal body the other. Let experience, therefore, judge from these samples. Nothing seems more delicate, with regard to its causes, than thought; and as these causes never operate in two persons after the same manner, so we never find two persons who think exactly alike. Nor indeed does the same person think exactly alike at any two different periods of time. A difference of age, of the disposition of his body, of weather, of food, of company, of books, of passions—any of these particulars, or others more minute, are sufficient to alter the curious machinery of thought and communicate to it very different movements and operations. As far as we can judge, vegetables and animal bodies are not more delicate in their motions, nor depend upon a greater variety or more curious adjustment of springs and principles.

How, therefore, shall we satisfy ourselves concerning the cause of that Being whom you suppose the Author of Nature, or, according to your system of anthropomorphism, the ideal world into which you trace the material? Have we not the same reason to trace that ideal world into another ideal world or new intelligent principle? But if we stop and go no farther, why go so far—why not stop at the material world? How can we satisfy ourselves without going on *in infinitum?* And, after all, what satisfaction is there in that infinite progression? Let us remember the story of the Indian philosopher and his elephant. It was never more applicable than to the present subject. If the material world rests upon a similar ideal world, this ideal world must rest upon some other, and so on without end. It were better, therefore, never to look beyond the present material world. By supposing it to contain the principle of its order within itself, we really assert it to be God; and the sooner we arrive at that Divine Being, so much the better. When you go one step beyond the mundane system, you only excite an inquisitive humor which it is impossible ever to satisfy.

To say that the different ideas which compose the reason of the Supreme Being fall into order of themselves and by their own nature is really to talk without any precise meaning. If it has a meaning, I would fain know why it is not as good sense to say that the parts of the material world fall into order of themselves and by their own nature. Can the one opinion be intelligible, while the other is not so?

We have, indeed, experience of ideas which fall into order of themselves and without any *known* cause. But, I am sure, we have a much larger experience of matter which does the same, as in all instances of generation and vegetation where the accurate analysis of the cause exceeds all human comprehension. We have also experience of particular systems of thought and of matter which have no order; of the first in madness, of the second in corruption. Why, then, should we think that order is more essential to one than the other? And if it requires a cause in both, what do we gain by your system, in tracing the universe of objects into a similar universe of ideas? The first step which we make leads us on forever. It were, therefore, wise in us to limit all our inquiries to the present world, without looking farther. No satisfaction can ever be attained by these speculations which so far exceed the narrow bounds of human understanding.

It was usual with the Peripatetics, you know, Cleanthes, when the cause of any phenomenon was demanded, to have recourse to their *faculties* or *occult qualities,* and to say, for instance, that bread nourished by its nutritive faculty, and senna purged by its purgative. But it has been discovered that this subterfuge was nothing but the disguise of ignorance, and that these philosophers, though less ingenuous, really said the same thing with the sceptics or the vulgar who fairly confessed that they knew not the cause of these phenomena. In like manner, when it is asked, what cause produces order in the ideas of the Supreme Being, can any other reason be assigned by you, anthropomorphites, than that it is a *rational* faculty, and that such is the nature of the Deity? But why a similar answer will not be equally satisfactory in accounting for the order of the world, without having recourse to any such intelligent creator as you insist on, may be difficult to determine. It is only to say that *such* is the nature of material objects, and that they are all originally possessed of a *faculty* of order and proportion. These are only more learned and elaborate ways of confessing our ignorance; nor has the one hypothesis any real advantage above the other, except in its greater conformity to vulgar prejudices.

You have displayed this argument with great emphasis, replied Cleanthes: You seem not sensible how easy it is to answer it. Even in common life, if I assign a cause for any event, is it any objection, Philo, that I cannot assign the cause of that cause, and answer every new question which may incessantly be started? And what philosophers could possibly submit to so rigid a rule? —philosophers who confess ultimate causes to be totally unknown, and are sensible that the most refined principles into which they trace the phenomena are still to them as inexplicable as these phenomena themselves are to the vulgar. The order and arrangement of nature, the curious adjustment of final causes, the plain use and intention of every part and organ—all of these bespeak in the clearest language an intelligent cause or author. The heavens and the earth join in the same testimony: The whole chorus of nature raises one hymn to the praises of its Creator. You alone, or almost alone, disturb this general harmony. You start abstruse doubts, cavils, and objections; you ask me what is the cause of this cause? I know not; I care not; that concerns not me. I have found a Deity; and here I stop my inquiry. Let those go farther who are wiser or more enterprising.

I pretend to be neither, replied Philo; and for that very reason I should never, perhaps, have attempted to go so far, especially when I am sensible that I must at least be contented to sit down with the same answer which, without further trouble, might have satisfied me from the beginning. If I am still to remain in utter ignorance of causes and can absolutely give an explication of nothing, I shall never esteem it any advantage to shove off for a moment a difficulty which you acknowledge must immediately, in its full force, recur upon me. Naturalists, indeed, very justly explain particular effects by more general causes, though these general causes themselves should remain in the end totally inexplicable; but they never surely thought it satisfactory to explain a particular effect by a particular cause which was no more to be accounted for than the effect itself. An ideal system, arranged of itself, without a precedent design, is not a whit more explicable than a material one which attains its order in a like manner; nor is there any more difficulty in the latter supposition than in the former.

Part V

But to show you still more inconveniences, continued Philo, in your anthropomorphism, please to take a new survey of your principles. *Like effects prove like causes.* This is the experimental argument; and this, you say too, is the sole theological argument. Now it is certain that the liker the effects are which are seen and the liker the causes which are inferred, the stronger is the argument. Every departure on either side diminishes the probability and renders the experiment less conclusive. You cannot doubt of the principle; neither ought you to reject its consequences.

All the new discoveries in astronomy which prove the immense grandeur and magnificence of the works of nature are so many additional arguments for a Deity, according to the true system of theism; but, according to your hypothesis of experi-

mental theism, they become so many objections, by removing the effect still farther
from all resemblance to the effects of human art and contrivance. For if Lucretius,[16]
even following the old system of the world could exclaim:

> Quis regere immensi summam, quis habere profundi
> Indu manu validas potis est moderanter habenas?
> Quis pariter coelos omnes convertere? et omnes
> Ignibus aetheriis terras suffire feraces?
> Omnibus inque locis esse omni tempore praesto?[17]

If Tully[18] esteemed this reasoning so natural as to put it into the mouth of his
Epicurean:

> Quibus enim oculis animi intueri potuit vester Plato fabricam illam tanti
> operis, qua construi a Deo atque aedificari mundum facit? quae molitio? quae
> ferramenta? qui vectes? quae machinae? qui ministri tanti muneris fuerunt?
> quemadmodum autem obedire et parere voluntati architecti aer, ignis, aqua,
> terra potuerunt?[19]

If this argument, I say, had any force in former ages, how much greater must it have
at present when the bounds of nature are so infinitely enlarged and such a magnificent scene is opened to us? It is still more unreasonable to form our idea of so
unlimited a cause from our experience of the narrow productions of human design
and invention.

The discoveries by microscopes, as they open a new universe in miniature, are
still objections, according to you; arguments, according to me. The further we push
our researches of this kind, we are still led to infer the universal cause of all to be
vastly different from mankind, or from any object of human experience and observation.

And what say you to the discoveries in anatomy, chemistry, botany? . . .
These surely are no objections, replied Cleanthes; they only discover new instances
of art and contrivance. It is still the image of mind reflected on us from innumerable
objects. Add a mind *like the human*, said Philo. I know of no other, replied
Cleanthes. And the liker, the better, insisted Philo. To be sure, said Cleanthes.

---

16. [Lucretius (c.99 B.C.–c.55 B.C.), a Roman poet and philosopher who espoused the Epicurean view
that the universe is composed of everlasting atoms that move in a void, the whole exhibiting beauty and
majesty but without purpose or divine providence.]

17. Lib. xi. 1094. [The quotation is from *On the Nature of the Universe.* "Who is able to rule the whole of
the immeasurable; who is able, with control, to hold in hand the strong reins of the boundless? Who
equally is able to turn all the heavens? And who is able to warm all fertile grounds with ethereal fire?
Who is able to be present in all places at every time?" (The translation is by William E. Mann.)]

18. [Regarding Tully (Cicero), see Hobbes's *Leviathan*, n. 11.]

19. *De Nat. Deor.*, lib. i. [The quotations is from *On the Nature of the Gods.* "For with which of the soul's
eyes has your [master] Plato been able to contemplate that fabrication of such great labor, by which he
establishes that the universe is furnished and even constructed by God? What preparation [was in-
volved]? What tools? What levers? What machines? What agents were there for such a great enterprise?
Moreover, how were air, fire, water, and earth able to obey and to come forth at the will of the
architect?" (The translation is by William E. Mann, whose amplifications are in brackets.)]

Now, Cleanthes, said Philo, with an air of alacrity and triumph, mark the consequences. *First,* by this method of reasoning you renounce all claim to infinity in any of the attributes of the Deity. For, as the cause ought only to be proportioned to the effect, and the effect, so far as it falls under our cognizance, is not infinite, what pretensions have we, upon your suppositions, to ascribe that attribute to the divine Being? You will still insist that, by removing him so much from all similarity to human creatures, we give in to the most arbitrary hypothesis, and at the same time weaken all proofs of his existence.

Secondly, you have no reason, on your theory, for ascribing perfection to the Deity, even in his finite capacity; or for supposing him free from every error, mistake, or incoherence, in his undertakings. There are many inexplicable difficulties in the works of nature which, if we allow a perfect author to be proved *a priori,* are easily solved, and become only seeming difficulties from the narrow capacity of man, who cannot trace infinite relations. But according to your method of reasoning, these difficulties become all real; and, perhaps, will be insisted on as new instances of likeness to human art and contrivance. At least, you must acknowledge that it is impossible for us to tell, from our limited views, whether this system contains any great faults or deserves any considerable praise if compared to other possible and even real systems. Could a peasant, if the *Aeneid* were read to him, pronounce that poem to be absolutely faultless, or even assign to it its proper rank among the productions of human wit, he who had never seen any other production?

But were this world ever so perfect a production, it must still remain uncertain whether all the excellences of the work can justly be ascribed to the workman. If we survey a ship, what an exalted idea must we form of the ingenuity of the carpenter who framed so complicated, useful, and beautiful a machine? And what surprise must we feel when we find him a stupid mechanic who imitated others, and copied an art which, through a long succession of ages, after multiplied trials, mistakes, corrections, deliberations, and controversies, had been gradually improving? Many worlds might have been botched and bungled, throughout an eternity, ere this system was struck out; much labor lost; many fruitless trials made; and a slow but continued improvement carried on during infinite ages in the art of world-making. In such subjects, who can determine where the truth, nay, who can conjecture where the probability lies, amidst a great number of hypotheses which may be proposed, and a still greater which may be imagined?

And what shadow of an argument, continued Philo, can you produce from your hypothesis to prove the unity of the Deity? A great number of men join in building a house or ship, in rearing a city, in framing a commonwealth; why may not several deities combine in contriving and framing a world? This is only so much greater similarity to human affairs. By sharing the work among several, we may so much further limit the attributes of each, and get rid of that extensive power and knowledge which must be supposed in one deity, and which, according to you, can only serve to weaken the proof of his existence. And if such foolish, such vicious creatures as man can yet often unite in framing and executing one plan, how much more those deities or demons, whom we may suppose several degrees more perfect?

To multiply causes without necessity is indeed contrary to true philosophy, but this principle applies not to the present case. Were one deity antecedently proved by your theory who were possessed of every attribute requisite to the production of the universe, it would be needless, I own (though not absurd), to suppose any other deity existent. But while it is still a question whether all these attributes are united in one subject or dispersed among several independent beings; by what phenomena in nature can we pretend to decide the controversy? Where we see a body raised in a scale, we are sure that there is in the opposite scale, however concealed from sight, some counterpoising weight equal to it; but it is still allowed to doubt whether that weight be an aggregate of several distinct bodies or one uniform united mass. And if the weight requisite very much exceeds anything which we have ever seen conjoined in any single body, the former supposition becomes still more probable and natural. An intelligent being of such vast power and capacity as is necessary to produce the universe—or, to speak in the language of ancient philosophy, so prodigious an animal—exceeds all analogy and even comprehension.

But further, Cleanthes, men are mortal, and renew their species by generation; and this is common to all living creatures. The two great sexes of male and female, says Milton, animate the world. Why must this circumstance, so universal, so essential, be excluded from those numerous and limited deities? Behold, then, the theogeny of ancient times brought back upon us.

And why not become a perfect anthropomorphite? Why not assert the deity or deities to be corporeal, and to have eyes, a nose, mouth, ears, etc? Epicurus maintained that no man had ever seen reason but in a human figure; therefore, the gods must have a human figure. And this argument, which is deservedly so much ridiculed by Cicero, becomes, according to you, solid and philosophical.

In a word, Cleanthes, a man who follows your hypothesis is able, perhaps, to assert or conjecture that the universe sometime arose from something like design; but beyond that position he cannot ascertain one single circumstance, and is left afterwards to fix every point of his theology by the utmost license of fancy and hypothesis. This world, for aught he knows, is very faulty and imperfect, compared to a superior standard; and was only the first rude essay of some infant deity who afterwards abandoned it, ashamed of his lame performance; it is the work only of some dependent, inferior deity, and is the object of derision to his superiors; it is the production of old age and dotage in some superannuated deity; and ever since his death has run on at adventures, from the first impulse and active force which it received from him. You justly give signs of horror, Demea, at these strange suppositions; but these, and a thousand more of the same kind, are Cleanthes' suppositions, not mine. From the moment the attributes of the Deity are supposed finite, all these have place. And I cannot, for my part, think that so wild and unsettled a system of theology is, in any respect, preferable to none at all.

These suppositions I absolutely disown, cried Cleanthes; they strike me, however, with no horror, especially when proposed in that rambling way in which they drop from you. On the contrary, they give me pleasure when I see that, by the utmost indulgence of your imagination, you never get rid of the hypothesis of design in the universe, but are obliged at every turn to have recourse to it. To this concession I adhere steadily; and this I regard as a sufficient foundation for religion.

Part VI

It must be a slight fabric, indeed, said Demea, which can be erected on so tottering a foundation. While we are uncertain whether there is one deity or many, whether the deity or deities, to whom we owe our existence, be perfect or imperfect, subordinate or supreme, dead or alive, what trust or confidence can we repose in them? What devotion or worship address to them? What veneration or obedience pay them? To all the purposes of life the theory of religion becomes altogether useless; and even with regard to speculative consequences its uncertainty, according to you, must render it totally precarious and unsatisfactory.

To render it still more unsatisfactory, said Philo, there occurs to me another hypothesis which must acquire an air of probability from the method of reasoning so much insisted on by Cleanthes. That like effects arise from like causes — this principle he supposes the foundation of all religion. But there is another principle of the same kind, no less certain and derived from the same source of experience, that, where several known circumstances are observed to be similar, the unknown will also be found similar. Thus, if we see the limbs of a human body, we conclude that it is also attended with a human head, though hid from us. Thus, if we see, through a chink in a wall, a small part of the sun, we conclude that were the wall removed we should see the whole body. In short, this method of reasoning is so obvious and familiar that no scruple can ever be made with regard to its solidity.

Now, if we survey the universe, so far as it falls under our knowledge, it bears a great resemblance to an animal or organized body, and seems actuated with a like principle of life and motion. A continual circulation of matter in it produces no disorder; a continual waste in every part is incessantly repaired; the closest sympathy is perceived throughout the entire system; and each part or member, in performing its proper offices, operates both to its own preservation and to that of the whole. The world, therefore, I infer, is an animal; and the Deity is the *soul* of the world, actuating it, and actuated by it.

You have too much learning, Cleanthes, to be at all surprised at this opinion which, you know, was maintained by almost all the theists of antiquity, and chiefly prevails in their discourses and reasonings. For though sometimes the ancient philosophers reason from final causes, as if they thought the world the workmanship of God, yet it appears rather their favorite notion to consider it as his body whose organization renders it subservient to him. And it must be confessed that, as the universe resembles more a human body than it does the works of human art and contrivance, if our limited analogy could ever, with any propriety, be extended to the whole of nature, the inference seems juster in favor of the ancient than the modern theory.

There are many other advantages, too, in the former theory which recommended it to the ancient theologians. Nothing more repugnant to all their notions — because nothing more repugnant to common experience — than mind without body; a mere spiritual substance which fell not under their senses nor comprehension, and of which they had not observed one single instance throughout all nature. Mind and body they knew because they felt both; an order, arrangement, organization, or internal machinery, in both they likewise knew, after the same manner; and it could not but seem reasonable to transfer this experience to the universe, and to suppose the divine mind and body to be also coeval and to have, both of them, order and arrangement naturally inherent in them and inseparable from them.

Here, therefore, is a new species of *anthropomorphism*, Cleanthes, on which you may deliberate; and a theory which seems not liable to any considerable difficulties. You are too much superior, surely, to *systematical prejudices* to find any more difficulty in supposing an animal body to be, originally, of itself or from unknown causes, possessed of order and organization, than in supposing a similar order to belong to mind. But the *vulgar prejudice* that body and mind ought always to accompany each other ought not, one should think, to be entirely neglected; since it is founded on *vulgar experience,* the only guide which you profess to follow in all these theological inquiries. And if you assert that our limited experience is an unequal standard by which to judge of the unlimited extent of nature, you entirely abandon your own hypothesis, and must thenceforward adopt our mysticism, as you call it, and admit of the absolute incomprehensibility of the Divine Nature.

This theory, I own, replied Cleanthes, has never before occurred to me, though a pretty natural one; and I cannot readily, upon so short an examination and reflection, deliver any opinion with regard to it. You are very scrupulous, indeed, said Philo; were I to examine any system of yours, I should not have acted with half that caution and reserve, in starting objections and difficulties to it. However, if anything occur to you, you will oblige us by proposing it.

Why then, replied Cleanthes, it seems to me that, though the world does, in many circumstances, resemble an animal body, yet is the analogy also defective in many circumstances the most material: no organs of sense, no seat of thought or reason; no one precise origin of motion and action. In short, it seems to bear a stronger resemblance to a vegetable than to an animal, and your inference would be so far inconclusive in favor of the soul of the world.

But, in the next place, your theory seems to imply the eternity of the world; and that is a principle which, I think, can be refuted by the strongest reasons and probabilities. I shall suggest an argument to this purpose which, I believe, has not been insisted on by any writer. Those who reason from the late origin of arts and sciences, though their inference wants not force, may perhaps be refuted by considerations derived from the nature of human society, which is in continual revolution between ignorance and knowledge, liberty and slavery, riches and poverty; so that it is impossible for us, from our limited experience, to foretell with assurance what events may or may not be expected. Ancient learning and history seem to have been in great danger of entirely perishing after the inundation of the barbarous nations; and had these convulsions continued a little longer, or been a little more violent, we should not probably have now known what passed in the world a few centuries before us. Nay, were it not for the superstition of the popes, who preserved a little jargon of Latin in order to support the appearance of an ancient and universal church, that tongue must have been utterly lost; in which case the Western world, being totally barbarous, would not have been in a fit disposition for receiving the Greek language and learning, which was conveyed to them after the sacking of Constantinople. When learning and books had been extinguished, even the mechanical arts would have fallen considerably to decay; and it is easily imagined that fable or tradition might ascribe to them a much later origin than the true one. This vulgar argument, therefore, against the eternity of the world seems a little precarious.

But here appears to be the foundation of a better argument. Lucullus was the first that brought cherry-trees from Asia to Europe; though that tree thrives so well in many European climates that it grows in the woods without any culture. Is it possible that, throughout a whole eternity, no European had ever passed into Asia and thought of transplanting so delicious a fruit into his own country? Or if the tree was once transplanted and propagated, how could it ever afterwards perish? Empires may rise and fall; liberty and slavery succeed alternately; ignorance and knowledge give place to each other; but the cherry-tree will still remain in the woods of Greece, Spain, and Italy, and will never be affected by the revolutions of human society.

It is not two thousand years since vines were transplanted into France, though there is no climate in the world more favorable to them. It is not three centuries since horses, cows, sheep, swine, dogs, corn, were known in America. Is it possible that during the revolutions of a whole eternity there never arose a Columbus who might open the communication between Europe and that continent? We may as well imagine that all men would wear stockings for ten thousand years, and never have the sense to think of garters to tie them. All these seem convincing proofs of the youth or rather infancy of the world, as being founded on the operation of principles more constant and steady than those by which human society is governed and directed. Nothing less than a total convulsion of the elements will ever destroy all the European animals and vegetables which are now to be found in the Western world.

And what argument have you against such convulsions? replied Philo. Strong and almost incontestable proofs may be traced over the whole earth that every part of this globe has continued for many ages entirely covered with water. And though order were supposed inseparable from matter, and inherent in it; yet may matter be susceptible of many and great revolutions, through the endless periods of eternal duration. The incessant changes to which every part of it is subject seem to intimate some such general transformations; though, at the same time, it is observable that all the changes and corruptions of which we have ever had experience are but passages from one state of order to another; nor can matter ever rest in total deformity and confusion. What we see in the parts, we may infer in the whole; at least, that is the method of reasoning on which you rest your whole theory. And were I obliged to defend any particular system of this nature, which I never willingly should do, I esteem none more plausible than that which ascribes an eternal, inherent principle of order to the world, though attended with great and continual revolutions and alterations. This at once solves all difficulties; and if the solution, by being so general, is not entirely complete and satisfactory, it is at least a theory that we must sooner or later have recourse to, whatever system we embrace. How could things have been as they are, were there not an original inherent principle of order somewhere, in thought or in matter? And it is very indifferent to which of these we give the preference. Chance has no place, on any hypothesis, sceptical or religious. Everything is surely governed by steady, inviolable laws. And were the inmost essence of things laid open to us, we should then discover a scene of which, at present, we can have no idea. Instead of admiring the order of natural beings, we should clearly see that it was absolutely impossible for them, in the smallest article, ever to admit of any other disposition.

Were anyone inclined to revive the ancient pagan theology which maintained, as we learn from Hesiod,[20] that this globe was governed by 30,000 deities, who arose from the unknown powers of nature, you would naturally object, Cleanthes, that nothing is gained by this hypothesis; and that it is as easy to suppose all men and animals, beings more numerous but less perfect, to have sprung immediately from a

20. [Regarding Hesiod, see Aristotle's *Ethics*, n. 3.]

like origin. Push the same inference a step further, and you will find a numerous society of deities as explicable as one universal deity who possesses within himself the
powers and perfections of the whole society. All these systems, then, of scepticism,
polytheism, and theism, you must allow, on your principles, to be on a like footing,
and that no one of them has any advantage over the others. You may thence learn
the fallacy of your principles.

Part VII

But here, continued Philo, in examining the ancient system of the soul of the world
there strikes me, all of a sudden, a new idea which, if just, must go near to subvert
all your reasoning, and destroy even your first inferences on which you repose such
confidence. If the universe bears a greater likeness to animal bodies and to vegetables than to the works of human art, it is more probable that its cause resembles the
cause of the former than that of the latter, and its origin ought rather to be
abscribed to generation or vegetation than to reason or design. Your conclusion,
even according to your own principles, is therefore lame and defective.

Pray open up this argument a little further, said Demea, for I do not rightly apprehend it in that concise manner in which you have expressed it.

Our friend Cleanthes, replied Philo, as you have heard, asserts that since no question of fact can be proved otherwise than by experience, the existence of a Deity
admits not of proof from any other medium. The world, says he, resembles the
works of human contrivance; therefore its cause must also resemble that of the
other. Here we may remark that the operation of one very small part of nature, to
wit, man, upon another very small part, to wit, that inanimate matter lying within
his reach, is the rule by which Cleanthes judges of the origin of the whole; and he
measures objects, so widely disproportioned, by the same individual standard. But
to waive all objections drawn from this topic, I affirm that there are other parts of
the universe (besides the machines of human invention) which bear still a greater
resemblance to the fabric of the world, and which, therefore, afford a better conjecture concerning the universal origin of this system. These parts are animals and
vegetables. The world plainly resembles more an animal or a vegetable than it does
a watch or a knitting-loom. Its cause, therefore, it is more probable, resembles the
cause of the former. The cause of the former is generation or vegetation. The cause,
therefore, of the world we may infer to be something similar or analogous to generation or vegetation.

But how is it conceivable, said Demea, that the world can arise from anything
similar to vegetation or generation?

Very easily, replied Philo. In like manner as a tree sheds its seed into the neigh-
boring fields and produces other trees; so the great vegetable, the world, or this
planetary system, produces within itself certain seeds which, being scattered into
the surrounding chaos, vegetate into new worlds. A comet, for instance, is the seed
of a world; and after it has been fully ripened, by passing from sun to sun, and star
to star, it is at last tossed into the unformed elements which everywhere surround
this universe, and immediately sprouts up into a new system.

Or if, for the sake of variety (for I see no other advantage) we should suppose this world to be an animal; a comet is the egg of this animal; and in like manner as an ostrich lays its egg in the sand, which, without any further care, hatches the egg and produces a new animal, so . . . I understand you, says Demea: But what wild, arbitrary suppositions are these? What *data* have you for such extraordinary conclusions? And is the slight, imaginary resemblance of the world to a vegetable or an animal sufficient to establish the same inference with regard to both? Objects which are in general so widely different; ought they to be a standard for each other?

Right, cries Philo: This is the topic on which I have all along insisted. I have still asserted that we have no *data* to establish any system of cosmogony. Our experience, so imperfect in itself and so limited both in extent and duration, can afford us no probable conjecture concerning the whole of things. But if we must needs fix on some hypothesis, by what rule, pray, ought we to determine our choice? Is there any other rule than the great similarity of the objects compared? And does not a plant or an animal, which springs from vegetation or generation, bear a stronger resemblance to the world than does any artificial machine, which arises from reason and design?

But what is this vegetation and generation of which you talk? said Demea. Can you explain their operations, and anatomize that fine internal structure on which they depend?

As much, at least, replied Philo, as Cleanthes can explain the operations of reason, or anatomize that internal structure on which *it* depends. But without any such elaborate disquisitions, when I see an animal, I infer that it sprang from generation; and that with as great certainty as you conclude a house to have been reared by design. These words *generation, reason* mark only certain powers and energies in nature whose effects are known, but whose essence is incomprehensible; and one of these principles, more than the other, has no privilege for being made a standard to the whole of nature.

In reality, Demea, it may reasonably be expected that the larger the views are which we take of things, the better will they conduct us in our conclusions concerning such extraordinary and such magnificent subjects. In this little corner of the world alone, there are four principles, *reason, instinct, generation, vegetation,* which are similar to each other, and are the causes of similar effects. What a number of other principles may we naturally suppose in the immense extent and variety of the universe could we travel from planet to planet, and from system to system, in order to examine each part of this mighty fabric? Any one of these four principles above mentioned (and a hundred others which lie open to our conjecture) may afford us a theory by which to judge of the origin of the world; and it is a palpable and egregious partiality to confine our view entirely to that principle by which our own minds operate. Were this principle more intelligible on that account, such a partiality might be somewhat excusable; but reason, in its internal fabric and structure, is really as little known to us as instinct or vegetation; and, perhaps, even that vague, undeterminate word *nature* to which the vulgar refer everything is not at the bottom more inexplicable. The effects of these principles are all known to us from experience; but the principles themselves and their manner of operation are totally unknown; nor is it less intelligible or less conformable to experience to say that the world arose by vegetation, from a seed shed by another world, than to say that it arose from a divine reason or contrivance, according to the sense in which Cleanthes understands it.

But methinks, said Demea, if the world had a vegetative quality and could sow the seeds of new worlds into the infinite chaos, this power would be still an additional argument for design in its author. For whence could arise so wonderful a faculty but from design? Or how can order spring from anything which perceives not that order which it bestows?

You need only look around you, replied Philo, to satisfy yourself with regard to this question. A tree bestows order and organization on that tree which springs from it, without knowing the order; an animal in the same manner on its offspring; a bird on its nest; and instances of this kind are even more frequent in the world than those of order which arise from reason and contrivance. To say that all this order in animals and vegetables proceeds ultimately from design is begging the question; nor can that great point be ascertained otherwise than by proving, *a priori*, both that order is, from its nature, inseparably attached to thought, and that it can never of itself or from original unknown principles belong to matter.

But further, Demea, this objection which you urge can never be made use of by Cleanthes, without renouncing a defence which he has already made against one of my objections. When I inquired concerning the cause of that supreme reason and intelligence into which he resolves everything, he told me that the impossibility of satisfying such inquiries could never be admitted as an objection in any species of philosophy. *We must stop somewhere,* says he; *nor is it ever within the reach of human capacity to explain ultimate causes or show the last connections of any objects. It is sufficient if any steps, so far as we go, are supported by experience and observation.* Now, that vegetation and generation, as well as reason, are experienced to be principles of order in nature is undeniable. If I rest my system of cosmogony on the former, preferably to the latter, it is at my choice. The matter seems entirely arbitrary. And when Cleanthes asks me what is the cause of my great vegetative or generative faculty, I am equally entitled to ask him the cause of his great reasoning principle. These questions we have agreed to forbear on both sides; and it is chiefly his interest on the present occasion to stick to this agreement. Judging by our limited and imperfect experience, generation has some privileges above reason; for we see every day the latter arise from the former, never the former from the latter.

Compare, I beseech you, the consequences on both sides. The world, say I, resembles an animal; therefore it is an animal, therefore it arose from generation. The steps, I confess, are wide; yet there is some small appearance of analogy in each step. The world, says Cleanthes, resembles a machine; therefore it is a machine, therefore it arose from design. The steps are here equally wide, and the analogy less striking. And if he pretends to carry on *my* hypothesis a step further, and to infer design or reason from the great principle of generation on which I insist, I may, with better authority, use the same freedom to push further *his* hypothesis, and infer a divine generation or theogony from his principle of reason. I have at least some faint shadow of experience, which is the utmost that can ever be attained in the present subject. Reason, in innumerable instances, is observed to arise from the principle of generation, and never to arise from any other principle.

Hesiod and all the ancient mythologists were so struck with this analogy that they universally explained the origin of nature from an animal birth, and copulation. Plato, too, so far as he is intelligible, seems to have adopted some such notion in his *Timaeus*.

The Brahmins[21] assert that the world arose from an infinite spider, who spun this whole complicated mass from his bowels, and annihilates afterwards the whole or any part of it, by absorbing it again and resolving it into his own essence. Here is a species of cosmogony which appears to us ridiculous because a spider is a little contemptible animal whose operations we are never likely to take for a model of the whole universe. But still here is a new species of analogy, even in our globe. And were there a planet wholly inhabited by spiders (which is very possible), this inference would there appear as natural and irrefragable as that which in our planet ascribes the origin of all things to design and intelligence, as explained by Cleanthes. Why an orderly system may not be spun from the belly as well as from the brain, it will be difficult for him to give a satisfactory reason.

I must confess, Philo, replied Cleanthes, that, of all men living, the task which you have undertaken, of raising doubts and objections, suits you best and seems, in a manner, natural and unavoidable to you. So great is your fertility of invention that I am not ashamed to acknowledge myself unable, on a sudden, to solve regularly such out-of-the-way difficulties as you incessantly start upon me; though I clearly see, in general, their fallacy and error. And I question not, but you are yourself, at present, in the same case, and have not the solution so ready as the objection; while you must be sensible that common sense and reason are entirely against you, and that such whimsies as you have delivered may puzzle but never can convince us.

Part VIII

What you ascribe to the fertility of my invention, replied Philo, is entirely owing to the nature of the subject. In subjects adapted to the narrow compass of human reason there is commonly but one determination which carries probability or conviction with it; and to a man of sound judgment all other suppositions but that one appear entirely absurd and chimerical. But in such questions as the present, a hundred contradictory views may preserve a kind of imperfect analogy, and invention has here full scope to exert itself. Without any great effort of thought, I believe that I could, in an instant, propose other systems of cosmogony which would have some faint appearance of truth; though it is a thousand, a million to one if either yours or any one of mine be the true system.

For instance, what if I should revive the old Epicurean hypothesis? This is commonly, and I believe justly, esteemed the most absurd system that has yet been proposed; yet I know not whether, with a few alterations, it might not be brought to bear a faint appearance of probability. Instead of supposing matter infinite, as Epicurus did, let us suppose it finite. A finite number of particles is only susceptible of finite transpositions, and it must happen, in an eternal duration, that every possible order or position must be tried an infinite number of times. This world, therefore, with all its events, even the most minute, has before been produced and destroyed, and will again be produced and destroyed, without any bounds and limitations. No one who has a conception of the powers of infinite, in comparison of finite, will ever scruple this determination.

21. [Brahmins are members of the highest Hindu caste.]

But this supposes, said Demea, that matter can acquire motion without any voluntary agent or first mover.

And where is the difficulty, replied Philo, of that supposition? Every event, before experience, is equally difficult and incomprehensible; and every event, after experience, is equally easy and intelligible. Motion, in many instances, from gravity, from elasticity, from electricity, begins in matter, without any known voluntary agent; and to suppose always, in these cases, an unknown voluntary agent is mere hypothesis—and hypothesis attended with no advantages. The beginning of motion in matter itself is as conceivable *a priori* as its communication from mind and intelligence.

Besides, why may not motion have been propagated by impulse through all eternity, and the same stock of it, or nearly the same, be still upheld in the universe? As much as is lost by the composition of motion, as much is gained by its resolution. And whatever the causes are, the fact is certain that matter is and always has been in continual agitation, as far as human experience or tradition reaches. There is not probably, at present, in the whole universe, one particle of matter at absolute rest.

And this very consideration, too, continued Philo, which we have stumbled on in the course of the argument suggests a new hypothesis of cosmogony that is not absolutely absurd and improbable. Is there a system, an order, an economy of things, by which matter can preserve that perpetual agitation which seems essential to it, and yet maintain a constancy in the forms which it produces? There certainly is such an economy, for this is actually the case with the present world. The continual motion of matter, therefore, in less than infinite transpositions, must produce this economy or order; and, by its very nature, that order, when once established, supports itself for many ages if not to eternity. But wherever matter is so poised, arranged, and adjusted, as to continue in perpetual motion, and yet preserve a constancy in the forms, its situation must, of necessity, have all the same appearance of art and contrivance which we observe at present. All the parts of each form must have a relation to each other and to the whole; and the whole itself must have a relation to the other parts of the universe, to the element in which the form subsists, to the materials with which it repairs its waste and decay, and to every other form which is hostile or friendly. A defect in any of these particulars destroys the form; and the matter of which it is composed is again set loose, and is thrown into irregular motions and fermentations till it unite itself to some other regular form. If no such form be prepared to receive it, and if there be a great quantity of this corrupted matter in the universe, the universe itself is entirely disordered, whether it be the feeble embryo of a world in its first beginnings that is thus destroyed or the rotten carcass of one languishing in old age and infirmity. In either case, a chaos ensues till finite though innumerable revolutions produce, at last, some forms whose parts and organs are so adjusted as to support the forms amidst a continued succession of matter.

Suppose (for we shall endeavor to vary the expression) that matter were thrown into any position by a blind, unguided force; it is evident that this first position must, in all probability, be the most confused and most disorderly imaginable, without any resemblance to those works of human contrivance which, along with a symmetry of parts, discover an adjustment of means to ends and a tendency to self-preservation. If the actuating force cease after this operation, matter must remain forever in disorder, and continue an immense chaos, without any proportion or activity. But suppose that the actuating force, whatever it be, still continues in matter, this first position will immediately give place to a second which will likewise, in all probability, be as disorderly as the first, and so on through many successions of changes and revolutions. No particular order or position ever continues a moment unaltered. The original force, still remaining in activity, gives a perpetual restlessness to matter. Every possible situation is produced, and instantly destroyed. If a glimpse or dawn of order appears for a moment, it is instantly hurried away and confounded by that never-ceasing force which actuates every part of matter.

Thus the universe goes on for many ages in a continued succession of chaos and disorder. But is it not possible that it may settle at last, so as not to lose its motion and active force (for that we have supposed inherent in it), yet so as to preserve a uniformity of appearance, amidst the continual motion and fluctuation of its parts? This we find to be the case with the universe at present. Every individual is perpetually changing, and every part of every individual; and yet the whole remains, in appearance, the same. May we not hope for such a position or rather be assured of it from the eternal revolutions of unguided matter; and may not this account for all the appearing wisdom and contrivance which is in the universe? Let us contemplate the subject a little, and we shall find this adjustment if attained by matter of a seeming stability in the forms, with a real and perpetual revolution or motion of parts, affords a plausible, if not a true, solution of the difficulty.

It is in vain, therefore, to insist upon the uses of the parts in animals or vegetables, and their curious adjustment to each other. I would fain know how an animal could subsist unless its parts were so adjusted? Do we not find that it immediately perishes whenever this adjustment ceases, and that its matter, corrupting, tries some new form? It happens indeed that the parts of the world are so well adjusted that some regular form immediately lays claim to this corrupted matter; and if it were not so, could the world subsist? Must it not dissolve, as well as the animal, and pass through new positions and situations till in great but finite succession it fall, at last, into the present or some such order?

It is well, replied Cleanthes, you told us that this hypothesis was suggested on a sudden, in the course of the argument. Had you had leisure to examine it, you would soon have perceived the insuperable objections to which it is exposed. No form, you say, can subsist unless it possess those powers and organs requisite for its subsistence; some new order or economy must be tried, and so on, without intermission, till at last some order which can support and maintain itself is fallen upon. But according to this hypothesis, whence arise the many conveniences and advantages which men and all animals possess? Two eyes, two ears are not absolutely necessary for the subsistence of the species. Human race might have been propagated and preserved without horses, dogs, cows, sheep, and those innumerable fruits and products which serve to our satisfaction and enjoyment. If no camels had been created for the use of man in the sandy deserts of Africa and Arabia, would the world have been dissolved? If no loadstone had been framed to give that wonderful and useful direction to the needle, would human society and the human kind have been immediately extinguished? Though the maxims of nature be in general very frugal, yet instances of this kind are far from being rare; and any one of them is sufficient proof of design—and of a benevolent design—which gave rise to the order and arrangement of the universe.

At least, you may safely infer, said Philo, that the foregoing hypothesis is so far incomplete and imperfect, which I shall not scruple to allow. But can we ever reasonably expect greater success in any attempts of this nature? Or can we ever hope to erect a system of cosmogony that will be liable to no exceptions, and will contain no circumstance repugnant to our limited and imperfect experience of the analogy of nature? Your theory itself cannot surely pretend to any such advantage; even though you have run into *anthropomorphism*, the better to preserve a conformity to common experience. Let us once more put it to trial. In all instances which we have ever seen, ideas are copied from real objects, and are ectypal, not archetypal, to express myself in learned terms. You reverse this order and give thought the precedence. In all instance which we have ever seen, thought has no influence upon matter except where that matter is so conjoined with it as to have an equal reciprocal influence upon it. No animal can move immediately anything but the members of its own body; and, indeed, the equality of action and reaction seems to be an universal law of nature; but your theory implies a contradiction to this experience. These instances, with many more which it were easy to collect (particularly the supposition of a mind or system of thought that is eternal or, in other words, an animal ingenerable and immortal)—these instances, I say, may teach all of us sobriety in condemning each other, and let us see that no system of this kind ought ever to be received from a slight analogy, so neither ought any to be rejected on account of a small incongruity. For that is an inconvenience from which we can justly pronounce no one to be exempted.

All religious systems, it is confessed, are subject to great and insuperable difficulties. Each disputant triumphs in his turn, while he carries on an offensive war, and exposes the absurdities, barbarities, and pernicious tenets of his antagonist. But all of them, on the whole, prepare a complete triumph for the *sceptic*, who tells them that no system ought ever to be embraced with regard to such subjects; for this plain reason, that no absurdity ought ever to be assented to with regard to any subject. A total suspense of judgment is here our only reasonable resource. And if every attack, as is commonly observed, and no defence among theologians is successful, how complete must be *his* victory who remains always, with all mankind, on the offensive, and has himself no fixed station or abiding city which he is ever, on any occasion, obliged to defend?

Part IX

But if so many difficulties attend the argument *a posteriori*, said Demea, had we not better adhere to that simple and sublime argument *a priori* which, by offering to us infallible demonstration, cuts off at once all doubt and difficulty? By this argument, too, we may prove the *infinity* of the Divine attributes, which, I am afraid, can never be ascertained with certainty from any other topic. For how can an effect which either is finite or, for aught we know, may be so—how can such an effect, I say, prove an infinite cause? The unity, too, of the Divine Nature it is very difficult, if not absolutely impossible, to deduce merely from contemplating the works of nature; nor will the uniformity alone of the plan, even were it allowed, give us any assurance of that attribute. Whereas the argument *a priori* . . .

You seem to reason, Demea, interposed Cleanthes, as if those advantages and conveniences in the abstract argument were full proofs of its solidity. But it is first proper, in my opinion, to determine what argument of this nature you choose to insist on; and we shall afterwards, from itself, better than from its *useful* consequences, endeavor to determine what value we ought to put upon it.

The argument, replied Demea, which I would insist on is the common one. Whatever exists must have a cause or reason of its existence, it being absolutely impossible for anything to produce itself or be the cause of its own existence. In mounting up, therefore, from effects to causes, we must either go on in tracing an infinite succession, without any ultimate cause at all, or must at last have recourse to some ultimate cause that is *necessarily* existent. Now, that the first supposition is absurd may be thus proved. In the infinite chain or succession of causes and effects, each single effect is determined to exist by the power and efficacy of that cause which immediately preceded; but the whole eternal chain or succession, taken together, is not determined or caused by anything; and yet it is evident that it requires a cause or reason, as much as any particular object which begins to exist in time. The question is still reasonable why this particular succession of causes existed from eternity, and not any other succession or no succession at all. If there be no necessarily existent being, any supposition which can be formed is equally possible; nor is there any more absurdity in nothing's having existed from eternity than there is in that succession of causes which constitutes the universe. What was it, then, which determined something to exist rather than nothing, and bestowed being on a particular possibility, exclusive of the rest? *External causes,* there are supposed to be none. *Chance* is a word without meaning. Was it *nothing?* But that can never produce anything. We must, therefore, have recourse to a necessarily existent Being who carries the *reason* of his existence in himself; and who cannot be supposed not to exist, without an express contradiction. There is, consequently, such a Being—that is, there is a Deity.

I shall not leave it to Philo, said Cleanthes (though I know that the starting objections is his chief delight), to point out the weakness of this metaphysical reasoning. It seems to me so obviously ill-grounded, and at the same time of so little consequence to the cause of true piety and religion, that I shall myself venture to show the fallacy of it.

I shall begin with observing that there is an evident absurdity in pretending to demonstrate a matter of fact, or to prove it by any arguments *a priori.* Nothing is demonstrable unless the contrary implies a contradiction. Nothing that is distinctly conceivable implies a contradiction. Whatever we conceive as existent, we can also conceive as non-existent. There is no being, therefore, whose non-existence implies a contradiction. Consequently there is no being whose existence is demonstrable. I propose this argument as entirely decisive, and am willing to rest the whole controversy upon it.

It is pretended that the Deity is a necessarily existent being; and this necessity of his existence is attempted to be explained by asserting that, if we knew his whole essence or nature, we should perceive it to be as impossible for him not to exist, as for twice two not to be four. But it is evident that this can never happen, while our faculties remain the same as at present. It will still be possible for us, at any time, to conceive the non-existence of what we formerly conceived to exist; nor can the mind ever lie under a necessity of supposing any object to remain always in being; in the same manner as we lie under a necessity of always conceiving twice two to be four. The words, therefore, *necessary existence* have no meaning; or, which is the same thing, none that is consistent.

But further, why may not the material universe be the necessarily existent Being, according to this pretended explication of necessity? We dare not affirm that we know all the qualities of matter; and, for aught we can determine, it may contain some qualities which, were they known, would make its non-existence appear as great a contradiction as that twice two is five. I find only one argument employed to prove that the material world is not the necessarily existent Being; and this argument is derived from the contingency both of the matter and the form of the world. "Any particle of matter," it is said, "may be *conceived* to be annihilated, and any form may be *conceived* to be altered. Such an annihilation or alteration, therefore, is not impossible."[22] But it seems a great partiality not to perceive that the same argument extends equally to the Deity, so far as we have any conception of him; and that the mind can at least imagine him to be non-existent, or his attributes to be altered. It must be some unknown, inconceivable qualities which can make his non-existence appear impossible or his attributes unalterable: And no reason can be assigned why these qualities may not belong to matter. As they are altogether unknown and inconceivable, they can never be proved incompatible with it.

Add to this that in tracing an eternal succession of objects it seems absurd to inquire for a general cause or first author. How can anything that exists from eternity have a cause, since that relation implies a priority in time and in a beginning of existence?

In such a chain, too, or succession of objects, each part is caused by that which preceded it, and causes that which succeeds it. Where then is the difficulty? But the *whole*, you say, wants a cause. I answer that the uniting of these parts into a whole, like the uniting of several distinct countries into one kingdom, or several distinct members into one body, is performed merely by an arbitrary act of the mind, and has no influence on the nature of things. Did I show you the particular causes of each individual in a collection of twenty particles of matter, I should think it very unreasonable should you afterwards ask me what was the cause of the whole twenty. This is sufficiently explained in explaining the cause of the parts.

Though the reasonings which you have urged, Cleanthes, may well excuse me, said Philo, from starting any further difficulties; yet I cannot forbear insisting still upon another topic. It is observed by arithmeticians that the products of 9 compose always either 9 or some lesser product of 9 if you add together all the characters of which any of the former products is composed. Thus, of 18, 27, 36, which are products of 9, you make 9 by adding 1 to 8, 2 to 7, 3 to 6. Thus 369 is a product also of 9; and if you add 3, 6, and 9, you make 18, a lesser product of 9.[23] To a superficial observer so wonderful a regularity may be admired as the effect either of chance or design; but a skilful algebraist immediately concludes it to be the work of necessity, and demonstrates that it must forever result from the nature of these numbers. Is it not probable, I ask, that the whole economy of the universe is conducted by a like necessity, though no human algebra can furnish a key which solves the difficulty? And instead of admiring the order of natural beings, may it not happen that, could

---

22. Dr. Clark. [The quotation is from *A Demonstration of the Being and Attributes of God* by Samuel Clarke, regarding whom see Hume's *Enquiry*, n. 37.]

23. *République des Lettres*, Août 1685. [The reference is to the *Nouvelles de la république des lettres*, a journal edited in Holland by Pierre Bayle, regarding whom see Leibniz's *Monadology*, n. 1. The article cited by Hume appeared not in the August issue, as he stated, but in the September issue and was written by Bernard le Bovier de Fontenelle (1657–1757), a French scientist and man of letters.]

we penetrate into the intimate nature of bodies, we should clearly see why it was absolutely impossible they could ever admit of any other disposition? So dangerous is it to introduce this idea of necessity into the present question! and so naturally does it afford an inference directly opposite to the religious hypothesis!

But dropping all these abstractions, continued Philo, and confining ourselves to more familiar topics, I shall venture to add an observation that the argument *a priori* has seldom been found very convincing, except to people of a metaphysical head who have accustomed themselves to abstract reasoning, and who, finding from mathematics that the understanding frequently leads to truth through obscurity, and contrary to first appearances, have transferred the same habit of thinking to subjects where it ought not to have place. Other people, even of good sense and the best inclined to religion, feel always some deficiency in such arguments, though they are not perhaps able to explain distinctly where it lies—a certain proof that men ever did and ever will derive their religion from other sources than from this species of reasoning.

Part X

It is my opinion, I own, replied Demea, that each man feels, in a manner, the truth of religion within his own breast; and, from a consciousness of his imbecility and misery rather than from any reasoning, is led to seek protection from that Being on whom he and all nature are dependent. So anxious or so tedious are even the best scenes of life that futurity is still the object of all our hopes and fears. We incessantly look forward and endeavor, by prayers, adoration, and sacrifice, to appease those unknown powers whom we find, by experience, so able to afflict and oppress us. Wretched creatures that we are! What resource for us amidst the innumerable ills of life did not religion suggest some methods of atonement, and appease those terrors with which we are incessantly agitated and tormented?

I am indeed persuaded, said Philo, that the best and indeed the only method of bringing everyone to a due sense of religion is by just representations of the misery and wickedness of men. And for that purpose a talent of eloquence and strong imagery is more requisite than that of reasoning and argument. For is it necessary to prove what everyone feels within himself? It is only necessary to make us feel it, if possible, more intimately and sensibly.

The people, indeed, replied Demea, are sufficiently convinced of this great and melancholy truth. The miseries of life, the unhappiness of man, the general corruptions of our nature, the unsatisfactory enjoyment of pleasures, riches, honors—these phrases have become almost proverbial in all languages. And who can doubt of what all men declare from their own immediate feeling and experience?

In this point, said Philo, the learned are perfectly agreed with the vulgar; and in all letters, *sacred* and *profane,* the topic of human misery has been insisted on with the most pathetic eloquence that sorrow and melancholy could inspire. The poets, who speak from sentiment, without a system, and whose testimony has therefore the more authority, abound in images of this nature. From Homer down to Dr. Young,[24] the whole inspired tribe have ever been sensible that no other representa-

24. [The reference is to Edward Young (1683–1765), an English poet.]

tion of things would suit the feeling and observation of each individual.

As to authorities, replied Demea, you need not seek them. Look round this library of Cleanthes. I shall venture to affirm that, except authors of particular sciences, such as chemistry or botany, who have no occasion to treat of human life, there is scarce one of those innumerable writers from whom the sense of human misery has not, in some passage or other, extorted a complaint and confession of it. At least, the chance is entirely on that side; and no one author has ever, so far as I can recollect, been so extravagant as to deny it.

There you must excuse me, said Philo: Leibniz has denied it, and is perhaps the first[25] who ventured upon so bold and paradoxical an opinion; at least, the first who made it essential to his philosophical system.

And by being the first, replied Demea, might he not have been sensible of his error? For is this a subject in which philosophers can propose to make discoveries especially in so late an age? And can any man hope by a simple denial (for the subject scarcely admits of reasoning) to bear down the united testimony of mankind, founded on sense and consciousness?

And why should man, added he, pretend to an exemption from the lot of all other animals? The whole earth, believe me, Philo, is cursed and polluted. A perpetual war is kindled amongst all living creatures. Necessity, hunger, want stimulate the strong and courageous; fear, anxiety, terror agitate the weak and infirm. The first entrance into life gives anguish to the new-born infant and to its wretched parent; weakness, impotence, distress attend each stage of that life, and it is, at last, finished in agony and horror.

Observe, too, says Philo, the curious artifices of nature in order to embitter the life of every living being. The stronger prey upon the weaker and keep them in perpetual terror and anxiety. The weaker, too, in their turn, often prey upon the stronger, and vex and molest them without relaxation. Consider that innumerable race of insects, which either are bred on the body of each animal or, flying about, infix their stings in him. These insects have others still less than themselves which torment them. And thus on each hand, before and behind, above and below, every animal is surrounded with enemies which incessantly seek his misery and destruction.

Man alone, said Demea, seems to be, in part, an exception to this rule. For by combination in society he can easily master lions, tigers, and bears, whose greater strength and agility naturally enable them to prey upon him.

On the contrary, it is here chiefly, cried Philo, that the uniform and equal maxims of nature are most apparent. Man, it is true, can, by combination, surmount all his *real* enemies and become master of the whole animal creation; but does he not immediately raise up to himself *imaginary* enemies, the demons of his fancy, who haunt him with superstitious terrors and blast every enjoyment of life? His pleasure, as he imagines, becomes in their eyes a crime; his food and repose give them umbrage and offence; his very sleep and dreams furnish new materials to anxious fear; and even death, his refuge from every other ill, presents only the dread of endless and innumerable woes. Nor does the wolf molest more the timid flock than superstition does the anxious breast of wretched mortals.

25. That sentiment had been maintained by Dr. King and some few others before Leibniz, though by none of so great fame as that German philosopher. [The reference is to William King (1650–1729), an Irish clergyman who wrote *De Origine Mali* (Of the Origin of Evil).]

Besides, consider, Demea: This very society by which we surmount those wild beasts, our natural enemies, what new enemies does it not raise to us? What woe and misery does it not occasion? Man is the greatest enemy of man. Oppression, injustice, contempt, contumely, violence, sedition, war, calumny, treachery, fraud—by these they mutually torment each other, and they would soon dissolve that society which they had formed were it not for the dread of still greater ills which must attend their separation.

But though these external insults, said Demea, from animals, from men, from all the elements, which assault us form a frightful catalogue of woes, they are nothing in comparison of those which arise within ourselves, from the distempered condition of our mind and body. How many lie under the lingering torment of diseases? Hear the pathetic enumeration of the great poet.

> Intestine stone and ulcer, colic-pangs,
> Demoniac frenzy, moping melancholy,
> And moon-struck madness, pining atrophy,
> Marasmus, and wide-wasting pestilence.
> Dire was the tossing, deep the groans: *Despair*
> Tended the sick, busiest from couch to couch.
> And over them triumphant *Death* his dart
> Shook: but delay'd to strike, though oft invok'd
> With vows, as their chief good and final hope.[26]

The disorders of the mind, continued Demea, though more secret, are not perhaps less dismal and vexatious. Remorse, shame, anguish, rage, disappointment, anxiety, fear, dejection, despair—who has ever passed through life without cruel inroads from these tormentors? How many have scarcely ever felt any better sensations? Labor and poverty, so abhorred by everyone, are the certain lot of the far greater number; and those few privileged persons who enjoy ease and opulence never reach contentment or true felicity. All the goods of life united would not make a very happy man, but all the ills united would make a wretch indeed; and any one of them almost (and who can be free from every one), nay, often the absence of one good (and who can possess all) is sufficient to render life ineligible.

Were a stranger to drop on a sudden into this world, I would show him, as a specimen of its ills, a hospital full of diseases, a prison crowded with malefactors and debtors, a field of battle strewed with carcases, a fleet foundering in the ocean, a nation languishing under tyranny, famine, or pestilence. To turn the gay side of life to him and give him a notion of its pleasures—whither should I conduct him? To a ball, to an opera, to court? He might justly think that I was only showing him a diversity of distress and sorrow.

There is no evading such striking instances, said Philo, but by apologies which still further aggravate the charge. Why have all men, I ask, in all ages, complained incessantly of the miseries of life? . . . They have no just reason, says one: These complaints proceed only from their discontented, repining, anxious disposition . . . And can there possibly, I reply, be a more certain foundation of misery than such a wretched temper?

---

26. [The quotation is from John Milton's *Paradise Lost*.]

But if they were really as unhappy as they pretend, says my antagonist, why do they remain in life? . . .

Not satisfied with life, afraid of death.

This is the secret chain, say I, that holds us. We are terrified, not bribed to the continuance of our existence.

It is only a false delicacy, he may insist, which a few refined spirits indulge, and which has spread these complaints among the whole race of mankind . . . And what is this delicacy, I ask, which you blame? Is it anything but a greater sensibility to all the pleasures and pains of life? And if the man of a delicate, refined temper, by being so much more alive than the rest of the world, is only so much more unhappy, what judgment must we form in general of human life?

Let men remain at rest, says our adversary, and they will be easy. They are willing artificers of their own misery. . . . No! reply I: An anxious languor follows their repose; disappointment, vexation, trouble, their activity and ambition.

I can observe something like what you mention in some others, replied Cleanthes; but I confess I feel little or nothing of it in myself, and hope that it is not so common as you represent it.

If you feel not human misery yourself, cried Demea, I congratulate you on so happy a singularity. Others, seemingly the most prosperous, have not been ashamed to vent their complaints in the most melancholy strains. Let us attend to the great, the fortunate emperor, Charles V,[27] when, tired with human grandeur, he resigned all his extensive dominions into the hands of his son. In the last harangue which he made on that memorable occasion, he publicly avowed *that the greatest prosperities which he had ever enjoyed had been mixed with so many adversities that he might truly say he had never enjoyed any satisfaction or contentment.* But did the retired life in which he sought for shelter afford him any greater happiness? If we may credit his son's account, his repentance commenced the very day of his resignation.

Cicero's fortune, from small beginnings, rose to the greatest luster and renown; yet what pathetic complaints of all ills of life do his familiar letters, as well as philosophical discourses, contain? And suitably to his own experience, he introduces Cato,[28] the great, the fortunate Cato protesting in his old age that had he a new life in his offer he would reject the present.

As yourself, ask any of your acquaintance, whether they would live over again the last ten or twenty years of their life. No! but the next twenty, they say, will be better:

And from the dregs of life, hope to receive
What the first sprightly running could not give.[29]

Thus, at last, they find (such is the greatness of human misery, it reconciles even

27. [Charles V (1500–1588) was king of Spain for forty years.]

28. [The reference is to Marcus Porcius Cato the Elder (234–149 B.C.), a Roman statesman.]

29. [The quotation is from John Dryden's *Aurengzebe.*]

contradictions) that they complain at once of the shortness of life and of its vanity and sorrow.

And is it possible, Cleanthes, said Philo, that after all these reflections, and infinitely more which might be suggested, you can still persevere in your anthropomorphism, and assert the moral attributes of the Deity, his justice, benevolence, mercy, and rectitude, to be of the same nature with these virtues in human creatures? His power, we allow, is infinite; whatever he wills is executed; but neither man nor any other animal is happy; therefore, he does not will their happiness. His wisdom is infinite; he is never mistaken in choosing the means to any end; but the course of nature tends not to human or animal felicity; therefore, it is not established for that purpose. Through the whole compass of human knowledge there are no inferences more certain and infallible than these. In what respect, then, do his benevolence and mercy resemble the benevolence and mercy of men?

Epicurus' old questions are yet unanswered.

Is he willing to prevent evil, but not able? then is he impotent. Is he able, but not willing? then is he malevolent. Is he both able and willing? whence then is evil?

You ascribe, Cleanthes (and I believe justly), a purpose and intention to nature. But what, I beseech you, is the object of that curious artifice and machinery which she has displayed in all animals—the preservation alone of individuals, and propagation of the species? It seems enough for her purpose, if such a rank be barely upheld in the universe, without any care or concern for the happiness of the members that compose it. No resource for this purpose: no machinery in order merely to give pleasure or ease: no fund of pure joy and contentment: no indulgence without some want or necessity accompanying it. At least, the few phenomena of this nature are overbalanced by opposite phenomena of still greater importance.

Our sense of music, harmony, and indeed beauty of all kinds, gives satisfaction, without being absolutely necessary to the preservation and propagation of the species. But what racking pains, on the other hand, arise from gouts, gravels, megrims, toothaches, rheumatisms, where the injury to the animal machinery is either small or incurable? Mirth, laughter, play, frolic seem gratuitous satisfactions which have no further tendency; spleen, melancholy, discontent, superstition are pains of the same nature. How then does the divine benevolence display itself, in the sense of you anthropomorphites? None but we mystics, as you were pleased to call us, can account for this strange mixture of phenomena, by deriving it from attributes infinitely perfect but incomprehensible.

And have you, at last, said Cleanthes smiling, betrayed your intentions, Philo? Your long agreement with Demea did indeed a little surprise me, but I find you were all the while erecting a concealed battery against me. And I must confess that you have now fallen upon a subject worthy of your noble spirit of opposition and controversy. If you can make out the present point, and prove mankind to be unhappy or corrupted, there is an end at once of all religion. For to what purpose establish the natural attributes of the Deity, while the moral are still doubtful and uncertain?

You take umbrage very easily, replied Demea, at opinions the most innocent and the most generally received, even amongst the religious and devout themselves; and nothing can be more surprising than to find a topic like this—concerning the wickedness and misery of man—charged with no less than atheism and profaneness. Have not all pious divines and preachers who have indulged their rhetoric on so fertile a subject; have they not easily, I say, given a solution of any difficulties which may attend it? This world is but a point in comparison of the universe; this life but a moment in comparison of eternity. The present evil phenomena, therefore, are rectified in other regions, and in some future period of existence. And the eyes of men, being then opened to larger views of things, see the whole connection of general laws, and trace, with adoration, the benevolence and rectitude of the Deity through all the mazes and intricacies of his providence.

No! replied Cleanthes, no! These arbitrary suppositions can never be admitted, contrary to matter of fact, visible and uncontroverted. Whence can any cause be known but from its known effects? Whence can any hypothesis be proved but from the apparent phenomena? To establish one hypothesis upon another is building entirely in the air; and the utmost we ever attain by these conjectures and fictions is to ascertain the bare possibility of our opinion, but never can we, upon such terms, establish its reality.

The only method of supporting divine benevolence—and it is what I willingly embrace—is to deny absolutely the misery and wickedness of man. Your representations are exaggerated; your melancholy views mostly fictitious; your inferences contrary to fact and experience. Health is more common than sickness; pleasure than pain; happiness than misery. And for one vexation which we meet with, we attain, upon computation, a hundred enjoyments.

Admitting your position, replied Philo, which yet is extremely doubtful, you must at the same time allow that, if pain be less frequent than pleasure, it is infinitely more violent and durable. One hour of it is often able to outweigh a day, a week, a month of our common insipid enjoyments; and how many days, weeks, and months are passed by several in the most acute torments? Pleasure, scarcely in one instance, is ever able to reach ecstasy and rapture; and in no one instance can it continue for any time at its highest pitch and altitude. The spirits evaporate, the nerves relax, the fabric is disordered, and the enjoyment quickly degenerates into fatigue and uneasiness. But pain often, good God, how often! rises to torture and agony; and the longer it continues, it becomes still more genuine agony and torture. Patience is exhausted, courage languishes, melancholy seizes us, and nothing terminates our misery but the removal of its cause or another event which is the sole cure of all evil, but which, from our natural folly, we regard with still greater horror and consternation.

But not to insist upon these topics, continued Philo, though most obvious, certain, and important, I must use the freedom to admonish you, Cleanthes, that you have put the controversy upon a most dangerous issue, and are unawares introducing a total scepticism into the most essential articles of natural and revealed theology. What! no method of fixing a just foundation for religion unless we allow the happiness of human life, and maintain a continued existence even in this world, with all our present pains, infirmities, vexations, and follies, to be eligible and desirable! But this is contrary to everyone's feeling and experience; it is contrary to an authority so established as nothing can subvert. No decisive proofs can ever be produced against this authority; nor is it possible for you to compute, estimate, and compare all the pains and all the pleasures in the lives of all men and of all animals; and thus, by your resting the whole system of religion on a point which, from its very nature, must forever be uncertain, you tacitly confess that that system is equally uncertain.

But allowing you what never will be believed, at least, what you never possibly can prove, that animal or, at least, human happiness in this life exceeds its misery, you have yet done nothing; for this is not, by any means, what we expect from infinite power, infinite wisdom, and infinite goodness. Why is there any misery at all in the world? Not by chance, surely. From some cause then. Is it from the intention of the Deity? But he is perfectly benevolent. Is it contrary to his intention? But he is almighty. Nothing can shake the solidity of this reasoning, so short, so clear, so decisive, except we assert that these subjects exceed all human capacity, and that our common measures of truth and falsehood are not applicable to them—a topic which I have all along insisted on, but which you have, from the beginning, rejected with scorn and indignation.

But I will be contented to retire still from this intrenchment, for I deny that you can ever force me in it. I will allow that pain or misery in man is *compatible* with infinite power and goodness in the Deity, even in your sense of these attributes: what are you advanced by all these concessions? A mere possible compatibility is not sufficient. You must *prove* these pure, unmixed and uncontrollable attributes from the present mixed and confused phenomena, and from these alone. A hopeful undertaking! Were the phenomena ever so pure and unmixed, yet, being finite, they would be insufficient for that purpose. How much more, where they are also so jarring and discordant!

Here, Cleanthes, I find myself at ease in my argument. Here I triumph. Formerly, when we argued concerning the natural attributes of intelligence and design, I needed all my sceptical and metaphysical subtilty to elude your grasp. In many views of the universe and of its parts, particularly the latter, the beauty and fitness of final causes strike us with such irresistible force that all objections appear (what I believe they really are) mere cavils and sophisms; nor can we then imagine how it was ever possible for us to repose any weight on them. But there is no view of human life or of the condition of mankind from which, without the greatest violence, we can infer the moral attributes or learn that infinite benevolence, conjoined with infinite power and infinite wisdom, which we must discover by the eyes of faith alone. It is your turn now to tug the laboring oar, and to support your philosophical subtilties against the dictates of plain reason and experience.

Part XI

I scruple not to allow, said Cleanthes, that I have been apt to suspect the frequent repetition of the word *infinite,* which we meet with in all theological writers, to savor more of panegyric than of philosophy, and that any purposes of reasoning, and even of religion, would be better served were we to rest contented with more accurate and more moderate expressions. The terms *admirable, excellent, superlatively great, wise,* and *holy*—these sufficiently fill the imaginations of men, and anything beyond, besides that it leads into absurdities, has no influence on the affections or sentiments. Thus, in the present subject, if we abandon all human analogy, as seems your intention, Demea, I am afraid we abandon all religion and retain no conception of the great object of our adoration. If we preserve human analogy, we must forever find it impossible to reconcile any mixture of evil in the universe with infinite attributes; much less can we ever prove the latter from the former. But supposing the Author of Nature to be finitely perfect, though far exceeding mankind, a satisfactory account may then be given of natural and moral evil, and every untoward phenomenon be explained and adjusted. A less evil may then be chosen in order to avoid a greater; inconveniences be submitted to in order to reach a desirable end; and, in a word, benevolence, regulated by wisdom and limited by necessity, may produce just such a world as the present. You, Philo, who are so prompt at starting views and reflections and analogies, I would gladly hear, at length, without interruption, your opinion of this new theory; and if it deserve our attention, we may afterwards, at more leisure, reduce it into form.

My sentiments, replied Philo, are not worth being made a mystery of; and, therefore, without any ceremony, I shall deliver what occurs to me with regard to the present subject. It must, I think, be allowed that, if a very limited intelligence whom we shall suppose utterly unacquainted with the universe were assured that it were the production of a very good, wise, and powerful being, however finite, he would, from his conjectures, form *beforehand* a different notion of it from what we find it to be by experience; nor would he ever imagine, merely from these attributes of the cause of which he is informed, that the effect could be so full of vice and misery and disorder, as it appears in this life. Supposing now that this person were brought into the world, still assured that it was the workmanship of such a sublime and benevolent being, he might, perhaps, be surprised at the disappointment, but would never retract his former belief if founded on any very solid argument, since such a limited intelligence must be sensible of his own blindness and ignorance, and must allow that there may be many solutions of those phenomena which will forever escape his comprehension. But supposing, which is the real case with regard to man, that this creature is not antecedently convinced of a supreme intelligence, benevolent, and powerful, but is left to gather such a belief from the appearances of things—this entirely alters the case, nor will he ever find any reason for such a conclusion. He may be fully convinced of the narrow limits of his understanding, but this will not help him in forming an inference concerning the goodness of superior powers, since he must form that inference from what he knows, not from what he is ignorant of. The more you exaggerate his weakness and ignorance, the more diffident you render him, and give him the greater suspicion that such subjects are beyond the reach of his faculties. You are obliged, therefore, to reason with him merely from the known phenomena, and to drop every arbitrary supposition or conjecture.

Did I show you a house or palace where there was not one apartment convenient or agreeable; where the windows, doors, fires, passages, stairs, and the whole economy of the building were the source of noise, confusion, fatigue, darkness, and the extremes of heat and cold, you would certainly blame the contrivance, without any further examination. The architect would in vain display his subtilty, and prove to you that, if this door or that window were altered, greater ills would ensue. What he says may be strictly true: The alteration of one particular, while the other parts of the building remain, may only augment the inconveniences. But still you would assert in general that, if the architect had had skill and good intentions, he might have formed such a plan of the whole, and might have adjusted the parts in such a manner as would have remedied all or most of these inconveniences. His ignorance, or even your own ignorance of such a plan, will never convince you of the impossibility of it. If you find any inconveniences and deformities in the building, you will always, without entering into any detail, condemn the architect.

In short, I repeat the question: Is the world, considered in general and as it appears to us in this life, different from what a man or such a limited being would, *beforehand,* expect from a very powerful, wise, and benevolent Deity? It must be strange prejudice to assert the contrary. And from thence I conclude that, however consistent the world may be, allowing certain suppositions and conjectures with the idea of such a Deity, it can never afford us an inference concerning his existence. The consistency is not absolutely denied, only the inference. Conjectures, especially where infinity is excluded from the divine attributes, may perhaps be sufficient to prove a consistency, but can never be foundations for any inference.

There seem to be *four* circumstances on which depend all or the greatest part of the ills that molest sensible creatures; and it is not impossible but all these circumstances may be necessary and unavoidable. We know so little beyond common life, or even of common life, that, with regard to the economy of a universe, there is no conjecture, however wild, which may not be just; nor any one, however plausible, which may not be erroneous. All that belongs to human understanding, in this deep ignorance and obscurity, is to be sceptical or at least cautious, and not to admit of any hypothesis whatever, much less of any which is supported by no appearance of probability. Now this I assert to be the case with regard to all the causes of evil and the circumstances on which it depends. None of them appear to human reason in the least degree necessary or unavoidable, nor can we suppose them such, without the utmost license of imagination.

The *first* circumstance which introduces evil is that contrivance or economy of the animal creation by which pains, as well as pleasures, are employed to excite all creatures to action, and make them vigilant in the great work of self-preservation. Now pleasure alone, in its various degrees, seems to human understanding sufficient for this purpose. All animals might be constantly in a state of enjoyment; but when urged by any of the necessities of nature, such as thirst, hunger, weariness; instead of pain, they might feel a diminution of pleasure by which they might be prompted to seek that object which is necessary to their subsistence. Men pursue pleasure as eagerly as they avoid pain; at least, they might have been so constituted. It seems, therefore, plainly possible to carry on the business of life without any pain. Why then is any animal ever rendered susceptible of such a sensation? If animals can be free from it an hour, they might enjoy a perpetual exemption from it, and it required as particular a contrivance of their organs to produce that feeling as to endow them with sight, hearing, or any of the senses. Shall we conjecture that such a contrivance was necessary, without any appearance of reason; and shall we build on that conjecture as on the most certain truth?

But a capacity of pain would not alone produce pain were it not for the *second* circumstance, viz., the conducting of the world by general laws; and this seems nowise necessary to a very perfect being. It is true, if everything were conducted by particular volitions, the course of nature would be perpetually broken, and no man could employ his reason in the conduct of life. But might not other particular violitions remedy this inconvenience? In short, might not the Deity exterminate all ill, wherever it were to be found, and produce all good, without any preparation or long progress of causes and effects?

Besides, we must consider that, according to the present economy of the world, the course of nature, though supposed exactly regular, yet to us appears not so, and many events are uncertain, and many disappoint our expectations. Health and sickness, calm and tempest, with an infinite number of other accidents whose causes are unknown and variable, have a great influence both on the fortunes of particular persons and on the prosperity of public societies; and indeed all human life, in a manner, depends on such accidents. A being, therefore, who knows the secret springs of the universe might easily, by particular volitions, turn all these accidents to the good of mankind and render the whole world happy, without discovering himself in any operation. A fleet whose purposes were salutary to society might always meet with a fair wind; good princes enjoy sound health and long life; persons born to power and authority be framed with good tempers and virtuous dispositions. A few such events as these, regularly and wisely conducted, would change the face of the world; and yet would no more seem to disturb the course of nature or confound human conduct than the present economy of things where the causes are secret and variable and compounded. Some small touches given to Caligula's[30] brain in his infancy might have converted him into a Trajan.[31] One wave, a little higher than the rest, by burying Caesar and his fortune in the bottom of the ocean, might have restored liberty to a considerable part of mankind. There may, for aught we know, be good reasons why Providence interposes not in this manner, but they are unknown to us; and, though the mere supposition that such reasons exist may be sufficient to *save* the conclusion concerning the divine attributes, yet surely it can never be sufficient to *establish* that conclusion.

If everything in the universe be conducted by general laws, and if animals be rendered susceptible of pain, it scarcely seems possible but some ill must arise in the various shocks of matter and the various concurrence and opposition of general laws; but this ill would be very rare were it not for the *third* circumstance which I proposed to mention, viz., the great frugality with which all powers and faculties are distributed to every particular being. So well adjusted are the organs and capacities of all animals, and so well fitted to their preservation, that, as far as history or tradition reaches, there appears not to be any single species which has yet been extinguished in the universe. Every animal has the requisite endowments, but these endowments are bestowed with so scrupulous an economy that any considerable diminution must entirely destroy the creature. Wherever one power is increased, there is a proportional abatement in the others. Animals which excel in swiftness are commonly defective in force. Those which possess both are either imperfect in some of their senses or are oppressed with the most craving wants. The human species, whose chief excellence is reason and sagacity, is of all others the most necessitous, and the most deficient in bodily advantages, without clothes, without arms, without food, without lodging, without any convenience of life, except what they owe to their own skill and industry. In short, nature seems to have formed an exact calculation of the necessities of her creatures; and, like a *rigid master,* has afforded them little more powers or endowments than what are strictly sufficient to supply those necessities. An *indulgent parent* would have bestowed a large stock in order to guard against accidents, and secure the happiness and welfare of the creature in the most unfortunate concurrence of circumstances. Every course of life would not have been so surrounded with precipices that the least departure from the true path, by

---

30. [Caligula (12–41) was a Roman emperor renowned for his cruelty.]

31. [Trajan (c.53–117) was a Roman emperor who pursued benevolent social policies.]

mistake or necessity, must involve us in misery and ruin. Some reserve, some fund, would have been provided to ensure happiness, nor would the powers and the necessities have been adjusted with so rigid an economy. The Author of Nature is inconceivably powerful; his force is supposed great, if not altogether inexhaustible; nor is there any reason, as far as we can judge, to make him observe this strict frugality in his dealings with his creatures. It would have been better, were his power extremely limited, to have created fewer animals, and to have endowed these with more faculties for their happiness and preservation. A builder is never esteemed prudent who undertakes a plan beyond what his stock will enable him to finish.

In order to cure most of the ills of human life, I require not that man should have the wings of the eagle, the swiftness of the stag, the force of the ox, the arms of the lion, the scales of the crocodile or rhinoceros; much less do I demand the sagacity of an angel or cherubim. I am contented to take an increase in one single power or faculty of his soul. Let him be endowed with a greater propensity to industry and labor, a more vigorous spring and activity of mind, a more constant bent to business and application. Let the whole species possess naturally an equal diligence with that which many individuals are able to attain by habit and reflection, and the most beneficial consequences, without any allay of ill, is the immediate and necessary result of this endowment. Almost all the moral as well as natural evils of human life arise from idleness; and were our species, by the original constitution of their frame, exempt from this vice or infirmity, the perfect cultivation of land, the improvement of arts and manufactures, the exact execution of every office and duty, immediately follow; and men at once may fully reach that state of society which is so imperfectly attained by the best regulated government. But as industry is a power, and the most valuable of any, nature seems determined, suitably to her usual maxims, to bestow it on men with a very sparing hand; and rather to punish him severely for his deficiency in it than to reward him for his attainments. She has so contrived his frame that nothing but the most violent necessity can oblige him to labor; and she employs all his other wants to overcome, at least in part, the want of diligence, and to endow him with some share of a faculty of which she has thought fit naturally to bereave him. Here our demands may be allowed very humble, and therefore the more reasonable. If we required the endowments of superior penetration and judgment, of a more delicate taste of beauty, of a nicer sensibility to benevolence and friendship, we might be told that we impiously pretend to break the order of nature, that we want to exalt ourselves into a higher rank of being, that the presents which we require, not being suitable to our state and condition, would only be pernicious to us. But it is hard, I dare to repeat it, it is hard that, being placed in a world so full of wants and necessities, where almost every being and element is either our foe or refuses its assistance . . . we should also have our own temper to struggle with, and should be deprived of that faculty which can alone fence against these multiplied evils.

The *fourth* circumstance whence arises the misery and ill of the universe is the inaccurate workmanship of all the springs and principles of the great machine of nature. It must be acknowledged that there are few parts of the universe which seem not to serve some purpose, and whose removal would not produce a visible defect and disorder in the whole. The parts hang all together, nor can one be touched without affecting the rest, in a greater or less degree. But at the same time, it must be observed that none of these parts or principles, however useful, are so accurately adjusted as to keep precisely within those bounds in which their utility consists; but they are, all of them, apt, on every occasion, to run into the one extreme or the other. One would imagine that this grand production had not received the last hand of the maker—so little finished is every part, and so coarse are the strokes with which it is executed. Thus the winds are requisite to convey the vapors along the surface of the globe, and to assist men in navigation; but how often, rising up to tempests and hurricanes, do they become pernicious? Rains are necessary to nourish all the plants and animals of the earth; but how often are they defective? how often excessive? Heat is requisite to all life and vegetation, but is not always found in the due proportion. On the mixture and secretion of the humors and juices of the body depend the health and prosperity of the animal; but the parts perform not regularly their proper function. What more useful than all the passions of the mind, ambition, vanity, love, anger? But how often do they break their bounds and cause the greatest convulsions in society? There is nothing so advantageous in the universe but what frequently becomes pernicious, by its excess or defect; nor has nature guarded, with the requisite accuracy, against all disorder or confusion. The irregularity is never perhaps so great as to destroy any species, but is often sufficient to involve the individuals in ruin and misery.

On the concurrence, then, of these *four* circumstances does all or the greatest part of natural evil depend. Were all living creatures incapable of pain, or were the world administered by particular volitions, evil never could have found access into the universe; and were animals endowed with a large stock of powers and faculties, beyond what strict necessity requires, or were the several springs and principles of the universe so accurately framed as to preserve always the just temperament and medium, there must have been very little ill in comparison of what we feel at present. What then shall we pronounce on this occasion? Shall we say that these circumstances are not necessary, and that they might easily have been altered in the contrivance of the universe? This decision seems too presumptuous for creatures so blind and ignorant. Let us be more modest in our conclusions. Let us allow that, if the goodness of the Deity (I mean a goodness like the human) could be established on any tolerable reasons *a priori*, these phenomena, however untoward, would not be sufficient to subvert that principle, but might easily, in some unknown manner, be reconcilable to it. But let us still assert that, as this goodness is not antecedently established but must be inferred from the phenomena, there can be no grounds for such an inference while there are so many ills in the universe, and while these ills might so easily have been remedied, as far as human understanding can be allowed to judge on such a subject. I am sceptic enough to allow that the bad appearances, notwithstanding all my reasonings, may be compatible with such attributes as you suppose, but surely they can never prove these attributes. Such a conclusion cannot result from scepticism, but must arise from the phenomena, and from our confidence in the reasonings which we deduce from these phenomena.

Look round this universe. What an immense profusion of beings, animated and organized, sensible and active! You admire this prodigious variety and fecundity. But inspect a little more narrowly these living existences, the only beings worth regarding. How hostile and destructive to each other! How insufficient all of them for their own happiness! How contemptible or odious to the spectator! The whole presents nothing but the idea of a blind nature, impregnated by a great vivifying principle, and pouring forth from her lap, without discernment or parental care, her maimed and abortive children!

Here the Manichaean[32] system occurs as a proper hypothesis to solve the difficulty; and, no doubt, in some respects it is very specious and has more probability than the common hypothesis, by giving a plausible account of the strange mixture of good and ill which appears in life. But if we consider, on the other hand, the perfect uniformity and agreement of the parts of the universe, we shall not discover in it any marks of the combat of a malevolent with a benevolent being. There is indeed an opposition of pains and pleasures in the feelings of sensible creatures; but are not all the operations of nature carried on by an opposition of principles, of hot and cold, moist and dry, light and heavy? The true conclusion is that the original source of all things is entirely indifferent to all these principles, and has no more regard to good above ill than to heat above cold, or to drought above moisture, or to light above heavy.

There may *four* hypotheses be framed concerning the first causes of the universe: that they are endowed with perfect goodness; that they have perfect malice; that they are opposite and have both goodness and malice; that they have neither goodness nor malice. Mixed phenomena can never prove the two former unmixed principles; and the uniformity and steadiness of general laws seem to oppose the third. The fourth, therefore, seems by far the most probable.

What I have said concerning natural evil will apply to moral with little or no variation; and we have no more reason to infer that the rectitude of the Supreme Being resembles human rectitude than that his benevolence resembles the human. Nay, it will be thought that we have still greater cause to exclude from him moral sentiments, such as we feel them, since moral evil, in the opinion of many, is much more predominant above moral good than natural evil above natural good.

But even though this should not be allowed, and though the virtue which is in mankind should be acknowledged much superior to the vice; yet, so long as there is any vice at all in the universe, it will very much puzzle you anthropomorphites how to account for it. You must assign a cause for it, without having recourse to the first cause. But as every effect must have a cause, and that cause another, you must either carry on the progression *in infinitum* or rest on that original principle, who is the ultimate cause of all things. . . .

Hold! hold! cried Demea: Whither does your imagination hurry you? I joined in alliance with you in order to prove the incomprehensible nature of the Divine Being, and refute the principles of Cleanthes, who would measure everything by human rule and standard. But I now find you running into all the topics of the greatest libertines and infidels, and betraying that holy cause which you seemingly espoused. Are you secretly, then, a more dangerous enemy than Cleanthes himself?

And are you so late in perceiving it? replied Cleanthes. Believe me, Demea, your friend Philo, from the beginning, has been amusing himself at both our expense; and it must be confessed that the injudicious reasoning of our vulgar theology has given him but too just a handle of ridicule. The total infirmity of human reason, the absolute incomprehensibility of the Divine Nature, the great and universal misery, and still greater wickedness of men — these are strange topics, surely, to be so fondly cherished by orthodox divines and doctors. In ages of stupidity and ignorance, indeed, these principles may safely be espoused; and perhaps no views of things are

---

32. [Regarding Manichaeism, see Berkeley's *Treatise*, n. 13.]

more proper to promote superstition than such as encourage the blind amazement, the diffidence, and melancholy of mankind. But at present . . .

Blame not so much, interposed Philo, the ignorance of these reverend gentlemen. They know how to change their style with the times. Formerly, it was a most popular theological topic to maintain that human life was vanity and misery, and to exaggerate all the ills and pains which are incident to men. But of late years, divines, we find, begin to retract this position and maintain, though still with some hesitation, that there are more goods than evils, more pleasures than pains, even in this life. When religion stood entirely upon temper and education, it was thought proper to encourage melancholy; as indeed, mankind never have recourse to superior powers so readily as in that disposition. But as men have now learned to form principles and to draw consequences, it is necessary to change the batteries, and to make use of such arguments as will endure at least some scrutiny and examination. This variation is the same (and from the same causes) with that which I formerly remarked with regard to scepticism.

Thus Philo continued to the last his spirit of opposition, and his censure of established opinions. But I could observe that Demea did not at all relish the latter part of the discourse; and he took occasion soon after, on some pretence or other, to leave the company.

Part XII

After Demea's departure, Cleanthes and Philo continued the conversation in the following manner. Our friend, I am afraid, said Cleanthes, will have little inclination to revive this topic of discourse while you are in company; and to tell the truth, Philo, I should rather wish to reason with either of you apart on a subject so sublime and interesting. Your spirit of controversy, joined to your abhorrence of vulgar superstition, carries you strange lengths when engaged in an argument; and there is nothing so sacred and venerable, even in your own eyes, which you spare on that occasion.

I must confess, replied Philo, that I am less cautious on the subject of Natural Religion than on any other; both because I know that I can never, on that head, corrupt the principles of any man of common sense and because no one, I am confident, in whose eyes I appear a man of common sense will ever mistake my intentions. You, in particular, Cleanthes, with whom I live in unreserved intimacy; you are sensible that, notwithstanding the freedom of my conversation and my love of singular arguments, no one has a deeper sense of religion impressed on his mind, or pays more profound adoration to the Divine Being, as he discovers himself to reason in the inexplicable contrivance and artifice of nature. A purpose, an intention, a design strikes everywhere the most careless, the most stupid thinker; and no man can be so hardened in absurd systems as at all times to reject it. *That nature does nothing in vain* is a maxim established in all the schools, merely from the contemplation of the works of nature, without any religious purpose; and, from a firm conviction of its truth, an anatomist who had observed a new organ or canal would never be satisfied till he had also discovered its use and intention. One great foundation of the Copernican system is the maxim *that nature acts by the simplest methods, and chooses the most proper means to any end;* and astronomers often, without thinking of it, lay this strong foundation of piety and religion. The same thing is observable in other parts of philosophy; and thus all the sciences almost lead us insensibly to acknowledge a first intelligent Author; and their authority is often so much the greater as they do not directly profess that intention.

It is with pleasure I hear Galen[33] reason concerning the structure of the human body. The anatomy of a man, says he, discovers above 600 different muscles; and whoever duly considers these will find that, in each of them, nature must have adjusted at least ten different circumstances in order to attain the end which she proposed: proper figure, just magnitude, right disposition of the several ends, upper and lower position of the whole, the due insertion of the several nerves, veins, and arteries; so that, in the muscles alone, above 6000 several views and intentions must have been formed and executed. The bones he calculates to be 284; the distinct purposes aimed at in the structure of each, above forty. What a prodigious display of artifice, even in these simple and homogeneous parts! But if we consider the skin, ligaments, vessels, glandules, humors, the several limbs and members of the body, how must our astonishment rise upon us, in proportion to the number and intricacy of the parts so artificially adjusted! The further we advance in these researches, we discover new scenes of art and wisdom; but descry still, at a distance, further scenes beyond our reach; in the fine internal structure of the parts, in the economy of the brain, in the fabric of the seminal vessels. All these artifices are repeated in every different species of animal, with wonderful variety, and with exact propriety, suited to the different intentions of nature in framing each species. And if the infidelity of Galen, even when these natural sciences were still imperfect, could not withstand such striking appearances, to what pitch of pertinacious obstinacy must a philosopher in this age have attained who can now doubt of a Supreme Intelligence!

Could I meet with one of this species (who, I thank God, are very rare), I would ask him: Supposing there were a God who did not discover himself immediately to our senses, were it possible for him to give stronger proofs of his existence than what appear on the whole face of nature? What indeed could such a Divine Being do but copy the present economy of things, render many of his artifices so plain that no stupidity could mistake them, afford glimpses of still greater artifices which demonstrate his prodigious superiority above our narrow apprehensions, and conceal altogether a great many from such imperfect creatures? Now, according to all rules of just reasoning, every fact must pass for undisputed when it is supported by all the arguments which its nature admits of, even though these arguments be not, in themselves, very numerous or forcible: How much more in the present case where no human imagination can compute their number, and no understanding estimate their cogency.

I shall further add, said Cleanthes, to what you have so well urged, that one great advantage of the principle of theism is that it is the only system of cosmogony which can be rendered intelligible and complete, and yet can throughout preserve a strong analogy to what we every day see and experience in the world. The comparison of the universe to a machine of human contrivance is so obvious and natural, and is justified by so many instances of order and design in nature, that it must immediately strike all unprejudiced apprehensions and procure universal approbation.

33. *De Formatione Foetus.* [Galen (c.130–c.200) was a Greek physician and devotee of philosophy who served at the court of Marcus Aurelius (regarding whom, see Hume's *Enquiry,* n. 58) and wrote prolifically, most notably in the fields of anatomy and physiology.]

Whoever attempts to weaken this theory cannot pretend to succeed by establishing in its place any other that is precise and determinate: It is sufficient for him if he start doubts and difficulties; and, by remote and abstract views of things reach that suspense of judgment which is here the utmost boundary of his wishes. But, besides that this state of mind is in itself unsatisfactory, it can never be steadily maintained against such striking appearances as continually engage us into the religious hypothesis. A false, absurd system, human nature, from the force of prejudice, is capable of adhering to with obstinacy and perseverance; but no system at all, in opposition to a theory supported by strong and obvious reason, by natural propensity, and by early education, I think it absolutely impossible to maintain or defend.

So little, replied Philo, do I esteem this suspense of judgment in the present case to be possible that I am apt to suspect there enters somewhat of a dispute of words into this controversy, more than is usually imagined. That the works of nature bear a great analogy to the productions of art is evident; and, according to all the rules of good reasoning, we ought to infer, if we argue at all concerning them, that their causes have a proportional analogy. But as there are also considerable differences, we have reason to suppose a proportional difference in the causes, and, in particular, ought to attribute a much higher degree of power and energy to the supreme cause than any we have ever observed in mankind. Here, then, the existence of a *Deity* is plainly ascertained by reason; and if we make it a question whether, on account of these analogies, we can properly call him a *mind* or *intelligence*, notwithstanding the vast difference which may reasonably be supposed between him and human minds; what is this but a mere verbal controversy? No man can deny the analogies between the effects: to restrain ourselves from inquiring concerning the causes is scarcely possible. From this inquiry the legitimate conclusion is that the causes have also an analogy; and if we are not contented with calling the first and supreme cause a *God* or *Deity*, but desire to vary the expression, what can we call him but *Mind* or *Thought*, to which he is justly supposed to bear a considerable resemblance?

All men of sound reason are disgusted with verbal disputes, which abound so much in philosophical and and theological inquiries; and it is found that the only remedy for this abuse must arise from clear definitions, from the precision of those ideas which enter into any argument, and from the strict and uniform use of those terms which are employed. But there is a species of controversy which, from the very nature of language and of human ideas, is involved in perpetual ambiguity, and can never, by any precaution or any definitions, be able to reach a reasonable certainty or precision. These are the controversies concerning the degrees of any quality or circumstance. Men may argue to all eternity whether Hannibal be a great, or a very great, or a superlatively great man, what degree of beauty Cleopatra possessed, what epithet of praise Livy or Thucydides[34] is entitled to, without bringing the controversy to any determination. The disputants may here agree in their sense and differ in the terms, or *vice versa*, yet never be able to define their terms so as to enter into each other's meaning; because the degrees of these qualities are not, like quantity or number, susceptible of any exact mensuration, which may be the standard in the controversy. That the dispute concerning theism is of this nature,

---

34. [Thucydides (c.460–400 B.C.) was the noted Greek historian who authored the *History of the Peloponnesian War.*]

and consequently is merely verbal, or, perhaps, if possible, still more incurably ambiguous, will appear upon the slightest inquiry. I ask the theist if he does not allow that there is a great and immeasurable, because incomprehensible, difference between the *human* and the *divine* mind: The more pious he is, the more readily will he assent to the affirmative, and the more will he be disposed to magnify the difference; he will even assert that the difference is of a nature which cannot be too much magnified. I next turn to the atheist, who, I assert, is only nominally so and can never possibly be in earnest, and I ask him whether, from the coherence and apparent sympathy in all the parts of this world, there be not a certain degree of analogy among all the operations of nature, in every situation and in every age; whether the rotting of a turnip, the generation of an animal, and the structure of human thought, be not energies that probably bear some remote analogy to each other. It is impossible he can deny it: He will readily acknowledge it. Having obtained this concession, I push him still further in his retreat, and I ask him if it be not probable that the principle which first arranged and still maintains order in this universe bears not also some remote inconceivable analogy to the other operations of nature and, among the rest, to the economy of human mind and thought. However reluctant, he must give his assent. Where then, cry I to both these antagonists, is the subject of your dispute? The theist allows that the original intelligence is very different from human reason; the atheist allows that the original principle of order bears some remote analogy to it. Will you quarrel, Gentlemen, about the degrees, and enter into a controversy which admits not of any precise meaning, nor consequently of any determination? If you should be so obstinate, I should not be surprised to find you insensibly change sides; while the theist, on the one hand, exaggerates the dissimilarity between the Supreme Being and frail, imperfect, variable, fleeting, and mortal creatures; and the atheist, on the other, magnifies the analogy among all the operations of nature, in every period, every situation, and every position. Consider then where the real point of controversy lies; and if you cannot lay aside your disputes, endeavor, at least, to cure yourselves of your animosity.

And here I must also acknowledge, Cleanthes, that, as the works of nature have a much greater analogy to the effects of *our* art and contrivance than to those of *our* benevolence and justice, we have reason to infer that the natural attributes of the Deity have a greater resemblance to those of men than his moral have to human virtues. But what is the consequence? Nothing but this, that the moral qualities of man are more defective in their kind than his natural abilities. For, as the Supreme Being is allowed to be absolutely and entirely perfect, whatever differs most from him departs the farthest from the supreme standard of rectitude and perfection.[35]

These, Cleanthes, are my unfeigned sentiments on this subject; and these senti-

---

35. It seems evident that the dispute between the sceptics and dogmatists is entirely verbal, or, at least, regards only the degrees of doubt and assurance which we ought to indulge with regard to all reasoning; and such disputes are commonly, at the bottom, verbal and admit not of any precise determination. No philosophical dogmatist denies that there are difficulties both with regard to the senses and to all science, and that these difficulties are, in a regular, logical method, absolutely insolvable. No sceptic denies that we lie under an absolute necessity, notwithstanding these difficulties, of thinking, and believing, and reasoning, with regard to all kinds of subjects, and even of frequently assenting with confidence and security. The only difference, then, between these sects, if they merit that name, is that the sceptic, from habit, caprice, or inclination, insists most on the difficulties, the dogmatist, for like reasons, on the necessity.

ments, you know, I have ever cherished and maintained. But in proportion to my veneration for true religion is my abhorrence of vulgar superstitions; and I indulge a peculiar pleasure, I confess, in pushing such principles sometimes into absurdity, sometimes into impiety. And you are sensible that all bigots, notwithstanding their great aversion to the latter above the former, are commonly equally guilty of both.

My inclination, replied Cleanthes, lies, I own, a contrary way. Religion, however corrupted, is still better than no religion at all. The doctrine of a future state is so strong and necessary a security to morals that we never ought to abandon or neglect it. For if finite and temporary rewards and punishments have so great an effect, as we daily find, how much greater must be expected from such as are infinite and eternal?

How happens it then, said Philo, if vulgar superstition be so salutary to society, that all history abounds so much with accounts of its pernicious consequences on public affairs? Factions, civil wars, persecutions, subversions of government, oppression, slavery—these are the dismal consequences which always attend its prevalence over the minds of men. If the religious spirit be ever mentioned in any historical narration, we are sure to meet afterwards with a detail of the miseries which attend it. And no period of time can be happier or more prosperous than those in which it is never regarded or heard of.

The reason of this observation, replied Cleanthes, is obvious. The proper office of religion is to regulate the hearts of men, humanize their conduct, infuse the spirit of temperance, order, and obedience; and, as its operation is silent and only enforces the motives of morality and justice, it is in danger of being overlooked and confounded with these other motives. When it distinguishes itself, and acts as a separate principle over men, it has departed from its proper sphere and has become only a cover to faction and ambition.

And so will all religion, said Philo, except the philosophical and rational kind. Your reasonings are more easily eluded than my facts. The inference is not just—because finite and temporary rewards and punishments have so great influence that therefore such as are infinite and eternal must have so much greater. Consider, I beseech you, the attachment which we have to present things, and the little concern which we discover for objects so remote and uncertain. When divines are declaiming against the common behavior and conduct of the world, they always represent this principle as the strongest imaginable (which indeed it is), and describe almost all human kind as lying under the influence of it, and sunk into the deepest lethargy and unconcern about their religious interests. Yet these same divines, when they refute their speculative antagonists, suppose the motives of religion to be so powerful that, without them, it were impossible for civil society to subsist; nor are they ashamed of so palpable a contradiction. It is certain, from experience, that the smallest grain of natural honesty and benevolence has more effect on men's conduct than the most pompous views suggested by theological theories and systems. A man's natural inclination works incessantly upon him; it is forever present to the mind, and mingles itself with every view and consideration; whereas religious motives, where they act at all, operate only by starts and bounds; and it is scarcely possible for them to become altogether habitual to the mind. The force of the greatest gravity, say the philosophers, is infinitely small, in comparison of that of the least impulse, yet it is certain that the smallest gravity will, in the end, prevail above a great impulse because no strokes or blows can be repeated with such constancy as attraction and gravitation.

Another advantage of inclination: It engages on its side all the wit and ingenuity of the mind, and, when set in opposition to religious principles, seeks every method and art of eluding them; in which it is almost always successful. Who can explain the heart of man, or account for those strange salvos and excuses with which people satisfy themselves when they follow their inclinations in opposition to their religious duty? This is well understood in the world; and none but fools ever repose less trust in a man because they hear that, from study and philosophy, he has entertained some speculative doubts with regard to theological subjects. And when we have to do with a man who makes a great profession of religion and devotion, has this any other effect upon several who pass for prudent than to put them on their guard, lest they be cheated and deceived by him?

We must further consider that philosophers, who cultivate reason and reflection, stand less in need of such motives to keep them under the restraint of morals; and that the vulgar, who alone may need them, are utterly incapable of so pure a religion as represents the Deity to be pleased with nothing but virtue in human behavior. The recommendations to the Divinity are generally supposed to be either frivolous observances or rapturous ecstasies or a bigoted credulity. We need not run back into antiquity or wander into remote regions to find instances of this degeneracy. Amongst ourselves, some have been guilty of that atrociousness, unknown to the Egyptian and Grecian superstitions, of declaiming, in express terms, against morality, and representing it as a sure forfeiture of the divine favor if the least trust or reliance be laid upon it.

But even though superstition or enthusiasm should not put itself in direct opposition to morality, the very diverting of the attention, the raising up a new and frivolous species of merit, the preposterous distribution which it makes of praise and blame, must have the most pernicious consequences, and weaken extremely men's attachment to the natural motives of justice and humanity.

Such a principle of action likewise, not being any of the familiar motives of human conduct, acts only by intervals on the temper, and must be roused by continual efforts in order to render the pious zealot satisfied with his own conduct and make him fulfil his devotional task. Many religious exercises are entered into with seeming fervor where the heart, at the time, feels cold and languid. A habit of dissimulation is by degrees contracted, and fraud and falsehood become the predominant principle. Hence the reason of that vulgar observation that the highest zeal in religion and the deepest hypocrisy, so far from being inconsistent, are often or commonly united in the same individual character.

The bad effects of such habits, even in common life, are easily imagined; but, where the interests of religion are concerned, no morality can be forcible enough to bind the enthusiastic zealot. The sacredness of the cause sanctifies every measure which can be made use of to promote it.

The steady attention alone to so important an interest as that of eternal salvation is apt to extinguish the benevolent affections, and beget a narrow, contracted selfishness. And when such a temper is encouraged, it easily eludes all the general precepts of charity and benevolence.

Thus the motives of vulgar superstition have no great influence on general conduct, nor is their operation favorable to morality, in the instances where they predominate.

Is there any maxim in politics more certain and infallible than that both the number and authority of priests should be confined within very narrow limits, and that the civil magistrate ought, for ever, to keep his *fasces* and *axes*[36] from such dangerous hands? But if the spirit of popular religion were so salutary to society, a contrary maxim ought to prevail. The greater number of priests and their greater authority and riches will always augment the religious spirit. And though the priests have the guidance of this spirit, why may we not expect a superior sanctity of life and greater benevolence and moderation from persons who are set apart for religion, who are continually inculcating it upon others, and who must themselves imbibe a greater share of it? Whence comes it then that, in fact, the utmost a wise magistrate can propose with regard to popular religions is, as far as possible, to make a saving game of it, and to prevent their pernicious consequences with regard to society? Every expedient which he tries for so humble a purpose is surrounded with inconveniences. If he admits only one religion among his subjects, he must sacrifice, to an uncertain prospect of tranquillity, every consideration of public liberty, science, reason, industry, and even his own independence. If he gives indulgence to several sects, which is the wiser maxim, he must preserve a very philosophical indifference to all of them and carefully restrain the pretensions of the prevailing sect; otherwise he can expect nothing but endless disputes, quarrels, factions, persecutions, and civil commotions.

True religion, I allow, has no such pernicious consequences; but we must treat of religion as it has commonly been found in the world, nor have I anything to do with that speculative tenet of theism which, as it is a species of philosophy, must partake of the beneficial influence of that principle, and, at the same time, must lie under a like inconvenience of being always confined to very few persons.

Oaths are requisite in all courts of judicature, but it is a question whether their authority arises from any popular religion. It is the solemnity and importance of the occasion, the regard to reputation, and the reflecting on the general interests of society, which are the chief restraints upon mankind. Customhouse oaths and political oaths are but little regarded even by some who pretend to principles of honesty and religion; and a Quaker's asseveration is with us justly put upon the same footing with the oath of any other person. I know that Polybius[37] ascribes the infamy of Greek faith to the prevalence of the Epicurean philosophy; but I know also that Punic faith had as bad a reputation in ancient times as Irish evidence has in modern, though we cannot account for these vulgar observations by the same reason. Not to mention that Greek faith was infamous before the rise of the Epicurean philosophy; and Euripides,[38] in a passage which I shall point out to you, has glanced a remarkable stroke of satire against his nation, with regard to this circumstance.

Take care, Philo, replied Cleanthes, take care; push not matters too far, allow not your zeal against false religion to undermine your veneration for the true. Forfeit not this principle—the chief, the only great comfort in life and our principal support amidst all the attacks of adverse fortune. The most agreeable reflection which it

36. [Rods and axes, a Roman symbol of authority.]

37. Lib. vi, cap. 54 [The reference is to the *Histories* of Polybius, regarding whom see Hume's *Enquiry*, n. 40.]

38. *Iphigenia in Tauride.*

is possible for human imagination to suggest is that of genuine theism, which represents us as the workmanship of a Being perfectly good, wise, and powerful; who created us for happiness; and who, having implanted in us immeasurable desires of good, will prolong our existence to all eternity, and will transfer us into an infinite variety of scenes, in order to satisfy those desires and render our felicity complete and durable. Next to such a Being himself (if comparison be allowed), the happiest lot which we can imagine is that of being under his guardianship and protection.

These appearances, said Philo, are most engaging and alluring; and, with regard to the true philosopher, they are more than appearances. But it happens here, as in the former case, that, with regard to the greater part of mankind, the appearances are deceitful, and that the terrors of religion commonly prevail above its comforts.

It is allowed that men never have recourse to devotion so readily as when dejected with grief or depressed with sickness. Is not this a proof that the religious spirit is not so nearly allied to joy as to sorrow?

But men, when afflicted, find consolation in religion, replied Cleanthes. Sometimes, said Philo; but it is natural to imagine that they will form a notion of those unknown beings, suitable to the present gloom and melancholy of their temper, when they betake themselves to the contemplation of them. Accordingly, we find the tremendous images to predominate in all religions; and we ourselves, after having employed the most exalted expression in our descriptions of the Deity, fall into the flattest contradiction in affirming that the damned are infinitely superior in number to the elect.

I shall venture to affirm that there never was a popular religion which represented the state of departed souls in such a light as would render it eligible for human kind that there should be such a state. These fine models of religion are the mere product of philosophy. For as death lies between the eye and the prospect of futurity, that event is so shocking to nature that it must throw a gloom on all the regions which lie beyond it; and suggest to the generality of mankind the idea of Cerberus[39] and Furies, devils, and torrents of fire and brimstone.

It is true, both fear and hope enter into religion because both these passions, at different times, agitate the human mind, and each of them forms a species of divinity suitable to itself. But when a man is in a cheerful disposition, he is fit for business, or company, or entertainment of any kind; and he naturally applies himself to these and thinks not of religion. When melancholy and dejected, he has nothing to do but brood upon the terrors of the invisible world, and to plunge himself still deeper in affliction. It may indeed happen that, after he has, in this manner, engraved the religious opinions deep into his thought and imagination, there may arrive a change of health or circumstances which may restore his good humor and, raising cheerful prospects of futurity, make him run into the other extreme of joy and triumph. But still it must be acknowledged that, as terror is the primary principle of religion, it is the passion which always predominates in it, and admits but of short intervals of pleasure.

Not to mention that these fits of excessive, enthusiastic joy, by exhausting the spirits, always prepare the way for equal fits of superstitious terror and dejection,

---

39. [According to Greek mythology, Cerberus was the monstrous dog who guarded the entrance to the underworld.]

nor is there any state of mind so happy as the calm and equable. But this state it is impossible to support where a man thinks that he lies in such profound darkness and uncertainty, between an eternity of happiness and an eternity of misery. No wonder that such an opinion disjoints the ordinary frame of mind and throws it into the utmost confusion. And though that opinion is seldom so steady in its operation as to influence all the actions; yet it is apt to make a considerable breach in the temper, and to produce that gloom and melancholy so remarkable in all devout people.

It is contrary to common sense to entertain apprehensions or terrors upon account of any opinion whatsoever, or to imagine that we run any risk hereafter, by the freest use of our reason. Such a sentiment implies both an *absurdity* and an *inconsistency*. It is an absurdity to believe that the Deity has human passions, and one of the lowest human passions, a restless appetite for applause. It is an inconsistency to believe that, since the Deity has this human passion, he has not others also; and, in particular, a disregard to the opinions of creatures so much inferior.

To know God, says Seneca,[40] *is to worship him.* All other worship is indeed absurd, superstitious, and even impious. It degrades him to the low condition of mankind, who are delighted with entreaty, solicitation, presents, and flattery. Yet is this impiety the smallest of which superstition is guilty. Commonly, it depresses the Deity far below the condition of mankind, and represents him as a capricious demon who exercises his power without reason and without humanity! And were that Divine Being disposed to be offended at the vices and follies of silly mortals, who are his own workmanship, ill would it surely fare with the votaries of most popular superstitions. Nor would any of human race merit his *favor* but a very few, the philosophical theists, who entertain or rather indeed endeavor to entertain suitable notions of his divine perfections. As the only persons entitled to his *compassion* and *indulgence* would be the philosophical sceptics, a sect almost equally rare, who, from a natural diffidence of their own capacity, suspend or endeavor to suspend all judgment with regard to such sublime and such extraordinary subjects.

If the whole of natural theology, as some people seem to maintain, resolves itself into one simple, though somewhat ambiguous, at least undefined, proposition, *That the cause or causes of order in the universe probably bear some remote analogy to human intelligence*—if this proposition be not capable of extension, variation, or more particular explication; if it affords no inference that affects human life, or can be the source of any action or forbearance; and if the analogy, imperfect as it is, can be carried no further than to the human intelligence, and cannot be transferred, with any appearance of probability, to the other qualities of the mind; if this really be the case, what can the most inquisitive, contemplative, and religious man do more than give a plain, philosophical assent to the proposition, as often as it occurs, and believe that the arguments on which it is established exceed the objections which lie against it? Some astonishment, indeed, will naturally arise from the greatness of the object: Some melancholy from its obscurity: Some contempt of human reason that it can give no solution more satisfactory with regard to so extraordinary and magnificent a question. But believe me, Cleanthes, the most natural sentiment which a

---

40. [Lucius Annaeus Seneca (c.3 B.C.−65 A.D.), born in Córdoba, Spain, was a Stoic philosopher who tutored the young Nero and became his political adviser, although later, having left the court, he was accused of conspiracy against the Emperor and forced to commit suicide.]

well-disposed mind will feel on this occasion is a longing desire and expectation that heaven would be pleased to dissipate, at least alleviate, this profound ignorance by affording some more particular revelation to mankind, and making discoveries of the nature, attributes, and operations of the divine object of our faith. A person, seasoned with a just sense of the imperfections of natural reason, will fly to revealed truth with the greatest avidity; while the haughty dogmatist, persuaded that he can erect a complete system of theology by the mere help of philosophy, disdains any further aid and rejects this adventitious instructor. To be a philosophical sceptic is, in a man of letters, the first and most essential step towards being a sound, believing Christian—a proposition which I would willingly recommend to the attention of Pamphilus; and I hope Cleanthes will forgive me for interposing so far in the education and instruction of his pupil.

Cleanthes and Philo pursued not this conversation much further; and as nothing ever made greater impression on me than all the reasonings of that day, so I confess that, upon a serious review of the whole, I cannot but think that Philo's principles are more probable than Demea's, but that those of Cleanthes approach still nearer to the truth.

IMMANUEL KANT—by Hans Veit Schnoor von Carolsfeld (1764-1841), in the Kupperstich Kabinett, Dresden

KÖNIGSBERG UNIVERSITY

KANT AND LUNCHEON GUESTS
(E. Doestling, 1893)

IMMANUEL KANT

Immanuel Kant (1724–1804) was born in Königsburg, East Prussia, a city he never left. His parents were simple people, and their moral and religious influence on him was profound. In 1740 Kant entered the University at Königsburg to study philology and classics, but he soon became interested in science and philosophy. In 1755 he bcame a lecturer at the University, and in 1770 was given the chair of logic and metaphysics.

Kant's early writing was scientific. His inaugural dissertation in Latin (1770) heralded the beginning of his own philosophical thought. For the next eleven years he struggled with the central doctrines of what was to become the *Critique of Pure Reason* (1781). With its careful, difficult, and painstaking analysis of the nature, extent, and limits of human knowledge, the *Critique* revolutionized philosophy. Disappointed with its somewhat tepid reception, Kant published in 1783 "for the benefit of teachers of philosophy" the work reprinted here, *Prolegomena to Any Future Metaphysics,* a simplified statement of the main points of the *Critique*. 1785 saw the publication of the other work of Kant reprinted here, *Fundamental Principles of the Metaphysic of Morals.* Kant rounded out his system with two more Critiques: the *Critique of Practical Reason* (1788), which developed his moral views further; and the *Critique of Judgment* (1790), which combined an analysis of aesthetic taste with a consideration of the principles of order and purpose in the world.

Kant claimed that Hume's skepticism awoke him from his dogmatic slumber. His answer to Hume's skepticism has three parts: (1) space and time are a priori intuitions of the human mind and provide the medium for our experience of objects; (2) the human mind has categories which organize our sensations into a unified, interconnected whole; (3) there is a distinction between the world of phenomena and the world of noumena.

By (1) Kant means that the objects we see have to conform to a purely human faculty of perception. If a person is to know an object, the object has to appear in space and time. But these are the conditions only of human knowledge, not necessarily of the knowledge of other rational beings.

(2) reflects Kant's conviction that in addition to space and time as the medium of experience, there must be active powers of the understanding, or categories, which give a unity, organization, and permanence to what we perceive. Without the categories, all that we perceive would be a chaotic, confused blob of sensation. The categories are ways the understanding gives form to the matter taken in by the senses. Both the categories and space and time are a priori, by which Kant means that they are not derived from experience, but are what we need in order to experience.

(3) shows that Kant agrees with Hume that we cannot have knowledge of ultimate reality. All the objects that we experience, Kant believes, are phenomena or appearances of things which underlie them. These things which are not in space and time, and consequently can never be known by us, Kant calls things-in-themselves. These have concepts or noumena which refer to them, like God, the substantial self, and other concepts whose objects we as human beings can never experience. Yet, for the purpose of morality and for increasing our knowledge and creating a unity of knowledge, we can think these concepts as long as we do not think that we have knowledge of their objects.

The *Foundations of the Metaphysic of Morals,* written not to present new ideas of morality but to elucidate and justify Kant's view of the supreme principle of morality, begins with an account of the view of morality held by the ordinary person. The kernel of that view is the concept of the good or moral will, which is morally right not because of its beneficial actions or the kind and generous motives which produce those actions, but because its maxims (rules governing actions) are adopted not only in accord with duty or morality but for the sake of morality. Moral action may result in advantageous results or produce pleasure, but these have nothing to do with the moral worth of the action.

After showing through its relation with duty what the concept of the good, or moral, will implies for the ordinary man, Kant provides a philosophical account of the supreme principle of practical or moral reason, the Categorical Imperative, which he develops through several formulations. The first and most important is: "Act only on that maxim whereby thou canst at the same time will that it should become a universal law." By this formulation Kant means that within the context that produced your moral maxim, any rational being would adopt that maxim. After discussing further formulations of the Categorical Imperative, Kant concludes his discussion by assuming for the justification of morality the postulate of freedom — a postulate, however, which affords us no knowledge of such an idea.

Useful and accessible general studies of Kant's philosophy are John Kemp, *The Philosophy of Kant* (New York: Oxford University Press, 1968); S. Körner, *Kant* (Baltimore: Penguin Books, 1955); and W.H. Werkmeister, *Kant: The Architectonic and Development of his Philosophy* (La Salle and London: Open Court, 1980). These studies would be useful preparation for those interested in tackling the *Critique of Pure Reason* and its exhaustive commentaries. The best study in English of the *Foundation of the Metaphysics of Morals* is H.J. Paton, *The Categorical Imperative* (1947: rpt. Philadelphia: University of Pennsylvania Press, 1971). A recent study of the same work is Robert Paul Wolff, *The Autonomy of Reason* (New York: Harper & Row, 1974).

R.W.H.

PROLEGOMENA TO
ANY FUTURE METAPHYSICS

PREFACE

These *Prolegomena* are not for the use of pupils but of future teachers, and even the latter should not expect that they will be serviceable for the systematic exposition of a ready-made science, but merely for the discovery of the science itself.

There are scholars for whom the history of philosophy (both ancient and modern) is philosophy itself; for these the present *Prolegomena* are not written. They must wait till those who endeavor to draw from the fountain of reason itself have completed their work; it will then be the turn of such scholars to inform the world of what has been done. Unfortunately, nothing can be said which, in their opinion, has not been said before, and truly the same prophecy applies to all future time; for since the human reason has for many centuries speculated upon innumerable objects in various ways, it is hardly to be expected that we should not be able to discover analogies for every new idea among the old sayings of past ages.

My object is to persuade all those who think metaphysics worth studying that it is absolutely necessary to pause a moment and, disregarding all that has been done, to propose first the preliminary question, "Whether such a thing as metaphysics be at all possible?"

If it is a science, how does it happen that it cannot, like other sciences, obtain universal and permanent recognition? If not, how can it maintain its pretensions and keep the human understanding in suspense with hopes never ceasing, yet never fulfilled? Whether then we demonstrate our knowledge or our ignorance in this field, we must come once for all to a definite conclusion respecting the nature of this so-called science, which cannot possibly remain on its present footing. It seems almost ridiculous, while every other science is continually advancing, that in this, which pretends to be wisdom incarnate, for whose oracle every one inquires, we should constantly move round the same spot, without gaining a single step. And so its supporters having melted away, we do not find that men who are confident of their ability to shine in other sciences venture their reputation here, where everybody, however ignorant in other matters, presumes to deliver a final verdict, inasmuch as in this domain there is as yet no standard weight and measure to distinguish soundness from shallow talk.

After all, it is nothing extraordinary in the elaboration of a science, when men begin to wonder how far it has advanced, that the question should at last occur as to whether and how in general such a science is possible? Human reason so delights in constructions that it has several times built up a tower and then razed it to examine

The Paul Carus translation (Chicago, 1902), extensively revised by James W. Ellington (University of Connecticut).

the nature of the foundation. It is never too late to become reasonable and wise; but if the insight comes late, there is always more difficulty in starting the change.

The question whether a science be possible presupposes a doubt as to its actuality. But such a doubt offends the man whose entire goods may perhaps consist in this supposed jewel; hence he who raises the doubt must expect opposition from all sides. Some, in the proud consciousness of their possessions, which are ancient and therefore considered legitimate, will take their metaphysical compendia in their hands and look down on him with contempt; others who never see anything except it be identical with what they have somewhere else seen before will not understand him, and everything will remain for a time as if nothing had happened to excite the concern or the hope for an impending change.

Nevertheless, I venture to predict that the independent reader of these *Prolegomena* will not only doubt his previous science, but ultimately be fully persuaded that it cannot exist unless the demands here stated on which its possibility depends be satisfied; and, as this has never been done, that there is, as yet, no such thing as metaphysics. But as it can never cease to be in demand[1]—since the interests of human reason in general are intimately interwoven with it—he must confess that a radical reform, or rather a rebirth of the science according to a new plan, is unavoidable, however much men may struggle against it for a while.

Since the *Essays* of Locke and Leibnitz, or rather since the origin of metaphysics so far as we know its history, nothing has ever happened which could have been more decisive to its fate than the attack made upon it by David Hume. He threw no light on this kind of knowledge; but he certainly struck a spark from which light might have been obtained, had it caught some inflammable substance and had its smouldering fire been carefully nursed and developed.

Hume started mainly from a single but important concept in metaphysics, namely, that of the connection of cause and effect (including its derivative concepts of force and action, etc.). He challenged reason, which pretends to have given birth to this concept of herself, to answer him by what right she thinks anything could be so constituted that if that thing be posited, something else also must necessarily be posited; for this is the meaning of the concept of cause. He demonstrated irrefutably that it was entirely impossible for reason to think *a priori* and by means of concepts such a combination as involves necessity. We cannot at all see why, in consequence of the existence of one thing, another must necessarily exist, or how the concept of such a combination can arise *a priori*. Hence he inferred that reason was altogether deluded with reference to this concept, which she erroneously considered as one of her children, whereas in reality it was nothing but a bastard of imagination, impregnated by experience, which subsumed certain representations under the law of association, and mistook a subjective necessity (custom) for an objective necessity arising from insight. Hence he inferred that reason had no power to think such connections, even in general, because her concepts would then be purely fictitious and all her pretended *a priori* cognitions nothing but common experiences marked with

---

1. Says Horace:

Rusticus expectat, dum defluat amnis, at ille
labitur et labetur in omne volubilis aevum.
["A peasant waits for the river to flow away,
but it flows on and will so flow forever."—J.W.E.]
Epistle I, 2, 42f.

a false stamp. This is as much as to say that there is not, and cannot be, any such thing as metaphysics at all.[2]

However hasty and mistaken Hume's conclusion may appear, it was at least founded upon investigation, and this investigation deserved the concentrated attention of the brighter spirits of his day as well as determined efforts on their part to discover, if possible, a happier solution of the problem in the sense proposed by him, all of which would have speedily resulted in a complete reform of the science.

But Hume suffered the usual misfortune of metaphysicians, of not being understood. It is positively painful to see how utterly his opponents, Reid, Oswald, Beattie, and lastly Priestley, missed the point of the problem; for while they were ever taking for granted that which he doubted, and demonstrating with zeal and often with impudence that which he never thought of doubting, they so misconstrued his valuable suggestion that everything remained in its old condition, as if nothing had happened. The question was not whether the concept of cause was right, useful, and even indispensable for our knowledge of nature, for this Hume had never doubted; but whether that concept could be thought by reason *a priori*, and consequently whether it possessed an inner truth, independent of all experience, implying a more widely extended usefulness, not limited merely to objects of experience. This was Hume's problem. It was a question concerning the *origin* of the concept, not concerning its indispensability in use. Were the former decided, the conditions of its use and the sphere of its valid application would have been determined as a matter of course.

But to satisfy the conditions of the problem, the opponents of the great thinker should have penetrated very deeply into the nature of reason, so far as it is concerned with pure thought—a task which did not suit them. They found a more convenient method of being defiant without any insight, viz., the appeal to *common sense*. It is indeed a great gift of heaven to possess right or (as they now call it) plain common sense. But this common sense must be shown in deeds by well-considered and reasonable thoughts and words, not by appealing to it as an oracle when no rational justification of oneself can be advanced. To appeal to common sense when insight and science fail, and no sooner—this is one of the subtle discoveries of modern times, by means of which the most superficial ranter can safely enter the lists with the most thorough thinker and hold his own. But as long as a particle of insight remains, no one would think of having recourse to this subterfuge. Seen in a clear light, it is but an appeal to the opinion of the multitude, of whose applause the philosopher is ashamed, while the popular charlatan glories and confides in it. I should think that Hume might fairly have laid as much claim to common sense as Beattie and, in addition, to a critical reason (such as the latter did not possess), which keeps common sense in check and prevents it from speculating, or, if speculations are under discussion, restrains the desire to decide because it cannot satisfy

---

2. Nevertheless Hume called such destructive philosophy metaphysics and attached to it great value. "Metaphysics and morals," he says, "are the most important branches of science; mathematics and natural philosophy are not half so important." [*Essays Moral, Politcal, and Literary* (edited by Green and Grose) vol. I, p. 187. Essay XIV: Of the Rise and Progress of the Arts and Sciences] But the acute man merely regarded the negative use arising from the moderation of extravagant claims of speculative reason, and the complete settlement of the many endless and troublesome controversies that mislead mankind. He overlooked the positive injury which results if reason be deprived of its most important prospects, which can alone supply to the will the highest aim for all its endeavors.

itself concerning its own principles. By this means alone can common sense remain sound. Chisels and hammers may suffice to work a piece of wood, but for etching we require an etcher's needle. Thus common sense and speculative understanding are both useful, but each in its own way: the former in judgments which apply immediately to experience; the latter when we judge universally from mere concepts, as in metaphysics, where sound common sense, so called in spite of the inappropriateness of the word, has no right to judge at all.

I openly confess that my remembering David Hume was the very thing which many years ago first interrupted my dogmatic slumber and gave my investigations in the field of speculative philosophy a quite new direction. I was far from following him in the conclusions to which he arrived by considering, not the whole of his problem, but a part, which by itself can give us no information. If we start from a well-founded, but undeveloped, thought which another has bequeathed to us, we may well hope by continued reflection to advance further than the acute man to whom we owe the first spark of light.

So I tried first whether Hume's objection could not be put into a general form, and soon found that the concept of the connection of cause and effect was by no means the only concept by which the understanding thinks the connection of things *a priori*, but rather that metaphysics consists altogether of such concepts. I sought to ascertain their number; and when I had satisfactorily succeeded in this by starting from a single principle, I proceeded to the deduction of these concepts, which I was now certain were not derived from experience, as Hume had tried, but sprang from the pure understanding. This deduction (which seemed impossible to my acute predecessor and had never even occured to any one else, though no one had hesitated to use the concepts without investigating the basis of their objective validity) was the most difficult task ever undertaken in the service of metaphysics; and the worst was that metaphysics, such as it then existed, could not assist me in the least because this deduction alone can render metaphysics possible. But as soon as I had succeeded in solving Hume's problem, not merely in a particular case, but with respect to the whole faculty of pure reason, I could proceed safely, though slowly, to determine the whole sphere of pure reason completely and from universal principles, in its boundaries as well as in its contents. This was required for metaphysics in order to construct its system according to a sure plan.

But I fear that the working out of Hume's problem in its widest extent (namely, my *Critique of Pure Reason*) will fare as the problem itself fared when first proposed. It will be misjudged because it is misunderstood, and misunderstood because men choose to skim through the book and not to think through it—a disagreeable task, because the work is dry, obscure, opposed to all ordinary notions, and moreover long-winded. Now I confess that I did not expect to hear from philosophers complaints of want of popularity, entertainment, and facility when the existence of a highly prized and indispensable cognition is at stake, which cannot be established otherwise than by the strictest rules of scholarly precision. Popularity may follow, but is inadmissible at the beginning. Yet as regards a certain obscurity, arising partly from the diffuseness of the plan, owing to which the principal points of the investigation are easily lost sight of, the complaint is just, and I intend to remove it by the present *Prolegomena*.

The first-mentioned work, which discusses the pure faculty of reason in its whole extent and bounds, will remain the foundation, to which the *Prolegomena*, as a preliminary exercise, refer; for that critique must exist as a science, systematic and complete as to its smallest parts, before we can think of letting metaphysics appear on the scene, or even have the most distant hope of so doing.

We have been long accustomed to seeing antiquated knowledge produced as new by taking it out of its former context, and fitting it into a systematic dress of any fancy pattern under new titles. Most readers will set out by expecting nothing else from the *Critique;* but these *Prolegomena* may persuade him that it is a perfectly new science, of which no one has ever even thought, the very idea of which was unknown, and for which nothing hitherto accomplished can be of the smallest use, except it be the suggestion of Hume's doubts. Yet even he did not suspect such a formal science, but ran his ship ashore, for safety's sake, landing on scepticism, there to let it lie and rot; whereas my object is rather to give it a pilot who, by means of safe navigational principles drawn from a knowledge of the globe and provided with a complete chart and compass, may steer the ship safely whither he listeth.

If in a new science that is wholly isolated and unique in its kind we started with the prejudice that we can judge of things by means of would-be knowledge previously acquired, even though this is precisely what has first to be called in question; then we should only fancy we saw everywhere what we had already known, because the expressions have a similar sound. Yet everything would appear utterly metamorphosed, senseless, and unintelligible, because we should have as a foundation our own thoughts, made by long habit a second nature, instead of the author's. However, the longwindedness of the work, so far as it depends on the science itself and not on the exposition, its consequent unavoidable dryness, and its scholastic precision are qualities which can only benefit the science, though they may discredit the book.

Few writers are gifted with the subtlety and, at the same time, with the grace of David Hume, or with the depth, as well as the elegance of, Moses Mendelssohn. Yet I flatter myself that I might have made my own exposition popular, if my object had been merely to sketch out a plan and leave its completion to others, instead of having my heart in the welfare of the science to which I had devoted myself so long; in truth, it required no little constancy, and even self-denial, to postpone the sweets of an immediate success to the prospect of a slower, but more lasting, reputation.

Making plans is often the occupation of an opulent and boastful mind, which thus obtains the reputation of a creative genius by demanding what it cannot itself supply, by censuring what it cannot improve, and by proposing what it knows not where to find. And yet something more should belong to a sound plan of a general critique of pure reason than mere conjectures, if this plan is to be other than the usual declamations of pious aspirations. But pure reason is a sphere so separate and self-contained that we cannot touch a part without affecting all the rest. We can therefore do nothing without first determining the position of each part and its relation to the rest. For inasmuch as our judgment cannot be corrected by anything outside of pure reason, so the validity and use of every part depends upon the relation in which it stands to all the rest within the domain of reason, just as in the structure of an organized body the end of each member can only be deduced from the full conception of the whole. It may, then, be said of such a critique that it is never trustworthy except it be perfectly complete, down to the smallest elements of pure reason. In the sphere of this faculty you can determine either everything or nothing.

But although a mere sketch preceding the *Critique of Pure Reason* would be unintelligible, unreliable, and useless, it is all the more useful as a sequel which enables us to grasp the whole, to examine in detail the chief points of importance in the science, and to improve in many respects our exposition, as compared with the first execution of the work.

That work being completed, I offer here such a plan which is sketched out after an analytical method, while the *Critique* itself had to be executed in the synthetical style, in order that the science may present all its articulations, as the structure of a peculiar cognitive faculty, in their natural combination. But should any reader find this plan, which I publish as the *Prolegomena to Any Future Metaphysics*, still obscure, let him consider that not every one is bound to study metaphysics, that many minds will succeed very well in the exact and even in deep sciences more closely allied to intuition while they cannot succeed in investigations dealing exclusively with abstract concepts. In such cases men should apply their talents to other subjects. But he who undertakes to judge or, still more, to construct a system of metaphysics must satisfy the demands here made, either by adopting my solution or by thoroughly refuting it and substituting another. To evade it is impossible. In conclusion, let it be remembered that this much-abused obscurity (frequently serving as a mere pretext under which people hide their own indolence or dullness) has its uses, since all who in other sciences observe a judicious silence speak authoritatively in metaphysics and make bold decisions, because their ignorance is not here contrasted with the knowledge of others. Yet it does contrast with sound critical principles, which we may therefore commend in the words of Virgil:

Ignavum, fucos, pecus a praesepibus arcent.[3]

PROLEGOMENA

PREAMBLE ON THE PECULIARITIES OF ALL METAPHYSICAL COGNITION

§ 1. Of the Sources of Metaphysics

If it becomes desirable to present any cognition as science, it will be necessary first to determine exactly its differentia, which no other science has in common with it and which constitutes its peculiarity; otherwise the boundaries of all sciences become confused, and none of them can be treated thoroughly according to its nature.

The peculiar features of a science may consist of a simple difference of object, or of the sources of cognition, or of the kind of cognition, or perhaps of all three conjointly. On these features, therefore, depends the idea of a possible science and its territory.

First, as concerns the sources of metaphysical cognition, its very concept implies that they cannot be empirical. Its principles (including not only its basic propositions but also its basic concepts) must never be derived from experience. It must not

3. ["They keep out of the hives the drones, an indolent bunch."] *Georgics*, IV, 168.

be physical but metaphysical knowledge, i.e., knowledge lying beyond experience. It can therefore have for its basis neither external experience, which is the source of physics proper, nor internal, which is the basis of empirical psychology. It is therefore *a priori* cognition, coming from pure understanding and pure reason.

But so far metaphysics would not be distinguishable from pure mathematics; it must therefore be called pure philosophical cognition; and for the meaning of this term I refer to the *Critique of Pure Reason* ("Methodology", Chap. I, Sec. 1), where the distinction between these two employments of reason is sufficiently explained. So much for the sources of metaphysical cognition.

§ 2. Concerning the Kind of Cognition Which Can Alone Be Called Metaphysical

a. Of the Distinction between Analytic and Synthetic Judgments in General. — The peculiarity of its sources demands that metaphysical cognition must consist of nothing but *a priori* judgments. But whatever be their origin or their logical form, there is a distinction in judgments, as to their content, according to which they are either merely *explicative,* adding nothing to the content of the cognition, or *ampliative,* increasing the given cognition: the former may be called *analytic,* the latter *synthetic,* judgments.

Analytic judgments express nothing in the predicate but what has been already actually thought in the concept of the subject, though not so clearly and with the same consciousness. If I say: "All bodies are extended," I have not amplified in the least my concept of body, but have only analysed it, as extension was really thought to belong to that concept before the judgment was made, though it was not expressed; this judgment is therefore analytic. On the other hand, this judgment, "All bodies have weight," contains in its predicate something not actually thought in the universal concept of body; it amplifies my knowledge by adding something to my concept, and must therefore be called synthetic.

b. The Common Principle of all Analytic Judgments is that of Contradiction. — All analytic judgments depend wholly on the principle of contradiction, and are in their nature *a priori* cognitions, whether the concepts that supply them with matter be empirical or not. For the predicate of an affirmative analytic judgment is already thought in the concept of the subject, of which it cannot be denied without contradiction. In the same way its opposite is necessarily denied of the subject in an analytic, but negative, judgment, by the same principle of contradiction. Such is the case of the judgments: "All bodies are extended," and "No bodies are unextended (i.e., simple)."

For this very reason all analytic judgments are *a priori* even when the concepts are empirical, as, for example, "Gold is a yellow metal"; for to know this I require no experience beyond my concept of gold, which contained the thought that this body is yellow and metal. It is, in fact, this thought that constituted my concept; and I need only analyze it, without looking beyond it elsewhere.

c. Synthetic Judgments Require a Different Principle from that of Contradiction. — There are synthetic *a posteriori* judgments of empirical origin; but there are also others which are certain *a priori,* and which spring from pure understanding and reason. Yet they both agree in this, that they cannot possibly spring from the principle of analysis, namely, the principle of contradiction, alone, but require another quite different principle. But whatever principle they may be deduced from, they must be subject to the principle of contradiction, which must never be violated, even though everything cannot be deduced from it. I shall first classify synthetic judgments.

1. *Judgments of Experience* are always synthetic. For it would be absurd to base an analytic judgment on experience, as our concept suffices for the purpose without requiring any testimony from experience. That a body is extended is a judgment which holds *a priori*, and is not a judgment of experience. For before appealing to experience, we already have all the conditions for the judgment in the concept, from which we have then but to elicit the predicate according to the principle of contradiction, and thereby to become conscious of the necessity of the judgment, which experience could not at all teach us.

2. *Mathematical Judgments* are all synthetic. This fact seems hitherto to have altogether escaped the observation of those who have analysed human reason; it even seems directly opposed to all their conjectures, though it is incontestably certain and most important in its consequences. For as it was found that the conclusions of mathematicians all proceed according to the principle of contradiction (as is demanded by all apodeictic certainty), men persuaded themselves that the fundamental propositions were known from the principle of contradiction. This was a great mistake, for a synthetic proposition can indeed be comprehended according to the principle of contradiction, but only by presupposing another synthetic proposition from which it follows, but never in and by itself.

First of all, we must observe that properly mathematical propositions are always judgments *a priori*, and not empirical, because they carry with them necessity, which cannot be obtained from experience. But if this be not conceded to me, very well; I shall confine my assertion to *pure mathematics*, the very concept of which implies that it contains pure *a priori* and not empirical cognition.

It might at first be thought that the proposition $7 + 5 = 12$ is a mere analytic judgment, following from the concept of the sum of seven and five, according to the principle of contradiction. But on closer examination it appears that the concept of the sum of $7 + 5$ contains merely their union in a single number, without its being at all thought what the particular number is that unites them. The concept of twelve is by no means thought by merely thinking of the combination of seven and five; and, analyze this possible sum as we may, we shall not discover twelve in the concept. We must go beyond these concepts by calling to our aid some intuition corresponding to one of them, i.e., either our five fingers or five points (as Segner[4] has it in his *Arithmetic*); and we must add successively the units of the five given in the intuition to the concept of seven. Hence our concept is really amplified by the proposition $7 + 5 = 12$, and we add to the first concept a second one not thought in it. Arithmetical judgments are therefore synthetic, and the more plainly according as we take larger numbers; for in such cases it is clear that, however closely we analyze our concepts without calling intuition to our aid, we can never find the sum by such mere analysis.

All principles of geometry are no less analytic. That a straight line is the shortest path between two points is a synthetic proposition. For my concept of straight contains nothing of quantity, but only a quality. The concept of the shortest is therefore altogether additional and cannot be obtained by any analysis of the concept of the

4. [J. A. Segner: *Elementa Arithmeticae et Geometriae*, Göttingen, 1739.]

straight line. Here, too, intuition must come to aid us. It alone makes the synthesis possible.

(Some other principles, assumed by geometers, are indeed actually analytic and depend on the principle of contradiction; but they only serve, as identical propositions, as a method of concatenation, and not as principles, e.g., $a = a$, the whole is equal to itself, or $a + b > a$, the whole is greater than its part. And yet even these, though they are recognised as valid from mere concepts, are only admitted in mathematics because they can be presented in some intuition.)

What actually makes us believe that the predicate of such apodeictic judgments is already contained in our concept, and that the judgment is therefore analytic, is the duplicity of the expression. We must think a certain predicate as joined to a given concept, and this necessity inheres in the concepts themselves. But the question is not what we must join in thought *to* the given concept, but what we actually think together with and in it, though obscurely; and so it is manifest that the predicate belongs to this concept necessarily indeed, yet not directly but indirectly by means of a necessarily present intuition.[5]

The essential and distinguishing feature of pure mathematical cognition among all other *a priori* cognitions is that it cannot at all proceed from concepts, but only by means of the construction of concepts (see *Critique of Pure Reason*, "Methodology", Chap. I, Sect. 1). As therefore in its judgments it must proceed beyond the concept to that which its corresponding intuition contains, these judgments neither can, nor ought to arise analytically, by dissecting the concept, but are all synthetic.

I cannot refrain from pointing out the disadvantage resulting to philosophy from the neglect of this easy and apparently insignificant observation. Hume, feeling the call (which is worthy of a philosopher) to cast his eye over the whole field of *a priori* cognitions in which human understanding claims such mighty possessions, heedlessly severed from it a whole, and indeed its most valuable, province, viz., pure mathematics. For he imagined that its nature, or, so to speak, the constitution of this province, depended on totally different principles, namely, on the principle of contradiction alone, and although he did not divide judgments in this manner formally and universally and did not use the same terminology as I have done here, what he said was equivalent to this: that pure mathematics contains only analytic, but metaphysics synthetic, *a priori* judgments. In this, however, he was greatly mistaken, and the mistake had a decidedly injurious effect upon his whole conception. But for this, he would have extended his question concerning the origin of our synthetic judgments far beyond the metaphysical concept of causality and included in it the possibility of mathematics *a priori* also; for this latter he must have assumed to be equally synthetic. And then he could not have based his metaphysical judgments on mere experience without subjecting the axioms of mathematics equally to experience, a thing which he was far too acute to do. The good company into which metaphysics would thus have been brought would have saved it from the danger of a contemptuous ill-treatment; for the thrust intended for it must have reached mathematics, which was not and could not have been Hume's intention. Thus that acute man would have been led into considerations which must needs be similar to those that now occupy us, but which would have gained inestimably from his inimitably elegant style.

5. [In the next several pages the order of the German text as it appears in the *Philosophische Bibliothek* Edition of Kant's *Works* is followed rather than the *Akademie* Edition.]

3. *Metaphysical Judgments*, properly so-called, are all synthetic. We must distinguish judgments belonging to metaphysics from metaphysical judgments properly so-called. Many of the former are analytic, but they only afford the means to metaphysical judgments, which are the whole aim of the science and which are always synthetic. For if there be concepts belonging to metaphysics (as, for example, that of substance), the judgments springing from simple analysis of them also belong to metaphysics, as, for example, substance is that which only exists as subject, etc. By means of several such analytic judgments we seek to arrive at the definition of a concept. But as the analysis of a pure concept of the understanding (such as metaphysics contains) does not proceed in any different manner from the dissection of any other, even empirical, concepts, not belonging to metaphysics (such as, air is an elastic fluid, the elasticity of which is not destroyed by any known degree of cold), it follows that the concept indeed, but not the analytic judgment, is properly metaphysical. This science has something special and peculiar to itself in the production of its *a priori* cognitions, which must therefore be distinguished from the features it has in common with other rational knowledge. Thus the judgment that all the substance in things is permanent is a synthetic and properly metaphysical judgment.

If the *a priori* concepts which constitute the materials and building blocks of metaphysics have first been collected according to fixed principles, then their analysis will be of great value. It might be taught as a particular part (as a *philosophia definitiva*), containing nothing but analytic judgments pertaining to metaphysics, and could be treated separately from the synthetic which constitute metaphysics proper. For indeed these analyses are not elsewhere of much value except in metaphysics, i.e., as regards the synthetic judgments which are to be generated out of these previously analyzed concepts.

The conclusion drawn in this section then is that metaphysics is properly concerned with synthetic propositions *a priori*, and these alone constitute its end, for which it indeed requires various dissections of its concepts, viz., analytic judgments, but wherein the procedure is not different from that in every other kind of cognition, in which we merely seek to render our concepts distinct by analysis. But the generation of *a priori* cognition by intuition as well as by concepts, in fine, of synthetic propositions *a priori* in philosophical cognition, constitutes the essential content of metaphysics.

§ 3. A Remark on the General Division of Judgments into Analytic and Synthetic

This division is indispensable as concerns the critique of human understanding and therefore deserves to be classical in it, though otherwise it is of little use. But this is the reason why dogmatic philosophers, who always seek the sources of metaphysical judgments in metaphysics itself and not outside of it in the pure laws of reason generally, altogether neglected this apparently obvious distinction. Thus the celebrated Wolff and his acute follower Baumgarten came to seek the proof of the principle of sufficient reason, which is clearly synthetic, in the principle of contradiction. In Locke's *Essay*, however, I find an indication of my division. For in the fourth book (chap. iii., § 9, seq.), having discussed the various connections of representations in judgments, and their sources, one of which he makes "identity or contradiction" (analytic judgments) and another the coexistence of representations in a subject (synthetic judgments), he confesses (§ 10) that our (*a priori*) knowledge of the latter is very narrow and almost nothing. But in his remarks on this species of cognition, there is so little of what is definite and reduced to rules that we cannot wonder if no one, not even Hume, was led to make investigations concerning judgments of this kind. For such universal and yet determinate principles are not easily learned from other men who have only had them obscurely in their minds. One must hit on them first by one's own reflection; then one finds them elsewhere, where one could not possibly have found them at first because the authors themselves did not know that such an idea lay at the basis of their observations. Men who never think independently have nevertheless the acuteness to discover everything, after it has been once shown them, in what was said long since, though no one could ever see it there before.

§ 4. The General Question of the Prolegomena: Is Metaphysics at All Possible?

Were a metaphysics, which could maintain its place as a science, really in existence, could we say: here is metaphysics, learn it, and it will convince you irresistibly and irrevocably of its truth? This question would be useless, and there would only remain that other question (which would rather be a test of our acuteness than a proof of the existence of the thing itself): how is the science possible, and how does reason come to attain it? But human reason has not been so fortunate in this case. There is no single book to which you can point, as you do to Euclid, and say: this is metaphysics; here you may find the noblest aim of this science, namely, the knowledge of a highest being, and of a future existence, proved from principles of pure reason. We can be shown indeed many judgments, apodeictically certain, and never questioned; but these are all analytic, and rather concern the materials and the scaffolding for metaphysics than the extension of knowledge, which is our proper object in studying it (§ 2). Even supposing you point to synthetic judgments (such as the principles of sufficient reason, which you have never proved, as you ought to, from pure reason *a priori*, though we gladly concede its truth), you lapse, when you try to use them for your principal purpose, into such inadmissible and uncertain assertions that in all ages one metaphysics has contradicted another, either in its assertions or their proofs, and thus has itself destroyed its own claim to lasting assent. Nay, the very attempts to set up such a science are the main cause of the early appearance of scepticism, a way of thinking in which reason treats itself with such violence that it could never have arisen save from complete despair of ever satisfying our most important aspirations. For long before men began to inquire into nature methodically, they consulted abstract reason, which had to some extent been exercised by means of ordinary experience; for reason is ever present, while laws of nature must usually be discovered with labor. So metaphysics floated to the surface, like foam, which dissolved the moment it was scooped off. But immediately there appeared a new supply on the surface, to be ever eagerly gathered up by some; while others, instead of seeking in the depths the cause of the phenomenon, thought they showed their wisdom by ridiculing the idle labor of their neighbors.

Weary therefore of dogmatism, which teaches us nothing, and of scepticism, which does not even promise us anything, not even to rest in permitted ignorance; disquieted by the importance of knowledge so much needed; and, lastly, rendered suspicious by long experience of all knowledge which we believe we possess or which offers itself under the title of pure reason—we have left but one critical question upon whose answer depends our future conduct, viz., *is metaphysics at all possi-*

ble? But this question must be answered not by sceptical objections to the asseverations of some actual system of metaphysics (for we do not as yet admit such a thing to exist), but from the conception, as yet only problematic, of a science of this sort.

In the *Critique of Pure Reason* I have treated this question synthetically, by making inquiries into pure reason itself and endeavoring in this source to determine the elements as well as the laws of its pure use according to principles. The task is difficult and requires a resolute reader to penetrate by degrees into a system based on no data except reason itself, and which therefore seeks, without resting upon any fact, to unfold knowledge from its original germs. These *Prolegomena,* however, are designed for preparatory exercises; they are intended to point out what must be done in order to make a science actual if it is possible, rather than to expound it. They must therefore rest upon something already known as trustworthy, from which we can set out with confidence and ascend to sources as yet unknown, the discovery of which will not only explain to us what we knew but exhibit a sphere of many cognitions which all spring from the same sources. The method of such *Prolegomena,* especially of those designed as a preparation for future metaphysics, is consequently analytical.

But it happens, fortunately, that though we cannot assume metaphysics to be an actual science, we can say with confidence that certain pure *a priori* synthetic cognitions are actual and given, namely, pure mathematics and pure physics; for both contain propositions which are everywhere recognized as apodeictically certain, partly by mere reason, partly by universal agreement from experience, and yet as independent of experience. We have therefore some, at least uncontested, synthetic knowledge *a priori,* and need not ask *whether* it be possible (for it is actual) but *how* it is possible, in order that we may deduce from the principle which makes the given knowledge possible the possibility of all the rest.

§ 5. The General Problem: How is Cognition from Pure Reason Possible?

We have above learned the significant distinction between analytic and synthetic judgments. The possibility of analytic propositions was easily comprehended, being entirely founded on the principle of contradiction. The possibility of synthetic *a posteriori* judgments, of those which are gathered from experience, also requires no special explanation; for experience is nothing but a continual joining together (synthesis) of perceptions. There remain therefore only synthetic propositions *a priori,* of which the possibility must be sought or investigated, because they must depend upon other principles than that of contradiction.

But here we need not first establish the possibility of such propositions so as to ask whether they are possible. For there are enough of them which indeed are of undoubted certainty, and as our present method is analytical, we shall start from the fact that such synthetic but purely rational cognition actually exists; but we must now inquire into the ground of this possibility and ask *how* such cognition is possible, in order that we may, from the principles of its possibility, be enabled to determine the conditions of its use, its sphere, and its limits. The proper problem upon which all depends, when expressed with scholastic precision, is therefore:

How are synthetic propositions a priori possible?

For the sake of popularity I have above expressed this problem somewhat differently, as an inquiry into purely rational cognition, which I could do for once without detriment to the desired insight, because, as we have only to do here with metaphysics and its sources, the reader will, I hope, after the foregoing remarks, keep in mind that when we speak of purely rational cognition we do not mean analytic but synthetic cognition.[6]

Metaphysics stands or falls with the solution of this problem; its very existence depends upon it. Let anyone make metaphysical assertions with ever so much plausibility, let him overwhelm us with conclusions; but if he has not first been able to answer this question satisfactorily, I have the right to say: this is all vain, baseless philosophy and false wisdom. You speak through pure reason and claim, as it were, to create cognitions *a priori* not only by dissecting given concepts, but also by asserting connections which do not rest upon the principle of contradiction, and which you believe you conceive quite independently of all experience; how do you arrive at this, and how will you justify such pretensions? An appeal to the consent of the common sense of mankind cannot be allowed, for that is a witness whose authority depends merely upon rumor. Says Horace:

Quodcunque ostendis mihi sic, incredulus odi.[7]

The answer to this question is as indispensable as it is difficult; and though the principal reason that it was not attempted long ago is that the possibility of the question never occurred to anybody, there is yet another reason, viz., that a satisfactory answer to this one question requires a much more persistent, profound, and painstaking reflection than the most diffuse work on metaphysics, which on its first appearance promised immortality to its author. And every intelligent reader, when he carefully reflects what this problem requires, must at first be struck with its difficulty, and would regard it as insoluble and even impossible did there not actually exist pure synthetic cognitions *a priori*. This actually happened to David Hume, though he did not conceive the question in its entire universality as is done here and as must be done, if the answer is to be decisive for all metaphysics. For how is it possible, says that acute man, that when a concept is given me I can go beyond it and connect with it another which is not contained in it, in such a manner as if the latter *necessarily* belonged to the former? Nothing but experience can furnish us with such connections (thus he concluded from the difficulty which he took to be an impossibility), and all that vaunted necessity or, what is the same thing, all cognition assumed to be *a priori* is nothing but a long habit of accepting something as true, and hence of mistaking subjective necessity for objective.

Should my reader complain of the difficulty and the trouble which I occasion him in the solution of this problem, he is at liberty to solve it himself in an easier way. Perhaps he will then feel under obligation to the person who has undertaken for

---

6. It is unavoidable that as knowledge advances certain expressions which have become classical after having been used since the infancy of science will be found inadequate and unsuitable, and a newer and more appropriate application of the terms will give rise to confusion. [This is the case with the term "analytic,"] The analytical method, insofar as it is opposed to the synthetical, is very different from an aggregate of analytic propositions. It signifies only that we start from what is sought, as if it were given, and ascend to the only conditions under which it is possible. In this method we often use nothing but synthetic propositions, as in mathematical analysis, and it were better to term it the regressive method, in contradistinction to the synthetic or progressive. A principal part of logic too is distinguished by the name of analytic, which here signifies the logic of truth in contrast to dialectic, without considering whether the cognitions belonging to it are analytic or synthetic.

7. ["Whatever is shown me thus, I do not believe and do hate."] *Epistle* II, 3, 188.

him a labor of so profound research and will rather be surprised at the facility with which, considering the nature of the subject, the solution has been attained. Yet it has cost years of work to solve the problem in its whole universality (using the term in the mathematical sense, viz., for that which is sufficient for all cases), and finally to exhibit it in the analytical form, as the reader will find it here.

All metaphysicians are therefore solemnly and legally suspended from their occupations till they shall have satisfactorily answered the question: *How are synthetic cognitions a priori possible?* For the answer contains the only credentials which they must show when they have anything to offer us in the name of pure reason. But if they do not possess these credentials, they can expect nothing else of reasonable people, who have been deceived so often, than to be dismissed without further ado.

If they, on the other hand, desire to carry on their business, not as a science, but as an art of wholesome persuasion suitable for the common sense of man, they cannot in fairness be prevented from pursuing this trade. They will then speak the modest language of a rational belief; they will grant that they are not allowed even to conjecture, far less to know, anything which lies beyond the bounds of all possible experience, but only to assume (not for speculative use, which they must abandon, but for practical use only) the existence of something that is possible and even indispensable for the guidance of the understanding and of the will in life. In this manner alone can they be called useful and wise men, and the more so as they renounce the title of metaphysicians. For the latter profess to be speculative philosophers; and since, when judgments *a priori* are under discussion, poor probabilities cannot be admitted (for what is declared to be known *a priori* is thereby announced as necessary), such men cannot be permitted to play with conjectures, but their assertions must be either science or else nothing at all.

It may be said that the entire transcendental philosophy, which necessarily precedes all metaphysics, is nothing but the complete solution of the problem here propounded, in systematic order and completeness, and that we have hitherto never had any transcendental philosophy. For what goes by its name is properly a part of metaphysics, whereas the former science has first to settle the possibility of the latter and must therefore precede all metaphysics. And it is not surprising that when a whole science, deprived of all help from other sciences and consequently in itself quite new, is required to answer a single question satisfactorily, we should find the answer troublesome and difficult, nay, even shrouded in obscurity.

As we now proceed to this solution according to the analytical method, in which we assume that such cognitions from pure reason actually exist, we can only appeal to two sciences of theoretical cognition (which alone is under consideration here), namely, pure mathematics and pure natural science. For these alone can exhibit to us objects in intuition and consequently (if there should occur in them a cognition *a priori*) can show the truth or conformity of the cognition to the object *in concreto*, that is, its actuality, from which we could proceed to the ground of its possibility by the analytical method. This facilitates our work greatly, for here universal considerations are not only applied to facts, but even start from them, while in a synthetic procedure they must strictly be derived *in abstracto* from concepts.

But in order to ascend from these actual and, at the same time, well-grounded pure cognitions *a priori* to a possible cognition of the kind that we are seeking, viz., to metaphysics as a science, we must comprehend that which occasions it, namely, the mere natural (though not above suspicion as to its truth) cognition *a priori* which lies at the foundation of that science, the elaboration of which without any critical investigation of its possibility is commonly called metaphysics. In a word, we must comprehend the natural conditions of such a science as a part of our inquiry, and thus the transcendental problem will be gradually answered by a division into four questions:

1. *How is pure mathematics possible?*
2. *How is pure natural science possible?*
3. *How is metaphysics in general possible?*
4. *How is metaphysics as a science possible?*

It may be seen that the solution of these problems, though chiefly designed to exhibit the essential content of the *Critique*, has yet something peculiar, which for itself alone deserves attention. This is the search for the sources of given sciences in reason itself, so that its faculty of knowing something *a priori* may by its own deeds be investigated and measured. By this procedure these sciences gain, if not with regard to their contents, yet as to their proper use; and while they throw light on the higher question concerning their common origin, they give, at the same time, an occasion for better explaining their own nature.

FIRST PART OF THE MAIN TRANSCENDENTAL QUESTION
HOW IS PURE MATHEMATICS POSSIBLE?

§ 6. Here is a great and established branch of knowledge, encompassing even now a wonderfully large domain and promising an unlimited extension in the future, and carrying with it thoroughly apodeictical certainty, i.e., absolute necessity, which therefore rests upon no empirical grounds. Consequently it is a pure product of reason, and moreover is thoroughly synthetic. [Here the question arises:] "How then is it possible for human reason to produce such cognition entirely *a priori?*" Does not this faculty [which produces mathematics], as it neither is nor can be based upon experience, presuppose some ground of cognition *a priori*, which lies deeply hidden but which might reveal itself by these its effects, if their first beginnings were but diligently ferreted out?

§ 7. But we find that all mathematical cognition has this peculiarity: it must first exhibit its concept in intuition, and do so *a priori*, in an intuition that is not empirical but pure. Without this mathematics cannot take a single step; hence its judgments are always *intuitive;* whereas philosophy must be satisfied with *discursive* judgments from mere concepts, and though it may illustrate its apodeictic doctrines through intuition, can never derive them from it. This observation on the nature of mathematics gives us a clue to the first and highest condition of its possibility, which is that some pure intuition must form its basis, in which all its concepts can be exhibited or constructed, *in concreto* and yet *a priori*.[8] If we can discover this pure intuition and its possibility, we may thence easily explain how synthetic propositions *a priori* are possible in pure mathematics, and consequently how this science itself is possible. For just as empirical intuition [viz., sense-perception] enables us without difficulty to enlarge the concept which we frame of an object of intuition by

8. [See *Critique of Pure Reason*, B 741.]

new predicates which intuition itself presents synthetically in experience, so pure intuition also does likewise, only with this difference: that in the latter case the synthetic judgment is *a priori* certain and apodeictic, in the former only *a posteriori* and empirically certain, because the *a posteriori* case contains only that which occurs in contingent empirical intuition, but the *a priori* case contains that which must necessarily be discovered in pure intuition. Here intuition, being an intuition *a priori*, is inseparably joined with the concept before all experience or particular perception.

§ 8. But with this step our perplexity seems rather to increase than to lessen. For the question now is, "How is it possible to intuit anything *a priori?*" An intuition is such a representation as would immediately depend upon the presence of the object. Hence it seems impossible to intuit anything *a priori* originally, because intuition would in that event have to take place without either a former or a present object to refer to, and hence could not be intuition. Concepts indeed are such that we can easily form some of them *a priori*, viz., such as contain nothing but the thought of an object in general; and we need not find ourselves in an immediate relation to the object. Take, for instance, the concepts of quantity, of cause, etc. But even these require, in order to be meaningful and significant, certain concrete use — that is, an application to some intuition by which an object of them is given us. But how can the intuition of the object precede the object itself?

§ 9. If our intuition had to be of such a nature as to represent things as they are in themselves, there would not be any intuition *a priori*, but intuition would be always empirical. For I can only know what is contained in the object in itself if it is present and given to me. It is indeed even then inconceivable how the intuition of a present thing should make me know this thing as it is in itself, as its properties cannot migrate into my faculty of representation. But even if this possibility be granted, an intuition of that sort would not take place *a priori*, that is, before the object were presented to me; for without this latter fact no ground of a relation between my representation and the object can be conceived, unless it rested on inspiration. Therefore in one way only can my intuition anticipate the actuality of the object, and be a cognition *a priori*, viz., *if my intuition contains nothing but the form of sensibility, which in me as subject precedes all the actual impressions through which I am affected by objects.* For that objects of sense can only be intuited according to this form of sensibility I can know *a priori*. Hence it follows that propositions which concern this form of sensuous intuition only are possible and valid for objects of the senses; as also, conversely, that intuitions which are possible *a priori* can never concern any other things than objects of our senses.

§ 10. Accordingly, it is only the form of sensuous intuition by which we can intuit things *a priori*, but by which we can know objects only as they *appear* to us (to our senses), not as they are in themselves; and this assumption is absolutely necessary if synthetic propositions *a priori* be granted as possible or if, in case they actually occur, their possibility is to be conceived and determined beforehand.

Now, the intuitions which pure mathematics lays at the foundation of all its cognitions and judgments which appear at once apodeictic and necessary are space and time. For mathematics must first present all its concepts in intuition, and pure mathematics in pure intuition, i.e., it must construct them. If it proceeded in any other way, it would be impossible to make a single step; for mathematics proceeds, not analytically by dissection of concepts, but synthetically, and if pure intuition be wanting there is nothing in which the matter for synthetic judgments *a priori* can be given. Geometry is based upon the pure intuition of space. Arithmetic attains its concepts of numbers by the successive addition of units in time, and pure mechanics especially can attain its concepts of motion only by employing the representation of time. Both representations, however, are merely intuitions; for if we omit from the empirical intuitions of bodies and their alterations (motion) everything empirical, i.e., belonging to sensation, space and time still remain, and are therefore pure intuitions that lie *a priori* at the basis of the empirical. Hence they can never be omitted; but at the same time, by their being pure intuitions *a priori*, they prove that they are mere forms of our sensibility, which must precede all empirical intuition, i.e., perception of actual objects, and in conformity with which objects can be known *a priori* but only as they appear to us.

§ 11. The problem of the present section is therefore solved. Pure mathematics, as synthetic cognition *a priori*, is possible only by referring to no other objects than those of the senses. At the basis of their empirical intuition lies a pure intuition (of space and time), which is *a priori*. This is possible because the latter intuition is nothing but the mere form of sensibility, which precedes the actual appearance of the objects, since in fact it makes them possible. Yet this faculty of intuiting *a priori* concerns not the matter of the appearance (that is, the sensation in it, for this constitutes what is empirical), but its form, viz., space and time. Should any man venture to doubt that both are not determinations of things in themselves but are merely determinations of their relation to sensibility, I should be glad to know how it can be possible to know *a priori* how their intuition will be characterized before we have any acquaintance with them and before they are presented to us. Such, however, is the case with space and time. But this is quite conceivable as soon as both count for nothing more than formal conditions of our sensibility, while the objects count merely as appearance; for then the form of the appearance, i.e., pure intuition, can by all means be represented as proceeding from ourselves, that is, *a priori*.

§ 12. In order to add something by way of illustration and confirmation, we need only watch the ordinary and unavoidably necessary procedure of geometers. All proofs of the complete congruence of two given figures (where the one can in every respect be substituted for the other) ultimately come down to the fact that they may be made to coincide. This is evidently nothing but a synthetic proposition resting upon immediate intuition; and this intuition must be pure and given *a priori*, else the proposition could not hold as apodeictically certain but would have empirical certainty only. In that case it could only be said that it is always found to be so and holds good only as far as our perception reaches. That complete space (which is not itself the boundary of another space) has three dimensions and that space in general cannot have more is based on the proposition that not more than three lines can intersect at right angles in one point. This proposition cannot at all be shown from concepts, but rests immediately on intuition, and indeed on pure intuition *a priori* because it is apodeictically certain. That we can require a line to be drawn to infinity (*in indefinitum*) or that a series of changes (for example, spaces traversed by motion) shall be infinitely continued presupposes a representation of space and time, which can only attach to intuition, namely, so far as it in itself is bounded by nothing, for from concepts it could never be inferred. Consequently, the basis of mathematics actually is pure intuitions, which make its synthetic and apodeictically valid propositions possible. Hence our transcendental deduction of the concepts of space and of time explains at the same time the possibility of pure mathematics. Without some such deduction its truth may be granted, but its existence could by no means be understood, and we must assume "that everything which can be given to our senses (to the external senses in space and to the internal sense in time) is intuited by us as it appears to us, not as it is in itself."

§ 13. Those who cannot yet rid themselves of the notion that space and time are actual qualities inherent in things in themselves may exercise their acumen on the following paradox. When they have in vain attempted its solution and are free from prejudices at least for a few moments, they will suspect that the reduction of space and time to mere forms of our sensuous intuition may perhaps be well founded.

If two things are quite equal in all respects as much as can be ascertained by all means possible, quantitatively and qualitatively, it must follow that the one can in all cases and under all circumstances replace the other, and this substitution would not occasion the least recognizable difference. This in fact is true of plane figures in geometry; but some spherical figures exhibit, notwithstanding a complete internal agreement, such a difference in their external relation that the one figure cannot possibly be put in the place of the other. For instance, two spherical triangles on opposite hemispheres which have an arc of the equator as their common base may be quite equal, both as regards sides and angles, so that nothing is to be found in either, if it be described for itself alone and completed, that would not equally be applicable to both; and yet the one cannot be put in the place of the other (on the opposite hemisphere). Here, then, is an internal difference between the two triangles; this difference our understanding cannot show to be internal but only manifests itself by external relations in space. But I shall adduce examples, taken from common life, that are more obvious still.

What can be more similar in every respect and in every part more alike to my hand and to my ear than their images in a mirror? And yet I cannot put such a hand as is seen in the mirror in the place of its original; for if this is a right hand, that in the mirror is a left one, and the image or reflection of the right ear is a left one, which never can serve as a substitute for the other. There are in this case no internal differences which our understanding could determine by thinking alone. Yet the differences are internal as the senses teach, for, notwithstanding their complete equality and similarity, the left hand cannot be enclosed in the same bounds as the right one (they are not congruent); the glove of one hand cannot be used for the other. What is the solution? These objects are not representations of things as they are in themselves, and as some pure understanding would cognize them, but sensuous intuitions, that is, appearances, whose possibility rests upon the relation of certain things unknown in themselves to something else, viz., to our sensibility. Space is the form of the external intuition of this sensibility, and the internal determination of any space is possible only by the determination of its external relation to the whole of space, of which it is a part (in other words, by its relation to external sense). That is to say, the part is possible only through the whole, which is never the case with things in themselves as objects of the mere understanding, but can well be the case with mere appearances. Hence the difference between similar and equal things which are not congruent (for instance, helices winding in opposite ways), cannot be made intelligible by any concept, but only by the relation to the right and the left hands, which immediately refers to intuition.

REMARK I

Pure mathematics, and especially pure geometry, can only have objective reality on condition that it refers merely to objects of sense. But in regard to the latter the principle holds good that our sense representation is not a representation of things in themselves, but of the way in which they appear to us. Hence it follows that the propositions of geometry are not determinations of a mere creation of our poetic imagination, which could therefore not be referred with assurance to actual objects; but rather that they are necessarily valid of space, and consequently of all that may be found in space, because space is nothing but the form of all external appearances, and it is this form alone in which objects of sense can be given to us. Sensibility, the form of which is the basis of geometry, is that upon which the possibility of external appearance depends. Therefore these appearances can never contain anything but what geometry prescribes to them. It would be quite otherwise if the senses were so constituted as to represent objects as they are in themselves. For then it would not by any means follow from the representation of space, which with all its properties serves the geometer as an *a priori* foundation, that this foundation together with what is inferred from it must be so in nature. The space of the geometer would be considered a mere fiction, and it would not be credited with objective validity because we cannot see how things must of necessity agree with an image of them which we make spontaneously and previous to our acquaintance with them. But if this image, or rather this formal intuition, is the essential property of our sensibility by means of which alone objects are given to us, and if this sensibility represents not things in themselves but their appearances, then we shall easily comprehend, and at the same time indisputably prove, that all external objects of our world of sense must necessarily coincide in the most rigorous way with the propositions of geometry. This is so because sensibility by means of its form of external intuition (space), with which the geometer is concerned, makes those objects possible as mere appearances. It will always remain a remarkable phenomenon in the history of philosophy that there was a time when even mathematicians who at the same time were philosophers began to doubt, not of the correctness of their geometrical propositions so far as they merely concerned space, but of their objective validity and the applicability to nature of this concept itself and all its geometrical determinations. They showed much concern whether a line in nature might not consist of physical points, and consequently that true space in the object might consist of simple parts, while the space which the geometer has in his mind cannot be such. They did not recognise that this thought space renders possible the physical space, i.e., the extension of matter itself, and that this pure space is not at all a quality of things in themselves but a form of our sensuous faculty of representation, and that furthermore all objects in space are mere appearances, i.e., not things in themselves but representations of our sensuous intuition. But such is the case, for the space of the geometer is exactly the form of sensuous intuition which we find *a priori* in us, and contains the ground of the possibility of all external appearances (according to their form); and the latter must necessarily and most precisely agree with the propositions of the geometer, which he draws not from any fictitious concept but from the subjective basis of all external appearances, viz., sensibility itself. In this and no other way can geometry be made secure as to the undoubted objective reality of its propositions against all the chicaneries of a shallow metaphysics, however strange this may seem to a metaphysics that does not go back to the sources of its concepts.

REMARK II

Whatever is given us as object must be given us in intuition. All our intuition, however, takes place only by means of the senses; the understanding intuits nothing but only reflects. And as we have just shown that the senses never and in no manner enable us to know things in themselves, but only their appearances, which are mere representations of the sensibility, we conclude that "all bodies, together with the space in which they are, must be considered nothing but mere representations in us, and exist nowhere but in our thoughts." Now is not this manifest idealism?

Idealism consists in the assertion that there are none but thinking beings; all other things which we believe are perceived in intuition are nothing but representations in the thinking beings, to which no object external to them in fact corresponds. On the contrary, I say that things as objects of our senses existing outside us are given, but we know nothing of what they may be in themselves, knowing only their appearances, i.e., the representations which they cause in us by affecting our senses. Consequently, I grant by all means that there are bodies without us, that is, things which, though quite unknown to us as to what they are in themselves, we yet know by the representations which their influence on our sensibility procures us, and which we call bodies. This word merely means the appearance of the thing, which is unknown to us but is not therefore less real. Can this be termed idealism? It is the very contrary.

Long before Locke's time, but assuredly since him, it has been generally assumed and granted without detriment to the actual existence of external things that many of their predicates may be said to belong, not to the things in themselves, but to their appearances, and to have no proper existence outside our representation. Heat, color, and taste, for instance, are of this kind. Now, if I go further and, for weighty reasons, rank as mere appearances also the remaining qualities of bodies, which are called primary—such as extension, place, and, in general, space, with all that which belongs to it (impenetrability or materiality, shape, etc.)—no one in the least can adduce the reason of its being inadmissible. As little as the man who admits colors not to be properties of the object in itself but only to be modifications of the sense of sight should on that account be called an idealist, so little can my doctrine be named idealistic merely because I find that more, nay, *all the properties which constitute the intuition of a body belong merely to its appearance.* The existence of the thing that appears is thereby not destroyed, as in genuine idealism, but it is only shown that we cannot possibly know it by the senses as it is in itself.

I should be glad to know what my assertions must be in order to avoid all idealism. Undoubtedly, I should say that the representation of space is not only perfectly conformable to the relation which our sensibility has to objects—that I have said— but that it is completely like the object—an assertion in which I can find as little meaning as if I said that the sensation of red has a similarity to the property of cinnabar which excites this sensation in me.

REMARK III

Hence we may at once dismiss an easily foreseen but futile objection, "that by our admitting the ideality of space and of time the whole sensible world would be turned into mere illusion." After all philosophical insight into the nature of sensuous cognition was spoiled by making the sensibility merely a confused mode of representation, according to which we still know things as they are, but without being able to reduce everything in this our representation to a clear consciousness; whereas on the contrary proof is offered by us that sensibility consists, not in this logical distinction of clearness and obscurity, but in the genetic one of the origin of cognition itself. For sensuous perception represents things not at all as they are, but only the mode in which they affect our senses; and consequently by sensuous perception appearances only, and not things themselves, are given to the understanding for reflection. After this necessary correction, an objection rises from an unpardonable and almost intentional misconception, as if my doctrine turned all the things of the world of sense into mere illusion.

When an appearance is given us, we are still quite free as to how we should judge the matter. The appearance depends upon the senses, but the judgment upon the understanding; and the only question is whether in the determination of the object there is truth or not. But the difference between truth and dreaming is not ascertained by the nature of the representations which are referred to objects (for they are the same in both cases), but by their connection according to those rules which determine the coherence of the representations in the concept of an object, and by ascertaining whether they can subsist together in experience or not. And it is not the fault of the appearances if our cognition takes illusion for truth, i.e., if the intuition, by which an object is given us, is taken for the concept of the thing or even of its existence, which the understanding only can think. The senses represent to us the paths of the planets as now progressive, now retrogressive; and herein is neither falsehood nor truth, because as long as we hold this to be nothing but appearance we do not judge of the objective nature of their motion. But as a false judgment may easily arise when the understanding is not on its guard against this subjective mode of representation being considered objective, we say they appear to move backward; it is not the senses however which must be charged with the illusion, but the understanding, whose province alone it is to make an objective judgment on appearances.

Thus, even if we did not at all reflect on the origin of our representations, whenever we connect our intuitions of sense (whatever they may contain) in space and in time, according to the rules of the coherence of all cognition in experience, illusion or truth will arise according as we are negligent or careful. It is merely a question of the use of sensuous representations in the understanding, and not of their origin. In the same way, if I consider all the representations of the senses, together with their form, space and time, to be nothing but appearances, and space and time to be a mere form of the sensibility, which is not to be met with in objects out of it, and if I make use of these representations in reference to possible experience only, there is nothing in my regarding them as appearances that can lead astray or cause illusion. For all that, they can correctly cohere according to rules of truth in experience. Thus all the propositions of geometry hold good of space as well as of all the objects of the senses, consequently, of all possible experience, whether I consider space as a mere form of the sensibility or as something adhering to the things themselves. In the former case, however, I comprehend how I can know *a priori* these propositions concerning all the objects of external intuition. Otherwise, everything else as regards all possible experience remains just as if I had not departed from the ordinary view.

But if I venture to go beyond all possible experience with my concepts of space and time, which I cannot refrain from doing if I proclaim them qualities inherent in things in themselves (for what should prevent me from letting them hold good of the same things, even though my senses might be different, and unsuited to them?), then a grave error may arise due to illusion, in which I proclaim to be universally valid what is merely a subjective condition of the intuition of things and certain only for all objects of sense, viz., for all possible experience; I would refer this condition to things in themselves, and not limit it to the conditions of experience.

My doctrine of the ideality of space and of time, therefore, far from reducing the whole sensible world to mere illusion, is the only means of securing the application of one of the most important cognitions (that which mathematics propounds *a priori*) to actual objects and of preventing its being regarded as mere illusion. For without this observation it would be quite impossible to make out whether the intuitions of space and time, which we borrow from no experience and which yet lie in our representation *a priori*, are not mere phantasms of our brain to which no objects correspond, at least not adequately; and, consequently, whether we have been able to show geometry's unquestionable validity with regard to all the objects of the sensible world just because they are mere appearances.

Secondly, though these my principles make appearances of the representations of the senses, they are so far from turning the truth of experience into mere illusion that they are rather the only means of preventing the transcendental illusion, by which metaphysics has been deceived hitherto and misled into childish efforts of catching at bubbles, because appearances, which are mere representations, were taken for things in themselves. Here originated the remarkable event of the antinomy of reason, which I shall mention later on and which is cancelled by the single observation that appearance, as long as it is employed in experience, produces truth, but the moment it transgresses the bounds of experience, and consequently becomes transcendent, produces nothing but illusion.

Inasmuch, therefore, as I leave to things as we obtain them by the senses their actuality and only limit our sensuous intuition of these things to this—that it represents in no respect, not even in the pure intuitions of space and of time, anything more than mere appearance of those things, but never their constitution in themselves—so is this position of mine not a sweeping illusion invented by me for nature. My protestation, too, against all charges of idealism is so valid and clear as even to seem superfluous, were there not incompetent judges who, while they would have an old name for every deviation from their perverse though common opinion and never judge of the spirit of philosophic nomenclature, but cling to the letter only, are ready to put their own conceits in the place of well-defined concepts, and thereby deform and distort them. I have myself given this my theory the name of transcendental idealism, but that cannot authorise anyone to confound it either with the empirical idealism of Descartes (indeed, his was only an insoluble problem, owing to which he thought every one at liberty to deny the existence of the corporeal world because it could never be proved satisfactorily), or with the mystical and visionary idealism of Berkeley (against which and other similar phantasms, our *Critique* contains the proper antidote). My idealism concerns not the existence of things (the doubting of which, however, constitutes idealism in the ordinary sense), since it never came into my head to doubt it; but it concerns the sensuous representation of things, to which space and time especially belong. Regarding space and time and, consequently, regarding all appearances in general, I have only shown that they are neither things (but are mere modes of representation) nor are they determinations belonging to things in themselves. But the word "transcendental," which for me never means a reference of our cognition to things, but only to our faculty of cognition, was meant to obviate this misconception. Yet rather than give further occasion to it by this word, I now retract it and desire this idealism of mine to be called "critical." But if it be really an objectionable idealism to convert actual things (not appearances) into mere representations, by what name shall we call that which, conversely, changes mere representations into things? It may, I think, be called *dreaming* idealism, in contradistinction to the former, which may be called *visionary* idealism, both of which are to be refuted by my transcendental, or better, *critical* idealism.

SECOND PART OF THE MAIN TRANSCENDENTAL QUESTION
HOW IS PURE NATURAL SCIENCE POSSIBLE?

§ 14. *Nature* is the *existence* of things, so far as it is determined according to universal laws. Should nature signify the existence of things in themselves, we could never cognise it either *a priori* or *a posteriori*. Not *a priori*, for how can we know what belongs to things in themselves, since this never can be done by the dissection of our concepts (in analytic judgments)? For I do not want to know what is contained in my concept of a thing (for that belongs to its logical being), but what in the actuality of the thing is superadded to my concept and by what the thing itself is determined in its existence outside the concept. My understanding and the conditions on which alone it can connect the determinations of things in their existence do not prescribe any rule to things in themselves; these do not conform to my understanding, but it would have to conform to them; they would therefore have to be first given to me in order to gather these determinations from them, wherefore they would not be cognised *a priori*.

A cognition of the nature of things in themselves *a posteriori* would be equally impossible. For if experience is to teach us laws to which the existence of things is subject, these laws, if they refer to things in themselves, would have to refer to them of necessity even outside our experience. But experience teaches us what exists and how it exists, but never that it must necessarily exist so and not otherwise. Experience therefore can never teach us the nature of things in themselves.

§ 15. We nevertheless actually possess a pure natural science in which are propounded, *a priori* and with all the necessity requisite to apodeictic propositions, laws to which nature is subject. I need only call to witness that propaedeutic to natural knowledge which, under the title of universal natural science,[9] precedes all physics (which is founded upon empirical principles). In it we have mathematics applied to appearances, and also merely discursive principles (from concepts),[10] which constitute the philosophical part of the pure cognition of nature. But there is much in it which is not quite pure and independent of empirical sources, such as the concept of *motion*, that of *impenetrability* (upon which the empirical concept of matter rests), that of *inertia*, and many others, which prevent its being called a quite pure

9. [Contained in Kant's *Metaphysical Foundations of Natural Science* (1786).]

10. [Rather than intuitive principles, like mathematics.]

[transcendental] natural science. Besides, it only refers to objects of the external senses, and therefore does not give an example of a universal natural science in the strict sense; for such a science must bring nature in general, whether it regards the object of the external senses or that of the internal sense (the object of physics as well as psychology), under universal laws. But among the principles of this universal physics there are a few which actually have the required universality; for instance, the propositions that "substance is permanent," and that "every event is determined by a cause according to constant laws," etc. These are actually universal laws of nature, which subsist completely *a priori.* There is then in fact a pure [transcendental] natural science, and the question arises: how is it possible?

§ 16. The word *nature* assumes yet another meaning, which determines the object, whereas in the former sense it only denotes the conformity to law of the determinations of the existence of things generally. Nature considered *materialiter* is the *totality of all objects of experience.* And with this only are we now concerned; for, besides, things which can never be objects of experience, if they were to be cognised as to their nature, would oblige us to have recourse to concepts whose meaning could never be given *in concreto* (by any example of possible experience). Consequently, we would have to form for ourselves a list of concepts of their nature, the reality whereof (i.e., whether they actually referred to objects or were mere creations of thought) could never be determined. The cognition of what cannot be an object of experience would be hyperphysical, and with things hyperphysical we are here not concerned, but only with the cognition of nature, the actuality of which can be confirmed by experience, though this cognition is possible *a priori* and precedes all experience.

§ 17. The formal aspect of nature in this narrower sense is therefore the conformity to law of all the objects of experience and, so far as it is cognised *a priori,* their necessary conformity. But it has just been shown that the laws of nature can never be cognised *a priori* in objects so far as they are considered, not in reference to possible experience, but as things in themselves. And our inquiry here extends, not to things in themselves (the properties of which we pass by), but to things as objects of possible experience, and the totality of these is properly what we here call nature. And now I ask, when the possibility of cognition of nature *a priori* is in question, whether it is better to arrange the problem thus: how can we cognise *a priori* that things as objects of experience necessarily conform to law? or thus: how is it possible to cognise *a priori* the necessary conformity to law of experience itself as regards all its objects generally?

Closely considered, the solution of the question represented in either way amounts, with regard to the pure cognition of nature (which is the point of the question at issue), entirely to the same thing. For the subjective laws, under which alone an empirical cognition of things is possible, hold good of these things as objects of possible experience (not as things in themselves, which are not considered here). Either of the following statements means quite the same: a judgement of perception can never rank as experience without the law that, whenever an event is observed, it is always referred to some antecedent, which it follows according to a universal rule; or else, everything of which experience teaches that it happens must have a cause.

It is, however, more convenient to choose the first formula. For we can *a priori* and before all given objects have a cognition of those conditions on which alone experience of them is possible, but never of the laws to which things may in themselves be subject, without reference to possible experience. We cannot, therefore, study the nature of things *a priori* otherwise than by investigating the conditions and the universal (though subjective) laws, under which alone such a cognition as experience (as to mere form) is possible, and we determine accordingly the possibility of things as objects of experience. For if I should choose the second formula and seek the *a priori* conditions under which nature as an object of experience is possible, I might easily fall into error and fancy that I was speaking of nature as a thing in itself, and then move round in endless circles, in a vain search for laws concerning things of which nothing is given me.

Accordingly, we shall here be concerned merely with experience and the universal conditions of its possibility, which are given *a priori*. Thence we shall determine nature as the whole object of all possible experience. I think it will be understood that I here do not mean the rules of the observation of a nature that is already given, for these already presuppose experience. I do not mean how (through experience) we can study the laws of nature; for these would not then be laws *a priori* and would yield us no pure natural science; but [I mean to ask] how the conditions *a priori* of the possibility of experience are at the same time the sources from which all the universal laws of nature must be derived.

§ 18. In the first place we must state that while all judgments of experience are empirical (i.e., have their ground in immediate sense-perception), yet conversely, all empirical judgments are not therefore judgments of experience; but, besides the empirical, and in general besides what is given to sensuous intuition, special concepts must yet be superadded—concepts which have their origin quite *a priori* in the pure understanding, and under which every perception must be first of all subsumed and then by their means changed into experience.

Empirical judgments, so far as they have objective validity, are *judgments of experience;* but those which are only subjectively valid I name mere *judgments of perception.* The latter require no pure concept of the understanding, but only the logical connection of perception in a thinking subject. But the former always require, besides the representation of the sensuous intuition, special *concepts originally generated in the understanding,* which make the judgment of experience objectively valid.

All our judgments are at first merely judgments of perception; they hold good only for us (i.e., for our subject), and we do not till afterwards give them a new reference (to an object) and want that they shall always hold good for us and in the same way for everybody else; for if a judgment agrees with an object, all judgments concerning the same object must likewise agree with one another, and thus the objective validity of the judgment of experience signifies nothing else than its necessary universal validity. And, conversely, if we have reason to hold a judgment to be necessarily universally valid (which never rests on perception, but on the pure concept of the understanding under which the perception is subsumed), we must consider it to be objective also, that is, that it expresses not merely a reference of our perception to a subject, but a quality of the object. For there would be no reason for the judgments of other men necessarily to agree with mine, if it were not the unity of the object to which they all refer and with which they accord; hence they must all agree with one another.

§ 19. Therefore objective validity and necessary universal validity (for everybody) are equivalent concepts, and though we do not know the object in itself, yet when we consider a judgment as universally valid, and hence necessary, we understand it thereby to have objective validity. By this judgment we cognise the object (though it remains unknown as it is in itself) by the universally valid and necessary connection of the given perceptions. As this is the case with all objects of sense, judgments of experience take their objective validity, not from the immediate cognition of the object (which is impossible), but merely from the condition of the universal validity of empirical judgments, which, as already said, never rests upon empirical or, in short, sensuous conditions, but upon a pure concept of the understanding. The object in itself always remains unknown; but when by the concept of the understanding the connection of the representations of the object, which are given by the object to our sensibility, is determined as universally valid, the object is determined by this relation, and the judgment is objective.

To illustrate the matter: when we say, "The room is warm, sugar sweet, and wormwood nasty,"[11] we have only subjectively valid judgments. I do not at all expect that I or any other person shall always find it as I now do; each of these sentences only expresses a reference of two sensations to the same subject, i.e., myself, and that only in my present state of perception; consequently, they are not intended to be valid of the object. Such are judgments of perception. Judgments of experience are of quite a different nature. What experience teaches me under certain circumstances, it must always teach me and everybody; and its validity is not limited to the subject nor to its state at a particular time. Hence I pronounce all such judgments as being objectively valid. For instance, when I say the air is elastic, this judgment is as yet a judgment of perception only—I do nothing but refer two sensations in my senses to one another. But if I would have it called a judgment of experience, I require this connection to stand under a condition which makes it universally valid. I desire therefore that I and everybody else should always necessarily connect the same perceptions under the same circumstances.

§ 20. We must therefore analyze experience in general in order to see what is contained in this product of the senses and of the understanding, and how the judgment of experience itself is possible. The foundation is the intuition of which I become conscious, i.e., perception (perceptio), which pertains merely to the senses. But in the next place, there is judging (which belongs only to the understanding). But this judging may be twofold: first, I may merely compare perceptions and connect them in a consciousness of my state; or, secondly, I may connect them in consciousness in general. The former judgment is merely a judgment of perception and is of subjective validity only; it is merely a connection of perceptions in my mental state, without reference to the object. Hence it is not, as is commonly imagined, enough for experience to compare perceptions and connect them in consciousness through judgment; there arises no universal validity and necessity, by virtue of which alone consciousness can become objectively valid and be called experience.

Quite another judgment therefore is required before perception can become experience. The given intuition must be subsumed under a concept which determines

---

11. I freely grant that these examples do not represent such judgments of perception as ever could become judgments of experience, even though a concept of the understanding were superadded, because they refer merely to feeling, which everybody knows to be merely subjective and which, of course, can never be attributed to the object and, consequently, never can become objective. I only wished to give here an example of a judgment that is merely subjectively valid, containing no ground for necessary universal validity and thereby for a relation to the object. An example of the judgments of perception which become judgments of experience by superadded concepts of the understanding will be given in the next note.

the form of judging in general with regard to the intuition, connects the empirical consciousness of the intuition in consciousness in general, and thereby procures universal validity for empirical judgments. A concept of this nature is a pure *a priori* concept of the understanding, which does nothing but determine for an intuition the general way in which it can be used for judging. Let the concept be that of cause; then it determines the intuition which is subsumed under it, e.g., that of air, with regard to judging in general, viz., the concept of air as regards its expansion serves in the relation of antecedent to consequent in a hypothetical judgment. The concept of cause accordingly is a pure concept of the understanding, which is totally disparate from all possible perception and only serves to determine the representation contained under it with regard to judging in general, and so to make a universally valid judgment possible.

Before, therefore, a judgment of perception can become a judgment of experience, it is requisite that the perception should be subsumed under some such concept of the understanding; for instance, air belongs under the concept of cause, which determines our judgment about it with regard to its expansion as hypothetical. [12] Thereby the expansion of the air is represented, not as merely belonging to the perception of the air in my present state or in several states of mine, or in the state of perception of others, but as belonging to it necessarily. The judgment that air is elastic becomes universally valid and a judgment of experience only because certain judgments precede it which subsume the intuition of air under the concepts of cause and effect; and they thereby determine the perceptions, not merely as regards one another in me, but as regards the form of judging in general (which is here hypothetical), and in this way they render the empirical judgment universally valid.

If all our synthetic judgments are analyzed so far as they are objectively valid, it will be found that they never consist of mere intuitions connected only (as is commonly supposed) by comparison into a judgment; but that they would be impossible were not a pure concept of the understanding superadded to the concepts abstracted from intuition, under which pure concept these latter concepts are subsumed and in this manner only combined into an objectively valid judgment. Even the judgments of pure mathematics in their simplest axioms are not exempt from this condition. The principle that a straight line is the shortest distance between two points presupposes that the line is subsumed under the concept of quantity, which certainly is no mere intuition but has its seat in the understanding alone and serves to determine the intuition (of the line) with regard to the judgments which may be made about it in respect to the quantity, that is, to plurality (as *judica plurativa*.)[13]

---

12. As an easier example, we may take the following: when the sun shines on the stone, it grows warm. This judgment, however often I and others may have perceived it, is a mere judgment of perception and contains no necessity; perceptions are only usually conjoined in this manner. But if I say: the sun warms the stone, I add to the perception a concept of the understanding, viz., that of cause, which necessarily connects with the concept of sunshine that of heat, and the synthetic judgment becomes of necessity universally valid, viz., objective, and is converted from a perception into experience.

13. This name seems preferable to the term *particularia*, which is used for these judgments in logic. For the latter already contains the thought that they are not universal. But when I start from unity (in singular judgments) and proceed to totality, I must not [even indirectly and negatively] include any reference to totality. I think plurality merely without totality, and not the exclusion of totality. This is necessary, if the logical moments are to underlie the pure concepts of the understanding. In logical usage one may leave things as they were.

For under them it is understood that in a given intuition there is contained a plurality of homogeneous parts.

§ 21. To prove, then, the possibility of experience so far as it rests upon pure *a priori* concepts of the understanding, we must first represent what belongs to judgments in general and the various moments (functions) of the understanding in them, in a complete table. For the pure concepts of the understanding must run parallel to these moments, inasmuch as such concepts are nothing more than concepts of intuitions in general, so far as these are determined by one or other of these moments of judging, in themselves, i.e., necessarily and universally. Hereby also the *a priori* principles of the possibility of all experience, as objectively valid empirical cognition, will be precisely determined. For they are nothing but propositions which subsume all perception (conformably to certain universal conditions of intuition) under those pure concepts of the understanding.

LOGICAL TABLE OF JUDGMENTS

1	2
As to Quantity	*As to Quality*
Universal	Affirmative
Particular	Negative
Singular	Infinite

3	4
As to Relation	*As to Modaltiy*
Categorical	Problematic
Hypothetical	Assertoric
Disjunctive	Apodeictic

TRANSCENDENTAL TABLE OF THE CONCEPTS OF THE UNDERSTANDING

1	2
As to Quantity	*As to Quality*
Unity (Measure)	Reality
Plurality (Quantity)	Negation
Totality (Whole)	Limitation

3	4
As to Relation	*As to Modality*
Substance	Possibility
Cause	Existence
Community	Necessity

PURE PHYSIOLOGICAL[14] TABLE OF THE UNIVERSAL PRINCIPLES OF NATURAL SCIENCE

1 Axioms of Intuition	2 Anticipations of Perception
3 Analogies of Experience	4 Postulates of Empirical Thought in General

§ 21a. In order to comprise the whole matter in one idea, it is first necessary to remind the reader that we are discussing, not the origin of experience, but what lies in experience. The former pertains to empirical psychology and would even then never be adequately developed without the latter, which belongs to the critique of cognition, and particularly of the understanding.

Experience consists of intuitions, which belong to the sensibility, and of judgments, which are entirely a work of the understanding. But the judgments which the understanding makes entirely out of sensuous intuitions are far from being judgments of experience. For in the one case the judgment connects only the perceptions as they are given in sensuous intuition, while in the other the judgments must express what experience in general and not what the mere perception (which possesses only subjective validity) contains. The judgment of experience must therefore add to the sensuous intuition and its logical connection in a judgment (after it has been rendered universal by comparison) something that determines the synthetic judgment as necessary and therefore as universally valid. This can be nothing but that concept which represents the intuition as determined in itself with regard to one form of judgment rather than another, viz., a concept of that synthetic unity of intuitions which can only be represented by a given logical function of judgments.

§ 22. The sum of the matter is this: the business of the senses is to intuit, that of the understanding is to think. But thinking is uniting representations in a consciousness. This unification originates either merely relative to the subject and is contingent and subjective, or it happens absolutely and is necessary or objective. The uniting of representations in a consciousness is judgment. Thinking therefore is the same as judging, or referring representations to judgments in general. Hence judgments are either merely subjective when representations are referred to a consciousness in one subject only and are united in it, or they are objective when they are united in a consciousness in general, that is, necessarily. The logical moments of all judgments are so many possible ways of uniting representations in consciousness. But if they serve as concepts, they are concepts of the necessary unification of representations in a consciousness and so are principles of objectively valid judgments. This uniting in a consciousness is either analytic by identity, or synthetic by the combination and addition of various representations one to another. Experience consists in the synthetic connection of appearances (perceptions) in consciousness, so far as this connection is necessary. Hence the pure concepts of the understanding are those under which all perceptions must first be subsumed before they can serve

14. [See last sentence of § 23.]

for judgments of experience, in which the synthetic unity of the perceptions is represented as necessary and universally valid.[15]

§ 23. Judgments, when considered merely as the condition of the unification of given representations in a consciousness, are rules. These rules, so far as they represent the unification as necessary, are rules *a priori*, and so far as they cannot be deduced from higher rules, are principles. But in regard to the possibility of all experience, merely in relation to the form of thinking in it, no conditions of judgments of experience are higher than those which bring the phenomena, according to the different form of their intuition, under pure concepts of the understanding, and render the empirical judgments objectively valid. These are therefore the *a priori* principles of possible experience.

The principles of possible experience are then at the same time universal laws of nature, which can be cognised *a priori*. And thus the problem in our second question: How is pure natural science possible? is solved. For the systematization which is required for the form of a science is to be met with in perfection here, because, beyond the above-mentioned formal conditions of all judgments in general and of all rules in general, that are offered in logic, no others are possible, and these constitute a logical system. The concepts grounded thereupon, which contain the *a priori* conditions of all synthetic and necessary judgments, accordingly constitute a transcendental system. Finally, the principles by means of which all appearances are subsumed under these concepts constitute a physiological system, that is, a system of nature, which precedes all empirical cognition of nature, first makes it possible, and hence may in strictness be called the universal and pure natural science.

§ 24. The first[16] of the physiological principles[17] subsumes all appearances, as intuitions in space and time, under the concept of *quantity*, and is so far a principle of the application of mathematics to experience. The second[18] subsumes the strictly empirical element, viz., sensation, which denotes the real in intuitions, not indeed directly under the concept of *quantity*, because sensation is not an intuition that *contains* either space or time, though it puts the object corresponding to sensation in both space and time. But still there is between reality (sense-representation) and zero, or total lack of intuition in time, a difference which has a quantity. For between any given degree of light and darkness, between any degree of heat and com-

---

15. But how does the proposition that judgments of experience contain necessity in the synthesis of perceptions agree with my statement so often before inculcated that experience, as cognition *a posteriori*, can afford contingent judgments only? When I say that experience teaches me something, I mean only the perception that lies in experience—for example, that heat always follows the shining of the sun on a stone; consequently, the proposition of experience is always so far contingent. That this heat necessarily follows the shining of the sun is contained indeed in the judgment of experience (by means of the concept of cause), yet is a fact not learned by experience; for, conversely, experience is first of all generated by this addition of the concept of the understanding (of cause) to perception. How perception attains this addition may be seen by referring in the *Critique* itself to the section on the transcendental faculty of judgment, B 176 *et seq.*

16. The three following paragraphs will hardly be understood unless reference be made to what the *Critique* itself says on the subject of the principles; they will, however, be of service in giving a general view of the principles, and in fixing the attention on the main moments. [See *Critique*, B 187–294.]

17. [The Axioms of Intuition. See *Critique*, B 202–207.]

18. [The Anticipations of Perception. See *ibid.*, B 207–218.]

plete cold, between any degree of weight and absolute lightness, between any degree of occupied space and of totally empty space, ever smaller degrees can be thought, just as even between consciousness and total unconsciousness (psychological darkness) ever smaller degrees obtain. Hence there is no perception that can show an absolute absence; for instance, no psychological darkness that cannot be regarded as a consciousness only surpassed by a stronger consciousness. This occurs in all cases of sensation; and so the understanding can anticipate sensations, which constitute the peculiar quality of empirical representations (appearances), by means of the principle that they all have a degree, consequently, that what is real in all appearance has a degree. Here is the second application of mathematics (*mathesis intensorum*) to natural science.

§ 25. As regards the relation of appearances merely with a view to their existence, the determination is not mathematical but dynamical, and can never be objectively valid and fit for experience, if it does not come under *a priori* principles[19] by which the cognition of experience relative to appearances first becomes possible. Hence appearances must be subsumed under the concept of substance, which as a concept of the thing itself is the foundation of all determination of existence; or, secondly—so far as a succession is found among appearances, that is, an event—under the concept of an effect with reference to cause; or, lastly—so far as coexistence is to be known objectively, that is, by a judgment of experience—under the concept of community (action and reaction). Thus *a priori* principles form the basis of objectively valid, though empirical, judgments—that is, of the possibility of experience so far as it must connect objects as existing in nature. These principles are properly the laws of nature, which may be called dynamical.

Finally[20] the cognition of the agreement and connection, not only of appearances among themselves in experience, but of their relation to experience in general, belongs to judgments of experience. This relation contains either their agreement with the formal conditions which the understanding cognises, or their coherence with the material of the senses and of perception, or combines both into one concept and consequently contains possibility, actuality, and necessity according to universal laws of nature. This would constitute the physiological doctrine of method (distinction between truth and hypotheses, and the bounds of the reliability of the latter).

§ 26. The third table of principles drawn from the nature of the understanding itself according to the critical method shows an inherent perfection, which raises it far above every other table which has hitherto, though in vain, been tried or may yet be tried by analyzing the objects themselves dogmatically. It exhibits all synthetic *a priori* principles completely and according to one principle, viz., the faculty of judging in general, which constitutes the essence of experience as regards the understanding, so that we can be certain that there are no more such principles. This affords a satisfaction such as can never be attained by the dogmatic method. Yet this is not all; there is a still greater merit in it.

We must carefully bear in mind the ground of proof which shows the possibility of this cognition *a priori* and, at the same time, limits all such principles to a condi-

---

19. [The Analogies of Experience. See *ibid.*, B 218–265.]

20. [The Postulates of Empirical Thought. See *ibid.*, B 265–294.]

tion which must never be lost sight of, if they are not to be misunderstood and extended in use beyond what is allowed by the original sense which the understanding places in them. This limit is that they contain nothing but the conditions of possible experience in general so far as it is subjected to laws *a priori*. Consequently, I do not say that things *in themselves* possess a quantity, that their reality possesses a degree, their existence a connection of accidents in a substance, etc. This nobody can prove, because such a synthetic connection from mere concepts, without any reference to sensuous intuition on the one side or connection of such intuition in a possible experience on the other, is absolutely impossible. The essential limitation of the concepts in these principles, then, is that all things stand necessarily *a priori* under the aforementioned conditions only *as objects of experience*.

Hence there follows, secondly, a specifically peculiar mode of proof of these principles; they are not directly referred to appearances and to their relation, but to the possibility of experience, of which appearances constitute the matter only, not the form. Thus they are referred to objectively and universally valid synthetic propositions, in which we distinguish judgments of experience from those of perception. This takes place because appearances, as mere intuitions *occupying a part of space and time,* come under the concept of quantity, which synthetically unites their multiplicity *a priori* according to rules. Again, insofar as the perception contains, besides intuition, sensation, and between the latter and nothing (i.e., the total disappearance of sensation), there is an ever-decreasing transition, it is apparent that the real in appearances must have a degree, so far as it (viz., the sensation) *does not itself occupy any part of space or of time.*[21] Still the transition to sensation from empty time or empty space is only possible in time. Consequently, although sensation, as the quality of empirical intuition in respect of its specific difference from other sensations, can never be cognised *a priori*, yet it can, in a possible experience in general, as a quantity of perception be intensively distinguished from every other similar perception. Hence the application of mathematics to nature, as regards the sensuous intuition by which nature is given to us, is first made possible and determined.

Above all, the reader must pay attention to the mode of proof of the principles which occur under the title of Analogies of Experience. For these do not refer to the generation of intuitions, as do the principles of applying mathematics to natural science in general, but to the connection of their existence in experience; and this can be nothing but the determination of their existence in time according to necessary laws, under which alone the connection is objectively valid and thus becomes experience. The proof, therefore, does not turn on the synthetic unity in the connection of things in themselves, but merely of perceptions, and of these, not in regard to their content, but to the determination of time and of the relation of their existence in it according to universal laws. If the empirical determination in relative time is indeed to be objectively valid (i.e., experience), these universal laws thus contain

---

21. Heat and light are in a small space just as large, as to degree, as in a large one; in like manner the internal representations, pain, consciousness in general, whether they last a short or a long time, need not vary as to the degree. Hence the quantity is here in a point and in a moment just as great as in any space or time, however great. Degrees are thus quantities not in intuition but in mere sensation (or the quantity of the content of an intuition). Hence they can only be estimated quantitatively by the relation of 1 to 0, viz., by their capability of decreasing by infinite intermediate degrees to disappearance, or of increasing from naught through infinite gradations to a determinate sensation in a certain time. *Quantitas qualitatis est gradus* [the quantity of quality is degree].

the necessity of the determination of existence in time generally (viz., according to a rule of the understanding *a priori*). Since these are prolegomena I cannot further descant on the subject, but my reader (who has probably long been accustomed to consider experience as a mere empirical synthesis of perceptions, and hence has not considered that it goes much beyond them since it imparts to empirical judgments universal validity, and for that purpose requires a pure and *a priori* unity of the understanding) is recommended to pay special attention to this distinction of experience from a mere aggregate of perceptions and to judge the mode of proof from this point of view.

§ 27. Now we are prepared to remove Hume's doubt. He justly maintains that we cannot comprehend by reason the possibility of causality, that is, of the reference of the existence of one thing to the existence of another which is necessitated by the former. I add that we comprehend just as little the concept of subsistence, that is, the necessity that at the foundation of the existence of things there lies a subject which cannot itself be a predicate of any other thing; nay, we cannot even form a concept of the possibility of such a thing (though we can point out examples of its use in experience). The very same incomprehensibility affects the community of things, as we cannot comprehend how from the state of one thing an inference to the state of quite another thing beyond it, and *vice versa*, can be drawn, and how substances which have each their own separate existence should depend upon one another necessarily. But I am very far from holding these concepts to be derived merely from experience, and the necessity represented in them to be fictitious and a mere illusion produced in us by long habit. On the contrary, I have amply shown that they and the principles derived from them are firmly established *a priori* before all experience and have their undoubted objective rightness, though only with regard to experience.

§ 28. Though I have no conception of such a connection of things in themselves, how they can either exist as substances, or act as causes, or stand in community with others (as parts of a real whole) and I can just as little think such properties in appearances as such (because those concepts contain nothing that lies in the appearances, but only what the understanding alone must think), we have yet a concept of such a connection of representations in our understanding and in judgments generally. This is the concept that representations belong in one sort of judgments as subject in relation to predicates; in another as ground in relation to consequent; and, in a third, as parts which constitute together a total possible cognition. Further we know *a priori* that without considering the representation of an object as determined with regard to one or the other of these moments, we can have no valid cognition of the object; and, if we should occupy ourselves with the object in itself, there is not a single possible attribute by which I could know that it is determined with regard to one or the other of these moments, that is, belonged under the concept of substance, or of cause, or (in relation to other substances) of community, for I have no conception of the possibility of such a connection of existence. But the question is not how things in themselves but how the empirical cognition of things is determined, as regards the above moments of judgments in general, that is, how things, as objects of experience, can and must be subsumed under these concepts of the understanding. And then it is clear that I completely comprehend, not only the possibility, but also the necessity, of subsuming all appearances under these concepts, that is, of using them as principles of the possibility of experience.

§ 29. In order to put to a test Hume's problematic concept (his *crux metaphysicorum*), the concept of cause, we have, in the first place, given *a priori* by means of logic the form of a conditional judgment in general, i.e., we have one given cognition as antecedent and another as consequent. But it is possible that in perception we may meet with a rule of relation which runs thus: that a certain appearance is constantly followed by another (though not conversely); and this is a case for me to use the hypothetical judgment and, for instance, to say that if the sun shines long enough upon a body it grows warm. Here there is indeed as yet no necessity of connection, or concept of cause. But I proceed and say that if this proposition, which is merely a subjective connection of perceptions, is to be a judgment of experience, it must be regarded as necessary and universally valid. Such a proposition would be that the sun is by its light the cause of heat. The empirical rule is now considered as a law, and as valid not merely of appearances but valid of them for the purposes of a possible experience which requires universal and therefore necessarily valid rules. I therefore easily comprehend the concept of cause as a concept necessarily belonging to the mere form of experience, and its possibility as a synthetic unification of perceptions in a consciousness in general; but I do not at all comprehend the possibility of a thing in general as a cause, inasmuch as the concept of cause denotes a condition not at all belonging to things, but to experience. For experience can only be an objectively valid cognition of appearances and of their succession, only so far as the antecedent appearances can be conjoined with the consequent ones according to the rule of hypothetical judgments.

§ 30. Hence if the pure concepts of the understanding try to go beyond objects of experience and be referred to things in themselves *(noumena)*, they have no meaning whatever. They serve, as it were, only to spell out appearances, so that we may be able to read them as experience. The principles which arise from their reference to the sensible world only serve our understanding for use in experience. Beyond this they are arbitrary combinations without objective reality; and we can neither cognise their possibility *a priori*, nor verify their reference to objects, let alone make such reference understandable, by any example, because examples can only be borrowed from some possible experience, and consequently the objects of these concepts can be found nowhere but in a possible experience.

This complete (though to its originator unexpected) solution of Hume's problem rescues for the pure concepts of the understanding their *a priori* origin and for the universal laws of nature their validity as laws of the understanding, yet in such a way as to limit their use to experience, because their possibility depends solely on the reference of the understanding to experience, but with a completely reversed mode of connection which never occurred to Hume: they are not derived from experience, but experience is derived from them.

This is, therefore, the result of all our foregoing inquiries: "All synthetic principles *a priori* are nothing more than principles of possible experience" and can never be referred to things in themselves, but only to appearances as objects of experience. And hence pure mathematics as well as pure natural science can never be referred to anything more than mere appearances, and can only represent either that which makes experience in general possible, or else that which, as it is derived from these principles, must always be capable of being represented in some possible experience.

§ 31. And thus we have at last something determinate upon which to depend in all metaphysical enterprises, which have hitherto, boldly enough but always at random, attempted everything without discrimination. That the goal of their exertions should be set up so close struck neither the dogmatic thinkers nor those who, confident in their supposed sound common sense, started with concepts and principles of pure reason (which were legitimate and natural, but destined for mere empirical use) in search of insights for which they neither knew nor could know any determinate bounds, because they had never reflected nor were able to reflect on the nature or even on the possibility of such a pure understanding.

Many a naturalist of pure reason (by which I mean the man who believes he can decide in matters of metaphysics without any science) may pretend that he, long ago, by the prophetic spirit of his sound sense, not only suspected but knew and comprehended what is here propounded with so much ado, or, if he likes, with prolix and pedantic pomp: "that with all our reason we can never reach beyond the field of experience." But when he is questioned about his rational principles individually, he must grant that there are many of them which he has not taken from experience and which are therefore independent of it and valid *a priori*. How then and on what grounds will he restrain both himself and the dogmatist, who makes use of these concepts and principles beyond all possible experience because they are recognised to be independent of it? And even he, this adept in sound sense, in spite of all his assumed and cheaply acquired wisdom, is not exempt from wandering inadvertently beyond objects of experience into the field of chimeras. He is often deeply enough involved in them, though in announcing everything as mere probability, rational conjecture, or analogy, he gives by his popular language a color to his groundless pretensions.

§ 32. Since the oldest days of philosophy, inquirers into pure reason have thought that, besides the things of sense, or appearances *(phenomena)*, which make up the sensible world, there were certain beings of the understanding *(noumena)*, which should constitute an intelligible world. And as appearance and illusion were by those men identified (a thing which we may well excuse in an undeveloped epoch), actuality was only conceded to the beings of the understanding.

And we indeed, rightly considering objects of sense as mere appearances, confess thereby that they are based upon a thing in itself, though we know not this thing as it is in itself but only know its appearances, viz., the way in which our senses are affected by this unknown something. The understanding therefore, by assuming appearances, grants also the existence of things in themselves, and thus far we may say that the representation of such things as are the basis of appearances, consequently of mere beings of the understanding, is not only admissible but unavoidable.

Our critical deduction by no means excludes things of that sort *(noumena)*, but rather limits the principles of the Aesthetic[22] in such a way that they shall not extend to all things (as everything would then be turned into mere appearance) but that they shall hold good only of objects of possible experience. Hereby, then, beings of the understanding are admitted, but with the inculcation of this rule which admits of no exception: that we neither know nor can know anything determinate whatever about these pure beings of the understanding, because our pure concepts of the understanding as well as our pure intuitions extend to nothing but objects of possible experience, consequently to mere things of sense; and as soon as

---

22. [The principles of sensibility (space and time). See *Critique* of *Pure Reason*, B 33–B 73.]

we leave this sphere, these concepts retain no meaning whatever.

§ 33. There is indeed something seductive in our pure concepts of the understanding which tempts us to a transcendent use—a use which transcends all possible experience. Not only are our concepts of substance, of power, of action, of reality, and others, quite independent of experience, containing nothing of sense appearance, and so apparently applicable to things in themselves *(noumena)*, but, what strengthens this conjecture, they contain a necessity of determination in themselves, which experience never attains. The concept of cause contains a rule according to which one state follows another necessarily; but experience can only show us that one state of things often or, at most, commonly follows another, and therefore affords neither strict universality nor necessity.

Hence concepts of the understanding seem to have a deeper meaning and content than can be exhausted by their merely empirical use, and so the understanding inadvertently adds for itself to the house of experience a much more extensive wing which it fills with nothing but beings of thought, without ever observing that it has transgressed with its otherwise legitimate concepts the bounds of their use.

§ 34. Two important and even indispensable, though very dry, investigations therefore became indispensable in the *Critique of Pure Reason* [viz., the two chapters "The Schematism of the Pure Concepts of the Understanding" and "The Ground of the Distinction of All Objects in General into Phenomena and Noumena"]. In the former there is shown that the senses furnish, not the pure concepts of the understanding *in concreto*, but only the schema for their use, and that the object conformable to it occurs only in experience (as the product of the understanding from materials of sensibility). In the latter there is shown that, although our pure concepts of the understanding and our principles are independent of experience, and despite the apparently greater sphere of their use, still nothing whatever can be thought by them beyond the field of experience, because they can do nothing but merely determine the logical form of the judgment with regard to given intuitions. But as there is no intuition at all beyond the field of sensibility, these pure concepts, since they cannot possibly be exhibited *in concreto,* are void of all meaning; consequently all these *noumena*, together with their sum total, the intelligible world,[23] are nothing but representations of a problem, the object of which in itself is quite possible but the solution, from the nature of our understanding, totally impossible. For our understanding is not a faculty of intuition but of the connection of given intuitions in an experience. Experience must therefore contain all the objects for our concepts; but beyond it no concepts have any meaning, since no intuition can be subsumed under them.

§ 35. The imagination may perhaps be forgiven for occasional vagaries and for not keeping carefully within the limits of experience, since it gains life and vigor by such flights and since it is always easier to moderate its boldness than to stimulate its languor. But the understanding which ought to *think* can never be forgiven for indulging in vagaries; for we depend upon it alone for assistance to set bounds, when necessary, to the vagaries of the imagination.

23. We speak of the "intelligible world," not (as the usual expression is) "intellectual world." For cognitions are intellectual through the understanding and refer to our world of sense also; but objects, insofar as they can be represented merely by the understanding, and to which none of our sensible intuitions can refer, are termed "intelligible." But as some possible intuition must correspond to every object, we would have to think an understanding that intuits things immediately; but of such we have not the least concept, nor of *beings of the understanding* to which it should be applied.

But the understanding begins its aberrations very innocently and modestly. It first discerns the elementary cognitions which inhere in it prior to all experience, but yet must always have their application in experience. It gradually drops these limits; and what is there to prevent it, inasmuch as it has quite freely derived its principles from itself? And then it proceeds first to newly thought out forces in nature, then to beings outside nature—in short, to a world for whose construction the materials cannot be wanting, because fertile fiction furnishes them abundantly, and though not confirmed is yet never refuted by experience. This is the reason why young thinkers are so partial to metaphysics in the truly dogmatical manner, and often sacrifice to it their time and their talents, which might be otherwise better employed.

But there is no use in trying to moderate these fruitless endeavors of pure reason by all manner of cautions as to the difficulties of solving questions so occult, by complaints of the limits of our reason, and by degrading our assertions into mere conjectures. For if their impossibility is not distinctly shown, and reason's knowledge of itself does not become a true science, in which the field of its right use is distinguished, so to say, with geometrical certainty from that of its worthless and idle use, these fruitless efforts will never be entirely abandoned.

§ 36. *How is nature itself possible?* This question—the highest point that transcendental philosophy can ever reach, and to which, as its boundary and completion, it must proceed—properly contains two questions.

First: How is nature possible in general in the *material* sense, i.e., according to intuition, as the totality of appearances; how are space, time, and that which fills both—the object of sensation—possible in general? The answer is: by means of the constitution of our sensibility, according to which it is in its special way affected by objects which are in themselves unknown to it and totally distinct from those appearances. This answer is given in the *Critique* itself in the Transcendental Aesthetic, and in these *Prolegomena* by the solution of the first main question.

Secondly: How is nature possible in the *formal* sense, as the totality of the rules under which all appearances must come in order to be thought as connected in an experience? The answer must be this: it is only possible by means of the constitution of our understanding, according to which all those representations of sensibility are necessarily referred to a consciousness, and by which the peculiar way in which we think (viz., by rules) and hence experience also are possible, but must be clearly distinguished from an insight into the objects in themselves. This answer is given in the *Critique* itself in the Transcendental Logic, and in these *Prolegomena* in the course of the solution of the second main question.

But how this peculiar property of our sensibility itself is possible, or that of our understanding and of the apperception which is necessarily its basis and also that of all thinking, cannot be further analyzed or answered, because it is of them that we are in need for all our answers and for all our thinking about objects.

There are many laws of nature which we can only know by means of experience; but conformity to law in the connection of appearances, i.e., nature in general, we cannot discover by any experience, because experience itself requires laws which are *a priori* at the basis of its possibility.

The possibility of experience in general is therefore at the same time the universal law of nature, and the principles of experience are the very laws of nature. For we know nature as nothing but the totality of appearances, i.e., of representations in us; and hence we can only derive the law of their connection from the principles of their connection in us, that is, from the conditions of their necessary unification in a consciousness, which constitutes the possibility of experience.

Even the main proposition expounded throughout this section—that universal laws of nature can be cognised *a priori*—leads of itself to the proposition that the highest legislation of nature must lie in ourselves, i.e., in our understanding; and that we must not seek the universal laws of nature in nature by means of experience, but conversely must seek nature, as to its universal conformity to law, in the conditions of the possibility of experience, which lie in our sensibility and in our understanding. For how would it otherwise be possible to know *a priori* these laws, as they are not rules of analytic cognition but truly synthetic extensions of it? Such a necessary agreement of the principles of possible experience with the laws of the possibility of nature can only proceed from one of two reasons: either these laws are drawn from nature by means of experience, or conversely nature is derived from the laws of the possibility of experience in general and is quite the same as the mere universal conformity to law of the latter. The former is self-contradictory, for the universal laws of nature can and must be cognised *a priori* (that is, independent of all experience) and be the foundation of all empirical use of the understanding; the latter alternative therefore alone remains.[24]

But we must distinguish the empirical laws of nature, which always presuppose particular perceptions, from the pure or universal laws of nature, which, without being based on particular perceptions, contain merely the conditions of their necessary unification in experience. With regard to the latter, nature and possible experience are quite the same, and as the conformity to law in the latter depends upon the necessary connection of appearances in experience (without which we cannot cognize any object whatever in the sensible world), consequently upon the original laws of the understanding, it seems at first strange, but is not the less certain, to say: *the understanding does not derive its laws (a priori) from, but prescribes them to, nature.*

§ 37. We shall illustrate this seemingly bold proposition by an example, which will show that laws which we discover in objects of sensuous intuition (especially when these laws are cognised as necessary) are already held by us to be such as have been placed there by the understanding, in spite of their being similar in all points to the laws of nature which we ascribe to experience.

§ 38. If we consider the properties of the circle, by which this figure at once combines into a universal rule so many arbitrary determinations of the space in it, we cannot avoid attributing a nature to this geometrical thing. Two lines, for example, which intersect each other and the circle, howsoever they may be drawn, are always divided so that the rectangle constructed with the segments of the one is equal to that constructed with the segments of the other. The question now is: Does this law lie in the circle or in the understanding? That is, does this figure, independently of the understanding, contain in itself the ground of the law; or does the understanding, having constructed according to its concepts (of the equality of the radii) the

---

24. Crusius alone thought of a compromise: that a spirit who can neither err nor deceive implanted these laws in us originally. But since false principles often intrude themselves, as indeed the very system of this man shows in not a few examples, we are involved in difficulties as to the use of such a principle in the absence of sure criteria to distinguish the genuine origin from the spurious, for we never can know certainly what the spirit of truth or the father of lies may have instilled into us.

figure itself, introduce into it this law of the chords intersecting in geometrical proportion? When we follow the proofs of this law, we soon perceive that it can only be derived from the condition on which the understanding founds the construction of this figure, viz., the equality of the radii. But if we enlarge this concept to pursue further the unity of manifold properties of geometrical figures under common laws and consider the circle as a conic section, which of course is subject to the same fundamental conditions of construction as other conic sections, we shall find that all the chords which intersect within the circle, ellipse, parabola, and hyperbola always intersect so that the rectangles of their segments are not indeed equal but always bear a constant ratio to one another. If we proceed still further to the fundamental doctrines of physical astronomy, we find a physical law of reciprocal attraction extending over the whole material nature, the rule of which is that it decreases inversely as the square of the distance from each attracting point, just as the spherical surfaces through which this force diffuses itself increase; and this law seems to be necessarily inherent in the very nature of things, so that it is usually propounded as cognisable *a priori*. Simple as the sources of this law are, merely resting upon the relation of spherical surfaces of different radii, its consequence is so excellent with regard to the variety and regularity of its agreement that not only are all possible orbits of the celestial bodies conic sections, but such a relation of these orbits to each other results that no other law of attraction than that of the inverse square of the distance can be thought as fit for a cosmical system.

Here, accordingly, is nature resting on laws which the understanding cognises *a priori*, and chiefly from universal principles of the determination of space. Now I ask: do the laws of nature lie in space, and does the understanding learn them by merely endeavoring to find out the enormous wealth of meaning that lies in space; or do they inhere in the understanding and in the way in which it determines space according to the conditions of the synthetic unity in which its concepts are all centered? Space is something so uniform and as to all particular properties so indeterminate that we should certainly not seek a store of laws of nature in it. Whereas that which determines space to assume the form of a circle, or the figures of a cone and a sphere is the understanding, so far as it contains the ground of the unity of their constructions. The mere universal form of intuition, called space, must therefore be the substratum of all intuitions determinable to particular objects; and in it, of course, the condition of the possibility and of the variety of these intuitions lies. But the unity of the objects is entirely determined by the understanding, and according to conditions which lie in its own nature; and thus the understanding is the origin of the universal order of nature, in that it comprehends all appearances under its own laws and thereby brings about, in an *a priori* way, experience (as to its form), by means of which whatever is to be cognised only by experience is necessarily subjected to its laws. For we are not concerned with the nature of things in themselves, which is independent of the conditions both of our sensibility and our understanding, but with nature as an object of possible experience; and in this case the understanding, because it makes experience possible, thereby insists that the sensuous world is either not an object of experience at all, or else is nature.

APPENDIX TO PURE NATURAL SCIENCE

§ 39. *Of the system of the categories.* There can be nothing more desirable to a philosopher than to be able to derive the scattered multiplicity of the concepts or the principles which had occurred to him in concrete use from a principle *a priori,* and to unite everything in this way in one cognition. He formerly only believed that those things which remained after a certain abstraction, and seemed by comparison among one another to constitute a particular kind of cognitions, were completely collected; but this was only an *aggregate.* Now he knows that just so many, neither more nor less, can constitute this kind of cognition, and perceives the necessity of his division; this constitutes comprehension. And only now has he attained a *system.*

To search in our ordinary knowledge for the concepts which do not rest upon particular experience and yet occur in all knowledge from experience, of which they constitute as it were the mere form of connection, presupposes neither greater reflection nor deeper insight than to detect in a language the rules of the actual use of words generally and thus to collect elements for a grammar (in fact both inquiries are very closely related), even though we are not able to give a reason why each language has just this and no other formal constitution, and still less why exactly so many, neither more nor less, of such formal determinations in general can be found in it.

Aristotle collected ten pure elementary concepts under the name of categories.[25] To these, which were also called predicaments, he found himself obliged afterwards to add five post-predicaments,[26] some of which however *(prius, simul,* and *motus)* are contained in the former; but this rhapsody must be considered (and commended) as a mere hint for future inquirers, not as a regularly worked out idea, and hence it has, in the present more advanced state of philosophy, been rejected as quite useless.

After long reflection on the pure elements of human knowledge (those which contain nothing empirical), I at last succeeded in distinguishing with certainty and in separating the pure elementary concepts of sensibility (space and time) from those of the understanding. Thus the 7th, 8th, and 9th categories had to be excluded from the old list. And the others were of no service to me because there was no principle on which the understanding could be fully mapped out and all the functions, whence its pure concepts arise, determined exhaustively and with precision.

But in order to discover such a principle, I looked about for an act of the understanding which comprises all the rest and is differentiated only by various modifications or moments, in bringing the manifold of representation under the unity of thinking in general. I found this act of the understanding to consist in judging. Here, then, the labors of the logicians were ready at hand, though not yet quite free from defects; and with this help I was enabled to exhibit a complete table of the pure functions of the understanding, which were however undetermined in regard to any object. I finally referred these functions of judging to objects in general, or rather to the condition of determining judgments as objectively valid; and so there arose the pure concepts of the understanding, concerning which I could make certain that these, and this exact number only, constitute our whole cognition of things from pure understanding. I was justified in calling them by their old name of *categories,* while I reserved for myself the liberty of adding, under the title of *predicables,* a complete list of all the concepts deducible from them by combinations, whether among themselves, or with the pure form of the appearance, i.e., space or time, or

25. 1. *Substantia.* 2. *Qualitas.* 3. *Quantitas.* 4. *Relatio.* 5. *Actio.* 6. *Passio.* 7. *Quando.* 8. *Ubi.* 9. *Situs.* 10. *Habitus.*

26. *Oppositum, Prius, Simul, Motus, Habere.*

with its matter, so far as it is not yet empirically determined (viz., the object of sensation in general), as soon as a system of transcendental philosophy should be completed, with the construction of which I was engaged in the *Critique of Pure Reason* itself.

Now the essential point in this system of categories, which distinguishes it from the old rhapsody (which proceeded without any principle) and for which point alone this system deserves to be considered as philosophy, consists in this: that, by means of it, the true meaning of the pure concepts of the understanding and the condition of their use could be exactly determined. For here it became obvious that they are themselves nothing but logical functions, and as such do not constitute the least concept of an object in itself, but require some sensuous intuition as a basis. These concepts, therefore, only serve to determine empirical judgments (which are otherwise undetermined and indifferent with respect to all functions of judging) as regards these functions, thereby procuring them universal validity, and by means of them, making judgments of experience in general possible.

Such an insight into the nature of the categories, which limits them at the same time to use merely in experience, never occurred either to their first author, or to any of his successors; but without this insight (which exactly depends upon their derivation or deduction), they are quite useless and only a miserable list of names, without explanation or rule for their use. Had the ancients ever conceived such a notion, doubtless the whole study of pure rational knowledge, which under the name of metaphysics has for centuries spoiled many a sound mind, would have reached us in quite another shape and would have enlightened the human understanding instead of actually exhausting it in obscure and vain subtleties and rendering it useless for true science.

This system of categories makes all treatment of every object of pure reason itself systematic, and affords a direction or clue how and through what points of inquiry any metaphysical consideration must proceed in order to be complete; for it exhausts all the moments of the understanding, under which every other concept must be brought. In like manner the table of principles has been formulated, the completeness of which we can only vouch for by the system of the categories. Even in the division of the concepts which are to go beyond the physiological application of the understanding,[27] it is still the same clue, which, as it must always be determined *a priori* by the same fixed points of the human understanding, always forms a closed circle. There is no doubt that the object of a pure concept, either of the understanding or of reason, so far as it is to be estimated philosophically and on *a priori* principles, can in this way be completely cognised. I could not therefore omit to make use of this clue with regard to one of the most abstract ontological divisions, viz., the various distinctions of the concepts of something and of nothing, and to construct accordingly[28] a regular and necessary table of their divisions.[29]

27. [Cf. *Critique of Pure Reason*, B 402 and B 442–3.]

28. [Cf. *ibid.*, B 348.]

29. On the table of the categories many neat observations may be made, for instance: (1) that the third arises from the first and the second, joined in one concept; (2) that in those of quantity and of quality there is merely a progress from unity to totality or from something to nothing (for this purpose the categories of quality must stand thus: reality, limitation, total negation), without *correlata* or *opposita*, whereas those of relation and of modality have them; (3) that, as in logic categorical judgments are the

And this system, like every other true one founded on a universal principle, shows its inestimable usefulness in that it excludes all foreign concepts which might otherwise intrude among the pure concepts of the understanding, and determines the place of every cognition. Those concepts, which under the name of *concepts of reflection* have been likewise arranged in a table according to the clue of the categories, intrude into ontology without having any privilege or legitimate claim to be among the pure concepts of the understanding. The latter are concepts of connection, and thereby of the objects themselves, whereas the former are only concepts of a mere comparison of concepts already given, and therefore are of quite another nature and use. By my systematic division[30] they are saved from this confusion. But the utility of this separate table of the categories will be still more obvious when, as will soon happen, we separate the table of the transcendental concepts of reason from the concepts of the understanding. The concepts of reason being of quite another nature and origin, their table must have quite another form from that of the concepts of understanding. This so necessary separation has never yet been made in any system of metaphysics, where as a rule, these ideas of reason are all mixed up with the concepts of the understanding, like children belonging to one family—a confusion that was unavoidable in the absence of a definite system of categories.

THIRD PART OF THE MAIN TRANSCENDENTAL QUESTION
HOW IS METAPHYSICS IN GENERAL POSSIBLE?

§ 40. Pure mathematics and pure natural science had no need for such a deduction (as has been made for both) for the sake of their own safety and certainty. For the former rests upon its own evidence, and the latter (though sprung from pure sources of the understanding) upon experience and its thorough confirmation. Pure natural science cannot altogether refuse and dispense with the testimony of experience; hence with all its certainty it can never, as philosophy, rival mathematics. Both sciences therefore stood in need of this inquiry, not for themselves, but for the sake of another science, namely, metaphysics.

Metaphysics has to do not only with concepts of nature, which always find their application in experience, but also with pure rational concepts, which never can be given in any possible experience whatsoever. Consequently, the objective reality of these concepts (viz., that they are not mere chimeras) and also the truth or falsity of metaphysical assertions cannot be discovered or confirmed by any experience. This part of metaphysics, however, is precisely what constitutes its essential end, to which the rest is only a means, and thus this science is in need of such a deduction

---

basis of all others, so the category of substance is the basis of all concepts of actual things; (4) that, as modality in a judgment is not a distinct predicate, so by the modal concepts a determination is not superadded to things, etc. Such observations are of great use. If we, besides, enumerate all the predicables, which we can find pretty completely in any good ontology (for example, Baumgarten's), and arrange them in classes under the categories, in which operation we must not neglect to add as complete a dissection of all these concepts as possible, there will then arise a merely analytic part of metaphysics, which does not contain a single synthetic proposition and might precede the second (the synthetic), and would, by its precision and completeness, be not only useful, but, in virtue of its system, be even to some extent elegant.

30. [See *Critique of Pure Reason*, B 316.]

for its own sake. The third question now proposed relates therefore, as it were, to the root and peculiarity of metaphysics, i.e., the occupation of reason merely with itself and the supposed knowledge of objects arising immediately from this brooding over its own concepts, without requiring experience or indeed being able to reach that knowledge through experience.[31]

Without solving this question, reason will never be satisfied. The empirical use to which reason limits the pure understanding does not fully satisfy reason's own proper destination. Every single experience is only a part of the whole sphere of its domain, but the absolute totality of all possible experience is itself not experience. Yet it is a necessary problem for reason, the mere representation of which requires concepts quite different from the pure concepts of the understanding, whose use is only immanent, i.e., refers to experience so far as it can be given. Whereas the concepts of reason aim at the completeness, i.e., the collective unity of all possible experience, and thereby go beyond every given experience. Thus they become *transcendent.*

As the understanding stands in need of categories for experience, reason contains in itself the ground of ideas, by which I mean necessary concepts whose object *cannot* be given in any experience. The latter are inherent in the nature of reason, as the former are in that of the understanding. While the ideas carry with them an illusion likely to mislead, this illusion is unavoidable though it certainly can be kept from misleading us.

Since all illusion consists in holding the subjective ground of our judgments to be objective, a self-knowledge of pure reason in its transcendent (hyperbolical) use is the only safeguard against the aberrations into which reason falls when it mistakes its destination, and transcendently refers to the object in itself that which only concerns reason's own subject and its guidance in all immanent use.

§ 41. The distinction of *ideas,* i.e., of pure concepts of reason, from the categories, or pure concepts of the understanding, as cognitions of a quite different species, origin, and use is so important a point in founding a science which is to contain the system of all these *a priori* cognitions that, without this distinction, metaphysics is absolutely impossible or is at best a random, bungling attempt to build a castle in the air without a knowledge of the materials or of their fitness for one purpose or another. Had the *Critique of Pure Reason* done nothing but first point out this distinction, it would thereby have contributed more to clear up our conception of, and to guide our inquiry in, the field of metaphysics than all the vain efforts which have hitherto been made to satisfy the transcendent problems of pure reason; for one never even suspected that he was in quite another field from that of the understanding, and hence that he was classing concepts of the understanding and those of reason together, as if they were of the same kind.

§ 42. All pure cognitions of the understanding have the feature that the concepts can be given in experience, and the principles can be confirmed by it; whereas the transcendent cognitions of reason cannot either, as ideas, be given in experience or, as propositions, ever be confirmed or refuted by it. Hence whatever errors may slip

31. If we can say that a science is actual, at least in the idea of all men, as soon as it appears that the problems which lead to it are proposed to everybody by the nature of human reason, and hence that at all times many (though faulty) endeavors are unavoidably made in its behalf; then we are bound to say that metaphysics is subjectively (and indeed necessarily) actual, and then we justly ask how is it (objectively) possible.

in unawares can only be discovered by pure reason itself—a discovery of much difficulty, because this very reason naturally becomes dialectical by means of its ideas; and this unavoidable illusion cannot be limited by any objective and dogmatic inquiries into things, but only by a subjective investigation of reason itself as a source of ideas.

§ 43. In the *Critique of Pure Reason* it was always my greatest care to endeavor, not only carefully to distinguish the several kinds of cognition, but to derive concepts belonging to each one of them from their common source. I did this in order that by knowing whence they originated, I might determine their use with safety and also have the invaluable, but never previously anticipated, advantage of knowing the completeness of my enumeration, classification, and specification of concepts *a priori*, and of knowing it according to principles. Without this, metaphysics is mere rhapsody, in which no one knows whether he has enough or whether and where something is still wanting. We can indeed have this advantage only in pure philosophy, but of this philosophy it constitutes the very essence.

As I had found the origin of the categories in the four logical functions of all judgments of the understanding, it was quite natural to seek the origin of the ideas in the three functions of syllogisms. For as soon as these pure concepts of reason (the transcendental ideas) are given, they could hardly, except they be held innate, be found anywhere else than in the same activity of reason, which, so far as it regards mere form, constitutes the logical element of syllogisms; but, so far as it represents judgments of the understanding as determined with respect to one or another form *a priori*, constitutes transcendental concepts of pure reason.

The formal difference of syllogisms makes their division into categorical, hypothetical, and disjunctive necessary. The concepts of reason founded on them contain therefore, first, the idea of the complete subject (the substantial); secondly, the idea of the complete series of conditions; thirdly, the determination of all concepts in the idea of a complete complex of that which is possible.[32] The first idea is psychological, the second cosmological, the third theological; and, as all three give occasion to dialectic, yet each in its own way, the division of the whole dialectic of pure reason into its paralogism, its antinomy, and its ideal was arranged accordingly. Through this derivation we may feel assured that all the claims of pure reason are completely represented and that none can be wanting, because the faculty of reason itself, whence they all take their origin, is thereby completely surveyed.

§ 44. In these general considerations it is also remarkable that the ideas of reason, unlike the categories, are of no service to the use of our understanding in experience, but quite dispensable, and become even an impediment to the maxims of a rational cognition of nature. Yet in another aspect still to be determined they are necessary. Whether the soul is or is not a simple substance is of no consequence to us in the explanation of its phenomena. For we cannot render the concept of a simple being understandable sensuously and concretely by any possible experience.

---

32. In disjunctive judgments we consider all possibility as divided in respect to a particular concept. By the ontological principle of the thoroughgoing determination of a thing in general, I understand the principle that either the one or the other of all possible contradictory predicates must be assigned to any object. This is at the same time the principle of all disjunctive judgments, constituting the foundation of the totality of all possibility, and in it the possibility of every object in general is considered as determined. This may serve as a brief explanation of the above proposition: that the activity of reason in disjunctive syllogisms is formally the same as that by which it fashions the idea of a totality of all reality, containing in itself the positive member of all contradictory predicates.

The concept is therefore quite void as regards all hoped-for insight into the cause of appearances and cannot at all serve as a principle of the explanation of that which internal or external experience supplies. Likewise the cosmological ideas of the beginning of the world or of its eternity *(a parte ante)* cannot be of any service to us for the explanation of any event in the world itself. And finally we must, according to a right maxim of the philosophy of nature, refrain from all explanation of the design of nature as being drawn from the will of a Supreme Being, because this would not be natural philosophy but an admission that we have come to the end of it. The use of these ideas, therefore, is quite different from that of those categories by which (and by the principles built upon which) experience itself first becomes possible. But our laborious analytic of the understanding would be superfluous if we had nothing else in view than the mere cognition of nature as it can be given in experience; for reason does its work, both in mathematics and in natural science, quite safely and well without any of this subtle deduction. Therefore our critique of the understanding combines with the ideas of pure reason for a purpose which lies beyond the empirical use of the understanding; but we have above declared the use of the understanding in this respect to be totally inadmissible and without any object or meaning. Yet there must be a harmony between the nature of reason and that of the understanding, and the former must contribute to the perfection of the latter and cannot possibly upset it.

The solution of this question is as follows. Pure reason does not in its ideas point to particular objects which lie beyond the field of experience, but only requires completeness of the use of the understanding in the complex of experience. But this completeness can be a completeness of principles only, not of intuitions and of objects. In order, however, to represent the ideas definitely, reason conceives them after the fashion of the cognition of an object. This cognition is, as far as these rules are concerned, completely determined; but the object is only an idea invented for the purpose of bringing the cognition of the understanding as near as possible to the completeness indicated by that idea.

Prefatory Remark to the Dialectic of Pure Reason

§ 45. We have above shown in §§ 33 and 34 that the purity of the categories from all admixture of sensuous determinations may mislead reason into extending their use beyond all experience to things in themselves; for though these categories themselves find no intuition which can give them meaning or sense *in concreto*, they, as mere logical functions, can represent a thing in general, but not give by themselves alone a determinate concept of anything. Such hyperbolical objects are distinguished by the appellation of *noumena*, or pure beings of the understanding (or better, beings of thought) —such as, for example, "substance," but conceived without permanence in time; or "cause," but not acting in time, etc. Here predicates that only serve to make the conformity-to-law of experience possible are applied to these concepts, and yet they are deprived of all the conditions of intuition on which alone experience is possible, and so these concepts lose all significance.

There is no danger, however, of the understanding spontaneously making an excursion so very wantonly beyond its own bounds into the field of the mere beings of thought, unless being impelled by alien laws. But when reason, which cannot be fully satisfied with any empirical use of the rules of the understanding, as being always conditioned, requires a completion of this chain of conditions, then the understanding is forced out of its sphere. And then reason partly represents objects of experience in a series so extended that no experience can grasp it, partly even (with a view to complete the series) it seeks entirely beyond experience *noumena*, to which it can attach that chain; and so, having at last escaped from the conditions of experience, reason makes its hold complete. These are then the transcendental ideas, which, (though in accord with the true but hidden ends of the natural determination of our reason) may aim, not at extravagant concepts, but at an unbounded extension of their empirical use, yet seduce the understanding by an unavoidable illusion to a transcendent use, which, though deceitful, cannot be restrained within the bounds of experience by any resolution, but only by scientific instruction and with much difficulty.

I. *The Psychological Ideas*[33]

§ 46. People have long since observed that in all substances the subject proper, that which remains after all the accidents (as predicates) are abstracted, hence the substantial itself, remains unknown, and various complaints have been made concerning these limits to our insight. But it will be well to consider that the human understanding is not to be blamed for its inability to know the substance of things, i.e., to determine it by itself, but rather for demanding to cognise it determinately as though it were a given object, it being a mere idea. Pure reason requires us to seek for every predicate of a thing its own subject, and for this subject, which is itself necessarily nothing but a predicate, its subject, and so on indefinitely (or as far as we can reach). But hence it follows that we must not hold anything at which we can arrive to be an ultimate subject, and that substance itself never can be thought by our understanding, however deep we may penetrate, even if all nature were unveiled to us. For the specific nature of our understanding consists in thinking everything discursively, i.e., by concepts, and so by mere predicates, to which, therefore, the absolute subject must always be wanting. Hence all the real properties by which we cognise bodies are mere accidents, not even excepting impenetrability, which we can only represent to ourselves as the effect of a force for which the subject is unknown to us.

Now we appear to have this substance in the consciousness of ourselves (in the thinking subject), and indeed in an immediate intuition; for all the predicates of an internal sense refer to the *ego*, as a subject, and I cannot conceive myself as the predicate of any other subject. Hence completeness in the reference of the given concepts as predicates to a subject—not merely an idea, but an object—that is, the *absolute subject* itself, seems to be given in experience. But this expectation is disappointed. For the ego is not a concept,[34] but only the indication of the object of the internal sense, so far as we cognise it by no further predicate. Consequently, it cannot be itself a predicate of any other thing; but just as little can it be a determinate concept of an absolute subject, but is, as in all other cases, only the reference of the internal phenomena to their unknown subject. Yet this idea (which serves very well

---

33. See *Critique of Pure Reason*, "The Paralogisms of Pure Reason," A 341/B 399 — A 405/B 432.

34. Were the representation of the apperception (the ego) a concept by which anything could be thought, it could be used as a predicate of other things or contain predicates in itself. But it is nothing more than the feeling of an existence without the slightest concept and is only the representation of that to which all thinking stands in relation *(relatione accidentis)*.

as a regulative principle totally to destroy all materialistic explanations of the internal phenomena of the soul) occasions by a very natural misunderstanding a very specious argument, which infers the nature of the soul from this supposed cognition of the substance of our thinking being. This argument is specious insofar as the knowledge of this substance falls quite without the complex of experience.

§ 47. But though we may call this thinking self (the soul) substance, as being the ultimate subject of thinking which cannot be further represented as the predicate of another thing, it remains quite empty and inconsequential if permanence—the quality which renders the concept of substances in experience fruitful—cannot be proved of it.

But permanence can never be proved of the concept of a substance as a thing in itself, but only for the purposes of experience. This is sufficiently shown by the first Analogy of Experience,[35] and whoever will not yield to this proof may try for himself whether he can succeed in proving, from the concept of a subject which does not exist itself as the predicate of another thing, that its existence is thoroughly permanent and that it cannot either in itself or by any natural cause come into being or pass out of it. These synthetic *a priori* propositions can never be proved in themselves, but only in reference to things as objects of possible experience.

§ 48. If, therefore, from the concept of the soul as a substance we would infer its permanence, this can hold good as regards possible experience only, not of the soul as a thing in itself and beyond all possible experience. Now life is the subjective condition of all our possible experience; consequently we can only infer the permanence of the soul in life, for the death of man is the end of all the experience that concerns the soul as an object of experience, except the contrary be proved—which is the very question in hand. The permanence of the soul can therefore only be proved (and no one cares for that) during the life of man, but not, as we desire to do, after death. This is so because the concept of substance, insofar as it is to be considered as necessarily combined with the concept of permanence, can be so combined only according to the principles of possible experience, and therefore for the purposes of experience only.[36]

§ 49. That there is something real outside us which not only corresponds but must correspond to our external perceptions can likewise be proved to be, not a connection of things in themselves, but for the sake of experience. This means that there is something empirical, i.e., some appearance in space outside us, that admits

35. Cf. *Critique*, B 224–232.

36. It is indeed very remarkable how carelessly metaphysicians have always passed over the principle of the permanence of substances without ever attempting a proof of it; doubtless because they found themselves abandoned by all proofs as soon as they began to deal with the concept of substance. Common sense, which felt distinctly that without this presupposition no union of perceptions in experience is possible, supplied the want by a postulate. From experience itself it never could derive such a principle, partly because material objects (substances) cannot be so traced in all their alterations and dissolutions that the matter can always be found undiminished, partly because the principle contains *necessity*, which is always the sign of an *a priori* principle. People then boldly applied this postulate to the concept of soul as a *substance*, and concluded a necessary continuance of the soul after the death of man (especially as the simplicity of this substance, which is inferred from the indivisibility of consciousness, secured it from destruction by dissolution). Had they found the genuine source of this principle—a discovery which requires deeper researches than they were ever inclined to make—they would have seen that the law of the permanence of substances finds a place for the purposes of experience only, and hence can hold good of things so far as they are to be cognised and conjoined with others in experience, but never independently of all possible experience, and consequently cannot hold good of the soul after death.

of a satisfactory proof; for we have nothing to do with other objects than those which belong to possible experience, because objects which cannot be given us in any experience are nothing for us. Empirically outside me is that which is intuited in space; and space, together with all the appearances which it contains, belongs to the representations whose connection, according to laws of experience, proves their objective truth, just as the connection of the appearances of the internal sense proves the actuality of my soul (as an object of the internal sense). By means of external experience I am conscious of the actuality of bodies as external appearances in space, in the same manner as by means of internal experience I am conscious of the existence of my soul in time; but this soul is cognised only as an object of the internal sense by appearances that constitute an internal state and of which the being in itself, which forms the basis of these appearances, is unknown. Cartesian idealism therefore does nothing but distinguish external experience from dreaming and the conformity to law (as a criterion of its truth) of the former from the irregularity and the false illusion of the latter. In both it presupposes space and time as conditions of the existence of objects, and it only inquires whether the objects of the external senses which we, when awake, put in space, are as actually to be found in it as the object of the internal sense, the soul, is in time; that is, whether experience carries with it sure criteria to distinguish it from imagination. This doubt, however, may easily be disposed of, and we always do so in common life by investigating the connection of appearances in both space and time according to universal laws of experience; and we cannot doubt, when the representation of external things throughout agrees therewith, that they constitute truthful experience. Material idealism, in which appearances are considered as such only according to their connection in experience may accordingly be very easily refuted; and it is just as sure an experience that bodies exist outside us (in space) as that I myself exist according to the representation of the internal sense (in time), for the concept "outside us" only signifies existence in space. However, as the ego in the proposition "I am" means not only the object of internal intuition (in time) but the subject of consciousness, just as body means not only external intuition (in space) but the thing in itself which is the basis of this appearance, then the question whether bodies (as appearances of the external sense) exist as bodies in nature apart from my thoughts may without any hesitation be denied. But the question whether I myself as an appearance of the internal sense (the soul according to empirical psychology) exist apart from my faculty of representation in time is an exactly similar question and must likewise be answered in the negative. And in this manner everything, when it is reduced to its true meaning, is decided and certain. The formal (which I have also called transcendental) actually abolishes the material, or Cartesian, idealism. For if space be nothing but a form of my sensibility, it is as a representation in me just as actual as I myself am, and nothing but the empirical truth of the appearances in it remains for consideration. But if this is not the case, if space and the appearances in it are something existing outside us, then all the criteria of experience outside our perception can never prove the actuality of these objects outside us.

II. *The Cosmological Ideas*[37]

§ 50. This product of pure reason in its transcendent use is its most remarkable phenomenon. It serves as a very powerful agent to rouse philosophy from its dog-

---

37. Cf. *Critique*, "The Antinomy of Pure Reason," B 432–595.

matic slumber and to stimulate it to the arduous task of undertaking a criticism of reason itself.

I term this idea cosmological because it always takes its object only from the sensible world and does not need any other world than that whose object is given to sense; consequently, it remains in this respect in its native home, does not become transcendent, and is therefore so far not an idea; whereas to conceive the soul as a simple substance, on the contrary, means to conceive such an object (the simple) as cannot be presented to the senses. Notwithstanding, the cosmological idea extends the connection of the conditioned with its condition (whether mathematical or dynamical) so far that experience never can keep up with it. It is therefore with regard to this point always an idea, whose object never can be adequately given in any experience.

§ 51. In the first place, the use of a system of categories becomes here so obvious and unmistakable that, even if there were not several other proofs of it, this alone would sufficiently prove it indispensable in the system of pure reason. There are only four such transcendent ideas, as many as there are classes of categories; in each of which, however, they refer only to the absolute completeness of the series of the conditions for a given conditioned. In conformity with these cosmological ideas, there are only four kinds of dialectical assertions of pure reason, which, being dialectical, prove that to each of them, on equally specious principles of pure reason, a contradictory assertion stands opposed. As all the metaphysical art of the most subtle distinction cannot prevent this opposition, it compels the philosopher to recur to the first sources of pure reason itself. This antinomy, not arbitrarily invented but founded in the nature of human reason, and hence unavoidable and never ceasing, contains the following four theses together with their antitheses:

1

Thesis

The world has, as to time and space, a beginning (limit).

Antithesis

The world is, as to time and space, infinite.

2

Thesis

Everything in the world is constituted out of the simple.

Antithesis

There is nothing simple, but everything is composite.

3

Thesis

There are in the world causes through freedom.

Antithesis

There is no freedom, but all is nature.

4

Thesis

In the series of world-causes there is some necessary being.

Antithesis
There is nothing necessary in the world, but in this series all is contingent.

§ 52a. Here is the most singular phenomenon of human reason, no other instance of which can be shown in its any other use. If we, as is commonly done, represent to ourselves the appearances of the sensible world as things in themselves, if we assume the principles of their combination as principles universally valid of things in themselves and not merely of experience, as is usually, nay, without our *Critique*, unavoidably done, there arises an unexpected conflict which never can be removed in the common dogmatic way; because the thesis, as well as the antithesis, can be shown by equally clear, evident, and irresistible proofs—for I pledge myself as to the correctness of all these proofs—and reason therefore perceives that it is divided against itself, a state at which the sceptic rejoices, but which must make the critical philosopher pause and feel ill at ease.

§ 52b. We may blunder in various ways in metaphysics without any fear of being detected in falsehood. For we never can be refuted by experience if we but avoid self-contradiction, which in synthetic though purely fictitious propositions may be done whenever the concepts which we connect are mere ideas that cannot be given (as regards their whole content) in experience. For how can we make out by experience whether the world is from eternity or had a beginning, whether matter is infinitely divisible or consists of simple parts? Such concepts cannot be given in any experience, however extensive, and consequently the falsehood either of the affirmative or the negative propostion cannot be discovered by this touchstone.

The only possible way in which reason could have revealed unintentionally its secret dialectic, falsely announced as dogmatics, would be when it were made to ground an assertion upon a universally admitted principle and to deduce the exact contrary with the greatest accuracy of inference from another which is equally granted. This is actually here the case with regard to four natural ideas of reason, whence four assertions on the one side and as many counter-assertions on the other arise, each consistently following from universally acknowledged principles. Thus they reveal, by the use of these principles, the dialectical illusion of pure reason, which would otherwise forever remain concealed.

This is therefore a decisive experiment, which must necessarily expose any error lying hidden in the assumptions of reason.[38] Contradictory propositions cannot both be false, unless the concept lying at the ground of both of them is self-contradictory; for example, the propositions, "A square circle is round," and "A square circle is not round," are both false. For, as to the former, it is false that the circle is round because it is quadrangular; and it is likewise false that it is not round, i.e., angular, because it is a circle. For the logical criterion of the impossibility of a concept consists in this, that if we presuppose it, two contradictory propositions both become false; consequently, as no middle between them is conceivable, nothing at all is thought by that concept.

---

38. I therefore would be pleased to have the critical reader to devote to this antinomy of pure reason his chief attention, because nature itself seems to have established it with a view to stagger reason in its daring pretentions and to force it to self-examination. For every proof which I have given both of the thesis and the antithesis, I pledge myself to be responsible, and thereby to show the certainty of the inevitable antinomy of reason. When the reader is brought by this curious phenomenon to fall back upon the proof of the presumption upon which it rests, he will feel himself obliged to investigate the ultimate foundation of all the cognition of pure reason with me more thoroughly.

§ 52c. The first two antinomies, which I call mathematical because they are concerned with the addition or division of the homogeneous, are founded on such a contradictory concept; and hence I explain how it happens that both the thesis and antithesis of the two are false.

When I speak of objects in time and in space, it is not of things in themselves, of which I know nothing, but of things in appearance, i.e., of experience, as a particular way of cognising objects which is only afforded to man. I must not say of that which I think in time or in space, that in itself, and independent of these my thoughts, it exists in space and in time, for in that case I would contradict myself, because space and time, together with the appearances in them, are nothing existing in themselves and outside of my representations, but are themselves only modes of representation, and it is palpably contradictory to say that a mere mode of representation exists outside our representation. Objects of the senses therefore exist only in experience, whereas to give them a self-subsisting existence apart from experience or prior to it is merely to represent to ourselves that experience actually exists apart from experience or prior to it.

Now if I ask about the magnitude of the world, as to space and time, it is equally impossible, with regard to all my concepts, to declare it infinite or to declare it finite. For neither assertion can be contained in experience, because experience either of an infinite space or of an infinite time elapsed, or again, of the boundary of the world by an empty space or by an antecedent empty time, is impossible; these are mere ideas. This magnitude of the world, be it determined in either way, would therefore have to exist in the world itself apart from all experience. But this contradicts the concept of a world of sense, which is merely a complex of the appearances whose existence and connection occur only in our representations, i.e., in experience; since this latter is not an object in itself but a mere mode of representation. Hence it follows that, as the concept of an absolutely existing world of sense is self-contradictory, the solution of the problem concerning its magnitude, whether attempted affirmatively or negatively, is always false.

The same holds of the second antinomy, which relates to the division of appearances. For these are mere representations; and the parts exist merely in their representation, consequently in the division (i.e., in a possible experience where they are given) and the division reaches only as far as such experience reaches. To assume that an appearance, e.g., that of a body, contains in itself before all experience all the parts which any possible experience can ever reach is to impute to a mere appearance, which can exist only in experience, an existence previous to experience. In other words, it would mean that mere representations exist before they can be found in our faculty of representation. Such an assertion is self-contradictory, as also every solution of our misunderstood problem, whether we maintain that bodies in themselves consist of an infinite number of parts or of a finite number of simple parts.

§ 53. In the first (the mathematical) class of antinomies the falsehood of the presupposition consists in representing in one concept something self-contradictory as if it were compatible (i.e., an appearance as an object in itself). But as to the second (the dynamical) class of antinomies, the falsehood of the presupposition consists in representing as contradictory what is compatible. Consequently, whereas in the first case the opposed assertions were both false, in this case, on the other hand, where they are opposed to one another by mere misunderstanding, they may both be true.

Any mathematical connection necessarily presupposes homogeneity of what is connected (in the concept of magnitude), while the dynamical one by no means requires this. When we have to deal with extended magnitudes, all the parts must be homogeneous with one another and with the whole. But in the connection of cause and effect homogeneity may indeed likewise be found but is not necessary, for the concept of causality (by means of which something is posited through something else quite different from it) does not in the least require it.

If the objects of the world of sense are taken for things in themselves and the above-mentioned laws of nature for the laws of things in themselves, the contradiction would be unavoidable. So also, if the subject of freedom were, like other objects, represented as mere appearance, the contradiction would be just as unavoidable; for the same predicate would at once be affirmed and denied of the same kind of object in the same sense. But if natural necessity is referred merely to appearances and freedom merely to things in themselves, no contradiction arises if we at the same time assume or admit both kinds of causality, however difficult or impossible it may be to make the latter kind conceivable.

In appearance every effect is an event, or something that happens in time; the effect must, according to the universal law of nature, be preceded by a determination of the causality of its cause (a state of the cause) on which the effect follows according to a constant law. But this determination of the cause to causal action must likewise be something that takes place or happens; the cause must have begun to act, otherwise no succession between it and the effect could be thought. Otherwise the effect, as well as the causality of the cause, would have always existed. Therefore the determination of the cause to act must also have originated among appearances and must consequently, just like its effect, be an event, which must again have its cause, and so on; hence natural necessity must be the condition according to which efficient causes are determined. Whereas if freedom is to be a property of certain causes of appearances, it must, as regards the latter as events, be a faculty of starting them spontaneously, i.e., without the causality of the cause itself needing to begin and hence needing no other ground to determine its beginning. But then the cause, as to its causality, must not stand under time-determinations of its state, i.e., it cannot be an appearance, and must be considered a thing in itself, while only its effects would be appearances.[39] If without contradiction we can think of the beings of understanding as exercising such an influence on appearances, then natural necessity will attach to all connections of cause and effect in the sensuous world, though, on the other hand, freedom can be granted to the cause which is itself not an appearance (but the foundation of appearance). Nature and freedom therefore can

---

39. The idea of freedom occurs only in the relation of the intellectual, as cause, to the appearance, as effect. Hence we cannot attribute freedom to matter in regard to the incessant action by which it fills its space, though this action takes place from an internal principle. We can likewise find no concept of freedom suitable to purely rational beings, for instance, to God, so far as his action is immanent. For his action, though independent of external determining causes, is determined in his eternal reason, that is, in the divine *nature*. It is only, if *something is to start* by an action, and so the effect occurs in the sequence of time, or in the world of sense (e.g., the beginning of the world), that we can put the question whether the causality of the cause must in its turn have been started or whether the cause can originate an effect without its causality itself beginning. In the former case the concept of this causality is a concept of natural necessity; in the latter, that of freedom. From this the reader will see that as I explained freedom to be the faculty of starting an event spontaneously, I have exactly hit the concept which is the problem of metaphysics.

without contradiction be attributed to the very same thing, but in different relations—on one side as an appearance, on the other as a thing in itself.

We have in us a faculty which not only stands in connection with its subjective determining grounds that are the natural causes of its actions and is so far the faculty of a being that itself belongs to appearances, but is also related to objective grounds that are only ideas so far as they can determine this faculty; this connection is expressed by *ought*. This faculty is called *reason*, and, so far as we consider a being (man) entirely according to this objectively determinable reason, he cannot be considered as a being of sense; but, rather, this property is that of a thing in itself, and we cannot comprehend the possibility of this property—I mean how the *ought* (which might never yet have taken place) should determine its activity and could become the cause of actions whose effect is an appearance in the sensible world. Yet the causality of reason would be freedom with regard to the effects in the sensuous world, so far as we can consider *objective grounds*, which are themselves ideas, as their determinants. For its action in that case would not depend upon subjective conditions, consequently not upon those of time, and of course not upon the law of nature which serves to determine them, because grounds of reason give the rule universally to actions, according to principles, without influence of the circumstances of either time or place.

What I adduce here is merely meant as an example to make the thing intelligible, and does not necessarily belong to our problem, which must be decided from mere concepts independently of the properties which we meet in the actual world.

Now I may say without contradiction that all the actions of rational beings, so far as they are appearances (encountered in some experience), are subject to the necessity of nature; but the same actions, as regards merely the rational subject and its faculty of acting according to mere reason, are free. For what is required for the necessity of nature? Nothing more than the determinability of every event in the world of sense according to constant laws, i.e., a reference to cause in the appearance; in this process the thing in itself at its foundation and its causality remain unknown. But, I say, the law of nature remains, whether the rational being is the cause of the effects in the sensuous world from reason, i.e., through freedom, or whether it does not determine them on grounds of reason. For if the former is the case, the action is performed according to maxims, the effect of which as appearance is always conformable to constant laws; if the latter is the case, and the action not performed on principles of reason, it is subject to the empirical laws of sensibility, and in both cases the effects are connected according to constant laws; more than this we do not require or know concerning natural necessity. But in the former case reason is the cause of these laws of nature, and therefore free; in the latter, the effects follow according to mere natural laws of sensibility, because reason does not influence it; but reason itself is not determined on that account by the sensibility (which is impossible) and is therefore free in this case too. Freedom is therefore no hindrance to natural law in appearances; neither does this law abrogate the freedom of the practical use of reason, which is connected with things in themselves as determining grounds.

Thus practical freedom, viz., the freedom in which reason possesses causality according to objectively determining grounds, is rescued; and yet natural necessity is not in the least curtailed with regard to the very same effects, as appearances. The same remarks will serve to explain what we had to say concerning transcendental freedom and its compatibility with natural necessity (in the same subject, but not taken in one and the same reference). For, as to this, every beginning of the action of a being from objective causes regarded as determining grounds is always a first beginning, though the same action is in the series of appearances only a subordinate beginning, which must be preceded by a state of the cause which determines it and is itself determined in the same manner by another immediately preceding. Thus we are able, in rational beings, or in beings generally so far as their causality is determined in them as things in themselves, to think of a faculty of beginning of themselves a series of states without falling into contradiction with the laws of nature. For the relation of the action to objective grounds of reason is not a time-relation; in this case that which determines the causality does not precede in time the action, because such determining grounds represent, not a reference to objects of sense, e.g., to causes in the appearances, but to determining causes as things in themselves, which do not stand under conditions of time. And in this way the action, with regard to the causality of reason, can be considered as a first beginning, while in respect to the series of appearances as a merely subordinate beginning. We may therefore without contradiction consider it in the former aspect as free, but in the latter (insofar as it is merely appearance) as subject to natural necessity.

As to the fourth antinomy, it is solved in the same way as the conflict of reason with itself in the third. For, provided the cause *in* the appearance is distinguished from the cause *of* the appearances (so far as it can be thought as a thing in itself), both propositions are perfectly reconcilable: the one, that there is nowhere in the sensuous world a cause (according to similar laws of causality) whose existence is absolutely necessary; the other, that this world is nevertheless connected with a necessary being as its cause (but of another kind and according to another law). The incompatibility of these two propositions rests entirely upon the misunderstanding of extending what is valid merely of appearances to things in themselves and in general of mixing both in one concept.

§ 54. This, then, is the exposition, and this is the solution of the whole antinomy in which reason finds itself involved in the application of its principles to the sensible world. The former alone (the mere exposition) would be a considerable service in the cause of our knowledge of human reason, even though the solution might fail to fully satisfy the reader, who has here to combat a natural illusion which has been but recently exposed to him and which he had hitherto always regarded as true. For one result at least is unavoidable. As it is quite impossible to prevent this conflict of reason with itself—so long as the objects of the sensible world are taken for things in themselves and not for mere appearances, which they are in fact—the reader is thereby compelled to examine over again the deduction of all our *a priori* cognition and the proof which I have given of my deduction in order to come to a decision on the question. This is all I require at present; for when in this occupation he shall have thought himself deep enough into the nature of pure reason, those concepts by which alone the solution of the conflict of reason is possible will become sufficiently familiar to him. Without this preparation I cannot expect an unreserved assent even from the most attentive reader.

III. *The Theological Idea*[40]

§ 55. The third transcendental idea, which affords material for the most important but, if pursued only speculatively, transcendent and thereby dialectical use of

---

40. Cf. *Critique*, "The Ideal of Pure Reason," B 595–670.

reason, is the ideal of pure reason. Reason in this case does not, as with the psychological and the cosmological ideas, start from experience and err by exaggerating its grounds in striving to attain, if possible, the absolute completeness of their series. Rather, it totally breaks with experience and from mere concepts of what constitutes the absolute completeness of a thing in general (hence by means of the idea of a most perfect primal being) proceeds to determine the possibility and therefore the actuality of all other things. And so the mere presupposition of a being which, although not in the series of experiences is thought for the purposes of experience and for the sake of conceiving its connection, order, and unity, i.e., the idea, is more easily distinguished from the concept of the understanding here than in the former cases. Hence we can easily expose the dialectical illusion which arises from our making the subjective conditions of our thinking objective conditions of objects themselves, and from making an hypothesis necessary for the satisfaction of our reason into a dogma. As the observations of the *Critique* on the pretensions of trancendental theology are intelligible, clear, and decisive, I have nothing more to add on the subject.

General Remark on the Transcendental Ideas

§ 56. The objects which are given us by experience are in many respects inconceivable, and many questions to which the law of nature leads us when carried beyond a certain point (though still quite conformably to the laws of nature) admit of no answer, as, for example, the question as to why material objects attract one another? But if we entirely quit nature or, in pursuing its combinations, exceed all possible experience, and so enter the realm of mere ideas, we cannot then say that the object is inconceivable and that the nature of things proposes to us insoluble problems. For we are not then concerned with nature or with given objects at all, but with mere concepts which have their origin solely in our reason, and with mere beings of thought; and all the problems that arise from our concepts of them must be solved, because of course reason can and must give a full account of its own procedure.[41] As the psychological, cosmological, and theological ideas are nothing but pure concepts of reason, which cannot be given in any experience, the questions which reason asks us about them are put to us, not by the objects, but by mere maxims of our reason for the sake of its own satisfaction. They must all be capable of satisfactory answers, which are provided by showing that they are principles which bring our use of the understanding into thorough agreement, completeness, and synthetical unity, and that they thus hold good of experience only, but of experience as a whole. Although an absolute whole of experience is impossible, the idea of a whole of cognition according to principles in general must impart to our knowledge a peculiar kind of unity, that of a system, without which it is nothing but piecework and cannot be used for the highest purpose (which is always only the system of

---

41. Herr Platner, in his *Aphorisms*, acutely says (§§ 728, 729), "If reason be a criterion, no concept which is incomprehensible to human reason can be possible. Incomprehensibility has place in what is actual only. Here incomprehensibility arises from the insufficiency of the acquired ideas." It sounds paradoxical, but is otherwise not strange to say that in nature there is much that is incomprehensible (e.g., the faculty of generation); but if we mount still higher and go even beyond nature, everything again becomes conceivable. For we then quit entirely the objects which can be given us and occupy ourselves merely about ideas, in which occupation we can easily conceive the law that reason prescribes by them to the understanding for its use in experience, because the law is reason's own product.

all purposes); I do not here refer only to the practical, but also to the highest purpose of the speculative use of reason.

The transcendental ideas therefore express the peculiar application of reason as a principle of systematic unity in the use of the understanding. Yet if we assume this unity of the mode of cognition to pertain to the object of cognition, if we regard that which is merely *regulative* to be *constitutive*, and if we persuade ourselves that we can by means of these ideas enlarge our cognition transcendently or far beyond all possible experience, while it only serves to render experience within itself as nearly complete as possible, i.e., to limit its progress by nothing that cannot belong to experience—if we do all this, then we suffer from a mere misunderstanding in our estimate of the proper application of our reason and of its principles and suffer from a dialectic which confuses the empirical use of reason and also sets reason at variance with itself.

CONCLUSION

ON THE DETERMINATION OF THE BOUNDS OF PURE REASON

§ 57. The clearest arguments having been adduced, it would be absurd for us to hope that we can know more of any object than belongs to the possible experience of it or lay claim to the least knowledge of how anything not assumed to be an object of possible experience is determined according to the constitution that it has in itself. For how could we determine anything in this way, since time, space, and all the concepts of the understanding, and still more all the concepts formed by empirical intuition (or perception) in the sensible world have and can have no other use than to make experience possible? And if this condition is omitted from the pure concepts of the understanding, they do not determine any object and have no meaning whatever.

But it would be, on the other hand, a still greater absurdity if we conceded no things in themselves or declared our experience to be the only possible mode of knowing things, our intuition of them in space and in time to be the only possible intuition, our discursive understanding to be the archetype of every possible understanding, and to have the principles of the possibility of experience taken for universal conditions of things in themselves.

Our principles, which limit the use of reason to possible experience, might in this way become transcendent and the limits of our reason be set up as limits of the possibility of things in themselves (as Hume's *Dialogues*[42] may illustrate) if a careful critique did not guard the bounds of our reason with respect to its empirical use and set a limit to its pretensions. Scepticism originally arose from metaphysics and its lawless dialectic. At first it might, merely to favor the empirical use of reason, announce everything that transcends this use as worthless and deceitful; but by and by, when it was perceived that the very same principles that are used in experience insensibly and apparently with the same right led still further than experience ex-

---

42. [David Hume, *Dialogues Concerning Natural Religion* (1779).]

tends, then men began to doubt even the propositions of experience. But here there is no danger, for common sense will doubtless always assert its rights. A certain confusion, however, arose in science, which cannot determine how far reason is to be trusted, and why only so far and no further; and this confusion can only be cleared up and all future relapses obviated by a formal determination, on principle, of the boundary of the use of our reason.

We cannot indeed, beyond all possible experience, form a definite notion of what things in themselves may be. Yet we are not at liberty to abstain entirely from inquiring into them; for experience never satisfies reason fully but, in answering questions, refers us further and further back and leaves us dissatisfied with regard to their complete solution. This anyone may gather from the dialectic of pure reason, which therefore has its good subjective grounds. Having acquired, as regards the nature of our soul, a clear conception of the subject, and having come to the conviction that its appearances cannot be explained materialistically, who can refrain from asking what the soul really is and, if no concept of experience suffices for the purpose, from accounting for it by a concept of reason (that of a simple immaterial being), though we cannot by any means prove its objective reality? Who can satisfy himself with mere empirical knowledge in all the cosmological questions of the duration and of the magnitude of the world, of freedom or of natural necessity, since every answer given on principles of experience begets a fresh question, which likewise requires its answer and thereby clearly shows the insufficiency of all physical modes of explanation to satisfy reason? Finally, who does not see in the thoroughgoing contingency and dependence of all his thoughts and assumptions on mere principles of experience the impossibility of stopping there? And who does not feel himself compelled, notwithstanding all interdictions against losing himself in transcendent ideas, to seek rest and contentment, beyond all the concepts which he can vindicate by experience, in the concept of a being, the possibility of which cannot be conceived but at the same time cannot be refuted, because it relates to a mere being of the understanding and without it reason must needs remain forever dissatisfied?

Bounds (in extended beings) always presuppose a space existing outside a certain definite place and inclosing it; limits do not require this, but are mere negations which affect a quantity so far as it is not absolutely complete. But our reason, as it were, sees in its surroundings a space for the cognition of things in themselves, though we can never have determinate concepts of them and are limited to appearances only.

As long as the cognition of reason is homogeneous, determinate bounds to it cannot be thought. In mathematics and natural science human reason admits of limits but not of bounds, viz., that something indeed lies outside it, at which it can never arrive, but not that it will at any point find completion in its internal progress. The enlarging of insights in mathematics and the possibility of new discoveries are infinite; and the same is the case with the discovery of new properties of nature, of new forces and laws, by continued experience and its rational unification. But limits cannot fail to be seen here; for mathematics refers to appearances only, and what cannot be an object of sensuous intuition (such as the concepts of metaphysics and of morals) lies entirely without its sphere. It can never lead to them, but neither does it require them. There is therefore a continuous progress and approach to these sciences; and there is, as it were, a point or line of contact. Natural science will never reveal to us the internal constitution of things, which, though not appearance, yet can serve as the ultimate ground for explaining appearances. Nor does that science need this for its physical explanations. Nay, even if such grounds should be offered from other sources (for instance, the influence of immaterial beings), they must be rejected and not used in the progress of its explanations. For these explanations must only be grounded upon that which as an object of sense can belong to experience, and be brought into connection with our actual perceptions according to empirical laws.

But metaphysics leads us towards bounds in the dialectical attempts of pure reason (not undertaken arbitrarily or wantonly, but stimulated thereto by the nature of reason itself). And the transcendental ideas, as they do not admit of evasion and yet are never capable of realisation, serve to point out to us actually not only the bounds of the use of pure reason, but also the way to determine them. Such is the end and the use of this natural predisposition of our reason, which has brought forth metaphysics as its favorite child, whose generation, like every other in the world, is not to be ascribed to blind chance but to an original germ, wisely organised for great ends. For metaphysics, in its fundamental features, perhaps more than any other science, is placed in us by nature itself and cannot be considered the production of an arbitrary choice or a casual enlargement in the progress of experience from which it is quite disparate.

Reason with all its concepts and laws of the understanding, which are adequate to it for empirical use, i.e., within the sensible world, finds for itself no satisfaction because ever-recurring questions deprive us of all hope of their complete solution. The transcendental ideas, which have that completion in view, are such problems of reason. But it sees clearly that the sensible world cannot contain this completion; neither, consequently, can all the concepts which serve merely for understanding the world of sense, e.g., space and time, and whatever we have adduced under the name of pure concepts of the understanding. The sensible world is nothing but a chain of appearances connected according to universal laws; it has therefore no subsistence by itself; it is not the thing in itself, and consequently must point to that which contains the basis of this appearance, to beings which cannot be cognised merely as appearances, but as things in themselves. In the cognition of them alone can reason hope to satisfy its desire for completeness in proceeding from the conditioned to its conditions.

We have above (§§ 33, 34) indicated the limits of reason with regard to all cognition of mere beings of thought. Now, since the transcendental ideas have urged us to approach them and thus have led us, as it were, to the spot where the occupied space (viz., experience) touches the void (that of which we can know nothing, viz., noumena), we can determine the bounds of pure reason. For in all bounds there is something positive (e.g., a surface is the boundary of corporeal space, and is therefore itself a space; a line is a space, which is the boundary of the surface, a point the boundary of the line, but yet always a place in space), whereas limits contain mere negations. The limits pointed out in those paragraphs are not enough after we have discovered that beyond them there still lies something (though we can never cognise what it is in itself). For the question now is, What is the attitude of our reason in this connection of what we know with what we do not, and never shall, know? This is an actual connection of a known thing with one quite unknown (and which will always remain so), and though what is unknown should not become the least more known—which we cannot even hope—yet the notion of this connection must be definite, and capable of being rendered distinct.

We must therefore think an immaterial being, a world of understanding, and a Supreme Being (all mere noumena), because in them only, as things in themselves, reason finds that completion and satisfaction, which it can never hope for in the derivation of appearances from their homogeneous grounds, and because these actually have reference to something distinct from them (and totally heterogeneous), as appearances always presuppose an object in itself and therefore suggest its existence whether we can know more of it or not.

But as we can never cognise these beings of understanding as they are in themselves, that is, determinately, yet must assume them as regards the sensible world and connect them with it by reason, we are at least able to think this connection by means of such concepts as express their relation to the world of sense. Yet if we represent to ourselves a being of the understanding by nothing but pure concepts of the understanding, we then indeed represent nothing determinate to ourselves, and consequently our concept has no significance; but if we think of it by properties borrowed from the sensible world, then it is no longer a being of understanding but is conceived as a phenomenon and belongs to the sensible world. Let us take an instance from the concept of the Supreme Being.

The deistic concept is quite a pure concept of reason, but represents only a thing containing all realities, without being able to determine any one of them; because for that purpose an example must be taken from the world of sense, in which case I should have an object of sense only, not something quite heterogeneous which can never be an object of sense. Suppose I attribute to the Supreme Being understanding, for instance; I have no concept of an understanding other than my own, one that must receive its intuitions by the senses and which is occupied in bringing them under rules of the unity of consciousness. Then the elements of my concept would always lie in the appearance; I should, however, by the insufficiency of the appearances be required to go beyond them to the concept of a being which neither depends upon appearances nor is bound up with them as conditions of its determination. But if I separate understanding from sensibility to obtain a pure understanding, then nothing remains but the mere form of thinking without intuition, by which form alone I can cognise nothing determinate and consequently no object. For that purpose I should have to think another understanding, such as would intuit its objects but of which I have not the least concept, because the human understanding is discursive, and can cognise only by means of general concepts. And the very same difficulties arise if we attribute a will to the Supreme Being; for I have this concept only by drawing it from my inner experience, and therefore from my dependence for satisfaction upon objects whose existence I require; and so the concept rests upon sensibility, which is wholly incompatible with the pure concept of the Supreme Being.

Hume's objections to deism are weak, and affect only the proofs, and not the deistic assertion itself. But as regards theism, which depends on a stricter determination of the concept of the Supreme Being, which in deism is merely transcendent, they are very strong and, as this concept is formed, in certain (in fact in all common) cases irrefutable. Hume always insists that by the mere concept of an original being to which we apply only ontological predicates (eternity, omnipresence, omnipotence) we think nothing determinate, and that properties which can yield a concept *in concreto* must be superadded. He insists also that it is not enough to say that it is cause, but we must explain the nature of its causality, e.g., that of an understanding and of a will. He then begins his attacks on the essential point itself, i.e., theism, as he had previously directed his battery only against the proofs of deism, an attack which is not very dangerous to it in its consequences. All his dangerous arguments refer to anthropomorphism, which he holds to be inseparable from theism and to make it contradictory in itself; but if the former can be abandoned, the latter must vanish with it and nothing remain but deism, of which nothing can come, which is of no value and which cannot serve as any foundation to religion or morals. If this anthropomorphism were really unavoidable, no proofs whatever of the existence of a Supreme Being, even were they all granted, could determine for us the concept of this Being without involving us in contradictions.

If we connect with the command to avoid all transcendent judgments of pure reason the command (which apparently conflicts with it) to proceed to concepts that lie beyond the field of its immanent (empirical) use, we discover that both can subsist together, but only at the boundary of all permitted use of reason. For this boundary belongs to the field of experience as well as to that of the beings of thought, and we are thereby taught how these remarkable ideas serve merely for marking the bounds of human reason. On the one hand, they give warning not boundlessly to extend cognition by experience, as if nothing but world remained for us to cognise, and yet, on the other hand, not to transgress the bounds of experience and to think of judging about things beyond them as things in themselves.

But we stop at this boundary if we limit our judgment merely to the relation which the world may have to a being whose very concept lies beyond all the cognition which we can attain within the world. For we then do not attribute to the Supreme Being any of the properties in themselves by which we represent objects of experience, and thereby avoid *dogmatic* anthropomorphism; but we attribute them to his relation to the world and allow ourselves a *symbolic* anthropomorphism, which in fact concerns language only and not the object itself.

If I say that we are compelled to consider the world *as if* it were the work of a Supreme Understanding and Will, I really say nothing more than that a watch, a ship, a regiment bears the same relation to the watchmaker, the shipbuilder, the commanding officer as the world of sense (or whatever constitutes the substratum of this complex of appearances) does to the unknown, which I do not hereby cognise as it is in itself but as it is for me, i.e., in relation to the world of which I am a part.

§ 58. Such a cognition is one of analogy and does not signify (as is commonly understood) an imperfect similarity of two things, but a perfect similarity of relations between two quite dissimilar things.[43] By means of this analogy, however,

---

43. Thus there is an analogy between the juridical relation of human actions and the mechanical relation of moving forces. I never can do anything to another man without giving him a right to do the same to me on the same conditions; just as no body can act with its moving force on another body without thereby causing the other to react equally against it. Here right and moving force are quite dissimilar things, but in their relation there is complete similarity. By means of such an analogy, I can obtain a relational concept of things which are absolutely unknown to me. For instance, as the promotion of the welfare of children (= a) is to the love of parents (= b), so the welfare of the human species (= c) is to that unknown in God (= x), which we call love; not as if it had the least similarity to any human inclination, but because we can posit its relation to the world to be similar to that which things of the world bear one another. But the relational concept in this case is a mere category, viz., the concept of cause, which has nothing to do with sensibility.

there remains a concept of the Supreme Being sufficiently determined *for us,* though we have left out everything that could determine it absolutely and *in itself;* for we determine it as regards the world and therefore as regards ourselves, and more do we not require. The attacks which Hume makes upon those who would determine this concept absolutely, by taking the materials for so doing from themselves and the world, do not affect us; and he cannot object to us that we have nothing left if we take away the objective anthropomorphism from our concept of the Supreme Being.

For let us assume at the outset (as Hume in his *Dialogues* makes Philo grant Cleanthes), as a necessary hypothesis, the deistic concept of the First Being, in which this Being is thought by the mere ontological predicates of substance, of cause, etc. This must be done because reason, actuated in the sensible world by mere conditions which are themselves in turn always conditioned, cannot otherwise have any satisfaction; and it therefore can be done without falling into anthropomorphism (which transfers predicates from the world of sense to a being quite distinct from the world) because those predicates are mere categories which, though they do not give a determinate concept of this being, yet give a concept not limited to any conditions of sensibility. Thus nothing can prevent our predicating of this being a causality through reason with regard to the world, and thus passing to theism, without being obliged to attribute to this being itself this kind of reason, as a property inhering in it. For as to the former, the only possible way of pushing the use of reason (as regards all possible experience in complete harmony with itself) in the world of sense to the highest point is to assume a supreme reason as a cause of all the connections in the world. Such a principle must be quite advantageous to reason and can hurt it nowhere in its application to nature. As to the latter, reason is thereby not transferred as a property to the First Being in itself, but only to its relation to the world of sense, and so anthropomorphism is entirely avoided. For nothing is considered here but the cause of the rational form which is found everywhere in the world, and reason is attributed to the Supreme Being so far as it contains the ground of this rational form in the world, but according to analogy only, i.e., so far as this expression shows merely the relation which the Supreme Cause, unknown to us, has to the world in order to determine everything in it conformably to reason in the highest degree. We are thereby kept from using reason as an attribute in order to think God, but not kept from thinking the world in such a manner as is necessary to have the greatest possible use of reason within it according to principle. We thereby acknowledge that the Supreme Being is quite inscrutable and even unthinkable in any determinate way as to what it is in itself. We are thereby kept, on the one hand, from making a transcendent use of the concepts which we have of reason as an efficient cause (by means of the will), in order to determine the Divine Nature by properties which are only borrowed from human nature, and from losing ourselves in gross and extravagant concepts; and, on the other hand, from deluging the contemplation of the world with hyperphysical modes of explanation according to our concepts of human reason which we transfer to God, and so from losing for this contemplation its proper role, according to which it should be a rational study of mere nature and not a presumptuous derivation of its appearances from a Supreme Reason. The expression suited to our feeble concepts is that we conceive the world *as if* it came, regarding its existence and its inner determination, from a Supreme Reason. By this conception we both cognise the constitution which belongs to the world itself without pretending to determine the nature of its cause in itself, and we transfer the ground of this constitution (of the rational form of the world) to the *relation* of the Supreme Cause to the world, without finding the world sufficient by itself for that purpose.[44]

Thus the difficulties which seem to oppose theism disappear by combining with Hume's principle, "not to carry the use of reason dogmatically beyond the field of all possible experience," this other principle, which he quite overlooked, "not to consider the field of experience as one which bounds itself in the eyes of our reason." The *Critique of Pure Reason* here points out the true mean between dogmatism, which Hume combats, and skepticism, which he would substitute for it—a mean which is not like other means that we find advisable to determine for ourselves as it were mechanically (by adopting something from one side and something from the other), and by which nobody is taught a better way, but such a one as can be exactly determined on principles.

§ 59. At the beginning of this note I made use of the metaphor of a boundary in order to establish the limits of reason in regard to its suitable use. The world of sense contains merely appearances, which are not things in themselves; but the understanding must assume these latter ones, viz., noumena, because it knows the objects of experience to be mere appearances. In our reason both are comprised together, and the question is, How does reason proceed to set boundaries to the understanding as regards both these fields? Experience, which contains all that belongs to the sensible world, does not bound itself; it only proceeds in every case from the conditioned to some other equally conditioned thing. Its boundary must lie quite without it, and this is the field of the pure beings of the understanding. But this field, so far as the determination of the nature of these beings is concerned, is an empty space for us; and if dogmatically determined concepts are being considered, we cannot pass beyond the field of possible experience. But as a boundary is itself something positive, which belongs to what lies within as well as to the space that lies without the given complex, it is still an actual positive cognition which reason only acquires by enlarging itself to this boundary, yet without attempting to pass it because it there finds itself in the presence of an empty space in which it can think forms of things but not things themselves. But the setting of a boundary to the field of experience by something which is otherwise unknown to reason, is still a cognition which belongs to it even at this point, and by which it is neither confined within the sensible nor strays beyond the sensible, but only limits itself, as befits the knowledge of a boundary, to the relation between what lies beyond it and what is contained within it.

Natural theology is such a concept at the boundary of human reason, being constrained to look beyond this boundary to the idea of a Supreme Being (and, for practical purposes, to that of an intelligible world also), not in order to determine anything relatively to this mere being of the understanding, which lies beyond the world of sense, but in order to guide the use of reason within the world of sense according to principles of the greatest possible (theoretical as well as practical) unity. For this purpose reason makes use of the reference of the world of sense to an inde-

---

44. I may say that the causality of the Supreme Cause holds the same place with regard to the world that human reason does with regard to its works of art. Here the nature of the Supreme Cause itself remains unknown to me; I only compare its effects (the order of the world), which I know, and their conformity to reason to the effects of human reason, which I also know; and hence I term the former reason, without attributing to it on that account what I understand in man by this term, or attaching to it anything else known to me as its property.

pendent reason as the cause of all that world's connections. Thereby reason does not merely invent a being, but, as beyond the sensible world there must be something that can be thought only by the pure understanding, reason determines that something in this particular way, though only of course according to analogy.

And thus there remains our original proposition, which is the result of the whole *Critique:* "that reason by all its *a priori* principles never teaches us anything more than objects of possible experience, and even of these nothing more than can be cognised in experience." But this limitation does not prevent reason from leading us to the objective boundary of experience, viz., to the reference to something which is not itself an object of experience but must be the highest ground of all experience. Reason does not, however, teach us anything concerning the thing in itself; it only instructs us as regards its own complete and highest use in the field of possible experience. But this is all that can be reasonably desired in the present case, and with it we have cause to be satisfied.

§ 60. Thus we have fully exhibited metaphysics according to its subjective possibility, as it is actually given in the natural predisposition of human reason and in that which constitutes the essential end of its pursuit. We have found that this merely natural use of such a predisposition of our reason, if no discipline arising only from a scientific critique bridles and sets limits to it, involves us in transcendent dialectical inferences, that are in part merely illusory and in part even self-contradictory, and that this fallacious metaphysics is not only unnecessary as regards the promotion of our knowledge of nature but even disadvantageous to it. There yet remains a problem worthy of inquiry, which is to find out the natural ends intended by this disposition to transcendent concepts in our reason, because everything that lies in nature must be originally intended for some useful purpose.

Such an inquiry is of a doubtful nature, and I acknowledge that what I can say about it is conjecture only, like every speculation about the first ends of nature. This conjecture may be allowed to me in this case alone, because the question does not concern the objective validity of metaphysical judgments but our natural predisposition to them, and therefore does not belong to the system of metaphysics but to anthropology.

When I compare all the transcendental ideas, the totality of which constitutes the particular problem of natural pure reason, compelling it to quit the mere contemplation of nature, to transcend all possible experience, and in this endeavor to produce the thing (be it knowledge or fiction) called metaphysics; I think I perceive that the aim of this natural tendency is to free our concepts from the fetters of experience and from the limits of the mere contemplation of nature so far as at least to open to us a field containing mere objects for the pure understanding which no sensibility can reach, not indeed for the purpose of speculatively occupying ourselves with them (for there we can find no ground to stand on), but in order that practical principles might find some such scope for their necessary expectation and hope and might expand to the universality which reason unavoidably requires from a moral point of view.

So I find that the psychological idea (however little it may reveal to me the nature of the human soul, which is elevated above all concepts of experience) shows the insufficiency of these concepts plainly enough and thereby deters me from materialism, a psychological concept which is unfit for any explanation of nature and which in addition confines reason in practical respects. The cosmological ideas, by the obvious insufficiency of all possible cognition of nature to satisfy reason in its legitimate inquiry, serve in the same manner to keep us from naturalism, which asserts nature to be sufficient for itself. Finally, all natural necessity in the sensible world is conditional, as it always presupposes the dependence of things upon others, and unconditional necessity must be sought only in the unity of a cause different from the world of sense. But as the causality of this cause, in its turn, were it merely nature, could never render the existence of the contingent (as its consequent) comprehensible, reason frees itself by means of the theological idea from fatalism (both as a blind natural necessity in the coherence of nature itself, without a first principle, and as a blind causality of this principle itself) and leads to the concept of a cause possessing freedom and hence of a Supreme Intelligence. Thus the transcendental ideas serve, if not to instruct us positively, at least to destroy the impudent and restrictive assertions of materialism, of naturalism, and of fatalism, and thus to afford scope for the moral ideas beyond the field of speculation. These considerations, I should think, explain in some measure the natural predisposition of which I spoke.

The practical value which a merely speculative science may have lies outside the bounds of this science, and can therefore be considered as a scholium merely, and like all scholia does not form part of the science itself. This application, however, surely lies within the bounds of philosophy, especially of philosophy drawn from the pure sources of reason, where its speculative use in metaphysics must necessarily be at one with its practical use in morals. Hence the unavoidable dialectic of pure reason, considered in metaphysics as a natural tendency, deserves to be explained not as a mere illusion, which is to be removed, but also, if possible, as a natural provision as regards its end, though this task, a work of supererogation, cannot justly be assigned to metaphysics proper.

The solutions of these questions which are treated in the *Critique*[45] should be considered a second scholium, which, however, has a greater affinity with the subject of metaphysics. For there certain rational principles are expounded which determine *a priori* the order of nature or rather of the understanding, which seeks nature's laws through experience. They seem to be constitutive and legislative with regard to experience, though they spring from mere reason, which cannot be considered, like the understanding, as a principle of possible experience. Now whether or not this harmony rests upon the fact that, just as nature does not inhere in appearances or in their source (the sensibility) itself, but only in the relation of the latter to the understanding, so also a thoroughgoing unity in the use of the understanding to bring about an entirety of all possible experience (in a system) can only belong to the understanding when in relation to reason, with the result that experience is in this way mediately subordinate to the legislation of reason: this question may be discussed by those who desire to trace the nature of reason even beyond its use in metaphysics into the general principles for making systematic a history of nature in general. I

---

45. *Critique of Pure Reason,* "The Regulative Employment of the Ideas of Pure Reason," B 670–696.

have presented this task as important, but not attempted its solution in the book itself.[46]

And thus I conclude the analytical solution of the main question which I had proposed: "How is metaphysics in general possible?" by ascending from the data of its actual use, at least in its consequences, to the grounds of its possibility.

SOLUTION OF THE GENERAL QUESTION OF THE *PROLEGOMENA* "HOW IS METAPHYSICS POSSIBLE AS SCIENCE?"

Metaphysics, as a natural disposition of reason, is actual; but if considered by itself alone (as the analytical solution of the third principal question showed), it is dialectical and illusory. If we think of taking principles from it, and in using them follow the natural, but on that account not less false, illusion, we can never produce science, but only a vain dialectical art, in which one school may outdo another but none can ever acquire a just and lasting approbation.

In order that as a science metaphysics may be entitled to claim, not mere fallacious plausibility, but insight and conviction, a critique of reason must itself exhibit the whole stock of *a priori* concepts, their division according to their various sources (sensibility, understanding, and reason), together with a complete table of them, the analysis of all these concepts, with all their consequences and especially the possibility of synthetic cognition *a priori* by means of the deduction of these concepts, the principles and bounds of their use, all in a complete system. Critique, therefore, and critique alone contains in itself the whole well-proved and well-tested plan, and even all the means required to establish metaphysics as a science; by other ways and means it is impossible. The question here, therefore, is not so much how this performance is possible as how to set it going and induce men of clear heads to quit their hitherto perverted and fruitless cultivation for one that will not deceive, and how such a union for the common end may best be directed.

This much is certain: whoever has once tasted critique will be ever after disgusted with all dogmatical twaddle which he formerly put up with because his reason had to have something and could find nothing better for its support. Critique stands in the same relation to the common metaphysics of the schools as chemistry does to alchemy, or as astronomy to the astrology of the fortune teller. I pledge myself that nobody who has thought through and grasped the principles of critique, even only in these *Prolegomena*, will ever return to that old and sophistical pseudoscience; but he will, rather, with a certain delight look forward to a metaphysics which is now indeed in his power, requiring no more preparatory discoveries, and now at last affording permanent satisfaction to reason. For here is an advantage upon which, of all possible sciences, metaphysics alone can with certainty reckon: that it can be brought to such completion and fixity as to require no further change or be capable of any augmentation by new discoveries, because here reason has the

---

46. Throughout in the *Critique* I never lost sight of the plan not to neglect anything, were it ever so recondite, that could render the inquiry into the nature of pure reason complete. Everybody may afterwards carry his researches as far as he pleases, when he has been merely shown what yet remains to be done. This can reasonably be expected of him who has made it his business to survey the whole field, in order to consign it to others for future cultivation and allotment. And to this branch both the scholia belong, which will hardly recommend themselves by their dryness to amateurs, and hence are added here for connoisseurs only.

sources of its knowledge in itself, not in objects and their observation, by which its stock of knowledge could be further increased. When, therefore, it has exhibited the fundamental laws of its faculty completely and so determinately as to avoid all misunderstanding, there remains nothing more for pure reason to cognise *a priori;* nay, there is even no ground to raise further questions. The sure prospect of knowledge so determinate and so compact has a peculiar charm, even though we should set aside all its advantages, of which I shall hereafter speak.

All false art, all vain wisdom, lasts its time but finally destroys itself, and its highest culture is also the epoch of its decay. That this time is come for metaphysics appears from the state into which it has fallen among all learned nations, despite all the zeal with which other sciences of every kind are prosecuted. The old arrangement of our university studies still preserves its shadow; now and then an academy of science tempts men by offering prizes to write essays on it, but it is no longer numbered among sound sciences; and let anyone judge for himself how a sophisticated man, if he were called a great metaphysician, would receive the compliment, which may be well meant but is scarcely envied by anybody.

Yet, though the period of the downfall of all dogmatic metaphysics has undoubtedly arrived, we are yet far from being able to say that the period of its regeneration is come by means of a thorough and complete critique of reason. All transitions from an inclination to its contrary pass through the stage of indifference, and this moment is the most dangerous for an author but, in my opinion, the most favorable for the science. For when party spirit has died out by a total dissolution of former connections, minds are in the best state to listen to several proposals for an organisation according to a new plan.

When I say that I hope these *Prolegomena* will excite investigation in the field of critique and afford a new and promising object to sustain the general spirit of philosophy, which seems on its speculative side to want sustenance, I can imagine beforehand that everyone whom the thorny paths of my *Critique* have tired and put out of humor will ask me upon what I found this hope. My answer is: upon the irresistible law of necessity.

That the human spirit will ever give up metaphysical researches is as little to be expected as that we should prefer to give up breathing altogether, in order to avoid inhaling impure air. There will, therefore, always be metaphysics in the world; nay, everyone, especially every reflective man, will have it and, for want of a recognised standard, will shape it for himself after his own pattern. What has hitherto been called metaphysics cannot satisfy any critical mind, but to forego it entirely is impossible; therefore a critique of pure reason itself must now be attempted or, if one exists, investigated and brought to the full test, because there is no other means of supplying this pressing want which is something more than mere thirst for knowledge.

Ever since I have come to know critique, whenever I finish reading a book of metaphysical contents which, by the determination of its concepts, by variety, order, and an easy style, was not only entertaining but also helpful, I cannot help asking, "Has this author indeed advanced metaphysics a single step?" The learned men whose works have been useful to me in other respects and always contributed to the culture of my mental powers will, I hope, forgive me for saying that I have never been able to find either their essays or my own less important ones (though self-love may recommend them to me) to have advanced the science of metaphysics in the least, and why? Here is the very obvious reason: metaphysics did not then exist as a science, nor can it be gathered piecemeal; but its germ must be fully preformed in critique. But in order to prevent all misconception, we must remember what has already been said—that by the analytic treatment of our concepts the understanding gains indeed a great deal, but the science (of metaphysics) is thereby not in the least advanced because these analyses of concepts are nothing but the materials from which the intention is to carpenter our science. Let the concepts of substance and of accident be ever so well analyzed and determined; all this is very well as a preparation for some future use. But if we cannot prove that in all which exists the substance endures and only the accidents vary, our science is not the least advanced by all our analyses. Metaphysics has hitherto never been able to prove *a priori* either this proposition or that of sufficient reason, still less any more complex theorem such as belongs to psychology or cosmology, or indeed any synthetic proposition. By all its analyzing, therefore, nothing is affected, nothing obtained or forwarded; and the science, after all this bustle and noise, still remains as it was in the days of Aristotle, though far better preparations were made for it than of old if only the clue to synthetic cognitions had been discovered.

If anyone thinks himself offended, he is at liberty to refute my charge by producing a single synthetic proposition belonging to metaphysics which he would prove dogmatically *a priori;* for until he has actually performed this feat, I shall not grant that he has truly advanced the science, even though this proposition should be sufficiently confirmed by common experience. No demand can be more moderate or more equitable and, in the (inevitably certain) event of its nonperformance, no assertion more just than that hitherto metaphysics has never existed as a science.

But there are two things which, in case the challenge be accepted, I must deprecate: first, trifling about probability and conjecture, which are suited as little to metaphysics as to geometry; and secondly, a decision by means of the magic wand of so-called sound common sense, which does not convince everyone but accommodates itself to personal peculiarities.

For as to the former, nothing can be more absurd than in metaphysics, a philosophy from pure reason, to try to ground our judgments upon probability and conjecture. Everything that is to be cognised *a priori* is thereby announced as apodeictically certain, and must therefore be proved in this way. We might as well try to ground geometry or arithmetic upon conjectures. As to the calculus of probabilities in the latter, it does not contain probable but perfectly certain judgments concerning the degree of the the possibility of certain cases under given uniform conditions, which, in the sum of all possible cases, must infallibly happen according to the rule, though it is not sufficiently determined as regards every single instance. Conjectures (by means of induction and analogy) can be suffered in an empirical natural science only, yet even there at least the possibility of what we assume must be quite certain.

The appeal to common sense is even more absurd, when concepts and principles are said to be valid, not insofar as they hold with regard to experience, but outside the conditions of experience. For what is common sense? It is normal good sense, so far as it judges right. What is normal good sense? It is the faculty of the knowledge and use of rules *in concreto,* as distinguished from the speculative understanding, which is a faculty of knowing rules *in abstracto.* Common sense can hardly understand the rule that every event is determined by means of its cause and can never comprehend it thus generally. It therefore demands an example from experience;

and when it hears that this rule means nothing but what it always thought when a pane was broken or a kitchen-utensil missing, it then understands the principle and grants it. Common sense, therefore, is only of use so far as it can see its rules (though they actually are *a priori*) confirmed by experience; consequently, to comprehend them *a priori,* or independently of experience, belongs to the speculative understanding and lies quite beyond the horizon of common sense. But the province of metaphysics is entirely confined to the latter kind of knowledge, and it is certainly a bad sign of common sense to appeal to it as a witness, for it cannot here form any opinion whatever, and men look down upon it with contempt until they are in trouble and can find in their speculation neither advice nor help.

It is a common subterfuge of those false friends of common sense (who occasionally prize it highly, but usually despise it) to say that there must surely be at all events some propositions which are immediately certain and of which there is no occasion to give any proof, or even any account at all, because we otherwise could never stop inquiring into the grounds of our judgments. But if we except the principle of contradiction, which is not sufficient to show the truth of synthetic judgments, they can never adduce, in proof of this privilege, anything else indubitable which they can immediately ascribe to common sense, except mathematical propositions, such as twice two make four, between two points there is but one straight line, etc. But these judgments are radically different from those of metaphysics. For in mathematics I can by thinking construct whatever I represent to myself as possible by a concept: I add to the first two the other two, one by one, and myself make the number four, or I draw in thought from one point to another all manner of lines, equal as well as unequal; yet I can draw one only which is like itself in all its parts. But I cannot, by all my power of thinking, extract from the concept of a thing the concept of something else whose existence is necessarily connected with the former, but I must call upon experience. And though my understanding furnishes me *a priori* (yet only in reference to possible experience) with the concept of such a connection (i.e., causation), I cannot exhibit it *a priori* in intuition, like the concepts of mathematics, and so show its possibility *a priori.* This concept, together with the principles of its application, always requires, if it is to hold *a priori*—as is requisite in metaphysics—a justification and deduction of its possibility, because we cannot otherwise know how far it holds good and whether it can be used in experience only or beyond it also. Therefore in metaphysics, as a speculative science of pure reason, we can never appeal to common sense, but may do so only when (in certain matters) we are forced to surrender it and renounce all pure speculative cognition, which must always be theoretic knowledge, and therefore are forced to forego metaphysics itself and its instruction for the sake of adopting a rational faith which alone may be possible for us, sufficient to our wants, and perhaps even more salutary than knowledge itself. For then the shape of the thing is quite altered. Metaphysics must be science, not only as a whole but in all its parts; otherwise it is nothing at all, because as speculation of pure reason it finds a hold only on universal insights. Beyond its field, however, probability and common sense may be used advantageously and justly, but on quite special principles, the importance of which always depends on their reference to the practical.

This is what I hold myself justified in requiring for the possibility of metaphysics as a science.

APPENDIX

ON WHAT CAN BE DONE TO MAKE
METAPHYSICS AS A SCIENCE ACTUAL

Since all the ways heretofore taken have failed to attain the goal, and since without a preceding critique of pure reason it is not likely ever to be attained, the attempt before us has a right to an accurate and careful examination, unless it be thought more advisable to give up all pretensions to metaphysics, to which, if men would but consistently adhere to their purpose, no objection can be made. If we take the course of things as it is, not as it ought to be, there are two sorts of judgments: (1) one a judgment which precedes investigation (in our case one in which the reader from his own metaphysics pronounces judgment on the *Critique of Pure Reason,* which was intended to discuss the very possibility of metaphysics); (2) the other a judgment subsequent to investigation. In the latter, the reader is enabled to ignore for a while the consequences of the critical researches that may be repugnant to his formerly adopted metaphysics, and first examines the grounds whence those consequences are derived. If what common metaphysics propounds were demonstrably certain (like geometry) the former way of judging would hold good. For if the consequences of certain principles are repugnant to established truths, these principles are false and without further inquiry to be repudiated. But if metaphysics does not possess a stock of indisputably certain (synthetic) propositions, and should it even be the case that there are a number of them, which, though among the most plausible, are by their consequences in mutual conflict, and if no sure criterion of the truth of peculiarly metaphysical (synthetic) propositions is to be met with in it, then the former way of judging is not admissible, but the investigation of the principles of the *Critique* must precede all judgments as to its value.

A SPECIMEN OF A JUDGMENT ABOUT THE CRITIQUE
PRIOR TO ITS EXAMINATION

Such a judgment is to be found in the *Göttingische gelehrte Anzeigen,* in the supplement to the third part, of January 19, 1782, pages 40 *et seq.*[47]

When an author who is familiar with the subject of his work and endeavors to present his independent reflections in its elaboration falls into the hands of a reviewer who, in his turn, is keen enough to discern the points on which the worth or worthlessness of the books rests, who does not cling to words but goes to the heart of the subject, sifting and testing the principles which the author takes as his point of departure, the severity of the judgment may indeed displease the author, but the public does not care, as it gains thereby. And the author himself may be satisfied at having an opportunity of correcting or explaining his positions at an early date by the examination of a competent judge, in such a manner that if he believes himself fundamentally right, he can remove in time any stumbling-block that might hurt the success of his work.

I find myself, with my reviewer, in quite another position. He seems not to see at

---

47. [This review was given by Christian Garve.]

all the real matter of the investigation, with which (successfully or unsuccessfully) I have been occupied. It is either impatience at thinking out a lengthy work, or vexation at a threatened reform of a science in which he believed he had brought everything to perfection long ago, or, what I am reluctant to suppose, real narrow-mindedness that prevents him from ever carrying his thoughts beyond his school metaphysics. In short, he passes impatiently in review a long series of propositons, of which, without knowing their premises, one can comprehend nothing, intersperses here and there his censure, the reason of which the reader understands just as little as the propositions against which it is directed; and hence [his report] can neither serve the public nor damage me in the judgment of experts. I should, for these reasons, have passed over this judgment altogether, were it not that it may afford me occasion for some explanations which may in some cases save the readers of these *Prolegomena* from a misconception.

In order to take a position from which my reviewer could most easily set the whole work in a most unfavorable light, without venturing to trouble himself with any special investigation, he begins and ends by saying: "This work is a system of transcendental (or, as he translates it, of higher[48]) idealism."

A glance at this line soon showed me the sort of criticism that I had to expect, much as though the reviewer were one who had never seen or heard of geometry, having found a Euclid and coming upon various figures in turning over its leaves, were to say, on being asked his opinion of it: "The work is a textbook of drawing; the author introduces a peculiar terminology in order to give dark, incomprehensible directions, which in the end teach nothing more than what everyone can effect by a fair natural accuracy of eye, etc."

Let us see, in the meantime, what sort of an idealism it is that goes through my whole work, although it does not by a long way constitute the soul of the system.

The dictum of all genuine idealists, from the Eleatic school to Bishop Berkeley, is contained in this formula: "All cognition through the senses and experience is nothing but sheer illusion, and only in the ideas of the pure understanding and reason is there truth."

The principle that throughout dominates and determines my idealism is, on the contrary: "All cognition of things merely from pure understanding or pure reason is nothing but sheer illusion, and only in experience is there truth."

But this is directly contrary to idealism proper. How came I then to use this expression for quite an opposite purpose, and how came my reviewer to see it everywhere?

The solution of this difficulty rests on something that could have been very easily understood from the context of the work, if the reader had only desired to do so. Space and time, together with all that they contain, are not things in themselves or

---

48. By no means "higher." High towers and metaphysically great men resembling them, round both of which there is commonly much wind, are not for me. My place is the fruitful bathos of experience; and the word "transcendental," the meaning of which is so often indicated by me but not once grasped by my reviewer (so carelessly has he regarded everything), does not signify something passing beyond all experience but something that indeed precedes it *a priori*, but that is intended simply to make cognition of experience possible. If these concepts overstep experience, their use is termed "transcendent," which must be distinguished from the immanent use, i.e., use restricted to experience. All misunderstandings of this kind have been sufficiently guarded against in the work itself, but my reviewer found his advantage in misunderstanding me.

their qualities but belong merely to the appearances of the things in themselves; up to this point I am one in confession with the above idealists. But these, and among them more particularly Berkeley, regarded space as a mere empirical representation that, like the appearances it contains, is, together with its determinations, known to us only by means of experience or perception. I, on the contrary, prove in the first place that space (and also time, which Berkeley did not consider) and all its determinations can be cognized *a priori* by us, because, no less than time, it inheres in us as a pure form of our sensibility before all perception of experience and makes possible all intuition of sensibility, and therefore all appearances. It follows from this that, as truth rests on universal and necessary laws as its criteria, experience, according to Berkeley, can have no criteria of truth because its appearances (according to him) have nothing *a priori* at their foundation, whence it follows that experience is nothing but sheer illusion; whereas with us, space and time (in conjunction with the pure concepts of the understanding) prescribe their law *a priori* to all possible experience and, at the same time, afford the certain criterion for distinguishing truth from illusion therein.[49]

My so-called (properly critical) idealism is of quite a special kind, in that it reverses the usual idealism and through my kind all *a priori* cognition, even that of geometry, first receives objective reality, which, without my demonstrated ideality of space and time, could not be maintained by the most zealous realists. This being the state of the case, I could wish, in order to avoid all misunderstanding, to have named this concept of mine otherwise, but to alter it altogether is probably impossible. It may therefore be permitted me in future, as has been above intimated, to term it "formal" or, better still, "critical" idealism, to distinguish it from the dogmatic idealism of Berkeley and from the skeptical idealism of Descartes.

Beyond this, I find nothing remarkable in the judgment of my book. The reviewer makes sweeping criticisms, a mode prudently chosen, since it does not betray one's own knowledge or ignorance; a single thorough criticism in detail, had it touched the main question, as is only fair, would have exposed either my error or my reviewer's measure of insight into this kind of inquiry. It was, moreover, not a badly conceived plan, in order at once to take from readers (who are accustomed to form their conceptions of books from newspaper reports) the desire to read the book itself, to pour out one after the other in one breath a number of propositions which, torn from their connection with their premises and explanations, must necessarily sound senseless, especially considering how antipathetic they are to all school-metaphysics; to exhaust the reader's patience *ad nauseam*, and then, having made me acquainted with the lucid propostion that persistent illusion is truth, to conclude with the crude paternal moralization: to what end, then, the quarrel with accepted language; to what end, and whence, the idealistic distinction? A judgment which seeks all that is characteristic of my book, first supposed to be metaphysically heterodox, in a mere innovation of the nomenclature proves clearly that my would-

---

49. Idealism proper always has a mystical tendency, and can have no other; but mine is solely designed for the purpose of comprehending the possibility of our *a priori* cognition of objects of experience, which is a problem never hitherto solved or even suggested. In this way all mystical idealism falls to the ground, for (as may be seen in Plato) it inferred from our cognitions *a priori* (even from those of geometry) another intuition different from that of the senses (namely, an intellectual intuition), because it never occurred to anyone that the senses themselves might intuit *a priori*.

be judge has understood nothing of the subject and, in addition, has not understood himself.[50]

My reviewer speaks like a man who is conscious of important and superior insight which he keeps hidden, for I am aware of nothing recent with respect to metaphysics that could justify his tone. But he is quite wrong to withhold his discoveries from the world, for there are doubtless many who, like myself, have not been able to find in all the fine things that have for long past been written in this department anything that has advanced the science by so much as a finger's breadth. We find indeed the giving a new point to definitions, the supplying of lame proofs with new crutches, the adding to the crazy-quilt of metaphysics fresh patches or changing its pattern; but all this is not what the world requires. The world is tired of metaphysical assertions; what is wanted is the possibility of this science, the sources from which certainty therein can be derived, and certain criteria by which it may distinguish the dialectical illusion of pure reason from truth. To this the critic seems to possess a key, otherwise he would never have spoken out in such a high tone.

But I am inclined to suspect that no such requirement of the science has ever entered his thoughts, for in that case he would have directed his judgment to this point, and even a mistaken attempt in such an important matter would have won his respect. If that be the case, we are once more good friends. He may penetrate as deeply as he likes into his metaphysics, without any one hindering him; only as concerns that which lies outside metaphysics, its sources, which are to be found in reason, he cannot form a judgment. That my suspicion is not without foundation is proved by the fact that he does not mention a word about the possibility of synthetic knowledge *a priori*, the special problem upon the solution of which the fate of metaphysics wholly rests and upon which my *Critique* (as well as the present *Prolegomena*) entirely hinges. The idealism he encountered and which he hung upon was only taken up in the doctrine as the sole means of solving the above problem (although it received its confirmation on other grounds), and hence he must have shown either that the above problem does not possess the importance I attribute to it (even in these *Prolegomena*) or that, by my concept of appearances, it is either not solved at all or can be better solved in another way; but I do not find a word of this in the criticism. The reviewer, then, understands nothing of my work and possibly also nothing of the spirit and essential nature of metaphysics itself; and it is not, what I would rather assume, the haste of a reviewer to finish his review, incensed at the labor of plodding through so many obstacles, that threw an unfavorable shadow over the work lying before him and made its fundamental features unrecognizable.

There is a great deal to be done before a learned journal, it matters not with what care its writers may be selected, can maintain its otherwise well-merited reputation in the field of metaphysics as elsewhere. Other sciences and branches of knowledge have their standard. Mathematics has it in itself, history and theology in secular or

50. The reviewer often fights with his own shadow. When I oppose the truth of experience to dream, he never thinks that I am here speaking simply of the well-known *somnio objective sumto* ["dreams taken objectively"—Christian Wolff's *German Metaphysics*, § 142] of the Wolffian philosophy, which is merely formal, and with which the distinction between sleeping and waking is in no way concerned—a distinction which can indeed have no place in a transcendental philosophy. For the rest, he calls my deduction of the categories and table of the principles of the understanding "common well-known axioms of logic and ontology, expressed in an idealistic manner." The reader need only consult these *Prolegomena* upon this point to convince himself that a more miserable and historically incorrect judgment could hardly be made.

sacred books, natural science and the art of medicine in mathematics and experience, jurisprudence in law books, and even matters of taste in the examples of the ancients. But for the judgment of the thing called metaphysics, the standard has yet to be found. I have made an attempt to determine it, as well as its use. What is to be done, then, until it be found, when works of this kind have to be judged? If they are of a dogmatic character, one may do what one likes; no one will play the master over others here for long before someone else appears to deal with him in the same manner. If, however, they are critical in character, not indeed with reference to other works but to reason itself, so that the standard of judgment cannot be assumed but has first of all to be sought for, then, though objection and blame may indeed be permitted, yet a certain degree of leniency is indispensable, since the need is common to us all and the lack of the necessary insight makes the high-handed attitude of judge unwarranted.

In order, however, to connect my defense with the interest of the philosophical commonwealth, I propose a test, which must be decisive as to the mode whereby all metaphysical investigations may be directed to their common purpose. This is nothing more that what mathematicians have done in establishing the advantage of their methods by competition. I challenge my critic to demonstrate, as is only just, on *a priori* grounds, in his own way, any single really metaphysical principle asserted by him. Being metaphysical, it must be synthetic and cognized *a priori* from concepts, but it may also be any one of the most indispensable propositions, as, for instance, the principle of the permanence of substance or of the necessary determination of events in the world by their causes. If he cannot do this (silence however is confession), he must admit that, since metaphysics without apodeictic certainty of propositions of this kind is nothing at all, its possibility or impossibility must before all things be established in a critique of pure reason. Thus he is bound either to confess that my principles in the *Critique* are correct, or he must prove their invalidity. But as I can already foresee that, confidently as he has hitherto relied on the certainty of his principles, when it comes to a strict test he will not find a single one in the whole range of metaphysics he can boldly bring forward, I will concede to him an advantageous condition, which can only be expected in such a competition, and will relieve him of the *onus probandi* by laying it on myself.

He finds in these *Prolegomena* and in my *Critique*[51] eight propositions, of which one in each pair contradicts the other, but each of which necessarily belongs to metaphysics, by which it must either be accepted or rejected (although there is not one that has not in its time been accepted by some philosopher). Now he has the liberty of selecting any one of these eight propositions at his pleasure and accepting it without any proof, of which I shall make him a present, but only one (for waste of time will be just as little serviceable to him as to me), and then of attacking my proof of the opposite proposition. If I can save this one and at the same time show that, according to principles which every dogmatic metaphysics must necessarily recognize, the contrary of the proposition adopted by him can be just as clearly proved, it is thereby established that metaphysics has an hereditary failing not to be explained, much less set aside, until we ascend to its birthplace, pure reason itself. And thus my *Critique* must either be accepted or a better one take its place; at least it must be studied, which is the only thing I now require. If, on the other hand, I

51. [The theses and antitheses of "The Antinomy of Pure Reason" in the *Critique,* B 454–489]

cannot save my demonstration, then a synthetic proposition *a priori* from dogmatic principles is to be reckoned to the score of my opponent, and I shall deem my impeachment of ordinary metaphysics unjust and pledge myself to recognize his censure of my *Critique* as justified (although this would not be the consequence by a long way). To this end it would be necessary, it seems to me, that he should step out of his incognito. Otherwise I do not see how it could be avoided that, instead of dealing with one, I should be honored or besieged by several challenges coming from anonymous and unqualified opponents.

PROPOSALS AS TO AN INVESTIGATION OF THE *CRITIQUE* UPON WHICH A JUDGMENT MAY FOLLOW

I feel obliged to the learned public even for the silence with which it for a long time honored my *Critique,* for this proves at least a postponement of judgment and some supposition that, in a work leaving all beaten tracks and striking out on a new path, in which one cannot at once perhaps so easily find one's way, something may perchance lie from which an important but at present dead branch of human knowledge may derive new life and productiveness. Hence may have originated a solicitude for the as yet tender shoot, lest it be destroyed by a hasty judgment. A specimen of a judgment, delayed for the above reasons, is now before my eye in the *Gothaische gelehrte Zeitung,*[52] the thoroughness of which (leaving out of account my praise, which might be suspicious) every reader will himself perceive from the clear and unperverted presentation of a fragment of one of the first principles of my work.

Since an extensive structure cannot be judged at once as a whole from a hurried glance, I propose that it be tested piece by piece from its foundation up, and in this, the present *Prolegomena* may be used as a general outline with which the work itself may conveniently be compared. This suggestion, if it were founded on nothing more than my conceit of importance, such as vanity ordinarily attributes to all of one's own productions, would be immodest and would deserve to be rejected with indignation. But now the interests of all speculative philosophy have arrived at the point of total extinction, while human reason hangs upon them with inextinguishable affection; and only after having been endlessly disappointed, does it vainly attempt to change this into indifference.

In our thinking age, it is not to be supposed but that many deserving men would use any good opportunity of working for the common interest of an ever more enlightened reason, if there were only some hope of attaining the goal. Mathematics, natural science, laws, arts, even morality, etc. do not completely fill the soul; there is always a space left over reserved for pure and speculative reason, the emptiness of which prompts us to seek in vagaries, buffooneries, and mysticism for what seems to be employment and entertainment, but what actually is mere pastime undertaken in order to deaden the troublesome voice of reason, which, in accordance with its nature, requires something that can satisfy it and does not merely subserve other ends or the interests of our inclinations. A consideration, therefore, which is concerned only with this extent of reason as it subsists for itself has, as I may reasonably suppose, a great fascination for everyone who has attempted thus to extend his concept, and I may even say a greater fascination than any other

---

52. [The issue of August 24, 1782]

theoretical branch of knowledge, for which he would not willingly exchange it because here all other branches of knowledge and even purposes must meet and unite themselves in a whole.

I offer, therefore, these *Prolegomena* as a plan and guide for this investigation, and not the work itself. Although I am even now perfectly satisfied with the latter as far as contents, order, and mode of presentation, and the care that I have expended in weighing and testing every sentence before writing it down are concerned (for it has taken me years to satisfy myself fully, not only as regards the whole, but in some cases even as to the sources of one particular proposition); yet I am not quite satisfied with my exposition in some sections of the Doctrine of Elements,[53] as for instance in the deduction of the concepts of the understanding or in the chapter on the paralogisms of pure reason,[54] because a certain diffuseness takes away from their clearness, and in place of them what is here said in the *Prolegomena* respecting these sections may be made the basis of the test.

It is the boast of the Germans that, where steady and continuous industry are requisite, they can carry things further than other nations. If this opinion be well founded, an opportunity, a task, presents itself; the successful issue of this task can scarcely be doubted and all thinking men can equally take part in it, though they have hitherto been unsuccessful in accomplishing it and in thus confirming the above good opinion. This is chiefly because the science in question is of such a special kind that it can all at once be brought to completion and to that permanent state beyond which it can never be developed, in the least degree enlarged by later discoveries, or changed if we leave out of account adornment by greater clearness in some places or additional utility for all sorts of purposes. This is an advantage no other science has or can have, because there is none so completely isolated and independent of others and so exclusively concerned with the faculty of cognition pure and simple. And the present moment seems not to be unfavorable to my expectation; for in Germany no one seems now to know how to occupy himself, apart from the so-called useful sciences, so as to pursue not mere play but a business possessing an enduring purpose.

To discover how the endeavors of the learned may be united in such a purpose I must leave to others. In the meantime, it is not my intention to persuade anyone merely to follow my theses or even to flatter me with the hope that he will do so; but attacks, repetitions, limitations, or confirmation, completion, and extension, as the case may be, should be appended. If the matter be but investigated from its foundation, it cannot fail that a system, albeit not my own, shall be erected that shall be a possession for future generations for which they may have reason to be grateful.

It would lead us too far here to show what kind of metaphysics may be expected when the principles of criticism have been perfected and how, though the old false feathers have been pulled out, it need by no means appear poor and reduced to an insignificant figure but may be in other respects richly and respectably adorned. But other and great uses which would result from such a reform strike one immediately. The ordinary metaphysics had its uses, in that it sought out the elementary concepts of the pure understanding in order to make them clear through analysis and determinate through explications. In this way it was a training for rea-

53. [The first part of the *Critique of Pure Reason*, the second part being the Methodology]

54. [These sections were almost entirely rewritten in the second edition of the *Critique* (1787).]

son, in whatever direction it might be turned. But this was all the good it did. This merit was subsequently destroyed when it favored conceit by venturesome assertions, sophistry by subtle dodges and prettifying, and shallowness by the ease with which it decided the most difficult problems by means of a little school wisdom, which is only the more seductive the more it has the choice, on the one hand, of taking on something of the language of science and, on the other, from that of popular discourse—thus being everything to everybody but in reality being nothing at all. By criticism, however, a standard is given to our judgment whereby knowledge may be with certainty distinguished from pseudo-knowledge and firmly founded, being brought into full operation in metaphysics—a mode of thought extending by degrees its beneficial influence over every other use of reason, at once infusing into it the true philosophical spirit. But the service that metaphysics performs also for theology, by making it independent of the judgment of dogmatic speculation and thereby securing it completely against the attacks of all such opponents, is certainly not to be valued lightly. For ordinary metaphysics, although it promised theology much advantage, could not keep this promise, and by summoning speculative dogmatics to its assistance did nothing but arm enemies against itself. Mysticism, which can prosper in a rationalistic age only when it hides itself behind a system of school metaphysics, under the protection of which it may venture to rave with a semblance of rationality, is driven from theology, its last hiding place, by critical philosophy. Last, but not least, it cannot be otherwise than important to a teacher of metaphysics to be able to say with universal assent that what he expounds is *science*, and that by it actual service will be rendered to the commonweal.

GROUNDING
FOR THE
METAPHYSICS OF MORALS
PREFACE

Ancient Greek philosophy was divided into three sciences: physics, ethics, and logic. This division is perfectly suitable to the nature of the subject, and the only improvement that can be made in it is perhaps only to supply its principle so that there will be a possibility on the one hand of insuring its completeness and on the other of correctly determining its necessary subdivisions.

All rational knowledge is either material and concerned with some object, or formal and concerned only with the form of understanding and of reason themselves and with the universal rules of thought in general without regard to differences of its objects. Formal philosophy is called logic. Material philosophy, however, has to do with determinate objects and with the laws to which these objects are subject; and such philosophy is divided into two parts, because these laws are either laws of nature or laws of freedom. The science of the former is called physics, while that of the latter is called ethics; they are also called doctrine of nature and doctrine of morals respectively.

Logic cannot have any empirical part, i.e., a part in which the universal and necessary laws of thought would be based on grounds taken from experience; for in that case it would not be logic, i.e., a canon for understanding and reason, which is valid for all thinking and which has to be demonstrated.[1] Natural and moral philosophy, on the contrary, can each have an empirical part. The former has to because it must determine the laws of nature as an object of experience, and the latter because it must determine the will of man insofar as the will is affected by nature. The laws of the former are those according to which everything does happen, while the laws of the latter are those according to which everything ought to happen, although these moral laws also consider the conditions under which what ought to happen frequently does not.

All philosophy insofar as it is founded on experience may be called empirical, while that which sets forth its doctrines as founded entirely on a priori principles may be called pure. The latter, when merely formal, is called logic; but when limited to determinate objects of the understanding, it is called metaphysics.

Reprinted by permission of the translator, James W. Ellington, from Kant, *Grounding for the Metaphysics of Morals* (Indianapolis, Hackett Publishing Company, 1981).

1. [Kant's *Logic* was first published in 1800 in a version edited by Gottlob Benjamin Jäsche, who was one of Kant's students. —J.W.E.]

In this way there arises the idea of a twofold metaphysics: a metaphysics of nature and a metaphysics of morals.[2] Physics will thus have its empirical part, but also a rational one. Ethics will too, though here the empirical part might more specifically be called practical anthropology,[3] while the rational part might properly be called morals.

All industries, crafts, and arts have gained by the division of labor, viz., one man does not do everything, but each confines himself to a certain kind of work that is distinguished from all other kinds by the treatment it requires, so that the work may be done with the highest perfection and with greater ease. Where work is not so distinguished and divided, where everyone is a jack of all trades, there industry remains sunk in the greatest barbarism. Whether or not pure philosophy in all its parts requires its own special man might well be in itself a subject worthy of consideration. Would not the whole of this learned industry be better off if those who are accustomed, as the public taste demands, to purvey a mixture of the empirical with the rational in all sorts of proportions unknown even to themselves and who style themselves independent thinkers, while giving the name of hair-splitters to those who apply themselves to the purely rational part, were to be given warning about pursuing simultaneously two jobs which are quite different in their technique, and each of which perhaps requires a special talent that when combined with the other talent produces nothing but bungling? But I only ask here whether the nature of science does not require that the empirical part always be carefully separated from the rational part. Should not physics proper (i.e., empirical physics) be preceded by a metaphysics of nature, and practical anthropology by a metaphysics of morals? Both of these metaphysics must be carefully purified of everything empirical in order to know how much pure reason can accomplish in each case and from what sources it draws its a priori teaching, whether such teaching be conducted by all moralists (whose name is legion) or only by some who feel a calling thereto.

Since I am here primarily concerned with moral philosophy, the foregoing question will be limited to a consideration of whether or not there is the utmost necessity for working out for once a pure moral philosophy that is wholly cleared of everything which can only be empirical and can only belong to anthropology. That there must be such a philosophy is evident from the common idea of duty and of moral laws. Everyone must admit that if a law is to be morally valid, i.e., is to be valid as a ground of obligation, then it must carry with it absolute necessity. He must admit that the command, "Thou shalt not lie," does not hold only for men, as if other rational beings had no need to abide by it, and so with all the other moral laws properly so called; and he must concede that the ground of obligation here must therefore be sought not in the nature of man nor in the circumstances of the world in which man is placed, but must be sought a priori solely in the concepts of pure reason; he must grant that every other precept which is founded on principles of mere experience — even a precept that may in certain respects be universal — insofar as it rests in the least on empirical grounds — perhaps only in its motive — can indeed be called a practical rule, but never a moral law.

Thus not only are moral laws together with their principles essentially different from every kind of practical cognition in which there is anything empirical, but all

---

2. [*The Metaphysical Foundations of Natural Science* was published in 1786. *The Metaphysics of Morals* appeared in 1797.]

3. [*Anthropology from a Pragmatic Point of View* first appeared in 1798.]

moral philosophy rests entirely on its pure part. When applied to man, it does not in the least borrow from acquaintance with him (anthropology) but gives a priori laws to him as a rational being. To be sure, these laws require, furthermore, a power of judgment sharpened by experience, partly in order to distinguish in what cases they are applicable, and partly to gain for them access to the human will as well as influence for putting them into practice. For man is affected by so many inclinations that, even though he is indeed capable of the idea of a pure practical reason, he is not so easily able to make that idea effective *in concreto* in the conduct of his life.

A metaphysics of morals is thus indispensably necessary, not merely because of motives of speculation regarding the source of practical principles which are present a priori in our reason, but because morals themselves are liable to all kinds of corruption as long as the guide and supreme norm for correctly estimating them are missing. For in the case of what is to be morally good, that it conforms to the moral law is not enough; it must also be done for the sake of the moral law. Otherwise that conformity is only very contingent and uncertain, since the non-moral ground may now and then produce actions that conform with the law but quite often produces actions that are contrary to the law. Now the moral law in its purity and genuineness (which is of the utmost concern in the practical realm) can be sought nowhere but in a pure philosophy. Therefore, pure philosophy (metaphysics) must precede; without it there can be no moral philosophy at all. That philosophy which mixes pure principles with empirical ones does not deserve the name of philosophy (for philosophy is distinguished from ordinary rational knowledge by its treatments in a separate science of what the latter comprehends only confusedly). Still less does it deserve the name of moral philosophy, since by this very confusion it spoils even the purity of morals and counteracts its own ends.

There must be no thought that what is required here is already contained in the propaedeutic that precedes the celebrated Wolff's moral philosophy, i.e., in what he calls *Universal Practical Philosophy*,[4] and that hence there is no need to break entirely new ground. Just because his work was to be a universal practical philosophy, it has not taken into consideration any special kind of will, such as one determined solely by a priori principles without any empirical motives and which could be called a pure will, but has considered volition in general, together with all the actions and conditions belonging to it under this general signification. And thereby does his propaedeutic differ from a metaphysics of morals in the same way that general logic, which expounds the acts and rules of thinking in general, differs from transcendental philosophy, which treats merely of the particular acts and rules of pure thinking, i.e., of that thinking whereby objects are cognized completely a priori. For the metaphysics of morals has to investigate the idea and principles of a possible pure will and not the actions and conditions of human volition as such, which are for the most part drawn from psychology. Moral laws and duty are discussed in this universal practical philosophy (though quite improperly), but this is no objection to what has been said about such philosophy. For the authors of this science remain true to their idea of it on the following point also: they do not distinguish the motives which, as such, are presented completely a priori by reason alone and are properly moral, from the empirical motives which the understanding raises to general concepts merely by the comparison of experiences. Rather, they consider motives irrespective of any dif-

---

4.[This work of Christian Wolff was published in 1738-39; this and other of his works served for many years as the standard philosophy textbooks in German universities. Wolff's philosophy was founded on that of Leibniz.]

ference in their source; and inasmuch as they regard all motives as being homogeneous, they consider nothing but their relative strength or weakness. In this way they frame their concept of obligation, which is certainly not moral, but is all that can be expected from a philosophy which never decides regarding the origin of all possible practical concepts whether they are a priori or merely a posteriori.

I intend some day to publish a metaphysics of morals,[5] but as a preliminary to that I now issue this *Grounding* [1785]. Indeed there is properly no other foundation for such a metaphysics than a critical examination of pure practical reason, just as there is properly no other foundation for a metaphysics [of nature] than the critical examination of pure speculative reason, which has already been published.[6] But, in the first place, the former critique is not so absolutely necessary as the latter one, because human reason can, even in the most ordinary mind, be easily brought in moral matters to a high degree of correctness and precision, while on the other hand in its theoretical but pure use it is wholly dialectical. In the second place, if a critical examination of pure practical reason is to be complete, then there must, in my view, be the possibility at the same time of showing the unity of practical and speculative reason in a common principle; for in the final analysis there can be only one and the same reason, which is to be differentiated solely in its application. But there is no possibility here of bringing my work to such completeness, without introducing considerations of an entirely different kind and without thereby confusing the reader. Instead of calling the present work a *Critique of Pure Practical Reason*, I have, therefore, adopted the title *Grounding for the Metaphysics of Morals* [*Grundlegung zur Metaphysik der Sitten.*][7]

But, in the third place, since a metaphysics of morals, despite the forbidding title, is nevertheless capable of a high degree of popularity and adaptation to the ordinary understanding, I find it useful to separate from the aforementioned metaphysics this preliminary work on its foundation [*Grundlage*] in order later to have no need to introduce unavoidable subtleties into doctrines that are easier to grasp.

The present *Grounding* [*Grundlegung*] is, however, intended for nothing more than seeking out and establishing the supreme principle of morality. This constitutes by itself a task which is complete in its purpose and should be kept separate from every other moral inquiry. The application of this supreme principle to the whole ethical system would, to be sure, shed much light on my conclusions regarding this central question, which is important but has not heretofore been at all satisfactorily discussed; and the adequacy manifested by the principle throughout such application would provide strong confirmation for the principle. Nevertheless, I must forego this advantage, which after all would be more gratifying for myself than helpful for others, since ease of use and apparent adequacy of a principle do not provide any certain proof of its soundness, but do awaken, rather, a certain bias which prevents any rigorous examination and estimation of it for itself, without any regard to its consequences.

5. [This appeared in 1797.]

6. [The first edition of the *Critique of Pure Reason* appeared in 1781, while the second edition appeared in 1787. The *Critique of Practical Reason* was published in 1788.]

7. [This might be translated as *Laying the Foundation for the Metaphysics of Morals*. But for the sake of brevity *Grounding for the Metaphysics of Morals* has been chosen.]

The method adopted in this work is, I believe, one that is most suitable if we proceed analytically from ordinary knowledge to a determination of the supreme principle and then back again synthetically from an examination of this principle and its sources to ordinary knowledge where its application is found. Therefore, the division turns out to be the following:

1. *First Section.* Transition from the Ordinary Rational Knowledge of Morality to the Philosophical.
2. *Second Section.* Transition from Popular Moral Philosophy to a Metaphysics of Morals.
3. *Third Section.* Final Step from a Metaphysics of Morals to a Critique of Pure Practical Reason.

FIRST SECTION

Transition from the Ordinary Rational Knowledge of Morality to the Philosophical

There is no possibility of thinking of anything at all in the world, or even out of it, which can be regarded as good without qualification, except a *good will*. Intelligence, wit, judgment, and whatever talents of the mind one might want to name are doubtless in many respects good and desirable, as are such qualities of temperament as courage, resolution, perseverance. But they can also become extremely bad and harmful if the will, which is to make use of these gifts of nature and which in its special constitution is called character, is not good. The same holds with gifts of fortune; power, riches, honor, even health, and that complete well-being and contentment with one's condition which is called happiness make for pride and often hereby even arrogance, unless there is a good will to correct their influence on the mind and herewith also to rectify the whole principle of action and make it universally conformable to its end. The sight of a being who is not graced by any touch of a pure and good will but who yet enjoys an uninterrupted prosperity can never delight a rational and impartial spectator. Thus a good will seems to constitute the indispensable condition of being even worthy of happiness.

Some qualities are even conducive to this good will itself and can facilitate its work. Nevertheless, they have no intrinsic unconditional worth; but they always presuppose, rather, a good will, which restricts the high esteem in which they are otherwise rightly held, and does not permit them to be regarded as absolutely good. Moderation in emotions and passions, self-control, and calm deliberation are not only good in many respects but even seem to constitute part of the intrinsic worth of a person. But they are far from being rightly called good without qualification (however unconditionally they were commended by the ancients). For without the principles of a good will, they can become extremely bad; the coolness of a villain makes him not only much more dangerous but also immediately more abominable in our eyes than he would have been regarded by us without it.

A good will is good not because of what it effects or accomplishes, nor because of its fitness to attain some proposed end; it is good only through its willing, i.e., it is good in itself. When it is considered in itself, then it is to be esteemed very much higher than anything which it might ever bring about merely in order to favor some inclination, or even the sum total of all inclinations. Even if, by some especially unfortunate fate or by the niggardly provision of stepmotherly nature, this will should be wholly lacking in the power to accomplish its purpose; if with the greatest effort it should yet achieve nothing, and only the good will should remain (not, to be sure, as a mere wish but as the summoning of all the means in our power), yet would it, like a jewel, still shine by its own light as something which has its full value in itself. Its usefulness or fruitlessness can neither augment nor diminish this value. Its usefulness would be, as it were, only the setting to enable us to handle it in ordinary dealings or to attract to it the attention of those who are not yet experts, but not to recommend it to real experts or to determine its value.

But there is something so strange in this idea of the absolute value of a mere will, in which no account is taken of any useful results, that in spite of all the agreement received even from ordinary reason, yet there must arise the suspicion that such an idea may perhaps have as its hidden basis merely some high-flown fancy, and that we may have misunderstood the purpose of nature in assigning to reason the governing of our will. Therefore, this idea will be examined from this point of view.

In the natural constitution of an organized being, i.e., one suitably adapted to the purpose of life, let there be taken as a principle that in such a being no organ is to be found for any end unless it be the most fit and the best adapted for that end. Now if that being's preservation, welfare, or in a word its happiness, were the real end of nature in the case of a being having reason and will, then nature would have hit upon a very poor arrangement in having the reason of the creature carry out this purpose. For all the actions which such a creature has to perform with this purpose in view, and the whole rule of his conduct would have been prescribed much more exactly by instinct; and the purpose in question could have been attained much more certainly by instinct than it ever can be by reason. And if in addition reason had been imparted to this favored creature, then it would have had to serve him only to contemplate the happy constitution of his nature, to admire that nature, to rejoice in it, and to feel grateful to the cause that bestowed it; but reason would not have served him to subject his faculty of desire to its weak and delusive guidance nor would it have served him to meddle incompetently with the purpose of nature. In a word, nature would have taken care that reason did not strike out into a practical use nor presume, with its weak insight, to think out for itself a plan for happiness and the means for attaining it. Nature would have taken upon herself not only the choice of ends but also that of the means, and would with wise foresight have entrusted both to instinct alone.

And, in fact, we find that the more a cultivated reason devotes itself to the aim of enjoying life and happiness, the further does man get away from true contentment. Because of this there arises in many persons, if only they are candid enough to admit it, a certain degree of misology, i.e., hatred of reason. This is especially so in the case of those who are the most experienced in the use of reason, because after calculating all the advantages they derive, I say not from the invention of all the arts of common luxury, but even from the sciences (which in the end seem to them to be also a luxury of the understanding), they yet find that they have in fact only brought more trouble on their heads than they have gained in happiness. Therefore, they come to envy, rather than despise, the more common run of men who are closer to the guidance of mere natural instinct and who do not allow their reason much influence on their conduct. And we must admit that the judgment of those who would temper, or even reduce below zero, the boastful eulogies on behalf of the advantages which reason is supposed to provide as regards the happiness and contentment of life is by no means morose or ungrateful to the goodness with which the world is governed. There lies at the root of such judgments, rather, the idea that existence has another and much more worthy purpose, for which, and not for happiness, reason is quite properly intended, and which must, therefore, be regarded as the supreme condition to which the private purpose of men must, for the most part, defer.

Reason, however, is not competent enough to guide the will safely as regards its objects and the satisfaction of all our needs (which it in part even multiplies); to this end would an implanted natural instinct have led much more certainly. But inasmuch as reason has been imparted to us as a practical faculty, i.e., as one which is to have influence on the will, its true function must be to produce a will which is not merely good as a means to some further end, but is good in itself. To produce a will good in itself reason was absolutely necessary, inasmuch as nature in distributing her capacities has everywhere gone to work in a purposive manner. While such a will may not indeed be the sole and complete good, it must, nevertheless, be the highest good and the condition of all the rest, even of the desire for happiness. In this case there is nothing inconsistent with the wisdom of nature that the cultivation of reason, which is requisite for the first and unconditioned purpose, may in many ways restrict, at least in this life, the attainment of the second purpose, viz., happiness, which is always conditioned. Indeed happiness can even be reduced to less than nothing, without nature's failing thereby in her purpose; for reason recognizes as its highest practical function the establishment of a good will, whereby in the attainment of this end reason is capable only of its own kind of satisfaction, viz., that of fulfilling a purpose which is in turn determined only by reason, even though such fulfilment should often interfere with the purposes of inclination.

The concept of a will estimable in itself and good without regard to any further end must now be developed. This concept already dwells in the natural sound understanding and needs not so much to be taught as merely to be elucidated. It always holds first place in estimating the total worth of our actions and constitutes the condition of all the rest. Therefore, we shall take up the concept of *duty*, which includes that of a good will, though with certain subjective restrictions and hindrances, which far from hiding a good will or rendering it unrecognizable, rather bring it out by contrast and make it shine forth more brightly.

I here omit all actions already recognized as contrary to duty, even though they may be useful for this or that end; for in the case of these the question does not arise at all as to whether they might be done from duty, since they even conflict with duty. I also set aside those actions which are really in accordance with duty, yet to which men have no immediate inclination, but perform them because they are impelled thereto by some other inclination. For in this [second] case to decide whether the action which is in accord with duty has been done from duty or from some selfish purpose is easy. This difference is far more difficult to note in the [third] case where the action accords with duty and the subject has in addition an immediate inclination to do the action. For example,[1] that a dealer should not overcharge an inexperienced purchaser certainly accords with duty; and where there is much commerce, the prudent merchant does not overcharge but keeps to a fixed price for everyone in general, so that a child may buy from him just as well as everyone else may. Thus customers are honestly served, but this is not nearly enough for making us believe that the merchant has acted this way from duty and from principles of honesty; his own advantage

---

1. [The ensuing example provides an illustration of the second case.]

required him to do it. He cannot, however, be assumed to have in addition [as in the third case] an immediate inclination toward his buyers, causing him, as it were, out of love to give no one as far as price is concerned any advantage over another. Hence the action was done neither from duty nor from immediate inclination, but merely for a selfish purpose.

On the other hand,[2] to preserve one's life is a duty; and, furthermore, everyone has also an immediate inclination to do so. But on this account the often anxious care taken by most men for it has no intrinsic worth, and the maxim of their action has no moral content. They preserve their lives, to be sure, in accordance with duty, but not from duty. On the other hand,[3] if adversity and hopeless sorrow have completely taken away the taste for life, if an unfortunate man, strong in soul and more indignant at his fate than despondent or dejected, wishes for death and yet preserves his life without loving it — not from inclination or fear, but from duty — then his maxim indeed has a moral content.[4]

To be beneficent where one can is a duty; and besides this, there are many persons who are so sympathetically constituted that, without any further motive of vanity or self-interest, they find an inner pleasure in spreading joy around them and can rejoice in the satisfaction of others as their own work. But I maintain that in such a case an action of this kind, however dutiful and amiable it may be, has nevertheless no true moral worth.[5] It is on a level with such actions as arise from other inclinations, e.g., the inclination for honor, which if fortunately directed to what is in fact beneficial and accords with duty and is thus honorable, deserves praise and encouragement, but not esteem; for its maxim lacks the moral content of an action done not from inclina-

---

2. [This next example illustrates the third case.]

3. [The ensuing example illustrates the fourth case.]

4. [Four different cases have been distinguished in the two foregoing paragraphs. Case 1 involves those actions which are contrary to duty (lying, cheating, stealing, etc.). Case 2 involves those which accord with duty but for which a person perhaps has no immediate inclination, though he does have a mediate inclination thereto (one pays his taxes not because he likes to but in order to avoid the penalties set for delinquents, one treats his fellows well not because he really likes them but because he wants their votes when at some future time he runs for public office, etc.). A vast number of so-called "morally good" actions actually belong to this case 2 — they accord with duty because of self-seeking inclinations. Case 3 involves those which accord with duty and for which a person does have an immediate inclination (one does not commit suicide because all is going well with him, one does not commit adultery because he considers his wife to be the most desirable creature in the whole world, etc.). Case 4 involves those actions which accord with duty but are contrary to some immediate inclination (one does not commit suicide even when he is in dire distress, one does not commit adultery even though his wife has turned out to be an impossible shrew, etc.). Now case 4 is the crucial test case of the will's possible goodness — but Kant does not claim that one : hould lead his life in such a way as to encounter as many such cases as possible in order constantly to test his virtue (deliberately marry a shrew so as to be able to resist the temptation to commit adultery). Life itself forces enough such cases upon a person without his seeking them out. But when there is a conflict between duty and inclination, duty should always be followed. Case 3 makes for the easiest living and the greatest contentment, and anyone would wish that life might present him with far more of these cases than with cases 2 or 4. But yet one should not arrange his life in such a way as to avoid case 4 at all costs and to seek out case 3 as much as possible (become a recluse so as to avoid the possible rough and tumble involved with frequent association with one's fellows, avoid places where one might encounter the sick and the poor so as to spare oneself the pangs of sympathy and the need to exercise the virtue of benefiting those in distress, etc.). For the purpose of philosophical analysis Kant emphasizes case 4 as being the test case of the will's possible goodness, but he is not thereby advocating puritanism.]

5. [This is an example of case 3.]

tion but from duty. Suppose then the mind of this friend of mankind to be clouded over with his own sorrow so that all sympathy with the lot of others is extinguished, and suppose him still to have the power to benefit others in distress, even though he is not touched by their trouble because he is sufficiently absorbed with his own; and now suppose that, even though no inclination moves him any longer, he nevertheless tears himself from this deadly insensibility and performs the action without any inclination at all, but solely from duty — then for the first time his action has genuine moral worth.[6] Further still, if nature has put little sympathy in this or that man's heart, if (while being an honest man in other respects) he is by temperament cold and indifferent to the sufferings of others, perhaps because as regards his own sufferings he is endowed with the special gift of patience and fortitude and expects or even requires that others should have the same; if such a man (who would truly not be nature's worst product) had not been exactly fashioned by her to be a philanthropist, would he not yet find in himself a source from which he might give himself a worth far higher than any that a good-natured temperament might have? By all means, because just here does the worth of the character come out; this worth is moral and incomparably the highest of all, viz., that he is beneficent, not from inclination, but from duty.[7]

To secure one's own happiness is a duty (at least indirectly); for discontent with one's condition under many pressing cares and amid unsatisfied wants might easily become a great temptation to transgress one's duties. But here also do men of themselves already have, irrespective of duty, the strongest and deepest inclination toward happiness, because just in this idea are all inclinations combined into a sum total.[8] But the precept of happiness is often so constituted as greatly to interfere with some inclinations, and yet men cannot form any definite and certain concept of the sum of satisfaction of all inclinations that is called happiness. Hence there is no wonder that a single inclination which is determinate both as to what it promises and as to the time within which it can be satisfied may outweigh a fluctuating idea; and there is no wonder that a man, e.g., a gouty patient, can choose to enjoy what he likes and to suffer what he may, since by his calculation he has here at least not sacrificed the enjoyment of the present moment to some possibly groundless expectations of the good fortune that is supposed to be found in health. But even in this case, if the universal inclination to happiness did not determine his will and if health, at least for him, did not figure as so necessary an element in his calculations; there still remains here, as in all other cases, a law, viz., that he should promote his happiness not from inclination but from duty, and thereby for the first time does his conduct have real moral worth.[9]

Undoubtedly in this way also are to be understood those passages of Scripture which command us to love our neighbor and even our enemy. For love as an inclination cannot be commanded; but beneficence from duty, when no inclination impels

---

6. [This is an example of case 4.]

7. [This is an even more extreme example of case 4.]

8. [This is an example of case 3.]

9. [This example is a weak form of case 4; the action accords with duty but is not contrary to some immediate inclination.]

us[10] and even when a natural and unconquerable aversion opposes such beneficence,[11] is practical, and not pathological, love. Such love resides in the will and not in the propensities of feeling, in principles of action and not in tender sympathy; and only this practical love can be commanded.

The second proposition[12] is this: An action done from duty has its moral worth, not in the purpose that is to be attained by it, but in the maxim according to which the action is determined. The moral worth depends, therefore, not on the realization of the object of the action, but merely on the principle of volition according to which, without regard to any objects of the faculty of desire, the action has been done. From what has gone before it is clear that the purposes which we may have in our actions, as well as their effects regarded as ends and incentives of the will, cannot give to actions any unconditioned and moral worth. Where, then, can this worth lie if it is not to be found in the will's relation to the expected effect? Nowhere but in the principle of the will, with no regard to the ends that can be brought about through such action. For the will stands, as it were, at a crossroads between its a priori principle, which is formal, and its a posteriori incentive, which is material; and since it must be determined by something, it must be determined by the formal principle of volition, if the action is done from duty—and in that case every material principle is taken away from it.

The third proposition, which follows from the other two, can be expressed thus: Duty is the necessity of an action done out of respect for the law. I can indeed have an inclination for an object as the effect of my proposed action; but I can never have respect for such an object, just because it is merely an effect and is not an activity of the will. Similarly, I can have no respect for inclination as such, whether my own or that of another. I can at most, if my own inclination, approve it; and, if that of another, even love it, i.e., consider it to be favorable to my own advantage. An object of respect can only be what is connected with my will solely as ground and never as effect—something that does not serve my inclination but, rather, outweighs it, or at least excludes it from consideration when some choice is made—in other words, only the law itself can be an object of respect and hence can be a command. Now an action done from duty must altogether exclude the influence of inclination and therewith every object of the will. Hence there is nothing left which can determine the will except objectively the law and subjectively pure respect for this practical law, i.e., the will can be subjectively determined by the maxim[13] that I should follow such a law even if all my inclinations are thereby thwarted.

Thus the moral worth of an action does not lie in the effect expected from it nor in any principle of action that needs to borrow its motive from this expected effect. For all these effects (agreeableness of one's condition and even the furtherance of other people's happiness) could have been brought about also through other causes and would not have required the will of a rational being, in which the highest and

10. [This is case 4 in its weak form.]

11. [This is case 4 in its strong form.]

12. [The first proposition of morality says that an action must be done from duty in order to have any moral worth. It is implicit in the preceding examples but was never explicitly stated.]

13. A maxim is the subjective principle of volition. The objective principle (i.e., one which would serve all rational beings also subjectively as a practical principle if reason had full control over the faculty of desire) is the practical law. [See below Kant's footnote at Ak. 420-21.]

unconditioned good can alone be found. Therefore, the pre-eminent good which is called moral can consist in nothing but the representation of the law in itself, and such a representation can admittedly be found only in a rational being insofar as this representation, and not some expected effect, is the determining ground of the will. This good is already present in the person who acts according to this representation, and such good need not be awaited merely from the effect.[14]

But what sort of law can that be the thought of which must determine the will without reference to any expected effect, so that the will can be called absolutely good without qualification? Since I have deprived the will of every impulse that might arise for it from obeying any particular law, there is nothing left to serve the will as principle except the universal conformity of its actions to law as such, i.e., I should never act except in such a way that I can also will that my maxim should become a universal law.[15] Here mere conformity to law as such (without having as its basis any law determining particular actions) serves the will as principle and must so serve it if duty is not to be a vain delusion and a chimerical concept. The ordinary reason of mankind in its practical judgments agrees completely with this, and always has in view the aforementioned principle.

For example, take this question. When I am in distress, may I make a promise with the intention of not keeping it? I readily distinguish here the two meanings which the question may have; whether making a false promise conforms with prudence or with duty. Doubtless the former can often be the case. Indeed I clearly see that escape from some present difficulty by means of such a promise is not enough. In addition I must carefully consider whether from this lie there may later arise far greater inconvenience for me than from what I now try to escape. Furthermore, the consequences of my false promise are not easy to forsee, even with all my supposed cunning; loss of confidence in me might prove to be far more disadvantageous than the misfortune which I now try to avoid. The more prudent way might be to act according to a universal maxim and to make it a habit not to promise anything without intending to keep it. But that such a maxim is, nevertheless, always based on nothing but a fear of consequences becomes clear to me at once. To be truthful from duty is, however, quite different from being truthful from fear of disadvantageous consequences; in the first case the concept of the action itself contains a law for me, while

---

14. There might be brought against me here an objection that I take refuge behind the word "respect" in an obscure feeling, instead of giving a clear answer to the question by means of a concept of reason. But even though respect is a feeling, it is not one received through any outside influence but is, rather, one that is self-produced by means of a rational concept; hence it is specifically different from all feelings of the first kind, which can all be reduced to inclination or fear. What I recognize immediately as a law for me, I recognize with respect; this means merely the consciousness of the subordination of my will to a law without the mediation of other influences upon my sense. The immediate determination of the will by the law, and the consciousness thereof, is called respect, which is hence regarded as the effect of the law upon the subject and not as the cause of the law. Respect is properly the representation of a worth that thwarts my self-love. Hence respect is something that is regarded as an object of neither inclination nor fear, although it has at the same time something analogous to both. The object of respect is, therefore, nothing but the law—indeed that very law which we impose on ourselves and yet recognize as necessary in itself. As law, we are subject to it without consulting self-love; as imposed on us by ourselves, it is a consequence of our will. In the former aspect, it is analogous to fear; in the latter, to inclination. All respect for a person is properly only respect for the law (of honesty, etc.) of which the person provides an example. Since we regard the development of our talents as a duty, we think of a man of talent as being also a kind of example of the law (the law of becoming like him by practice), and that is what constitutes our respect for him. All so-called moral interest consists solely in respect for the law.

15. [This is the first time in the *Grounding* that the categorical imperative is stated.]

in the second I must first look around elsewhere to see what are the results for me that might be connected with the action. For to deviate from the principle of duty is quite certainly bad; but to abandon my maxim of prudence can often be very advantageous for me, though to abide by it is certainly safer. The most direct and infallible way, however, to answer the question as to whether a lying promise accords with duty is to ask myself whether I would really be content if my maxim (of extricating myself from difficulty by means of a false promise) were to hold as a universal law for myself as well as for others, and could I really say to myself that everyone may promise falsely when he finds himself in a difficulty from which he can find no other way to extricate himself. Then I immediately become aware that I can indeed will the lie but can not at all will a universal law to lie. For by such a law there would really be no promises at all, since in vain would my willing future actions be professed to other people who would not believe what I professed, or if they over-hastily did believe, then they would pay me back in like coin. Therefore, my maxim would necessarily destroy itself just as soon as it was made a universal law.[16]

Therefore, I need no far-reaching acuteness to discern what I have to do in order that my will may be morally good. Inexperienced in the course of the world and incapable of being prepared for all its contingencies, I only ask myself whether I can also will that my maxim should become a universal law. If not, then the maxim must be rejected, not because of any disadvantage accruing to me or even to others, but because it cannot be fitting as a principle in a possible legislation of universal law, and reason exacts from me immediate respect for such legislation. Indeed I have as yet no insight into the grounds of such respect (which the philosopher may investigate). But I at least understand that respect is an estimation of a worth that far outweighs any worth of what is recommended by inclination, and that the necessity of acting from pure respect for the practical law is what constitutes duty, to which every other motive must give way because duty is the condition of a will good in itself, whose worth is above all else.

Thus within the moral cognition of ordinary human reason we have arrived at its principle. To be sure, such reason does not think of this principle abstractly in its universal form, but does always have it actually in view and does use it as the standard of judgment. It would here be easy to show how ordinary reason, with this compass in hand, is well able to distinguish, in every case that occurs, what is good or evil, in accord with duty or contrary to duty, if we do not in the least try to teach reason anything new but only make it attend, as Socrates did, to its own principle—and thereby do we show that neither science nor philosophy is needed in order to know what one must do to be honest and good, and even wise and virtuous. Indeed we might even have conjectured beforehand that cognizance of what every man is obligated to do, and hence also to know, would be available to every man, even the most ordinary. Yet we cannot but observe with admiration how great an advantage the power of practical judgment has over the theoretical in ordinary human understanding. In the theoretical, when ordinary reason ventures to depart from the laws of experience and the perceptions of sense, it falls into sheer inconceivabilities and self-contradictions, or at least into a chaos of uncertainty, obscurity, and instability. In the practical, however, the power of judgment first begins to show itself to advantage

16. [This means that when you tell a lie, you merely take exception to the general rule that says everyone should always tell the truth and believe that what you are saying is true. When you lie, you do not thereby will that everyone else lie and not believe that what you are saying is true, because in such a case your lie would never work to get you what you want.]

when ordinary understanding excludes all sensuous incentives from practical laws. Such understanding then becomes even subtle, whether in quibbling with its own conscience or with other claims regarding what is to be called right, or whether in wanting to determine correctly for its own instruction the worth of various actions. And the most extraordinary thing is that ordinary understanding in this practical case may have just as good a hope of hitting the mark as that which any philosopher may promise himself. Indeed it is almost more certain in this than even a philosopher is, because he can have no principle other than what ordinary understanding has, but he may easily confuse his judgment by a multitude of foreign and irrelevant considerations and thereby cause it to swerve from the right way. Would it not, therefore, be wiser in moral matters to abide by the ordinary rational judgment or at most to bring in philosophy merely for the purpose of rendering the system of morals more complete and intelligible and of presenting its rules in a way that is more convenient for use (especially in disputation), but not for the purpose of leading ordinary human understanding away from its happy simplicity in practical matters and of bringing it by means of philosophy into a new path of inquiry and instruction?

Innocence is indeed a glorious thing; but, unfortunately, it does not keep very well and is easily led astray. Consequently, even wisdom—which consists more in doing and not doing than in knowing—needs science, not in order to learn from it, but in order that wisdom's precepts may gain acceptance and permanence. Man feels within himself a powerful counterweight to all the commands of duty, which are presented to him by reason as being so pre-eminently worthy of respect; this counterweight consists of his needs and inclinations, whose total satisfaction is summed up under the name of happiness. Now reason irremissibly commands its precepts, without thereby promising the inclinations anything; hence it disregards and neglects these impetuous and at the same time so seemingly plausible claims (which do not allow themselves to be suppressed by any command). Hereby arises a natural dialectic, i.e., a propensity to quibble with these strict laws of duty, to cast doubt upon their validity, or at least upon their purity and strictness, and to make them, where possible, more compatible with our wishes and inclinations. Thereby are such laws corrupted in their very foundations and their whole dignity is destroyed—something which even ordinary practical reason cannot in the end call good.

Thus is ordinary human reason forced to go outside its sphere and take a step into the field of practical philosophy, not by any need for speculation (which never befalls such reason so long as it is content to be mere sound reason) but on practical grounds themselves. There it tries to obtain information and clear instruction regarding the source of its own principle and the correct determination of this principle in its opposition to maxims based on need and inclination, so that reason may escape from the perplexity of opposite claims and may avoid the risk of losing all genuine moral principles through the ambiguity into which it easily falls. Thus when ordinary practical reason cultivates itself, there imperceptibly arises in it a dialectic which compels it to seek help in philosophy. The same thing happens in reason's theoretical use; in this case, just as in the other, peace will be found only in a thorough critical examination of our reason.

SECOND SECTION

Transition from Popular Moral Philosophy to a Metaphysics of Morals

If we have so far drawn our concept of duty from the ordinary use of our practical reason, one is by no means to infer that we have treated it as a concept of experience. On the contrary, when we pay attention to our experience of the way human beings act, we meet frequent and — as we ourselves admit — justified complaints that there cannot be cited a single certain example of the disposition to act from pure duty; and we meet complaints that although much may be done that is in accordance with what duty commands, yet there are always doubts as to whether what occurs has really been done from duty and so has moral worth. Hence there have always been philosophers who have absolutely denied the reality of this disposition in human actions and have ascribed everything to a more or less refined self-love. Yet in so doing they have not cast doubt upon the rightness of the concept of morality. Rather, they have spoken with sincere regret as to the frailty and impurity of human nature, which they think is noble enough to take as its precept an idea so worthy of respect but yet is too weak to follow this idea: reason, which should legislate for human nature, is used only to look after the interest of inclinations, whether singly or, at best, in their greatest possible harmony with one another.

In fact there is absolutely no possibility by means of experience to make out with complete certainty a single case in which the maxim of an action that may in other respects conform to duty has rested solely on moral grounds and on the representation of one's duty. It is indeed sometimes the case that after the keenest self-examination we can find nothing except the moral ground of duty that could have been strong enough to move us to this or that good action and to such great sacrifice. But there cannot with certainty be at all inferred from this that some secret impulse of self-love, merely appearing as the idea of duty, was not the actual determining cause of the will. We like to flatter ourselves with the false claim to a more noble motive; but in fact we can never, even by the strictest examination, completely plumb the depths of the secret incentives of our actions. For when moral value is being considered, the concern is not with the actions, which are seen, but rather with their inner principles, which are not seen.

Moreover, one cannot better serve the wishes of those who ridicule all morality as being a mere phantom of human imagination getting above itself because of self-conceit than by conceding to them that the concepts of duty must be drawn solely from experience (just as from indolence one willingly persuades himself that such is the case as regards all other concepts as well). For by so conceding, one prepares for them a sure triumph. I am willing to admit out of love for humanity that most of our actions are in accordance with duty; but if we look more closely at our planning and striving, we everywhere come upon the dear self, which is always turning up, and upon which the intent of our actions is based rather than upon the strict command of duty (which would often require self-denial). One need not be exactly an enemy of virtue, but only a cool observer who does not take the liveliest wish for the good to be straight off its realization, in order to become doubtful at times whether any true virtue is actually to be found in the world. Such is especially the case when years increase and one's power of judgment is made shrewder by experience and keener in observation. Because of these things nothing can protect us from a complete falling away from our ideas of duty and preserve in the soul a well-grounded respect for duty's law except the clear conviction that, even if there never have been actions springing from such pure sources, the question at issue here is not whether this or that has happened but that reason of itself and independently of all experience commands what ought to happen. Consequently, reason unrelentingly commands actions of which the world has perhaps hitherto never provided an example and whose feasibility might well be doubted by one who bases everything upon experience; for instance, even though there might never yet have been a sincere friend, still pure sincerity in friendship is nonetheless required of every man, because this duty, prior to all experience, is contained as duty in general in the idea of a reason that determines the will by means of a priori grounds.

There may be noted further that unless we want to deny to the concept of morality all truth and all reference to a possible object, we cannot but admit that the moral law is of such widespread significance that it must hold not merely for men but for all rational beings generally, and that it must be valid not merely under contingent conditions and with exceptions but must be absolutely necessary. Clearly, therefore, no experience can give occasion for inferring even the possibility of such apodeictic laws. For with what right could we bring into unlimited respect as a universal precept for every rational nature what is perhaps valid only under the contingent conditions of humanity? And how could laws for the determination of our will be regarded as laws for the determination of a rational being in general and of ourselves only insofar as we are rational beings, if these laws were merely empirical and did not have their source completely a priori in pure, but practical, reason?

Moreover, worse service cannot be rendered morality than that an attempt be made to derive it from examples. For every example of morality presented to me must itself first be judged according to principles of morality in order to see whether it is fit to serve as an original example, i.e., as a model. But in no way can it authoritatively furnish the concept of morality. Even the Holy One of the gospel must first be compared with our ideal of moral perfection before he is recognized as such. Even he says of himself, "Why do you call me (whom you see) good? None is good (the archetype of the good) except God only (whom you do not see)." But whence have we the concept of God as the highest good? Solely from the idea of moral perfection, which reason frames a priori and connects inseparably with the concept of a free will. Imitation has no place at all in moral matters. And examples serve only for encouragement, i.e., they put beyond doubt the feasibility of what the law commands and they make visible what the practical rule expresses more generally. But examples can never justify us in setting aside their true original, which lies in reason, and letting ourselves be guided by them.

If there is then no genuine supreme principle of morality that must rest merely on pure reason, independently of all experience, I think it is unnecessary even to ask whether it is a good thing to exhibit these concepts generally (*in abstracto*), which, along with the principles that belong to them, hold a priori, so far as the knowledge involved is to be distinguished from ordinary knowledge and is to be called philosophical. But in our times it may well be necessary to do so. For if one were to take a vote as to whether pure rational knowledge separated from everything empirical, i.e., metaphysics of morals, or whether popular practical philosophy is to be preferred, one can easily guess which side would be preponderant.

This descent to popular thought is certainly very commendable once the ascent to the principles of pure reason has occurred and has been satisfactorily accomplished. That would mean that the doctrine of morals has first been grounded on metaphysics and that subsequently acceptance for morals has been won by giving it a popular character after it has been firmly established. But it is quite absurd to try for popularity in the first inquiry, upon which depends the total correctness of the principles. Not only can such a procedure never lay claim to the very rare merit of a true philosophical popularity, inasmuch as there is really no art involved at all in being generally intelligible if one thereby renounces all basic insight, but such a procedure turns out a disgusting mishmash of patchwork observations and half-reasoned principles in which shallowpates revel because all this is something quite useful for the chitchat of everyday life. Persons of insight, on the other hand, feel confused by all this and turn their eyes away with a dissatisfaction which they nevertheless cannot cure. Yet philosophers, who quite see through the delusion, get little hearing when they summon people for a time from this pretended popularity in order that they may be rightfully popular only after they have attained definite insight.

One need only look at the attempts to deal with morality in the way favored by popular taste. What he will find in an amazing mixture is at one time the particular constitution of human nature (but along with this also the idea of a rational nature in general), at another time perfection, at another happiness; here moral feeling, and there the fear of God; something of this, and also something of that. But the thought never occurs to ask whether the principles of morality are to be sought at all in the knowledge of human nature (which can be had only from experience). Nor does the thought occur that if these principles are not to be sought here but to be found, rather, completely a priori and free from everything empirical in pure rational concepts only, and are to be found nowhere else even to the slightest extent — then there had better be adopted the plan of undertaking this investigation as a separate inquiry, i.e., as pure practical philosophy or (if one may use a name so much decried) as a metaphysics[1] of morals. It is better to bring this investigation to full completeness entirely by itself and to bid the public, which demands popularity, to await the outcome of this undertaking.

But such a completely isolated metaphysics of morals, not mixed with any anthropology, theology, physics, or hyperphysics, and still less with occult qualities (which might be called hypophysical), is not only an indispensable substratum of all theoretical and precisely defined knowledge of duties, but is at the same time a desideratum of the highest importance for the actual fulfillment of their precepts. For the pure thought of duty and of the moral law generally, unmixed with any extraneous addition of empirical inducements, has by the way of reason alone (which first becomes aware hereby that it can of itself be practical) an influence on the human heart so much more powerful than all other incentives[2] which may be derived from the empirical field that reason in the consciousness of its dignity despises such

1. Pure philosophy of morals (metaphysics) may be distinguished from the applied (viz., applied to human nature) just as pure mathematics is distinguished from applied mathematics and pure logic from applied logic. By this designation one is also immediately reminded that moral principles are not grounded on the peculiarities of human nature but must subsist a priori of themselves, and that from such principles practical rules must be derivable for every rational nature, and accordingly for human nature.

2. I have a letter from the late excellent Sulzer [Johann Georg Sulzer (1720–1779), an important Berlin savant, who translated Hume's *Inquiry Concerning the Principles of Morals* into German in 1755] in which he asks me why it is that moral instruction accomplishes so little, even though it contains so much that is convincing to reason. My answer was delayed so that I might make it complete. But it is just that the teachers themselves have not purified their concepts: since they try to do too well by looking everywhere for motives for being morally good, they spoil the medicine by trying to make it really strong. For the most or-

incentives and is able gradually to become their master. On the other hand, a mixed moral philosophy, compounded both of incentives drawn from feelings and inclinations and at the same time of rational concepts, must make the mind waver between motives that cannot be brought under any principle and that can only by accident lead to the good but often can also lead to the bad.

It is clear from the foregoing that all moral concepts have their seat and origin completely a priori in reason, and indeed in the most ordinary human reason just as much as in the most highly speculative. They cannot be abstracted from any empirical, and hence merely contingent, cognition. In this purity of their origin lies their very worthiness to serve us as supreme practical principles; and to the extent that something empirical is added to them, just so much is taken away from their genuine influence and from the absolute worth of the corresponding actions. Moreover, it is not only a requirement of the greatest necessity from a theoretical point of view, when it is a question of speculation, but also of the greatest practical importance, to draw these concepts and laws from pure reason, to present them pure and unmixed, and indeed to determine the extent of this entire practical and pure rational cognition, i.e., to determine the whole faculty of pure practical reason. The principles should not be made to depend on the particular nature of human reason, as speculative philosophy may permit and even sometimes finds necessary; but, rather, the principles should be derived from the universal concept of a rational being in general, since moral laws should hold for every rational being as such. In this way all morals, which require anthropology in order to be applied to humans, must be entirely expounded at first independently of anthropology as pure philosophy, i.e., as metaphysics (which can easily be done in such distinct kinds of knowledge). One knows quite well that unless one is in possession of such a metaphysics, then the attempt is futile, I shall not say to determine exactly for speculative judgment the moral element of duty in all that accords with duty, but that the attempt is impossible, even in ordinary and practical usage, especially in that of moral instruction, to ground morals on their genuine principles and thereby to produce pure moral dispositions and engraft them on men's minds for the promotion of the highest good in the world.

In this study we must advance by natural stages not merely from ordinary moral judgment (which is here ever so worthy of respect) to philosophical judgment, as has already been done, but also from popular philosophy, which goes no further than it can get by groping about with the help of examples, to metaphysics (which does not permit itself to be held back any longer by what is empirical, and which, inasmuch as it must survey the whole extent of rational knowledge of this kind, goes right up to ideas, where examples themselves fail us). In order to make such an advance, we must follow and clearly present the practical faculty of reason from its universal rules of determination to the point where the concept of duty springs from it.

Everything in nature works according to laws. Only a rational being has the power to act according to his conception of laws, i.e., according to principles, and thereby has he a will. Since the derivation of actions from laws requires reason, the will is

---

dinary observation shows that when a righteous act is represented as being done with a steadfast soul and sundered from all view to any advantage in this or another world, and even under the greatest temptations of need or allurement, it far surpasses and eclipses any similar action that was in the least affected by any extraneous incentive; it elevates the soul and inspires the wish to be able to act in this way. Even moderately young children feel this impression, and duties should never be represented to them in any other way.

nothing but practical reason. If reason infallibly determines the will, then in the case of such a being actions which are recognized to be objectively necessary are also subjectively necessary, i.e., the will is a faculty of choosing only that which reason, independently of inclination, recognizes as being practically necessary, i.e., as good. But if reason of itself does not sufficiently determine the will, and if the will submits also to subjective conditions (certain incentives) which do not always agree with objective conditions; in a word, if the will does not in itself completely accord with reason (as is actually the case with men), then actions which are recognized as objectively necessary are subjectively contingent, and the determination of such a will according to objective laws is necessitation. That is to say that the relation of objective laws to a will not thoroughly good is represented as the determination of the will of a rational being by principles of reason which the will does not necessarily follow because of its own nature.

The representation of an objective principle insofar as it necessitates the will is called a command (of reason), and the formula of the command is called an imperative.

All imperatives are expressed by an *ought* and thereby indicate the relation of an objective law of reason to a will that is not necessarily determined by this law because of its subjective constitution (the relation of necessitation). Imperatives say that something would be good to do or to refrain from doing, but they say it to a will that does not always therefore do something simply because it has been represented to the will as something good to do. That is practically good which determines the will by means of representations of reason and hence not by subjective causes, but objectively, i.e., on grounds valid for every rational being as such. It is distinguished from the pleasant as that which influences the will only by means of sensation from merely subjective causes, which hold only for this or that person's senses but do not hold as a principle of reason valid for everyone.[3]

A perfectly good will would thus be quite as much subject to objective laws (of the good), but could not be conceived as thereby necessitated to act in conformity with law, inasmuch as it can of itself, according to its subjective constitution, be determined only by the representation of the good. Therefore no imperatives hold for the divine will, and in general for a holy will; the *ought* is here out of place, because the *would* is already of itself necessarily in agreement with the law. Consequently, imperatives are only formulas for expressing the relation of objective laws of willing in general to the subjective imperfection of the will of this or that rational being, e.g., the human will.

---

3. The dependence of the faculty of desire on sensations is called inclination, which accordingly always indicates a need. The dependence of a contingently determinable will on principles of reason, however, is called interest. Therefore an interest is found only in a dependent will which is not of itself always in accord with reason; in the divine will no interest can be thought. But even the human will can take an interest in something without thereby acting from interest. The former signifies practical interest in the action, while the latter signifies pathological interest in the object of the action. The former indicates only dependence of the will on principles of reason by itself, while the latter indicates the will's dependence on principles of reason for the sake of inclination, i.e., reason merely gives the practical rule for meeting the need of inclination. In the former case the action interests me, while in the latter case what interests me is the object of the action (so far as this object is pleasant for me). In the First Section we have seen that in the case of an action done from duty regard must be given not to the interest in the object, but only to interest in the action itself and in its rational principle (viz., the law).

Now all imperatives command either hypothetically or categorically. The former represent the practical necessity of a possible action as a means for attaining something else that one wants (or may possibly want). The categorical imperative would be one which represented an action as objectively necessary in itself, without reference to another end.

Every practical law represents a possible action as good and hence as necessary for a subject who is practically determinable by reason; therefore all imperatives are formulas for determining an action which is necessary according to the principle of a will that is good in some way. Now if the action would be good merely as a means to something else, so is the imperative hypothetical. But if the action is represented as good in itself, and hence as necessary in a will which of itself conforms to reason as the principle of the will, then the imperative is categorical.

An imperative thus says what action possible by me would be good, and it presents the practical rule in relation to a will which does not forthwith perform an action simply because it is good, partly because the subject does not always know that the action is good and partly because (even if he does know it is good) his maxims might yet be opposed to the objective principles of practical reason.

A hypothetical imperative thus says only that an action is good for some purpose, either possible or actual. In the first case it is a problematic practical principle; in the second case an assertoric one. A categorical imperative, which declares an action to be of itself objectively necessary without reference to any purpose, i.e., without any other end, holds as an apodeictic practical principle.

Whatever is possible only through the powers of some rational being can be thought of as a possible purpose of some will. Consequently, there are in fact infinitely many principles of action insofar as they are represented as necessary for attaining a possible purpose achievable by them. All sciences have a practical part consisting of problems saying that some end is possible for us and of imperatives telling us how it can be attained. These can, therefore, be called in general imperatives of skill. Here there is no question at all whether the end is reasonable and good, but there is only a question as to what must be done to attain it. The prescriptions needed by a doctor in order to make his patient thoroughly healthy and by a poisoner in order to make sure of killing his victim are of equal value so far as each serves to bring about its purpose perfectly. Since there cannot be known in early youth what ends may be presented to us in the course of life, parents especially seek to have their children learn many different kinds of things, and they provide for skill in the use of means to all sorts of arbitrary ends, among which they cannot determine whether any one of them could in the future become an actual purpose for their ward, though there is always the possibility that he might adopt it. Their concern is so great that they commonly neglect to form and correct their children's judgment regarding the worth of things which might be chosen as ends.

There is, however, one end that can be presupposed as actual for all rational beings (so far as they are dependent beings to whom imperatives apply); and thus there is one purpose which they not merely can have but which can certainly be assumed to be such that they all do have by a natural necessity, and this is happiness. A hypothetical imperative which represents the practical necessity of an action as means for the promotion of happiness is assertoric. It may be expounded not simply as necessary to an uncertain, merely possible purpose, but as necessary to a purpose which can be presupposed a priori and with certainty as being present in everyone because it belongs to his essence. Now skill in the choice of means to one's own greatest well-being can be called prudence[4] in the narrowest sense. And thus the imperative that refers to the choice of means to one's own happiness, i.e., the precept of prudence, still remains hypothetical; the action is commanded not absolutely but only as a means to a further purpose.

Finally, there is one imperative which immediately commands a certain conduct without having as its condition any other purpose to be attained by it. This imperative is categorical. It is not concerned with the matter of the action and its intended result, but rather with the form of the action and the principle from which it follows; what is essentially good in the action consists in the mental disposition, let the consequences be what they may. This imperative may be called that of morality.

Willing according to these three kinds of principles is also clearly distinguished by dissimilarity in the necessitation of the will. To make this dissimilarity clear I think that they are most suitably named in their order when they are said to be either *rules of skill, counsels of prudence,* or *commands (laws) of morality.* For law alone involves the concept of a necessity that is unconditioned and indeed objective and hence universally valid, and commands are laws which must be obeyed, i.e., must be followed even in opposition to inclination. Counsel does indeed involve necessity, but involves such necessity as is valid only under a subjectively contingent condition, viz., whether this or that man counts this or that as belonging to his happiness. On the other hand, the categorical imperative is limited by no condition, and can quite properly be called a command since it is absolutely, though practically, necessary. The first kind of imperatives might also be called technical (belonging to art), the second kind pragmatic[5] (belonging to welfare), the third kind moral (belonging to free conduct as such, i.e., to morals).

The question now arises: how are all of these imperatives possible?[6] This question does not seek to know how the fulfillment of the action commanded by the imperative can be conceived, but merely how the necessitation of the will expressed by the imperative in setting a task can be conceived. How an imperative of skill is possible requires no special discussion. Whoever wills the end, wills (so far as reason has decisive influence on his actions) also the means that are indispensably necessary to his actions and that lie in his power. This proposition, as far as willing is concerned, is analytic. For in willing an object as my effect there is already thought the causality of myself as an acting cause, i.e., the use of means. The imperative derives the concept of actions necessary to this end from the concept of willing this end. (Synthetic propositions are indeed required for determining the means to a proposed end; but such propositions are concerned not with the ground, i.e., the act of the will, but only with the way to

---

4. The word "prudence" is used in a double sense: firstly, it can mean worldly wisdom, and, secondly, private wisdom. The former is the skill of someone in influencing others so as to use them for his own purposes. The latter is the sagacity to combine all these purposes for his own lasting advantage. The value of the former is properly reduced to the latter, and it might better be said of one who is prudent in the former sense but not in the latter that he is clever and cunning, but on the whole imprudent.

5. It seems to me that the proper meaning of the word "pragmatic" could be defined most accurately in this way. For those sanctions are called pragmatic which properly flow not from the law of states as necessary enactments but from provision for the general welfare. A history is pragmatically written when it teaches prudence, i.e., instructs the world how it can provide for its interests better than, or at least as well as, has been done in former times.

6. [That is, why should one let his actions be determined at various times by one or the other of these three kinds of imperatives?]

realize the object of the will.) Mathematics teaches by nothing but synthetic propositions that in order to bisect a line according to a sure principle I must from each of its extremities draw arcs such that they intersect. But when I know that the proposed result can come about only by means of such an action, then the proposition (if I fully will the effect, then I also will the action required for it) is analytic. For it is one and the same thing to conceive of something as an effect that is possible in a certain way through me and to conceive of myself as acting in the same way with regard to the aforesaid effect.

If it were only as easy to give a determinate concept of happiness, then the imperatives of prudence would exactly correspond to those of skill and would be likewise analytic. For there could be said in this case just as in the former that whoever wills the end also wills (necessarily according to reason) the sole means thereto which are in his power. But, unfortunately, the concept of happiness is such an indeterminate one that even though everyone wishes to attain happiness, yet he can never say definitely and consistently what it is that he really wishes and wills. The reason for this is that all the elements belonging to the concept of happiness are unexceptionally empirical, i.e., they must be borrowed from experience, while for the idea of happiness there is required an absolute whole, a maximum of well-being in my present and in every future condition. Now it is impossible for the most insightful and at the same time most powerful, but nonetheless finite, being to frame here a determinate concept of what it is that he really wills. Does he want riches? How much anxiety, envy, and intrigue might he not thereby bring down upon his own head! Or knowledge and insight? Perhaps these might only give him an eye that much sharper for revealing that much more dreadfully evils which are at present hidden but are yet unavoidable, or such an eye might burden him with still further needs for the desires which already concern him enough. Or long life? Who guarantees that it would not be a long misery? Or health at least? How often has infirmity of the body kept one from excesses into which perfect health would have allowed him to fall, and so on? In brief, he is not able on any principle to determine with complete certainty what will make him truly happy, because to do so would require omniscience. Therefore, one cannot act according to determinate principles in order to be happy, but only according to empirical counsels, e.g., of diet, frugality, politeness, reserve, etc., which are shown by experience to contribute on the average the most to well-being. There follows from this that imperatives of prudence, strictly speaking, cannot command at all, i.e., present actions objectively as practically necessary. They are to be taken as counsels (*consilia*) rather than as commands (*praecepta*) of reason. The problem of determining certainly and universally what action will promote the happiness of a rational being is completely insoluble. Therefore, regarding such action no imperative that in the strictest sense could command what is to be done to make one happy is possible, inasmuch as happiness is not an ideal of reason but of imagination. Such an ideal rests merely on empirical grounds; in vain can there be expected that such grounds should determine an action whereby the totality of an infinite series of consequences could be attained. This imperative of prudence would, nevertheless, be an analytic practical proposition if one assumes that the means to happiness could with certainty be assigned; for it differs from the imperative of skill only in that for it the end is given while for the latter the end is merely possible. Since both, however, command only the means to what is assumed to be willed as an end, the imperative commanding him who wills the end to will likewise the means thereto is in both cases analytic. Hence there is also no difficulty regarding the possibility of an imperative of prudence.

On the other hand, the question as to how the imperative of morality is possible is undoubtedly the only one requiring a solution. For it is not at all hypothetical; and hence the objective necessity which it presents cannot be based on any presupposition, as was the case with the hypothetical imperatives. Only there must never here be forgotten that no example can show, i.e., empirically, whether there is any such imperative at all. Rather, care must be taken lest all imperatives which are seemingly categorical may nevertheless be covertly hypothetical. For instance, when it is said that you should not make a false promise, the assumption is that the necessity of this avoidance is no mere advice for escaping some other evil, so that it might be said that you should not make a false promise lest you ruin your credit when the falsity comes to light. But when it is asserted that an action of this kind must be regarded as bad in itself, then the imperative of prohibition is therefore categorical. Nevertheless, it cannot with certainty be shown by means of an example that the will is here determined solely by the law without any other incentive, even though such may seem to be the case. For it is always possible that secretly there is fear of disgrace and perhaps also obscure dread of other dangers; such fear and dread may have influenced the will. Who can prove by experience that a cause is not present? Experience only shows that a cause is not perceived. But in such a case the so-called moral imperative, which as such appears to be categorical and unconditioned, would actually be only a pragmatic precept which makes us pay attention to our own advantage and merely teaches us to take such advantage into consideration.

We shall, therefore, have to investigate the possibility of a categorical imperative entirely a priori, inasmuch as we do not here have the advantage of having its reality given in experience and consequently of thus being obligated merely to explain its possibility rather than to establish it. In the meantime so much can be seen for now: the categorical imperative alone purports to be a practical law, while all the others may be called principles of the will but not laws. The reason for this is that whatever is necessary merely in order to attain some arbitrary purpose can be regarded as in itself contingent, and the precept can always be ignored once the purpose is abandoned. Contrariwise, an unconditioned command does not leave the will free to choose the opposite at its own liking. Consequently, only such a command carries with it that necessity which is demanded from a law.

Secondly, in the case of this categorical imperative, or law of morality, the reason for the difficulty (of discerning its possibility) is quite serious. The categorical imperative is an a priori synthetic practical proposition;[7] and since discerning the possibility of propositions of this sort involves so much difficulty in theoretic knowledge, there may readily be gathered that there will be no less difficulty in practical knowledge.

In solving this problem, we want first to inquire whether perhaps the mere concept of a categorical imperative may not also supply us with the formula containing the proposition that can alone be a categorical imperative. For even when we know the

---

7. I connect a priori, and therefore necessarily, the act with the will without presupposing any condition taken from some inclination (though I make such a connection only objectively, i.e., under the idea of a reason having full power over all subjective motives). Hence this is a practical proposition which does not analytically derive the willing of an action from some other willing already presupposed (for we possess no such perfect will) but which connects the willing of an action immediately with the concept of the will of a rational being as something which is not contained in this concept.

purport of such an absolute command, the question as to how it is possible will still require a special and difficult effort, which we postpone to the last section.[8]

If I think of a hypothetical imperative in general, I do not know beforehand what it will contain until its condition is given. But if I think of a categorical imperative, I know immediately what it contains. For since, besides the law, the imperative contains only the necessity that the maxim[9] should accord with this law, while the law contains no condition to restrict it, there remains nothing but the universality of a law as such with which the maxim of the action should conform. This conformity alone is properly what is represented as necessary by the imperative.

Hence there is only one categorical imperative and it is this: Act only according to that maxim whereby you can at the same time will that it should become a universal law.[10]

Now if all imperatives of duty can be derived from this one imperative as their principle, then there can at least be shown what is understood by the concept of duty and what it means, even though there is left undecided whether what is called duty may not be an empty concept.

The universality of law according to which effects are produced constitutes what is properly called nature in the most general sense (as to form), i.e., the existence of things as far as determined by universal laws. Accordingly, the universal imperative of duty may be expressed thus: Act as if the maxim of your action were to become through your will a universal law of nature.[11]

We shall now enumerate some duties, following the usual division of them into duties to ourselves and to others and into perfect and imperfect duties.[12]

1. A man reduced to despair by a series of misfortunes feels sick of life but is still so far in possession of his reason that he can ask himself whether taking his own life would not be contrary to his duty to himself.[13] Now he asks whether the maxim of his action could become a universal law of nature. But his maxim is this: from self-love I make as my principle to shorten my life when its continued duration threatens more evil than it promises satisfaction. There only remains the question as to whether this

---

8. [See below Ak. 446-63.]

9. A maxim is the subjective principle of acting and must be distinguished from the objective principle, viz., the practical law. A maxim contains the practical rule which reason determines in accordance with the conditions of the subject (often his ignorance or his inclinations) and is thus the principle according to which the subject does act. But the law is the objective principle valid for every rational being, and it is the principle according to which he ought to act, i.e., an imperative.

10. [This formulation of the categorical imperative is often referred to as the formula of universal law.]

11. [This is often called the formula of the law of nature.]

12. There should be noted here that I reserve the division of duties for a future *Metaphysics of Morals* [in Part II of the *Metaphysics of Morals*, entitled *The Metaphysical Principles of Virtue*, Ak. 417-474]. The division presented here stands as merely an arbitrary one (in order to arrange my examples). For the rest, I understand here by a perfect duty one which permits no exception in the interest of inclination. Accordingly, I have perfect duties which are external [to others], while other ones are internal [to oneself]. This classification runs contrary to the accepted usage of the schools, but I do not intend to justify it here, since there is no difference for my purpose whether this classification is accepted or not.

13. [Not committing suicide is an example of a perfect duty to oneself. See *Metaphysical Principles of Virtue*, Ak. 422-24.]

principle of self-love can become a universal law of nature. One sees at once a contradiction in a system of nature whose law would destroy life by means of the very same feeling that acts so as to stimulate the furtherance of life, and hence there could be no existence as a system of nature. Therefore, such a maxim cannot possibly hold as a universal law of nature and is, consequently, wholly opposed to the supreme principle of all duty.

2. Another man in need finds himself forced to borrow money. He knows well that he won't be able to repay it, but he sees also that he will not get any loan unless he firmly promises to repay it within a fixed time. He wants to make such a promise, but he still has conscience enough to ask himself whether it is not permissible and is contrary to duty to get out of difficulty in this way. Suppose, however, that he decides to do so. The maxim of his action would then be expressed as follows: when I believe myself to be in need of money, I will borrow money and promise to pay it back, although I know that I can never do so. Now this principle of self-love or personal advantage may perhaps be quite compatible with one's entire future welfare, but the question is now whether it is right.[14] I then transform the requirement of self-love into a universal law and put the question thus: how would things stand if my maxim were to become a universal law? He then sees at once that such a maxim could never hold as a universal law of nature and be consistent with itself, but must necessarily be self-contradictory. For the universality of a law which says that anyone believing himself to be in difficulty could promise whatever he pleases with the intention of not keeping it would make promising itself and the end to be attained thereby quite impossible, inasmuch as no one would believe what was promised him but would merely laugh at all such utterances as being vain pretenses.

3. A third finds in himself a talent whose cultivation could make him a man useful in many respects. But he finds himself in comfortable circumstances and prefers to indulge in pleasure rather than to bother himself about broadening and improving his fortunate natural aptitudes. But he asks himself further whether his maxim of neglecting his natural gifts, besides agreeing of itself with his propensity to indulgence, might agree also with what is called duty.[15] He then sees that a system of nature could indeed always subsist according to such a universal law, even though every man (like South Sea Islanders) should let his talents rust and resolve to devote his life entirely to idleness, indulgence, propagation, and, in a word, to enjoyment. But he cannot possibly will that this should become a universal law of nature or be implanted in us as such a law by a natural instinct. For as a rational being he necessarily wills that all his faculties should be developed, inasmuch as they are given him for all sorts of possible purposes.

4. A fourth man finds things going well for himself but sees others (whom he could help) struggling with great hardships; and he thinks: what does it matter to me? Let everybody be as happy as Heaven wills or as he can make himself; I shall take nothing from him nor even envy him; but I have no desire to contribute anything to his well-being or to his assistance when in need. If such a way of thinking were to become a universal law of nature, the human race admittedly could very well subsist and doubtless could subsist even better than when everyone prates about sympathy and benevolence and even on occasions exerts himself to practice them but, on the other

14. [Keeping promises is an example of a perfect duty to others. See *ibid.*, Ak. 423–31.]

15. [Cultivating one's talents is an example of an imperfect duty to oneself. See *ibid.*, Ak. 444–46.]

hand, also cheats when he can, betrays the rights of man, or otherwise violates them. But even though it is possible that a universal law of nature could subsist in accordance with that maxim, still it is impossible to will that such a principle should hold everywhere as a law of nature.[16] For a will which resolved in this way would contradict itself, inasmuch as cases might often arise in which one would have need of the love and sympathy of others and in which he would deprive himself, by such a law of nature springing from his own will, of all hope of the aid he wants for himself.

These are some of the many actual duties, or at least what are taken to be such, whose derivation from the single principle cited above is clear. We must be able to will that a maxim of our action become a universal law; this is the canon for morally estimating any of our actions. Some actions are so constituted that their maxims cannot without contradiction even be thought as a universal law of nature, much less be willed as what should become one. In the case of others this internal impossibility is indeed not found, but there is still no possibility of willing that their maxim should be raised to the universality of a law of nature, because such a will would contradict itself. There is no difficulty in seeing that the former kind of action conflicts with strict or narrow [perfect] (irremissible) duty, while the second kind conflicts only with broad [imperfect] (meritorious) duty.[17] By means of these examples there has thus been fully set forth how all duties depend as regards the kind of obligation (not the object of their action) upon the one principle.

If we now attend to ourselves in any transgression of a duty, we find that we actually do not will that our maxim should become a universal law — because this is impossible for us — but rather that the opposite of this maxim should remain a law universally.[18] We only take the liberty of making an exception to the law for ourselves (or just for this one time) to the advantage of our inclination. Consequently, if we weighed up everything from one and the same standpoint, namely, that of reason, we would find a contradiction in our own will, viz., that a certain principle be objectively necessary as a universal law and yet subjectively not hold universally but should admit of exceptions. But since we at one moment regard our action from the standpoint of a will wholly in accord with reason and then at another moment regard the very same action from the standpoint of a will affected by inclination, there is really no contradiction here. Rather, there is an opposition (*antagonismus*) of inclination to the precept of reason, whereby the universality (*universalitas*) of the principle is changed into a mere generality (*generalitas*) so that the practical principle of reason may meet the maxim halfway. Although this procedure cannot be justified in our own impartial judgment, yet it does show that we actually acknowledge the validity of the categorical imperative and (with all respect for it) merely allow ourselves a few exceptions which, as they seem to us, are unimportant and forced upon us.

We have thus at least shown that if duty is a concept which is to have significance and real legislative authority for our actions, then such duty can be expressed only in categorical imperatives but not at all in hypothetical ones. We have also — and this is

16. [Benefiting others is an example of an imperfect duty to others. See *ibid.*, Ak. 452-54.]

17. [Compare *ibid.*, Ak. 390-94, 410-11, 421-51.]

18. [This is to say, for example, that when you tell a lie, you do so on the condition that others are truthful and believe that what you are saying is true, because otherwise your lie will never work to get you what you want. When you tell a lie, you simply take exception to the general rule that says everyone should always tell the truth.]

already a great deal—exhibited clearly and definitely for every application what is the content of the categorical imperative, which must contain the principle of all duty (if there is such a thing at all). But we have not yet advanced far enough to prove a priori that there actually is an imperative of this kind, that there is a practical law which of itself commands absolutely and without any incentives, and that following this law is duty.

In order to attain this proof there is the utmost importance in being warned that we must not take it into our mind to derive the reality of this principle from the special characteristics of human nature. For duty has to be a practical, unconditioned necessity of action; hence it must hold for all rational beings (to whom alone an imperative is at all applicable) and for this reason only can it also be a law for all human wills. On the other hand, whatever is derived from the special natural condition of humanity, from certain feelings and propensities, or even, if such were possible, from some special tendency peculiar to human reason and not holding necessarily for the will of every rational being—all of this can indeed yield a maxim valid for us, but not a law. This is to say that such can yield a subjective principle according to which we might act if we happen to have the propensity and inclination, but cannot yield an objective principle according to which we would be directed to act even though our every propensity, inclination, and natural tendency were opposed to it. In fact, the sublimity and inner worth of the command are so much the more evident in a duty, the fewer subjective causes there are for it and the more they oppose it; such causes do not in the least weaken the necessitation exerted by the law or take away anything from its validity.

Here philosophy is seen in fact to be put in a precarious position, which should be firm even though there is neither in heaven nor on earth anything upon which it depends or is based. Here philosophy must show its purity as author of its laws, and not as the herald of such laws as are whispered to it by an implanted sense or by who knows what tutelary nature. Such laws may be better than nothing at all, but they can never give us principles dictated by reason. These principles must have an origin that is completely a priori and must at the same time derive from such origin their authority to command. They expect nothing from the inclination of men but, rather, expect everything from the supremacy of the law and from the respect owed to the law. Without the latter expectation, these principles condemn man to self-contempt and inward abhorrence.

Hence everything empirical is not only quite unsuitable as a contribution to the principle of morality, but is even highly detrimental to the purity of morals. For the proper and inestimable worth of an absolutely good will consists precisely in the fact that the principle of action is free of all influences from contingent grounds, which only experience can furnish. This lax or even mean way of thinking which seeks its principle among empirical motives and laws cannot too much or too often be warned against, for human reason in its weariness is glad to rest upon this pillow. In a dream of sweet illusions (in which not Juno but a cloud is embraced) there is substituted for morality some bastard patched up from limbs of quite varied ancestry and looking like anything one wants to see in it but not looking like virtue to him who has once beheld her in her true form.[19]

19. To behold virtue in her proper form is nothing other than to present morality stripped of all admixture of what is sensuous and of every spurious adornment of reward or self-love. How much she then eclipses all else that appears attractive to the inclinations can be easily seen by everyone with the least effort of his reason, if it be not entirely ruined for all abstraction.

Therefore, the question is this: is it a necessary law for all rational beings always to judge their actions according to such maxims as they can themselves will that such should serve as universal laws? If there is such a law, then it must already be connected (completely a priori) with the concept of a rational being in general. But in order to discover this connection we must, however reluctantly, take a step into metaphysics, although into a region of it different from speculative philosophy, i.e., we must enter the metaphysics of morals. In practical philosophy the concern is not with accepting grounds for what happens but with accepting laws of what ought to happen, even though it never does happen — that is, the concern is with objectively practical laws. Here there is no need to inquire into the reasons as to why something pleases or displeases, how the pleasure of mere sensation differs from taste, and whether taste differs from a general satisfaction of reason, upon what does the feeling of pleasure and displeasure rest, and how from this feeling desires and inclinations arise, and how, finally, from these there arise maxims through the cooperation of reason. All of this belongs to an empirical psychology, which would constitute the second part of the doctrine of nature, if this doctrine is regarded as the philosophy of nature insofar as this philosophy is grounded on empirical laws. But here the concern is with objectively practical laws, and hence with the relation of a will to itself insofar as it is determined solely by reason. In this case everything related to what is empirical falls away of itself, because if reason entirely by itself determines conduct (and the possibility of such determination we now wish to investigate), then reason must necessarily do so a priori.

The will is thought of as a faculty of determining itself to action in accordance with the representation of certain laws, and such a faculty can be found only in rational beings. Now what serves the will as the objective ground of its self-determination is an end; and if this end is given by reason alone, then it must be equally valid for all rational beings. On the other hand, what contains merely the ground of the possibility of the action, whose effect is an end, is called the means. The subjective ground of desire is the incentive; the objective ground of volition is the motive. Hence there arises the distinction between subjective ends, which rest on incentives, and objective ends, which depend on motives valid for every rational being. Practical principles are formal when they abstract from all subjective ends; they are material, however, when they are founded upon subjective ends, and hence upon certain incentives. The ends which a rational being arbitrarily proposes to himself as effects of this action (material ends) are all merely relative, for only their relation to a specially constituted faculty of desire in the subject gives them their worth. Consequently, such worth cannot provide any universal principles, which are valid and necessary for all rational beings and, furthermore, are valid for every volition, i.e., cannot provide any practical laws. Therefore, all such relative ends can be grounds only for hypothetical imperatives.

But let us suppose that there were something whose existence has in itself an absolute worth, something which as an end in itself could be a ground of determinate laws. In it, and in it alone, would there be the ground of a possible categorical imperative, i.e., of a practical law.

Now I say that man, and in general every rational being, exists as an end in himself and not merely as a means to be arbitrarily used by this or that will. He must in all his actions, whether directed to himself or to other rational beings, always be regarded at the same time as an end. All the objects of inclinations have only a conditioned value; for if there were not these inclinations and the needs founded on them, then their object would be without value. But the inclinations themselves, being sources of needs, are so far from having an absolute value such as to render them desirable for their own sake that the universal wish of every rational being must be, rather, to be wholly free from them. Accordingly, the value of any object obtainable by our action is always conditioned. Beings whose existence depends not on our will but on nature have, nevertheless, if they are not rational beings, only a relative value as means and are therefore called things. On the other hand, rational beings are called persons inasmuch as their nature already marks them out as ends in themselves, i.e., as something which is not to be used merely as means and hence there is imposed thereby a limit on all arbitrary use of such beings, which are thus objects of respect. Persons are, therefore, not merely subjective ends, whose existence as an effect of our actions has a value for us; but such beings are objective ends, i.e., exist as ends in themselves. Such an end is one for which there can be substituted no other end to which such beings should serve merely as means, for otherwise nothing at all of absolute value would be found anywhere. But if all value were conditioned and hence contingent, then no supreme practical principle could be found for reason at all.

If then there is to be a supreme practical principle and, as far as the human will is concerned, a categorical imperative, then it must be such that from the conception of what is necessarily an end for everyone because this end is an end in itself it constitutes an objective principle of the will and can hence serve as a practical law. The ground of such a principle is this: rational nature exists as an end in itself. In this way man necessarily thinks of his own existence; thus far is it a subjective principle of human actions. But in this way also does every other rational being think of his existence on the same rational ground that holds also for me;[20] hence it is at the same time an objective principle, from which, as a supreme practical ground, all laws of the will must be able to be derived. The practical imperative will therefore be the following: Act in such a way that you treat humanity, whether in your own person or in the person of another, always at the same time as an end and never simply as a means.[21] We now want to see whether this can be carried out in practice.

Let us keep to our previous examples.[22]

First, as regards the concept of necessary duty to oneself, the man who contemplates suicide will ask himself whether his action can be consistent with the idea of humanity as an end in itself. If he destroys himself in order to escape from a difficult situation, then he is making use of his person merely as a means so as to maintain a tolerable condition till the end of his life. Man, however, is not a thing and hence is not something to be used merely as a means; he must in all his actions always be regarded as an end in himself. Therefore, I cannot dispose of man in my own person by mutilating, damaging, or killing him. (A more exact determination of this principle so as to avoid all misunderstanding, e.g., regarding the amputation of limbs in order to save oneself, or the exposure of one's life to danger in order to save it, and so on, must here be omitted; such questions belong to morals proper.)

Second, as concerns necessary or strict duty to others, the man who intends to make

---

20. This proposition I here put forward as a postulate. The grounds for it will be found in the last section. [See below Ak. 446-63.]

21. [This oft-quoted version of the categorical imperative is usually referred to as the formula of the end in itself.]

22. [See above Ak. 422-23.]

a false promise will immediately see that he intends to make use of another man merely as a means to an end which the latter does not likewise hold. For the man whom I want to use for my own purposes by such a promise cannot possibly concur with my way of acting toward him and hence cannot himself hold the end of this action. This conflict with the principle of duty to others becomes even clearer when instances of attacks on the freedom and property of others are considered. For then it becomes clear that a transgressor of the rights of men intends to make use of the persons of others merely as a means, without taking into consideration that, as rational beings, they should always be esteemed at the same time as ends, i.e., be esteemed only as beings who must themselves be able to hold the very same action as an end.[23]

Third, with regard to contingent (meritorious) duty to oneself, it is not enough that the action does not conflict with humanity in our own person as an end in itself; the action must also harmonize with this end. Now there are in humanity capacities for greater perfection which belong to the end that nature has in view as regards humanity in our own person. To neglect these capacities might perhaps be consistent with the maintenance of humanity as an end in itself, but would not be consistent with the advancement of this end.

Fourth, concerning meritorious duty to others, the natural end that all men have is their own happiness. Now humanity might indeed subsist if nobody contributed anything to the happiness of others, provided he did not intentionally impair their happiness. But this, after all, would harmonize only negatively and not positively with humanity as an end in itself, if everyone does not also strive, as much as he can, to further the ends of others. For the ends of any subject who is an end in himself must as far as possible be my ends also, if that conception of an end in itself is to have its full effect in me.

This principle of humanity and of every rational nature generally as an end in itself is the supreme limiting condition of every man's freedom of action. This principle is not borrowed from experience, first, because of its universality, inasmuch as it applies to all rational beings generally, and no experience is capable of determining anything about them; and, secondly, because in experience (subjectively) humanity is not thought of as the end of men, i.e., as an object that we of ourselves actually make our end which as a law ought to constitute the supreme limiting condition of all subjective ends (whatever they may be); and hence this principle must arise from pure reason [and not from experience]. That is to say that the ground of all practical legislation lies objectively in the rule and in the form of universality, which (according to the first principle) makes the rule capable of being a law (say, for example, a law of nature). Subjectively, however, the ground of all practical legislation lies in the end; but (according to the second principle) the subject of all ends is every rational being as an end in himself. From this there now follows the third practical principle of the will as the supreme condition of the will's conformity with universal practical reason, viz., the idea of the will of every rational being as a will that legislates universal law.[24]

23. Let it not be thought that the trivial *quod tibi non vis fieri, etc.* [do not do to others what you do not want done to yourself] can here serve as a standard or principle. For it is merely derived from our principle, although with several limitations. It cannot be a universal law, for it contains the ground neither of duties to oneself nor of duties of love toward others (for many a man would gladly consent that others should not benefit him, if only he might be excused from benefiting them). Nor, finally, does it contain the ground of strict duties toward others, for the criminal would on this ground be able to dispute with the judges who punish him; and so on.

24. [This is usually called the formula of autonomy.]

According to this principle all maxims are rejected which are not consistent with the will's own legislation of universal law. The will is thus not merely subject to the law but is subject to the law in such a way that it must be regarded also as legislating for itself and only on this account as being subject to the law (of which it can regard itself as the author).

In the previous formulations of imperatives, viz., that based on the conception of the conformity of actions to universal law in a way similar to a natural order and that based on the universal prerogative of rational beings as ends in themselves, these imperatives just because they were thought of as categorical excluded from their legislative authority all admixture of any interest as an incentive. They were, however, only assumed to be categorical because such an assumption had to be made if the concept of duty was to be explained. But that there were practical propositions which commanded categorically could not itself be proved, nor can it be proved anywhere in this section. But one thing could have been done, viz., to indicate that in willing from duty the renunciation of all interest is the specific mark distinguishing a categorical imperative from a hypothetical one and that such renunciation was expressed in the imperative itself by means of some determination contained in it. This is done in the present (third) formulation of the principle, namely, in the idea of the will of every rational being as a will that legislates universal law.

When such a will is thought of, then even though a will which is subject to law may be bound to this law by means of some interest, nevertheless a will that is itself a supreme lawgiver is not able as such to depend on any interest. For a will which is so dependent would itself require yet another law restricting the interest of its self-love to the condition that such interest should itself be valid as a universal law.

Thus the principle that every human will as a will that legislates universal law in all its maxims,[25] provided it is otherwise correct, would be well suited to being a categorical imperative in the following respect: just because of the idea of legislating universal law such an imperative is not based on any interest, and therefore it alone of all possible imperatives can be unconditional. Or still better, the proposition being converted, if there is a categorical imperative (i.e., a law for the will of every rational being), then it can only command that everything be done from the maxim of such a will as could at the same time have as its object only itself regarded as legislating universal law. For only then are the practical principle and the imperative which the will obeys unconditional, inasmuch as the will can be based on no interest at all.

When we look back upon all previous attempts that have been made to discover the principle of morality, there is no reason now to wonder why they one and all had to fail. Man was viewed as bound to laws by his duty; but it was not seen that man is subject only to his own, yet universal, legislation and that he is bound only to act in accordance with his own will, which is, however, a will purposed by nature to legislate universal laws. For when man is thought as being merely subject to a law (whatever it might be), then the law had to carry with it some interest functioning as an attracting stimulus or as a constraining force for obedience, inasmuch as the law did not arise as a law from his own will. Rather, in order that his will conform with law, it had to be necessitated by something else to act in a certain way. By this absolutely necessary conclusion, however, all the labor spent in finding a supreme ground for duty was ir-

---

25. I may here be excused from citing instances to elucidate this principle inasmuch as those which were first used to elucidate the categorical imperative and its formula can all serve the same purpose here. [See above Ak. 421–23, 429–30.]

retrievably lost; duty was never discovered, but only the necessity of acting from a certain interest. This might be either one's own interest or another's, but either way the imperative had to be always conditional and could never possibly serve as a moral command. I want, therefore, to call my principle the principle of the autonomy of the will, in contrast with every other principle, which I accordingly count under heteronomy.

The concept of every rational being as one who must regard himself as legislating universal law by all his will's maxims, so that he may judge himself and his actions from this point of view, leads to another very fruitful concept, which depends on the aforementioned one, viz., that of a kingdom of ends.

By "kingdom" I understand a systematic union of different rational beings through common laws. Now laws determine ends as regards their universal validity; therefore, if one abstracts from the personal differences of rational beings and also from all content of their private ends, then it will be possible to think of a whole of all ends in systematic connection (a whole both of rational being as ends in themselves and also of the particular ends which each may set for himself); that is, one can think of a kingdom of ends that is possible on the aforesaid principles.

For all rational beings stand under the law that each of them should treat himself and all others never merely as means but always at the same time as an end in himself. Hereby arises a systematic union of rational beings through common objective laws, i.e., a kingdom that may be called a kingdom of ends (certainly only an ideal), inasmuch as these laws have in view the very relation of such beings to one another as ends and means.[26]

A rational being belongs to the kingdom of ends as a member when he legislates in it universal laws while also being himself subject to these laws. He belongs to it as sovereign, when as legislator he is himself subject to the will of no other.

A rational being must always regard himself as legislator in a kingdom of ends rendered possible by freedom of the will, whether as member or as sovereign. The position of the latter can be maintained not merely through the maxims of his will but only if he is a completely independent being without needs and with unlimited power adequate to his will.

Hence morality consists in the relation of all action to that legislation whereby alone a kingdom of ends is possible. This legislation must be found in every rational being and must be able to arise from his will, whose principle then is never to act on any maxim except such as can also be a universal law and hence such as the will can thereby regard itself as at the same time the legislator of universal law. If now the maxims do not by their very nature already necessarily conform with this objective principle of rational beings as legislating universal laws, then the necessity of acting on that principle is called practical necessitation, i.e., duty. Duty does not apply to the sovereign in the kingdom of ends, but it does apply to every member and to each in the same degree.

The practical necessity of acting according to this principle, i.e., duty, does not rest at all on feelings, impulses, and inclinations, but only on the relation of rational beings to one another, a relation in which the will of a rational being must always be regarded at the same time as legislative, because otherwise he could not be thought of as an end in himself. Reason, therefore, relates every maxim of the will as legislating

26. [This is usually called the formula of the kingdom of ends.]

universal laws to every other will and also to every action toward oneself; it does so not on account of any other practical motive or future advantage but rather from the idea of the dignity of a rational being who obeys no law except what he at the same time enacts himself.

In the kingdom of ends everything has either a price or a dignity. Whatever has a price can be replaced by something else as its equivalent; on the other hand, whatever is above all price, and therefore admits of no equivalent, has a dignity.

Whatever has reference to general human inclinations and needs has a market price; whatever, without presupposing any need, accords with a certain taste, i.e., a delight in the mere unpurposive play of our mental powers,[27] has an affective price; but that which constitutes the condition under which alone something can be an end in itself has not merely a relative worth, i.e., a price, but has an intrinsic worth, i.e., dignity.

Now morality is the condition under which alone a rational being can be an end in himself, for only thereby can he be a legislating member in the kingdom of ends. Hence morality and humanity, insofar as it is capable of morality, alone have dignity. Skill and diligence in work have a market price; wit, lively imagination, and humor have an affective price; but fidelity to promises and benevolence based on principles (not on instinct) have intrinsic worth. Neither nature nor art contain anything which in default of these could be put in their place; for their worth consists, not in the effects which arise from them, nor in the advantage and profit which they provide, but in mental dispositions, i.e., in the maxims of the will which are ready in this way to manifest themselves in action, even if they are not favored with success. Such actions also need no recommendation from any subjective disposition or taste so as to meet with immediate favor and delight; there is no need of any immediate propensity or feeling toward them. They exhibit the will performing them as an object of immediate respect; and nothing but reason is required to impose them upon the will, which is not to be cajoled into them, since in the case of duties such cajoling would be a contradiction. This estimation, therefore, lets the worth of such a disposition be recognized as dignity and puts it infinitely beyond all price, with which it cannot in the least be brought into competition or comparison without, as it were, violating its sanctity.

Now there follows incontestably from this that every rational being as an end in himself must be able to regard himself with reference to all laws to which he may be subject as being at the same time the legislator of universal law, for just this very fitness of his maxims for the legislation of universal law distinguishes him as an end in himself. There follows also that his dignity (prerogative) of being above all the mere things of nature implies that his maxims must be taken from the viewpoint that regards himself, as well as every other rational being, as being legislative beings (and hence are they called persons). In this way there is possible a world of rational beings (*mundus intelligibilis*) as a kingdom of ends, because of the legislation belonging to all persons as members. Therefore, every rational being must so act as if he were through his maxim always a legislating member in the universal kingdom of ends. The formal principle of these maxims is this: So act as if your maxims were to serve at the same time as a universal law (for all rational beings). Thus a kingdom of ends is possible only on the analogy of a kingdom of nature; yet the former is possible only through maxims, i.e., self-imposed rules, while the latter is possible only through laws

27. [See Kant, *Critique of Aesthetic Judgment*, §'s 1-5.]

of efficient causes necessitated from without. Regardless of this difference and even though nature as a whole is viewed as a machine, yet insofar as nature stands in a relation to rational beings as its ends, it is on this account given the name of a kingdom of nature. Such a kingdom of ends would actually be realized through maxims whose rule is prescribed to all rational beings by the categorical imperative, if these maxims were universally obeyed. But even if a rational being himself strictly obeys such a maxim, he cannot for that reason count on everyone else's being true to it, nor can he expect the kingdom of nature and its purposive order to be in harmony with him as a fitting member of a kingdom of ends made possible by himself, i.e., he cannot expect the kingdom of nature to favor his expectation of happiness. Nevertheless, the law: Act in accordance with the maxims of a member legislating universal laws for a merely possible kingdom of ends, remains in full force, since it commands categorically. And just in this lies the paradox that merely the dignity of humanity as rational nature without any further end or advantage to be thereby gained—and hence respect for a mere idea—should yet serve as an inflexible precept for the will; and that just this very independence of the maxims from all such incentives should constitute the sublimity of maxims and the worthiness of every rational subject to be a legislative member in the kingdom of ends, for otherwise he would have to be regarded as subject only to the natural law of his own needs. And even if the kingdom of nature as well as the kingdom of ends were thought of as both united under one sovereign so that the latter kingdom would thereby no longer remain a mere idea but would acquire true reality, then indeed the kingdom of ends would gain the addition of a strong incentive, but never any increase in its intrinsic worth. For this sole absolute legislator must, in spite of all this, always be thought of as judging the worth of rational beings solely by the disinterested conduct prescribed to themselves by means of this idea alone. The essence of things is not altered by their external relations; and whatever without reference to such relations alone constitutes the absolute worth of man is also what he must be judged by, whoever the judge may be, even the Supreme Being. Hence morality is the relation of actions to the autonomy of the will, i.e., to the possible legislation of universal law by means of the maxims of the will. That action which is compatible with the autonomy of the will is permitted; that which is not compatible is forbidden. That will whose maxims are necessarily in accord with the laws of autonomy is a holy, or absolutely good, will. The dependence of a will which is not absolutely good upon the principle of autonomy (i.e., moral necessitation) is obligation, which cannot therefore be applied to a holy will. The objective necessity of an action from obligation is called duty.

What then is it that entitles the morally good disposition, or virtue, to make such lofty claims? It is nothing less than the share which such a disposition affords the rational being of legislating universal laws, so that he is fit to be a member in a possible kingdom of ends, for which his own nature has already determined him as an end in himself and therefore as a legislator in the kingdom of ends. Thereby is he free as regards all laws of nature, and he obeys only those laws which he gives to himself. Accordingly, his maxims can belong to a universal legislation to which he at the same time subjects himself. For nothing can have any worth other than what the law determines. But the legislation itself which determines all worth must for that very reason have dignity, i.e., unconditional and incomparable worth; and the word "respect" alone provides a suitable expression for the esteem which a rational being must have for it. Hence autonomy is the ground of the dignity of human nature and of every rational nature.

The aforementioned three ways of representing the principle of morality are at bottom only so many formulas of the very same law: one of them by itself contains a combination of the other two. Nevertheless, there is a difference in them, which is subjectively rather than objectively practical, viz., it is intended to bring an idea of reason closer to intuition (in accordance with a certain analogy) and thereby closer to feeling. All maxims have, namely,

1. A form, which consists in universality; and in this respect the formula of the moral imperative is expressed thus: maxims must be so chosen as if they were to hold as universal laws of nature.

2. A matter, viz., an end; and here the formula says that a rational being, inasmuch as he is by his very nature an end and hence an end in himself, must serve in every maxim as a condition limiting all merely relative and arbitrary ends.

3. A complete determination of all maxims by the formula that all maxims proceeding from his own legislation ought to harmonize with a possible kingdom of ends as a kingdom of nature.[28] There is a progression here through the categories of the *unity* of the form of the will (its universality), the *plurality* of its matter (its objects, i.e., its ends), and the *totality* or completeness of its system of ends. But one does better if in moral judgment he follows the rigorous method and takes as his basis the universal formula of the categorical imperative: Act according to that maxim which can at the same time make itself a universal law. But if one wants also to secure acceptance for the moral law, it is very useful to bring one and the same action under the three aforementioned concepts and thus, as far as possible, to bring the moral law nearer to intuition.

We can now end where we started in the beginning, viz., the concept of an unconditionally good will. That will is absolutely good which cannot be evil, i.e., whose maxim, when made into a universal law, can never conflict with itself. This principle is therefore also its supreme law: Act always according to that maxim whose universality as a law you can at the same time will. This is the only condition under which a will can never be in conflict with itself, and such an imperative is categorical. Inasmuch as the validity of the will as a universal law for possible actions is analogous to the universal connection of the existence of things in accordance with universal laws, which is the formal aspect of nature in general, the categorical imperative can also be expressed thus: Act according to maxims which can at the same time have for their object themselves as universal laws of nature. In this way there is provided the formula for an absolutely good will.

Rational nature is distinguished from the rest of nature by the fact that it sets itself an end. This end would be the matter of every good will. But in the idea of an absolutely good will—good without any qualifying condition (of attaining this or that end)—complete abstraction must be made from every end that has to come about as an effect (since such would make every will only relatively good). And so the end must here be conceived, not as an end to be effected, but as an independently existing end. Hence it must be conceived only negatively, i.e., as an end which should never be acted against and therefore as one which in all willing must never be regarded merely

28. Teleology considers nature as a kingdom of ends; morals regards a possible kingdom of ends as a kingdom of nature. In the former the kingdom of ends is a theoretical idea for explaining what exists. In the latter it is a practical idea for bringing about what does not exist but can be made actual by our conduct, i.e., what can be actualized in accordance with this very idea.

as means but must always be esteemed at the same time as an end. Now this end can be nothing but the subject of all possible ends themselves, because this subject is at the same time the subject of a possible absolutely good will; for such a will cannot without contradiction be subordinated to any other object. The principle: So act in regard to every rational being (yourself and others) that he may at the same time count in your maxim as an end in himself, is thus basically the same as the principle: Act on a maxim which at the same time contains in itself its own universal validity for every rational being. That in the use of means for every end my maxim should be restricted to the condition of its universal validity as a law for every subject says just the same as that a subject of ends, i.e., a rational being himself, must be made the ground for all maxims of actions and must thus be used never merely as means but as the supreme limiting condition in the use of all means, i.e., always at the same time as an end.

From what has just been said, there can now easily be explained how it happens that, although in the concept of duty we think of subjection to the law, yet at the same time we thereby ascribe a certain dignity and sublimity to the person who fulfills all his duties. For not insofar as he is subject to the moral law does he have sublimity, but rather has it only insofar as with regard to this very same law he is at the same time legislative, and only thereby is he subject to the law. We have also shown above[29] how neither fear nor inclination, but solely respect for the law, is the incentive which can give an action moral worth. Our own will, insofar as it were to act only under the condition of its being able to legislate universal law by means of its maxims — this will, ideally possible for us, is the proper object of respect. And the dignity of humanity consists just in its capacity to legislate universal law, though with the condition of humanity's being at the same time itself subject to this very same legislation.

Autonomy of the Will
As the Supreme Principle of Morality

Autonomy of the will is the property that the will has of being a law to itself (independently of any property of the objects of volition). The principle of autonomy is this: Always choose in such a way that in the same volition the maxims of the choice are at the same time present as universal law. That this practical rule is an imperative, i.e., that the will of every rational being is necessarily bound to the rule as a condition, cannot be proved by merely analyzing the concepts contained in it, since it is a synthetic proposition. For proof one would have to go beyond cognition of objects to a critical examination of the subject, i.e. go to a critique of pure practical reason, since this synthetic proposition which commands apodeictically must be capable of being cognized completely a priori. This task, however, does not belong to the present section. But that the above principle of autonomy is the sole principle of morals can quite well be shown by mere analysis of the concepts of morality; for thereby the principle of morals is found to be necessarily a categorical imperative, which commands nothing more nor less than this very autonomy.

Heteronomy of the Will
As the Source of All Spurious Principles
of Morality

If the will seeks the law that is to determine it anywhere but in the fitness of its

---

29. [Ak. 400-402.]

maxims for its own legislation of universal laws, and if it thus goes outside of itself and seeks this law in the character of any of its objects, then heteronomy always results. The will in that case does not give itself the law, but the object does so because of its relation to the will. This relation, whether it rests on inclination or on representations of reason, admits only of hypothetical imperatives: I ought to do something because I will something else. On the other hand, the moral, and hence categorical, imperative says that I ought to act in this way or that way, even though I did not will something else. For example, the former says that I ought not to lie if I would maintain my reputation; the latter says that I ought not to lie even though lying were to bring me not the slightest discredit. The moral imperative must therefore abstract from every object to such an extent that no object has any influence at all on the will, so that practical reason (the will) may not merely minister to an interest not belonging to it but may merely show its own commanding authority as the supreme legislation. Thus, for example, I ought to endeavor to promote the happiness of others, not as though its realization were any concern of mine (whether by immediate inclination or by any satisfaction indirectly gained through reason), but merely because a maxim which excludes it cannot be comprehended as a universal law in one and the same volition.

Classification of All Possible Principles of Morality Founded upon the Assumed Fundamental Concept of Heteronomy

Here as elsewhere human reason in its pure use, so long as it lacks a critical examination, first tried every possible wrong way before it succeeded in finding the only right way.

All principles that can be taken from this point of view are either empirical or rational. The first kind, drawn from the principle of happiness, are based upon either physical or moral feeling. The second kind, drawn from the principle of perfection, are based upon either the rational concept of perfection as a possible effect of our will or else upon the concept of an independent perfection (the will of God) as a determining cause of our will.

Empirical principles are wholly unsuited to serve as the foundation for moral laws. For the universality with which such laws ought to hold for all rational beings without exception (the unconditioned practical necessity imposed by moral laws upon such beings) is lost if the basis of these laws is taken from the particular constitution of human nature or from the accidental circumstances in which such nature is placed. But the principle of one's own happiness is the most objectionable. Such is the case not merely because this principle is false and because experience contradicts the supposition that well-being is always proportional to well-doing, nor yet merely because this principle contributes nothing to the establishment of morality, inasmuch as making a man happy is quite different from making him good and making him prudent and sharp-sighted for his own advantage quite different from making him virtuous. Rather, such is the case because this principle of one's own happiness bases morality upon incentives that undermine it rather than establish it and that totally destroy its sublimity, inasmuch as motives to virtue are put in the same class as motives to vice and inasmuch as such incentives merely teach one to become better at calculation, while the specific difference between virtue and vice is entirely obliterated. On the other hand, moral feeling, this alleged special sense,[30] remains closer to morality than does the aforementioned principle of one's own happiness. Yet the appeal to the principle of moral feeling is superficial, since men who cannot think believe that they will be helped out by feeling, even when the question is solely one of universal laws. They do so even though feelings naturally differ from one another by an infinity of degrees, so that feelings are not capable of providing a uniform measure of good and evil; furthermore, they do so even though one man cannot by his feeling judge validly at all for other men. Nevertheless, the principle of moral feeling is closer to morality and its dignity than is the principle of one's own happiness inasmuch as the former principle pays virtue the honor of ascribing to her directly the satisfaction and esteem that is held for her, and does not, as it were, tell her to her face that our attachment to her rests not on her beauty but only on our advantage.

Among the rational principles of morality (or those arising from reason rather than from feeling) there is the ontological concept of perfection. It is empty, indeterminate, and hence of no use for finding in the immeasurable field of possible reality the maximum sum suitable for us. Furthermore, in attempting to distinguish specifically between the reality just mentioned and every other, it exhibits an inevitable tendency for turning about in a circle and cannot avoid tacitly presupposing the morality that it has to explain. Nevertheless, it is better than the theological concept, whereby morality is derived from a divine and most perfect will. It is better not merely because we cannot intuit divine perfection but can only derive it from our own concepts, among which morality is foremost; but also because if it is not so derived (and being thus derived would involve a crudely circular explanation), then the only remaining concept of God's will is drawn from such characteristics as desire for glory and dominion combined with such frightful representations as those of might and vengeance. Any system of morals based on such notions would be directly opposed to morality.

But if I had to choose between the concept of moral sense and that of perfection in general (both of which at least do not weaken morality, even though they are not at all capable of serving as its foundation), I would decide for the latter because it at least withdraws the decision of the question from sensibility and brings it to the court of pure reason, though it does not even here get any decision. Furthermore, I would choose the concept of perfection in general because it preserves the indeterminate idea (of a will good in itself) free from falsity until it can be more precisely determined.

For the rest, I believe that I may be excused from a lengthy refutation of all these doctrines. Such a refutation would be merely superfluous labor, since it is so easy and is presumably so well understood even by those whose office requires them to declare themselves for one of these theories (since their hearers would not tolerate suspension of judgment). But what interests us more here is to know that these principles never lay down anything but heteronomy of the will as the first ground of morality and that they must, consequently, necessarily fail in their purpose.

---

30. I count the principle of moral feeling under that of happiness, because every empirical interest promises to contribute to our well-being through the amenity afforded by something, whether immediately and without any reference to advantage or with reference to advantage. Similarly, the principle of sympathy for the happiness of others must with Hutcheson be counted along with the principle of moral sense as adopted by him. [Francis Hutcheson (1694-1747) was Professor of Moral Philosophy in the University of Glasgow, Scotland. He was the main proponent of the doctrine of moral sense.]

In every case where an object of the will must be laid down as the foundation for prescribing a rule to determine the will, there the rule is nothing but heteronomy. The imperative is then conditioned, viz., if or because one wills this object, one should act thus or so. Hence the imperative can never command morally, i.e., categorically. Now the object may determine the will by means of inclination, as in the case of the principle of one's own happiness, or by means of reason directed to objects of our volition in general, as in the case of the principle of perfection. Yet in both cases the will never determines itself immediately by the thought of an action, but only by the incentive that the anticipated effect of the action has upon the will: I ought to do something because I will something else. And here must yet another law be assumed in me the subject, whereby I necessarily will this something else; this other law in turn requires an imperative to restrict this maxim. For the impulse which the representation of an object that is possible by means of our powers is to exert upon the will of a subject in accordance with his natural constitution belongs to the nature of the subject, whether to his sensibility (his inclination and taste) or to his understanding and reason, whose employment on an object is by the particular arrangement of their nature attended with satisfaction; consequently, the law would, properly speaking, be given by nature. This law, insofar as it is a law of nature, must be known and proved through experience and is therefore in itself contingent and hence is not fit to be an apodeictic practical rule, such as a moral rule must be. The law of nature under discussion is always merely heteronomy of the will; the will does not give itself the law, but a foreign impulse gives the law to the will by means of the subject's nature, which is adapted to receive such an impulse.

An absolutely good will, whose principle must be a categorical imperative, will therefore be indeterminate as regards all objects and will contain merely the form of willing; and indeed that form is autonomy. This is to say that the fitness of the maxims of every good will to make themselves universal laws is itself the only law that the will of every rational being imposes on itself, without needing to assume any incentive or interest as a basis.

How such a synthetic practical a priori proposition is possible and why it is necessary are problems whose solution does not lie any longer within the bounds of a metaphysics of morals. Furthermore, we have not here asserted the truth of this proposition, much less professed to have within our power a proof of it. We simply showed by developing the universally accepted concept of morality that autonomy of the will is unavoidably bound up with it, or rather is its very foundation. Whoever, then, holds morality to be something real, and not a chimerical idea without any truth, must also admit the principle here put forward. Hence this section, like the first, was merely analytic. To show that morality is not a mere phantom of the brain, which morality cannot be if the categorical imperative, and with it the autonomy of the will, is true and absolutely necessary as an a priori principle, we require a possible synthetic use of pure practical reason. But we must not venture on this use without prefacing it with a critical examination of this very faculty of reason. In the last section we shall give the main outlines of this critical examination as far as sufficient for our purpose.[31]

31. [The ensuing Third Section is difficult to grasp. Kant expressed himself more clearly regarding the topics discussed there in the *Critique of Practical Reason*, Part I, Book I ("Analytic of Pure Practical Reason").]

THIRD SECTION

TRANSITION FROM A METAPHYSICS OF MORALS TO A CRITIQUE OF PURE PRACTICAL REASON

The Concept of Freedom Is the Key for an Explanation of the Autonomy of the Will

The will is a kind of causality belonging to living beings insofar as they are rational; freedom would be the property of this causality that makes it effective independent of any determination by alien causes. Similarly, natural necessity is the property of the causality of all non-rational beings by which they are determined to activity through the influence of alien causes.

The foregoing explanation of freedom is negative and is therefore unfruitful for attaining an insight regarding its essence; but there arises from it a positive concept, which as such is richer and more fruitful. The concept of causality involves that of laws according to which something that we call cause must entail something else—namely, the effect. Therefore freedom is certainly not lawless, even though it is not a property of will in accordance with laws of nature. It must, rather, be a causality in accordance with immutable laws, which, to be sure, is of a special kind; otherwise a free will would be something absurd. As we have already seen [in the preceding paragraph], natural necessity is a heteronomy of efficient causes, inasmuch as every effect is possible only in accordance with the law that something else determines the efficient cause to exercise its causality. What else, then, can freedom of the will be but autonomy, i.e., the property that the will has of being a law to itself? The proposition that the will is in every action a law to itself expresses, however, nothing but the principle of acting according to no other maxim than that which can at the same time have itself as a universal law for its object. Now this is precisely the formula of the categorical imperative and is the principle of morality. Thus a free will and a will subject to moral laws are one and the same.

Therefore if freedom of the will is presupposed, morality (together with its principle) follows by merely analyzing the concept of freedom. However, the principle of morality is, nevertheless, a synthetic proposition: viz., an absolutely good will is one whose maxim can always have itself as content when such maxim is regarded as a universal law; it is synthetic because this property of the will's maxim can never be found by analyzing the concept of an absolutely good will. Now such synthetic propositions are possible only as follows—two cognitions are bound together through their connection with a third in which both of them are to be found. The positive concept of freedom furnishes this third cognition, which cannot, as is the case with physical causes, be the nature of the world of sense (in whose concept is combined the concept of something as cause in relation to something else as effect). We cannot here yet show straight away what this third cognition is which freedom indicates to us and of which we have an a priori idea, nor can we as yet conceive of the deduction of the concept of freedom from pure practical reason and therewith also the possibility of a categorical imperative. Rather, we require some further preparation.

Freedom Must Be Presupposed as a Property of the Will of All Rational Beings

It is not enough to ascribe freedom to our will, on whatever ground, if we have not also sufficient reason for attributing it to all rational beings. For inasmuch as morality serves as a law for us only insofar as we are rational beings, it must also be valid for all rational beings. And since morality must be derived solely from the property of freedom, one must show that freedom is also the property of the will of all rational beings. It is not enough to prove freedom from certain alleged experiences of human nature (such a proof is indeed absolutely impossible, and so freedom can be proved only a priori). Rather, one must show that freedom belongs universally to the activity of rational beings endowed with a will. Now I say that every being who cannot act in any way other than under the idea of freedom is for this very reason free from a practical point of view. This is to say that for such a being all the laws that are inseparably bound up with freedom are valid just as much as if the will of such a being could be declared to be free in itself for reasons that are valid for theoretical philosophy.[1] Now I claim that we must necessarily attribute to every rational being which has a will also the idea of freedom, under which only can such a being act. For in such a being we think of a reason that is practical, i.e., that has causality in reference to its objects. Now we cannot possibly think of a reason that consciously lets itself be directed from outside as regards its judgments; for in that case the subject would ascribe the determination of his faculty of judgment not to his reason, but to an impulse. Reason must regard itself as the author of its principles independent of foreign influences. Therefore as practical reason or as the will of a rational being must reason regard itself as free. This is to say that the will of a rational being can be a will of its own only under the idea of freedom, and that such a will must therefore, from a practical point of view, be attributed to all rational beings.

Concerning the Interest Attached to the Ideas of Morality

We have finally traced the determinate concept of morality back to the idea of freedom, but we could not prove freedom to be something actual in ourselves and in human nature. We saw merely that we must presuppose it if we want to think of a being as rational and as endowed with consciousness of its causality as regards actions, i.e., as endowed with a will. And so we find that on the very same ground we must attribute to every being endowed with reason and a will this property of determining itself to action under the idea of its own freedom.

Now there resulted from the presupposition of this idea of freedom also the consciousness of a law of action: that the subjective principles of actions, i.e., maxims, must always be so adopted that they can also be valid objectively, i.e., universally, as principles, and can therefore serve as universal laws of our own legislation. But why, then, should I subject myself to this principle simply as a rational being and by so doing also subject to this principle all other beings endowed with reason? I am willing to grant that no interest impels me to do so, because this would not give a categorical imperative. But nonetheless I must necessarily take an interest in it and discern how

---

1. I adopt this method of assuming as sufficient for our purpose that freedom is presupposed merely as an idea by rational beings in their actions in order that I may avoid the necessity of having to prove freedom from a theoretical point of view as well. For even if this latter problem is left unresolved, the same laws that would bind a being who was really free are valid equally for a being who cannot act otherwise than under the idea of its own freedom. Thus we can relieve ourselves of the burden which presses on the theory.

this comes about, for this *ought* is properly a *would* which is valid for every rational being, provided that reason is practical for such a being without hindrances. In the case of beings who, like ourselves, are also affected by sensibility, i.e., by incentives of a kind other than the purely rational, and who do not always act as reason by itself would act, this necessity of action is expressed only as an *ought,* and the subjective necessity is to be distinguished from the objective.

It therefore seems as if we have in the idea of freedom actually only presupposed the moral law, namely, the principle of the autonomy of the will, and as if we could not prove its reality and objective necessity independently. In that case we should indeed still have gained something quite considerable by at least determining the genuine principle more exactly than had previously been done. But as regards its validity and the practical necessity of subjecting oneself to it, we would have made no progress. We could give no satisfactory answer if asked the following questions: why must the universal validity of our maxim taken as a law be a condition restricting our actions; upon what do we base the worth that we assign to this way of acting—a worth that is supposed to be so great that there can be no higher interest; how does it happen that by this alone does man believe that he feels his own personal worth, in comparison with which that of an agreeable or disagreeable condition is to be regarded as nothing.

Indeed we do sometimes find that we can take an interest in a personal characteristic which involves no interest in any [external] condition but only makes us capable of participating in the condition in case reason were to effect the allotment. This is to say that the mere worthiness of being happy can of itself be of interest even without the motive of participating in this happiness. This judgment, however, is in fact only the result of the importance that we have already presupposed as belonging to moral laws (when by the idea of freedom we divorce ourselves from all empirical interest). However, in this way we are not as yet able to have any insight into why it is that we should divorce ourselves from such interest, i.e., that we should consider ourselves as free in action and yet hold ourselves as subject to certain laws so as to find solely in our own person a worth that can compensate us for the loss of everything that gives worth to our condition. We do not see how this is possible and hence how the moral law can obligate us.

One must frankly admit that there is here a sort of circle from which, so it seems, there is no way to escape. In the order of efficient causes we assume that we are free so that we may think of ourselves as subject to moral laws in the order of ends. And we then think of ourselves as subject to these laws because we have attributed to ourselves freedom of the will. Freedom and self-legislation of the will are both autonomy and are hence reciprocal concepts. Since they are reciprocal, one of them cannot be used to explain the other or to supply its ground, but can at most be used only for logical purposes to bring seemingly different conceptions of the same object under a single concept (just as different fractions of the same value are reduced to lowest terms).

However, one recourse still remains open to us, namely, to inquire whether we do not take one point of view when by means of freedom we think of ourselves as a priori efficient causes, and another point of view when we represent ourselves with reference to our actions as effects which we see before our eyes.

No subtle reflection is required for the following observation, which even the commonest understanding may be supposed to make, though it does so in its own fashion through some obscure discrimination of the faculty of judgment which it calls feeling:

all representations that come to us without our choice (such as those of the senses) enable us to know objects only as they affect us; what they may be in themselves remains unknown to us. Therefore, even with the closest attention and the greatest clarity that the understanding can bring to such representations, we can attain to a mere knowledge of appearances but never to knowledge of things in themselves. Once this distinction is made (perhaps merely as a result of observing the difference between representations which are given to us from without and in which we are passive from those which we produce entirely from ourselves and in which we show our own activity), then there follows of itself that we must admit and assume that behind the appearances there is something else which is not appearance, namely, things in themselves. Inasmuch as we can never cognize them except as they affect us [through our senses], we must admit that we can never come any nearer to them nor ever know what they are in themselves. This must provide a distinction, however crude, between a world of sense and a world of understanding; the former can vary considerably according to the difference of sensibility [and sense impressions] in various observers, while the latter, which is the basis of the former, remains always the same. Even with regard to himself, a man cannot presume to know what he is in himself by means of the acquaintance which he has through internal sensation. For since he does not, as it were, create himself and since he acquires the concept of himself not a priori but empirically, it is natural that he can attain knowledge even about himself only through inner sense and therefore only through the appearance of his nature and the way in which his consciousness is affected. But yet he must necessarily assume that beyond his own subject's constitution as composed of nothing but appearances there must be something else as basis, namely, his ego as constituted in itself. Therefore with regard to mere perception and the receptivity of sensations, he must count himself as belonging to the world of sense; but with regard to whatever there may be in him of pure activity (whatever reaches consciousness immediately and not through affecting the senses) he must count himself as belonging to the intellectual world, of which he has, however, no further knowledge.

Such a conclusion must be reached by a reflective man regarding all the things that may be presented to him. It is presumably to be found even in the most ordinary understanding, which, as is well known, is quite prone to expect that behind objects of the senses there is something else invisible and acting of itself. But such understanding spoils all this by making the invisible again sensible, i.e., it wants to make the invisible an object of intuition; and thereby does it become not a bit wiser.

Now man really finds in himself a faculty which distinguishes him from all other things and even from himself insofar as he is affected by objects. That faculty is reason, which as pure spontaneity is elevated even above understanding. For although the latter is also spontaneous and does not, like sense, merely contain representations that arise only when one is affected by things (and is therefore passive), yet understanding can produce by its activity no other concepts than those which merely serve to bring sensuous representations [intuitions] under rules and thereby to unite them in one consciousness. Without this use of sensibility, understanding would think nothing at all. Reason, on the other hand, shows such a pure spontaneity in the case of what are called ideas that it goes far beyond anything that sensibility can offer and shows its highest occupation in distinguishing the world of sense from the world of understanding, thereby prescribing limits to the understanding itself.

Therefore a rational being must regard himself qua intelligence (and hence not from the side of his lower powers) as belonging not to the world of sense but to the world of understanding. Therefore he has two standpoints from which he can regard himself and know laws of the use of his powers and hence of all his actions: first, insofar as he belongs to the world of sense subject to laws of nature (heteronomy); secondly, insofar as he belongs to the intelligible world subject to laws which, independent of nature, are not empirical but are founded only on reason.

As a rational being and hence as belonging to the intelligible world, can man never think of the causality of his own will except under the idea of freedom; for independence from the determining causes of the world of sense (an independence which reason must always attribute to itself) is freedom. Now the idea of freedom is inseparably connected with the concept of autonomy, and this in turn with the universal principle of morality, which ideally is the ground of all actions of rational beings, just as natural law is the ground of all appearances.

The suspicion that we raised earlier is now removed, viz., that there might be a hidden circle involved in our inference from freedom to autonomy, and from this to the moral law — this is to say that we had perhaps laid down the idea of freedom only for the sake of the moral law in order subsequently to infer this law in its turn from freedom, and that we had therefore not been able to assign any ground at all for this law but had only assumed it by begging a principle which well-disposed souls would gladly concede us but which we could never put forward as a demonstrable proposition. But now we see that when we think of ourselves as free, we transfer ourselves into the intelligible world as members and know the autonomy of the will together with its consequence, morality; whereas when we think of ourselves as obligated, we consider ourselves as belonging to the world of sense and yet at the same time to the intelligible world.

How Is a Categorical Imperative Possible?

The rational being counts himself, qua intelligence, as belonging to the intelligible world, and only insofar as he is an efficient cause belonging to the intelligible world does he call his causality a will. But on the other side, he is conscious of himself as being also a part of the world of sense, where his actions are found as mere appearances of that causality. The possibility of these actions cannot, however, be discerned through such causality, which we do not know; rather, these actions as belonging to the world of sense must be viewed as determined by other appearances, namely, desires and inclinations. Therefore, if I were solely a member of the intelligible world, then all my actions would perfectly conform to the principle of the autonomy of a pure will; if I were solely a part of the world of sense, my actions would have to be taken as in complete conformity with the natural law of desires and inclinations, i.e., with the heteronomy of nature. (My actions would in the first case rest on the supreme principle of morality, in the second case on that of happiness.) But the intelligible world contains the ground of the world of sense and therefore also the ground of its laws; consequently, the intelligible world is (and must be thought of as) directly legislative for my will (which belongs wholly to the intelligible world). Therefore, even though on the one hand I must regard myself as a being belonging to the world of sense, yet on the other hand shall I have to know myself as an intelligence and as subject to the law of the intelligible world, i.e., to reason, which contains this law in the idea of freedom, and hence to know myself as subject to the autonomy of the will. Consequently, I must regard the laws of the intelligible world as imperatives for me, and the actions conforming to this principle as duties.

And thus are categorical imperatives possible because the idea of freedom makes me a member of an intelligible world. Now if I were a member of only that world, all my actions *would* always accord with autonomy of the will. But since I intuit myself at the same time as a member of the world of sense, my actions *ought* so to accord. This categorical *ought* presents a synthetic a priori proposition, whereby in addition to my will as affected by sensuous desires there is added further the idea of the same will, but as belonging to the intelligible world, pure and practical of itself, and as containing the supreme condition of the former will insofar as reason is concerned. All this is similar to the way in which concepts [categories] of the understanding, which of themselves signify nothing but the form of law in general, are added to intuitions of the world of sense and thus make possible synthetic a priori propositions, upon which all knowledge of nature rests.

The practical use of ordinary human reason bears out the correctness of this deduction. There is no one, not even the meanest villain, provided only that he is otherwise accustomed to the use of reason, who, when presented with examples of honesty of purpose, of steadfastness in following good maxims, and of sympathy and general benevolence (even when involved with great sacrifices of advantages and comfort) does not wish that he might also possess these qualities. Yet he cannot attain these in himself only because of his inclinations and impulses; but at the same time he wishes to be free from such inclinations which are a burden to him. He thereby proves that by having a will free of sensuous impulses he transfers himself in thought into an order of things entirely different from that of his desires in the field of sensibility. Since he cannot expect to obtain by the aforementioned wish any gratification of his desires or any condition that would satisfy any of his actual or even conceivable inclinations (inasmuch as through such an expectation the very idea that elicited the wish would be deprived of its preeminence) he can only expect a greater intrinsic worth of his own person. This better person he believes himself to be when he transfers himself to the standpoint of a member of the intelligible world, to which he is involuntarily forced by the idea of freedom, i.e., of being independent of determination by causes of the world of sense. From this standpoint he is conscious of having a good will, which by his own admission constitutes the law for the bad will belonging to him as a member of the world of sense—a law whose authority he acknowledges even while he transgresses it. The moral *ought* is, therefore, a necessary *would* insofar as he is a member of the intelligible world, and is thought by him as an *ought* only insofar as he regards himself as being at the same time a member of the world of sense.

Concerning the Extreme Limit of All Practical Philosophy

All men think of themselves as free as far as their will is concerned. Hence arise all judgments upon actions as being such as ought to have been done, even though they were not done. But this freedom is not a concept of experience, nor can it be such, since it always holds, even though experience shows the opposite of those requirements represented as necessary under the presupposition of freedom. On the other hand, it is just as necessary that whatever happens should be determined without any exception according to laws of nature; and this necessity of nature is likewise no concept of experience, just because it involves the concept of necessity and thus of a priori knowledge. But this concept of nature is confirmed by experience and must inevitably be presupposed if there is to be possible experience, which is coherent knowledge of the objects of sense in accordance with universal laws. Freedom is, therefore, only an idea of reason whose objective reality is in itself questionable; but nature is a concept of the understanding, which proves, and necessarily must prove, its reality by examples from experience.

There arises from this a dialectic of reason, since the freedom attributed to the will seems to contradict the necessity of nature. And even though at this parting of the ways reason for speculative purposes finds the road of natural necessity much better worn and more serviceable than that of freedom, yet for practical purposes the footpath of freedom is the only one upon which it is possible to make use of reason in our conduct. Therefore, it is just as impossible for the most subtle philosophy as for the most ordinary human reason to argue away freedom. Hence philosophy must assume that no real contradiction will be found between freedom and natural necessity in the same human actions, for it cannot give up the concept of nature any more than that of freedom.

Nevertheless, even though one might never be able to comprehend how freedom is possible, yet this apparent contradiction must at least be removed in a convincing manner. For if the thought of freedom contradicts itself or nature, which is equally necessary, then freedom would have to be completely given up in favor of natural necessity.

It would, however, be impossible to escape this contradiction if the subject, deeming himself free, were to think of himself in the same sense or in the very same relationship when he calls himself free as when he assumes himself subject to the law of nature regarding the same action. Therefore, an unavoidable problem of speculative philosophy is at least to show that its illusion regarding the contradiction rests on our thinking of man in a different sense and relation when we call him free from when we regard him as being a part of nature and hence as subject to the laws of nature. Hence it must show not only that both can coexist very well, but that both must be thought of as necessarily united in the same subject; for otherwise no explanation could be given as to why reason should be burdened with an idea which involves us in a perplexity that is sorely embarrassing to reason in its theoretic use, even though it may without contradiction be united with another idea that is sufficiently established. This duty, however, is incumbent solely on speculative philosophy in order that it may clear the way for practical philosophy. Thus the philosopher has no option as to whether he will remove the apparent contradiction or leave it untouched; for in the latter case the theory regarding this could be *bonum vacans*,[2] into the possession of which the fatalist can justifiably enter and chase all morality out of its supposed property as occupying it without title.

Nevertheless, one cannot here say as yet that the boundary of practical philosophy begins. For the settlement of the controversy does not belong to practical philosophy; the latter only requires speculative reason to put an end to the dissension in which it is entangled as regards theoretical questions in order that practical reason may have rest and security from external attacks that might make disputable the ground upon which it wants to build.

The just claim to freedom of the will made even by ordinary human reason is founded on the consciousness and the admitted presupposition that reason is independent of mere subjective determination by causes which together make up what

2. [vacant property]

belongs only to sensation and comes under the general designation of sensibility. Regarding himself in this way as intelligence, man thereby puts himself into another order of things. And when he thinks of himself as intelligence endowed with a will and consequently with causality, he puts himself into relation with determining grounds of a kind altogether different from the kind when he perceives himself as a phenomenon in the world of sense (as he really is also) and subjects his causality to external determination according to laws of nature. Now he soon realizes that both can — and indeed must — hold good at the same time. For there is not the slightest contradiction involved in saying that a thing as appearance (belonging to the world of sense) is subject to certain laws, while it is independent of those laws when regarded as a thing or being in itself. That man must represent and think of himself in this twofold way rests, on the one hand, upon the consciousness of himself as an object affected through the senses and, on the other hand, upon the consciousness of himself as intelligence, i.e., as independent of sensuous impulses in his use of reason (and hence as belonging to the intelligible world).

And hence man claims that he has a will which reckons to his account nothing that belongs merely to his desires and inclinations, and which, on the contrary, thinks of actions that can be performed only by disregarding all desires and sensuous incitements as being possible and as indeed being necessary for him. The causality of such actions lies in man as intelligence and lies in the laws of such effects and actions as are in accordance with principles of an intelligible world, of which he knows nothing more than that in such a world reason alone, and indeed pure reason independent of sensibility, gives the law. Furthermore, since he is in such a world his proper self only as intelligence (whereas regarded as a human being he is merely an appearance of himself), those laws apply to him immediately and categorically. Consequently, incitements from inclinations and impulses (and hence from the whole nature of the world of sense) cannot impair the laws of his willing insofar as he is intelligence. Indeed he does not even hold himself responsible for such inclinations and impulses or ascribe them to his proper self, i.e., his will, although he does ascribe to his will any indulgence which he might extend to them if he allowed them any influence on his maxims to the detriment of the rational laws of his will.

When practical reason thinks itself into an intelligible world, it does not in the least thereby transcend its limits, as it would if it tried to enter it by intuition or sensation. The thought of an intelligible world is merely negative as regards the world of sense. The latter world does not give reason any laws for determining the will and is positive only in this single point, viz., it simultaneously combines freedom as negative determination with a positive faculty and even a causality of reason. This causality is designated as a will to act in such a way that the principle of actions may accord with the essential character of a rational cause, i.e., with the condition that the maxim of these actions have universal validity as a law. But if practical reason were to bring in an object of the will, i.e., a motive of action, from the intelligible world, then it would overstep its boundaries and pretend to be acquainted with something of which it knows nothing. The concept of an intelligible world is thus only a point of view which reason sees itself compelled to take outside of appearances in order to think of itself as practical. If the influences of sensibility were determining for man, reason would not be able to take this point of view, which is nonetheless necessary if he is not to be denied the consciousness of himself as intelligence and hence as a rational cause that is active through reason, i.e., free in its operation. This thought certainly involves the idea of an order and a legislation different from that of the mechanism of nature which applies to the world of sense; and it makes necessary the concept of an intelligible world (i.e., the whole of rational beings as things in themselves). But it makes not the slightest claim to anything more than to think of such a world as regards merely its formal condition—i.e., the universality of the will's maxims as laws and thus the will's autonomy, which alone is consistent with freedom. On the contrary, all laws determined by reference to an object yield heteronomy, which can be found only in laws of nature and can apply only to the world of sense.

But reason would overstep all its bounds if it undertook to explain how pure reason can be practical. This is exactly the same problem as explaining how freedom is possible.

For we can explain nothing but what we can reduce to laws whose object can be given in some possible experience. But freedom is a mere idea, whose objective reality can in no way be shown in accordance with laws of nature and consequently not in any possible experience. Therefore, the idea of freedom can never admit of comprehension or even of insight, because it cannot by any analogy have an example falling under it. It holds only as a necessary presupposition of reason in a being who believes himself conscious of a will, i.e., of a faculty distinct from mere desire (namely, a faculty of determining himself to action as intelligence and hence in accordance with laws of reason independently of natural instincts). But where determination according to laws of nature ceases, there likewise ceases all explanation and nothing remains but defense, i.e., refutation of the objections of those who profess to have seen deeper into the essence of things and thereupon boldly declare freedom to be impossible. One can only show them that their supposed discovery of a contradiction lies nowhere but here: in order to make the law of nature applicable to human actions, they have necessarily had to regard man as an appearance; and now when they are required to think of man qua intelligence as thing in himself as well, they still persist in regarding him as appearance. In that case, to be sure, the exemption of man's causality (i.e., his will) from all the natural laws of the world of sense would, as regards one and the same subject, give rise to a contradiction. But this disappears if they would but bethink themselves and admit, as is reasonable, that behind appearances there must lie as their ground also things in themselves (though hidden) and that the laws of their operations cannot be expected to be the same as those that govern their appearances.

The subjective impossibility of explaining freedom of the will is the same as the impossibility of discovering and explaining an interest[3] which man can take in moral laws. Nevertheless, he does indeed take such an interest, the basis of which in us is called moral feeling. Some people have falsely construed this feeling to be the standard of our moral judgment, whereas it must rather be regarded as the subjective effect that the law exercises upon the will, while reason alone furnishes the objective grounds of such moral feeling.

---

3. Interest is that by which reason becomes practical, i.e., a cause determining the will. Therefore one says of rational beings only that they take an interest in something; non-rational creatures feel only sensuous impulses. Reason takes an immediate interest in the action only when the universal validity of the maxim of the action is a sufficient determining ground of the will. Such an interest alone is pure. But when reason is able to determine the will only by means of another object of desire or under the presupposition of some special feeling in the subject, then reason takes only a mediate interest in the action. And since reason of itself alone without the help of experience can discover neither objects of the will nor a special feeling underlying the will, the latter interest would be only empirical and not a pure rational interest. The logical interest of reason (viz., to extend its insights) is never immediate, but presupposes purposes for which reason might be used.

In order to will what reason alone prescribes as an *ought* for sensuously affected rational beings, there certainly must be a power of reason to infuse a feeling of pleasure or satisfaction in the fulfillment of duty, and hence there has to be a causality of reason to determine sensibility in accordance with rational principles. But it is quite impossible to discern, i.e., to make a priori conceivable, how a mere thought which itself contains nothing sensuous can produce a sensation of pleasure or displeasure. For here is a special kind of causality regarding which, as with all causality, we can determine nothing a priori but must consult experience alone. However, experience can provide us with no relation of cause and effect except between two objects of experience. But in this case pure reason by means of mere ideas (which furnish no object at all for experience) is to be the cause of an effect that admittedly lies in experience. Consequently, there is for us men no possibility at all for an explanation as to how and why the universality of a maxim as a law, and hence morality, interests us. This much only is certain: the moral law is valid for us not because it interests us (for this is heteronomy and the dependence of practical reason on sensibility, viz., on an underlying feeling whereby reason could never be morally legislative); but, rather, the moral law interests us because it is valid for us as men, since it has sprung from our will as intelligence and hence from our proper self. But what belongs to mere appearance is necessarily subordinated by reason to the nature of the thing in itself.

Thus the question as to how a categorical imperative is possible can be answered to the extent that there can be supplied the sole presupposition under which such an imperative is alone possible—namely, the idea of freedom. The necessity of this presupposition is discernible, and this much is sufficient for the practical use of reason, i.e., for being convinced as to the validity of this imperative, and hence also of the moral law; but how this presupposition itself is possible can never be discerned by any human reason. However, on the presupposition of freedom of the will of an intelligence, there necessarily follows the will's autonomy as the formal condition under which alone the will can be determined. To presuppose this freedom of the will (without involving any contradiction with the principle of natural necessity in the connection of appearances in the world of sense) is not only quite possible (as speculative philosophy can show), but is without any further condition also necessary for a rational being conscious of his causality through reason and hence conscious of a will (which is different from desires) as he makes such freedom in practice, i.e., in idea, the underlying condition of all his voluntary actions. But how pure reason can be practical by itself without other incentives taken from whatever source—i.e., how the mere principle of the universal validity of all reason's maxims as laws (which would certainly be the form of a pure practical reason) can by itself, without any matter (object) of the will in which some antecedent interest might be taken, furnish an incentive and produce an interest which could be called purely moral; or, in other words, how pure reason could be practical: to explain all this is quite beyond the power of human reason, and all the effort and work of seeking such an explanation is wasted.

It is just the same as if I tried to find out how freedom itself is possible as causality of a will. For I thereby leave the philosophical basis of explanation, and I have no other basis. Now I could indeed flutter about in the world of intelligences, i.e., in the intelligible world still remaining to me. But even though I have an idea of such a world—an idea which has its own good grounds—yet I have not the slightest acquaintance with such a world and can never attain such acquaintance by all the efforts of my natural faculty of reason. This intelligible world signifies only a something that remains over when I have excluded from the determining grounds of my will everything that belongs to the world of sense, so as to restrict the principle of having all motives come from the field of sensibility. By so doing I set bounds to this field and show that it does not contain absolutely everything within itself but that beyond it there is still something more, regarding which, however, I have no further acquaintance. After the exclusion of all matter, i.e., cognition of objects, from pure reason which thinks this ideal, nothing remains over for me except such reason's form, viz., the practical law of the universal validity of maxims; and in conformity with this law I think of reason in its relation to a pure intelligible world as a possible efficient cause, i.e., as a cause determining the will. An incentive must in this case be wholly absent; this idea of an intelligible world would here have to be itself the incentive or have to be that in which reason originally took an interest. But to make this conceivable is precisely the problem that we cannot solve.

Here then is the extreme limit of all moral inquiry. To determine this limit is of great importance for the following considerations. On the one hand, reason should not, to the detriment of morals, search around in the world of sense for the supreme motive and for some interest that is conceivable but is nonetheless empirical. On the other hand, reason should not flap its wings impotently, without leaving the spot, in a space that for it is empty, namely, the space of transcendent concepts that is called the intelligible world, and thereby lose itself among mere phantoms of the brain. Furthermore, the idea of a pure intelligible world regarded as a whole of all intelligences to which we ourselves belong as rational beings (even though we are from another standpoint also members of the world of sense) remains always a useful and permissible idea for the purpose of a rational belief, although all knowledge ends at its boundary. This idea produces in us a lively interest in the moral law by means of the splendid ideal of a universal kingdom of ends in themselves (rational beings), to which we can belong as members only if we carefully conduct ourselves according to maxims of freedom as if they were laws of nature.

Concluding Remark

The speculative use of reason with regard to nature leads to the absolute necessity of some supreme cause of the world. The practical use of reason with reference to freedom leads also to absolute necessity, but only to the necessity of the laws of the actions of a rational being as such. Now it is an essential principle of all use of our reason to push its knowledge to a consciousness of its necessity (for without necessity there would be no rational knowledge). But there is an equally essential restriction of the same reason that it cannot have insight into the necessity either of what is or of what does happen or of what should happen, unless there is presupposed a condition under which it is or does happen or should happen. In this way, however, the satisfaction of reason is only further and further postponed by the continual inquiry after the condition. Reason, therefore, restlessly seeks the unconditionally necessary and sees itself compelled to assume this without having any means of making such necessity conceivable; reason is happy enough if only it can find a concept which is compatible with this assumption. Hence there is no fault in our deduction of the supreme principle of morality, but rather a reproach which must be made against human reason generally, involved in the fact that reason cannot render conceivable the absolute necessity of an unconditioned practical law (such as the categorical imperative must be). Reason cannot be blamed for not being willing to explain this necessity by means of a condition, namely, by basing it on some underlying interest, because in that case the law would no longer be moral, i.e., a supreme law of freedom. And so even though we do not indeed grasp the practical unconditioned necessity of the moral imperative, we do nevertheless grasp its inconceivability. This is all that can be fairly asked of a philosophy which strives in its principles to reach the very limit of human reason.

JOHN STUART MILL—engraving

JEREMY BENTHAM (J. Watts)

AVIGNON, PALACE OF THE POPES

JOHN STUART MILL

John Stuart Mill (1806–1873) was born in London, the son of a well-known philosopher, James Mill. He was extremely well educated by his father, beginning his studies of Greek and Latin at the ages of three and eight, and subsequently reading widely in the classics, history, philosophy, logic, and mathematics. In 1826, at the age of twenty, he underwent a period of acute depression: his ability to feel emotion, he believed, had been weakened by his intensive analytic training. He responded to this crisis by turning to the arts, taking special solace in the poetry of Wordsworth. Eventually he recovered fully. Hired as a clerk by the East India Company in 1823, he supported himself by working for this concern in various capacities until his retirement in 1858. In 1831 he met Harriet Taylor, a merchant's wife with whom he fell in love. Mill and Harriet Taylor were close and constant friends for many years, collaborating on many literary enterprises and finally marrying in 1851 after her husband's death. In his later years, Mill served a term in Parliament (1865–1868).

Mill's contributions to philosophy and social thoughts are varied. *A System of Logic* (1843) and *An Examination of Sir William Hamilton's Philosophy* (1865) deal with questions of logic and epistemology. *On Liberty* (1859) is a well known discussion of the extent to which society may interfere with individuals' liberties. In *Utilitarianism* (first published in *Fraser's Magazine,* 1861), Mill expounds his own version of utilitarian ethics. Other topics of social importance are discussed in *Principles of Political Economy* (1848), *Considerations on Representative Government* (1861), *August Comte and Positivism* (1865), and *The Subjection of Women* (1869). His *Autobiography* (1873) presents a fascinating picture of his life.

Like the earlier empiricists, Mill believed that sensation and the mind's awareness of its own activity are the sole sources of all knowledge. However, his empiricism differs from earlier versions on a number of important issues, among them the nature of ordinary objects and the role of induction. Mill accepted Berkeley's contention that ordinary objects are collections of sense-impressions but rejected his contention that the continuous existence of these objects is due mainly to God's continuing perception of them. Rather, Mill argued, the continuous existence of tables, chairs, and other objects resides entirely in the fact that we *could* perceive them at any moment. Ordinary objects are just "permanent possibilities of sensation." Concerning induction, or reasoning which extrapolates from known regularities to conclusions about what is likely to happen in unknown instances, Mill did not share Hume's skepticism. Inductive reasoning, he argued, is licensed by a general axiom of nature's uniformity (itself arrived at inductively), and is the fundamental element in all forms of inference, including deductive inference. Even the truths of mathematics and geometry, generally held to be known a priori, are actually determined by generalizing from past experience.

Mill's moral philosophy is known as utilitarianism. Its fundamental principle is that we should always perform those acts which will bring the most happiness or, failing that, the least unhappiness to the most people. This "greatest happiness principle" did not originate with Mill but was pioneered by Jeremy Bentham (1748–1832), the English philosopher and social reformer. However, Mill's essay *Utilitarianism* is the principle's best-known formulation. In support of the greatest happiness principle, Mill argued that "the sole evidence it is possible to produce that anything is desirable is that people do actually desire it"; and that, as a matter of fact, happiness is the one and only thing that people desire. When they seem to desire other things, such as wealth or virtue, it is always because these things are either means to their happiness or "part of their happiness." Given this reasoning, Mill naturally differed with Bentham over the values of different types of pleasure. Bentham had held that the intensity of a pleasure is the only criterion of its worth. For him, sublime moments of intellect or sentiment were worth no more than equally intense moments of animal gratification. For Mill, however, pleasures of equal intensity could differ in worth. Anyone who has experienced both the pleasures of the brute and the pleasures of the civilized person will prefer the latter to the former; and so, according to Mill, the civilized pleasures must be preferable.

At first glance, Mill's greatest-happiness principle may seem to imply that society should interfere with people's liberties whenever such interference will maximize overall happiness. However, Mill did not take any such position. Rather, he argued in *On Liberty* that "the only purpose for which power can be rightfully exercised over any member of a civilised community, against his will, is to prevent harm to others. His own good, either physical or moral, is not a sufficient warrant." In support of this principle, Mill cited the varied benefits of liberty in self-regarding actions. Such liberty, he argued, leads to the discovery of useful new truths and modes of life; confirms and strengthens the insights we already possess; and promotes the happiness of each individual more surely than any enforced and uniform standard can. In this and other ways, Mill attempted to reconcile his utilitarianism with the plurality of values which we possess.

For general discussion of Mill's work, see R.P. Anschutz, *The Philosophy of John Stuart Mill* (Oxford: Oxford University Press, 1953), and Alan Ryan, *J.S. Mill* (London: Routledge & Kegan Paul, 1974). For shorter essays, see J.P. Schneewind, ed., *Mill: A Collection of Critical Essays* (Garden City: Doubleday, 1968); Peter Radcliff, ed., *Limits of Liberty* (Belmont, Calif: Wadsworth, 1966); and Samuel Gorovitz, ed., *Utilitarianism with Critical Essays* (Indianapolis: Bobbs-Merrill, 1971). A clear general discussion of utilitarianism can be found in J.J.C. Smart and Bernard Williams, *Utilitarianism: For and Against* (Cambridge: Cambridge University Press, 1973).

G.S.

UTILITARIANISM

CHAPTER I

GENERAL REMARKS

There are few circumstances among those which make up the present condition of human knowledge more unlike what might have been expected, or more significant of the backward state in which speculation on the most important subjects still lingers, than the little progress which has been made in the decision of the controversy respecting the criterion of right and wrong. From the dawn of philosophy, the question concerning the *summum bonum,* or, what is the same thing, concerning the foundation of morality, has been accounted the main problem in speculative thought, has occupied the most gifted intellects and divided them into sects and schools carrying on a vigorous warfare against one another. And after more than two thousand years the same discussions continue, philosophers are still ranged under the same contending banners, and neither thinkers nor mankind at a large seem nearer to being unanimous on the subject than when the youth Socrates listened to the old Protagoras[1] and asserted (if Plato's dialogue be grounded on a real conversation) the theory of utilitarianism against the popular morality of the so-called sophist.

It is true that similar confusion and uncertainty and, in some cases, similar discordance exist respecting the first principles of all the sciences, not excepting that which is deemed the most certain of them—mathematics, without much impairing, generally indeed without impairing at all, the trustworthiness of the conclusions of those sciences. An apparent anomaly, the explanation of which is that the detailed doctrines of a science are not usually deduced from, nor depend for their evidence upon, what are called its first principles. Were it not so, there would be no science more precarious, or whose conclusions were more insufficiently made out, than algebra, which derives none of its certainty from what are commonly taught to learners as its elements, since these, as laid down by some of its most eminent teachers, are as full of fictions as English law, and of mysteries as theology. The truths which are ultimately accepted as the first principles of a science are really the last results of metaphysical analysis practiced on the elementary notions with which the science is conversant; and their relation to the science is not that of foundations to an edifice, but of roots to a tree, which may perform their office equally well though they be never dug down to and exposed to light. But though in science the particular truths precede the general theory, the contrary might be expected to be the case with a practical art, such as morals or legislation. All action is for the sake of some end, and rules of action, it seems natural to suppose, must take their whole character and color from the end to which they are subservient. When we engage in pursuit, a clear and precise conception of what we are pursuing would seem to be the first thing we need, instead of the last we are to look forward to. A test of right

1. [Regarding Protagoras, see Hume's *Enquiry,* n.72. —S.M.C.]

and wrong must be the means, one would think, of ascertaining what is right or wrong, and not a consequence of having already ascertained it.

The difficulty is not avoided by having recourse to the popular theory of a natural faculty, a sense of instinct, informing us of right and wrong. For—besides that the existence of such a moral instinct is itself one of the matters in dispute—those believers in it who have any pretensions to philosophy have been obliged to abandon the idea that it discerns what is right or wrong in the particular case in hand, as our other senses discern the sight or sound actually present. Our moral faculty, according to all those of its interpreters who are entitled to the name of thinkers, supplies us only with the general principles of moral judgments; it is a branch of our reason, not of our sensitive faculty, and must be looked to for the abstract doctrines of morality, not for perception of it in the concrete. The intuitive, no less than what may be termed the inductive, school of ethics insists on the necessity of general laws. They both agree that the morality of an individual action is not a question of direct perception, but of the application of a law to an individual case. They recognize also, to a great extent, the same moral laws, but differ as to their evidence and the source from which they derive their authority. According to the one opinion, the principles of morals are evident *a priori*, requiring nothing to command assent except that the meaning of the terms be understood. According to the other doctrine, right and wrong, as well as truth and falsehood, are questions of observation and experience. But both hold equally that morality must be deduced from principles; and the intuitive school affirm as strongly as the inductive that there is a science of morals. Yet they seldom attempt to make out a list of the *a priori* principles which are to serve as the premises of the science; still more rarely do they make any effort to reduce those various principles to one first principle or common ground of obligation. They either assume the ordinary precepts of morals as of *a priori* authority, or they lay down as the common groundwork of those maxims some generality much less obviously authoritative than the maxims themselves, and which has never succeeded in gaining popular acceptance. Yet to support their pretensions there ought either to be some one fundamental principle or law at the root of all morality, or, if there be several, there should be a determinate order of precedence among them; and the one principle, or the rule for deciding between the various principles when they conflict, ought to be self-evident.

To inquire how far the bad effects of this deficiency have been mitigated in practice, or to what extent the moral beliefs of mankind have been vitiated or made uncertain by the absence of any distinct recognition of an ultimate standard, would imply a complete survey and criticism of past and present ethical doctrine. It would, however, be easy to show that whatever steadiness or consistency these moral beliefs have attained has been mainly due to the tacit influence of a standard not recognized. Although the nonexistence of an acknowledged first principle has made ethics not so much a guide as a consecration of men's actual sentiments, still, as men's sentiments, both of favor and of aversion, are greatly influenced by what they suppose to be the effects of things upon their happiness, the principle of utility, or, as Bentham latterly called it, the greatest happiness principle, has had a large share in forming the moral doctrines even of those who most scornfully reject its authority. Nor is there any school of thought which refuses to admit that the influence of actions on happiness is a most material and even predominant consideration in many of the details of morals, however unwilling to acknowledge it as the fundamental principle of morality and the source of moral obligation. I might go much further and say that to all those *a priori* moralists who deem it necessary to argue at all, utilitarian arguments are indispensable. It is not my present purpose to criticize these thinkers; but I cannot help referring, for illustration, to a systematic treatise by one of the most illustrious of them, the *Metaphysics of Ethics* by Kant. This remarkable man, whose system of thought will long remain one of the landmarks in the history of philosophical speculation, does, in the treatise in question, lay down a universal first principle as the origin and ground of moral obligation; it is this: "So act that the rule on which thou actest would admit of being adopted as a law by all rational beings." But when he begins to deduce from this precept any of the actual duties of morality, he fails, almost grotesquely, to show that there would be any contradiction, any logical (not to say physical) impossibility, in the adoption by all rational beings of the most outrageously immoral rules of conduct. All he shows is that the *consequences* of their universal adoption would be such as no one would choose to incur.

On the present occasion, I shall, without further discussion of the other theories, attempt to contribute something toward the understanding and appreciation of the "utilitarian" or "happiness" theory, and toward such proof as it is susceptible of. It is evident that this cannot be proof in the ordinary and popular meaning of the term. Questions of ultimate ends are not amenable to direct proof. Whatever can be proved to be good must be so by being shown to be a means to something admitted to be good without proof. The medical art is proved to be good by its conducing to health; but how is it possible to prove that health is good? The art of music is good, for the reason, among others, that it produces pleasure; but what proof is it possible to give that pleasure is good? If, then, it is asserted that there is a comprehensive formula, including all things which are in themselves good, and that whatever else is good is not so as an end but as a means, the formula may be accepted or rejected, but is not a subject of what is commonly understood by proof. We are not, however, to infer that its acceptance or rejection must depend on blind impulse or arbitrary choice. There is a larger meaning of the word "proof," in which this question is as amenable to it as any other of the disputed questions of philosophy. The subject is within the cognizance of the rational faculty; and neither does that faculty deal with it solely in the way of intuition. Considerations may be presented capable of determining the intellect either to give or withhold its assent to the doctrine; and this is equivalent to proof.

We shall examine presently of what nature are these considerations; in what manner they apply to the case, and what rational grounds, therefore, can be given for accepting or rejecting the utilitarian formula. But it is a preliminary condition of rational acceptance or rejection that the formula should be correctly understood. I believe that the very imperfect notion ordinarily formed of its meaning is the chief obstacle which impedes its reception, and that, could it be cleared even from only the grosser misconceptions, the question would be greatly simplified and a large proportion of its difficulties removed. Before, therefore, I attempt to enter into the philosophical grounds which can be given for assenting to the utilitarian standard, I shall offer some illustrations of the doctrine itself, with the view of showing more clearly what it is, distinguishing it from what it is not, and disposing of such of the practical objections to it as either originate in, or are closely connected with, mistaken interpretations of its meaning. Having thus prepared the ground, I shall afterwards endeavor to throw such light as I can call upon the question considered as one of philosophical theory.

CHAPTER II

WHAT UTILITARIANISM IS

A passing remark is all that needs be given to the ignorant blunder of supposing that those who stand up for utility as the test of right and wrong use the term in that restricted and merely colloquial sense in which utility is opposed to pleasure. An apology is due to the philosophical opponents of utilitarianism for even the momentary appearance of confounding them with anyone capable of so absurd a misconception; which is the more extraordinary, inasmuch as the contrary accusation, of referring everything to pleasure, and that, too, in its grossest form, is another of the common charges against utilitarianism: and, as has been pointedly remarked by an able writer, the same sort of persons, and often the very same persons, denounce the theory "as impracticably dry when the word 'utility' precedes the word 'pleasure,' and as too practicably voluptuous when the word 'pleasure' precedes the word 'utility.' " Those who know anything about the matter are aware that every writer, from Epicurus to Bentham, who maintained the theory of utility meant by it, not something to be contradistinguished from pleasure, but pleasure itself, together with exemption from pain; and instead of opposing the useful to the agreeable or the ornamental, have always declared that the useful means these, among other things. Yet the common herd, including the herd of writers, not only in newspapers and periodicals, but in books of weight and pretension, are perpetually falling into this shallow mistake. Having caught up the word "utilitarian," while knowing nothing whatever about it but its sound, they habitually express by it the rejection or the neglect of pleasure in some of its forms: of beauty, of ornament, or of amusement. Nor is the term thus ignorantly misapplied solely in disparagement, but occasionally in compliment, as though it implied superiority to frivolity and the mere pleasures of the moment. And this perverted use is the only one in which the word is popularly known, and the one from which the new generation are acquiring their sole notion of its meaning. Those who introduced the word, but who had for many years discontinued it as a distinctive appellation, may well feel themselves called upon to resume it if by doing so they can hope to contribute anything toward rescuing it from this utter degradation.[2]

The creed which accepts as the foundation of morals "utility" or the "greatest

2. The author of this essay has reason for believing himself to be the first person who brought the word "utilitarian" into use. He did not invent it, but adopted it from a passing expression in Mr. Galt's *Annals of the Parish*. [John Galt (1779–1839) was a Scottish novelist.] After using it as a designation for several years, he and others abandoned it from a growing dislike to anything resembling a badge or watchword of sectarian distinction. But as a name for one single opinion, not a set of opinions—to denote the recognition of utility as a standard, not any particular way of applying it—the term supplies a want in the language, and offers, in many cases, a convenient mode of avoiding tiresome circumlocutions.

happiness principle" holds that actions are right in proportion as they tend to promote happiness; wrong as they tend to produce the reverse of happiness. By happiness is intended pleasure and the absence of pain; by unhappiness, pain and the privation of pleasure. To give a clear view of the moral standard set up by the theory, much more requires to be said; in particular, what things it includes in the ideas of pain and pleasure, and to what extent this is left an open question. But these supplementary explanations do not affect the theory of life on which this theory of morality is grounded—namely, that pleasure and freedom from pain are the only things desirable as ends; and that all desirable things (which are as numerous in the utilitarian as in any other scheme) are desirable either for pleasure inherent in themselves or as means to the promotion of pleasure and the prevention of pain.

Now such a theory of life excites in many minds, and among them in some of the most estimable in feeling and purpose, inveterate dislike. To suppose that life has (as they express it) no higher end than pleasure—no better and nobler object of desire and pursuit—they designate as utterly mean and groveling, as a doctrine worthy only of swine, to whom the followers of Epicurus were, at a very early period, contemptuously likened; and modern holders of the doctrine are occasionally made the subject of equally polite comparisons by its German, French, and English assailants.

When thus attacked, the Epicureans have always answered that it is not they, but their accusers, who represent human nature in a degrading light, since the accusation supposes human beings to be capable of no pleasures except those of which swine are capable. If this supposition were true, the charge could not be gainsaid, but would then be no longer an imputation; for if the sources of pleasure were precisely the same to human beings and to swine, the rule of life which is good enough for the one would be good enough for the other. The comparison of the Epicurean life to that of beasts is felt as degrading, precisely because a beast's pleasures do not satisfy a human being's conceptions of happiness. Human beings have faculties more elevated than the animal appetites and, when once made conscious of them, do not regard anything as happiness which does not include their gratification. I do not indeed, consider the Epicureans to have been by any means faultless in drawing out their scheme of consequences from the utilitarian principle. To do this in any sufficient manner, many Stoic, as well as Christian, elements require to be included. But there is no known Epicurean theory of life which does not assign to the pleasures of the intellect, of the feelings and imagination, and of the moral sentiments a much higher value as pleasures than to those of mere sensation. It must be admitted, however, that utilitarian writers in general have placed the superiority of mental over bodily pleasures chiefly in the greater permanency, safety, uncostliness, etc., of the former—that is, in their circumstantial advantages rather than in their intrinsic nature. And on all these points utilitarians have fully proved their case; but they might have taken the other and, as it may be called, higher ground with entire consistency. It is quite compatible with the principle of utility to recognize the fact that some kinds of pleasure are more desirable and more valuable than others. It would be absurd that, while in estimating all other things quality is considered as well as quantity, the estimation of pleasure should be supposed to depend on quantity alone.

If I am asked what I mean by difference of quality in pleasures, or what makes one pleasure more valuable than another, merely as a pleasure, except its being greater in amount, there is but one possible answer. Of two pleasures, if there be one to which all or almost all who have experience of both give a decided preference, irrespective of any feeling of moral obligation to prefer it, that is the more desirable pleasure. If one of the two is, by those who are competently acquainted with both, placed so far above the other that they prefer it, even though knowing it to be attended with a greater amount of discontent, and would not resign it for any quantity of the other pleasure which their nature is capable of, we are justified in ascribing to the preferred enjoyment a superiority in quality so far outweighing quantity as to render it, in comparison, of small account.

Now it is an unquestionable fact that those who are equally acquainted with and equally capable of appreciating and enjoying both do give a most marked preference to the manner of existence which employs their higher faculties. Few human creatures would consent to be changed into any of the lower animals for a promise of the fullest allowance of a beast's pleasures; no intelligent human being would consent to be a fool, no instructed person would be an ignoramus, no person of feeling and conscience would be selfish and base, even though they should be persuaded that the fool, the dunce, or the rascal is better satisfied with his lot than they are with theirs. They would not resign what they possess more than he for the most complete satisfaction of all the desires which they have in common with him. If they ever fancy they would, it is only in cases of unhappiness so extreme that to escape from it they would exchange their lot for almost any other, however undesirable in their own eyes. A being of higher faculties requires more to make him happy, is capable probably of more acute suffering, and certainly accessible to it at more points, than one of an inferior type; but in spite of these liabilities, he can never really wish to sink into what he feels to be a lower grade of existence. We may give what explanation we please of this unwillingness; we may attribute it to pride, a name which is given indiscriminately to some of the most and to some of the least estimable feelings of which mankind are capable; we may refer it to the love of liberty and personal independence, an appeal to which was with the Stoics one of the most effective means for the inculcation of it; to the love of power or to the love of excitement, both of which do really enter into and contribute to it; but its most appropriate appellation is a sense of dignity, which all human beings possess in one form or other, and in some, though by no means in exact, proportion to their higher faculties, and which is so essential a part of the happiness of those in whom it is strong that nothing which conflicts with it could be otherwise than momentarily an object of desire to them. Whoever supposes that this preference takes place at a sacrifice of happiness—that the superior being, in anything like equal circumstances, is not happier than the inferior—confounds the two very different ideas of happiness and content. It is indisputable that the being whose capacities of enjoyment are low has the greatest chance of having them fully satisfied; and a highly endowed being will always feel that any happiness which he can look for, as the world is constituted, is imperfect. But he can learn to bear its imperfections, if they are at all bearable; and they will not make him envy the being who is indeed unconscious of the imperfections, but only because he feels not at all the good which those imperfections qualify. It is better to be a human being dissatisfied than a pig satisfied; better to be Socrates dissatisfied than a fool satisfied. And if the fool, or the pig, are of a different opinion, it is because they only know their own side of the question. The other party to the comparison knows both sides.

It may be objected that many who are capable of the higher pleasures occasionally, under the influence of temptation, postpone them to the lower. But this is quite compatible with a full appreciation of the intrinsic superiority of the higher. Men often, from infirmity of character, make their election for the nearer good, though they know it to be the less valuable; and this no less when the choice is between two bodily pleasures than when it is between bodily and mental. They pursue sensual indulgences to the injury of health, though perfectly aware that health is the greater good. It may be further objected that many who begin with youthful enthusiasm for everything noble, as they advance in years, sink into indolence and selfishness. But I do not believe that those who undergo this very common change voluntarily choose the lower description of pleasures in preference to the higher. I believe that, before they devote themselves exclusively to the one, they have already become incapable of the other. Capacity for the nobler feelings is in most natures a very tender plant, easily killed, not only by hostile influences, but by mere want of sustenance; and in the majority of young persons it speedily dies away if the occupations to which their position in life has devoted them, and the society into which it has thrown them, are not favorable to keeping that higher capacity in exercise. Men lose their high aspirations as they lose their intellectual tastes, because they have not time or opportunity for indulging them; and they addict themselves to inferior pleasures, not because they deliberately prefer them, but because they are either the only ones to which they have access or the only ones which they are any longer capable of enjoying. It may be questioned whether anyone who has remained equally susceptible to both classes of pleasures ever knowingly and calmly preferred the lower, though many, in all ages, have broken down in an ineffectual attempt to combine both.

From this verdict of the only competent judges, I apprehend there can be no appeal. On a question which is the best worth having of two pleasures, or which of two modes of existence is the most grateful to the feelings, apart from its moral attributes and from its consequences, the judgment of those who are qualified by knowledge of both, or, if they differ, that of the majority among them, must be admitted as final. And there needs be the less hesitation to accept this judgment respecting the quality of pleasures, since there is no other tribunal to be referred to even on the question of quantity. What means are there of determining which is the acutest of two pains, or the intensest of two pleasurable sensations, except the general suffrage of those who are familiar with both? Neither pains nor pleasures are homogeneous, and pain is always heterogeneous with pleasure. What is there to decide whether a particular pleasure is worth purchasing at the cost of a particular pain, except the feelings and judgment of the experienced? When, therefore, those feelings and judgment declare the pleasures derived from the higher faculties to be preferable *in kind,* apart from the question of intensity, to those of which the animal nature, disjoined from the higher faculties, is susceptible, they are entitled on this subject to the same regard.

I have dwelt on this point as being a necessary part of a perfectly just conception of utility or happiness considered as the directive rule of human conduct. But it is by no means an indispensable condition to the acceptance of the utilitarian standard; for that standard is not the agent's own greatest happiness, but the greatest amount of happiness altogether; and if it may possibly be doubted whether a noble character is always the happier for its nobleness, there can be no doubt that it makes other people happier, and that the world in general is immensely a gainer by it.

Utilitarianism, therefore, could only attain its end by the general cultivation of nobleness of character, even if each individual were only benefited by the nobleness of others, and his own, so far as happiness is concerned, were a sheer deduction from the benefit. But the bare enunciation of such an absurdity as this last renders refutation superfluous.

According to the greatest happiness principle, as above explained, the ultimate end, with reference to and for the sake of which all other things are desirable — whether we are considering our own good or that of other people — is an existence exempt as far as possible from pain, and as rich as possible in enjoyments, both in point of quantity and quality; the test of quality and the rule for measuring it against quantity being the preference felt by those who, in their opportunities of experience, to which must be added their habits of self-consciousness and self-observation, are best furnished with the means of comparison. This, being according to the utilitarian opinion the end of human action, is necessarily also the standard of morality, which may accordingly be defined "the rules and precepts for human conduct," by the observance of which an existence such as has been described might be, to the greatest extent possible, secured to all mankind; and not to them only, but, so far as the nature of things admits, to the whole sentient creation.

Against this doctrine, however, arises another class of objectors who say that happiness, in any form, cannot be the rational purpose of human life and action; because, in the first place, it is unattainable; and they contemptuously ask, What right hast thou to be happy? — a question which Mr. Carlyle[3] clinches by the addition, What right, a short time ago, hadst thou even *to be?* Next they say that men can do *without* happiness; that all noble human beings have felt this, and could not have become noble but by learning the lesson of *Entsagen,* or renunciation; which lesson, thoroughly learned and submitted to, they affirm to be the beginning and necessary condition of all virtue.

The first of these objections would go to the root of the matter were it well founded; for if no happiness is to be had at all by human beings, the attainment of it cannot be the end of morality or of any rational conduct. Though, even in that case, something might still be said for the utilitarian theory, since utility includes not solely the pursuit of happiness, but the prevention or mitigation of unhappiness; and if the former aim be chimerical, there will be all the greater scope and more imperative need for the latter, so long at least as mankind think fit to live and do not take refuge in the simultaneous act of suicide recommended under certain conditions by Novalis.[4] When, however, it is thus positively asserted to be impossible that human life should be happy, the assertion, if not something like a verbal quibble, is at least an exaggeration. If by happiness be meant a continuity of highly pleasurable excitement, it is evident enough that this is impossible. A state of exalted pleasure lasts only moments or in some cases, and with some intermissions, hours or days, and is the occasional brilliant flash of enjoyment, not its permanent and steady flame. Of this the philosophers who have taught that happiness is the end of life were as fully aware as those who taunt them. The happiness which they meant was

3. [Thomas Carlyle (1795–1881) was a Scottish author and social critic who wrote a multivolume history of the French Revolution. His theistic view stressed the essential spirituality of the world and its leaders.]

4. [Pseudonym of Friedrich Leopold Freiherr von Hardenberg (1771–1801), a German romantic poet.]

not a life of rapture, but moments of such, in an existence made up of few and transitory pains, many and various pleasures, with a decided predominance of the active over the passive, and having as the foundation of the whole not to expect more from life than it is capable of bestowing. A life thus composed, to those who have been fortunate enough to obtain it, has always appeared worthy of the name of happiness. And such an existence is even now the lot of many during some considerable portion of their lives. The present wretched education and wretched social arrangements are the only real hindrance to its being attainable by almost all.

The objectors perhaps may doubt whether human beings, if taught to consider happiness as the end of life, would be satisfied with such a moderate share of it. But great numbers of mankind have been satisfied with much less. The main constituents of a satisfied life appear to be two, either of which by itself is often found sufficient for the purpose: tranquillity and excitement. With much tranquillity, many find that they can be content with very little pleasure; with much excitement, many can reconcile themselves to a considerable quantity of pain. There is assuredly no inherent impossibility of enabling even the mass of mankind to unite both, since the two are so far from being incompatible that they are in natural alliance, the prolongation of either being a preparation for, and exciting a wish for, the other. It is only those in whom indolence amounts to a vice that do not desire excitement after an interval of respose; it is only those in whom the need of excitement is a disease that feel the tranquillity which follows excitement dull and insipid, instead of pleasurable in direct proportion to the excitement which preceded it. When people who are tolerably fortunate in their outward lot do not find in life sufficient enjoyment to make it valuable to them, the cause generally is caring for nobody but themselves. To those who have neither public nor private affections, the excitements of life are much curtailed, and in any case dwindle in value as the time approaches when all selfish interests must be terminated by death; while those who leave after them objects of personal affection, and especially those who have also cultivated a fellow-feeling with the collective interests of mankind, retain as lively an interest in life on the eve of death as in the vigor of youth and health. Next to selfishness, the principal cause which makes life unsatisfactory is want of mental cultivation. A cultivated mind—I do not mean that of a philosopher, but any mind to which the fountains of knowledge have been opened, and which has been taught, in any tolerable degree, to exercise its faculties—finds sources of inexhaustible interest in all that surrounds it: in the objects of nature, the achievements of art, the imaginations of poetry, the incidents of history, the ways of mankind, past and present, and their prospects in the future. It is possible, indeed, to become indifferent to all this, and that too without having exhausted a thousandth part of it, but only when one has had from the beginning no moral or human interest in these things and has sought in them only the gratification of curiosity.

Now there is absolutely no reason in the nature of things why an amount of mental culture sufficient to give an intelligent interest in these objects of contemplation should not be the inheritance of everyone born in a civilized country. As little is there an inherent necessity that any human being should be a selfish egotist, devoid of every feeling or care but those which center in his own miserable individuality. Something far superior to this is sufficiently common even now, to give ample earnest of what the human species may be made. Genuine private affections and a sincere interest in the public good are possible, though in unequal degrees, to every rightly brought up human being. In a world in which there is so much to interest, so much to enjoy, and so much also to correct and improve, everyone who has this moderate amount of moral and intellectual requisites is capable of an existence which may be called enviable; and unless such a person, through bad laws or subjection to the will of others, is denied the liberty to use the sources of happiness within his reach, he will not fail to find this enviable existence, if he escapes the positive evils of life, the great sources of physical and mental suffering—such as indigence, disease, and the unkindness, worthlessness, or premature loss of objects of affection. The main stress of the problem lies, therefore, in the contest with these calamities from which it is a rare good fortune entirely to escape; which, as things now are, cannot be obviated, and often cannot be in any material degree mitigated. Yet no one whose opinion deserves a moment's consideration can doubt that most of the great positive evils of the world are in themselves removable, and will, if human affairs continue to improve, be in the end reduced within narrow limits. Poverty, in any sense implying suffering, may be completely extinguished by the wisdom of society combined with the good sense and providence of individuals. Even that most intractable of enemies, disease, may be indefinitely reduced in dimensions by good physical and moral education and proper control of noxious influences, while the progress of science holds out a promise for the future of still more direct conquests over this detestable foe. And every advance in that direction relieves us from some, not only of the chances which cut short our own lives, but, what concerns us still more, which deprive us of those in whom our happiness is wrapt up. As for vicissitudes of fortune and other disappointments connected with wordly circumstances, these are principally the effect either of gross imprudence, of ill-regulated desires, or of bad or imperfect social institutions. All the grand sources, in short, of human suffering are in a great degree, many of them almost entirely, conquerable by human care and effort; and though their removal is grievously slow—though a long succession of generations will perish in the breach before the conquest is completed, and this world becomes all that, if will and knowledge were not wanting, it might easily be made—yet every mind sufficiently intelligent and generous to bear a part, however small and inconspicuous, in the endeavor will draw a noble enjoyment from the contest itself, which he would not for any bribe in the form of selfish indulgence consent to be without.

And this leads to the true estimation of what is said by the objectors concerning the possibility and the obligation of learning to do without happiness. Unquestionably it is possible to do without happiness; it is done involuntarily by nineteen-twentieths of mankind, even in those parts of our present world which are least deep in barbarism; and it often has to be done voluntarily by the hero or the martyr, for the sake of something which he prizes more than his individual happiness. But this something, what is it, unless the happiness of others or some of the requisites of happiness? It is noble to be capable of resigning entirely one's own portion of happiness, or chances of it; but, after all, this self-sacrifice must be for some end; it is not its own end; and if we are told that its end is not happiness but virtue, which is better than happiness, I ask, would the sacrifice be made if the hero or martyr did not believe that it would earn for others immunity from similar sacrifices? Would it be made if he thought that his renunciation of happiness for himself would produce no fruit for any of his fellow creatures, but to make their lot like his and place them also in the condition of persons who have renounced happiness? All honor to those who can abnegate for themselves the personal enjoyment of life when by such renunciation they contribute worthily to increase the amount of happiness in the world; but he who does it or professes to do it for any other purpose is no more deserving of admiration than the ascetic mounted on his pillar. He may be an inspiriting proof of what men *can* do, but assuredly not an example of what they *should.*

Though it is only in a very imperfect state of the world's arrangements that any-one can best serve the happiness of others by the absolute sacrifice of his own, yet, so long as the world is in that imperfect state, I fully acknowledge that the readiness to make such a sacrifice is the highest virtue which can be found in man. I will add that in this condition of the world, paradoxical as the assertion may be, the con-scious ability to do without happiness gives the best prospect of realizing such hap-piness as is attainable. For nothing except that consciousness can raise a person above the chances of life by making him feel that, let fate and fortune do their worst, they have not power to subdue him; which, once felt, frees him from excess of anx-iety concerning the evils of life and enables him, like many a Stoic in the worst times of the Roman Empire, to cultivate in tranquillity the sources of satisfaction accessi-ble to him, without concerning himself about the uncertainty of their duration any more than about their inevitable end.

Meanwhile, let utilitarians never cease to claim the morality of self-devotion as a possession which belongs by as good a right to them as either to the Stoic or to the Transcendentalist.[5] The utilitarian morality does recognize in human beings the power of sacrificing their own greatest good for the good of others. It only refuses to admit that the sacrifice is itself a good. A sacrifice which does not increase or tend to increase the sum total of happiness, it considers as wasted. The only self-renuncia-tion which it applauds is devotion to the happiness, or to some of the means of hap-piness, of others, either of mankind collectively or of individuals within the limits imposed by the collective interests of mankind.

I must again repeat what the assailants of utilitarianism seldom have the justice to acknowledge, that the happiness which forms the utilitarian standard of what is right in conduct is not the agent's own happiness but that of all concerned. As be-tween his own happiness and that of others, utilitarianism requires him to be as strictly impartial as a disinterested and benevolent spectator. In the golden rule of Jesus of Nazareth, we read the complete spirit of the ethics of utility. "To do as you would be done by," and "to love your neighbor as yourself," constitute the ideal perfection of utilitarian morality. As the means of making the nearest approach to this ideal, utility would enjoin, first, that laws and social arrangements should place the happiness or (as, speaking practically, it may be called) the interest of every in-dividual as nearly as possible in harmony with the interest of the whole; and, sec-ondly, that education and opinion, which have so vast a power over human character, should so use that power as to establish in the mind of every individual an indissoluble association between his own happiness and the good of the whole, espe-cially between his own happiness and the practice of such modes of conduct, nega-tive and positive, as regard for the universal happiness prescribes; so that not only he may be unable to conceive the possibility of happiness to himself, consistently with conduct opposed to the general good, but also that a direct impulse to promote the general good may be in every individual one of the habitual motives of action,

5. [Transcendentalism was a literary and philosophical movement that flourished in New England from about 1835 to 1860. It emphasized intuition as the source of knowledge and enlightened individu-alism as the basis of ethics. Its leading spokesmen were Ralph Waldo Emerson (1803–1882) and Henry David Thoreau (1817–1862).]

and the sentiments connected therewith may fill a large and prominent place in every human being's sentient existence. If the impugners of the utilitarian morality represented it to their own minds in this its true character, I know not what recommendation possessed by any other morality they could possibly affirm to be wanting to it; what more beautiful or more exalted developments of human nature any other ethical system can be supposed to foster, or what springs of action, not accessible to the utilitarian, such systems rely on for giving effect to their mandates.

The objectors to utilitarianism cannot always be charged with representing it in a discreditable light. On the contrary, those among them who entertain anything like a just idea of its disinterested character sometimes find fault with its standard as being too high for humanity. They say it is exacting too much to require that people shall always act from the inducement of promoting the general interests of society. But this is to mistake the very meaning of a standard of morals and confound the rule of action with the motive of it. It is the business of ethics to tell us what are our duties, or by what test we may know them; but no system of ethics requires that the sole motive of all we do shall be a feeling of duty; on the contrary, ninety-nine hundredths of all our actions are done from other motives, and rightly so done if the rule of duty does not condemn them. It is the more unjust to utilitarianism that this particular misapprehension should be made a ground of objection to it, inasmuch as utilitarian moralists have gone beyond almost all others in affirming that the motive has nothing to do with the morality of the action, though much with the worth of the agent. He who saves a fellow creature from drowning does what is morally right, whether his motive be duty or the hope of being paid for his trouble; he who betrays the friend that trusts him is guilty of a crime, even if his object be to serve another friend to whom he is under greater obligations.[6] But to speak only of actions done from the motive of duty, and in direct obedience to principle: it is a misapprehension of the utilitarian mode of thought to conceive it as implying that people should fix their minds upon so wide a generality as the world, or society at large. The great majority of good actions are intended not for the benefit of the world, but for that of

---

6. An opponent, whose intellectual and moral fairness it is a pleasure to acknowledge (the Rev. J. Llewellyn Davies), has objected to this passage, saying, "Surely the rightness or wrongness of saving a man from drowning does depend very much upon the motive with which it is done. Suppose that a tyrant, when his enemy jumped into the sea to escape from him, saved him from drowning simply in order that he might inflict upon him more exquisite tortures, would it tend to clearness to speak of that rescue as 'a morally right action'? Or suppose again, according to one of the stock illustrations of ethical inquiries, that a man betrayed a trust received from a friend, because the discharge of it would fatally injure that friend himself or someone belonging to him, would utilitarianism compel one to call the betrayal 'a crime' as much as if it had been done from the meanest motive?"

I submit that he who saves another from drowning in order to kill him by torture afterwards does not differ only in motive from him who does the same thing from duty or benevolence; the act itself is different. The rescue of the man is, in the case supposed, only the necessary first step of an act far more atrocious than leaving him to drown would have been. Had Mr. Davies said, "The rightness or wrongness of saving a man from drowning does depend very much" — not upon the motive, but — "upon the intention," no utilitarian would have differed from him. Mr. Davies, by an oversight too common not to be quite venial, has in this case confounded the very different ideas of Motive and Intention. There is no point which utilitarian thinkers (and Bentham pre-eminently) have taken more pains to illustrate than this. The morality of the action depends entirely upon the intention — that is, upon what the agent *wills to do*. But the motive, that is, the feeling which makes him will so to do, if it makes no difference in the act, makes none in the morality: though it makes a great difference in our moral estimation of the agent, especially if it indicates a good or a bad habitual *disposition* — a bent of character from which useful, or from which hurtful actions are likely to arise.

[This note appeared in the second edition of *Utilitarianism* but not in subsequent ones.]

individuals, of which the good of the world is made up; and the thoughts of the most virtuous man need not on these occasions travel beyond the particular persons concerned, except so far as is necessary to assure himself that in benefiting them he is not violating the rights, that is, the legitimate and authorized expectations, of anyone else. The multiplication of happiness is, according to the utilitarian ethics, the object of virtue: the occasions on which any person (except one in a thousand) has it in his power to do this on an extended scale—in other words, to be a public benefactor—are but exceptional; and on these occasions alone is he called on to consider public utility; in every other case, private utility, the interest or happiness of some few persons, is all he has to attend to. Those alone the influence of whose actions extends to society in general need concern themselves habitually about so large an object. In the case of abstinences indeed—of things which people forbear to do from moral considerations, though the consequences in the particular case might be beneficial—it would be unworthy of an intelligent agent not to be consciously aware that the action is of a class which, if practiced generally, would be generally injurious, and that this is the ground of the obligation to abstain from it. The amount of regard for the public interest implied in this recognition is no greater than is demanded by every system of morals, for they all enjoin to abstain from whatever is manifestly pernicious to society.

The same considerations dispose of another reproach against the doctrine of utility, founded on a still grosser misconception of the purpose of a standard of morality and of the very meaning of the words "right" and "wrong." It is often affirmed that utilitarianism renders men cold and unsympathizing; that it chills their moral feelings toward individuals; that it makes them regard only the dry and hard consideration of the consequences of actions, not taking into their moral estimate the qualities from which those actions emanate. If the assertion means that they do not allow their judgment respecting the rightness or wrongness of an action to be influenced by their opinion of the qualities of the person who does it, this is a complaint not against utilitarianism, but against any standard or morality at all; for certainly no known ethical standard decides an action to be good or bad because it is done by a good or bad man, still less because done by an amiable, a brave, or a benevolent man, or the contrary. These considerations are relevant, not to the estimation of actions, but of persons; and there is nothing in the utilitarian theory inconsistent with the fact that there are other things which interest us in persons besides the rightness and wrongness of their actions. The Stoics, indeed, with the paradoxical misuse of language which was part of their system, and by which they strove to raise themselves above all concern about anything but virtue, were fond of saying that he who has that has everything; that he, and only he, is rich, is beautiful, is a king. But no claim of this description is made for the virtuous man by the utilitarian doctrine. Utilitarians are quite aware that there are other desirable possessions and qualities besides virtue, and are perfectly willing to allow to all of them their full worth. They are also aware that a right action does not necessarily indicate a virtuous character, and that actions which are blamable often proceed from qualities entitled to praise. When this is apparent in any particular case, it modifies their estimation, not certainly of the act, but of the agent. I grant that they are, notwithstanding, of opinion that in the long run the best proof of a good character is good actions; and resolutely refuse to consider any mental disposition as good of which the predominant tendency is to produce bad conduct. This makes them unpopular with many people, but it is an unpopularity which they must share with everyone who regards the distinction between right and wrong in a serious light; and the reproach is not one which a conscientious utilitarian need be anxious to repel.

If no more be meant by the objection than that many utilitarians look on the morality of actions, as measured by the utilitarian standards, with too exclusive a regard, and do not lay sufficient stress upon the other beauties of character which go toward making a human being lovable or admirable, this may be admitted. Utilitarians who have cultivated their moral feelings, but not their sympathies, nor their artistic perceptions, do fall into this mistake; and so do all other moralists under the same conditions. What can be said in excuse for other moralists is equally available for them, namely, that, if there is to be any error, it is better that it should be on that side. As a matter of fact, we may affirm that among utilitarians, as among adherents of other systems, there is every imaginable degree of rigidity and of laxity in the application of their standard; some are even puritanically rigorous, while others are as indulgent as can possibly be desired by sinner or by sentimentalist. But on the whole, a doctrine which brings prominently forward the interest that mankind have in the repression and prevention of conduct which violates the moral law is likely to be inferior to no other in turning the sanctions of opinion against such violations. It is true, the question "What does violate the moral law?" is one on which those who recognize different standards of morality are likely now and then to differ. But difference of opinion on moral questions was not first introduced into the world by utilitarianism, while that doctrine does supply, if not always an easy, at all events a tangible and intelligible, mode of deciding such differences.

It may not be superfluous to notice a few more of the common misapprehensions of utilitarian ethics, even those which are so obvious and gross that it might appear impossible for any person of candor and intelligence to fall into them; since persons, even of considerable mental endowment, often give themselves so little trouble to understand the bearings of any opinion against which they entertain a prejudice, and men are in general so little conscious of this voluntary ignorance as a defect that the vulgarest misunderstandings of ethical doctrines are continually met with in the deliberate writings of persons of the greatest pretensions both to high principle and to philosophy. We not uncommonly hear the doctrine of utility inveighed against a *godless* doctrine. If it be necessary to say anything at all against so mere an assumption, we may say that the question depends upon what idea we have formed of the moral character of the Deity. If it be a true belief that God desires, above all things, the happiness of his creatures, and that this was his purpose in their creation, utility is not only not a godless doctrine, but more profoundly religious than any other. If it be meant that utilitarianism does not recognize the revealed will of God as the supreme law of morals, I answer that a utilitarian who believes in the perfect goodness and wisdom of *God* necessarily believes that whatever God has thought fit to reveal on the subject of morals must fulfill the requirements of utility in a supreme degree. But others besides utilitarians have been of opinion that the Christian revelation was intended, and is fitted, to inform the hearts and minds of mankind with a spirit which should enable them to find for themselves what is right, and incline them to do it when found, rather than to tell them, except in a very general way, what it is; and that we need a doctrine of ethics, carefully followed out, to *interpret* to us the will of God. Whether this opinion is correct or not, it is superfluous here to discuss; since whatever aid religion, either natural or revealed, can afford to ethical investigation is as open to the utilitarian moralist as to any other. He can use it as the testimony of God to the usefulness or hurtfulness of any given course of action by as good a right as others can use it for the indication of a transcendental law having no connection with usefulness or with happiness.

Again, utility is often summarily stigmatized as an immoral doctrine by giving it the name of "expediency," and taking advantage of the popular use of that term to contrast it with principle. But the expedient, in the sense in which it is opposed to the right, generally means that which is expedient for the particular interest of the agent himself; as when a minister sacrifices the interests of his country to keep himself in place. When it means anything better than this, it means that which is expedient for some immediate object, some temporary purpose, but which violates a rule whose observance is expedient in a much higher degree. The expedient, in this sense, instead of being the same thing with the useful, is a branch of the hurtful. Thus it would often be expedient, for the purpose of getting over some momentary embarrassment, or attaining some object immediately useful to ourselves or others, to tell a lie. But inasmuch as the cultivation in ourselves of a sensitive feeling on the subject of veracity is one of the most useful, and the enfeeblement of that feeling one of the most hurtful, things to which our conduct can be instrumental; and inasmuch as any, even unintentional, deviation from truth does that much toward weakening the trustworthiness of human assertion, which is not only the principal support of all present social well-being, but the insufficiency of which does more than any one thing that can be named to keep back civilization, virtue, everything on which human happiness on the largest scale depends—we feel that the violation, for a present advantage, of a rule of such transcendent expediency is not expedient, and that he who, for the sake of convenience to himself or to some other individual, does what depends on him to deprive mankind of the good, and inflict upon them the evil, involved in the greater or less reliance which they can place in each other's word, acts the part of one of their worst enemies. Yet that even this rule, sacred as it is, admits of possible exceptions is acknowledged by all moralists; the chief of which is when the withholding of some fact (as of information from a malefactor, or of bad news from a person dangerously ill) would save an individual (especially an individual other than oneself) from great and unmerited evil, and when the withholding can only be effected by denial. But in order that the exception may not extend itself beyond the need, and may have the least possible effect in weakening reliance on veracity, it ought to be recognized and, if possible, its limits defined; and, if the principle of utility is good for anything, it must be good for weighing these conflicting utilities against one another and marking out the region within which one or the other preponderates.

Again, defenders of utility often find themselves called upon to reply to such objections as this—that there is not time, previous to action, for calculating and weighing the effects of any line of conduct on the general happiness. This is exactly as if anyone were to say that it is impossible to guide our conduct by Christianity because there is not time, on every occasion on which anything has to be done, to read through the Old and New Testaments. The answer to the objection is that there has been ample time, namely, the whole past duration of the human species. During all that time mankind have been learning by experience the tendencies of actions; on which experience all the prudence as well as all the morality of life are dependent. People talk as if the commencement of this course of experience had hitherto been put off, and as if, at the moment when some man feels tempted to meddle with the property or life of another, he had to begin considering for the first time whether murder and theft are injurious to human happiness. Even then I do not think that he would find the question very puzzling; but, at all events, the matter is now done to his hand. It is truly a whimsical supposition that, if mankind were agreed in considering utility to be the test of morality, they would remain without any agreement as to what *is* useful, and would take no measures for having their notions on the subject taught to the young and enforced by law and opinion. There is no difficulty in proving any ethical standard whatever to work ill if we suppose universal idiocy to be conjoined with it; but on any hypothesis short of that, mankind must by this time have acquired positive beliefs as to the effects of some actions on their happiness; and the beliefs which have thus come down are the rules of morality for the multitude, and for the philosopher until he has succeeded in finding better. That philosophers might easily do this, even now, on many subjects; that the received code of ethics is by no means of divine right; and that mankind have still much to learn as to the effects of actions on the general happiness, I admit or rather earnestly maintain. The corollaries from the principle of utility, like the precepts of every practical art, admit of indefinite improvement, and, in a progressive state of the human mind, their improvement is perpetually going on. But to consider the rules of morality as improvable is one thing; to pass over the intermediate generalization entirely and endeavor to test each individual action directly by the first principle is another. It is a strange notion that the acknowledgment of a first principle is inconsistent with the admission of secondary ones. To inform a traveler respecting the place of his ultimate destination is not to forbid the use of landmarks and direction-posts on the way. The proposition that happiness is the end and aim of morality does not mean that no road ought to be laid down to that goal, or that persons going thither should not be advised to take one direction rather than another. Men really ought to leave off talking a kind of nonsense on this subject, which they would neither talk nor listen to on other matters of practical concernment. Nobody argues that the art of navigation is not founded on astronomy because sailors cannot wait to calculate the Nautical Almanac. Being rational creatures, they go to sea with it ready calculated; and all rational creatures go out upon the sea of life with their minds made up on the common questions of right and wrong, as well as on many of the far more difficult questions of wise and foolish. And this, as long as foresight is a human quality, it is to be presumed they will continue to do. Whatever we adopt as the fundamental principle of morality, we require subordinate principles to apply it by; the impossibility of doing without them, being common to all systems, can afford no argument against any one in particular; but gravely to argue as if no such secondary principles could be had, and as if mankind had remained till now, and always must remain, without drawing any general conclusions from the experience of human life is as high a pitch, I think, as absurdity has every reached in philosophical controversy.

The remainder of the stock arguments against utilitarianism mostly consist in laying to its charge the common infirmities of human nature, and the general difficulties which embarrass conscientious persons in shaping their course through life. We are told that a utilitarian will be apt to make his own particular case an exception to moral rules, and, when under temptation, will see a utility in the breach of a rule, greater than he will see in its observance. But is utility the only creed which is able to furnish us with excuses for evil-doing and means of cheating our own conscience? They are afforded in abundance by all doctrines which recognize as a fact in morals the existence of conflicting considerations, which all doctrines do that have been believed by sane persons. It is not the fault of any creed, but of the complicated nature of human affairs, that rules of conduct cannot be so framed as to require no exceptions, and that hardly any kind of action can safely be laid down as either always obligatory or always condemnable. There is no ethical creed which does not temper the rigidity of its laws by giving a certain latitude, under the moral responsibility of the agent, for accommodation to peculiarities of circumstances; and under every creed, at the opening thus made, self-deception and dishonest casuistry get in. There exists no moral system under which there do not arise unequivocal cases of conflicting obligation. These are the real difficulties, the knotty points both in the theory of ethics and in the conscientious guidance of personal conduct. They are overcome practically, with greater or with less success, according to the intellect and virtue of the individual; but it can hardly be pretended that anyone will be the less qualified for dealing with them, from possessing an ultimate standard to which conflicting rights and duties can be referred. If utility is the ultimate source of moral obligations, utility may be invoked to decide between them when their demands are incompatible. Though the application of the standard may be difficult, it is better than none at all; while in other systems, the moral laws all claiming independent authority, there is no common umpire entitled to interfere between them; their claims to precedence one over another rest on little better than sophistry, and, unless determined, as they generally are, by the unacknowledged influence of consideration of utility, afford a free scope for the action of personal desires and partialities. We must remember that only in these cases of conflict between secondary principles is it requisite that first principles should be appealed to. There is no case of moral obligation in which some secondary principle is not involved; and if only one, there can seldom be any real doubt which one it is, in the mind of any person by whom the principle itself is recognized.

CHAPTER III

OF THE ULTIMATE SANCTION
OF THE PRINCIPLE OF UTILITY

The question is often asked, and properly so, in regard to any supposed moral standard—What is its sanction? what are the motives to obey? or, more specifically, what is the source of its obligation? whence does it derive its binding force? It is a necessary part of moral philosophy to provide the answer to this question, which, though frequently assuming the shape of an objection to the utilitarian morality, as if it had some special applicability to that above others, really arises in regard to all standards. It arises, in fact, whenever a person is called on to *adopt* a standard, or refer morality to any basis on which he has not been accustomed to rest it. For the customary morality, that which education and opinion have consecrated, is the only one which presents itself to the mind with the feeling of being *in itself* obligatory; and when a person is asked to believe that this morality *derives* its obligation from some general principle round which custom has not thrown the same halo, the assertion is to him a paradox; the supposed corollaries seem to have a more binding force than the original theorem; the superstructure seems to stand better without than with what is represented as its foundation. He says to himself, I feel that I am bound not to rob or murder, betray or deceive; but why am I bound to promote the general happiness? If my own happiness lies in something else, why may I not give that the preference?

If the view adopted by the utilitarian philosophy of the nature of the moral sense be correct, this difficulty will always present itself until the influences which form moral character have taken the same hold of the principle which they have taken of some of the consequences—until, by the improvement of education, the feeling of unity with our fellow creatures shall be (what it cannot be denied that Christ intended it to be) as deeply rooted in our character, and to our own consciousness as completely a part of our nature, as the horror of crime is in an ordinarily well-brought up young person. It the meantime, however, the difficulty has no peculiar application to the doctrine of utility, but is inherent in every attempt to analyze morality and reduce it to principles; which, unless the principle is already in men's minds invested with as much sacredness as any of its applications, always seems to divest them of a part of their sanctity.

The principle of utility either has, or there is no reason why it might not have, all the sanctions which belong to any other system of morals. Those sanctions are either external or internal. Of the external sanctions it is not necessary to speak at any length. They are the hope of favor and the fear of displeasure from our fellow creatures or from the Ruler of the universe, along with whatever we may have of sympathy or affection for them, or of love and awe of Him, inclining us to do His will independently of selfish consequences. There is evidently no reason why all these motives for observance should not attach themselves to the utilitarian morality as completely and as powerfully as to any other. Indeed, those of them which refer to our fellow creatures are sure to do so, in proportion to the amount of general intelligence; for whether there be any other ground of moral obligation than the general happiness or not, men do desire happiness; and however imperfect may be their own practice, they desire and commend all conduct in others toward themselves by which they think their happiness is promoted. With regard to the religious motive, if men believe, as most profess to do, in the goodness of God, those who think that conduciveness to the general happiness is the essence or even only the criterion of good must necessarily believe that it is also that which God approves. The whole force therefore of external reward and punishment, whether physical or moral, and whether proceeding from God or from our fellow men, together with all that the capacities of human nature admit of disinterested devotion to either, become available to enforce the utilitarian morality, in proportion as that morality is recognized; and the more powerfully, the more the appliances of education and general cultivation are bent to the purpose.

So far as to external sanctions. The internal sanction of duty, whatever our standard of duty may be, is one and the same—a feeling in our own mind; a pain, more or less intense, attendant on violation of duty, which in properly cultivated moral natures rises, in the more serious cases, into shrinking from it as an impossibility. This feeling, when disinterested and connecting itself with the pure idea of duty, and not with some particular form of it, or with any of the merely accessory circumstances, is the essence of conscience; though in that complex phenomenon as it actually exists, the simple fact is in general all encrusted over with collateral associations derived from sympathy, from love, and still more from fear; from all the forms of religious feeling; from the recollections of childhood and of all our past life; from self-esteem, desire of the esteem of others, and occasionally even self-abasement. This extreme complication is, I apprehend, the origin of the sort of mystical character which, by a tendency of the human mind of which there are many other examples, is apt to be attributed to the idea of moral obligation, and which leads people to believe that the idea cannot possibly attach itself to any other objects than those which, by a supposed mysterious law, are found in our present experience to excite it. Its binding force, however, consists in the existence of a mass of feeling which must be broken through in order to do what violates our standard of right, and which, if we do nevertheless violate that standard, will probably have to be encountered afterwards in the form of remorse. Whatever theory we have of the nature or origin of conscience, this is what essentially constitutes it.

The ultimate sanction, therefore, of all morality (external motives apart) being a subjective feeling in our own minds, I see nothing embarrassing to those whose standard is utility in the question, What is the sanction of that particular standard? We may answer, the same as of all other moral standards—the conscientious feelings of mankind. Undoubtedly this sanction has no binding efficacy on those who do not possess the feelings it appeals to; but neither will these persons be more obedient to any other moral principle than to the utilitarian one. On them morality of any kind has no hold but through the external sanctions. Meanwhile the feelings exist, a fact in human nature, the reality of which, and the great power with which they are capable of acting on those in whom they have been duly cultivated, are proved by experience. No reason has ever been shown why they may not be cultivated to as great intensity in connection with the utilitarian as with any other rule of morals.

There is, I am aware, a disposition to believe that a person who sees in moral obligation a transcendental fact, an objective reality belonging to the province of "things in themselves," is likely to be more obedient to it than one who believes it to be entirely subjective, having its seat in human consciousness only. But whatever a person's opinion may be on this point of ontology, the force he is really urged by is his own subjective feeling, and is exactly measured by its strength. No one's belief that duty is an objective reality is stronger than the belief that God is so; yet the belief in God, apart from the expectation of actual reward and punishment, only operates on conduct through, and in proportion to, the subjective religious feeling. The sanction, so far as it is disinterested, is always in the mind itself; and the notion, therefore, of the transcendental moralists must be that this sanction will not exist *in* the mind unless it is believed to have its root out of the mind; and that if a person is able to say to himself, "That which is restraining me and which is called my conscience is only a feeling in my own mind," he may possibly draw the conclusion that when the feeling ceases the obligation ceases, and that if he find the feeling inconvenient, he may disregard it and endeavor to get rid of it. But is this danger confined to the utilitarian morality? Does the belief that moral obligation has its seat outside the mind make the feeling of it too strong to get rid of? The fact is so far otherwise that all moralists admit and lament the ease with which, in the generality of minds, conscience can be silenced or stifled. The question, "Need I obey my conscience?" is quite as often put to themselves by persons who never heard of the principle of utility as by its adherents. Those whose conscientious feelings are so weak as to allow of their asking this question, if they answer it affirmatively, will not do so because they believe in the transcendental theory, but because of the external sanctions.

It is not necessary, for the present purpose, to decide whether the feeling of duty is innate or implanted. Assuming it to be innate, it is an open question to what objects it naturally attaches itself; for the philosophic supporters of that theory are now agreed that the intuitive perception is of principles of morality and not of the details. If there be anything innate in the matter, I see no reason why the feeling which is innate should not be that of regard to the pleasures and pains of others. If there is any principle of morals which is intuitively obligatory, I should say it must be that. If so, the intuitive ethics would coincide with the utilitarian, and there would be no further quarrel between them. Even as it is, the intuitive moralists, though they believe that there are other intuitive moral obligations, do already believe this to be one; for they unanimously hold that a large *portion* of morality turns upon the consideration due to the interests of our fellow creatures. Therefore, if the belief in the transcendental origin of moral obligation gives any additional efficacy to the internal sanction, it appears to me that the utilitarian principle has already the benefit of it.

On the other hand, if, as is my own belief, the moral feelings are not innate but acquired, they are not for that reason the less natural. It is natural to man to speak, to reason, to build cities, to cultivate the ground, though these are acquired faculties. The moral feelings are not indeed a part of our nature in the sense of being in any perceptible degree present in all of us; but this, unhappily, is a fact admitted by those who believe the most strenuously in their transcendental origin. Like the other acquired capacities above referred to, the moral faculty, if not a part of our nature, is a natural outgrowth from it; capable, like them, in a certain small degree, of springing up spontaneously; and susceptible of being brought by cultivation to a high degree of development. Unhappily it is also susceptible, by a sufficient use of the external sanctions and of the force of early impressions, of being cultivated in almost any direction, so that there is hardly anything so absurd or so mischievous that it may not, by means of these influences, be made to act on the human mind with all the authority of conscience. To doubt that the same potency might be given by the same means to the principle of utility, even if it had no foundation in human nature, would be flying in the face of all experience.

But moral associations which are wholly of artificial creation, when the intellectual culture goes on, yield by degrees to the dissolving force of analysis; and if the feeling of duty, when associated with utility, would appear equally arbitrary; if there were no leading department of our nature, no powerful class of sentiments, with which that association would harmonize, which would make us feel congenial and incline us not only to foster it in others (for which we have abundant interested motives), but also to cherish it in ourselves—if there were not, in short, a natural basis of sentiment for utilitarian morality, it might well happen that this association also, even after it had been implanted by education, might be analyzed away.

But there *is* this basis of powerful natural sentiment; and that it is which, when once the general happiness is recognized as the ethical standard, will constitute the strength of the utilitarian morality. This firm foundation is that of the social feelings of mankind—the desire to be in unity with our fellow creatures, which is already a powerful principle in human nature, and happily one of those which tend to become stronger, even without express inculcation, from the influences of advancing civilization. The social state is at once so natural, so necessary, and so habitual to man, that, except in some unusual circumstances or by an effort of voluntary abstraction, he never conceives himself otherwise than as a member of a body; and this association is riveted more and more, as mankind are further removed from the state of savage independence. Any condition, therefore, which is essential to a state of society becomes more and more an inseparable part of every person's conception of the state of things which he is born into, and which is the destiny of a human being. Now society between human beings, except in the relation of master and slave, is manifestly impossible on any other footing than that the interests of all are to be consulted. Society between equals can only exist on the understanding that the interests of all are to be regarded equally. And since in all states of civilization, every person, except an absolute monarch, has equals, everyone is obliged to live on these terms with somebody; and in every age some advance is made toward a state in which it will be impossible to live permanently on other terms with anybody. In this way people grow up unable to conceive as possible to them a state of total disregard of other people's interests. They are under a necessity of conceiving themselves as at least abstaining from all the grosser injuries, and (if only for their own protection) living in a state of constant protest against them. They are also familiar with the fact of co-operating with others and proposing to themselves a collective, not an individual, interest as the aim (at least for the time being) of their actions. So long as they are co-operating, their ends are identified with those of others; there is at least a temporary feeling that the interests of others are their own interests. Not only does all strengthening of social ties, and all healthy growth of society, give to each individual a stronger personal interest in practically consulting the welfare of others, it also leads him to identify his *feelings* more and more with their good, or at least with an even greater degree of practical consideration for it. He comes, as though instinctively, to be conscious of himself as a being who *of course* pays regard to others. The good of others becomes to him a thing naturally and necessarily to be attended to, like any of the physical conditions of our existence. Now, whatever amount of this feeling a person has, he is urged by the strongest motives both of interest and of sympathy to demonstrate it, and to the utmost of his power encourage it in others; and even if he has none of it himself, he is as greatly interested as anyone else that others should have it. Consequently, the smallest germs of the feeling are laid hold of and nourished by the contagion of sympathy and the influences of education; and a complete web of corroborative association is woven round it by the powerful agency of the external sanctions. This mode of conceiving ourselves and human life, as civilization goes on, is felt to be more and more natural. Every step in political improvement renders it more so, by removing the sources of opposition of interest and leveling those inequalities of legal privilege between individuals or classes, owing to which there are large portions of mankind whose happiness it is still practicable to disregard. In an improving state of the human mind, the influences are constantly on the increase which tend to generate in each individual a feeling of unity with all the rest; which, if perfect, would make him never think of, or desire, any beneficial condition for himself in the benefits of which they are not included. If we now suppose this feeling of unity to be taught as a religion, and the whole force of education, of institutions, and of opinion directed, as it once was in the case of religion, to make every person grow up from infancy surrounded on all sides both by the profession and the practice of it, I think that no one who can realize this conception will feel any misgiving about the sufficiency of the ultimate sanction for the happiness morality. To any ethical student who finds the realization difficult, I recommend, as a means of facilitating it, the second of M. Comte's two principal works, the *Traité de politique positive*.[7] I entertain the strongest objections to the system of politics and morals set forth in that treatise, but I think it has superabundantly shown the possibility of giving to the service of humanity, even without the aid of belief in a Providence, both the psychological power and the social efficacy of a religion, making it take hold of human life, and color all thought, feeling, and action in a manner of which the greatest ascendancy ever exercised by any religion may be but a type and foretaste; and of which the danger is, not that it should be insufficient, but that it should be so excessive as to interfere unduly with human freedom and individuality.

Neither is it necessary to the feeling which constitutes the binding force of the utilitarian morality on those who recognize it to wait for those social influences which would make its obligation felt by mankind at large. In the comparatively early state of human advancement in which we now live, a person cannot, indeed, feel that entireness of sympathy with all others which would make any real discordance in the general direction of their conduct in life impossible, but already a person in whom the social feeling is at all developed cannot bring himself to think of the rest of his fellow creatures as struggling rivals with him for the means of happiness, whom he must desire to see defeated in their object in order that he may succeed in his. The deeply rooted conception which every individual even now has of himself as a social being tends to make him feel it one of his natural wants that there should be harmony between his feelings and aims and those of his fellow creatures. If differences of opinion and of mental culture make it impossible for him to share many of their actual feelings—perhaps make him denounce and defy those feelings—he still needs to be conscious that his real aim and theirs do not conflict; that he is not opposing himself to what they really wish for, namely, their own good, but is, on the contrary, promoting it. This feeling in most individuals is much inferior in strength to their selfish feelings, and is often wanting altogether. But to those who have it, it possesses all the characters of a natural feeling. It does not present itself to their minds as a superstition of education or a law despotically imposed by the power of society, but as an attribute which it would not be well for them to be without. This conviction is the ultimate sanction of the greatest happiness morality. This it is which makes any mind of well-developed feelings work with, and not against, the outward motives to care for others, afforded by what I have called the external sanctions; and, when those sanctions are wanting or act in an opposite direction, constitutes in itself a powerful internal binding force, in proportion to the sensitiveness and thoughtfulness of the character, since few but those whose mind is a moral blank could bear to lay out their course of life on the plan of paying no regard to others except so far as their own private interest compels.

---

7. [Auguste Comte (1798–1857) was the French philosopher who founded positivism, a view that denies the sense of speculative metaphysics and stresses the role of scientific observation in achieving understanding. As a social reformer he called for a moral order in which all people and nations could live in harmony. The work referred to is his *Treatise of Positive Polity*.]

CHAPTER IV

OF WHAT SORT OF PROOF
THE PRINCIPLE OF UTILITY IS SUSCEPTIBLE

It has already been remarked that questions of ultimate ends do not admit of proof, in the ordinary acceptation of the term. To be incapable of proof by reasoning is common to all first principles, to the first premises of our knowledge, as well as to those of our conduct. But the former, being matters of fact, may be the subject of a direct appeal to the faculties which judge of fact—namely, our senses and our internal consciousness. Can an appeal be made to the same faculties on questions of practical ends? Or by what other faculty is cognizance taken of them?

Questions about ends are, in other words, questions what things are desirable. The utilitarian doctrine is that happiness is desirable, and the only thing desirable, as an end; all other things being only desirable as means to that end. What ought to be required of this doctrine, what conditions is it requisite that the doctrine should fulfill—to make good its claim to be believed?

The only proof capable of being given that an object is visible is that people actually see it. The only proof that a sound is audible is that people hear it; and so of the other sources of our experience. In like manner, I apprehend, the sole evidence it is possible to produce that anything is desirable is that people do actually desire it. If the end which the utilitarian doctrine proposes to itself were not, in theory and in practice, acknowledged to be an end, nothing could ever convince any person that it was so. No reason can be given why the general happiness is desirable, except that each person, so far as he believes it to be attainable, desires his own happiness. This, however, being a fact, we have not only all the proof which the case admits of, but all which it is possible to require, that happiness is a good, that each person's happiness is a good to that person, and the general happiness, therefore, a good to the aggregate of all persons. Happiness has made out its title as *one* of the ends of conduct and, consequently, one of the criteria of morality.

But it has not, by this alone, proved itself to be the sole criterion. To do that, it would seem, by the same rule, necessary to show, not only that people desire happiness, but that they never desire anything else. Now it is palpable that they do desire things which, in common language, are decidedly distinguished from happiness. They desire, for example, virtue and the absence of vice no less really than pleasure and the absence of pain. The desire of virtue is not as universal, but it is as authentic a fact as the desire of happiness. And hence the opponents of the utilitarian standard deem that they have a right to infer that there are other ends of human action besides happiness, and that happiness is not the standard of approbation and disapprobation.

But does the utilitarian doctrine deny that people desire virtue, or maintain that virtue is not a thing to be desired? The very reverse. It maintains not only that virtue is to be desired, but that it is to be desired disinterestedly, for itself. Whatever may be the opinion of utilitarian moralists as to the original conditions by which virtue is made virtue, however they may believe (as they do) that actions and dispositions are only virtuous because they promote another end than virtue, yet this being granted, and it having been decided, from considerations of this description, what *is* virtuous, they not only place virtue at the very head of the things which are good as means to the ultimate end, but they also recognize as a psychological fact the possibility of its being, to the individual, a good in itself, without looking to any end beyond it; and hold that the mind is not in a right state, not in a state conformable to utility, not in the state most conducive to the general happiness, unless it does love virtue in this manner — as a thing desirable in itself, even although, in the individual instance, it should not produce those other desirable consequences which it tends to produce, and on account of which it is held to be virtue. This opinion is not, in the smallest degree, a departure from the happiness principle. The ingredients of happiness are very various, and each of them is desirable in itself, and not merely when considered as swelling an aggregate. The principle of utility does not mean that any given pleasure, as music, for instance, or any given exemption from pain, as for example health, is to be looked upon as means to a collective something termed happiness, and to be desired on that account. They are desired and desirable in and for themselves; besides being means, they are a part of the end. Virtue, according to the utilitarian doctrine, is not naturally and originally part of the end, but it is capable of becoming so; and in those who live it disinterestedly it has become so, and is desired and cherished, not as a means to happiness, but as a part of their happiness.

To illustrate this further, we may remember that virtue is not the only thing originally a means, and which if it were not a means to anything else would be and remain indifferent, but which by association with what it is a means to comes to be desired for itself, and that too with the utmost intensity. What, for example, shall we say of the love of money? There is nothing originally more desirable about money than about any heap of glittering pebbles. Its worth is solely that of the things which it will buy; the desires for other things than itself, which it is a means of gratifying. Yet the love of money is not only one of the strongest moving forces of human life, but money is, in many cases, desired in and for itself; the desire to possess it is often stronger than the desire to use it, and goes on increasing when all the desires which point to ends beyond it, to be compassed by it, are falling off. It may, then, be said truly that money is desired not for the sake of an end, but as part of the end. From being a means to happiness, it has come to be itself a principal ingredient of the individual's conception of happiness. The same may be said of the majority of the great objects of human life: power, for example, or fame, except that to each of these there is a certain amount of immediate pleasure annexed, which has at least the semblance of being naturally inherent in them — a thing which cannot be said of money. Still, however, the strongest natural attraction, both of power and of fame, is the immense aid they give to the attainment of our other wishes; and it is the strong association thus generated between them and all our objects of desire which gives to the direct desire of them the intensity it often assumes, so as in some characters to surpass in strength all other desires. In these cases the means have become a part of the end, and a more important part of it than any of the things which they are means to. What was once desired as an instrument for the attainment of happiness has come to be desired for its own sake. In being desired for its own sake it is, however, desired as *part* of happiness. The person is made, or thinks he would be made, happy by its mere possession; and is made unhappy by failure to obtain it. The desire of it is not a different thing from the desire of happiness any more than the love of music or the desire of health. They are included in happiness.

They are some of the elements of which the desire of happiness is made up. Happiness is not an abstract idea but a concrete whole; and these are some of its parts. And the utilitarian standard sanctions and approves their being so. Life would be a poor thing, very ill provided with sources of happiness, if there were not this provision of nature by which things originally indifferent, but conducive to, or otherwise associated with, the satisfaction of our primitive desires, become in themselves sources of pleasure more valuable than the primitive pleasures, both in permanency, in the space of human existence that they are capable of covering, and even in intensity.

Virtue, according to the utilitarian conception, is a good of this description. There was no original desire of it, or motive to it, save its conduciveness to pleasure, and especially to protection from pain. But through the association thus formed it may be felt a good in itself, and desired as such with as great intensity as any other good; and with this difference between it and the love of money, of power, or of fame — that all of these may, and often do, render the individual noxious to the other members of the society to which he belongs, whereas there is nothing which makes him so much a blessing to them as the cultivation of the disinterested love of virtue. And consequently, the utilitarian standard, while it tolerates and approves those other acquired desires, up to the point beyond which they would be more injurious to the general happiness than promotive of it, enjoins and requires the cultivation of the love of virtue up to the greatest strength possible, as being above all things important to the general happiness.

It results from the preceding considerations that there is in reality nothing desired except happiness. Whatever is desired otherwise than as a means to some end beyond itself, and ultimately to happiness, is desired as itself a part of happiness, and is not desired for itself until it has become so. Those who desire virtue for its own sake desire it either because the consciousness of it is a pleasure, or because the consciousness of being without it is a pain, or for both reasons united; as in truth the pleasure and pain seldom exist separately, but almost always together — the same person feeling pleasure in the degree of virtue attained, and pain in not having attained more. If one of these gave him no pleasure, and the other no pain, he would not love or desire virtue, or would desire it only for the other benefits which it might produce to himself or to persons whom he cared for.

We have now, then, an answer to the question, of what sort of proof the principle of utility is susceptible. If the opinion which I have now stated is psychologically true — if human nature is so constituted as to desire nothing which is not either a part of happiness or a means of happiness — we can have no other proof, and we require no other, that these are the only things desirable. If so, happiness is the sole end of human action, and the promotion of it the test by which to judge of all human conduct; from whence it necessarily follows that it must be the criterion of morality, since a part is included in the whole.

And now to decide whether this is really so, whether mankind do desire nothing for itself but that which is a pleasure to them, or of which the absence is a pain, we have evidently arrived at a question of fact and experience, dependent, like all similar questions, upon evidence. It can only be determined by practiced self-consciousness and self-observation, assisted by observation of others. I believe that these sources of evidence, impartially consulted, will declare that desiring a thing and finding it pleasant, aversion to it and thinking of it as painful, are phenomena entirely inseparable or, rather, two parts of the same phenomenon—in strictness of language, two different modes of naming the same psychological fact; that to think of an object as desirable (unless for the sake of its consequences) and to think of it as pleasant are one and the same thing; and that to desire anything except in proportion as the idea of it is pleasant is a physical and metaphysical impossibility.

So obvious does this appear to me that I expect it will hardly be disputed; and the objection made will be, not that desire can possibly be directed to anything ultimately except pleasure and exemption from pain, but that the will is a different thing from desire; that a person of confirmed virtue or any other person whose purposes are fixed carries out his purposes without any thought of the pleasure he has in contemplating them or expects to derive from their fulfillment, and persists in acting on them, even though these pleasures are much diminished by changes in his character or decay of his passive sensibilities, or are outweighed by the pains which the pursuit of the purposes may bring upon him. All this I fully admit and have stated it elsewhere as positively and emphatically as anyone. Will, the active phenomenon, is a different thing from desire, the state of passive sensibility, and, though originally an offshoot from it, may in time take root and detach itself from the parent stock, so much so that in the case of a habitual purpose, instead of willing the thing because we desire it, we often desire it only because we will it. This, however, is but an instance of that familiar fact, the power of habit, and is nowise confined to the case of virtuous actions. Many indifferent things which men originally did from a motive of some sort they continue to do from habit. Sometimes this is done unconsciously, the consciousness coming only after the action; at other times with conscious volition, but volition which has become habitual and is put in operation by the force of habit, in opposition perhaps to the deliberate preference, as often happens with those who have contracted habits of vicious or hurtful indulgence. Third and last comes the case in which the habitual act of will in the individual instance is not in contradiction to the general intention prevailing at other times, but in fulfillment of it, as in the case of the person of confirmed virtue and of all who pursue deliberately and consistently any determinate end. The distinction between will and desire thus understood is an authentic and highly important psychological fact; but the fact consists solely in this—that will, like all other parts of our constitution, is amenable to habit, and that we may will from habit what we no longer desire for itself, or desire only because we will it. It is not the less true that will, in the beginning, is entirely produced by desire, including in that term the repelling influence of pain as well as the attractive one of pleasure. Let us take into consideration no longer the person who has a confirmed will to do right, but him in whom that virtuous will is still feeble, conquerable by temptation, and not to be fully relied on; by what means can it be strengthened? How can the will to be virtuous, where it does not exist in sufficient force, be implanted or awakened? Only by making the person *desire* virtue—by making him think of it in a pleasurable light, or of its absence in a painful one. It is by associating the doing right with pleasure, or the wrong with pain, or by eliciting and impressing and bringing home to the person's experience the pleasure naturally involved in the one or the pain in the other, that it is possible to call forth that will to be virtuous which, when confirmed, acts without any thought of either pleasure or pain. Will is the child of desire, and passes out of the dominion of its parent only to come under that of habit. That which is the result of habit affords no presumption of being intrinsically good; and there would be no reason for wishing that the purpose of virtue should become independent of pleasure and pain were it not that the influence of the pleasurable and painful associations which prompt to virtue is not sufficiently to be depended on for unerring constancy of action until it has acquired the support of habit. Both in feeling and in conduct, habit is the only thing which imparts certainty; and it is because of the importance to others of being able to rely absolutely on one's feelings and conduct, and to oneself of being able to rely on one's own, that the will to do right ought to be cultivated into this habitual independence. In other words, this state of the will is a means to good, not intrinsically a good; and does not contradict the doctrine that nothing is a good to human beings but in so far as it is either itself pleasurable or a means of attaining pleasure or averting pain.

But if this doctrine be true, the principle of utility is proved. Whether it is so or not must now be left to the consideration of the thoughtful reader.

CHAPTER V

ON THE CONNECTION BETWEEN JUSTICE AND UTILITY

In all ages of speculation one of the strongest obstacles to the reception of the doctrine that utility or happiness is the criterion of right and wrong has been drawn from the idea of justice. The powerful sentiment and apparently clear perception which that word recalls with a rapidity and certainty resembling an instinct have seemed to the majority of thinkers to point to an inherent quality in things; to show that the just must have an existence in nature as something absolute, generically distinct from every variety of the expedient and, in idea, opposed to it, though (as is commonly acknowledged) never, in the long run, disjoined from it in fact.

In the case of this, as of our other moral sentiments, there is no necessary connection between the question of its origin and that of its binding force. That a feeling is bestowed on us by nature does not necessarily legitimate all its promptings. The feeling of justice might be a peculiar instinct, and might yet require, like our other instincts, to be controlled and enlightened by a higher reason. If we have intellectual instincts leading us to judge in a particular way, as well as animal instincts that prompt us to act in a particular way, there is no necessity that the former should be more infallible in their sphere than the latter in theirs; it may as well happen that wrong judgments are occasionally suggested by those, as wrong actions by these. But though it is one thing to believe that we have natural feelings of justice, and another to acknowledge them as an ultimate criterion of conduct, these two opinions are very closely connected in point of fact. Mankind are always predisposed to believe that any subjective feeling, not otherwise accounted for, is a revelation of some objective reality. Our present object is to determine whether the reality to which the feeling of justice corresponds is one which needs any such special revelation, whether the justice or injustice of an action is a thing intrinsically peculiar and distinct from all its other qualities or only a combination of certain of those qualities presented under a peculiar aspect. For the purpose of this inquiry it is practically important to consider whether the feeling itself, of justice and injustice, is *sui generis* like our sensations of color and taste or a derivative feeling formed by a combination of others. And this it is the more essential to examine, as people are in general willing enough to allow that objectively the dictates of justice coincide with a part of the field of general expediency; but inasmuch as the subjective mental feeling of justice is different from that which commonly attaches to simple expediency, and, except in the extreme cases of the latter, is far more imperative in its demands, people find it difficult to see in justice only a particular kind or branch of general utility, and think that its superior binding force requires a totally different origin.

To throw light upon this question, it is necessary to attempt to ascertain what is the distinguishing character of justice, or of injustice; what is the quality, or whether there is any quality, attributed in common to all modes of conduct designated as unjust (for justice, like many other moral attributes, is best defined by its opposite), and distinguishing them from such modes of conduct as are disapproved, but without having that particular epithet of disapprobation applied to them. If in everything which men are accustomed to characterize as just or unjust some one common attribute or collection of attributes is always present, we may judge whether this particular attribute or combination of attributes would be capable of gathering round it a sentiment of that peculiar character and intensity by virtue of the general laws of our emotional constitution, or whether the sentiment is inexplicable and requires to be regarded as a special provision of nature. If we find the former to be the case, we shall, in resolving this question, have resolved also the main problem; if the latter, we shall have to seek for some other mode of investigating it.

To find the common attributes of a variety of objects, it is necessary to begin by surveying the objects themselves in the concrete. Let us therefore advert successively to the various modes of action and arrangements of human affairs which are classed, by universal or widely spread opinion, as just or as unjust. The things well known to excite the sentiments associated with those names are of a very multifarious character. I shall pass them rapidly in review, without studying any particular arrangement.

In the first place, it is mostly considered unjust to deprive anyone of his personal liberty, his property, or any other thing which belongs to him by law. Here, therefore, is one instance of the application of the terms "just" and "unjust" in a perfectly definite sense, namely, that it is just to respect, unjust to violate, the *legal rights* of anyone. But this judgment admits of several exceptions, arising from the other forms in which the notions of justice and injustice present themselves. For example, the person who suffers the deprivation may (as the phrase is) have *forfeited* the rights which he is so deprived of—a case to which we shall return presently. But also—

Secondly, the legal rights of which he is deprived may be rights which *ought* not to have belonged to him; in other words, the law which confers on him these rights may be a bad law. When it is so or when (which is the same thing for our purpose) it is supposed to be so, opinions will differ as to the justice or injustice of infringing it. Some maintain that no law, however bad, ought to be disobeyed by an individual citizen; that his opposition to it, if shown at all, should only be shown in endeavoring to get it altered by competent authority. This opinion (which condemns many of the most illustrious benefactors of mankind, and would often protect pernicious institutions against the only weapons which, in the state of things existing at the time, have any chance of succeeding against them) is defended by those who hold it on grounds of expediency, principally on that of the importance to the common inter-est of mankind, of maintaining inviolate the sentiment of submission to law. Other persons, again, hold the directly contrary opinion that any law, judged to be bad, may blamelessly be disobeyed, even though it be not judged to be unjust but only inexpedient, while others would confine the license of disobedience to the case of unjust laws; but, again, some say that all laws which are inexpedient are unjust, since every law imposes some restriction on the natural liberty of mankind, which restriction is an injustice unless legitimated by tending to their good. Among these diversities of opinion it seems to be universally admitted that there may be unjust laws, and that law, consequently, is not the ultimate criterion of justice, but may give to one person a benefit, or impose on another an evil, which justice condemns. When, however, a law is thought to be unjust, it seems always to be regarded as being so in the same way in which a breach of law is unjust, namely, by infringing somebody's right, which, as it cannot in this case be a legal right, receives a different appellation and is called a moral right. We may say, therefore, that a second case of injustice consists in taking or withholding from any person that to which he has a *moral right*.

Thirdly, it is universally considered just that each person should obtain that (whether good or evil) which he *deserves*, and unjust that he should obtain a good or be made to undergo an evil which he does not deserve. This is, perhaps, the clearest and most emphatic form in which the idea of justice is conceived by the general mind. As it involves the notion of desert, the question arises what constitutes desert? Speaking in a general way, a person is understood to deserve good if he does right, evil if he does wrong; and in a more particular sense, to deserve good from those to whom he does or has done good, and evil from those to whom he does or has done evil. The precept of returning good for evil has never been regarded as a case of the fulfillment of justice, but as one in which the claims of justice are waived, in obedience to other considerations.

Fourthly, it is confessedly unjust to *break faith* with anyone: to violate an engage-ment, either express or implied, or disappoint expectations raised by our own con-duct, at least if we have raised those expectations knowingly and voluntarily. Like the other obligations of justice already spoken of, this one is not regarded as absolute, but as capable of being overruled by a stronger obligation of justice on the other side, or by such conduct on the part of the person concerned as is deemed to absolve us from our obligation to him and to constitute a *forfeiture* of the benefit which he has been led to expect.

Fifthly, it is, by universal admission, inconsistent with justice to be *partial*—to show favor or preference to one person over another in matters to which favor and preference do not properly apply. Impartiality, however, does not seem to be re-garded as a duty in itself, but rather as instrumental to some other duty; for it is admitted that favor and preference are not always censurable, and, indeed, the cases in which they are condemned are rather the exception than the rule. A person would be more likely to be blamed than applauded for giving his family or friends no superiority in good offices over strangers when he could do so without violating any other duty; and no one thinks it unjust to seek one person in preference to another as a friend, connection, or companion. Impartiality where rights are con-cerned is of course obligatory, but this is involved in the more general obligation of giving to everyone his right. A tribunal, for example, must be impartial because it is bound to award, without regard to any other consideration, a disputed object to the one of two parties who has the right to it. There are other cases in which impartiality means being solely influenced by desert, as with those who, in the capacity of judges, preceptors, or parents, administer reward and punishment as such. There are cases, again, in which it means being solely influenced by consideration for the public interest, as in making a selection among candidates for a government employment. Impartiality, in short, as an obligation of justice, may be said to mean being exclusively influenced by the considerations which it is supposed ought to influence the particular case in hand, and resisting solicitation of any motives which prompt to conduct different from what those considerations would dictate.

Nearly allied to the idea of impartiality is that of *equality*, which often enters as a component part both into the conception of justice and into the practice of it, and, in the eyes of many persons, constitutes its essence. But in this, still more than in any other case, the notion of justice varies in different persons, and always conforms in its variations to their notion of utility. Each person maintains that equality is the dictate of justice, except where he thinks that expediency requires inequality. The justice of giving equal protection to the rights of all is maintained by those who support the most outrageous inequality in the rights themselves. Even in slave countries it is theoretically admitted that the rights of the slave, such as they are, ought to be as sacred as those of the master, and that a tribunal which fails to enforce them with equal strictness is wanting in justice; while, at the same time, institutions which leave to the slave scarcely any rights to enforce are not deemed unjust because they are not deemed inexpedient. Those who think that utility requires distinctions of rank do not consider it unjust that riches and social privileges should be unequally dispensed; but those who think this inequality inexpedient think it unjust also. Whoever thinks that government is necessary sees no injustice in as much inequality as is constituted by giving to the magistrate powers not granted to other people. Even among those who hold leveling doctrines, there are differences of opinion about expediency. Some communists consider it unjust that the produce of the labor of the community should be shared on any other principle than that of exact equality; others think it just that those should receive most whose wants are greatest; while others hold that those who work harder, or who produce more, or whose services are more valuable to the community, may justly claim a larger quota in the division of the produce. And the sense of natural justice may be plausibly appealed to in behalf of every one of these opinions.

Among so many diverse applications of the term "justice," which yet is not regarded as ambiguous, it is a matter of some difficulty to seize the mental link which holds them together, and on which the moral sentiment adhering to the term essentially depends. Perhaps, in this embarrassment, some help may be derived from the history of the word, as indicated by its etymology.

In most if not in all languages, the etymology of the word which corresponds to "just" points distinctly to an origin connected with the ordinances of law. *Justum* is a form of *jussum*, that which has been ordered. *Dikaion* comes directly from *dike*, a suit at law. *Recht*, from which came *right* and *righteous*, is synonymous with law. The courts of justice, the administration of justice, are the courts and the administration of law. *La justice*, in French, is the established term for judicature. I am not committing the fallacy, imputed with some show of truth to Horne Tooke,[8] of assuming

---

8. [John Horne Tooke (1736–1812) was an English politician and philologist who supported both the American and French Revolutions.]

that a word must still continue to mean what it originally meant. Etymology is slight evidence of what the idea now signified is, but the very best evidence of how it sprang up. There can, I think, be no doubt that the *idée mère*, the primitive element, in the formation of the notion of justice was conformity to law. It constituted the entire idea among the Hebrews, up to the birth of Christianity; as might be expected in the case of a people whose laws attempted to embrace all subjects on which precepts were required, and who believed those laws to be a direct emanation from the Supreme Being. But other nations, and in particular the Greeks and Romans, who knew that their laws had been made originally, and still continued to be made, by men, were not afraid to admit that those men might make bad laws; might do, by law, the same things, and from the same motives, which if done by individuals without the sanction of law would be called unjust. And hence the sentiment of injustice came to be attached, not to all violations of law, but only to violations of such laws as *ought* to exist, including such as ought to exist but do not, and to laws themselves if supposed to be contrary to what ought to be law. In this manner the idea of law and of its injunctions was still predominant in the notion of justice, even when the laws actually in force ceased to be accepted as the standard of it.

It is true that mankind consider the idea of justice and its obligations as applicable to many things which neither are, nor is it desired that they should be, regulated by law. Nobody desires that laws should interfere with the whole detail of private life; yet everyone allows that in all daily conduct a person may and does show himself to be either just or unjust. But even here, the idea of the breach of what ought to be law still lingers in a modified shape. It would always give us pleasure, and chime in with our feelings of fitness, that acts which we deem unjust should be punished, though we do not always think it expedient that this should be done by the tribunals. We forego that gratification on account of incidental inconveniences. We should be glad to see just conduct enforced and injustice repressed, even in the minutest details, if we were not, with reason, afraid of trusting the magistrate with so unlimited an amount of power over individuals. When we think that a person is bound in justice to do a thing, it is an ordinary form of language to say that he ought to be compelled to do it. We should be gratified to see the obligation enforced by anybody who had the power. If we see that its enforcement by law would be inexpedient, we lament the impossibility, we consider the impunity given to injustice as an evil, and strive to make amends for it by bringing a strong expression of our own and the public disapprobation to bear upon the offender. Thus the idea of legal constraint is still the generating idea of the notion of justice, though undergoing several transformations before that notion as it exists in an advanced state of society becomes complete.

The above is, I think, a true account, as far as it goes, of the origin and progressive growth of the idea of justice. But we must observe that it contains as yet nothing to distinguish that obligation from moral obligation in general. For the truth is that the idea of penal sanction, which is the essence of law, enters not only into the conception of injustice, but into that of any kind of wrong. We do not call anything wrong unless we mean to imply that a person ought to be punished in some way or other for doing it—if not by law, by the opinion of his fellow creatures; if not by opinion, by the reproaches of his own conscience. This seems the real turning point of the distinction between morality and simple expediency. It is a part of the notion of duty in every one of its forms that a person may rightfully be compelled to fulfill it. Duty is a thing which may be *exacted* from a person, as one exacts a debt. Unless we think that it may be exacted from him, we do not call it his duty. Reasons of prudence, or the interest of other people, may militate against actually exacting it, but the person himself, it is clearly understood, would not be entitled to complain. There are other things, on the contrary, which we wish that people should do, which we like or admire them for doing, perhaps dislike or despise them for not doing, but yet admit that they are not bound to do; it is not a case of moral obligation; we do not blame them, that is, we do not think that they are proper objects of punishment. How we come by these ideas of deserving and not deserving punishment will appear, perhaps, in the sequel; but I think there is no doubt that this distinction lies at the bottom of the notions of right and wrong; that we call any conduct wrong, or employ, instead, some other term of dislike or disparagement, according as we think that the person ought, or ought not, to be punished for it; and we say it would be right to do so and so, or merely that it would be desirable or laudable, according as we would wish to see the person whom it concerns compelled, or only persuaded and exhorted, to act in that manner.[9]

This, therefore, being the characteristic difference which marks off, not justice, but morality in general from the remaining provinces of expediency and worthiness, the character is still to be sought which distinguishes justice from other branches of morality. Now it is known that ethical writers divide moral duties into two classes, denoted by the ill-chosen expressions, duties of perfect and of imperfect obligation; the latter being those in which, though the act is obligatory, the particular occasions of performing it are left to our choice, as in the case of charity or beneficence, which we are indeed bound to practice but not toward any definite person, nor at any prescribed time. In the more precise language of philosophic jurists, duties of perfect obligation are those duties in virtue of which a correlative *right* resides in some person or persons; duties of imperfect obligation are those moral obligations which do not give birth to any right. I think it will be found that this distinction exactly coincides with that which exists between justice and the other obligations of morality. In our survey of the various popular acceptations of justice, the term appeared generally to involve the idea of a personal right—a claim on the part of one or more individuals, like that which the law gives when it confers a proprietary or other legal right. Whether the injustice consists in depriving a person of a possession, or in breaking faith with him, or in treating him worse than he deserves, or worse than other people who have no greater claims—in each case the supposition implies two things: a wrong done, and some assignable person who is wronged. Injustice may also be done by treating a person better than others; but the wrong in this case is to his competitors, who are also assignable persons. It seems to me that this feature in the case—a right in some person, correlative to the moral obligation—constitutes the specific difference between justice and generosity of beneficence. Justice implies something which it is not only right to do, and wrong not to do, but which some individual person can claim from us as his moral right. No one has a moral right to our generosity or beneficence because we are not morally bound to practice those virtues toward any given individual. And it will be found with respect to this as to every correct definition that the instances which seem to

9. See this point enforced and illustrated by Professor Bain, in an admirable chapter (entitled "The Ethical Emotions, or the Moral Sense"), of the second of the two treatises composing his elaborate and profound work on the Mind. [Alexander Bain (1818–1903) was a Scottish philosopher and psychologist. The work referred to is his *The Emotions and the Will.*]

conflict with it are those which most confirm it. For if a moralist attempts, as some have done, to make out that mankind generally, though not any given individual, have a right to all the good we can do them, he at once, by that thesis, includes generosity and beneficence within the category of justice. He is obliged to say that our utmost exertions are *due* to our fellow creatures, thus assimilating them to a debt; or that nothing less can be a sufficient *return* for what society does for us, thus classing the case as one of gratitude; both of which are acknowledged cases of justice, and not of the virtue of beneficence; and whoever does not place the distinction between justice and morality in general, where we have now placed it, will be found to make no distinction between them at all, but to merge all morality in justice.

Having thus endeavored to determine the distinctive elements which enter into the composition of the idea of justice, we are ready to enter on the inquiry whether the feeling which accompanies the idea is attached to it by a special dispensation of nature, or whether it could have grown up, by any known laws, out of the idea itself; and, in particular, whether it can have originated in considerations of general expediency.

I conceive that the sentiment itself does not arise from anything which would commonly or correctly be termed an idea of expediency, but that, though the sentiment does not, whatever is moral in it does.

We have seen that the two essential ingredients in the sentiment of justice are the desire to punish a person who has done harm and the knowledge or belief that there is some definite individual or individuals to whom harm has been done.

Now it appears to me that the desire to punish a person who has done harm to some individual is a spontaneous outgrowth from two sentiments, both in the highest degree natural and which either are or resemble instincts: the impulse of self-defense and the feeling of sympathy.

It is natural to resent and to repel or retaliate any harm done or attempted against ourselves or against those with whom we sympathize. The origin of this sentiment it is not necessary here to discuss. Whether it be an instinct or a result of intelligence, it is, we know, common to all animal nature; for every animal tries to hurt those who have hurt, or who it thinks are about to hurt, itself or its young. Human beings, on this point, only differ from other animals in two particulars. First, in being capable of sympathizing, not solely with their offspring, or, like some of the more noble animals, with some superior animal who is kind to them, but with all human, and even with all sentient, beings; secondly, in having a more developed intelligence, which gives a wider range to the whole of their sentiments, whether self-regarding or sympathetic. By virtue of his superior intelligence, even apart from his superior range of sympathy, a human being is capable of apprehending a community of interest between himself and the human society of which he forms a part, such that any conduct which threatens the security of the society generally is threatening to his own, and calls forth his instinct (if instinct it be) of self-defense. The same superiority of intelligence, joined to the power of sympathizing with human beings generally, enables him to attach himself to the collective idea of his tribe, his country, or mankind in such a manner that any act hurtful to them raises his instinct of sympathy and urges him to resistance.

The sentiment of justice, in that one of its elements which consists of the desire to punish, is thus, I conceive, the natural feeling of retaliation or vengeance, rendered by intellect and sympathy applicable to those injuries, that is, to those hurts, which wound us through, or in common with, society at large. This sentiment, in itself, has nothing moral in it; what is moral is the exclusive subordination of it to the social sympathies, so as to wait on and obey their call. For the natural feeling would make us resent indiscriminately whatever anyone does that is disagreeable to us; but, when moralized by the social feeling, it only acts in the directions conformable to the general good: just persons resenting a hurt to society, though not otherwise a hurt to themselves, and not resenting a hurt to themselves, however painful, unless it be of the kind which society has a common interest with them in the repression of.

It is no objection against this doctrine to say that, when we feel our sentiment of justice outraged, we are not thinking of society at large or of any collective interest, but only of the individual case. It is common enough, certainly, though the reverse of commendable, to feel resentment merely because we have suffered pain; but a person whose resentment is really a moral feeling, that is, who considers whether an act is blamable before he allows himself to resent it—such a person, though he may not say expressly to himself that he is standing up for the interest of society, certainly does feel that he is asserting a rule which is for the benefit of others as well as for his own. If he is not feeling this, if he is regarding the act solely as it affects him individually, he is not consciously just; he is not concerning himself about the justice of his actions. This is admitted even by anti-utilitarian moralists. When Kant (as before remarked) propounds as the fundamental principle of morals, "So act that thy rule of conduct might be adopted as a law by all rational beings," he virtually acknowledges that the interest of mankind collectively, or at least of mankind indiscriminately, must be in the mind of the agent when conscientiously deciding on the morality of the act. Otherwise he uses words without a meaning; for that a rule even of utter selfishness could not *possibly* be adopted by all rational beings— that there is any insuperable obstacle in the nature of things to its adoption—cannot be even plausibly maintained. To give any meaning to Kant's principle, the sense put upon it must be that we ought to shape our conduct by a rule which all rational beings might adopt *with benefit to their collective interest.*

To recapitulate: the idea of justice supposes two things—a rule of conduct and a sentiment which sanctions the rule. The first must be supposed common to all mankind and intended for their good. The other (the sentiment) is a desire that punishment may be suffered by those who infringe the rule. There is involved, in addition, the conception of some definite person who suffers by the infringement, whose rights (to use the expression appropriated to the case) are violated by it. And the sentiment of justice appears to me to be the animal desire to repel or retaliate a hurt or damage to oneself or to those with whom one sympathizes, widened so as to include all persons, by the human capacity of enlarged sympathy and the human conception of intelligent self-interest. From the latter elements the feeling derives its morality; from the former, its peculiar impressiveness and energy of self-assertion.

I have, throughout, treated the idea of a *right* residing in the injured person and violated by the injury, not as a separate element in the composition of the idea and sentiment, but as one of the forms in which the other two elements clothe themselves. These elements are a hurt to some assignable person or persons, on the one hand, and a demand for punishment, on the other. An examination of our own minds, I think, will show that these two things include all that we mean when we speak of violation of a right. When we call anything a person's right, we mean that he has a valid claim on society to protect him in the possession of it, either by the force of law or by that of education and opinion. If he has what we consider a sufficient claim, on whatever account, to have something guaranteed to him by society, we say that he has a right to it. If we desire to prove that anything does not belong to him by right, we think this done as soon as it is admitted that society ought not to take measure for securing it to him, but should leave him to chance or to his own exertions. Thus a person is said to have a right to what he can earn in fair professional competition, because society ought not to allow any other person to hinder him from endeavoring to earn in that manner as much as he can. But he has not a right to three hundred a year, though he may happen to be earning it; because society is not called on to provide that he shall earn that sum. On the contrary, if he owns ten thousand pounds three-per-cent stock, he *has* a right to three hundred a year because society has come under an obligation to provide him with an income of that amount.

To have a right, then, is, I conceive, to have something which society ought to defend me in the possession of. If the objector goes on to ask why it ought, I can give him no other reason than general utility. If that expression does not seem to convey a sufficient feeling of the strength of the obligation, nor to account for the peculiar energy of the feeling, it is because there goes to the composition of the sentiment, not a rational only but also an animal element—the thirst for retaliation; and this thirst derives its intensity, as well as its moral justification, from the extraordinarily important and impressive kind of utility which is concerned. The interest involved is that of security, to everyone's feelings the most vital of all interests. All other earthly benefits are needed by one person, not needed by another; and many of them can, if necessary, be cheerfully foregone or replaced by something else; but security no human being can possibly do without; on it we depend for all our immunity from evil and for the whole value of all and every good, beyond the passing moment, since nothing but the gratification of the instant could be of any worth to us if we could be deprived of everything the next instant by whoever was momentarily stronger than ourselves. Now this most indispensable of all necessaries, after physical nutriment, cannot be had unless the machinery for providing it is kept unintermittedly in active play. Our notion, therefore, of the claim we have on our fellow creatures to join in making safe for us the very groundwork of our existence gathers feelings around it so much more intense than those concerned in any of the more common cases of utility that the difference in degree (as is often the case in psychology) becomes a real difference in kind. The claim assumes that character of absoluteness, that apparent infinity and incommensurability with all other considerations which constitute the distinction between the feeling of right and wrong and that of ordinary expediency and inexpediency. The feelings concerned are so powerful, and we count so positively on finding a responsive feeling in others (all being alike interested) that *ought* and *should* grow into *must*, and recognized indispensability becomes a moral necessity, analogous to physical, and often not inferior to it in binding force.

If the preceding analysis, or something resembling it, be not the correct account of the notion of justice—if justice be totally independent of utility, and be a standard *per se*, which the mind can recognize by simple introspection of itself—it is hard to understand why that internal oracle is so ambiguous, and why so many things appear either just or unjust, according to the light in which they are regarded.

We are continually informed that utility is an uncertain standard, which every different person interprets differently, and that there is no safety but in the immutable, ineffaceable, and unmistakable dictates of justice, which carry their evidence in themselves and are independent of the fluctuations of opinion. One would suppose from this that on questions of justice there could be no controversy; that, if we take that for our rule, its application to any given case could leave us in as little doubt as a mathematical demonstration. So far is this from being the fact that there is as much difference of opinion, and as much discussion, about what is just as about what is useful to society. Not only have different nations and individuals different notions of justice, but in the mind of one and the same individual, justice is not some one rule, principle, or maxim, but many which do not always coincide in their dictates, and, in choosing between which, he is guided either by some extraneous standard or by his own personal predilections.

For instance, there are some who say that it is unjust to punish anyone for the sake of example to others, that punishment is just only when intended for the good of the sufferer himself. Others maintain the extreme reverse, contending that to punish persons who have attained years of discretion, for their own benefit, is despotism and injustice, since, if the matter at issue is solely their own good, no one has a right to control their own judgment of it; but that they may justly be punished to prevent evil to others, this being the exercise of the legitimate right of self-defense. Mr. Owen,[10] again, affirms that it is unjust to punish at all, for the criminal did not make his own character; his education and the circumstances which surrounded him have made him a criminal, and for these he is not responsible. All these opinions are extremely plausible; and so long as the question is argued as one of justice simply, without going down to the principles which lie under justice and are the source of its authority, I am unable to see how any of these reasoners can be refuted. For in truth every one of the three builds upon rules of justice confessedly true. The first appeals to the acknowledged injustice of singling out an individual and making him a sacrifice, without his consent, for other people's benefit. The second relies on the acknowledged justice of self-defense and the admitted injustice of forcing one person to conform to another's notions of what constitutes his good. The Owenite invokes the admitted principle that it is unjust to punish anyone for what he cannot help. Each is triumphant so long as he is not compelled to take into consideration any other maxims of justice than the one he has selected; but as soon as their several maxims are brought face to face, each disputant seems to have exactly as much to say for himself as the others. No one of them can carry out his own notion of justice without trampling upon another equally binding. These are difficulties; they have always been felt to be such; and many devices have been invented to turn rather than to overcome them. As a refuge from the last of the three, men imagined what they called the freedom of the will—fancying that they could not justify punishing a man whose will is in a thoroughly hateful state unless it be supposed to have come into that state through no influence of anterior circumstances. To escape from the other difficulties, a favorite contrivance has been the fiction of a contract whereby at some unknown period all the members of society engaged to obey the laws and consented to be punished for any disobedience to them, thereby giving to their legislators the right, which it is assumed they would not otherwise

10. [Robert Owen (1771–1858) was a British social reformer who believed that individual character is determined by environment. He proposed the formation of self-sufficient cooperative communities, one of which was established in 1825 in New Harmony, Indiana, but lasted only a few years.]

have had, of punishing them, either for their own good or for that of society. This happy thought was considered to get rid of the whole difficulty and to legitimate the infliction of punishment, in virtue of another received maxim of justice, *volenti non fit injuria*—that is not unjust which is done with the consent of the person who is supposed to be hurt by it. I need hardly remark that, even if the consent were not a mere fiction, this maxim is not superior in authority to the others which it is brought in to supersede. It is, on the contrary, an instructive specimen of the loose and irregular manner in which supposed principles of justice grow up. This particular one evidently came into use as a help to the coarse exigencies of courts of law, which are sometimes obliged to be content with very uncertain presumptions, on account of the greater evils which would often arise from any attempt on their part to cut finer. But even courts of law are not able to adhere consistently to the maxim, for they allow voluntary engagements to be set aside on the ground of fraud, and sometimes on that of mere mistake or misinformation.

Again, when the legitimacy of inflicting punishment is admitted, how many conflicting conceptions of justice come to light in discussing the proper apportionment of punishments to offenses. No rule on the subject recommends itself so strongly to the primitive and spontaneous sentiment of justice as the *lex talionis,* an eye for an eye and a tooth for a tooth. Though this principle of the Jewish and of the Mohammedan law has been generally abandoned in Europe as a practical maxim, there is, I suspect, in most minds, a secret hankering after it; and when retribution accidentally falls on an offender in that precise shape, the general feeling of satisfaction evinced bears witness how natural is the sentiment to which this repayment in kind is acceptable. With many, the test of justice in penal infliction is that the punishment should be proportioned to the offense, meaning that it should be exactly measured by the moral guilt of the culprit (whatever be their standard for measuring moral guilt), the consideration what amount of punishment is necessary to deter from the offense having nothing to do with the question of justice, in their estimation; while there are others to whom that consideration is all in all, who maintain that it is not just, at least for man, to inflict on a fellow creature, whatever may be his offenses, any amount of suffering beyond the least that will suffice to prevent him from repeating, and others from imitating, his misconduct.

To take another example from a subject already once referred to. In co-operative industrial association, is it just or not that talent or skill should give a title to superior remuneration? On the negative side of the question it is argued that whoever does the best he can deserves equally well, and ought not in justice to be put in a position of inferiority for no fault of his own; that superior abilities have already advantages more than enough, in the admiration they excite, the personal influence they command, and the internal sources of satisfaction attending them, without adding to these a superior share of the world's goods; and that society is bound in justice rather to make compensation to the less favored for this unmerited inequality of advantages than to aggravate it. On the contrary side it is contended that society receives more from the more efficient laborer; that, his services being more useful, society owes him a larger return for them; that a greater share of the joint result is actually his work, and not to allow his claim to it is a kind of robbery; that, if he is only to receive as much as others, he can only be justly required to produce as much, and to give a smaller amount of time and exertion, proportioned to his superior efficiency. Who shall decide between these appeals to conflicting principles of justice? Justice has in this case two sides to it, which it is impossible to bring into harmony, and the two disputants have chosen opposite sides; the one looks to what it is just that the individual should receive, the other to what it is just that the community should give. Each, from his own point of view, is unanswerable; and any choice between them, on grounds of justice, must be perfectly arbitrary. Social utility alone can decide the preference.

How many, again, and how irreconcilable are the standards of justice to which reference is made in discussing the repartition of taxation. One opinion is that payment to the state should be in numerical proportion to pecuniary means. Others think that justice dictates what they term graduated taxation—taking a higher percentage from those who have more to spare. In point of natural justice a strong case might be made for disregarding means altogether, and taking the same absolute sum (whenever it could be got) from everyone; as the subscribers to a mess or to a club all pay the same sum for the same privileges, whether they can all equally afford it or not. Since the protection (it might be said) of law and government is afforded to and is equally required by all, there is no injustice in making all buy it at the same price. It is reckoned justice, not injustice, that a dealer should charge to all customers the same price for the same article, not a price varying according to their means of payment. This doctrine, as applied to taxation, finds no advocates because it conflicts so strongly with man's feelings of humanity and of social expediency; but the principle of justice which it invokes is as true and as binding as those which can be appealed to against it. Accordingly it exerts a tacit influence on the line of defense employed for other modes of assessing taxation. People feel obliged to argue that the state does more for the rich man than for the poor, as a justification for its taking more from them, though this is in reality not true, for the rich would be far better able to protect themselves, in the absence of law or government, than the poor, and indeed would probably be successful in converting the poor into their slaves. Others, again, so far defer to the same conception of justice as to maintain that all should pay an equal capitation tax for the protection of their persons (these being of equal value to all), and an unequal tax for the protection of their property, which is unequal. To this others reply that the all of one man is as valuable to him as the all of another. From these confusions there is no other mode of extrication than the utilitarian.

Is, then, the difference between the just and the expedient a merely imaginary distinction? Have mankind been under a delusion in thinking that justice is a more sacred thing than policy, and that the latter ought only to be listened to after the former has been satisfied? By no means. The exposition we have given of the nature and origin of the sentiment recognizes a real distinction; and no one of those who profess the most sublime contempt for the consequences of actions as an element in their morality attaches more importance to the distinction than I do. While I dispute the pretensions of any theory which sets up an imaginary standard of justice not grounded on utility, I account the justice which is grounded on utility to be the chief part, and incomparably the most sacred and binding part, of all morality. Justice is a name for certain classes of moral rules which concern the essentials of human well-being more nearly, and are therefore of more absolute obligation, than any other rules for the guidance of life; and the notion which we have found to be of the essence of the idea of justice—that of a right residing in an individual—implies and testifies to this more binding obligation.

The moral rules which forbid mankind to hurt one another (in which we must never forget to include a wrongful interference with each other's freedom) are more vital to human well-being than any maxims, however important, which only point out the best mode of managing some department of human affairs. They have also the peculiarity that they are the main element in determining the whole of the social feelings of mankind. It is their observance which alone preserves peace among human beings; if obedience to them were not the rule, and disobedience the exception, everyone would see in everyone else an enemy against whom he must be perpetually guarding himself. What is hardly less important, these are the precepts which mankind have the strongest and the most direct inducements for impressing upon one another. By merely giving to each other prudential instruction or exhortation, they may gain, or think they gain, nothing; in inculcating on each other the duty of positive beneficence, they have an unmistakable interest, but far less in degree; a person may possibly not need the benefits of others, but he always needs that they should not do him hurt. Thus the moralities which protect every individual from being harmed by others, either directly or by being hindered in his freedom of pursuing his own good, are at once those which he himself has most at heart and those which he has the strongest interest in publishing and enforcing by word and deed. It is by a person's observance of these that his fitness to exist as one of the fellowship of human beings is tested and decided; for on that depends his being a nuisance or not to those with whom he is in contact. Now it is these moralities primarily which compose the obligations of justice. The most marked cases of injustice, and those which give the tone to the feeling of repugnance which characterizes the sentiment, are acts of wrongful aggression or wrongful exercise of power over someone; the next are those which consist in wrongfully withholding from him something which is his due—in both cases inflicting on him a positive hurt, either in the form of direct suffering or of the privation of some good which he had reasonable ground, either of a physical or of a social kind, for counting upon.

The same powerful motives which command the observance of these primary moralities enjoin the punishment of those who violate them; and as the impulses of self-defense, of defense of others, and of vengeance are all called forth against such persons, retribution, or evil for evil, becomes closely connected with the sentiment of justice, and is universally included in the idea. Good for good is also one of the dictates of justice; and this, though its social utility is evident, and though it carries with it a natural human feeling, has not at first sight that obvious connection with hurt or injury which, existing in the most elementary cases of just and unjust, is the source of the characteristic intensity of the sentiment. But the connection, though less obvious, is not less real. He who accepts benefits and denies a return of them when needed inflicts a real hurt by disappointing one of the most natural and reasonable of expectations, and one which he must at least tacitly have encouraged, otherwise the benefits would seldom have been conferred. The important rank, among human evils and wrongs, of the disappointment of expectation is shown in the fact that it constitutes the principal criminality of two such highly immoral acts as a breach of friendship and a breach of promise. Few hurts which human beings can sustain are greater, and none wound more, than when that on which they habitually and with full assurance relied fails them in the hour of need; and few wrongs are greater than this mere withholding of good; none excite more resentment, either in the person suffering or in a sympathizing spectator. The principle, therefore, of giving to each what they deserve, that is, good for good as well as evil for evil, is not only included within the idea of justice as we have defined it, but is a proper object of that intensity of sentiment which places the just human estimation above the simply expedient.

Most of the maxims of justice current in the world, and commonly appealed to in its transactions, are simply instrumental to carrying into effect the principles of justice which we have now spoken of. That a person is only responsible for what he has done voluntarily, or could voluntarily have avoided, that it is unjust to condemn any person unheard; that the punishment ought to be proportioned to the offense, and the like, are maxims intended to prevent the just principle of evil for evil from being perverted to the infliction of evil without that justification. The greater part of these common maxims have come into use from the practice of courts of justice, which have been naturally led to a more complete recognition and elaboration than was likely to suggest itself to others, of the rules necessary to enable them to fulfill their double function—of inflicting punishment when due, and of awarding to each person his right.

That first of judicial virtues, impartiality, is an obligation of justice, partly for the reason last mentioned, as being a necessary condition of the fulfillment of other obligations of justice. But this is not the only source of the exalted rank, among human obligations, of those maxims of equality and impartiality, which, both in popular estimation and in that of the most enlightened, are included among the precepts of justice. In one point of view, they may be considered as corollaries from the principles already laid down. If it is a duty to do to each according to his deserts, returning good for good, as well as repressing evil by evil, it necessarily follows that we should treat all equally well (when no higher duty forbids) who have deserved equally well of *us*, and that society should treat all equally well who have deserved equally well of *it*, that is, who have deserved equally well absolutely. This is the highest abstract standard of social and distributive justice, toward which all institutions and the efforts of all virtuous citizens should be made in the utmost possible degree to converge. But this great moral duty rests upon a still deeper foundation, being a direct emanation from the first principle of morals, and not a mere logical corollary from secondary or derivative doctrines. It is involved in the very meaning of utility, or the greatest happiness principle. That principle is a mere form of words without rational signification unless one person's happiness, supposed equal in degree (with the proper allowance made for kind), is counted for exactly as much as another's. Those conditions being supplied, Bentham's dictum "everybody to count for one, nobody for more than one," might be written under the principle of utility as an explanatory commentary.[11] The equal claim of everybody to happiness, in the estimation of the moralist and of the legislator, involves an equal claim to all the

---

11. This implication, in the first principle of the utilitarian scheme, of perfect impartiality between persons is regarded by Mr. Herbert Spencer (in his *Social Statics*) as a disproof of the pretensions of utility to be a sufficient guide to right; since (he says) the principle of utility presupposes the anterior principle that everybody has an equal right to happiness. It may be more correctly described as supposing that equal amounts of happiness are equally desirable, whether felt by the same or different persons. This, however, is not a *pre*supposition, not a premise needful to support the principle of utility, but the very principle itself; for what is the principle of utility if it be not that "happiness" and "desirable" are synonymous terms? If there is any anterior principle implied, it can be no other than this, that the truths of arithmetic are applicable to the valuation of happiness, as of all other measurable quantities.

(Mr. Herbert Spencer, in a private communication on the subject of the preceding note, objects to being considered an opponent of utilitarianism and states that he regards happiness as the ultimate end of morality; but deems that end only partially attainable by empirical generalizations from the observed

means of happiness except in so far as the inevitable conditions of human life and the general interest in which that of every individual is included set limits to the maxim; and those limits ought to be strictly construed. As every other maxim of justice, so this is by no means applied or held applicable universally; on the contrary, as I have already remarked, it bends to every person's ideas of social expediency. But in whatever case it is deemed applicable at all, it is held to be the dictate of justice. All persons are deemed to have a *right* to equality of treatment, except when some recognized social expediency requires the reverse. And hence all social inequalities which have ceased to be considered expedient assume the character, not of simple inexpediency, but of injustice, and appear so tyrannical that people are apt to wonder how they ever could have been tolerated—forgetful that they themselves, perhaps, tolerate other inequalities under an equally mistaken notion of expediency, the correction of which would make that which they approve seem quite as monstrous as what they have at last learned to condemn. The entire history of social improvement has been a series of transitions by which one custom or institution after another, from being a supposed primary necessity of social existence, has passed into the rank of a universally stigmatized injustice and tyranny. So it has been with the distinctions of slaves and freemen, nobles and serfs, patricians and plebeians; and so it will be, and in part already is, with the aristocracies of color, race, and sex.

It appears from what has been said that justice is a name for certain moral requirements which, regarded collectively, stand higher in the scale of social utility, and are therefore of more paramount obligation, than any others, though particular cases may occur in which some other social duty is so important as to overrule any one of the general maxims of justice. Thus, to save a life, it may not only be allowable, but a duty, to steal or take by force the necessary food or medicine, or to kidnap and compel to officiate the only qualified medical practitioner. In such cases, as we do not call anything justice which is not a virtue, we usually say, not that justice must give way to some other moral principle, but that what is just in ordinary cases is, by reason of that other principle, not just in the particular case. By this useful accommodation of language, the character of indefeasibility attributed to justice is kept up, and we are saved from the necessity of maintaining that there can be laudable injustice.

The considerations which have not been adduced resolve, I conceive, the only real difficulty in the utilitarian theory of morals. It has always been evident that all cases of justice are also cases of expediency; the difference is in the peculiar senti-

---

results of conduct, and completely attainable only by deducing, from the laws of life and the conditions of existence, what kinds of action necessarily tend to produce happiness, and what kinds to produce unhappiness. With the exception of the word "necessarily," I have no dissent to express from this doctrine; and (omitting that word) I am not aware that any modern advocate of utilitarianism is of a different opinion. Bentham, certainly, to whom in the *Social Statics* Mr. Spencer particularly referred, is, least of all writers, chargeable with unwillingness to deduce the effect of actions on happiness from the laws of human nature and the universal conditions of human life. The common charge against him is of relying too exclusively upon such deductions and declining altogether to be bound by the generalizations from specific experience which Mr. Spencer thinks that utilitarians generally confine themselves to. My own opinion (and, as I collect, Mr. Spencer's) is that in ethics, as in all other branches of scientific study, the consilience of the results of both these processes, each corroborating and verifying the other, is requisite to give to any general proposition the kind and degree of evidence which constitutes scientific proof.)

ment which attaches to the former, as contradistinguished from the latter. If this characteristic sentiment has been sufficiently accounted for; if there is no necessity to assume for it any peculiarity of origin; if it is simply the natural feeling of resentment, moralized by being made co-extensive with the demands of social good; and if this feeling not only does but ought to exist in all the classes of cases to which the idea of justice corresponds—that idea no longer presents itself as a stumbling block to the utilitarian ethics. Justice remains the appropriate name for certain social utilities which are vastly more important, and therefore more absolute and imperative, than any others are as a class (though not more so than others may be in particular cases); and which, therefore, ought to be, as well as naturally are, guarded by a sentiment, not only different in degree, but also in kind; distinguished from the milder feeling which attaches to the mere idea of promoting human pleasure or convenience at once by the more definite nature of its commands and by the sterner character of its sanctions.

ON LIBERTY

The grand, leading principle, towards which every argument unfolded in these pages directly converges, is the absolute and essential importance of human development in its richest diversity.—Wilhelm von Humboldt: *Sphere and Duties of Government.*[1]

To the beloved and deplored memory of her who was the inspirer, and in part the author, of all that is best in my writings—the friend and wife whose exalted sense of truth and right was my strongest incitement, and whose approbation was my chief reward—I dedicate this volume. Like all that I have written for many years, it belongs as much to her as to me; but the work as it stands has had, in a very insufficient degree, the inestimable advantage of her revision; some of the most important portions having been reserved for a more careful re-examination, which they are now never destined to receive. Were I but capable of interpreting to the world one half the great thoughts and noble feelings which are buried in her grave, I should be the medium of a greater benefit to it, than is ever likely to arise from anything that I can write, unprompted and unassisted by her all but unrivaled wisdom.

CHAPTER I

INTRODUCTORY

The subject of this essay is not the so-called "liberty of the will," so unfortunately opposed to the misnamed doctrine of philosophical necessity; but civil, or social liberty: the nature and limits of the power which can be legitimately exercised by society over the individual. A question seldom stated, and hardly ever discussed in general terms, but which profoundly influences the practical controversies of the age by its latent presence, and is likely soon to make itself recognized as the vital question of the future. It is so far from being new that, in a certain sense, it has divided mankind almost from the remotest ages; but in the stage of progress into which the more civilized portions of the species have now entered, it presents itself under new conditions and requires a different and more fundamental treatment.

The struggle between liberty and authority is the most conspicuous feature in the portions of history with which we are earliest familiar, particularly in that of Greece, Rome, and England. But in old times this contest was between subjects, or some classes of subjects, and the government. By liberty was meant protection against the tyranny of the political rulers. The rulers were conceived (except in

---

1. [Wilhelm Freiherr von Humboldt (1767–1835), German statesman and philologist, was a liberal reformer and a founder of the University of Berlin. —S.M.C.]

some of the popular governments of Greece) as in a necessarily antagonistic position to the people whom they ruled. They consisted of a governing One, or a governing tribe or caste, who derived their authority from inheritance or conquest, who, at all events, did not hold it at the pleasure of the governed, and whose supremacy men did not venture, perhaps did not desire, to contest, whatever precautions might be taken against its oppressive exercise. Their power was regarded as necessary, but also as highly dangerous; as a weapon which they would attempt to use against their subjects, no less than against external enemies. To prevent the weaker members of the community from being preyed upon by innumerable vultures, it was needful that there should be an animal of prey stronger than the rest, commissioned to keep them down. But as the king of the vultures would be no less bent upon preying on the flock than any of the minor harpies, it was indispensable to be in a perpetual attitude of defense against his beak and claws. The aim, therefore, of patriots was to set limits to the power which the ruler should be suffered to exercise over the community; and this limitation was what they meant by liberty. It was attempted in two ways. First, by obtaining a recognition of certain immunities, called political liberties or rights, which it was to be regarded as a breach of duty in the ruler to infringe, and which if he did infringe, specific resistance or general rebellion was held to be justifiable. A second, and generally a later, expedient was the establishment of constitutional checks by which the consent of the community, or of a body of some sort, supposed to represent its interests, was made a necessary condition to some of the more important acts of the governing power. To the first of these modes of limitation, the ruling power, in most European countries, was compelled, more or less, to submit. It was not so with the second; and, to attain this, or, when already in some degree possessed, to attain it more completely, became everywhere the principal object of the lovers of liberty. And so long as mankind were content to combat one enemy by another, and to be ruled by a master on condition of being guaranteed more or less efficaciously against his tyranny, they did not carry their aspirations beyond this point.

A time, however, came, in the progress of human affairs, when men ceased to think it a necessity of nature that their governors should be an independent power opposed in interest to themselves. It appeared to them much better that the various magistrates of the state should be their tenants or delegates, revocable at their pleasure. In that way alone, it seemed, could they have complete security that the powers of government would never be abused to their disadvantage. By degrees this new demand for elective and temporary rulers became the prominent object of the exertions of the popular party wherever any such party existed, and superseded, to a considerable extent, the previous efforts to limit the power of rulers. As the struggle proceeded for making the ruling power emanate from the periodical choice of the ruled, some persons began to think that too much importance had been attached to the limitation of the power itself. *That* (it might seem) was a resource against rulers whose interests were habitually opposed to those of the people. What was now wanted was that the rulers should be identified with the people, that their interest and will should be the interest and will of the nation. The nation did not need to be protected against its own will There was no fear of its tyrannizing over itself. Let the rulers be effectually responsible to it, promptly removable by it, and it could afford to trust them with power of which it could itself dictate the use to be made. Their power was but the nation's own power, concentrated and in a form convenient for exercise. This mode of thought, or rather perhaps of feeling, was common among the last generation of European liberalism, in the Continental section of which it still apparently predominates. Those who admit any limit to what a government may do, except in the case of such governments as they think ought not to exist, stand out as brilliant exceptions among the political thinkers of the Continent. A similar tone of sentiment might by this time have been prevalent in our country if the circumstances which for a time encouraged it had continued unaltered.

But, in political and philosophical theories as well as in persons, success discloses faults and infirmities which failure might have concealed from observation. The notion that the people have no need to limit their power over themselves might seem axiomatic, when popular government was a thing only dreamed about, or read of as having existed at some distant period of the past. Neither was that notion necessarily disturbed by such temporary aberrations as those of the French Revolution, the worst of which were the work of a usurping few, and which, in any case, belonged, not to the permanent working of popular institutions, but to a sudden and convulsive outbreak against monarchical and aristocratic despotism. In time, however, a democratic republic came to occupy a large portion of the earth's surface and made itself felt as one of the most powerful members of the community of nations;[2] and elective and responsible government became subject to the observations and criticisms which wait upon a great existing fact. It was now perceived that such phrases as "self-government," and "the power of the people over themselves," do not express the true state of the case. The "people" who exercise the power are not always the same people with those over whom it is exercised; and the "self-government" spoken of is not the government of each by himself, but of each by all the rest. The will of the people, moreover, practically means the will of the most numerous or the most active *part* of the people—the majority, or those who succeed in making themselves accepted as the majority; the people, consequently, *may* desire to oppress a part of their number, and precautions are as much needed against this as against any other abuse of power. The limitation, therefore, of the power of government over individuals loses none of its importance when the holders of power are regularly accountable to the community, that is, to the strongest party therein. This view of things, recommending itself equally to the intelligence of thinkers and to the inclination of those important classes in European society to whose real or supposed interests democracy is adverse, has had no difficulty in establishing itself; and in political speculations "the tyranny of the majority" is now generally included among the evils against which society requires to be on its guard.

Like other tyrannies, the tyranny of the majority was at first, and is still vulgarly, held in dread, chiefly as operating through the acts of the public authorities. But reflecting persons perceived that when society is itself the tyrant—society collectively over the separate individuals who compose it—its means of tyrannizing are not restricted to the acts which it may do by the hands of its political functionaries. Society can and does execute its own mandates; and if it issues wrong mandates instead of right, or any mandates at all in things with which it ought not to meddle, it practices a social tyranny more formidable than many kinds of political oppression, since, though not usually upheld by such extreme penalties, it leaves fewer means of escape, penetrating much more deeply into the details of life, and enslaving the soul itself. Protection, therefore, against the tyranny of the magistrate is not enough;

2. [The reference is to the United States.]

there needs protection also against the tyranny of the prevailing opinion and feeling, against the tendency of society to impose, by other means than civil penalties, its own ideas and practices as rules of conduct on those who dissent from them; to fetter the development and, if possible, prevent the formation of any individuality not in harmony with its ways, and compel all characters to fashion themselves upon the model of its own. There is a limit to the legitimate interference of collective opinion with individual independence; and to find that limit, and maintain it against encroachment, is as indispensable to a good condition of human affairs as protection against political despotism.

But though this proposition is not likely to be contested in general terms, the practical question where to place the limit—how to make the fitting adjustment between individual independence and social control—is a subject on which nearly everything remains to be done. All that makes existence valuable to anyone depends on the enforcement of restraints upon the actions of other people. Some rules of conduct, therefore, must be imposed—by law in the first place, and by opinion on many things which are not fit subjects for the operation of law. What these rules should be is the principal question in human affairs; but if we except a few of the most obvious cases, it is one of those which least progress has been made in resolving. No two ages, and scarcely any two countries, have decided it alike; and the decision of one age or country is a wonder to another. Yet the people of any given age and country no more suspect any difficulty in it than if it were a subject on which mankind had always been agreed. The rules which obtain among themselves appear to them self-evident and self-justifying. This all but universal illusion is one of the examples of the magical influence of custom, which is not only, as the proverb says, a second nature but is continually mistaken for the first. The effect of custom, in preventing any misgiving respecting the rules of conduct which mankind impose on one another, is all the more complete because the subject is one on which it is not generally considered necessary that reasons should be given, either by one person to others or by each to himself. People are accustomed to believe, and have been encouraged in the belief by some who aspire to the character of philosophers, that their feelings on subjects of this nature are better than reasons and render reasons unnecessary. The practical principle which guides them to their opinions on the regulation of human conduct is the feeling in each person's mind that everybody should be required to act as he, and those with whom he sympathizes, would like them to act. No one, indeed, acknowledges to himself that his standard of judgment is his own liking; but an opinion on a point of conduct, not supported by reasons, can only count as one person's preference; and if the reasons, when given, are a mere appeal to a similar preference felt by other people, it is still only many people's liking instead of one. To an ordinary man, however, his own preference, thus supported, is not only a perfectly satisfactory reason but the only one he generally has for any of his notions of morality, taste, or propriety, which are not expressly written in his religious creed, and his chief guide in the interpretation even of that. Men's opinions, accordingly, on what is laudable or blamable are affected by all the multifarious causes which influence their wishes in regard to the conduct of others, and which are as numerous as those which determine their wishes on any other subject. Sometimes their reason; at other times their prejudices or superstitions; often their social affections, not seldom their antisocial ones, their envy or jealousy, their arrogance or contemptuousness; but most commonly their desires or fears for themselves—their legitimate or illegitimate self-interest. Wherever there is an ascendant class, a large portion of the morality of the country emanates from its class interests and its feelings of class superiority. The morality between Spartans and Helots,[3] between planters and Negroes, between princes and subjects, between nobles and roturiers,[4] between men and women has been for the most part the creation of these class interests and feelings; and the sentiments thus generated react in turn upon the moral feelings of the members of the ascendant class, in their relations among themselves. Where, on the other hand, a class, formerly ascendant, has lost its ascendancy, or where its ascendancy is unpopular, the prevailing moral sentiments frequently bear the impress of an impatient dislike of superiority. Another grand determining principle of the rules of conduct, both in act and forbearance, which have been enforced by law or opinion, has been the servility of mankind toward the supposed preferences or aversions of their temporal masters or of their gods. This servility, though essentially selfish, is not hypocrisy; it gives rise to perfectly genuine sentiments of abhorrence; it made men burn magicians and heretics. Among so many baser influences, the general and obvious interests of society have, of course, had a share, and a large one, in the direction of the moral sentiments; less, however, as a matter of reason, and on their own account, than as a consequence of the sympathies and antipathies which grew out of them; and sympathies and antipathies which had little or nothing to do with the interests of society have made themselves felt in the establishment of moralities with quite as great force.

The likings and dislikings of society, or of some powerful portion of it, are thus the main thing which has practically determined the rules laid down for general observance, under the penalties of law or opinion. And in general, those who have been in advance of society in thought and feeling have left this condition of things unassailed in principle, however they may have come into conflict with it in some of its details. They have occupied themselves rather in inquiring what things society ought to like or dislike than in questioning whether its likings or dislikings should be a law to individuals. They preferred endeavoring to alter the feelings of mankind on the particular points on which they were themselves heretical rather than make common cause in defense of freedom with heretics generally. The only case in which the higher ground has been taken on principle and maintained with consistency, by any but an individual here and there, is that of religious belief: a case instructive in many ways, and not least so as forming a most striking instance of the fallibility of what is called the moral sense; for the *odium theologicum*,[5] in a sincere bigot, is one of the most unequivocal cases of moral feeling. Those who first broke the yoke of what called itself the Universal Church were in general as little willing to permit difference of religious opinion as that church itself. But when the heat of the conflict was over, without giving a complete victory to any party, and each church or sect was reduced to limit its hopes to retaining possession of the ground it already occupied, minorities, seeing that they had no chance of becoming majorities, were under the necessity of pleading to those whom they could not convert for permission to differ. It is accordingly on this battlefield, almost solely, that the rights of the individual against society have been asserted on broad grounds of principle, and the claim of society to exercise authority over dissentients openly controverted. The

---

3. [Helots were Spartan state serfs alloted to landowners.]

4. [Roturiers are plebeians, persons of low rank.]

5. [Hatred engendered by bitter theological controversy.]

great writers to whom the world owes what religious liberty it possesses have mostly
asserted freedom of conscience as an indefeasible right, and denied absolutely that a
human being is accountable to others for his religious belief. Yet so natural to
mankind is intolerance in whatever they really care about that religious freedom
has hardly anywhere been practically realized, except where religious indifference,
which dislikes to have its peace disturbed by theological quarrels, has added its
weight to the scale. In the minds of almost all religious persons, even in the most tolerant countries, the duty of toleration is admitted with tacit reserves. One person
will bear with dissent in matters of church government, but not of dogma; another
can tolerate everybody, short of a Papist or a Unitarian; another, everyone who believes in revealed religion; a few extend their charity a little further, but stop at the
belief in a God and in a future state. Wherever the sentiment of the majority is still
genuine and intense, it is found to have abated little of its claim to be obeyed.

In England, from the peculiar circumstances of our political history, though the
yoke of opinion is perhaps heavier, that of law is lighter than in most other countries
of Europe; and there is considerable jealousy of direct interference by the legislative
or the executive power with private conduct, not so much from any just regard for
the independence of the individual as from the still subsisting habit of looking on
the government as representing an opposite interest to the public. The majority
have not yet learned to feel the power of the government their power, or its opinions
their opinions. When they do so, individual liberty will probably be as much exposed to invasion from the government as it already is from public opinion. But, as
yet, there is a considerable amount of feeling ready to be called forth against any attempt of the law to control individuals in things in which they have not hitherto
been accustomed to be controlled by it; and this with very little discrimination as to
whether the matter is, or is not, within the legitimate sphere of legal control; insomuch that the feeling, highly salutary on the whole, is perhaps quite as often
misplaced as well grounded in the particular instances of its application. There is, in
fact, no recognized principle by which the propriety or impropriety of government
interference is customarily tested. People decide according to their personal preferences. Some, whenever they see any good to be done, or evil to be remedied, would
willingly instigate the government to undertake the business, while others prefer to
bear almost any amount of social evil rather than add one to the departments of
human interests amenable to governmental control. And men range themselves on
one or the other side in any particular case, according to this general direction of
their sentiments, or according to the degree of interest which they feel in the particular thing which it is proposed that the government should do, or according to the
belief they entertain that the government would, or would not, do it in the manner
they prefer; but very rarely on account of any opinion to which they consistently
adhere, as to what things are fit to be done by a government. And it seems to me
that in consequence of this absence of rule or principle, one side is at present as
often wrong as the other; the interference of government is, with about equal frequency, improperly invoked and improperly condemned.

The object of this essay is to assert one very simple principle, as entitled to govern
absolutely the dealings of society with the individual in the way of compulsion and
control, whether the means used be physical force in the form of legal penalties or
the moral coercion of public opinion. That principle is that the sole end for which
mankind are warranted, individually or collectively, in interfering with the liberty
of action of any of their number is self-protection. That the only purpose for which

power can be rightfully exercised over any member of a civilized community, against his will, is to prevent harm to others. His own good, either physical or moral, is not a sufficient warrant. He cannot rightfully be compelled to do or forbear because it will be better for him to do so, because it will make him happier, because, in the opinions of others, to do so would be wise or even right. These are good reasons for remonstrating with him, or reasoning with him, or persuading him, or entreating him, but not for compelling him or visiting him with any evil in case he do otherwise. To justify that, the conduct from which it is desired to deter him must be calculated to produce evil to someone else. The only part of the conduct of anyone for which he is amenable to society is that which concerns others. In the part which merely concerns himself, his independence is, of right, absolute. Over himself, over his own body and mind, the individual is sovereign.

It is, perhaps, hardly necessary to say that this doctrine is meant to apply only to human beings in the maturity of their faculties. We are not speaking of children or of young persons below the age which the law may fix as that of manhood or womanhood. Those who are still in a state to require being taken care of by others must be protected against their own actions as well as against external injury. For the same reason we may leave out of consideration those backward states of society in which the race itself may be considered as in its nonage. The early difficulties in the way of spontaneous progress are so great that there is seldom any choice of means for overcoming them; and a ruler full of the spirit of improvement is warranted in the use of any expedients that will attain an end perhaps otherwise unattainable. Despotism is a legitimate mode of government in dealing with barbarians, provided the end be their improvement and the means justified by actually effecting that end. Liberty, as a principle, has no application to any state of things anterior to the time when mankind have become capable of being improved by free and equal discussion. Until then, there is nothing for them but implicit obedience to an Akbar[6] or a Charlemagne, if they are so fortunate as to find one. But as soon as mankind have attained the capacity of being guided to their own improvement by conviction or persuasion (a period long since reached in all nations with whom we need here concern ourselves), compulsion, either in the direct form or in that of pains and penalties for noncompliance, is no longer admissible as a means to their own good, and justifiable only for the security of others.

It is proper to state that I forego any advantage which could be derived to my argument from the idea of abstract right as a thing independent of utility. I regard utility as the ultimate appeal on all ethical questions; but it must be utility in the largest sense, grounded on the permanent interests of man as a progressive being. Those interests, I contend, authorize the subjection of individual spontaneity to external control only in respect to those actions of each which concern the interest of other people. If anyone does an act hurtful to others, there is a *prima facie* case for punishing him by law or, where legal penalties are not safely applicable, by general disapprobation. There are also many positive acts for the benefit of others which he may rightfully be compelled to perform, such as to give evidence in a court of justice, to bear his fair share in the common defense or in any other joint work necessary to the interest of the society of which he enjoys the protection, and to perform certain acts of individual beneficence, such as saving a fellow creature's life or interposing to protect the defenseless against ill usage—things which whenever it is

---

6. [Akbar (1542–1605) was a Mogol emperor of India.]

obviously a man's duty to do he may rightfully be made responsible to society for not doing. A person may cause evil to others not only by his actions but by his inaction, and in either case he is justly accountable to them for the injury. The latter case, it is true, requires a much more cautious exercise of compulsion than the former. To make anyone answerable for doing evil to others is the rule; to make him answerable for not preventing evil is, comparatively speaking, the exception. Yet there are many cases clear enough and grave enough to justify that exception. In all things which regard the external relations of the individual, he is *de jure* amenable to those whose interests are concerned, and, if need be, to society as their protector. There are often good reasons for not holding him to the responsibility; but these reasons must arise from the special expediencies of the case: either because it is a kind of case in which he is on the whole likely to act better when left to his own discretion than when controlled in any way in which society have it in their power to control him; or because the attempt to exercise control would produce other evils, greater than those which it would prevent. When such reasons as these preclude the enforcement of responsibility, the conscience of the agent himself should step into the vacant judgment seat and protect those interests of others which have no external protection; judging himself all the more rigidly, because the case does not admit of his being made accountable to the judgment of his fellow creatures.

But there is a sphere of action in which society, as distinguished from the individual, has, if any, only an indirect interest: comprehending all that portion of a person's life and conduct which affects only himself or, if it also affects others, only with their free, voluntary, and undeceived consent and participation. When I say only himself, I mean directly and in the first instance; for whatever affects himself may affect others through himself: and the objection which may be grounded on this contingency will receive consideration in the sequel. This, then, is the appropriate region of human liberty. It comprises, first, the inward domain of consciousness, demanding liberty of conscience in the most comprehensive sense, liberty of thought and feeling, absolute freedom of opinion and sentiment on all subjects, practical or speculative, scientific, moral, or theological. The liberty of expressing and publishing opinions may seem to fall under a different principle, since it belongs to that part of the conduct of an individual which concerns other people, but, being almost of as much importance as the liberty of thought itself and resting in great part on the same reasons, is practically inseparable from it. Secondly, the principle requires liberty of tastes and pursuits, of framing the plan of our life to suit our own character, of doing as we like, subject to such consequences as may follow, without impediment from our fellow creatures, so long as what we do does not harm them, even though they should think our conduct foolish, perverse, or wrong. Thirdly, from this liberty of each individual follows the liberty, within the same limits, of combination among individuals; freedom to unite for any purpose not involving harm to others: the persons combining being supposed to be of full age and not forced or deceived.

No society in which these liberties are not, on the whole, respected is free, whatever may be its form of government; and none is completely free in which they do not exist absolute and unqualified. The only freedom which deserves the name is that of pursuing our own good in our own way, so long as we do not attempt to deprive others of theirs or impede their efforts to obtain it. Each is the proper guardian of his own health, whether bodily *or* mental and spiritual. Mankind are greater gainers by suffering each other to live as seems good to themselves than by compelling each to live as seems good to the rest.

Though this doctrine is anything but new and, to some persons, may have the air of a truism, there is no doctrine which stands more directly opposed to the general tendency of existing opinion and practice. Society has expended fully as much effort in the attempt (according to its lights) to compel people to conform to its notions of personal as of social excellence. The ancient commonwealths thought themselves entitled to practice, and the ancient philosophers countenanced, the regulation of every part of private conduct by public authority, on the ground that the State had a deep interest in the whole bodily and mental discipline of every one of its citizens—a mode of thinking which may have been admissible in small republics surrounded by powerful enemies, in constant peril of being subverted by foreign attack or internal commotion, and to which even a short interval of relaxed energy and self-command might so easily be fatal that they could not afford to wait for the salutary permanent effects of freedom. In the modern world, the greater size of political communities and, above all, the separation between spiritual and temporal authority (which placed the direction of men's consciences in other hands than those which controlled their worldly affairs) prevented so great an interference by law in the details of private life; but the engines of moral repression have been wielded more strenuously against divergence from the reigning opinion in self-regarding than even in social matters; religion, the most powerful of the elements which have entered into the formation of moral feeling, having almost always been governed either by the ambition of a hierarchy seeking control over every department of human conduct, or by the spirit of Puritanism. And some of those modern reformers who have placed themselves in strongest opposition to the religions of the past have been noway behind either churches or sects in their assertion of the right of spiritual domination: M. Comte,[7] in particular, whose social system, as unfolded in his *Système de Politique Positive,* aims at establishing (though by moral more than by legal appliances) a despotism of society over the individual surpassing anything contemplated in the political ideal of the most rigid disciplinarian among the ancient philosophers.

Apart from the peculiar tenets of individual thinkers, there is also in the world at large an increasing inclination to stretch unduly the powers of society over the individual both by the force of opinion and even by that of legislation; and as the tendency of all the changes taking place in the world is to strengthen society and diminish the power of the individual, this encroachment is not one of the evils which tend spontaneously to disappear, but, on the contrary, to grow more and more formidable. The disposition of mankind, whether as rulers or as fellow citizens, to impose their own opinions and inclinations as a rule of conduct on others is so energetically supported by some of the best and by some of the worst feelings incident to human nature that it is hardly ever kept under restraint by anything but want of power; and as the power is not declining, but growing, unless a strong barrier of moral conviction can be raised against the mischief, we must expect, in the present circumstances of the world, to see it increase.

It will be convenient for the argument if, instead of at once entering upon the general thesis, we confine ourselves in the first instance to a single branch of it on which the principle here stated is, if not fully, yet to a certain point, recognized by

7. [Regarding Comte, see Mill's *Utilitarianism*, n. 7. The work referred to is the *System of Positive Polity*.]

the current opinions. This one branch is the Liberty of Thought, from which it is impossible to separate the cognate liberty of speaking and of writing. Although these liberties, to some considerable amount, form part of the political morality of all countries which profess religious toleration and free institutions, the grounds, both philosophical and practical, on which they rest are perhaps not so familiar to the general mind, nor so thoroughly appreciated by many, even of the leaders of opinion, as might have been expected. Those grounds, when rightly understood, are of much wider application than to only one division of the subject, and a thorough consideration of this part of the question will be found the best introduction to the remainder. Those to whom nothing which I am about to say will be new may therefore, I hope, excuse me if on a subject which for now three centuries has been so often discussed I venture on one discussion more.

CHAPTER II

OF THE LIBERTY OF THOUGHT AND DISCUSSION

The time, it is to be hoped, is gone by when any defense would be necessary of the "liberty of the press" as one of the securities against corrupt or tyrannical government. No argument, we may suppose, can now be needed against permitting a legislature or an executive, not identified in interest with the people, to prescribe opinions to them and determine what doctrines or what arguments they shall be allowed to hear. This aspect of the question, besides, has been so often and so triumphantly enforced by preceding writers that it needs not be specially insisted on in this place. Though the law of England, on the subject of the press, is as servile to this day as it was in the time of the Tudors, there is little danger of its being actually put in force against political discussion except during some temporary panic when fear of insurrection drives ministers and judges from their propriety;[8] and, speaking generally,

---

8. These words had scarcely been written when, as if to give them an emphatic contradition, occurred the Government Press Prosecutions of 1858. That ill-judged interference with the liberty of public discussion has not, however, induced me to alter a single word in the text, nor has it at all weakened my conviction that, moments of panic excepted, the era of pains and penalties for political discussion has, in our own country, passed away. For, in the first place, the prosecutions were not persisted in; and, in the second, they were never, properly speaking, political prosecutions. The offense charged was not that of criticizing institutions or the acts or persons of rulers, but of circulating what was deemed as immoral doctrine, the lawfulness of tyrannicide.

If the arguments of the present chapter are of any validity, there ought to exist the fullest liberty of professing and discussing, as a matter of ethical conviction, any doctrine, however immoral it may be considered. It would, therefore, be irrelevant and out of place to examine here whether the doctrine of tyrannicide deserves that title. I shall content myself with saying that the subject has been at all times one of the open questions of morals; that the act of a private citizen in striking down a criminal who, by raising himself above the law, has placed himself beyond the reach of legal punishment or control has been accounted by whole nations, and by some of the best and wisest of men, not a crime but an act of exalted virtue; and that, right or wrong, it is not of the nature of assassination, but of civil war. As such, I hold that the instigation to it, in a specific case, may be a proper subject of punishment, but only if an overt act has followed, and at least a probable connection can be established between the act and the instigation. Even then it is not a foreign government but the very government assailed which alone, in the exercise of self-defense, can legitimately punish attacks directed against its own existence.

it is not, in constitutional countries, to be apprehended that the government, whether completely responsible to the people or not, will often attempt to control the expression of opinion, except when in doing so it makes itself the organ of the general intolerance of the public. Let us suppose, therefore, that the government is entirely at one with the people, and never thinks of exerting any power of coercion unless in agreement with what it conceives to be their voice. But I deny the right of the people to exercise such coercion, either by themselves or by their government. The power itself is illegitimate. The best government has no more title to it than the worst. It is as noxious, or more noxious, when exerted in accordance with public opinion than when in opposition to it. If all mankind minus one were of one opinion, mankind would be no more justified in silencing that one person than he, if he had the power, would be justified in silencing mankind. Were an opinion a personal possession of no value except to the owner, if to be obstructed in the enjoyment of it were simply a private injury, it would make some difference whether the injury was inflicted only on a few persons or on many. But the peculiar evil of silencing the expression of an opinion is that it is robbing the human race, posterity as well as the existing generation—those who dissent from the opinion, still more than those who hold it. If the opinion is right, they are deprived of the opportunity of exchanging error for truth; if wrong, they lose, what is almost as great a benefit, the clearer perception and livelier impression of truth produced by its collision with error.

It is necessary to consider separately these two hypotheses, each of which has a distinct branch of the argument corresponding to it. We can never be sure that the opinion we are endeavoring to stifle is a false opinion; and if we were sure, stifling it would be an evil still.

First, the opinion which it is attempted to suppress by authority may possibly be true. Those who desire to suppress it, of course, deny its truth; but they are not infallible. They have no authority to decide the question for all mankind and exclude every other person from the means of judging. To refuse a hearing to an opinion because they are sure that it is false is to assume that *their* certainty is the same thing as *absolute* certainty. All silencing of discussion is an assumption of infallibility. Its condemnation may be allowed to rest on this common argument, not the worse for being common.

Unfortunately for the good sense of mankind, the fact of their fallibility is far from carrying the weight in their practical judgment which is always allowed to it in theory; for while everyone well knows himself to be fallible, few think it necessary to take any precautions against their own fallibility, or admit the supposition that any opinion of which they feel very certain may be one of the examples of the error to which they acknowledge themselves to be liable. Absolute princes, or others who are accustomed to unlimited deference, usually feel this complete confidence in their own opinions on nearly all subjects. People more happily situated, who sometimes hear their opinions disputed and are not wholly unused to be set right when they are wrong, place the same unbounded reliance only on such of their opinions as are shared by all who surround them, or to whom they habitually defer; for in proportion to a man's want of confidence in his own solitary judgment does he usually repose, with implicit trust, on the infallibility of "the world" in general. And the world, to each individual, means the part of it with which he comes in contact: his party, his sect, his church, his class of society; the man may be called, by comparison, almost liberal and large-minded to whom it means anything so comprehensive as his own country or his own age. Nor is his faith in this collective authority at all shaken by his being aware that other ages, countries, sects, churches, classes, and parties have thought, and even now think, the exact reverse. He devolves upon his own world the responsibility of being in the right against the dissentient worlds of other people; and it never troubles him that mere accident has decided which of these numerous worlds is the object of his reliance, and that the same causes which make him a churchman in London would have made him a Buddhist or a Confucian in Peking. Yet it is as evident in itself, as any amount of argument can make it, that ages are no more infallible than individuals—every age having held many opinions which subsequent ages have deemed not only false but absurd; and it is as certain that many opinions, now general, will be rejected by future ages, as it is that many, once general, are rejected by the present.

The objection likely to be made to this argument would probably take some such form as the following. There is no greater assumption of infallibility in forbidding the propagation of error than in any other thing which is done by public authority on its own judgment and responsibility. Judgment is given to men that they may use it. Because it may be used erroneously, are men to be told that they ought not to use it at all? To prohibit what they think pernicious is not claiming exemption from error, but fulfilling the duty incumbent on them, although fallible, of acting on their conscientious conviction. If we were never to act on our opinions, because those opinions may be wrong, we should leave all our interests uncared for, and all our duties unperformed. An objection which applies to all conduct can be no valid objection to any conduct in particular. It is the duty of governments, and of individuals, to form the truest opinions they can; to form them carefully, and never impose them upon others unless they are quite sure of being right. But when they are sure (such reasoners may say), it is not conscientiousness but cowardice to shrink from acting on their opinions and allow doctrines which they honestly think dangerous to the welfare of mankind, either in this life or in another, to be scattered abroad without restraint, because other people, in less enlightened times, have persecuted opinions now believed to be true. Let us take care, it may be said, not to make the same mistake; but governments and nations have made mistakes in other things which are not denied to be fit subjects for the exercise of authority: they have laid on bad taxes, made unjust wars. Ought we therefore to lay on no taxes and, under whatever provocation, make no wars? Men and governments must act to the best of their ability. There is no such thing as absolute certainty, but there is assurance sufficient for the purposes of human life. We may, and must, assume our opinion to be true for the guidance of our own conduct; and it is assuming no more when we forbid bad men to pervert society by the propagation of opinions which we regard as false and pernicious.

I answer, that it is assuming very much more. There is the greatest difference between presuming an opinion to be true because, with every opportunity for contesting it, it has not been refuted, and assuming its truth for the purpose of not permitting its refutation. Complete liberty of contradicting and disproving our opinion is the very condition which justifies us in assuming its truth for purposes of action; and on no other terms can a being with human faculties have any rational assurance of being right.

When we consider either the history of opinion or the ordinary conduct of human life, to what is it to be ascribed that the one and the other are no worse than they are? Not certainly to the inherent force of the human understanding, for on any matter not self-evident there are ninety-nine persons totally incapable of judging of

it for one who is capable; and the capacity of the hundredth person is only comparative, for the majority of the eminent men of every past generation held many opinions now known to be erroneous, and did or approved numerous things which no
one will now justify. Why is it, then, that there is on the whole a preponderance
among mankind of rational opinions and rational conduct? If there really is this
preponderance—which there must be unless human affairs are, and have always
been, in an almost desperate state—it is owing to a quality of the human mind, the
source of everything respectable in man either as an intellectual or as a moral being,
namely, that his errors are corrigible. He is capable of rectifying his mistakes by discussion and experience. Not by experience alone. There must be discussion to show
how experience is to be interpreted. Wrong opinions and practices gradually yield
to fact and argument; but facts and arguments, to produce any effect on the mind,
must be brought before it. Very few facts are able to tell their own story, without
comments to bring out their meaning. The whole strength and value, then, of
human judgment depending on the one property, that it can be set right when it is
wrong, reliance can be placed on it only when the means of setting it right are kept
constantly at hand. In the case of any person whose judgment is really deserving of
confidence, how has it become so? Because he has kept his mind open to criticism of
his opinions and conduct. Because it has been his practice to listen to all that could
be said against him; to profit by as much of it as was just, and to expound to himself,
and upon occasion to others, the fallacy of what was fallacious. Because he has felt
that the only way in which a human being can make some approach to knowing the
whole of a subject is by hearing what can be said about it by persons of every variety
of opinion, and studying all modes in which it can be looked at by every character of
mind. No wise man ever acquired his wisdom in any mode but this; nor is it in the
nature of human intellect to become wise in any other manner. The steady habit of
correcting and completing his own opinion by collating it with those of others, so
far from causing doubt and hesitation in carrying it into practice, is the only stable
foundation for a just reliance on it; for, being cognizant of all that can, at least
obviously, be said against him, and having taken up his position against all gainsayers—knowing that he has sought for objections and difficulties instead of avoiding them, and has shut out no light which can be thrown upon the subject from any
quarter—he has a right to think his judgment better than that of any person, or any
multitude, who have not gone through a similar process.

It is not too much to require that what the wisest of mankind, those who are best
entitled to trust their own judgment, find necessary to warrant their relying on it,
should be submitted to by that miscellaneous collection of a few wise and many
foolish individuals called the public. The most intolerant of churches, the Roman
Catholic Church, even at the canonization of a saint admits, and listens patiently to,
a "devil's advocate." The holiest of men, it appears, cannot be admitted to
posthumous honors until all that the devil could say against him is known and
weighed. If even the Newtonian philosophy were not permitted to be questioned,
mankind could not feel as complete assurance of its truth as they now do. The
beliefs which we have most warrant for have no safeguard to rest on but a standing
invitation to the whole world to prove them unfounded. If the challenge is not accepted, or is accepted and the attempt fails, we are far enough from certainty still,
but we have done the best that the existing state of human reason admits of: we
have neglected nothing that could give the truth a chance of reaching us; if the lists
are kept open, we may hope that, if there be a better truth, it will be found when the

human mind is capable of receiving it; and in the meantime we may rely on having attained such approach to truth as is possible in our own day. This is the amount of certainty attainable by a fallible being, and this the sole way of attaining it.

Strange it is that men should admit the validity of the arguments for free discussion, but object to their being "pushed to an extreme," not seeing that unless the reasons are good for an extreme case, they are not good for any case. Strange that they should imagine that they are not assuming infallibility when they acknowledge that there should be free discussion on all subjects which can possibly be *doubtful,* but think that some particular principle or doctrine should be forbidden to be questioned because it is so *certain,* that is, because *they are certain* that it is certain. To call any proposition certain, while there is anyone who would deny its certainty if permitted, but who is not permitted, is to assume that we ourselves, and those who agree with us, are the judges of certainty, and judges without hearing the other side.

In the present age—which has been described as "destitute of faith, but terrified at skepticism"[9]—in which people feel sure, not so much that their opinions are true as that they should not know what to do with them—the claims of an opinion to be protected from public attack are rested not so much on its truth as on its importance to society. There are, it is alleged, certain beliefs so useful, not to say indispensable, to well-being that it is as much the duty of governments to uphold those beliefs as to protect any other of the interests of society. In a case of such necessity, and so directly in the line of their duty, something less than infallibility may, it is maintained, warrant, and even bind, governments to act on their own opinion confirmed by the general opinion of mankind. It is also often argued, and still oftener thought, that none but bad men would desire to weaken these salutary beliefs; and there can be nothing wrong, it is thought, in restraining bad men and prohibiting what only such men would wish to practice. This mode of thinking makes the justification of restraints on discussion not a question of the truth of doctrines but of their usefulness, and flatters itself by that means to escape the responsibility of claiming to be an infallible judge of opinions. But those who thus satisfy themselves do not perceive that the assumption of infallibility is merely shifted from one point to another. The usefulness of an opinion is itself matter of opinion—as disputable, as open to discussion, and requiring discussion as much as the opinion itself. There is the same need of an infallible judge of opinions to decide an opinion to be noxious as to decide it to be false, unless the opinion condemned has full opportunity of defending itself. And it will not do to say that the heretic may be allowed to maintain the utility or harmlessness of his opinion, though forbidden to maintain its truth. The truth of an opinion is part of its utility. If we would know whether or not it is desirable that a proposition should be believed, is it possible to exclude the consideration of whether or not it is true? In the opinion, not of bad men, but of the best men, no belief which is contrary to truth can be really useful; and can you prevent such men from urging that plea when they are charged with culpability for denying some doctrine which they are told is useful, but which they believe to be false? Those who are on the side of received opinions never fail to take all possible advantage of this plea; you do not find *them* handling the question of ability as if it could be completely abstracted from that of truth; on the contrary, it is, above all, because their doctrine is "the truth" that the knowledge or the belief of it is held to be so

___

9. [The quotation is from Thomas Carlyle's "Memoirs of the Life of Scott," reprinted in his *Critical and Miscellaneous Essays.* Regarding Carlyle, see Mill's *Utilitarianism,* n. 3.]

indispensable. There can be no fair discussion of the question of usefulness when an argument so vital may be employed on one side, but not on the other. And in point of fact, when law or public feeling do not permit the truth of an opinion to be disputed, they are just as little tolerant of a denial of its usefulness. The utmost they allow is an extenuation of its absolute necessity, or of the positive guilt of rejecting it.

In order more fully to illustrate the mischief of denying a hearing to opinions because we, in our own judgment, have condemned them, it will be desirable to fix down the discussion to a concrete case; and I choose, by preference, the cases which are least favorable to me—in which the argument against freedom of opinion, both on the score of truth and on that of utility, is considered the strongest. Let the opinions impugned be the belief in a God and in a future state, or any of the commonly received doctrines of morality. To fight the battle on such ground gives a great advantage to an unfair antagonist, since he will be sure to say (and many who have no desire to be unfair will say it internally), Are these the doctrines which you do not deem sufficiently certain to be taken under the protection of law? Is the belief in a God one of the opinions to feel sure of which you hold to be assuming infallibility? But I must be permitted to observe that it is not the feeling sure of a doctrine (be it what it may) which I call an assumption of infallibility. It is the undertaking to decide that question *for others*, without allowing them to hear what can be said on the contrary side. And I denounce and reprobate this pretension not the less if put forth on the side of my most solemn convictions. However positive anyone's persuasion may be, not only of the falsity but of the pernicious consequences—not only of the pernicious consequences, but (to adopt expressions which I altogether condemn) the immorality and impiety of an opinion—yet if, in pursuance of that private judgment, though backed by the public judgment of his country or his contemporaries, he prevents the opinion from being heard in its defense, he assumes infallibility. And so far from the assumption being less objectionable or less dangerous because the opinion is called immoral or impious, this is the case of all others in which it is most fatal. These are exactly the occasions on which the men of one generation commit those dreadful mistakes which excite the astonishment and horror of posterity. It is among such that we find the instances memorable in history, when the arm of the law has been employed to root out the best men and the noblest doctrines; with deplorable success as to the men, though some of the doctrines have survived to be (as if in mockery) invoked in defense of similar conduct toward those who dissent from *them,* or from their received interpretation.

Mankind can hardly be too often reminded that there was once a man called Socrates, between whom and the legal authorities and public opinion of his time there took place a memorable collision. Born in an age and country abounding in individual greatness, this man has been handed down to us by those who best knew both him and the age as the most virtuous man in it; while *we* know him as the head and prototype of all subsequent teachers of virtue, the source equally of the lofty inspiration of Plato and the judicious utilitarianism of Aristotle, *"i maestri di color che sanno,"*[10] the two headsprings of ethical as of all other philosophy. This acknowledged master of all the eminent thinkers who have since lived—whose fame, still growing after more than two thousand years, all but outweighs the whole remainder of the names which make his native city illustrious—was put to death by

10. [The master of them that know.]

his countrymen, after a judicial conviction, for impiety and immorality. Impiety, in denying the gods recognized by the State; indeed, his accuser asserted (see the *Apologia*) that he believed in no gods at all. Immorality, in being, by his doctrines and instructions, a "corruptor of youth." Of these charges the tribunal, there is every ground for believing, honestly found him guilty, and condemned the man who probably of all then born had deserved best of mankind to be put to death as a criminal.

To pass from this to the only other instance of judicial iniquity, the mention of which, after the condemnation of Socrates, would not be an anticlimax: the event which took place on Calvary rather more than eighteen hundred years ago. The man who left on the memory of those who witnessed his life and conversation such an impression of his moral grandeur that eighteen subsequent centuries have done homage to him as the Almighty in person, was ignominiously put to death, as what? As a blasphemer. Men did not merely mistake their benefactor, they mistook him for the exact contrary of what he was and treated him as that prodigy of impiety which they themselves are now held to be for their treatment of him. The feelings with which mankind now regard these lamentable transactions, especially the later of the two, render them extremely unjust in their judgment of the unhappy actors. These were, to all appearance, not bad men—not worse than men commonly are, but rather the contrary; men who possessed in a full, or somewhat more than a full measure, the religious, moral, and patriotic feelings of their time and people: the very kind of men who, in all times, our own included, have every chance of passing through life blameless and respected. The high priest who rent his garments when the words were pronounced, which, according to all the ideas of his country, constituted the blackest guilt, was in all probability quite as sincere in his horror and indignation as the generality of respectable and pious men now are in the religious and moral sentiments they profess; and most of those who now shudder at his conduct, if they had lived in his time, and been born Jews, would have acted precisely as he did. Orthodox Christians who are tempted to think that those who stoned to death the first martyrs must have been worse men than they themselves are ought to remember that one of those persecutors was Saint Paul.

Let us add one more example, the most striking of all, if the impressiveness of an error is measured by the wisdom and virtue of him who falls into it. If ever anyone possessed of power had grounds for thinking himself the best and most enlightened among his contemporaries, it was the Emperor Marcus Aurelius.[11] Absolute monarch of the whole civilized world, he preserved through life not only the most unblemished justice, but what was less to be expected from his Stoical breeding, the tenderest heart. The few failings which are attributed to him were all on the side of indulgence, while his writings, the highest ethical product of the ancient mind, differ scarcely perceptibly, if they differ at all, from the most characteristic teachings of Christ. This man, a better Christian in all but the dogmatic sense of the word than almost any of the ostensibly Christian sovereigns who have since reigned, persecuted Christianity. Placed at the summit of all the previous attainments of humanity, with an open, unfettered intellect, and a character which led him of himself to embody in his moral writings the Christian ideal, he yet failed to see that Christianity was to be a good and not an evil to the world, with his duties to which he was so deeply penetrated. Existing society he knew to be in a deplorable

11. [Regarding Marcus Aurelius, see Hume's *Enquiry*, n. 58.]

state. But such as it was, he saw, or thought he saw, that it was held together, and prevented from being worse, by belief and reverence of the received divinities. As a ruler of mankind, he deemed it his duty not to suffer society to fall in pieces; and saw not how, if its existing ties were removed, any others could be formed which could again knit it together. The new religion openly aimed at dissolving these ties; unless, therefore, it was his duty to adopt that religion, it seemed to be his duty to put it down. Inasmuch then as the theology of Christianity did not appear to him true or of divine origin, inasmuch as this strange history of a crucified God was not credible to him, and a system which purported to rest entirely upon a foundation to him so wholly unbelievable, could not be foreseen by him to be that renovating agency which, after all abatements, it has in fact proved to be; the gentlest and most amiable of philosophers and rulers, under a solemn sense of duty, authorized the persecution of Christianity. To my mind this is one of the most tragical facts in all history. It is a bitter thought how different a thing the Christianity of the world might have been if the Christian faith had been adopted as the religion of the empire under the auspices of Marcus Aurelius instead of those of Constantine. But it would be equally unjust to him and false to truth to deny that no one plea which can be urged for punishing anti-Christian teaching was wanting to Marcus Aurelius for punishing, as he did, the propagation of Christianity. No Christian more firmly believes that atheism is false and tends to the dissolution of society than Marcus Aurelius believed the same things of Christianity; he who, of all men then living, might have been thought the most capable of appreciating it. Unless anyone who approves of punishment for the promulgation of opinions flatters himself that he is a wiser and better man than Marcus Aurelius—more deeply versed in the wisdom of his time, more elevated in his intellect above it, more earnest in his search for truth, or more single-minded in his devotion to it when found—let him abstain from that assumption of the joint infallibility of himself and the multitude which the great Antoninus made with so unfortunate a result.

Aware of the impossibility of defending the use of punishment for restraining irreligious opinions by any argument which will not justify Marcus Antoninus, the enemies of religious freedom, when hard pressed, occasionally accept this consequence and say, with Dr. Johnson,[12] that the persecutors of Christianity were in the right, that persecution is an ordeal through which truth ought to pass, and always passes successfully, legal penalties being, in the end, powerless against truth, though sometimes beneficially effective against mischievous errors. This is a form of the argument for religious intolerance sufficiently remarkable not to be passed without notice.

A theory which maintains that truth may justifiably be persecuted because persecution cannot possibly do it any harm cannot be charged with being intentionally hostile to the reception of new truths; but we cannot commend the generosity of its dealing with the persons to whom mankind are indebted for them. To discover to the world something which deeply concerns it, and of which it was previously ignorant, to prove to it that it had been mistaken on some vital point of temporal or spiritual interest, is as important a service as a human being can render to his fellow creatures, and in certain cases, as in those of the early Christians and of the Reform-ers, those who think with Dr. Johnson believe it to have been the most precious gift

---

12. [Samuel Johnson (1709–1784) was the leading literary critic of his time and author of the *Diction-ary of the English Language* (1755).]

which could be bestowed on mankind. That the authors of such splendid benefits should be requited by martyrdom, that their reward should be to be dealt with as the vilest of criminals, is not, upon this theory, a deplorable error and misfortune for which humanity should mourn in sackcloth and ashes, but the normal and justifiable state of things. The propounder of a new truth, according to this doctrine, should stand, as stood, in the legislation of the Locrians,[13] the proposer of a new law, with a halter round his neck, to be instantly tightened if the public assembly did not, on hearing his reasons, then and there adopt his proposition. People who defend this mode of treating benefactors cannot be supposed to set much value on the benefit; and I believe this view of the subject is mostly confined to the sort of persons who think that new truths may have been desirable once, but that we have had enough of them now.

But, indeed, the dictum that truth always triumphs over persecution is one of those pleasant falsehoods which men repeat after one another till they pass into commonplaces, but which all experience refutes. History teems with instances of truth put down by persecution. If not suppressed forever, it may be thrown back for centuries. To speak only of religious opinions: the Reformation broke out at least twenty times before Luther, and was put down. Arnold of Brescia[14] was put down. Fra Dolcino[15] was put down. Savonarola[16] was put down. The Albigeois[17] were put down. The Vaudois[18] were put down. The Lollards[19] were put down. The Hussites[20] were put down. Even after the era of Luther, wherever persecution was persisted in, it was successful. In Spain, Italy, Flanders, the Austrian empire, Protestantism was

13. [The Locrians, Greek colonists in southern Italy, adopted in the seventh century, B.C. the earliest written legal code. It was drafted by the lawgiver Zaleucus and was known for its extreme severity.]

14. [Arnold of Brescia (c.1090–1155), Italian monk and reformer, was exiled and his books burned for opposing the Church's possession of property. He defended the people of Rome who wished liberty and other democratic rights. He was executed as a political rebel.]

15. [Fra Dolcino of Novario (d. 1307), leader of an ascetic religious sect that urged purification of the Church, was tortured to death.]

16. [Girolamo Savonarola (1452–1498), Italian religious reformer, severely condemned what he considered the degeneration of spiritual and moral values in his time. He was hanged for schism and heresy.]

17. [Albigensianism, a medieval French religious movement which maintained the existence of both God and the Evil One, was condemned as heretical by the Church and stamped out in the thirteenth century by the papal Inquisition.]

18. [The Waldensians, known in French as "Vaudois," were a medieval religious sect who proclaimed the Bible as the sole guide of life and rejected the claims of the papacy. In 1184 the Church condemned them as heretics, and many were burned at the stake, but the group survived in weakened form and became affiliated with Protestantism.]

19. [Lollardry, a medieval English movement for ecclesiastical reform led by John Wycliff (1320–1384), considered the Bible, as interpreted by each person for himself, the standard of holiness. Severe repressive measures were begun against it by the Church about 1400, but surviving remnants contributed to the development of Protestantism.]

20. [The Hussites, followers of the Czech religious reformer John Huss (c. 1369–1415), demanded the abolition of the feudal system and limitations on the powers of the Church. Huss, a champion of his countrymen, was burned at the stake for heresy, but the movement helped pave the way for the Protestant Reformation and the rise of modern nationalism.]

rooted out; and, most likely, would have been so in England had Queen Mary lived or Queen Elizabeth died. Persecution has always succeeded save where the heretics were too strong a party to be effectually persecuted. No reasonable person can doubt that Christianity might have been extirpated in the Roman Empire. It spread and became predominant because the persecutions were only occasional, lasting but a short time, and separated by long intervals of almost undisturbed propagandism. It is a piece of idle sentimentality that truth, merely as truth, has any inherent power denied to error of prevailing against the dungeon and the stake. Men are not more zealous for truth than they often are for error, and a sufficient application of legal or even of social penalties will generally succeed in stopping the propagation of either. The real advantage which truth has consists in this, that when an opinion is true, it may be extinguished once, twice, or many times, but in the course of ages there will generally be found persons to rediscover it, until some one of its reappearances falls on a time when from favorable circumstances it escapes persecution until it has made such head as to withstand all subsequent attempts to suppress it.

It will be said that we do not now put to death the introducers of new opinions: we are not like our fathers who slew the prophets; we even build sepulchers to them. It is true we no longer put heretics to death; and the amount of penal infliction which modern feeling would probably tolerate, even against the most obnoxious opinions, is not sufficient to extirpate them. But let us not flatter ourselves that we are yet free from the stain even of legal persecution. Penalties for opinion, or at least for its expression, still exist by law; and their enforcement is not, even in these times, so unexampled as to make it at all incredible that they may some day be revived in full force. In the year 1857, at the summer assizes[21] of the county of Cornwall, an unfortunate man, said to be of unexceptionable conduct in all relations of life, was sentenced to twenty-one months' imprisonment for uttering, and writing on a gate, some offensive words concerning Christianity.[22] Within a month of the same time, at the Old Bailey, two persons, on two separate occasions,[23] were rejected as jurymen, and one of them grossly insulted by the judge and by one of the counsel, because they honestly declared that they had no theological belief; and a third, a foreigner,[24] for the same reason, was denied justice against a thief. This refusal of redress took place in virtue of the legal doctrine that no person can be allowed to give evidence in a court of justice who does not profess belief in a God (any god is sufficient) and in a future state, which is equivalent to declaring such persons to be outlaws, excluded from the protection of the tribunals; who may not only be robbed or assaulted with impunity, if no one but themselves, or persons of similar opinions, be present, but anyone else may be robbed or assaulted with impunity if the proof of the fact depends on their evidence. The assumption on which this is grounded is that the oath is worthless of a person who does not believe in a future state—a proposition which betokens much ignorance of history in those who assent to it (since it is historically true that a large proportion of infidels in all ages

21. [Assizes are civil or criminal courts held periodically in English counties.]

22. Thomas Pooley, Bodmin Assizes, July 31, 1857. In December following, he received a free pardon from the Crown.

23. George Jacob Holyoake, August 17, 1857; Edward Truelove, July, 1857.

24. Baron de Gleichen, Marlborough Street Police Court, August 4, 1857.

have been persons of distinguished integrity and honor), and would be maintained by no one who had the smallest conception how many of the persons in greatest repute with the world, both for virtues and attainments, are well known, at least to their intimates, to be unbelievers. The rule, besides, is suicidal and cuts away its own foundation. Under pretense that atheists must be liars, it admits the testimony of all atheists who are willing to lie, and rejects only those who brave the obloquy of publicly confessing a detested creed rather than affirm a falsehood. A rule thus self-convicted of absurdity so far as regards its professed purpose can be kept in force only as a badge of hatred, a relic of persecution—a persecution, too, having the peculiarity that the qualification for undergoing it is the being clearly proved not to deserve it. The rule and the theory it implies are hardly less insulting to believers than to infidels. For if he who does not believe in a future state necessarily lies, it follows that they who do believe are only prevented from lying, if prevented they are, by the fear of hell. We will not do the authors and abettors of the rule the injury of supposing that the conception which they have formed of Christian virtue is drawn from their own consciousness.

These, indeed, are but rags and remnants of persecution, and may be thought to be not so much an indication of the wish to persecute, as an example of that very frequent infirmity of English minds, which makes them take a preposterous pleasure in the assertion of a bad principle, when they are no longer bad enough to desire to carry it really into practice. But unhappily there is no security in the state of the public mind that the suspension of worse forms of legal persecution, which has lasted for about the space of a generation, will continue. In this age the quiet surface of routine is as often ruffled by attempts to resuscitate past evils as to introduce new benefits. What is boasted of at the present time as the revival of religion is always, in narrow and uncultivated minds, at least as much the revival of bigotry; and where there is the strong permanent leaven of intolerance in the feelings of a people, which at all times abides in the middle classes of this country, it needs but little to provoke them into actively persecuting those whom they have never ceased to think proper objects of persecution.[25] For it is this—it is the opinions men entertain, and the feelings they cherish, respecting those who disown the beliefs they deem important which makes this country not a place of mental freedom. For a long time past, the chief mischief of the legal penalties is that they strengthen the social

---

25. Ample warning may be drawn from the large infusion of the passions of a persecutor, which mingled with the general display of the worst parts of our national character on the occasion of the Sepoy insurrection. The ravings of fanatics or charlatans from the pulpit may be unworthy of notice; but the heads of the Evangelical party have announced as their principle for the government of Hindus and Mohammedans that no schools be supported by public money in which the Bible is not taught, and by necessary consequence that no public employment be given to any but real or pretended Christians. An Undersecretary of State, in a speech delivered to his constituents on the 12th of November, 1857, is reported to have said: "Toleration of their faith" (the faith of a hundred millions of British subjects), "the superstition which they call religion, by the British Government, had had the effect of retarding the ascendancy of the British name, and preventing the salutary growth of Christianity. . . Toleration was the great cornerstone of the religious liberties of this country; but do not let them abuse that precious word 'toleration.' As he understood it, it meant the complete liberty to all, freedom of worship, *among Christians, who worshiped upon the same foundation.* It meant toleration of all sects and denominations of *Christians who believed in the one mediation.*" I desire to call attention to the fact that a man who has been deemed fit to fill a high office in the government of this country under a liberal ministry maintains the doctrine that all who do not believe in the divinity of Christ are beyond the pale of toleration. Who, after this imbecile display, can indulge the illusion that religious persecution has passed away, never to return?

stigma. It is that stigma which is really effective, and so effective is it that the profession of opinions which are under the ban of society is much less common in England than is, in many other countries, the avowal of those which incur risk of judicial punishment. In respect to all persons but those whose pecuniary circumstances make them independent of the good will of other people, opinion, on this subject, is as efficacious as law; men might as well be imprisoned as excluded from the means of earning their bread. Those whose bread is already secured, and who desire no favors from men in power, or from bodies of men, or from the public, have nothing to fear from the open avowal of any opinions but to be ill-thought of and ill-spoken of, and this it ought not to require a very heroic mold to enable them to bear. There is no room for any appeal *ad misericordiam* in behalf of such persons. But though we do not now inflict so much evil on those who think differently from us as it was formerly our custom to do, it may be that we do ourselves as much evil as ever by our treatment of them. Socrates was put to death, but the Socratic philosophy rose like the sun in heaven and spread its illumination over the whole intellectual firmament. Christians were cast to the lions, but the Christian church grew up a stately and spreading tree, overtopping the older and less vigorous growths, and stifling them by its shade. Our merely social intolerance kills no one, roots out no opinions, but induces men to disguise them or to abstain from any active effort for their diffusion. With us, heretical opinions do not perceptibly gain, or even lose, ground in each decade or generation; they never blaze out far and wide, but continue to smolder in the narrow circles of thinking and studious persons among whom they originate, without ever lighting up the general affairs of mankind with either a true or a deceptive light. And thus is kept up a state of things very satisfactory to some minds, because, without the unpleasant process of fining or imprisoning anybody, it maintains all prevailing opinions outwardly undisturbed, while it does not absolutely interdict the exercise of reason by dissentients afflicted with the malady of thought. A convenient plan for having peace in the intellectual world, and keeping all things going on therein very much as they do already. But the price paid for this sort of intellectual pacification is the sacrifice of the entire moral courage of the human mind. A state of things in which a large portion of the most active and inquiring intellects find it advisable to keep the general principles and grounds of their convictions within their own breasts, and attempt, in what they address to the public, to fit as much as they can of their own conclusions to premises which they have internally renounced, cannot send forth the open, fearless characters and logical, consistent intellects who once adorned the thinking world. The sort of men who can be looked for under it are either mere conformers to commonplace, or timeservers for truth, whose arguments on all great subjects are meant for their hearers, and are not those which have convinced themselves. Those who avoid this alternative do so by narrowing their thoughts and interest to things which can be spoken of without venturing within the region of principles, that is, to small practical matters which would come right of themselves, if but the minds of mankind were strengthened and enlarged, and which will never be made effectually right until then, while that which would strengthen and enlarge men's minds—free and daring speculation on the highest subjects—is abandoned.

Those in whose eyes this reticence on the part of heretics is no evil should consider, in the first place, that in consequence of it there is never any fair and thorough discussion of heretical opinions; and that such of them as could not stand such a discussion, though they may be prevented from spreading, do not disappear. But it is not the minds of heretics that are deteriorated most by the ban placed on all inquiry which does not end in the orthodox conclusions. The greatest harm done is to those who are not heretics, and whose whole mental development is cramped and their reason cowed by the fear of heresy. Who can compute what the world loses in the multitude of promising intellects combined with timid characters, who dare not follow out any bold, vigorous, independent train of thought, lest it should land them in something which would admit of being considered irreligious or immoral? Among them we may occasionally see some man of deep conscientiousness and subtle and refined understanding, who spends a life in sophisticating with an intellect which he cannot silence, and exhausts the resources of ingenuity in attempting to reconcile the promptings of his conscience and reason with orthodoxy, which yet he does not, perhaps, to the end succeed in doing. No one can be a great thinker who does not recognize that as a thinker it is his first duty to follow his intellect to whatever conclusions it may lead. Truth gains more even by the errors of one who, with due study and preparation, thinks for himself than by the true opinions of those who only hold them because they do not suffer themselves to think. Not that it is solely, or chiefly, to form great thinkers that freedom of thinking is required. On the contrary, it is as much and even more indispensable to enable average human beings to attain the mental stature which they are capable of. There have been, and may again be, great individual thinkers in a general atmosphere of mental slavery. But there never has been, nor ever will be, in that atmosphere an intellectually active people. Where any people has made a temporary approach to such a character, it has been because the dread of heterodox speculation was for a time suspended. Where there is a tacit convention that principles are not to be disputed, where the discussion of the greatest questions which can occupy humanity is considered to be closed, we cannot hope to find that generally high scale of mental activity which has made some periods of history so remarkable. Never when controversy avoided the subjects which are large and important enough to kindle enthusiasm was the mind of a people stirred up from its foundations, and the impulse given which raised even persons of the most ordinary intellect to something of the dignity of thinking beings. Of such we have had an example in the condition of Europe during the times immediately following the Reformation; another, though limited to the Continent and to a more cultivated class, in the speculative movement of the latter half of the eighteenth century; and a third, of still briefer duration, in the intellectual fermentation of Germany during the Goethian and Fichtean period.[26] These periods differed widely in the particular opinions which they developed, but were alike in this, that during all three the yoke of authority was broken. In each, an old mental despotism had been thrown off, and no new one had yet taken its place. The impulse given at these three periods has made Europe what it now is. Every single improvement which has taken place either in the human mind or in institutions may be traced distinctly to one or other of them. Appearances have for some time indicated that all three impulses are well-nigh spent; and we can expect no fresh start until we again assert our mental freedom.

Let us now pass to the second division of the argument, and dismissing the supposition that any of the received opinions may be false, let us assume them to be true and examine into the worth of the manner in which they are likely to be held

---

26. [Johann Fichte (1762–1814) was a post-Kantian German philosopher.]

when their truth is not freely and openly canvassed. However unwillingly a person who has a strong opinion may admit the possibility that his opinion may be false, he ought to be moved by the consideration that, however true it may be, if it is not fully, frequently, and fearlessly discussed, it will be held as a dead dogma, not a living truth.

There is a class of persons (happily not quite so numerous as formerly) who think it enough if a person assents undoubtingly to what they think true, though he has no knowledge whatever of the grounds of the opinion and could not make a tenable defense of it against the most superficial objections. Such persons, if they can once get their creed taught from authority, naturally think that no good, and some harm, comes of its being allowed to be questioned. Where their influence prevails, they make it nearly impossible for the received opinion to be rejected wisely and considerately, though it may still be rejected rashly and ignorantly; for to shut out discussion entirely is seldom possible, and when it once gets in, beliefs not grounded on conviction are apt to give way before the slightest semblance of an argument. Waiving, however, this possibility—assuming that the true opinion abides in the mind, but abides as a prejudice, a belief independent of, and proof against, argument—this is not the way in which truth ought to be held by a rational being. This is not knowing the truth. Truth, thus held, is but one superstition the more, accidentally clinging to the words which enunciate a truth.

If the intellect and judgment of mankind ought to be cultivated, a thing which Protestants at least do not deny, on what can these faculties be more appropriately exercised by anyone than on the things which concern him so much that it is considered necessary for him to hold opinions on them? If the cultivation of the understanding consists in one thing more than in another, it is surely in learning the grounds of one's own opinions. Whatever people believe, on subjects on which it is of the first importance to believe rightly, they ought to be able to defend against at least the common objections. But, someone may say, "Let them be *taught* the grounds of their opinions. It does not follow that opinions must be merely parroted because they are never heard controverted. Persons who learn geometry do not simply commit the theorems to memory, but understand and learn likewise the demonstrations; and it would be absurd to say that they remain ignorant of the grounds of geometrical truths because they never hear anyone deny and attempt to disprove them." Undoubtedly: and such teaching suffices on a subject like mathematics, where there is nothing at all to be said on the wrong side of the question. The peculiarity of the evidence of mathematical truths is that all the argument is on one side. There are no objections, and no answers to objections. But on every subject on which difference of opinion is possible, the truth depends on a balance to be struck between two sets of conflicting reasons. Even in natural philosophy, there is always some other explanation possible of the same facts; some geocentric theory instead of heliocentric, some phlogiston instead of oxygen; and it has to be shown why that other theory cannot be the true one; and until this is shown, and until we know how it is shown, we do not understand the grounds of our opinion. But when we turn to subjects infinitely more complicated, to morals, religion, politics, social relations, and the business of life, three-fourths of the arguments for every disputed opinion consist in dispelling the appearances which favor some opinion different from it. The greatest orator, save one, of antiquity, has left it on record that he always studied his adversary's case with as great, if not still greater, intensity than even his own. What Cicero[27] practiced as the means of forensic success requires to be imitated by all who study any subject in order to arrive at the truth. He who knows only his own side of the case knows little of that. His reasons may be good, and no one may have been able to refute them. But if he is equally unable to refute the reasons on the opposite side, if he does not so much as know what they are, he has no ground for preferring either opinion. The rational position for him would be suspension of judgment, and unless he contents himself with that, he is either led by authority or adopts, like the generality of the world, the side to which he feels most inclination. Nor is it enough that he should hear the arguments of adversaries from his own teachers, presented as they state them, and accompanied by what they offer as refutations. That is not the way to do justice to the arguments or bring them into real contact with his own mind. He must be able to hear them from persons who actually believe them, who defend them in earnest and do their very utmost for them. He must know them in their most plausible and persuasive form; he must feel the whole force of the difficulty which the true view of the subject has to encounter and dispose of, else he will never really possess himself of the portion of truth which meets and removes that difficulty. Ninety-nine in a hundred of what are called educated men are in this condition, even of those who can argue fluently for their opinions. Their conclusion may be true, but it might be false for anything they know; they have never thrown themselves into the mental position of those who think differently from them, and considered what such persons may have to say; and, consequently, they do not, in any proper sense of the word, know the doctrine which they themselves profess. They do not know those parts of it which explain and justify the remainder—the considerations which show that a fact which seemingly conflicts with another is reconcilable with it, or that, of two apparently strong reasons, one and not the other ought to be preferred. All that part of the truth which turns the scale and decides the judgment of a completely informed mind, they are strangers to; nor is it ever really known but to those who have attended equally and impartially to both sides and endeavored to see the reasons of both in the strongest light. So essential is this discipline to a real understanding of moral and human subjects that, if opponents of all-important truths do not exist, it is indispensable to imagine them and supply them with the strongest arguments which the most skillful devil's advocate can conjure up.

To abate the force of these considerations, an enemy of free discussion may be supposed to say that there is no necessity for mankind in general to know and understand all that can be said against or for their opinions by philosophers and theologians. That it is not needful for common men to be able to expose all the misstatements or fallacies of an ingenious opponent. That it is enough if there is always somebody capable of answering them, so that nothing likely to mislead uninstructed persons remains unrefuted. That simple minds, having been taught the obvious grounds of the truths inculcated in them, may trust to authority for the rest and, being aware that they have neither knowledge nor talent to resolve every difficulty which can be raised, may repose in the assurance that all those which have been raised have been or can be answered by those who are specially trained to the task.

Conceding to this view of the subject the utmost that can be claimed for it by

27. [Regarding Cicero, see Hobbes's *Leviathan*, n. 11.]

those most easily satisfied with the amount of understanding of truth which ought to accompany the belief of it, even so, the argument for free discussion is noway weakened. For even this doctrine acknowledges that mankind ought to have a rational assurance that all objections have been satisfactorily answered; and how are they to be answered if that which requires to be answered is not spoken? Or how can the answer be known to be satisfactory if the objectors have no opportunity of showing that it is unsatisfactory? If not the public, at least the philosophers and theologians who are to resolve the difficulties must make themselves familiar with those difficulties in their most puzzling form; and this cannot be accomplished unless they are freely stated and placed in the most advantageous light which they admit of. The Catholic Church has its own way of dealing with this embarrassing problem. It makes a broad separation between those who can be permitted to receive its doctrines on conviction and those who must accept them on trust. Neither, indeed, are allowed any choice as to what they will accept; but the clergy, such at least as can be fully confided in, may admissibly and meritoriously make themselves acquainted with the arguments of opponents, in order to answer them, and may, therefore, read heretical books; the laity, not unless by special permission, hard to be obtained. This discipline recognizes a knowledge of the enemy's case as beneficial to the teachers, but finds means, consistent with this, of denying it to the rest of the world, thus giving to the *élite* more mental culture, though not more mental freedom, than it allows to the mass. By this device it succeeds in obtaining the kind of mental superiority which its purposes require; for though culture without freedom never made a large and liberal mind, it can make a clever *nisi prius*[28] advocate of a cause. But in countries professing Protestantism, this resource is denied, since Protestants hold, at least in theory, that the responsibility for the choice of a religion must be borne by each for himself and cannot be thrown off upon teachers. Besides, in the present state of the world, it is practically impossible that writings which are read by the instructed can be kept from the uninstructed. If the teachers of mankind are to be cognizant of all that they ought to know, everything must be free to be written and published without restraint.

If, however, the mischievous operation of the absence of free discussion, when the received opinions are true, were confined to leaving men ignorant of the grounds of those opinions, it might be thought that this, if an intellectual, is no moral evil and does not affect the worth of the opinions, regarded in their influence on the character. The fact, however, is that not only the grounds of the opinion are forgotten in the absence of discussion, but too often the meaning of the opinion itself. The words which convey it cease to suggest ideas, or suggest only a small portion of those they were originally employed to communicate. Instead of a vivid conception and a living belief, there remain only a few phrases retained by rote; or, if any part, the shell and husk only of the meaning is retained, the finer essence being lost. The great chapter in human history which this fact occupies and fills cannot be too earnestly studied and meditated on.

It is illustrated in the experience of almost all ethical doctrines and religious creeds. They are all full of meaning and vitality to those who originate them, and to the direct disciples of the originators. Their meaning continues to be felt in undiminished strength, and is perhaps brought out into even fuller consciousness,

---

28. [A term, adopted from English legal proceedings, meaning that existing law is to be presumed valid until demonstrated otherwise.]

so long as the struggle lasts to give the doctrine or creed an ascendancy over other creeds. At last it either prevails and becomes the general opinion, or its progress stops; it keeps possession of the ground it has gained, but ceases to spread further. When either of these results has become apparent, controversy on the subject flags, and gradually dies away. The doctrine has taken its place, if not as a received opinion, as one of the admitted sects or divisions of opinion; those who hold it have generally inherited, not adopted it; and conversion from one of these doctrines to another, being now an exceptional fact, occupies little place in the thoughts of their professors. Instead of being, as at first, constantly on the alert either to defend themselves against the world or to bring the world over to them, they have subsided into acquiescence and neither listen, when they can help it, to arguments against their creed, nor trouble dissentients (if there be such) with arguments in its favor. From this time may usually be dated the decline in the living power of the doctrine. We often hear the teachers of all creeds lamenting the difficulty of keeping up in the minds of believers a lively apprehension of the truth which they nominally recognize, so that it may penetrate the feelings and acquire a real mastery over the conduct. No such difficulty is complained of while the creed is still fighting for its existence; even the weaker combatants then know and feel what they are fighting for, and the difference between it and other doctrines; and in that period of every creed's existence not a few persons may be found who have realized its fundamental principles in all the forms of thought, have weighed and considered them in all their important bearings, and have experienced the full effect on the character which belief in that creed ought to produce in a mind thoroughly imbued with it. But when it has come to be an hereditary creed, and to be received passively, not actively—when the mind is no longer compelled, in the same degree as at first, to exercise its vital powers on the questions which its belief presents to it, there is a progressive tendency to forget all of the belief except the formularies, or to give it a dull and torpid assent, as if accepting it on trust dispensed with the necessity of realizing it in consciousness, or testing it by personal experience, until it almost ceases to connect itself at all with the inner life of the human being. Then are seen the cases, so frequent in this age of the world as almost to form the majority, in which the creed remains as it were outside the mind, incrusting and petrifying it against all other influences addressed to the higher parts of our nature; manifesting its power by not suffering any fresh and living conviction to get in, but itself doing nothing for the mind or heart except standing sentinel over them to keep them vacant.

To what an extent doctrines intrinsically fitted to make the deepest impression upon the mind may remain in it as dead beliefs, without being ever realized in the imagination, the feelings, or the understanding, is exemplified by the manner in which the majority of believers hold the doctrines of Christianity. By Christianity, I here mean what is accounted such by all churches and sects—the maxims and precepts contained in the New Testament. These are considered sacred, and accepted as laws, by all professing Christians. Yet it is scarcely too much to say that not one Christian in a thousand guides or tests his individual conduct by reference to those laws. The standard to which he does refer it is the custom of his nation, his class, or his religious profession. He has thus, on the one hand, a collection of ethical maxims which he believes to have been vouchsafed to him by infallible wisdom as rules for his government; and, on the other, a set of everyday judgments and practices which go a certain length with some of those maxims, not so great a length with others, stand in direct opposition to some, and are, on the whole, a compromise between the

Christian creed and the interests and suggestions of worldly life. To the first of these standards he gives his homage; to the other his real allegiance. All Christians believe that the blessed are the poor and humble, and those who are ill-used by the world; that it is easier for a camel to pass through the eye of a needle than for a rich man to enter the kingdom of heaven; that they should judge not, lest they be judged; that they should swear not at all; that they should love their neighbor as themselves; that if one take their cloak, they should give him their coat also; that they should take no thought for the morrow; that if they would be perfect they should sell all that they have and give it to the poor. They are not insincere when they say that they believe these things. They do believe them, as people believe what they have always heard lauded and never discussed. But in the sense of that living belief which regulates conduct, they believe these doctrines just up to the point to which it is usual to act upon them. The doctrines in their integrity are serviceable to pelt adversaries with; and it is understood that they are to be put forward (when possible) as the reasons for whatever people do that they think laudable. But anyone who reminded them that the maxims require an infinity of things which they never even think of doing would gain nothing but to be classed among those very unpopular characters who affect to be better than other people. The doctrines have no hold on ordinary believers—are not a power in their minds. They have an habitual respect for the sound of them, but no feeling which spreads from the words to the things signified and forces the mind to take *them* in and make them conform to the formula. Whenever conduct is concerned, they look round for Mr. A and B to direct them how far to go in obeying Christ.

Now we may be well assured that the case was not thus, but far otherwise, with the early Christians. Had it been thus, Christianity never would have expanded from an obscure sect of the despised Hebrews into the religion of the Roman empire. When their enemies said, "See how these Christians love one another" (a remark not likely to be made by anybody now), they assuredly had a much livelier feeling of the meaning of their creed than they have ever had since. And to this cause, probably, it is chiefly owing that Christianity now makes so little progress in extending its domain, and after eighteen centuries is still nearly confined to Europeans and the descendants of Europeans. Even with the strictly religious, who are much in earnest about their doctrines and attach a greater amount of meaning to many of them than people in general, it commonly happens that the part which is thus comparatively active in their minds is that which was made by Calvin, or Knox,[29] or some such person much nearer in character to themselves. The sayings of Christ coexist passively in their minds, producing hardly any effect beyond what is caused by mere listening to words so amiable and bland. There are many reasons, doubtless, why doctrines which are the badge of a sect retain more of their vitality than those common to all recognized sects, and why more pains are taken by teachers to keep their meaning alive; but one reason certainly is that the peculiar doctrines are more questioned and have to be oftener defended against open gainsayers. Both teachers and learners go to sleep at their post as soon as there is no enemy in the field.

The same thing holds true, generally speaking, of all traditional doctrines—those of prudence and knowledge of life as well as of morals or religion. All languages and literatures are full of general observations on life, both as to what it is and how to

---

29. [John Knox (c. 1514–1572) was the religious reformer who founded Scottish Presbyterianism.]

conduct oneself in it—observations which everybody knows, which everybody repeats or hears with acquiescence, which are received as truisms, yet of which most people first truly learn the meaning when experience, generally of a painful kind, has made it a reality to them. How often, when smarting under some unforeseen misfortune or disappointment, does a person call to mind some proverb or common saying, familiar to him all his life, the meaning of which, if he had ever before felt it as he does now, would have saved him from the calamity. There are indeed reasons for this, other than the absence of discussion; there are many truths of which the full meaning *cannot* be realized until personal experience has brought it home. But much more of the meaning even of these would have been understood, and what was understood would have been far more deeply impressed on the mind, if the man had been accustomed to hear it argued *pro* and *con* by people who did understand it. The fatal tendency of mankind to leave off thinking about a thing when it is no longer doubtful is the cause of half their errors. A contemporary author has well spoken of "the deep slumber of a decided opinion."

But what! (it may be asked), Is the absence of unanimity an indispensable condition of true knowledge? Is it necessary that some part of mankind should persist in error to enable any to realize the truth? Does a belief cease to be real and vital as soon as it is generally received—and is a proposition never thoroughly understood and felt unless some doubt of it remains? As soon as mankind have unanimously accepted a truth, does the truth perish within them? The highest aim and best result of improved intelligence, it has hitherto been thought, is to unite mankind more and more in the acknowledgment of all-important truths; and does the intelligence only last as long as it has not achieved its object? Do the fruits of conquest perish by the very completeness of the victory?

I affirm no such thing. As mankind improve, the number of doctrines which are no longer disputed or doubted will be constantly on the increase; and the well-being of mankind may almost be measured by the number and gravity of the truths which have reached the point of being uncontested. The cessation, on one question after another, of serious controversy is one of the necessary incidents of the consolidation of opinion—a consolidation as salutary in the case of true opinions as it is dangerous and noxious when the opinions are erroneous. But though this gradual narrowing of the bounds of diversity of opinion is necessary in both senses of the term, being at once inevitable and indispensable, we are not therefore obliged to conclude that all its consequences must be beneficial. The loss of so important an aid to the intelligent and living apprehension of a truth as is afforded by the necessity of explaining it to, or defending it against, opponents, though not sufficient to outweigh, is no trifling drawback from the benefit of its universal recognition. Where this advantage can no longer be had, I confess I should like to see the teachers of mankind endeavoring to provide a substitute for it—some contrivance for making the difficulties of the question as present to the learner's consciousness as if they were pressed upon him by a dissentient champion, eager for his conversion.

But instead of seeking contrivances for this purpose, they have lost those they formerly had. The Socratic dialectics, so magnificently exemplified in the dialogues of Plato, were a contrivance of this description. They were essentially a negative discussion of the great questions of philosophy and life, directed with consummate skill to the purpose of convincing anyone who had merely adopted the commonplaces of received opinion that he did not understand the subject—that he as yet attached no definite meaning to the doctrines he professed; in order that, becoming aware of his ignorance, he might be put in the way to obtain a stable belief, resting on a clear apprehension both of the meaning of doctrines and of their evidence. The school disputations of the Middle Ages had a somewhat similar object. They were intended to make sure that the pupil understood his own opinion, and (by necessary correlation) the opinion opposed to it, and could enforce the grounds of the one and confute those of the other. These last-mentioned contests had indeed the incurable defect that the premises appealed to were taken from authority, not from reason; and, as a discipline to the mind, they were in every respect inferior to the powerful dialectics which formed the intellects of the *"Socratici viri"*;[30] but the modern mind owes far more to both than it is generally willing to admit, and the present modes of education contain nothing which in the smallest degree supplies the place either of the one or of the other. A person who derives all his instruction from teachers or books, even if he escape the besetting temptation of contenting himself with cram, is under no compulsion to hear both sides; accordingly it is far from a frequent accomplishment, even among thinkers, to know both sides; and the weakest part of what everybody says in defense of his opinion is what he intends as a reply to antagonists. It is the fashion of the present time to disparage negative logic—that which points out weaknesses in theory or errors in practice without establishing positive truths. Such negative criticism would indeed be poor enough as an ultimate result, but as a means to attaining any positive knowledge or conviction worthy the name it cannot be valued too highly; and until people are again systematically trained to it, there will be few great thinkers and a low general average of intellect in any but the mathematical and physical departments of speculation. On any other subject no one's opinions deserve the name of knowledge, except so far as he has either had forced upon him by others or gone through of himself the same mental process which would have been required of him in carrying on an active controversy with opponents. That, therefore, which, when absent, it is so indispensable, but so difficult, to create, how worse than absurd it is to forego when spontaneously offering itself! If there are any persons who contest a received opinion, or who will do so if law or opinion will let them, let us thank them for it, open our minds to listen to them, and rejoice that there is someone to do for us what we otherwise ought, if we have any regard for either the certainty or the vitality of our convictions, to do with much greater labor for ourselves.

It still remains to speak of one of the principal causes which make diversity of opinion advantageous, and will continue to do so until mankind shall have entered a stage of intellectual advancement which at present seems at an incalculable distance. We have hitherto considered only two possibilities: that the received opinion may be false, and some other opinion, consequently, true; or that, the received opinion being true, a conflict with the opposite error is essential to a clear apprehension and deep feeling of its truth. But there is a commoner case than either of these: when the conflicting doctrines, instead of being one true and the other false, share the truth between them, and the nonconforming opinion is needed to supply the remainder of the truth of which the received doctrine embodies only a part. Popular opinions, on subjects not palpable to sense, are often true, but seldom or never the whole truth. They are a part of the truth, sometimes a greater, sometimes a smaller part, but exaggerated, distorted, and disjointed from the truths by which they

---

30. [The pupils and followers of Socrates.]

ought to be accompanied and limited. Heretical opinions, on the other hand, are generally some of these suppressed and neglected truths, bursting the bonds which kept them down, and either seeking reconciliation with the truth contained in the common opinion, or fronting it as enemies, and setting themselves up, with similar exclusiveness, as the whole truth. The latter case is hitherto the most frequent, as, in the human mind, one-sidedness has always been the rule, and many-sidedness the exception. Hence, even in revolutions of opinion, one part of the truth usually sets while another rises. Even progress, which ought to superadd, for the most part only substitutes one partial and incomplete truth for another; improvement consisting chiefly in this, that the new fragment of truth is more wanted, more adapted to the needs of the time than that which it displaces. Such being the partial character of prevailing opinions, even when resting on a true foundation, every opinion which embodies somewhat of the portion of truth which the common opinion omits ought to be considered precious, with whatever amount of error and confusion that truth may be blended. No sober judge of human affairs will feel bound to be indignant because those who force on our notice truths which we should otherwise have overlooked, overlook some of those which we see. Rather, he will think that so long as popular truth is one-sided, it is more desirable than otherwise that unpopular truth should have one-sided assertors, too, such being usually the most energetic and the most likely to compel reluctant attention to the fragment of wisdom which they proclaim as if it were the whole.

Thus, in the eighteenth century, when nearly all the instructed, and all those of the uninstructed who were led by them, were lost in admiration of what is called civilization, and of the marvels of modern science, literature, and philosophy, and while greatly overrating the amount of unlikeness between the men of modern and those of ancient times, indulged the belief that the whole of the difference was in their own favor; with what a salutary shock did the paradoxes of Rousseau explode like bombshells in the midst, dislocating the compact mass of one-sided opinion and forcing its elements to recombine in a better form and with additional ingredients. Not that the current opinions were on the whole farther from the truth than Rousseau's were; on the contrary, they were nearer to it; they contained more of positive truth, and very much less of error. Nevertheless there lay in Rousseau's doctrine, and has floated down the stream of opinion along with it, a considerable amount of exactly those truths which the popular opinion wanted; and these are the deposit which was left behind them when the flood subsided. The superior worth of simplicity of life, the enervating and demoralizing effect of the trammels and hypocrisies of artificial society are ideas which have never been entirely absent from cultivated minds since Rousseau wrote; and they will in time produce their due effect, though at present needing to be asserted as much as ever, and to be asserted by deeds; for words, on this subject, have nearly exhausted their power.

In politics, again, it is almost a commonplace that a party of order or stability and a party of progress or reform are both necessary elements of a healthy state of political life, until the one or the other shall have so enlarged its mental grasp as to be a party equally of order and of progress, knowing and distinguishing what is fit to be preserved from what ought to be swept away. Each of these modes of thinking derives its utility from the deficiencies of the other; but it is in a great measure the opposition of the other that keeps each within the limits of reason and sanity. Unless opinions favorable to democracy and to aristocracy, to property and to equality, to co-operation and to competition, to luxury and to abstinence, to sociality and individuality, to liberty and discipline, and all the other standing antagonisms of practical life, are expressed with equal freedom and enforced and defended with equal talent and energy, there is no chance of both elements obtaining their due; one scale is sure to go up, and the other down. Truth, in the great practical concerns of life, is so much a question of the reconciling and combining of opposites that very few have minds sufficiently capacious and impartial to make the adjustment with an approach to correctness, and it has to be made by the rough process of a struggle between combatants fighting under hostile banners. On any of the great open questions just enumerated, if either of the two opinions has a better claim than the other, not merely to be tolerated, but to be encouraged and countenanced, it is the one which happens at the particular time and place to be in a minority. That is the opinion which, for the time being, represents the neglected interests, the side of human well-being which is in danger of obtaining less than its share. I am aware that there is not, in this country, any intolerance of differences of opinion on most of these topics. They are adduced to show, by admitted and multiplied examples, the universality of the fact that only through diversity of opinion is there, in the existing state of human intellect, a chance of fair play to all sides of the truth. When there are persons to be found who form an exception to the apparent unanimity of the world on any subject, even if the world is in the right, it is always probable that dissentients have something worth hearing to say for themselves, and that truth would lose something by their silence.

It may be objected, "But *some* received principles, especially on the highest and most vital subjects, are more than half-truths. The Christian morality, for instance, is the whole truth on that subject, and if anyone teaches a morality which varies from it, he is wholly in error." As this is of all cases the most important in practice, none can be fitter to test the general maxim. But before pronouncing what Christian morality is or is not, it would be desirable to decide what is meant by Christian morality. If it means the morality of the New Testament, I wonder that any one who derives his knowledge of this from the book itself can suppose that it was announced, or intended, as a complete doctrine of morals. The Gospel always refers to a pre-existing morality and confines its precepts to the particulars in which that morality was to be corrected or superseded by a wider and higher, expressing itself, moreover, in terms most general, often impossible to be interpreted literally, and possessing rather the impressiveness of poetry or eloquence than the precision of legislation. To extract from it a body of ethical doctrine has never been possible without eking it out from the Old Testament, that is, from a system elaborate indeed, but in many respects barbarous, and intended only for a barbarous people. St. Paul, a declared enemy to this Judaical mode of interpreting the doctrine and filling up the scheme of his Master, equally assumes a pre-existing morality, namely that of the Greeks and Romans; and his advice to Christians is in a great measure a system of accommodation to that, even to the extent of giving an apparent sanction to slavery. What is called Christian, but should rather be termed theological, morality was not the work of Christ or the Apostles, but is of much later origin, having been gradually built up by the Catholic Church of the first five centuries, and though not implicitly adopted by moderns and Protestants, has been much less modified by them than might have been expected. For the most part, indeed, they have contented themselves with cutting off the additions which had been made to it in the Middle Ages, each sect supplying the place by fresh additions, adapted to its own character and tendencies. That mankind owe a great debt to this morality, and to its early teachers, I should be the last person to deny, but I do not scruple to say of it that it is, in many important points, incomplete and one-sided, and that, unless ideas and feelings not sanctioned by it had contributed to the formation of European life and character, human affairs would have been in a worse condition than they now are. Christian morality (so called) has all the characters of a reaction; it is, in great part, a protest against paganism. Its ideal is negative rather than positive; passive rather than active; innocence rather than nobleness; abstinence from evil rather than energetic pursuit of good; in its precepts (as has been well said) "thou shalt not" predominates unduly over "though shalt." In its horror of sensuality, it made an idol of asceticism which has been gradually compromised away into one of legality. It holds out the hope of heaven and the threat of hell as the appointed and appropriate motives to a virtuous life: in this falling far below the best of the ancients, and doing what lies in it to give to human morality an essentially selfish character, by disconnecting each man's feelings of duty from the interests of his fellow creatures, except so far as a self-interested inducement is offered to him for consulting them. It is essentially a doctrine of passive obedience; it inculcates submission to all authorities found established; who indeed are not to be actively obeyed when they command what religion forbids, but who are not to be resisted, far less rebelled against, for any amount of wrong to ourselves. And while, in the morality of the best pagan nations, duty to the State holds even a disproportionate place, infringing on the just liberty of the individual, in purely Christian ethics that grand department of duty is scarcely noticed or acknowledged. It is in the Koran, not the New Testament, that we read the maxim: "A ruler who appoints any man to an office, when there is in his dominions another man better qualified for it, sins against God and against the State." What little recognition the idea of obligation to the public obtains in modern morality is derived from Greek and Roman sources, not from Christian; as, even in the morality of private life, whatever exists of magnanimity, high-mindedness, personal dignity, even the sense of honor, is derived from the purely human, not the religious part of our education, and never could have grown out of a standard of ethics in which the only worth, professedly recognized, is that of obedience.

I am as far as anyone from pretending that these defects are necessarily inherent in the Christian ethics in every manner in which it can be conceived, or that the many requisites of a complete moral doctrine which it does not contain do not admit of being reconciled with it. Far less would I insinuate this out of the doctrines and precepts of Christ himself. I believe that the sayings of Christ are all that I can see any evidence of their having been intended to be; that they are irreconcilable with nothing which a comprehensive morality requires; that everything which is excellent in ethics may be brought within them, with no greater violence to their language than has been done to it by all who have attempted to deduce from them any practical system of conduct whatever. But it is quite consistent with this to believe that they contain, and were meant to contain, only a part of the truth; that many essential elements of the highest morality are among the things which are not provided for, nor intended to be provided for, in the recorded deliverances of the Founder of Christianity, and which have been entirely thrown aside in the system of ethics erected on the basis of those deliverances by the Christian Church. And this being so, I think it a great error to persist in attempting to find in the Christian doctrine that complete rule for our guidance which its Author intended it to sanction and enforce, but only partially to provide. I believe, too, that this narrow theory is becoming a grave practical evil, detracting greatly from the moral training and instruction which so many well-meaning persons are now at length exerting themselves to promote. I much fear that by attempting to form the mind and feelings on an exclusively religious type, and discarding those secular standards (as for want of a better name they may be called) which heretofore coexisted with and supplemented the Christian ethics, receiving some of its spirit, and infusing into it some of theirs, there will result, and is even now resulting, a low, abject, servile type of character which, submit itself as it may to what it deems the Supreme Will, is incapable of rising to or sympathizing in the conception of Supreme Goodness. I believe that other ethics than any which can be evolved from exclusively Christian sources must exist side by side with Christian ethics to produce the moral regeneration of mankind; and that the Christian system is no exception to the rule that in an imperfect state of the human mind the interests of truth require a diversity of opinions. It is not necessary that in ceasing to ignore the moral truths not contained in Christianity men should ignore any of those which it does contain. Such prejudice or oversight, when it occurs, is altogether an evil, but it is one from which we cannot hope to be always exempt, and must be regarded as the price paid for an inestimable good. The exclusive pretension made by a part of the truth to be the whole must and ought to be protested against; and if a reactionary impulse should make the protestors unjust in their turn, this one-sidedness, like the other, may be lamented but must be tolerated. If Christians would teach infidels to be just to Christianity, they should themselves be just to infidelity. It can do truth no service to blink the fact, known to all who have the most ordinary acquaintance with literary history, that a large portion of the noblest and most valuable moral teaching has been the work, not only of men who did not know, but of men who knew and rejected, the Christian faith.

I do not pretend that the most unlimited use of the freedom of enunciating all possible opinions would put an end to the evils of religious or philosophical sectarianism. Every truth which men of narrow capacity are in earnest about is sure to be asserted, inculcated, and in many ways even acted on, as if no other truth existed in the world, or at all events none that could limit or qualify the first. I acknowledge that the tendency of all opinions to become sectarian is not cured by the freest discussion, but is often heightened and exacerbated thereby; the truth which ought to have been, but was not, seen, being rejected all the more violently because proclaimed by persons regarded as opponents. But it is not on the impassioned partisan, it is on the calmer and more disinterested bystander, that this collision of opinions works its salutary effect. Not the violent conflict between parts of the truth, but the quiet suppression of half of it, is the formidable evil; there is always hope when people are forced to listen to both sides; it is when they attend only to one that errors harden into prejudices, and truth itself ceases to have the effect of truth by being exaggerated into falsehood. And since there are few mental attributes more rare than that judicial faculty which can sit in intelligent judgment between two sides of a question, of which only one is represented by an advocate before it, truth has no chance but in proportion as every side of it, every opinion which embodies any fraction of the truth, not only finds advocates, but is so advocated as to be listened to.

We have now recognized the necessity to the mental well-being of mankind (on which all their other well-being depends) of freedom of opinion, and freedom of the expression of opinion, on four distinct grounds, which we will now briefly recapitulate:

First, if any opinion is compelled to silence, that opinion may, for aught we can certainly know, be true. To deny this is to assume our own infallibility.

Secondly, though the silenced opinion be an error, it may, and very commonly does, contain a portion of truth; and since the general or prevailing opinion on any subject is rarely or never the whole truth, it is only by the collision of adverse opinions that the remainder of the truth has any chance of being supplied.

Thirdly, even if the received opinion be not only true, but the whole truth; unless it is suffered to be, and actually is, vigorously and earnestly contested, it will, by most of those who receive it, be held in the manner of a prejudice, with little comprehension or feeling of its rational grounds. And not only this, but, fourthly, the meaning of the doctrine itself will be in danger of being lost or enfeebled, and deprived of its vital effect on the character and conduct: the dogma becoming a mere formal profession, inefficacious for good, but cumbering the ground and preventing the growth of any real and heartfelt conviction from reason or personal experience.

Before quitting the subject of freedom of opinion, it is fit to take some notice of those who say that the free expression of all opinions should be permitted on condition that the manner be temperate, and do not pass the bounds of fair discussion. Much might be said on the impossibility of fixing where these supposed bounds are to be placed; for if the test be offense to those whose opinions are attacked, I think experience testifies that this offense is given whenever the attack is telling and powerful, and that every opponent who pushes them hard, and whom they find it difficult to answer, appears to them, if he shows any strong feeling on the subject, an intemperate opponent. But this, though an important consideration in a practical point of view, merges in a more fundamental objection. Undoubtedly, the manner of asserting an opinion, even though it be a true one, may be very objectionable and may justly incur severe censure. But the principal offenses of the kind are such as it is mostly impossible, unless by accidental self-betrayal, to bring home to conviction. The gravest of them is, to argue sophistically, to suppress facts or arguments, to misstate the elements of the case, or misrepresent the opposite opinion. But all this, even to the most aggravated degree, is so continually done in perfect good faith by persons who are not considered, and in many other respects may not deserve to be considered, ignorant or incompetent, that it is rarely possible, on adequate grounds, conscientiously to stamp the misrepresentation as morally culpable, and still less could law presume to interfere with this kind of controversial misconduct. With regard to what is commonly meant by intemperate discussion, namely invective, sarcasm, personality, and the like, the denunciation of these weapons would deserve more sympathy if it were ever proposed to interdict them equally to both sides; but it is only desired to restrain the employment of them against the prevailing opinion; against the unprevailing they may not only be used without general disapproval, but will be likely to obtain for him who uses them the praise of honest zeal and righteous indignation. Yet whatever mischief arises from their use is greatest when they are employed against the comparatively defenseless; and whatever unfair advantage can be derived by any opinion from this mode of asserting it accrues almost exclusively to received opinions. The worst offense of this kind which can be committed by a polemic is to stigmatize those who hold the contrary opinion as bad and immoral men. To calumny of this sort, those who hold any unpopular opinion are peculiarly exposed, because they are in general few and uninfluential, and nobody but themselves feels much interested in seeing justice done them; but this weapon is, from the nature of the case, denied to those who attack a prevailing opinion: they can neither use it with safety to themselves, nor, if they could, would it do anything but recoil on their own cause. In general, opinions contrary to those commonly received can only obtain a hearing by studied moderation of language and the most cautious avoidance of unnecesary offense, from which they hardly ever deviate even in a slight degree without losing ground, while unmeasured vituperation employed on the side of the prevailing opinion really does deter people from professing contrary opinions and from listening to those who profess them. For the interest, therefore, of truth and justice it is far more important to restrain this employment of vituperative language than the other; and, for example, if it were necessary to choose, there would be much more need to discourage offensive attacks on infidelity than on religion. It is, however, obvious that law and authority have no business with restraining either, while opinion ought, in every instance, to determine its verdict by the circumstances of the individual case—condemning everyone, on whichever side of the argument he places himself, in whose mode of advocacy either want of candor, or malignity, bigotry, or intolerance of feeling manifest themselves; but not inferring these vices from the side which a person takes, though it be the contrary side of the question to our own; and giving merited honor to everyone, whatever opinion he may hold, who has calmness to see and honesty to state what his opponents and their opinions really are, exaggerating nothing to their discredit, keeping nothing back which tells, or can be supposed to tell, in their favor. This is the real morality of public discussion; and if often violated, I am happy to think that there are many controversialists who to a great extent observe it, and a still greater number who conscientiously strive toward it.

CHAPTER III

OF INDIVIDUALITY, AS ONE OF
THE ELEMENTS OF WELL-BEING

Such being the reasons which make it imperative that human beings should be free to form opinions and to express their opinions without reserve; and such the baneful consequences to the intellectual, and through that to the moral nature of man, unless this liberty is either conceded or asserted in spite of prohibition; let us next examine whether the same reasons do not require that men should be free to act upon their opinions—to carry these out in their lives without hindrance, either physical or moral, from their fellow men, so long as it is at their own risk and peril. This last proviso is of course indispensable. No one pretends that actions should be as free as opinions. On the contrary, even opinions lose their immunity when the circumstances in which they are expressed are such as to constitute their expression a positive instigation to some mischievous act. An opinion that corn dealers are starvers of the poor, or that private property is robbery, ought to be unmolested when simply circulated through the press, but may justly incur punishment when delivered orally to an excited mob assembled before the house of a corn dealer, or when handed about among the same mob in the form of a placard. Acts, of whatever kind, which without justifiable cause do harm to others may be, and in the more important cases absolutely require to be, controlled by the unfavorable sentiments, and, when needful, by the active interference of mankind. The liberty of the individual must be thus far limited; he must not make himself a nuisance to other people. But if he refrains from molesting others in what concerns them, and merely acts according to his own inclination and judgment in things which concern himself, the same reasons which show that opinion should be free prove also that he should be allowed, without molestation, to carry his opinions into practice at his own cost. That mankind are not infallible; that their truths, for the most part, are only half-truths; that unity of opinion, unless resulting from the fullest and freest comparison of opposite opinions, is not desirable, and diversity not an evil, but a good, until mankind are much more capable than at present of recognizing all sides of the truth, are principles applicable to men's modes of action not less than to their opinions. As it is useful that while mankind are imperfect there should be different opinions, so it is that there should be different experiments of living; that free scope should be given to varieties of character, short of injury to others; and that the worth of different modes of life should be proved practically, when anyone thinks fit to try them. It is desirable, in short, that in things which do not primarily concern others individuality should assert itself. Where not the person's own character but the traditions or customs of other people are the rule of conduct, there is wanting one of the principal ingredients of human happiness, and quite the chief ingredient of individual and social progress.

In maintaining this principle, the greatest difficulty to be encountered does not lie in the appreciation of means toward an acknowledged end, but in the indifference of persons in general to the end itself. If it were felt that the free development of individuality is one of the leading essentials of well-being; that it is not only a co-ordinate element with all that is designated by the terms civilization, instruction, education, culture, but is itself a necessary part and condition of all those things, there would be no danger that liberty should be undervalued, and the adjustment of the boundaries between it and social control would present no extraordinary difficulty. But the evil is that individual spontaneity is hardly recognized by the common modes of thinking as having any intrinsic worth, or deserving any regard on its own account. The majority, being satisfied with the ways of mankind as they now are (for it is they who make them what they are), cannot comprehend why those ways should not be good enough for everybody; and what is more, spontaneity forms no part of the ideal of the majority of moral and social reformers, but is rather looked on with jealousy, as a troublesome and perhaps rebellious obstruction to the general acceptance of what these reformers, in their own judgment, think would be best for mankind. Few persons, out of Germany, even comprehend the meaning of the doctrine which Wilhelm von Humboldt, so eminent both as a *savant* and as a politician, made the text of a treatise—that "the end of man, or that which is prescribed by the eternal or immutable dictates of reason, and not suggested by vague and transient desires, is the highest and most harmonious development of his powers to a complete and consistent whole"; that, therefore, the object "toward which every human being must ceaselessly direct his efforts, and on which especially those who design to influence their fellow men must ever keep their eyes, is the individuality of power and development"; that for this there are two requisites, "freedom, and variety of situations"; and that from the union of these arise "individual vigor and manifold diversity," which combine themselves in "originality."[31]

Little, however, as people are accustomed to a doctrine like that of von Humboldt, and surprising as it may be to them to find so high a value attached to individuality, the question, one must nevertheless think, can only be one of degree. No one's idea of excellence in conduct is that people should do absolutely nothing but copy one another. No one would assert that people ought not to put into their mode of life, and into the conduct of their concerns, any impress whatever of their own judgment or of their own individual character. On the other hand, it would be absurd to pretend that people ought to live as if nothing whatever had been known in the world before they came into it; as if experience had as yet done nothing toward showing that one mode of existence, or of conduct, is preferable to another. Nobody denies that people should be so taught and trained in youth as to know and benefit by the ascertained results of human experience. But it is the privilege and proper condition of a human being, arrived at the maturity of his faculties, to use and interpret experience in his own way. It is for him to find out what part of recorded experience is properly applicable to his own circumstances and character. The traditions and customs of other people are, to a certain extent, evidence of what their experience has taught *them*—presumptive evidence, and as such, have a claim to his deference: but, in the first place, their experience may be too narrow, or they may have not interpreted it rightly. Secondly, their interpretation of experience may be correct, but unsuitable to him. Customs are made for customary circumstances and customary characters; and his circumstances or his character may be uncustomary. Thirdly, though the customs be both good as customs and suitable to him, yet to conform to custom merely *as* custom does not educate or develop in him any of the qualities which are the distinctive endowment of a human being. The human faculties of perception, judgment, discriminative feeling, mental activity, and even moral preference are exercised only in making a choice. He who does anything because it is the custom makes no choice. He gains no practice either in discerning or in desiring what is best. The mental and moral, like the muscular, powers are improved only by being used. The faculties are called into no exercise by doing a thing merely because others do it, no more than by believing a thing only because others believe it. If the grounds of an opinion are not conclusive to the person's own reason, his reason cannot be strengthened, but is likely to be weakened, by his adopting it: and if the inducements to an act are not such as are consentaneous to his own feelings and character (where affection, or the rights of others, are not concerned), it is so much done toward rendering his feelings and character inert and torpid instead of active and energetic.

He who lets the world, or his own portion of it, choose his plan of life for him has no need of any other faculty than the ape-like one of imitation. He who chooses his plan for himself employs all his faculties. He must use observation to see, reasoning and judgment to foresee, activity to gather materials for decision, discrimination to decide, and when he has decided, firmness and self-control to hold to his deliberate decision. And these qualities he requires and exercises exactly in proportion as the

---

31. *The Sphere and Duties of Government*, from the German of Baron Wilhelm von Humboldt, pp. 11–13.

part of his conduct which he determines according to his own judgment and feelings is a large one. It is possible that he might be guided in some good path, and kept out of harm's way, without any of these things. But what will be his comparative worth as a human being? It really is of importance, not only what men do, but also what manner of men they are that do it. Among the works of man which human life is rightly employed in perfecting and beautifying, the first in importance surely is man himself. Supposing it were possible to get houses built, corn grown, battles fought, causes tried, and even churches erected and prayers said by machinery—by automatons in human form—it would be a considerable loss to exchange for these automatons even the men and women who at present inhabit the more civilized parts of the world, and who assuredly are but starved specimens of what nature can and will produce. Human nature is not a machine to be built after a model, and set to do exactly the work prescribed for it, but a tree, which requires to grow and develop itself on all sides, according to the tendency of the inward forces which make it a living thing.

It will probably be conceded that it is desirable people should exercise their understandings, and that an intelligent following of custom, or even occasionally an intelligent deviation from custom, is better than a blind and simply mechanical adhesion to it. To a certain extent it is admitted that our understanding should be our own; but there is not the same willingness to admit that our desires and impulses should be our own likewise, or that to possess impulses of our own, and of any strength, is anything but a peril and a snare. Yet desires and impulses are as much a part of a perfect human being as beliefs and restraints; and strong impulses are only perilous when not properly balanced, when one set of aims and inclinations is developed into strength, while others, which ought to coexist with them, remain weak and inactive. It is not because men's desires are strong that they act ill; it is because their consciences are weak. There is no natural connection between strong impulses and a weak conscience. The natural connection is the other way. To say that one person's desires and feelings are stronger and more various than those of another is merely to say that he has more of the raw material of human nature and is therefore capable, perhaps of more evil, but certainly of more good. Strong impulses are but another name for energy. Energy may be turned to bad uses; but more good may always be made of an energetic nature than of an indolent and impassive one. Those who have most natural feeling are always those whose cultivated feelings may be made the strongest. The same strong susceptibilities which make the personal impulses vivid and powerful are also the source from whence are generated the most passionate love of virtue and the sternest self-control. It is through the cultivation of these that society both does its duty and protects its interests, not by rejecting the stuff of which heroes are made, because it knows not how to make them. A person whose desires and impulses are his own—are the expression of his own nature, as it has been developed and modified by his own culture—is said to have a character. One whose desires and impulses are not his own has no character, no more than a steam engine has a character. If, in addition to being his own, his impulses are strong and are under the government of a strong will, he has an energetic character. Whoever thinks that individuality of desires and impulses should not be encouraged to unfold itself must maintain that society has no need of strong natures—is not the better for containing many persons who have much character—and that a high general average of energy is not desirable.

In some early states of society, these forces might be, and were, too much ahead of the power which society then possessed of disciplining and controlling them. There has been a time when the element of spontaneity and individuality was in excess, and the social principle had a hard struggle with it. The difficulty then was to induce men of strong bodies or minds to pay obedience to any rules which required them to control their impulses. To overcome this difficulty, law and discipline, like the Popes struggling against the Emperors, asserted a power over the whole man, claiming to control all his life in order to control his character—which society had not found any other sufficient means of binding. But society has now fairly got the better of individuality; and the danger which threatens human nature is not the excess, but the deficiency, of personal impulses and preferences. Things are vastly changed since the passions of those who were strong by station or by personal endowment were in a state of habitual rebellion against laws and ordinances, and required to be rigorously chained up to enable the persons within their reach to enjoy any particle of security. In our times, from the highest class of society down to the lowest, everyone lives as under the eye of a hostile and dreaded censorship. Not only in what concerns others, but in what concerns only themselves, the individual or the family do not ask themselves, what do I prefer? or, what would suit my character and disposition? or, what would allow the best and highest in me to have fair play and enable it to grow and thrive? They ask themselves, what is suitable to my position? what is usually done by persons of my station and pecuniary circumstances? or (worse still) what is usually done by persons of a station and circumstances superior to mine? I do not mean that they choose what is customary in preference to what suits their own inclination. It does not occur to them to have any inclination except for what is customary. Thus the mind itself is bowed to the yoke: even in what people do for pleasure, conformity is the first thing thought of; they like in crowds; they exercise choice only among things commonly done; peculiaritiy of taste, eccentricity of conduct are shunned equally with crimes, until by dint of not following their own nature they have no nature to follow: their human capacities are withered and starved; they become incapable of any strong wishes or native pleasures, and are generally without either opinions or feelings of home growth, or properly their own. Now is this, or is it not, the desirable condition of human nature?

It is so, on the Calvinistic theory. According to that, the one great offense of man is self-will. All the good of which humanity is capable is comprised in obedience. You have no choice; thus you must do, and no otherwise: "Whatever is not a duty is a sin." Human nature being radically corrupt, there is no redemption for anyone until human nature is killed within him. To one holding this theory of life, crushing out any of the human faculties, capacities, and susceptibilities is no evil: man needs no capacity but that of surrendering himself to the will of God; and if he uses any of his faculties for any other purpose but to do that supposed will more effectually, he is better without them. This is the theory of Calvinism; and it is held, in a mitigated form, by many who do not consider themselves Calvinists; the mitigation consisting in giving a less ascetic interpretation to the alleged will of God, asserting it to be his will that mankind should gratify some of their inclinations, of course not in the manner they themselves prefer, but in the way of obedience, that is, in a way prescribed to them by authority, and, therefore, by the necessary condition of the case, the same for all.

In some such insidious form there is at present a strong tendency to this narrow theory of life, and to the pinched and hidebound type of human character which it patronizes. Many persons, no doubt, sincerely think that human beings thus cramped and dwarfed are as their Maker designed them to be, just as many have thought that trees are a much finer thing when clipped into pollards, or cut out into figures of animals, than as nature made them. But if it be any part of religion to believe that man was made by a good Being, it is more consistent with that faith to believe that this Being gave all human faculties that they might be cultivated and unfolded, not rooted out and consumed, and that he takes delight in every nearer approach made by his creatures to the ideal conception embodied in them, every increase in any of their capabilities of comprehension, of action, or of enjoyment. There is a different type of human excellence from the Calvinistic: a conception of humanity as having its nature bestowed on it for other purposes than merely to be abnegated. "Pagan self-assertion" is one of the elements of human worth, as well as "Christian self-denial." [32] There is a Greek ideal of self-development, which the Platonic and Christian ideal of self-government blends with, but does not supersede. It may be better to be a John Knox than an Alcibiades,[33] but it is better to be a Pericles[34] than either; nor would a Pericles, if we had one in these days, be without anything good which belonged to John Knox.

It is not by wearing down into uniformity all that is individual in themselves, but by cultivating it and calling it forth, within the limits imposed by the rights and interests of others, that human beings become a noble and beautiful object of contemplation; and as the works partake the character of those who do them, by the same process human life also becomes rich, diversified, and animating, furnishing more abundant aliment to high thoughts and elevating feelings, and strengthening the tie which binds every individual to the race, by making the race infinitely better worth belonging to. In proportion to the development of his individuality, each person becomes more valuable to himself, and is, therefore, capable of being more valuable to others. There is a greater fullness of life about his own existence, and when there is more life in the units there is more in the mass which is composed of them. As much compression as is necessary to prevent the stronger specimens of human nature from encroaching on the rights of others cannot be dispensed with; but for this there is ample compensation even in the point of view of human development. The means of development which the individual loses by being prevented from gratifying his inclinations to the injury of others are chiefly obtained at the expense of the development of other people. And even to himself there is a full equivalent in the better development of the social part of his nature, rendered possible by the restraint put upon the selfish part. To be held to rigid rules of justice for the sake of others develops the feelings and capacities which have the good of others for their object. But to be restrained in things not affecting their good, by their mere displeasure, develops nothing valuable except such force of character as may unfold itself in resisting the restraint. If acquiesced in, it dulls and blunts the whole nature. To give any fair play to the nature of each, it is essential that different persons should be allowed to lead different lives. In proportion as this latitude has been ex-

32. Sterling's *Essays*. [John Sterling (1806–1844) was a British essayist and poet. The reference is to his *Essays and Tales*.]

33. [Alcibiades (c. 450–404 B.C.) was an ambitious Athenian general who, according to some historians, was largely responsible for the decline of Athens.]

34. [Regarding Pericles, see Aristotle's *Ethics*, n. 52.]

ercised in any age has that age been noteworthy to posterity. Even despotism does not produce its worst effects so long as individuality exists under it; and whatever crushes individuality is despotism, by whatever name it may be called and whether it professes to be enforcing the will of God or the injunctions of men.

Having said that the individuality is the same thing with development, and that it is only the cultivation of individuality which produces, or can produce, well-developed human beings, I might here close the argument; for what more or better can be said of any condition of human affairs than that it brings human beings themselves nearer to the best thing they can be? Or what worse can be said of any obstruction to good than that it prevents this? Doubtless, however, these considerations will not suffice to convince those who most need convincing; and it is necessary further to show that these developed human beings are of some use to the undeveloped—to point out to those who do not desire liberty, and would not avail themselves of it, that they may be in some intelligible manner rewarded for allowing other people to make use of it without hindrance.

In the first place, then, I would suggest that they might possibly learn something from them. It will not be denied by anybody that originality is a valuable element in human affairs. There is always need of persons not only to discover new truths and point out when what were once truths are true no longer, but also to commence new practices and set the example of more enlightened conduct and better taste and sense in human life. This cannot well be gainsaid by anybody who does not believe that the world has already attained perfection in all its ways and practices. It is true that this benefit is not capable of being rendered by everybody alike; there are but few persons, in comparison with the whole of mankind, whose experiments, if adopted by others, would be likely to be any improvement on established practice. But these few are the salt of the earth; without them, human life would become a stagnant pool. Not only is it they who introduce good things which did not before exist; it is they who keep the life in those which already exist. If there were nothing new to be done, would human intellect cease to be necessary? Would it be a reason why those who do the old things should forget why they are done, and do them like cattle, not like human beings? There is only too great a tendency in the best beliefs and practices to degenerate into the mechanical; and unless there were a succession of persons whose ever-recurring originality prevents the grounds of those beliefs and practices from becoming merely traditional, such dead matter would not resist the smallest shock from anything really alive, and there would be no reason why civilization should not die out, as in the Byzantine Empire. Persons of genius, it is true, are, and are always likely to be, a small minority; but in order to have them, it is necessary to preserve the soil in which they grow. Genius can only breathe freely in an *atmosphere* of freedom. Persons of genius are, *ex vi termini*,[35] more individual than any other people—less capable, consequently, of fitting themselves, without hurtful compression, into any of the small number of molds which society provides in order to save its members the trouble of forming their own character. If from timidity they consent to be forced into one of these molds, and to let all that part of themselves which cannot expand under the pressure remain unexpanded, society will be little the better for their genius. If they are of a strong character and break their fetters, they become a mark for the society which has not succeeded in reducing them to commonplace, to point out with solemn warnings as "wild," "erratic,"

35. [By definition.]

and the like—much as if one should complain of the Niagara river for not flowing smoothly between its banks like a Dutch canal.

I insist thus emphatically on the importance of genius and the necessity of allowing it to unfold itself freely both in thought and in practice, being well aware that no one will deny the position in theory, but knowing also that almost everyone, in reality, is totally indifferent to it. People think genius a fine thing if it enables a man to write an exciting poem or paint a picture. But in its true sense, that of originality in thought and action, though no one says that it is not a thing to be admired, nearly all, at heart, think that they can do very well without it. Unhappily this is too natural to be wondered at. Originality is the one thing which unoriginal minds cannot feel the use of. They cannot see what it is to do for them: how should they? If they could see what it would do for them, it would not be originality. The first service which originality has to render them is that of opening their eyes: which being once fully done, they would have a chance of being themselves original. Meanwhile, recollecting that nothing was ever done which someone was not the first to do, and that all good things which exist are the fruits of originality, let them be modest enough to believe that there is something still left for it to accomplish, and assure themselves that they are more in need of originality, the less they are conscious of the want.

In sober truth, whatever homage may be professed, or even paid, to real or supposed mental superiority, the general tendency of things throughout the world is to render mediocrity the ascendant power among mankind. In ancient history, in the Middle Ages, and in a diminishing degree through the long transition from feudality to the present time, the individual was a power in himself; and if he had either great talents or a high social position, he was a considerable power. At present individuals are lost in the crowd. In politics it is almost a triviality to say that public opinion now rules the world. The only power deserving the name is that of masses, and of governments while they make themselves the organ of the tendencies and instincts of masses. This is as true in the moral and social relations of private life as in public transactions. Those whose opinions go by the name of public opinion are not always the same sort of public: in America, they are the whole white population; in England, chiefly the middle class. But they are always a mass, that is to say, collective mediocrity. And what is a still greater novelty, the mass do not now take their opinions from dignitaries in Church or State, from ostensible leaders, or from books. Their thinking is done for them by men much like themselves, addressing them or speaking in their name, on the spur of the moment, through the newspapers. I am not complaining of all this. I do not assert that anything better is compatible, as a general rule, with the present low state of the human mind. But that does not hinder the government of mediocrity from being mediocre government. No government by a democracy or a numerous aristocracy, either in its political acts or in the opinions, qualities, and tone of mind which it fosters, ever did or could rise above mediocrity except in so far as the sovereign. Many have let themselves be guided (which in their best times they always have done) by the counsels and influence of a more highly gifted and instructed *one* or *few*. The initiation of all wise or noble things comes and must come from individuals; generally at first from some one individual. The honor and glory of the average man is that he is capable of following that initiative; that he can respond internally to wise and noble things, and be led to them with his eyes open. I am not countenancing the sort of "hero-worship" which applauds the strong man of genius for forcibly seizing on the government of the world and making it do his bidding in spite of itself. All he can claim is freedom to point out the way. The power of compelling others into it is not only inconsistent with the freedom and development of all the rest, but corrupting to the strong man himself. It does seem, however, that when the opinions of masses of merely average men are everywhere become or becoming the dominant power, the counterpoise and corrective to that tendency would be the more and more pronounced individuality of those who stand on the higher eminences of thought. It is in these circumstances most especially that exceptional individuals, instead of being deterred, should be encouraged in acting differently from the mass. In other times there was no advantage in their doing so, unless they acted not only differently but better. In this age, the mere example of nonconformity, the mere refusal to bend the knee to custom, is itself a service. Precisely because the tyranny of opinion is such as to make eccentricity a reproach, it is desirable, in order to break through that tyranny, that people should be eccentric. Eccentricity has always abounded when and where strength of character has abounded; and the amount of eccentricity in a society has generally been proportional to the amount of genius, mental vigor, and moral courage it contained. That so few now dare to be eccentric marks the chief danger of the time.

I have said that it is important to give the freest scope possible to uncustomary things, in order that it may in time appear which of these are fit to be converted into customs. But independence of action and disregard of custom are not solely deserving of encouragement for the chance they afford that better modes of action, and customs more worthy of general adoption, may be struck out; nor is it only persons of decided mental superiority who have a just claim to carry on their lives in their own way. There is no reason that all human existence should be constructed on some one or some small number of patterns. If a person possesses any tolerable amount of common sense and experience, his own mode of laying out his existence is the best, not because it is the best in itself, but because it is his own mode. Human beings are not like sheep; and even sheep are not undistinguishably alike. A man cannot get a coat or a pair of boots to fit him unless they are either made to his measure or he has a whole warehouseful to choose from; and is it easier to fit him with a life than with a coat, or are human beings more like one another in their whole physical and spiritual conformation than in the shape of their feet? If it were only that people have diversities of taste, that is reason enough for not attempting to shape them all after one model. But different persons also require different conditions for their spiritual development; and can no more exist healthily in the same moral than all the variety of plants can in the same physical, atmosphere and climate. The same things which are helps to one person toward the cultivation of his higher nature are hindrances to another. The same mode of life is a healthy excitement to one, keeping all his faculties of action and enjoyment in their best order, while to another it is a distracting burden which suspends or crushes all internal life. Such are the differences among human beings in their sources of pleasure, their susceptibilities of pain, and the operation on them of different physical and moral agencies that, unless there is a corresponding diversity in their modes of life, they neither obtain their fair share of happiness, nor grow up to the mental, moral, and aesthetic stature of which their nature is capable. Why then should tolerance, as far as the public sentiment is concerned, extend only to tastes and modes of life which extort acquiescence by the multitude of their adherents? Nowhere (except in some monastic institutions) is diversity of taste entirely unrecognized; a person may, without blame, either like or dislike rowing, or smoking, or music, or athletic exercises, or chess, or cards, or study, because both those who like each of these things and those who dislike them are too numerous to be put down. But the man, and still more the woman, who can be accused either of doing "what nobody does," or of not doing "what everybody does," is the subject of as much depreciatory remark as if he or she had committed some grave moral delinquency. Persons require to possess a title, or some other badge of rank, or of the consideration of people of rank, to be able to indulge somewhat in the luxury of doing as they like without detriment to their estimation. To indulge somewhat, I repeat: for whoever allow themselves much of that indulgence incur the risk of something worse than disparaging speeches—they are in peril of a commission *de lunatico* and of having their property taken from them and given to their relations.[36]

There is one characteristic of the present direction of public opinion peculiarly calculated to make it intolerant of any marked demonstrations of individuality. The general average of mankind are not only moderate in intellect, but also moderate in inclinations; they have no tastes or wishes strong enough to incline them to do anything unusual, and they consequently do not understand those who have, and class all such with the wild and intemperate whom they are accustomed to look down upon. Now, in addition to this fact which is general, we have only to suppose that a strong movement has set in toward the improvement of morals, and it is evident what we have to expect. In these days such a movement has set in; much has actually been effected in the way of increased regularity of conduct and discouragement of excesses; and there is a philanthropic spirit abroad for the exercise of which there is no more inviting field than the moral and prudential improvement of our fellow creatures. These tendencies of the times cause the public to be more disposed than at most former periods to prescribe general rules of conduct and endeavor to make everyone conform to the approved standard. And that standard, express or tacit, is to desire nothing strongly. Its ideal of character is to be without any marked character—to maim by compression, like a Chinese lady's foot, every part of human nature which stands out prominently and tends to make the person markedly dissimilar in outline to commonplace humanity.

As is usually the case with ideals which exclude one-half of what is desirable, the present standard of approbation produces only an inferior imitation of the other half. Instead of great energies guided by vigorous reason and strong feelings strongly controlled by a conscientious will, its result is weak feelings and weak energies,

---

36. There is something both contemptible and frightful in the sort of evidence on which, of late years, any person can be judicially declared unfit for the management of his affairs; and after his death, his disposal of his property can be set aside if there is enough of it to pay the expenses of litigation—which are charged on the property itself. All the minute details of his daily life are pried into, and whatever is found which, seen through the medium of the perceiving and describing faculties of the lowest of the low, bears an appearance unlike absolute commonplace, is laid before the jury as evidence of insanity, and often with success; the jurors being little, if at all, less vulgar and ignorant than the witnesses, while the judges, with that extraordinary want of knowledge of human nature and life which continually astonishes us in English lawyers, often help to mislead them. These trials speak volumes as to the state of feeling and opinion among the vulgar with regard to human liberty. So far from setting any value on individuality—so far from respecting the right of each individual to act, in things indifferent, as seems good to his own judgment and inclinations, judges and juries cannot even conceive that a person in a state of sanity can desire such freedom. In former days, when it was proposed to burn atheists, charitable people used to suggest putting them in a madhouse instead; it would be nothing surprising nowadays were we to see this done, and the doers applauding themselves because, instead of persecuting for religion, they had adopted so humane and Christian a mode of treating these unfortunates, not without a silent satisfaction at their having thereby obtained their deserts.

which therefore can be kept in outward conformity to rule without any strength either of will or of reason. Already energetic characters on any large scale are becoming merely traditional. There is now scarcely any outlet for energy in this country except business. The energy expended in this may still be regarded as considerable. What little is left from that employment is expended on some hobby, which may be a useful, even a philanthropic, hobby, but is always some one thing, and generally a thing of small dimensions. The greatness of England is now all collective; individually small, we only appear capable of anything great by our habit of combining; and with this our moral and religious philanthropists are perfectly contented. But it was men of another stamp than this that made England what it has been; and men of another stamp will be needed to prevent its decline.

The despotism of custom is everywhere the standing hindrance to human advancement, being in unceasing antagonism to that disposition to aim at something better than customary, which is called, according to circumstances, the spirit of liberty, or that of progress or improvement. The spirit of improvement is not always a spirit of liberty, for it may aim at forcing improvements on an unwilling people; and the spirit of liberty, in so far as it resists such attempts, may ally itself locally and temporarily with the opponents of improvement; but the only unfailing and permanent source of improvement is liberty, since by it there are as many possible independent centers of improvement as there are individuals. The progressive principle, however, in either shape, whether as the love of liberty or of improvement, is antagonistic to the sway of custom, involving at least emancipation from that yoke; and the contest between the two constitutes the chief interest of the history of mankind. The greater part of the world has, properly speaking, no history, because the despotism of Custom is complete. This is the case over the whole East. Custom is there, in all things, the final appeal; justice and right mean conformity to custom; the argument of custom no one, unless some tyrant intoxicated with power, thinks of resisting. And we see the result. Those nations must once have had originality; they did not start out of the ground populous, lettered, and versed in many of the arts of life; they made themselves all this, and were then the greatest and most powerful nations of the world. What are they now? The subjects or dependents of tribes whose forefathers wandered in the forests when theirs had magnificent palaces and gorgeous temples, but over whom custom exercised only a divided rule with liberty and progress. A people, it appears, may be progressive for a certain length of time, and then stop: when does it stop? When it ceases to possess individuality. If a similar change should befall the nations of Europe, it will not be in exactly the same shape: the despotism of custom with which these nations are threatened is not precisely stationariness. It proscribes singularity, but it does not preclude change, provided all change together. We have discarded the fixed costumes of our forefathers; everyone must still dress like other people, but the fashion may change once or twice a year. We thus take care that when there is a change, it shall be for change's sake, and not from any idea of beauty or convenience; for the same idea of beauty or convenience would not strike all the world at the same moment, and be simultaneously thrown aside by all at another moment. But we are progressive as well as changeable: we continually make new inventions in mechanical things, and keep them until they are again superseded by better; we are eager for improvement in politics, in education, even in morals, though in this last our idea of improvement chiefly consists in persuading or forcing other people to be as good as ourselves. It is not progress that we object to; on the contrary, we flatter ourselves that we are the most progressive people who ever lived. It is individuality that we war against: we should think we had done wonders if we had made ourselves all alike, forgetting that the unlikeness of one person to another is generally the first thing which draws the attention of either to the imperfection of his own type and the superiority of another, or the possibility, by combining the advantages of both, of producing something better than either. We have a warning example in China—a nation of much talent and, in some respects, even wisdom, owing to the rare good fortune of having been provided at an early period with a particularly good set of customs, the work, in some measure, of men to whom even the most enlightened European must accord, under certain limitations, the title of sages and philosophers. They are remarkable, too, in the excellence of their apparatus for impressing, as far as possible, the best wisdom they possess upon every mind in the community, and securing that those who have appropriated most of it shall occupy the posts of honor and power. Surely the people who did this have discovered the secret of human progressiveness and must have kept themselves steadily at the head of the movement of the world. On the contrary, they have become stationary—have remained so for thousands of years; and if they are ever to be further improved, it must be by foreigners. They have succeeded beyond all hope in what English philanthropists are so industriously working at—in making a people all alike, all governing their thoughts and conduct by the same maxims and rules; and these are the fruits. The modern *régime* of public opinion is, in an unorganized form, what the Chinese educational and political systems are in an organized; and unless individuality shall be able successfully to assert itself against this yoke, Europe, not-withstanding its noble antecedents and its professed Christianity, will tend to become another China.

What is it that has hitherto preserved Europe from this lot? What has made the European family of nations an improving, instead of a stationary, portion of mankind? Not any superior excellence in them, which, when it exists, exists as the effect, not as the cause, but their remarkable diversity of character and culture. Individuals, classes, nations have been extremely unlike one another: they have struck out a great variety of paths, each leading to something valuable; and although at every period those who traveled in different paths have been intolerant of one another, and each would have thought it an excellent thing if all the rest could have been compelled to travel his road, their attempts to thwart each other's development have rarely had any permanent success, and each has in time endured to receive the good which the others have offered. Europe is, in my judgment, wholly indebted to this plurality of paths for its progressive and many-sided development. But it already begins to possess this benefit in a considerably less degree. It is decidedly advancing toward the Chinese idea of making all people alike. M. de Tocqueville,[37] in his last important work, remarks how much more the Frenchmen of the present day resemble one another than did those even of the last generation. The same remark might be made of Englishmen in a far greater degree. In a passage already quoted from Wilhelm von Humboldt, he points out two things as necessary conditions of human development—because necessary to render people unlike one another—namely, freedom and variety of situations. The second of these two conditions is in this country every day diminishing. The circumstances which surround different classes and individuals, and shape their characters, are daily becoming more assimilated. Formerly, different ranks, different neighborhoods, different

---

37. [Alexis de Tocqueville (1805–1859) was the French writer who authored *Democracy in America*, perhaps the single most impressive sociological study of American democratic life. The work referred to is *The Old Régime and the French Revolution.*]

trades and professions lived in what might be called different worlds; at present, to a great degree in the same. Comparatively speaking, they now read the same things, listen to the same things, see the same things, go to the same places, have their hopes and fears directed to the same objects, have the same rights and liberties, and the same means of asserting them. Great as are the differences of position which remain, they are nothing to those which have ceased. And the assimilation is still proceeding. All the political changes of the age promote it, since they all tend to raise the low and to lower the high. Every extension of education promotes it, because education brings people under common influences and gives them access to the general stock of facts and sentiments. Improvement in the means of communication promotes it, by bringing the inhabitants of distant places into personal contact, and keeping up a rapid flow of changes of residence between one place and another. The increase of commerce and manufactures promotes it, by diffusing more widely the advantages of easy circumstances and opening all objects of ambition, even the highest, to general competition, whereby the desire of rising becomes no longer the character of a particular class, but of all classes. A more powerful agency than even all these, in bringing about a general similarity among mankind, is the complete establishment, in this and other free countries, of the ascendancy of public opinion in the State. As the various social eminences which enabled persons entrenched on them to disregard the opinion of the multitude gradually become leveled; as the very idea of resisting the will of the public, when it is positively known that they have a will, disappears more and more from the minds of practical politicians, there ceases to be any social support for nonconformity—any substantive power in society which, itself opposed to the ascendancy of numbers, is interested in taking under its protection opinions and tendencies at variance with those of the public.

The combination of all these causes forms so great a mass of influences hostile to individuality that it is not easy to see how it can stand its ground. It will do so with increasing difficulty unless the intelligent part of the public can be made to feel its value—to see that it is good there should be differences, even though not for the better, even though, as it may appear to them, some should be for the worse. If the claims of individuality are ever to be asserted, the time is now while much is still wanting to complete the enforced assimilation. It is only in the earlier stages that any stand can be successfully made against the encroachment. The demand that all other people shall resemble ourselves grows by what it feeds on. If resistance waits till life is reduced *nearly* to one uniform type, all deviations from that type will come to be considered impious, immoral, even monstrous and contrary to nature. Mankind speedily become unable to conceive diversity when they have been for some time unaccustomed to see it.

CHAPTER IV

OF THE LIMITS TO THE AUTHORITY OF SOCIETY OVER THE INDIVIDUAL

What, then, is the rightful limit to the sovereignty of the individual over himself?

Where does the authority of society begin? How much of human life should be assigned to individuality, and how much to society?

Each will receive its proper share if each has that which more particularly concerns it. To individuality should belong the part of life in which it is chiefly the individual that is interested; to society, the part which chiefly interests society.

Though society is not founded on a contract, and though no good purpose is answered by inventing a contract in order to deduce social obligations from it, everyone who receives the protection of society owes a return for the benefit, and the fact of living in society renders it indispensable that each should be bound to observe a certain line of conduct toward the rest. This conduct consists, first, in not injuring the interests of one another, or rather certain interests which, either by express legal provision or by tacit understanding, ought to be considered as rights; and secondly, in each person's bearing his share (to be fixed on some equitable principle) of the labors and sacrifices incurred for defending the society or its members from injury and molestation. These conditions society is justified in enforcing at all costs to those who endeavor to withhold fulfillment. Nor is this all that society may do. The acts of an individual may be hurtful to others or wanting in due consideration for their welfare, without going to the length of violating any of their constituted rights. The offender may then be justly punished by opinion, though not by law. As soon as any part of a person's conduct affects prejudicially the interests of others, society has jurisdiction over it, and the question whether the general welfare will or will not be promoted by interfering with it becomes open to discussion. But there is no room for entertaining any such question when a person's conduct affects the interests of no persons besides himself, or needs not affect them unless they like (all the persons concerned being of full age and the ordinary amount of understanding). In all such cases, there should be perfect freedom, legal and social, to do the action and stand the consequences.

It would be a great misunderstanding of this doctrine to suppose that it is one of selfish indifference which pretends that human beings have no business with each other's conduct in life, and that they should not concern themselves about the well-doing or well-being of one another, unless their own interest is involved. Instead of any diminution, there is need of a great increase of disinterested exertion to promote the good of others. But disinterested benevolence can find other instruments to persuade people to their good than whips and scourges, either of the literal or the metaphorical sort. I am the last person to undervalue the self-regarding virtues; they are only second in importance, if even second, to the social. It is equally the business of education to cultivate both. But even education works by conviction and persuasion as well as by compulsion, and it is by the former only that, when the period of education is passed, the self-regarding virtues should be inculcated. Human beings owe to each other help to distinguish the better from the worse, and encouragement to choose the former and avoid the latter. They should be forever stimulating each other to increased exercise of their higher faculties and increased direction of their feelings and aims toward wise instead of foolish, elevating instead of degrading, objects and contemplations. But neither one person, nor any number of persons, is warranted in saying to another human creature of ripe years that he shall not do with his life for his own benefit what he chooses to do with it. He is the person most interested in his own well-being: the interest which any other person, except in cases of strong personal attachment, can have in it is trifling compared with that which he himself has; the interest which society has in him individually (except as to his conduct to others) is fractional and altogether indirect, while with respect to his own feelings and circumstances the most ordinary man or woman has means of knowledge immeasurably surpassing those that can be possessed by anyone else. The interference of society to overrule his judgment and purposes in what only regards himself must be grounded on general presumptions which may be altogether wrong and, even if right, are as likely as not to be misapplied to individual cases, by persons no better acquainted with the circumstances of such cases than those are who look at them merely from without. In this department, therefore, of human affairs, individuality has its proper field of action. In the conduct of human beings toward one another it is necessary that general rules should for the most part be observed in order that people may know what they have to expect; but in each person's own concerns his individual spontaneity is entitled to free exercise. Considerations to aid his judgment, exhortations to strengthen his will may be offered to him, even obtruded on him, by others; but he himself is the final judge. All errors which he is likely to commit against advice and warning are far outweighed by the evil of allowing others to constrain him to what they deem his good.

I do not mean that the feelings with which a person is regarded by others ought not to be in any way affected by his self-regarding qualities or deficiencies. This is neither possible nor desirable. If he is eminent in any of the qualities which conduce to his own good, he is, so far, a proper object of admiration. He is so much the nearer to the ideal perfection of human nature. If he is grossly deficient in those qualities, a sentiment the opposite of admiration will follow. There is a degree of folly, and a degree of what may be called (though the phrase is not unobjectionable) lowness or depravation of taste, which, though it cannot justify doing harm to the person who manifests it, renders him necessarily and properly a subject of distaste, or, in extreme cases, even of contempt: a person could not have the opposite qualities in due strength without entertaining these feelings. Though doing no wrong to anyone, a person may so act as to compel us to judge him, and feel to him, as a fool or as a being of an inferior order; and since this judgment and feeling are a fact which he would prefer to avoid, it is doing him a service to warn him of it beforehand, as of any other disagreeable consequence to which he exposes himself. It would be well, indeed, if this good office were much more freely rendered than the common notions of politeness at present permit, and if one person could honestly point out to another that he thinks him in fault, without being considered unmannerly or presuming. We have a right, also, in various ways, to act upon our unfavorable opinion of anyone, not to the oppression of his individuality, but in the exercise of ours. We are not bound, for example, to seek his society; we have a right to avoid it (though not to parade the avoidance), for we have a right to choose the society most acceptable to us. We have a right, and it may be our duty, to caution others against him if we think his example or conversation likely to have a pernicious effect on those with whom he associates. We may give others a preference over him in optional good offices, except those which tend to his improvement. In these various modes a person may suffer very servere penalties at the hands of others for faults which directly concern only himself; but he suffers these penalties only in so far as they are the natural and, as it were, the spontaneous consequences of the faults themselves, not because they are purposely inflicted on him for the sake of punishment. A person who shows rashness, obstinacy, self-conceit—who cannot live within moderate means; who cannot restrain himself from hurtful indulgence;

who pursues animal pleasures at the expense of those of feeling and intellect—must expect to be lowered in the opinion of others, and to have a less share of their favorable sentiments; but of this he has no right to complain unless he has merited their favor by special excellence in his social relations and has thus established a title to their good offices, which is not affected by his demerits toward himself.

What I contend for is that the inconveniences which are strictly inseparable from the unfavorable judgment of others are the only ones to which a person should ever be subjected for that portion of his conduct and character which concerns his own good, but which does not affect the interest of others in their relations with him. Acts injurious to others require a totally different treatment. Encroachment on their rights; infliction on them of any loss or damage not justified by his own rights; falsehood or duplicity in dealing with them; unfair or ungenerous use of advantages over them; even selfish abstinence from defending them against injury—these are fit objects of moral reprobation and, in grave cases, of moral retribution and punishment. And not only these acts, but the dispositions which lead to them, are properly immoral and fit subjects of disapprobation which may rise to abhorrence. Cruelty of disposition; malice and ill-nature; that most antisocial and odious of all passions, envy; dissimulation and insincerity, irascibility on insufficient cause, and resentment disproportioned to the provocation; the love of domineering over others; the desire to engross more than one's share of advantages (the *pleonexia*[38] of the Greeks); the pride which derives gratification from the abasement of others; the egotism which thinks self and its concerns more important than everything else, and decides all doubtful questions in its own favor—these are moral vices and constitute a bad and odious moral character; unlike the self-regarding faults previously mentioned, which are not properly immoralities and, to whatever pitch they may be carried, do not constitute wickedness. They may be proofs of any amount of folly or want of personal dignity and self-respect, but they are only a subject of moral reprobation when they involve a breach of duty to others, for whose sake the individual is bound to have care for himself. What are called duties to ourselves are not socially obligatory unless circumstances render them at the same time duties to others. The term duty to oneself, when it means anything more than prudence, means self-respect or self-development, and for none of these is anyone accountable to his fellow creatures, because for none of them is it for the good of mankind that he be held accountable to them.

The distinction between the loss of consideration which a person may rightly incur by defect of prudence or of personal dignity, and the reprobation which is due to him for an offense against the rights of others, is not a merely nominal distinction. It makes a vast difference both in our feelings and in our conduct toward him whether he displeases us in things in which we think we have a right to control him or in things in which we know that we have not. If he displeases us, we may express our distaste, and we may stand aloof from a person as well as from a thing that displeases us; but we shall not therefore feel called on to make his life uncomfortable. We shall reflect that he already bears, or will bear, the whole penalty of his error; if he spoils his life by mismanagement, we shall not, for that reason, desire to spoil it still further; instead of wishing to punish him, we shall rather endeavor to alleviate his punishment by showing him how he may avoid or cure the evils his conduct tends to bring upon him. He may be to us an object of pity, perhaps of dislike, but

38. [Greed.]

not of anger or resentment; we shall not treat him like an enemy of society; the worst we shall think ourselves justified in doing is leaving him to himself, if we do not interfere benevolently by showing interest or concern for him. It is far otherwise if he has infringed the rules necessary for the protection of his fellow creatures, individually or collectively. The evil consequences of his acts do not then fall on himself, but on others; and society, as the protector of all its members, must retaliate on him, must inflict pain on him for the express purpose of punishment, and must take care that it be sufficiently severe. In the one case, he is an offender at our bar, and we are called on not only to sit in judgment on him, but, in one shape or another, to execute our own sentence; in the other case, it is not our part to inflict any suffering on him, except what may incidentally follow from our using the same liberty in the regulation of our own affairs which we allow to him in his.

The distinction here pointed out between the part of a person's life which concerns only himself and that which concerns others, many persons will refuse to admit. How (it may be asked) can any part of the conduct of a member of society be a matter of indifference to the other members? No person is an entirely isolated being; it is impossible for a person to do anything seriously or permanently hurtful to himself without mischief reaching at least to his near connections, and often far beyond them. If he injures his property, he does harm to those who directly or indirectly derived support from it, and usually diminishes, by a greater or less amount, the general resources of the community. If he deteriorates his bodily or mental faculties, he not only brings evil upon all who depended upon him for any portion of their happiness, but disqualifies himself for rendering the services which he owes to his fellow creatures generally, perhaps becomes a burden on their affection or benevolence; and if such conduct were very frequent hardly any offense that is committed would detract more from the general sum of good. Finally, if by his vices or follies a person does no direct harm to others, he is nevertheless (it may be said) injurious by his example, and ought to be compelled to control himself for the sake of those whom the sight or knowledge of his conduct might corrupt or mislead.

And even (it will be added) if the consequences of misconduct could be confined to the vicious or thoughtless individual, ought society to abandon to their own guidance those who are manifestly unfit for it? If protection against themselves is confessedly due to children and persons under age, is not society equally bound to afford it to persons of mature years who are equally incapable of self-government? If gambling, or drunkenness, or incontinence, or idleness, or uncleanliness are as injurious to happiness, and as great a hindrance to improvement, as many or most of the acts prohibited by law, why (it may be asked) should not law, so far as is consistent with practicability and social convenience, endeavor to repress these also? And as a supplement to the unavoidable imperfections of law, ought not opinion at least to organize a powerful police against these vices and visit rigidly with social penalties those who are known to practice them? There is no question here (it may be said) about restricting individuality, or impeding the trial of new and original experiments in living. The only things it is sought to prevent are things which have been tried and condemned from the beginning of the world until now—things which experience has shown not to be useful or suitable to any person's individuality. There must be some length of time and amount of experience after which a moral or prudential truth may be regarded as established; and it is merely desired to prevent generation after generation from falling over the same precipice which has been fatal to their predecessors.

I fully admit that the mischief which a person does to himself may seriously affect, both through their sympathies and their interests, those nearly connected with him and, in a minor degree, society at large. When, by conduct of this sort, a person is led to violate a distinct and assignable obligation to any other person or persons, the case is taken out of the self-regarding class and becomes amenable to moral disapprobation in the proper sense of the term. If, for example, a man, through intemperance or extravagance, becomes unable to pay his debts, or, having undertaken the moral responsibility of a family, becomes from the same cause incapable of supporting or educating them, he is deservedly reprobated and might be justly punished; but it is for the breach of duty to his family or creditors, not for the extravagance. If the resources which ought to have been devoted to them had been diverted from them for the most prudent investment, the moral culpability would have been the same. George Barnwell[39] murdered his uncle to get money for his mistress, but if he had done it to set himself up in business, he would equally have been hanged. Again, in the frequent case of a man who causes grief to his family by addiction to bad habits, he deserves reproach for his unkindness or ingratitude; but so he may for cultivating habits not in themselves vicious, if they are painful to those with whom he passes his life, or who from personal ties are dependent on him for their comfort. Whoever fails in the consideration generally due to the interests and feelings of others, not being compelled by some more imperative duty, or justified by allowable self-preference, is a subject of moral disapprobation for that failure, but not for the cause of it, nor for the errors, merely personal to himself, which may have remotely led to it. In like manner, when a person disables himself, by conduct purely self-regarding, from the performance of some definite duty incumbent on him to the public, he is guilty of a social offense. No person ought to be punished simply for being drunk; but a soldier or a policeman should be punished for being drunk on duty. Whenever, in short, there is a definite damage, or a definite risk of damage, either to an individual or to the public, the case is taken out of the province of liberty and placed in that of morality or law.

But with regard to the merely contingent or, as it may be called, constructive injury which a person causes to society by conduct which neither violates any specific duty to the public, nor occasions perceptible hurt to any assignable individual except himself, the inconvenience is one which society can afford to bear, for the sake of the greater good of human freedom. If grown persons are to be punished for not taking proper care of themselves, I would rather it were for their own sake than under pretense of preventing them from impairing their capacity or rendering to society benefits which society does not pretend it has a right to exact. But I cannot consent to argue the point as if society had no means of bringing its weaker members up to its ordinary standard of rational conduct, except waiting till they do something irrational, and then punishing them, legally or morally, for it. Society has had absolute power over them during all the early portion of their existence; it has had the whole period of childhood and nonage in which to try whether it could make them capable of rational conduct in life. The existing generation is master both of the training and the entire circumstances of the generation to come; it cannot indeed make them perfectly wise and good, because it is itself so lamentably deficient in goodness and wisdom; and its best efforts are not always, in individual cases, its most successful ones; but it is perfectly well able to make the rising genera-

_____

39. [A character in an English ballad.]

tion, as a whole, as good as, and a little better than, itself. If society lets any con-siderable number of its members grow up mere children, incapable of being acted on by rational consideration of distant motives, society has itself to blame for the consequences. Armed not only with all the powers of education, but with the ascendancy which the authority of a received opinion always exercises over the minds who are least fitted to judge for themselves, and aided by the *natural* penalties which cannot be prevented from falling on those who incur the distaste or the con-tempt of those who know them—let not society pretend that it needs, besides all this, the power to issue commands and enforce obedience in the personal concerns of individuals in which, on all principles of justice and policy, the decision ought to rest with those who are to abide the consequences. Nor is there anything which tends more to discredit and frustrate the better means of influencing conduct than a resort to the worse. If there be among those whom it is attempted to coerce into pru-dence or temperance any of the material of which vigorous and independent charac-ters are made, they will infallibly rebel against the yoke. No such person will ever feel that others have a right to control him in his concerns, such as they have to pre-vent him from injuring them in theirs; and it easily comes to be considered a mark of spirit and courage to fly in the face of such usurped authority and do with osten-tation the exact opposite of what it enjoins, as in the fashion of grossness which suc-ceeded, in the time of Charles II, to the fanatical moral intolerance of the Puritans. With respect to what is said of the necessity of protecting society from the bad ex-ample set to others by the vicious or the self-indulgent, it is true that bad example may have a pernicious effect, especially the example of doing wrong to others with impunity to the wrong-doer. But we are now speaking of conduct which, while it does no wrong to others, is supposed to do great harm to the agent himself; and I do not see how those who believe this can think otherwise than that the example, on the whole, must be more salutary than hurtful, since, if it displays the misconduct, it displays also the painful or degrading consequences which, if the conduct is justly censured, must be supposed to be in all or most cases attendant on it.

But the strongest of all the arguments against the interference of the public with purely personal conduct is that, when it does interfere, the odds are that it interferes wrongly and in the wrong place. On questions of social morality, of duty to others, the opinion of the public, that is, of an over-ruling majority, though often wrong, is likely to be still oftener right, because on such questions they are only required to judge of their own interests, of the manner in which some mode of conduct, if allowed to be practiced, would affect themselves. But the opinion of a similar major-ity, imposed as a law on the minority, on questions of self-regarding conduct is quite as likely to be wrong as right, for in these cases public opinion means, at the best, some people's opinion of what is good or bad for other people, while very often it does not even mean that—the public, with the most perfect indifference, passing over the pleasure or convenience of those whose conduct they censure and consider-ing only their own preference. There are many who consider as an injury to them-selves any conduct which they have a distaste for, and resent it as an outrage to their feelings; as a religious bigot, when charged with disregarding the religious feelings of others, has been known to retort that they disregard his feelings by persisting in their abominable worship or creed. But there is no parity between the feeling of a person for his own opinion and the feeling of another who is offended at his holding it, no more than between the desire of a thief to take a purse and the desire of the right owner to keep it. And a person's taste is as much his own peculiar concern as his opinion or his purse. It is easy for anyone to imagine an ideal public which leaves the freedom and choice of individuals in all uncertain matters undisturbed and only requires them to abstain from modes of conduct which universal experience has condemned. But where has there been seen a public which set any such limit to its censorship? Or when does the public trouble itself about universal experience? In its interferences with personal conduct it is seldom thinking of anything but the enormity of acting or feeling differently from itself; and this standard of judgment, thinly disguised, is held up to mankind as the dictate of religion and philosophy by nine-tenths of all moralists and speculative writers. These teach that things are right because they are right; because we feel them to be so. They tell us to search in our own minds and hearts for laws of conduct binding on ourselves and on all others. What can the poor public do but apply these instructions and make their own personal feelings of good and evil, if they are tolerably unanimous in them, obligatory on all the world?

The evil here pointed out is not one which exists only in theory; and it may perhaps be expected that I should specify the instances in which the public of this age and country improperly invests its own preferences with the character of moral laws. I am not writing an essay on the aberrations of existing moral feeling. That is too weighty a subject to be discussed parenthetically, and by way of illustration. Yet examples are necessary to show that the principle I maintain is of serious and practical moment, and that I am not endeavoring to erect a barrier against imaginary evils. And it is not difficult to show, by abundant instances, that to extend the bounds of what may be called moral police until it encroaches on the most unquestionably legitimate liberty of the individual is one of the most universal of all human propensities.

As a first instance, consider the antipathies which men cherish on no better grounds than that persons whose religious opinions are different from theirs do not practice their religious observances, especially their religious abstinences. To cite a rather trivial example, nothing in the creed or practice of Christians does more to envenom the hatred of Mohammedans against them than the fact of their eating pork. There are few acts which Christians and Europeans regard with more unaffected disgust than Mussulmans regard this particular mode of satisfying hunger. It is in the first place, an offense against their religion; but this circumstance by no means explains either the degree or the kind of their repugnance; for wine also is forbidden by their religion, and to partake of it is by all Mussulmans accounted wrong, but not disgusting. Their aversion to the flesh of the "unclean beast" is, on the contrary, of that peculiar character, resembling an instinctive antipathy, which the idea of uncleanness, when once it thoroughly sinks into the feelings, seems always to excite even in those whose personal habits are anything but scrupulously cleanly, and of which the sentiment of religious impurity, so intense in the Hindus, is a remarkable example. Suppose now that in a people of whom the majority were Mussulmans, that majority should insist upon not permitting pork to be eaten within the limits of the country. This would be nothing new in Mohammedan countries.[40] Would it be a legitimate exercise of the moral authority

40. The case of the Bombay Parsees is a curious instance in point. When this industrious and enterprising tribe, the descendants of the Persian fire-worshipers, flying from their native country before the Caliphs, arrived in western India, they were admitted to toleration by the Hindu sovereigns, on condition of not eating beef. When those regions afterward fell under the dominion of Mohammedan conquerors, the Parsees obtained from them a continuance of indulgence, on condition of refraining from

of public opinion, and if not, why not? The practice is really revolting to such a public. They also sincerely think that it is forbidden and abhorred by the Deity. Neither could the prohibition be censured as religious persecution. It might be religious in its origin, but it would not be persecution for religion, since nobody's religion makes it a duty to eat pork. The only tenable ground of condemnation would be that with the personal tastes and self-regarding concerns of individuals the public has no business to interfere.

To come somewhat nearer home: the majority of Spaniards consider it a gross impiety, offensive in the highest degree to the Supreme Being, to worship him in any other manner than the Roman Catholic; and no other public worship is lawful on Spanish soil. The people of all southern Europe look upon a married clergy as not only irreligious, but unchaste, indecent, gross, disgusting. What do Protestants think of these perfectly sincere feelings, and of the attempt to enforce them against non-Catholics? Yet, if mankind are justified in interfering with each other's liberty in things which do not concern the interests of others, on what principle is it possible consistently to exclude these cases? Or who can blame people for desiring to suppress what they regard as a scandal in the sight of God and man? No stronger case can be shown for prohibiting anything which is regarded as a personal immorality than is made out for suppressing these practices in the eyes of those who regard them as impieties; and unless we are willing to adopt the logic of persecutors, and to say that we may persecute others because we are right, and that they must not persecute us because they are wrong, we must beware of admitting a principle of which we should resent as a gross injustice the application to ourselves.

The preceding instances may be objected to, although unreasonably, as drawn from contingencies impossible among us—opinion, in this country, not being likely to enforce abstinence from meats or to interfere with people for worshiping and for either marrying or not marrying, according to their creed or inclination. The next example, however, shall be taken from an interference with liberty which we have by no means passed all danger of. Wherever the Puritans have been sufficiently powerful, as in New England, and in Great Britain at the time of the Commonwealth, they have endeavored, with considerable success, to put down all public, and nearly all private, amusements: especially music, dancing, public games, or other assemblages for purposes of diversion, and the theater. There are still in this country large bodies of persons by whose notions of morality and religion these recreations are condemned; and those persons belonging chiefly to the middle class, who are the ascendant power in the present social and political condition of the kingdom, it is by no means impossible that persons of these sentiments may at some time or other command a majority in Parliament. How will the remaining portion of the community like to have the amusements that shall be permitted to them regulated by the religious and moral sentiments of the stricter Calvinists and Methodists? Would they not, with considerable peremptoriness, desire these intrusively pious members of society to mind their own business? This is precisely what should be said to every government and every public who have the pretension that no person shall enjoy any pleasure which they think wrong. But if the principle of the pre-

---

pork. What was at first obedience to authority became a second nature, and the Parsees to this day abstain both from beef and pork. Though not required by their religion, the double abstinence has had time to grow into a custom of their tribe; and custom, in the East, is a religion.

tension be admitted, no one can reasonably object to its being acted on in the sense of the majority, or other preponderating power in the country; and all persons must be ready to conform to the idea of a Christian commonwealth as understood by the early settlers in New England, if a religious profession similar to theirs should ever succeed in regaining its lost ground, as religions supposed to be declining have so often been known to do.

To imagine another contingency, perhaps more likely to be realized than the one last mentioned. There is confessedly a strong tendency in the modern world toward a democratic constitution of society, accompanied or not by popular political institutions. It is affirmed that in the country where this tendency is most completely realized—where both society and the government are most democratic: the United States—the feeling of the majority, to whom any appearance of a more showy or costly style of living than they can hope to rival is disagreeable, operates as a tolerably effectual sumptuary law, and that in many parts of the Union it is really difficult for a person possessing a very large income to find any mode of spending it which will not incur popular disapprobation. Though such statements as these are doubtless much exaggerated as a representation of existing facts, the state of things they describe is not only a conceivable and possible, but a probable result of democratic feeling combined with the notion that the public has a right to a veto on the manner in which individuals shall spend their incomes. We have only further to suppose a considerable diffusion of Socialist opinions, and it may become infamous in the eyes of the majority to possess more property than some very small amount, or any income not earned by manual labor. Opinions similar in principle to these already prevail widely among the artisan class and weigh oppressively on those who are amenable to the opinion chiefly of that class, namely, its own members. It is known that the bad workmen who form the majority of the operatives in many branches of industry are decidedly of opinion that bad workmen ought to receive the same wages as good, and that no one ought to be allowed, through piecework or otherwise, to earn by superior skill or industry more than others can without it. And they employ a moral police, which occasionally becomes a physical one, to deter skillful workmen from receiving, and employers from giving, a larger remuneration for a more useful service. If the public have any jurisdiction over private concerns, I cannot see that these people are in fault, or that any individual's particular public can be blamed for asserting the same authority over his individual conduct which the general public asserts over people in general.

But, without dwelling upon supposititious cases, there are, in our own day, gross usurpations upon the liberty of private life actually practiced, and still greater ones threatened with some expectation of success, and opinions propounded which assert an unlimited right in the public not only to prohibit by law everything which it thinks wrong, but, in order to get at what it thinks wrong, to prohibit a number of things which it admits to be innocent.

Under the name of preventing intemperance, the people of one English colony, and of nearly half the United States, have been interdicted by law[41] from making any use whatever of fermented drinks, except for medical purposes, for prohibition of their sale is in fact, as it is intended to be, prohibition of their use. And though the impracticability of executing the law has caused its repeal in several of the States

41. [The reference is to the Maine Liquor Law of 1815.]

which had adopted it, including the one from which it derives its name, an attempt has notwithstanding been commenced, and is prosecuted with considerable zeal by many of the professed philanthropists, to agitate for a similar law in this country. The association, or "Alliance," as it terms itself, which has been formed for this purpose, has acquired some notoriety through the publicity given to a correspondence between its secretary and one of the very few English public men who hold that a politician's opinions ought to be founded on principles. Lord Stanley's[42] share in this correspondence is calculated to strengthen the hopes already built on him by those who know how rare such qualities as are manifested in some of his public appearances unhappily are among those who figure in political life. The organ of the Alliance, who would "deeply deplore the recognition of any principle which could be wrested to justify bigotry and persecution," undertakes to point out the "broad and impassable barrier" which divides such principles from those of the association. "All matters relating to thought, opinion, conscience, appear to me," he says, "to be without the sphere of legislation; all pertaining to social act, habit, relation, subject only to a discretionary power vested in the State itself, and not in the individual, to be within it." No mention is made of a third class, different from either of these, viz., acts and habits which are not social, but individual; although it is to this class, surely that the act of drinking fermented liquors belongs. Selling fermented liquors, however, is trading, and trading is a social act. But the infringement complained of is not on the liberty of the seller, but on that of the buyer and consumer; since the State might just as well forbid him to drink wine as purposely make it impossible for him to obtain it. The secretary, however, says, "I claim, as a citizen, a right to legislate whenever my social rights are invaded by the social act of another." And now for the definition of these "social rights": "If anything invades my social rights, certainly the traffic in strong drink does. It destroys my primary right of security by constantly creating and stimulating social disorder. It invades my right of equality by deriving a profit from the creation of a misery I am taxed to support. It impedes my right to free moral and intellectual development by surrounding my path with dangers and by weakening and demoralizing society, from which I have a right to claim mutual aid and intercourse." A theory of "social rights" the like of which probably never before found its way into distinct language: being nothing short of this—that it is the absolute social right of every individual that every other individual shall act in every respect exactly as he ought; that whosoever fails thereof in the smallest particular violates my social right and entitles me to demand from the legislature the removal of the grievance. So monstrous a principle is far more dangerous than any single interference with liberty; there is no violation of liberty which it would not justify; it acknowledges no right to any freedom whatever, except perhaps to that of holding opinions in secret, without ever disclosing them; for the moment an opinion which I consider noxious passes anyone's lips, it invades all the "social rights" attributed to me by the Alliance. The doctrine ascribes to all mankind a vested interest in each other's moral, intellectual, and even physical perfection, to be defined by each claimant according to his own standard.

Another important example of illegitimate interference with the rightful liberty of the individual, not simply threatened, but long since carried into triumphant effect, is Sabbatarian legislation. Without doubt, abstinence on one day in the week,

42. [Edward Henry Stanley (1826–1893), fifteenth Earl of Derby, served as undersecretary of state for foreign affairs, first secretary of state for India, and foreign secretary.]

so far as the exigencies of life permit, from the usual daily occupation, though in no respect religiously binding on any except Jews, is a highly beneficial custom. And inasmuch as this custom cannot be observed without a general consent to that effect among the industrious classes, therefore, in so far as some persons by working may impose the same necessity on others, it may be allowable and right that the law should guarantee to each the observance by others of the custom, by suspending the greater operations of industry on a particular day. But this justification, grounded on the direct interest which others have in each individual's observance of the practice, does not apply to the self-chosen occupations in which a person may think fit to employ his leisure, nor does it hold good, in the smallest degree, for legal restrictions on amusements. It is true that the amusement of some is the day's work of others; but the pleasure, not to say the useful recreation, of many is worth the labor of a few, provided the occupation is freely chosen and can be freely resigned. The operatives are perfectly right in thinking that if all worked on Sunday, seven days' work would have to be given for six days' wages; but so long as the great mass of employments are suspended, the small number who for the enjoyment of others must still work obtain a proportional increase of earnings; and they are not obliged to follow those occupations if they prefer leisure to emolument. If a further remedy is sought, it might be found in the establishment by custom of a holiday on some other day of the week for those particular classes of persons. The only ground, therefore, on which restrictions on Sunday amusements can be defended must be that they are religiously wrong—a motive of legislation which can never be too earnestly protested against. "*Deorum injuriae Diis curae.*"[43] It remains to be proved that society or any of its officers holds a commission from on high to avenge any supposed offense to Omnipotence which is not also a wrong to our fellow creatures. The notion that it is one man's duty that another should be religious was the foundation of all the religious persecutions ever perpetrated, and, if admitted, would fully justify them. Though the feeling which breaks out in the repeated attempts to stop railway traveling on Sunday, in the resistance to the opening of museums, and the like, has not the cruelty of the old persecutors, the state of mind indicated by it is fundamentally the same. It is a determination not to tolerate others in doing what is permitted by their religion, because it is not permitted by the persecutor's religion. It is a belief that God not only abominates the act of the misbeliever, but will not hold us guiltless if we leave him unmolested.

I cannot refrain from adding to these examples of the little account commonly made of human liberty the language of downright persecution which breaks out from the press of this country whenever it feels called on to notice the remarkable phenomenon of Mormonism. Much might be said on the unexpected and instructive fact that an alleged new revelation and a religion founded on it—the product of palpable imposture, not even supported by the *prestige* of extraordinary qualities in its founder—is believed by hundreds of thousands, and has been made the foundation of a society in the age of newspapers, railways, and the electric telegraph. What here concerns us is that this religion, like other and better religions, has its martyrs: that its prophet and founder was, for his teaching, put to death by a mob; that others of its adherents lost their lives by the same lawless violence; that they were forcibly expelled, in a body, from the country in which they first grew up,

---

43. [Injustices to the gods are the concern of the gods. The quotation is from the *Annals* of Tacitus, regarding whom see Hume's *Enquiry*, n. 41.]

while, now that they have been chased into a solitary recess in the midst of a desert, many in this country openly declare that it would be right (only that it is not convenient) to send an expedition against them and compel them by force to conform to the opinions of other people. The article of the Mormonite doctrine which is the chief provocative to the antipathy which thus breaks through the ordinary restraints of religious tolerance is its sanction of polygamy; which, though permitted to Mohammedans, and Hindus, and Chinese, seems to excite unquenchable animosity when practiced by persons who speak English and profess to be a kind of Christians. No one has a deeper disapprobation than I have of this Mormon institution; both for other reasons and because, far from being in any way countenanced by the principle of liberty, it is a direct infraction of that principle, being a mere riveting of the chains of one half of the community, and an emancipation of the other from reciprocity of obligation toward them. Still, it must be remembered that this relation is as much voluntary on the part of the women concerned in it, and who may be deemed the sufferers by it, as is the case with any other form of the marriage institution; and however surprising this fact may appear, it has its explanation in the common ideas and customs of the world, which, teaching women to think marriage the one thing needful, make it intelligible that many a woman should prefer being one of several wives to not being a wife at all. Other countries are not asked to recognize such unions, or release any portion of their inhabitants from their own laws on the score of Mormonite opinions. But when the dissentients have conceded to the hostile sentiments of others far more than could justly be demanded; when they have left the countries to which their doctrines were unacceptable and established themselves in a remote corner of the earth, which they have been the first to render habitable to human beings, it is difficult to see on what principles but those of tyranny they can be prevented from living there under what laws they please, provided they commit no aggression on other nations and allow perfect freedom of departure to those who are dissatisfied with their ways. A recent writer, in some respects of considerable merit, proposes (to use his own words) not a crusade, but a *civilizade*, against this polygamous community, to put an end to what seems to him a retrograde step in civilization. It also appears so to me, but I am not aware that any community has a right to force another to be civilized. So long as the sufferers by the bad law do not invoke assistance from other communities, I cannot admit that persons entirely unconnected with them ought to step in and require that a condition of things with which all who are directly interested appear to be satisfied should be put an end to because it is a scandal to persons some thousands of miles distant who have no part or concern in it. Let them send missionaries, if they please, to preach against it; and let them, by any fair means (of which silencing the teachers is not one), oppose the progress of similar doctrines among their own people. If civilization has got the better of barbarism when barbarism had the world to itself, it is too much to profess to be afraid lest barbarism, after having been fairly got under, should revive and conquer civilization. A civilization that can thus succumb to its vanquished enemy must first have become so degenerate that neither its appointed priests and teachers, nor anybody else, has the capacity, or will take the trouble, to stand up for it. If this be so, the sooner such a civilization receives notice to quit, the better. It can only go on from bad to worse until destroyed and regenerated (like the Western Empire) by energetic barbarians.

CHAPTER V

APPLICATIONS

The principles asserted in these pages must be more generally admitted as the basis for discussion of details before a consistent application of them to all the various departments of government and morals can be attempted with any prospect of advantage. The few observations I propose to make on questions of detail are designed to illustrate the principles rather than to follow them out to their consequences. I offer not so much applications as specimens of application, which may serve to bring into greater clearness the meaning and limits of the two maxims which together form the entire doctrine of this essay, and to assist the judgment in holding the balance between them in the cases where it appears doubtful which of them is applicable to the case.

The maxims are, first, that the individual is not accountable to society for his actions in so far as these concern the interests of no person but himself. Advice, instruction, persuasion, and avoidance by other people, if thought necessary by them for their own good, are the only measures by which society can justifiably express its dislike or disapprobation of his conduct. Secondly, that for such actions as are prejudicial to the interests of others, the individual is accountable and may be subjected either to social or to legal punishment if society is of opinion that the one or the other is requisite for its protection.

In the first place, it must by no means be supposed, because damage, or probability of damage, to the interests of others can alone justify the interference of society, that therefore it always does justify such interference. In many cases an individual, in pursuing a legitimate object, necessarily and therefore legitimately causes pain or loss to others, or intercepts a good which they had a reasonable hope of obtaining. Such oppositions of interest between individuals often arise from bad social institutions, but are unavoidable while those institutions last; and some would be unavoidable under any institutions. Whoever succeeds in an overcrowded profession or in a competitive examination, whoever is preferred to another in any contest for an object which both desire, reaps benefit from the loss of others, from their wasted exertion and their disappointment. But it is, by common admission, better for the general interest of mankind that persons should pursue their objects undeterred by this sort of consequences. In other words, society admits no right, either legal or moral, in the disappointed competitors to immunity from this kind of suffering, and feels called on to interfere only when means of success have been employed which it is contrary to the general interest to permit—namely, fraud or treachery, and force.

Again, trade is a social act. Whoever undertakes to sell any description of goods to the public does what affects the interest of other persons, and of society in general; and thus his conduct, in principle, comes within the jurisdiction of society; accordingly, it was once held to be the duty of governments, in all cases which were considered of importance, to fix prices and regulate the processes of manufacture. But it is now recognized, though not till after a long struggle, that both the cheapness and the good quality of commodities are most effectually provided for by leaving the producers and sellers perfectly free, under the sole check of equal freedom to the buyers for supplying themselves elsewhere. This is the so-called doctrine of "free trade," which rests on grounds different from, though equally solid with, the principle of individual liberty asserted in this essay. Restrictions on trade, or on production for purposes of trade, are indeed restraints; and all restraint, *qua* restraint, is an evil; but the restraints in question affect only that part of conduct which society is competent to restrain, and are wrong solely because they do not really produce the results which it is desired to produce by them. As the principle of individual liberty is not involved in the doctrine of free trade, so neither is it in most of the questions which arise respecting the limits of that doctrine, as, for example, what amount of public control is admissible for the prevention of fraud by adulteration; how far sanitary precautions, or arrangements to protect workpeople employed in dangerous occupations, should be enforced on employers. Such questions involve considerations of liberty only in so far as leaving people to themselves is always better, *caeteris paribus,* than controlling them; but that they may be legitimately controlled for these ends is in principle undeniable. On the other hand, there are questions relating to interference with trade which are essentially questions of liberty, such as the Maine Law, already touched upon; the prohibition of the importation of opium into China; the restriction of the sale of poisons—all cases, in short, where the object of the interference is to make it impossible or difficult to obtain a particular commodity. These interferences are objectionable, not as infringements on the liberty of the producer or seller, but on that of the buyer.

One of these examples, that of the sale of poisons, opens a new question: the proper limits of what may be called the functions of police; how far liberty may legitimately be invaded for the prevention of crime, or of accident. It is one of the undisputed functions of government to take precautions against crime before it has been committed, as well as to detect and punish it afterwards. The preventive function of government, however, is far more liable to be abused, to the prejudice of liberty, than the punitory function; for there is hardly any part of the legitimate freedom of action of a human being which would not admit of being represented, and fairly, too, as increasing the facilities for some form or other of delinquency. Nevertheless, if a public authority, or even a private person, sees anyone evidently preparing to commit a crime, they are not bound to look on inactive until the crime is committed, but may interfere to prevent it. If poisons were never bought or used for any purpose except the commission of murder, it would be right to prohibit their manufacture and sale. They may, however, be wanted not only for innocent but for useful purposes, and restrictions cannot be imposed in the one case without operating in the other. Again, it is a proper office of public authority to guard against accidents. If either a public officer or anyone else saw a person attempting to cross a bridge which had been ascertained to be unsafe, and there were no time to warn him of his danger, they might seize him and turn him back, without any real infringement of his liberty; for liberty consists in doing what one desires, and he does not desire to fall into the river. Nevertheless, when there is not a certainty, but only a danger of mischief, no one but the person himself can judge of the sufficiency of the motive which may prompt him to incur the risk; in this case, therefore (unless he is a child, or delirious, or in some state of excitement or absorption incompatible with the full use of the reflecting faculty), he ought, I conceive, to be only warned of the danger; not forcibly prevented from exposing himself to it. Similar considerations, applied to such a question as the sale of poisons, may enable us to decide which among the possible modes of regulation are or are not contrary to principle. Such a precaution, for example, as that of labeling the drug with some word expressive of its dangerous character may be enforced without violation of liberty: the buyer cannot wish not to know that the thing he possesses has poisonous qualities. But to require in all cases the certificate of a medical practitioner would make it sometimes impossible, always expensive, to obtain the article for legitimate uses. The only mode apparent to me, in which difficulties may be thrown in the way of crime committed through this means, without any infringement worth taking into account upon the liberty of those who desire the poisonous substance for other purposes, consists in providing what, in the apt language of Bentham, is called "preappointed evidence." This provision is familiar to everyone in the case of contracts. It is usual and right that the law, when a contract is entered into, should require as the condition of its enforcing performance that certain formalities should be observed, such as signatures, attestation of witnessess, and the like, in order that in case of subsequent dispute there may be evidence to prove that the contract was really entered into, and that there was nothing in the circumstances to render it legally invalid, the effect being to throw great obstacles in the way of fictitious contracts, or contracts made in circumstances which, if known, would destroy their validity. Precautions of a similar nature might be enforced in the sale of articles adapted to be instruments of crime. The seller, for example, might be required to enter in a register the exact time of the transaction, the name and address of the buyer, the precise quality and quantity sold; to ask the purpose for which it was wanted, and record the answer he received. When there was no medical prescription, the presence of some third person might be required to bring home the fact to the purchaser, in case there should afterwards be reason to believe that the article had been applied to criminal purposes. Such regulations would in general be no material impediment to obtaining the article, but a very considerable one to making an improper use of it without detection.

The right inherent in society to ward off crimes against itself by antecedent precautions suggests the obvious limitations to the maxim that purely self-regarding misconduct cannot properly be meddled with in the way of prevention or punishment. Drunkenness, for example, in ordinary cases, is not a fit subject for legislative interference, but I should deem it perfectly legitimate that a person who had once been convicted of any act of violence to others under the influence of drink should be placed under a special legal restriction, personal to himself; that if he were afterwards found drunk, he should be liable to a penalty, and that if, when in that state, he committed another offense, the punishment to which he would be liable for that other offense should be increased in severity. The making himself drunk, in a person whom drunkenness excites to do harm to others, is a crime against others. So, again, idleness, except in a person receiving support from the public, or except when it constitutes a breach of contract, cannot without tyranny be made a subject of legal punishment; but if, either from idleness or from any other avoidable cause, a man fails to perform his legal duties to others, as for instance to support his children, it is no tyranny to force him to fulfill that obligation by compulsory labor if no other means are available.

Again, there are many acts which, being directly injurious only to the agents themselves, ought not to be legally interdicted, but which, if done publicly, are a violation of good manners and, coming thus within the category of offenses against others, may rightly be prohibited. Of this kind are offenses against decency; on which it is unnecessary to dwell, the rather as they are only connected indirectly with our subject, the objection to publicity being equally strong in the case of many actions not in themselves condemnable, nor supposed to be so.

There is another question to which an answer must be found, consistent with the principles which have been laid down. In cases of personal conduct supposed to be blamable, but which respect for liberty precludes society from preventing or punishing because the evil directly resulting falls wholly on the agent; what the agent is free to do, ought other persons to be equally free to counsel or instigate? This question is not free from difficulty. The case of a person who solicits another to do an act is not strictly a case of self-regarding conduct. To give advice or offer inducements to anyone is a social act and may, therefore, like actions in general which affect others, be supposed amenable to social control. But a little reflection corrects the first impression, by showing that if the case is not strictly within the definition of individual liberty, yet the reasons on which the principle of individual liberty is grounded are applicable to it. If people must be allowed, in whatever concerns only themselves, to act as seems best to themselves, at their own peril, they must equally be free to consult with one another about what is fit to be so done; to exchange opinions, and give and receive suggestions. Whatever it is permitted to do, it must be permitted to advise to do. The question is doubtful only when the instigator derives a personal benefit from his advice, when he makes it his occupation, for subsistence or pecuniary gain, to promote what society and the State consider to be an evil. Then, indeed, a new element of complication is introduced—namely, the existence of classes of persons with an interest opposed to what is considered as the public weal, and whose mode of living is grounded on the counteraction of it. Ought this to be interfered with, or not? Fornication, for example, must be tolerated, and so must gambling; but should a person be free to be a pimp, or to keep a gambling house? The case is one of those which lie on the exact boundary line between two principles, and it is not at once apparent to which of the two it properly belongs. There are arguments on both sides. On the side of toleration it may be said that the fact of following anything as an occupation, and living or profiting by the practice of it, cannot make that criminal which would otherwise be admissible; that the act should either be consistently permitted or consistently prohibited; that if the principles which we have hitherto defended are true, society has no business, *as* society, to decide anything to be wrong which concerns only the individual; that it cannot go beyond dissuasion, and that one person should be as free to persuade as another to dissuade. In opposition to this it may be contended that, although the public, or the State, are not warranted in authoritatively deciding, for purposes of repression or punishment, that such or such conduct affecting only the interests of the individual is good or bad, they are fully justified in assuming, if they regard it as bad, that its being so or not is at least a disputable question: that, this being supposed, they cannot be acting wrongly in endeavoring to exclude the influence of solicitations which are not disinterested, of instigators who cannot possibly be impartial—who have a direct personal interest on one side, and that side the one which the State believes to be wrong, and who confessedly promote it for personal objects only. There can surely, it may be urged, be nothing lost, no sacrifice of good, by so ordering matters that persons shall make their election, either wisely or foolishly, on their own prompting, as free as possible from the arts of persons who stimulate their inclinations for interested purposes of their own. Thus (it may be said), though the statutes respecting unlawful games are utterly indefensible—

though all persons should be free to gamble in their own or each other's houses, or in any place of meeting established by their own subscriptions and open only to the members and their visitors—yet public gambling houses should not be permitted. It is true that the prohibition is never effectual, and that, whatever amount of tyrannical power may be given to the police, gambling houses can always be maintained under other pretenses; but they may be compelled to conduct their operations with a certain degree of secrecy and mystery, so that nobody knows anything about them but those who seek them; and more than this society ought not to aim at. There is considerable force in these arguments. I will not venture to decide whether they are sufficient to justify the moral anomaly of punishing the accessory when the principal is (and must be) allowed to go free; of fining or imprisoning the procurer, but not the fornicator—the gambling-house keeper, but not the gambler. Still less ought the common operations of buying and selling to be interfered with on analogous grounds. Almost every article which is bought and sold may be used in excess, and the sellers have a pecuniary interest in encouraging that excess; but no argument can be founded on this in favor, for instance, of the Maine Law; because the class of dealers in strong drinks, though interested in their abuse, are indispensably required for the sake of their legitimate use. The interest, however, of these dealers in promoting intemperance is a real evil and justifies the State in imposing restrictions and requiring guarantees which, but for that justification, would be infringements of legitimate liberty.

A further question is whether the State, while it permits, should nevertheless indirectly discourage conduct which it deems contrary to the best interests of the agent; whether, for example, it should take measures to render the means of drunkenness more costly, or add to the difficulty of procuring them by limiting the number of the places of sale. On this, as on most other practical questions, many distinctions require to be made. To tax stimulants for the sole purpose of making them more difficult to be obtained is a measure differing only in degree from their entire prohibition, and would be justifiable only if that were justifiable. Every increase of cost is a prohibition to those whose means do not come up to the augmented price; and to those who do, it is a penalty laid on them for gratifying a particular taste. Their choice of pleasures and their mode of expending their income, after satisfying their legal and moral obligations to the State and to individuals, are their own concern and must rest with their own judgment. These considerations may seem at first sight to condemn the selection of stimulants as special subjects of taxation for purposes of revenue. But it must be remembered that taxation for fiscal purposes is absolutely inevitable; that in most countries it is necessary that a considerable part of that taxation should be indirect; that the State, therefore, cannot help imposing penalties, which to some persons may be prohibitory, on the use of some articles of consumption. It is hence the duty of the State to consider, in the imposition of taxes, what commodities the consumers can best spare; and *a fortiori*, to select in preference those of which it deems the use, beyond a very moderate quantity, to be positively injurious. Taxation, therefore, of stimulants up to the point which produces the largest amount of revenue (supposing that the State needs all the revenue which it yields) is not only admissible, but to be approved of.

The question of making the sale of these commodities a more or less exclusive privilege must be answered differently, according to the purposes to which the restriction is intended to be subservient. All places of public resort require the restraint of a police, and places of this kind peculiarly, because offenses against society are especially apt to originate there. It is, therefore, fit to confine the power of selling these commodities (at least for consumption on the spot) to persons of known or vouched-for respectability of conduct; to make such regulations respecting hours of opening and closing as may be requisite for public surveillance, and to withdraw the license if breaches of the peace repeatedly take place through the connivance or incapacity of the keeper of the house, or if it becomes a rendezvous for concocting and preparing offenses against the law. Any further restriction I do not conceive to be, in principle, justifiable. The limitation in number, for instance, of beer and spirit houses, for the express purpose of rendering them more difficult of access and diminishing the occasions of temptation, not only exposes all to an inconvenience because there are some by whom the facility would be abused, but is suited only to a state of society in which the laboring classes are avowedly treated as children or savages, and placed under an education of restraint, to fit them for future admission to the privileges of freedom. This is not the principle on which the laboring classes are professedly governed in any free country; and no person who sets due value on freedom will give his adhesion to their being so governed, unless after all efforts have been exhausted to educate them for freedom and govern them as freemen, and it has been definitively proved that they can only be governed as children. The bare statement of the alternative shows the absurdity of supposing that such efforts have been made in any case which needs be considered here. It is only because the institutions of this country are a mass of inconsistencies, that things find admittance into our practice which belong to the system of despotic, or what is called paternal, government, while the general freedom of our institutions precludes the exercise of the amount of control necessary to render the restraint of any real efficacy as a moral education.

It was pointed out in an early part of this essay that the liberty of the individual, in things wherein the individual is alone concerned, implies a corresponding liberty in any number of individuals to regulate by mutual agreement such things as regard them jointly, and regard no persons but themselves. This question presents no difficulty so long as the will of all the persons implicated remains unaltered; but since that will may change it is often necessary, even in things in which they alone are concerned, that they should enter into engagements with one another; and when they do, it is fit, as a general rule, that those engagements should be kept. Yet, in the laws, probably, of every country, this general rule has some exceptions. Not only persons are not held to engagements which violate the rights of third parties, but it is sometimes considered a sufficient reason for releasing them from an engagement that it is injurious to themselves. In this and most other civilized countries, for example, an engagement by which a person should sell himself, or allow himself to be sold, as a slave would be null and void, neither enforced by law nor by opinion. The ground for thus limiting his power of voluntarily disposing of his own lot in life is apparent, and is very clearly seen in this extreme case. The reason for not interfering, unless for the sake of others, with a person's voluntary acts is consideration for his liberty. His voluntary choice is evidence that what he so chooses is desirable, or at least endurable, to him, and his good is on the whole best provided for by allowing him to take his own means of pursuing it. But by selling himself for a slave, he abdicates his liberty; he foregoes any future use of it beyond that single act. He therefore defeats, in his own case, the very purpose which is the justification of allowing him to dispose of himself. He is no longer free, but is thenceforth in a position which has no longer the presumption in its favor that would be afforded by his voluntarily remaining in it. The principle of freedom cannot require that he should be free not to be free. It is not freedom to be allowed to alienate his freedom. These reasons, the force of which is so conspicuous in this peculiar case, are evidently of far wider application, yet a limit is everywhere set to them by the necessities of life, which continually require, not indeed that we should resign our freedom, but that we should consent to this and the other limitation of it. The principle, however, which demands uncontrolled freedom of action in all that concerns only the agents themselves requires that those who have become bound to one another, in things which concern no third party, should be able to release one another from the engagement; and even without such voluntary release there are perhaps no contracts or engagements, except those that relate to money or money's worth, of which one can venture to say that there ought to be no liberty whatever of retraction. Baron Wilhelm von Humboldt, in the excellent essay from which I have already quoted, states it as his conviction that engagements which involve personal relations or services should never be legally binding beyond a limited duration of time; and that the most important of these engagements, marriage, having the peculiarity that its objects are frustrated unless the feelings of both the parties are in harmony with it, should require nothing more than the declared will of either party to dissolve it. This subject is too important and too complicated to be discussed in a parenthesis, and I touch on it only so far as is necessary for purposes of illustration. If the conciseness and generality of Baron Humboldt's dissertation had not obliged him in this instance to content himself with enunciating his conclusion without discussing the premises, he would doubtless have recognized that the question cannot be decided on grounds so simple as those to which he confines himself. When a person, either by express promise or by conduct, has encouraged another to rely upon his continuing to act in a certain way — to build expectations and calculations, and stake any part of his plan of life upon that supposition — a new series of moral obligations arises on his part toward that person, which may possibly be overruled, but cannot be ignored. And again, if the relation between two contracting parties has been followed by consequences to others; if it has placed third parties in any peculiar position, or, as in the case of marriage, has even called third parties into existence, obligations arise on the part of both the contracting parties toward those third persons, the fulfillment of which, or at all events the mode of fulfillment, must be greatly affected by the continuance or disruption of the relation between the original parties to the contract. It does not follow, nor can I admit, that these obligations extend to requiring the fulfillment of the contract at all costs to the happiness of the reluctant party; but they are a necessary element in the question; and, even if, as von Humboldt maintains, they ought to make no difference in the *legal* freedom of the parties to release themselves from the engagement (and I also hold that they ought not to make *much* difference), they necessarily make a great difference in the *moral* freedom. A person is bound to take all these circumstances into account before resolving on a step which may affect such important interests of others; and if he does not allow proper weight to those interests, he is morally responsible for the wrong. I have made these obvious remarks for the better illustration of the general principle of liberty, and not because they are at all needed on the particular question, which, on the contrary, is usually discussed as if the interest of children was everything, and that of grown persons nothing.

I have already observed that, owing to the absence of any recognized general principles, liberty is often granted where it should be withheld, as well as withheld where it should be granted; and on of the cases in which, in the modern European world, the sentiment of liberty is the strongest is a case where, in my view, it is altogether misplaced. A person should be free to do as he likes in his own concerns, but he ought not to be free to do as he likes in acting for another, under the pretext that the affairs of the other are his own affairs. The State, while it respects the liberty of each in what specially regards himself, is bound to maintain a vigilant control over his exercise of any power which it allows him to possess over others. This obligation is almost entirely disregarded in the case of the family relations—a case, in its direct influence on human happiness, more important than all others taken together. The almost despotic power of husbands over wives needs not be enlarged upon here, because nothing more is needed for the complete removal of the evil than that wives should have the same rights and should receive the protection of law in the same manner as all other persons; and because, on this subject, the defenders of established injustice do not avail themselves of the plea of liberty but stand forth openly as the champions of power. It is in the case of children that misapplied notions of liberty are a real obstacle to the fulfillment by the State of its duties. One would almost think that a man's children were supposed to be literally, and not metaphorically, a part of himself, so jealous is opinion of the smallest interference of law with his absolute and exclusive control over them, more jealous than of almost any interference with his own freedom of action: so much less do the generality of mankind value liberty than power. Consider, for example, the case of education. Is it not almost a self-evident axiom that the State should require and compel the education, up to a certain standard, of every human being who is born its citizen? Yet who is there that is not afraid to recognize and assert this truth? Hardly anyone, indeed, will deny that it is one of the most sacred duties of the parents (or, as law and usage now stand, the father), after summoning a human being into the world, to give to that being an education fitting him to perform his part well in life toward others and toward himself. But while this is unanimously declared to be the father's duty, scarcely anybody, in this country, will bear to hear of obliging him to perform it. Instead of his being required to make any exertion or sacrifice for securing education to his child, it is left to his choice to accept it or not when it is provided gratis! It still remains unrecognized that to bring a child into existence without a fair prospect of being able, not only to provide food for its body, but instruction and training for its mind is a moral crime, both against the unfortunate offspring and against society; and that if the parent does not fulfill this obligation, the State ought to see it fulfilled at the charge, as far as possible, of the parent.

Were the duty of enforcing universal education once admitted there would be an end to the difficulties about what the State should teach, and how it should teach, which now convert the subject into a mere battlefield for sects and parties, causing the time and labor which should have been spent in educating to be wasted in quarreling about education. If the government would make up its mind to require for every child a good education, it might save itself the trouble of providing one. It might leave to parents to obtain the education where and how they pleased, and content itself with helping to pay the school fees of the poorer classes of children, and defraying the entire school expenses of those who have no one else to pay for them. The objections which are urged with reason against State education do not apply to the enforcement of education by the State, but to the State's taking upon itself to direct that education; which is a totally different thing. That the whole or any large part of the education of the people should be in State hands, I go as far as anyone in deprecating. All that has been said of the importance of individuality of character, and diversity in opinions and modes of conduct, involves, as of the same unspeakable importance, diversity of education. A general State education is a mere contrivance for molding people to be exactly like one another; and as the mold in which it casts them is that which pleases the predominant power in the government—whether this be a monarch, a priesthood, an aristocracy, or the majority of the existing generation—in proportion as it is efficient and successful, it establishes a despotism over the mind, leading by natural tendency to one over the body. An education established and controlled by the State should only exist, if it exist at all, as one among many competing experiments, carried on for the purpose of example and stimulus to keep the others up to a certain standard of excellence. Unless, indeed, when society in general is in so backward a state that it could not or would not provide for itself any proper institutions of education unless the government undertook the task, then, indeed, the government may, as the less of two great evils, take upon itself the business of schools and universities, as it may that of joint stock companies when private enterprise in a shape fitted for undertaking great works of industry does not exist in the country. But in general, if the country contains a sufficient number of persons qualified to provide education under government auspices, the same persons would be able and willing to give an equally good education on the voluntary principle, under the assurance of remuneration afforded by a law rendering education compulsory, combined with State aid to those unable to defray the expense.

The instrument for enforcing the law could be no other than public examinations, extending to all children and beginning at an early age. An age might be fixed at which every child must be examined, to ascertain if he (or she) is able to read. If a child proves unable, the father, unless he has some sufficient ground of excuse, might be subjected to a moderate fine, to be worked out, if necessary, by his labor, and the child might be put to school at his expense. Once in every year the examination should be renewed, with a graduallly extending range of subjects, so as to make the universal acquisition and, what is more, retention of a certain minimum of general knowledge virtually compulsory. Beyond that minimum there should be voluntary examinations on all subjects, at which all who come up to a certain standard of proficiency might claim a certificate. To prevent the State from exercising, through these arrangements, an improper influence over opinion, the knowledge required for passing an examination (beyond the merely instrumental parts of knowledge, such as languages and their use) should, even in the higher classes of examinations, be confined to facts and positive science exclusively. The examinations on religion, politics, or other disputed topics should not turn on the truth or falsehood of opinions, but on the matter of fact that such and such an opinion is held, on such grounds, by such authors, or schools, or churches. Under this system, the rising generation would be no worse off in regard to all disputed truths than they are at present; they would be brought up either churchmen or dissenters as they now are, the State merely taking care that they should be instructed churchmen, or instructed dissenters. There would be nothing to hinder them from being taught religion, if their parents chose, at the same schools where they were taught other things. All attempts by the State to bias the conclusions of its citizens on disputed subjects are evil; but it may very properly offer to ascertain and certify that a person possesses the knowledge requisite to make his conclusions on any given subject worth attending to. A student of philosophy would be the better for being able to stand an examination both in Locke and in Kant, whichever of the two he takes up with, or even if with neither: and there is no reasonable objection to examining an atheist in the evidences of Christianity, provided he is not required to profess a belief in them. The examinations, however, in the higher branches of knowledge should, I conceive, be entirely voluntary. It would be giving too dangerous a power to governments were they allowed to exclude anyone from professions, even from the profession of teacher, for alleged deficiency of qualifications; and I think, with Wilhelm von Humboldt, that degrees or other public certificates of scientific or professional acquirements should be given to all who present themselves for examination and stand the test, but that such certificates should confer no advantage over competitors other than the weight which may be attached to their testimony by public opinion.

It is not in the matter of education only that misplaced notions of liberty prevent moral obligations on the part of parents from being recognized, and legal obligations from being imposed, where there are the strongest grounds for the former always, and in many cases for the latter also. The fact itself, of causing the existence of a human being, is one of the most responsible actions in the range of human life. To undertake this responsibility—to bestow a life which may be either a curse or a blessing—unless the being on whom it is to be bestowed will have at least the ordinary chances of a desirable existence, is a crime against that being. And in a country, either overpeopled or threatened with being so, to produce children, beyond a very small number, with the effect of reducing the reward of labor by their competition is a serious offense against all who live by the remuneration of their labor. The laws which, in many countries on the Continent, forbid marriage unless the parties can show that they have the means of supporting a family do not exceed the legitimate powers of the State; and whether such laws be expedient or not (a question mainly dependent on local circumstances and feelings), they are not objectionable as violations of liberty. Such laws are interferences of the State to prohibit a mischievous act—an act injurious to others, which ought to be a subject of reprobation and social stigma, even when it is not deemed expedient to superadd legal punishment. Yet the current ideas of liberty, which bend so easily to real infringements of the freedom of the individual in things which concern only himself, would repel the attempt to put any restraint upon his inclinations when the consequence of their indulgence is a life or lives of wretchedness and depravity to the offspring, with manifold evils to those sufficiently within reach to be in any way affected by their actions. When we compare the strange respect of mankind for liberty with their strange want of respect for it, we might imagine that a man had an indispensable right to do harm to others, and no right at all to please himself without giving pain to anyone.

I have reserved for the the last place a large class of questions respecting the limits of government interference, which, though closely connected with the subject of this essay, do not, in strictness, belong to it. These are cases in which the reasons against interference do not turn upon the principle of liberty: the question is not about restraining the actions of individuals, but about helping them; it is asked whether the government should do, or cause to be done, something for their benefit instead of leaving it to be done by themselves, individually or in voluntary combination.

The objections to government interference, when it is not such as to involve infringement of liberty, may be of three kinds:

The first is when the thing to be done is likely to be better done by individuals than by the government. Speaking generally, there is no one so fit to conduct any business, or to determine how or by whom it shall be conducted, as those who are personally interested in it. This principle condemns the interferences, once so common, of the legislature, or the officers of government, with the ordinary processes of industry. But this part of the subject has been sufficiently enlarged upon by political economists, and is not particularly related to the principles of this essay.

The second objection is more nearly allied to our subject. In many cases, though individuals may not do the particular thing so well, on the average, as the officers of government, it is nevertheless desirable that it should be done by them, rather than by the government, as a means to their own mental education—a mode of strengthening their active faculties, exercising their judgment, and giving them a familiar knowledge of the subjects with which they are thus left to deal. This is a principal, though not the sole, recommendation of jury trial (in cases not political); of free and popular local and municipal institutions; of the conduct of industrial and philanthropic enterprises by voluntary associations. These are not questions of liberty, and are connected with that subject only by remote tendencies, but they are questions of development. It belongs to a different occasion from the present to dwell on these things as parts of national education, as being, in truth, the peculiar training of a citizen, the practical part of the political education of a free people, taking them out of the narrow circle of personal and family selfishness, and accustoming them to the comprehension of joint interests, the management of joint concerns—habituating them to act from public or semi-public motives, and guide their conduct by aims which unite instead of isolating them from one another. Without these habits and powers, a free constitution can neither be worked nor preserved, as is exemplified by the too-often transitory nature of political freedom in countries where it does not rest upon a sufficient basis of local liberties. The management of purely local business by the localities, and of the great enterprises of industry by the union of those who voluntarily supply the pecuniary means, is further recommended by all the advantages which have been set forth in this essay as belonging to individuality of development and diversity of modes of action. Government operations tend to be everywhere alike. With individuals and voluntary associations, on the contrary, there are varied experiments and endless diversity of experience. What the State can usefully do is to make itself a central depository, and active circulator and diffuser, of the experience resulting from many trials. Its business is to enable each experimentalist to benefit by the experiments of others, instead of tolerating no experiments but its own.

The third and most cogent reason for restricting the interference of government is the great evil of adding unnecessarily to its power. Every function superadded to those already exercised by the government causes its influence over hopes and fears to be more widely diffused, and converts, more and more, the active and ambitious part of the public into hangers-on of the government, or of some party which aims at becoming the government. If the roads, the railways, the banks, the insurance offices, the great joint-stock companies, the universities, and the public charities were all of them branches of the government; if, in addition, the municipal corporations and local boards, with all that now devolves on them, became departments of the central administration; if the employees of all these different enterprises were appointed and paid by the government and looked to the government for every rise in life, not all the freedom of the press and popular constitution of the legislature would make this or any other country free otherwise than in name. And the evil would be greater, the more efficiently and scientifically the administrative machinery was constructed—the more skillful the arrangements for obtaining the best qualified hands and heads with which to work it. In England it has of late been proposed that all the members of the civil service of government should be selected by competitive examination, to obtain for these employments the most intelligent and instructed persons procurable; and much has been said and written for and against this proposal. One of the arguments most insisted on by its opponents is that the occupation of a permanent official servant of the State does not hold out sufficient prospects of emolument and importance to attract the highest talents, which will always be able to find a more inviting career in the professions or in the service of companies and other public bodies. One would not have been surprised if this argument had been used by the friends of the proposition as as an answer to its principal difficulty. Coming from the opponents it is strange enough. What is urged as an objection is the safety valve of the proposed system. If, indeed, all the high talent of the country *could* be drawn into the service of the government, a proposal tending to bring about that result might well inspire uneasiness. If every part of the business of society which required organized concert, or large and comprehensive views, were in the hands of the government, and if government offices were universally filled by the ablest men, all the enlarged culture and practiced intelligence in the country, except the purely speculative, would be concentrated in a numerous bureaucracy, to whom alone the rest of the community would look for all things—the multitude for direction and dictation in all they had to do; the able and aspiring for personal advancement. To be admitted into the ranks of this bureaucracy, and when admitted, to rise therein, would be the sole objects of ambition. Under this *régime* not only is the outside public ill-qualified, for want of practical experience, to criticize or check the mode of operation of the bureaucracy, but even if the accidents of despotic or the natural working of popular institutions occasionally raise to the summit a ruler or rulers of reforming inclinations, no reform can be effected which is contrary to the interest of the bureaucracy. Such is the melancholy condition of the Russian empire, as shown in the accounts of those who have had sufficient opportunity of observation. The Czar himself is powerless against the bureaucratic body; he can send any one of them to Siberia, but he cannot govern without them, or against their will. On every decree of his they have a tacit veto, by merely refraining from carrying it into effect. In countries of more advanced civilization and of a more insurrectionary spirit, the public, accustomed to expect everything to be done for them by the State, or a least to do nothing for themselves without asking from the State not only leave to do it, but even how it is to be done, naturally hold the State responsible for all evil which befalls them, and when the evil exceeds their amount of patience, they rise against the government and make what is called a revolution; whereupon somebody else, with or without legitimate authority from the nation, vaults into the seat, issues his orders to the bureaucracy, and everything goes on much as it did before; the bureaucracy being unchanged, and nobody else being capable of taking their place.

A very different spectacle is exhibited among a people accustomed to transact their own business. In France, a large part of the people, having been engaged in military service, many of whom have held at least the rank of noncommissioned officers, there are in every popular insurrection several persons competent to take the lead and improvise some tolerable plan of action. What the French are in military affairs, the Americans are in every kind of civil business; let them be left without a government, every body of Americans is able to improvise one and to carry on that or any other public business with a sufficient amount of intelligence, order, and decision. This is what every free people ought to be; and a people capable of this is certain to be free; it will never let itself be enslaved by any man or body of men because these are able to seize and pull the reins of the central administration. No bureaucracy can hope to make such a people as this do or undergo anything that they do not like. But where everything is done through the bureaucracy, nothing to which the bureaucracy is really adverse can be done at all. The constitution of such countries is an organization of the experience and practical ability of the nation into a disciplined body for the purpose of governing the rest; and the more perfect that organization is in itself, the more successful in drawing to itself and educating for itself the persons of greatest capacity from all ranks of the community, the more complete is the bondage of all, the members of the bureaucracy included. For the governors are as much the slaves of their organization and discipline as the governed are of the governors. A Chinese mandarin is as much the tool and creature of a despotism as the humblest cultivator. An individual Jesuit is to the utmost degree of abasement the slave of his order, though the order itself exists for the collective power and importance of its members.

It is not, also, to be forgotten that the absorption of all the principal ability of the country into the governing body is fatal, sooner or later, to the mental activity and progressiveness of the body itself. Banded together as they are—working a system which, like all systems, necessarily proceeds in a great measure by fixed rules—the official body are under the constant temptation of sinking into indolent routine, or, if they now and then desert that mill-horse round, of rushing into some half-examined crudity which has struck the fancy of some leading member of the corps; and the sole check to these closely allied, though seemingly opposite, tendencies, the only stimulus which can keep the ability of the body itself up to a high standard, is liability to the watchful criticism of equal ability outside the body. It is indispensable, therefore, that the means should exist, independently of the government, of forming such ability and furnishing it with the opportunities and experience necessary for a correct judgment of great practical affairs. If we would possess permanently a skillful and efficient body of functionaries—above all a body able to originate and willing to adopt improvements—if we would not have our bureaucracy degenerate into a pedantocracy, this body must not engross all the occupations which form and cultivate the faculties required for the government of mankind.

To determine the point at which evils, so formidable to human freedom and advancement, begin, or rather at which they begin to predominate over the benefits attending the collective application of the force of society, under its recognized chiefs, for the removal of the obstacles which stand in the way of its well-being; to secure as much of the advantages of centralized power and intelligence as can be had without turning into governmental channels too great a proportion of the general activity—is one of the most difficult and complicated questions in the art of government. It is, in a great measure, a question of detail in which many and various considerations must be kept in view, and no absolute rule can be laid down. But I believe that the practical principle in which safety resides, the ideal to be kept in view, the standard by which to test all arrangements intended for overcoming the difficulty, may be conveyed in these words: the greatest dissemination of power consistent with efficiency; but the greatest possible centralization of information and diffusion of it from the center. Thus, in municipal administration, there would be, as in the New England states, a very minute division among separate officers, chosen by the localities, of all business which is not better left to the persons directly interested; but besides this, there would be, in each department of local affairs, a central superintendence, forming a branch of the general government. The organ of this superintendence would concentrate, as in a focus, the variety of information and experience derived from the conduct of that branch of public business in all the localities, from everything analogous which is done in foreign countries, and from the general principles of political science. This central organ should have a right to know all that is done, and its special duty should be that of making the knowledge acquired in one place available for others. Emancipated from the petty prejudices and narrow views of a locality by its elevated position and comprehensive sphere of observation, its advice would naturally carry much authority; but its actual power, as a permanent institution, should, I conceive, be limited to compelling the local officers to obey the laws laid down for their guidance. In all things not provided for by general rules, those officers should be left to their own judgment, under responsibility to their constituents. For the violation of rules, they should be responsible to law, and the rules themselves should be laid down by the legislature; the central administrative authority only watching over their execution and, if they were not properly carried into effect, appealing, according to the nature of the case, to the tribunals to enforce the law, or to the constituencies to dismiss the functionaries who had not executed it according to its spirit. Such, in its general conception, is the central superintendence which the Poor Law Board is intended to exercise over the administrators of the Poor Rate throughout the country. Whatever powers the Board exercises beyond this limit were right and necessary in that peculiar case, for the cure of rooted habits of maladministration in matters deeply affecting not the localities merely, but the whole community; since no locality has a moral right to make itself by mismanagement a nest of pauperism, necessarily overflowing into other localities and impairing the moral and physical condition of the whole laboring community. The powers of administrative coercion and subordinate legislation possessed by the Poor Law Board (but which, owing to the state of opinion on the subject, are very scantily exercised by them), though perfectly justifiable in a case of first-rate national interest, would be wholly out of place in the superintendence of interests purely local. But a central organ of information and instruction for all the localities would be equally valuable in all departments of administration. A government cannot have too much of the kind of activity which does not impede, but aids and stimulates, individual exertion and development. The mischief begins when, instead of calling forth the activity and powers of individuals and bodies, it substitutes its own activity for theirs; when, instead of informing, advising, and, upon occasion, denouncing, it makes them work in fetters, or bids them stand aside and does their work instead of them. The worth of a State, in the long run, is the worth of the individuals composing it; and a State which postpones the interests of *their* mental expansion and elevation to a little more of administrative skill, or of that semblance of it which practice gives in the details of business; a State which dwarfs its men, in order that they may be more docile instruments in its hands even for beneficial purposes—will find that with small men no great thing can really be accomplished; and that the perfection of machinery to which it has sacrificed everything will in the end avail it nothing, for want of the vital power which, in order that the machine might work more smoothly, it has preferred to banish.

The text and display lines of this book have been set in Baskerville type on a computerized phototypesetting system by Compolith Typesetting of Indianapolis, Indiana. The book was printed and bound by R. R. Donnelley & Sons Company, of Chicago, Illinois.

identical, they may actually differ in gain by an appreciable amount. The gain measured in this case is

$$G_0 = \sqrt{G_{01}G_{02}} \qquad (15\text{-}14)$$

where G_{01} = gain of antenna 1 of the "identical" pair
$\quad\;\; G_{02}$ = gain of antenna 2 of the "identical" pair
both gains referred to an isotropic source. To find G_{01} and G_{02}, the above measurement is supplemented by a comparison of each of the antennas with a third reference antenna whose gain need not be known. This gives a gain ratio between "identical" antennas of

$$G' = \frac{G_1}{G_2} \qquad (15\text{-}15)$$

where G_1 = gain of antenna 1 over reference antenna
$\quad\;\; G_2$ = gain of antenna 2 over reference antenna
Then since

$$G' = \frac{G_1}{G_2} = \frac{G_{01}}{G_{02}} \qquad (15\text{-}16)$$

we have

$$G_{01} = G_0 \sqrt{G'} \qquad (15\text{-}17)$$

and

$$G_{02} = \frac{G_0}{\sqrt{G'}} \qquad (15\text{-}18)$$

15-7. Terminal Impedance Measurements. The terminal impedance of UHF antennas is conveniently measured by transmission-line methods. The antenna terminals are connected to the end of a transmission line energized by a transmitter or oscillator as shown in Fig. 15-14. Measurement of the SWR of voltage or current along the line and of the distance d between either a current minimum or a voltage minimum and the antenna terminals permits a determination of the terminal impedance by well known methods.[1] This is done simply with a Smith chart.[2] The impedance values

---

[1] F. E. Terman, "Radio Engineering," 3d ed., McGraw-Hill Book Company, Inc., New York, 1947, pp. 94–98.

F. E. Terman, "Radio Engineers' Handbook," McGraw-Hill Book Company, Inc., New York, 1943, pp. 172–197.

Chap. 2 by Nelson, Lazarus, Christensen, and Buss, "Very High Frequency Techniques," McGraw-Hill Book Company, Inc., New York, 1947.

Chap. 8 by J. F. Reintjes, "Principles of Radar," by M.I.T. Radar School Staff, McGraw-Hill Book Company, Inc., New York, 1946.

R. W. P. King, H. R. Mimno, and A. H. Wing, "Transmission Lines, Antennas, and Wave Guides," McGraw-Hill Book Company, Inc., New York, 1945, Chap. 1.

J. C. Slater, "Microwave Transmission," McGraw-Hill Book Company, Inc., New York, 1943, Chap. 1.

[2] P. H. Smith, Transmission Line Calculator, *Electronics*, **12**, 29–31, January, 1939.

so obtained at each frequency of measurement may be connected to form an impedance-vs.-frequency curve. The shape of this curve on a Smith chart is a function of the characteristic impedance of the transmission line. To avoid this dependence, it is sometimes desirable to replot the impedance values on a simple R vs. X diagram such as Fig. 8-12 or Fig. 9-9.

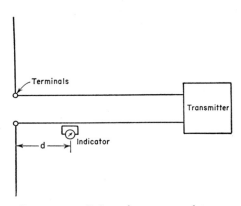

On balanced antennas with two-wire transmission lines the measurement of the SWR and of the current minimum point are conveniently made with a small loop connected to a current indicator as in Fig. 15-14. The indicating device may be a crystal rectifier (square law) with current meter, or it may be a thermocouple meter. The indicator can be coupled to one wire of the line as shown. By measuring both wires, the amount of unbalance of the transmission line can also be measured.

FIG. 15-14. Balanced antenna and transmission line for impedance measurements.

On antennas fed with unbalanced or coaxial transmission lines the impedance measurements can be made with a slotted coaxial line as in Fig. 15-15. Usually a voltage probe is used to give the SWR and distance to a voltage minimum.

Measurements on balanced antennas can often be conveniently made with a slotted coaxial line and ground-plane arrangement (Fig. 15-15) by

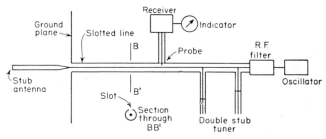

FIG. 15-15. Stub antenna and ground (image) plane with typical coaxial line for impedance measurements.

measuring one-half the antenna and then multiplying the measured impedance values by 2. Thus, instead of measuring a balanced $\frac{1}{2}$-wavelength dipole with a two-wire transmission line (Fig. 15-14), measurements are made of one-half the dipole as a $\frac{1}{4}$-wavelength stub antenna with a large ground plane (Fig. 15-15). Ideally the ground plane should be perfectly

conducting and infinite in extent to produce a perfect image of the stub antenna. The ground plane of finite extent used in practice should, therefore, be as large as possible. Even though the ground plane is several wavelengths in diameter, the measured impedance of a stub antenna varies appreciably as a function of the diameter.[1] This variation is reduced as the ground-plane diameter is increased. Meier and Summers[1] found that a large square ground plane results in about half the variation of impedance observed with a circular ground plane of approximately the same size. The antennas were mounted symmetrically on both ground planes. The reduced variation with the square ground plane is presumably due to the partial cancellation of waves reflected to the antenna terminals from the edge of the ground plane. These waves travel different distances on a square ground plane, and, hence, all cannot arrive in the same phase. The ratio of the longest to the shortest distance is the ratio of the diagonal of a square to the length of one side (1.41). With a circular ground plane and symmetrically located antenna, all the waves reflected from the edge return in the same phase.

The ground (image) plane technique can also be used to advantage in measuring the terminal impedance of slot antennas. A sheet with a half slot (equal in length to the full slot but of one-half the width) is butted against an image plane placed perpendicular to the slot plane. The half slot is energized by a coaxial line with the inner conductor connected to the terminal of the slot and the outer conductor terminated in the image plane. The terminal impedance of the full slot is twice the impedance of the half slot. The impedance $Z_{s/2}$ of the half slot is related to the impedance $Z_{d/2}$ of the complementary stub antenna or $\frac{1}{2}$ dipole by $Z_{s/2} = 8,869/Z_{d/2}$.

With horn or slot antennas that are fed with a wave guide, measurements of the field in the guide can be made with a slotted wave guide and probe arrangement. In this way measurements of the SWR, reflection coefficient, and equivalent load impedance may be obtained in a manner analogous to that used with a coaxial line.[2]

15-8. Radiation Resistance by Reflection Method. The method of Sec. 15-7 requires that the antenna terminals be available for the connection of a transmission line. In the case of a short-circuited resonant element (such as a parasitic element), however, no terminals are available. To measure the relative radiation resistance of such an element, a reflection method[3] can be employed. Consider that the antenna is a $\frac{1}{2}$-

[1] A. S. Meier and W. P. Summers, Measured Impedance of Vertical Antennas Over Finite Ground Planes, *Proc. I.R.E.*, **37**, 609–616, June, 1949.

[2] See, for example, "Very High Frequency Techniques," Radio Research Laboratory Staff, McGraw-Hill Book Company, Inc., New York, 1947, pp. 39–46.

[3] Edwin Istvanffy, Antenna Impedance Measurement by Reflection Method, *Proc. I.R.E.*, **37**, 604–608, June, 1949.

wavelength element that has been adjusted in length to resonance. As shown in Fig. 15-16, the antenna is placed in the field of a transmitting

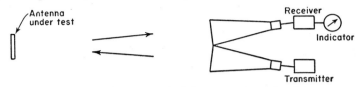

Fig. 15-16.   Reflection method for comparison of resistances.

antenna and the reflected power that is received by another antenna is measured.   The power the antenna under test reradiates is

$$W_1 = k \frac{(E_t l_{e1})^2}{R_1}$$ (15-19)

where E_t = field of transmitting antenna at antenna under test (test antenna 1)

l_{e1} = effective length of resonant test antenna 1

R_1 = radiation resistance of resonant test antenna 1

k = constant involving the distance between antennas

For another resonant $\frac{1}{2}$-wavelength element (test antenna 2) of different thickness and, hence, different effective length l_{e2} but of substantially the same pattern, the reflected power is

$$W_2 = k \frac{(E_t l_{e2})^2}{R_2}$$ (15-20)

where R_2 is the radiation resistance of the resonant test antenna 2 and k is the same constant as in (15-19).   Then dividing (15-19) by (15-20)

$$\frac{R_2}{R_1} = \frac{W_1}{W_2} \left(\frac{l_{e2}}{l_{e1}}\right)^2$$ (15-21)

Assuming that for small changes in length the effective length is proportional to the physical length,

$$\frac{l_1}{l_2} = \frac{l_{e1}}{l_{e2}}$$ (15-22)

where l_1 = physical length of test antenna 1

l_2 = physical length of test antenna 2

Thus,

$$\frac{R_2}{R_1} = \frac{W_1}{W_2} \left(\frac{l_2}{l_1}\right)^2$$ (15-23)

The ratio W_1/W_2 can be conveniently measured as the ratio $(V_1/V_2)^2$ where V_1 is the voltage received when test antenna 1 is observed and V_2

is the voltage received when test antenna 2 is observed. Thus, from the ratio W_1/W_2 or $(V_1/V_2)^2$ and the length ratio (l_2/l_1), the relative radiation resistance of one resonant antenna with respect to another can be evaluated. To determine the absolute value of the resistance requires that the resistance of one of the antennas be known.

15-9. Current-distribution Measurements. In many cases it is important to know the current distribution along an antenna. For example, if both the magnitude and phase of the current is known at all points along an antenna, the far field of the antenna can be calculated.

The measurement of current distributions is based on a current sampling method. A small pickup loop is placed close to the antenna conductor. A current is induced in the loop proportional to the adjacent antenna current. If the wavelength is sufficiently long, the loop and indicating meter can be combined in a single unit as in Fig. 15-17a. At very high frequencies the indicating instrument may be too large to be placed near the antenna without seriously disturbing the field, so that an arrangement

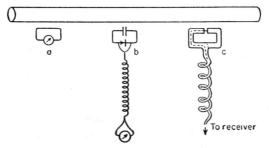

FIG. 15-17.   Sampling loops for current distribution measurements.

such as illustrated in Fig. 15-17b is resorted to. Here the indicating meter is remote from the pickup loop. The loop is connected to a crystal rectifier. Very fine insulated output wires from the rectifier are twisted together and then wound as a helical choke on a dielectric rod which may act as a handle or support for the loop probe. The diameter of the choke is about $\lambda/50$ with a spacing about equal to the diameter. The choke minimizes the current induced on the output wires by the field near the antenna. Hence, this reduces the reaction of the probe on the antenna. A by-pass condenser in the loop prevents a d-c short circuit on the crystal. A current distribution measured by a loop of the above construction is presented in Fig. 15-18.[1]

[1] Bhupendra N. Bhargava, "A Study of Current Distribution on Long Radiators," master's thesis, Department of Electrical Engineering, The Ohio State University, Columbus, Ohio, 1947.

Another type of sampling loop is shown in Fig. 15-17c. This loop is constructed of small diameter coaxial cable.[1] The loop is of balanced

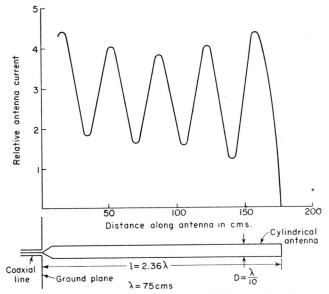

FIG. 15-18. Relative current distribution on long thick cylindrical antenna. (*After Bhargava.*)

construction. The cable leading away from the loop is wound into a helical choke of small diameter (about λ/50 diameter).

In order to remove completely the leads between loop and indicator

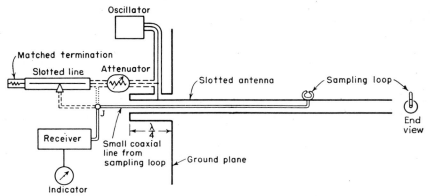

FIG. 15-19a. Slotted antenna and sampling loop.

[1] For microwave frequencies, coaxial cable as small as 0.042 in. outside diameter is obtainable from Precision Tube Co., 3824 Terrace St., Philadelphia, Pa.

from the field of the antenna, the arrangement shown in Fig. 15-19a can be employed.[1] In this method a narrow longitudinal slot is cut in the hollow cylindrical antenna conductor. The loop projects through the slot. The output cable from the loop is confined within the antenna conductor and is brought out through the end of a grounded stub as shown.

On broadcast-station arrays the current can be monitored with a loop in this manner as shown in Fig. 15-19b. A loop is mounted permanently in place on each tower of the array and the relative phase of the outputs of the loops monitored in the station to ensure that the field pattern does not shift.

The variation of current magnitude as a function of position on an antenna can be measured with any of the types of sampling loops shown in Fig. 15-17 by moving the loop along the antenna. If in addition it is desired to measure the phase variation, a comparison must be made between the phase of the sampled current and a reference current. This may be done, for example, as indicated by adding the dashed connections shown in the schematic diagram of Fig. 15-19a. Here the signal picked up by the sampling loop is mixed with a signal of approximately equal amplitude extracted by a probe on a matched slotted line. With the antenna sampling loop fixed, the line probe is moved to give a minimum indication. When the antenna sampling loop is displaced to a new location, the line probe is moved so as to maintain

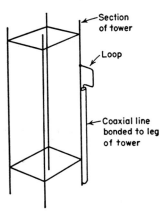

FIG. 15-19b. Current sampling loop on broadcast-station tower.

a minimum indication. The phase shift between the line-probe positions then equals the phase shift between the two antenna sampling-loop locations. The phase shift is a linear function of distance on a line with matched termination. Assuming the phase velocity equals that of light in free space, the phase shift θ along the line in degrees per unit length is given by $360°/\lambda$ where λ is the free-space wavelength of the applied signal. The phase change between two points on the line is then the distance between the points multiplied by θ.

The phase velocity v along the antenna is given by $v = \lambda_0 f$ where f is the frequency and λ_0 is the wavelength measured along the antenna.

---

[1] Milton Aronoff, "Measured Phase Velocity and Current Distribution Characteristics of Helical Beam Antennas Radiating in the Beam Mode," master's thesis, Department of Electrical Engineering, The Ohio State University, 1948.

Giorgio Barzilai, Experimental Determination of the Distribution of Current and Charge Along Cylindrical Antennas, *Proc. I.R.E.*, **37**, 825–829, July, 1949.

This is the length for a 360° shift in phase along the antenna. This may be determined from a phase-vs.-length curve measured as above. Or the measurement may be simplified by measuring only the distance intervals for a 360° phase shift. In this case the slotted matched line can be dispensed with and the reference voltage fed directly to the junction J, as indicated by the dotted line in Fig. 15-19a. The distance along the antenna between successive minimum readings on the indicator corresponds to 1 wavelength λ_0. This method is suitable when the current amplitude distribution is relatively uniform. If the SWR is very large, this method is difficult to apply and it may be simpler to take λ_0 as equal to twice the distance between successive current minima, excluding the minimum at the end of the antenna. The phase-velocity curve of Fig. 7-19 was measured on a slotted helix using the probe arrangement of Fig. 15-19a (without slotted line) and a combination of the above phase-velocity methods. At low frequencies the SWR on the helix is large, and twice the distance between successive current minima was taken for λ_0. At axial mode frequencies the current amplitude is more uniform along the helix, and λ_0 was measured as a 360° phase shift.

15-10. Wave Polarization. With some antennas it is of interest to measure the nature of the polarization. This may be measured at one frequency as a function of the space angles θ and ϕ (see Fig. 15-2). Or it may be measured at one angular position (θ_0, ϕ_0) as a function of the frequency. Such measurements are desirable where the dominant radiation is circularly or elliptically polarized. Before describing methods of measuring the polarization (Sec. 15-17), the general subject of wave polarization will be reviewed.

It is convenient to consider linear polarization and circular polarization as special cases of elliptical polarization. The electric field vectors for a *linearly polarized wave*[1] are shown in Fig. 15-20a. The magnitude and direction of the electric field $\mathbf{E}$ are indicated as a function of distance for a given instant of time. In Fig. 15-20b the wave is viewed from the direction of the positive z axis (wave approaching reader). The electric field $\mathbf{E}$ varies in magnitude between positive and negative E_2, the direction of $\mathbf{E}$ being confined to the y direction. In Fig. 15-20c the instantaneous space distribution of $\mathbf{E}$ is presented for an *elliptically polarized wave* traveling in the positive z direction. As viewed from the positive z axis, the tip of the electric field vector $\mathbf{E}$ at a fixed position z describes an ellipse with major and minor semiaxes E_2 and E_1 as shown in Fig. 15-20d. The special case of the linearly polarized wave of Fig. 15-20a and b occurs

---

[1] A linearly polarized wave is sometimes called a "plane-polarized" wave. However, "plane" is used here in another sense; so to avoid confusion the term linearly polarized will be employed.

when $E_1 = 0$. On the other hand, when $E_1 = E_2$, the ellipse becomes a circle and we have another special case of elliptical polarization called *circular polarization*. The variation of **E** for a circularly polarized wave is illustrated by Fig. 15-20e and *f*.

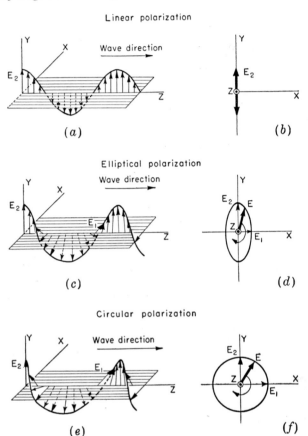

Fig. 15-20. Linear, elliptical, and circular polarization.

An elliptically polarized wave may be regarded from two points of view: (1) as the resultant of two linearly polarized waves of the same frequency and (2) as the resultant of two circularly polarized waves of the same frequency but having opposite rotation directions. Both points of view will be discussed, the former being taken up first.

15-11. Elliptical Polarization as Produced by Two Linearly Polarized Waves.[1] In this section an elliptically polarized wave is considered as the

[1] Max Born, "Optik," Verlag Julius Springer, Berlin, 1933, p. 21.

resultant of two linearly polarized waves of the same frequency. Assume that both waves are traveling in the positive z direction and that the *plane of polarization*[1] of one wave is in the x direction and the other in the y direction as in Fig. 15-21. If x is horizontal, the wave with **E** in the x direction may also be called a horizontally polarized wave and the wave with **E** in the y direction a vertically polarized wave.

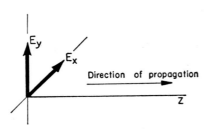

FIG. 15-21. Linearly polarized components of an elliptically polarized wave.

Let the instantaneous electric field of the horizontally polarized wave be designated E_x and the instantaneous electric field of the vertically polarized wave be designated as E_y. Then as a function of time and distance,

$$E_x = E_1 \sin(\omega t - \beta z) \tag{15-24}$$

and

$$E_y = E_2 \sin(\omega t - \beta z + \delta) \tag{15-25}$$

where E_1 = amplitude of horizontally polarized wave
E_2 = amplitude of vertically polarized wave
δ = time-phase angle by which E_y leads E_x (the horizontally polarized wave is taken as the reference for phase)

The component of the field in the z direction is everywhere zero ($E_z = 0$). The instantaneous values of the fields may also be expressed as the imaginary part (Im) of a complex function. Thus,

$$E_x = \text{Im } \dot{E}_x = E_1 \text{ Im } e^{j(\omega t - \beta z)} = E_1 \sin(\omega t - \beta z) \tag{15-26a}$$

and

$$E_y = \text{Im } \dot{E}_y = E_2 \text{ Im } e^{j(\omega t - \beta z + \delta)} = E_2 \sin(\omega t - \beta z + \delta) \tag{15-26b}$$

where[2]

$$\dot{E}_x = E_1 e^{j(\omega t - \beta z)} \tag{15-27a}$$

and

$$\dot{E}_y = E_2 e^{j(\omega t - \beta z + \delta)} \tag{15-27b}$$

The instantaneous value of the total field **E** resulting from the two linearly polarized waves is

$$\mathbf{E} = \mathbf{i}E_1 \sin(\omega t - \beta z) + \mathbf{j}E_2 \sin(\omega t - \beta z + \delta) \tag{15-28}$$

[1] The direction of the **E** vector (E plane) is usually taken as the direction of the "plane of polarization" of a linearly polarized wave.
[2] The dot (˙) indicates that $\dot{E}_x$ and $\dot{E}_y$ are complex functions of t, z, and δ but a scalar space component of the total field vector **E**. In general, the instantaneous value of the field is

$$\mathbf{E} = \mathbf{i} \text{ Im } \dot{E}_x + \mathbf{j} \text{ Im } \dot{E}_y + \mathbf{k} \text{ Im } \dot{E}_z$$

At $z = 0$, (15-28) reduces to

$$\mathbf{E} = \mathbf{i}E_1 \sin \omega t + \mathbf{j}E_2 \sin (\omega t + \delta) \tag{15-29}$$

Evaluating (15-29) as a function of time t and plotting the values of the total field $\mathbf{E}$, the time variation of $\mathbf{E}$ in the x-y plane is obtained. In general the tip of the vector $\mathbf{E}$ describes a locus that is an ellipse. If $E_1 = E_2$ and $\delta = 90°$, the ellipse becomes a circle.

The fact that, in general, the locus is an ellipse may be shown in another way by proving that (15-24) and (15-25) with $z = 0$ are the parametric equations of an ellipse. Thus, we have

$$E_x = E_1 \sin \omega t \tag{15-30}$$

$$E_y = E_2 \sin (\omega t + \delta) \tag{15-31}$$

where ωt is the independent variable. The procedure used in the proof will be to eliminate ωt and rearrange the resulting expression into the form of the equation for an ellipse. First we expand (15-31). That is,

$$E_y = E_2 (\sin \omega t \cos \delta + \cos \omega t \sin \delta) \tag{15-32}$$

From (15-30)

$$\sin \omega t = \frac{E_x}{E_1} \tag{15-33}$$

We also can write

$$\cos \omega t = \sqrt{1 - \sin^2 \omega t} = \sqrt{1 - \left(\frac{E_x}{E_1}\right)^2} \tag{15-34}$$

Substituting (15-33) and (15-34) in (15-32) and rearranging and squaring yields,

$$\frac{E_x^2}{E_1^2} - \frac{2E_x E_y \cos \delta}{E_1 E_2} + \frac{E_y^2}{E_2^2} = \sin^2 \delta \tag{15-35}$$

Dividing by $\sin^2 \delta$, (15-35) can be reduced to

$$aE_x^2 - bE_x E_y + cE_y^2 = 1 \tag{15-36}$$

where $a = 1/E_1^2 \sin^2 \delta$

$b = 2 \cos \delta / E_1 E_2 \sin^2 \delta$

$c = 1/E_2^2 \sin^2 \delta$

Equation (15-36) may be recognized as the equation for an ellipse in its most general form, the axes of the polarization ellipse not, in general, coinciding with the x and y axes (Fig. 15-22). This is the general case of elliptical polarization. The line segment OA is the semimajor axis, and the line segment OB is the semiminor axis of the ellipse. The ratio OA to

OB is called the *axial ratio* (AR) *of the polarization ellipse* or simply the *axial ratio.*[1] Thus

$$\text{Axial ratio} = \frac{OA}{OB} \qquad (15\text{-}37)$$

Returning now to (15-35), three special cases will be considered.

Case 1. First consider the case where E_y is either exactly in phase or 180° out of phase with E_x. Then $\delta = k\pi$, where $k = 0, 1, 2, 3, \cdots$ and Eq. (15-35) then reduces to

$$\frac{E_x^2}{E_1^2} \pm \frac{2E_x E_y}{E_1 E_2} + \frac{E_y^2}{E_2^2} = 0 \qquad (15\text{-}38)$$

which may be rewritten as

$$\left(\frac{E_x}{E_1} \pm \frac{E_y}{E_2}\right)^2 = 0 \qquad (15\text{-}39)$$

or

$$E_y = \pm\frac{E_2}{E_1} E_x \qquad (15\text{-}40)$$

Equation (15-40) is the equation of a straight line of the form

$$E_y = mE_x \qquad (15\text{-}41)$$

where $m = $ the slope equal to $\pm E_2/E_1$

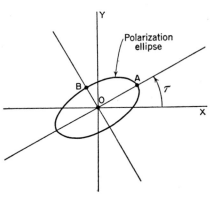

Fig. 15-22. Polarization ellipse.

When k is even ($\delta = 0, 2\pi, 4\pi$, etc.), the slope is positive, and when k is odd ($\delta = \pi, 3\pi, 5\pi$, etc.) the slope is negative.

Thus, when the two linearly polarized component waves are exactly in phase or 180° out of phase, the resultant wave is linearly polarized with $\mathbf{E}$, in general, not in the x or y direction. However, if $E_2 = 0$, $\mathbf{E}$ is in the x direction and the resultant wave is horizontally polarized. If $E_1 = 0$, $\mathbf{E}$ is in the y direction and the wave is vertically polarized. If $E_1 = E_2$ and $\delta = 0$, then $m = +1$ and $\mathbf{E}$ is at a 45° angle with respect to the positive x axis (Fig. 15-23a). If $E_1 = E_2$ and $\delta = \pi$, then $m = -1$ and $\mathbf{E}$ is at a negative 45° angle with respect to the positive x axis (Fig. 15-23b). The angle τ (Fig. 15-23a and 23b) is related to the slope m by

$$\tau = \arctan m \qquad (15\text{-}42)$$

---

[1] The term *ellipticity* is also used synonymously with axial ratio. However, *ellipticity* also may mean the ratio of the difference of the major and minor axes to the major axis. Another term used in connection with ellipses is *eccentricity*. The *eccentricity* of an ellipse is the ratio of the distance between a focus and the center to the slant distance between a focus and the end of the minor axis.

Case 2. Next consider the situation where E_x and E_y are in time phase quadrature. That is,

$$\delta = \frac{1 + 2k}{2}\,\pi \tag{15-43}$$

where $k = 0, 1, 2, 3 \ldots$
Then the cross-product term in (15-35) disappears and (15-35) reduces to

$$\frac{E_x^2}{E_1^2} + \frac{E_y^2}{E_2^2} = 1 \tag{15-44}$$

This is the standard form of the equation for an ellipse, that is, an ellipse with its axes coincident with the coordinate axes. This is a special case

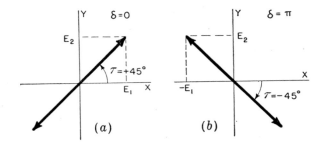

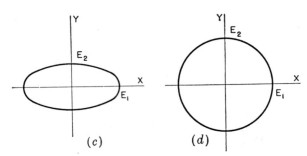

Fig. 15-23. Examples of linearly, elliptically, and circularly polarized waves.

of elliptical polarization. For example if $E_2 = \frac{1}{2}E_1$ the polarization ellipse is as shown in Fig. 15-23c.

Case 3. Finally consider Case 2 for the special condition of $E_1 = E_2$. Then (15-44) becomes

$$E_x^2 + E_y^2 = E_1^2 \tag{15-45}$$

This is the equation of a circle (Fig. 15-23d). Hence, when the two linearly polarized component waves are in time phase quadrature and also are equal in amplitude, the resultant wave is circularly polarized.

15-12. Clockwise and Counterclockwise Circular Polarization. Let us now consider the case of circular polarization (Case 3, Sec. 15-11) in more detail. According to (15-45) the locus of the tip of the vector **E** is a circle. That is, at a fixed position on the z axis the resultant electric field vector **E** is constant in magnitude and rotates uniformly with time in the x-y plane completing one revolution each cycle. However, (15-45) gives no information as to the direction in which **E** rotates, that is, clockwise or counterclockwise. To determine the rotation direction, let us rewrite (15-30) and (15-31) for the special case we are considering, namely,

$$\delta = \frac{1 + 2k}{2} \pi \quad \text{and} \quad E_1 = E_2$$

where $k = 0, 1, 2 \ldots$
Then, when k is even

$$E_x = +E_1 \sin \omega t \tag{15-46}$$

$$E_y = +E_1 \cos \omega t \tag{15-47}$$

and when k is odd E_x is the same but

$$E_y = -E_1 \cos \omega t \tag{15-48}$$

Consider first the case where k is even ($\delta = \pi/2$, $5\pi/2$, etc.). When $t = 0$, $E_x = 0$, and $E_y = +E_1$ so that **E** is in the positive y direction. One-quarter of a cycle later $E_x = +E_1$ and $E_y = 0$ so that **E** is in the

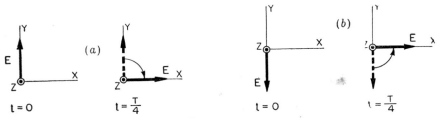

FIG. 15-24. Examples of clockwise rotation of **E** (a) and counterclockwise rotation (b).

One-quarter of a cycle later $E_x = +E_1$ and $E_y = 0$ so that **E** is in the positive x direction. Hence, at a fixed position on the z axis the resultant electric field vector **E** rotates in a clockwise direction as illustrated in Fig. 15-24a.

Next consider the case for k odd ($\delta = 3\pi/2$, $7\pi/2$, etc.). When $t = 0$, $E_x = 0$, and $E_y = -E_1$ so that **E** is in the negative y direction. One

quarter cycle later $E_x = +E_1$ and $E_y = 0$ so that **E** is in the positive x direction. Hence, at a fixed position on the z axis the resultant electric field vector **E** rotates in a counterclockwise direction as illustrated in Fig. 15-24b. The wave is traveling in the positive z direction (out of page) in both this case and the one illustrated by Fig. 15-24a. To avoid any uncertainty as to the wave direction, we can call the first case (Fig. 15-24a) "clockwise circular polarization wave approaching" and the second case (Fig. 15-24b) "counterclockwise circular polarization wave approaching."

If the electric vector appears to rotate clockwise with the wave approaching, the electric vector of the same wave appears to rotate counterclockwise when the wave is viewed from the opposite direction, that is, with the wave receding from the observer. Hence, we may say that "clockwise circular polarization wave approaching" is the same as "counterclockwise circular polarization wave receding."

According to the usage of classical physics, "clockwise circular polarization wave approaching" is called "right-circular polarization." However, according to the IRE Standards[1] "clockwise circular polarization *wave receding*" is called "right-circular polarization." Where the terms "right-circular" or "left-circular" are used in the following discussion, the IRE definition will be employed because of the convenient relation for helical beam antennas. Thus, a *right-handed helical beam antenna* transmits or receives *right-circular polarization*.

The two types of circular polarization and the various terms used to describe them are summarized in Table 15-1.

TABLE 15-1

Polarization	Classical physics usage	I.R.E. definition (1942)	Type of helical beam antenna for generating or receiving polarization
Clockwise wave approaching or Counterclockwise wave receding	Right	Left	Left-handed
Counterclockwise wave approaching or Clockwise wave receding	Left	Right	Right-handed

15-13. Clockwise and Counterclockwise Elliptical Polarization. In the general situation where the resultant wave is elliptically polarized, it is

[1] I.R.E. Standards on Radio Wave Propagation (definition of terms) 1942, p. 2, Supplement to *Proc. I.R.E.*, **30**, No. 7, Part III.

also of interest to know the direction of rotation of **E**. This can be determined by plotting **E** for several instants of time as calculated from E_x and E_y in (15-30) and (15-31). Or we can proceed in the following manner. Divide (15-27b) by (15-27a) obtaining

$$\frac{\dot{E}_y}{\dot{E}_x} = \frac{E_2}{E_1} e^{j\delta} \tag{15-49}$$

Equation (15-49) will now be applied to several special cases as illustrations.

Case 1. When $\dot{E}_y$ and $\dot{E}_x$ are in phase, $\delta = 0$. Then (15-49) reduces to

$$\frac{\dot{E}_y}{\dot{E}_x} = +\frac{E_2}{E_1} \qquad \text{or} \qquad \dot{E}_y = +\frac{E_2}{E_1}\dot{E}_x \tag{15-50}$$

When $\dot{E}_y$ and $\dot{E}_x$ are 180° out of phase, $\delta = \pi$. Then (15-49) becomes

$$\frac{\dot{E}_y}{\dot{E}_x} = -\frac{E_2}{E_1} \qquad \text{or} \qquad \dot{E}_y = -\frac{E_2}{E_1}\dot{E}_x \tag{15-51}$$

Both (15-50) and (15-51) are equations of straight lines, the resultant wave being linearly polarized.

Case 2. Next consider the situation where $\dot{E}_y$ leads $\dot{E}_x$ by 90° or $\delta = \pi/2$. Then (15-49) reduces to

$$\frac{\dot{E}_y}{\dot{E}_x} = +j\frac{E_2}{E_1} \tag{15-52}$$

This is the case of *clockwise elliptical polarization* (wave approaching).[1] The axial ratio of the polarization ellipse is in this instance E_2/E_1. If the axial ratio is unity ($E_2 = E_1$), then

$$\frac{\dot{E}_y}{\dot{E}_x} = +j \tag{15-53}$$

This is the case of *clockwise circular polarization* (wave approaching). It should be noted that the ratio E_2/E_1 equals the axial ratio only when $\delta = \pm\pi/2$.

Case 3. Finally consider the situation where $\dot{E}_y$ lags $\dot{E}_x$ by 90° or $\delta = -\pi/2$. Then (15-49) becomes

$$\frac{\dot{E}_y}{\dot{E}_x} = -j\frac{E_2}{E_1} \tag{15-54}$$

---

[1] According to the IRE definition this would be called "left-elliptical polarization."

This is the case of *counter clockwise elliptical polarization* (wave approaching). When $E_2 = E_1$ (15-54) reduces to

$$\frac{\dot{E}_y}{\dot{E}_x} = -j \qquad (15\text{-}55)$$

This is the case of *counterclockwise circular polarization* (wave approaching). Thus, from Cases 2 and 3 we can conclude that a $+j$ indicates clockwise rotation while a $-j$ indicates counterclockwise rotation of **E** (wave approaching).

15-14. Polarization as a Function of E_2/E_1 and δ. In the previous sections we have seen that the ratio E_2/E_1 (or E_1/E_2) and the phase angle determine the type of polarization of the resultant wave produced by two linearly polarized component waves (with their planes of polarization at right angles). The polarization ellipses for **E** of the resultant wave as a function of E_2/E_1 and δ are presented in Fig. 15-25 for E_2/E_1 values of ∞,

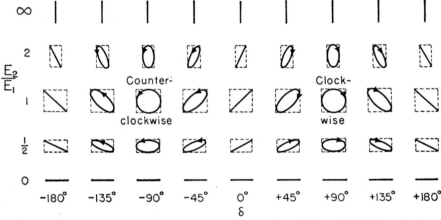

FIG. 15-25. Chart of polarization ellipses as a function of the ratio E_2/E_1 and phase angle δ (wave approaching).

2, 1, 0.5, and 0 and δ values of $0°$, $\pm 45°$, $\pm 90°$, $\pm 135°$, and $\pm 180°$. The direction of rotation of **E** is indicated. It is clockwise for positive values of δ and counterclockwise for negative values of δ (wave approaching).

Referring to Fig. 15-25, the resultant wave is linearly polarized and vertical for all values of δ when $E_2/E_1 = \infty$, that is, when $E_1 = 0$. When $E_2/E_1 = 0$, that is, when $E_2 = 0$, the wave is linearly polarized and horizontal for all values of δ. The wave is also linearly polarized when $\delta = 0$ or $\pm 180°$, the plane of polarization (horizontal, slant, or vertical) depending on the ratio E_2/E_1. Circular polarization occurs only for the case where $E_2/E_1 = 1$ and $\delta = \pm 90°$. When $\delta = +90°$, the rotation direction

is clockwise (wave approaching), and when $\delta = -90°$, the rotation direction is counterclockwise (wave approaching). All these situations are special limiting cases of the general situation in which the wave is elliptically polarized. In Fig. 15-25 there are 16 cases of elliptical polarization.

In Fig. 15-25 we note that for a given value of E_2/E_1 all polarization

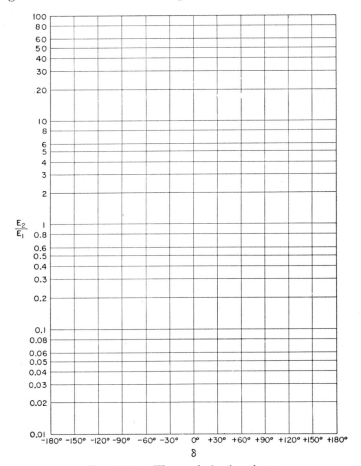

Fig. 15-26.   Wave polarization chart.

ellipses are contained within a rectangle (dashed lines) of height-to-width ratio equal to E_2/E_1. For $E_2/E_1 = 0$ or ∞ the rectangle degenerates to a line.

Two linearly polarized antennas oriented at right angles and energized with equal voltages in phase quadrature are sometimes employed to produce circular polarization. If the voltages are unequal or the phase rela-

tion is not 90°, the polarization becomes elliptical. By means of polarization measurements of the radiated wave (Sec. 15-17) it is possible to determine what adjustments should be made on the antenna to obtain circular polarization. For example, suppose that one of the linearly polarized antennas is vertical and the other is horizontal. Then if the polarization is elliptical, with the major axis of the polarization ellipse either vertical or horizontal, the phasing is ±90° but the two antennas are radiating unequal powers (see Fig. 15-25). If the major axis of the polarization ellipse is at $\tau = \pm45°$, it indicates that the two antennas are radiating the same power but the phase is not ±90°. For other ellipses, the power division and phasing can be estimated with the aid of Fig. 15-25.

To present wave polarization data, a chart with coordinates similar to those in Fig. 15-25 is useful. A chart of this type is presented in Fig. 15-26. The ordinate is the ratio E_2/E_1, and the abscissa is the phase angle δ. A point on the chart defines the polarization uniquely. Thus, the point $E_2/E_1 = 1$ and $\delta = +90°$ corresponds to clockwise circular polarization (wave approaching). If the polarization of an antenna is observed to change as a function of frequency, this variation can be plotted as a line on the chart of Fig. 15-26. The values of E_2/E_1 and δ can also be conveniently presented on the charts of Fig. 15-33 discussed in Sec. 15-17.

15-15. Orientation of Polarization Ellipse with Respect to Coordinates. It is often of interest to know the angle of tilt τ of the major axis of the polarization ellipse with respect to the reference axis. The angle τ will be called the *tilt angle*. It may be determined graphically from the polarization ellipse as evaluated from (15-30) and (15-31) as a function of time. Or τ can be obtained explicitly as a function of E_1, E_2, and δ in the following manner.

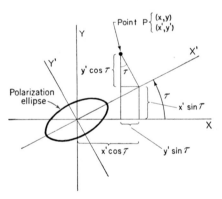

FIG. 15-27. Construction for finding the angle τ between the x axis and the major or minor axis of the polarization ellipse.

The reference axes are X, Y as shown in Fig. 15-27. Let a new set of axes X', Y' also be constructed. The coordinates of any point P may then be expressed in the new coordinates as

$$x = x' \cos \tau - y' \sin \tau \qquad (15\text{-}56)$$

$$y = x' \sin \tau + y' \cos \tau \qquad (15\text{-}57)$$

Therefore, the electric field components (E_x and E_y) can be expressed in terms of new field components ($E_{x'}$ and $E_{y'}$) as follows,

$$E_x = E_{x'} \cos \tau - E_{y'} \sin \tau \qquad (15\text{-}58)$$

$$E_y = E_{y'} \sin \tau + E_{y'} \cos \tau \qquad (15\text{-}59)$$

Now substituting (15-58) and (15-59) into (15-35) yields

$$\left. \begin{array}{l} \dfrac{1}{E_1^2} (E_{x'}^2 \cos^2 \tau - 2E_{x'}E_{y'} \sin \tau \cos \tau + E_{y'}^2 \sin^2 \tau) \\[2mm] - \dfrac{2 \cos \delta}{E_1 E_2} [(E_{x'}^2 - E_{y'}^2) \sin \tau \cos \tau + E_{x'}E_{y'}(\cos^2 \tau - \sin^2 \tau)] \\[2mm] + \dfrac{1}{E_2^2} (E_{x'}^2 \sin^2 \tau + 2E_{x'}E_{y'} \sin \tau \cos \tau + E_{y'}^2 \cos^2 \tau) = \sin^2 \delta \end{array} \right\} \quad (15\text{-}60)$$

Equation (15-60) is the general relation for an ellipse involving the field components in the direction of the new coordinate axes and the angle τ between the old and new x axes. If τ is adjusted so that the new coordinate axes coincide with the major and minor axes of the polarization ellipse, as in Fig. 15-27, then the sum of the cross-product terms in (15-60) is zero. This relation can then be solved for τ. Thus, setting the sum of the cross-product terms equal to zero,

$$\frac{2E_{x'}E_{y'} \sin \tau \cos \tau}{E_2^2} - \frac{2E_{x'}E_{y'} \sin \tau \cos \tau}{E_1^2}$$
$$- \frac{2E_{x'}E_{y'} \cos \delta}{E_1 E_2} (\cos^2 \tau - \sin^2 \tau) = 0 \qquad (15\text{-}61)$$

Solving (15-61) for the tilt angle τ yields[1]

$$\tan 2\tau = \frac{2E_1 E_2 \cos \delta}{E_1^2 - E_2^2} \qquad (15\text{-}62)$$

or

$$\tau = \frac{1}{2} \arctan \frac{2E_1 E_2 \cos \delta}{E_1^2 - E_2^2} \qquad (15\text{-}63)$$

By means of (15-63) the tilt angle τ between the major or minor axis of the polarization ellipse and the positive x axis can be calculated from a knowledge of the phase angle δ and the amplitudes E_1 and E_2 in the x and y directions. The angle τ as given by (15-63) is the angle between the x axis and *either* the major *or* minor axis of the ellipse since (15-61) is true whether the ellipse is as shown in Fig. 15-27 or turned through 90° so that its major axis is in the y' direction.

---

[1] Max Born, "Optik," Verlag Julius Springer, Berlin, 1933, p. 23.

Consider an example. For equal in-phase component fields $\delta = 0$ and $E_1 = E_2$, we find from (15-63) that $\tau = 45°$. This is the case of linear polarization at a slant (45°) angle. From (15-63) it is also apparent that $\tau = \pm 45°$ when $E_1 = E_2$ for all values of δ (see Fig. 15-25, row for $E_2/E_1 = 1$). As another example, take the case for $\delta = 45°$ and $E_2 = 2E_1$. Then $\tau = -21.7°$. This is the angle between the x axis and the minor axis of the ellipse (see ellipse at $\delta = 45°$ and $E_2/E_1 = 2$ in Fig. 15-25). The angle to the major axis is $90° - 21.7° = +68.3°$.

15-16. Elliptical Polarization as Produced by Two Circularly Polarized Waves. In this section an elliptically polarized wave will be regarded from the point of view that it is the resultant of two circularly polarized waves. The circularly polarized waves are of the opposite rotation direction and, in general, of unequal amplitude.

When the amplitudes are equal, the resultant wave is linearly polarized (Fig. 15-28a). The plane of polarization depends on the phase relation

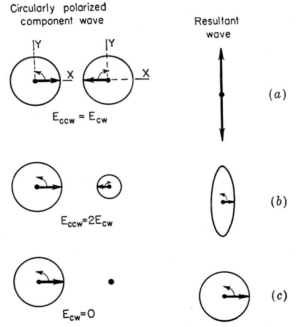

FIG. 15-28. Circularly polarized components of linearly, elliptically, and circularly polarized waves.

between the two circularly polarized waves. In the example of Fig. 15-28a the **E** vectors for both component waves are in the positive y direction at the same instant. Hence, the resultant wave is vertically polarized.

When the amplitudes are unequal, the resultant wave is elliptically polarized. If, for example, the counterclockwise rotating wave has twice the amplitude of the clockwise rotating wave ($E_{ccw} = 2E_{cw}$), the resultant wave is elliptically polarized as illustrated in Fig. 15-28b. Since the **E** vector of both waves is in the positive y direction at the same instant, the major axis of the polarization ellipse is vertical. The rotation direction is counterclockwise, the same as for the larger component wave.

If one of the component waves becomes zero, we have a limiting case and the resultant wave is equal to the other component wave (Fig. 15-28c).

The fact that the resultant of two circularly polarized waves (of opposite rotation direction) is, in general, an elliptically polarized wave can also be demonstrated analytically as follows.

Let the **E** vector of the counterclockwise rotating component wave be expressed by

$$\mathbf{E}_{ccw} = E_3 e^{j\omega t} \tag{15-64}$$

and for the clockwise component by

$$\mathbf{E}_{cw} = E_4 e^{-j(\omega t + \delta')} \tag{15-65}$$

The instantaneous x and y components of the resultant wave are then

$$E_x = \mathrm{Re}\ (\mathbf{E}_{ccw} + \mathbf{E}_{cw}) \tag{15-66}$$

and

$$E_y = \mathrm{Im}\ (\mathbf{E}_{ccw} + \mathbf{E}_{cw}) \tag{15-67}$$

Therefore,

$$E_x = E_3 \cos \omega t + E_4 \cos (\omega t + \delta') \tag{15-68}$$

and

$$E_y = E_3 \sin \omega t - E_4 \sin (\omega t + \delta') \tag{15-69}$$

Equations (15-68) and (15-69) are the parametric equations of an ellipse since by eliminating ωt they can be reduced to an equation for an ellipse of the form

$$q E_x^2 + p E_x E_y + r E_y^2 = 1 \tag{15-70}$$

where q, p, and r are functions of E_3, E_4, and δ.

The electric vector of a circularly polarized wave rotates with a uniform angular velocity. For a linearly polarized wave, **E** is in a fixed direction for one half cycle and then is in the opposite direction for the next half cycle. The situation for elliptical polarization is between these extremes. The angular velocity of **E** for an elliptically polarized wave is smaller when **E** is in the direction of the major axis of the polarization ellipse and larger when it is in the direction of the minor axis. The angular velocity is such that the rate of sweeping out the area of the polarization ellipse is constant.

15-17. Polarization Measurements. Three methods by which the polarization characteristics of a wave can be measured are:

1. By measuring the polarization pattern with a linear antenna and also observing the direction of rotation of **E**. This will be called the *polarization-pattern method*.
2. By measuring the amplitudes (E_1 and E_2) of two perpendicular linearly polarized components of the wave and the phase angle δ between them. This will be called the *linear-component method*.
3. By measuring the amplitudes (E_3 and E_4) of the two circularly polarized components (of opposite rotation direction) of the wave and the phase angle δ' between them. This will be called the *circular-component method*.

15-17a. *Polarization-pattern Method.* In this method a rotatable linearly polarized antenna, such as the $\frac{1}{2}$-wavelength antenna in Fig. 15-29, is connected to a receiver calibrated to read relative field intensity.[1]   Let

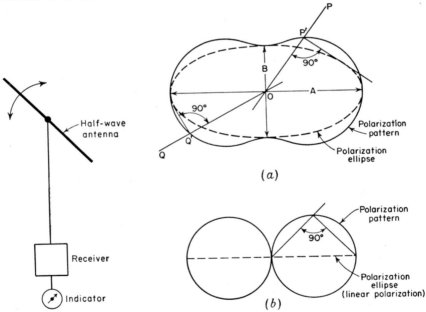

FIG. 15-29. Schematic arrangement of rotatable linearly polarized antenna for measuring polarization pattern.

FIG. 15-30. Relation of polarization ellipse to polarization pattern for elliptical polarization (a) and linear polarization (b).

[1] In practice a linearly polarized antenna of considerable directivity would be preferred to a $\frac{1}{2}$-wavelength type. Precautions must also be taken that the transmission line does not affect the antenna polarization characteristics.

the wave be approaching (out of page). Then as the antenna is rotated in the plane of the page, the field intensity observed at each position is proportional to the maximum component of **E** in the direction of the antenna. Such measurements of the incident wave with a rotatable linearly polarized antenna do not yield the *polarization ellipse* of the wave but rather its *polarization pattern* (Fig. 15-30a). Thus, if the tip of the electric vector **E** describes the *polarization ellipse* shown in Fig. 15-30a (dashed curve), the variation measured with a linearly polarized receiving antenna is given by the *polarization pattern* in Fig. 15-30a (solid line). For a given orientation OP of the linearly polarized antenna, the response is proportional to the greatest ellipse dimension measured normally to OP. As shown in Fig. 15-30a, this is the length OP'. If the linearly polarized antenna orientation is OQ, the response is proportional to the length OQ'. For the case of linear polarization, the polarization ellipse degenerates to a straight line and the corresponding polarization pattern is a figure of eight as indicated in Fig. 15-30b. By graphical construction as in Fig. 15-30, the polarization ellipse can be constructed if the polarization pattern is known or vice versa.[1] To determine the direction of rotation of **E** an auxiliary measurement is necessary. For example, the output of two circularly polarized antennas could be compared, one responsive to clockwise and the other to counterclockwise rotation. The rotation direction of **E** then corresponds to the polarization of the antenna with the larger response.

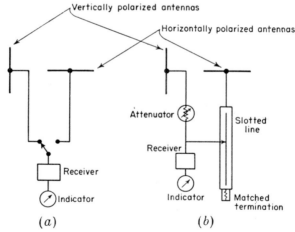

FIG. 15-31. Schematic arrangement of linearly polarized antennas for measuring ratio E_2/E_1 (a) and for measuring phase angle δ in linear-component method (b).

[1] See, for example, Chap. 6 by G. Stavis and A. Dorne, "Very High Frequency Techniques," Radio Research Laboratory Staff, McGraw-Hill Book Co., Inc., New York, 1947, p. 158.

Thus, by this method the polarization ellipse can be drawn and the rotation direction indicated (see Figs. 15-30 and 15-25). Although such a diagram completely describes the polarization characteristics of a wave, it is simpler to measure merely the maximum amplitude $A/2$ and the minimum amplitude $B/2$ and take the ratio of the two amplitudes which, as indicated in Sec. 15-11, is called the *axial ratio of the polarization ellipse* or simply the *axial ratio* (AR). The axial ratio is usually expressed so that it is equal to or greater than unity. The axial ratio of the polarization ellipse of Fig. 15-30a is

$$\text{AR} = \frac{A}{B}$$

Thus, by specifying AR, τ, and the rotation direction of **E** the polarization characteristics are completely described.

15-17b.   *Linear-component Method.*
In this method two fixed linearly polarized antennas can be mounted at right angles, like the two $\frac{1}{2}$-wavelength antennas in Fig. 15-31a. The wave is approaching normally out of the page. By connecting the receiver first to the terminals of one antenna and then the other, as in Fig. 15-31a, the ratio E_2/E_1 can be measured. Then, by connecting both antennas to a phase comparator, the angle δ can be measured. This may be done as in Fig. 15-31b, using a matched slotted line. From a knowledge of E_1, E_2, and δ the polarization ellipse can be calculated from (15-35) or from (15-30) and (15-31) and the direction of rotation **E** determined from (15-30) and (15-31) (see Fig. 15-25). The values of E_2/E_1 (or E_1/E_2) and δ can be plotted on the charts of Fig. 15-26 or 15-33.

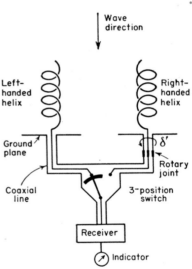

Fig. 15-32.   Arrangement for measuring left and right circular components of wave and phase angle δ' between them in circular component method.

15-17c.   *Circular-component Method.*   In this method two circularly polarized antennas of opposite rotation direction are connected successively to the receiver and the amplitudes E_3 and E_4 of the circularly polarized component waves measured. The antennas can very conveniently consist of two long helical beam antennas[1] one wound left-handed and the other wound right-handed as in Fig. 15-32. The left-handed helix responds to

[1] J. D. Kraus, The Helical Antenna, *Proc. I.R.E.*, **37**, 263–272, March, 1949.

left-circular polarization and the right-handed helix to right-circular polarization (IRE definition). The left-circular component E_L of the wave is measured with the switch to the left as in Fig. 15-32 so that the receiver is connected to the left-handed helix. The right-circular component E_R of the wave is measured with the switch thrown to the right so that the receiver is connected to the right-handed helix. The axial ratio (AR) of the received wave is then given by

$$AR = \frac{E_R + E_L}{E_R - E_L} \tag{15-71}$$

According to (15-71) the axial ratio may have values between $+1$ and $+\infty$ and between -1 and $-\infty$. For positive values of AR the wave is right-elliptical and for negative values is left-elliptical. The tilt angle τ of the polarization ellipse may be measured by finding the direction of maximum **E** with a rotable linearly polarized antenna. Or τ may be determined with the helical antennas of Fig. 15-32 by rotating one helix on its axis with both helices connected in parallel to the receiver (switch segment up in Fig. 15-32). Assuming that the axes of the helices are in a horizontal plane, let the helix rotation angle be δ' and let its reference point ($\delta' = 0$) be taken when the receiver output is a minimum for a horizontally

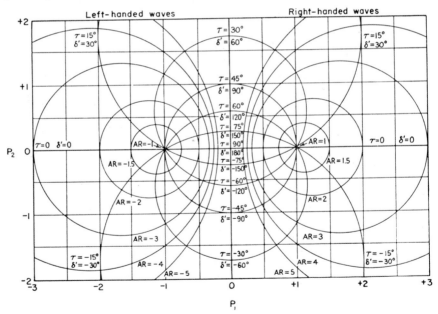

FIG. 15-33a. Rumsey and Tice type of wave polarization chart.

polarized incident wave. Then for any type of polarization with the polarization ellipse at a tilt angle τ to the horizontal, $\tau = \delta'/2$. Thus, three measurements E_L, E_R, and δ' with the helical antennas determine the polarization characteristics of the received wave completely.

The circular-component method using helical beam antennas is probably the most practical of the three methods, especially for measurements over a considerable frequency range. The accuracy depends on the circularity of polarization of the helices. This is improved (AR nearer unity) by making the helices long since by (7-48)

$$\text{AR} = \frac{2n + 1}{2n} \tag{15-72}$$

where n = the number of turns of the helix

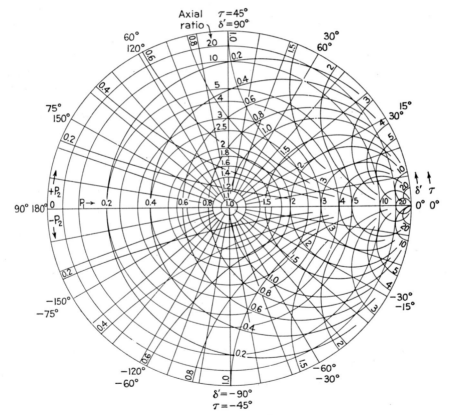

FIG. 15-33b. Rumsey and Tice type of wave polarization chart.

Rumsey and Tice have devised the very convenient presentation for wave-polarization data shown in Fig. 15-33a. This presentation employs a chart similar to a bipolar impedance chart except that AR takes the place of SWR and the tilt angle τ of the polarization ellipse takes the place of line length. The right half of the chart is for right-handed waves and the left half is for left-handed waves. The rectangular coordinates P_1 and P_2 are the real and imaginary parts of a complex polarization parameter P that is related to the linearly polarized components E_1 and E_2 of the wave and the phase angle δ between them (see Sec. 15-14) by the equation

$$P = P_1 + jP_2 = j\frac{E_1}{E_2}\angle\delta \qquad (15\text{-}73)$$

A circle diagram similar to a Smith chart can also be used for this type of presentation as shown in Fig. 15-33b. Here the chart is limited to either left- or to right-handed waves, unless some convention is adopted as, for example, that measurements of left-handed waves be plotted as circles and right-handed as crosses. Either of the charts in Fig. 15-33 is especially convenient for plotting polarization data measured by the circular-component method.

15-18. Antenna Rotation Experiments. Consider the radio circuit shown in Fig. 15-34a in which both the transmitting and receiving an-

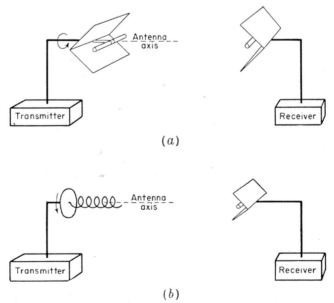

FIG. 15-34.   Arrangements for antenna rotation experiments.

tennas are linearly polarized. If either of the antennas is rotated about its axis at a frequency f (rps), the received signal is *amplitude modulated* at this frequency. The direction of rotation is immaterial.

Consider next the radio circuit shown in Fig. 15-34b in which one antenna is circularly polarized and the other is linearly polarized. If one of the antennas is rotated about its axis at a frequency f (rps), the received signal is shifted to $F \pm f$, where F is the transmitter frequency. This experiment may also be conducted with two circularly polarized antennas of the same type. The frequency f is added or subtracted from F depending on the direction of antenna rotation relative to the rotation direction of **E**.

15-19. Model Measurements. Pattern and impedance measurements of actual antennas are often difficult or impractical because of the large size of the antenna system. In such cases a scale model of the antenna system may be built to a convenient size and then measurements made on the properties of the model.[1] This technique is especially useful in measuring patterns of antennas mounted on aircraft. Although the antenna proper may be small, it may excite currents over much of the airplane surface so that the entire airplane becomes part of the antenna system, and, hence, the measurements must be made of the airplane *with* antenna. Another advantage is that the patterns of antennas on aircraft in flight (remote from the ground) can be easily simulated by the model technique by placing the model on a suitable tower. To measure such patterns on actual aircraft is both tedious and expensive.

Let the scale factor for the model be p. Then any length dimension L_m on the model is related to the corresponding dimension L on the actual antenna by

$$L_m = \frac{L}{p} \tag{15-74}$$

Then the frequency f_m used to measure the model must be related to the frequency f used with the actual antenna by

$$f_m = pf \tag{15-75}$$

A further requirement of an accurate model for pattern and impedance measurements is that the conductivity of the antenna metal be scaled according to the relation

$$\sigma_m = p\sigma \tag{15-76}$$

[1] George Sinclair, Theory of Models of Electromagnetic Systems, *Proc. I.R.E.*, **36**, 1364–1370, November, 1948.

G. H. Brown and Ronald King, High-frequency Models in Antenna Investigations, *Proc. I.R.E.*, **22**, 457–480, April, 1934.

where σ_m = conductivity of metal in model

σ = conductivity of metal in actual antenna

However, if σ is large enough, the metal can be considered to be a "perfect conductor" ($\sigma = \infty$) and the conductivity need not be modeled. Thus, actual antennas of copper can usually be modeled in copper. It is assumed that ferromagnetic materials are excluded from both actual antenna and model and that the model is measured in air. A detailed discussion of the model problem is given by Sinclair.[1]

PROBLEMS

15-1. A wave traveling normally out of the page (toward reader) has two linearly polarized components

$$E_x = 2 \cos \omega t$$
$$E_y = 3 \cos (\omega t + 90°)$$

a. What is the axial ratio of the resultant wave?

b. What is the tilt angle τ of the major axis of the polarization ellipse?

c. Does **E** rotate clockwise or counterclockwise?

15-2. A wave traveling normally outward from the page (toward reader) is the resultant of two elliptically polarized waves, one with **E**-vector components given by

$$E_y' = 2 \cos \omega t$$
$$E_x' = 6 \cos \left(\omega t + \frac{\pi}{2} \right)$$

and the other with components given by

$$E_y'' = 1 \cos \omega t$$
$$E_x'' = 3 \cos \left(\omega t - \frac{\pi}{2} \right)$$

a. What is the axial ratio of the resultant wave?

b. Does **E** rotate clockwise or counterclockwise?

15-3. An elliptically polarized plane wave traveling normally out of the page (toward reader) has linearly polarized components E_x and E_y. Given that $E_x = E_y = 1$ volt/meter and that E_y leads E_x by 72°.

a. Calculate and sketch the polarization ellipse.

b. What is the axial ratio?

c. What is the angle τ between the major axis and the x axis?

15-4. Answer the same questions as in Prob. 3 for the case where E_y leads E_x by 72° as before but $E_x = 2$ volts/meter and $E_y = 1$ volt/meter.

[1] George Sinclair, Theory of Models of Electromagnetic Systems, *Proc. I.R.E.*, **36**, 1364–1370, November, 1948.

15-5. Verify the relation (15-63) for the angle τ between the x axis and the direction of a major or minor axis of the polarization ellipse by expressing (15-35) in polar coordinates (r, θ). That is, let $E_x = E_r \cos \theta$ and $E_y = E_r \sin \theta$. Then apply the condition that $dE_r/d\theta = 0$ for a maximum or minimum value of E_r.

15-6. Two circularly polarized waves intersect at the origin. One (y wave) is traveling in the positive y direction with **E** rotating clockwise as observed from a point on the positive y axis. The other (x wave) is traveling in the positive x direction with **E** rotating clockwise as observed from a point on the positive x axis. At the origin, **E** for the y wave is in the positive z direction at the same instant that **E** for the x wave is in the negative z direction. What is the locus of the resultant **E** vector at the origin?

15-7. Prove that the instantaneous Poynting vector of a plane traveling wave is a constant when the wave is circularly polarized.

15-8. Prove that the average Poynting vector of a circularly polarized wave is twice that of a linearly polarized wave if the maximum field intensity is the same for both waves.

BOOKS FOR REFERENCE

BOOKS ON ELECTROMAGNETIC THEORY AND ON TRANSMISSION LINES, WAVE GUIDES, AND ANTENNAS

ABRAHAM, M., and R. BECKER: "Electricity and Magnetism," G. E. Stechert & Company, New York, 1932.

AHARONI, J., "Antennae," Oxford University Press, London, 1946.

"A. R. R. L. Antenna Book," 1949 ed., American Radio Relay League, Inc., West Hartford, Conn., 1949.

ATTWOOD, S. S., "Electric and Magnetic Fields," 3d ed., John Wiley & Sons, Inc., New York, 1949.

BOAST, W. B., "Principles of Electric and Magnetic Fields," Harper & Brothers, New York, 1948.

BRAINERD, J. G., G. KOEHLER, H. J. REICH, and L. F. WOODRUFF, "Ultra-high-frequency Techniques," D. Van Nostrand Company, Inc., New York, 1942.

BRONWELL, A. B., and R. E. BEAM, "Theory and Application of Microwaves," McGraw-Hill Book Company, Inc., New York, 1947.

BRÜCKMANN, H., "Antennen, ihre Theorie und Technik," S. Hirzel, Leipzig, 1939.

CADY, W. M., M. B. KARELITZ, and L. A. TURNER, "Radar Scanners and Radomes," McGraw-Hill Book Company, Inc., New York, 1948.

CULLWICK, E. G., "The Fundamentals of Electro-magnetism," The Macmillan Company, New York, 1939.

EVERITT, W. L., "Communication Engineering," McGraw-Hill Book Company, Inc., New York, 1937.

FARADAY, Michael, "Experimental Researches in Electricity," B. Quaritch, London, 1839, 1855.

HALLÉN, Erik, "Teoretisk Electricitetslära," Skrivbyran Standard, Stockholm, 1945.

HARNWELL, G. P., "Principles of Electricity and Electromagnetism," McGraw-Hill Book Company, Inc., New York, 1938.

HARPER, A. E., "Rhombic Antenna Design," D. Van Nostrand Company, Inc., New York, 1941.

HEAVISIDE, O., "Electromagnetic Theory," Ernest Benn, Ltd., London, 1893.

HENNEY, K., "Radio Engineering Handbook," 4th ed., McGraw-Hill Book Company, Inc., New York, 1950.

HERTZ, H. R., "Electric Waves," Macmillan & Co., Ltd., London, 1900.

HOLLMANN, H. E., "Physik und Technik der ultrakurzen Wellen," vol. 2, lithoreprint by Edwards Bros., Inc., Ann Arbor, Mich., 1943.

HOUSTON, W. V., "Principles of Mathematical Physics," McGraw-Hill Book Company, Inc., New York, 1948.

JEANS, Sir James, "The Mathematical Theory of Electricity and Magnetism," Cambridge University Press, London, 1933.

KIMBARK, E. W., "Electrical Transmission of Power and Signals," John Wiley & Sons, Inc., New York, 1949.

KING, R. W. P., "Electromagnetic Engineering," McGraw-Hill Book Company, Inc., New York, 1945.

KING, R. W. P., H. R. MIMNO, and A. H. WING, "Transmission Lines, Antennas, and Wave Guides," McGraw-Hill Book Company, Inc., New York, 1945.

LAMONT, R. L., "Wave Guides," Methuen & Co., Ltd., London, 1942.

LOEB, L. B., "Fundamentals of Electricity and Magnetism," John Wiley and Sons, Inc., New York, 1947.

MARCHAND, N., "Ultrahigh Frequency Transmission and Radiation," John Wiley & Sons, Inc., New York, 1947.

MAXWELL, J. C., "A Treatise on Electricity and Magnetism," Oxford University Press, New York, 2 vols., 1873, 3d ed. 1904.

PAGE, L., and N. I. ADAMS, Jr., "Principles of Electricity," D. Van Nostrand Company, Inc., New York, 1931.

PAGE, L., and N. I. ADAMS, Jr., "Electrodynamics," D. Van Nostrand Company, Inc., New York, 1940.

PIDDUCK, F. B., "Currents in Aerials and High-frequency Networks," Oxford University Press, New York, 1946.

POOR, V. C., "Electricity and Magnetism," John Wiley & Sons, Inc., New York, 1931.

POYNTING, J. H., and Sir J. J. THOMSON, "Textbook of Physics, Electricity and Magnetism," Charles Griffen & Co., Ltd., London, 1932.

"Principles of Radar" by M.I.T. Radar School Staff, J. F. Reintjes, editor, McGraw-Hill Book Company, Inc., New York, 1946.

"Radio Handbook," Editors and Engineers, Ltd., Santa Barbara, Calif., 1948.

RAMO, S., and J. R. WHINNERY, "Fields and Waves in Modern Radio," John Wiley & Sons, Inc., New York, 1946.

SARBACHER, R. I., and W. A. EDSON, "Hyper and Ultrahigh Frequency Engineering," John Wiley & Sons, Inc., New York, 1943.

SCHELKUNOFF, S. A., "Electromagnetic Waves," D. Van Nostrand Company, Inc., New York, 1943.

SCHUMANN, W. O., "Elektrische Wellen," Carl Hanser Verlag, Munich, 1948.

SILVER, S., "Microwave Antenna Theory and Design," McGraw-Hill Book Company, Inc., New York, 1949.

SKILLING, H. H., "Fundamentals of Electric Waves," 2d ed., John Wiley & Sons, Inc., New York, 1948.

SLATER, J. C., "Microwave Transmission," McGraw-Hill Book Company, Inc., New York, 1942.

SMITH, C. E., "Directional Antennas," Cleveland Institute of Radio Electronics, Cleveland, Ohio, 1946.

SMITH, C. E., "Theory and Design of Directional Antenna Systems," Natl. Assn. Broadcasters, 1949.

SMITH, W. W., "Antenna Manual," Editors and Engineers, Ltd., Santa Barbara, Calif., 1948.

SMYTHE, W. R., "Static and Dynamic Electricity," McGraw-Hill Book Company, Inc., New York, 1939.

STARLING, S. G., "Electricity and Magnetism," Longmans, Green & Co., Inc., New York, 1937.

STRATTON, J. A., "Electromagnetic Theory," McGraw-Hill Book Company, Inc., New York, 1941.

TERMAN, F. E., "Radio Engineers' Handbook," McGraw-Hill Book Company, Inc., New York, 1943.

TERMAN, F. E., "Radio Engineering," 3d ed., McGraw-Hill Book Company, Inc., New York, 1947.

"Very High Frequency Techniques" by Radio Research Laboratory Staff, vol. 1, H. J. Reich, editor, McGraw-Hill Book Company, Inc., New York, 1947.

VILBIG, F., and J. ZENNECK, editors, "Fortschritte der Hochfrequenztechnik," lithoreprint by Edwards Bros., Inc., Ann Arbor, Mich., 1945.

WATSON, W. H., "The Physical Principles of Wave Guide Transmission and Antenna Systems," Oxford University Press, New York, 1947.

BOOKS ON MATHEMATICS

BYERLY, W. E., "An Elementary Treatise on Fourier Series," Ginn & Company, Boston, 1893.

COFFIN, J. G., "Vector Analysis," John Wiley & Sons, Inc., New York, 1911.

COHEN, A., "An Elementary Treatise on Differential Equations," D. C. Heath and Company, Boston, 1906.

CHURCHILL, R. V., "Fourier Series and Boundary Value Problems," McGraw-Hill Book Company, Inc., New York, 1941.

CHURCHILL, R. V., "Modern Operational Mathematics in Engineering," McGraw-Hill Book Company, Inc., New York, 1944.

FRANKLIN, P., "Differential Equations for Electrical Engineers," John Wiley & Sons, Inc., 1933.

FRANK and von MISES, editors, "Differential und Integralgleichungen der Mechanik und Physik," Friedrich Vieweg & Sohn, Brunswick, 1935.

LOVITT, W. V., "Linear Integral Equations," McGraw-Hill Book Company, Inc., New York, 1924.

McLACHLAN, N. W., "Bessel Functions for Engineers," Oxford University Press, New York, 1934.

MARGENAU, H., and G. M. MURPHY, "The Mathematics of Physics and Chemistry," D. Van Nostrand Company, Inc., New York, 1943.

MELLOR, J. W., "Higher Mathematics for Students of Chemistry and Physics," 4th ed. Longmans, Green & Co., Inc., New York, 1931. Lithoreprint by Dover Publications, Inc., New York, 1947.

PHILLIPS, H. B., "Vector Analysis," John Wiley & Sons, Inc., New York, 1933.

REDDICK, H. W., and F. H. MILLER, "Advanced Mathematics for Engineers," John Wiley & Sons, Inc., New York, 1947.

SCHELKUNOFF, S. A., "Applied Mathematics for Engineers and Scientists," D. Van Nostrand Company, Inc., New York, 1948.

SOKOLNIKOFF, I. S., and E. S. SOKOLNIKOFF, "Higher Mathematics for Engineers and Physicists," McGraw-Hill Book Company, Inc., New York, 1941.

WHITTAKER, E. T., and G. N. WATSON, "A Course of Modern Analysis," The Macmillan Company, New York, 1944.

WILSON, E. B., "Gibbs' Vector Analysis," Yale University Press, New Haven, 1901.

APPENDIX

A number of useful tables, formulas, and charts are given on the following pages.

1. Table of Units. In this book the *rationalized mks system of units* is used.[1] The rationalized system has the advantage that the factor 4π does not appear in Maxwell's equations although it does appear in certain other relations.

In the following table the units that are commonly used in electromagnetics are listed. In the first column the name of the dimension or quantity is given and in the second column the common symbol for designating it. In the third column (Description) the dimension is described in terms of the fundamental dimensions (mass, length, time, and electric charge) or other secondary dimensions. The fourth column lists the rationalized mks unit for the dimension, and the fifth column gives equivalent units. The last column indicates the fundamental dimensions by means of the symbols M (mass), L (length), T (time), and Q (electric charge).

---

[1] To be more explicit, the rationalized mksc (meter-kilogram-second-coulomb) system is employed. However, the choice of the coulomb instead of the ampere or ohm as the fourth fundamental unit does not affect the size of the units. Hence, the system will usually be referred to simply as the rationalized mks system.

Name of dimension or quantity	Symbol	Description	Mks unit	Equivalent units	Fundamental dimensions
Length	L		meter	100 centimeter	L
Mass	M		kilogram	1000 gram	M
Time	T, t		second	$\frac{1}{60}$ minute $= \frac{1}{3,600}$ hour $= \frac{1}{86,400}$ day	T
Frequency	f	cycles/second	cps (hertz)		$\frac{1}{T}$
Area			meter^2		L^2
Volume			meter^3		L^3
Velocity	v	$\frac{\text{length}}{\text{time}}$	$\frac{\text{meter}}{\text{second}}$		$\frac{L}{T}$
Acceleration	a	$\frac{\text{velocity}}{\text{time}} = \frac{\text{length}}{\text{time}^2}$	$\frac{\text{meter}}{\text{second}^2}$		$\frac{L}{T^2}$
Force	F	mass $\times$ acceleration	newton	$\frac{\text{kilogram-meter}}{\text{second}^2} = \frac{\text{joule}}{\text{meter}} = 10^5$ dynes	$\frac{ML}{T^2}$
Momentum		mass $\times$ velocity $=$ force $\times$ time $= \frac{\text{energy}}{\text{velocity}}$	newton-seconds	$\frac{\text{kilogram-meter}}{\text{second}} = \frac{\text{joule-second}}{\text{meter}}$	$\frac{ML}{T}$

Name of dimension or quantity	Symbol	Description	Mks unit	Equivalent units	Fundamental dimensions
Energy or work		force × length = power × time	joule	newton-meter = watt-second = volt-coulomb = 10^7 ergs = 10^7 dyne centimeter	$\dfrac{ML^2}{T^2}$
Energy density	w	$\dfrac{\text{energy}}{\text{volume}}$	$\dfrac{\text{joule}}{\text{meter}^3}$		$\dfrac{M}{LT^2}$
Power	W	$\dfrac{\text{force} \times \text{length}}{\text{time}}$ = $\dfrac{\text{energy}}{\text{time}}$	watt	$\dfrac{\text{joule}}{\text{second}} = \dfrac{\text{newton-meter}}{\text{second}}$ = $\dfrac{\text{kilogram-meter}^2}{\text{second}^3}$	$\dfrac{ML^2}{T^3}$
Charge	Q, q	current × time or $\int (\text{current})\, dt$	coulomb	6.29×10^{18} electroncharges = ampere-second = 3×10^9 cgs esu* = 0.1 cgs emu†	Q
Electric flux	ψ	$\iint \mathbf{D} \cdot d\mathbf{s}$	coulombs	ampere-second	Q
Current	I, i	$\dfrac{\text{charge}}{\text{time}}$	ampere	$\dfrac{\text{coulomb}}{\text{second}} = 3 \times 10^9$ cgs esu = 0.1 cgs emu	$\dfrac{Q}{T}$
Current density	J	$\dfrac{\text{current}}{\text{area}}$	$\dfrac{\text{ampere}}{\text{meter}^2}$	$\dfrac{\text{coulomb}}{\text{second meter}^2}$	$\dfrac{Q}{TL^2}$

* cgs esu = centimeter-gram-second electrostatic unit (stat unit).
† cgs emu = centimeter-gram-second electromagnetic unit (ab unit).

Name of dimension or quantity	Symbol	Description	Mks unit	Equivalent units	Fundamental dimensions
Linear charge density	ρ_L	$\dfrac{\text{charge}}{\text{length}}$	$\dfrac{\text{coulombs}}{\text{meter}}$	$\dfrac{\text{ampere-second}}{\text{meter}}$	$\dfrac{Q}{L}$
Surface charge density	ρ_S	$\dfrac{\text{charge}}{\text{area}}$	$\dfrac{\text{coulomb}}{\text{meter}^2}$	$\dfrac{\text{ampere-second}}{\text{meter}^2}$	$\dfrac{Q}{L^2}$
D vector (displacement) (flux density)	D	$\dfrac{\text{charge}}{\text{area}}$	$\dfrac{\text{coulomb}}{\text{meter}^2}$	$\dfrac{\text{ampere-second}}{\text{meter}^2} = \dfrac{\text{ampere}}{\text{meter}^2/\text{second}}$	$\dfrac{Q}{L^2}$
Charge (volume) density	ρ	$\dfrac{\text{charge}}{\text{volume}}$	$\dfrac{\text{coulomb}}{\text{meter}^3}$	$\dfrac{\text{ampere-second}}{\text{meter}^3}$	$\dfrac{Q}{L^3}$
Electric (scalar) potential	V	$\dfrac{\text{work}}{\text{charge}}$	volt	$\dfrac{\text{joule}}{\text{coulomb}} = \dfrac{\text{newton-meter}}{\text{coulomb}}$ $= \dfrac{\text{watt-second}}{\text{coulomb}} = \dfrac{\text{watt}}{\text{ampere}} = \dfrac{\text{weber}}{\text{second}}$ $= \dfrac{1}{300}$ cgs esu $= 10^8$ cgs emu	$\dfrac{ML^2}{T^2Q}$
Emf	V	$\int \mathbf{E} \cdot d\mathbf{l}$	volt		$\dfrac{ML^2}{T^2Q}$
E vector (electric field intensity)	E	$\dfrac{\text{potential}}{\text{length}} = \dfrac{\text{force}}{\text{charge}}$	$\dfrac{\text{volt}}{\text{meter}}$	$\dfrac{\text{newton}}{\text{coulomb}} = \dfrac{\text{joule}}{\text{coulomb-meter}}$ $= \tfrac{1}{3} \times 10^{-4}$ cgs esu $= 10^6$ cgs emu	$\dfrac{ML}{T^2Q}$

Name of dimension or quantity	Symbol	Description	Mks unit	Equivalent units	Fundamental dimensions
Electric dipole moment	ql	charge $\times$ length	$\dfrac{\text{coulomb-}}{\text{meter}}$	ampere-second-meter	LQ
Electric polarization	P	$\dfrac{\text{dipole moment}}{\text{volume}}$	$\dfrac{\text{coulomb}}{\text{meter}^2}$	$\dfrac{\text{ampere-second}}{\text{meter}^2}$	$\dfrac{Q}{L^2}$
Dielectric constant (permittivity) (for vacuum, $\epsilon_0 = 8.85 \times 10^{-12}$ $= 10^{-9}/36\pi$ farad/meter)	ϵ	$\dfrac{\text{capacitance}}{\text{length}}$	$\dfrac{\text{farad}}{\text{meter}}$	$\dfrac{\text{coulomb}}{\text{volt meter}}$	$\dfrac{T^2Q^2}{ML^3}$
Relative dielectric constant (relative permittivity)	ϵ_r	Ratio $\dfrac{\epsilon}{\epsilon_0}$			Dimensionless
Capacitance	C	$\dfrac{\text{charge}}{\text{potential}}$	farad	$\dfrac{\text{coulomb}}{\text{volt}} = \dfrac{\text{coulomb}^2}{\text{joule}}$ $= 9 \times 10^{11}$ cm (cgs esu) $= \dfrac{\text{ampere-second}}{\text{volt}}$	$\dfrac{T^2Q^2}{ML^2}$
Resistance	R	$\dfrac{\text{potential}}{\text{current}}$	ohm	$\dfrac{\text{volt}}{\text{ampere}} = \dfrac{\text{joule-second}}{\text{coulomb}^2}$ $= \dfrac{1}{9} \times 10^{-11}$ cgs esu $= 10^{-9}$ cgs emu	$\dfrac{ML^2}{TQ^2}$

Name of dimension or quantity	Symbol	Description	Mks unit	Equivalent units	Fundamental dimensions
Conductance	G	$\dfrac{1}{\text{resistance}}$	mho (siemens)	$\dfrac{\text{ampere}}{\text{volt}} = \dfrac{\text{coulomb}^2}{\text{joule-second}}$	$\dfrac{TQ^2}{ML^2}$
Reactance	X	$\dfrac{\text{potential}}{\text{current}}$	ohm	$\dfrac{\text{volt}}{\text{ampere}}$	$\dfrac{ML^2}{TQ^2}$
Susceptance	B	$\dfrac{1}{\text{reactance}}$	mho	$\dfrac{\text{ampere}}{\text{volt}}$	$\dfrac{TQ^2}{ML^2}$
Impedance	Z	$\dfrac{\text{potential}}{\text{current}}$	ohm	$\dfrac{\text{volt}}{\text{ampere}}$	$\dfrac{ML^2}{TQ^2}$
Admittance	Y	$\dfrac{1}{\text{impedance}}$	mho	$\dfrac{\text{ampere}}{\text{volt}}$	$\dfrac{TQ^2}{ML^2}$
Resistivity (specific resistance)	S	resistance × length	ohm meter	$\dfrac{\text{volt-meter}}{\text{ampere}}$	$\dfrac{ML^3}{TQ^2}$
Conductivity	σ	$\dfrac{1}{\text{resistivity}}$	$\dfrac{\text{mho}}{\text{meter}}$	$\dfrac{1}{\text{ohm meter}} = \dfrac{1}{100}$ mho/centimeter	$\dfrac{TQ^2}{ML^3}$
"Magnetic charge"	m	"magnetic current" × time = pole strength × permeability	weber	volt-second = 10^8 maxwell (cgs emu)	$\dfrac{ML^2}{TQ}$
"Magnetic current"	I_m	$\dfrac{\text{"magnetic charge"}}{\text{time}}$	volt	$\dfrac{\text{weber}}{\text{second}}$	$\dfrac{ML^2}{T^2Q}$

Name of dimension or quantity	Symbol	Description	Mks unit	Equivalent units	Fundamental dimensions
"Magnetic current density"	J_m	$\dfrac{\text{"magnetic current"}}{\text{area}}$	$\dfrac{\text{volt}}{\text{meter}^2}$	$\dfrac{\text{weber}}{\text{second meter}^2}$	$\dfrac{M}{T^2Q}$
"Magnetic charge volume density"	ρ_m	$\dfrac{\text{"magnetic charge"}}{\text{volume}}$	$\dfrac{\text{weber}}{\text{meter}^3}$	$\dfrac{\text{volt-second}}{\text{meter}}$	$\dfrac{M}{TQL}$
Magnetic pole strength	Q_m, q_m	electric current $\times$ length	$\dfrac{\text{ampere-}}{\text{meter}}$	$\dfrac{\text{coulomb-meter}}{\text{second}}$	$\dfrac{QL}{T}$
Magnetic flux	ψ_m	$\iint \mathbf{B} \cdot d\mathbf{s}$	weber	volt-second $= 10^8$ maxwell (cgs emu)	$\dfrac{ML^2}{TQ}$
B vector (magnetic flux density)	B	$\dfrac{\text{magnetic flux}}{\text{area}}$ $= \dfrac{\text{force}}{\text{pole}}$	$\dfrac{\text{weber}}{\text{meter}^2}$	$\dfrac{\text{volt-second}}{\text{meter}^2} = 10^4$ gauss (cgs emu) $= \dfrac{\text{newton}}{\text{ampere-meter}}$	$\dfrac{M}{TQ}$
Magnetic scalar potential (for H)	U_h	$\dfrac{\text{work}}{\text{"magnetic charge"}}$	ampere (ampere turn)	$\dfrac{\text{joule}}{\text{weber}} = \dfrac{\text{watt}}{\text{volt}} = \dfrac{\text{coulomb}}{\text{second}}$ $= \dfrac{4\pi}{10}$ gilberts (cgs emu)	$\dfrac{Q}{T}$
Magnetic scalar potential (for B) $(U_b = \mu_0 U_h)$	U_b	$\dfrac{\text{work}}{\text{pole}}$	$\dfrac{\text{weber}}{\text{meter}}$	$\dfrac{\text{joules}}{\text{ampere-meter}}$	$\dfrac{ML}{TQ}$

Name of dimension or quantity	Symbol	Description	Mks unit	Equivalent units	Fundamental dimensions
Mmf	U	$\int \mathbf{H} \cdot dl$	ampere (ampere turn)		$\dfrac{Q}{T}$
H vector (magnetic field intensity)	H	$\dfrac{\text{mmf}}{\text{length}} = \dfrac{\text{force}}{\text{"magnetic charge"}}$	$\dfrac{\text{ampere}}{\text{meter}}$ $\left[\dfrac{\text{ampere turn}}{\text{meter}}\right]$	$\dfrac{\text{newton}}{\text{weber}} = \dfrac{\text{watt}}{\text{volt-meter}}$ $= 4\pi \times 10^{-3}$ oersteds (cgs emu) $= 4\pi \times 100$ gammas	$\dfrac{Q}{TL}$
Magnetic (dipole) moment		magnetic pole strength × length	ampere-meter²		$\dfrac{QL^2}{T}$
Magnetization (magnetic polarization)	M	$\dfrac{\text{magnetic moment}}{\text{volume}}$	$\dfrac{\text{ampere}}{\text{meter}}$		$\dfrac{Q}{TL}$
Permeability (magnetic inductive capacity) for vacuum, $\mu_0 = 4\pi \times 10^{-7} = 1.257 \times 10^{-6}$ henry/meter	μ	$\dfrac{\text{inductance}}{\text{length}}$	$\dfrac{\text{henry}}{\text{meter}}$	$\dfrac{\text{weber}}{\text{ampere-meter}} = \dfrac{\text{volt-second}}{\text{ampere-meter}}$	$\dfrac{ML}{Q^2}$
Relative permeability	μ_r	Ratio $\dfrac{\mu}{\mu_0}$			Dimensionless
Inductance	L	$\dfrac{\text{magnetic flux}}{\text{current}}$	henry	$\dfrac{\text{weber}}{\text{ampere}} = \dfrac{\text{joule}}{\text{ampere}^2} = \dfrac{1}{9} \times 10^{-11}$ cgs esu $= 10^9$ centimeters (cgs emu)	$\dfrac{ML^2}{Q^2}$

Name of dimension or quantity	Symbol	Description	Mks unit	Equivalent units	Fundamental dimensions
Reluctance		$\dfrac{\text{mmf}}{\text{magnetic flux}}$	$\dfrac{1}{\text{henry}}$	$\dfrac{\text{ampere}}{\text{weber}}$	$\dfrac{Q^2}{ML^2}$
Permeance		$\dfrac{\text{magnetic flux}}{\text{mmf}}$	henry	$\dfrac{\text{weber}}{\text{ampere}}$	$\dfrac{ML^2}{Q^2}$
Vector potential	A	electric current $\times$ permeability	$\dfrac{\text{weber}}{\text{meter}}$		$\dfrac{ML}{TQ}$
Poynting vector (power surface density)	P	$\dfrac{\text{power}}{\text{area}}$	$\dfrac{\text{watts}}{\text{meter}^2}$		$\dfrac{M}{T^3}$

2. Tables of Maxwell's Equations.   Maxwell's equations are summarized in the tables.   The first table gives Maxwell's equations in differential form and the second table in integral form.   The equations are stated for the general case, free-space case, harmonic-variation case, steady case (static fields but with conduction currents), and static case (static fields with no currents).   In the table giving the integral form, the equivalence is also indicated between the various equations and the electric potential or emf V, the magnetic potential or mmf U, the electric current I, the electric flux ψ, and the magnetic flux ψ_m.

MAXWELL'S EQUATIONS IN DIFFERENTIAL FORM

Case \ Dimensions	From Ampère $\dfrac{\text{Electric current}}{\text{area}}$	From Faraday $\dfrac{\text{Electric potential}}{\text{area}}$	From Gauss $\dfrac{\text{Electric flux}}{\text{volume}}$	From Gauss $\dfrac{\text{Magnetic flux}}{\text{volume}}$
General	$\nabla \times \mathbf{H} = \mathbf{J} + \dfrac{\partial \mathbf{D}}{\partial t}$	$\nabla \times \mathbf{E} = -\dfrac{\partial \mathbf{B}}{\partial t}$	$\nabla \cdot \mathbf{D} = \rho$	$\nabla \cdot \mathbf{B} = 0$
Free space	$\nabla \times \mathbf{H} = \dfrac{\partial \mathbf{D}}{\partial t}$	$\nabla \times \mathbf{E} = -\dfrac{\partial \mathbf{B}}{\partial t}$	$\nabla \cdot \mathbf{D} = 0$	$\nabla \cdot \mathbf{B} = 0$
Harmonic variation	$\nabla \times \mathbf{H} = (\sigma + j\omega\epsilon)\mathbf{E}$	$\nabla \times \mathbf{E} = -j\omega\mu\mathbf{H}$	$\nabla \cdot \mathbf{D} = \rho$	$\nabla \cdot \mathbf{B} = 0$
Steady	$\nabla \times \mathbf{H} = \mathbf{J}$	$\nabla \times \mathbf{E} = 0$	$\nabla \cdot \mathbf{D} = \rho$	$\nabla \cdot \mathbf{B} = 0$
Static	$\nabla \times \mathbf{H} = 0$	$\nabla \times \mathbf{E} = 0$	$\nabla \cdot \mathbf{D} = \rho$	$\nabla \cdot \mathbf{B} = 0$

MAXWELL'S EQUATIONS IN INTEGRAL FORM

Dimensions / Case	From Ampère — Magnetic potential (amperes)	From Faraday — Electric potential (volts)	From Gauss — Electric flux (coulombs)	From Gauss — Magnetic flux (webers)
General	$U = \oint \mathbf{H} \cdot d\mathbf{l} = \iint \left(\mathbf{J} + \frac{\partial \mathbf{D}}{\partial t} \right) \cdot d\mathbf{s} = I_{\text{total}}$	$V = \oint \mathbf{E} \cdot d\mathbf{l} = -\iint \frac{\partial \mathbf{B}}{\partial t} \cdot d\mathbf{s}$	$\psi = \iint \mathbf{D} \cdot d\mathbf{s} = \iiint \rho \, d\tau$	$\psi_m = \iint \mathbf{B} \cdot d\mathbf{s} = 0$
Free space	$U = \oint \mathbf{H} \cdot d\mathbf{l} = \iint \frac{\partial \mathbf{D}}{\partial t} \cdot d\mathbf{s} = I_{\text{disp}}$	$V = \oint \mathbf{E} \cdot d\mathbf{l} = -\iint \frac{\partial \mathbf{B}}{\partial t} \cdot d\mathbf{s}$	$\psi = \iint \mathbf{D} \cdot d\mathbf{s} = 0$	$\psi_m = \iint \mathbf{B} \cdot d\mathbf{s} = 0$
Harmonic variation	$U = \oint \mathbf{H} \cdot d\mathbf{l} = (\sigma + j\omega\epsilon) \iint \mathbf{E} \cdot d\mathbf{s} = I_{\text{total}}$	$V = \oint \mathbf{E} \cdot d\mathbf{l} = -j\omega\mu \iint \mathbf{H} \cdot d\mathbf{s}$	$\psi = \iint \mathbf{D} \cdot d\mathbf{s} = \iiint \rho \, d\tau$	$\psi_m = \iint \mathbf{B} \cdot d\mathbf{s} = 0$
Steady	$U = \oint \mathbf{H} \cdot d\mathbf{l} = \iint \mathbf{J} \cdot d\mathbf{s} = I_{\text{cond}}$	$V = \oint \mathbf{E} \cdot d\mathbf{l} = 0$	$\psi = \iint \mathbf{D} \cdot d\mathbf{s} = \iiint \rho \, d\tau$	$\psi_m = \iint \mathbf{B} \cdot d\mathbf{s} = 0$
Static	$U = \oint \mathbf{H} \cdot d\mathbf{l} = 0$	$V = \oint \mathbf{E} \cdot d\mathbf{l} = 0$	$\psi = \iint \mathbf{D} \cdot d\mathbf{s} = \iiint \rho \, d\tau$	$\psi_m = \iint \mathbf{B} \cdot d\mathbf{s} = 0$

Mks units

3. Formulas for Input Impedance of Terminated Transmission Line.

Formulas for the input impedance Z_x appearing at a distance x from a load or terminating impedance Z on a transmission line of characteristic impedance Z_0 as shown in the figure are listed in the table for three-load

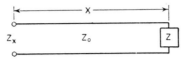

conditions: (1) any value of impedance Z, (2) $Z = 0$ or short-circuited line, and (3) $Z = \infty$ or open-circuited line. For each load condition there are columns for two cases: (1) the general case in which attentuation is present on the line ($\alpha \neq 0$), and (2) the lossless case where the line losses are negligible ($\alpha = 0$).

Load condition	General case $(\alpha \neq 0)$	Lossless case $(\alpha = 0)$
Any value Z	$Z_x = Z_0 \dfrac{Z + Z_0 \tanh \gamma x}{Z_0 + Z \tanh \gamma x}$	$Z_x = Z_0 \dfrac{Z + jZ_0 \tan \beta x}{Z_0 + jZ \tan \beta x}$ $Z_x = Z_0^2/Z^*$
$Z = 0$ Short-circuited line	$Z_x = Z_0 \tanh \gamma x$ $= Z_0 \dfrac{\tanh \alpha x + j \tan \beta x}{1 + j \tanh \alpha x \tan \beta x}$ $Z_x = Z_0 \coth \alpha x^*$	$Z_x = jZ_0 \tan \beta x$
$Z = \infty$ Open-circuited line	$Z_x = Z_0 \coth \gamma x$ $= Z_0 \dfrac{1 + j \tanh \alpha x \tan \beta x}{\tanh \alpha x + j \tan \beta x}$ $Z_x = Z_0 \tanh \alpha x^*$	$Z_x = -jZ_0 \cot \beta x$

* When $\beta x = n\pi/2$ where $n = 1, 3, 5, \ldots$
In the table $\gamma = \alpha + j\beta$ where $\alpha = $ attenuation constant and $\beta = 2\pi/\lambda$.

4. Reflection and Transmission Coefficients and SWR.

For a transmission line of characteristic impedance Z_0 terminated in a load impedance Z, the reflection coefficient for voltage ρ_v, the reflection coefficient for current ρ_i, the transmission coefficient for voltage or relative voltage at the load τ_v, the transmission coefficient for current or relative current at the load τ_i, and the SWR are given by

$$\rho_v = \frac{Z - Z_0}{Z + Z_0} = \text{reflection coefficient for voltage}$$

$$\rho_i = \frac{Z_0 - Z}{Z_0 + Z} = \text{reflection coefficient for current}$$

$$\tau_v = \frac{2Z}{Z_0 + Z} = 1 + \rho_v = \text{transmission coefficient for voltage}$$

$$\tau_i = \frac{2Z_0}{Z_0 + Z} = 1 + \rho_i = \text{transmission coefficient for current}$$

$$\text{SWR} = \frac{1 + |\rho_v|}{1 - |\rho_v|} = \frac{1 + |\rho_i|}{1 - |\rho_i|} = \text{standing wave ratio}$$

5. Formulas for the Characteristic Impedance of Transmission Lines.

In the following table the characteristic impedance Z_0 of a transmission line is given for three cases: (1) general case where losses are present, (2) special case where losses are small, and (3) lossless case. In the table

Z_0 = characteristic impedance, ohms
R_0 = characteristic resistance, ohms
Z = series impedance, ohms per meter
R = series resistance, ohms per meter
L = series inductance, henrys per meter
Y = shunt admittance, mhos per meter
G = shunt conductance, mhos per meter
C = shunt capacitance, farads per meter
$Z = R + j\omega L$
$Y = G + j\omega C$

General case	$Z_0 = \sqrt{\dfrac{Z}{Y}} = \sqrt{\dfrac{R + j\omega L}{G + j\omega C}}$
Small losses	$Z_0 = \sqrt{\dfrac{L}{C}}\left[1 + j\left(\dfrac{G}{2\omega C} - \dfrac{R}{2\omega L}\right)\right]$
Lossless case* $R = 0,\ G = 0$	$Z_0 = \sqrt{\dfrac{L}{C}} = R_0$

*Also holds approximately for case where losses are not zero but $\omega L \gg R$ and $\omega C \gg G$.

6. Trigonometric Relations

$$\sin(x \pm y) = \sin x \cos y \pm \cos x \sin y$$
$$\cos(x \pm y) = \cos x \cos y \mp \sin x \sin y$$
$$\sin(x + y) + \sin(x - y) = 2 \sin x \cos y$$

$$\cos (x + y) + \cos (x - y) = 2 \cos x \cos y$$

$$\sin (x + y) - \sin (x - y) = 2 \cos x \sin y$$

$$\cos (x + y) - \cos (x - y) = -2 \sin x \sin y$$

$$\sin 2x = 2 \sin x \cos x$$

$$\cos 2x = \cos^2 x - \sin^2 x = 2 \cos^2 x - 1 = 1 - 2 \sin^2 x$$

$$\cos x = 2 \cos^2 \tfrac{1}{2}x - 1 = 1 - 2 \sin^2 \tfrac{1}{2}x$$

$$\sin x = 2 \sin \tfrac{1}{2}x \cos \tfrac{1}{2}x$$

$$\sin^2 x + \cos^2 x = 1$$

$$\tan (x + y) = \frac{\tan x + \tan y}{1 - \tan x \tan y}$$

$$\tan (x - y) = \frac{\tan x - \tan y}{1 + \tan x \tan y}$$

$$\tan 2x = \frac{2 \tan x}{1 - \tan^2 x}$$

$$\pi = 3.1416$$

$$\pi^2 = 9.8696$$

$$1 \text{ rad} = 57.296°$$

7. Hyperbolic Relations

$$\sinh x = \frac{e^x - e^{-x}}{2} = x + \frac{x^3}{3!} + \frac{x^5}{5!} + \frac{x^7}{7!} + \cdots$$

$$\cosh x = \frac{e^x + e^{-x}}{2} = 1 + \frac{x^2}{2!} + \frac{x^4}{4!} + \frac{x^6}{6!} + \cdots$$

$$\tanh x = \frac{\sinh x}{\cosh x}$$

$$\coth x = \frac{\cosh x}{\sinh x} = \frac{1}{\tanh x}$$

$$\sinh (x \pm jy) = \sinh x \cos y \pm j \cosh x \sin y$$

$$\cosh (x \pm jy) = \cosh x \cos y \pm j \sinh x \sin y$$

$$\left.\begin{array}{l} \cosh (jx) = \tfrac{1}{2}(e^{+ix} + e^{-ix}) = \cos x \\ \sinh (jx) = \tfrac{1}{2}(e^{+ix} - e^{-ix}) = j \sin x \\ e^{\pm ix} = \cos x \pm j \sin x \end{array}\right\} \text{de Moivre's theorem}$$

$$\cosh x = \cos jx$$

$$j \sinh x = \sin jx$$

$$\tanh (x \pm jy) = \frac{\sinh 2x}{\cosh 2x + \cos 2y} \pm j \frac{\sin 2y}{\cosh 2x + \cos 2y}$$

$$\coth (x \pm jy) = \frac{\sinh 2x}{\cosh 2x - \cos 2y} \pm j \frac{\sin 2y}{\cosh 2x - \cos 2y}$$

8. Logarithmic Relations

$$\log_{10} x = \log x$$
$$\log_e x = \ln x$$
$$\log_{10} x = 0.4343 \log_e x = 0.4343 \ln x$$
$$\ln x = \log_e x = 2.3026 \log_{10} x$$
$$e = 2.7183$$

9. Approximation Formulas for Small Quantities

(δ is a small quantity compared to unity)

$$(1 \pm \delta)^2 = 1 \pm 2\delta$$
$$(1 \pm \delta)^n = 1 \pm n\delta$$
$$\sqrt{1 + \delta} = 1 + \tfrac{1}{2}\delta$$
$$\frac{1}{\sqrt{1 + \delta}} = 1 - \frac{1}{2}\delta$$
$$e^\delta = 1 + \delta$$
$$\ln(1 + \delta) = \delta$$
$$J_n(\delta) = \frac{\delta^n}{n!2^n} \qquad (\text{for } |\delta| \ll 1)$$

where J_n is Bessel function of order n

Thus, $J_1(\delta) = \dfrac{\delta}{2}$

10. Series

Binomial: $(x + y)^n = x^n + nx^{n-1}y + \dfrac{n(n-1)}{2!} x^{n-2}y^2$

$$+ \frac{n(n-1)(n-2)}{3!} x^{(n-3)}y^3 + \cdots$$

Taylor's: $f(x + y) = f(x) + f'(x)\dfrac{y}{1} + f''(x)\dfrac{y^2}{2!} + f'''(x)\dfrac{y^3}{3!} + \cdots$

11. Solution of Quadratic Equation

If $ax^2 + bx + c = 0$ then

$$x = \frac{-b \pm \sqrt{b^2 - 4ac}}{2a}$$

12. Pascal's Triangle.

The coefficients of the binomial series for $(a + b)^{n-1}$ are conveniently presented by the rows of Pascal's triangle. Any

inside number in the triangle is equal to the sum of the adjacent numbers in the row above.

$n=$							1						
$n=1:$							1						
$n=2:$						1		1					
$n=3:$					1		2		1				
$n=4:$				1		3		3		1			
$n=5:$			1		4		6		4		1		
$n=6:$		1		5		10		10		5		1	
$n=7:$	1		6		15		20		15		6		1
$n=8:$	1	7		21		35		35		21		7	1
$n=9:$	1	8	28		56		70		56		28	8	1
$n=10:$	1	9	36	84		126		126		84	36	9	1

13. Vector Identities (f and g are scalar functions; **F**, **G**, and **H** are vectors)

$$\nabla \cdot (\nabla \times \mathbf{F}) = 0$$
$$\nabla \cdot \nabla f = \nabla^2 f$$
$$\nabla \times \nabla f = 0$$
$$\nabla(f + g) = \nabla f + \nabla g$$
$$\nabla \cdot (\mathbf{F} + \mathbf{G}) = \nabla \cdot \mathbf{F} + \nabla \cdot \mathbf{G}$$
$$\nabla \times (\mathbf{F} + \mathbf{G}) = \nabla \times \mathbf{F} + \nabla \times \mathbf{G}$$
$$\nabla fg = g\nabla f + f\nabla g$$
$$\nabla \cdot f\mathbf{G} = \mathbf{G} \cdot (\nabla f) + f(\nabla \cdot \mathbf{G})$$
$$\nabla \times f\mathbf{G} = \nabla f \times \mathbf{G} + f(\nabla \times \mathbf{G})$$
$$\nabla \times (\nabla \times \mathbf{F}) = \nabla(\nabla \cdot \mathbf{F}) - \nabla^2 \mathbf{F}$$
$$\nabla \cdot (\mathbf{F} \times \mathbf{G}) = \mathbf{G} \cdot (\nabla \times \mathbf{F}) - \mathbf{F} \cdot (\nabla \times \mathbf{G})$$
$$\mathbf{F} \cdot (\mathbf{G} \times \mathbf{H}) = \mathbf{G} \cdot (\mathbf{H} \times \mathbf{F}) = \mathbf{H} \cdot (\mathbf{F} \times \mathbf{G})$$

14. Gradient, Divergence, Curl, and Laplacian in Rectangular, Cylindrical, and Spherical Coordinates (f is a scalar function; **F** is a vector function)

a. *Rectangular Coordinates* (unit vectors are **i**, **j**, **k**; the vector $\mathbf{F} = \mathbf{i}F_x + \mathbf{j}F_y + \mathbf{k}F_z$)

$$\nabla f = \mathbf{i}\frac{\partial f}{\partial x} + \mathbf{j}\frac{\partial f}{\partial y} + \mathbf{k}\frac{\partial f}{\partial z}$$

$$\nabla \cdot \mathbf{F} = \frac{\partial F_x}{\partial x} + \frac{\partial F_y}{\partial y} + \frac{\partial F_z}{\partial z}$$

$$\nabla \times \mathbf{F} = \mathbf{i}\left(\frac{\partial F_z}{\partial y} - \frac{\partial F_y}{\partial z}\right) + \mathbf{j}\left(\frac{\partial F_x}{\partial z} - \frac{\partial F_z}{\partial x}\right) + \mathbf{k}\left(\frac{\partial F_y}{\partial x} - \frac{\partial F_x}{\partial y}\right)$$

$$= \begin{vmatrix} \mathbf{i} & \mathbf{j} & \mathbf{k} \\ \dfrac{\partial}{\partial x} & \dfrac{\partial}{\partial y} & \dfrac{\partial}{\partial z} \\ F_x & F_y & F_z \end{vmatrix}$$

$$\nabla^2 f = \frac{\partial^2 f}{\partial x^2} + \frac{\partial^2 f}{\partial y^2} + \frac{\partial^2 f}{\partial z^2}$$

$$\nabla^2 \mathbf{F} = \mathbf{i}\nabla^2 F_x + \mathbf{j}\nabla^2 F_y + \mathbf{k}\nabla^2 F_z$$

b. *Cylindrical Coordinates* (unit vectors are $\mathbf{a}_r$, $\mathbf{a}_\theta$, $\mathbf{a}_z$; the vector $\mathbf{F} = \mathbf{a}_r F_r + \mathbf{a}_\theta F_\theta + \mathbf{a}_z F_z$) (related to rectangular coordinates by $x = r \cos\theta$, $y = r \sin\theta$, $z = z$)

$$\nabla f = \mathbf{a}_r \frac{\partial f}{\partial r} + \mathbf{a}_\theta \frac{1}{r}\frac{\partial f}{\partial \theta} + \mathbf{a}_z \frac{\partial f}{\partial z}$$

$$\nabla \cdot \mathbf{F} = \frac{1}{r}\frac{\partial}{\partial r}(rF_r) + \frac{1}{r}\frac{\partial F_\theta}{\partial \theta} + \frac{\partial F_z}{\partial z}$$

$$\nabla \times \mathbf{F} = \mathbf{a}_r\left(\frac{1}{r}\frac{\partial F_z}{\partial \theta} - \frac{\partial F_\theta}{\partial z}\right) + \mathbf{a}_\theta\left(\frac{\partial F_r}{\partial z} - \frac{\partial F_z}{\partial r}\right) + \mathbf{a}_z\left(\frac{1}{r}\frac{\partial(rF_\theta)}{\partial r} - \frac{1}{r}\frac{\partial F_r}{\partial \theta}\right)$$

$$\nabla^2 f = \frac{1}{r}\frac{\partial}{\partial r}\left(r\frac{\partial f}{\partial r}\right) + \frac{1}{r^2}\frac{\partial^2 f}{\partial \theta^2} + \frac{\partial^2 f}{\partial z^2}$$

c. *Spherical Coordinates* (unit vectors are $\mathbf{a}_r$, $\mathbf{a}_\theta$, $\mathbf{a}_\phi$; the vector $\mathbf{F} = \mathbf{a}_r F_r + \mathbf{a}_\theta F_\theta + \mathbf{a}_\phi F_\phi$) (related to rectangular coordinates by $x = r \sin\theta \cos\phi$, $y = r \sin\theta \sin\phi$, $z = r \cos\theta$)

$$\nabla f = \mathbf{a}_r \frac{\partial f}{\partial r} + \mathbf{a}_\theta \frac{1}{r}\frac{\partial f}{\partial \theta} + \mathbf{a}_\phi \frac{1}{r \sin\theta}\frac{\partial f}{\partial \phi}$$

$$\nabla \cdot \mathbf{F} = \frac{1}{r^2}\frac{\partial}{\partial r}(r^2 F_r) + \frac{1}{r \sin\theta}\frac{\partial}{\partial \theta}(F_\theta \sin\theta) + \frac{1}{r \sin\theta}\frac{\partial F_\phi}{\partial \phi}$$

$$\nabla \times \mathbf{F} = \mathbf{a}_r \frac{1}{r \sin\theta}\left(\frac{\partial}{\partial \theta}(F_\phi \sin\theta) - \frac{\partial F_\theta}{\partial \phi}\right)$$
$$+ \mathbf{a}_\theta \frac{1}{r}\left(\frac{1}{\sin\theta}\frac{\partial F_r}{\partial \phi} - \frac{\partial}{\partial r}(rF_\phi)\right)$$
$$+ \mathbf{a}_\phi \frac{1}{r}\left(\frac{\partial}{\partial r}(rF_\theta) - \frac{\partial F_r}{\partial \theta}\right)$$

$$\nabla^2 f = \frac{1}{r^2}\frac{\partial}{\partial r}\left(r^2\frac{\partial f}{\partial r}\right) + \frac{1}{r^2 \sin\theta}\frac{\partial}{\partial \theta}\left(\sin\theta\frac{\partial f}{\partial \theta}\right) + \frac{1}{r^2 \sin^2\theta}\frac{\partial^2 f}{\partial \phi^2}$$

15. Radians, Degrees, and Turns. In this book the arguments of trigonometric functions are generally expressed in radians or degrees as is

the usual custom. Much time and effort may often be saved, however, by expressing the argument in *turns* instead of in radians or degrees. Radians, degrees, and turns are related as follows:

$$2\pi \text{ rad} = 360° = 1 \text{ turn}$$

The symbol ^{T} is used to designate turns in the same way that ° designates degrees. Thus,

$$2\pi \text{ rad} = 360° = 1^T$$

To take advantage of the simplification afforded by using turns, a table of trigonometric functions of arguments expressed in decimal fractions of a turn is needed. A table of this kind with argument increments of 0.005 of a turn (1.8°) is given in Sec. 16. For smaller increments, reference may be made to Tölke's[1] table in which the argument increment is 0.001 of a turn (0.36°).

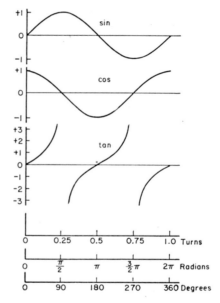

To convert an argument from radians to degrees, we let

$$2\pi \text{ rad} = 360°$$

To convert an argument from radians to turns, we let

$$2\pi \text{ rad} = 1^T$$

[1] F. Tölke, "Praktische Funktionlehre," lithoreprint by Edwards Bros., Inc., Ann Arbor, Mich., 1945.

That is, the conversion from radians to turns is made by dropping the factor 2π.*

Trigonometric quantities as a function of turns, radians, and degrees are shown graphically in the figure.

To illustrate a case where it is an advantage to use turns, let us find the value of

$$y = \sin \frac{2\pi}{\lambda} L$$

where $L = 0.615\,\lambda$
by using turns and also by using radians or degrees.

By the *turn method*, we find from the table below that

$$y = \sin \left(\frac{L}{\lambda}\right)^T = \sin 0.615^T = -0.6613^1$$

By the *radian or degree method*, we write

$$y = \sin (2\pi \times 0.615)$$

Since tables of trigonometric functions in degrees are more common than tables in radians, we usually convert to degrees. Thus,

$$y = \sin (360 \times 0.615) = \sin 221.4°$$

Since tables generally do not give functions for arguments exceeding 90°, we must convert the argument to a value less than 90°. Thus,

$$221.4° - 180° = 41.4°$$

Then, from a trigonometric table

$$\sin 41.4° = 0.6613$$

However, we must note that 221.4° is in the third quadrant so that the sine is negative and the result is

$$y = -0.6613$$

With the turn method the result is obtained in a single step, whereas with the radian or degree method several steps are required. Each extra step not only takes time but also increases the probability of introducing an error.

The trigonometric function of an argument is unchanged by subtracting or adding an integral number of turns. Thus, any argument can be con-

*In expressing an angle in turns it may be said that the angle is *rationalized*, that is, the factor 2π does not appear.

[1] Note that $(L/\lambda)^T$ is numerically equal to L_λ, the length in wavelengths ($L_\lambda = L/\lambda$).

verted to a value between 0 and $+1$, as in the table, by subtracting or adding the appropriate integer to the argument. For any positive number of turns we can disregard the number to the left of the decimal in using the table. Thus,

$$\sin 7.615^T = \sin 0.615^T = -0.6613$$

Although in this book the arguments of trigonometric functions are usually expressed in radians, it should be kept in mind that calculations will often be facilitated by dividing the argument by 2π to convert it to turns.

16. Table of Trigonometric Functions for Decimal Fractions of a Turn

Turns	Sin	Cos	Tan	Cot
0.00	0.0000	1.0000	0.0000	∞
0.005	0.0314	0.9995	0.0314	31.8214
0.010	0.0628	0.9980	0.0629	15.8947
0.015	0.0941	0.9956	0.0945	10.5787
0.020	0.1253	0.9921	0.1263	7.9160
0.025	0.1564	0.9877	0.1584	6.3139
0.030	0.1874	0.9823	0.1978	5.2422
0.035	0.2181	0.9759	0.2235	4.4738
0.040	0.2487	0.9686	0.2568	3.8947
0.045	0.2790	0.9603	0.2905	3.4420
0.050	0.3090	0.9511	0.3249	3.0777
0.055	0.3387	0.9409	0.3600	2.7776
0.060	0.3681	0.9298	0.3959	2.5256
0.065	0.3972	0.9178	0.4327	2.3108
0.070	0.4258	0.9048	0.4706	2.1251
0.075	0.4540	0.8910	0.5095	1.9626
0.080	0.4818	0.8763	0.5498	1.8190
0.085	0.5090	0.8607	0.5914	1.6909
0.090	0.5358	0.8443	0.6346	1.5757
0.095	0.5621	0.8271	0.6796	1.4715
0.100	0.5878	0.8090	0.7266	1.3764
0.105	0.6129	0.7902	0.7757	1.2892
0.110	0.6374	0.7705	0.8273	1.2088
0.115	0.6613	0.7501	0.8816	1.1343
0.120	0.6846	0.7290	0.9391	1.0649
0.125	0.7071	0.7071	1.0000	1.0000
0.130	0.7290	0.6846	1.0649	0.9391
0.135	0.7501	0.6613	1.1343	0.8816
0.140	0.7705	0.6374	1.2088	0.8273
0.145	0.7902	0.6129	1.2892	0.7757
0.150	0.8090	0.5878	1.3764	0.7266
0.155	0.8271	0.5621	1.4715	0.6796
0.160	0.8443	0.5358	1.5757	0.6346
0.165	0.8607	0.5090	1.6909	0.5914
0.170	0.8763	0.4818	1.8190	0.5498
0.175	0.8910	0.4540	1.9626	0.5092
0.180	0.9048	0.4258	2.1251	0.4706
0.185	0.9187	0.3972	2.3108	0.4327
0.190	0.9298	0.3681	2.5258	0.3959
0.195	0.9409	0.3387	2.7776	0.3600
0.200	0.9511	0.3090	3.0777	0.3249
0.205	0.9603	0.2790	3.4420	0.2905
0.210	0.9686	0.2487	3.8947	0.2568
0.215	0.9759	0.2181	4.4738	0.2235
0.220	0.9823	0.1874	5.2422	0.1908
0.225	0.9877	0.1564	6.3139	0.1584

Turns	Sin	Cos	Tan	Cot
0.230	0.9921	0.1253	7.9160	0.1263
0.235	0.9956	0.0941	10.5787	0.0945
0.240	0.9980	0.0628	15.8947	0.0629
0.245	0.9995	0.0314	31.8214	0.0314
0.250	1.0000	0.0000	± ∞	0.0000
0.255	0.9995	−0.0314	−31.8214	−0.0314
0.260	0.9980	−0.0628	−15.8947	−0.0629
0.265	0.9956	−0.0941	−10.5787	−0.0945
0.270	0.9921	−0.1253	−7.9160	−0.1263
0.275	0.9877	−0.1564	−6.3139	−0.1584
0.280	0.9823	−0.1874	−5.2422	−0.1908
0.285	0.9759	−0.2181	−4.4738	−0.2235
0.290	0.9686	−0.2487	−3.8947	−0.2568
0.295	0.9603	−0.2790	−3.4420	−0.2905
0.300	0.9511	−0.3090	−3.0777	−0.3249
0.305	0.9409	−0.3387	−2.7776	−0.3600
0.310	0.9298	−0.3681	−2.5258	−0.3959
0.315	0.9178	−0.3972	−2.3108	−0.4327
0.320	0.9048	−0.4258	−2.1251	−0.4706
0.325	0.8910	−0.4540	−1.9626	−0.5095
0.330	0.8763	−0.4818	−1.8190	−0.5498
0.335	0.8607	−0.5090	−1.6909	−0.5914
0.340	0.8443	−0.5358	−1.5757	−0.6346
0.345	0.8271	−0.5621	−1.4715	−0.6796
0.350	0.8090	−0.5878	−1.3764	−0.7266
0.355	0.7902	−0.6129	−1.2892	−0.7757
0.360	0.7705	−0.6374	−1.2088	−0.8273
0.365	0.7501	−0.6613	−1.1343	−0.8816
0.370	0.7290	−0.6846	−1.0649	−0.9391
0.375	0.7071	−0.7071	−1.0000	−1.0000
0.380	0.6846	−0.7290	−0.9391	−1.0649
0.385	0.6613	−0.7501	−0.8816	−1.1343
0.390	0.6374	−0.7705	−0.8273	−1.2088
0.395	0.6129	−0.7902	−0.7757	−1.2892
0.400	0.5878	−0.8090	−0.7266	−1.3764
0.405	0.5621	−0.8271	−0.6796	−1.4715
0.410	0.5358	−0.8443	−0.6346	−1.5757
0.415	0.5090	−0.8607	−0.5914	−1.6909
0.420	0.4818	−0.8763	−0.5498	−1.8190
0.425	0.4340	−0.8910	−0.5095	−1.9626
0.430	0.4258	−0.9048	−0.4706	−2.1251
0.435	0.3972	−0.9178	−0.4327	−2.3108
0.440	0.3681	−0.9298	−0.3959	−2.5258
0.445	0.3387	−0.9409	−0.3600	−2.7776
0.450	0.3090	−0.9511	−0.3249	−3.0777
0.455	0.2790	−0.9603	−0.2905	−3.4420
0.460	0.2487	−0.9686	−0.2568	−3.8947
0.465	0.2181	−0.9759	−0.2235	−4.4738

Turns	Sin	Cos	Tan	Cot
0.470	0.1874	−0.9823	−0.1908	−5.2422
0.475	0.1564	−0.9877	−0.1584	−6.3139
0.480	0.1253	−0.9921	−0.1263	−7.9160
0.485	0.0941	−0.9956	−0.0945	−10.5787
0.490	0.0628	−0.9980	−0.0629	−15.8947
0.495	0.0314	−0.9995	−0.0314	−31.8214
0.500	0.0000	−1.0000	0.0000	∓ ∞
0.505	−0.0314	−0.9995	+0.0314	+31.8214
0.510	−0.0628	−0.9980	0.0629	15.8947
0.515	−0.0941	−0.9956	0.0945	10.5787
0.520	−0.1253	−0.9921	0.1263	7.9160
0.525	−0.1564	−0.9877	0.1584	6.3139
0.530	−0.1874	−0.9823	0.1908	5.2422
0.535	−0.2181	−0.9759	0.2235	4.4738
0.540	−0.2487	−0.9686	0.2568	3.8947
0.545	−0.2790	−0.9603	0.2905	3.4420
0.550	−0.3090	−0.9510	0.3249	3.0777
0.555	−0.3387	−0.9408	0.3600	2.7776
0.560	−0.3681	−0.9298	0.3959	2.5258
0.565	−0.3972	−0.9178	0.4327	2.3108
0.570	−0.4258	−0.9048	0.4706	2.1251
0.575	−0.4540	−0.8910	0.5095	1.9626
0.580	−0.4818	−0.8763	0.5498	1.8190
0.585	−0.5090	−0.8607	0.5914	1.6909
0.590	−0.5358	−0.8443	0.6346	1.5757
0.595	−0.5621	−0.8271	0.6796	1.4715
0.600	−0.5878	−0.8090	0.7266	1.3764
0.605	−0.6129	−0.7902	0.7757	1.2892
0.610	−0.6374	−0.7705	0.8273	1.2088
0.615	−0.6613	−0.7501	0.8816	1.1343
0.620	−0.6846	−0.7290	0.9391	1.0649
0.625	−0.7071	−0.7071	1.0000	1.0000
0.630	−0.7290	−0.6846	1.0649	0.9391
0.635	−0.7501	−0.6613	1.1343	0.8816
0.640	−0.7705	−0.6374	1.2088	0.8273
0.645	−0.7902	−0.6129	1.2892	0.7757
0.650	−0.8090	−0.5878	1.3764	0.7266
0.655	−0.8271	−0.5621	1.4715	0.6796
0.660	−0.8443	−0.5358	1.5757	0.6346
0.665	−0.8607	−0.5090	1.6909	0.5914
0.670	−0.8763	−0.4818	1.8190	0.5498
0.675	−0.8910	−0.4540	1.9626	0.5095
0.680	−0.9048	−0.4258	2.1251	0.4706
0.685	−0.9178	−0.3972	2.3108	0.4327
0.690	−0.9298	−0.3681	2.5258	0.3959
0.695	−0.9409	−0.3388	2.7776	0.3600
0.700	−0.9511	−0.3090	3.0777	0.3249
0.705	−0.9603	−0.2790	3.4420	0.2905

Turns	Sin	Cos	Tan	Cot
0.710	−0.9686	−0.2487	3.8947	0.2568
0.715	−0.9759	−0.2181	4.4738	0.2235
0.720	−0.9823	−0.1874	5.2422	0.1908
0.725	−0.9877	−0.1564	6.3139	0.1584
0.730	−0.9921	−0.1253	7.9160	0.1263
0.735	−0.9956	−0.0941	10.5787	0.0945
0.740	−0.9980	−0.0628	15.8947	0.0629
0.745	−0.9995	−0.0314	31.8214	0.0314
0.750	−1.0000	0.0000	± ∞	0.0000
0.755	−0.9995	0.0314	−31.8214	−0.0314
0.760	−0.9980	0.0628	−15.8947	−0.0629
0.765	−0.9956	0.0941	−10.5787	−0.0945
0.770	−0.9921	0.1253	−7.9160	−0.1263
0.775	−0.9877	0.1564	−6.3139	−0.1584
0.780	−0.9823	0.1874	−5.2422	−0.1908
0.785	−0.9759	0.2181	−4.4738	−0.2235
0.790	−0.9686	0.2487	−3.8947	−0.2568
0.795	−0.9603	0.2790	−3.4420	−0.2905
0.800	−0.9510	0.3090	−3.0777	−0.3249
0.805	−0.9409	0.3387	−2.7776	−0.3600
0.810	−0.9298	0.3681	−2.5256	−0.3959
0.815	−0.9178	0.3972	−2.3108	−0.4327
0.820	−0.9048	0.4258	−2.1251	−0.4706
0.825	−0.8910	0.4540	−1.9626	−0.5095
0.830	−0.8763	0.4818	−1.8190	−0.5498
0.835	−0.8607	0.5090	−1.6909	−0.5914
0.840	−0.8443	0.5358	−1.5757	−0.6346
0.845	−0.8271	0.5621	−1.4717	−0.6796
0.850	−0.8090	0.5878	−1.3764	−0.7266
0.855	−0.7902	0.6129	−1.2892	−0.7759
0.860	−0.7705	0.6374	−1.2088	−0.8273
0.865	−0.7501	0.6613	−1.1343	−0.8816
0.870	−0.7290	0.6846	−1.0649	−0.9391
0.875	−0.7071	0.7071	−1.0000	−1.0000
0.880	−0.6846	0.7290	−0.9391	−1.0649
0.885	−0.6613	0.7501	−0.8816	−1.1343
0.890	−0.6374	0.7705	−0.8273	−1.2088
0.895	−0.6129	0.7902	−0.7757	−1.2892
0.900	−0.5878	0.8090	−0.7266	−1.3764
0.905	−0.5621	0.8271	−0.6796	−1.4715
0.910	−0.5358	0.8443	−0.8346	−1.5757
0.915	−0.5090	0.8607	−0.5914	−1.6909
0.920	−0.4818	0.8763	−0.5498	−1.8190
0.925	−0.4540	0.8910	−0.5095	−1.9626
0.930	−0.4258	0.9048	−0.4706	−2.1251
0.935	−0.3972	0.9178	−0.4327	−2.3108
0.940	−0.3681	0.9298	−0.3959	−2.5258
0.945	−0.3387	0.9409	−0.3600	−2.7776

Turns	Sin	Cos	Tan	Cot
0.950	−0.3090	0.9511	−0.3249	−3.0777
0.955	−0.2790	0.9603	−0.2905	−3.4420
0.960	−0.2487	0.9686	−0.2568	−3.8947
0.965	−0.2181	0.9759	−0.2235	−4.4738
0.970	−0.1874	0.9823	−0.1908	−5.2422
0.975	−0.1564	0.9877	−0.1584	−6.3139
0.980	−0.1253	0.9921	−0.1263	−7.9160
0.985	−0.0941	0.9956	−0.0945	−10.5787
0.990	−0.0628	0.9980	−0.0629	−15.8947
0.995	−0.0314	0.9995	−0.0314	−31.8214
1.000	0.0000	1.0000	0.0000	∞

17. Universal Pattern Charts. A universal field pattern chart for linear arrays of n isotropic point sources of equal amplitude and spacing is presented in Fig. 4-20 for $n = 1, 2, 3, 4, 5, 10,$ and 20. The following charts give n for all integral values from 1 through 24.[1] The abscissa is given in both turns and degrees. The array factor is normalized for all patterns for which the range of ψ includes zero.

It is sometimes advantageous to employ a graphical method with these charts in order to be able to observe at a glance the range of ψ as a function of ϕ. This method may be illustrated by the following example. A linear array consists of five isotropic point sources of equal amplitude and spacing. The spacing d between sources is 0.25 λ, and the phase difference is $\delta^T = -0.3$. The angle between the radius vector to a distant point and the array axis is ϕ (see Fig. 4-18). Then the value of ψ in turns is

$$\psi^T = d_\lambda \cos \phi - \delta^T$$

or

$$-\psi^T = 0.3 - 0.25 \cos \phi$$

The value δ^T is laid off along the abscissa of the universal pattern chart for $n = 5$ and a circle of radius d_λ constructed as shown in the figure. For $\phi = 30°$ the value of $d_\lambda \cos \phi$ is then the projection of the radius on the abscissa as in the figure on p. 520. Continuing the projection to the $n = 5$ curve gives the array factor E at $\phi = 30°$ as equal to 0.75. To have sufficient space for making the graphical construction it may be most convenient to first trace the $n = 5$ curve and as much of the coordinates as required on a sheet of tracing paper with large margins.

In extensive pattern calculations that do not employ the above graphical method it is desirable, as in calculations of any type, to systematize the

---

[1] These curves were furnished by J. C. Williamson.

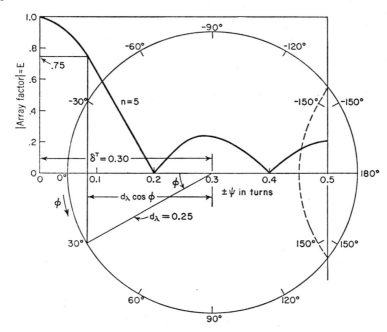

calculation by tabulating the work. This both facilitates the calculation and reduces the probability of introducing an error. For example, a sample calculation of the array factor for the above example is given below:

(1) ϕ	(2) $\cos(1)$ $\cos\phi$	(3) d_λ	(4) $(3) \times (2)$	(5) δ^T	(6) $(5) - (4)$ ψ^T	(7) E
0	1.000	0.25	0.250	0.30	−0.050	0.902
10	0.985	0.25	0.246	0.30	−0.054	0.885
20	0.940	0.25	0.235	0.30	−0.065	0.84
30	0.866	0.25	0.217	0.30	−0.083	0.75
Etc.						

Column (7) is evaluated by referring to the universal pattern chart for $n = 5$.

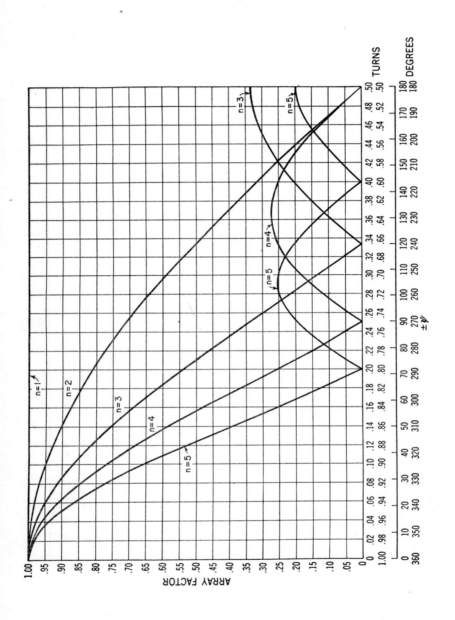

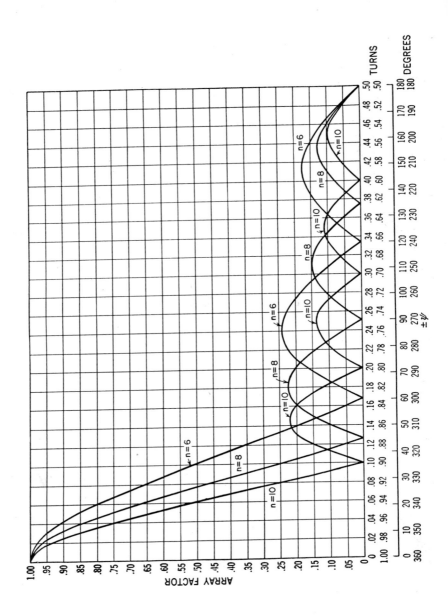

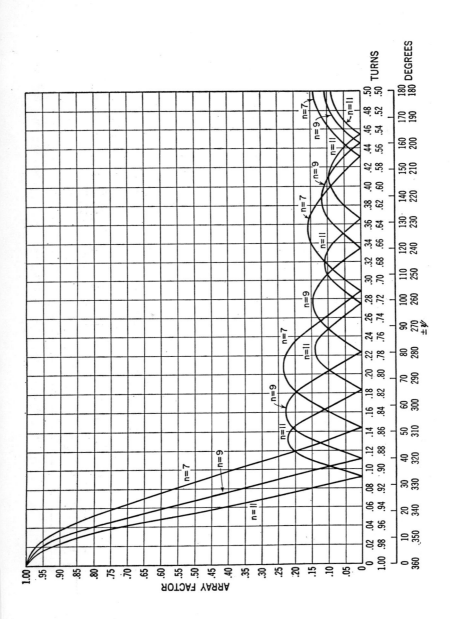

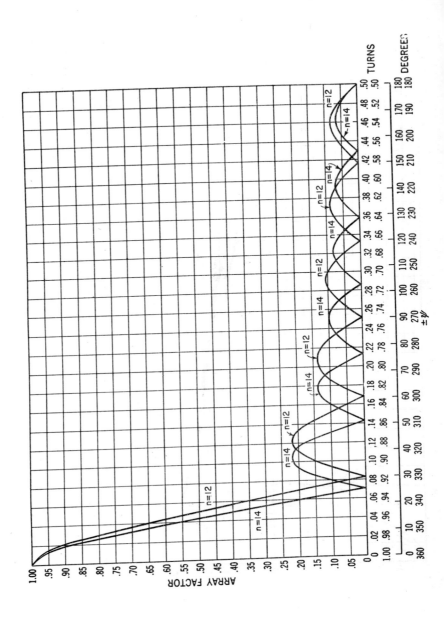

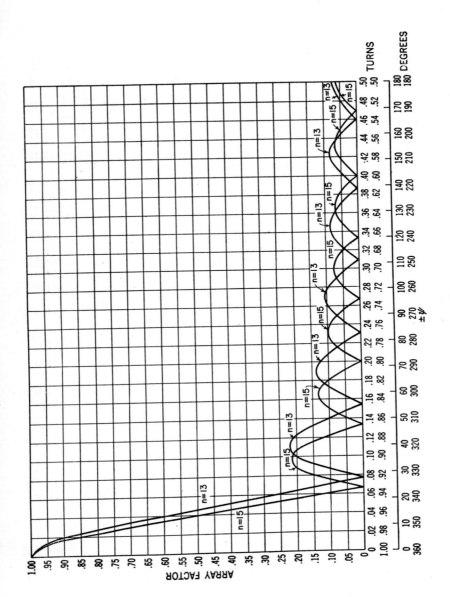

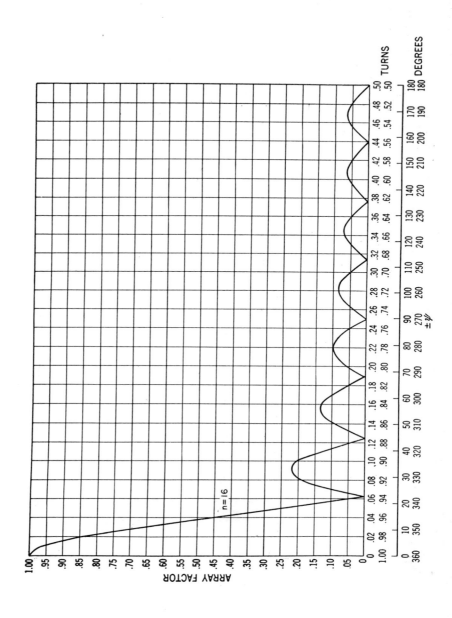

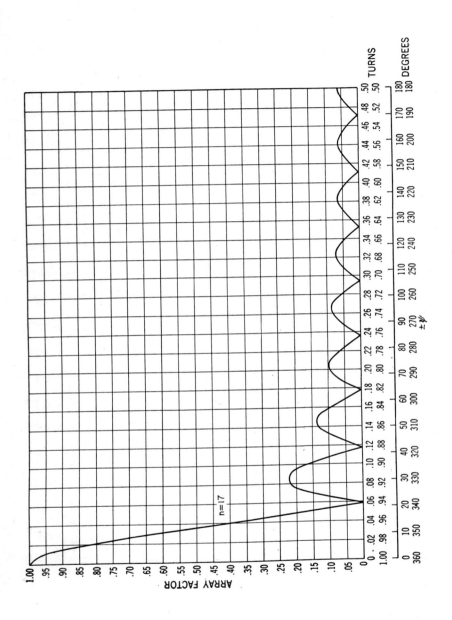

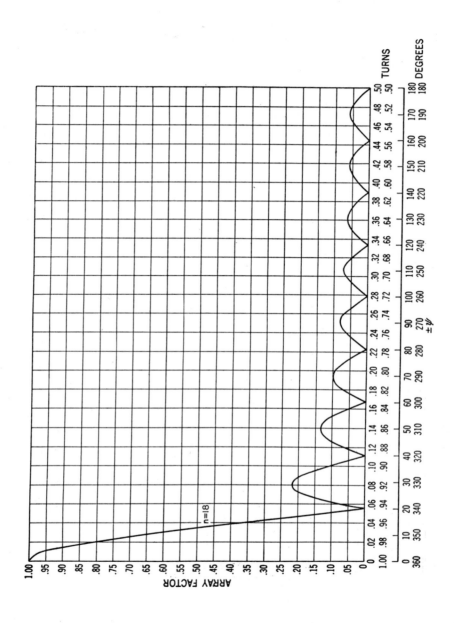

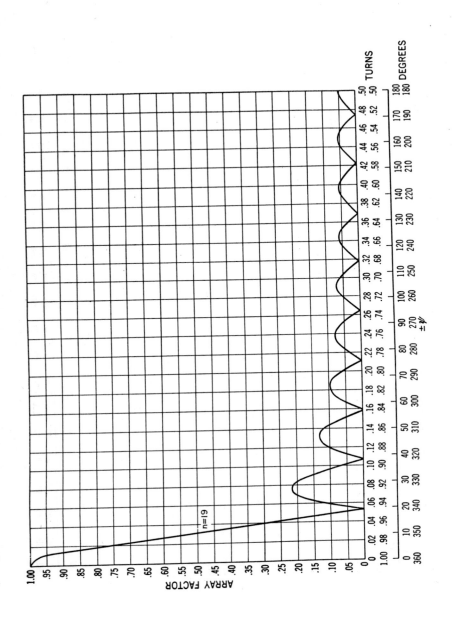

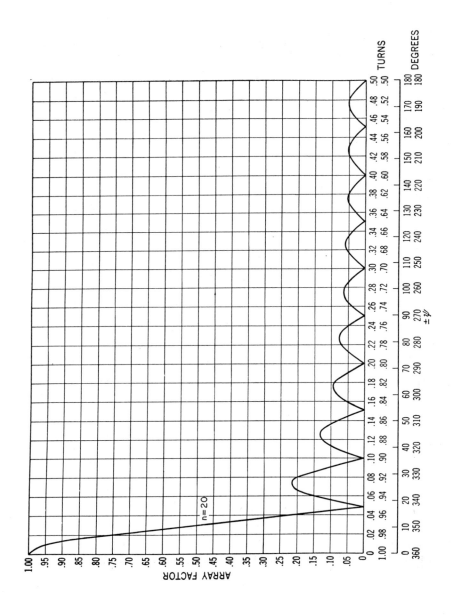

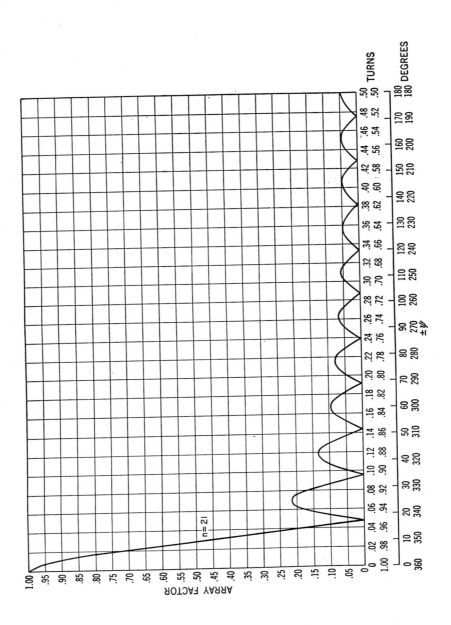

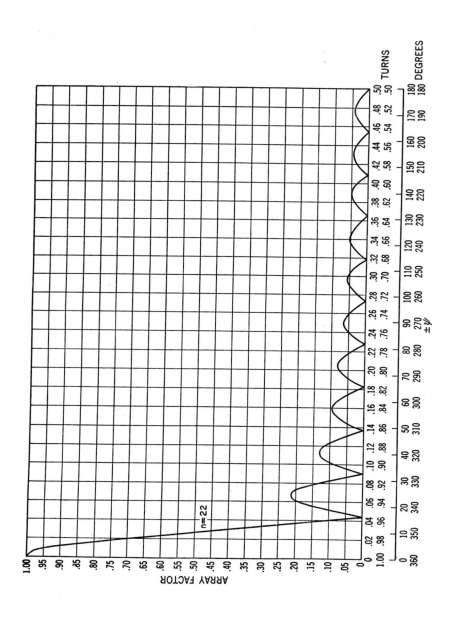

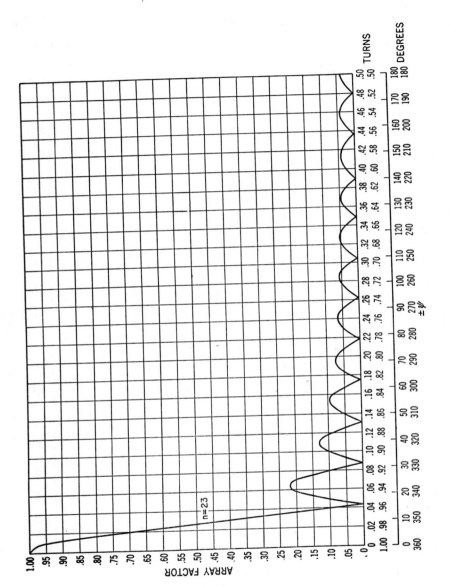

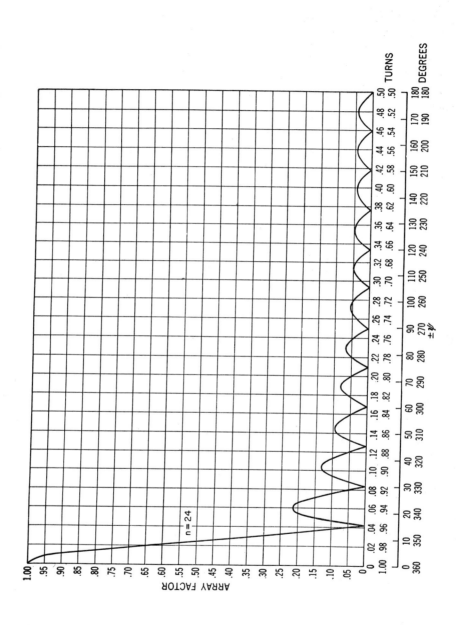

18. Sine, Cosine, and Exponential Integral Relations

$$\text{Ci}(x) = \int_{\infty}^{x} \frac{\cos u}{u}\, du = \text{cosine integral}$$

$$\text{Ci}(x) = \ln \gamma x - \frac{x^2}{2!2} + \frac{x^4}{4!4} - \frac{x^6}{6!6} + \cdots$$

where
$$\gamma = e^c = 1.781$$
$$\ln \gamma = C = 0.577 = \text{Euler's constant}$$

$$\text{Ci}(x) = 0.577 + \ln x - \frac{x^2}{2!2} + \frac{x^4}{4!4} - \frac{x^6}{6!6} + \cdots$$

When $x < 0.2$, $\quad \text{Ci}(x) \simeq 0.577 + \ln x$

When $x \gg 1$, $\quad \text{Ci}(x) \simeq \dfrac{\sin x}{x}$

$$\text{Cin}(x) = \int_{0}^{x} \frac{1 - \cos u}{u}\, du$$

$$\text{Cin}(x) = \ln \gamma x - \text{Ci}(x)$$

$$\text{Cin}(x) = \frac{x^2}{2!2} - \frac{x^4}{4!4} + \frac{x^6}{6!6} - \cdots$$

$$\text{Ci}(x) = \ln \gamma x - \text{Cin}(x)$$

Curves for Ci (x), ln γx, and Cin (x) are compared in the graph.

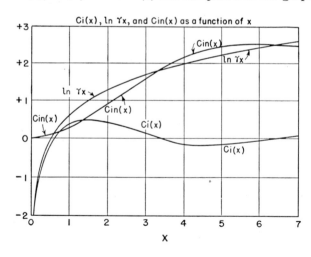

Ci(x), ln ϒx, and Cin(x) as a function of x

$$\text{Si}(x) = \int_{0}^{x} \frac{\sin u}{u}\, du = \text{sine integral}$$

$$\text{Si}(x) = x - \frac{x^3}{3!3} + \frac{x^5}{5!5} - \frac{x^7}{7!7} + \cdots$$

When $x < 0.5$, $\mathrm{Si}(x) \simeq x$

When $x \gg 1$, $\mathrm{Si}(x) \simeq \dfrac{\pi}{2} - \dfrac{\cos x}{2}$

$$\mathrm{Ein}(z) = \int_0^z \frac{1 - e^{-u}}{u}\, du = \text{exponential integral}$$

where $z = x + jy$

$$\mathrm{Ein}(jy) = \int_0^{jy} \frac{1 - e^{-u}}{u}\, du$$
$$\mathrm{Ein}(jy) = \mathrm{Cin}(y) + j\, \mathrm{Si}(y)$$
$$Ei(\pm jy) = Ci(y) \pm j\, Si(y)$$

19. Tables of Sine and Cosine Integrals. The following tables give values for the sine integral $\mathrm{Si}(x)$, the cosine integral $\mathrm{Ci}(x)$, and for $\mathrm{Cin}(x)$ for values of x from 0 to 50. Most of the entries in the tables have been compiled from various sources[1] but a considerable number, not to be found elsewhere, were calculated.

[1] F. E. Terman, "Radio Engineers' Handbook," McGraw-Hill Book Company, Inc., New York, 1943, pp. 16–17. Gives $\mathrm{Si}(x)$ and $\mathrm{Cin}(x)$ [listed as $S_1(x)$].

E. Jahnke and F. Emde, "Tables of Functions," lithoreprint by Dover Publications, New York, 1943, pp. 6–9. Gives $\mathrm{Si}(x)$ and $\mathrm{Ci}(x)$.

K. Tani, "Tables of $\mathrm{si}(x)$ and $\mathrm{ci}(x)$," Naval Experimental and Research Establishment, Tokyo, 1931. [$\mathrm{si}(x) = \mathrm{Si}(x) - \pi/2$, and $\mathrm{ci}(x) = \mathrm{Ci}(x)$].

"Tables of Sine, Cosine, and Exponential Integrals," vol. 2, Federal Works Agency, Works Projects Administration, for the City of New York, 1940. Gives $\mathrm{Si}(x)$ and $\mathrm{Ci}(x)$ in increments of 0.001 but only up to $x = 10$.

TABLE OF Si(x)

x	Si(x)	x	Si(x)	x	Si(x)	x	Si(x)
0.0	0.0000	8.0	1.5742	16.0	1.6313	24.0	1.5547
0.2	0.1996	8.2	1.5981	16.2	1.6266	24.2	1.5476
0.4	0.3965	8.4	1.6198	16.4	1.6197	24.4	1.5415
0.6	0.5881	8.6	1.6386	16.6	1.6111	24.6	1.5367
0.8	0.7721	8.8	1.6538	16.8	1.6011	24.8	1.5333
1.0	0.9461	9.0	1.6650	17.0	1.5901	25.0	1.5315
1.2	1.1081	9.2	1.6721	17.2	1.5787	26.0	1.5449
1.4	1.2562	9.4	1.6747	17.4	1.5671	27.0	1.5803
1.6	1.3892	9.6	1.6732	17.6	1.5560	28.0	1.6047
1.8	1.5058	9.8	1.6676	17.8	1.5457	29.0	1.5973
2.0	1.6054	10.0	1.6584	18.0	1.5366	30.0	1.5668
2.2	1.6876	10.2	1.6460	18.2	1.5291	31.0	1.5418
2.4	1.7525	10.4	1.6311	18.4	1.5234	32.0	1.5442
2.6	1.8004	10.6	1.6144	18.6	1.5197	33.0	1.5703
2.8	1.8321	10.8	1.5965	18.8	1.5181	34.0	1.5953
3.0	1.8487	11.0	1.5783	19.0	1.5186	35.0	1.5969
3.2	1.8514	11.2	1.5604	19.2	1.5212	36.0	1.5751
3.4	1.8419	11.4	1.5436	19.4	1.5257	37.0	1.5708
3.6	1.8220	11.6	1.5284	19.6	1.5319	38.0	1.5455
3.8	1.7933	11.8	1.5154	19.8	1.5395	39.0	1.5633
4.0	1.7582	12.0	1.5050	20.0	1.5482	40.0	1.5870
4.2	1.7184	12.2	1.4976	20.2	1.5577	41.0	1.5949
4.4	1.6758	12.4	1.4933	20.4	1.5674	42.0	1.5808
4.6	1.6325	12.6	1.4922	20.6	1.5771	43.0	1.5708
4.8	1.5900	12.8	1.4943	20.8	1.5864	44.0	1.5481
5.0	1.5499	13.0	1.4994	21.0	1.5949	45.0	1.5587
5.2	1.5137	13.2	1.5071	21.2	1.6023	46.0	1.5798
5.4	1.4823	13.4	1.5172	21.4	1.6082	47.0	1.5918
5.6	1.4567	13.6	1.5291	21.6	1.6126	48.0	1.5845
5.8	1.4374	13.8	1.5423	21.8	1.6153	49.0	1.5651
6.0	1.4247	14.0	1.5562	22.0	1.6161	50.0	1.5516
6.2	1.4187	14.2	1.5704	22.2	1.6151		
6.4	1.4192	14.4	1.5841	22.4	1.6124		
6.6	1.4258	14.6	1.5970	22.6	1.6081		
6.8	1.4379	14.8	1.6085	22.8	1.6023		
7.0	1.4546	15.0	1.6182	23.0	1.5955		
7.2	1.4751	15.2	1.6258	23.2	1.5877		
7.4	1.4983	15.4	1.6309	23.4	1.5795		
7.6	1.5233	15.6	1.6336	23.6	1.5710		
7.8	1.5489	15.8	1.6337	23.8	1.5626		

TABLE OF Ci(x)

x	Ci(x)	x	Ci(x)	x	Ci(x)	x	Ci(x)
0.01	−4.0280	5.40	−0.1544	14.40	0.0677	23.40	−0.0417
0.02	−3.3349	5.60	−0.1287	14.60	0.0628	23.60	−0.0423
0.03	−2.9296	5.80	−0.0994	14.80	0.0555	23.80	−0.0411
0.04	−2.6421	6.00	−0.0681	15.00	0.0463	24.00	−0.0383
0.05	−2.4191	6.20	−0.0359	15.20	0.0354	24.20	−0.0341
0.10	−1.7279	6.40	−0.0042	15.40	0.0234	24.40	−0.0286
0.15	−1.3255	6.60	0.0258	15.60	0.0108	24.60	−0.0220
0.20	−1.0422	6.80	0.0531	15.80	−0.0019	24.80	−0.0149
0.25	−0.8247	7.00	0.0767	16.00	−0.0142	25.00	−0.0068
0.30	−0.6492	7.20	0.0960	16.20	−0.0257	26.00	0.0283
0.35	−0.5031	7.40	0.1104	16.40	−0.0358	27.00	0.0357
0.40	−0.3788	7.60	0.1196	16.60	−0.0443	28.00	0.0109
0.45	−0.2715	7.80	0.1236	16.80	−0.0509	29.00	−0.0219
0.50	−0.1778	8.00	0.1224	17.00	−0.0552	30.00	−0.0330
0.55	−0.0953	8.20	0.1164	17.20	−0.0573	31.00	−0.0140
0.60	−0.0223	8.40	0.1061	17.40	−0.0571	32.00	0.0164
0.65	0.0427	8.60	0.0919	17.60	−0.0546	33.00	0.0303
0.70	0.1005	8.80	0.0747	17.80	−0.0500	34.00	0.0163
0.75	0.1522	9.00	0.0553	18.00	−0.0435	35.00	−0.0115
0.80	0.1983	9.20	0.0345	18.20	−0.0354	36.00	−0.0274
0.85	0.2394	9.40	0.0133	18.40	−0.0261	37.00	−0.0179
0.90	0.2761	9.60	−0.0077	18.60	−0.0160	38.00	0.0071
0.95	0.3086	9.80	−0.0275	18.80	−0.0054	39.00	0.0245
1.00	0.3374	10.00	−0.0455	19.00	0.0052	40.00	0.0190
1.20	0.4205	10.20	−0.0609	19.20	0.0153	41.00	−0.0033
1.40	0.4620	10.40	−0.0733	19.40	0.0246	42.00	−0.0216
1.60	0.4717	10.60	−0.0824	19.60	0.0327	43.00	−0.0196
1.80	0.4568	10.80	−0.0878	19.80	0.0394	44.00	−0.0001
2.00	0.4230	11.00	−0.0896	20.00	0.0444	45.00	0.0186
2.20	0.3751	11.20	−0.0877	20.20	0.0476	46.00	0.0198
2.40	0.3173	11.40	−0.0824	20.40	0.0487	47.00	0.0031
2.60	0.2533	11.60	−0.0740	20.60	0.0480	48.00	−0.0157
2.80	0.1865	11.80	−0.0630	20.80	0.0453	49.00	−0.0196
3.00	0.1196	12.00	−0.0498	21.00	0.0409	50.00	−0.0056
3.20	0.0553	12.20	−0.0350	21.20	0.0349		
3.40	−0.0045	12.40	−0.0194	21.40	0.0277		
3.60	−0.0580	12.60	−0.0034	21.60	0.0195		
3.80	−0.1038	12.80	0.0121	21.80	0.0107		
4.00	−0.1410	13.00	0.0268	22.00	0.0016		
4.20	−0.1690	13.20	0.0399	22.20	−0.0073		
4.40	−0.1877	13.40	0.0510	22.40	−0.0159		
4.60	−0.1970	13.60	0.0598	22.60	−0.0236		
4.80	−0.1976	13.80	0.0660	22.80	−0.0303		
5.00	−0.1900	14.00	0.0694	23.00	−0.0367		
5.20	−0.1753	14.20	0.0699	23.20	−0.0395		

TABLE OF Cin(x)

x	Cin(x)	x	Cin(x)	x	Cin(x)	x	Cin(x)
0.0	0.0000	8.0	2.5342	16.0	3.3640	24.0	3.7936
0.2	0.0100	8.2	2.5649	16.2	3.3879	24.2	3.7977
0.4	0.0397	8.4	2.5994	16.4	3.4103	24.4	3.8004
0.6	0.0887	8.6	2.6370	16.6	3.4310	24.6	3.8020
0.8	0.1558	8.8	2.6772	16.8	3.4495	24.8	3.8027
1.0	0.2398	9.0	2.7191	17.0	3.4657	25.0	3.8030
1.2	0.3391	9.2	2.7619	17.2	3.4795	26.0	3.8070
1.4	0.4517	9.4	2.8047	17.4	3.4908	27.0	3.8373
1.6	0.5755	9.6	2.8467	17.6	3.4997	28.0	3.8985
1.8	0.7082	9.8	2.8871	17.8	3.5064	29.0	3.9664
2.0	0.8474	10.0	2.9253	18.0	3.5111	30.0	4.0118
2.2	0.9906	10.2	2.9605	18.2	3.5140	31.0	4.0252
2.4	1.1354	10.4	2.9923	18.4	3.5157	32.0	4.0265
2.6	1.2794	10.6	3.0205	18.6	3.5163	33.0	4.0434
2.8	1.4204	10.8	3.0446	18.8	3.5165	34.0	4.0873
3.0	1.5562	11.0	3.0647	19.0	3.5166	35.0	4.1441
3.2	1.6851	11.2	3.0808	19.2	3.5169	36.0	4.1881
3.4	1.8055	11.4	3.0932	19.4	3.5179	37.0	4.2060
3.6	1.9161	11.6	3.1023	19.6	3.5200	38.0	4.2077
3.8	2.0160	11.8	3.1083	19.8	3.5235	39.0	4.2163
4.0	2.1045	12.0	3.1119	20.0	3.5285	40.0	4.2471
4.2	2.1813	12.2	3.1137	20.2	3.5354	41.0	4.2941
4.4	2.2465	12.4	3.1143	20.4	3.5440	42.0	4.3365
4.6	2.3003	12.6	3.1144	20.6	3.5546	43.0	4.3580
4.8	2.3434	12.8	3.1145	20.8	3.5669	44.0	4.3615
5.0	2.3767	13.0	3.1154	21.0	3.5809	45.0	4.3653
5.2	2.4011	13.2	3.1175	21.2	3.5963	46.0	4.3860
5.4	2.4180	13.4	3.1214	21.4	3.6129	47.0	4.4243
5.6	2.4287	13.6	3.1275	21.6	3.6304	48.0	4.4641
5.8	2.4345	13.8	3.1358	21.8	3.6484	49.0	4.4886
6.0	2.4370	14.0	3.1469	22.0	3.6666	50.0	4.4948
6.2	2.4376	14.2	3.1605	22.2	3.6847		
6.4	2.4377	14.4	3.1768	22.4	3.7022		
6.6	2.4385	14.6	3.1955	22.6	3.7188		
6.8	2.4411	14.8	3.2163	22.8	3.7343		
7.0	2.4464	15.0	3.2390	23.0	3.7484		
7.2	2.4553	15.2	3.2631	23.2	3.7609		
7.4	2.4683	15.4	3.2881	23.4	3.7717		
7.6	2.4858	15.6	3.3136	23.6	3.7807		
7.8	2.5078	15.8	3.3391	23.8	3.7880		

20. General Poynting Vector and Directivity Formulas. The derivation of a number of special Poynting vector relations used in the text from the more general relations is given in this section. Their application to radiated power and directivity formulas is also considered.

The instantaneous Poynting vector $\mathbf{P}_i$ is given by

$$\mathbf{P}_i = \mathbf{E} \times \mathbf{H} \tag{1}$$

In the far field, the field components are transverse so that (see coordinates of Fig. 2-16)

$$\mathbf{E} = \mathbf{a}_\phi E_\phi + \mathbf{a}_\theta E_\theta = \mathbf{a}_\phi E_{\phi 0} \cos \omega t + \mathbf{a}_\theta E_{\theta 0} \cos (\omega t + \delta) \tag{2}$$

and

$$\mathbf{H} = -\mathbf{a}_\theta H_\theta + \mathbf{a}_\phi H_\phi = -\mathbf{a}_\theta H_{\theta 0} \cos (\omega t + \xi) + \mathbf{a}_\phi H_{\phi 0} \cos (\omega t + \delta + \xi) \tag{3}$$

The instantaneous Poynting vector is then

$$\mathbf{P}_i = -\mathbf{a}_\phi \times \mathbf{a}_\theta E_\phi H_\theta + \mathbf{a}_\theta \times \mathbf{a}_\phi E_\theta H_\phi = \mathbf{a}_r (E_\phi H_\theta + E_\theta H_\phi) \tag{4}$$

and its radial component is

$$P_{ri} = E_\phi H_\theta + E_\theta H_\phi \tag{5}$$

The average value P_r is obtained by the integration of (5) over one cycle as given by

$$P_r = \frac{1}{2\pi} \int_0^{2\pi} (E_\phi H_\theta + E_\theta H_\phi) \, d(\omega t) \tag{6}$$

from which

$$P_r = \tfrac{1}{2} E_{\phi 0} H_{\theta 0} \cos \xi + \tfrac{1}{2} E_{\theta 0} H_{\phi 0} \cos \xi \tag{7}$$

The magnitudes of the far-field components are related by

$$\frac{E_\phi}{H_\theta} = \frac{E_\theta}{H_\phi} = Z \tag{8}$$

so (7) can be written

$$P_r = \tfrac{1}{2} H_{\theta 0}^2 Z \cos \xi + \tfrac{1}{2} H_{\phi 0}^2 Z \cos \xi \tag{9}$$

But $Z \cos \xi = \text{Re } Z$. In free space $Z = Z_0 = 120\pi$, which is real, so $\text{Re } Z = Z_0$ and

$$P_r = \frac{Z_0}{2} (H_{\theta 0}^2 + H_{\phi 0}^2) = 60\pi (H_{\theta 0}^2 + H_{\phi 0}^2) \tag{10}$$

or

$$P_r = \frac{E_{\phi 0}^2 + E_{\theta 0}^2}{2Z_0} = \frac{E_{\phi 0}^2 + E_{\theta 0}^2}{240\pi} \tag{11}$$

The above derivation may also be made using complex notation as follows. The complex Poynting vector is

$$\tilde{\mathbf{P}} = \tfrac{1}{2}\mathbf{E} \times \mathbf{H}^* \tag{12}$$

In the far field, the field components are transverse so that

$$\mathbf{E} = \mathbf{a}_\phi E_\phi + \mathbf{a}_\theta E_\theta = \mathbf{a}_\phi E_{\phi 0} e^{j\omega t} + \mathbf{a}_\theta E_{\theta 0} e^{j(\omega t + \delta)} \tag{13}$$

$$\mathbf{H}^* = -\mathbf{a}_\theta H_\theta^* + \mathbf{a}_\phi H_\phi^* = -\mathbf{a}_\theta H_{\theta 0} e^{-j(\omega t + \xi)} + \mathbf{a}_\phi H_{\phi 0} e^{-j(\omega t + \delta + \xi)} \tag{14}$$

The average Poynting vector (time average) is given by

$$\mathbf{P} = \tfrac{1}{2}\operatorname{Re}(\mathbf{E} \times \mathbf{H}^*) = \tfrac{1}{2}\mathbf{a}_r \operatorname{Re}(E_\phi H_\theta^* + E_\theta H_\phi^*)$$
$$= \tfrac{1}{2}\mathbf{a}_r (E_{\phi 0} H_{\theta 0} \cos \xi + E_{\theta 0} H_{\phi 0} \cos \xi) \tag{15}$$

The radial component of the average Poynting vector is then

$$P_r = \tfrac{1}{2}E_{\phi 0}H_{\theta 0} \cos \xi + \tfrac{1}{2}E_{\theta 0}H_{\phi 0} \cos \xi \tag{16}$$

as in (7) and, hence, in free space P_r reduces to the same form as in (10) and (11).

The total power W radiated through a large sphere is then

$$\left. \begin{aligned} W = \iint P_r \, ds &= \tfrac{1}{2}r^2 \int_0^{2\pi} \int_0^\pi \operatorname{Re}(E_\phi H_\theta^* + E_\theta H_\phi^*) \sin \theta \, d\theta \, d\phi \\ &= \tfrac{1}{2}r^2 \int_0^{2\pi} \int_0^\pi \operatorname{Re}(E_\phi H_\theta^* + E_\theta H_\phi^*) \, d\Omega \end{aligned} \right\} \tag{17}$$

where $d\Omega = \sin \theta \, d\theta \, d\phi = $ element of solid angle
From (17)

$$W = \tfrac{1}{2}r^2 Z_0 \int_0^{2\pi} \int_0^\pi (H_{\theta 0}^2 + H_{\phi 0}^2) \, d\Omega = \frac{r^2}{2Z_0} \int_0^{2\pi} \int_0^\pi (E_{\phi 0}^2 + E_{\theta 0}^2) \, d\Omega \tag{18}$$

In general $E_{\phi 0}$ and $E_{\theta 0}$ may be different functions of θ and ϕ. Thus,

$$E_{\phi 0} = E_1 F_1(\theta, \phi) \tag{19}$$

and

$$E_{\theta 0} = E_2 F_2(\theta, \phi) \tag{20}$$

The directivity D of an antenna is given by

$$D = \frac{U_m}{U_0} = \frac{4\pi U_m}{4\pi U_0} = \frac{4\pi r^2 P_{rm}}{W} \tag{21}$$

where P_{rm} is the value of the radial component of the average Poynting

vector in the direction from the source in which it is a maximum. From (11)

$$P_{rm} = \frac{[E_{\phi 0}^2 + E_{\theta 0}^2]_{max}}{2Z_0} = \frac{[E_1^2 F_1^2(\theta, \phi) + E_2^2 F_2^2(\theta, \phi)]_{max}}{2Z_0} \tag{22}$$

From (18) and (19)

$$W = \frac{r^2}{2Z_0} \int_0^{2\pi} \int_0^{\pi} [E_1^2 F_1^2(\theta, \phi) + E_2^2 F_2^2(\theta, \phi)] \, d\Omega \tag{23}$$

Introducing (22) and (23) in (21), the directivity of an antenna of any polarization is

$$D = \frac{4\pi}{\dfrac{\displaystyle\int_0^{2\pi} \int_0^{\pi} [E_1^2 F_1^2(\theta, \phi) + E_2^2 F_2^2(\theta, \phi)] \, d\Omega}{[E_1^2 F_1^2(\theta, \phi) + E_2^2 F_2^2(\theta, \phi)]_{max}}} = \frac{4\pi}{B} \tag{24}$$

where $B =$ beam area
Equation (24) may also be expressed

$$D = \frac{4\pi}{\dfrac{\displaystyle\int_0^{2\pi} \int_0^{\pi} F^2(\theta, \phi) \, d\Omega}{F^2(\theta, \phi)_{max}}} \tag{24a}$$

where $F(\theta, \phi) =$ total field pattern
For $F(\theta, \phi)_{max} = 1$, (24a) reduces to (15-6). If both field components have identical patterns

$$F_1(\theta, \phi) = F_2(\theta, \phi) \tag{25}$$

so that

$$D = \frac{4\pi}{\dfrac{\displaystyle\int_0^{2\pi} \int_0^{\pi} F_1^2(\theta, \phi) \, d\Omega}{F_1^2(\theta, \phi)_{max}}} \tag{26}$$

Whenever (25) is fulfilled, the directivity of a source of any polarization is a function of the space pattern of only a single field component. If also $F_1(\theta, \phi)_{max} = 1$, (26) reduces to

$$D = \frac{4\pi}{\displaystyle\int_0^{2\pi} \int_0^{\pi} F_1^2(\theta, \phi) \, d\Omega} \tag{27}$$

In the denominator of (24) the integrand divided by the denominator is equal to the relative radiation intensity pattern $[f(\theta, \phi)/f(\theta, \phi)_{max}]$ so that (24) reduces to (2-39).

The above expressions apply to fields of any polarization. It is to be noted that the relations are independent of the time-phase difference δ between E_ϕ and E_θ.

If the field is linearly polarized, for example, let it be everywhere horizontally polarized, $E_{\theta 0} = H_{\phi 0} = E_2 = 0$, and (24) reduces to (26).

INDEX

71